To Shannon

For the love, fun, beauty, and sheer joy you bring to our lives.

CONTENTS

PREFACE

In this text we focus on criminal behavior and antisocial behavior (because antisocial behavior is not always criminal) from a psychological perspective. More specifically, adults and juveniles who violate the law or who act antisocially are portrayed as embedded in and continually influenced by multiple systems within the psychosocial environment. Meaningful theory, well-executed research, and skillful application of knowledge to the "crime problem" require an understanding of the many levels of events that influence a person's life course—from the individual to the individual's family, peers, schools, neighborhoods, community, culture, and society as a whole.

The psychological study of crime has taken a decidedly developmental approach, while retaining its interest in cognitive-based explanations for antisocial behavior. Scholars from various academic disciplines have engaged in pathways-to-crime research, for example. A very common conclusion is that there are multiple developmental pathways to criminal offending; some begin to offend very early while others begin offending in adulthood. In addition, a variety of risk factors enable antisocial behavior, and protective factors insulate the individual from such behavior. The pathways approach does not always focus on psychological factors, but it coexists very well with psychological theories of child and adolescent development. In addition to developmental and cognitive research, much contemporary work is focusing on biopsychology and crime, or the way in which a range of genetic and biological factors may affect one's behavior, particularly aggressive behavior.

We do not consider all offenders psychologically flawed, and only some have diagnosable mental illnesses or disorders. Persons with serious mental disorders sometimes commit crimes, but the vast majority do not, and crimes that are committed by the mentally disordered are most typically minor offenses. The exceptional cases, such as some mass murders or other particularly shocking crimes, attract media attention and lead many people to draw unwarranted conclusions about the dangerousness of the mentally ill. Many offenders do have substance abuse problems and these may co-occur with mental disorders. In addition, emotionally healthy people break the law, and sometimes emotionally healthy people end up on probation or in jails and prisons. Like the earlier editions of this book, the 11th edition views the criminal offender as existing on a continuum, ranging from the occasional offender who offends at some point during the life course, usually during adolescence, to the serious, repetitive offender who usually begins his or her criminal career at a very early age, or the one-time, serious offender.

The book reviews contemporary research, theory, and practice concerning the psychology of crime as completely and accurately as possible. The very long list of references at the end of the book should attest to its comprehensive nature. Nevertheless, it is impossible to do justice to the wide swath of behavior that is defined as crime, nor to the many models and approaches used in studying it. We have selected representative crimes and representative research. If your favorite crime, theory, model, or prevention or treatment program is not found here, we hope you will still appreciate what is offered.

An early chapter sets the stage by defining crime and describing how it is measured. It is important to stress that crime rates in the United States have gone down for most serious offenses, something which rarely comes to public attention. Then, the book is organized from broad to specific content. Early chapters discuss individual and social risk factors, developmental principles, and the psychology of aggression, including its biological basis. We include a complete chapter on psychopathy, because it remains arguably one of the most heavily researched topics in the psychology of crime. The specific crimes covered in the latter part of the book are both very common ones and crimes that are rare but attract media and research attention because of their serious nature.

NEW TO THIS EDITION

The 11th edition was completed with the help of extensive reviews of the previous edition. The most significant changes reflect recent theoretical developments and models in criminology as well as ongoing psychological research on specific topics and offenses. Every chapter includes updated citations and illustrations. We have retained the 16-chapter structure used in the past few editions. However, some topics have been deleted and others added, as we explain below.

- We have provided more coverage of contemporary antisocial behavior, including crimes that are facilitated by the Internet, such as cyberstalking and cyberbullying, as well as cybercrimes like computer intrusions.
- Several changes in UCR definitions are relevant to the gathering of statistics and the measurement of crime. They are indicated in the early chapters of the book.
- The chapter on individual risk factors includes information about specific environmental toxins (e.g., lead, cadmium, mercury, manganese) that can negatively affect brain development in young children.
- Two sex offending chapters have been revised extensively. This required the updating of information on the dominant sex offender classification systems and addressing sex offender typologies.
- All material relating to the DSM is updated to conform to its latest edition, the DSM-5. Diagnoses that are relevant to discussions of mental disorder and crime comport with diagnoses listed in the DSM.
- Early in the book we discuss cumulative risk and developmental cascade models, and reiterate throughout the book that risk factors for antisocial behavior both accumulate and interact with one another in a dynamic fashion during the life course.
- Material on juveniles continues to form a separate chapter, but it is also interspersed throughout the text in sections of many chapters (e.g., juvenile substance abuse, sex offenders, juveniles who kill).
- Intimate Partner Violence (IPV) is discussed in a separate section of the chapter that also includes family violence, to reflect increasing research interest in this area. This edition covers IPV in specific populations, such as the elderly, non-heterosexual couples, and law enforcement and military families.
- In addition to cumulative risk and dynamic cascade models, several other models are highlighted, including Steinberg's dual systems model of adolescent brain development, the dual-process model of psychopathy, and the three-path model of sexual offending. While new general theories of criminal behavior have not been proposed, new models for illustrating theoretical concepts have appeared and are recognized when relevant.
- New models of why people join terrorist groups and act as lone wolves are introduced in the chapter on terrorism.
- Material on substance abuse and crime has been substantially updated to encompass ongoing changes in substance use patterns and dangers therein.
- Every chapter includes at least one box, and most often two. Box topics were chosen thematically: the boxes either illustrate a contemporary issue (e.g., Internet-facilitated crime), a research project (e.g., research on bystander apathy), or a program (e.g., treatment program for juvenile sex offenders). As a pedagogical aid, boxes include questions for discussion.

In addition to the boxes, pedagogical materials include 68 tables, all of which are either author-created or available from public documents, and 16 figures. As for other recent editions, chapter objectives are listed at the beginning of each chapter, and key concepts and review questions are included at the end.

The book includes updated examples and illustrations of the crimes and concepts being discussed, but retains illustrations of some past events that reflect many of the psychological concepts discussed (e.g., hostage taking, school shootings; sniper events). However, over half of the examples used refer to significant recent events, such as cases involving the insanity defense, mass murders, acts of terrorism, and corporate crime.

In addition to the above listed new features, the eleventh edition includes:

- More attention to female offending.
- More information on prescription drug abuse, especially among juveniles.
- Greater coverage of the role of neuropsychological factors in the development of antisocial behavior.
- Better presentation of structured professional judgment in risk assessment approaches.
- More emphasis on the importance of pre-school experiences for preventing antisocial behavior.

Readers familiar with previous recent editions of the text also may want to take note of the following:

As in the last two editions, there is less information on the juvenile justice process and the history of juvenile justice, and there is little delinquency material in Chapter 1. As noted above, however, a separate chapter is devoted to research on pathways to delinquency, and juvenile-related material is found in many other chapters. We have removed sections on boot camps for juveniles in favor of more coverage of evidence-based programs like Multisystemic Therapy, Functional Family Therapy, and the closely watched Fast Track experiment.

Also as in the 10th edition, we did not discuss some sex offenses such as prostitution and exhibitionism, nor did we cover in detail psychologically relevant issues relating to prisons and jails, such as violence, the effects of overcrowding, or conditions of confinement. Likewise, little attention is given to political crimes committed by agents of government, although we have included a box on this topic. Nevertheless, in light of their continued importance, we hope professors will find a way to incorporate some of these topics in their course content.

Criminal Behavior is designed to be a core text in undergraduate and graduate courses in criminal behavior, criminology, the psychology of crime, crime and delinquency, and forensic psychology. The material contained in this book was classroom-tested for over 30 years. Its emphasis on psychological theory and concepts makes it distinctive from other fine textbooks on crime, many of which are more sociologically based. The book's major goal is to encourage an appreciation of the many complex issues surrounding criminal behavior by citing relevant, contemporary research.

Once again, we have benefited from the encouragement and help of many individuals in completing this very long project. We cherish our main sources of emotional support—Gina, Ian, Soraya, Jim, Kai, Maddie, Darya, and Shannon. They are always there for us, and we continue to be awed by their goodness, their wit, their fun-loving spirit, the love they display, and their many accomplishments in so many different realms.

On the professional side, we are most grateful to the management, production, and distribution staff at Pearson Education/Prentice Hall, particularly Executive Editor Gary Bauer and his assistants Holly and Tara; Project Manager Susan Hannahs; Valerie Iglar-Mobley; Patricia Gutierrez; Marketing Coordinator Elizabeth Mackenzie Lamb; and editorial assistant Lynda Cramer. Philip Alexander and Sivakumar Krishnamoorthy, Project Managers at Integra Software Services led us to the finish line in a patient and professional manner.

Finally, we wish to acknowledge the following professors and scholars who reviewed the 10th edition of the book and provided many helpful suggestions for improvement: Larry Bench, University of Utah; Tomasina Cook, Erie Community College; Phyllis Gerstenfeld, California State University—Stanislaus; Edward Keane, Housatonic Community College; Kelly Roth, McCann School of Business & Technology; Christopher Salvatore, Montclair State University; Jeffrey Segal, College of Saint Elizabeth; and Ben Stevenson, University of Maryland University College. Our sincere thanks to all.

Curt R. Bartol
Anne M. Bartol

INSTRUCTOR SUPPLEMENTS

Instructor's Manual with Test Bank. Includes content outlines for classroom discussion, teaching suggestions, and answers to selected end-of-chapter questions from the text. This also contains a Word document version of the test bank.

TestGen. This computerized test generation system gives you maximum flexibility in creating and administering tests on paper, electronically, or online. It provides state-of-the-art features for viewing and editing test bank questions, dragging a selected question into a test you are creating, and printing sleek, formatted tests in a variety of layouts. Select test items from test banks included with TestGen for quick test creation, or write your own questions from scratch. TestGen's random generator provides the option to display different text or calculated number values each time questions are used.

PowerPoint Presentations. Our presentations offer clear, straightforward outlines and notes to use for class lectures or study materials. Photos, illustrations, charts, and tables from the book are included in the presentations when applicable.

To access supplementary materials online, instructors need to request an instructor access code. Go to **www.pearsonhighered.com/irc,** where you can register for an instructor access code. Within 48 hours after registering, you will receive a confirming email, including an instructor access code. Once you have received your code, go to the site and log on for full instructions on downloading the materials you wish to use.

Introduction to Criminal Behavior

CHAPTER OBJECTIVES

- Emphasize that criminal behavior has multiple causes, manifestations, and developmental pathways.
- Identify the different perspectives of human nature that underlie the theoretical development and research of criminal behavior.
- Introduce various theories that may help explain crime.
- Describe the three major disciplines in criminology: sociological, psychological, and psychiatric.
- Point out that the study of criminal behavior and delinquency, from a psychological perspective, has shifted from a personality toward a more cognitive and developmental focus.
- Define criminal behavior and juvenile delinquency.
- Introduce the reader to the various measurements of criminal and delinquent behavior.

Crime intrigues people. Sometimes it attracts us, sometimes it repels us, and occasionally, it does both at once. It can amuse, as when we read that two men dressed as "Spider-Man" and "Batman" were arrested after a brawl in Times Square in 2014. Many people chuckled, as well, at a YouTube video of a burglar who was sprawled and napping on a bed in the victims' home, next to a bag containing jewelry he had stolen. Presumably, no one was seriously injured by the conduct in either of these instances (though some children may have been devastated that their heroes acted less than nobly), but the homeowners likely suffered emotional distress and faced inconveniences that accompany being victims of a crime. Although readers will cite some exceptions, you are likely to agree that most crime leaves victims in its wake; most crime harms.

Crime can frighten, especially if we believe that what happened to one victim might happen to us or those we love. News of a child abduction or even an attempted one places parents at heightened alert. Crime can also anger, as when a beloved community member is brutally killed, a person or animal is subjected to heinous abuse, or individuals have had their credit card data compromised or have been deprived of their life savings by fraudulent schemes. Fatal accidents caused by inebriated drivers are noteworthy for the anger they arouse—and the anger may be directed at the friends of the driver who did not stop him from driving, as well as the driver himself.

What is crime? Legally, it is defined as conduct or failure to act in violation of the law forbidding or commanding it, and for which a range of possible penalties exist upon conviction. Criminal behavior, then, is behavior in violation of the criminal code. To be convicted of crime, a person must have acted intentionally and without justification or excuse. For example, even an intentional killing may be justified under certain circumstances, as in defense of one's life. Although there is a very narrow range of offenses that do not require criminal intent (called strict liability offenses), the vast majority of crime requires it. Obviously, this legal definition encompasses a great variety of acts, ranging from murder to petty offenses.

While interest in crime has always been high, understanding why it occurs and what to do about it has always been a problem. Public officials, politicians, various experts, and many people in the general public continue to offer simple and incomplete solutions for obliterating crime, particularly violent and street crime: more police officers, video cameras and state-of-the-art surveillance equipment, armed teachers and more guns, sturdy locks, self-defense classes, stiff penalties, speedy imprisonment, or capital punishment. Some of these approaches may be effective in the short term, but the overall problem of crime persists. Solutions that attack what are believed to be root causes of crime—such as reducing economic inequality, improving educational opportunities, or offering substance abuse treatment—have considerable merit, but they require public commitment, energy, and financial resources.

Our inability to prevent crime is also partly because we have trouble understanding criminal behavior and identifying and agreeing upon its many causes. Explanations of crime require complicated, involved answers, and psychological research indicates that most people have limited tolerance for complexity and ambiguity. We apparently want simple, straightforward answers, no matter how complex the issue. Parents become impatient when psychologists answer questions about child rearing by saying, "It depends"—on the situation, on the parents' reactions to it, or on any number of possible influences. Today, the preference for simplicity is aided by the vast array of information available in the media, including the Internet and social media. Search engines provide instant access to a multitude of both reputable and questionable sources. Discerning students are well served by this information explosion; they can find up-to-date research on virtually all topics covered in this book, for example. However, many people acquire information—but not necessarily knowledge—by clicking links, entering chat rooms, reading blogs and accompanying comments, and following friends and "friends" and friends of friends who may or may not be providing legitimate data. Thus, the selective and careful use of information technology is a crucial skill for all students to acquire.

Criminal behavior may be seen as a vastly complex, sometimes difficult-to-understand phenomenon. Our focus is the *psychological perspective*, although other viewpoints are also described. However, it is important to stress that there is no all-encompassing psychological explanation for crime, any more than there is a sociological, anthropological, psychiatric, economic, or historic one. In fact, it is unlikely that sociology, psychology, or any other discipline can formulate basic "truths" about crime without help from other disciplines and well-designed research. Criminology—the scientific study of crime—needs all the interdisciplinary help it can get to explain and control criminal behavior. To review accurately and adequately the plethora of studies and theories from each relevant discipline is far beyond the scope of this text, however. Our primary goal is to review and integrate recent scholarship and research in the psychology of crime, compare it with traditional approaches, and discuss strategies that have been offered to prevent and modify criminal behavior. We cannot begin to accomplish this task without first calling attention to philosophical questions that underlie any study of human behavior, including criminal behavior.

THEORIES OF CRIME

In everyday conversation, the term "theory" is used loosely. It may refer to personal experiences, observations, traditional beliefs, a set of opinions, or a collection of abstract thoughts. Almost everyone has personal theories about human behavior, and these extend to criminal behavior. To illustrate, some people have a personal theory that the world is a just place, where one gets what one deserves. "Just-worlders," as they are called, believe that things do not happen to people without a reason that is closely related to their own actions; for example, individuals who experience financial difficulties probably brought these on themselves. In 2008–2009, when many homeowners in the United States were facing foreclosure because they could not afford high mortgage payments, a just-worlder would be likely to say this was more their own fault than the fault of bank officers who enticed them into paying high interest rates.

In reference to crime, just-worlders may believe both that a burglar deserved a severe penalty and that the victims did not protect their property sufficiently. Because the world is a just place, the battered spouse must have provoked a beating. The man who sent in a $500 deposit to claim his million dollar prize should have known: if it's too good to be true, it isn't.

The above beliefs represent individual "theories" or assumptions about how the world works. However, psychologists have also developed a somewhat more elaborate *scientific theory* based on just-world ideas, and they have developed scales to measure one's just-world orientation (Lerner, 1980; Lerner & Miller, 1978). A variety of hypotheses—sometimes discussed under the umbrella term **just-world hypothesis**—have been proposed and tested. For example, people identified as just-worlders on the basis of their scores on the scales have been shown to favor capital punishment and to be nonsupportive of many social programs intended to reduce economic disparity between social groups (Sutton & Douglas, 2005).

Interestingly, the most recent research on just-world theory has identified two tracks: belief in a general just-world—described above—and belief in a personal just-world (Dalbert, 1999; Sutton & Douglas, 2005). Belief in a personal just-world ("I usually get what I deserve") is considered adaptive and helpful in coping with dire circumstances in one's life. For example, Dalbert and Filke (2007) found that prisoners with a high personal just-world orientation evaluated their prison experiences more positively and reported better overall well-being than those without such an orientation. Belief in a general just-world, however, seems to be far more problematic because it is associated with less compassion for others and even a derogation of victims of crime.

Scientific theories like the above are based on logic and research, but they vary widely in complexity. A scientific theory is "a set of interrelated constructs (concepts), definitions, and propositions that present a systematic view of phenomena by specifying relations among variables, with the purpose of explaining and predicting the phenomena" (Kerlinger, 1973, p. 9). A scientific theory of crime, therefore, should provide a general explanation that encompasses and *systematically* connects many different social, economic, and psychological variables to criminal behavior, and it should be supported by well-executed research. Moreover, the terms in any scientific theory must be as precise as possible, their meaning and usage clear and unambiguous, so that it can be meaningfully tested by observation and analysis. The process of theory testing is called **theory verification**. If the theory is not verified—indeed, if any of its propositions is not verified—the end result is **falsification** (Popper, 1968). For example, a theory of child sexual abuse that includes the proposition that all child sex offenders were sexually abused as children would be falsified as soon as one nonabused offender was encountered.

The primary purpose of theories of crime is to identify the causes or precursors of criminal behavior. Some theories are broad and encompassing, whereas others are narrow and specific. Basically, theories of criminal behavior are summary statements of a collection of research findings. Perhaps, more importantly, they provide direction for further research. If one component of a theory is falsified or not supported, the theory is not necessarily rejected outright, however. It can be modified and retested. In addition, each theory of crime has implications for policy or decisions made by society to prevent crime.

Over the past few decades, many researchers have been interested in proposing models to accompany various theories. A **model** is a graphic representation of a theory or a concept, designed to enhance its understanding. Throughout the text, you will encounter different models pertaining to criminal and delinquent behavior.

Models are relatively new, but theories of crime have been around for centuries. During the eighteenth century, the Italian philosopher Cesare Beccaria (1738–1794) developed a theory that human behavior is fundamentally driven by a choice made by weighing the amount of pleasure gained against the amount of pain or punishment expected. Beccaria argued that in order to reduce or stop criminal offending in any given society, the punishment should be swift, certain, and severe enough to deter people from the criminal (pleasure-seeking) act. If people realized in advance that severe punishment would be forthcoming, and coming soon, regardless of their social status or privileges, they would choose not to engage in illegal behavior. This theoretical thinking, which emphasizes free will as the hallmark of human behavior, has become known as

classical theory. Both criminal and civil law are rooted in the belief that individuals are masters of their fate, the possessors of free will and freedom of choice. Many of today's approaches to crime prevention are consistent with classical theory, which in its modern form is also known as **deterrence theory** (Nagin, 2007). For example, surveillance cameras on the streets, shoulder cameras on police officers, and harsh sentences assume that individuals choose to commit crime but may be persuaded not to under the threat of being discovered or being punished with long prison time. However, even if people are not deterred by the prospect of long sentences, they must still be punished, because crime was an expression of their free will.

Another thread of theoretical thought originated with **positivist theory**, which is closely aligned with the idea of determinism. From that view, free will cannot be the major explanation for our behavior. Antecedents—prior experiences or influences—*determine* how we will act. The earliest positive theories of crime considered biological antecedents, such as one's sex, one's race, or even the size of one's brain. An early theorist from the positivist perspective, Cesare Lombroso (1876) conducted elaborate measurements on the skulls of both dead and live prisoners and drew conclusions about their criminal tendencies. Later, positivists saw social antecedents, such as negative early life experiences or lack of educational opportunity, as the culprits. According to the positivist school, human behavior is governed by causal laws, and free will is undermined. Many contemporary theories of criminology are positivist because they search for causes beyond free will. Furthermore, many approaches to crime prevention are consistent with a positivist orientation: They try to "fix" the antecedents of criminal activity, such as by providing support services for youth believed to be at risk of engaging in crime.

In summary, the classical view of crime holds that the decision to violate the law is largely a result of free will. The positivist or deterministic perspective argues that most criminal behavior is a result of social, psychological, and even biological influences. It does not deny the importance of free will, and it does not suggest that individuals should not be held responsible for their actions. However, it maintains that these actions can be explained by more than "free will." This latter perspective, then, seeks to identify causes, predict and prevent criminal behavior, and rehabilitate (or habilitate) offenders.

THEORETICAL PERSPECTIVES ON HUMAN NATURE

All theories of crime have underlying assumptions about or perspectives on human nature. Three major ones can be identified. The **conformity perspective** views humans as creatures of conformity who want to do the "right" thing. To a large extent, this assumption represents the foundation of the humanistic perspectives in psychology. Human beings are basically "good" people trying to live to their fullest potential. Similarly, the branch of psychology called "positive psychology" focuses on studying the individual characteristics that make life worth living, such as contentment and intimacy (Peterson, 2006; Seligman & Csikszentmihalyi, 2000). Thus, positive psychology is very much in tune with a conformity perspective.

An excellent example of the conformity perspective in criminology is **strain theory**, which originated in the work of sociologist Robert K. Merton (1957) and continues today in the theory of Robert Agnew (1992, 2006) and his followers. Merton's original strain theory argued that humans are fundamentally conforming beings who are strongly influenced by the values and attitudes of the society in which they live. In short, most members of a given society desire what the other members of the society desire. In many societies and cultures, the accumulation of wealth or status is all important, representing symbols that all members should strive for. Unfortunately, access to these goals is not equally available. While some have the education, social network, personal contacts, and family influence to attain them, others are deprived of the opportunity. Thus, Merton's strain theory predicted that crime and delinquency would occur when there is a perceived discrepancy between the materialistic values and goals cherished and held in high esteem by a society and the availability of the legitimate means for reaching these goals. Under these conditions, a strain between the goals of wealth and power and the means for reaching them develops. Groups and individuals experiencing a high level of this strain are forced to decide whether to violate norms and laws to attain some of this sought-after wealth or power, or give up on their dream and go through the motions, withdraw, or rebel. Note that, although the original strain theory was formulated on American society, it can be applied on a global basis.

Following Merton's seminal work, other strain theorists emphasized that crimes of the rich and powerful also can be explained by strain theory. Even though these individuals have greater access to the legitimate means of reaching goals, they have a continuing need to accumulate even greater wealth and power and maintain their privileged status in society (Messner & Rosenfeld, 1994).

In developing his General Strain Theory (Strain Theory, 1992), Agnew used the word "strain" in a slightly different way, seeing strains as events and conditions that are disliked by individuals. The inability to achieve one's goals was only one such condition; others were losing something of value, or being treated negatively by others (2006). General Strain Theory, which has attracted much research and commentary, is continually being tested and evaluated and will be discussed again in Chapter 5; the point we make here is that it remains under the umbrella of a strain theory, representative of the conformity perspective on human nature.

A second perspective—the **nonconformist perspective**—assumes that human beings are basically undisciplined creatures, who, without the constraints of the rules and regulations of a given society, would flout society's conventions and commit crime indiscriminately. This perspective sees humans as fundamentally "unruly" and deviant, needing to be held in check. For example, the biological and neurobiological theories discussed in Chapter 3 identify genetic or other biological features or deficiencies in some individuals that predispose them to antisocial behavior, like aggressive actions. In recent years, some criminologists have emphasized the importance of biological influences on behavior, not as exclusive determinants of behavior but rather as factors that should be taken into consideration (DeLisi, 2009). They may be present at birth or appear during one's early formative years. It is important to point out that a nonconformity perspective does not blame people for their deviance. As readers will learn in Chapter 3, many theorists now believe that certain behaviors, such as aggressive actions, have their genesis in malnutrition and exposure to harmful elements in the environment. These are provocative claims that should ensure debate and discussion among readers.

Another good illustration of the nonconformist perspective is Travis Hirschi's (1969) social control theory. **Social control theory** contends that crime and delinquency occur when an individual's ties to the conventional order or normative standards are weak or largely nonexistent. In other words, the socialization that usually holds one's basic human nature in check is incomplete or faulty. This position perceives human nature as fundamentally "bad," "antisocial," or at least "imperfect." These innate tendencies must be *controlled* by society. Years after developing social control theory, Hirschi teamed with Michael Gottfredson to develop a **General Theory of Crime** (GTC; Gottfredson & Hirschi, 1990). This theory, also referred to as **self-control theory (SCT)**, represents one of the more prominent perspectives in criminology today. It suggests that a deficit of self-control or self-regulation is the key factor in explaining crime and delinquency. One controversial aspect of the theory is its contention that self-control is a stable trait that is fully in place in childhood, usually by the age of eight and is not likely to change thereafter. Many researchers have tested this aspect of SCT and have found that self-control can develop at later ages (e.g., Arnett, 2000; Sweeten & Simons, 2014; Zimmermann & Iwanski, 2014).

The third perspective—the **learning perspective**—sees human beings as born neutral (neither inherently conforming nor unruly) and subject to developmental changes throughout the life course. This perspective argues that humans learn virtually all their behavior, beliefs, and tendencies from the social environment. The learning perspective is exemplified most comprehensively by **social learning theory**, to be a main topic in Chapter 4, and the **differential association theory** of sociologist Edwin H. Sutherland (1947). Social learning theory emphasizes such concepts as imitation of models and reinforcements one gains from one's behavior. According to differential association theory, criminal behavior is learned, as is all social behavior, through social interactions with other people. It is not the result of emotional disturbance, mental illness, or innate qualities of "goodness" or "badness." Rather, people learn to be criminal as a result of messages they get from others who were also taught to be criminal. The conventional wisdom that bad company promotes bad behavior, therefore, finds validity in this theory.

TABLE 1-1	Perspectives of Human Nature	
Perspective of Behavior	**Theory Example**	**Humans Are...**
Conformity perspective	Strain theory (Merton) General strain (Agnew)	Basically good; strongly influenced by the values and attitudes of society
Nonconformist perspective	Social control theory (Hirschi) Biological theories of crime General theory of crime/ self-control theory	Basically undisciplined; individual's ties to social order are weak; innate tendencies must be controlled by society; individual lack of self-control
Learning perspective	Differential association theory (Sutherland) Social learning theory (Rotter, Bandura) Developmental criminology	Born neutral; behavior is learned through social interactions with other people; changes over the life span affect behavior

From the mid-twentieth century to the present, many criminologists have embraced a developmental approach, viewing crime and other antisocial activity as behavior that begins in early childhood and proceeds to and sometimes through one's adult years. Developmental psychologists as a group identify periods in human development across the life course, sometimes conceived of as stages. Those interested in the study of antisocial behavior often examine these stages as they relate to crime. Over the past decade, emerging adulthood has been identified as a period covering the time between adolescence and adulthood—roughly ages 18 to the late 20s, with a particular focus on 18–25 (Arnett, 2000, 2014). Emerging adulthood is a time when people are generally expected to be independent from parental and other institutional controls but are still searching for self-identity. Thus, they may be carefree and exploring their options but also may be struggling to achieve adult status. Many emerging adults have not yet settled on a career choice or chosen a partner. As we discuss later in the book, emerging adulthood has prompted considerable research relating to antisocial behavior.

Developmental criminologists also have studied the life paths or "pathways" people take that lead to criminal behavior. For example, some begin antisocial activity at very early ages, while others begin in adolescence or later. Developmental criminologists identify risk factors to be addressed and protective factors to be encouraged. Some have learned that girls and women, as a group, take pathways that are quite different from those taken by boys and men, as a group, though researchers differ on the extent to which these differences occur. It is possible that cultural groups may differ in the pathways to crime, though this is not as intensely studied as gender differences.

Table 1-1 summarizes the three perspectives—conformity, noncomformist, and learning—and provides illustrations of each. Developmental criminology cannot be placed firmly in any of the three categories, although it would seem to be most at home in the learning perspective, so we place it there. Nevertheless, aspects of each perspective can be detected in the research and writing of developmental criminologists (e.g., Farrington, Ttofi, & Coid, 2009; Le Blanc & Loeber, 1998; Moffitt, 1993a, 1993b; Odgers et al., 2008; Patterson, 1982). We discuss these theories in some detail in Chapter 6.

DISCIPLINARY PERSPECTIVES IN CRIMINOLOGY

Criminology is the multidisciplinary study of crime. As noted above, several theories we cited were framed by sociologists. Over the years, the study of crime has been dominated by sociology, psychology, and psychiatry, but in recent years more disciplines and subdisciplines have been involved. These include, but are not limited to, anthropology, biology, neurology, political science, and economics.

Although our main concern in this text is with *psychological principles*, concepts, theory, and research relevant to criminal behavior, considerable attention is placed on the research knowledge of the other disciplines, particularly sociology, psychiatry, and biology. In fact, some psychologists today have extensive backgrounds in biology and the workings of the brain, and many specialize in the rapidly expanding fields of biopsychology and neuropsychology. It is not easy to make sharp demarcations between disciplines, because they often overlap in focus and practice. It is fair to say that all try to develop, examine, and evaluate strategies and interventions that have the potential to prevent or reduce criminal and antisocial behavior.

In addition, what distinguishes a given theory as sociological, psychological, or psychiatric is sometimes simply the stated professional affiliation of its proponent. Furthermore, alignments are not clear cut, because theorists and researchers today often work hand in hand with those from other disciplines: They obtain grants together, conduct studies, teach together, form consulting agencies, and even write books together. Finally, condensing any major discipline into a few pages hardly does it justice. To obtain a more adequate overview, the interested reader should consult texts and articles within those disciplines. **Table 1-2** summarizes the three dominant disciplinary perspectives.

Sociological Criminology

Sociological criminology has a rich tradition in examining the relationships of demographic and group variables to crime. Variables such as age, race, gender, socioeconomic status, and ethnic-cultural affiliation have been shown to have significant relationships with certain categories and patterns of crimes. Sociological criminology, for example, has allowed us to conclude that juveniles as a group are overrepresented in nonviolent property offenses. Young black males from disadvantaged backgrounds are overrepresented as both perpetrators and victims of homicide. White males are overrepresented in political and corporate crimes. The many reasons for this are reflected in the various perspectives and research findings that are covered in the book. Sociological criminology also probes the situational or environmental factors that are most conducive to criminal action, such as the time, place, kind of weapons used, and the circumstances surrounding the crime.

Many sociologists today are divided into structuralist and culturalist groups. With reference to crime, structuralists are more likely to look at the underlying foundation of society, such as lack of employment and educational activities or the quality of health services offered in a community. Culturalists view the values and patterns of living within a given group of people. In recent years, some dissension between the two groups has occurred, particularly relating to the issue of race in American society (Sanneh, 2015).

Another major contribution of sociological criminology is the attention it directs to topics that reflect unequal distribution of power in society. This often takes the form of examining how crime is defined and how laws are enforced. The sale of "street" drugs has been monitored more

TABLE 1-2	The Three Major Disciplinary Perspectives in Criminology	
Perspective	**Influence**	**Focus**
Sociological criminology	Sociology Anthropology	Examines relationships of demographic and group variables to crime: focuses on the structure of society and the culture of groups and how these influence criminal behavior
Psychological criminology	Psychology	Focuses on individual criminal behavior; the science of the behavior, emotional, and mental processes of the criminal
Psychiatric criminology	Psychiatry	The contemporary perspective examines the interplay between psychobiological determinants of behavior and the social environment; traditional perspectives look for the unconscious and biological determinates of criminal behavior

closely than the sale of "suite" drugs, although they may be equally potent. The actions of corporate officials—for example, allowing environmental and workplace hazards that produce serious harm—are often not defined as crimes. Political crime, such as corruption, bribery, and abuse of power, is studied by sociologists much more than by other disciplines, although psychologists have begun to explore this area more in recent years. Sociological criminology also has a stronger tradition of addressing the underlying social conditions that may encourage criminal behavior, such as inequities in educational and employment opportunities. Conflict theories in sociology are particularly influential in questioning how crime is defined, who is subject to punishment, and in attempting to draw attention to the crimes of the rich and powerful.

Psychological Criminology

Psychology is the science of behavior and mental processes. **Psychological criminology**, then, is the science of the behavior and mental processes of the person who commits crime. While sociological criminology focuses primarily on groups and society as a whole, and how they influence criminal activity, psychological criminology focuses on individual criminal behavior—how it is acquired, evoked, maintained, and modified.

In the psychology of crime, both social and personality influences on criminal behavior are considered, along with the mental processes that mediate that behavior. Personality refers to all the biological influences, psychological traits, and cognitive features of the human being that psychologists have identified as important in the mediation and control of behavior. Recently, although interest in personality differences among offenders continues, psychological criminology has shifted its focus in several ways. First, it has taken a more cognitive approach to studying criminal behavior. Second, it has paid more attention to biological and neuropsychological factors. Third, it has adopted a developmental approach to studying criminal behavior among both individuals and groups.

COGNITIVE APPROACH. **Cognitions** refer to the attitudes, beliefs, values, and thoughts that people hold about the social environment, interrelations, human nature, and themselves. In serious criminal offenders, these cognitions are often distorted. Beliefs that children must be severely physically disciplined or that victims are not really hurt by fraud or burglary are good examples of cognitions that may lead to criminal activity. Prejudice is also a cognition that involves distortions of social reality. They include erroneous generalizations and oversimplification about others. Hate or bias crimes—highlighted in **Box 1-1**—are generally rooted in prejudice and cognitive distortions held by perpetrators. Many serial rapists also distort social reality to the point where they may

CONTEMPORARY ISSUES

BOX 1-1   Hate or Bias Crimes

Crimes committed against individuals out of bias, hatred, or racial, religious, and ethnic prejudice are nothing new; they are well documented in the history of virtually every nation. What is relatively new in the United States is the effort to keep track of such crimes and impose harsh penalties on those who commit them. This has been done with varying degrees of success. Bias crimes are widely underreported, not often prosecuted, and seldom punished.

Nevertheless, toward the end of the twentieth century, Congress and many states began to address the crucial problem of crimes—especially violent crimes—committed out of hatred, prejudice, or bias against someone because of their race, religion, sexual orientation, or ethnicity. Eventually,

characteristics such as gender, physical or mental disability, advanced age, and military status were added to the list of protected categories. Laws were passed requiring the gathering of statistics on these offenses and/or allowing enhanced sentences for someone convicted of a hate or bias crime. The first such federal law, the **Hate Crime Statistics Act** of 1990, required the collection of data on violent attacks, intimidation, arson, or property damage that are directed at people because of their race, religion, sexual orientation, or ethnicity. The law was amended in 1994 to include crimes motivated by bias against persons with disabilities and in late 2009 to include crimes of prejudice based on gender or gender identity (Langton & Planty, 2011).

(continued)

Recent official crime statistics (FBI, 2014a, reporting on crimes in 2013), indicate that 49.3 percent of the victims of bias-motivated crimes were targeted because of their race, 20.2 percent because of their sexual orientation, 16.9 percent because of their religion, and 11.4 percent because of their ethnicity. Percentages of other victims were below 2 percent. (See **Figure 1-1** on page 13 for additional data.) More than half of the bias crime victims—61.2 percent—were victims of crimes against persons, specifically intimidation, assault, rape, and murder, in decreasing order.

Relatedly, the Southern Poverty Law Center (SPLC) has reported significant increases in hate groups in the United States. The SPLC identified 602 hate groups in the year 2000; in 2014, the number was placed at 939 (www.splcenter.org). Known hate groups included neo-Nazis, Klansmen, white nationalists, neo-confederatists, racist skinheads, black separatists, and border vigilantes, among others.

Hate groups are those whose beliefs or practices attack or malign an entire class of people, such as members of a given race, ethnicity, or sexual orientation. The activities of hate groups are not necessarily criminal; in fact, they are more likely to involve rallies, marches, meetings, and distributing leaflets rather than perpetrating violence. However, people who commit hate crimes are sympathetic to their message, even though they do not always belong to an organized group. The man accused of killing nine people at a prayer meeting at the historic Mother Emanuel AME church in Charleston, South Carolina, in June 2015 had made comments about wanting to start a race war. The gunman who opened fire in a Sikh Temple in Wisconsin in August 2012, killing six people and wounding others, had ties to a neo-Nazi skinhead group.

Langton and Planty (2011) analyzed hate crime victimizations from 2003 to 2009 derived from both official data and accounts of victims. Following are a few of their findings:

- More than four of five hate crime victimizations involved violence; about 23 percent were serious violent crimes.
- In about 37 percent of violent hate crimes, the offender knew the victim; in violent nonhate crimes, half of all victims knew the offender.
- Eight hate crime homicides occurred in 2009. In 2013, five murders and 21 rapes were counted as hate crimes. It should be noted, as well, that the murders of the Emanuel 9 in Charleston were charged as federal hate crimes.
- Police were notified of fewer than half (45%) of all hate crime victimizations.
- In 2009, 85.9 percent of the law enforcement agencies participating in the Hate Crime Statistics Program reported that no hate crimes occurred in their jurisdiction.

The last bullet point should lead readers to be very cautious in accepting uncritically official reports of hate crime. Psychological concepts that might help us to understand why individuals would perpetrate these offenses are discussed in Chapter 4.

Questions for Discussion

1. It is not unusual for law enforcement agencies to report no hate crime in their jurisdiction. As noted above, 85.9 percent of agencies in 2009 reported none. Why might this be?
2. Victims of hate crimes, such as assaults, do not often report their victimization to law enforcement. Discuss reasons for this.

assault only victims who they perceive "deserve it." Some sex offenders even persuade themselves that they are not harming their victims, and white-collar offenders sometimes justify their crimes as what they have to do in order to stay in business. The importance of offender cognitions in understanding criminal behavior will be stressed throughout the book.

BIOLOGICAL OR NEUROLOGICAL APPROACH.   Many criminologists who identify themselves as psychologists—and some who identify themselves as sociologists—are recognizing that advances in the broad biological sciences are finding links between biology (including neuropsychology) and human behavior (Wright & Boisvert, 2009). The biological approach often focuses on aggression and violent behavior. For example, neurologists interested in criminology study to what extent damage, deficits, or abnormality of the brain may be related to antisocial behavior, particularly violent behavior. A traumatic brain injury (TBI), such as one that might occur in a traffic accident, may produce personality changes, including increased aggressive behavior (Gurley & Marcus, 2008). In early chapters of the book, we will learn that antisocial behavior can be reduced by practices and programs designed to improve neuropsychological functioning and prevent neuropsychological impairment early in life.

DEVELOPMENTAL APPROACH.   Learning how criminal behavior begins and progresses is extremely important. A **developmental approach** examines the changes and influences across a person's lifetime that may contribute to the formation of antisocial and criminal behavior. These are usually called "risk factors." Examples are poor nutrition, the loss of a parent, early school failure, or substandard housing. However, the developmental approach also searches for "protective factors," or influences that provide individuals with a buffer against the risk factors. A caring adult mentor and good social skills are examples of protective factors. If we are able to identify those changes and influences that occur across the developmental pathways of life that divert a person from becoming caring, sensitive, and prosocial, as well as those that steer a person away from a life of persistent and serious antisocial behavior, we gain invaluable information about how to prevent and change delinquent and criminal behavior.

TRAIT APPROACH.   In the past, psychologists assumed that they could best understand human behavior by searching for stable, consistent personality dispositions or traits that exerted widely generalized effects on behavior. A **trait** or **disposition** is a relatively stable and enduring tendency to behave in a particular way, and it distinguishes one person from another. For example, one person may be extroverted and have a consistent tendency to socialize and meet others, while another may be shy and introverted and demonstrate a tendency to socialize with only very close friends. In recent years, researchers (e.g., Frick & White, 2008) have given considerable attention to some traits—collectively termed "callous-unemotional traits"—that are often associated with psychopaths, individuals (see Chapter 7) who may (and may not) be responsible for many serious crimes. Callous-unemotional traits are characterized by a lack of empathy and concern for the welfare of others, and they often lead to a persistent and aggressive pattern of antisocial behavior. As noted above, self-control is another trait that has received considerable attention in the criminological world.

Trait theories hold that people show consistent behavior across time and place, and that these behaviors characterize personality. Many psychologists studying crime, therefore, assumed they should search for the personality traits or variables underlying criminal behavior. They paid less attention to the person's environment or situation. Presumably, once personality variables were identified, it would be possible to determine and predict which individual was most likely to engage in criminal behavior.

As you will learn, however, the search for any *single* personality type of the murderer, rapist, abuser, or burglar has not been fruitful. Contemporary perspectives in the psychology of crime still include personality or behavior traits in their explanations of crime, as we will see in our discussion of callous-unemotional traits, but they also include cognitions, neuropsychology, and developmental factors in these explanations. Thus, while trait psychology standing alone has lost favor, some aspects of this approach have survived.

Psychiatric Criminology

The terms "psychology" and "psychiatry" are often confused by the layperson and even by professionals and scholars in other disciplines. Many psychiatrists, like psychologists, work in a variety of settings that bring them into contact with persons accused of or convicted of crime. They assess defendants, provide expert testimony in court, and offer treatment in the community or in correctional facilities. Psychiatrists and psychologists who are closely associated with the courts and other legal arenas are often referred to as forensic psychiatrists or forensic psychologists.

Psychiatric concepts and theories are often believed to be accepted tenets in the field of psychology. However, the two professions often see things quite differently and approach explanations of criminal behavior along a different course. Part of this difference is due to the dissimilarity in the educational requirements for the two professions. Unlike psychologists, who have earned a PhD, a PsyD, or an EdD and who often complete specialized training in research and some area of psychology, psychiatrists first earn a medical degree (MD or a DO) and complete a medical internship, as other physicians do. Then, during an average four-year residency program in psychiatry, they receive specific training in psychiatry, often focusing on the diagnosis and treatment of individuals in forensic settings, such as court clinics or mental hospitals with special units for mentally disordered individuals accused of crime. Understandably, this medical training encourages a biochemical and neurological approach to explanations of human behavior, and this is often reflected in the psychiatric theories of criminal behavior.

By contrast, psychologists who are interested in being certified and licensed as a clinical or counseling psychologist receive a one-year internship focusing on clinical training which includes methods and techniques for the diagnosis and treatment of various psychological disorders. This clinical training is sometimes followed by a one- to three-year postdoctoral program—sometimes longer—focusing on both research and practice. The emphasis of this training is *usually* far more on the cognitive (thought processes), developmental, and learned behavior of human action and less on the biochemical or neurological influences. As we saw above, however, biology is receiving much more attention in the science of behavior, and increasingly more psychologists today pursue training that is more biologically focused. Clinical neuropsychologists, for example, receive extensive training in the neurological and cognitive aspects of injury and disease.

Psychiatrists are medical doctors and, by definition, are able to prescribe drugs, most often psychoactive drugs. Psychoactive drugs represent a group of drugs that have significant effects on psychological processes, such as emotions and mental states of well-being. Currently, a great majority of states in the United States do not extend such prescription privileges to psychologists. In 2002, New Mexico became the first state in the United States to allow psychologists with specified training to prescribe psychoactive drugs (drugs designed to treat psychological problems). Louisiana became the second state, in 2004; those qualified to prescribe are called "medical psychologists." In 2014, Illinois became the third state to extend limited prescription privileges to authorized clinical psychologists with advanced specialized training. The privileges are limited in that they cannot prescribe to children, adolescents, or adults aged 66 or older, or to certain groups of people, like pregnant women or persons with intellectual or developmental disabilities.

Psychologists in the military also have prescription privileges. Twelve states have *rejected* such privileges, however, and at this point there appears to be a lull in additional efforts to gain the privileges. The powerful medical establishment has often fought these prescription privileges, saying they would lead to abuse and would decrease the quality of patient care. Even psychologists themselves disagree on this issue, but surveys suggest that most are in favor of extending privileges to those who want them and are suitably trained, particularly because this would increase the availability of mental health services for individuals who might not otherwise access them (Ax et al., 2007; Baird, 2007). Nevertheless, some worry that this could lead to a heavier reliance on medication for the treatment of mental disorder than is warranted.

In past years, psychiatric criminology has *traditionally* followed the Freudian, psychoanalytic, or psychodynamic tradition. The father of the psychoanalytical theory of human behavior was the physician-neurologist Sigmund Freud (1856–1939), whose followers are called Freudians. Many contemporary psychoanalysts subscribe to a modified version of the orthodox Freudian position and are therefore called neo-Freudians. Still other psychoanalysts follow the tenets of Alfred Adler and Carl Jung, who broke away from Freud and developed different theories about the human condition. A very influential psychoanalyst in more recent times is Erik Erikson, who developed a theory of development that included eight sequential stages. According to Erikson, ego identity is gradually achieved by facing positive goals and negative risks during eight stages across the life span. The degree of achievement in ego identity—or the progress one has made in reaching the various stages—may influence the tendency to commit crime.

Contemporary psychiatrists interested in the study of criminal behavior are less likely to be psychoanalytic in orientation, however. Many are research based and work in teams with psychologists and other mental health professionals. Psychiatrists, with some exceptions (e.g., Szasz, 1974, and his followers), are heavily influenced by the medical model of mental illness. Most subscribe to diagnostic categories outlined in the *Diagnostic and Statistical Manual of Mental Disorders*, 5th edition *(DSM-5)* (American Psychiatric Association, 2013) or a similar categorical scheme, the *International Classification of Disease (ICD)*, published by the World Health Organization. As we will discuss in later chapters, some diagnoses are associated with specific types of crimes, but it should not be presumed that persons with these mental disorders are more crime prone than those not so diagnosed. Furthermore, when crime is committed by individuals with mental disorders, it is likely that—for most—other risk factors such as substance abuse or past violent behavior prior to mental disorder were present (Peterson, Skeem, Kennealy, Bray, & Zvonkovic, 2014). Researchers have estimated that less than 10 percent of the crime committed by mentally disordered individuals was a product of their illness (Peterson et al., 2014).

DEFINING AND MEASURING CRIME

As defined at the beginning of the chapter, crime is intentional behavior that violates a criminal code, intentional in that it did not occur accidentally or without justification or excuse. Since crime encompasses so many types of behavior, should we restrict ourselves to a legal definition and study only those individuals who have been convicted of behaviors legally defined as crime? Or should we include individuals who indulge in antisocial behaviors but have not been detected by the criminal justice system? Perhaps our study should include persons predisposed to be criminal—if such persons can be identified.

As a review of criminology textbooks and literature attests, there is no universal agreement as to what group or groups should be targeted for study. If we abide strictly by the legal definition of crime and base research and discussion only on those people who have committed crimes, do we consider only those who have been convicted and incarcerated or serving a sentence in the community, or do we include those who may have broken the criminal law but were only arrested, not convicted? While some of these individuals are "truly criminal," an undetermined number of others were arrested but were not truly guilty. And, as is becoming more apparent in recent years, the innocent are sometimes convicted and sent to prison. On the basis of new DNA evidence, for example, as of early 2014, 312 prisoners had been exonerated after being wrongfully convicted (Innocence Project, 2014). Eighteen of these individuals had been sentenced to death. And, how can we include individuals who violate the law but escape detection or those who come to the attention of law enforcement officials but are never arrested or charged because they receive favorable treatment? Finally, many actions that qualify as crimes are not handled by the criminal justice system for example, financial exploitation and even physical abuse of the elderly are often referred to social service agencies rather than to police.

In sum, trying to study crime and criminal behavior presents many problems for social scientists. The subjects of study are most typically captive, such as prisoners or delinquents in institutions. They are not necessarily representative of the true criminal population. Likewise, the universe of crime itself defies any attempt at determining "how much" occurs. As we see below, although various methods have been used to do this, none provides sufficient and comprehensive information.

With respect to obtaining data on the incidence, prevalence, and characteristics of crime, there are many pitfalls. Crime is usually measured in one of the following three ways, and none is perfect:

1. Official police reports of reported crime and arrests, such as those tabulated and forwarded to the Federal Bureau of Investigation (FBI) for publication in its annual national statistical report on crime, the **Uniform Crime Reports (UCR)** and its accompanying **National Incident-Based Reporting System (NIBRS)**
2. Self-report (SR) studies, whereby members of a sample population are asked what offenses they have committed and how often
3. National or regional victimization studies, which sample a population of households or businesses asking respondents whether and how often they have been victims of specified crimes

We provide a brief review of each of these methods, along with their strengths and shortcomings, below.

Uniform Crime Reporting System

The FBI's UCR compiled since 1930 is the most cited source of U.S. crime statistics. The UCR program publishes an annual document containing accounts of crimes known to police and information on arrests received on a voluntary basis from local and state law enforcement agencies throughout the United States. Monthly reports also are available. The UCR data can be found on the FBI website (www.fbi.gov). Interestingly, federal law enforcement agencies do not report through the traditional UCR Program, but they do through the NIBRS, to be described below.

The UCR program is the only major data source permitting a comparison of national data broken down by age, sex, race, and offense. Its main component is the summary reporting system (SRS), which provides basic statistics on crimes that are of most concern. A *Supplementary Homicide Report* contains data on victim and offender demographics, the offender–victim relationship, the weapon used, and the circumstances surrounding the homicide. Additionally, the FBI provides special reports, such as those on hate crimes mentioned in **Box 1-1**, campus crimes, and law enforcement officers killed in the line of duty. A special report was also prepared to cover the events of September 11, 2001. (See **Figure 1-1** for additional information on bias-motivated crimes.)

The UCR provides a variety of information relating to crimes that come to the attention of police, along with the city and region where the crime was committed. Arrest data include the age, gender, and race of persons arrested. Crimes are divided into two major groups, which until recently were referred to as Part I and Part II crimes. Although that designation has been de-emphasized in the latest FBI reports, we continue to use it periodically, including in some tables, because it is a convenient way to distinguish the offenses and the data that are gathered for each group. Until approximately 2004, the crimes in the first group were also called index crimes. They are divided into violent and property offenses. (See **Table 1-3** for definitions of these eight crimes as well as other common crimes.)

Violent crime comprises four offenses: murder and nonnegligent manslaughter, rape, robbery, and aggravated assault. As noted in **Table 1-3**, the definition of rape has been broadened to specify particular actions and to include males as victims. Because the change is so recent, some law enforcement agencies still used the old or "legacy" definition in reporting crimes—so it is important to keep this in mind when assessing UCR data related to this crime.

The property crimes are burglary, larceny-theft, motor vehicle theft, and arson. The primary objective of the offender in property crime is the taking or destruction of money or property. Arson is included in property crime because it involves the destruction of property, but it may result in the loss of life or serious injury. It should be noted that only arsons that were known to be willfully or maliciously set are included; fires of suspicious origins are not.

For these eight crimes, the UCR provides information on the crime known to police (reported crime or crimes they have observed in progress), as well as arrests. Only arrest data are provided for

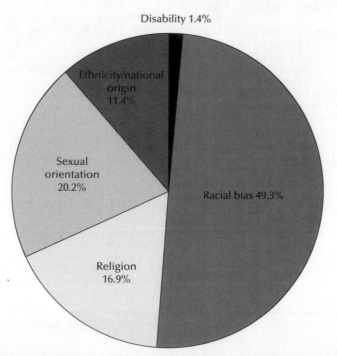

FIGURE 1-1   Percentage Distribution of Bias-Motivated Offenses, 2013   *Source*: Federal Bureau of Investigation (2014a). Crime in the United States 2013: Uniform Crime Reports. Washington, DC: U.S. Department of Justice.

TABLE 1-3	Definitions of Violent, Property, and Various Common Crimes in the Uniform Crime Reports, 2014

Violent Crimes	Definitions
Murder and nonnegligent manslaughter	The willful (nonnegligent) killing of one human being by another
Rape*	Penetration, no matter how slight, of the vagina or anus with any body part or object, or oral penetration by a sex organ of another person, without the consent of the victim. This includes the offenses of rape, sodomy, and sexual assault with an object. Fondling, incest, and statutory rape are included in a separate category, crimes against persons, other.
Robbery	The taking or attempting to take anything of value from the care, custody, or control of a person or persons by force or threat of force or violence and/or by putting the victim in fear
Aggravated assault	An unlawful attack by one person on another for the purpose of inflicting severe or aggravated bodily injury; attempts to inflict injury are also included

Property Crimes	Definitions
Motor vehicle theft	The theft or attempted theft of a motor vehicle, defined as self-propelled vehicle that runs on land and not on rails. It includes sport utility vehicles, automobiles, trucks, buses, motorcycles, motor scooters, all-terrain vehicles, and snowmobiles.
Burglary	The unlawful entry of a structure to commit a felony or theft
Larceny-theft	The unlawful taking, carrying, leading, or riding away with of property from the possession or constructive possession of another; includes crimes such as shoplifting, pocket picking, purse snatching, thefts from motor vehicles, and bicycle thefts
Arson	Any willful or malicious burning or attempt to burn, with or without intent to defraud, a dwelling house, public building, motor vehicle or aircraft, or personal property of another

Other Common Offenses**	Definitions
Simple assault	Assault and attempted assault in which no weapon is used and which does not result in serious or aggravated injury to victim
Forgery and counterfeiting	Making, altering, uttering, or possessing, with intent to defraud, anything false in the semblance of that which is true
Fraud	Fraudulent conversion and obtaining money or property by false pretenses
Embezzlement	Misappropriation or misapplication of money entrusted to one's care, custody, or control
Stolen property	Buying, receiving, and possessing stolen property, including attempts to do so
Offenses against the family and children	Unlawful nonviolent acts by a family member that threaten the physical, mental, or economic well-being or morals of another family member; does not include assault or sex offenses
Sex offenses	Statutory rape, fondling, and incest
Drug abuse violations	State and/or local offenses relating to the unlawful possession, sale, use, growing, and manufacture of drugs
Gambling	Promoting, permitting, or engaging in illegal gambling
Vandalism	Willful or malicious destruction, injury, disfigurement, or defacement of any public or private property, real or personal, without the consent of the owner or persons having custody or control

Source: Federal Bureau of Investigation (2014a). Crime in the United States 2013: Uniform Crime Reports. Washington, DC: U.S. Department of Justice.

*This is the new definition of rape, adopted for the current UCR. The previous definition, which is now referred to as the "legacy definition," was called forcible rape (to distinguish it from statutory rape) and was limited to rape of females.

**This is not an inclusive list.

other crimes, such as those included in **Table 1-3** under other common offenses. In order to appear in the UCR as one of the eight dominant, a crime must, at a minimum, meet the following requirements:

- Be experienced by the victim or observed by someone else
- Be defined as a crime by the victim or the observer
- In some way become known to a law enforcement agency as a crime
- Be defined by that law enforcement agency as a crime
- Be accurately recorded by the law enforcement agency
- Be reported to the FBI compilation center

It should be emphasized that the UCR provides *crime rate* data on only these eight crimes. The **crime rate** is the percentage of crime known to police per 100,000 population. For example, in 2013, the murder rate was 4.5, meaning there were 4.5 murders known to police for every 100,000 population. Because the UCR keeps track of trends in offending, the FBI was able to report that the 2013 murder figure represented an 18.3 percent decrease since 2004 (Federal Bureau of Investigation, 2014a). The decrease in crime since 2004 is found for all major crimes, a fact that often does not come to public attention. The decrease in crime is even more noticeable when we compare recent data to statistics from the early 1990s, a high-crime period in the United States.

For all offenses other than the eight listed above, only arrest data are included in the UCR. For example, if a victim reports a simple assault but no perpetrator is located, that assault would not be included in the *crime rate*. However, the *arrest* of one or more individuals for that simple assault would appear in the UCR. Note that an *aggravated* assault would be included in the crime rate.

On a regular yearly basis, if we look at crimes known to police, the property crime of lar-ceny-theft, which usually comprises approximately 60 percent of the Part I crimes, is the most frequently occurring of the eight offenses (see **Figure 1-2**). The violent crime of murder occurs the least frequently, accounting for only 0.1 percent of the total for these eight crimes. In addition, again looking at crimes known to police, recent data indicate that in 2013 violent crimes were down 14.5 percent from 2004, and the property crime rate was 22.3 percent below the 2004 rate (Federal Bureau of Investigation, 2014a). These are of course national figures. If we examine UCR

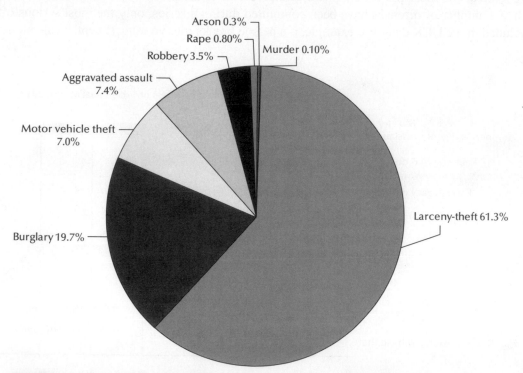

FIGURE 1-2 Percentage Distribution of Violent and Property Crimes, 2013
Source: Federal Bureau of Investigation (2014a). Crime in the United States 2013: Uniform Crime Reports. Washington, DC: U.S. Department of Justice.

breakdowns for different regions or metropolitan areas, we see variations in crime rates and trends. For example, murder rates in many major cities increased in 2015.

The UCR also reports the **clearance rate** of all eight major crime categories. An offense is cleared when at least one person is arrested, charged with the commission of the offense, and remanded to the court for prosecution. An offense may also be cleared by exceptional means when something happens to an offender outside the control of the reporting law enforcement agency. For example, if a person about to be arrested for rape commits suicide, the crime will likely be cleared. As another example, when a youth accused of burglary is cited to appear in juvenile court or before other juvenile authorities, the incident is considered cleared by arrest, even though a physical arrest may not have occurred. In 2013, 48.1 percent of violent crimes in the United States and 19.7 percent of property offenses were cleared by arrest or exceptional means. Usually, murder has the highest clearance rate. In 2013, law enforcement agencies cleared 64.1 percent of murders; by contrast, burglary and motor vehicle theft have low clearance rates (13.1% and 14.2%, respectively). (See **Figure 1-3** for illustrations of other clearance rates.)

Finally, arrest data should be distinguished from reported crime and clearance data. One crime may result in the arrest of five individuals, for example, or the arrest of one individual may clear or solve many crimes. An arrest is recorded for each separate instance in which a person is arrested, cited, or summoned for an offense, meaning that an actual physical taking into custody is not required. If a person turns himself in to police, this is counted as an arrest. In recent years, the highest number of arrests were for drug abuse violations and larceny-theft. Like crime rates, recent arrest trends show decreases in arrests of both juveniles and adults for violent crime and property crime.

UCR PROBLEMS.   Although it is not disputed that the crimes measured by the UCR have declined since the 1990s, it is also recognized that official statistics have always underestimated most criminal offenses. The overall number of criminal offenses that go undetected or are unknown by law enforcement agencies, known as the **dark figure**, is difficult to estimate. In addition, official data like the UCR program are routinely criticized for errors and omissions, so the data can be misleading. One of the most frequently mentioned problems is the **hierarchy rule**, which stipulates that when a number of offenses have been committed during a series, only the most serious offense is included in the UCR data. For example, if a person breaks into your apartment, steals money, kicks

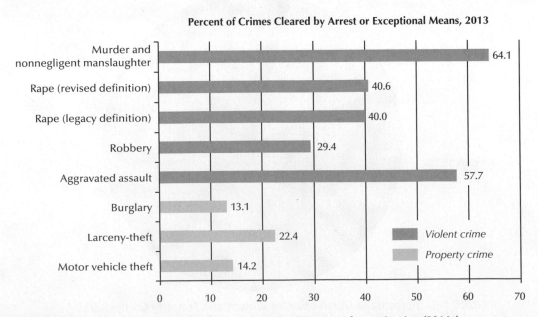

Percent of Crimes Cleared by Arrest or Exceptional Means, 2013

Murder and nonnegligent manslaughter	64.1
Rape (revised definition)	40.6
Rape (legacy definition)	40.0
Robbery	29.4
Aggravated assault	57.7
Burglary	13.1
Larceny-theft	22.4
Motor vehicle theft	14.2

Violent crime
Property crime

FIGURE 1-3   Clearance Rates 2013   *Source*: Federal Bureau of Investigation (2014a).

your cat, kills your roommate, and runs off in your car, only the murder will appear in the UCR. The exception to the hierarchy rule is arson, which is always reported even if accompanied by a violent offense (e.g., murder).

The compilation center also relies on the accuracy and compliance of local and state agencies to report crime statistics. When definitions of crimes change—such as the definition of rape described above—there is bound to be at least some temporary confusion in reporting instances. Partly in response to this, the most recent UCR often distinguishes between rape reported under the "legacy" definition and the new definition (Federal Bureau of Investigation, 2014a). UCR data also cannot take into account early discretionary decision making by law enforcement officers, such as a decision not to "found" a crime when it is reported by a member of the public or a decision not to arrest an individual. In addition, the major crime categories emphasize street crime to the neglect of the equally serious "white-collar" crime, which includes a wide variety of offenses such as corporate, political, and professional crimes. Very often these crimes are federal offenses and thus would not appear in the UCR. Finally, many crimes that fall under the general category of cybercrime or Internet-facilitated crime (see **Box 1-2**) do not appear in the UCR, primarily because they are federal offenses but also because they simply are not detected by the law enforcement community.

THE NATIONAL INCIDENT-BASED REPORTING SYSTEM (NIBRS). During the late 1970s, the law enforcement community called for the expanded use of the UCR and more detailed information on crime than the summary statistics offered in the UCR. In response, the NIBRS was initiated as a supplement to the UCR. Although the NIBRS was initially intended to replace the SRS, this has not yet happened, but progress has been made. The FBI reports that as of 2012, 15 states submit all of their crime data through NIBRS, and thirty-three state UCR programs are certified to submit in that matter (Federal Bureau of Investigation, 2014a). It is also important to note that federal law enforcement agencies are required to report crime data through NIBRS.

Through NIBRS, the FBI collects data on two categories of offenses: Group A, which includes 46 serious offense categories such as arson, assault, homicide, fraud, embezzlement,

CONTEMPORARY ISSUES

BOX 1-2   The Problem of Internet-Facilitated Crime

As noted in the chapter, the crime rate overall, including the violent crime rate, has declined since the mid-1990s. Some specific crimes, though, are on the increase. Included in this group are nontraditional crimes associated with technology, which often are not reflected in crime statistics. Attempts to obtain an accurate account of the crime picture are hampered by the limitations inherent in gathering information about these crimes. For example, authorities can only estimate the number of individuals whose credit card data have been compromised, or whose health data, including Social Security numbers, have been obtained illegally as a result of computer hacking.

In a 2014 interview, FBI Director James Comey pointed to the rise in Internet-based crime as the biggest change he has seen in recent years (Graff, 2014). Facilitated by the Internet, people across the globe have engaged in criminal activities across a wide range, including terrorist threats, fraudulent schemes, hacking, cyberstalking, distribution of child pornography, and human trafficking, to name but a few. Comey was quoted as saying, "That's where bad people come to do harm across those dimensions—people who want to hurt my kids, steal my identity, damage our infrastructure, steal our secrets"

(Graff, 2014, p. 4). And, in her first public speech after taking office in April 2015, U.S. Attorney General Loretta Lynch identified cybercrime as among the priorities to be addressed during her tenure.

Some of the crimes listed above (e.g., cyberstalking, accessing child pornography, hacking, and human trafficking) will be covered later in the book as we discuss psychological concepts that might help to explain them. Relevant to the measurement of crime covered in this chapter, however, it is important to be aware that these offenses are not likely to be adequately represented in statistics.

Questions for Discussion

1. Evaluate the following statement: It is not difficult to name crimes that are, or that can be, facilitated by the Internet; it is more of a challenge to name crimes that cannot be.
2. In the article cited above, the FBI director referred to the evil layer cake of Internet crime, placing the worst crimes at the top and the least serious at the bottom. Is this a good metaphor for Internet crime? If no, why not? If yes, how would you label each layer?

55555

larceny-theft, and sex offenses; and Group B, which includes 11 less serious offenses, such as passing bad checks, driving under the influence of alcohol, engaging in disorderly conduct, drunkenness, nonviolent family offenses, and liquor law violations (see **Table 1-4** for a list of Group A offenses). There is always danger in labeling crimes serious or not serious, however. Just from the above list, it is likely that readers may challenge some of the categorizations. The important thing to keep in mind is that the extent of the data gathered by the FBI differs according to the group in which the crime falls. Since its inception, NIBRS also has examined more closely bias crimes, the presence of gang activity in communities, crimes against law enforcement officers, and data on cargo theft (Federal Bureau of Investigation, 2014a).

TABLE 1-4 National Incident-Based Reporting System (NIBRS) Group A Offenses

Arson	Homicide offenses
Assault offenses	Murder/nonnegligent manslaughter
Aggravated assault	Negligent manslaughter
Simple assault	Justifiable homicide
Intimidation	Kidnapping/abduction
Bribery	Larceny-theft offenses
Burglary/breaking and entering	Pocket picking
Counterfeiting/forgery	Purse snatching
Destruction/damage/vandalism of property	Shoplifting
Drug/narcotic offenses	Theft from building
Drug/narcotic violations	Theft from coin-operated machines
Drug/equipment violations	Theft from motor vehicle
Embezzlement	Theft of motor vehicle parts/accessories
Extortion/blackmail	Motor vehicle theft
Fraud offenses	Pornography/obscene materials
False pretenses/swindle/confidence game	Prostitution offenses
Credit card/ATM fraud	Prostitution
Impersonation	Assisting or promoting prostitution
Welfare fraud	Robbery
Wire fraud	Sex offenses, forcible
Gambling offenses	Forcible rape
Betting/wagering	Forcible sodomy
Operating/promoting/assisting gambling	Sexual assault with an object
Gambling equipment violations	Forcible fondling
Sports tampering	Sex offenses, nonforcible
	Stolen property offenses
	Weapon law violations

Source: Based on information from *The National Center for the Analysis of Violent Crime, Annual Report, 1992* (Quantico, VA: FBI Academy, 1992), p. 22.

In the *Group A Incident Report* information, a crime is viewed along with all its aspects. For example, the report of a crime includes information about the victim, weapon, location of the crime, alcohol/drug influence, type of criminal activity, relationship of victim to alleged offender, residence of victims and arrestees (if someone was arrested), and a description of property and its value. Presumably, this added information is an indispensable tool for law enforcement agencies and researchers because it provides them with detailed data about when and where specific types of crime take place, what forms they take, and the characteristics of their victims and perpetrators. Reporting for Group B offenses is less detailed, reflecting the lesser degree of seriousness of these crimes.

Self-Report Studies

Many researchers believe that **self-report (SR) data** provide a more accurate estimate of actual offenses than do UCR or NIBRS statistics, which are based on data provided by law enforcement. In SR research, people report their own criminal or otherwise antisocial activity to researchers. Although respondents may inflate or deflate reports of their own criminal activity, proponents of this research strategy maintain that self-reporting offers a better approximation of criminal activity. Early SR surveys are often cited in criminology history (Short & Nye, 1957; Wallerstein & Wyle, 1947). Wallerstein and Wyle found that 91 percent of nearly 1,700 respondents admitted they had committed one or more offenses for which they might have received jail or prison sentences, with the average number of offenses for each person being 18. No one in the sample had served an actual prison sentence.

Short and Nye administered questionnaires to three thousand high school students and found that, across all socioeconomic classes, they, too, reported high incidences of unlawful behavior, although most of it was minor and not all qualified as crime. For example, one item included in their measure of delinquency was disobedience to parents; another referred to skipping school without a legitimate excuse. In the years since these earliest studies, researchers added more serious items, and generally have learned that violations of the law are common across all levels of society, though serious offending is less common.

Most SR investigations focus on delinquency rather than adult offending, however, and current studies focus primarily on risk-taking behaviors that are associated with physical or mental health. A study that is receiving extensive research attention is the National Longitudinal Study of Adolescent Health, which collected initial data on some 19,000 students in grades 7–12 at 132 schools. The self-reported information related to a variety of health issues, including those associated with criminal activity (e.g., illegal drug possession and use). A subgroup of the original participants, about 15,000, was recontacted as young adults. Several different studies were developed from the data obtained from this survey and will be mentioned in later chapters.

A recent federally funded study on dating behavior (Taylor & Mumford, in press) also used SR methodology. A nationwide sample of 667 youths aged 12–18 who dated during the past year responded online to questions about their relationships. The researchers found high levels of violence as well as psychological abuse in dating relationships, with a majority of both boys and girls describing themselves as both victims and perpetrators of abusive behavior. The abuse was primarily psychological—such as insults—but nearly 20 percent of the respondents said they were victims of physical and sexual abuse in their relationships.

With the exception of substance use, to be discussed below, studies of self-reported criminal activity are conducted primarily with adults who are incarcerated. Researchers often ask inmates about the extent of their past offending. Not all respondents are convicted individuals, however. In an early study of employee theft, for example, researchers found that about one-third of employees who returned surveys admitted to stealing from their employers (Hollinger, 1986). An SR survey of income tax evasion found 10 percent of the respondents admitting to cheating on their taxes (Tittle, 1980). College students also are often queried about their criminal behavior, including drug use and sexual assaults.

SR data are gathered through either interviews (personal or telephone) or questionnaires. Increasingly more are now collected online, which raises additional questions about validity.

Although a larger sample of respondents can be obtained, online responding presents challenges to quality control or, in research terminology, reliability and validity.

As another change, SR research is often imbedded in larger, longitudinal studies, where researchers follow up a group of individuals over many years and track both official contacts with police and their own self-reported illegal activity. A good example of this is the ADD-Health study mentioned above. Another is the Project on Human Development in Chicago Neighborhoods (PHDCN), which began in the 1990s and continues to this day (Sampson, 2012). Numerous studies have been published using data obtained from this project, which followed more than 6,000 children, adolescents, and young adults (e.g., Hawkins et al., 2009; Piquero, Farrington, & Blumstein, 2003).

Still, we must be careful about drawing far-reaching conclusions based on the information from SR research unless the nature of the questions is known, as well as who was asked, why, and how. Because some people arc likely not to be honest in reporting their own antisocial activities, we must be guarded in reviewing the data obtained from SR studies, perhaps most particularly those conducted over the Internet. The best studies recognize this problem themselves and include reliability checks in their methodology—such as by cross-checking the information against other sources. At this point, SR studies do suggest that minor criminal activity is extensive and widespread, at least among youth. Furthermore, SR studies continually show that the number of individuals involved in serious crimes is relatively small, but those few who do engage in serious criminal activity commit many crimes. Moreover, persistent, repetitive offenders do not specialize in any one crime (such as larceny) but show considerable versatility in criminal involvement, committing a wide variety of offenses, violent as well as nonviolent.

DRUG USE SELF-REPORT SURVEYS.   Several nationwide SR surveys collect data specifically on drug use and abuse in the United States. The major surveys are the National Survey on Drug Use and Health (NSDUH), formerly called the *National Household Survey on Drug Abuse (NHSDA)*; **Monitoring the Future (MTF)**; and the *Arrestees Drug Abuse Monitoring Program (ADAM and ADAM II)*.

NSDUH is an ongoing survey of a random sample of the noninstitutionalized population of the United States, 12 years old or older. The survey, sponsored by the federal government, is conducted by a private research firm that collects and analyzes the data and issues annual reports. Approximately seventy thousand individuals across the United States are asked about their use of tobacco, alcohol, illicit drugs, and mental health. Mental health questions are included in recognition that substance use and mental health are often related. Individuals are visited in their homes or in neutral locations, such as a community center. Those surveyed enter responses into a computer, and the answers are coded and amassed with other data shortly thereafter. Confidentially is assured and is guaranteed by federal law. The survey is intended to provide accurate data, track trends in drug and substance use, assess their consequences, and identify groups at risk for use and abuse. Data from the NSDUH are available on the Internet and are used extensively by academic researchers, journalists, and government agencies, as well as organizations dedicated to the prevention of substance abuse. The 2013 survey, for example, found that about 24.6 million people are current illicit drug users, including 2.2 million adolescents age 12–17. One in 10 adolescents reported a major depressive episode in the past year, and 1 in 5 adults said they had a mental illness.

MTF is a nationwide survey of eighth grade and high school students in the United States conducted at the Institute for Social Research at the University of Michigan and sponsored by research grants from the National Institute of Drug Abuse. Each year, since 1991, about fifty thousand 8th, 10th, and 12th grade students are surveyed. MTF also conducts a follow-up survey of a sample of each graduating class for a number of years after their initial participation, so that college students and young adults are represented in the data. The mission of MTF is to predict future trends of drug abuse based on current youth drug use. Current data indicated that 1 in 20 college students reported that they got high or near high daily on marijuana, indicating that marijuana remains the highest second used substance by young people besides alcohol

(Johnston, O'Malley, Miech, Bachman, & Schulenberg, 2015). We describe these surveys and their informative results in more detail in Chapter 16.

The ADAM II is a continuation of a National Institute of Justice program—ADAM—that collected data from adult males and females who were arrested in 35 sites in the United States between 2000 and 2003, when it was terminated for lack of funding. In 2007, ADAM II, sponsored by the federal Office of National Drug Control Policy (ONDCP), took up the data collection, focusing on 10 sites. The ADAM II utilizes both urinalysis and self-report data to identify the level of recent drug use by the arrestees. The individuals arrested provide information about the types of drugs they use, as well as how they obtained them. The urinalysis provides a validity check on the openness of the arrestees in providing information about their drug abuse. Urine specimens are analyzed for the presence of 10 drugs. The ADAM projects, both ADAM and ADAM II, offer invaluable insight into drug use of persons arrested in representative areas of the country. Again, latest findings are discussed in Chapter 16.

Victimization Surveys

Additional sources of data on offending are victimization surveys, in which victims provide information on the crimes committed against them. The main source of victimization data on crime is the **National Crime Victimization Survey** (NCVS), originally called the National Crime Survey (NCS). Workers for the Bureau of the Census interview—in person or by phone—a large national sample of households (approximately 42,000) representing over 76,000 persons over the age of 12. The same households are interviewed every six months for a period of three years, and during each session, they are asked about crime they had experienced over the past six months. Persons living in group quarters such as dormitories, rooming houses, and religious group dwellings are included, but persons in institutions or in military barracks are not. Crimes committed against children below age 12 are not counted for privacy reasons and because the designers of the survey believe that younger respondents, compared with adults, are not as likely to provide accurate information. Additionally, because young children may be victims of crime within their own households, the topic would be too sensitive to broach. The NCVS provides the largest national forum for victims to describe the impact of crime and characteristics of violent offenders. Its reports, including detailed information about the methodology used to conduct the interviews and analyze the data, are available on the Bureau of Justice Statistics (BJS) website, http://www.bjs.gov.

The survey is currently designed to measure the extent to which households and individuals are victims of rape and other sexual assault, robbery, aggravated assault, simple assault, household burglary, motor vehicle theft, and theft. It also provides many details about the victims (such as age, race, sex, marital status, education, income, and whether the victim and the offender were related to each other) and about the crimes themselves. Recent versions of the NCVS also ask respondents whether they perceived they were victims of a hate crime. Among other things, the NCVS interviewer wants to know the following about all victimization:

- Exactly what happened
- When and where the offense occurred
- Whether any injury or loss was suffered
- Whether the crime was reported to the police and, if not, why
- The victim's perception of the offender's gender, race, and age

According to the NCVS, victimization incidents have decreased in recent years (see, generally, BJS, 2012). In 2009, about five and one half million total violent victimizations were experienced, while just under 5 million were experienced in 2010. By far the greatest number was for simple assault, with about three and a half million experienced in 2009 and 3,241,148 in 2010.

There are several possible explanations for these downward trends. The most optimistic is that victimizations are indeed decreasing, which in itself could be attributed to numerous factors. As reported earlier in the chapter, crime rates themselves have fallen quite dramatically since the early 1990s high-crime era. However, many crime victims continue to be reluctant to report victimizations to police, to workers from the Census Bureau (which conducts the NCVS), or to private researchers. Again, there are numerous reasons for this: They may know who victimized them and not wish to implicate the individual; they may fear retribution from the perpetrator; they may not want the attention; they may be embarrassed; they may not trust the agents of government; they may believe nothing can be done. In recent years, many undocumented workers have been reluctant to come forward and report victimization out of fear of being deported.

The NCVS data consistently show demographic differences in victimization rates. Males and American Indian or Alaskan Natives are victims of violent crime at rates greater than those of whites and persons of other races (Rennison & Rand, 2003; Truman, 2011). (See **Table 1-5**.) For the first time since the NCVS began reporting victimizations by sex, males and females had similar rates of victimization. Persons of age group 12–24 sustain violent victimization at rates higher than individuals of all other ages, with the 18–20 age group being especially vulnerable. Persons of age group 18–20 experienced overall violence, rape/sexual assault, and assault at rates higher than rates for persons in other age categories. However, we also know that much abuse suffered by certain populations—such as younger children, the elderly, transgender individuals, undocumented immigrants, the intellectually disabled—is hidden. These patterns have continued in recent years, as we will see later in the book when specific crimes are covered.

TABLE 1-5   Violent Victimizations per 1,000 Persons Age 12 or Older

Demographic Characteristics of Victim	Total	Rape/Sexual Assault	Robbery	Aggravated Assault	Simple Assault
Total	14.9	0.7	1.9	2.8	9.5
Sex					
Male	15.7	0.11	2.4	3.4	9.7
Female	14.2	1.3	1.4	2.3	9.2
Race/Hispanic Origin					
White	13.6	0.7	1.4	2.6	9.0
Black	20.8	1.11	3.6	4.7	11.4
Hispanic	15.6	0.81	2.7	2.3	9.8
American Indian or Alaskan Native	42.2	0.0	4.3	19.5	18.3
Asian or Pacific Islander	6.3	0.6	1.1	0.5	4.0
Two or more races	52.6	1.2	8.0	8.5	34.9
Age (years)					
12–14	27.5	2.7	0.7	5.8	18.3
15–17	23.0	1.7	2.7	5.8	18.3
18–20	33.9	1.1	5.9	6.9	20.0
21–24	26.9	1.5	3.7	8.0	13.7
25–34	18.8	1.3	2.5	3.3	11.7
35–49	12.6	0.6	1.5	1.9	8.6
50–64	10.9	0.0	1.3	2.1	7.6
65 or older	2.4	0.1	0.6	0.2	1.5

Source: Data derived from Truman (2011). Truman, J. L. (2011, September). National Crime Victimization Survey: Criminal Victimization, 2010. Washington, DC: U.S. Department of Justice, Bureau of Justice Statistics.

Relationship patterns are also important in understanding victimization, particularly violent victimization. Females are most often victimized by someone they know, while males are more likely to be victimized by strangers (Rennison & Rand, 2003; Truman, 2011). Female victims report that most offenders are friends and acquaintances, followed by intimate partners or former intimates (Catalano, 2013). By contrast, male victims report that strangers are the most likely perpetrators, followed by friends or acquaintances. Very few males report being victimized by intimate partners. These patterns have been consistent, varying slightly from survey to survey. Specific statistics will be provided in later chapters.

As suggested above, a good amount of victimization occurs at the hands of intimate partners. In 2000, Rennison and Welchans noted that every year, about 1 million violent crimes are committed against persons by their current or former spouses, boyfriends, or girlfriends. This **intimate partner violence (IPV)** is committed primarily against women. Black women are subject to intimate partner violence at a rate 35 percent higher than white women and approximately 2.5 times higher than the rate for women of other races. However, other group variations might be important to consider as well. For example, women in many ethnic groups are reluctant to report such violence, as we will learn in Chapter 9. In addition, spouses or partners of abusers who work in law enforcement or professional sports or are otherwise in the public eye may resist bringing attention to this crime.

The NCVS, similar to all national surveys, has its problems in accurately portraying victimization data. In addition to reluctance to report their victimization, some individuals may not be truthful or may recall victimization that may have occurred outside of the time period being studied. Other people are not represented in the data because they are homeless or live in institutional settings that may not be reached by the researchers (Rennison & Welchans, 2000).

Despite their shortcomings, victimization surveys are considered a good source of information about crime incidents, independent of data collected by law enforcement agencies throughout the country. Often the offending trends reported through NCVS data procedures differ substantially from those found in police data (Ohlin & Tonry, 1989). Although we have focused on the government-conducted NCVS to illustrate victimization data, be aware that independent researchers also survey victims of crime, often with grants from government agencies or private foundations. One noteworthy example is the National Violence Against Women Survey, conducted by the Center for Policy Research (Tjaden, 1997), which included an examination of the extent and nature of violence and stalking in American society. That survey and others like it will be covered later in the text.

JUVENILE DELINQUENCY

The definitions of crime and the methods of gathering crime data discussed above relate to both adults and juveniles. Like adult crime, juvenile crime overall has decreased since the 1990s. As we will learn in Chapter 6, which is devoted exclusively to juvenile delinquency, juveniles do commit a disproportionate amount of crime, but it is not necessarily the most serious offenses. The school shootings by juveniles that are depicted in the media are tragic but atypical. Furthermore, crimes committed by juveniles may be treated very differently from those committed by adults. In addition to the focus on delinquency in Chapter 6, we include special sections devoted to juvenile offenders and victims in other chapters. At this point, however, it is important to mention a few other preliminary distinctions.

First, not all offenses committed by juveniles are technically crimes. Some behaviors—referred to as juvenile **status offenses**—are forbidden only to juveniles because of their age. The prime examples are running away from home, curfew violations, underage drinking, skipping school on a regular basis (truancy), and—in some states—"incorrigibility." Many criminologists argue that juvenile-status offenses should not be criminalized in the same way that true crimes are for various reasons. For example, status offenses label children delinquents for behavior that is not harmful to others, and they are often indicative of problems in the child's environment (e.g., the runaway child may be running away from victimization). Other criminologists argue that it is important to keep track of status offenders in order to provide them with help that they may need; additionally, some, though not all, status offenders commit "real crimes" like burglary and theft. What to do with status offenders is a controversial area, as we will see in Chapter 6.

Another distinction between adult and juvenile criminal behavior is that data gathering on juvenile offending is even more imperfect than data gathering on adult crime. The nature and extent of delinquent behavior—both what is reported and what is unreported to law enforcement agencies—is essentially an unknown area (Krisberg, 1995). Nonetheless, information from a variety of sources, including the UCR, self-report, court records, and data from juvenile corrections, provides us some insight into the nature and extent of juvenile offending.

Third, much of the crime (and status offenses) committed by juveniles may be regarded as a "rite of passage" to adulthood. Self-report data indicate that offending among juveniles is more widespread than among adults but—as with adult offending—most people eventually stop. In the case of juveniles, most stop committing crime once they reach adulthood and have a stake in prosocial behavior. Juveniles may act out in high school or slightly beyond, but then they get full-time jobs, go to college, enter into significant relationships, get married, or join the military. It is common to assert, then, that most juveniles age out of crime. From a psychological perspective, however, we need to be particularly concerned with two groups of juveniles: those who continue offending, particularly serious offending, well into their adult years; and those who commit a very serious crime during their juvenile years. The former group typically demonstrated problem behavior very early in their lives. The latter group—those who commit a one-time, very serious offense—receives extensive media attention (e.g., juvenile school shooters, or juvenile murderers), but this type of one-time offending is rare. Continued serious offending, though, is more problematic. Many theories of crime describe antisocial behavior as having its origins in childhood. Over the past few decades, developmental psychologists in particular have conducted extensive research on children and adolescents who begin offending early and continue into adulthood. This is the main topic of Chapter 2.

RECAP: DEFINING CRIME AND DELINQUENCY

A major challenge faced by the authors in preparing this book has been striking the balance between antisocial behavior and criminal behavior, or between antisocial individuals and legally defined criminals. Some scholars have long argued (e.g., Sellin, 1970; Tappan, 1947)—and the law agrees—that one who engages in undetected criminal activity is not a criminal in the strictest or operational sense, because a criminal is by definition one who has been detected, arrested or cited to appear in court, and convicted. However, from a psychological point of view, we encounter problems when we limit ourselves to studying persons legally defined as criminals or behavior legally defined as crime. Legal classifications are determined by that which society, at some point in time, considers socially harmful. It may or may not also be considered morally wrong. Therefore, because each society has a different and changing set of values, what may be judged a criminal act in one may not meet the criteria in another or even in the same society at a later time. Many states in the United States differ significantly in their criminal codes and are continually revising them. This is illustrated by the patchwork of marijuana legislation: Some states allow the drug for medicinal purposes, some have decriminalized its possession in small amounts, and a few allow it to be purchased legally for recreational use. Illegal gambling, prostitution, and dissemination of obscene material are examples of other activities that generate ever-changing statutes. In recent years, use of handheld cell phones or text messaging while driving has been banned in some jurisdictions, with criminal penalties sometimes prescribed. Although we do not condone text messaging while driving, we are not interested in focusing on the psychology of the text messager. The more serious crimes, those we are most concerned with in this text, are more likely to be universally recognized as unacceptable. Nevertheless, we also pay attention to offenses that may not be seen as universally serious or even wrong, but that can have psychological implications for offenders and victims. Shoplifting and minor fraud are examples.

Furthermore, members of every society (and consequently every society's legal system) perceive and process violators of the criminal code with some disparity, so that the offender's background, economic circumstances, social status, personality, motivation, sex, age, race, ethnicity, and legal counsel, as well as the circumstances surrounding the offense, may all affect the criminal justice process. Few of us would dispute the observation that selective enforcement of the law is a reality. It is highly likely that individuals who have been arrested, convicted, and punished represent a distinctly different sample from those who participate in illegal activity but avoid detection, arrest, conviction, or punishment.

Approximately one-fifth of those arrested go to trial, according to Sarbin (1979), who describes the legal process of becoming labeled a criminal. First, the agents of social control (usually the police) identify the individual as a suspect. Next, they may decide that the suspect should be arrested. Third, the arrested party may be charged with a crime, at which point he or she becomes a defendant. Fourth, the defendant may plead guilty or be tried and convicted, at which point he or she becomes an offender (a felon or a misdemeanant, depending on the seriousness of the crime). Finally, the offender may be incarcerated in a correctional facility and be labeled a convict, inmate, prisoner, or criminal. Alternatively, the offender may be placed on probation, effectively serving a sentence in the community. At each step in the process, there is a funneling effect that shows that fewer and fewer individuals reach each subsequent step in the criminal justice process. This funneling process is prominently displayed in numerous criminal justice texts to illustrate how the system operates.

It is generally acknowledged, therefore, that those individuals sentenced to jail or prison are not representative of the "true" criminal population, because many true criminals go undetected and/or unpunished. Furthermore, as we have long suspected but only recently documented with the increasing availability of DNA evidence or reinvestigation of cases, convicted persons are not even necessarily true criminals (The Innocence Project, 2014). Yet, researchers studying the "criminal mind" often use as participants those individuals who have reached the final stage of the legal process—inmates in correctional institutions or convicted offenders serving their sentences in the community. Consequently, if we discuss only legally determined criminals, we will be neglecting a considerable segment of the population that actually breaks the law. To some extent, we have little choice but to do just that. Because this book is based on research, the kinds and amounts of available empirical data dictate to a great extent what will be covered.

Additionally, if we discuss only behavior that is legally defined as crime, we omit a sizable segment of behavior that is clearly relevant to our concerns. For example, a vast body of psychological research deals with topics like aggression and antisocial behavior. Because of their implications for the eventual development of behavior that is legally defined as crime, we will be covering these areas in the text.

The great majority of crime in the United States and other countries is not violent. In 2013, the highest numbers of arrests were for drug abuse violations, driving under the influence, and larceny-theft. The great majority of persons arrested are not serious offenders (Federal Bureau of Investigation, 2014a). Psychological criminology, however, is most concerned about the minority. Therefore, the main focus of the book is the persistent, repetitive *offender*—or the persistent, repetitive antisocial *behavior*—whether detected or undetected by the criminal justice system. In other words, in this text, we concentrate on the individual who has frequently committed serious crimes or antisocial acts over an extended period of time (at least several years). Nevertheless, we give attention to the one-time serious offender—the mass murderer, for example, or the juvenile offender who commits a heinous crime.

For all of the above reasons, many psychologists and other mental health professionals prefer the term "antisocial behavior" to "crime" or "criminal behavior" to refer to the more serious habitual actions that violate personal rights, laws, and/or widely held social norms. **Antisocial behavior** includes both the legal designations delinquency and criminal behavior, and the actions that violate standards of society but are not necessarily defined as crimes. Not all antisocial behavior is criminal. Furthermore, many antisocial behaviors that are criminal—probably most—go undetected. Consequently, we use antisocial behavior frequently throughout the text, especially when discussing the development of behavior that has not yet been legally designated delinquent or criminal behavior but is likely to lead to such designation. It should be mentioned that many psychologists also use the term "externalizing behavior" to refer to antisocial behavior, but—depending on the context—the term often has surplus meaning. For example, when some psychologists use the term, they intend to include a spectrum of behaviors such as delinquency, hyperactivity, acting out, hostility, aggression, and attention deficient/hyperactivity disorder. We prefer to use the more straightforward term "antisocial behavior" throughout the book. However, we will also cover—separately and in some detail—the other concepts often included in externalizing behavior.

SUMMARY AND CONCLUSIONS

Crime intrigues people, harms people, angers people, and sometimes amuses and entertains people. Overall, despite media accounts of sensational crimes, crime in the United States has fallen in the early years of the twenty-first century. This is good news, but it does not imply that efforts to reduce it further are not needed, nor can crime rates of the future be predicted with confidence. There is continuing need to study and prevent the behavior that is defined as criminal, but this is a complex undertaking. It involves theorizing, data gathering, and the development of strategies for its prevention and control, as well as treatment of individuals who engage in criminal activity.

This chapter introduces readers to the major theoretical viewpoints on crime and the dominant methods used to measure it. We have also discussed the difficulty in defining criminal behavior for purposes of examining it from a psychological perspective. Although criminology is an interdisciplinary enterprise, one that benefits from input from various disciplines, the approach in this text is predominantly psychological, with research and theory in that field emphasized throughout the book.

Theories of crime can be divided into classical and positivist schools. The classical school emphasizes free will as the primary cause of crime: Unless they are robbed of their free will (as by being seriously mentally disordered), people choose to commit criminal behavior. The positive school looks for determinants or influences over and above free will. According to those who adopt a positivist approach, people still choose to commit crime, but their choice is influenced by numerous predetermining factors. These may be in the social environment, such as a crime-ridden neighborhood or a deviant peer group, or within the individual, such as lack of empathy. Psychologists studying criminal behavior have focused primarily on the learning experiences or the cognitive constructs of people who commit crime, but in recent years some have focused on biological influences, including traumatic brain injuries or exposure to environmental contaminants. Developmental psychologists have studied the pathways various individuals take as they engage in and desist from antisocial behavior. All of these themes will be developed in the chapters ahead.

We reviewed the dominant methods of measuring crime, emphasizing that each has its strengths and weaknesses. The U.S. government's major measures—the summary system of the UCR and the NIBRS—are readily available in monthly reports. They allow us to conclude that crime rates have decreased dramatically since the high-crime era of the early and mid-1990s, though this is no reason for complacency. Victimization rates, measured by the NCVS as well as by nongovernmental surveys, also have decreased. Victimization data continually indicate that most crimes are never reported to police. Likewise, self-report data, in which people report their own offending, indicate that much criminal behavior is never unearthed. Thus, the "dark figure" of crime remains a reality. Early SR studies focused primarily on behavior of juveniles, but contemporary SR research tends to focus heavily on substance use and, to a lesser extent, violence in interpersonal relationships. Official, victimization, and SR data sources like the above will be revisited throughout the text as they relate to specific crimes.

Finally, we addressed briefly the topic of juvenile delinquency, which will be discussed in Chapter 6. Antisocial behavior by juveniles is not unusual and has at times been exaggerated in media accounts. Though juveniles are responsible for a disproportionate amount of crime, most of the crime they commit is nonviolent. Nevertheless, violent and other serious crimes by juveniles remain a concern and will be addressed in later chapters.

Key Concepts

Antisocial behavior
Classical theory
Clearance rate
Cognitions
Conformity perspective
Crime rate
Criminology
Dark figure
Deterrence theory
Developmental approach
Differential association theory
Falsification
General Theory of Crime
Hate Crime Statistics Act
Hierarchy rule
Intimate partner violence (IPV)
Just-world hypothesis
Learning perspective
Model

Monitoring the Future (MTF)
National Crime Victimization Survey (NCVS)
National Incident-Based Reporting System (NIBRS)
Nonconformist perspective
Positivist theory
Psychiatric criminology
Psychological criminology
Self-control theory
Self-report (SR) data
Social control theory
Social learning theory
Sociological criminology
Status offenses
Strain theory
Theory verification
Trait or disposition
Uniform Crime Reports (UCR)

Review Questions

1. Briefly explain the difference between psychological criminology and sociological criminology. How do these differ from a psychiatric approach to the study of criminal behavior?
2. Provide examples of crime control or crime prevention policies—other than those mentioned in the chapter—that are consistent with (a) classical theories of crime and (b) positivist theories.
3. Define and provide examples of the conformity, nonconformist, and learning perspectives of human nature.
4. Identify and provide one example of each of the three predominant methods of measuring crime.

5. How does the NIBRS differ from the UCR's Summary Report Statistics (SRS)?
6. List the strengths and weaknesses of self-report surveys.
7. What are status offenses and how do they differ from other juvenile offenses?
8. Compare and contrast the FBI's Uniform Crime Reports and the National Crime Victimization Survey, focusing on (a) how the data are obtained and (b) what type of information is available from each.

2

Origins of Criminal Behavior: Developmental Risk Factors

CHAPTER OBJECTIVES

- Introduce cumulative risk and developmental cascade models.
- Identify social, family, and psychological developmental risk factors that lead to delinquency and crime.
- Demonstrate how early preschool experiences can lead to a life of antisocial behavior.
- Emphasize the extensive influence of peer rejection on child and youth behavior.
- Stress the connection between cognitive abilities and delinquency and crime.
- Discuss attention deficit hyperactivity disorder (ADHD), conduct disorder (CD), and oppositional defiant disorder (ODD) as possible contributors to delinquent and criminal behavior.

As a preschooler, Trent was the child most known for shoving other children, stepping on their toes, and refusing to comply with the instructions of his teachers. In early grade school, he became the classroom bully; at age eight, he began to steal—from other children, from storekeepers, from teachers, and from his parents. By middle school, he was experimenting with alcohol and other drugs. He was suspended from high school on four separate occasions, all relating to violent behavior, and he dropped out at 16. Trent was convicted of robbery at age 19.

Antisocial behavior, including criminal behavior, in adults can often be traced to their childhoods. If we look back at the childhoods of chronic offenders, for example, we typically see signs portending problems in adulthood, although this is not invariably so. As noted in Chapter 1, many theories of criminology propose that the roots of serious criminal behavior appear in childhood or early adolescence. This highlights the importance of identifying both factors that put children at risk of becoming antisocial and those that might protect otherwise vulnerable children from this fate.

Each person follows a **developmental pathway**, the characteristics of which often can be identified at a very early age. The developmental perspective views the life course of all humans as following a path (or trajectory) that may be littered with risk factors. Some risk factors can be described as experiences that are common in the background of many repeat offenders, such as school failure, abuse of alcohol, antisocial peers, or childhood victimization. Some experts believe that the more risks a person is exposed to, the greater is the probability that person will participate in antisocial behavior throughout his or her lifetime (Wasserman & Seracini, 2001). In studies of both adult and juvenile offenders, researchers have identified a number of distinct pathways, which we will cover in later chapters. For example, some children follow a pathway leading to serious delinquency and crime, while others follow one that may lead to only minor juvenile offending which stops as they approach adulthood. Some children display antisocial behavior early; others wait until adolescence. For some children, there is no offending at all.

Contemporary researchers also stress the value of a nurturing environment to protect children against the onslaught of potential risk factors in their lives (Biglan, Flay, Embry, & Sandler, 2012). They identify protective factors, which are characteristics or experiences that can shield children from serious antisocial behavior. Warm and caring parents and a high-quality educational experience are examples. In general, a nurturing and healthy environment minimizes biologically and socially toxic conditions that influence healthy development (Biglan et al., 2012). Though we recognize the importance of protective factors, the goal in this chapter is to identify the origins and causes of delinquency and criminal behavior; thus, the focus is on factors that place individuals at risk for offending.

The risk factors we are most concerned with in this chapter are the social, family, and psychological experiences that are believed to increase the probability that an individual will engage in persistent criminal behavior. In Chapter 3 we will focus again on individual attributes, but they will be largely biologically based. Examples of *social risk factors* are poverty and limited resources, antisocial peers, peer rejection, and preschool or school experiences. *Parental and family risk factors* include faulty or inadequate parenting, sibling influences, and child maltreatment or abuse. Examples of *psychological risk factors* are inadequate cognitive and language ability, lack of empathy, poor interpersonal and social skills, and behavioral disorders. Psychological risk factors that are more biologically based, such as a troublesome temperament or prenatal exposure to neurotoxins, will be discussed in Chapter 3.

It is important that we learn about these risk factors and how they influence the developmental pathway, especially during the early stages of development. Early identification will help improve the effectiveness of prevention and intervention programs designed to eliminate or, at least, reduce delinquent and criminal behavior. As noted by Terrie Moffitt (2005a), we know that certain risk factors are closely linked to delinquency and criminal behavior, but how or why they are linked is largely unknown.

We must be careful not to imply that all criminal behavior has its origins in childhood, however. Pathways researchers emphasize that some individuals begin their criminal offending in adulthood (Farrington, Ttofi, & Cold, 2009) and that this may or may not be precipitated by childhood experiences. For example, some researchers have documented a pathway consisting of adult-onset female offenders whose criminal careers began when they engaged in dysfunctional relationships with male offenders (Salisbury & Van Voorhis, 2009). Nonetheless, risk factors are so often present in the childhoods of both juvenile and adult offenders that we must give them careful attention. It should be emphasized though, that *it is unlikely that any single risk factor, by itself, causes antisocial, aggressive, or violent behavior*. This leads us to a discussion of two main models used to explain how risk factors might operate.

CUMULATIVE RISK MODEL

Researchers are beginning to understand that exposure to *multiple risk factors* is most likely to increase the probability that a child, adolescent, or adult develops antisocial behavior and other maladaptive behaviors (Evans, Li, & Whipple, 2013). "Probably the most important reason for the widespread use of multiple risk factor metrics in developmental psychology today is the robust finding that multiple relative to single risk exposures have worse developmental consequences" (Evans et al., 2013, p. 1343). For example, living in poverty is a recognized risk factor, but poverty alone does not "cause" antisocial behavior. Most poor children are not antisocial. However, living in poverty can encompass a spectrum of other risk factors ranging from environmental risk factors (e.g., substandard housing and education, exposure to chemical toxins, high-crime neighborhoods) to psychosocial risk factors, such as exposure to violence, parental substance abuse, parental discord, and separation or divorce. Note that these psychosocial factors also can be present in the lives of children from economically advantaged families. "All these factors affect a child's development and the confluence of risk factors has been shown to have higher explanatory power compared to individual risk factors considered in isolation" (Doan, Dich, & Evans, 2014, p. 1402).

The **cumulative risk (CR) model** is favored by many developmental researchers, who believe that this accumulation of risk factors in the absence of sufficient protective factors results in negative behavioral, emotional, and cognitive outcomes (Doan, Fuller-Rowell, & Evans, 2012; Rutter, 1979). Furthermore, the CR model predicts that the greater the number of risks experienced by a child or adolescent, the greater the prevalence of mental health, cognitive deficits, and behavioral problems they may have (Whitson, Bernard, & Kaufman, 2013). It is the number of different risk factors experienced that is important. As mentioned by Evans et al. (2013), "[b]ecause of its simplicity (simply count the number of risk factors), the CR metric is readily understood and easily communicated to laypersons and policymakers" (p. 1386). In addition, some researchers prefer to represent cumulative risk as an index. As noted by Wade and his associates (in press), for example, "[c]umulative risk indices have been constructed to test the idea that development is affected by the accumulation of environmental risks rather than the level of a single and specific risk" (italics in original quote, p. 12). There is a good amount of empirical evidence that these indices are useful for identifying social risks that affect developmental patterns, including antisocial behavior (Wade et al., in press). The total number of risks identified and added essentially form the index. Because multiple risk exposure nearly always has greater impact than single risk exposure, the identification of children who encounter multiple risks during early development is likely to reveal those most in need of intervention services (Evans et al., 2013).

As stated above, protective factors can dampen the effect of risk factors. Supportive caretakers and healthy school environments are examples of protective factors. Many children raised in high-crime neighborhoods, even when other risk factors are present, have become successful adults with the help of loving parents and encouraging teachers. Consequently, researchers have focused in recent years on exploring the effectiveness of protective factors in mitigating or eliminating the negative influences of risk factors (Whitson et al., 2013).

DEVELOPMENTAL CASCADE MODEL

A similar but more complicated model is the **developmental cascade model** (also known as the **dynamic cascade model**), which was first introduced by several developmental psychologists but perhaps most prominently by Kenneth Dodge et al. (2008) and Ann Masten (2006, 2014). Like the cumulative risk model, it has significantly changed the way researchers look at the causes of antisocial behavior and, most particularly, of aggression and violent behavior. Although the dynamic cascade model could be considered a form of cumulative risk model because it refers to multiple risks, it is distinct in that it emphasizes the *interaction* among risk factors and their effect on outcomes over the course of development (see **Table 2-1**). According to the cascade model, the person's developmental skills or deficits enhance, affect, or determine the next skill or deficit

TABLE 2-1 Key Aspects of Cumulative Risk and Developmental Cascade Models

Cumulative Risk Model	Developmental Cascade Model
Also called multiple risk model	Also called dynamic cascade model
Predicts negative emotional and mental health outcomes in the life span	Predicts negative behavioral outcomes in the life span but also predicts positive outcomes
Additive approach in assessing overall effects of risks in development	Interactive approach in assessing effects of risks in developmental pathways
Focuses on the harmful environmental, psychological, and social influences which heighten the risk of maladaptive development	Focuses on the development of competence and resilience to reduce maladaptive development
Emphasizes identification of children confronted by multiple risk factors and development of ways to reduce those factors	Emphasizes well-timed and targeted interventions designed to promote positive cascades through development of competence and resilience

along a life-course trajectory. The term "snowballing" could also be used to describe the cascading effect. The cascade and the cumulative models both argue that early negative experiences can alter a child's developmental trajectory and interfere with accomplishment of normal developmental milestones, such as the formation of peer relationships, interpersonal skills, academic achievement, and cognitive development (Lynne-Landsman, Bradshaw, & Ialongo, 2010). However, the developmental cascade model also focuses heavily on the development and enhancement of positive cascades.

Although the cascade model initially focused on children from low-income families, it is now applied across the economic spectrum. To illustrate, the model starts with children who are born into a family where parents are absent or uncaring or may lack parenting skills. In an effort to control their young children, they resort to harsh or inconsistent discipline. Harsh and inconsistent parental disciplinary strategies have a high risk of preventing the child from acquiring social and cognitive skills that are necessary for school social and academic success. "These skill deficits include vocabulary deficits, poor social problem solving, hostile attributional biases, and emotion recognition deficits" (Dodge et al., 2008, p. 1921). Note that the above can occur regardless of the parents' economic situation.

Lacking the necessary social and academic skills to achieve during the early school years, the child begins to show conduct problems soon after entry into school, signaling the early start of antisocial behavior across the life course. Next in the cascade is school social and academic failure as a result of disinterest in school, which may or may not be accompanied by conduct disorder (CD), which we discuss later in the chapter. Rejection by prosocial peers—a factor also to be covered shortly—sets in during this time. As the youth approaches early adolescence, parental monitoring of his or her activities and whereabouts is virtually nonexistent, accelerating academic failure and poor relationships with nondelinquent peers. Consequently, deviant peer associates become important and highly influential, and this often leads to persistent antisocial and violent behavior.

The Dodge et al. research team was also able to determine that girls follow largely similar developmental pathways as boys. The researchers did recognize that males are more likely than females to become seriously violent due to biological and socialization differences. However, they found little evidence to support the view that females as a group, when they do engage in violent behavior, take a different developmental path from males. In other words, they did not find a gender-specific developmental pathway. The pathway was similar, but the type of antisocial behavior displayed was not.

After describing the dynamic cascade model, Dodge and his associates (2008) conclude with this crucial statement:

> An important implication of the current findings is that it is premature to conclude that an early-starting antisocial 5-year-old is unequivocally destined for a life persistent path toward violent outcomes. Although the risk is substantial, it is by no means certain. The findings reported here indicate that trajectories can be deflected at each subsequent era in development, through interactions with peers, school, and parents along the way. (p. 1922)

Both the cumulative risk and developmental cascade models provide targets for intervention and prevention at specific periods in development, and both stress the importance of protective factors. Teaching effective parenting skills or offering after-school drop-in centers are examples of intervention. A supportive extended family is an example of a protective factor. However, because new risks arise with each developmental period, prevention and intervention cannot be deemed completed until the child passes through adolescence.

The developmental cascade model, while recognizing the importance of effective, positive parenting, also strongly emphasizes the importance of developing cognitive competence (often measured by academic achievement or intellectual ability) and resilience (Masten & Cicchetti, 2010). Competence in this context refers to the capacity to adapt and successfully achieve developmental tasks and challenges. In commenting about competence, Masten and Cicchetti write, "effectiveness in one domain of competence in one period of life becomes the scaffold on which later competence in newly emerging domains develop: in other words, *competence begets competence*" (Masten & Cicchetti, 2010, p 492; italics in the original quote). Success in early developmental tasks of childhood is likely to foster competence in subsequent developmental tasks.

The concept of resilience emerged when it was noticed by many researchers that there are always a number of children who appear to develop well, despite their high-risk status and the challenges they encounter (Coatsworth, nd). "Resilience is inferred when individuals experience a significant threat to development or adaptation but continue to 'do well' despite the threat" (Coatsworth, nd, p. 9). Basically, resilience is the ability to bounce back quickly and adaptively from negative emotional experiences. Children who show resilience at one stage of their lives tend to show resilience across the entire life span. And it is far more common in children than originally supposed (Masten, 2014).

In this and the next two chapters, we will focus on the many early risk factors most often confronted by children and youth in their daily lives. In addition, we will address some of the protective factors that have the power to reduce the impact of these cumulative risk factors.

SOCIAL ENVIRONMENT RISK FACTORS

Poverty

It is difficult to lead off with poverty, because the poor too often get blamed for society's ills. Yet, the association between economic strain and childhood development leading to crime is too robust to ignore. It must be continually emphasized, however, that to be poor is not to be criminal, and that many criminals are far from economically deprived.

Poverty refers to a situation in which the basic resources to maintain an average standard of living within a specific geographic region are lacking. This typically includes the absence of sufficient income to meet basic necessities of life. Approximately 20 percent of children in the United States live in families that have incomes that fall below the poverty line, currently defined as $22,000 per year for a family of four (Duncan, 2012; Yoshikawa et al., 2012). Another 20 percent of children are "near poor," living in families very near the poverty line (Yoshikawa et al., 2012).

The research literature is substantial in underscoring the adverse effects of poverty on child development. As summarized by Blair and Raver (2012): "It is well established that the material and psychosocial contexts of poverty adversely affect multiple aspects of development in children" (p. 310). Some researchers (Hubbs-Tait, Nation, Krebs, & Bellinger, 2005) underscore that "[L]ower family income has long been associated with poorer cognitive functioning and, to a lesser extent, poorer socioeconomic functioning" (p. 73).

The overall effects of poverty on human development are often severe. Moreover, the effects of poverty are not only cumulative but also interactive, in that the effects at one stage can hinder development at later stages (Yoshikawa et al., 2012). There is also little doubt that poverty has a strong connection to persistent, violent offending, as measured by official, victimization, and self-report data on both adult and juvenile offenders. The connection between poverty and nonviolent offending is not quite as strong, but still existent. Accumulating research evidence indicates that poverty is one of the most robust predictors of adolescent violence for both males and females (Beyers, Bates, Pettit, & Dodge, 2003; Shaw & Shelleby, 2014; Stouthamer-Loeber, Loeber, Wei, Farrington, & Wikström, 2002), and the indigence of defendants processed in criminal courts is well documented.

However, we must be extremely cautious both in interpreting these data and in making decisions about how to prevent future offending. Furthermore, it should be emphasized that this strong connection holds whether we are referring to victims or offenders. Children and youth living under dire economic conditions are more likely to be victims as well as offenders. Preschool children living in a low-income family characterized by poor housing and unemployment are especially at high risk to become delinquent and/or to become victimized (Dodge, 1993b; Farrington, 1991). Adults living in substandard housing are more likely to be victims of crime than those living in more advantageous conditions.

The exact nature of the relationship between poverty and violence is not well understood. This is because poverty is intertwined with a large number of influences that are called poverty cofactors (Yoshikawa et al., 2012). For example, Hubbs-Tait et al. (2005) emphasize that the consistently reported connection between low income and crime is most likely linked to the panoply of circumstances that usually accompany poverty, which fits in with both the cumulative risks and developmental cascade models. Poverty is often accompanied not only by inequities in resources but also by discrimination, racism, family disruption, unsafe living conditions, poor nutrition, joblessness, social isolation, and limited social support systems (Evans, 2004; Hill, Soriano, Chen, & LaFromboise, 1994; Sampson & Lauritsen, 1994). Youth living under poverty conditions are more likely to attend inadequate schools, to drop out of school, to be unemployed, to be victimized, and to be a witness to a variety of violent events. They live in social environments with low-quality health care, "greater exposure to pesticides, higher noise levels, fewer open spaces in which to play, and greater exposure to lead and other neurotoxicants" (Hubbs-Tait et al., 2005, p. 73). Therefore, many risk factors other than one's economic situation come into play.

Poverty influences the family in many ways, not the least of which is the impact on parents' behavior toward children. For instance, the stress that accompanies poverty is believed to diminish some parents' capacity for supportive and consistent parenting (Blair & Raver, 2012; Dodge, Greenberg, Malone, and Conduct Problems Prevention Research Group, 2008; Hammond & Yung, 1994). This situation may lead to coercive and highly aggressive methods of child control. Living in conditions where lack of social support, lack of resources, and lack of opportunity are prevalent make it difficult for some parents to avoid harsh and inconsistent discipline with their young children. Coercive methods of child control are more direct, immediate, and easy to administer. They require less time and energy to administer, compared with parenting that emphasizes sensitivity, interpersonal skills, and patient understanding. It is much "easier" to slap a child than it is to utilize more thoughtful parenting strategies, but the consequences of slapping can be severe. A pattern of slapping or hitting a child to punish or to maintain control promotes a negative self-concept in the child. Furthermore, parenting that utilizes aggressive and violent tactics often provides models and a violent context that can carry the cycle of violence into the next generation. Living in a disadvantaged environment accompanied by physical punishment may also lead to the belief that economic survival and social status depend greatly on being aggressive and violent to others.

Important caveats must be repeated in any discussion of serious delinquency and economic status. First, the connection between low socioeconomic class and delinquency does not mean that poverty causes or inevitably leads to serious, chronic offending. The great majority of poor children and adults are law-abiding citizens, and children and adults from families of high economic status do engage in serious delinquency and crime. Both self-report and victimization data indicate that sexual assault, serious drug use, theft, and fraud are perpetrated by juveniles and adults across all social classes. Second, in many communities, children from the lower socioeconomic class are targeted by law enforcement practices more than children of the middle and upper classes. They are more likely to be taken into custody by police, referred to juvenile courts, and adjudicated delinquent. Thus, they appear in the government statistics that serve as the official measures of crime covered in Chapter 1. Third, children of the poor are taken into a system that may itself promote delinquent behavior or adult crime, particularly when they are institutionalized with other offenders. Victimization in these facilities is common as well. Children from more economically advantaged families, by contrast, are more likely to be handled informally, provided with legal assistance, or placed by their parents in private facilities for the treatment of their problem behavior (Chesney-Lind, 2002; Chesney-Lind & Shelden, 1998; Schwartz, 1989).

Peer Rejection and Association with Antisocial Peers

Developmental researchers have continually found that children's peer relations make unique and essential contributions to their social and emotional development (Bagwell, 2004; Blandon et al., 2010; Newcomb, Bukowksi, & Pattee, 1993). During adolescence, there is an increase in susceptibility to peer influence and a decline in susceptibility to parental influence (Mounts, 2002). In addition, numerous investigators have found that peer influence is a strong predictor of adolescent substance use and delinquent behavior (Coie & Miller-Johnson, 2001; Mounts, 2002). Not surprisingly, many members of most societies believe that this connection is obvious. The folk wisdom to "avoid bad companions" has long been the traditional admonition from parents and other concerned adults. The link between childhood peer *rejection* and antisocial behavior and delinquency is not so obvious, however, and requires a closer examination.

One of the strongest predictors of later involvement in antisocial behavior is early rejection by peers (Dodge, 2003; Lansford, Malone, Dodge, Pettit, & Bates, 2010; Parker & Asher, 1987; Trentacosta & Shaw, 2009). In elementary school, being liked and accepted by the peer group is a crucial developmental task, generally leading to healthy psychological and social development (Rubin, Bukowski, & Parker, 1998). Social rejection by peers in the elementary school grades, on the other hand, presents a very powerful risk factor for delinquency in adolescence and antisocial behavior throughout the life course (Dodge, Coie, & Lynam, 2006; Laird, Jordan, Dodge, Pettit, & Bates, 2001). Research has consistently demonstrated that peer rejection by first-grade peers is significantly linked to the development of antisocial behavior by the fourth grade (Cowan & Cowan, 2004; Miller-Johnson et al., 2002). Furthermore, those children who were rejected for at least two or three years by second grade had a 50 percent chance of displaying clinically significant antisocial behavior later in adolescence, in contrast with just a 9 percent chance for those children who managed to avoid early peer rejection (Dodge & Pettit, 2003). Some researchers also find evidence of a "cascade effect," whereby conduct disorders lead to peer rejection and then to depressive symptoms in elementary school children (Gooren, van Lier, Stegge, Terwogt, & Koot, 2011).

Interestingly, the quality of parent–child and marital relationships seems to play a significant role in whether a child is rejected or not by peers early in his or her life. Research by Cowan and Cowan (2004) demonstrates that "negative qualities in marital- and parent–child relationships in both prekindergarten and kindergarten are risk factors for low social skills, aggressive behavior, and rejection in the early years of elementary school" (p. 173).

Peer-rejected children frequently interact with one another or gravitate to antisocial peers (Laird, Pettit, Dodge, & Bates, 2005). During the adolescent years, involvement with antisocial peers shows a robust and consistent relationship to delinquency, drug use, and a range of other problematic behaviors (Laird et al., 2005). Consequently, we would expect that both peer rejection *and* involvement with antisocial peers would be characteristic of those youngsters exhibiting antisocial or delinquent behavior early in their social development.

WHY ARE SOME CHILDREN REJECTED BY THEIR PEERS?   Children are rejected by their peers for a variety of reasons, often because they are perceived as being "different" from others. For example, children diagnosed with Asperger's or other disorders on the autism spectrum are often ostracized by peers because of their ineffective social interaction skills. They may be bright and knowledgeable, but they often do not maintain eye contact with others and may have occasional tantrums. They typically are not physically aggressive, but they often say what they think, even if it results in insulting others. Consequently, they have difficulty maintaining friendships and often face rejection. Other children are rejected because they do not wear the right clothes or because a family member is incarcerated.

For many rejected children, however, their own aggressive behavior appears to be a prominent reason for the rejection (Lansford et al., 2010). Children tend to reject those peers who frequently use forms of physical and verbal aggression as their preferred way of dealing with others. These findings prompted many social scientists to conclude that aggressive children are more likely than nonaggressive children to be rejected by peers. Ongoing research indicates, however, that the relationship may not be that straightforward. First, peers also may reject peers whom they perceive as shy, socially withdrawn, or "different." Second, not all aggressive children are rejected by peers; some are liked, accepted, and sought as friends. In fact, research finds that many popular youngsters are often dominant, arrogant, and physically and relationally aggressive (Cillessen & Mayeux, 2004; Rose, Swenson, & Waller, 2004). Thus, if the children are rejected, it is not *always* because they are aggressive.

On the other hand, aggression *combined with* peer rejection does appear to lead to serious antisocial or delinquent behavior. Stated another way, children who are *both* physically aggressive and socially rejected by their peers have a high probability of becoming serious delinquents during adolescence and violent offenders during early adulthood. Researchers Coie and Miller-Johnson (2001), for example, conclude from their extensive review of the research literature that "those aggressive children who are rejected by peers are at a significantly greater risk for chronic antisocial behavior than those who are not rejected" (Cillessen & Mayeux, 2004; Rose, Swenson, & Waller, 2004, p 201).

An important question still remains: Why are some aggressive children rejected in the first place and others not? Coie (2004) points out that there are three important differences between the two. First, peer-rejected, aggressive boys are more impulsive and have problems sustaining attention and staying on task. Consequently, they are more likely to be disruptive of ongoing activities in the classroom or during group play. Second, peer-rejected, aggressive boys are aroused to anger more readily and probably have more difficulty calming down. This emotional rage is more likely to result in physical and verbal attacks on peers, which in turn encourages peers to avoid them altogether. Third, rejected, aggressive youngsters have fewer social and interpersonal skills for making friends and maintaining positive relationships with peers. In addition, they probably have acquired fewer social and interpersonal skills because they have had limited opportunities to practice these skills on nonrejected peers.

In summary, peer-rejected children often, though not invariably, are aggressive, but they also tend to be more argumentative, inattentive, and disruptive than others, and generally have poorer social skills. These behaviors are characteristic of attention deficit hyperactivity disorder (ADHD), to be discussed in more detail later in the chapter under psychological risks. The observation that peer-rejected boys demonstrate inattentive, impulsive, disruptive behavior suggests that ADHD may contribute to some of the peer rejection. A study by Erhardt and Hinshaw (1994) underscores this possibility.

The study involved 25 boys with ADHD and 24 other boys who participated in a summer school program, all of whom did not know one another at the beginning of the program. The boys ranged in ages from 6 to 12 years. As early as the first day of social interactions between the two groups, the ADHD and comparison boys showed clear differences in social behaviors, with the ADHD youngsters displaying socially noxious and noncompliance-disruptive behaviors. More important, within the first day, the ADHD youngsters were overwhelmingly rejected by their peers. Other studies have found similar results, with ADHD symptoms and aggression showing a close link to eventual antisocial behavioral patterns (Coie, 2004; Miller-Johnson et al., 2002). Again, this topic is discussed in more detail later in the chapter.

GENDER DIFFERENCES IN PEER REJECTION.   Most of the research and theoretical work examining the effects of peer rejection, aggression, and delinquent behavior has focused on boys. Among girls, little is known about the combined effects of aggression and peer rejection. In one of the few studies focusing on girls, Prinstein and La Greca (2004) found that the development of antisocial and delinquent behavior in girls, as in boys, can be predicted by early involvement in aggressive behavior with peers. However, in a national sample of 413 children and adolescents, Higgins, Piquero, and Piquero (2011) found high peer rejection was related to high delinquency and crime in males but not in females.

There is also some evidence to suggest that relationally aggressive girls are more likely than nonaggressive girls to be peer rejected (Crick, 1995). Relational aggression is the tendency to hurt others and diminish their social status by words, shunning, or other nonphysical methods. Prinstein and La Greca discovered—as did Crick—that peer rejection among girls in elementary school increased aggression but also was associated with increased substance abuse and other delinquent behaviors during adolescence. On the other hand, peer acceptance reduced and even eliminated the risk of aggression and other delinquent behaviors later on. More specifically, the effects of childhood aggression and antisocial behavior were mollified under conditions of high acceptance by peers.

GANG OR DEVIANT GROUP INFLUENCES ON REJECTED YOUTH.   There are three major perspectives on the influence of peer groups on antisocial and delinquent behavior. One perspective argues that youngsters become delinquent as a direct result of association with deviant peer groups.

According to this view, almost any child is susceptible to the negative influences of participating in a deviant peer group. A second perspective contends that antisocial, peer-rejected youths seek out greater contact with similar peer-rejected and socially unskillful peers. A third perspective is somewhat between these two positions. Peer-rejected, antisocial children are drawn to deviant groups with members similar to themselves, and this encourages and amplifies *already existing* antisocial tendencies. Current research evidence is in favor of the third perspective. It appears that childhood peer rejection encourages children to participate in deviant peer groups that then *amplify* tendencies to become more deviant and antisocial. That is, deviant group membership or gangs encourage and increase the already existing antisocial patterns in children and adolescents. As noted by Coie (2004): "The impact of deviant peer group influences on the *crystallization of an antisocial developmental trajectory* [emphasis added] has been solidly documented" (Crick, 1995, p 257).

An important aspect of peer rejection that has come to light in recent years is that rejected children and youth do not usually have the opportunity to learn social and interpersonal skills for getting along with others. In addition, children who have been rejected by their peers are often denied opportunities for learning competent ways of processing social situations (Lansford et al., 2010). "That is, children who are not able accurately to encode social cues, who misinterpret their peers' intentions, who are not able to generate competent solutions to peer dilemmas, and who favorably evaluate noncompetent solutions to social problems are likely to behave in ways (aggressive or not) that make them less desirable social partners" (Lansford et al., 2010, p. 595). These deficits in social information processing account for at least part of the link between peer rejection and aggression. More importantly, Lansford and her colleagues emphasize that social information processing offers a promising target for intervention designed to neutralize the effects of peer rejection and correct the individual's misinterpretations of the social world. We will return to this point in Chapter 5 on aggression when we discuss hostile attribution and other problems in social information processing.

Preschool Experiences

Over the past three decades, children as a group have been shifted gradually from home to center-based day care or nursery school. The proportion of mothers participating in the workforce has increased substantially over that time; because mothers have traditionally been the primary caretakers, this is a significant change. The percentage of mothers with children under age six working outside the home increased from 12 percent in 1947, to 31 percent in 1975, to 64 percent in 1997 (Tran & Weinraub, 2006). In 2003, more than half the mothers with infants less than one year old were in the labor force (Tran & Weinraub, 2006). Recent data indicate that over 60 percent of children under the age of five are in some form of day care or nonparental care on a regular basis (U.S. Bureau of the Census, 2014).

The quality of care provided by child-care centers is highly variable, in large part due to low wages and high staff turnover in many facilities. Nonetheless, licensed centers, which are expected to meet minimal standards for nutrition, programming, and staffing, are often more adequate than individual care providers whom some parents must rely upon. However it occurs, poor-quality child care has been reported to put children's development at risk for poorer language, cognitive development, and lower ratings of social and emotional adjustment (Tran & Weinraub, 2006). Unfortunately, children from families led by single employed mothers with low incomes are more likely to be found in lower-quality care.

The reality of multiple child-care arrangements has only recently come to attention. The nation's economic crisis of 2009 resulted in many parents assuming second jobs—such as low-paying part-time work on weekends—to keep the family financially afloat. This may necessitate "juggling" child-care duties among day-care centers, relatives, babysitters, and neighbors. Unfortunately, recent research suggests that these multiple arrangements have negative impacts on children's social adjustment (Morrissey, 2009). Being placed in different homes, day-care centers, classrooms, or peer groups on a weekly basis increases problem behavior and decreases prosocial behavior.

More encouragingly, there is evidence that improving out-of-home care for children can have long-term beneficial effects. Low-income children who experience high-quality infant and preschool care show better school achievement and socialized behavior in later years than similar children without child-care experience or with experience in lower-quality care. For low-income children, quality child care offers learning opportunities and social and emotional supports that many would not experience at home. Again, this is not to say that low-income parents do not or cannot offer these opportunities to their children; however, the stress associated with maintaining the household under stringent economic conditions may make it difficult to do so.

According to Goldstein Arnold, Rosenberg, Stowe, and Ortiz (2001), day-care teachers worry about aggression in their toddlers more than any other behavioral problem, and they report disruptive behavior as their greatest classroom challenge. These concerns may be important, as aggressive tendencies at three years of age predict aggressive behavior later in life (Goldstein et al., 2001). Accumulating evidence indicates that the amount of exposure that a child has to aggressive peers in day care or preschool is predictive of later child aggressive behavior, perhaps because of modeling effects (Dodge & Pettit, 2003).

After-School Care

The quality of after-school care has been closely associated with the development of antisocial behavior (Flannery, Williams, & Vazsonyi, 1999; Posner & Vandell, 1999; Vandell & Posner, 1999). In the 1990s, the term "latch-key" children was applied to children who returned from school to an empty house and remained on their own until their parents or guardians finished their own work day. Children who spend fairly large amounts of time in unsupervised after-school self-care in the early elementary grades are at elevated risk for behavior problems in early adolescence (Pettit, Laird, Bates, & Dodge, 1997). Moreover, such children are more likely to spend time in unsupervised activity with peers in early adolescence (Colwell, Pettit, Meece, Bates, & Dodge, 2001). Antisocial children seek out niches that involve association with antisocial peers and environments with minimal adult supervision (Snyder, Reid, & Patterson, 2003). Day-care centers that open their doors to children after school hours or community groups that offer after-school programs in troubled neighborhoods can make a positive difference.

Academic Failure

Academic failure and school dropout rates remain discouragingly high in the United States, with estimates of over 25 percent of public school students failing to earn a diploma (Casillas et al., 2012; Stillwell, 2009). In some communities, these rates exceed 50 percent (Casillas et al., 2012). Early academic failure is also linked to antisocial development and delinquency (Dodge & Pettit, 2003). As early as kindergarten, behavioral problems are strongly associated with academic failure in later grades (Ansary & Luthar, 2009; Duncan et al., 2007).

Studies examining the education level of inmates in correctional facilities found that 75 percent of state prison inmates, 59 percent of federal inmates, and 69 percent of jail inmates did not complete high school (Harlow, 2003). Many had only attained an eighth-grade education or less. Moreover, the data further revealed that dropping out of school increases the odds of being arrested during a lifetime by over 350 percent.

Early academic failure appears to set up a cascading series of events that increase incremental risks. For example, research indicates that retention or failure to be promoted in kindergarten and in the early school grades has long-term detrimental effects on mental and psychological development, in spite of its immediate academic benefits (Dodge & Pettit, 2003; Holmes, 1989; Sameroff, Peck, & Eccles, 2004). On the other hand, *delaying entry* into kindergarten does not appear to have the same effects. It is the "staying back" label that prompts retained children to be seen negatively and socially rejected and ridiculed by their peers (Plummer & Graziano, 1987).

In fact, early academic failure seems to be strongly associated with delinquency and adult criminal behavior. Some researchers discovered that the odds of severe delinquent behavior in eight-year-old-male children who were failing in school were nearly double those of other male children (Loeber, Farrington, Stouthamer-Loeber, & Van Kammen, 1998).

Regardless of race, socioeconomic status, or ethnic background, reading achievement appears to play a prominent role in academic failure. In fact, not only is poor reading achievement closely associated with school failure, but it also predicts later arrest and criminal activity in boys (Coley & Barton, 2006; Petras et al., 2004). On the other hand, a high level of reading achievement seems to prevent at-risk youth from engaging in later antisocial behavior. More specifically, a high level of reading achievement brings more acceptance from mainstream peers, greater attachment to school, enhanced job prospects in young adulthood, and better cognitive resources for anticipating the negative consequences of engaging in criminal activity (Petras et al., 2004). In that sense, high reading achievement could be considered a protective factor.

In summary, the most prominent social risk factors that have been identified in the development of criminal behavior include the many disadvantages of living in poverty, peer rejection combined with association with antisocial peers, poor-quality child care during the preschool years, and academic failure. In line with a cumulative model, the more social risk factors a child experiences during his or her early life, the higher the probability a child will follow a developmental pathway toward delinquent and criminal behavior. The developmental cascade model would emphasize that there were factors that feed into one another. For example, the cofactors of living in poverty may intensify the likelihood that a child will be rejected by peers. Parental and family risk factors may play an even more prominent role in the development of antisocial behavior.

PARENTAL AND FAMILY RISK FACTORS

The family, particularly the nuclear family, has long been identified in criminology literature as a crucial factor in a child or adolescent's antisocial behavior, or lack of it. In the past decade, though, social science researchers have examined more closely the process variables (e.g., quality of parenting) rather than the structural variables (e.g., single-parent households). It is well recognized that the family has a critically important role in providing a healthy environment for children and adolescents (see, generally, Biglan et al., 2012 for an excellent review of this literature). Much of this attention is directed at identifying aversive events, such as abuse, criticism, insults, and coercive interactions among parents and children and among family members as a group. Once the events have been identified, treatment programs or interventions are attempted, with the goal to establishing a nurturing family environment. As Biglan et al. note: "Reducing aversive conditions such as harsh and inconsistent discipline and parental rejection is a core component of virtually every experimentally evaluated parenting intervention" (p. 259). Despite the emphasis on process variables, though, some structural variables continue to be highlighted in the literature, as we see below.

Single-Parent Households

According to the last completed census figures, over 12 million American families with children are maintained by only one parent (Vespa, Lewis, & Kreider, 2013). In 2012, 28 percent of all children in the United States lived with one parent; 88 percent of these children were with their mothers. Early studies based on official data found that delinquents were more likely than nondelinquents to come from homes where parents were divorced or separated (Eaton & Polk, 1961; Glueck & Glueck, 1950; Monahan, 1957; Rodman & Grams, 1967). This led to conclusions that the single-parent home—or the "broken home" as it was then called—could be blamed for much delinquency and thus could be considered a risk factor. Beginning in the 1970s, when self-report data indicated that delinquent behavior was widespread, criminologists began to question these conclusions. Today, as noted above, researchers are more likely to examine accompanying factors such as the quality of the relationship between the child and the custodial parent, the quality of the relationship between the child and the noncustodial parent if he or she remains in the child's life, the family's economic status, and the degree of emotional support provided to the family by other adults, such as extended family members or community agents.

A wide variety of circumstances can lead to a single-parent home. The home may have started that way, as when an unmarried woman gives birth to or adopts a child. Additionally, two-parent homes may be "broken" by a wide variety of circumstances—death, desertion, divorce, or separation. Such separations do not affect all families the same way. Furthermore, there is evidence that children from single-parent homes that are relatively conflict free are less likely to be delinquent than children from conflict-ridden "intact" homes. The composition of the home (e.g., grandparents, stepparent, relatives, significant others, and friends) also must be considered. The "nontraditional" family has become a fixture in today's society. Many researchers define family as individuals related by blood or by legal arrangements (i.e., adoptions, legal guardianships, civil unions). Others point out that individuals who live together in long-term committed relationships—either as friends or as sexual partners—and who may be caring for their own or other people's children are also family.

While the relationship between single-parent homes and delinquency continues to be commonly reported, we are far from explaining it—and it may be pointless to try. If the single-parent home is a risk factor, it is probably influenced by other interacting variables and a host of risk factors. Rather than concentrating on the *structure* of the family, a focus on the *process* is far more desirable. As Flynn (1983, p. 13) asserts: "One point is indisputably clear in the literature: A stable, secure, and mutually supportive family is exceedingly important in delinquency prevention." However family is defined, it should include at least one competent, caring adult with primary responsibility for the well-being of the child.

Parental Styles and Practices

Parental styles and practices pertain to the ways in which parents or caregivers interact with their children. Some parental (or caregiver) styles and practices appear to be more likely than others to lead to delinquency, and thus can be called risk factors. **Parental practices** are strategies employed by parents to achieve specific academic, social, or athletic goals across different contexts and situations (Hart, Nelson, Robinson, Olsen, & McNeilly-Choque, 1998). That is, when parents use parenting practices, their focus is on affecting some particular aspect of the child (Mounts, 2002). Giving a child a weekly allowance with the hope of teaching her to manage money is an example of a practice. Reading with children, attending their sports events, or serving as room parents in school are other examples. Parenting practices have a direct effect on the development of specific child behaviors (from table manners to academic performance) and characteristics (such as acquisition of particular values or high self-esteem).

While parental practices refer to parental behavioral patterns, **parental styles** refer to parent–child interactions characterized by parental *attitudes* toward the child and the emotional climate of the parent–child relationship (Baumrind, 1991a; Mounts, 2002). Behaviors such as gestures, tone of voice, or the spontaneous expression of emotion are examples of parental style. For example, responsive parent–child interactions are described as warm, playful, accepting, and engaging. Studies reveal that a responsive parenting style often leads to social competence, peer acceptance, and less antisocial behavior (Hart et al., 1998). As emphasized by Gallitto (2014): "It is through sensitive and responsive parenting behavior that parents fulfill the child's basic needs for physical proximity, interpersonal relatedness, and intimacy, which are essential to the promotion of children's emotional, social, and intellectual growth" (p. 1).

FOUR TYPES OF PARENTAL STYLES.   Diana Baumrind (1991a) identified four parental styles: (1) authoritarian, (2) permissive, (3) authoritative, and (4) neglecting (see **Table 2-2**). Those parents who use an **authoritarian style** try to shape, control, and evaluate the behavior of their children in accordance with some preestablished, absolute standard. The authoritarian household has numerous rules and regulations which must be rigidly observed, often without question or explanation. Authoritarian parents discourage any verbal exchanges that imply equality between parent and child; the parent is the authority in all important matters, as well as many unimportant ones. Authoritarian parents expect their children to be obedient and unquestioningly respectful of authority. These parents are often referred to as "running a tight ship." Deviations and transgressions are met with punitive, forceful measures, which may or may not include physical punishment.

TABLE 2-2	Summary of Baumrind's Parental Styles
Style	**Intent or Emphasis**
Authoritarian	To shape and control child's life
Permissive	No control and extremely few restrictions
Authoritative	To be rational and apply reasonable restrictions
Neglecting	Detached and unengaged in child's life

Years ago, a student, who was the youngest in a family of five children, revealed to the class one of the most memorable experiences of his childhood. An older brother—then a high school junior—had arrived home shortly after midnight, heavily under the influence of alcohol. The father of the family woke each of the younger children and had them watch as he placed the oldest son face down across a chair and whipped his backside. He then told the other children, "This is what will happen to you if I ever see you come home like this." Asked about the outcome of this incident, the student said, "We all turned out fine; we knew our father loved us and we still know it now." Obviously, many of us would not agree with this approach. In fact, brought to public attention it could result in child abuse charges, as we saw in 2014 in the case of a noted professional football player who used a switch on his young child. Despite this, and the fact that corporal punishment has negative physical and psychological effects, the authoritarian parent is not the one most closely associated with criminal behavior in his or her offspring.

Parents who adopt a **permissive style** display tolerant, nonpunitive, accepting attitudes toward their children's behavior, including expressions of aggressive and sexual impulses. Permissive parents generally avoid asserting authority or imposing social controls or restrictions on the child's behavior. In this type of family, parents see themselves as "resource persons" to be consulted if needed. Permissive parents allow children to set their own time schedule for eating, sleeping, watching television, playing video games, leaving the home, and meeting with friends, and they employ little parental monitoring. They are, in essence, ineffectual in their socializing roles. While this may seem a harsh appraisal, and while these parents may suggest that children learn from their own mistakes, research indicates that permissiveness is not the recommended approach (Jackson & Foshee, 1998).

In the **authoritative style**, parents try to direct their children's activities in a rational, issue-oriented manner. There are frequent decision-making exchanges and a general spirit of open communication between parents and children. The hallmark of the family led by authoritative parents is reasoned discussion punctuated with social controls. Authoritative parents expect age-related "mature" behavior from the child, and they apply firm, consistent enforcement of family rules and standards. At the same time, they encourage independence and individuality. In the illustration given above, an authoritative parent might have allowed the high school junior to go to bed—perhaps even tucked him in—but would likely have reasoned with the son the next day and applied some penalty to the unacceptable behavior.

Finally, in the **neglecting style**, parents demonstrate detachment and very little involvement in their children's life or activities. They are neither demanding nor responsive. "They do not structure or monitor, and are not supportive, but may be actively rejecting or else neglect their childrearing responsibilities altogether" (Baumrind, 1991b, p. 62). Basically, the parent or parents respond minimally to either the child's needs or the child's behavior (Brenner & Fox, 1999). They are far more than permissive; they simply have no interest in controlling the child's behavior or monitoring the child's activities. In its extreme form, this style of parenting qualifies as child neglect. It should come as no surprise that Hoeve et al. (2007) found neglecting parenting was one of the strongest risk factors identified with delinquency and a life of crime. Baumrind (1991b) found that adolescents from unengaged families were far more likely than their adolescent peers to be antisocial, lacking self-regulation, social responsibility, and cognitive competence.

Baumrind's typology of parenting styles is not without its problems. Many parents, for example, vacillate between permissiveness and authoritativeness, and some vary their styles according to the age of the child. Authoritative parents may allow their children to set their own eating and sleeping schedules and choose their modes of dress, but may demand extensive input into decisions related to school, careers, or work. Likewise, some parents may be generally permissive in style, but suddenly erupt into anger and demand that their children abide by a newly announced rule. Despite its shortcomings, "Baumrind's conceptualization of parenting style has produced a remarkably consistent picture of the type of parenting conducive to the successful socialization of children…" (Darling & Steinberg, 1993, p. 487).

ENMESHED AND LAX PARENTAL STYLES.   James Snyder and Gerald Patterson (1987) conclude that two parental styles contribute directly or indirectly to delinquency. They label the two styles "enmeshed" and "lax," and these are very similar to Baumrind's authoritarian and permissive styles. In the **enmeshed style**, parents see an unusually large number of minor behaviors as problematic, and they use ineffective, authoritarian strategies to deal with them. "These parents don't ignore even very trivial excessive behaviors. They issue more and poorer commands, use verbal threats, disapproval, and cajoling more frequently, but fail to consistently and effectively back up these verbal reprimands with nonviolent, nonphysical punishment" (Snyder & Patterson, 1987, p. 221). The ineffective use of coercive punishment sets up a reverberating pattern of family interactions, "which elicits, maintains, and exacerbates the aggressive behavior of all family members" (p. 221). When one family member in this coercive interaction acts aversively, other family members react the same way, escalating the exchange. Cathy reacts strongly to her brother's loud music by suddenly screaming at him to turn it off. He screams back at her to "stick it." Cathy bangs violently on his door. He screams louder. The father screams at both, telling them to "shut up" or else. Cathy screams louder and proceeds to kick in her brother's door. She throws a vase at him, just missing. He runs after her, throwing a book. Eventually, the child sometimes "wins" this escalating confrontation when parents "give in" to demands, reinforcing this highly aversive interpersonal strategy. For example, father kicks a chair and "orders" the brother to turn the loud music off. Thus, parents and children "teach" each other that this harsh tactic works in social interactions, a pattern that soon extends to members outside the family.

Enmeshed parents also sometimes dispense authoritarian, harsh punishment, although it is inconsistent and ineffective. However, they probably do not have the energy to apply punishments to each and every behavior they perceive as problematic. Consequently, there are many instances where aversive behavior goes unpunished, such as in the preceding example. This pattern results in an intermittent, inconsistent punishment schedule that, in the long run, does little to discourage antisocial behavior.

The **lax style** employs strategies that are the opposite of the above. According to Snyder and Patterson (1987), lax parents are not sufficiently attuned to what constitutes problematic or antisocial behavior in children. Consequently, they allow much of it to slip by, without disciplinary actions. For a variety of reasons, they fail to recognize or accept the fact that their children are involved in deviant, antisocial, or even violent actions. They simply do not believe it is happening, or they convince themselves that there is very little they can do about it. Lax parents may pretend they are unaware that their son is hosting a drug fest in the back field or fail to see the danger in the weaponry he is collecting.

It appears that overcontrolling parental behaviors—those associated with enmeshed and authoritarian styles—are closely connected to the development of aggression and antisocial behavior in children and adolescents (Blitstein, Murray, Lytle, Birnhaum, & Perry, 2005; Ruchkin, 2002). By contrast, an authoritative style has the opposite effect. Blitstein et al. (2005) report evidence that violent behavior and antisocial behavior among girls may be buffered by the presence of a warm, responsive (i.e., authoritative) mother, although the same result was not found for boys. In short, authoritative mothers seem to play a more significant role for the prevention of antisocial behavior in girls than in boys (Hollister-Wagner, Foshee, & Jackson, 2001).

Of all the parenting styles discussed in this section, neglecting style is most closely associated with antisocial behavior and delinquency. Although this is not surprising, having a neglecting parent does not automatically lead to serious antisocial behavior. Alternative adult role models, such as relatives, teachers, coaches, or mentors, may be available. Other parental styles, though, are also tied to delinquency. These include Baumrind's permissive and Snyder and Patterson's lax style. The children brought up with these styles often have very low levels of self-reliance and great difficulty controlling their impulses. Permissive parents have long been faulted both for lack of discipline and for lack of supervision. They may treat their children as adults, pushing them into adult behaviors or responsibilities far before they are ready and without needed direction from adult authority figures.

Parental Monitoring

Closely related to parental styles and antisocial, deviant behavior is the issue of parental supervision or monitoring. **Parental monitoring** "refers to parents' awareness of their child's peer associates, free-time activities, and physical whereabouts when outside the home" (Snyder & Patterson, 1987, pp. 225–226). Research continues to demonstrate that monitored youths are less likely to participate in drug and alcohol use or engage in delinquent behavior (Fosco, Stormshak, Dishion, & Winter, 2012; Kilgore, Snyder, & Lentz, 2000; Tilton-Weaver, Burk, Kerr, & Stattin, 2013). Fosco et al. write, "parents who stay informed about their child's activities, attend to their child's behavior, and structure their child's environment have children with better outcomes" (p. 203).

Parental monitoring appears to be especially important during the middle school years, an observation that has received substantial support from several studies (Fosco et al., 2012; Laird, Pettit, Bates, & Dodge, 2003; Slesnick et al., 2012). During this time, youth begin "to spend less time with their families, feel less close to them, and receive less supervision and monitoring from their parents" (Fosco et al., 2012, p. 202). For the most part, problem behaviors (including substance use and delinquent behavior) during the middle school years occur within the peer context. Peers are especially powerful agents during this period. Effective parenting is certainly protective against deviant peer influences, but often it is not enough. A growing body of research (e.g., Fosco et al., 2012; Slesnick et al., 2012) indicates that it is the nature of the relationships within the family that matters in reducing deviant peer risk factors. (See **Box 2-1**.)

CONTEMPORARY RESEARCH FOCUS

BOX 2-1 Monitoring, Middle School, and Family Relationships

Parental monitoring has been well established as a good approach to guide children as they approach and negotiate the challenges of adolescence. Broadly viewed, monitoring involves being aware of one's children's activities, maintaining structure, and setting reasonable restrictions. As noted in the text, a substantial amount of research documents that monitoring "works."

To be most effective, though, monitoring should be accompanied by a positive parent–child relationship. In fact, some research indicates that the quality of the relationship is a good predictor of problem behaviors in youth, even if good parenting practices are in effect (Bronte-Tinkew, Moore, & Carrano, 2006). This should not be surprising: Children who perceive themselves as having a good relationship with their parents or caretakers are more likely to inform them of their important activities and be more willing to accept the oversight that accompanies monitoring. Therefore, it is likely that the combination of

monitoring and good family relationships will reduce the likelihood that children will participate in antisocial activities. Families are complex, however, and until recently specific relationships between family members (e.g., child and father, child and mother, child and siblings) have not been studied extensively.

One exception is a study by Fosco, Stormshak, Dishion, and Winter (2012), who examined parental monitoring and various family relationships in families of middle school students. As the researchers noted: "There is good reason to believe that youths have unique and meaningful relationships with their mother, father, and siblings, and each likely contributes to adolescents' development" (p. 203).

Middle school for many children is a risky period, one in which they may begin drifting away from family norms and toward the influence of peers. In their longitudinal study, the researchers followed an ethnically diverse sample of male and female youth from 6th to 8th grades, measuring through surveys and interviews both parental monitoring and the connectedness the youths felt with up to five caring adults in their lives. They also assessed antisocial behavior, substance use, and association with deviant peers.

Consistent with other research, parental monitoring was found to be associated with decreasing levels of problem behavior from 6th through 8th grades. Scrutinizing family relationships added another interesting dimension, however. Specifically, both connectedness with the father and conflict with a sibling had significant predictive effects on problem behavior. Strong father–child connectedness predicted decreases in problem behavior, and conflict with siblings predicted increasing problem behavior. Mother–child connectedness was not a significant predictor of change, but the researchers urged caution in interpreting this finding. Also interestingly, the connectedness with father was crucial whether or not the father lived in the home, and it did not differ whether the youth was male or female.

Fosco et al. emphasized the need for replicating their findings. However, they also suggested that reducing conflict among siblings and encouraging father–child bonds during adolescence—even when the father was not living in the home—had merit for promoting healthy adolescent development.

Questions for Discussion

1. Note that the researchers urged caution in interpreting the findings regarding mother–child connectedness, primarily because these findings are inconsistent with previous research. Given that caution is warranted, what might be possible explanations for those findings?
2. Suggest reasons why conflicts with a sibling would result in more problem behavior in early adolescence.
3. What kind of questions would you use in a survey or an interview to measure "connectedness" with a caring adult as perceived by a middle schooler?

Studies consistently reveal that parents gain knowledge primarily from adolescent disclosure rather than from parental monitoring alone (Tilton-Weaver et al., 2013). This is because it is difficult to "monitor" activities if the youth does not inform the adult of where he or she is going. Therefore, the better the relationships and connectedness within the family, especially between the parents and the youth, the more impactful the parental monitoring will be. Youth who feel close and connected to their parents or caregivers are more likely to value their opinions and are more willing to seek their advice and guidance for difficult and troubling situations (Fosco et al., 2012)

Interestingly, preliminary research suggests that a positive relationship and sense of connectedness between the father and the middle school child—regardless of gender—appears to be particularly important in preventing associations with deviant peers and the development of problem behaviors (Fosco et al., 2012; see Box 2-1). This finding appears to hold whether the father resides with the child or is separated from the family. Thus, when parents are separated or divorced and the mother has custody, the ideal situation is for the father to remain a steady presence in the children's lives.

In essence, the research suggests that problem behavior in adolescence is significantly reduced by balanced parental monitoring combined with positive parent–youth relationships. The phrase "balanced parental monitoring" is important to note because adolescents often view some forms of monitoring and peer management as intrusive (Kakihara, Tilton-Weaver, Kerr, & Stattin, 2010; Tilton-Weaver et al., 2013). Adolescents who feel overcontrolled may become less willing "to accept parental authority over their friendships and leisure activities than those who feel less controlled by their parents" (Tilton-Weaver et al., 2013, p. 2068). This conflict appears to be more likely to occur during early adolescence and become less of an issue in later adolescence, however. Overall, the effectiveness of monitoring depends on the nature of the family relationships, timing of its use, and whether the adolescent feels overcontrolled by parents.

The amount and quality of parental monitoring are also influenced by a number of things. For example, divorce, serious financial distress, loss of job, parental psychological disorders, substance abuse, or death may significantly affect family dynamics and parental or caregiver monitoring. However, monitoring does not necessarily require the physical presence of the parent. Other adult caretakers or after-school programs also could provide suitable monitoring. In addition, we cannot underestimate the importance of *neighborhood* monitoring. For example, some researchers have found lower rates of delinquency and crime in communities where adults monitor the actions of young people and speak up when they see misbehavior (Sampson, Morenoff, & Gannon-Rowley, 2002). As has been frequently asserted: "It takes a village to raise a child."

Influence of Siblings

While parental monitoring and family and parent–youth relationships are important considerations in cumulative risk factors and developmental cascade processes, siblings also play a crucial role in the development of youth problem behaviors.

Siblings imitate each other, and most often younger children imitate their older siblings rather than the reverse (Fosco et al., 2012; Garcia, Shaw, Winslow, & Yaggi, 2000; Whiteman, Jensen, & Maggs, 2014). The modeling of the older sibling by the younger sibling(s) is not always the case, however. Whiteman and associates (2014) found that in about a third of their sibling sample, the younger sibling, who was close in age to the older sibling, actually tried to be different from the older sibling in behavior and attitude. Overall, though, since siblings generally spend so much time together, it is reasonable to assume that they play a role in shaping the development of aggression and antisocial behavior. This area has not been researched as heavily as other peer influences, but the few studies available indicate that adolescents with high rates of delinquency are also more likely to have siblings with high rates of delinquency (Buist, 2010; Coie & Miller-Johnson, 2001; Samek & Rueter, 2011; Whiteman et al., 2014).

Rowe and Gulley (1992) suggest that older siblings who engage in delinquent behavior reinforce antisocial behavior in younger siblings when there is a close and warm relationship between the youths. If the siblings are not close, the opposite effect may occur. That is, the nonaggressive younger sibling may make it a point not to be like his or her older aggressive or antisocial sibling.

Extensive conflict between siblings also affects the family dynamics, and it may drive a child away from the family and toward the peer group, including deviant peers. Fosco and his colleagues (Fosco et al., 2012) found that siblings who frequently argued or engaged in physical fights with each other reported increased problem behaviors by eighth grade, "independent of the effects of parental monitoring and parent–youth relationships" (p. 211). Moreover, the impact of the sibling conflict did not differ as a function of the gender composition of the sibling pairs. Fosco et al. concluded: "These study findings are consistent with the view that the sibling subsystem may contribute to the overall family environment by creating greater coercion, conflict, and hostility" (Fosco, his colleagues, 2012, p 211). In summary, a small but growing body of research is beginning to demonstrate that the relationship between siblings often has an enormous influence on the family atmosphere and development (or nondevelopment) of problem behaviors, substance use, and delinquency.

Parental Psychopathology

Children of parents who are clinically depressed—especially mothers—are at increased risk for a range of socioemotional and behavioral problems, including antisocial behavior, emotion dysregulation, and poor cognitive development (Bennett, Bendersky, & Lewis, 2002; Mazulis, Hyde, & Clark, 2004; Nelson, Hammen, Brennan, & Ullman, 2003). As they grow older, children whose mothers were depressed during pregnancy or during the child's infancy continue to display behavioral problems and often engage in various kinds of criminal behavior. Mothers are singled out because they tend to be the dominant caretakers. However, the risk for developing problem behaviors appears to be magnified if both parents are depressed during early childhood.

Parental alcoholism elevates risk for a variety of negative child outcomes, including behavioral difficulties, antisocial behavior, and subsequent alcoholism (Loukas, Zucker, Fitzgerald, & Krull, 2003; Zucker et al., 2000). Interestingly, Loukas and her colleagues (2003) found that the presence of paternal alcoholism in the family may be more important than maternal alcoholism in contributing to a son's antisocial behavior and maladjustment.

The aggressive behavior that is demonstrated in domestic violence is clearly a form of parental psychopathology. However, this topic is discussed more fully in Chapter 9 under family violence.

PSYCHOLOGICAL RISK FACTORS

Lack of Attachment

According to John Bowlby (1969), the early relationship between an infant and a caregiver largely determines the quality of social relationships later in life. Bowlby's **attachment theory** has been discussed extensively in the psychological literature and may be extended to the study of criminal behavior. Although it is essentially a psychological risk factor within the individual, it also fits in well with the family and parental issues discussed above.

Some infants, when placed in a strange and unfamiliar environment, show *secure attachment*. They play comfortably in their parent's presence and demonstrate curiosity about their new and challenging environment. When the parent leaves, the child becomes distressed, but when she or he returns, the child beams with delight. These infants use their parent or caregiver as a secure base from which to explore. Other infants may show an *insecure attachment*, which is often divided into two attachment styles: *anxious/ambivalent* and *avoidant*. The anxious/ambivalent-attached child becomes intensely distressed and anxious by separation, and in new environments, they often cling anxiously to their parent without much exploration (Ainsworth, 1979). When the parent returns after separation, they may become indifferent and even hostile. These infants may push the returning parent away, stiffen up, or cry when picked up. The *avoidant attachment* style is characterized by little distress on the part of the infant, whether the parent is present or not. They rarely cry during separation or reunion. Avoidant attachment in infancy and childhood is associated with dismissing attachment in adulthood (Adshead, 2002).

Problems with attachment apparently are related to deficiencies in caregiving by adults in the child's life. The DSM-5 (American Psychiatric Association, 2013) includes diagnoses of reactive attachment disorder and disinhibited social engagement disorder, both of which are precipitated by the absence of adequate caregiving during infancy or early childhood. In the case of reactive attachment disorder, the social neglect results in the child demonstrating "a consistent pattern of inhibited, emotionally withdrawn behavior toward adult caregivers" (p. 265). Disinhibited social engagement disorder is indicated by "a pattern of behavior in which a child actively approaches and interacts with unfamiliar adults..." (p. 268). In the latter case, merely conversing with an unfamiliar adult is not cause for alarm. Other criteria must be present, such as evidence of insufficient care by the child's own caregivers and a willingness to go off with an unfamiliar adult without hesitation.

Mary Ainsworth (1979) observed that caregivers who are sensitive, affectionate, and responsive, and who create in their babies a basic trust of the world, typically have securely attached infants. Children with a secure attachment base usually develop into psychologically healthy people. As adults, they form good relationships, empathize with others, and generally show good self-regulation (Ansbro, 2008). "Later on, they emerge as more competent and more sympathetic in interaction with peers" (Ainsworth, 1979, p. 936). It is also commonly believed that our attachments in infancy play a powerful role in romantic relationships as adults.

According to Ainsworth and her colleagues (Ainsworth et al., 1979), infants with avoidant attachment style often have parents who are aloof, distant, and prefer to avoid intimacy with their children. Consequently, these children as adults have difficulty forming intimate relationships. Infants with anxious/ambivalent attachment usually have parents who are overbearing and inconsistent in their affection and intimacy. These infants never know when and how their parents will respond to their needs. As adults, they want to have close relationships but continually worry about their partners and relationships returning the affection. They tend to become obsessive and preoccupied with their relationships, especially spouses and intimate partners.

Ward and his associates (1995) hypothesize that many sex offenders probably had parents who were inconsistently affectionate and poor at identifying their child's needs. In essence, the sex offenders demonstrate the dismissing (avoidant) attachment style in their adult relationships. Gwen Adshead (2002) reports evidence for insecure attachment in her study of violent offenders. She notes that many victims of interpersonal violence are part of the violent offender's attachment network: a child, a parent, a partner, or ex-partner. Fear of loss or separation can generate strong feelings of anxiety and rage in the offender, often resulting in violent actions. Adshead found that a majority of offenders showed a dismissing attachment style, suggesting a diminished capacity for empathy toward their victims or relationships.

It is extremely important, however, to distinguish the healthy psychological attachment discussed in this section with "attachment parenting," a heavily used phrase in contemporary pop culture. Attachment parenting—similar to the phrase "helicopter parenting"—refers to an approach in which parents seek to be completely involved in every phase of their children's lives, into adolescence and beyond. It is not unheard of for adults who embrace attachment parenting to show up frequently and unexpectedly at their children's dormitory suite or try to intercede and resolve every relationship problem their adolescent child may be having. These practices are not reflective of a positive parent–child attachment.

Discussion of the attachment process serves as a good link between the social risk factors reviewed above and the psychological factors. (For a summary of all of the developmental risk factors, see **Table 2-3**.) While attachment has a connection with parenting styles, the attachment process also reflects a characteristic of the individual offender. However, though attachment may be an important component, it is only one of many and is unlikely to be a major factor. Furthermore, the factors covered below have received more research attention with respect to the development of antisocial behavior.

Lack of Empathy

Anyone observing a group of children playing together can notice differences among them if one child gets hurt and begins to cry. Some children will ignore the crying child and continue with their play; others will become solicitous and want to be sure the child is alright. Although this is a simplistic example, we might say that the children in the second group are more empathetic than those in the first.

TABLE 2-3   Developmental Risk Factors for Delinquency*

Social Risk Factors

- Poverty
- Early peer rejection
- Association with antisocial peers
- Inadequate preschool child care
- Inadequate after-school care
- Academic failure

Parental and Family Risk Factors

- Single-parent household
- Permissive or lax parental style
- Minimal parental monitoring
- Parental psychopathology
- Physical and emotional abuse/neglect
- Domestic violence and/or substance abuse
- Antisocial siblings

Psychological Risk Factors

- Lack of empathy
- Attachment disorder
- Animal cruelty
- Cognitive and language deficiencies
- Low IQ scores or psychometric intelligence
- ADHD
- CD
- ODD

*Although some of these factors may have a stronger effect than others, none should be considered a sole risk factor for antisocial behavior.

In practice and research, empathy is perceived as existing along two dimensions: affective and cognitive. Affective empathy is "an emotional response characterized by feelings of concern for another and a desire to alleviate that person's distress" (Young, Fox, & Zahn-Waxler, 1999, p. 1189). Cognitive empathy refers to the ability to understand a person from his or her frame of reference rather than simply from one's own point of view. Jolliffe and Farrington (2007) note that affective empathy is the ability to *experience* another person's emotions, whereas cognitive empathy is the ability to *understand* another's emotions. These terms are not mutually exclusive, however. In other words, one can possess both affective and cognitive empathy.

Deficiencies in empathy have long been considered characteristic of persistently aggressive and antisocial individuals (Cohen & Strayer, 1996; Hastings, Zahn-Waxler, Usher, Robinson, & Bridges, 2000; Hawes & Dadds, 2012; Marshall & Marshall, 2011). For example, low affective empathy is hypothesized to be a central ingredient of psychopathy, which is a combination of psychological and behavioral factors related to an increased tendency to engage in antisocial and violent behavior. Interestingly, psychopaths are believed to be able to understand the emotions of others (cognitive empathy), but show a remarkable inability to experience them. We return to the topic of psychopathy in greater detail in Chapter 7. Empathy deficiencies are also believed to be central behavioral features of both CDs—to be discussed below—and antisocial personality disorder (Vachon, Lynam, & Johnson, 2014), which is covered in chapters 6 and 7.

Girls generally show both dimensions of empathy earlier than boys, beginning in the second year of life and continuing at least through adolescence (Eisenberg & Fabes, 1998; Hastings et al., 2000; Hawes & Dadds, 2012). We urge caution in adopting a strict binary approach in any discussion of gender research, however. While biological differences between girls and boys may be apparent, gender exists on a continuum, and features associated with girls are present in many boys, and vice-versa. Distinctions among age groups are more clearcut. For example, the relationship between a lack of empathy and antisocial or excessively aggressive behavior is discernible in children during the early to middle elementary school years (Hastings et al., 2000; Tremblay, Vitaro, Gagnon, Piche, & Royer, 1992) and seems to become stronger with age (Miller & Eisenberg, 1988). Children who display little empathy in the third grade exhibit even less in the eighth grade.

Although researchers have generally found deficiencies in both dimensions of empathy (affective and cognitive), recent studies have generally found that a deficiency in affective (or emotional) empathy appears to be most strongly related to violence and persistent criminal behavior (Jolliffe & Farrington, 2007; de Kemp, Overbeek, de Wied, Engels, & Scholte, 2007; Schaffer, Clark, & Jeglic, 2009; van Langen et al., 2014; Van Vugt et al., 2011). "It...appears that it is the inability to *experience the emotions of others*, which is related to violence for both males and females rather than the inability to *understand* other people's emotions" (Jolliffe & Farrington, 2007, p. 281, emphasis added). In addition, "[b]oth high-frequency male and female offenders showed lower affective empathy (but not cognitive empathy) than low-rate offenders" (Jolliffe & Farrington, 2007, p. 281). Essentially, people who engage in violence and/or a large variety of serious offenses appear to have a significant inability to feel the pain of their victims. However, in a recent comprehensive study of the link between empathy and aggression, Vachon et al. (2014) concluded that the relationship may not be nearly as strong as previously reported in the research literature. Consequently, Vachon et al. recommended caution before making firm conclusions at this point in our knowledge. Their findings were especially pertinent concerning affective empathy. Logically, it makes sense to assume that a lack of empathy might predispose a person to be more aggressive and even violent toward others, but it also makes sense that a number of cumulating, escalating influences probably play a more significant role in the formation of frequent aggressive or violent behavior across the life span.

ANIMAL CRUELTY.   Some research has shown an interesting association between lack of empathy and animal cruelty. Cruelty to animals, defined as "socially unacceptable behavior that intentionally causes unnecessary pain, suffering, or distress to and/or death of an animal" (Guymer, Mellor, Luk, & Pearse, 2001, p. 1057) is a behavior that demonstrates a lack of empathy; if it occurs in childhood, it can signify serious problem behavior. Swatting a fly does not qualify as cruelty (although torture of insects, birds, frogs, etc. would qualify). Cruelty to dogs, cats, and other household pets is considered significant. Cruelty as defined here does not refer to chasing the family cat and gently pulling its tail, but swinging the cat by the tail or setting its ears on fire is another matter.

Several studies have found a strong association between animal cruelty and violent behavior toward humans. The aphorism "People who abuse animals rarely stop there" appears to have validity. For example, Stouthamer-Loeber and her associates (2004) followed young males from the ages of 13 to 25 and discovered that cruelty to animals was one of the strongest predictors of serious, violent criminal behavior. Lucia and Killias (2011) discovered, in their sample of 3,600 Swiss students (grades 7 to 9), that 12 percent admitted animal cruelty (17% of boys and 8% of girls). More importantly, the researchers found that youths who have been cruel to animals were three times more likely to have committed serious interpersonal violence, compared to youths with no reported history of animal cruelty. Wright and Hensley (2003) found a possible link between childhood cruelty to animals and later serial murders. In fact, the five serial murderers studied by Wright and Hensley, which included the infamous Jeffrey Dahmer, used the same method of torture and killing on their human victims as they had used on their animal victims. Merz-Perez, Heide, and Silverman (2001) reported a similar finding. Arluke and Madfis (2014) found that 43 percent of school shooters were often cruel to animals, and that the cruelty was most often directed against cats and dogs in a vicious, personal, and up-close manner. A similar pattern was uncovered by Levin and Arluke (2009) in their investigation of serial killers.

Current research has reported that the supposed link between animal abuse and violence has not been strong enough to use it as the sole predictor of violent crime, however, even though it certainly is one factor to consider. Furthermore, while animal cruelty may serve as an early warning sign for antisocial and violent behavior toward humans, it should not be used in isolation to predict future serious offending (Walters, 2013, 2014). Other factors should be included in the prediction assessment, such as cognitive and personality variables, the intensity of the animal abuse, and the age at which the abuse began. In other words, as in the study of empathy, rarely does a single risk factor lead to a lifelong commitment to aggression and violence.

Cognitive and Language Deficiencies

Cognitive and language impairments increase the risk of behavior problems and antisocial behavior, at least in boys (Brownlie et al., 2004; Petersen et al., 2013). For example, a high percentage of children and adolescents diagnosed and treated for antisocial behavior and CD demonstrate language impairments (Cohen et al., 1998; Giddan, Milling, & Campbell, 1996). **Language impairment** usually refers to problems expressing or understanding language, and some research has even traced these problems as far back as very early childhood. In an important study of Swedish children, Stattin and Klackenberg-Larson (1993) discovered that poor language development during the second year of life was a significant predictor of adult criminal behavior. Brownlie et al. (2004) also found that boys diagnosed with a language impairment at age five were far more likely to exhibit delinquent behavior at age 19 than a group of boys without early indications of a language impairment. This relationship held even when controlling for verbal IQ, demographic, and family variables. Brownlie et al. speculated, though, that the association may be largely due to the negative impact that language impairments have on the child's schooling and academic performance in general. In other words, language impairment appears to produce a serious cascading effect on healthy academic and social development. In essence, language deficiency often makes school a painful and unappealing enterprise, leading to poor or disinterested performance on academic tasks.

Furthermore, poor language and communication skills may also interfere with socialization and the ability to get along with others (Petersen et al., 2013). Language-impaired children are often rejected by peers and are frequently viewed negatively by their teachers. As we saw earlier in the chapter, peer rejection is one of the social risk factors for delinquency.

The use of language in the form of private and self-directed speech not only helps guide behavior to facilitate problem solving and academic performance, but it also helps children develop and maintain self-control and self-regulation (Petersen et al., 2013). After all, language enables a person to "talk to oneself" about what to do in challenging or conflictual situations. According to Dionne (2005), "Emotion regulation and self-regulation are generally viewed as requiring complex linguistic tools such as the ability to analyze social situations, organize thoughts about one's own emotions, and plan behavior according to social roles" (p. 346).

Language problems also increase frustration levels in children who have difficulty expressing their points of view, which is so necessary for reasonable resolutions of conflict. This frustration, if not self-regulated, is likely to lead to aggressive and disruptive behavior at home and at school.

Intelligence and Delinquency

For some time, criminologists have been eager to label the relationship between intelligence and delinquency and crime as misguided and unsubstantiated. Even to mention the connection may prompt a derisive reaction. As Hirschi and Hindelang (1977, p. 572) wrote some years ago, "Textbooks in crime and delinquency ignore IQ or impatiently explain to the reader that IQ is no longer taken seriously by knowledgeable students simply because no differences worth considering have been revealed by research." Hirschi and Hindelang maintained that these textbooks were misleading, because the delinquency literature consistently reported that delinquents do, as a group, score lower on standard intelligence tests than nondelinquents.

In their 1977 paper, Hirschi and Hindelang hypothesized that an *indirect* causal relationship exists between IQ and delinquency. That is, a low IQ leads to poor performance and negative attitudes toward school, which in turn leads to school failure and ultimately to delinquency. Low IQ does not directly lead to delinquency. A high IQ, on the other hand, leads to good performance and positive attitudes toward school, which in turn leads to the internal acceptance of conventional values and conformity (nondelinquency). The essential point, according to Hirschi and Hindelang, is that the inverse relationship between IQ scores and delinquency continues to be documented by research.

Why does this relationship exist? To address this question, it is necessary to consider the meaning of IQ and to stress that it is not identical to "intelligence." The term "IQ" is an abbreviation of *intelligence quotient*, derived from a numerical score on a so-called *intelligence* test, and it originated out of what is now called the **psychometric approach**. The word "psychometric" means "psychological measurement." Traditionally, the psychometric approach has searched for unique differences in persons through the use of psychological tests, including intelligence tests, scholastic aptitude tests (e.g., SAT), school achievement tests, personality inventories, and other specific abilities tests. The various tests are used for many purposes, such as selection, diagnosis, and evaluation. The psychometric approach continues to be widely used by practicing psychologists and mental health professionals. However, the term **psychometric intelligence (PI)**—which was preferred by some psychologists (Neisser et al., 1996) in the 1990s—has not caught on. Consequently, the traditional term "IQ" continues to be used today, and one hears of someone scoring 70 or scoring 160 on an IQ test. Although scores can work to the advantage of the person who was tested (e.g., by providing access to a program for the intellectually disabled or a program for the gifted), they may also be disadvantageous, if the individual is wrongfully labeled as intellectually deficient.

Satisfactory performance on a vast majority of intelligence tests depends greatly on language acquisition and verbal development. Usually, a person must have considerable experience using and defining words—particularly English words—to do well on most IQ tests. The examinee must be able to make conventional connections and see distinctions between verbal concepts. The examinee must also know the facts that the test designer deems important to know within mainstream culture. At the very least, almost all intelligence tests measure some aspect of academic skills that are taught in school or that predict success in school. A vast majority of psychologists today would agree that IQ scores are strongly influenced by social, educational, and cultural experiences. In short, all intelligence tests are culturally biased, regardless of their claims.

More importantly, IQ scores and the concept of intelligence should not be confused. The term "IQ" merely refers to a standardized score from a test. *Intelligence, on the other hand, is a broad, all-encompassing ability that defies any straightforward or simple definition.* It means many things to different people. Overall, intelligence is generally associated with competence and is a good marker for adaptive success in modern society (Masten, 2014). There is also considerable evidence that intelligence is a protective factor against high lifetime adversity exposure (Masten, 2014). More specifically, though, intelligence includes ability ranging from musical talent to logical mathematical skills. The term may also include wisdom, intuition, judgment, and even humor. While delinquents, as a group, do score lower on intelligence *tests*, this observation should not be construed as documenting that delinquents are less intelligent than nondelinquents. For example, Brazilian street children are masters at doing the math required for survival in their street business even though they have failed mathematics in school (Carraher, Carraher, & Schliemann, 1985; Neisser et al., 1996). Likewise, institutionalized delinquents often display artistic and verbal skills and a sense of humor that are not tapped by traditional IQ scores.

Nevertheless, the relationship between IQ test scores and school performance is strong and consistent. "Wherever it has been studied, children with high scores on tests of intelligence tend to learn more of what is taught in school than their lower-scoring peers" (Neisser et al., 1996, p. 82). Schools help develop certain intellectual skills and attitudes. Quality schools generally have positive effects on IQ. Preschool programs (e.g., Headstart) show significant positive effects on children during their early school years, and recent research shows that these gains do not fade when the program is over, provided there is periodic intervention during the child's middle school years (Masten, 2014).

IQ AND ETHNICITY. Average IQ scores do vary among racial and ethnic groups. For example, many studies using different tests and samples typically show African Americans scoring significantly lower than whites (Neisser et al., 1996; Suzuki, Naqvi, & Hill, 2014). Studies show, however, that this IQ gap has been consistently decreasing since 1980 (Nisbett, 2005). Asian Americans and whites, on average, score about the same on IQ tests; Native Americans score slightly lower than other groups on verbal skills, but this slight difference may be the result of chronic middle-ear infections common among Native American children (McShane & Plas, 1984a, 1984b). Latinos, who make up the second largest and fastest-growing minority group in the United States, typically score somewhere between African Americans and whites. It is unclear what these reported differences mean, but there is no scientific evidence to support the view that racial or ethnic differences in psychometric intelligence are due to genetics or biological factors (Sternberg, Grigorenko, & Kidd, 2005). Although genetics may play a role in *individual* differences in psychometric intelligence, there is little evidence for ethnic *group* differences.

SUMMARY. The association between IQ scores and delinquency is controversial and troubling, but it is a persistent finding. Group differences often can be explained by social influences, such as the quality of education or correlates of poverty that were discussed earlier in the chapter. Poor nutrition, inadequate prenatal care, lack of adequate child-care facilities, and inaccessibility to occupational and training opportunities also play critical but largely unknown roles in the assessment of intelligence. IQ scores are crude indices of mainstream language skills that are heavily influenced by experience and exposure to cumulative risk factors. In general, rich and varied experiences increase IQ scores, and limited experience decreases them (Garbarino & Asp, 1981; Neisser et al., 1996). School experiences, if positive, may increase language skills; if negative, they may stagnate, or even decrease, language skills. IQ scores are also strongly influenced by the type of test used, its content, the many characteristics of testing situations, and the training and skill of the examiner.

Still, even with these many variations, the inverse relationship between IQ scores and the tendency toward delinquency is consistently reported (e.g., Koenen et al., 2006; Nigg & Huang-Pollock, 2003; Parker & Morton, 2009; Simonoff et al., 2004; Sorge, Skilling, & Toplak, in press). As IQ scores go down, the probability of misconduct increases, and vice versa. Children with low IQ scores are at a higher risk for delinquent behavior, and as Anne Crocker and Sheilagh Hodgins (1997, p. 434) write, "To our knowledge, no study has failed to confirm this relation." The relationship is particularly strong for verbal IQ scores (Culberton, Feral, & Gabby, 1989; Kandel et al.,

1988; Parker & Morton, 2009). Furthermore, as noted by Crocker and Hodgins (1997), the relationship between low IQ scores and delinquency appears to be independent of socioeconomic status, race, and detection by the police (Koenen et al., 2006; Lynam, Moffitt, & Stouthamer-Loeber, 1993; Moffitt, 1990b). Moreover, it should be emphasized that this relationship is not specific to delinquency; the relationship is equally robust for adult offenders. Interestingly, it has been suggested that many adult-onset offenders have low intelligence but did not offend as juveniles because they were protected by supportive families or schools. As these cognitively limited individuals reached adulthood, they were unable to transition successfully to adult roles (Thornberry & Krohn, 2005).

Very low IQ scores—those that indicate intellectual disability—are of particular concern. Estimates indicate that at least 4 percent of the U.S. prison population qualify as being intellectually or cognitively disabled (Ashford, Sales, & Reid, 2001). Jails are believed to hold an even higher percentage. It should be noted that intellectual disability (formerly called mental retardation) is distinct from mental disorder or mental illness. Intellectual disability is a cognitive impairment that cannot be reversed, although persons with this disability can be educated, trained, and supported to lead productive lives. Mental disorder or illness is emotional, and it may or may not have a biological basis. It can be addressed with therapy or medication, but psychologists as a group far prefer the former. These conditions as they relate to criminal behavior will be discussed in more detail in Chapter 8.

What does the relationship between IQ scores and delinquency and crime mean exactly? It probably means that delinquents *as a group*, particularly serious delinquents, have had limited experiences in mainstream society, ineffective parenting, restricted cognitive and language development, and poor school experiences, but it does not necessarily mean that they are not intelligent. An undetermined proportion of delinquents are cognitively impaired to the extent that they could be called intellectually disabled, but so many factors are involved in an ultimate IQ score that a simple causal connection between low IQ and delinquency is unwarranted.

Related to the IQ question is the issue of "learning disabilities," a term that is also not synonymous with intelligence. Educational psychologists have identified a variety of learning disabilities, including some that may be associated with brain injuries and perceptual difficulties. Many, if not most, children with learning disabilities are not cognitively impaired. However, there is considerable empirical evidence that juvenile delinquents have a far greater incidence of learning disabilities than nondelinquents (Brier, 1989; Lombardo & Lombardo, 1991; Mallett, 2014; Scaret & Wilgosh, 1989). According to Mallett (2014), approximately 28 to 43 percent of detained and incarcerated young offenders have some form of learning disability. The most common problem appears to be reading comprehension (Rucklidge, McLean, & Bateup, 2009). While learning disabilities clearly exist, it is believed that they are overdiagnosed or misdiagnosed in many children, who then acquire a label that may follow them through the educational system. Like the IQ question, it is very unclear what the relationship between delinquency and learning disability truly means.

Attention Deficit Hyperactivity Disorder

Children are born with a wide range of genetic influences, neurological predispositions, and different temperaments, although the social and physical environments may alter them. These are all biological factors, and some appear to play a major role in the development of crime and delinquency.

The term "hyperactive syndrome" (also called minimal brain dysfunction, hyperkinesis, attention deficit disorder, or, currently, **attention deficit hyperactivity disorder [ADHD]**) includes a variety of behaviors. The central three are (1) inattention (does not seem to listen, or is easily distracted), (2) impulsivity (acts before thinking, shifts quickly from one activity to another), and (3) excessive motor activity (cannot sit still, fidgets, runs about, is talkative and noisy). Some scholars (e.g., Frick & Nigg, 2012) conclude from the research literature that ADHD's core is basically two-dimensional rather than three, represented by (1) inattention and (2) hyperactivity/impulsivity.

ADHD is the leading psychological diagnosis for American children (Cowley, 1993; Staller, 2006). (See **Box 2-2**.) Symptoms of the disorder often emerge in preschool and mostly in boys by a ratio of 3 to 1 over girls (Egger, Kondo, & Angold, 2006; Frick & Nigg, 2012; Sjöwall, Backman, & Thorell, in press). Educators note that children who have been diagnosed with ADHD have difficulty staying on task, remaining cognitively organized, sustaining academic achievement in the school setting, and maintaining control over their behavior. Although the common belief is that one eventually outgrows hyperactivity, the evidence is that the key symptomatic features of hyperactivity persist into adulthood (Frick & Nigg, 2012; Molina, & Pelham, 2014). It should be emphasized, however, that many children diagnosed with ADHD grow up to lead highly successful lives, and most do not follow a life course of serious delinquency and crime. There is a long list of scientists, entertainers, politicians, artists, musicians, athletes, and other public figures who were once diagnosed with or are now suspected of having had ADHD, including Albert Einstein, Dwight D. Eisenhower, Whoopi Goldberg, Bill Gates, Michael Phelps, Steven Spielberg, Walt Disney, John Lennon, Ann Bancroft, Terry Bradshaw, Richard Byrd, Andrew Carnegie, Robin Williams, Agatha Christie, and Ludwig Beethoven.

CONTEMPORARY ISSUES

BOX 2-2   ADHD: Which Treatment to Use?

According to the Center for Disease Control and Prevention (2014), almost 11 percent of school-aged children in the United States have received a diagnosis of ADHD. Many mental health professionals believe that the disorder is over-diagnosed, particularly among preschool children, because the markers (e.g., excessive movement and difficulty staying on task) represent normal early childhood behavior. Despite these concerns, early diagnosis is helpful in anticipating and addressing problems the child who truly has ADHD might encounter in school.

Regardless of the age of the child, parents and caretakers faced with this diagnosis must not only obtain accurate information about the disorder but also make decisions on how it should be treated. The three dominant methods are medication, diet, and behavioral treatment, sometimes in combination.

The typical medication prescribed for ADHD is in the form of stimulants, such as Ritalin®, Adderall®, and Daytrana® (methylphenidate). By stimulating chemicals in the brain to help a person restrain behavior, these medications should inhibit the excessive motor activity that characterizes ADHD and help the person concentrate. Although there are likely side effects, such as loss of appetite or problems sleeping, these side effects should dissipate once the person adjusts to the medication. Parents are often concerned that the use of stimulants will lead to substance abuse in teenage years, but this is a misconception unsubstantiated by research (Sciutto, 2015). However, many critics are concerned about the untested long-term effects of medication, and many believe they are definitely not appropriate for use with young children (Clay, 2013).

The typical dietary restriction is a reduction or total elimination of sugar, an approach which has shown little positive effect. Some parents also adopt caffeine as a supplementary diet, because of its stimulant effects. The dietary approach is not harmful to the child, but neither the medical nor psychological professions recommend it as the sole option.

Many, if not most, psychologists prefer the third option: research-based behavioral treatment. Such treatment typically falls into three categories: parent programs, teacher programs, and therapeutic recreation programs. Parents and teachers can be taught to use strategies that will reward the child for attentiveness and concentration at home and in the classroom, as well as lessen the likelihood of disruptive behavior. ADHD researchers (e.g., Fabiano, 2009) have described many interventions that have produced good results and obviated the need for medication, particularly for very young children. They range from providing praise for appropriate behavior to assuring that the child has sufficient sleep. Recreation programs are typically offered over weeks at a time and involve exercise, crafts, physical activities, and some form of mild behavioral training for the children participating. Behavioral treatment as a whole requires commitment on the part of parents and teachers, but it may be preferable to stimulants if one is concerned about the long-term effects of chemical manipulation.

Questions for Discussion

1. Is it likely that children with ADHD would benefit from counseling or psychotherapy? Why or why not?
2. The percentage of children and adolescents diagnosed with ADHD has increased in recent years. What are the possible reasons for this increase?
3. Which of the treatment approaches discussed above would you recommend for a nine-year-old boy who has just been diagnosed with ADHD?

As mentioned in **Box 2-2**, ADHD affects an estimated 11 percent of school-age children (17 years of age and younger) in the United States, and boys tend to outnumber girls by a ratio of 3 to 1 (Centers for Disease Control and Prevention, 2014). The percentage of children with an ADHD diagnosis has increased in recent years, from 7.8 percent in 2003, to 9.5 percent in 2007, and to 11.0 percent in 2011 (Centers for Disease Control and Prevention, 2014). In the general adult population, the incidence is also about 5 percent (Kessler et al., 2006). Furthermore, ADHD is diagnosed more frequently in children who have a close biological relative with ADHD than in the general population, suggesting there may be a significant biological component involved. ADHD appears to be largely a disorder of self-control and emotional regulation related to problems in brain functioning (Connor, Ford, Chapman, & Banga, 2012). Antisocial and aggressive behavior stemming from ADHD is most often impulsive and a reaction to frustration or perceived threat (Connor et al., 2012). Boys with ADHD are at increased risk for engaging in delinquent and antisocial behavior. "As they grow older, children with untreated ADHD…may abuse drugs or alcohol, engage in antisocial behavior, and suffer physical injury at higher rates than the general population" (Stern, 2001, p. 1).

ADHD is a puzzling problem, the cause of which is largely unknown. Some scientists contend that ADHD children are born with a biological predisposition toward hyperactivity; others maintain that some children are exposed to environmental factors that damage the nervous system. Rolf Loeber (1990) demonstrates how exposure to toxic substances during the preschool years often retards children's neurological development or otherwise influences it in a negative way, often resulting in symptoms of ADHD. For example, children exposed to low levels of lead toxicity (e.g., from paint or contaminated soil) are more hyperactive and impulsive, and are easily distracted and frustrated. They also show discernible problems in following simple instructions. The causal factors of ADHD are probably multiple, complicated, and extremely difficult to identify.

Some researchers observe that children with ADHD do not possess effective strategies and cognitive organization with which to deal with the daily demands of school. ADHD children also seem to lack cognitively organized ways for dealing with new knowledge. The core problem appears to center around executive functions, or what can be termed "self-regulation skills" (Douglas, 2004). **Self-regulation** refers to the ability to control one's own behavior. According to Virginia Douglas (2004), it is not so much "not knowing" as "not doing." Attention, inhibition, and organizing are ways of "doing" or working on cognitive processes. Stimulant drugs, Douglas argues, enable ADHD children to improve on self-regulation processes. These drugs themselves, though, are extremely controversial and are themselves widely believed to be overprescribed (see again **Box 2-2**).

Although many behaviors have been identified as accompanying ADHD, another overriding theme is that ADHD children are perceived as annoying and aversive to those around them. Although ADHD children are continually seeking and prolonging interpersonal contacts, they eventually manage to irritate and frustrate those people with whom they interact (Henker & Whalen, 1989). They are often rejected by peers, especially if they are perceived as aggressive (Henker & Whalen, 1989). Parents report ADHD children are 10 times more likely to have difficulties developing friendships with peers than non-ADHD children (Centers for Disease Control and Prevention, 2014). This pattern of peer rejection appears to continue throughout the developmental years (Murray-Close et al., 2010; Reid, 1993). According to research data, approximately 52 to 82 percent of children with ADHD are rejected by peers (Hoza et al., 2005; Murray-Close et al., 2010).

ADHD and Criminal Behavior

Some researchers (e.g., Pfiffner, McBurnett, Rathouz, & Judice, 2005) estimate about one-fourth of all children with ADHD engage in serious antisocial behavior during childhood and adolescence and criminal behavior as adults. Terrie Moffitt (Moffitt, 1993b; Moffitt & Silva, 1988) observes that a very large number of ADHD children self-report delinquent behaviors by early adolescence. She also found that children between the ages of five and seven who display the characteristics of both ADHD and delinquent behavior not only have special difficulty with social relationships but also have a high probability of consistent serious antisocial behavior into adolescence and beyond (Lee & Hinshaw, 2004; Moffitt, 1990b; Sibley et al., 2011). Experts generally agree that the most common problem associated with ADHD is delinquency and substance abuse. The data strongly suggest that youth with symptoms of both ADHD and antisocial behavior are at very high risk for developing lengthy and serious criminal careers (Moffitt, 1990b; Satterfield, Swanson, Schell, & Lee, 1994). David Farrington (1991), in his well-cited research, also found that violent offenders often have a history of hyperactivity, impulsivity, and attention deficit problems.

It should be noted that "the prevalence rates for ADHD are 3 to 10 times higher in secure correctional facilities than are found in the general population" (Connor et al., 2012, p. 727). More specifically, ADHD rates are between 11.7 percent and 45 percent for incarcerated males, and 10 percent and 18.5 percent for incarcerated females, compared to around 5 percent in the general population (Connor et al., 2012). In addition, incarcerated individuals with ADHD are more likely to engage in disruptive, rule-violating, and impulsive aggressive behaviors than others in secure correctional facilities. "ADHD youth in juvenile justice and secure treatment settings are at risk for rehabilitative failure, academic failure, occupational failure, continued antisocial behavior, substance abuse, comorbid psychiatric and learning disorders, and impulsive aggression" (Connor et al., 2012, p. 743).

Conduct Disorder

ADHD frequently co-occurs with a diagnostic category called "conduct disorders" (Connor et al., 2012; Offord, Boyle, & Racine, 1991; Reid, 1993), but the two should be considered separate entities. However, it should also be mentioned that the often-observed progression from childhood ADHD to early-onset CD is accounted for, in part, by ineffective and coercive parenting (Beauchaine, Hinshaw, & Pang, 2010; Meier, Slutske, Heath, & Martin, 2009). Research demonstrates that certain disorders occur together often as a result of psychological and biological vulnerabilities interacting with environmental conditions, such as the quality of parenting. In other words, childhood and adult disorders are a result of developmental cascading factors.

The term **conduct disorder (CD)** represents a cluster of behaviors characterized by persistent misbehavior, including bullying, fighting, using or threatening weapon use on others, physical cruelty to people and animals, destruction of property, chronic deceitfulness, sexual assaults, and serious violations of rules (American Psychiatric Association, 2013). CD is also associated with a variety of psychological problems across the life span (Frick & Nigg, 2012). "This includes mental health problems (e.g., substance abuse), legal problems (e.g., risk for arrest), educational problems (dropping out of school), social problems (e.g., poor marital adjustment), occupation problems (e.g., poor job performance), and physical health problems (e.g., poor respiratory function)" (Frick & Nigg, 2012, p. 93). Youth conduct problems frequently result in significant disruptions at home and school, and can lead to violence and other serious crimes (McMahon, Witkiewitz, Kotler, & The Conduct Problems Prevention Research Group, 2010). Examples of this misbehavior include stealing, fire setting, running away from home, skipping school, destroying property, fighting, frequently telling lies, and cruelty to animals and people. According to the DSM-5 (American Psychiatric Association, 2013), the central feature of CD is a *repetitive* and *persistent* pattern of behavior that violates the basic rights of others or violates major age-appropriate societal norms. CD can range from mild forms of expression (such as minimal harm to persons or property) to severe forms of behavior, such as substantial harm to persons, and significant damage to property.

In the DSM-5, CD is separated into two main categories. If the misconduct begins before age 10, it is called CD: childhood-onset type. If it begins in adolescence, it is called CD: adolescent-onset type. The childhood-onset group frequently begins showing mild conduct problems as early as preschool or early elementary school, and then increases in rate and severity throughout childhood and through adolescence (Frick & Nigg, 2012). According to the DSM-5, although the onset of CD can occur in preschool years, "the first significant symptoms usually emerge during the period from middle childhood through middle adolescence, and onset is rare after age 16 years" (p. 473).

If CD emerges during early childhood, the child may be destined for an exposure to a wide spectrum of risk factors that result in a life of trouble and difficulty. If onset occurs during adolescence, the individual often matures into a life without involvement in serious or violent criminal behavior.

As noted by Frick and Nigg, childhood-onset CD appears to be strongly related to neuropsychological and cognitive deficits, compounded by family conflict and instability, and faulty parenting. This process disrupts the child's socialization and development of interpersonal skills for getting along with others within and outside the family.

Overall, between 2 percent and 10 percent of children and adolescents in the United States show behavioral patterns that may be diagnosed as a CD (American Psychiatric Association, 2013; Eddy, 2003; Frick, 2006). Boys outnumber girls by about four-to-one before adolescence, and by about two-to-one during adolescence (Frick, 2006). In addition, CD is the diagnostic label most often placed on youths who appear before the juvenile courts (Lahey et al., 1995). A study by Anna Bardone and her colleagues (Bardone, Moffitt, & Caspi, 1996) found that CD patterns in girls are a strong predictor of a lifetime of problems, including poor interpersonal relations with partners/spouses and peers, criminal activity, early pregnancy without supportive partners, and frequent job loss and firings. Similar to CD boys, CD girls appear destined for a life of interpersonal conflict with the social environment.

Oppositional Defiant Disorder

CD and **oppositional defiant disorder (ODD)** are often classified as **disruptive behavior disorders (DBD)**, though they involve both behaviors and emotions. Sometimes ADHD is also included as a disruptive behavior disorder. (See **Table 2-4** for features associated with these three diagnoses.)

TABLE 2-4 Features of ADHD, CD, and ODD

Attention Deficit Hyperactivity Disorder
- Most common psychological diagnosis of children
- Characterized by inattention, impulsivity, excessive motor activity
- Typically manifested early, preschool period
- Boys outnumber girls, usually by 3:1 ratio
- About 11 percent of school-aged children in the United States now have this diagnosis
- About one-half retain the diagnosis into adulthood
- Difficulty developing friendships with peers—perceived as aversive or annoying
- Cause unknown; theories range from genetic to toxins in environment
- Misdiagnosis not uncommon

Conduct Disorder
- Repetitive and persistent patterns of violating rights of others
- Typical behaviors include bullying, destroying property, cruelty to animals, theft
- Problems controlling behavior, but also emotions
- Divided into childhood-onset and adolescent-onset types
- Childhood onset most serious, associated with problems across the life span
- Boys outnumber girls by ratio of 4:1 (childhood) and 2:1 (adolescence)
- Most common diagnosis recorded in juvenile courts
- May co-occur with ADHD

Oppositional Defiant Disorder
- Characterized by problems controlling emotions and behavior
- Least frequently diagnosed of the three
- Negative, hostile, vindictive, defiant demeanor
- May display irritability
- Problems not generally long lasting
- May predict adjustment problems in adolescence and adulthood if begins early

According to the DSM-5 (American Psychiatric Association, 2013), ODD represents problems in self-control of emotions and behaviors, while CD represents more problems in control of behavior, but also some problems in controlling emotions. The DSM-5 describes the child with ODD as negative, hostile, vindictive, and defiant, more than is expected for his or her age, with these behaviors lasting for at least six months. According to the DSM, children and adolescents with ODD display a persistent pattern of angry outbursts, arguments, vindictiveness, resentment, and disobedience. Some researchers have suggested that irritability be added as a core dimension of the disorder (Burke et al., 2014). These behavioral and emotional patterns may be directed at parents, teachers, classmates, friends, or other authority figures. In order to receive this diagnosis, the intensity and frequency of the negative pattern should exceed what is normative for the individual's age, gender, and culture. In clinical practice, CD sometimes occurs without the accompanying characteristics of ODD. Furthermore, although ODD is a challenging condition during childhood, it is a diagnosis that is not highly associated with *lasting* conduct or behavioral problems. To some, ODD is just "normal child and teenage behavior." In general, the symptoms of ODD appear to decline as the child gets older (Maughan, Rowe, Messer, Goodman, & Meltzer, 2004). Although there is some research that suggests that early signs of ODD predict early onset of CD (Frick & Nigg, 2012), it is largely unknown if ODD predicts criminal behavior over the long run (Burke et al., 2014; Burke, Waldman, & Lahey, 2010). Some recent research suggests ODD does not lead to long-term antisocial or serious criminal behavior (Leadbetter & Homel, in press). However, ODD in childhood has been shown to predict adjustment problems in adolescence and adulthood (Frick & Nigg, 2012). The complex relationship between ADHD, CD, ODD, and criminal behavior is perhaps best summarized by the following quote: "…delinquent adult boys usually traverse a developmental pathway that begins with severe hyperactive/impulsive behaviors as early as toddlerhood, followed by ODD in preschool, early-onset CD in elementary school, substance abuse disorders (SUDs) in adolescence, and antisocial personality in adulthood" (Beauchaine et al., 2010, p. 328). While this developmental trajectory may be typical for some youth, we hasten to add that research has yet to establish that anyone of the disorders (AHDH, CD, or ODD) automatically leads to another. After all, there are often a number of intervening protective factors that occur during the life course that may neutralize or mitigate future negative outcomes.

Finally, as suggested earlier in the chapter, a cumulative risk or a cascade effect of early onset of ADHD, CD, or ODD may precipitate a series of social and developmental setbacks, which may then snowball into a variety of psychological and antisocial behaviors later on if preventive strategies are not implemented early.

SUMMARY AND CONCLUSIONS

In this chapter, we began to examine some of the social and psychological risk factors associated with crime and delinquency, often focusing on the work of developmental psychologists. They examine developmental pathways or trajectories that lead to little or no offending, minor juvenile offending that begins and ends around mid- to late adolescence, and offending that begins early in childhood and continues on to serious offending into adulthood, among other pathways. In addition, psychologists have searched for effective intervention strategies for children and families, with a goal to promoting a healthy, nurturing environment. Unfortunately, effective treatment strategies are more elusive, although approaches such as reducing coercive family interactions have had promising results (Biglan et al., 2012).

Researchers can now point with confidence to a large list of risk factors associated with juvenile delinquency and criminal behavior. No single risk factor is particularly at fault; rather, it is believed that multiple factors lead to serious offending by juveniles. Two important and similar models proposed in recent years are the cumulative risk and developmental cascade models, both of which emphasize that antisocial behavior can be attributed to an accumulation of risk factors during a child's development. At the same time, there is a shortage or a complete absence of protective variables that might offset the negative effects of the risk factors.

Many theories of criminology trace the roots of offending to childhood and early adolescence. An adverse economic environment must be considered within the context of the many influences that impinge on young lives. Features often associated with poverty—discrimination, inadequate schools, unsafe living conditions, and joblessness—may play roles in the formation of crime and delinquency, but it is important not to focus on poverty alone.

One risk factor that appears increasingly in the literature on delinquency is early peer rejection, even during the elementary school years. This can occur regardless of a child's socioeconomic status. Children who are rejected by peers are often aggressive, but aggression alone is not the major explanation. Rather, they also tend to be disruptive, impulsive, and/or have few interpersonal skills. Research has demonstrated consistently that antisocial adolescents, particularly those who displayed highly aggressive behavior, experienced significant peer rejection during their childhoods. In addition, they often associate with other rejected peers and form groups or gangs engaging in antisocial activity. In girls, substance abuse and other delinquent behaviors in adolescence have been associated with peer rejection in elementary school.

Preschool experiences are also increasingly being recognized as possible risk factors. Poor-quality child care places children at risk for poorer language and cognitive development, as well as deficiencies in social skills. Unfortunately, inadequate child care is often associated with low socioeconomic class. On the other hand, high-quality day care has been shown to improve the chances that children from economically deprived families will do well both behaviorally and in school settings.

It is important to stress that delinquency is clearly not limited to youths from any one socioeconomic group. Self-report data suggest that social class differences become smaller when youths are asked to report their own offending. If poverty and the conditions it generates are not an issue for these youth, we must look to other risk factors, such as parenting styles and practices, the influence of antisocial peers, and the more individual factors such as CDs, ADHD, intelligence, and gender.

Among the parental and family risk factors discussed in the chapter are single-parent households, which have too often been blamed for antisocial behavior of children. We stressed process variables rather than structure variables were more likely risk factors. For example, researchers have found associations between certain parental styles and antisocial behavior in children. Styles are typically identified as authoritarian, permissive, authoritative, or neglecting (Baumrind, 1991a) or as enmeshed or lax (Snyder & Patterson, 1987). Although many parents may well vary their styles across situations and as children get older, in general one style dominates. The permissive and lax styles—characterized by little or no control over the children and extremely few restrictions—are highly correlated with delinquent behavior. In similar fashion, parental monitoring or supervision of the child's activities, particularly from the ages of nine to mid-adolescence, is crucial to the development of prosocial behavior. In addition, community or neighborhood monitoring should be promoted.

We covered psychological risk factors—those that are unique to the child—as factors on the road to delinquency. Low IQ scores have consistently been associated with delinquency, not necessarily directly but more likely because children with low scores do not do well in school, and school failure is also commonly associated with antisocial behavior. We stressed, though, that a low score on an "intelligence" test does not mean that a child is not intelligent. In addition, we know not only that many delinquents are intelligent despite scoring below normal on IQ tests but also that other delinquents score high on IQ tests. Therefore, the IQ–delinquency connection must be expressed very cautiously.

Children with ADHD are at some risk of antisocial behavior both as juveniles and adults. This disorder apparently affects 3 to 5 percent of school-aged children, though in some communities the percentages are even higher, leading to questions about misdiagnoses. ADHD appears to be a disorder affecting social relationships; the children have difficulty staying on task, they get easily distracted, are impulsive, display excessive motor activity, and are annoying to others. These features often lead to peer rejection. Although ADHD is routinely treated with medication, this in itself is a controversial issue, and critics recommend the use of other approaches, including physical exercise and outdoor activities. Untreated, ADHD children are at risk for delinquency and substance abuse.

CD is somewhat of a catch-all category that is characterized by persistent misbehavior, including stealing, running away, fighting, telling lies, and cruelty. Signs of CD may occur as early as age three, but it most often emerges in late childhood or adolescence. Not surprisingly, CD is also associated with peer rejection. Finally, ODD is often associated with antisocial behavior, but not everyone agrees that it merits the attention it has received. Although a diagnosis of ODD in childhood is associated with adjustment problems in adolescence and adulthood, the association between ODD and ongoing or serious criminal activity has not been established.

Key Concepts

Attachment theory
Attention deficit hyperactivity
　　disorder (ADHD)
Authoritarian style
Authoritative style
Conduct disorder (CD)
Cumulative risk (CR) model
Developmental cascade model
　　(also dynamic cascade model)
Developmental pathway
Disruptive behavior disorders (DBD)
Enmeshed style

Language impairment
Lax style
Neglecting style
Oppositional defiant disorder
　　(ODD)
Parental monitoring
Parental practices
Parental styles
Permissive style
Psychometric approach
Psychometric intelligence (PI)
Self-regulation

Review Questions

1. Compare and contrast the cumulative risk and developmental cascade model.
2. What three categories of risk factors are covered in this chapter? Name and explain briefly any two factors falling into each category.
3. Discuss the relevance of peer rejection to ongoing antisocial behavior.

4. Describe each of Baumrind's four parental styles.
5. What is attachment theory, and how might it relate to juvenile delinquency and adult criminal behavior?
6. Describe the features of ADHD that create problems for the child who has this disorder.
7. Explain the differences among ODD, ADHD, and conduct disorder.

Origins of Criminal Behavior: Biological Factors

CHAPTER OBJECTIVES

- Explore the genetic and biological aspects of criminal behavior.
- Provide an overview of behavior genetics and molecular genetics as they pertain to antisocial behavior.
- Provide an overview of twin and adoption studies and their relation to theories of crime.
- Discuss temperament and its effects on the behavior of children and their caretakers.
- Identify environmental risk factors that play a role in the psychobiological aspects of criminal behavior.
- Summarize the current research on environmental neurotoxins that present the greatest risk for healthy neurodevelopment.
- Summarize recent research on child and adolescent brain development, including fetal exposure to nicotine and drugs, effects of malnutrition, and traumatic brain injury and their relationship to antisocial and criminal behavior.

Cross the threshold of any preschool or kindergarten classroom, and you are likely to encounter a flurry of activity—little people scurrying around the room, or restless and energetic tykes eager to move to a different location or position. You are also likely to observe a fair amount of pushing and shoving, despite a teacher's efforts to keep these behaviors under control. "Trent," described at the beginning of Chapter 2, was probably not that atypical as a preschooler or even as an early grade school student.

A common research finding is that many, if not most, children, especially boys, exhibit high levels of physical aggression in preschool or kindergarten, but in most cases, they typically show significant reductions of these behaviors as the school years progress due to the effects of socialization and parenting (Bongers, Koot, van der Ende, & Verhulst, 2003; Séguin, Nagin, Asaad, & Tremblay, 2004). The pushing and shoving observed in kindergarten should dissipate within the next few years. Another common finding, however, is that certain brain and biochemical characteristics appear to *predispose* some children to exhibit higher levels of aggression than that exhibited by their peers, and if these are not neutralized by socialization and competent parenting, many of these children grow up to follow a life path characterized by high levels of aggression and violence. Youngsters who follow an early onset of persistent antisocial behavior often exhibit biological/neurological abnormalities or deficits, while late-onset offending appears to be more influenced by social factors (Moffitt, Lynam, & Silva, 1994; Rutter, 1997; Rutter, Giller, & Hagell, 1998).

Thus, many—perhaps most—contemporary criminologists would agree that genetics and biological factors may play some role in criminality, but the social environment is the most important determinant of criminal behavior. Greed, desire for power, the glorification of violence, economic inequality, high unemployment, substandard education, faulty parenting, and group values that deviate from society's norms are often considered the major culprits in producing crime. Heredity-based or physiologically based components have been traditionally scoffed at, and their possible role in criminality is often dismissed. In recent years, however, with more research, the interaction between biological factors and the environment is receiving more positive attention (Wright & Boisvert, 2009). Whereas genetic and other biological factors were initially considered negligible by contemporary criminologists, they are now given respectable status, though certainly not center stage.

Adrian Raine (2008), a prominent biopsychologist, has remarked: "Despite strong resistance in many quarters, there is now little scientific doubt that genes play a significant role in antisocial behavior" (p. 323). According to Raine, the more challenging questions today are twofold: (1) determining how much of antisocial behavior is influenced by genes and (2) deciding which specific genes predispose a person to which kinds of antisocial behavior.

Biopsychologists (psychologists who study the biological aspects of behavior) try to determine which genetic and neurophysiological variables play a part in criminal behavior, how important they are, and what can be done to modify them. Biopsychologists do not believe that genetic or neurophysiological components are the sole or even primary causal agents of human behavior. Most would say that understanding the social environment is as important as understanding the biological one. In the words of one group of biopsychologists, "The social world, as well as the organization and operation of the brain, shapes and modulates genetic and biological processes, and accordingly, knowledge of biological and social domains is necessary to develop comprehensive theories in either domain" (Cacioppo, Berntson, Sheridan, & McClintock, 2000, p. 833). In this chapter, we concentrate on the biological relationships to criminal behavior, while, at the same time, continually appreciating the enormous influence of the social environment on the neurological and biological processes.

The chapter first explores the genetic aspects of crime, including findings from twin and adoption studies and from molecular biology. We then move on to discuss physiological and environmental health factors that can lead to antisocial behavior.

GENETICS AND ANTISOCIAL BEHAVIOR

From the late twentieth century to today, two categories of genetics research have been featured prominently in studies of human behavior, including antisocial and criminal behavior. They are **behavior genetics** and **molecular genetics**. Behavior genetics focuses on examining the role genes play in the formation and development of human and animal behavior. It is the branch of biology that investigates the relationship between genes and the environment in determining individual differences in behavior. It has the advantage of "clearly distinguishing genetic from environmental influences and estimating their relative magnitudes" (Rhee & Waldman, 2011, p. 143). The method used in behavior genetics is especially powerful for disentangling genetic from environmental influences in twin and adoption studies.

Molecular genetics is the field of biology that studies the structure and function of genes at the molecular level. Contemporary molecular biology has focused on specific genes as foundations for certain patterns of behavior. Further, "a central precept of molecular biology is that all the information needed to construct a mammalian body, whether human or mouse, is contained in the approximately 100,000 genes of mammalian DNA and that a set of master genes activates the DNA necessary to produce the appropriate proteins for development and behavior" (Cacioppo et al., 2000, p. 833). Molecular genetics studies how the genes are transferred from generation to generation and generally concentrates on the long polymers of deoxyribonucleic acid (DNA).

Behavior Genetics

Traditional behavior genetics views behavioral differences as springing from three genetic or environmental sources: (1) those influences attributable to genetic effects; (2) environmental influences shared by siblings (e.g., family environments); and (3) influences that arise from unshared environmental experiences that makes siblings differ from one another (Dick & Rose, 2002). The magnitude of these genetic and environmental influences is usually obtained from statistical analyses that compare identical twins with fraternal twins, who like ordinary siblings share one-half of their genes. Identical twins share the same genes. Therefore, one way to determine the role of genetics in criminality is to compare the incidence and type of delinquency or criminal convictions among identical (monozygotic) and fraternal (dizygotic) twins. **Dizygotic (DZ) twins** (also called **fraternal twins**) develop from two different fertilized eggs and are no more genetically alike than nontwin siblings. They are, though, equally susceptible to prenatal environmental influences, such as nicotine or alcohol use by the mother during that particular pregnancy. **Monozygotic (MZ) twins** (or **identical twins**) develop from a single egg; they are always the same sex and share the same genes. Presumably, then, if genes are determinative, identical twins should display highly similar behavior. If they do not, then we may infer that the behavioral differences are due to environmental factors. Because MZ twins share 100 percent of their genes, it can be inferred that a child's genetic risk for antisocial behavior is high if his or her co-twin shows antisocial behavior and low if the MZ co-twin does not.

However, to complicate matters a bit, approximately two-thirds of MZ twins are monochorionic (share the same chorion), and one-third of the MZ pair is dichorionic (two different chorions) (Rhee & Waldman, 2002). The chorion is the outer membrane enclosing the embryo. Therefore, some identical twins develop in slightly different prenatal environments, which may contribute to some individual differences that may emerge as the twins develop into maturity. In fact, several studies have found that monochorionic, MZ twins are more similar in personality and cognitive ability than dichorionic, MZ twins (Rhee & Waldman, 2002). Theoretically, however, by comparing fraternal twins and identical twins, researchers should be able to identify the relative contributions of genes compared with environmental factors in the development of personality, cognitive ability, and behavior in general.

Studies of Twins

Twin studies—and some adoption studies—provide some support for the heritability of antisocial behavior. Over 100 such studies involving a total of more than 77,000 families have examined the relationship between genes and antisocial behavior (Moffitt, 2005a, 2005b; Raine, 2008). Twin research has included as many as 800,000 pairs of twins (Johnson, Turkheimer, Gottesman, & Bouchard, 2009). The data from these studies have allowed researchers to conclude that genes influence approximately 50 percent of the population variation in antisocial behavior, suggesting that genetics plays a significant role in its development (Burt, 2009; Raine, 2013). Similar results have been reported for specifically aggressive and violent behavior (Rhee & Waldman, 2011) and for serious, chronic juvenile offenders (Barnes, Beaver, & Boutwell, 2011). The presence of genetic influences does not mean, however, that genes directly *cause* the behavior to the exclusion of other influences (Johnson et al., 2009). Genes are not fixed, static, and immutable. Environmental influences early in human development can directly change gene expression, in turn altering brain functioning and resulting in antisocial and other forms of deviant behavior; or environmental influences can have the opposite effect, producing a positive change on genes that might otherwise be problematic. Psychosocial influences can result in structural modifications to DNA that have profound influences on neuronal functioning and behavior. These complex interactions underscore the importance of understanding developmental cascade effects.

Moreover, if genes influence half of the total variation in antisocial behavior, this still leaves considerable room for environmental influences on the formation of behavior. Peer and sibling interactions, child neglect and abuse, social modeling, and brain injuries or disease can also have negative influences. On the positive side, warm, supportive parenting can effectively neutralize or shift a child's behavior toward more prosocial and nonantisocial behavior, even in those children who are most genetically vulnerable toward criminal behavior (Kim-Cohen & Gold, 2009).

Several concepts should be recognized before a good understanding of twin studies can be achieved. They are shared environments, nonshared environments, and concordance.

SHARED AND NONSHARED ENVIRONMENTS. **Shared environments**, sometimes referred to as common environments, include prenatal and life experiences affecting both twins in the same way. For example, twins raised by the same biological parents share a common hereditary and home environment. Shared environments in this sense are apt to promote high trait or behavioral similarity between twin pairs, especially for identical twins. This is especially the case for antisocial behavioral patterns, even in siblings who are not twins (Kendler, Prescott, Myers, & Neale, 2003; Moffitt, 2005a). Antisocial-prone parents tend to produce antisocial-prone offspring. Compared to genes, which account for about 50 percent of the variation in antisocial behavior, shared environments contribute about 15 to 20 percent of the variation (Moffitt, 2005a; Rhee & Waldman, 2002).

Nonshared environments, on the other hand, include living experiences that are different for each twin, such as being raised in a different home environment, participating in different activities, or even attending different schools. Parents sometimes want to preserve the uniqueness of each twin by encouraging them to join separate groups or pursue separate hobbies and activities. Therefore, in order to determine the relative influence of genes and the environment on behavior, shared and nonshared aspects must be considered. The available research suggests that nonshared environments account for approximately 30 percent of the variation in antisocial behavior (Moffitt, 2005a). However, research suggests that developmental factors also play a critical role. For example, twin research indicates that, for a variety of traits, the magnitude of genetic and nonshared environmental influences increases as a person gets older, whereas the magnitude of shared environmental influences decreases (Loehlin, 1992; Plomin, 1986; Rhee & Waldman, 2002). That is, as the child begins to spend more time outside the family circle, especially when he or she becomes a young adult, the influence of the shared environment (family) tends to wane, whereas the influence of genetics and nonshared environments (e.g., peers) becomes more discernible. Rhee and Waldman (2002) describe a longitudinal study by Matheny (1989) which revealed that the temperaments (e.g., emotional tone, fearfulness, approach, and avoidance toward others) became more similar for identical pairs than for fraternal pairs as they grew older. Thus, we might expect that developmental age of the subjects in any twin study may play an important role in determining the influences of genetics compared with the environment. We return to this point shortly.

Some investigators suggest that identical twins are so physically alike that they probably elicit similar social responses from their environment (shared environment), more so than fraternal twins. In this sense, they are more likely to develop similar personalities. There may be merit to this viewpoint, but research does not yet support it. When reared together, identical twins or their parents may make a conscious effort to accentuate their individual identities, whereas when reared apart, they may have less need to be different.

CONCORDANCE. A key concept in twin study research, **concordance** is the term used in genetics for the degree to which related pairs of subjects both show a particular behavior or condition. It is usually expressed in percentages. Assume that we want to determine the concordance of intelligence among 20 pairs of identical twins and 20 pairs of fraternals. If we find that 10 pairs of the identical twins have approximately the same IQ score, but only five pairs of the fraternals obtain the same score, our concordance is 50 percent for identicals and 25 percent for fraternals. The concordance for identicals would be twice that of fraternals, suggesting that hereditary factors play an important role in intelligence. If, however, the two concordances were about the same, we would conclude that genetics is irrelevant, at least as represented in our sample and measured by our methods.

Numerous early twin studies using this concordance method have indicated that heredity may be a powerful determinant of intelligence, schizophrenia, depressions, neurotic disorders, alcoholism, and criminal behavior (Claridge, 1973; Hetherington & Parke, 1975; McClearn & DeFries, 1973; Rosenthal, 1970, 1971). The first such study relative to criminality was reported by the Munich physician Johannes Lange (1929) in his book *Crime as Destiny* (Christiansen, 1977; Rosenthal, 1971). The title reflects Lange's conviction that criminal conduct is a predetermined fate dictated by heredity. He found a criminality concordance of 77 percent for 13 pairs of adult identical twins and only 12 percent for 17 pairs of adult fraternal twins. Auguste Marcel Legras (1932) then found a 100 percent criminal concordance for five pairs of identicals. Note that both of these studies used small samples. Subsequent studies, using more sophisticated designs and methods of twin identification and sampling, continued to find a substantially higher criminal concordance for identical twins when compared with fraternals. The levels were not as high as those reported by either Lange or Legras, however. Although these tabulated investigations differed in method and definitions of criminality, the combined concordance levels demonstrate that, where criminal behavior is concerned, identical twins seem better matched than fraternal twins.

The Twins' Early Development Study

One of the most closely watched series of twin studies is the ongoing longitudinal research being conducted in the United Kingdom involving a large sample of twins born in 1994, 1995, and 1996 in England and Wales. Called the **Twins' Early Development Study (TEDS)**, it explores behavior problems as well as problematic development in language, cognition, and academic abilities from early childhood through adolescence (Haworth, Davis, & Plomin, 2012; Oliver & Plomin, 2007; Trouton, Spinath, & Plomin, 2002). Although there has been some attrition since data were first collected, over 13,000 pairs of twins have remained involved in the research. It should be noted that between January 2012 and December 2014, all of the TEDS twins turned age 18, enabling the researchers to examine the developmental pathways of twins from early childhood to young adulthood. Consequently, the study offers one of the most extensive investigations of the developmental patterns of twins to date. The sample currently consists of 10,000 twin pairs (Haworth et al., 2012). The ongoing project is based at King's College London and is under the leadership of Professor Robert Plomin.

As we indicate throughout this chapter, both nature and nurture contribute to human behavior, and—not surprisingly—this is supported in TEDS research studies. However, TEDS research indicates that nature has considerable influence over some behavior problems (e.g., ADHD; autism spectrum disorder). With respect to antisocial behavior, which is our main concern, the TEDS data suggest heritability seems to play a modest role. Nevertheless, at least one personality feature that has been associated with antisocial behavior—the callous-unemotional trait—shows very high heritability and little shared environmental influence (Oliver & Plomin, 2007; Viding, Blair, James, Moffitt, & Plomin, 2005). Callous-unemotional traits will be discussed again in Chapter 6.

In a study facilitated by the TEDS database, Jaffee and her colleagues (2005) used MZ and DZ twin pairs to study the interplay between genetic and environmental risks on the development of antisocial behavior in a cohort of 1,116 five-year-old twin pairs and their families. These participants are members of the Environmental Risk (E-Risk) Longitudinal Twin Study. The Jaffee researchers ascertained the children's antisocial behavior through interviews with parents, assessments of the children, and questionnaires administered to teachers. The environmental risk factor in the study was the amount of maltreatment the child reportedly received from parents, because research shows that early maltreatment often leads to antisocial behavior (Lansford et al., 2002). Not surprisingly, Jaffee et al. (2005) discovered that the effect of maltreatment on the risk to develop antisocial behavior was strongest among those at higher genetic risk. In other words, those children with a genetic predisposition to become troublesome and antisocial were especially likely to be that way if they were mistreated. These findings and the findings of many other studies continue to support the general consensus that environmental changes turn genetic influences on and off during the developmental years, and that biological factors and environmental influences do interact (Raine, 2002, 2013). There is emerging evidence that suggests the social environment (e.g., parenting) can affect people who are at genetic risk more strongly than previously appreciated (Hou et al., 2013; Maes et al., 2006; Moffitt, 2005a).

As mentioned previously, these environmental influences seem to wane somewhat as a person moves into adulthood. For example, there is emerging evidence that the magnitude of familial or parental influences on aggressive behavior decreases with increasing age, and genetic factors increasingly play a prominent role in the stability of aggression and antisocial behavior across the life span (Rhee & Waldman, 2002; van Beijsterveldt, Bartels, Hudziak, & Boomsma, 2003). This effect seems to be particularly strong in males. Female aggressive behavior, on the other hand, seems to be more strongly affected by the family environment (van Beijsterveldt et al., 2003). In other words, family influences appear to be more powerful in the inhibition of antisocial behavior in girls than in boys, particularly as the girls approach adolescence and early adulthood.

Twin Study of Child and Adolescent Development

Another longitudinal research project is the Twin Study of Child and Adolescent Development (TCHAD), using data from the Swedish Twin Registry. Tuvblad, Eley, and Lichtenstein (2005), studying 1,226 twin pairs, employed a well-researched behavioral scale to measure parental-reported aggression in children ages eight and nine. They then asked the same group of children to report their own delinquent behavior eight years later. The researchers used both MZ and DZ twins in their effort to disentangle genetic factors from environmental factors. They found that genetic factors played an important role in the early onset of aggressive behavior in children, but appeared to play a less important role in the development of delinquent behavior as reported by male adolescents. A similar finding was reported by Taylor, Iacono, and McGue (2000), who found that genetics played a more prominent role in early-onset delinquency (life-course-persistent offenders), whereas the social environment (e.g., delinquent peers) was more influential in late-onset delinquency (adolescent-limited offenders). The subjects in the study were all boys. Surprisingly, genetics appeared to play a much more prominent role in development of *both* aggressive behavior and delinquency in girls in the Tuvblad et al. (2005) study. These results appear to be in contrast to the study of Rhee and Waldman (2002), who concluded that the magnitude of genetic and environmental influences on antisocial behavior is equal for both genders. It is clear from these two contrasting studies that further research on the relative influence of genes on gender differences in antisocial behavior is warranted.

Adoption Studies

Another method used to identify crucial variables in the interaction between heredity and environment is the adoption study, which helps identify environments most conducive to criminality. The adoption study capitalizes on the assumption that adoptive parents and their adopted children are not genetically related (Jaffee, Strait, & Odgers, 2012). There have been exceedingly few such investigations, however, and those few have been fraught with methodological problems.

One of the first adoption studies was carried out in Denmark by Schulsinger (1972), who explored the incidence of psychopathy in the biological relatives of adopted adults. Schulsinger compared 57 adopted adults whom he diagnosed psychopathic to a control group of 57 nonpsychopathic adopted adults. The two groups were matched for sex, age, social class, and age of transfer to the adopting family. The study's direct implications for criminal behavior are questionable, because Schulsinger defined psychopathy by his own loose criteria. Individuals who were impulse ridden and who exhibited acting-out behavior qualified. As we will see in Chapter 7, these descriptions do not necessarily connote either psychopathy or criminality. Nevertheless, impulsivity is associated with some forms of criminal behavior, so the study has some relevance.

Schulsinger found that 3.9 percent of the biological relatives of psychopathic adoptees could also be classified as psychopathic, whereas only 1.4 percent of the control group's biological relatives could. The results just failed to reach statistical significance, indicating that we should be very cautious about accepting their implications. It is interesting, though, that psychopathy—even given its loose definition—was about two and a half times greater in the family backgrounds of acting-out adoptees.

Crowe (1974) conducted a better-designed study, a follow-up of 52 persons relinquished for early adoption by female offenders. Ninety percent of the biological mothers were felons at the time of the adoptive placement, the most common offenses being forgery and passing bad checks. Twenty-five of the adoptees were female, and all were white. Another 52 adoptees with no evidence of criminal family background were selected as a control group and matched for sex, race, and age at the time of adoption.

For the follow-up phase of the study, Crowe selected 37 index and 37 control subjects who had by then reached age 18. (Index subjects in research are those subjects who are of major concern.) Seven of the index adoptees had arrest records: As adults, all seven had at least one conviction, four had multiple arrests, two had multiple convictions, and three were felons. Of the 37 matching controls, two had adult arrest records and only one of these had been convicted. Each subject's personality was diagnosed by three clinicians based on test results and data gathered in an interview; no family background was included. The clinicians made their diagnoses independently of one another and without knowing the subject's group. Six of the adoptees born of female offenders were labeled "antisocial personality"; one control group subject was labeled "probable antisocial personality."

Crowe found a positive correlation between the tendency of the index group to be antisocial and two other variables: the child's age at the time of adoptive placement and the length of time the child had spent in temporary care (orphanages and foster homes) prior to that placement. The older the child of an offender upon adoptive placement and the longer the temporary placement, the more likely the child would grow up antisocial. The control group members were not affected by these conditions. This suggests either that the two adoptee groups responded differently to similar environmental conditions or that the adoption agency placed the offspring of female offenders in less desirable homes—and there was no indication that this selective placement had occurred.

Hutchings and Mednick (1975) also conducted a study examining the effects of genetics and environment. They reasoned that if there is a genetic basis for criminality, then there should be a significant relationship between the criminal tendencies of biological parents and those of their children who were adopted by someone else. In 1971, using Copenhagen adoption files, Hutchings and Mednick identified 1,145 male adoptees, who were by then 30 to 44 years old. They were matched with an equal number of nonadoptee controls on sex, age, occupational status of fathers, and residence. The researchers learned that 185 adoptees (16.2%) had criminal records, compared with 105 nonadoptees (8.9%). A check on the biological fathers of the adoptees revealed that they were nearly three times more likely to be involved in criminal activity than were either the adoptees' adoptive fathers or the fathers of the nonadopted controls. Furthermore, there was a significant relationship between the criminality of the sons and that of the fathers. Where the biological father had a criminal record and the adoptive father had none, a significant number of adoptees still became criminal (22%), but where the biological father had no record and the adoptive father had a criminal record, the number of adoptees who pursued criminal activities was lower (11.5%). If both the biological and adoptive fathers were criminal, the chances were much greater that the adoptee would also be criminal than if only one man was criminal. Hutchings and Mednick concluded that genetic factors continue to exert strong influences in the tendency toward criminality, even though environmental factors also play important roles.

One serious limitation to the Hutchings-Mednick data, as well as to any adoption study, is that agencies often try to match the adopted child with the adoptive family on the basis of the child's biological and sometimes socioeconomic background as well. The Crowe study involving the children of offenders found no evidence of this, but the Danish agency used in the Hutchings-Mednick investigation confirmed that this was done. The researchers not only recognized this problem but also admonished that extrapolations to American society should be made cautiously, since Danish society at the time was more homogeneous in cultural values and race.

The most comprehensive adoption study to date was conducted some years ago by Mednick, Gabrielli, and Hutchings (1984, 1987). These researchers compared the court convictions of 14,427 adoptees (adopted between the years 1927 and 1947) in a small European country with conviction records of their biological and adoptive parents. The study showed a significant relationship between the conviction history of the adoptees (for both males and females) and their biological parents. Specifically, if either biological parent had been convicted of a crime, the risk of criminality in the adoptee (the biological child) increased significantly. This relationship was especially strong for male adoptees who were chronic or persistent offenders. As we might expect, chronic offenders accounted for a disproportionate share of the total offending for the entire cohort. Interestingly, there was no evidence that the type of crime committed by the biological parent had any relation to the type of crime committed by the biological child. Both the biological parent and biological child tended to engage in crime but selected different kinds of crime. There was also no indication that the adopted children knew about the criminality of their biological parents. The researchers concluded that some factor transmitted by criminal parents increased the probability that their children would engage in criminal behavior. Elsewhere, Gabrielli and Mednick (1983, p. 63) commented: "It is reasonable...to conclude that some people inherit biological characteristics which permit them to be antisocial more readily than others."

In summary, both twin and adoption studies suggest that genetic components may contribute moderately to a tendency to become criminal, but they have also found that environment is highly important (Raine, 2002). According to biopsychologists, the available data so far indicate that some people may be born with a biological predisposition to behavior that runs counter to social values and norms, but environmental factors may either inhibit or facilitate it. For example, adoptees at genetic risk for antisocial behavior because their biological parents were antisocial are more likely to become antisocial themselves if their adoptive parents provided stressful home environments, such as by abusing them (Johnson, 2007; Raine, 2002). Genes may not influence criminal behavior directly, but genes may act to influence people's susceptibility or resistance to environmental risk factors.

Molecular Genetics

Molecular genetics attempts to answer such questions as, "Which genes predispose to which kinds of antisocial behavior?" (Raine, 2008, p. 323). Some answers are beginning to emerge. For example:

> If the monoamine oxidase A (MAOA) gene is knocked out (neutralized) in mice, they become highly aggressive, becoming "knock-out" fighters themselves. Knock the gene back in, and they return to their normal behavior patterns. (Raine, 2008, p. 323)

The **MAOA** gene appears to play an instrumental role in preventing antisocial behavior in humans (Kim-Cohen et al., 2006). Interestingly, the low activity form of the MAOA gene (abbreviated MAOA-L) which has been commonly linked to aggression and violence, has been nicknamed "the warrior gene" by some researchers in the field (McDermott, Tingley, Cowden, Frassetto, & Johnson, 2009). It is estimated that **MAOA-L** is carried by roughly one-third of the population in some societies and usually comes into play after some form of provocation (McDermott et al., 2009). In a recent study, those persons with the MAOA-L gene who were exposed to adversity in their childhoods were significantly more likely to report offending in late adolescence and early adulthood (Fergusson, Boden, Horwood, Miller, & Kennedy, 2012). Again, this study highlights the importance of considering the effects of the environment on genes rather than simply assuming that genes directly cause behavior.

Raine further notes that at least seven genes have been identified by molecular genetic research to be associated with antisocial behavior in humans. In most cases, these genes appear to contribute to impairments in brain structure and function which, in turn, result in antisocial or abnormal aggressive behavior. Structural or functional problems in the prefrontal cortex are associated with impulsively violent offenders. For example, some research has discovered reduced glucose metabolism in the prefrontal cortex of convicted murderers (Raine, Buschsbaum, & LaCasse, 1997) and a reduction of gray matter in the prefrontal cortex of criminal psychopaths (Yang et al., 2005). Both studies found no obvious evidence that these brain abnormalities were due to trauma or disease, but seemed to reflect the influence of genes.

PSYCHOPHYSIOLOGICAL FACTORS

Psychophysiology is the study of the dynamic interactions between behavior and the autonomic nervous system. The autonomic nervous system is the subdivision of the peripheral nervous system that regulates involuntary functions, such as heartbeat, blood pressure, breathing, and digestion, and is closely connected to the genetic makeup of the individual. Heart rates (cardiovascular activity)

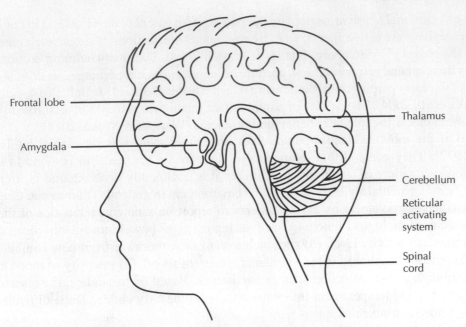

FIGURE 3-1   Brain Diagram Displaying Frontal Lobe and Other Subcortical Structures

and electrical conductance in the skin (electrodermal activity) are the usual measures of psycho-physiological investigations examining the relationship between antisocial behavior and autonomic activity. Autonomic arousal theory of crime hypothesizes that persistent, chronic offenders compared with those with no or little offending history, will exhibit low levels of autonomic arousal across a wide variety of situations and conditions. Presumably, low levels of arousal predispose a person to crime because this produces some degree of fearlessness and also because it encourages antisocial stimulation (excitement) seeking (Raine, 2002). That is, persistent offenders experience little anxiety and fear and are not troubled about getting caught and punished. Furthermore, they find certain aspects of crime exciting and challenging. On the other hand, high levels of autonomic arousal, in light of the amount of fear and anxiety involved, encourage childhood socialization because of fear of disapproval and punishment. According to DeLisi, Umphress, and Vaughn (2009), the **amygdala** is a brain structure that is particularly important to consider in light of its role in regulating fear and other emotional responses. (See **Figure 3-1** for a view of the structure of the brain.) The amygdala, they contend, is crucially related to psychopathy and to the callous-unemotional traits that are often associated with persons who engage in chronic antisocial activity.

Some studies reveal that antisocial boys and criminal psychopaths do appear to have lower levels of physiological arousal (as measured by electrodermal and cardiovascular activity) than their nonantisocial counterparts (Raine, 2002; Raine, Venables, & Williams, 1995, 1996). We cover this in more detail when we discuss the psychopath in Chapter 7.

Temperament

A child's **temperament**—defined as a "natural" mood disposition determined largely by genetics and biological influences—may offer important clues about criminal behavior. How we approach and interact with our social environment influences how that environment will interact with us. This is true even of infants and very young children. Parents, teachers, physicians, and caretakers know very well that infants and young children differ in activity, emotionality, and general sensitivity to stimuli. A smiling, relaxed, socially interactive child is apt to initiate and maintain a different social response than a fussy, tense, and withdrawn one. A consistently ill-tempered child may become so frustrating to his parents that they feel overwhelmed and helpless in dealing with him. The parents' resulting irritability may feed into the behavior of the child in a reciprocal fashion, producing a serious disruption in the parent–child relationship. Frustration may progress into physical or emotional abuse or neglect by the parent(s). In essence, the child and his or her parents or other caregivers are active agents, who, by continuous transactions, cocreate their emerging relationship (Kochanska, Friesenborg, Lange, & Martel, 2004). The overwhelming consensus among experts is that parental responsiveness, nurturance, and warmth have emerged as critical core determinants of the early parent–child relationship (Chen, Deater-Deckard, & Bell, 2014; Gallitto, 2014; Kochanska et al., 2004). The quality of parent–infant relationships play a pivotal role in preventing children from cascading into later behavioral problems (Winsper & Woke, 2014).

One of the most influential perspectives on temperament was developed by Thomas and Chess (1977). They contend that temperament is an innate readiness to respond to events and objects across a variety of situations. In addition, it is continually evolving and is strongly influenced by family, parental styles, and the social environment in general. Thomas and Chess systematically studied temperament by asking parents to report on nine characteristics of their infants: (1) rhythmicity of biological functions, such as regularity of bowel movements, sleep cycles, and feeding times, (2) activity level, (3) approach toward or withdrawal from new stimuli, (4) adaptability, (5) sensory thresholds, (6) predominant quality of mood, (7) intensity of mood expression, (8) distractibility, and (9) attention span or persistence. Based on these data, the researchers were able to classify child temperament into three styles: (1) the easy child, (2) the difficult child, and (3) the slow-to-warm-up child.

Table 3-1 summarizes the characteristics of each style. The easy child is characterized by high rhythmicity, positive moods, high approachability, high adaptability, and low intensity of mood expression. The difficult child shows the opposite patterns: irregular biological functioning, initial aversion, and slow adaptability to environmental changes, high intensity of emotional expression, and generally a negative mood. It is important to note that many children exhibit these patterns, particularly in infancy, and not all can be said to have a difficult temperament. For example, it is estimated that approximately 20 percent of all infants show symptoms of excessive crying and sleeping or feeding problems during the first year, but a much smaller number (1 to 2%) qualify as truly difficult (Winsper & Woke, 2014). The slow-to-warm-up child displays high activity, withdrawal from new stimuli and people, low adaptability, negative mood, and low intensity. According to Thomas and Chess, it is the difficult children who have the specific cluster of inborn temperamental attributes that make child rearing more challenging for many parents or caregivers.

It is suggested here that temperament increases or decreases the *probability* of antisocial behavior, not that it determines directly whether an individual will or will not engage in antisocial behavior. That is, the concurrence of these temperaments and certain kinds of family environments and parenting style may lead to delinquent or criminal outcomes. Studies have continually discovered significant *links* between children's "difficult" temperament and the occurrence of persistent antisocial behavior (e.g., Bates, Pettit, Dodge, & Ridge, 1998; Chen et al., 2014; Gallitto, 2014; Rubin, Burgess, Dwyer, & Hastings, 2003; Shaw, Owens, Giovannelli, & Winslow, 2001). Usually, temperament is measured from reports from parents or caregivers.

FEATURES OF TEMPERAMENT. As it is currently used in the research and scholarly literature, "temperament" is assumed to (1) have a constitutional or biological basis, (2) appear in infancy and

TABLE 3-1 Thomas & Chess Categories of Child Temperaments			
Behavioral Characteristics	**Easy Child**	**Difficult Child**	**Slow-to-Warm-Up Child**
Rhythmicity	Regular	Irregular	Regular
Moods	Positive	Negative	Negative
Approach to others	High	Low	Low
Adaptability	Rapid	Slow	Slow
Intensity	Low	High	Low

Source: Thomas, A., & Chess, S. (1977). Temperament and development. New York: Brunner/Mazel.

continue throughout life, and (3) be influenced by the environment (Bates & McFadyen-Ketchum, 2000). Most developmental experts believe that temperament has biological underpinnings that are best identified at birth (Bates, Pettit, Dodge, & Ridge, 1998; Dodge & Pettit, 2003; Lahey & Waldman, 2003). Else-Quest, Hyde, Goldsmith, and Van Hulle (2006) write: "Temperament reflects biologically based emotional and behavioral consistencies that appear early in life and predict— often in conjunction with other factors—patterns and outcomes in numerous other domains such as psychopathology and personality" (p. 33). Most of the contemporary research on temperament, therefore, focuses on the infant, because the connection between temperament and behavior seems uncomplicated at this stage and becomes more complex as the child matures and interacts with the psychosocial environment.

Contemporary research also suggests that differential temperamental characteristics reflect different susceptibility to socializing influences (Chen et al., 2014). "Generally, children with difficult temperaments are more susceptible to their rearing environment and it is claimed that difficult temperaments reflect high neural sensitivity to both positive and negative environmental influences" (Chen et al., 2014, p. 1252). This suggests that children with difficult temperaments not only respond more poorly to negative parenting than other children but also may benefit even more from warm, sensitive parenting.

Currently, most developmental experts agree that activity and emotionality are two of the behaviors that are strong indicators of temperament. Activity, the most widely studied, refers to gross motor movement across a variety of settings and times, such as the movement of arms and legs, squirming, crawling, or walking. Emotionality refers to such features as irritability, sensitivity, ability to be soothed, and general intensity of emotional reactions. Self-regulation (a technical term for controlling impulsivity) is another behavior which is often included in descriptions of temperament. As covered in Chapter 2, self-regulation refers to the extent that a child controls his or her own behavior, independent of the control of others and the social environment. Highly impulsive and unmanageable children (poor self-regulators) move into (and often against) their environments at a higher pace and more aggressively than less impulsive children. Research has shown a strong connection between poor self-regulation and antisocial behavior across different social situations (Olson, Sameroff, Kerr, Lopez, & Wellman, 2005).

Failure to acknowledge these dispositional or temperamental variables may leave researchers and practitioners with an incomplete picture of the development of antisocial behavior, especially in cases of individuals who demonstrate a persistent pattern of violent or serious offending. Else-Quest et al. (2006) report that girls temperamentally seem better able than boys to manage and regulate their attention and inhibit their impulses (self-regulation). Henry, Caspi, Moffitt, and Silva (1996) found that children considered temperamentally explosive and lacking in self-control were more likely to become violent adolescents compared with their more temperamentally stable peers. In a recent study, Honomichl and Donnellan (2012) found that preschoolers with difficult temperaments (characterized by negative moodiness and low soothability) demonstrated a significantly higher incidence of antisocial problems and reckless risk-taking at age 15 compared to their peers. However, although temperament is present at birth, it must be emphasized that its manifestations can be modified by the social environment, especially by parents and significant caregivers. As noted in this section, difficult temperaments can be challenging, but a nurturing and warm parenting style, in which rules are firmly laid out and appropriate self-regulation is encouraged, can prevent, change, or eliminate antisocial behavior in children (Moffitt, 2005; Veenstra, Lindenberg, Oldehinkel, De Winter, & Ormel, 2006). On the other hand, a difficult temperament combined with parental rejection or parental coercion offers a high risk for antisocial behavior (Dekovic, Janssens, & Van As, 2003; Veenstra et al., 2006).

Likewise, the temperament of parents must also be considered as a possible component in the development of the criminal behavior. Moffitt (1993b) suggests that parents and their offspring often resemble each other in temperament and personality. An irritable, temperamental child may have a high probability of being born to highly irritable, temperamental parents. Thus, parents of difficult children often lack the necessary psychological and emotional resources to cope effectively with a difficult child. Cultural differences may also play a role in the interaction between parenting and temperament, but the research on the parent–child–temperament interaction is relatively too recent to make advanced, even tentative, conclusions (Porter et al., 2005; Russell, Hart, Robinson, & Olsen, 2003).

In the next section, we will take a closer look at additional environmental factors that may facilitate or inhibit antisocial tendencies. These are distinct from the social environmental risk factors covered in Chapter 2, in that they are more likely to influence the child's physiological and neurological makeup. These factors include prenatal influences, postnatal diseases and experiences, and inadequate nutrition and medical care. Although we referred to malnutrition and inadequate medical care as social risk factors in Chapter 2, they are discussed here relative to their effect on the child's physical well-being.

ENVIRONMENTAL RISK FACTORS

In addition to genetic and temperamental factors, in utero experiences may also play a role in the predisposition toward criminal behavior. During pregnancy, the fetus is exposed to various influences that may adversely affect development, leading to potential risks for serious antisocial behaviors later in life. Exposure to a toxic or diseased prenatal environment is one example. "Fetuses exposed to opiates or methadone are at heightened risk for conduct problems 10 to 13 years later, as are fetuses exposed to alcohol, marijuana, and cigarette by-products during pregnancy" (Dodge & Pettit, 2003, p. 351). **Fetal alcohol spectrum disorder (FASD)**—which we discuss in more detail later in the chapter—is another example. This is a broad term for several serious medical conditions that result from prenatal exposure to alcohol (Brown, Connor, & Adler, 2012). Youth on the FASD continuum are linked to a high rate of self-regulation problems, antisocial behavior, and conduct disorders (Brown et al., 2012). However, one of the greatest early dangers to the developing brain (especially but not exclusively children and adolescents living in poverty) is prenatal and postnatal exposure to environmental pollutants and toxic materials, such as neurotoxins.

Neurotoxins

"Neurotoxins are trace elements, pesticides, chemicals, and biological elements that have toxic effects on the human nervous system" (Hubbs-Tait et al., 2005, p. 58). These toxic effects may damage, destroy, or impair neurons (nerve cells), which produce changes in behavior, emotions, and cognitive ability. However, the stage of human development at which exposure to neurotoxins occurs is a critical variable. The fetus and children less than two years of age appear to be the most vulnerable, because this is the time when central nervous system development is most active. The extent of exposure to these neurotoxins is also important.

Neurotoxins are relevant because their effects on the nervous system have been linked to a variety of behavior disorders and antisocial acts, including aggression and violence. Basically, neurotoxins have the potential of producing neurocognitive dysfunction which predisposes individuals to antisocial behavior and violence (Raine, 2013). We emphasize, however, that while neurotoxins may play a role in the development of such behavior, it takes an amalgam of a wide spectrum of factors to directly produce it. No one single neurotoxin is likely a causal factor by itself. On the other hand, an accumulation of exposure to neurotoxins, poor nutrition, and an inadequate social environment can lead to deleterious effects on memory, learning, and self-regulation, and may also lead to behavioral disorders in children, adolescents, and young adults. Poor nutrition usually involves a deficiency in micronutrients (especially iron, calcium, zinc, and selenium), which have the ability to neutralize the negative effects of many neurotoxins on the human nervous system. We will discuss micronutrients in more detail later in the chapter.

Three neurotoxins have received sufficient research to connect them to the development of antisocial behavior: lead, cadmium, and manganese. Of the three, lead has drawn the greatest amount of research attention. Two additional prominent neurotoxins, mercury and polychlorinated biphenyls (PCBs), have been linked to nervous system problems, but current evidence has yet to connect them significantly to cognitive and behavioral outcomes related to criminal behavior.

Lead

Over the past three decades, a large segment of the research on neurotoxins has focused on the effects of exposure to lead, both before and after birth. Research is very clear that abnormal levels of lead in the human body predict a variety of academic, emotional, and cognitive problems in children (Biglan, Flay, Embry, & Sandler, 2012). In fact, Raine (2013) asserts that lead is a leading candidate for some of the structural and functional impairments found in the brain. Citing a number of studies, Biglan et al. (2012) conclude that "lead exposure is associated with an increased lifetime burden of special education, attention deficit disorder, crime, and even homicide" (p. 260). Raine asserts that lead exposure is a strong environmental risk factor for antisocial and aggressive behavior in delinquent children and violence in adults. Several other studies have found a strong connection between high lead levels and antisocial behavior and delinquency (Dietrich et al., 2001; Needleman, 2004; Needleman et al., 2002; Nevin, 2000, 2007; Olympio et al., 2009, 2010; Wright et al., 2008). A recent summary of the research literature on the topic (Yolton, Cornelius, Ornoy, McGough, Makris, & Schnatz, 2014) concluded:

> A large body of research implicates lead in a multitude of health and neurobehavioral disorders. The findings on neurobehavior include clearly identified links to behavior problems and ADHD, as well as delinquency and criminal activity. (p. 40)

Where is lead found in the everyday environment? In 1977, the U.S. Consumer Product Safety Commission banned the sale of leaded paint (Cole & Winsler, 2010). The ban, however, does not extend to buildings and houses built or painted before 1977, meaning that children living in old houses continue to be exposed to lead-paint particles and dust if steps are not taken to remove these contaminants. In 1996, the sale of all leaded gasoline in the United States was banned, although leaded jet fuel was not affected by the regulation. Despite these regulations and other attempts at eliminating lead, it continues to be present in soil, air, and water (Narag, Pizarro, & Gibbs, 2009). For example, lead residue still lingers in the soil near major roads and expressways many years after leaded gasoline was banned (Raine, 2013). Because lead continues to be widely used in other countries, it can also be found in car batteries, toys, toy jewelry, tobacco, leaded-coated ceramic pottery, crystal baby bottles, imported cosmetics, imported spices, herbal medicines, and imported plastic containers that come into contact with food (Advisory Committee on Childhood Lead Poisoning Prevention [ACCLPP], 2012; Cole & Winsler, 2010; Olympio et al., 2010). More importantly, another source of lead exposure today is tap water. "Lead leeches into tap water through contact with lead-based piping or through the corrosion of pipes in water treatment systems and household plumbing" (Cole & Winsler, 2010, p.12). This potential danger is especially prevalent in older housing.

Although there have been serious attempts to remove lead contaminates, many children continue to show some lead exposure. In one comprehensive study, Apostolou et al. (2012) conclude: "Despite a dramatic overall decline in lead levels in children and young adults over the last few decades, inner-city children and young adults of low socioeconomic status continue to experience high lead exposure" (p. 717). The researchers discovered that one surprising source of lead exposure in children and adolescents is second-hand tobacco smoke. Children who live with one, two, or more smokers had higher blood lead levels (BLL) than children who lived in nonsmoking households.

How high is too high in BLL? For years the "level of concern" standard for the Centers of Disease Control (CDC) was BLL of 10μg/dl (10 micrograms per deciliter) and above. With new federal standards in place, BLL has decreased dramatically in recent years. The percentage of children with BLLs higher than 10μg/dl reported to the Centers for Disease Control decreased from 7.6 percent in 1997 to 3.1 percent in 2001 (ACCLPP, 2012). In 2008, the percentage was down to 0.83 percent. Although 10μg/dl was considered a "level of concern," many studies conducted after this standard was set found that significant and troubling behavioral and health effects occurred at lower levels (Biglan et al., 2012; Federal Interagency Forum on Child and Family Statistics, 2005; Min, Singer, Kirchner, Minnes, Short, Hussain et al., 2009). Significant amounts of research have revealed that blood levels less than 5µg/dl are associated with deficient cognitive development, behavioral problems, and poor academic performance (ACCLPP, 2012; Min et al., 2009). Based on the extensive research literature that found no level of blood lead is without its effects on health and neurological development, the ACCLPP (2012) concluded: "Because no measureable level of blood lead is known to be without deleterious effects, and because once engendered, the effects appear to be irreversible in the absence of any other interventions, environmental and housing policies should encourage prevention of *all exposure to lead*" (p. 5; italics added).

Many children continue to have BLLs at or above 5µg/dl, and these children are predominantly in homes with incomes below poverty level (Dietrich, Ris, Succop, Berger, & Bornschien, 2001; Needleman, McFarland, Ness, Fienberg, & Tobin, 2002). Some racial and ethnic groups may be particularly susceptible (e.g., African American children, 19%; Mexican American children, 7%). These differences can be traced to disparities in housing quality, environmental conditions, nutrition, and other factors. In addition, childhood studies published since 2005 have established the connections between low BLLs and reductions in cognitive functioning, especially memory and learning ability (ACCLPP, 2012).

Cadmium

In his review of neurotoxins and violence, Raine (2013) concludes that high levels of cadmium in the body have been linked to violent behavior in a number of studies. He summarizes studies that show that hair samples from violent offenders often indicate they have significantly more cadmium in their tissues than nonviolent offenders. Raine further notes that high hair cadmium levels are also found in U.S. elementary school children with behavioral problems. Scalp hair analysis is considered a decent measure of the accumulation of neurotoxins, because hair incorporates toxins during its growth cycle and provides a permanent record of toxin levels in the body at the time of hair growth (LeClair & Quig, 2001).

Extensive cadmium exposure during development appears to be related to learning difficulties and lower cognitive functioning in children and adolescents (Hubbs-Tait et al., 2005). Learning difficulties and deficient cognitive functioning pose lifelong and widespread difficulties in holding employment, learning new skills, and working with others (Koger, Schettler, & Weiss, 2005). The learning disabled may be "more likely to enter the criminal justice system for delinquency and adult criminal behavior...possibly because of academic difficulties that lead many to drop out of school..." (Koger et al., 2005, p. 243, citing the research).

Cadmium is a soft, malleable metal used largely in the production of nickel-cadmium rechargeable batteries and as corrosion-protection coating for iron and steel (Occupational Safety and Health Administration, 2014). Currently, about three-fourths of the world's cadmium is used in the manufacture of nickel-cadmium batteries, which are found in almost every electronic device used today (Haider et al., 2014). It is considered a toxic environmental and industrial pollutant that that has been linked to several biochemical and neurological disorders in animals and humans. It is also found in significant amounts in tobacco products.

In humans, cadmium gains entry into the body via three *primary* sources: (1) maternal smoking during pregnancy; (2) postnatal exposure to environmental tobacco smoke; and (3) and exposure to smoke and particles from the burning of fossil fuels and the incineration of municipal and industrial waste (Environmental Protection Agency, 2000; Hubbs-Tait et al., 2005). To some extent, food may have traces of cadmium, but research is lacking for determining whether food sources present a significant danger. Smoking is probably the major source of cadmium in humans today. For example, some research indicates that smokers have approximately twice as much cadmium in their bodies as do nonsmokers (Paschal et al., 2000). In children who have been exposed to maternal smoking in utero and environmental tobacco smoke during postnatal development, cadmium levels may be distressingly high.

In children and adolescents, cadmium has been linked to deficiencies in intellectual functioning. For example, Hubbs-Tait et al. (2005) find that "...recent investigations have shown that children who live near waste sites and who have higher body burdens of cadmium are at increased risk for learning disorders" (p. 99). Raine (2013) cites a study conducted in Guangdong province, China (Bao, Lu, Song, Wang, Ling et al., 2009). The researchers found schoolchildren living downstream from a cadmium mine had heavy concentrations of the metal in their scalp hair. The children with high amounts of hair cadmium demonstrated higher rates of aggression and delinquency than their low cadmium counterparts.

Manganese

Environmental exposure to manganese presents a complicated challenge to investigators. The metal is both an essential trace element and a potent neurotoxin (Abdelouahab, Huel, Suvorov, Foliguet, Goua, Debotte et al., 2010). Major food sources of this essential element are nuts, tea, legumes, pineapple, and grains—the consumption of which is a good thing. However, toxicity comes into play when there is an excessive intake or exposure to the element, such as may occur in some occupations, like welding. Welding aerosols may contain high amounts of manganese, depending on the welding method and consumables used (Ellingsen et al., 2014). Several studies reveal that welders who have been at the occupation for some time often exhibit a variety of neurological problems (Ellingsen et al., 2014). Raine (2013) writes: "perhaps it's not too surprising that *fifteen studies* on workers exposed to manganese in all corners of the world—including Chile, Great Britain, Egypt, Poland, Brazil, the United States, Scotland, and Canada—without exception report significant mood disruption, including aggression, hostility, irritability, and emotional disturbances" (p. 230, italics in original quote). Moreover, antisocial acts committed by workers exposed to high amounts of manganese are often due to brain impairment and are characterized by poor emotional regulation and impulsivity (Raine, 2013).

In children, overexposure to manganese may come prenatally and from infant feeding. In utero, manganese passes easily through the placenta of the pregnant woman, depending on her level of exposure. However, this is most apt to happen when the pregnant woman has a deficiency of iron. Women who have a deficiency of the micronutrient iron absorb about four times more manganese than women with sufficient iron levels (Finley, 1999). Therefore, excessive manganese exposure is highly likely to find its way into the developing fetus. Maternal exposure may include living near a manufacturing plant which engages in toxic-chemical release and manganese-containing pesticides and fungicides. Municipal drinking water may also contain manganese, depending on certain bedrock formations and pollution levels in the local environment.

The nervous system is the principal target of manganese, especially the central nervous system (Ellingsen et al., 2014; EPA, 2007). Excessive manganese accumulation in the child's nervous system may result in poorer brain functioning, lower intellectual functioning, and a tendency toward aggression and violence during adolescence and adulthood (Raine, 2013).

Erickson and his colleagues (Erickson et al., 2007) discovered that prenatal exposure to manganese, as measured in tooth enamel deposits dating to the 20th gestational week, is significantly associated with childhood behavioral outcomes. Specifically, the researchers found: "Children with higher levels of prenatal manganese were more impulsive, inattentive, aggressive, defiant, disobedient, destructive, and hyperactive" (p. 185). Raine (2013) reviews several studies that have found that many violent offenders have higher levels of manganese in their scalp hair samples than nonviolent people.

Mercury (Methlymercury)

A vast number of behavioral disturbances are associated with mercury exposure, especially memory, cognition, and learning problems (Freire et al., 2010; Hubbs-Tait et al., 2005). Mercury is toxic and damaging to the brain and other body organs (Raine, 2013). Human exposure to mercury comes primarily from eating mercury-contaminated fish and marine mammals and to a much lesser extent from dental fillings. A *direct* link of mercury exposure to criminal or antisocial behavior has yet to be established, primarily because of the inconsistency of research findings (Raine, 2013). Raine refers to mercury as "mysterious mercury" because—for a variety of reasons—its effect on human health and behavior is extremely difficult to measure accurately.

Although the criminal behavior–mercury exposure link has not been established, the mercury connection to neurodevelopmental deficits in children has been a relatively consistent finding (Grandjean et al., 2014; Oken et al., 2008). Mercury from contaminated seafood consumption by a pregnant woman easily crosses the placenta and rapidly passes through the blood–brain barrier to the developing fetus (Karagas et al., 2012). High levels of mercury are known to contribute to extreme fetal abnormalities and neurotoxicity among infants, including microcephaly, blindness, and severe mental and physical developmental retardation (Karaga et al., 2012). It is also known to act directly in the central nervous system by destroying or damaging nerve cells (Koger, Schettler, & Weiss, 2005). Lower levels of mercury exposure have been found to be associated with decrements in memory, attention, language, intelligence, and visual–motor skills in children (Freire et al., 2010; Karagas et al., 2012). Freire and associates (2010) write: "Our results support the findings of some studies that higher mercury exposure in young child is associated with lower cognition, even at relatively low-exposure levels" (p. 101). Several other studies have also discovered that low-level mercury exposure in U.S. populations can contribute to childhood neurodevelopmental problems, especially if exposure occurs during the prenatal period (Oken et al., 2012). Consequently, it is safe to assume—in line with the cumulative risk model—that mercury exposure from eating contaminated food may play some role in the formation of behavioral problems in children, adolescents, and adults. For example, mercury is not the only neurotoxic substance found in certain kinds of fish. Other pollutants, such as PCBs, other heavy metals, pharmaceuticals, and other damaging compounds, are often found in sea foods as well.

Fish has long been believed to be a healthy food, providing protein and other nutrients, and for many reasons it is unlikely that it will be eliminated from most diets. Scientists who are concerned about its harmful effects indicate that consumers must seek information about which fish to eat and which to avoid, along with supporting efforts to eliminate the sources of contamination—such as mercury and other toxic materials in the world's oceans. Information about sustainable seafood initiatives is widely available to the public and is often summarized in research reports (e.g., Oken et al., 2012). (See **Table 3-2** for summary of the four neurotoxins discussed in this section.)

Protective Properties of Micronutrients

Although the above material may suggest that environmental contaminants create irrevocable damage to human development, the situation is not that dire, even from purely physiological and neurological standpoints. One positive factor is the presence of trace elements in the human body.

TABLE 3-2	A List of Neurotoxins That Present the Strongest Connections to Aggressive and Violent Behavior
Neurotoxin	**Effects**
Manganese	Depletes the neurotransmitters of dopamine, serotonin, and norepinephrine. Long-term negative effects on brain and nervous system development and functioning. Excessive exposure has been linked to poor attention, poor impulse control, and other neurological deficits.
Cadmium	Has a nonspecific effect on most neurotransmitters. Restricts calcium-mediated release of the transmitters. Long-term negative effects on brain development and intelligence. Excessive exposure may lead to aggression and violence.
Lead	Damages functioning of neurotransmitters and destroys neurons relevant to learning, memory, cognition, and self-regulation. Especially affects the prefrontal cortex. Exposure is associated with a variety of behavioral problems including distractibility, poor organization skills, violence, delinquency, and criminal behavior.
Mercury	Damages functioning of neurotransmitters. Adversely affects functioning and development of central nervous system. Research suggests it contributes to problems in vision, learning, memory, attention, and behavioral control. At high doses, it appears to damage wide areas of brain functioning.

The trace elements represent essential micronutrients found in the human body in small amounts (Hubbs-Tait et al., 2005). "The trace minerals for which a mammalian requirement has been established include iron, zinc, iodine, selenium, copper, manganese, fluoride, chromium, and molybdenum" (Hubbs-Tait et al., 2005, p. 58). Although each of these trace elements may be toxic and neurologically destructive in excessive amounts, at low amounts they also may serve as protective factors for healthy outcomes. For example, iron and zinc are essential micronutrients in cognitive development in children. Adequate intake of zinc, iron, and calcium in the diet appears to reduce the effects and accumulation of neurotoxins cadmium and lead in the body, especially the brain (Hubbs-Tait et al., 2005). Selenium modifies the neurological influences of mercury. Iron appears to reduce the negative effects of excessive levels of manganese.

One of the effects of living in poverty is that children (and adults) often have insufficient dietary intake of these important micronutrients, rendering them subject to a greater impact of the pollutants and neurotoxicants in their environments. Diets supplemented with micronutrients will at least have the effect of reducing the accumulating risk factors that accompany a child's exposure to the many chemicals inherent in a polluted environment.

Prenatal and Postnatal Malnutrition

Malnutrition affects the neurodevelopment of 167.2 million preschool-aged children worldwide (Waber et al., 2014). As noted by Waber and her associates (2014), pre- and postnatal nutritional deprivation can result in long-term changes or alteration of brain development. Pertinent to our discussion here, several studies have indicated that prenatal and early childhood malnutrition "is associated with adverse outcomes in school-aged children and adolescents, including an increased prevalence of conduct problems and aggressive behaviors" (Galler et al., 2012, p. 239). For example, one early well-cited study (Neugebauer, Hoek, & Susser, 1999) found that maternal malnutrition during pregnancy in combination with adverse caregiving conditions may also be closely linked to violent behavior in the offspring. Recently, the Barbados Nutrition Study (BNS) represents one of the most comprehensive studies on the effects of malnutrition on child development ever undertaken. The BNS has followed over the course of decades the development of a group of Barbadian children with normal birth weights who experienced moderate to severe malnutrition during their first year of life. (See **Box 3-1** for further description.) From their analysis of the data, Galler and her associates (2012) discovered that conduct problems and aggressive behavior were significantly elevated when these children reached preadolescence and adolescence, despite improvements in diet after the first year. The earlier study by Neugebauer et al. (1999) reported similar results, showing that those children exposed to intrauterine malnutrition demonstrated high levels of antisocial behavior in adulthood.

RESEARCH FOCUS

BOX 3-1   Malnutrition in Infants

The first years of a child's life are crucial to healthy brain development. Although negative events and experiences during those first years rarely cause irreversible damage, some are likely to lead to cognitive and behavioral impairments, including conduct problems, decreased attention, and lower IQ (Galler et al., 2011). Malnutrition during the first year of life appears to be one of these negative events.

As part of a series of longitudinal studies mentioned in the text, Galler and her colleagues studied a cohort of Barbadian children of normal birth weight who experienced protein-energy malnutrition during their first year and were hospitalized as a result. The researchers followed the children from their first year of life (Time 1) up to age 17 and compared them to a matched control group of healthy children from the same classrooms and neighborhoods. The malnourished children had no evidence of malnutrition after their first year, and they had reached the same level of physical growth as the control group by the end of puberty.

However, the malnourished group demonstrated cognitive deficits and an impairment in fine motor skills when they

(*continued*)

were 9 to 15 years old (Time 2) and again two years later, when they were 11 to 17 years old (Time 3). Teachers and parents reported that they demonstrated attention and behavioral problems in school and at home, including problems relating with peers. Aggression was prominent at the younger ages, but was reported less among the 11- to 17-year-olds.

Significantly, the research by Galler et al. determined that the differences in executive function and early aggression could not be explained by sex, age, or the home environments of the children. When the researchers controlled for socioeconomic disadvantage and maternal depression—two factors that were suspected to affect the children's behavioral and cognitive difficulties—the differences between the malnourished children and the control group persisted. Galler et al. noted that their research was consistent with many other studies indicating that early malnutrition leads to a host of subsequent problems, ranging from hyperactivity to attention deficit disorders later in life.

How much later in life might the effect of early malnutrition persist? The research group is presently following their sample into adulthood to study their adjustment in areas such as employment and social relationships. "Data collected when these individuals were children and adolescents will provide an essential platform for understanding the lifelong consequences of early malnutrition" (Galler et al., 2011, p. 142).

Questions for Discussion

1. Teachers and parents reported less aggression at Time 3 (11 to 17 years) than at Time 2 (9 to 15 years). What might explain this finding?
2. Why do you think there was no evidence of malnutrition after the first year?
3. Do the findings as reported above suggest that the negative effects of malnutrition during the first year are irreversible? Explain your answer.

Other researchers also have associated infant and early-childhood malnutrition with deficits in cognitive functioning down the line. For example, Liu and associates (2004) found that malnutrition at age three predisposes a child to neurocognitive deficits, which in turn predispose a child to persistent antisocial behaviors throughout childhood and adolescence. Malnutrition, then, has been indicted as a crucial factor impeding both cognitive functioning and prosocial behavior into adulthood.

Although infant and child malnutrition may be linked with cognitive impairment, malnutrition by itself is unlikely to be the sole cause of a lifetime of serious, aggressive, or violent behavior. Galler and associates express the same cautions. They write: "Later vulnerability to increased conduct problems appears to be mediated by the proximal neurobehavioral effects of malnutrition on cognitive function and by adverse condition in the early home environment" (Galler et al., 2012, p. 186). Recall from **Box 3-1**, though, that the researchers controlled for some adverse conditions, such as maternal depression and family standard of living. Nonetheless, some observers have noted that the children in the Barbados Nutrition Study differed in their physical and social environments from the better nourished group and likely were exposed to a different set of cumulating risk (Waber et al., 2014).

The BNS study examined cognitive difficulties, deficiencies in executive function, and acting out behaviors among children, not serious violent behavior. Throughout this text we emphasize that most serious, violent and antisocial behavior is a result of cumulative and cascading factors, not just one factor. There are exceptions, of course, such as serious brain damage due to trauma that may promote aggressive outbursts, but malnourishment usually represents only one potentially damaging link in a chain of events that can lead to aggressive and violent behavior. It is more likely the malnutrition–*violence* relationship requires the presence of negative environmental circumstances and additional heightened psychosocial risks in general. For example, *chronic* malnutrition during early childhood is most likely to have a negative impact on children's abilities to learn to self-regulate their behavior. In addition, the hungry or malnourished child is unlikely to be able to concentrate in school and achieve success in the academic realm. Clearly, school breakfast and lunch programs, which provide nutrition to students who might not otherwise have adequate food, are an important component of educational services.

Nicotine, Alcohol, and Drug Exposure

There is substantial literature on the effects of prenatal exposure to drugs on child development in general. However, the prenatal effects of substance and alcohol abuse on antisocial behavioral development have received relatively little attention, although a few studies have examined these effects. According to Raine (2002, p. 317), "The effects of fetal exposure to alcohol in increasing risk for conduct disorders is well known, but recently a spate of studies has established beyond reasonable doubt a significant link between smoking during pregnancy and later conduct disorder and violent offending." As mentioned earlier in the chapter, youth with diagnoses associated with exposure to alcohol in utero are far more likely to exhibit aggressive behavior, violence, and other conduct problems than the general youth population (Brown et al., 2012). In fact, some studies suggest that "a large percentage of youth in confinement suffer from undiagnosed FASD" (Brown et al., 2012, p. 773).

FASD is an umbrella term for a continuum of conditions that result from alcohol exposure in utero. Specific medical diagnoses include fetal alcohol syndrome (FAS), partial fetal alcohol syndrome (pFAS), alcohol-related neurodevelopmental disorder (ARND), and alcohol-related birth defects (ARBD). All may produce cognitive and behavioral problems, such as difficulty with memory, reasoning, and abstract language, as well as problems engaging in activities of daily living. It is important to stress that, although conduct disorder and violence are mentioned above, they are not the only effects of FASD and are probably not the major ones for most FASD children. It should not be assumed that a child with FASD is destined to be aggressive; it is likely, however, that he or she will experience some degree of difficulty in neurological functioning.

The evidence for the relationship between maternal smoking during pregnancy and antisocial behavior in her children is quite strong for boys, but weak for girls (Wakschlag & Hans, 2002). In addition, women who stopped smoking during their pregnancy gave birth to children who demonstrated lower levels of antisocial behavior in life than women who did not quit smoking (Jaffee, Strait, & Odgers, 2012; Robinson et al., 2010). One study (Brennan, Grekin, & Mednick, 1999), using a birth cohort of 4,169 males, found a strong connection between adult violent offending and smoking by their mothers during their pregnancy. On average, the mothers smoked 20 cigarettes a day. This relationship was especially strong (increasing by fivefold) when the offspring were both exposed to nicotine and had birth complications. In another study that used a large sample from the general population of Finland, Räsänen et al. (1998) found that, compared with the sons of mothers who did not smoke, the sons of mothers who smoked during pregnancy had more than a twofold risk of having committed a violent crime or having repeatedly committed crimes. This finding held even when other biopsychological risk factors were controlled. The available evidence suggests that smoking during pregnancy may contribute to brain deficits that have been frequently found in adult offenders (Raine, 2002).

However, Jaffee et al. (2012) caution that, despite the consistency across studies, it remains difficult to firmly conclude that maternal smoking promotes or *causes* antisocial behavior in children. They point out that mothers who smoke during pregnancy are different in many aspects from those who do not. Mothers who smoke tend to have less income, less education, are of lower socioeconomic status, and experience more stress in pregnancy than nonsmoking mothers. In addition, smokers are more likely to have a history of antisocial behavior themselves compared to nonsmokers (Jaffee et al., 2012). As with all other risk factors, one factor alone is not responsible for antisocial behavior. It is clear, though, that the infants of smoking mothers have significant health problems, including slower brain development (Roza et al., 2007; Shah & Braken, 2000).

Exposure to secondhand smoke—such as might occur when someone other than the pregnant woman smokes in close quarters—is also a risk factor. For example, since 1964, approximately 2.5 million nonsmokers have died from health problems primarily caused by exposure to secondhand smoke (Centers for Disease Control and Prevention, 2015). Secondhand smoke is also believed to be responsible for sudden infant death syndrome (SIDS).

Maternal substance abuse during pregnancy does show a link to substance abuse by their offspring during adolescence, but it is difficult to determine whether this link is due to a shared genetic predisposition between parent and child, the child modeling the parents' behavior, or the in utero effects of the substances themselves (Allen, Lewinsohn, & Seeley, 1998). Identifying the differential effects of maternal substance abuse of specific drugs is also daunting because the drug-abusing mother rarely uses a drug in isolation. That is, abusers usually use multiple substances. Nonetheless, there is some strong evidence to suggest that prenatal cocaine use by mothers adversely affects emotional and attention regulation in infants and preschool-aged children (Mayes, 1999). This finding is significant because cocaine or crack continued to be used by some pregnant women at least into the 1990s. For example, in some urban areas, nearly 50 percent of women giving birth reported or tested positive for cocaine use at the time of delivery (Mayes, 1999).

Traumatic Brain Injury

Whether it occurs in children or adults, **traumatic brain injury (TBI)** is frequently associated with neuropathological changes in cognition, emotion, and behavior. It is also often linked to serious and violent behavior (Colantonio et al., 2014; Ishikawa & Raine, 2004; Raine, 2013) and other antisocial behaviors (Scott, McKinlay et al., 2015). It appears that this connection is particularly relevant in the case of pathological violence (such as impulsive violence occurring in the context of emotional arousal and provocation) (Siever, 2008).

Approximately 60 percent of the incarcerated population in the United States is believed to have some evidence of TBI in their background (Shiroma, Ferguson, & Pickelsimer, 2010), compared to 8.5 percent in the general population (Piccolino & Solberg, 2014; Wald, Helgeson, & Langlois, 2008). Some researchers (e.g., Piccolino & Solberg, 2014) have reported data suggesting that as many as 82 percent of offenders meet the criteria for having incurred a TBI at some point in their lives.

The offending TBI link is especially strong if the brain dysfunction is located in the frontal lobe (Cusimano et al., 2014), which comprises about one-third of the front part of the human brain (see **Figure 3-1**). Organized thought, planning, and self-regulation are located in this area.

The importance of the frontal portion of the brain was revealed in the classic case of Phineas Gage. In September 1848, Gage worked as a construction foreman for the Rutland & Burlington Railroad in Vermont. The work crew was blasting rock while clearing the roadbed for a new rail line. During the preparation for the next blast, something suddenly went wrong. A premature explosion sent an iron rod, used for tampering the gunpowder into the blasting hole, into Gage's head. The 3-foot iron, which Gage was using, entered the side of his face, shattering the upper jaw, passing through the frontal lobe, out the top of his head, and flew another 50 feet in the air. The frontal lobe area of his brain was badly damaged. Surprisingly, Gage spoke within a few minutes after the blast, walked with little or no assistance, and sat in a cart that took him to the town doctors. Although Gage lived for another 12 years, the accident dramatically changed his personality. Prior to the accident, Gage was controlled, playful, friendly, and competent. He was a responsible and dependable employee for the railroad. After the accident, he became hostile, ill-tempered, profane, highly unreasonable, and showed poor social judgment. He demonstrated uncontrolled anger, a pattern which led to his inability to hold down a job. Although one could argue that anyone having experienced this trauma might display some personality changes, the extent of the changes and their radical nature were attributed to the physical damage to his brain.

We do not have to go back more than a century to find other examples of individuals with frontal lobe damage and subsequent personality change, however. TBI is widely believed to affect one's personality, not infrequently leading to increased aggression (Barash, Tranel, & Anderson, 2000). Researchers studying Vietnam War veterans found that those with head injuries scored higher than those without such injuries on tests of violence (Grafman et al., 1996). Numerous studies indicate that veterans of later conflicts, such as wars in Iraq and Afghanistan, were even more likely to experience and survive TBIs (see, e.g., Christy, Clark, Frei, & Rynearson-Moody, 2012, and references therein). Based on available research, it has been clearly established that individuals with frontal lobe damage are far more likely to use physical intimidation and violence in conflict situations (Grafman et al., 1996; Siever, 2008). This is especially the case in impulsive violence, where self-regulation and self-control appear to be lacking. Lately, attention has been brought to head injuries associated with some sports, particularly football, soccer, and boxing. Such injuries may lead to brain damage that could facilitate personality changes and aggressive behavior.

Although research has not addressed this issue, it is possible that domestic violence committed by professional athletes might be explained, at least in part, by concussions experienced in the past. This is not to excuse the behavior, nor is to say that other factors (like the learning factors to be considered in Chapter 4) are not relevant or even more significant. Like all other risk factors, TBI is neither a necessary nor a sufficient condition for antisocial behavior; however, it may be one among several cumulative factors in the developmental sequence of some offenders.

Brain Development Abnormalities

While brain damage due to accidents and physical trauma can result in a propensity toward impulsive violence, the quality of the prenatal environment is also clearly important in brain development. The brain is highly vulnerable to intrinsic hazards (cell development gone wrong) and to external insults resulting from viral infection, drug or alcohol exposure, malnutrition, or other teratogens. Nutritional adequacy is crucial for both prenatal and postnatal brain development because of the growing brain's reliance on folic acid, iron, vitamins, and other nutrients. As noted previously, malnutrition is a biological risk to which the developing infant brain is especially vulnerable. Other hazards include fetal exposure to maternal viruses like HIV and rubella, illicit drugs such as cocaine and heroin, maternal alcohol ingestion, exposure to environmental neurotoxins, pollutants, pesticides, and other teratogens. The developing brain's vulnerability to many of these risk factors continues throughout the early years after birth. As we learned in the beginning of this section, unsafe lead levels found in the paint of older homes or in the environment may be a contributing factor in the development of serious antisocial behavior.

Another area of the brain, the *limbic system*, which consists of a diverse group of loosely connected brain structures and circuitry, has also emerged as an important component associated with impulsive violence. The most important brain structure in the limbic system involved in aggressive behavior is the amygdala (see **Figure 3-1**). The amygdala is a small, almond-shaped group of nerve cells that appears to play a major role in learning, memory, and the experience of emotions. Impulsive aggression and violence appear to be related to activity in the amygdala (DeLisi et al., 2009; Jones et al., 2009; Siever, 2008). Developmental influences that adversely affect the amygdala (and the limbic system generally) are very likely to affect various emotional responses, especially anger.

BRAIN PLASTICITY.   After birth, early experiences are crucial in shaping the cultivation and pruning of neural synapses that underlie the functional capabilities of the developing brain (Thompson & Nelson, 2001). Studies of humans and other species have made it clear that the developing brain is profoundly responsive to experience (Nelson & Bloom, 1997). Both structure and function are affected by experience, a characteristic known as **plasticity**. In fact, the plasticity and compensational capacities of the developing brain is perhaps the most remarkable discovery found in the developmental sciences to date (Lidzba & Staudt, 2008).

Among the most important of early experiences in the developing infant is nurturing, sensitive care. Although there are few relevant human neuroscience data, parents and caregivers are encouraged to talk and sing to, play with, read to, and sensitively nurture young children because of how these contingent sensory experiences provide stimulation for the brain (Thompson & Nelson, 2001). On the other hand, when caregivers are unable to provide these multisensory stimulations, brain development is likely to be delayed, either temporarily or permanently depending on the timing and quality of the intervention.

The first three to four years of life are significant in the prevention of antisocial behavior and persistent, serious criminal behavior throughout life, but other developmental periods are also important. There is some evidence, for example, that by the 4th year of life, the plasticity of the brain for language development begins to decrease (Chilosi et al., 2008), suggesting that language stimulation of the developing brain is most important during the first four or five years of life. But this does not mean that brain stimulation after age five is not necessary for brain growth and development. Research demonstrates that the brain retains its capacity to grow throughout life (Thompson & Nelson, 2001). Brain development can be facilitated not only during the first four years but also at other developmental stages. This suggests that early deprivation and harm can be treated and modified during later years, even in adults.

Hormones and Neurotransmitters

Neurotransmitters are chemicals, manufactured in the brain, that are intimately involved in biochemical activity and transmission of messages in the nervous system. Research has consistently suggested that the neurotransmitter **serotonin** may play the most significant role in aggression and violence (Coscina, 1997; Lesch & Merschdorf, 2000; Loeber & Stouthamer-Loeber, 1998; Moffitt et al., 1997; Vaughn, DeLisi, Beaver, & Wright, 2009). Serotonin exists in large amounts in the frontal lobe, which we have learned is involved in planning and self-regulation. It has been commonly concluded in the biopsychology literature that a deficiency in serotonin in the forebrain is largely responsible for aggressive, antisocial, and violent behavior. "This *serotonin deficiency hypothesis* of human aggression has been tested hundreds of times over the past several decades and remains the most common hypothesis of serotonin's role in pathological aggression" (Duke, Bègue, Bell, & Eisenlhr-Moul, 2013, p. 1148; italics in the original quote). In fact, one well-cited author (Fishbein, 2001) proclaimed the relationship between serotonin and aggression "perhaps the most reliable finding in the history of psychiatry" (p. 15). Levels of serotonin also were believed to explain to some extent the general differences in physical aggression between men and women (Verona, Joiner, Johnson, & Bender, 2006).

Duke and his colleagues (2013) comprehensively examined 144 published and unpublished studies that investigated the serotonin deficiency hypothesis over the past three decades. Combined, the studies included over 6,500 participants. Their findings, however, were not promising. The researchers found a very weak relationship between a deficiency in serotonin and aggression, anger, and hostility. Consequently, the researchers concluded that the relation between serotonin and human aggression as well as the validity of the serotonin deficiency hypothesis remain open to debate. They point out that "[O]ver the past several decades, rapid advances in technology and copious amount of research have led to a much clearer understanding of serotonin's role in the brain; however, with increased understanding has come an increased awareness of the complexity of serotonin's role in regulating behavior" (p. 1162). In other words, serotonin's role in aggression and other behavior is far more complicated and mysterious than previously assumed. In addition, as emphasized previously, focusing on a single risk factor, such as serotonin levels, rather than multiple risk factors, is likely to result in an incomplete understanding of the development and maintenance of antisocial behavior

The neurotransmitter dopamine has also been considered a possible candidate for involvement in human aggression and violence (Pihl & Benkelfat, 2005; Raine, 2013). However, the research has been not been as extensive as the research on serotonin, and the jury is still out as to whether dopamine plays a significant role in aggressive or antisocial behavior. Several other neurotransmitters (e.g., norepinephrine, gamma-aminobutyric acid [GABA]) have also been suggested as contributors to antisocial behavior, aggression, and violence, but the evidence remains inconclusive (Pihl & Benkelfat, 2005).

NEUROPSYCHOLOGICAL FACTORS

Neuropsychological deficits in combination with certain family risk factors are often found in persistent, serious, violent offenders (Moffitt, 1993a). As described in the previous sections, neuropsychological deficits, especially those associated with executive function problems in the frontal lobe, are reasonably well-established risk factors for antisocial behavior in children, adolescents, and adults (Raine, 2002). **Executive function** refers to the higher levels of cognitive processes that organize and plan behavior, including logic and abstract reasoning. Executive function also prioritizes the steps necessary for solving problems and is closely involved in self-control and self-regulation. As we saw above in our discussion of malnutrition, moderate and severe malnutrition has negative effects on executive function. Several studies of school-age children and adolescents have found a significant relationship between deficits in executive functions and antisocial behavior (Morgan & Lilienfeld, 2000; Piehler et al., 2014; Syngelaki, Moore, Savage, Fairchild, & Van Goozen, 2009; Tremblay, 2003).

Acting without thinking, sometimes referred to simply as risk-taking, is also believed to be closely associated with deficits in executive function (Romer, 2010; Romer et al., 2011). Acting without thinking is "characterized by hyperactivity without evidence of deliberation or attention to the environment" (Romer, 2010, p. 265). Acting without thinking is a form of impulsiveness that is the focus of neurobehavioral theories of early risk for substance abuse problems and other types of risk-taking behavior in adolescents. Interestingly, although acting without thinking can occur at any age, it appears to be a component of the normal adolescent development process. A prominent, contemporary approach to explaining delinquency today, the dual developmental model of brain development (Steinberg, 2008, 2010) focuses on the impulsivity that characterizes the teenage years. We will discuss this model in Chapter 6.

SUMMARY AND CONCLUSIONS

Realizing that crime, like all human behavior, may result from an interaction among heredity, neurophysiology, and the environment, we have in this chapter looked at the research on the genetic and biological makeup of persons who engage in persistent antisocial behavior, particularly that which is defined as criminal. The biopsychological approaches of today are far more sophisticated compared with very early efforts to link biology with criminal behavior. These early efforts associated criminal activity with (for example) the size of one's skull or one's physique. Contemporary biopsychologists assert that, while some people may be predisposed toward aggressive behavior or behavior that indicates a need for stimulation, socialization or medication can keep inappropriate expressions of those behaviors in check. However, although the past decade has seen a resurgence of interest in this biosocial perspective, many criminologists resist any notion of biological or genetic predispositions. Some, while veering away from predispositions, do agree that factors like toxins, hormones, or brain injuries can influence one's behavior, however.

The genetic factor has been explored in twin and adoption studies and in the work of molecular biologists. Despite the continuing research, such as the TEDS and TCHAD twin studies discussed in the chapter, it is difficult to draw firm conclusions about the magnitude of genetic and environmental influences on antisocial behavior. Some empirical studies, however, have found a high concordance rate between identical twins engaged in crime, lending some credence to genetic predisposition. These studies have shown that even when separated at birth, identical twins tend to be similar in their pursuit of criminal careers. However, researchers continually have difficulty separating the social environment (shared or nonshared) from the nature–nurture equation, and it is becoming increasingly clear that the social and biological approaches to understanding human behavior are complementary rather than antagonistic (Cacioppo et al., 2000). There have been relatively few adoption studies conducted, primarily because of the inaccessibility of records. Researchers in this area, who say their research supports the genetic viewpoint, admonish that the social environment can either stimulate or inhibit any inborn tendency toward antisocial behavior.

In the field of molecular genetics, researchers have isolated genes that they believe are particularly significant in predisposing individuals to violent or other antisocial behavior. The prominent biopsychologist Adrian Raine has stated that at least seven genes are associated with antisocial behavior. For example, a low form of the MAOA gene (known as MAOL-L) is associated with aggression, and some polymorphisms are associated with low self-control.

Considerable research also has explored temperament, a mood disposition determined largely by genetics and biological influences, and its relationship with antisocial or criminal behavior. Temperament appears in infancy and continues throughout one's life. Irritable babies, according to these researchers, are a challenge to parents or caretakers who may become highly frustrated dealing with them. Likewise, a child who is impulsive is a poor self-regulator who often comes into conflict with the environment. On the other hand, nurturing and warm caretakers can override the effects of such difficult temperaments.

The structure of the brain, and specifically the amygdala, also has been scrutinized. The frontal lobe of the human brain, which includes the amygdala, is the location for organized thought, planning, and self-regulation. Faulty brain development in utero or trauma to the brain in child-hood may predispose someone to behaviors linked with criminality, including low impulse control, callous-unemotional traits, or poor self-regulation. Some environmental hazards that have been studied include exposure to lead and other toxic substances, maternal smoking and alcohol use, and malnutrition. In recent years, scientists have focused on the deleterious effects of environmental toxins like cadmium, manganese, and mercury on the developing brain. Brain injuries in later life, which have received increasing attention in recent years because of survival rates of veterans who have experienced such trauma, can also contribute to aggressive behavior.

We emphasize that most studies in this area, with respect to adult criminality, focus on vio-lent crime or aggressive antisocial behavior and, with just a few exceptions, have not focused on nonviolent crimes. The interest is mainly on exploring the relationship between "violence and the brain." However, assigning a *major* role in the causation of such behavior to diverse neurological deficits and nervous system functioning is unwarranted.

Key Concepts

Amygdala
Behavior genetics
Biopsychologists
Concordance
Executive function
Fetal alcohol spectrum disorder (FASD)
Fraternal twins (dizygotic (DZ) twins)
Identical twins (monozygotic (MZ) twins)
MAOA
MAOA-L

Molecular genetics
Neurotransmitters
Nonshared environments
Plasticity
Psychophysiology
Serotonin
Shared environments
Temperament
Traumatic brain injury (TBI)
Twins' Early Development Study (TEDS)

Review Questions

1. Briefly describe behavior genetics and how it differs from molecular genetics.
2. Summarize findings from the TEDS and TCHAD research.
3. Summarize the findings of adoption studies on the interac-tion between heredity and environment.
4. Define and explain the significance of the following: con-cordance, plasticity, serotonin, and executive function.
5. What is meant by the term "shared environment" and why is it important in genetic research on crime?

6. Explain how temperament plays a role in the development of antisocial behavior.
7. Provide examples of any three environmental hazards that have been linked with aggressive behavior.
8. What are some of the effects of traumatic brain injury on behavior?

4

Origins of Criminal Behavior: Learning and Situational Factors

CHAPTER OBJECTIVES

- Present learning and cognitive factors as key elements in the development of delinquent and criminal behavior.
- Review the historical background of behaviorism and its contributions to understanding human learning of delinquent and criminal behavior.
- Define and describe classical conditioning, operant conditioning, and social learning.
- Review the fundamental principles of social learning and its contributions to understanding antisocial behavior.
- Introduce frustration-induced crime.
- Describe the power of the social situation, authority, and deindividuation in instigating criminal actions.
- Discuss and review research on the bystander effect.
- Provide overview of recent research on moral development and moral disengagement.

People do not come into situations empty-headed. Unless they have experienced memory loss (e.g., as the result of a brain injury or some form of dementia), they remember what just happened and what has happened in the more distant past. They also have a store of living experiences and an extensive repertoire of strategies for reacting to events. Up to this point, we have not highlighted these cognitive strategies, concentrating instead on various individual, family, and social risk factors that can contribute to the development of criminal behavior.

A basic premise of this text is that criminal behavior is learned. Traditionally, psychologists have delineated three major types of learning: **classical** or **Pavlovian conditioning**, **instrumental learning** or **operant conditioning**, and **social learning**. The reader with a background in introductory psychology will recall Ivan Pavlov's famous experiments with dogs that learned to salivate at the sound of a bell, because the bell had been associated with the arrival of food. Even when the food was not presented, the dogs salivated when the bell was rung. When classical conditioning is applied to people, it suggests that they, too, can "learn" if they have been rewarded or punished for behavior. Biological factors, such as those discussed in Chapter 3, appear to account in part for individual differences in susceptibility to classical conditioning (Eysenck, 1967). The classical conditioning perspective presumes, however, that the human being is an automaton and acts in a monotonous routine manner without active intelligence. Pair a neutral stimulus with a closely following rewarding or painful event and the alert, intact robot will eventually, and automatically, connect the stimulus with the reward or the pain. This sequence may be a powerful factor in some behaviors, but certainly not in all or even most. Conditioning is only one of several factors involved in the acquisition (or avoidance) of criminal behavior. We will discuss classical conditioning again later in the chapter.

In instrumental learning, the process is quite different. Here, the learner must do something to the environment in order to obtain a reward or, in some cases, to avoid punishment. Instrumental learning is based on learning the consequences of behavior: If you do something, there is some probability that a certain rewarding event (or perhaps an avoidance of punishment) will occur. A child may learn, for example, that one parent will give her a piece of candy to quell a temper tantrum; the other parent will not yield. The child will eventually learn to use temper tantrums when one parent is around, but not the other.

Social learning is more complex than either classical conditioning or instrumental learning, because it involves learning from watching others and organizing social experiences in the brain. Of the three types of learning, social learning is the most representative of contemporary psychology. It enables us to integrate knowledge from varied aspects of a person's environment and to consider—not only the biological and social environment that was discussed in the previous chapters—but also the cognitive environment. In this chapter, we will revisit classical and instrumental learning, but we focus primarily on social learning.

In order to understand criminal behavior in some depth, it is crucial that we regard all individuals—whether or not they violate the rules of society—as *active* problem solvers who perceive, process, interpret, and respond uniquely to their environments. For the moment, think of unlawful behavior as subjectively adaptable rather than deviant. In this sense, unlawful conduct or antisocial behavior is a response pattern that a person has found to be effective, or thinks will be effective, in certain circumstances.

Violent crimes like aggravated assault and homicide are sometimes called "irrational," "uncontrollable," or "motiveless," but in reality they usually are not. We know that crimes, including violent crimes, are often planned. By the early twenty-first century, it had become chillingly clear to the public that some violence is planned, controlled, and motivated. Those who entered the Paris offices of the satirical publication Charlie Hebdo in January 2015 and killed 12 people had methodically planned their actions, as became apparent from recorded videos of their behavior prior to and after the incident. Similar comments could be made of other shocking incidents, such as individual murders and mass killings of school children, café patrons, theater goers, or marathon fans. Furthermore, even when a decision to act violently is a quick one—as would be the case when an armed gunman shoots an unanticipated witness or a police officer shoots an unarmed suspect in the back—the action is not uncontrollable.

Engaging in criminal behavior, violent or nonviolent, might be one person's way of adapting or surviving under physically, socially, financially, or psychologically dire conditions. For another person, the behavior reflects a belief that what one is doing is justified. Although terrorist activities immediately come to mind, this should not be limited to a terrorist context. Child abusers may say they were teaching a child a lesson. White collar criminals may say their illegal activities are common and are not really wrong. Political figures may justify torture in the name of national security. Even behavior that can be attributed to a severe mental disorder may be adaptive, though it may not be legally culpable, something we will discuss in Chapter 8. In all these cases, the person is choosing what he or she believes is the best alternative for that particular situation (although real choice may be illusory in the case of the person who is severely mentally disordered). It is not, of course, necessarily the alternative that others would choose, nor what society condones.

Besides susceptibility to classical conditioning, what accounts for the choice to act in a violent or otherwise antisocial manner? In a very general sense, learning—both operant (or instrumental) and social learning—is an extremely important component in the behavioral equation. Because these concepts spring from the school of psychological thought called behaviorism, we will begin our discussion there.

BEHAVIORISM

Behaviorism officially began in 1913 with the publication of a now classic paper by John B. Watson (1878–1958), "Psychology as the Behaviorist Views It." The paper, which appeared in the journal *Psychological Review*, is considered the first definitive statement on behaviorism, and Watson is acknowledged as the school's founder. However, Watson was by no means the first to discuss the basic elements of behaviorism. Its roots can be traced back at least to Aristotle (Diserens, 1925). Watson's behaviorism represents a recurring phase in the cyclical history of psychology. A psychology of consciousness or mind is followed by a psychology of action and behavior (behaviorism), from which a psychology of mind and consciousness reemerges. Today psychology is immersed once again in a psychology of mind, especially cognitive processes and the neuropsychological aspects of the brain. **Cognitive processes** are those internal mental processes that enable humans to imagine, to gain knowledge, to reason, and to evaluate information. Although some theorists have suggested that cognitive psychology does not sufficiently recognize the importance of self-reflectiveness or self-agency (Bandura, 2001), to others cognitive psychology does encompass these aspects. Interestingly, contemporary psychology also is embracing biological and developmental influences on human behavior, as we learned in Chapter 3. For the moment, however, let's return to Watsonian behaviorism, which has heavily influenced psychological interpretations of criminal behavior.

Watson frequently declared that psychology was the science of behavior. He believed that psychologists should eliminate the "mind" and all of its related vague concepts from scientific consideration because they could not be observed or measured. He was convinced that the fundamental goal of psychology was to understand, predict, and control human behavior, and that only a rigidly scientific approach could accomplish this.

Watson was greatly influenced by Pavlov's famous research on classical conditioning, alluded to briefly above. Pavlov (1849–1936) was a Russian physiologist interested in studying the digestive system. His subjects were dogs. He strapped them in harnesses, placed different types of food in their mouths, and then measured the flow of saliva through a tube he had surgically placed in their cheek. During these experiments, he began to notice a curious fact. The dogs began to salivate *before* they received the food. He observed that some began to salivate at the mere sight of the container where their food was kept, and some salivated at the sight of the caretaker who usually fed the dogs. Dog owners will easily recognize this pairing. A dog will become excited—some even start slobbering—as you begin opening a bag of dog chow or shaking a box of dog biscuits. Pavlov quickly recognized the importance of this connection and spent the rest of his life studying it.

Pavlov expanded his laboratory conditions by controlling the dog's associations between events or things and the delivery of food. He began to present a neutral event (an event not previously associated with food) just before food delivery. In his well-known laboratory conditions, he presented a bell just before meat powder. The meat powder was termed the *unconditioned stimulus* because its ability to produce salivation was innate and did not depend on the dog's having to learn the response. Likewise, the salivation was an unconditioned response because it too does not depend on learning. The bell became the *conditioned stimulus*, because the dog quickly learned that the sound of the bell (or even the presence of the bell) preceded the treat. Similarly, salivation to the bell became the *conditioned response* because the association was learned. As we will learn in later chapters, classical conditioning is relevant to the understanding of some crimes, particularly some sexual offenses.

Watson thought that psychology should focus exclusively on the interplay between stimulus and response. A **stimulus** is a person, object, or event that elicits behavior. A **response** is the elicited behavior. Watson was convinced that all behavior—both animal and human—was controlled by the external environment in a way similar to that described by Pavlov in his initial study—stimulus produces response (sometimes called S-R psychology). Therefore, for Watson, classical (or Pavlovian) conditioning was the key to understanding, predicting, and controlling behavior, and its practical applicability was unlimited.

The chief spokesperson for behaviorism for several decades was B. F. Skinner (1904–1990), who was the most influential psychologist in the United States in the twentieth century.

The Skinnerian perspective especially dominated the application of behavior modification or behavior therapy in the correctional system and in many institutions for the intellectually disabled or mentally disordered. Patients or offenders earned rewards for good behavior and lost items or points when good behavior was not forthcoming. As the history of such settings demonstrates, there were many abuses associated with these practices; for example, some rewards were basic necessities, such as adequate food or clothing, which should have been provided regardless of one's behavior (Rothman, 1980). In addition, "good behavior" within an institutional setting did not necessarily carry over to the outside world.

Later theories on criminal behavior (e.g., Akers, 1985) tried to integrate Skinnerian behaviorism with sociological perspectives. Concepts associated with behaviorism are entrenched in many other theories as well. It is worthwhile, therefore, to spend some time sketching the Skinnerian approach to human behavior in general before assessing its impact on the study of criminal behavior.

Skinner's Theory of Behavior

Like Watson, Skinner believed that the primary goal of psychology is the prediction and control of behavior. And like Watson, he believed that environmental or external stimuli are the primary—if not the sole—determinants of all behavior, both human and animal. The environmental stimuli become **independent variables**, and the behaviors they elicit the **dependent variables**. In the behavioral sciences, a **variable** is any entity (or behavior) that can be measured. A behavior (or response) is called "dependent" because it is under the control of (or dependent on) one or more independent variables. The consistent relationships between independent and dependent variables (stimulus and response) are scientific laws. Thus, according to Skinner, the goal of behavioristic psychology is to uncover these laws, making possible the prediction and control of human behavior, including criminal behavior.

Unlike Watson, Skinner did not deny the existence and sometimes usefulness of private mental events or cognitive processes. He emphasized, however, that these stimuli are not needed by a *science* of behavior, since the products of mental activity can be explained in ways that do not require allusion to unobserved mental states. Specifically, mental activity can be explained by observing what a person does, and it is what a person does that counts. Watson, remember, insisted that consciousness and mind simply do not exist. Thought, to Watson, was little more than tiny movements of the speech apparatus. To Skinner, thought and cognitive processes existed, but studying them is unlikely to lead to the "hard" science of behavior. Consequently, in order to understand and modify criminal behavior, the thoughts, values, decisions, and intentions of a criminal mind are irrelevant. According to Skinner, to understand the development of delinquency and criminal behavior, we must focus on environmental stimuli, observable behavior, and rewards.

Behaviorism as a Method of Science

At this point, we must emphasize the need to distinguish between behaviorism as a *method of science* and as a *perspective on human nature*. As a method of science, behaviorism posits that knowledge about human behavior can be best advanced if scientists use referents that have a physical basis and can be *publicly observed* by others. Since private events that happen inside our heads cannot be seen by others, they cannot be subjected to the rules of science. According to Skinner, behavioral science data must be comparable to be verified or disconfirmed. Otherwise, psychology would remain a philosophical exercise steeped in armchair speculation and untestable opinions. Some psychologists, psychiatrists, and other professionals could continue to assert that shoplifting and gambling are addictions, without being taken to task about the validity of their statements. Only a well-executed, systematic study in which the terms *shoplifting, gambling,* and *addiction* are clearly spelled out and rigorously tested will advance our knowledge about the accuracy of the addiction connection. Therefore, every psychological experiment, every sentence written into a psychological report, should be anchored to something that we can all observe, or that is testable by another professional. Rather than merely saying that someone is anxious or angry, we must identify the precise behaviors that prompt us to make these interpretations. This offers a basis for others, including the person being observed, to agree or disagree with us.

Behaviorism as a Perspective of Human Nature

Concerning behaviorism as a perspective of human nature, Skinner—and a majority of psychologists with a strong behavioristic leaning—embraced the view that humans differ only in degree from their animal ancestry. The behavior of humans follows the same basic natural laws as that of all animals. Like Darwin, Skinner saw no radical differences between humans and animals. Even human language and conceptual thinking are nondistinctive. Verbal behavior "is a very special kind of behavior, but there is nothing by way of processes involved that would distinguish it from non-verbal behavior and hence [verbal behavior] would not distinguish man from the [other] animals" (Skinner, 1964, p. 156). To Skinner, therefore, research on subhumans such as monkeys, rats, and pigeons had great value; if carefully done, it would reveal lawful relationships between all organisms and their environments.

Clearly, Skinner was also a strong situationist. **Situationism** refers to the belief that all behavior is at the mercy of stimuli in the environment, and individuals have virtually no control or self-determination. Independent thinking and free will are myths. Animals, including humans, react, like complicated robots, to their environments. The environmental stimuli and the range of reactions are complex and infinite, but with careful research, this complexity is not unmanageable. Complex human behavior can be broken down into more simple behavior, a procedure sometimes referred to as **reductionism**. In other words, complicated behavior can be best understood by examining the simplest stimulus-response chains of behavior. This point brings us to the issue of operant conditioning and other Skinnerian concepts.

Skinnerian Concepts

OPERANT CONDITIONING.   Skinner accepted the basic tenets of classical conditioning, but asserted that we need an additional type of conditioning to account more fully for all forms of behavior. In Pavlov's experiments on classical conditioning, the dogs did not operate on their environments to receive rewards; the event (food) occurred regardless of what they did. Skinner called this "responding conditioning" and contrasted it with a situation in which a subject does something that affects the situation. In other words, subjects—now called participants in psychological experiments—behave in such a way that reinforcement is forthcoming. To uncover this operant conditioning principle, Skinner established an association between *behavior* and its *consequences.* He trained pigeons (apparently less troublesome and less expensive than dogs) to peck at keys or push levers for food. The pecking or pushing are operations on the environment. **Operant conditioning**, then, is learning to either make or withhold a particular response because of its consequences. Operant conditioning (or operant learning) is a fundamental learning process that is acquired (or eliminated) by the consequences that follow the behavior. Recall the child who learned the effectiveness of the temper tantrum in the company of one parent but not the other. Children often operate on their environments in this way, "learning" the effectiveness of certain behaviors as they go along—but so do adults. You may have learned that complimenting a coworker improves the quality of your day, while being the office grump drives people away. If you prefer to be a loner, however, the office grump strategy could be effective.

The learning that comes about through operant conditioning was described before Skinner's time, but he is credited with drawing contemporary attention to it and studying it scientifically. In the late eighteenth and early nineteenth centuries, for example, philosophers like Cesare Beccaria and Jeremy Bentham observed that human conduct was motivated by the seeking of pleasure and the avoidance of pain. We alluded to this in Chapter 1 when the classical school of criminology was mentioned. Through the exercise of their free will, people choose their actions. In essence, this is what is meant by operant learning. It assumes that people do things solely to receive rewards and avoid punishment. The rewards may be physical (e.g., material goods, money), psychological (e.g., feelings of importance or control over one's fate), or social (e.g., improved status, acceptance).

REINFORCEMENT.   Skinner called rewards **reinforcement**, defining that term as anything that increases the probability of future responding. Furthermore, reinforcement may be either positive or negative. In **positive reinforcement**, we *gain* something we desire as a consequence of certain behavior. We spend hours practicing a difficult piece on the keyboard or perfecting a ski jump and are rewarded by praise from listeners or a gold medal in the Olympics. In **negative reinforcement**, we *avoid* an unpleasant event or stimulus as a consequence of certain behavior. For example, if as a child you were able to avoid the unpleasantness of certain school days by feigning illness, your malingering was negatively reinforced. Therefore, you were more likely to engage in it again at a future date, under similar circumstances—you were "sick" on high school dress-up day, class discussion day in a difficult college course, or the day the district supervisor was scheduled to visit the office. Thus, both positive and negative reinforcement can increase the likelihood of future behavior.

PUNISHMENT AND EXTINCTION.   Negative reinforcement is to be distinguished from punishment and extinction. In **punishment**, an organism receives noxious or painful stimuli as consequences of behavior, such as being slapped or hit for "being bad." In **extinction**, a person or animal receives neither reinforcement nor punishment (see **Table 4-1**). Skinner argued that punishment is a less effective way to eliminate behavior, because it merely suppresses it temporarily. At a later time, under the right conditions, the response is very likely to reoccur. Extinction is far more effective, because once the organism learns that a behavior brings no reinforcement, the behavior will be dropped from the repertoire of possible responses for that set of circumstances.

According to Nietzel (1979), C. R. Jeffrey (1965) was one of the first criminologists to suggest that criminal behavior was learned according to principles of Skinnerian operant conditioning. Shortly afterward, Burgess and Akers (1966) agreed with this, and further hypothesized that criminal behavior was both acquired and maintained through operant conditioning. But, as Nietzel points out, most of the direct evidence for this claim comes from experiments with nonhuman animals. Evidence that the same occurs in humans is scarce and replete with possible alternate interpretations.

Nevertheless, neither Jeffrey nor Burgess and Akers relied exclusively on Skinnerian theory. Rather, they combined sociologist Edwin Sutherland's principles of social learning with operant conditioning, particularly the reinforcement aspect, to suggest explanations for criminal behavior (Williams & McShane, 2004). We will return to Sutherland's theory shortly.

Operant Learning and Crime

The premise that operant conditioning is the basis for the origin of criminal behavior is deceptively simple: Criminal behavior is learned and strengthened because of the reinforcements it brings. According to Skinner, human beings are born neutral—neither good nor bad. Culture, society, and the environment shape behavior. Therefore, behavior will be labeled good, bad, or indifferent, as society chooses. What is judged "good" behavior in one society or culture may be labeled "bad" in another. Members of one group in a society may believe that it is "bad" for a child to masturbate or to pretend that a block of wood is a toy truck and "good" to hit the child to stop these behaviors. To others, the behavior of the adults who hit the child is "bad." Depending on the severity of the

TABLE 4-1	Skinner's Basic Principles of Operant Learning	
	Goal	**Action**
Positive reinforcement	Increases a desired behavior	Introduction of a pleasant stimulus following a desired behavior
Negative reinforcement	Increases a desired behavior	Removal of aversive stimulus following a desired behavior
Punishment	Decreases undesired behavior	Introduction of aversive stimulus following undesired behavior
Extinction	Eliminates undesired behavior	No reinforcement or punishment for undesired behavior

punishment, it may also be aggravated assault, a crime as defined in the law. In fact, even corporal punishment that is not severe—such as a slap—qualifies as criminal activity according to the legal definition of simple assault. To many it is "bad," not because it is a crime, but because of its effect on the child's development.

Skinner was convinced that searches for individual dispositions or personalities that lead to criminal conduct are fruitless, because people are ultimately determined by the environment in which they live. He did not completely discount the role of genetics in the formation of behavior, but he saw it as a very minor one; the dominant player is operant conditioning. According to Skinner and his followers, if we wish to eliminate crime, we must change society through behavioral engineering based on a *scientific* conception of humans. Having agreed on rules and regulations (having defined what behaviors constitute antisocial or criminal offenses), we must design a society in which members learn very early that positive reinforcement will not occur if they transgress against these rules and regulations, but will occur if they abide by them.

This is a tall order, since the reinforcements for antisocial behavior are already occurring, are not always obvious, and may actually be highly complex. Property crimes such as shoplifting and burglary, or violent crimes such as robbery, appear to be motivated in many cases by a desire for physical rewards. However, they may also be prompted by a desire for social and psychological reinforcements, such as increased status among peers, self-esteem, feelings of competence, or simply for the thrill of it. It is a safe bet that much criminal behavior is undertaken for reinforcement purposes, positive or negative. The problem then becomes, how do we identify those reinforcements and how do we prevent them from happening, or at least minimize their value?

Contemporary psychology still embraces a behavioristic orientation toward the *scientific* study of behavior, but has grown very cool toward the Skinnerian perspective of human nature. All behaviorists are not Skinnerians. Many (if not most) find Skinner's brand of behaviorism too limiting and find the many facets of social learning—to be discussed below—far more appealing. While they agree that a stimulus can elicit a reflexive response (classical conditioning) and that a behavior produces consequences that influence subsequent responding (operant conditioning), they are also convinced that additional factors must be introduced to explain human behavior.

This brings us to the topic of mental states and cognitive processes, which Skinner urged all behavioral scientists to shun. In recent years, many psychologists have been examining the roles played by self-reinforcement, anticipatory reinforcement, vicarious reinforcement, and all the symbolic processes that occur within the human brain. To avoid confusion, we must now begin to distinguish Skinnerian behaviorism from other forms, including social behaviorism (social learning) and differential association-reinforcement.

SOCIAL LEARNING

Early learning theorists worked in the laboratory, using nonhumans as their primary subjects. Pavlov's, Watson's, and Skinner's theories, for example, were based on careful, painstaking observations and experiments with nonhuman animals. The learning principles gleaned from their work were generalized to a wide variety of human behaviors. In many cases, this was a valid process. Few psychologists would dispute the contention that the concept of reinforcement is one of the most soundly established principles in psychology today.

However, behaviorists also suggested that since all human behavior is learned, it can also be changed, using the same principles by which it was acquired. This generated a plethora of behavior therapies or behavior modification techniques. Use learning principles to establish conditions that change or maintain targeted behaviors and voilà! Therapeutic success! The apparent simplicity of the procedures and methods was especially appealing to many clinicians and other professionals working in the criminal justice system, and behavior modification packages sometimes guaranteed to modify criminal behavior were rushed to various institutions, including facilities for juveniles. Patients as well as prisoners (and juveniles) would be rewarded for good behavior with such incentives as cigarettes, canteen privileges, or an extra shower. As noted above, the incentives were sometimes basic necessities that should have been available to them as a matter of course, such as a towel or a mattress to sleep on. But oversimplification is dangerous when we deal with human complexity. Human beings do respond to reinforcement and punishment, and behavior therapy based on learning principles can change certain elements of behavior. Moreover, humans can be classically conditioned, although there are individual differences in their susceptibility. When we lose sight of the person and overemphasize the environmental or external determinants of behavior, however, we may be overlooking a critical level of explanation. Remember that human beings are, in large part, active problem solvers who perceive, encode, interpret, and make decisions on the basis of what the environment has to offer. Thus, internal factors, as well as external ones, may play significant roles in behavior. This is the essence of **social learning theory**, which suggests that to understand criminal behavior we must examine perceptions, thoughts, expectancies, competencies, and values. Each person has his or her own version of the world and lives by that version.

To explain human behavior, social learning theorists place great emphasis on cognitive processes, which are the internal processes we commonly call thinking and remembering. Classical and operant conditioning ignore what transpires between the time the organism perceives a stimulus and the time it responds or reacts. Skinnerian behaviorists claim, "If we can account for the facts by using observable behavior, why worry about the labyrinths of internal processes?" Social behaviorists, however, counter that this perspective offers an incomplete picture of human behavior.

The term *social learning* reflects the theory's strong assumption that we learn primarily by observing and listening to people around us—the social environment. In fact, social learning theorists believe that the social environment is the most important factor in the *acquisition* of most human behavior. Humans are basically social creatures. These theorists do accept the necessity of reinforcement for the *maintenance* of behavior, however. Criminal behavior, for example, may initially be acquired through association and through observation, but whether or not it is maintained will depend primarily upon reinforcement (operant conditioning). For example, if a boy sees someone he admires (i.e., a role model) successfully pilfering from the local sporting goods store, the boy may try some pilfering of his own. Whether he continues that behavior, however, will depend on the personal reinforcement or value it assumes. If no reinforcement is forthcoming (he fails to pocket a baseball because someone else walked into the store, or he finds that the gym shorts he stole do not fit), then the behavior will probably drop out of his response repertoire (extinction). If the behavior brings aversive results (punishment), this might inhibit or suppress future similar behavior, but the suppression or inhibition is unlikely to be long lasting.

Several clusters of psychologists are enrolled in the social learning school of thought. Additionally, the discipline of sociology has its own social learning school. We will focus first on the work of two prominent representatives, psychologists Julian Rotter and Albert Bandura, since they seem to have the most to offer to the study of criminal behavior from the social learning perspective.

Expectancy Theory

Julian Rotter is best known for drawing attention to the importance of expectations (cognitions) about the consequences (outcomes) of behavior, including the reinforcement that will be gained from it. In other words, before doing anything, we ask, "What has happened to me before in this situation, and what will I gain this time?" According to Rotter, whether a specific pattern of behavior occurs will depend on our expectancies and how much we value the outcomes. To predict whether someone will behave a certain way, we must estimate that person's expectancies and the importance he or she places on the rewards gained by the behavior. Often, the person will develop "generalized expectancies" that are stable and consistent across relatively similar situations (Mischel, 1976). **Expectancy theory**, therefore, argues that a person's performance level is based on that person's *expectation* that behaving in a particular way will lead to a given outcome.

The hypothesis that people enter situations with generalized expectancies about the outcomes of their behavior is an important one for students of crime. Applying Rotter's theory to criminal behavior, we would say that when people engage in unlawful conduct, they *expect* to gain something in the form of status, power, security, affection, material goods, or living conditions. The violent person, for example, may elect to behave that way in the belief that something will be gained; the serial murderer might believe that his god has sent him on a mission to eliminate all "loose" women, and thus by doing so he pleases this god; the father who physically abuses his children thinks they will comply with his wishes or learn to respect adults; the woman who poisons an abusive husband looks for an improvement in her life situation. Simply to label a violent person impulsive, crazy, or lacking in ego control fails to include other essential ingredients in the act. Although self-regulation and moral development are involved, people who act unlawfully perceive and interpret the situation and select what they consider to be the most effective behavior under the circumstances. Usually, when people act violently, they do so because that approach has been used successfully in the past (at least they believe it has been successful). Less frequently, they have simply observed someone else gain by employing a violent approach, and they try it for themselves. This brings us to Bandura's imitational model of social learning.

Imitational Aspects of Social Learning

A person may acquire ways of doing something simply by watching others do it; direct reinforcement is not necessary. Bandura (1973b) introduced this idea, which he called **observational learning** or **modeling**, to the social learning process. Bandura contends that much of our behavior is initially acquired by watching others, who are called models. **Models** are those significant persons in the social environment that provide cues for how to do something. For example, a child may learn how to shoot a gun by imitating television or video characters. He or she then rehearses and fine-tunes this behavioral pattern by practicing with toy guns. The behavior is likely to be maintained if peers also play with guns and reinforce one another for doing so. Even if the children have not pulled the triggers on real guns, they have acquired a close approximation of shooting someone by observing others do it. It is likely that just about every adult and older child in the United States knows how to shoot a gun, even if they have never actually done so: "You aim and pull the trigger." Of course, shooting safely and accurately is much more complicated, but the rudimentary know-how has been acquired through **imitational learning** (also called modeling or observational learning). The behavioral pattern exists in our repertoires, even if we have never received direct reinforcement for acquiring it.

According to Bandura, the more significant and respected the models, the greater their impact on our behavior. Relevant models include parents, teachers, siblings, friends, and peers, as well as symbolic models like literary characters or television, video, or movie personages. Rock stars and athletes are modeled by many young people, which is one reason we are exposed to so many public figures touting cosmetics, reverse mortgages, smart phones, weight-loss programs, and brands of yogurt. Well-known individuals also appear in public service announcements, such as those promoting a drug-free life or telling viewers that domestic violence is "not o.k." Interestingly, these public service advertisements often miss the point. In observational learning, it is not so much what the model says as what the model does that is effective. Accounts of popular public figures engaging and allegedly engaging in domestic violence, animal abuse, substance abuse, rape, assault, tax evasion, and illegal gambling suggest to some observers that such behavior is normative, and these accounts may counteract any positive message promoted by public service announcements.

The observed behavior of the model is also more likely to be imitated if the observer sees the model receive a reward, such as fame plus millions of dollars per year. It is less likely to be imitated if the model is punished, such as receiving a prison sentence. Thus, according to social learning principles, convictions of sports and entertainment figures charged with the crimes mentioned above would suggest that the behaviors will not be imitated. On the other hand, if they serve little or no time and write a best-selling book about their experiences, or subsequently received a lucrative contract to play professional sports, an observer might not perceive this as a punishment. Bandura believes—much like Rotter—that once a person decides to use a newly acquired behavior, whether he or she performs or maintains it will depend on the situation and the expectancies for potential gain. This potential gain may come from outside (the praise of others, financial gain) or it may come from within (self-reinforcement for a job the individual perceives as well done).

Much of Bandura's original research was directed at the learning of aggressive and violent behavior through modeling. We will be returning to his theory, therefore, in Chapter 5 on aggression and violence. At this point, however, be aware that a substantial body of experimental findings gives impressive support to his theory. In a classic study, preschool children who watched a film of an adult assaulting an inflated plastic rubber doll were significantly more likely to imitate that behavior than were a comparable group who viewed more passive behavior (Bandura & Huston, 1961; Bandura, Ross, & Ross, 1963). Many studies employing variations of this basic procedure report similar results, strengthening the hypothesis that observing aggression leads to hostility in both children and adults (Walters & Grusec, 1977). This research has been extended to viewing media violence and playing violent video games (Dodge & Pettit, 2003). While the research in these areas is not totally conclusive, the growing evidence is that people who observe aggressive acts not only imitate the observed behavior but also become generally more hostile and aggressive themselves (Anderson & Prot, 2011; Bryant & Zillmann, 2002; Huesmann, Moise-Titus, Podolski, & Eron, 2003).

To some extent, social learning, as it is discussed by Rotter and Bandura, humanizes the Skinnerian viewpoint, because it provides clues about what transpires inside the human brain, especially the cognitive processes involved. It draws our attention to the cognitive aspects of behavior, while classical and operant conditioning focus exclusively on the environment. Social learning theorists use environment in the social sense, which includes the internal as well as the external environment. Skinnerians prefer to limit relevant stimuli to external surroundings.

Differential Association-Reinforcement Theory

Ronald Akers (1977, 1985; Burgess & Akers, 1966) proposed a social learning theory of deviance that tries to integrate the core ingredients of Skinnerian behaviorism, the social learning theory as outlined by Bandura, and the differential association theory of criminologist Edwin H. Sutherland (1947). Akers called his theory **differential association-reinforcement (DAR)**. Briefly, the theory states that people learn to commit deviant acts through interpersonal interactions with their social environment.

To understand DAR theory, we must grasp Sutherland's differential association theory, which dominated the field of sociological criminology for over four decades. It was first set forth in the 3rd edition (1939) of Sutherland's *Principles of Criminology* and restated in 1947. Although Sutherland died in 1950, the theory was left intact in Donald R. Cressey's subsequent revisions of the original text (Sutherland & Cressey, 1978; Sutherland, Cressey, & Luckenbill, 1992).

Sutherland, a sociologist, believed that criminal or deviant behavior is learned the same way that all behavior is learned. The crucial factors are with whom a person associates, for how long, how frequently, how personally meaningful the associations, and how early they occur in the person's development. According to Sutherland, in our intimate personal groups, we all learn definitions, or normative meanings (messages or values), favorable or unfavorable to law violation. A person becomes delinquent or criminal "because of an excess of definitions favorable to violation of law over definitions unfavorable to violation of law. This is the principle of differential association" (Sutherland & Cressey, 1974, pp. 80–81).

Note that criminal behavior does not invariably develop out of association or contacts with "bad companions" or a criminal element. The messages, not the contacts themselves, are crucial. Furthermore, in order for the person to be influenced toward delinquent behavior, the deviant messages or values from the "bad companions" must outweigh conventional ones. Therefore, Sutherland also believed that criminal behavior may develop even if association with criminal groups is minimal. For example, law-abiding groups—such as parents—may communicate subtly or bluntly that it is all right to cheat, or that everyone is basically dishonest. This is an extremely important point that will be reiterated when we discuss moral disengagement later in the chapter. Nevertheless, contemporary reviews of differential association theory emphasize that the associations with deviant peer groups have a major effect on illegal behavior (Williams & McShane, 2004). What is not known is which comes first: the behavior or the associations (Williams & McShane, 2004).

Sutherland's theory is probably popular among social scientists because, as one writer put it, "it attempts a logical, systematic formulation of the chain of interrelations that makes crime reasonable and understandable as normal, learned behavior without having to resort to assumptions of biological or psychological deviance" (Vold, Theoretical Criminology (New York: Oxford University Press, 1958), p. 192). However, the theory is also ambiguous; because of this feature, it did not at first draw much empirical research (see Gibbons, 1977, pp. 221–228). How are a person's contacts to be measured and weighed? Also, as Cressey (Sutherland & Cressey, 1974) admits, the theory does not specify what kinds of learning are important (e.g., operant, classical, modeling). Neither does it adequately consider individual differences in the learning process. Among some sociologists, however, differential association theory remains popular and continues to attract research interest (Hunt, 2010; Williams & McShane, 2004).

Akers (1985) tries to correct some of the problems with differential association theory by reformulating it to dovetail with Skinnerian and social learning principles. He proposes that most deviant behavior is learned according to principles outlined in Skinner's operant conditioning, with classical conditioning playing a secondary role. Furthermore, the strength of deviant behavior is a direct function of the amount, frequency, and probability of reinforcement the individual has experienced by performing that behavior in the past. The reinforcement may be positive or negative in the Skinnerian meanings of the terms.

Crucial to the Akers position is the role played by *social* and *nonsocial reinforcement*, the former being the more important. "Most of the learning relevant to deviant behavior is the result of social interactions or exchanges in which the words, responses, presence, and behavior of other persons make reinforcers available, and provide the setting for reinforcement" (Akers, 1985, p. 45). It is also important to note that most of these social reinforcements are symbolic and verbal rewards for participating or for agreeing with group norms and expectations. For example, doing something in accordance with group or subcultural norms is rewarded with "Way to go," "Great job," a pat on the back, a high five, a fist bump, or a friendly grin. Nonsocial reinforcement refers primarily to physiological factors or material acquisition that may be relevant for some crimes, such as drug-related offenses or burglary.

Deviant or antisocial behavior, then, is most likely to develop as a result of social reinforcements given by significant others, usually within one's peer group. The group first adopts its own *normative definitions* about what conduct is good or bad, right or wrong, justified or unjustified. These normative definitions become internal, cognitive guides to what is appropriate and will most likely be reinforced by the group. In this sense, normative definitions operate as **discriminative stimuli**—social signals transmitted by subcultural or peer groups to indicate whether certain kinds of behavior will be rewarded or punished within a particular social context.

According to Akers, two classes of discriminative stimuli operate in promoting deviant behavior. First, positive discriminative stimuli are the signals (verbal or nonverbal) that communicate that certain behaviors are encouraged by the subgroup. Not surprisingly, they follow the principle of positive reinforcement: The individual engaging in them gains social rewards from the group. The second type of social cue, *neutralizing* or *justifying discriminative stimuli*, neutralizes the warnings communicated by society at large that certain behaviors are inappropriate or unlawful. According to Akers, they "make the behavior, which others condemn and which the person himself may initially define as bad, seem all right, justified, excusable, necessary, the lesser of two evils, or not 'really' deviant after all" (Akers, 1977, p. 521). Statements like "Everyone has a price," "I can't help myself," "Everyone else does it," or "She deserved it" reflect the influence of neutralizing stimuli.

The more people define their behavior as positive or at least justified, the more likely they are to engage in it. If deviant activity (as defined by society at large) has been reinforced more than conforming behavior, and if it has been justified, it is likely that deviant behavior will be maintained. In essence, our behavior is guided by the norms we have internalized and for which we expect to be continually socially reinforced by significant others.

Akers accepts the validity of Bandura's modeling as a necessary factor in the initial acquisition of deviant behavior. But its continuation will depend greatly on the frequency and personal significance of *social reinforcement*, which comes from association with others.

Akers's social learning theory has received its share of criticism. Some scholars consider it circular and difficult to follow: Behavior occurs because it is reinforced, but it is reinforced because it occurs. Kornhauser (1978) asserted that there was no empirical support for the theory. During the 1980s and 1990s, though, Akers himself—along with research colleagues—published a number of studies supportive of his theory, particularly as it related to drug use (e.g., Akers & Cochran, 1985; Akers & Lee, 1996; Krohn, Akers, Radosevich, & Lanza-Kaduce, 1982). Like Sutherland's differential association theory, Akers's approach retains respectability within sociological criminology (Chappell & Piquero, 2004).

FRUSTRATION-INDUCED CRIMINALITY

Several learning investigators (e.g., Amsel, 1958; Brown & Farber, 1951) have noted that when organisms—including humans—are prevented from responding in a way that had previously produced rewards, their behavior often becomes more energetic and vigorous. Cats bite, scratch, snarl, and become irritable; humans may snarl and become irritable and rambunctious (and may also bite and scratch). Researchers assume that these responses result from an aversive internal state of arousal that they call **frustration**.

Thus, when behavior directed at a specific goal is blocked, arousal increases, and the individual experiences a drive to reduce it. Behavior is energized, but more significantly the responses that lead to a reduction in the arousal may be strengthened or reinforced. This suggests that people who employ violence to reduce frustration will, under extreme frustration, become more vigorous than usual, possibly even resorting to murder and other violent actions. It also suggests that violent behavior directed at reducing frustration will be reinforced, since it reduces unpleasant arousal by altering the precipitating event or stimuli.

The Socialized and Individual Offender

Leonard Berkowitz (1962) conducted numerous studies relating frustration to criminality. He divided criminal personalities into two main classifications: the **socialized** and the **individual offender**. You have already met socialized offenders. We have discussed them throughout this chapter as products of learning, conditioning, and modeling. They offend because they have learned to, or expect rewards, as a result of their interactions with the social environment. The individual offender, by contrast, is the product of a long, possibly intense series of frustrations resulting from unmet needs. According to Berkowitz, both modeling and frustration are involved in the development of criminal behavior, but one set of life experiences favors a particular criminal style. "Most lawbreakers may have been exposed to some combination of frustrations and aggressively antisocial models, with the thwartings being particularly important in the development of 'individual' offenders and the antisocial models being more influential in the formulation of the 'socialized' criminals" (Berkowitz, 1962, p. 303).

Berkowitz adds an important dimension to frustration, suggesting that it is particularly intense if an individual has high expectancy of reaching a goal (Berkowitz, 1969). People who anticipate reaching a goal, and who feel they have some personal control over their lives, are more likely to react strongly to interference than those who feel hopeless. In the first case, delay or blockage may generate intense anger and even a violent response, if the frustrated individual believes that type of response will eliminate the interference. The power of frustration may well have been what Maslow (1954) was referring to when he stated that crime and delinquency represent a legitimate revolt against exploitation, injustice, and unfairness. The frustration hypothesis also fits neatly into theories offered by radical or conflict criminologists. Individuals who feel suppressed by the power elite and feel they have a right to reap society's benefits may well experience intense frustration at continuing domination. These criminologists would prefer, though, that the focus be on those who hold the power rather than on those who commit crime out of possible frustration.

Frustration-Induced Riots

The frustration-induced theory helps to explain the behavior of looters during unexpected events like floods, fires, or electrical blackouts. The theory is also cited when criminal activity occurs following controversial decisions associated with the criminal justice system. For example, after a jury in 1993 acquitted four Los Angeles police officers of aggravated assault in the beating of Rodney King, four days of rioting and looting ensued, 58 people were killed, and damage was estimated to be at least $1 billion dollars. The LA riots were widely perceived to be a reflection of frustration with what was perceived to be a racist criminal justice system. Although many of the rioters were black, not all were. People of all ages and diverse racial and ethnic backgrounds stole food, alcohol, firearms, and electronics. (Later, a federal jury convicted two of the four officers on federal charges.)

Twenty years later, in the fall of 2014, much of the nation's attention was riveted on Ferguson, Missouri, after the shooting of an unarmed young black man by a white police officer. Tensions were high as competing accounts of what had occurred appeared in the media. A grand jury refused to indict the officer. Marches, protests, and public demonstrations marked the weeks following the incident as well as the days following the grand jury's decision. But the widespread violence and looting that had been feared never materialized, though some violence did occur. Similarly, when an unarmed black man in Staten Island was confronted for selling loose cigarettes and was subsequently placed in an illegal choke hold by police and died, and when a grand jury again declined to indict, there were numerous protests and marches, but they were by and large peaceful. In both of these situations, as well as many others, the theory of frustration-induced criminality would have predicted more criminal activity, including violence, but it did not materialize.

Violence did materialize in Baltimore, Maryland in April and May 2015, after a young black man was arrested by police, placed in restraints, and taken in a van to the police station. He suffered severe spinal injuries, was hospitalized, and subsequently died. In this case both peaceful protests and violence erupted, particularly on one afternoon and evening. Peaceful marchers streamed through city streets, but cars were also set afire, businesses looted and destroyed, and police officers were injured from bricks thrown at them. National Guard troops were called in, and the violence was followed by appeals for calm from many segments of the community. Citizens were seen cleaning up the streets following the effects of the looting and burning. The Baltimore prosecutor's office investigating the incident quickly filed many criminal charges against six police officers, noting that the medical examiner had ruled the death a homicide.

A grand jury subsequently indicted all six officers on various charges, including second degree "depraved heart" murder, manslaughter, second degree assault, reckless endangerment, and misconduct in office. Not all charges pertained to each officer.

In sum, there have been numerous accounts of peaceful demonstrations and protests after a perceived injustice, even when major disruptions or even riots had been feared. The perceived injustices did not always involve police activity. In the fall of 2011 the Occupy Wall Street movement that began in New York City spread rapidly across the United States as well as in other countries. It was fueled by intense disenchantment with financial markets and corporate greed. Despite the large numbers of individuals who turned out for these protests, there was no widespread looting or violence, although there were reports of minor vandalism, disruption of traffic, and property damage. Likewise, in the aftermath of the 2012 death of a 17-year-old unarmed black youth by a white (Hispanic) neighborhood watch volunteer in Florida, many protests occurred across the nation. The protests were held to bring attention to the fact that no arrest had been made many weeks after the boy's death. The neighborhood watch volunteer was subsequently brought to trial and was acquitted by a six-member jury. Again, violent protests were predicted as a result, but they did not occur. As a general rule, the protests and marches that did happen were peaceful and nonviolent.

There is no question that frustration played a large role in prompting all of the above protests. In the case of the young black men, frustration was directed at perceived racial profiling, delay in attending appropriately to victims, disrespect of the deceased person's body, and the apparent reluctance of the criminal justice system to promptly investigate the deaths. The Occupy protesters were frustrated at the nation's economic systems and policies. Nevertheless, the frustration aggression hypothesis would not be supported in these instances because frustration was turned into something more positive—peaceful and dignified marches to bring public attention to injustice and to call for change. On the other hand, frustration may play an important role in explaining crime committed by individuals, as we discuss below.

Frustration and Crime

The role of frustration in criminal behavior can be complex, and it may be a matter of degree. Berkowitz hypothesizes that the more intense and frequent the thwarting or frustration in a person's life, the more susceptible and sensitive the person is to subsequent frustration. Thus, the individual who frequently strikes out at society in unlawful or deviant ways may have encountered numerous severe frustrating incidents, especially during early development, but has not given up hope. In support of this argument, Berkowitz cites early research findings on delinquency (e.g., Bandura & Walters, 1959; Glueck & Glueck, 1950; McCord, McCord, & Zola, 1959), revealing that delinquent children, compared with nondelinquents, have been considerably more deprived and frustrated during their lifetime.

Berkowitz also suggests that parental neglect or failure to meet the child's needs for dependency and affection are internal, frustrating circumstances that germinate distrust of all others within the social environment. This generalized distrust is carried into the streets and school, and the youngster may exhibit a "chip on the shoulder." The frustration of not having dependency needs met prevents the child from establishing emotional attachments to other people. The individual may thus become resentful, angry, and hostile toward other people in general.

Current psychological approaches to delinquency would not disagree, but would place far less blame on the parent. They are more likely to recognize the restrictions that parents face as a result of social problems like racism and economic inequality. As described in Chapter 2, for example, over 20 percent of children under the age of 18 in the United States live in households below the official poverty line, and another 20 percent are near poor (Yoshikawa et al., 2012). The negative effects of poverty on the mental, emotional, and behavioral health of children are well recognized, as we noted in chapters 2 and 3. In addition, contemporary psychologists recognize the influences of other social systems in the juvenile's life, including peers and the educational system.

SITUATIONAL INSTIGATORS AND REGULATORS OF CRIMINAL BEHAVIOR

Most contemporary theories and research support the view that human behavior results from a mutual interaction between personality and situational variables. However, several behavioral and social scientists (e.g., Alison, Bennell, Ormerod, & Mokros, 2002; Gibbons, 1977; Mischel, 1976) have observed that much crime research and theory neglects situational variables in favor of dispositional factors. They contend that criminality in many cases may simply reflect being in the wrong place at the wrong time with the wrong people. For example, Gibbons comments, "In many cases, criminality may be a response to nothing more temporal than the provocations and attractions bound up in the immediate circumstances out of which deviant acts arise" (Gibbons, 1977, p. 229). Skinner, of course, exemplifies the position that behavior is controlled by environmental contingencies and events.

Haney (1983) discusses **fundamental attribution error**, which refers to a common human tendency to discount the influence of the situation and explain behavior by referring to the personality of the actor instead. Fundamental attribution error is a concept that applies to making attributions about others, not ourselves. For example, when correctional counselors were asked why inmates had committed the crimes that put them in prison, the counselors attributed the causes almost exclusively to dispositional or personality factors (such as laziness, or meanness) rather than to environmental factors (such as upbringing, economic circumstances, or other social factors) (Saulnier & Perlman, 1981). The inmates, on the other hand, said that factors they believed landed them in prison were largely external in nature, such as poverty, poor employment opportunities, and physical and sexual abuse. When it comes to ourselves, we engage in **self-serving biases**, in which we tend to attribute good things about ourselves to dispositional factors, and bad things to events and forces outside ourselves. For example, when we do well on an exam, we tend to attribute the cause to our intelligence and study habits. On the other hand, when we do poorly, we tend to attribute the cause to a poorly designed, unfair, or "tricky" exam.

Haney believes that personality or internal states account very little for how we act. He contends that the important determining influence is the situation in which we find ourselves. In essence, Haney is arguing that, given the appropriate circumstances, anyone might engage in culpable criminal behavior—that we all have our price.

Situations are rarely static. Our behavior influences them to some extent, and they in turn influence our behavior. This reciprocal interaction between person and environment is one reason students of crime are beginning to pay more attention to victimology—victims often influence the course of criminal actions, particularly violent ones. **Victimology** is the scientific study of the causes, circumstances, individual characteristics, and social context of becoming a victim of a crime. Although victimologists are very careful not to blame victims for the crimes perpetrated against them, they do note that certain actions can facilitate, precipitate, and sometimes even provoke others to commit crime (Karmen, 2009). We will address this again later in the book, particularly in Chapter 9. At this point we will turn our attention to two situational factors that seem to play a particularly important role in antisocial behavior: obedience to authority and deindividuation.

Authority as an Instigator of Criminal Behavior

Sometimes, people behave a certain way because someone with power told them they must, even though the actions do not "set right" with their own principles. Kelman and Hamilton (1989) refer to this phenomenon as **crimes of obedience**. "A crime of obedience is an act performed in response to orders from authority that is considered illegal or immoral by the larger community" (Kelman & Hamilton, 1989, p. 46). Crimes of obedience have occurred throughout human history. Nazi concentration camps and orders to kill innocent civilians in wartime are two horrifying examples, but destructive crimes of obedience also occur in corporate business practices, such as were illustrated in the criminal cases of Enron, WorldCom, and Arthur Anderson (Carsten & Uhl-Bien, 2013). The classic example of the influence of authority is the military order to kill indiscriminately or to commit some other atrocity, such as then-Lieutenant William Calley's carrying out the massacre of villagers at My Lai in the Vietnam War. An example of crimes of obedience in a political/bureaucratic context is the Watergate scandal, when, on June 17, 1972, a group of men under the auspices of the Nixon administration burglarized the Democratic National Headquarters in the Watergate apartment complex. The concept also came to mind in the midst of scrutinizing the national security interrogations and the treatment of detainees in the wake of September 11.

In an attempt to delineate some of the variables involved in obedience to authority, Stanley Milgram (1977) designed a series of experiments. Participants were persons who volunteered (for money) in response to a newspaper ad. The experiments, which eventually received intensive public scrutiny and are now cited in nearly every introductory psychology textbook, studied the amount of electrical shock people were willing to administer to others when ordered to do so by an apparent authority figure.

Participants were adult males, ages 20 to 50, who represented a cross section of the socioeconomic classes. They were told that the researchers were studying the effects of punishment on memory. The experiment required a "teacher" and a "victim." Unknown to the volunteers, the victim was part of the experiment, a confederate who had been trained to act in a certain manner as part of the experimental design. In a rigged coin toss, the naive participant (the volunteer) always became the teacher and the confederate the victim. The victim-learner was taken to an adjacent room and strapped into an "electric chair" in the presence of the "naive" teacher.

Next, the teacher was led back to a room where he saw a simulated shock generator—a frightening apparatus with 30 toggle switches presumably capable of delivering 30 levels of electric shock to the learner in the adjacent room. Each level was marked in volts ranging from 15 to 450 and accompanied by a switch. In addition, labels indicated "slight shock," "danger: severe shock," and beyond, to an "XXX" level. Each time the learner gave an incorrect answer to a learning task, the teacher was instructed to administer a stronger level of shock. The victim, who did not of course receive any shock at all, purposefully gave incorrect answers; he had also been trained to scream in agony, plead with the subject to stop, and pound on the wall when the higher levels of shock were administered.

Milgram wanted to discover how far people would go under the orders of an apparent authority figure (the experimenter). He may have found more than he bargained for. Almost two-thirds of the subjects obeyed the experimenter and administered the maximum shock levels. When the participant resisted giving the shock, the experimenter was instructed to pressure them with a graded series of prods. For example, if a participant hesitated, the experimenter would say "please continue." A second hesitation would prompt the experimenter to admonish "The experiment requires that you continue," and so on. The strongest and final prod demanded "You have no other choice; you must go on." For many of the participants who refused to continue, the last prompt generated even more resistance from them and they immediately stopped.

In subsequent experiments, using similar experimental conditions but different participants (including both males and females), Milgram continued to find similar results. (See Blass (2009) for a detailed review of the Milgram experiments.) Interestingly, when Milgram originally asked mental health experts to predict the outcome of this experiment, the majority of them thought that only a pathological few would obey the experimenter's commands to incrementally increase the shock to dangerous levels (Tsang, 2002). The experts apparently discounted the enormous pressures that the experiment placed on participants and committed the fundamental attribution error, assuming that "the obedient person who obeys evil commands is sadistic and ill" (Tsang, 2002, p. 27).

Many of Milgram's participants, while obeying the experimenter's instructions, demonstrated considerable tension and discomfort. Some stuttered, bit their lips, twisted their hands, laughed nervously, sweated profusely, or dug their fingernails into their flesh, especially after the victim began pounding the wall in protest (Milgram, 1963). As noted by Reicher and his colleagues (2012), "Listening to any of the sessions, one is struck by the ways in which participants struggle to reconcile the unreconcilable, the ways in which they shift from one position to another, and their deep ambivalence about what to do" (p. 319). After the experiment, some reported that they wanted to stop punishing the victim but continued to do so because the experimenter would not let them stop. Milgram (1977, p. 118) concluded, "The individual, upon entering the laboratory, becomes integrated into a situation that carries its own momentum."

As noted above, Milgram conducted more research, which modified his original study. In approximately 30 additional studies (Reicher, Haslam, & Smith, 2012), he not only included women but also tried to determine more precisely what conditions inhibited or promoted this extreme obedience. For example, he varied the psychological and physical distance between the participant and the victim. To increase the psychological distance between the two, Milgram eliminated the cries of the victim that had been programmed into the original experiment. In another experiment, to minimize the physical and psychological distance between them, the participant sat next to the victim.

In general, Milgram found that the participants obeyed the experimenter less as physical, visual, and auditory contact with the victim increased. However, the nearer the *experimenter* got to the "teacher," the more likely the teacher was to obey. Milgram found no evidence of significant personality or gender differences in the studies as far as shocking behavior was concerned, but he did find that female teachers were more distressed about their task than their male counterparts.

The psychological and physical distance variable suggests some interesting implications. If we were to analogize between Milgram's studies and violent actions, we would expect that the more impersonal the weapon or situation (psychological and physical distance), the greater the likelihood for destruction and serious violence. Certainly, killing someone with a firearm at a distance versus killing someone point-blank are two different tasks, although more sophisticated weaponry allows a distant sniper, for example, to have extremely close access to a victim. And both methods differ from choking someone to death with one's bare hands. It would appear that the firearm offers a more impersonal and possibly easier way to eliminate someone, and thus is more likely to lead to violent behavior. Admittedly, this suggestion makes some quantum jumps from a psychological experiment in an artificial setting, but it is a point worth considering when we discuss the relationship between weapons and violence later in the book.

In assessing the profound influence of commands from an authority figure, we should also pay close attention to the reactions of the participants in Milgram's study. As noted above, individual differences were detected in the way they reacted to the situation, but not in their actual willingness to shock. Although some refused to continue with the experiment when they believed that they were hurting the victim, most (about 65%) administered the full range of shock levels. Most also displayed anxiety and conflict.

Milgram noted a curious dissociation between word and action. Many participants said they could not go on, but nevertheless they did. Some justified their action by concluding that the experimenter would not permit any harm to come to the victim. "He must know what he is doing." Others expressed different interpretations and expectancies, such as the belief that the scientific knowledge gained in the experiment justified the method. It is interesting to note that people who have not undergone the ordeal are quite convinced that they would be members of the defiant group who refused to deliver the extreme levels of shock. Later studies conducted both in the United States and abroad confirmed Milgram's findings, however (Burger, 2009; Penrod, 1983).

Milgram hypothesized that the obedient behavior could be explained by a shift in the perceived role played by the participant. He referred to this shift in role as an "agentic state," where "a person sees himself as an agent for carrying out another's wishes" (Milgram, 1974, p. 133). In other words, the person believes he is no longer acting on his own accord but for another authorized agent. Tsang (2002, p. 28) notes that Bandura (1999) also theorizes "that many individuals in an obedient situation have a shift in attention from their responsibility as *moral agents* to their duty as obedient subordinates" [italics added]. Similar points of view have been expressed by Kelman and Hamilton (1989) and Blumenthal (1999). Milgram suggested that our culture may not provide adequate models for disobedience to authority. Likewise, Kelman and Hamilton (1989) argued that it was important for schools to provide all children with opportunities to develop leadership skills and encourage them to be critical thinkers and to question authority in an effective manner. This is similar to the concept of moral agency discussed by Bandura (1999). Milgram admonished (1977, p. 120) that his studies raise the possibility that human nature or, more specifically, the kind of character produced in American democratic society, cannot be counted on to insulate its citizens from brutality and inhumane treatment at the direction of malevolent authority. A substantial proportion of people do what they are told to do, irrespective of the context of the act and without limitations of conscience, so long as they perceive that the command comes from a legitimate authority.

Some years after Milgram's experiments, Burger (2009) replicated the original work in an effort to discover if people today would still obey commands from authority figures if they were uncomfortable about doing what was asked. He discovered that obedience rates were only slightly lower than those Milgram had found 45 years earlier. In addition, contrary to expectations, participants who witnessed another person refusing to obey the experimenter's instructions obeyed just as often as those who did not witness another person refusing to obey. Moreover, men and women did not differ in their rates of obedience. The findings suggest that the same situational factors appear to be operating today. Burger also found that individuals who were high in empathy expressed a reluctance to continue to obey earlier than those who were low in empathy. However, even though they expressed reluctance, these participants continued to follow procedure.

Milgram's original experiment was controversial for a number of reasons, but most particularly for deceiving its participants and not adequately deprogramming them after the experiment had ended. There are a number of other ethical concerns expressed by scholars in recent years (see Nicholson (2011) for comprehensive review of these concerns). Over the years, some participants have stated that they suffered emotionally as a result of their willingness to harm others, even though they were told the shocking had been a ruse. In his replication, Burger (2009) took a few additional precautions. He excluded people with a history of psychological or emotional problems from the study. He also stopped the experiment at 150 volts for all participants. In addition, participants who had at least three college-level psychology classes were excluded because there was high probability they would know the results of the original experiment.

Milgram's theory—supported by Burger's research—may account to some extent for immoral or despicable acts committed under the influence of authority. At the beginning of his presidency, President Barack Obama announced his intention to close the military detention center at Guantanamo Bay in Cuba. Due to political opposition this has yet to occur, although the population of the center has been reduced. The announcement was made after extensive publicity about interrogation tactics and humiliating treatment used at Guantanamo, Abu Ghraib prison in Iraq, and other detention centers, and it accompanied the President's condemnation of torture. Some of the soldiers and nonmilitary personnel who were guards came forward to reveal actions they took under orders from supervisors. (See **Box 4-1** for a discussion on psychology's role in coercive interrogation techniques.)

CONTEMPORARY ISSUES

BOX 4-1   National Security Interrogations—Psychology's Role

The interrogation tactics used in military detention centers across the world have come under intense scrutiny in recent years. Declassified government reports, media accounts, and independent investigations all have revealed that many different techniques—some questionable, some illegal—were used in an attempt to extract information from individuals suspected of direct involvement in terrorist activities, or with knowledge of such activities. Among the most controversial techniques have been waterboarding; sleep deprivation; confinement in small, cage-like structures; desecration of religious symbols; loud, piped-in aversive music; forced feeding of detainees who refused to eat; sexual shaming and degradation; and threats of harm to loved ones. The widely circulated photos of hooded detainees at Abu Ghraib standing on boxes with nooses around their necks, or detainees on the floor while guards urinated on them were a shock to many consciences.

Until very recently—as will be noted shortly—psychologists have worked in these settings, both as military psychologists and consultants. Typically they have not been directly involved in interrogation. Nevertheless, some psychologists have given advice on how to break down the spirit of detainees. For example, in a declassified Senate report on the CIA interrogation program, made public in the fall of 2014, two psychologists were said to devise a list of brutal interrogation methods. They were paid millions of dollars to run interrogation programs for the U.S. government in secret prisons in countries like Poland, Lithuania, and Romania. Although

pseudonyms were used in the report (Grayson Swigert and Hammond Dunbar), the real names (James Mitchell and Bruce Jessen) have been widely publicized since.

Prior to the Senate report, and realizing that some psychologists were complicit with or did not speak out against practices that many defined as physical or psychological torture, the Board of Directors of the American Psychological Association (APA) issued a policy statement condemning the participation of psychologists in questionable interrogation tactics (APA, 2009). However, the organization did not issue a complete ban at that time, and many questions were left unanswered. Shortly thereafter, following a series of news stories and a damaging book by investigative reporter James Risen (Risen, 2014), the APA commissioned former federal prosecutor David Hoffman to conduct an independent investigation. Risen had suggested that the APA had been complicit with the Bush administration in facilitating abusive interrogation techniques, including torture, and that high officials in the organization had protected psychologists who had contributed to the interrogation process. The Hoffman report, which was delivered to the APA Board of Directors in late June of 2015, confirmed much, but not all, of the damning material reported by Risen.

As a result of the Hoffman report, as well as the strong and fervent activism of members of the APA, that group's Council of Representatives issued a total ban on psychologists' participation in national security interrogations—including noncoercive interrogations—conducted by military or intelligence entities, including private contractors working on their behalf. This new policy was approved by the general membership at their annual convention in August 2015. The policy allows psychologists to be present in detention settings that have been deemed to be in violation of international law only if they are working directly for detainees or for an independent third party working to protect human rights. They also may be in these settings for purposes of providing treatment to military personnel.

Review Questions

1. Obtain more information about the Hoffman report and the APA's subsequent response. (The full report is available at www.nationalpsychologist.com.) Do you believe the ban on psychologists' participation in national security interrogations is an appropriate action? Why or why not? To whom does the ban apply?
2. It appears that psychologists named in the many documents thus far released did not directly interrogate detainees. If they devised interrogation tactics and suggested how far the interrogators could go, does that make them more or less blameworthy?
3. Shifting from the role of psychologists to the actions of the interrogators themselves, which psychological concepts covered in this chapter are relevant to the behavior of these individuals?

Generalizations from the psychological laboratory to the real-world scenarios of destructive or violent obedience must remain tentative for the time being, but the relevance of the Milgram-type studies to actual situations cannot be overlooked. Milgram appeared convinced that situational factors normally override individual factors, and he would probably find personality or the morality of the individual fundamentally irrelevant in the explanation of the behavior. Other theorists, however, argue that it is precisely personality or moral development that account for resistance to authority. Kelman and Hamilton (1989) suggested that one's behavior in high authority situations most likely is a result of an interaction between one's personality characteristics and the roles played. Philip Zimbardo (1970, 1973; Haney & Zimbardo, 1998), on the other hand, is more closely aligned with Milgram, believing that the situation—including the overwhelming power of roles—is the most likely determinant of the behavior. Zimbardo demonstrated this in the famous Stanford Prison Experiment, and more broadly through the concept of deindividuation, which we discuss next. In addition, in recent years, Zimbardo, along with other researchers, has focused on moral disengagement, which we also discuss shortly.

Deindividuation

Deindividuation theory is based on the classic crowd theory of Gustave Le Bon. The theory, formulated in Le Bon's book *The Crowd: A Study of the Popular Mind* (1885/1995) was introduced into mainstream social psychology by Festinger, Pepitone, and Newcomb in 1952 (Postmes & Spears, 1998) using the concept of deindividuation. According to Festinger et al. (1952), many people lose their sense of individuality when in a crowd or group, remove self-imposed controls, and neutralize their internalized moral restraints. Thus, "deindividuation was closely associated with the feeling of not being scrutinized or accountable when submerged in the group" (Postmes & Spears, 1998, p. 240). Philip Zimbardo (1970) extended and further developed deindividuation theory in a number of well-known research projects. For Zimbardo, deindividuation involved feelings of reduced self-observation, and he sought to identify the things that could induce that state (Postmes & Spears, 1998).

Deindividuation, Zimbardo hypothesized, usually follows a complex chain of events. First, the presence of many other persons encourages feelings of anonymity. Then the individual feels he or she loses identity and becomes part of the group. Under these conditions, he or she can no longer be singled out and held responsible for his or her behavior. Apparently, this feeling then generates a "loss of self-awareness, reduced concern over evaluations from others, and a narrowed focus of attention" (Baron & Byrne, 1977, pp. 581–582). When combined, these processes lower restraints against antisocial or criminal behavior and appear to be basic ingredients in mass violence. However, they also may be at work in nonviolent offenses, such as looting.

In one early experiment, Zimbardo (1970) purchased two used cars, left one abandoned on a street in Manhattan, New York, and the other on a street in Palo Alto, California (about 55,000 population in the late 1960s). Zimbardo's deindividuation hypothesis predicted that, due to the large population of New York, people would more likely lose their identity and feel less responsible for their actions. Consequently, New Yorkers would be more likely to loot the abandoned vehicle. This is exactly what happened. Within 26 hours, the New York car was stripped of battery, radiator, air cleaner, radio antenna, windshield wipers, side chrome, all four hubcaps, a set of jumper cables, a can of car wax, a gas can, and the only tire worth taking. On the other hand, the car in Palo Alto was untouched during the seven days it was left abandoned. At one point during a rainstorm, a passerby actually lowered the hood to prevent the motor from getting wet. Why such a dramatic difference?

Zimbardo suggests that the anonymity of the New York residents worked in combination with situational cues, implying that they could get by without repercussions. Zimbardo's hypothesis contends that in high population areas, who cares what you are doing as long as you are not bothering others or damaging a concerned party's property? Passersby in New York even stopped and chatted with the looters, some of whom were even families. In Palo Alto, people could be more easily identified. Moreover, a person engaging in this kind of behavior would expect to be the target of social disapproval or gossip.

Deindividuation is a commonly used concept to explain various expressions of collective behavior such as violent crowds, mindless hooligans, and lynch mobs, as well as widespread social atrocities such as genocide (Postmes & Spears, 1998). As we saw from the car experiment, deindividuation is not necessarily associated with crowds. Nor is a massive population required. The effect may be achieved by a disguise, a mask, or a uniform also worn by others, or it may be achieved by darkness (Zimbardo, 1970). Research data suggest that people may be more abusive, aggressive, and violent when their identity is hidden. This phenomenon might explain why, throughout history, war paints, masks, and costumes have been donned by warriors preparing for battle (Watson, 1973). Even contemporary soldiers, guerrillas, and military advisors are deindividuated by their uniforms. Deindividuation also helps explain the apparent ease with which members of groups such as the Ku Klux Klan regressed from being apparently respectable citizens by day to violent, hooded terrorizers by night. Again, however, it is too simplistic to assume that no dispositional or other factors are at work.

In another widely cited experiment, Zimbardo manipulated two variables: feelings of anonymity and features about the victim. He randomly assigned female college students to deindividuation and "identifiable" groups. Those in the deindividuation group wore shapeless white lab coats and hoods over their heads and worked in dimly lit conditions. The experimenters avoided using their names. By contrast, participants in the identifiable groups felt anything but anonymous. They wore large name tags, were greeted by name, worked under fully illuminated conditions, and wore their own clothes with no added lab coats or hoods.

The participants were told the project was set up to study empathy. The real purpose, of course, was to study the relationship between deindividuation and aggression. Each one listened to a five-minute recorded interview between her future "victim" and the experimenter. Some victims were portrayed as warm, sincere, honest persons, while others were obnoxious, self-centered, conceited, and critical. After each interview, the participants were allowed to administer shock to the interviewees they had heard on tape. They were allowed to observe the reactions of their victims by way of a one-way mirror. Aggressive behavior was measured by the length of time a painful electrical shock was administered. "Victims"—who actually received no shock—were trained to writhe, twist, and grimace.

Recall now that Zimbardo was manipulating two variables: anonymity (loss of personal identity) and features of the victim (environmental stimuli). Thus, some participants were hooded, others were well identified. Some victims were pleasant and likable, others were obnoxious. Zimbardo reasoned that members of the deindividuation group would administer shocks of longer duration because of the diffusion of responsibility and loss of personal identity. He also hypothesized that victim features would be irrelevant, because the heightened arousal experienced under deindividuation would interfere with the ability to discriminate between the victims. Put another way, the excitement and resulting arousal engendered by shocking someone without the threat of any repercussions would prevent discernment of the target (the person receiving the shock).

One additional hypothesis was tested. Zimbardo predicted that participants in the deindividuation group would administer longer shocks as the experiment progressed. He believed the act of administering shock without responsibility would be exciting and reinforcing for its own sake (what he called "affective proprioceptive feedback"). Zimbardo predicted that members of the deindividuation group would increase the duration of shock administered to the victim as the experiment progressed. In brief, the person finds that doing the antisocial behavior feels "so good" each time the person does it that the behavior builds on itself in intensity (vigor) and frequency.

Results of the experiment supported all three hypotheses. The deindividuation group shocked victims twice as long as the identifiable group. The deindividuation group also administered the same levels of shock, regardless of the victim's personality features. And, finally, this group shocked for longer periods as the experiment progressed. Essentially, Zimbardo argued that deindividuated aggression is not controlled by the social environment; it is unresponsive to both the situation and the state or characteristics of the victim.

Zimbardo's research design, like that of Milgram, has been criticized extensively for its questionable use of deception and shock (albeit simulated) and its focus on the negative aspects of human behavior. In a sense, these types of experiments constitute a form of psychological entrapment. Would people really act this way if not prompted by an experimenter? In the wake of such experiments, the National Institute of Mental Health, the American Psychological Association, and other organizations have adopted ethical guidelines that are applied to the funding and approval of research. Experiments like Zimbardo's, therefore, are unlikely to be replicated, although we learned above that Milgram's experiment was replicated with modifications that rendered it more ethically acceptable. Moreover, the possible implications of the results of these research studies cannot be ignored.

The Stanford Prison Experiment

The disguise aspect of deindividuation was vividly illustrated in still another sobering Zimbardo experiment (1973) known as the **Stanford Prison Experiment**. Some scholars posit that the experiment is arguably the most famous experiment in the history of psychology (Griggs, 2014; Griggs & Whitehead, 2014). It has even been made into an independent documentary, which debuted at Sundance Film Festival in January 2015, winning several awards. It began to appear in theaters, usually for limited engagements, later that year.

Zimbardo and his colleagues simulated a prison environment in the basement of the psychology building at Stanford University, with physical and psychological trappings supposedly representative of an actual prison: bars, prison uniforms, identification numbers, uniformed guards, and other features that encouraged identity slippage. The facility actually represented a jail more than a prison. Furthermore, as critics of the experiment have noted, the simulation lacked authenticity in a number of ways, including the sack-like uniforms and stocking caps worn by the "prisoners" and the mirrored sunglasses worn by "guards" (Johnson, 1996). Corrections officers in real prisons and jails also undergo training and are not given the unlimited power that Zimbardo placed in the hands of his experimental subjects, although they certainly wield power.

Student volunteers were screened through clinical interviews and psychological tests to ensure that they were emotionally stable and mature. According to Zimbardo, the participants finally selected were "normal," intelligent college students from middle-class homes throughout the United States and Canada. They were paid $15 a day for participating.

The experiment required two roles, guard and prisoner, which were assigned by random coin toss. The randomization assured that there were no significant differences between the two groups. The "prisoners" were unexpectedly "arrested" and brought to the simulated prison in a police car. There they were handcuffed, searched, fingerprinted, booked, stripped, showered, given a number, and issued a prison uniform. Each prisoner was then placed in a six-by-nine-foot cell with two other inmates.

The guards wore standard uniforms and mirrored sunglasses to encourage deindividuation, but as noted, they were not representative of the attire worn by real corrections officers. In addition, they carried symbols of power: a night stick (which real officers do not always carry), keys to the cells, whistles, and handcuffs. Before the prisoners could do even routine things (e.g., write a letter, smoke a cigarette), they had to obtain permission. Guards drew up their own formal rules for maintaining law and order in the prison (16 rules in all) and were free to improvise new ones.

Within six days, both guards and prisoners had completely absorbed their roles:

Three prisoners had to be released during the first four days because of hysterical crying, confusion in thinking, and severe depression. Many others begged to be paroled, willing to forfeit the money they had earned for participating in the experiment.

About a third of the guards abused their power and were brutal and demeaning. Other subjects did their jobs as tough but fair correctional guards, but none of these supported the prisoners by urging the brutal guards to ease off. The realism of the prison was apparently striking. "The consultant for our prison…an ex-convict with sixteen years of imprisonment in California's jails, would get so depressed and furious each time he visited our prison, because of its psychological similarity to his experiences, that he would have to leave." (Zimbardo, 1973, p. 164)

The situation became such that Zimbardo decided to terminate the experiment during the sixth day, instead of proceeding through the planned two weeks. Zimbardo believed that due to the power of demands of the situation, the participating college students had actually assumed the role of guards and prisoners, largely independent of personality or individual differences among the participants. Essentially, the situation forcibly overrode individual differences. Interestingly, in recent years (Zimbardo, 2007) he has commented that the brutality reported in the Stanford study explains the treatment of detainees by U.S. military, intelligence representatives, and government contractors at detention centers worldwide (see **Box 4-1**). Zimbardo argues that the situation into which they were thrown forced them to do brutal, unthinkable things to other human beings.

Zimbardo's Stanford study prompted him to conclude, "Many people, perhaps the majority, can be made to do almost anything when put into psychologically compelling situations— regardless of their morals, ethics, values, attitudes, beliefs, or personal convictions" (1973, p. 164). Much the same conclusion had been reached by Milgram with respect to the influence of authority figures. Although the Stanford Prison Experiment underscores the crucial importance of situational variables in determining behavior, there were still significant individual differences in the way the participants responded to the conditions. For example, only one-third of the guards became brutally enthralled with their power. Rather than making far-reaching conclusions on the basis of how a total of 21 participants (both guards and prisoners) responded, it would be much more fruitful to give some attention to individual variables. For example, it would have been helpful to examine the values, expectancies, competencies, and moral development of the participants, in combination with the situational factors. What developmental factors most likely predisposed people to act the way they did, and exactly how did they perceive the situation? What did they expect to gain by their behavior?

The BBC Prison Study

The Stanford Prison Study is cited in virtually every introductory psychology textbook and social psychology textbook, and is often mentioned in criminal justice literature as well. A more recent study is also instructive and relevant to deindividuation. In December 2001, Alexander Haslam and Stephen Reicher (2012), in conjunction with the documentaries unit of the British Broadcasting Corporation, conducted the BBC Prison Study. Although some of the procedures were similar, the BBC project was not intended to replicate the Stanford study. Rather, it was designed to revisit some of the questions raised by the Stanford study. The researchers were particularly interested in testing Zimbardo's conclusion that the demands of the situation strongly dictate what a person will do, to the exclusion of individual differences, personality, or character.

Fifteen participants were selected from a pool of 322 obtained in response to a newspaper advertisement. The 15 were selected after the entire sample went through three stages of careful screening. Members of the selected group were then randomly assigned to play the role as either a "guard" or a "prisoner."

As one departure from the methodology of the Stanford study, the BBC experimenters were careful not to take a leadership role and tell the guards how they should behave. They also did not allow the guards to set their own rules. Furthermore, the BBC experimenters were interested in "investigating the conditions under which prisoners would either adapt to or challenge the inequalities of the prison system" (Haslam & Reicher, 2012, p. 158).

The findings of the BBC Prison Study differed markedly from those of the Stanford experiment. For one thing, there was no evidence that the guards assumed their roles naturally or uncritically. Many were reluctant to exercise their authority and disagreed among each other on how their roles should be interpreted. In essence, major individual differences emerged, and the "guard" group lost cohesion and became increasingly incapable of maintaining order over the prisoners. In addition, compared to the Stanford study, the BBC prisoner behavior was substantially different. For instance, Zimbardo (2007) asserted that the Stanford prisoners became "zombie-like in yielding to the whims of the ever-escalating guard-power" (p. 196). In the BBC study, "Rather than the scenes of guard brutality witnessed in Stanford, the prisoners began to mock, challenge, and undermine the guards" (Haslam & Reicher, 2012, p. 159). In summary, neither the guards nor the prisoners conformed blindly or mindlessly to their assigned roles as some participants did in the Stanford study.

Even though the BBC project found major differences in the behavior of the participants, these findings by no means should undermine the importance of the Zimbardo study. The Stanford experiment clearly underscores the dangers that can be created when conditions controlled by a powerful, respected authority (Professor Zimbardo) at a prestigious university (Stanford University) are established for trustful, unsuspecting students who volunteered for an experiment. The Stanford experiment, however, does not confirm that *all* powerful situations override the personalities and individual differences of all those persons in the situation. Some do, and some do not.

Deindividuation and Crowd Violence

The powerful effects of crowds on individual behavior has interested social scientists since the early 1900s. Crowd influence is usually studied under the rubric of negative *collective behavior*, which includes riots, gang rapes, panics, lynchings, and violent demonstrations and revolutions. Collective behavior also can have a positive connotation, however, as is the case with peaceful protests, demonstrations, marches, sit-ins, tent-ins, and their variants. For our purposes, we are concerned with collective behavior as it affects the instigation and maintenance of violence or illegal activities, such as looting. Recall that earlier in the chapter we discussed the role of frustration as a possible instigator of riots or other antisocial behavior displayed in group situations. Here, we focus on a different component, the likelihood that, in a crowd, individuals may lose their individual identity and adopt the behavior of those around them.

Most of us have seen dramatizations of a "berserk" mob clamoring for the destruction of some political, social, or physical institution or for swift "justice" for an individual or group. Descriptions of mob actions often liken them to brush fires that grow in intensity and are quickly out of control. There are numerous anecdotal accounts of vandalism and assaults that occur in some communities, often alcohol related and associated with parties, festivals, or celebrations. On one college campus, students raided "free book" bins placed outside the library and had a middle-of-the night book-burning. Ten to twenty percent of the students were allegedly part of the unruly crowd. In other cases, fans have displayed antisocial behavior after sports events (both when their teams won and when their teams lost). In recent years, controversial judicial decisions (a not-guilty verdict or a failure to indict) were followed by both peaceful and violent protests. As we noted earlier in the chapter, although observers had feared and predicted days of violence in these cases, the crowds did not turn into violent "mobs," however.

True "mob" actions—those that include extensive violence—are a rare occurrence. In the many police shootings of black men that were publicized in 2014 and 2015 and discussed above, for example, respected public figures as well as average citizens encouraged peaceful protesting and pleaded for calm. Nevertheless, disturbing and disruptive crowd behavior remains a reality in some circumstances, such as the lootings and arsons mentioned above. They cannot be explained only by the presence of alcohol, which is often the explanation given for disruptive group activities on college campuses, festivals, or other celebrations.

However, since true mob actions are naturally occurring and spontaneous events, it is difficult to place them under the scrutiny of scientific, systematic investigation. The processes involved in mob action are still not well understood. Some social psychologists (e.g., Diener, 1980; Zimbardo, 1970) attempted laboratory studies of mob or group violence, generally by approximating conditions that might bring out aggression and positing that, if allowed to continue, the aggression would likely result in violence. Obviously, they must stop far short of actual violence, so whether it would have occurred remains speculative. The procedure of trying to mimic an event under laboratory conditions is called a **simulation**.

Zimbardo (1970) believed that deindividuation accounts for much of the tendency of otherwise "tame" individuals to engage in antisocial, violent behavior. Recall that deindividuation includes a reduction in personal distinctiveness, identifiability, and personal responsibility. You don't stand out, you cannot be identified, and you bear no personal responsibility. Furthermore, in a crowd, the threshold of normally restrained behavior is lowered. In other words, because people feel anonymous and less responsible for their behavior, they are less inhibited. According to Zimbardo, these conditions encourage the antisocial behavior associated with selfishness, greed, hostility, lust, cruelty, and destruction.

Diener's (1980) perspective is a bit different. According to Diener, because deindividuated individuals do not pay attention to their internal processes, including their self-regulatory capabilities, they depend more on environmental cues for behavioral direction. Thus, when aggressive and violent cues are present, they are far more likely than usual to engage in violence. It is Diener's contention that if the victim of a mob action could, in some way, be "humanized," the crowd might stop its brutality. In other words, the perpetrators' attention should be directed toward the suffering or fear expressed by the victim rather than the violence being displayed by other actors. Diener also believes that participants in a mob action can be made to pay closer attention to their own internal regulation norms. His hypothesis deserves to be tested by further research. Of course, whether the cries and pleas of the victim during an attack actually could alter the crowd behavior is a question unlikely to be answered by laboratory research. Furthermore, because the theories of Zimbardo and Diener are based on laboratory studies, we cannot conclude that they generalize to actual situations. They do, however, suggest possible explanations for violent mob behavior.

The Bystander Effect

The process of deindividuation and diffusion of responsibility may also play significant roles in emergencies, such as decisions as to whether to help a victim of a violent crime. The classic example is the case of Catherine (Kitty) Genovese, which has been recounted in both the media and social psychology textbooks since the incident occurred in 1964. However, as we note below, the actual case was quite different from what has been presented for over half a century. (See also **Box 4-2.**)

During the early morning hours of March 13, 1964, 28-year-old Genovese was walking home from work to her apartment in Queens, New York. Realizing she was being followed by a strange man, she began running but was unable to get away. He caught her, slammed her to the ground, and stabbed her twice in the back. She screamed for help, but although lights went on in adjacent apartments, no one came to her aid. The assailant retreated for a short time, but when he realized no one was coming to help her, he returned and stabbed her to death. The incident took approximately 45 minutes, and, according to newspaper reports, none of 38 witnesses helped her during the entire time. The media publicized the case extensively, and people were shocked and disappointed at the apparent insensitivity and lack of courage shown by the witnesses. Kitty Genovese's attacker (Winston Moseley) was eventually found, arrested, tried, and convicted by a jury. At age 79, Moseley was reported as being the longest-serving inmate in the New York prison system (Lemann, 2014).

The Genovese incident prompted social psychologists John Darley and Bibb Latané (1968) to conduct an extensive series of experiments designed to determine why there appeared to be so much apathy and callousness displayed by the witnesses. The research, known as the **bystander effect** project, discovered that there are a complicated set of factors that determine who will assist in life-threatening or dangerous situations. For example, a person intervening when another is being stabbed by a third party risks harm and injury. Even to call the police is "getting involved" and risking threats. In addition, seeing an actual violent or criminal event is so unusual that a majority of people are not prepared for appropriate action and have considerable difficulty in deciding on the best course of action. Perhaps the most important finding of the bystander effect studies is that the presence of other persons tends to inhibit one from taking responsibility for doing something for the victim. The basic conclusion of the Darley and Latané research: "The story of the 38 witnesses in psychology tells of the malign influence of others to overwhelm the will of the individual" (Manning, Levine, & Collins, 2007, p. 535). What's more, they found that the more bystanders there are in dangerous situation, the less likely someone will volunteer to help. The research at that time continually indicated that crowds remove personal responsibility and individual differences and character. "In this tradition, crowds are a dangerous threat to social stability; crowds and people in crowds lack rationality; the irrationality of crowds reveals a primitive nature stripped of constraints usually provided by other psychological qualities; people in crowds lose their sense of individuality and so on" (Manning et al., 2007, p. 560).

Bystander apathy, or nonintervention, is a reality, but unfortunately the 38 witnesses to the original crime against Kitty Genovese "got a bad rap," as documented in various recent accounts (Cook, 2014; Manning et al., 2007; Pelonero, 2014). The most significant inaccuracy was the conclusion that no one came to the aid of the victim or bothered to call the police. However, evidence gathered by the police, revealed in court documents, and entered at the trial of the assailant revealed that several witnesses did indeed call the police. At least one said that the police did not respond quickly, or did not respond at all because the call was inadvertently made to the wrong precinct. One neighbor yelled, "Leave that girl alone," causing the attacker to leave the scene temporarily, only to later return to complete the assault. Another neighbor courageously left her apartment to go to the crime scene and hold Genovese in her arms, even though she had no way of knowing that the attacker had fled (Lemann, 2014). These were certainly not examples of bystander apathy. Many of the witnesses said that though they heard screams, they could not see what was going on because their apartment location obstructed their view. The second attack occurred inside part of a building where very few witnesses could see the incident (Manning et al., 2007). There were, however, at least two men who actively refused to help, even though they saw the murder at close range, all of which highlights the spectrum of individual differences that often occur in emergencies.

Despite inaccuracies in reporting the original crime against Kitty Genovese, recent research demonstrates that the bystander effect does occur, but particularly in relatively nonlife threatening emergency situations. However, it is far more complicated and contingent on more factors than supposed in earlier social psychological studies (Fischer et al., 2011). There appears to be very little bystander apathy in dangerous emergencies (Fischer et al., 2006, 2011). People generally come to the aid of a victim in clearly violent events, such as a rape or assault. It is interesting to note that students who had learned about the bystander effect in class were more likely to intervene in an emergency at a later date than were students who were not informed (Beaman, Barnes, Klentz, & McQuirk, 1978; Fischer et al., 2011). Furthermore, some research has investigated other ways in

RESEARCH FOCUS

BOX 4-2 Do Security Cameras Affect Bystander Apathy?

Since the concept of bystander apathy was first introduced by Latané and Darley (1970), a large body of research has studied this interesting phenomenon (Fischer et al., 2011). In general, the presence of others is believed to diminish prosocial behavior. "Someone else will jump in or call police. Let them do it." Furthermore, bystander apathy (or nonintervention) seems to increase as the size of a crowd increases, presumably because responsibility is diffused over a greater number of people. However, bystander apathy is less likely to occur during an emergency or serious situation, even when the situation involves criminal activity. People are more likely to come to the aid of someone who is being stabbed than someone whose backpack is being snatched.

As noted in the text, earlier accounts of the Kitty Genovese killing in 1968 were incorrect. It was widely reported at the time—and repeated in both academic and popular literature over the years—that people in the vicinity did not respond to the victim's pleas for help. Over the years, the record has been corrected. Although two individuals walking by did not come to her assistance, many others did try to intervene in a number of ways, including calling police and shouting out to stop the assailant. One person ran out of her apartment and cradled the victim while she was dying. Many people who lived in the vicinity where the attack occurred did not have a direct view of the incident and could not have heard or seen what was happening.

Even though the Genovese incident itself was not what it first appeared to be, it did prompt a line of research on the conditions under which bystander nonintervention is most likely to occur. As a recent example, Marco van Bommel and his colleagues (van Bommel, van Prooijen, Elffers, & van Lange, 2014) posited that apathy might be influenced by still another factor—specifically, the desire to maintain a positive image. If we are being watched, are we more likely to help others, even if we are not obliged to, in the desire to achieve or maintain a good reputation?

The researchers set up an experimental situation in which participants observed someone try to steal money from the experimenter's desk during a brief period when the experimenter had left the room. In one condition, three participants were in the room waiting for the experimenter; in another condition, two participants were in the room. However, in both conditions, there was only one "true" participant, because others were confederates of the experimenter. One confederate played the role of "thief."

Then, there were two camera conditions—in one condition, no security camera was present. In another, a camera was very visibly displayed in the participant's line of sight.

Consistent with other research on bystander apathy, participants tended not to intervene when even one other participant was present. Although the group was a small one, the diffusion of responsibility still seemed to occur. Also consistent with other research, if no other bystander was present, the participant was more likely to intervene by saying something to the "thief" or reporting the incident to the experimenter. In the camera condition, though, the presence of the camera made it even less likely that bystander apathy would occur. As the researchers had hypothesized, when a camera was present, intervention was more likely whether or not another bystander was present. The researchers concluded that the cameras promoted prosocial behavior in the participants, encouraging them to intervene because there was an audience (behind the camera or eventually on video) to impress.

Questions for Discussion

1. Based on the above brief description, the study does not suggest that security cameras reduce crime, but rather that cameras discourage bystander apathy and encourage intervention. What one component is essential in order for this to happen?

2. Form a hypothesis and propose a study to further examine the effect of security cameras on bystander apathy.

3. Security cameras as well as private cameras are ubiquitous today. What are advantages and disadvantages of having cameras record criminal events? Does it matter whether the cameras are (a) stationary surveillance cameras; (b) cameras worn by police or mounted on patrol cars; or (c) hand-held cameras carried by private citizens?

which bystander intervention can be encouraged, such as—perhaps surprisingly—the installation of on-street cameras (see **Box 4-2**).

The Genovese incident also has had far-reaching consequences besides the research it engendered. It was instrumental in the push to establish 911 as an easy to remember emergency number nationwide (Lemann, 2014). It also helped in the adoption of good Samaritan laws across the country (Getlen, 2014) as well as similar laws. These laws either require certain individuals to come to the aid of a victim or protect people from civil penalties if they intervene in a crime or an accident and the intervention is ineffective or someone is hurt.

MORAL DISENGAGEMENT

The prominent social psychologist Albert Bandura (1990, 1991) theorized that through social learning people internalize moral principles, and that these promote self-worth when they are maintained and self-condemnation when they are violated. **Moral agency**—essentially behaving in a moral manner—requires that one distinguishes right from wrong and refrains from doing the wrong thing (Caprara et al., 2013). Bandura also proposed the concept of **moral disengagement** to explain why people do things that they know are not "right," both on their own and when ordered to do so by some higher authority or under high social pressure. At times the acts are not universally recognized as immoral, but are more in keeping with their occupational roles, such as part of the corporate culture or the culture of the military or law enforcement. In such situations, they "disengage" or detach themselves from what would be their usual moral principles, primarily to avoid self-condemnation. Thus, it is not the situation alone that determines the person's behavior; rather the personal attribute—the ability to detach oneself from moral principles—is critical. (In the prison experiments discussed above, we would say that some participants were more likely than others to employ moral disengagement.) Specifically, "effective moral disengagement…frees one from the restraints of self-censure experienced as anticipative guilt from detrimental conduct" (Bandura, Caprara, Barbaranelli, Pastorelli, & Regalia, 2001, p. 125).

Research on moral development and moral disengagement continued into the 1990s and beyond (Caprara et al., 2013). Disengagement can occur, for example, when people justify their actions or when they dehumanize their victims. They may tell themselves they are doing something they would otherwise consider immoral, but doing it for the greater good. Or they may dehumanize their victims, for example, by saying they deserved their fate. Bandura, Barbaranelli, Caprara, and Pastorelli (1996) found that delinquents who displayed aggressive behavior toward others often used these methods of moral disengagement. Dehumanization refers to the process of maintaining beliefs that strip people of human qualities or invests them with demonic or bestial qualities (Bandura et al., 2001). "The victims are then seen as subhuman, without the same feelings or hopes as the perpetrators, and thus one can rationalize that normal moral principles do not apply" (Tsang, 2002, p. 41). Dehumanization is covered in more detail in Chapter 11.

Bandura and his associates (Bandura et al., 2001) found some gender differences in the extent to which juveniles disengaged from their moral principles. Specifically, male adolescents were "more prone to disengage moral self-sanctions from detrimental conduct, were quicker to rouse themselves to anger through hostile rumination, and were less prosocially oriented" (p. 131). These results, the researchers conclude, lend support to the influence of social learning as a major determinant of the frequently reported gender differences in detrimental or immoral conduct. "Girls are substantially more consoling, sharing, helpful, and affectionately demonstrative" (Bandura et al., 2001, p. 131). Boys, on the other hand, tend to be far less likely to engage peers in discussions of their negative feelings and hostility toward others. These assertions may not be representative of contemporary society, when statements about sex differences must be tempered with the recognition that generalizations about boys and girls, women and men, males and females, are often unwarranted. Nevertheless, Bandura's studies underscore the importance of considering the situation *and* the personal attributes of the person in understanding why people do what they do.

Moral disengagement has remained a provocative topic for contemporary researchers interested in social-cognitive psychology, particularly as it relates to aggressive behavior. Many researchers focus on adolescents, as did Bandura (e.g., Gini, 2006; Paciello, Fida, Tramontano, Lupinetti, & Caprara, 2008; Shulman, Cauffman, Piquero, & Fagan, 2011). Others focus on young adults (e.g., Caprara et al., 2013). There are interesting exceptions. For example, Osofsky, Bandura, and Zimbardo (2005) studied moral disengagement among prison personnel in facilities where the death penalty was carried out. They included executioners, support teams for the condemned inmates and their families, and corrections officers who were not directly involved in the execution process. They found that the executioners displayed the highest levels of disengagement, as well as dehumanization of the condemned prisoners and justification for their work. Members of the support teams were the least likely to display moral disengagement.

Studies of moral disengagement among adolescents indicate that it often declines with age, and this finding is associated with an accompanying decline in antisocial behavior (Paciello et al., 2008). Thus, in their longitudinal study of 1,169 adolescent felony offenders, Shulman et al. found that as the youths grew older, their attitudes toward wrongdoing also changed in a positive direction—that is they were less likely to condone it—and their offending behavior desisted. The reasons for this, the authors note, remain to be explored, although some preliminary research is available. "Understanding what contributes to this change in delinquent youths' attitudes toward wrongdoing is a worthwhile aim for future studies" (Shulman et al., 2011, p. 1630).

Up to this point, though, social psychologists have focused almost exclusively on aggressive behavior among adolescents and young adults. Moral disengagement is a topic that should be relevant to white-collar offenses, including both political crimes and those in the corporate sphere. We return to this topic in Chapter 11.

SUMMARY AND CONCLUSIONS

This chapter has led us away from the biologically oriented approaches of Chapter 3 to the perspective that all behavior, including antisocial behavior, is learned as a result of interactions with the environment—after, not before birth. According to the theories discussed in this chapter, people are not born with a predisposition to violence or deficient conditionability; rather they become that way as a result of social experiences. Furthermore, criminal behavior, again like all behavior, is an individual's way of adapting to his or her environment.

We have reviewed Skinnerian behaviorism, a theory based on the psychology of J. B. Watson and Ivan Pavlov. Together, Skinnerian, Watsonian, and Pavlovian psychology provided the field with some of its most fundamental concepts, such as classical conditioning, operant conditioning, reinforcement, punishment, and extinction. Today, most behaviorists may applaud the basic premise that stimuli elicit responses (classical conditioning), and behavior produces consequences that influence subsequent responses (operant conditioning). However, they also believe other factors must be introduced to explain human behavior. Thus, social learning theorists have focused on cognitions, attitudes, beliefs, and other mental processes that must be taken into consideration.

We covered the expectancy theory of Rotter, the observational learning theory of Bandura, and the social learning theories of Sutherland and Akers to illustrate these mental processes. Sutherland, a sociologist with antipathy toward psychology, probably would not want to be included in this group, but his is still an important learning theory. Berkowitz's frustration theory, and Zimbardo's concept of deindividuation and accompanying research were also discussed. Each of these emphasizes to varying degrees the importance of learning in the development *and maintenance* of criminal behavior. Most of them also outline the external reinforcements involved in this maintenance, or alternately, its cessation. People who engage in persistent antisocial behavior get tangible rewards, as well as social and psychological ones. Collectively, external reinforcements that bring us material, social, or psychological gain are called positive reinforcements. Behaviors that enable us to avoid unpleasant circumstances are negatively reinforced.

Also included in the regulation of behavior is vicarious reinforcement, which consists of both observed reward and observed punishment. When we observe others (models) receiving rewards or punishments for certain behavior, we tend to alter our behavior correspondingly. Models are extremely important in the acquisition and regulation of criminal behavior. They are reference points for what we should and can do in a particular set of circumstances. Therefore, models may act as inhibitors or facilitators of behavior. People internalize the actions and philosophies of significant models, thereby making them part of their own behavioral repertoire and cognitive structure. Research in recent years has focused extensively on the models available in the media, violent video games, and Internet sites. There is growing evidence that *some* people who observe aggressive acts to a great degree themselves become more violent and aggressive.

In addition to models, situational factors can be important contributors to criminal behavior. To some theorists, frustration plays a significant role in violent criminality. When children are frustrated at not having their needs met by parents or caretakers, for example, this promotes distrust of other adults and prevents the forming of emotional attachments. Individuals who strike out at society have encountered severe frustration, according to this approach.

We also discussed the influence of authority figures and the environmental factors involved in the process of deindividuation. People sometimes engage in illegal or violent conduct because they are told or ordered to do so, as Milgram's classic shocking experiment demonstrated. It is interesting that Burger (2009) found results very similar to Milgram's. There are many anecdotal illustrations as well in the military, in law enforcement, and in places of business. Some psychologists have searched for individual differences that might predict the extent to which a person will or will not obey an order perceived to be immoral or illegal, such as differences in personality or moral development, a topic that will be covered in Chapter 11. In recent years, researchers have focused on moral disengagement, a process by which people are able to separate themselves from their normal codes of conduct in order to engage in illegal or morally ambivalent behavior. On the other hand, other researchers point to the powerful influence of roles, illustrated by Zimbardo's Stanford experiment. Interestingly, the less-well-known BBC Prison Study suggests that individual attributes can strongly challenge situational demands.

The phenomenon of bystander apathy—or bystander nonintervention—remains a fascinating topic of study for contemporary researchers. Over 30 years of research has documented that original assumptions of widespread nonintervention in crisis situations were unwarranted. People do come to the aid of others, but this is most likely to occur in serious situations. In addition, the size of a crowd of witnesses appears to decrease the likelihood that a given bystander will intervene. In recent years, some research has suggested that coming to the rescue may increase if it would improve or maintain one's standing in the community. Bystander response is a complex issue, however, and merits additional study.

Key Concepts

Behaviorism	Moral agency
Bystander effect	Moral disengagement
Classical or Pavlovian conditioning	Negative reinforcement
Cognitive processes	Observational learning (modeling)
Crimes of obedience	Positive reinforcement
Deindividuation	Punishment
Dependent variables	Reductionism
Differential Association-Reinforcement (DAR) Theory	Reinforcement
Discriminative stimuli	Response
Expectancy theory	Self-serving biases
Extinction	Simulation
Frustration	Situationism
Fundamental attribution error	Social learning
Imitational learning	Socialized offender
Independent variable	Stanford Prison Experiment
Individual offender	Stimulus
Instrumental learning/operant conditioning	Variable
Models	Victimology

Review Questions

1. Describe the process of operant conditioning and give an example of how criminal behavior is acquired.
2. Explain the difference between differential association theory and differential association-reinforcement theory.
3. Explain the concept of deindividuation and illustrate by describing any one experiment in social psychology.
4. What is "frustration-induced criminality"? Provide an illustration.
5. Compare and contrast the behaviorism promoted by B. F. Skinner with the modern behaviorism promoted by Bandura.
6. Describe and discuss the situational factors that can influence criminal behavior. In addition to those mentioned in this chapter, what others might be identified?
7. What is meant by crimes of obedience? Give examples.
8. What is meant by bystander apathy, and under what circumstances is it most likely to occur?
9. Explain the concept of moral disengagement and discuss its relevance to antisocial or morally ambivalent behavior.

5

Human Aggression and Violence

CHAPTER OBJECTIVES

- Explore the various ways of defining and identifying aggressive behavior.
- Review the major theories on the development of aggression and violence.
- Emphasize the importance of cognitive processes in aggressive behavior.
- Explore the interactions of biology and cognitive processes in aggressive behavior and violence.
- Outline important key concepts in understanding aggression and violence, such as weapons effect, modeling, and hostile attribution bias.
- Introduce the General Aggression Model and I^3 Theory.
- Review the effects of digital, electronic, and other media on aggression and violence.
- Examine the current research on copycat (contagion effect) crime.

There is ample evidence of the long history of human involvement in aggression and violence. Over 5,600 years of recorded human history, for example, include 14,600 wars, a rate of more than 2.6 per year (Baron, 1983; Montagu, 1976). Today, many people fear additional wars, terrorist attacks, or mass shootings. In reality, violence is more likely to occur in people's homes or in high-crime areas on the streets. Nevertheless, as we noted in Chapter 1, the violent crime rate in the United States has decreased steadily since the early 1990s (Federal Bureau of Investigation, 2014a).

Violence and aggression go hand in hand, but—as will be demonstrated in this chapter—not all aggression is violent in the physical sense of that word. Some writers argue that aggression has been instrumental in helping people survive. Through centuries of experience, humans learned that aggressive behavior enabled them to obtain material goods, land, and treasures; to protect property and family; and to gain prestige, status, and power. Although some might wonder whether the human species could have survived had it not used aggression, others are quick to point out that both historically and in the present, aggressive behavior is at the root of numerous social and individual problems.

Aggression—a psychological concept that we will define shortly—warrants an entire chapter because it is the basic ingredient in violent crime. By studying aggression, psychologists have made substantial contributions to society's efforts to understand both violent and nonviolent crime, as well as violent behavior that may not necessarily be defined as crime (e.g., legitimate uses of force). Is human aggression instinctive, biological, learned, or some combination of these characteristics? If it results from an innate, biological mechanism, the methods designed to control, reduce, or eliminate aggressive behavior will differ significantly from methods used if aggression is learned.

Perspectives of human nature emerge very clearly from the scholarly and research literature on aggression. Some writers and researchers believe that aggressive behavior is basically biological and genetic in origin, a strong residue of our evolutionary past. This physiological, genetic contention is accompanied by compelling evidence that explanations of human aggressive behavior may be found in the animal kingdom as a whole. On the other hand, researchers who subscribe to the learning viewpoint believe that, while some species of animals may be genetically programmed to behave aggressively, human beings learn to be aggressive from the social environment. The learning position also offers cogent evidence to support its theory. Other researchers remain on a theoretical fence, accepting and rejecting some aspects of each argument. Research does indicate, however, that the level of aggressive behavior demonstrated by an eight-year-old appears to remain largely unchanged well into adulthood for many individuals, regardless of gender (Kokko & Pulkkinen, 2005).

If aggression and violence represent a built-in, genetically programmed aspect of human nature, we may be forced, as Baron (1983) suggests, toward a pessimistic conclusion. At best, we can only hope to hold our natural, aggressive urges and drives temporarily in check. Furthermore, we should design the environment and society in such a way as to discourage violence, including administering immediate and aversive consequences (punishment) when it is displayed. Even better—and setting aside ethical or legal considerations for the moment—we might consider psychosurgery, electrode implants, and drug control—all effective methods for the reduction, if not the elimination, of violence.

If, on the other hand, we believe that aggression is learned and is influenced by a wide range of situational, social, and environmental variables, we can be more optimistic. Aggression is not an inevitable aspect of human life. Once we understand what factors play major roles in its acquisition and maintenance, we will be able to reduce its occurrence by addressing these factors. There are, of course, both positive and negative aspects of human aggression. Many individuals who play in competitive sports, hunt for sport, serve in the military, and work for law enforcement engage in socially permissible forms of aggression that may be necessary or that enhance their quality of life as well as that of others. To some extent, aggression is also valued in politics and in the corporate world. What we are concerned with in this chapter is the inappropriate expression of aggression, particularly as displayed in violent behavior. In other words, the focus in this chapter is on the negative aspects, or the forms of aggression that are not socially approved.

DEFINING AGGRESSION

The task of defining human aggression is surprisingly difficult, as many social psychologists have discovered. Forcibly jabbing someone in the midsection is certainly defining it by example—or is it? Now what about jabbing someone more softly, in jest? Would everyone consider football and boxing aggressive behaviors? If someone pointedly ignores a question, is that an example of aggression? What if someone spreads malicious gossip? If someone interrupts a public speaker by shouting invectives, is that an example of displaying aggressive behavior? If a burglar breaks into your home and you reach for a gun, aim it at the intruder, and pull the trigger, is yours an act of aggression? Is it any less so if the gun does not fire? If someone sits passively on a doorstep and purposefully blocks your entry, is this aggression?

Some social psychologists define aggression as the intent and attempt to harm another individual, physically or socially, or, in some cases, to destroy an object. This definition seems adequate for many situations, but it has several limitations. Refusing to speak does not fit well, since it is not an active attempt to harm someone, nor is blocking someone's entry. Most psychologists place these two behaviors in a special category of aggressive responses and call them **passive-aggressive behaviors**, since they are generally interpreted as aggressive in intent, although the behavior is passive and indirect.

As fascinating as passive-aggressive behavior may be, it is generally irrelevant when we discuss crime, since the aggression we are concerned about is the type that manifests itself directly in violent or antisocial behavior. We might stretch the point by suggesting that the doorstep sitter is trespassing, in which case he or she might be charged with a criminal offense. Likewise, there are other situations in which passive-aggressive behavior could lead to various types of crime.

TABLE 5-1 Varieties of Human Aggression

	Active		Passive	
	Direct	**Indirect**	**Direct**	**Indirect**
Physical	Punching Hitting	Practical joke Booby trap	Obstructing passage	Refusing to perform a necessary task
Verbal	Insulting the victim	Malicious gossip	Refusing to speak	Refusing consent

Source: Bartol, Curt R., Bartol, Anne M., Criminal Behavior: A Psychological Approach, 10e, Copyright © 2014. Pearson Education, Upper Saddle River, NJ.

Refusing to file income tax because one is intensely dissatisfied with the policies of the government is one example. In general, however, the aggressive behavior we wish to focus on in this chapter is not of the passive-aggressive kind.

In an effort to conceptualize the many varieties of human aggression, Buss (1971) tried to classify them based on the apparent motivation of the aggressor, although his classification does not refer specifically to motivations (see **Table 5-1**). You may easily find exceptions and overlapping categories in the Buss scheme, but that emphasizes how difficult it is to compartmentalize human aggressive behavior. It also epitomizes the many definitional dilemmas that hamper social psychologists studying aggression. Still, the Buss classification system is very useful for any meaningful discussion of aggression as well as research on its various forms. For example, researchers have learned that males employ more direct forms of aggression, especially toward other males, whereas females tend to rely more on indirect aggression, regardless of the gender of the target of their aggression (Richardson, 2005, 2014).

Hostile and Instrumental Aggression

Before finally settling on a satisfactory definition of aggression (and we will get there), it may be useful to recognize two types of aggression, **hostile** and **instrumental**, a distinction first made by Feshbach (1964). They are distinguished by their goals, or the rewards they offer the perpetrator. Hostile (or expressive) aggression, which we are most concerned with in this chapter, occurs in response to anger-inducing conditions, such as real or perceived insults, physical attacks, or one's own failures. The aggressor's goal is to make a victim suffer. Most criminal homicides, rapes, and other violent crimes directed at harming the victim are precipitated by hostile aggression. The behavior is characterized by the intense and disorganizing emotion of anger, with anger defined as an arousal state elicited by certain stimuli, particularly those evoking attack or frustration. (See **Box 5-1**, for discussion of contemporary cases relevant to this issue.)

CONTEMPORARY ISSUES

BOX 5-1 Aggression in Recent High Profile Cases

Over the past few years, as noted in Chapter 4, several high-profile cases involving deaths of unarmed black men have prompted public discussions and debates about use of force, law enforcement tactics, weapons, race relations, and the criminal justice system. We discuss four of these cases here, not with respect to these important broad concerns, but rather because they illustrate concepts discussed in this chapter.

In February 2012, 17-year-old Trayvon Martin, a black youth, was walking in a gated community in Sanford, Florida, unarmed and carrying a box of Skittles and a bottled iced tea he had just purchased from a convenience store. George Zimmerman, a white (Hispanic) neighborhood watch volunteer—not a sworn police officer—pursued Martin after calling 911 to report what he believed to be a suspicious individual. Despite being advised by the 911 dispatcher not to follow Martin, Zimmerman did so. At some point a scuffle ensued and Trayvon Martin was fatally shot in the chest at close distance.

(continued)

Following extensive media publicity about the case, Zimmerman was arrested six weeks after the shooting and charged with second-degree murder. Second-degree murder indicates an intention to kill but no premeditation, whereas first-degree murder involves both premeditation and intention. Zimmerman, claiming that he feared for his safety and shot Martin in self-defense, was found not guilty by a six-person jury.

In Ferguson, Missouri, Michael Brown was shot and killed in 2014 by police officer Darren Wilson, who claimed Brown reached into the officer's patrol car and tried to grab his gun. Witnesses differed in their accounts of the incident, some saying Brown approached the police car with his hands in the air, others saying he approached with a threatening gesture. A grand jury declined to indict the officer, prompting protests both in that town and nationwide.

Shortly after the Brown case, officers on Staten Island confronted Eric Garner, a black man who was selling loose cigarettes on the street, a misdemeanor. In a video that went viral on the Internet, Garner was seen being taken down by several officers, with one applying a chokehold and Garner stating that he could not breathe. Again, a grand jury refused to return any indictments.

In North Charleston, South Carolina, 50-year-old Walter Scott—also unarmed—was shot in the back by police officer Michael Slager as he was fleeing after being stopped for driving with a broken tail-light. The stop was captured on a police-cruiser dashboard camera, but the shooting itself—which occurred after the officer used a taser—was filmed by a passerby. The officer was quickly charged with murder and is held without bond in protective custody.

We bring attention to these cases to consider concepts associated with aggression discussed in the chapter.

- In two of the cases, Zimmerman's and Wilson's, the person who survived and the victim were involved in a physical fight. Bruises were found on all. In Garner's case, he resisted arrest verbally and by some thrashing, but he did not assault arresting officers. He, of course, was taken down and was placed in a chokehold. Scott was shot in the back. Therefore, the four cases all illustrate both aggression and *violence*.
- In accordance with Buss's typology, *direct, active aggression* of a *physical* sort occurred in all four cases. It is likely that there was *direct, active, verbal aggression*, as well, but we do not know this without more information.
- *Hostile aggression* occurred in three of the four cases— and each individual was both a victim and a perpetrator.

It is not clear whether Scott responded with hostile aggression. Recall that hostile aggression does not equate to crime, however.

- It is likely that Bushman and Anderson's (2001) continuum of aggression is involved; that is, some of the aggression displayed may have been more *automatic* than controlled. Would the decision to place Garner in a chokehold qualify?

In addition, the following concepts from the chapter might be relevant to these cases. You may agree or disagree.

- Weapons effect: The sight of a gun in Zimmerman's hands could have prompted Martin to act aggressively, either in anger or in self-defense. Michael Brown was unarmed, but he also may have been prompted to act aggressively by the sight of Wilson's gun.
- Cognitive scripts: All of these men had ample cognitive scripts that might be associated with violence. As a neighborhood watch volunteer (and criminal justice major) Zimmerman was familiar with scenarios that might predispose him to play out a scene whereby he would capture someone he perceived to be "up to no good." The officer in the Brown case may have had cognitive scripts in which he foresaw himself in a dangerous situation. Martin, Brown, Garner, and Scott, as black males, knew that black males are often wrongfully profiled and sometimes harmed physically by law enforcement officers. They could easily envision a scenario whereby their lives were in danger.

Questions for Discussion

1. What are the relative merits of hostile attribution bias and racial bias as explanations for what occurred in the above incidents?
2. Each of the above incidents is a continuing saga, particularly with respect to civil litigation. In one case (the Martin case), the person who killed has attracted additional media attention. In another case (the Scott shooting) the former officer remained in jail awaiting trial as of mid-September 2015. Obtain updated information and discuss if and how updated information has changed your view of these cases.
3. What roles might anger, fear, and frustration play in the above four incidents? Should we expect law enforcement officers to control their own anger, fear, and frustration more than "ordinary citizens"?

Instrumental aggression begins with competition or the desire for some object or status possessed by another person—jewelry, money, territory. The perpetrator tries to obtain the desired object regardless of the cost. Instrumental aggression is usually a factor in robbery, burglary, larceny, and various white-collar crimes. The perpetrator's obvious goal in a robbery is to obtain items of value. Usually, there is no intent to harm anyone. However, if someone or something interferes with the perpetrator's objective, he or she may feel forced to harm the victim or risk losing the desired goal. In that sense, a robbery may lead to murder, but the aggression represented is still instrumental. Instrumental aggression is also usually a feature of calculated murder committed by a hired, impersonal killer. Although psychologists make the distinction between hostile and instrumental aggression, the law does not, insofar as responsibility for the crime is concerned. However, certain factors associated with hostile aggression (e.g., if the crime is committed in a particularly heinous fashion) can affect the criminal sentence. On the other hand, a contract killer's instrumental aggression may also bring a longer sentence if information about prior offenses comes to light at sentencing.

It should be mentioned, however, that some scholars (e.g., Bushman & Anderson, 2001) find fault with a strict hostile-instrumental dichotomy. Bushman and Anderson point out that this two-category division fails to take into account that many aggressive acts have multiple motives. Furthermore, they say, aggressive acts can be better understood if they are placed somewhere along a continuum that runs from controlled aggression at one pole to automatic (impulsive or thoughtless) aggression at the other pole. Bushman and Anderson believe that, although the dichotomy was useful during the early stages of theory development, it is time to move to a more cognitive approach to understanding the various types of aggressive behavior. This is discussed more fully in the section on the cognitive models of aggression later in the chapter.

Interpretation by Victim

As Bandura (1973a) noted, most definitions of aggression imply that aggression revolves around the behaviors and intentions residing within the perpetrator (or performer). Going a step further, he suggests that an adequate definition of aggression must consider both the "injurious behavior" of the perpetrator and the "social judgment" of the victim. Thus, a soft poke in the belly may qualify as aggression if it is both done derisively and the recipient interprets it that way. A textbook on criminal behavior, however, must focus on aggression as manifested in conduct, not as it is perceived by a victim; it is the actions of the perpetrator that are critical. For our purposes, therefore, we define **aggression** as *behavior perpetrated or attempted with the intention of harming one or more individuals physically or psychologically or to destroy an object.* The psychological harm would cover aggressive actions that do not involve physical force but are still criminally accountable, such as intimidation, threats, or stalking. This definition encompasses all the behaviors described in Buss's typology. Note, however, that aggressive behavior will not *always* qualify as criminal. A law enforcement officer using *reasonable* force against a criminal suspect is displaying aggressive behavior, but it is not criminal. A hunter shooting a deer (in season) falls into the same category. A person who reasonably perceives him- or herself in grave danger of serious bodily harm and defends him- or herself against an aggressor, *without using disproportionate force*, is not committing a crime.

Furthermore, we define **violence** as *destructive physical aggression intentionally directed at harming other persons or things.* Violence may be methodical or random, sustained or fleeting, intensive or uncontrolled. It always harms or destroys the recipient or is intended to do so (Daniels & Gilula, 1970). Therefore, all violent behavior is aggressive behavior, but not all aggressive behavior is violent. Spreading malicious, false information about someone or stalking are cases in point. Both are aggressive, one is also criminal in most jurisdictions, but neither is violent.

THEORETICAL PERSPECTIVES ON AGGRESSION

Behavioral and social scientists have debated for over a half century whether humans are born aggressive and naturally violent, or born relatively free of aggressive tendencies. Several theories have been developed that try to provide some answers. The aggression debate, alluded to at the beginning of the chapter, is part of a wider controversy about the respective merits of nature and nurture. According to the first perspective, humans are programmed aggressive to defend themselves, family, and territory from intruders. According to the second, humans become violent by acquiring aggressive models and actions from society. In this section, the topics will move from the instinctive and biological perspectives to the more learning-based perspectives.

Psychoanalytical/Psychodynamic Viewpoint

Psychodynamic theorists assume that humans, by their very nature, will always be prone to aggressive impulses and hence are likely to commit violent acts if these impulses are not appropriately managed or held in check. Sigmund Freud, the father of psychoanalysis and a physician by training, was convinced that human beings are susceptible from birth to a buildup of aggressive energy, which must be dissipated or drained off before it reaches dangerous levels. This is known as the **psychodynamic or hydraulic model** since it bears a close resemblance to pressure buildup in a container. If excessive pressure accumulates in the container—the human psyche—an explosion is likely to occur, as demonstrated by tirades that may involve violence. According to the traditional Freudian perspective, people who have tirades are blowing off the excess steam of aggressive energy.

Freud suggested that violence in all of its forms is a manifestation of this aggressive energy discharge. Internal energy accumulates to dangerous levels when people have not discharged it appropriately through a process called catharsis, one of the most important concepts in psychoanalytic psychotherapy. Catharsis may be accomplished by actual behavior (e.g., playing football) or may occur vicariously (watching football). The Freudian-psychodynamic position predicts that children who participate in or avidly watch school sports will ultimately be less aggressive than children who do not. Freudian psychodynamic followers also maintain that people who engage in violent crime (particularly hostile aggression) have not had sufficient opportunity to "blow off steam" and keep their aggressive energies at manageable levels.

According to the psychoanalytical viewpoint, if violent crime is to be controlled, the human animal must be provided with multiple but appropriate channels for catharsis (e.g., adequate recreational facilities). In this way, children and adults presumably learn to dissipate aggression in socially approved, appropriate ways. Psychotherapy is one such channel, because it encourages catharsis under the guidance of a therapist.

Ethological Viewpoints

Ethology is the study of animal behavior in relation to the animal's natural habitat, and it compares that behavior to human behavior. In the mid-1960s, a number of ethologists published books and articles about aggression that interested and appealed to the general public. Three especially popular books were Konrad Lorenz's *On Aggression* (1966), Robert Ardrey's *The Territorial Imperative* (1966), and Desmond Morris's *The Naked Ape* (1967). Before his death, Lorenz was the chief spokesperson for a theoretical formulation of ethology as it relates to aggression.

A Nobel laureate in biology, Lorenz believed that aggression is an inherited instinct of both humans and animals. (Although humans are part of the animal kingdom, we make the distinction between humans and non-human animals throughout this section.) One of its main purposes is to enable the animal—and the human being—to defend "staked out" territory, a territory that ensures sufficient food, water, and space to roam and reproduce. If this space is violated, Lorenz argued, the instinctive or genetically programmed response is to attack, or at least to increase aggressive behavior toward the intruder, thus preventing further territory violation. The tendency to attack space violators is referred to as **territoriality**. Lorenz believed it is an innate propensity developed through the lengthy, complex process of evolution. This innate aggressive behavior among members of the same animal species (intraspecific aggression) prevents overcrowding and ensures the best and most powerful mates for the young.

The more deadly the animals' evolutionarily developed weaponry (e.g., fangs, claws, size, and strength), the more intense the innate inhibitions against engaging in physical combat with members of its own species. This innately programmed inhibition is a form of insurance for species survival, Lorenz believed, since constant intraspecific physical combat would eventually extinguish the species. Intraspecies aggression is accomplished, therefore, not by actual combat but by complicated displays of force and superiority, such as a show of teeth, size, or color array. These displays are referred to as **ritualized aggression**. Through an intricate communication system, the animals transmit signals, after which the more powerful, dominant animal generally wins out. The losing animal demonstrates defeat by various appeasement behaviors, such as rolling over on its back (characteristic of puppies), lowering its tail or head, and emitting cries of defeat. The weaker animal then leaves the territory of the dominant one.

What does all of this have to do with human aggression? Lorenz and other ethologists believe that it is important to understand animal aggression before we try to understand human aggression, since humans are part of the animal world and probably follow many of its basic principles. Efran and Cheyne (1974), for example, observed after studying invasion of personal space among humans that "human society may operate through mechanisms which are less uniquely human than is currently fashionable to suggest" (p. 225).

Lorenz raised another issue that, if valid, is more significant to criminal behavior, however. He maintained that human beings have outdistanced the evolutionary process of inhibiting aggression. Instead of developing natural weapons and the species-preserving function of ritualized aggression, humans have developed technological weaponry. Thus, he and many other ethologists believed they could provide at least a partial answer to why human beings wantonly maim and kill members of their own species: They have not developed the ability to engage in the species-preserving behavior of ritualized aggression. Instead, through superior learning ability, they have developed the capacity to annihilate.

The ethological position is intriguing, but it has not been supported by human aggression research (Bandura, 1983; Montagu, 1973; Zillmann, 1983). Zoologists, biologists, and psychologists have tried with little success to apply the Lorenzian tenets to humans. One problem is that the ethological position relies on a strong analogy between animals and humans. Lorenz argued, for example, that the Greylag goose is remarkably similar to the human species (Berkowitz, 1973). However, the human brain makes us remarkably unlike the Greylag goose and considerably less likely to rely on instinct for determining behavior. Research has yet to delineate any instinctive or invariant genetically programmed behavior determinant in humans. Furthermore, "the capacity to exercise control over one's own thought processes, motivation, and action is a distinctively human characteristic" (Bandura, 1989, p. 1175).

Ethologists also fail to acknowledge and interpret the vast body of existing scientific research that has tested their position and found it wanting. This curious response—or nonresponse—undermines the validity of their whole presentation. Some critics have referred to ethological theorizing as "scientific-sounding misinformation" (Leach, 1973). To date, therefore, there is little evidence to justify portraying humans as *innately* dangerous and brutal or as controlled by instinct. Some contemporary theories do adopt a biological perspective on violence, however, as we discuss later in the chapter.

The ethological perspective has evolved into what is referred to today as **evolutionary psychology**. Evolutionary psychology is the study of the evolution of behavior using the principles of natural selection. It argues that human evolutionary history provides the fundamental framework for understanding human cognition and behavior. An important point to remember here is that evolutionary psychology does not see aggression as pathology, but something that is normal. The evolutionary perspective views aggression as an adaptive behavior that has been naturally selected over the course of human evolution (Bjorklund & Hawley, 2014). In recent years, evolutionary psychology has taken hold of an increasing number of criminologists as providing cogent explanations for violence in contemporary human societies (Pinker, 2014).

Frustration-Aggression Hypothesis

Around the time of Freud's death in 1939, a group of psychologists at Yale University proposed that aggression is a direct result of frustration (Dollard, Doob, Miller, Mowrer, & Sears, 1939). According to John Dollard and his colleagues, people who are frustrated, thwarted, annoyed, or threatened will behave aggressively, since aggression is a natural, almost automatic response to frustrating circumstances. Moreover, people who exhibit aggressive behavior are frustrated, thwarted, annoyed, or threatened. "Aggression is always a consequence of frustration" (Dollard et al., 1939, p. 1).

Because of its simplicity and important implications, the **frustration-aggression hypothesis** drew much research, along with much criticism. Psychologists found it difficult not only to decide what frustration was, but also to determine how it could be measured accurately. Researchers also learned that aggression was a much more complex phenomenon than Dollard and his associates had postulated. Frustration does not always lead to aggression, and aggressive behavior does not always signify "frustration." Experiments in social psychology have indicated that people respond to frustration and anger differently. Some do indeed respond with aggression, but others display a wide variety of responses.

Led by Leonard Berkowitz (1962, 1969, 1973), whose general views on some of the causes of criminality were presented in Chapter 4, researchers began to propose a revised version of the frustration-aggression hypothesis. According to Berkowitz, frustration increases the probability that an individual will become angry and soon act aggressively. In short, frustration facilitates the performance of aggressive behavior. The behavior may be overt (physical or verbal) or implicit (wishing someone dead). Anger, however, is not the only emotion that potentially leads to aggression. Aversive conditions, such as pain, or pleasant states, such as sexual arousal, may also lead to aggressive behavior (Berkowitz, 1973). We will return to this subject shortly.

As we learned in Chapter 4, an important component of the revised frustration-aggression hypothesis is the concept of anticipated goals or expectations. When a behavior directed at a specific goal is thwarted, frustration is likely to result. Thus, the person must have been expecting or anticipating the attainment of a goal or achievement. Mere deprivation of goods will not necessarily lead to frustration. People who are living under deprived conditions may not be frustrated unless they actually expect something better. "Poverty-stricken groups who have never dreamed of having automobiles, washing machines, or new homes are not frustrated because they have been deprived of these things; they are frustrated only after they have begun to hope" (Berkowitz, 1969, p. 15).

Aggression, Berkowitz says, is only one possible response to frustration. The individual may learn others, like withdrawal, doing nothing, or trying to alter the situation by getting out of the situation completely or by compromising. With this approach, Berkowitz not only emphasizes the importance of learning but also stresses the role of individual differences in response to frustrating circumstances.

The revised frustration-aggression hypothesis, therefore, suggests the following steps: (1) the person is blocked from obtaining an expected goal, (2) frustration results, generating anger, and (3) anger *predisposes* or readies the person to behave aggressively. Whether the person actually engages in aggressive actions will depend in part on his or her learning history, interpretation of the event, and individual way of responding to frustration. It will also depend, however, on the presence of aggression-eliciting stimuli in the environment.

Weapons Effect

Berkowitz notes that the presence of aggressive stimuli in the external environment (or internal environment represented by thoughts) increases the probability of aggressive responses. A weapon is a good example of such a stimulus. Most people in our society associate firearms with aggression. Consider the concern many people have about laws that allow people with pistol permits to carry these weapons openly on the streets. Berkowitz (1983) likens the firearm to a conditioned stimulus in that the weapon conjures aggressive associations, facilitating overt aggression. A gun, even when not used, is more likely to generate aggressive action than is a neutral object. "The mere sight of the weapon might elicit ideas, images, and expressive reactions that had been linked with aggression in the past" (Berkowitz, 1983, p. 124).

In one early experiment designed to test this hypothesis (Berkowitz & LePage, 1967), angry male subjects were more likely to engage in aggressive action in the presence of a gun than a comparable group of angry subjects in the presence of a badminton racket. This suggests that a visible weapon (such as a law enforcement officer might carry) may actually facilitate, rather than inhibit, a violent response in some people. This is not to say that sworn law enforcement officers should not carry weapons. However, the carrying of weapons by others—such as private citizens, neighborhood watch volunteers, campus police in some colleges and universities, and private security officers—is often a controversial issue. Although the U.S. Supreme Court has ruled that the Second Amendment right to bear arms is a private right (*District of Columbia v. Heller*, 2008), restrictions on that right are possible. Most communities, therefore, do not allow "open carry" of weapons by persons not legally authorized to enforce the law.

The Berkowitz–LePage finding generated much controversy as to whether weapons actually do provoke aggressive behavior. A number of studies tried to replicate the finding, but failed to find evidence of a **weapons effect**. Some researchers believed that many of the participants used in some of the studies "saw through" the purpose of the study, a research flaw called demand characteristics. However, a comprehensive review of the research literature found strong evidence that the weapons effect does—in fact—exist (Carlson, Marcus-Newhall, & Miller, 1990). Carlson et al., concluded, "Aggression-related cues present in experimental settings act to increase aggressive responding. This cue effect occurs more strongly when subjects have been negatively aroused before their exposure to aggression-facilitating cues" (p. 632). The weapons effect has also been found in other countries, including Belgium, Croatia, Italy, and Sweden (Berkowitz, 1994).

Cognitive-Neoassociation Model

In his reformulation of the frustration-aggression hypothesis, Berkowitz has emphasized the importance of cognitive factors. The reformulation, referred to as the **cognitive-neoassociation model**, operates in the following manner: During the earlier stages, an aversive event produces a negative affect (discomfort). This negative affect may be due to physical pain or psychological discomfort. Physical pain as an aversive circumstance is clear, but psychological discomfort needs further elaboration. Being verbally insulted is a good example. While there is no physical pain, personal insults or demeaning comments engender anger, depression, or sadness—all negative affects—in just about everyone. Unpleasant feelings or negative affects presumably then give rise, almost automatically, to a variety of feelings, thoughts, and memories that are associated with flight (fear) and fight (anger) tendencies. During this early stage, mediating cognitive processes have little influence beyond the immediate appraisal that the situation is aversive. Some people may act quickly on the basis of these initial emotions without further deliberation or forethought, sometimes engaging in violence. Berkowitz emphasizes that any unpleasant feeling or arousal can evoke aggressive, even violent responses. A driver may lash out in anger and assault the person who rear-ended his new car. A boy cut from a sports team due to poor grades may violently lash out at authority by stabbing the school guidance counselor.

Most of us get past the initial stages of frustration, however. During the later stages, cognitive appraisal may go into operation and substantially influence the subsequent emotional reactions and experiences after the initial, automatic responses. These cognitions mediate and evaluate a proper course of action. During the later stages, roused people make causal attributions about the unpleasant experience, think about the nature of their feelings, and perhaps try to control their feelings and actions. Thus, what began as an angry reaction to someone's critical comments develops into a careful consideration of their merits or a conclusion that they are not worth being concerned about.

Excitation Transfer Theory

Zillmann (1988) has proposed a theory to explain how physiological arousal can generalize from one situation to another. Called **excitation transfer theory**, it is based on the assumption that physiological arousal, however produced, dissipates slowly over time. For example, a person who receives some anger-producing criticism at work is likely to have some residual arousal from that criticism when he or she arrives home later that evening. Encountering some annoying event at home, the person is apt to "fly off the handle" and overreact to the minor home incident. "You're taking it out on me," or "You're taking it out on the kids" are familiar statements in some homes.

Consequently, the combination of preexisting arousal, plus anger generated by the irritation at home, may increase the likelihood of aggression. The transfer of arousal from one situation to another is most likely to occur if the person is unaware that he or she is still carrying some arousal from a previous situation to a new, unrelated one.

Displaced Aggression Theory

Closely related to the excitation transfer theory is **displaced aggression theory**, especially the recent model proposed by Bushman, Anderson, Miller, and their colleagues (Anderson & Bushman, 2002; Bushman, Bonacci, Pederson, Vasquez, & Miller, 2005; Miller, Pedersen, Earleywine, & Pollack, 2003). According to Bushman et al. (2005), "Aggression is *displaced* when the target is innocent of any wrongdoing but is simply in the wrong place at the wrong time" (p. 969). Displaced aggression can occur when an individual cannot aggress against a source of provocation, such as a boss at work, but feels less constrained about being aggressive toward an innocent, nonprovoking, or mildly provoking individual (or pet). The displaced aggression is probably more likely to be directed at a person (or pet) who emits a mildly annoying act—the cat that tips over the water dish, for example. Bushman et al. refer to this phenomenon as *triggered displaced aggression*. "Following an initial provocation, the target commits a minor provocation, the triggering event, which in turn prompts an aggressive response" (p. 970). The "displaced" aggressive response is usually far in excess of what might be expected to be directed at the minor provocation but probably is in proportion to the perceived severity of the initial provocation. One may believe the boss deserves a good kick for not appreciating one's hard work on a project; since one can't kick the boss, the cat bears the brunt of the anger.

Bushman et al. (2005) take the model one step further by working into the equation the concept of rumination. **Rumination** refers to self-focused attention toward one's thoughts and feelings. In other words, the person keeps thinking about the incident long after it is over. More importantly, ruminative thought can harbor and maintain angry feelings over a period of time, far removed from the initial provocation. It is, according to Bushman et al., the ruminative thoughts that can promote subsequent aggression against someone who is mildly annoying but not highly deserving of an aggressive attack.

SOCIAL LEARNING FACTORS IN AGGRESSION AND VIOLENCE

Why do some people behave aggressively when intensely frustrated, while others change their tactics, withdraw, or seem not to be affected? One major factor may be past learning experiences. The human being, as we noted in Chapter 4, is very adept at learning and maintaining behavior patterns that have worked in the past, even if they only worked occasionally. This learning process begins in early childhood. Children develop many behaviors merely by watching their parents and significant others in their environment, a process we have called modeling or observational learning. A child's behavior pattern, therefore, is often acquired through the modeling or imitation of other people, real and imagined, in the child's environment (Bandura, 1973a). In fact, available research reveals that the conditions most conducive to the learning of aggression are those in which the child (1) has many opportunities to observe aggression, (2) is reinforced for his or her own aggression, or (3) is often the object of aggression (Huesmann, 1988).

Suppose Harris's father returns home feeling harried after a hot and humid day during which he accomplished nothing (frustration). He finds an official-looking letter from the IRS in the mailbox. He opens it, perhaps muttering mild obscenities under his breath, and finds that the IRS apparently suspects he has shortchanged the U.S. government by several hundred dollars, although he knows he has not (more frustration). He is invited for an audit (even more frustration). In response, he slams his fist on the table, exclaims "Damn it!" or some colorful variation, and kicks the nearest chair (just enough not to damage his toe, since he has learned the painful consequences from past similar episodes). Unknown to father, three-year-old Harris has observed this whole scenario. An hour later, when his tower of blocks crumbles, Harris pounds his fist, kicks a chair, and curses, "Damn it!"

Modeling

Many years ago, Albert Bandura (1965) conducted what is now considered a classic study in psychology. Sixty-six nursery school children (33 girls and 33 boys) were divided into three groups and shown one of three five-minute films. All three films depicted an adult verbally and physically assault a Bobo doll, a large plastic, inflatable clown with a sand base which bounces back after being pushed down. (A common household toy in the 1950s and 1960s, the Bobo doll has now morphed into inflatable superhero and supervillain characters that are available on the toy market of today.) In the film, the adult punched, kicked, and hit the clown with a mallet. One group saw the adult model being rewarded with candy and a soda after displaying aggressive behavior. A second group observed the model being spanked (with a rolled-up magazine) and reprimanded verbally. A third group witnessed a situation in which the model received neither punishment nor reward.

After the children saw the film, they were permitted to free play for 10 minutes in a playroom of toys, including a Bobo doll. The group that had witnessed the adult model being rewarded for aggressive behavior exhibited more aggression than the other two groups. In addition, boys were more aggressive than girls. The group that saw the adult model being punished exhibited the lowest amount of aggression in the playroom.

Bandura's subsequent research, which included variations on this basic study design, consistently demonstrated this modeling effect. Furthermore, numerous follow-up studies not only replicated his findings but also suggested that media violence (TV, movies, video games) may have a strong influence on real life in many situations (Baron, 1977). We cover this in a separate section below.

When a child's imitative behavior is reinforced or rewarded by praise and encouragement from significant models, the probability that the behavior will occur in the future is increased. There is evidence that American parents (consciously or inadvertently) encourage or reinforce aggressive behavior in their children, particularly in their sons. For example, the behavior of Harris described above might have been reinforced if his parents drew attention to it by laughing. In a future episode, the kicking behavior might be directed at the family cat. Furthermore, while kicking chairs and towers may seem relatively mild, the same behavior becomes very sobering if the parent's anger is taken out on a family member, as too many Harrises in our society have observed. Other children are "merely" expected or encouraged to be hard-hitting linebackers and to hold their own against neighborhood bullies, provided they are approximately the same size. They learn that the child who aggresses successfully against others is often rewarded by status, prestige, and the most attractive toys or material goods.

TYPES OF MODELS.   Bandura (1983) identifies three major types of models: family members, members of one's subculture, and symbolic models provided by the mass media. As we noted in Chapter 2, family members, particularly parents, can be very powerful models up until early adolescence. Beginning in early adolescence, peer models are likely to dominate. Not surprisingly, the highest incidence of aggression is found in communities and groups in which aggressive models abound and fighting prowess is regarded as a valued attribute (Bandura, 1983; Lacourse, Nagin, Tremblay, Vitaro, & Claes, 2003; Thornberry & Burch, 1997).

The mass media, including television, movies, magazines, newspapers, and books, provide abundant symbolic models. Video games and the Internet have vastly expanded this collection. Television, videos, and electronic devices pervade the life of the growing child, even the very young one, and offer hundreds of potentially powerful aggressive and violent models in a variety of formats, ranging from Saturday morning cartoon film festivals to triple-X-rated cable movies. The effects these models have on children are a highly debated issue, as we will note later in this chapter.

Since parents are powerful models, we would expect aggressive or antisocial parents to have aggressive or antisocial children. In an old but classic study, Sears, Maccoby, and Levin (1957) interviewed four hundred mothers of kindergarten children about their disciplinary techniques, their attitudes about children's aggressiveness, and the children's expressions of aggression toward peers, siblings, and parents. One of the major findings was that physical punishment by parents was related to aggressiveness in the children. This was especially true when physical discipline was supplemented by high permissiveness toward aggression. In support of this finding, some researchers found that preschoolers played more aggressively when they were watched by a permissive adult than when no adult was visible (Siegel & Kohn, 1959).

Bandura (1973a) argues persuasively that aggressive behavior can be most productively understood and modified if we give attention to the learning principles like those alluded to earlier. As psychologists learn more about human behavior, many are beginning to agree with him.

Social learning theory hypothesizes that the rudiments of aggressive behavior are initially acquired through observing aggressive models or on the basis of direct experience; aggression is then gradually refined and maintained by reinforcement. Therefore, people may have an aggressive behavioral pattern, but may rarely express it if it has no functional value or is not condoned by significant others in their social environment. Social learning theory acknowledges that biological structures can set limits on the types of aggressive responses that can be learned, and that genetic endowment influences the rate at which learning progresses (Bandura, 1973a). Biology does not program the individual to specific aggressive behavior, however. These behaviors are learned by observation, either deliberately or inadvertently; they become refined through reinforced practice.

Observation Modeling

In addition, mere exposure to aggressive models does not guarantee that the observer will try to engage in similar aggressive action at a later date. First, a variety of conditions may prevent observational learning from even taking place. Individuals differ widely in their ability to learn from observation. Some people may fail to notice the essential features of the model's behavior or may have a poor symbolic or visual memory. Alternately, they may not want to imitate the model. Bandura suggests also that one important component of observational learning may be the motivation to rehearse what has been observed. He notes that a mass murderer, for example, may get an idea from descriptive accounts of another mass killing. The incident remains prominent in his mind long after it has been forgotten by others. He continues to think about the crime and to rehearse the brutal scenario mentally until, under appropriate conditions, it serves as a script for his own murderous actions.

Another restriction on observational learning is what happens to the observed model. If the model is reprimanded or punished either during or immediately after an aggressive episode, this will probably inhibit the observer's behavior. The "bad guy" should not get away with violence, if we are to discourage antisocial behavior via the entertainment media.

If aggressive behavior is to be maintained, it needs periodic reinforcement. According to social learning theory, aggression is maintained by instrumental learning. In the initial stage of learning, observation is important, but in the later stages, reinforcement is essential. The reinforcement may be positive, as when the individual gains material or social rewards, or it may be negative, if it allows the individual to alter or avoid aversive conditions. If aggressive behavior brings rewards in either of these ways, the person is likely to continue it. Research has consistently discovered that aggressive children anticipate more positive outcomes and fewer negative outcomes following their aggressive acts (Hubbard, Dodge, Cillessen, Coie, & Schwartz, 2001). "When compared with average peers, aggressive children are more likely to believe that aggression will produce tangible rewards, reduce aversive treatment by others, make themselves and peers feel good, increase self-esteem, and help to avoid a negative image" (Hubbard et al., 2001, p. 268).

A youngster subjected to unmerciful harassment or bullying because of his unusual name or where he lives may be able to stop the teasing with his fists. The reinforcement he gets from his newly found aggressive behavior is highly rewarding and is likely to continue in the future. Aggression can also allow the individual to feel in control of a situation if things have not been going his or her way. A more extreme example is when a student who is constantly bullied by peers decides to put a stop to the aversive circumstances by using a firearm on all those who are perceived as participants as well as on bystanders. The psychological reinforcement offered by feeling in control is an extremely powerful component in any human behavior, especially aggressive or violent behavior.

COGNITIVE MODELS OF AGGRESSION

Recent cognitive models for learning aggression have hypothesized that, while observational learning is important in the process, the individual's cognitive capacities and information processing strategies are equally important. Two major cognitive models have emerged in recent years. One that has been proposed by Rowell Huesmann (1997) is a hypothesis called the **cognitive scripts model**. The other model has been developed by Kenneth Dodge and his colleagues (Dodge, 1986; Dodge & Coie, 1987), and is called the **hostile attribution model**.

Cognitive Scripts Model

According to Huesmann (1988), social behavior in general, and aggressive behavior in particular, is controlled largely by cognitive scripts learned and memorized through daily experiences. "A script suggests what events are to happen in the environment, how the person should behave in response to these events, and what the likely outcome of those behaviors would be" (Huesmann, 1988, p. 15). Scripts may be learned by direct experience or by observing significant others (Bushman & Anderson, 2001). Once learned, the script is usually followed. Each script is different and unique to each person, but once established, it becomes resistant to change and may persist into adulthood. For a script to become established, it must be rehearsed from time to time. With practice the script will not only become encoded and maintained in memory, but it will also be more easily retrieved and used when the individual faces a problem. "Scripts can be viewed as cognitive programs that have been acquired over time and are stored in a person's memory and are used as guides for behavior and social problem solving" (Huesmann, Dubow, & Boxer, 2011, p. 128). Furthermore, the individual's "evaluation of the 'appropriateness' of a script plays an important role in determining which scripts are stored in memory, in determining which scripts are retrieved and utilized, and which scripts continue to be utilized" (Huesmann, 1988, p. 19). Emotions play a role too, as they influence script selection and the evaluation of scripts. For example, script selection is likely to be different when the person is angry compared to when that same person is happy.

Parents too play an important role. "In the short run, when children see their parents behave aggressively, schemas, scripts, and normative beliefs associated with aggression are primed in the children's minds" (Huesmann et al., 2011, p. 131). Since parents provide suitable models, children are likely to mimic their parents' aggressive behaviors almost immediately, as we saw in the example with Harris earlier in the chapter. However, children do not simply mimic the immediate behavior; they tend to encode into their own repertoire of scripts their parents' scripts, as well as their parents' views and beliefs about the world. As the child grows older, the evaluation process includes the confidence that he or she has in predicting outcomes of the script, the extent to which an individual judges himself or herself capable of executing the script, and the extent to which the script is seen as congruent with the person's self-regulating internal standards. Scripts that are inconsistent or violate one's internalized standards are unlikely to be stored or utilized. An individual with poorly integrated internal standards against aggression, or who is convinced that aggressive behavior is a way of life, is more likely to incorporate aggressive scripts for behavior. Importantly, the aggressive child is apt to instigate aggressive reactions from others, confirming his or her beliefs about the aggressiveness of human nature in a circular, perpetuating fashion.

Hostile Attribution Model

Kenneth Dodge and his colleagues discovered that highly aggressive and violent youth often have a **hostile attribution bias**. That is, youth (and adults) prone toward violence are more likely to interpret ambiguous actions as hostile and threatening than are their less aggressive counterparts

(Dodge, 1993b). For example, a foot casually and innocently positioned near a school desk may be interpreted as a deliberate attempt to trip. As Dill, Anderson, Anderson, and Deuser (1997, p. 275) put it, people described as having hostile attribution bias "tend to view the world through blood-red tinted glasses." Children with a hostile attribution bias are twice as likely as average children to see aggressive actions from others where there are none (Hubbard et al., 2001). As noted by Dodge (2011), "when a respondent infers that the act was committed with hostile intent (*a hostile attribution*), the probability that the respondent will react aggressively is high (about .76), whereas when the same respondent infers that the act was committed benignly, the probability of an aggressive behavior is low (about .25)" (p. 165).

Hostile attribution bias is believed to be present in both boys and girls (Vitale, Newman, Serin, & Bolt, 2005), but it appears to be stronger for boys than for girls (Cillessen, Lansu, & Van Den Berg, 2014). Cillessen and his colleagues also discovered that hostile attribution bias was significantly stronger for children with a low status within their peer group compared to children who have a high status in the group.

Research consistently indicates that violent youth "typically define social problems in hostile ways, adopt hostile goals, and seek few additional facts, generate few alternative solutions, anticipate few consequences for aggression, and give higher priority to their aggressive solutions" (Eron & Slaby, 1994, p. 10). Similarly, Serin and Preston (2001, p. 259) conclude, "Aggressive juvenile offenders have been found to be deficient in social problem-solving skills and to espouse many beliefs supporting aggression. Specifically, they tend to define problems in hostile ways, adopt hostile goals, seek less confirmatory information, generate fewer alternative solutions, anticipate fewer consequences for aggressive solutions, and choose less effective solutions."

Research indicates that this hostile attribution bias begins to develop during the preschool years. For some children, the bias seems to be a stable attribute that is still present into adulthood (Dodge, 2011; Dodge et al., 2002; Nigg & Huang-Pollock, 2003). Most children, however, outgrow it. Preschoolers with more advanced social-cognitive skills (good language skills and the ability to understand different emotions and intentions) quickly outgrow hostile attribution biases during early childhood (Choe, Lane, Grabell, & Olson, 2013). Choe et al. write: "We found that preschoolers who were better able to *explain* others' behavior in terms of underlying false beliefs, those who were better at identifying others' emotional states that were *inconsistent* with their own, and those with greater verbal aptitude made fewer hostile attributions two to three years later" (p. 2251, italics in the original).

Peer rejection also appears to play an important role in the development and maintenance of hostile attribution bias. Dodge (1993b) reports that when children were followed from elementary school to middle school, a child's tendency to attribute hostile intentions to others showed a significant relationship between peer rejection during elementary school and increased aggression during middle school. Coie (2004) asserts, "The fact that rejected, aggressive males show persistently higher tendencies toward hostile attribution biases, as well as other social cognitive deficits related to aggression, fits with their pattern of higher involvement in violent delinquent acts in adolescence and their tendency to persist in violent behavior into the early adult years" (p. 255).

There is further research to suggest that some children are especially primed to develop hostile expectations of peers because of earlier exposure to family abuse and maltreatment (DeWall, Twenge, Gitter, & Baumeister, 2009; Dodge, Bates, & Pettit, 1990; Hubbard et al., 2001). "Children develop basic trust through interaction with caring adults, and violation of that trust through extreme or ongoing maltreatment is hypothesized to lead to schemas, scripts, knowledge structures, and working models that others will act maliciously" (Dodge, 2011, p. 173). Studies have revealed that children exposed to maltreatment early in their lives become "hypervigilant toward hostile social cues, perceptually ready to perceive hostility in others' intentions, and quick to generate aggressive retaliatory responses to even mild provocations" (Dodge, 2001, p. 65). In addition, peer-rejected children with hostile attribution bias are frequently targets of physical assault by others, prompting them to be more suspicious of the motives of others (Coie & Miller-Johnson, 2001). These children appear to be especially quick at developing hostile attribution biases against a wide range of peers, including new acquaintances. "These children come to have a generalized set of social cognitions that dispose them to draw hostile inferences from the behavior of new peer acquaintances more quickly than their peers do" (Hubbard et al., 2001, p. 277). Some other children, although prone to hostile attribution bias, tend to be specific in who they identify as hostile, probably due to certain behavioral patterns or interests they find threatening.

Ronald Blackburn (1998) also reports research evidence that suggests that persistent lawbreaking by adults represents attempts to master a social environment perceived as hostile and threatening. Blackburn hypothesizes that chronic offenders approach the world with a well-developed hostile-dominance interpersonal style. That is, rather than be simply a reflection of deficits in conscience or self-control, frequent criminal behavior may represent an ongoing attempt to control and dominate others in the social environment. According to Blackburn, chronic criminality can be understood as "an attempt to maintain status or mastery of a social environment from which they feel alienated" (1998, p. 174). The well-rehearsed cognitive script of persistent, lifelong offenders, therefore, is to dominate—often in a hostile manner—social environments they perceive as hostile.

Blackburn's observations have been supported by later research by Vitale et al. (2005) who investigated the extent of hostile attribution in 150 incarcerated males, some of whom were labeled psychopaths. The researchers discovered that psychopaths were significantly more likely to exhibit hostile attribution bias than non-psychopaths in a variety of situations. The study also supported the hypothesis that there may be different antisocial pathways associated with hostile attributions. That is, hostile attribution bias was also prevalent in those prisoners who held negative thoughts about themselves, other people, and the world in general even though they were not identified as psychopaths.

In summary, hostile attribution bias involves the tendency to view the behavior of others as provocative, harmful, hostile, or wrongful even when it is not. Some individuals demonstrate this tendency more strongly than others. Consequently, attribution bias or style should be viewed as existing along a continuum. At its extreme level, the bias represents a cognitive deficit in processing that distorts social information so dramatically that the individual is literally unable to process that information accurately (Fontaine, 2008). In some cases, some people may engage in extreme violence toward others they interpret as trying to do them harm. In the chapters on criminal homicide (Chapters 9 and 10), we will return to this topic as it applies to murder, including serial and mass murder.

AGGRESSIVE BEHAVIOR: SIMPLE AND EASY TO USE. Aggression is a simple, direct way of solving immediate conflicts. If something is not going your way, approaching the social environment in a threatening, hostile manner is the most direct way (though not the most effective in the long run) of confronting your tormentors. On the other hand, prosocial solutions and alternative nonaggressive scripts are less direct and more complex than aggressive solutions. In essence, they are more difficult to apply. Theoretically, the more cognitively "simple" individual would be more inclined to pursue simplistic and direct solutions to problems. In addition, because prosocial solutions are more complicated and more difficult to apply, they also require effective social skills. However, the development of effective social skills takes time, and those skills will have a spotty reinforcement history until perfected. Aggressive behavior, on the other hand, often receives immediate reinforcement for the aggressor, and therefore is more likely to be retained in one's arsenal of strategies for immediate solutions of conflictful situations.

After a 22-year longitudinal study, Eron and Huesmann (1984) concluded that diminished intellectual competence and poor social skills have an early effect in increasing the likelihood that a child will adopt characteristically more aggressive styles of behavior to resolve conflicts. For example, research has repeatedly documented the fact that juveniles who are serious sexual offenders have significant deficits in social competence, such as inadequate social skills, poor peer relationships, and social isolation from peers (Righthand & Welch, 2001). Further, the evidence indicates that this aggressive style will persist across situations and time and become a preferred style throughout adulthood. But the relationship is not simply one-way, with limited intellectual competence and inadequate skills promoting aggressive behavior. Rather it appears to be interactive. Aggressive behavior may interfere with positive social interactions with teachers and peers for intellectual and social advancement, perpetuating a chain of mutually influencing events: aggressive behavior influencing the social environment, and the social environment, in turn, influencing aggressive behavior.

Dolf Zillmann (1988) proposes a similar idea to the cognitive script theory, but, like Berkowitz, emphasizes the importance of physiological arousal and its interaction with cognitions. Zillmann agrees with Hebb (1955, p. 249) that arousal "is an energizer, but not a guide, an engine but not a steering gear." Cognition provides the steering and direction to the energizing effects of anger, fear, or frustration. Cognition is essentially the manager of emotions. Experiments demonstrate that "anger and anger control are particularly important with regards to understanding the aggressive behavior of offenders" (Roberton, Daffern, & Bucks, 2015, p. 79). Furthermore, it is a person's ability to control the outward expression of anger, rather than their ability to control their inner angry feelings, that predicts aggression and violent behavior (Roberton et al., 2015). Put another way, it is understandable if one feels angry at being denied a promotion that one believes was richly deserved; it is not acceptable to stab the individual responsible for making the promotion decision.

A long-standing observation in the study of aggression is that when the organism recognizes or perceives a threat to its welfare and well-being, it can either fight or flee. Following this "recognition of endangerment," physiological arousal quickly sets in, preparing the organism for fight or flight. The "recognition of endangerment," Zillmann reminds us, can be immediate, and the response can be reflex-like. What happens then is also highly dependent on cognition, especially in humans. Very likely, this is when cognitive scripts come in.

If the arousal is moderate, the individual with skills and well-integrated standards of prosocial values will probably pursue nonaggressive scripts, even though the person may have been angry or threatened at first. However, very *high* levels of arousal interfere with the complex cognitive processes that mediate our consideration of our internal codes of conduct, as well as our ability to assess the intentions of others and the mitigating circumstances around the incident (Zillmann, 1988). Think of a very stressful or frightening situation that has happened to you, and how difficult it was to think clearly. Or think of a time when you became extremely angry and said or did things you wish you hadn't. At high levels of arousal, our cognitions seem to become narrower and more restricted, almost incapacitated at times. Generally, under these high states of arousal, we resort to strongly established habits to guide and dominate our behavior. In essence, we become "impulsive" and largely unthinking, and cognitions that mediate the diminution of hostile or even violent actions are substantially reduced. However, if we have practiced or rehearsed nonviolent or nonaggressive behaviors as solutions, these cognitive scripts are likely to be the habits we resort to under high stress, fear, and high arousal. Psychological treatment programs directed at anger management help people learn to recognize the physiological responses that accompany their anger and identify strategies for controlling it. (See **Box 5-2** for description of programs directed at anger management.)

TREATMENT PROGRAM FOCUS

BOX 5-2 Dealing with Anger—What Works and for Whom?

Anger is a normal emotion, one which most people experience, sometimes frequently and on a regular basis. It is recognized as both a personality trait and an emotional state. Anger becomes problematic when it interferes with one's relationships, interferes with daily activities of living, affects one's physical health, or leads to harming others, such as through violent behavior. In a state of anger, parents may abuse their children, spouses may batter their partners, or motorists may harm pedestrians or other drivers. Anger also may be a contributing factor to depression and to suicide.

Anger management treatment (AMT) is a common approach taken by psychologists and other mental health practitioners for dealing with individuals whose persistent anger places them at risk of self-harm or committing crime, or who have already done so. It is available both as a one-on-one treatment approach and in group sessions, known as anger management group treatment or therapy (AMGT). AMGT in particular is widely used in dealing with domestic or intimate partner abusers, juveniles who have committed violent crimes, and veterans with PTSD.

Anger management also may be addressed in programs that address dating violence, and in school-based programs in which whole classrooms are targeted, although in these latter contexts it is considered to be a prevention rather than a treatment program (see Shorey et al., 2014, and McWhirter & McWhirter, 2010, for examples).

A typical AMGT program involves cognitive-behavior therapy (CBT) provided by one or two therapists, who may or may not be PhD psychologists. The treatment usually includes the following components at a minimum:

- Weekly 90-minute sessions for approximately 12 weeks
- Reading assignments, group discussion, skill-based exercises
- Training in recognizing physiological indicators of anger (e.g., increased heart rate)
- Training in recognizing anger triggers (e.g., a child's crying; alcohol misuse)
- Training in methods to handle anger (e.g., timeouts, breathing exercises, relaxation techniques)

Anger management programs have been shown to be effective in numerous research studies, but not surprisingly, their effectiveness varies in degree as well as according to target audience. Some programs have also been effective at changing cognitions but less at reducing anger-related conduct. Researchers continue to search for the individual differences that explain why some people respond well to these programs and others show little or no change in behavior. For example, AMGT has not had great success with persons with Antisocial Personality Disorder (APD) (Marshall et al., 2010 and references therein).

Questions for Discussion

1. What part, if any, does a person's social environment play in regulating anger as a human emotion?
2. What distinct challenges might be found in AMT with (a) domestic abusers; (b) veterans with PTSD; and (c) juveniles?
3. What are the advantages and disadvantages of initiating a school-based program that addresses anger management for all students?

The General Aggression Model

In an attempt to integrate the common features of previous theories of aggression, Nathan DeWall and Craig Anderson (DeWall & Anderson, 2011; DeWall, Anderson, & Bushman, 2011) propose the **general aggression model (GAM)**. According to DeWall and Anderson (2011), "GAM provides the only theoretical framework of aggression and violence that explicitly incorporates biological, personality development, social processes, basic cognitive processes, short-term and long-term processes, and decision processes" (p. 255). Although the model attempts to include most if not all the factors that can influence aggression and violence, it draws heavily on social-cognitive and social learning theories that have been developed over the past 40 years by social, personality, cognitive, and developmental psychologists. According to the model, aggression and violence depend on how an individual perceives and interprets the social environment, expectations about the likelihood of various outcomes, knowledge and beliefs about how people usually respond in certain situations, and the degree to which a person believes he or she has the ability to respond effectively. Although the cognitive process is initially complicated, judgments and choices in the process become automatized through cultural teachings and repeated experiences. Ultimately, they require little mental effort or conscious awareness. For instance, through repeated experiences and cultural teachings, some individuals quickly and thoughtlessly interpret that others—because of their appearance, religion, or national origin—are hostile and pose a physical threat.

GAM also posits that violence often occurs because of an escalation cycle, which begins with an initial triggering event that may be serious or relatively benign "The triggering event can influence any kind of dyad, including two people, two groups, two religions, or two nations" (DeWall & Anderson, 2011, p. 23). In these situations, one person or group considers retaliation for the incident to be justified or mild, whereas the other group believes the retaliation to be unjustified and severe. The person or group that believes the retaliation was unjustified often retaliates back. The cycle often persists through several iterations of violent actions. DeWall and Anderson hypothesize that one explanation for the persistence of the retaliation cycle is fundamental attribution error, discussed in Chapter 4. In fundamental attribution error—you will recall—people describe the negative behaviors of others as due to dispositional factors (he's mean), and their own negative behavior as due to situational factors (it was the right thing to do, considering the circumstances). DeWall and Anderson (2011) write: "people become caught in a web in which members perceive the other party as acting out of malice or evil and perceive their own behavior as appropriate responses to the situation at hand" (p. 24).

Beyond the escalation cycle, DeWall and Anderson contend that aggression and violence spring from a wide range of factors. "If you want to create people who are predisposed to aggression and violence, begin by depriving them of resources necessary to meet basic needs—physical, emotional, psychological, and social" (p. 26). Then, provide them with multiple examples and models of aggression and violence, especially examples that appear to work. And then, provide them with cognitive beliefs and values that dehumanize potential human targets, especially groups of people who are unlike the in-group. Then expose them to various forms of violence and destruction to the point where they become desensitized to it. Finally, provide the proper behavioral-cognitive scripts, and you should have the desired level of violence (DeWall & Anderson, 2011).

I³ Theory

In an expansion of the GAM, **I³ Theory** (pronounced "I-cubed theory") has been recently developed. Similar to GAM, I³ Theory is designed to provide an organized structure for understanding: (a) the process by which a given factor promotes aggression, and (b) how multiple risk factors inter-relate to create or reduce aggression (Slotter & Finkel, 2011). I³ Theory organizes the many aggression risk factors into three categories: (1) *instigating* triggers, which are discrete incidents that arouse tendencies or predispositions that are conducive to aggression; (2) *impelling* forces, which are forces that increase the likelihood of an aggressive action following the instigating trigger; and (3) *inhibiting* forces, which are factors that increase the likelihood that aggression will be mitigated or contained (Shaver & Mikulincer, 2011). I³ Theory differs from GAM in that it incorporates recent research on self-regulation as a core emphasis of the theory, and it specifies different, novel ways in which aggression risk factors produce aggression and violence (Slotter & Finkel, 2011). Recent research by Maldonado, DiLillo, and Hoffman (2015) found that I³ theory provides a very promising strategy for dealing with intimate partner aggression and violence, especially the emotion regulation aspects of the theory.

GAM and I³ Theory represent the new, emerging meta-theories that have been formulated to organize and integrate the many mini-theories that have been discussed in earlier sections of the chapter. Both provide an excellent frame of reference for future research on human aggression and violence.

OVERT AND COVERT ACTS OF AGGRESSION

Rolf Loeber and Magda Stouthamer-Loeber (1998) recommend that researchers on aggression and violence be mindful of two types of aggressive actions: overt and covert. According to Loeber and Stouthamer-Loeber, the two forms of aggression are different in (1) behavior patterns, (2) emotions, (3) cognitions, and (4) development (See **Table 5-2**). Behaviorally, overt aggression usually involves direct confrontation with victims and the administration of physical harm or threats of physical harm. Covert aggression, on the other hand, does not involve direct confrontation but relies on concealment, dishonesty, or sneaky behavior. It is similar to the passive-aggressive behavior discussed earlier in the chapter. In many instances, overt aggression decreases with age, while covert aggression increases

TABLE 5-2 Overt and Covert Aggressive Actions

Aggression	Behavior Patterns	Emotions	Cognitions	Development
Overt	Direct confrontation with victims; generally decreases with age.	Anger, high level of arousal and violence.	Lacks social cognitions for coming up with nonaggressive solutions.	Aggression begins early, especially in boys.
Covert	Concealment, dishonesty, sneaky behavior; increases with age.	Less emotion; crimes such as fraud, larceny, and theft.	Relies on cognitive capabilities, such as planfulness, deceitfulness.	Can evolve as well-learned strategy to escape punishment.

with age (Loeber, Lahey, & Thomas, 1991; Stanger, Achenbach, & Verhulst, 1997). However, children who exhibit serious forms of overt aggression (violence) tend to increase their violence as they get older, and often commit both violent and property crimes as adults (Loeber & Stouthamer-Loeber, 1998).

Emotionally, anger is usually an important ingredient in most overt acts of aggression, while more neutral emotions are characteristic of covert actions. Violent actions are usually accompanied by high levels of arousal brought on by anger. Covert actions, on the other hand, tend to be less emotional in nature. They include, for example, fraud, theft, embezzlement, burglary, and other white-collar or property offenses. Covert and overt aggression can also be distinguished on the basis of the cognitions that accompany them. As we explained in this chapter, violent persons (overt aggression) tend to have cognitive deficiencies that make it difficult for them to come up with nonaggressive solutions to interpersonal conflicts and disputes. Overt aggressors also have hostile attributional biases that contribute to violence-prone cognitive processing. On the other hand, people who use covert aggression as a preferred strategy do not demonstrate the degree of cognitive deficiencies in solving their interpersonal problems, nor do they manifest a hostile attributional bias. "Instead, it is postulated that most covert acts are facilitated by specific cognitive capabilities, such as planfulness (i.e., casing situations prior to theft), preoccupations with consumables and property, and lying to escape detection" (Loeber & Stouthamer-Loeber, 1998, p. 250). Occupationally related crimes, such as theft of company property, the misuse of information, or software piracy, are often committed with planning and forethought. Some crime committed through the use of computers, called cybercrime, is also a good example of covert actions of aggression. Examples are computer intrusion (hacking), cyberstalking, and cyberbullying, all discussed more fully in Chapter 15.

Developmentally, overt aggression generally begins early, especially in boys, as seen, for example, in the case of life-course-persistent offenders. However, Loeber and Stouthamer-Loeber suggest that development of overt aggressive behavior does not necessarily parallel the development of covert actions. Instead, "some children have never been socialized by their parents to be honest and to respect the property of others. This is common among neglectful parents or parents who hold an indistinct or a weak moral stance in these respects" (1998, p. 251). Honesty and respect for the property of others are instilled by parents' or caretakers' teaching and the prosocial models they offer their children. Some covert actions, especially lying, can also evolve as a well-learned strategy that serves to minimize the chances of detection and punishment by adults.

It should be emphasized that not all overt aggressors who engage in violence start early. As Loeber and Stouthamer-Loeber note, "It is necessary to account for the emergence of violence in individuals during adulthood who do not have a history of aggression earlier in their lives" (1998, p. 246). These *late-onset types* represent a minority of adult violent offenders, but the hypothesis does suggest that not all highly aggressive and violent individuals manifested aggression in childhood.

Reactive and Proactive Forms of Aggression

Kenneth Dodge and his colleagues (Dodge, Lochman, Harnish, Bates, & Pettit, 1997) have suggested that another way of classifying aggression in children (and adults) is to make a distinction between reactive aggression and proactive aggression. **Reactive aggression** includes anger expressions, temper tantrums, and vengeful hostility, and more generally "hot-blooded" aggressive acts. **Proactive aggression**, on the other hand, includes bullying, domination, teasing, name-calling, and coercive acts—in other words, more "cold-blooded" aggressive actions. Reactive aggression appears to be a reaction to frustration and is associated with a lack of control due to high states of arousal. In general, reactive aggression is a hostile act displayed in response to a perceived threat or provocation. Proactive aggression, by contrast, is less emotional, and more driven by expectations of rewards. "Proactive aggression is unprovoked, deliberate, goal-directed behavior used to influence or coerce a peer" (Hubbard et al., 2001, p. 269). Reactive aggression has its theoretical roots in the frustration-aggression model proposed by Berkowitz (1989) discussed earlier. The theoretical roots of proactive aggression are found in social learning theory, which, as we learned previously, states that aggression is acquired behavior that is controlled and maintained by reinforcement. It is highly similar to the concept of instrumental aggression. Reliable observations of these two forms of aggression have been found in children (as young as three to six years of age) through teacher ratings, peer ratings, clinical psychiatric records, and direct observations of peer interactions by researchers (Dodge & Coie, 1987; Dodge et al., 1997; Poulin & Boivin, 2000).

Reactively aggressive children, compared with proactively aggressive children, display greater problems in social and psychological adjustment (Dodge et al., 1997). Psychological adjustment problems include a lack of emotional control when angry, accompanied by sleep disorders, depressive symptoms, and personality disorders. On average, these problems emerged around age four to five. In addition, reactive aggression is related to the tendency to over attribute hostile intent to peers in ambiguous provocation situations (hostile attribution bias) (Hubbard et al., 2001). That is, when a reactive aggressive child interprets a peer's behavior as intentionally harmful or aggressive, he is far more likely to respond with angry retaliation or even violence.

Dodge (1991) proposed that reactive and proactive aggression originate from different social experiences and develop independently. According to Dodge, reactive aggression develops in reaction to a harsh, threatening, and unpredictable environment or abusive or cold parenting (Vitaro, Brendgen, & Barker, 2006). Proactive aggression, on the other hand, develops as a result of exposure to aggressive role models who value the use of aggression to resolve conflict or advance personal interests (Vitaro et al., 2006). However, Vitaro et al. are quick to point out that both proactive and reactive aggression may not only be fostered by different social environments but may also be influenced by differences in temperamental and genetic factors. That is, reactive aggression appears to be associated with a temperamental disposition toward anxiety, angry reactivity, emotional impulsiveness, and inattention. Proactive aggression appears to be less affected by temperament and is more based on beliefs that aggressive behavior will bring rewards and positive outcomes. Furthermore, preliminary research results suggest that reactive aggression develops earlier in the life span than proactive aggression, and the two types of aggression seem to follow different developmental trajectories (Vitaro & Brendgen, 2005).

Gender Differences in Aggression

While boys engage in more overt aggression and direct confrontation as they grow up, it is not clear if boys are generally more aggressive than girls. Furthermore, contemporary thought cautions against adopting a simple gender binary or division. Although researchers consistently identify participants as boys or girls, men or women, and males or females, it is clear today that gender exists on a continuum. Boys who identify themselves as boys may still possess feminine characteristics, and girls who identify themselves as girls may still possess masculine characteristics. Furthermore, some individuals prefer to consider themselves gender neutral or to self-identify with the gender other than that which was ascribed to them at birth. With these cautions in mind, it is nonetheless apparent that *physical* aggression is more prevalent among males than females, and this consistent finding holds across hundreds of studies and across nations (Archer, 2004; Campbell, 2006; Shaver & Mikulincer, 2011). What about other forms of aggression?

The current work of cognitive psychologists suggests that there may be socialized differences in the way girls and boys construct their worlds. Social learning theorists have long held that girls are "socialized" differently than boys, or taught not to be overtly aggressive. Anne Campbell (1993, p. 19) argued that "boys are not simply more aggressive than girls; they are aggressive in a different way." Other researchers concur with this observation (Hawkins, Pepler, & Craig, 2001; Lumley, McNeil, Herschell, & Bahl, 2002; Wood, Cowan, & Baker, 2002). According to Campbell, boys and girls are born with the potential to be equally aggressive, but girls are socialized not to be overtly aggressive, whereas boys are encouraged to be overtly aggressive "to defend" themselves.

Interestingly, research supports the observation that boys and girls are equally physically aggressive toward their peers when they are toddlers, but that this pattern soon changes as they grow older and enter their elementary school years (Xie, Farmer, & Cairns, 2003). Loeber and

Stouthamer-Loeber (1998, p. 253) conclude from their review of the research that "in general, gender differences in aggression, as expressed by frustration and rage, are not documented in infancy." They note that only in the preschool period (three to five years of age) do observable gender differences begin to emerge, with boys displaying more overt aggression than girls. Overt aggression becomes especially prominent in boys from elementary school age onward. Boys are taught to be tough, not to cry, to take on the bullies and physically defend themselves. However, many researchers report that girls are more likely to engage in relationship or interpersonal forms of aggression rather than the physical forms of pushing and hitting (Casey-Cannon, Hayward, & Gowen, 2001; Crick & Zahn-Waxler, 2003; Prinstein, Boergers, & Vernberg, 2001). For example, researchers (Björkqvist, Lagerspetz, & Kaukianinen, 1992; Cairns, Cairns, Neckerman, Ferguson, & Gariépy, 1989) find that girls and women tend to use more covert, indirect, and verbal forms of aggression, such as character defamation and ostracism. Other researchers report that girls are far more likely to employ *relational aggression*, such as abandoning one friend in favor of another, spreading malicious gossip, or ridiculing another's physical traits (e.g., their facial features, weight, or general demeanor) (Crick, 1995; Crick & Grotpeter, 1995; Crick & Zahn-Waxler, 2003; Garside & Klimes-Dougan, 2002; Loeber & Stouthamer-Loeber, 1998).

Some researchers (e.g., Moffitt, Caspi, Rutter, & Silva, 2001) hypothesize that the gender differences in aggression and antisocial behavior develop because of a higher exposure of boys to cumulative risk factors. On the other hand, other researchers (e.g., Ribeaud & Eisner, 2010) conclude from their research that, although boys are exposed to a higher cumulative risks than girls, boys also seem to be more vulnerable because they are expected to be more aggressive and "masculine" in many ways. Even though girls are increasingly involved in aggressive activities, such as some competitive sports, there are subtle differences in the manner in which coaches, parents, and spectators respond to their actions. For example, girls are more likely than boys to be given a hug or a high five for a job well done.

In conclusion, there is growing recognition that gender differences in aggression are not simply due to biology, but are primarily due to cultural and socialization processes that promote different kinds of aggression. Environmental cues are also important in cognitive scripts and in the aggressive strategies individuals employ for various situations. Which script or strategy an individual employs is dependent on which environmental cues are present.

EFFECTS OF MEDIA VIOLENCE

Youth today are growing up in a media-saturated environment (Gentile & Walsh, 2002), and much of this environment has a violence theme. In the first nationwide survey of video game play in the United States, researchers learned that 97 percent of adolescents (ages 12 to 17 years) play computer, Web, portable, tablet, or console video games (Lenhart et al., 2008; Willoughby, Adachi, & Good, 2011). Ninety-nine percent of boys and 94 percent of girls play the games (Lenhart et al., 2008). Nearly half of the teens play video games on a mobile device, such as a cell phone, I-pad, I-pod, or other handheld systems. Nearly a third play on a daily basis, and another 21 percent play at least several times a week. An estimated 80 percent of teens play five or more different game genres, and 40 percent play eight or more types of games (Lenhart et al., 2008). Most significantly for this chapter, content analyses of video games indicate that approximately 90 percent of them contain some violent content, and that half of the games include serious violent actions directed at others (Surette & Maze, 2014). With the variety of portable, wireless devices available today, youth and adults have access to games at all times, unless they are in a location where use is restricted, such as at school.

Even before the video game explosion, surveys estimated that the average American child sees more than 100,000 violent episodes and some 20,000 murders on television before reaching adolescence (Myers, 1996). Other studies estimated there were four scenes of violence portrayed on network television to every one scene expressing affection. Note that this does not include the huge range of "non-network" programming that offers an increasing number of options for viewers. A three-year study (1994–1997) by four universities on violence on American television revealed that 90 percent of movies shown on television include violence (National Cable Television Association, 1998). Violence was found most frequently on subscription television (85% on premium cable and 59% on basic cable), while the lowest incidence of violence (18%) was found on Public Broadcasting Service (PBS) stations. Across three years of the study, nearly 40 percent of the violent incidents on television were initiated by "good" characters, who are likely perceived as attractive role models. In 67 percent of the programs, violence was portrayed within a humorous context. In general, the study found that most media violence is glamorized and that the long-term negative consequences of violent behavior are rarely depicted. Nearly three-quarters of violent scenes contain no remorse, criticism, punishment, or emotional reactions from the perpetrators. Overall, the survey found that the percentage of programs on television that contain some violence remained unchanged over the three-year period of study. In a special report, the Parents Television Council (2007) concluded that television violence increased between the years 1998 and 2006 by 309 percent, and there is reason to believe the amount of violence has further increased in recent years.

The research community is sharply divided on the long-term effects of violent media on aggressive behavior. To date, however, the overwhelming bulk of the research *suggests* that portrayals of violence on television and movies may have a significant effect on the frequency and type of aggressive behavior expressed by America's youth (Bushman, Gollwitzer, & Cruz, 2015). Media violence appears to encourage, stimulate, and reinforce aggressive behavior in some individuals. Over the past 45 years, research has periodically demonstrated that media violence *viewing* is a contributing factor to the development of aggression and violence in *some* children, adolescents, and young adults (Huesmann, Moise-Titus, Podolski, & Eron, 2003).

Media violence does appear to influence children more strongly than adults, as they seem to be more susceptible to its long-term effects. Interestingly, the Huesmann et al. (2003) study discovered that violent films and TV programs that have the most deleterious effects on children are not always the ones that adults perceive as the most violent. Research suggests that violent scenes in which children can identify with the perpetrator of the violence, and those in which the perpetrator gets rewarded for the violence, have the greatest negative impact on children. It is not necessarily the level of violence per se.

Viewing violence and playing violent games are separate activities, however. Although violence is a common theme in the movie, TV, and video game media, game playing is an active enterprise. Is it more or less likely to have a negative effect on those who play? A survey by Bushman et al. (2015) found that 8 of 10 media researchers believe that violent media *games* increase aggression. The survey also indicated that both pediatricians and parents agree.

Although the largest body of research on media violence thus far has concentrated on televised violence, the research community in recent years has shifted its attention to violent video games (Murray, 2008). Similar to studies on violent film and TV programs, recent research consistently suggests that heavy exposure to violent video games may be significantly linked to increases in aggressive behavior, aggressive thoughts, aggressive feelings, and decreases in helping behavior (Anderson, 2004; Anderson & Bushman, 2001; Anderson et al., 2008; Dill & Dill, 1998). As we see shortly, not all researchers agree with these conclusions.

Before proceeding with this discussion, it is important to distinguish between short-term and long-term effects of violent media on aggressive behavior. Research indicates that different cognitive processes are involved (Huesmann, 2007). Although there is compelling evidence that exposure to violent electronic media has both short-term and long-term effects, we are particularly concerned here about long-term effects. They occur as a result of observational learning, desensitization, and storing violent and aggressive material into the thought process. Young children are especially open to new learning, and these early experiences often have a greater impact during the early development years than learning events that occur during adulthood. Thus, if young children learn that violence or aggressive behavior is acceptable, this information is likely to follow them to and through adulthood. To this effect, Huesmann et al. (2003) write, "In recent theorizing, long-term relations have been ascribed mainly to acquisition through observation learning of three social-cognitive structures: schemas about a hostile world, scripts for social problem solving that focus on aggression, and normative beliefs that aggression is acceptable" (p. 201). Over time, and with frequent exposure to aggressive behavior, children develop beliefs (schemas) that the world is basically a hostile place, that aggression is an acceptable social behavior, and that the best way to solve conflicts and to get things is to be aggressive. These aspects may actually become part of the personality over the long run.

Research by Krahé and Möller (2004) supports these hypotheses. They found that adolescents were more likely to condone aggression and to display hostile attribution bias toward ambiguous cues if they were frequently exposed to violent electronic games. Another study (i.e., Funk, Baldacci, Pasold, & Baumgardner, 2004) demonstrated that high exposure to violent electronic games is associated with lower levels of empathy and more positive attitudes toward violent behavior in general. This study also indicated that violent video games may have greater impact than other forms of violent entertainment media, such as films or television programs. This is likely due to the interactive component of video games, whereby the individual is a virtual participant rather than a passive observer of the violence.

Huesmann and his colleagues (2003) reported that strong long-term effects of media violence observed in early childhood appear to carry over into adulthood. They concluded:

> Overall, these results suggest that both males and females from all social strata and all levels of initial aggressiveness are placed at increased risk for the development of adult aggressive and violent behavior when they view a high and steady diet of violent TV shows in early childhood. (p. 128)

The effects of violent video or electronic games on the development of aggressive behavior received considerable scrutiny after a series of school shootings by avid players of such games occurred during the late 1990s and early 2000s. In April 1999, public concern was especially strong after 13 persons were murdered and 23 were wounded during a shooting spree by two students at Columbine High School in Colorado. The two assailants were considered social outcasts and seemed preoccupied with the violence presented in the media, music, and video games. In the years since that tragedy, reports of other highly publicized shootings indicated that the perpetrators frequently played violent video games. For example, the young man responsible for the Newtown, Connecticut school massacre in 2012 apparently spent hours in his room at that activity. The impact of violent electronic games is not restricted to the United States. It occurs in other countries as well, for example, Japan (Anderson, 2004; Anderson et al., 2008). In another example, Krahé and Möller (2004) described an incident that occurred in Germany in April 2002, in which 17 people were killed in a shooting spree by an expelled student who had spent much of his time playing violent electronic games.

However, similar to the effects of TV and movies, the research community is divided about the long-term effects of violent video games, and the empirical evidence has been challenged at many levels. Some scholars argue that many of the studies on video games are inconclusive and can be criticized on methodological grounds (Elson & Ferguson, 2014; Ferguson et al., 2008; Grimes & Bergen, 2008; Gunter, 2008; Savage, 2008; Savage & Yancey, 2008). Certainly, the overwhelming majority of individuals who play violent video games do not commit violent acts. Therefore, the oversimplified position that violent video media or games cause or even promote violence must be tempered. It may well be that exposure to media violence does increase violence and aggressive behavior for individuals who are already aggressive and prone toward violence. Media violence may not do the same for those individuals less prone toward physical aggression and violence.

In October 2002, ten people in Washington, D.C., were killed at random over a 23-day period. One of the shooters was 17-year-old Lee Malvo. Malvo's defense team argued that the youth had been brainwashed and trained to kill while playing violent video games depicting sniper attacks (Olson, 2004). While this may appear to be anecdotal evidence that extensive exposure to violent video games is harmful, it should also be noted that Malvo had been exposed to a wide variety of risk factors throughout his early life, including apparent rejection by his biological father and instability in his home life. He had also demonstrated a variety of antisocial actions, such as cruelty to animals, including apparently killing at least 20 cats (Olson, 2004).

Thus, if there is a research consensus emerging, it is that violent video games may be one risk factor, and when coupled with other risk factors, it may contribute to antisocial or even violent behavior. It is unlikely that video games contribute directly to make a child grow up to be a killer or even become excessively aggressive. "A review of both aggregate studies and experimental evidence does not provide support for the supposition that exposure to media violence causes criminally violent behavior" (Savage & Yancey, 2008, p. 786). However, a recent review of the research literature concluded: "The evidence strongly suggests that exposure to violent video games is a causal risk factor for increased aggressive behavior, aggressive cognition, and aggressive affect and for decreased empathy and prosocial behavior" (Anderson, Shibuya, Ihori, Swing, Bushman, et al., 2010, p. 151). Willoughby et al. (2011) found that adolescents who play violent video games across their high school years demonstrated steeper increases in aggression over time compared to those who reported less violent video game playing, The authors concluded that "violent video game play may influence an individual's level of direct aggression by promoting aggressive beliefs and attitudes and creating aggressive schema, aggressive behavioral scripts, and aggressive expectations" (p. 11). Adding to the controversy, one study (Adachi & Willoughby, 2011) found that it was the video game competitiveness—not the violent content—that may be responsible for encouraging aggressive behavior, at least in the short term.

Whether the exposure directly leads to increased *violence* remains an unanswered question. Willoughby et al. speculate that the long-term relationship between violent video play and aggression may be different for adolescents and adults (25 years or older) because of changes in brain development during adolescence and into young adulthood. As we learned in Chapter 3, brain development and self-regulation maturation are not complete until sometime after age 25 and beyond. These brain changes are likely to reduce violent behavior patterns as one gets older, for most but not all. Another contributing factor may be that each upcoming generation is more sophisticated about electronics in general, and for them the "fantasy factor" may have less impact on their real-life view of the world. One aspect that demands further investigation, however, is the possibility that certain personalities may be significantly more susceptible to the effects of violent media than others, regardless of age (Bettencourt, Talley, Benjamin, & Valentine, 2006).

In addition, research to date on the effects of violent games has largely concentrated on content to the neglect of other factors in digital or electronic games (Breuer, Scharkow, & Quandt, 2015). These include the social context in which the games are played (e.g., with aggressive peers), the outcome of the game, and how the games are played (interactive or passive) (Breuer et al., 2015). For example, highly competitive people usually do not like losing, even in digital games, and this might increase hostility and later aggression toward the winning gamer. Interestingly, approximately two-thirds of the U.S. gamers frequently played with other gamers in person (Breuer et al., 2015). Also, some video games are an active process where the player cocreates the violent content; others are passive games in which the gamer watches the violence but plays very little role in creating it (Surette & Maze, 2015). According to Surette and Maze, active participation in video games may be important: "The argument is that people are more likely to learn when they are actively involved and therefore video games players would learn aggressive and criminal behaviors more readily" (p. 360).

Therefore, future research that focuses on other factors besides content may help settle the debate on the effects of violent digital media. Although the research is trending toward the negative effects of violent media on certain individuals, an expansion of the research focus may bring the debate closer toward a tentative conclusion. Finally, as video games have become more life-like and interactive, the concern has grown that they may engender increased levels of copycat aggressive and criminal behavior in the young. (See **Box 5-3** for discussion of a study on this topic.)

Copycat Crime or Contagion Effect

To this point we have focused upon the effects of violence in the entertainment media. However, even news reports of violence may be problematic. Like entertainment media, the news media may provide aggressive models or may produce a **copycat or contagion effect**. This is a tendency in

RESEARCH FOCUS

BOX 5-3   Copycat Gamers

Video games are so common in today's culture that some observers have predicted that they already have or will eventually replace the board games of old. Gamers, both male and female, self-report spending hours at a time on various electronic devices, challenging their opponents, or placing themselves in the character of a hero or a wrongdoer.

Also common is the criticism of video games, particularly those that extoll crime, violence, or sexism. Video game playing is different than simply watching media portrayals, because game playing is not a passive activity, even though some games require more participation than others. In many games, the participants "kill" others; in some they steal, rape, or torture. Surette and Maze (2015, p. 361) observed that "As video games have become more life-like, concern over their ability to generate copycat crime has also grown." As mentioned in the text, however, there is dispute about the extent of a direct link between game playing and actual behavior outside of the gaming context.

In one of the few experimental studies examining copycat crime among inmates, Surette and Maze (2015) compared individuals who were self-identified video gamers (65.5%) to those who labeled themselves as nonvideo game players (34.5%). Participants—249 adults who were incarcerated in a county correctional facility—were diverse in age, gender, race, and ethnicity. All were asked whether they had attempted something against the law that they had learned from any media source—in other words, the researchers were trying to measure whether their participants had engaged in copycat crime. About 25 percent said they had. To determine the extent to which factors other than simply game playing might influence crime, the researchers also examined their participants' real-world crime models, their need for fame, their empathy, their identification with media characters, their criminal innovativeness, and their immersion in media content.

Surette and Maze found there were no statistical differences in either committing or trying a copycat crime between the gamers and the nongamers. Those who did commit copycat crimes tended to be males with prior arrests and, interestingly, fewer family and friends as criminal models. The copycat criminals also identified more closely with the media characters in video games, felt more immersed in the media content, and saw themselves as being innovative and empathic more than their noncopycat counterparts. Surette and Maze conclude that "The combination of immersion and identification is hypothesized to raise the risk of committing a copycat crime for media engaged criminally predisposed individuals" (p. 371).

The study was exploratory and had a number of limitations, as recognized by the researchers. Nevertheless, they noted that it should prompt further study of copycat crimes. The inmates who were influenced by media typically said they had copied a crime early in their criminal careers, often as teenagers. The empathy finding also suggests that people who engage in copycat crime may be more apt to identify with the characters they adopt while gaming.

Questions for Discussion

1. Choose three crime-related video games that are commonly played (e.g., Grand Theft Auto). Do these games include characters who are likeable as well as unlikeable? Do they suggest unusual crime scenarios that might prompt a person to want to attempt similar actions?
2. What is the significance of the finding that participants reported copycat crime during their early criminal careers?
3. What is the significance of the finding of no differences in copycat crime between gamers and nongamers? In the case of nongamers who reported committing copycat crime, what were they copying?

some people to model or copy an activity portrayed in the entertainment or news media. It is similar to social learning discussed earlier in the chapter, in which people imitate the behavior—such as hitting or punching—of a model in their day-to-day environment. In this case, however, the models usually are media or news figures who typically receive wide-spread attention. "Copycat followers" often seek similar widespread recognition and significance.

Contagion effect is said to occur when action depicted in the media or digital games is assessed by certain individuals as a good idea and then mimicked. An ingenious bank robbery, dramatized on television, might be imitated. A person immersed in a video game may be prompted to try out his escapades in real life. The video game *Grand Theft Auto*—now in its fifth iteration, published by Rockstar Games—presents a case in point. Its three main characters carry out various heist missions in their efforts to avoid law enforcement authorities, and players control their actions through ever challenging sequences across expansive geographical territory, both on foot and employing different and creative modes of transportation. The highly acclaimed game has been referred to as the best action game of all time and the most immersive, and it has won numerous awards for its artistic and graphical design. *Grand Theft Auto* also has been heavily criticized for its portrayal of women, torture, and violence.

SCHOOL-SHOOTER COPYCATS.   Another media-related tragic illustration of the copycat effect can be found in a series of school shootings, discussed briefly earlier and again in Chapter 10, that began in 1997. In October of that year, a 16-year-old, having just stabbed his mother to death, arrived at the high school in Pearl, Mississippi, and began randomly shooting his class-mates, killing two and wounding seven. Less than two months later, a 14-year-old boy opened fire on a group of fellow high school students participating in a prayer circle in West Paducah, Kentucky. He killed two schoolmates and wounded five others. The West Paducah incident received worldwide media coverage for several weeks, accompanied by extensive stories about the shooter. A few months later, on March 24, 1998, two boys, ages 13 and 11, armed with seven handguns and three rifles, opened fire on their classmates as they gathered on the school play-ground in Jonesboro, Arkansas, killing four very young girls and their teacher and wounding 10 others. Of the 15 killed or wounded, only one was male, suggesting that the young shooters were aiming specifically at girls.

After Jonesboro and exactly one month later, a 14-year-old male student in Edinboro, Pennsylvania, began shooting during a school dance, killing a teacher. This incident was followed by another shooting less than a month later in Fayetteville, Tennessee, resulting in the death of a student. A week later, a 15-year-old male in Springfield, Oregon, walked into the high school cafeteria and began shooting randomly at fellow students, firing 50 rounds from a .22-caliber semi-automatic rifle in less than a minute. As he stopped to reload, the young shooter was tackled and disarmed by a varsity wrestler. During that one minute, however, he managed to kill two classmates and wounded 22 others. He had also shot both his parents prior to leaving for school. Less than two weeks later, on June 15, 1998, a 14-year-old student, armed with a .32-caliber semiautomatic handgun, opened fire in the hallway of a high school as students took final exams, wounding a bas-ketball coach and a volunteer aide. All of these young shooters had an inordinate interest in guns, had troubled backgrounds, knew the details of the previous school shootings, and had a strong fas-cination with violence presented through the media. Thus, both media violence and the contagion or copycat effect seem to be implicated, along with other factors, in line with a cumulative risk model or cascade developmental model of offending.

Note that all of the above incidents occurred before the 1999 Columbine incident, which involved two shooters and ended in 13 deaths and multiple injuries. That incident is unique in that it involved so many deaths but also was publicized extensively, even as it was occurring: broadcast cameras were focused on the school property, and images of students signaling from windows or being guided out of the school buildings were widely disseminated, as were photos of the locations where the shootings occurred and images of the two shooters holding their guns. Perhaps because of the widespread publicity, the copycat effect may have been especially strong in that case. The incident in some sense set up a cultural script for others to imitate (Larkin, 2009). For example, since the Columbine shooting, researchers studying school shootings have found that a significant number of them have been modeled after the Columbine incident (Larkin, 2009). In Salt Lake City in January, 2012, police arrested two youths who had allegedly planned to plant bombs in their school; they learned that one of the youths had actually traveled to Littleton to interview the prin-cipal of Columbine to learn more about that attack. In other thwarted attempts, students indicated they wanted to carry out "another Columbine."

COPYCAT TERRORISTS.   The copycat effect may also play a role in terrorism. For instance, Surette (2014) observes that "the consensus regarding copycat terrorism is that it is especially strong following a well-publicized, successful act using a novel approach" (p. 706). Not all perpetrators are directly associated with a known terrorist organization, although some have obtained some degree of training or have attempted to join a group. About a month after two brothers entered the offices of the satirical publication Charlie Hebdo in Paris and killed 17 people there and at a kosher grocery store, a person shot to death a film director in an Internet café in Copenhagen as well as a security guard at a nearby synagogue. The brothers in the first incident allegedly received terrorist training; in the second incident, the perpetrator was said to be disaffected, had expressed allegiance to the terrorist group ISIS, and had intense hatred for Denmark. In 2015, two men were planning a mass attack against people attending a cultural event in Texas, at which images of the Prophet Mohammed were displayed. The men shot a security guard but were themselves killed before they were able to carry out their crime. Incidents such as this are widely publicized, but the media cannot be blamed for getting this information out. The opposite of a contagion effect is a deterrent effect; we never know how many similar crimes are prevented because someone is discouraged from carrying them out as a result of the media report.

In summary, exposure to media-portrayed violence and interactive digital games does not automatically promote aggression, but there is also little evidence of a "catharsis" or "letting off steam" effect. Some individuals are affected by media violence more than others. However, it is clear that no one causal factor alone accounts for more than a small proportion of variance of individual differences in aggressive behavior (Bartholow, Sestir, & Davis, 2005; Huesmann, 1998). Researchers have found evidence that positive parental models are likely to override violent models on television (Goldstein, 1975; Huesmann et al., 2003). Moreover, media violence seems to have substantially less effect on families in which the parents do not rely on aggressive behavior for solving problems (Wright et al., 2001). Overall, though, most of the information on the copycat effect comes from anecdotal accounts, similar to what has been portrayed above. The preliminary research by Surette and Maze (2015), highlighted in **Box 5-3** above, is an exception. Since copycat crimes are not counted in any systematic way, there is considerable debate concerning the extent to which they occur (Surette, 2014). Based on his research, however, Surette estimates that one in four at-risk individuals have engaged in copycat crime.

Interestingly, in recent years there has been a renewed interest in investigating whether a certain proportion of firesetters may be especially prone to be copycat offenders (Doley, Ferguson, & Surette, 2013; Lambie, Randel, & McDowell, 2014). The topic of firesetting will be covered in Chapter 15.

SUMMARY AND CONCLUSIONS

In this chapter, we reviewed the major psychological perspectives on aggression and violence. Answers to what can be done about aggression and violent crime rest ultimately on one's perspective of human nature. If one believes that aggression is innate and part of our evolutionary heritage, a position held by mainstream psychoanalytic and ethological thought, then the conclusion must be that aggression is part of life, and that little can be done to alter this basic ingredient of human nature. Clues for reducing aggression are found in the behavior demonstrated throughout the animal kingdom. If, on the other hand, one believes that human aggression is acquired, then the key becomes principles of human learning and thought, and hope that one can change this acquired behavior for the betterment of humankind. The distinction between the innate and learning viewpoints has been somewhat oversimplified, but most contemporary theories on aggression fall within one or the other camp. At this point, the learning perspective has garnered considerably more empirical support than the innate perspective. Cognitive factors are especially important in explanations of human aggression.

Complicating the above, though, is the increasing amount of research being done in the biological sciences, most particularly relating to the brain and to human genetics. Researchers are acquiring extensive information about the contribution of genes to physical characteristics and susceptibility to medical problems. Many believe that they will eventually link genes to a variety of behavioral problems and mental disorders as well. It is crucial to keep in mind, though, that although some genes may *predispose* individuals to certain disorders that may lead to violence or other antisocial behavior, genes do not *determine* behavior.

Furthermore, as more research data are published, even the *learning* perspective becomes increasingly complex, and additional factors must be considered. For one thing, physiological arousal certainly plays a major role in aggressive and violent behavior, as suggested by Berkowitz (1989). High levels of arousal seem to *facilitate* (again, not cause) aggressive behavior in certain situations. Extremely high arousal seems to interfere with our sense of self-awareness and internal control, rendering us more susceptible to environmental cues and to mindless or habitual behaviors. In this sense, under very high arousal, we may not stop to consider the consequences of our violent behavior.

The different classifications of aggressive behavior were also emphasized in this chapter. Overt and covert forms of aggression must be considered in any discussion of crime. Overt aggressors are more likely to be involved in violent crimes, whereas covert aggressors are more prone to be involved in property offenses. And although the conventional wisdom has been that boys are more likely to commit highly aggressive crimes, the evidence suggests that girls may be equally involved in aggressive behavior of a different kind. Gender differences in aggressive behavior are believed to be mainly due to socialization factors.

Situational and neurophysiological factors also contribute significantly to aggressive behavior. Aggressive stimuli, including weapons, crowds, pollution, temperature, and central nervous system pathology all must be entertained as possible contributors. Social learning theorists also note that the media and the models they provide substantially affect our attitudes, values, and overall impressions about violence as well as our behavior. Attitudes, beliefs, and thoughts refer to the cognitive processes that are beginning to emerge as contenders for a leading role in the psychological explanation of criminal behavior. Operant and classical conditioning remain important, but they do not adequately address the many intricacies of criminal behavior.

The controversial topic of violence in the entertainment and news media was addressed. In light of rapid developments in technology, it is impossible to shelter children and adolescents from violent images in a realistic manner, though it is possible to place limits on that exposure. Media violence, though, is only one of many risk factors in the development of violent behavior. Nevertheless, for some children, excessive exposure to such images can have significant negative effects on their development. With children and adolescents increasingly exposed to video games, including violent games, researchers are avidly exploring the effects of this exposure. The overwhelming evidence points to negative effects for some children and adolescents. These effects include both aggressive behavior and an insensitivity or indifference to violence. Although there are individual differences in reactions to violent images and games, research results thus far suggest there is cause for concern that excessive exposure to violence of this sort cannot be good for the emotional health of children and adolescents.

Key Concepts

Aggression
Cognitive-neoassociation model
Cognitive scripts model
Contagion effect (copycat effect)
Displaced aggression theory
Evolutionary psychology
Excitation transfer theory
Frustration-aggression hypothesis
General aggression model
Hostile aggression
Hostile attribution bias
Hostile attribution model

I^3 Theory
Instrumental aggression
Passive-aggressive behaviors
Proactive aggression
Psychodynamic model (hydraulic model)
Reactive aggression
Ritualized aggression
Rumination
Territoriality
Violence
Weapons effect

Review Questions

1. What physiological factors have been associated with aggression?
2. What accounts for gender differences in aggression? Cite relevant research findings.
3. Define cognitive scripts and how they may be applied in situations where spontaneous violence could occur.
4. Define weapons effect and discuss how it may account for some of the violence in today's society.
5. Define hostile attribution bias and discuss how it might explain chronic aggression in young children.
6. Explain the difference between each of the following: overt and covert acts of aggression, cognitive scripts model and hostile attribution model; and reactive and proactive aggression.
7. Review the research presented in this chapter on the effects of the mass media on violence.
8. Does playing violent video games increase the probability that children and adolescents will behave in a violent manner?

6

Juvenile Delinquency

CHAPTER OBJECTIVES

- Contrast legal, social, and psychological definitions of delinquency.
- Identify the categories and extent of juvenile offending, including status and serious offending.
- Describe Moffitt's developmental theory of delinquency.
- Describe the dual systems model of risk taking among adolescents.
- Describe Patterson's coercion developmental theory.
- Introduce callous-unemotional traits as features of serious delinquency.
- Summarize features of effective programs for juvenile offenders.
- Explore primary and secondary prevention strategies.
- Highlight Multisystemic Therapy (MST) and Functional Family Therapy (FFT) as effective community-based approaches.

Juveniles may well be the most maligned age group in our society. Myths abound about their contribution to crime and the extent of damage for which they are responsible. During the last quarter of the twentieth century, it was common to read accounts of skyrocketing juvenile crime, young super-predators in our midst, declining morality in youth, and the woeful state of family life that was seen as a major contributor to juvenile vandalism, drug use, thievery, and violence. To some extent, these accounts were supported by statistics, particularly during the 1980s and early 1990s. However, fears were also fueled by atypical illustrations of juvenile crime, such as a particularly heinous account of a murder committed by a juvenile or those associated with a number of school shootings.

The first decade of the new century continued to see such atypical accounts, including school shootings, which have increased along with incidents of gun violence perpetrated by adults. Most recently, bullying, cyberbullying, which we discuss in more detail in Chapter 15, sexual assault, and dating violence have attracted media scrutiny. There is reason to be concerned about these activities and juvenile crime in general, although the behaviors may be less widespread than they appear to be based on media accounts. Juvenile crime is troubling, but it is not intractable. Since the mid-1990s, we have seen a decrease in crime committed by youths across most crime categories, including both property and violent crime, but there are periodic upward spikes. In addition, drug use has seen significant increases.

Juveniles as a group are responsible for a small percentage of arrests compared with adults, but they are arrested disproportionately compared with other age groups. This may be due to their naiveté at committing crime as well as the fact that they often commit crime in groups. Moreover, the typical juvenile is far more likely to be the victim than the perpetrator of a violent crime. Nevertheless, a significant number of juveniles do victimize one another, drug use persists, and the problem of youth violence has not disappeared. Thus, though we have made strides in understanding the factors leading to these behaviors and developing strategies for prevention and treatment, much work remains to be done.

In this chapter, we review the incidence, prevalence, and nature of delinquency and the developmental theories that have been proposed to explain it. We also discuss prevention and treatment strategies. In later chapters, we give some attention to treatment issues relating to specific juvenile offenders, such as juveniles who kill, juveniles with psychopathic characteristics, juvenile sex offenders, and juvenile firesetters.

DEFINITIONS OF DELINQUENCY

"Juvenile delinquency" is an imprecise and nebulous term for a wide variety of law- and norm-violating behavior. It can be viewed from a legal, social, or psychological perspective, and its definition varies according to the perspective.

Legal Definition

At first glance, a simple legal definition seems to suffice: *Delinquency is behavior against the criminal code committed by an individual who has not reached adulthood, as defined by state or federal law.* But the term "delinquency" has different connotations beyond this one sentence definition. As we noted in Chapter 1, the legal definition in some states also includes juvenile status offending, which is not behavior against the criminal code but is behavior prohibited only for juveniles. For example, running away, violating curfew laws, and truancy, all qualify as **status offenses**.

Even age is not a simple issue in the legal definition of delinquency. Although no state considers anyone above 18 a delinquent, some have provisions for "youthful offenders," who have not reached the age of 21 or may even be in their early twenties. Youthful offenders are processed in criminal courts, but sentencing options are typically more lenient for them. It is noteworthy that several high-profile cases involving accused school shooters across the United States receive little publicity after the initial reports, primarily because the youth are considered juveniles and their cases are not heard by criminal courts. In many states, teens under 18 charged with crimes begin in family or juvenile court, regardless of the seriousness of the crime, but prosecutors or judges have the authority to transfer the case to criminal court. As a recent example, seven high school football players in New Jersey, ranging in age from 15 to 17, were charged with hazing and sexual abuse of freshmen players. They were initially sent to family court, as required in that state. Prosecutors then announced that they would not transfer their cases to criminal court but would try their cases in family court, where publicity is unlikely to occur. It should be mentioned that teens convicted of sex crimes are required to register as sex offenders for at least 15 years, regardless of the type of court that convicted them.

A minority of states give criminal courts, rather than juvenile courts, *automatic* jurisdiction over juveniles at age 16 or 17. This includes two states, New York and North Carolina, in which the age is 16; in others it is 17. In that minority of states, cases in which 16- and 17-year-olds are charged are presumptively heard in criminal courts, but judges are given some leeway to transfer them to the juvenile system. Furthermore, all states *allow* juveniles—some as young as age seven—to be tried as adults in criminal courts under certain conditions and for certain offenses. To repeat then, even age is not a simple issue in the legal definition of delinquency.

In the 1990s, virtually all states enacted or expanded their transfer provisions, resulting in more transfers to criminal courts (Puzzanchera & Addie, 2014). Increasingly, more and more young offenders are moved to adult court in this manner. Under the legal definition of delinquency, a 14-year-old transferred to a criminal court is not a delinquent. Nevertheless, many criminal cases involving juveniles are still heard in juvenile or family courts. Interestingly, some researchers have noticed a trend in juvenile courts nationwide to be tougher on juveniles, not only being more willing to transfer them to criminal courts but also meting out harsher sentences than in the past (Viljoen, McLachlan, Wingrove, & Penner, 2010).

The decision about where a case will be heard—juvenile or criminal court—has important consequences for the juvenile. Juvenile courts—which are part of the family court system in many states—typically are more informal than adversarial, more rehabilitative than punitive, and they are generally closed to the public and the media. In the New Jersey high school football player case mentioned above, representatives of the news media sued—thus far unsuccessfully—for access to transcripts of the proceedings. The youths processed in juvenile courts have the same 6th Amendment Constitutional rights as adults except for the right to a jury trial, although some states allow jury trials in these courts as well. By comparison, a youth processed in criminal court faces the glare of publicity and the possibility of a long prison sentence if convicted. T. J. Lane, a school shooter in Ohio who killed three fellow students in a high school cafeteria in 2012, was convicted in criminal court and is serving three life sentences. In 2014, he briefly escaped from prison but was captured shortly thereafter (Outhall, 2014). On the other hand, a youth "convicted" in juvenile court may be incarcerated in a juvenile facility for rehabilitation purposes until he reaches adulthood, while a youth convicted of the same offense in criminal court may receive probation or a short sentence. On the whole, however, research indicates that juveniles sentenced in criminal courts get longer sentences than those in juvenile courts for similar crimes (Redding, 2010).

Many states do not have a legally defined age of criminal responsibility, that is, a minimum age of arrest for children (Snyder, Espiritu, Huizinga, Loeber, & Petechuk, 2003). The minimum age will also indicate at which point the child can be brought before a juvenile court for delinquency proceedings. When the minimum is specified, it varies from age six to age 10, depending on the state. Another interesting and rarely mentioned issue is that of the intellectually disabled individual. The shoplifter or exhibitionist with a mental age of 10 and a chronological age of 33 is not eligible for delinquency status, yet his mental abilities resemble those of children far more than those of adults. On the other hand, an eight-year-old "genius" with a mental age of 25 could presumably not be tried in criminal court in most states simply because of his mental age, though he could be tried on the basis of the crime he was alleged to have committed.

Social Definition

Social and psychological definitions of delinquency may overlap considerably, just as each overlaps with legal definitions. Social delinquency consists of a wide variety of youthful behaviors considered inappropriate, such as aggressive behavior, intimidation of others, truancy, bullying, petty theft, vandalism, or substance abuse. Note that not all are considered criminal. In addition, the behavior may or may not have come to the attention of the police. It is not unusual for "social delinquents" to be referred to community social service agencies or to juvenile courts, but they never legally become delinquents until and unless they are found in a hearing to have committed the crime for which they are charged, if a crime has indeed been committed. For example, a juvenile court intake officer may place a juvenile on "informal probation," giving him a second chance to be supervised in the community rather than formally referred to juvenile court where he faces the possibility of being adjudicated delinquent. Other options for dealing with social delinquents are diversion programs, whereby juveniles are steered away from formal court proceedings if they admit their offenses and participate in various programs, such as substance abuse treatment, restitution, or community service.

Psychological Definitions

Psychological definitions of delinquency usually include conduct disorder, antisocial behavior, externalizing disorder, or some form of mental disorder. In other words, from a psychological perspective, a "delinquent" would have a conduct disorder or would display serious antisocial behavior, such as firesetting or the sexual abuse of young children. **Conduct disorder**, discussed in Chapter 2, is a diagnostic term used to represent a group of behaviors characterized by *habitual* misbehavior, such as stealing, setting fires, running away from home, skipping school, destroying property, fighting, being cruel to animals and people, and frequently telling lies. Like the social delinquent, the psychological delinquent may or may not have been arrested for these behaviors.

Some of the behaviors, in fact, are not even against the criminal law. Likewise, behaviors associated with ODD or with ADHD, both discussed in Chapter 2, might not be against the criminal law.

The clinical term **antisocial behavior** is sometimes used rather than conduct disorder, ODD, or ADHD, particularly when clinicians prefer not to use formal diagnoses, or when a child or adolescent may not fit the criteria for these disorders. However, antisocial behavior is not much different. It, too, is reserved for more serious *habitual* misbehavior, especially a behavioral pattern that involves direct and harmful actions against others. Though it is similar to conduct disorder, it should be distinguished from the term *antisocial personality disorder,* a diagnostic label reserved for *adults*, many if not most of whom displayed conduct disorders as children or adolescents and continued serious offending well into adulthood. We discuss antisocial personality disorders in more detail in Chapter 7.

Finally, some juvenile offenders may be plagued with mental disorders, such as paraphilias (sexual disorders), severe depression, or psychotic disorders, which may be associated with delinquent behavior. It is important to point out that, in some instances, the mental disorder develops as a result of being held in juvenile correctional facilities. The connection between mental disorder and crime will be discussed in Chapter 8.

NATURE AND EXTENT OF JUVENILE OFFENDING

In 2013, just over half a million persons under age 18 were arrested by law enforcement officers in the United States (Federal Bureau of Investigation, 2014a). This number represents a 45.7 percent decline from 2004, and is consistent with data on adult arrests as well. As emphasized in Chapter 1, the crime rate overall has declined in recent years.

Interestingly, a good number of children taken into custody or arrested in this manner are under the age of 12. At the turn of the twenty-first century, the term *child delinquent* appeared in child development literature and some media accounts. **Child delinquents** are juveniles between ages 7 and 12, who have committed a delinquent act according to criminal law (Loeber, Farrington, & Petechuk, 2003). Child delinquents often attract the attention of the mass media and public officials, especially after some particularly violent incident that involves a very young offender—for example, an eight-year-old who kills a four-year-old. Beginning in the mid- to late-1990s, the number of child delinquents handled by juvenile courts increased substantially. Overall, children younger than age 13 have comprised about 9 percent of all juvenile arrests (Federal Bureau of Investigation, 2014a; Snyder, Espiritu, et al., 2003). According to Loeber et al. (2003), child delinquents are two or three times more likely to become serious, violent, and chronic offenders than adolescents who begin offending in their teens. Because child delinquents are also referred to as early onset offenders, we will discuss them again later in the chapter, in sections on developmental theories of delinquency.

Table 6-1 gives an overview of serious crimes for which juveniles under 18 were taken into custody in 2004 and 2013, as well as the percentage change during that time period. Note that arrests were down for all crimes. **Figure 6-1** provides an overview of percentage distribution of all crimes for which juveniles were arrested in 2007.

Other revealing figures are those related to delinquency cases in juvenile courts. Between 1960 and 2008, delinquency caseloads in these courts increased more than 300 percent, from 400,000 to over 1,600,000 (Puzzanchera, Adams, & Sickmund, 2011). Nonetheless, juvenile crimes declined over the past decade, and court caseloads decreased 12 percent from their peak in 1997 to 2008 (Puzzanchera et al., 2011). Most recent figures indicate that the decline has persisted (Hockenberry & Puzzanchera, 2014). On average, nearly two-thirds of the cases involve youths age 15 or younger at the time of referral. Trends between 1985 and 2011 indicate early increases but then decreases in person, drug, and public order offenses. Property offenses declined overall (Hockenberry & Puzzanchera, 2014). Juvenile courts also saw an increase in female delinquency cases, up from 19 percent in 1985 to 27 percent in 2008. However, girls continue to represent a smaller proportion of youths whose cases are heard in juvenile court. In 2011, for example, 345,100 girls were processed in these courts compared to 891,100 boys.

TABLE 6-1	Juvenile Arrests for Violent and Property Crimes, 2004 and 2013		
Offense	2004	2013	Percent Change
Total all crimes	1,226,865	666,263	−45.7
Murder/Nonnegligent homicide	643	492	−23.5
Rape	2,414	1,484	−38.5
Robbery	14,936	12,340	−17.4
Aggravated assault	35,912	19,351	−46.1
Burglary	49,721	27,960	−43.8
Larceny-theft	198,071	117,141	−40.9
Motor vehicle theft	22,784	7,367	−67.7
Arson	4,593	2,370	−48.4

Source: Federal Bureau of Investigation (2014a). Crime in the United States 2013: Uniform Crime Reports. Washington, DC: U.S. Department of Justice.

The nature and extent of delinquent behavior—both what is reported and what is *unreported* to law enforcement agencies—are essentially unknown (Krisberg, 1995; Krisberg & Schwartz, 1983), even more so than adult crime. We simply do not have complete data on the national incidence of juvenile delinquency, broadly defined. We do have some statistics collected by law enforcement agencies (e.g., through the UCR system described in Chapter 1), the courts, and facilities for delinquents. The government regularly publishes reports on juvenile court statistics and on children in custody in both detention and treatment facilities, such as those cited above. Nevertheless, as for adult crime, there is a huge dark figure. As Barry Krisberg (1992, p. 2) notes, "Put simply, the amount of crime committed by juveniles is unknown and perhaps unknowable."

Percent of arrests involving juveniles

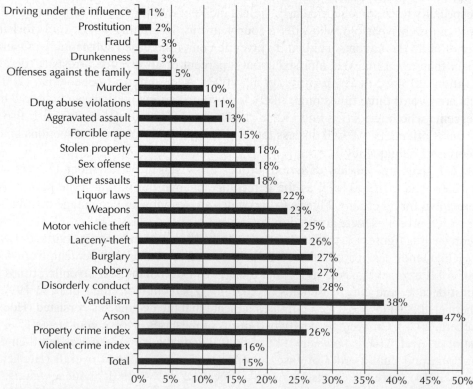

FIGURE 6-1 Juvenile Arrests, 2007 *Source:* Puzzanchera, C. M. (2009, April). Juvenile arrests 2007. Washington, DC: U.S. Department of Justice, Office of Juvenile Justice and Delinquency Prevention.

TABLE 6-2 Categories of Juvenile Offending	
Unlawful Acts	**Definition**
Unlawful acts against persons	Violent crimes, similar to those crimes committed by adults, such as aggravated assault, robbery, and sexual assault.
Unlawful acts against property	Property crimes, similar to those crimes committed by adults, such as burglary, larceny-theft, and vandalism.
Drug offenses	Possession, distribution, and/or manufacture of drugs.
Public order offenses	Nuisance crimes against society, such as noise violations or public intoxication.
Juvenile status offenses	Acts only juveniles can commit, such as violation of curfew, running away, and school truancy.

Usually, unlawful acts committed by delinquents are placed into five major categories: unlawful acts against persons, unlawful acts against property, drug offenses, public order offenses, and status offenses. They are defined in **Table 6-2**.

The first four categories are comparable in definition with crimes committed by adults and are discussed shortly. Before we turn to these criminal acts, it is important to focus briefly on the fifth category, the troubling issue of juvenile status offending.

Status Offenses

Juvenile status offenses are acts that only juveniles can commit and that are typically handled only in a juvenile or family court. As mentioned earlier, status offenses range from misbehavior, such as violations of curfew, running away from home, and truancy, to offenses that are interpreted subjectively, such as unruliness, unmanageability, or incorrigibility. However, only four status offenses are tabulated by the National Center for Juvenile Justice, a governmental research group affiliated with the Office of Juvenile Justice and Delinquency Prevention. They are running away, truancy, ungovernability (also known as incorrigibility or being beyond the control of one's parents or guardians), and underage liquor law violations (e.g., a minor in possession of alcohol, underage drinking). Although a number of other behaviors are often considered status offenses (e.g., curfew violations, tobacco offenses), they are usually not discussed in governmental reports.

The juvenile system has historically supported differential treatment of male and female status offenders. Adolescent girls, for example, have often been detained for incorrigibility or running away from home, when the same behavior in adolescent boys was ignored or tolerated. Until recently, about three times as many girls were detained for status offenses as boys (U.S. Department of Justice, 1988). In recent years, as a result of suits brought on behalf of juveniles, many courts have put authorities on notice that this discriminatory approach is unwarranted. Even so, figures indicate that girls are still more likely than boys to be arrested as runaways (Hockenberry & Puzzanchera, 2015; National Center for Juvenile Justice, 2003; Snyder, Sickmund, & Poe-Yamagata, 2000). Beginning in January 2011, the UCR SRS program discontinued the collection of arrest data for the category of runaways. The National Incident Based Reporting System (NIBRS) will continue to report runaway data using the Group B Arrest Report (Code 90I).

It has long been argued that, because status offenses lend themselves to so much subjectivity, they should be removed from the purview of all state juvenile courts (American Bar Association, 1979). Many states have clearly moved in this direction. On the other hand, while they do not label status offenders "delinquents," they do allow their detention and/or supervision because they are presumed to be in need of protection either from their own rash behavior or the behavior of others. The statutes allowing this are usually referred to as PINS or CHINS laws (person or child in need of supervision). Under these laws, runaways or incorrigible youngsters are subject to juvenile or family court jurisdiction, sometimes at the instigation of their parents, even though they may not have committed an act comparable with a crime. In reality, status offenders often do commit crimes, particularly property offenses such as theft or burglary. However, PINS or CHINS laws also allow juvenile and family courts to address the needs of neglected and dependent children, so it should not be assumed that a child who has been labeled a "CHINS" has displayed problem behaviors or has committed crimes.

In this text, although status offending and minor delinquent crime are considered, our focus is on violent offending and more serious property offending. We are particularly interested in the developmental trajectories that lead to serious delinquency and in many but not all cases to persistent offending into adulthood. In recent years, developmental psychologists have conducted extensive research on this topic.

The Serious Delinquent

Both self-report studies and official data indicate that only a small percentage of the juvenile population engages in serious delinquent behavior, whether it is defined legally, socially, or psychologically. Nevertheless, those who do commit a variety of antisocial behaviors often escape detection. An early self-report study (Weis & Sederstrom, 1981) indicated that only about 3–15 percent of serious offenses ever result in "police contact." Likewise, Elliott, Dunford, and Huizinga (1987) suggested that serious, repetitive juvenile offenders escaped detection 86 percent of the time over a five-year period. These figures further suggest that the incidence of offending may be substantially underestimated by official arrest data. In other words, a small percentage of youth are committing a substantial amount of offenses that do not come to the attention of police. This group of youths—when they do enter the justice system—tend to be high in recidivism, or repeat offending. In addition, frequent offenders do not specialize in any one particular kind of offending, such as theft or larceny. Instead, they tend to be involved in a wide variety of offenses, ranging from minor property crimes to highly violent ones. Longitudinal research also indicates that repetitive offenders as a group were unusually troublesome in school, earned poor grades, and had inadequate or poor social skills. Furthermore, these troublesome behaviors often began at an early age, and the more serious the offender, the earlier these childhood patterns appeared. Serious or habitual juvenile offenders rarely restrict their behaviors to one type of offense category.

A number of pessimistic conclusions about serious delinquents have been challenged as a result of an ongoing, longitudinal study of 1,354 predominately male, serious juvenile offenders for seven years after their conviction (Mulvey, 2011). The highly cited and continuing "Pathways to Delinquency" research sponsored by the Office of Juvenile Justice and Delinquency Prevention (OJJDP) indicates that most serious offenders reduce their offending over time, *particularly when monitored in the community after short-term incarceration*. As a general principle, long incarceration is ineffective at reducing recidivism among young offenders. The research, which followed youth in two metropolitan areas in Phoenix, Arizona, and Philadelphia County, Pennsylvania, also indicated that substance abuse treatment was effective in reducing both substance use and criminal offending. In the words of chief investigator Edward P. Mulvey, "The most important conclusion of the study is that even adolescents who have committed serious offenses are not necessarily on track for adult criminal careers" (2011, p. 3).

Other recent studies also have documented that serious juvenile offenders can benefit from intensive treatment when it is provided, particularly in community rather than institutional settings (Skeem, Scott, & Mulvey, 2014). We will return to this topic later in the chapter.

Gender Differences in Juvenile Offending

Over the years, boys have far outnumbered girls in most types of offending, but most particularly in violent offending. Victimization data, self-report data, and official data (both police records and court statistics) all have supported this gender gap.

Recent data on juvenile arrests suggest, however, that this gender gap may be closing somewhat and for some offenses. Between 1996 and 2009, arrests of juvenile females generally increased more (or decreased less) than male arrests in most categories (Puzzanchera & Adams, 2011; Snyder, 2008; Zahn, Hawkins, Chiancone, & Whitworth, 2008). In 2009, girls accounted for

30 percent of the juvenile arrests (Puzzanchera & Adams, 2011). They accounted for 18 percent of arrests for juvenile violent crime, 38 percent of arrests for juvenile property crime, and 45 percent of juvenile larceny-theft arrests. Furthermore, as noted above, the proportion of female delinquency case heard in juvenile courts rose from 19 percent in 1985 to 27 percent in 2008 (Puzzanchera et al., 2011). Nevertheless, when it comes to juveniles who are at high risk of serious offending, the vast majority are boys.

The connection between juvenile running away and prostitution is a sobering one. Recent arrest figures indicate that the runaway figures are about equal for girls and boys (Puzzanchera, 2009; Puzzanchera & Hockenberry, 2013). Nevertheless, girls are believed to be far more likely than boys to run away because of victimization in the home and ultimately to take up prostitution to survive. In fact, a history of violent victimization, in or outside the home, seems to haunt both juvenile and adult female offenders (Acoca & Austin, 1996) and is apparent in much of the current literature on women's pathways to offending (Salisbury & Van Voorhis, 2009). According to one study (Acoca & Dedel, 1998), 92 percent of juvenile female offenders reported that they had been subjected to some form of emotional, physical, and/or sexual abuse in or outside the home. Twenty-five percent reported they had been shot or stabbed one or more times.

In the late twentieth century, we knew far too little about girls' crime, the reasons it was committed, and the social and developmental factors that precipitate it (Broidy et al., 2003; Chesney-Lind & Shelden, 1998). Even more recent studies based on large samples, such as the Pathways study referred to above, either did not include girls or studied them in much smaller numbers. (The Pathways study followed 1,170 males and 184 females.) Partly to rectify this imbalance, and partly in response to rising arrest rates of female juveniles in the 1990s, the Office of Juvenile Justice and Delinquency Prevention convened the *Girls Study Group* (GSG) in 2004. This is a comprehensive research project designed to gain a better understanding of girls' delinquency and recommend effective prevention programs directed specifically at girls, a population whose needs are too often overlooked. The GSG consists of an interdisciplinary group of scholars and practitioners from the fields of sociology, psychology, criminology, and gender studies as well as legal practitioners and girls' program development coordinators.

In addition to investigating the extent of delinquency, the GSG seeks to answer the following questions: Which girls become delinquent? What factors protect girls from delinquency? What factors put girls at risk of delinquency? What developmental pathways lead to girls' delinquency? What factors are most effective in preventing girls' delinquency?

One of the earliest studies published by researchers associated with the group focused on whether violence is increasing among girls. Zahn, Brumbaugh, et al. (2008) found, based on arrest victimization and self-report data, that "although girls are arrested more for simple assault than previously, the actual incidence of being seriously violent has not changed much over the past two decades" (p. 15). They concluded that "there is no burgeoning national crisis of increasing serious violence among adolescent girls" (p. 15).

The researchers surmised that the increases in arrests for girls *may* be attributed more to changes in enforcement policies than to changes in girls' behavior. For example, as a result of mandatory arrest policies in domestic violence, girls involved in family altercations may be more likely to be arrested than to be provided with mediation services (Zahn, Hawkins, et al., 2008). Zahn, Brumbaugh, et al. (2008, p. 15) further concluded that when girls' violence did occur, it was usually for the following reasons:

- *Peer violence.* Girls come to blows with peers to gain status, for self-defense against sexual harassment, to defend themselves against bullying, or to defend their sexual reputation.
- *Violence within schools.* Fighting by girls in school may represent anger against teachers or school administrators, or may reflect a general feeling of hopelessness. Furthermore, schools' zero-tolerance policies probably increases the number of arrests and referrals for fights involving girls (Zahn, Hawkins, et al., 2008). Although these policies may increase the likelihood of arrests for both boys and girls, the effects seem to be stronger for girls.
- *Violence within disadvantaged neighborhoods.* Under these conditions, girls may become violent to protect themselves from being victimized.

- *Girls in gangs.* Girls join gangs for a variety of reasons. Violent behavior may be an expectation, or girls in gangs may fight for any of the reasons listed under peer violence.
- *Family violence.* It appears that girls fight more frequently at home with parents than do boys. Girls fight with parents for a variety of reasons. For some, it represents striking back against what they perceive as an overly controlling parental style; for others, it is defense or anger reaction to some form of abuse (emotional, physical, and/or sexual) by members in the household. It is important to note that some status offenses involving a domestic dispute between a girl and her parent or sibling—and which formerly might have been labeled "incorrigibility"—could now be classified as a simple assault and could result in an arrest (Zahn, Hawkins, et al., 2008).

The GSG group has also studied the many intervention programs offered for girls by the juvenile justice system. Although there were positive findings, for the great majority of programs there was insufficient evidence to conclude that they were effective or ineffective. In addition, there were not enough resources available for conducting rigorous evaluations of these programs (Zahn, Hawkins, et al., 2008). Additional material on the work of the GSG is available at http://girlsstudygroup.rti.org.

Research by developmental psychologists has shed considerable light on the gender difference in juvenile offending. Biology is *not* a significant factor in explaining the gender differences in offending, including violent offending (Adams, 1992; Pepler & Slaby, 1994). Research by Eleanor Maccoby (1986), for example, indicates that girls and boys learn different types of prosocial behavior, with girls being more accommodating than boys. The current work of cognitive psychologists suggests that there may be socialized and cultural differences in the way boys and girls perceive their worlds. Social learning theorists have long held that girls are socialized differently from boys, or taught not to be aggressive. Boys and girls may be born with the potential to be equally aggressive, but girls have been taught not to be overtly aggressive, whereas boys were encouraged to be aggressive (Campbell, 1993). The slight change in the ratio of violent offending, coupled with the overall decrease in juvenile violent crime discussed earlier in the chapter, suggests that the socialization of girls and boys is becoming more comparable. On the one hand, girls today are likely receiving the same aggression-supporting messages as boys (e.g., from media), and also have fewer restrictions on their behavior than they have had in the past. On the other hand, both genders are being encouraged to make good decisions and look for socially acceptable ways of channeling aggressive tendencies.

It remains to be seen whether the gender gap in offending will close even more, increase, or remain stable in the years ahead. In addition to psychosocial development, numerous societal factors affect the patterns of offending for both juveniles and adults. There is some indication that boys and girls share similar risk factors for delinquency (Zahn, Hawkins, et al., 2008). These include the economy, community disorganization, the actions of police, the quality of schools, the resources available to courts and to correctional agencies, and the adequacy of health and social services, to name but a few. In addition, however, girls may experience risk factors over and above those experienced by boys, such as a greater likelihood of sexual victimization and issues of self-esteem. Zahn et al. (2010) also found that girls were at particular risk for delinquency when factors such as early puberty, family conflict, and living in unstable neighborhoods (e.g., high unemployment and single-parent households) were present in their lives. In research comparing predictors of delinquency in males and females, Steketee, Junger, and Junger-Tas (2013) found that family disruption and the deviant behavior of friends were the greatest risk factors for girls, while lack of self-control was strongly related to delinquency among boys.

Other recent research has found certain mental health conditions to be associated with delinquency in girls. Barret, Ju, Katsiyannis, and Zhang (2013) compared background variables in approximately 34,000 female juvenile offenders and a similar-size control group of girls without histories of delinquency, matched on age and race. The juvenile offenders were significantly more likely to have been diagnosed with a disorder involving impulse control or aggression; of those so diagnosed, 60 percent had received the diagnosis before any involvement with the juvenile justice system. Barret et al. were interested in examining factors that lead to recidivism and found that a history of drug use and disruption in parent–child relationships were significant.

Another heavily cited longitudinal study, the Pittsburg Girls Study (PGS) (Hipwell et al., 2002; Keenan et al., 2010) has yielded important findings about delinquency in girls. The study began in 1999, recording data on approximately 3,000 girls who were between ages five and eight at that time. A number of research projects were developed from this sample (e.g., Miller, Loeber, & Hipwell, 2009; Henneberger et al., 2014). Henneberger et al. (2014) examined the confluence of parental versus peer influence and found that harsh parenting and peer delinquency had independent influence on the delinquency of girls during mid-adolescence. Put another way, when parental practices were punitive (e.g., screaming, negative name-calling, corporal punishment) as opposed to positive and accepting (e.g., offering praise, giving approval), there was greater likelihood that the girl would exhibit antisocial behavior. Likewise, when girls associated with delinquent peers, they were more likely to themselves be delinquent in their mid-adolescence. Henneberger et al. conclude that prevention and intervention programs for girls should target both parental practices and peer associations.

DEVELOPMENTAL THEORIES OF DELINQUENCY

It should be clear by now that a considerable amount of contemporary research has focused on understanding the *developmental processes* leading to aggression, antisocial behavior, and delinquency during the elementary school years and into adolescence for both boys and girls. Contemporary research has consistently demonstrated that the offender population consists of various distinct subgroups, each following an identifiable developmental pathway that is associated with different risks and outcomes (Wiesner & Windle, 2004).

As we learned in Chapter 2, studying the developmental process of individuals requires an examination of the trajectory of that development. A trajectory in this sense refers to the developmental changes a person shows over his or her lifetime. Examining differences in developmental trajectories or pathways of individuals over time adds a deeper understanding of delinquency than focusing on differences among individuals at any one point in time. A developmental trajectory or pathway reflects the changes in someone's cognitive, emotional, and social growth as he or she grows into adulthood. Included in the pathways are numerous experiences that may be encountered, such as early childhood victimization, exposure to environmental toxins, academic failure, the loss of a parent during childhood, or association with antisocial peers. As we discussed in earlier chapters, this is consistent with a cumulative risk model or a dynamic cascade model, both of which emphasize that multiple factors are involved in the production of antisocial behavior. No single risk factor, standing alone, predicts delinquency. In addition, protective factors—those that cushion the path—are also crucial to consider. In a recent study published by the GSG discussed above, researchers found that girls who reported having caring adults in their lives were less likely to report committing crimes, status offenses, and membership in gangs during adolescence (Hawkins, Graham, Williams, & Zahn, 2009). Theories that use developmental trajectories as models can identify a sequential chain of events that suggest how antisocial behavior is shaped and sustained (Kazdin, 1989).

Research has led to the striking consensus that children and adolescents follow different developmental pathways in their offending and nonoffending careers. Some children engage in stubborn, defiant, and disobedient behavior at very young ages, progressing to mild and then more severe forms of violence and criminal behavior during adolescence and young adulthood (Dahlberg & Potter, 2001). Some children exhibit cruelty to animals, aggressive behavior toward peers, bullying, and substance abuse at a very early age and continue this antisocial pathway far into adulthood. Other children show very few signs of antisocial behavior at very young ages, but during adolescence, they engage in various forms of delinquent behavior. Still others avoid engaging in any significant antisocial behavior over their lifetimes.

Despite these different developmental pathways, there is good evidence that most serious, persistent delinquency and crime patterns usually begin early and worsen with age, although as the research also indicates (Mulvey, 2011; Skeem et al., 2014), we cannot assume that all serious juvenile offenders will continue their criminal activity into adulthood. *Some* serious juvenile offenders will not continue into adulthood, but many will do so. In addition, the availability of intervention for juveniles on a path toward chronic serious offending is critical. Researchers also have noted early childhood differences in impulsiveness, social skills, and feelings for others among those children who become seriously antisocial and those children who stay on a prosocial life course. Contemporary developmental psychologists have begun targeting the development of antisocial behavior even during the preschool years.

Moffitt's Developmental Theory

A major impetus for the developmental perspective as an explanation for delinquency has been the theory and ongoing research of psychologist Terrie Moffitt (1993a, 1993b, 2003, 2006) and her colleagues. Originally, Moffitt's developmental theory identified two developmental paths, but as we note shortly, the theory was expanded to accommodate more than these basic two, which are described here.

LIFE-COURSE PERSISTENT OFFENDERS. On one path, the Moffitt group placed a small group of children who begin a lifelong pattern of delinquency and adult crime at a very early age, probably around age three or even younger. Moffitt (1993a, p. 679) wrote, "Across the life course, these individuals exhibit changing manifestations of antisocial behavior: biting and hitting at age four, shoplifting and truancy at age ten, selling drugs and stealing cars at age sixteen, robbery and rape at age twenty-two, and fraud and child abuse at age thirty." These individuals, whom Moffitt called **life-course-persistent (LCP) offenders**, continue their antisocial ways across all kinds of conditions and situations. Moffitt reported that many LCP offenders exhibit neurological problems during their childhoods, such as difficult temperaments as infants, attention deficit/hyperactive disorder (ADHD) as children, and learning problems during their later school years. Judgment and problem-solving deficiencies, mental health problems, and legal problems of various sorts are often apparent when LCP children reach adulthood (Jaffee & Odgers, 2013). LCP offenders generally commit a wide assortment of aggressive and violent crimes over their lifetimes.

LCPs as children miss opportunities to acquire and practice prosocial and interpersonal skills at each stage of development. They often display elevated aggressive behavior at home and in school, and consequently are rejected and avoided by their childhood peers. In addition, parents, teachers, and caretakers become frustrated and may even give up on them (Coie, Belding, & Underwood, 1988; Coie & Dodge, 1998; Coie, Dodge, & Kupersmith, 1990; Moffitt, 1993a). According to Moffitt (1993a, p. 684), "If social and academic skills are not mastered in childhood, it is very difficult to later recover from lost opportunities." Furthermore, as noted previously, disadvantaged homes, inadequate schools, and violent neighborhoods are factors that are very likely to exacerbate the ongoing and developing antisocial behavioral pattern of LCPs.

LCPs are plagued by various psychological and antisocial problems throughout their lifetimes (Jaffee & Odgers, 2013). Numerous studies report that early-onset antisocial behavior is typically associated with pervasive mental, physical, economic, interpersonal, and legal problems across the life span (Caspi, Wright, Moffitt, & Silva, 1998; Farrington, 1995; Moffitt, Caspi, Harrington, & Milne, 2002). Wiesner, Kim, and Capaldi (2005) write, "Developmental theories posit that antisocial behavior that onsets early in childhood is likely to lead to a cascade of secondary problems, including academic failure, involvement with deviant peers, substance abuse, depressive symptoms, health risk sexual behavior, and work failure" (p. 252). It appears as though LCPs become entrapped in a deviant lifestyle right out of the developmental gate. They are embedded in a social context that further increases their risk status (van Lier, Vuijk, & Crijen, 2005).

Other researchers have consistently reported that a small minority of children (about 5% to 10%) follow a high antisocial developmental trajectory (Fontaine, Carbonneau, Vitaro, Barker, & Tremblay, 2009; van Lier et al., 2005; van Lier, Wanner, & Vitaro, 2007). They are almost exclusively males. Recent research suggests that only about 1–2 percent of girls show this persistent, early-onset pattern (Fontaine et al., 2009). In addition, the level of antisocial behavior of LCPs seems to diverge from their less antisocial counterparts across time (van Lier et al., 2005). In other words, LCPs actually increase their offending as they grow older. The reasons for this may be due, at least in part, to their exposure to the learning, practicing, and reinforcement of antisocial behavior through the affiliation with similarly diverging antisocial peers. Basically, antisocial youth progressively affiliate with similarly antisocial peers (van Lier et al., 2005).

Nevertheless, it is important to stress that many children with early-onset conduct problems (e.g., bullying) and other high-risk features (e.g., callous-unemotional traits) do not continue their antisocial activity into adulthood (Piquero et al., 2013; Skeem, Scott, & Mulvey, 2014). In recent years, research on high-risk juveniles has taken a decidedly more positive turn. Rather than viewing early onset of antisocial behavior as a seemingly inevitable path toward a lifetime of offending, the research indicates that many juveniles considered at high risk for chronic criminal behavior desist, either during or following adolescence. In addition, risk-assessment measures have been designed for better delineation of the risk factors in a particular juvenile's life, and treatment approaches targeting them have been identified (Mulvey, 2011; Vincent, Guy, & Grisso, 2012). We discuss this further later in the chapter.

ADOLESCENCE-LIMITED OFFENDERS.   The great majority of juvenile offenders are those individuals who follow a second developmental path: They begin offending during their adolescent years and generally stop offending somewhere around their 18th birthday. Moffitt labels these youth **adolescent-limited (AL) offenders**. Their developmental histories do not demonstrate the early and persistent antisocial problems that members of the LCP group manifest. However—and this point is important—the frequency, and in some cases, the violence level of offending during the teen years may be as high as that of the LCP youth. In effect, the teenage offending patterns of the AL and that of the LCP may be highly similar during the adolescent years (Moffitt, Caspi, Dickson, Silva, & Stanton, 1996). "The two types cannot be discriminated on most indicators of antisocial and problem behavior in adolescence; boys on the LCP and AL paths are similar on parent-, self-, and official records of offending, peer delinquency, substance abuse, unsafe sex, and dangerous driving" (Moffitt et al., 1996, p. 400). Accordingly, mental health workers and criminal justice experts could not easily identify the group classification (AL or LCP) simply by examining juvenile arrest records, self-reports, or the information provided by parents during the teen years.

Nevertheless, the AL delinquent is most likely, during the teen years, to be involved in offenses that symbolize adult privilege and demonstrate autonomy from parental control. Examples include vandalism, drug and alcohol offenses, theft, and "status" offenses such as running away or truancy. In addition, AL delinquents are likely to engage in crimes that are profitable or rewarding, but they also have the ability to abandon these actions when prosocial styles become more rewarding. For example, the onset of young adulthood brings on opportunities not attainable during the teen years, such as leaving high school for college, obtaining a full-time job, and entering a relationship with a prosocial person. AL delinquents are quick to learn that they have something to lose if they continue offending into adulthood. During childhood, in contrast to the LCP child, the AL youngster has learned to get along with others. It should also be emphasized that "the theory of AL antisocial behavior regards it as an adaptation response to modern teens' social context, not the product of a cumulative history of pathological maldevelopment" (Moffitt & Caspi, 2001, p. 370). They normally have a satisfactory repertoire of academic, social, and interpersonal skills that enable them to "get ahead." Therefore, the developmental histories and personal dispositions of the AL youth allow him or her the option of exploring new life pathways, an opportunity not usually afforded the LCP youth. In short, Moffitt's theory hypothesizes that most young persons who become adolescence-limited delinquents are able to desist from crime when they age into maturity, turning gradually to a more conventional lifestyle (Moffitt & Caspi, 2001).

ADDITIONAL PATHWAYS.   Interestingly, in one of their follow-up studies, Moffitt et al. (2002) discovered that many ALs, at age 26, were still in trouble. "Although AL men fared better overall than LCP men, they fared poorly relative to the 'unclassified' men, who represented males with no remarkable delinquency history" (Moffitt et al., 2002, p. 199). The researchers found that AL men accounted for twice their share of the property and drug convictions during adulthood, compared with men without a delinquency history. It seemed as though some AL men relied on crime to supplement their incomes. The researchers further state that "the very name 'adolescence-limited' reveals that this much offending by AL men at age 26 was not anticipated by our theory" (p. 200). The researchers, in an effort to explain the discrepancy, speculated that perhaps adulthood in contemporary society may begin after 25 years of age. Therefore, this new developmental stage prolongs the crime-promoting conditions of adolescence. Moffitt et al. (2002, p. 200) observe that "This stage is characterized by roleless floundering, in which young people neither perceive themselves to be adults, nor choose to occupy any adult roles historically favored by people in their twenties (e.g., parenthood, marriage)." This would suggest that they too will eventually cease offending just as did their AL counterparts who stopped offending earlier.

Developmental psychologists have recently proposed a life stage that is very similar to Moffitt's above description. Called "emerging adulthood" (Arnett, 2000, 2014), the stage characterizes individuals between the ages of 18 and 25 (or 18 and 28 in some conceptions) who have not yet reached adult status in society. In some cases, they are actively seeking adulthood and struggling to achieve it, but in other cases they are carefree and enjoying their time of exploration. Thus, emerging adulthood can be a stressful period or a period of freedom from the institutions that restricted them in the past, such as family and educational systems. The concept of emerging adulthood was not intended as an explanation for antisocial behavior, but much of the research conducted on the topic has relevance to criminality. (See **Box 6-1** for further discussion.)

RESEARCH FOCUS

BOX 6-1   Emerging Adulthood as a Developmental Stage

Adolescence—the developmental stage that is primarily addressed in this chapter—typically spans the ages 10 to 18. Once one reaches 18, adulthood sets in—people can vote, join the military, buy guns legally, make many decisions independent of their parents, and enter into legal contracts, though they still cannot purchase most legal drugs. Although this 18-year-old line of demarcation can be flexible (e.g., some adolescents become "emancipated minors," and 17-year-olds may still go to adult prisons and join the military with parental consent), the line that separates adolescence from adulthood is well accepted in Western society.

As noted in the text, some researchers now argue that for many individuals there is a distinct developmental stage between adolescence and adulthood, called emerging adulthood (Arnett, 2000, 2014). For some it is a time for carefree exploration and self-discovery; for others a struggle to achieve adult status in society. At times it can be both. Emerging adulthood is not necessarily associated with criminal or antisocial behavior, but it may well be.

The acclaimed 2013 film *Fruitvale Station*, based on a true incident, provides a good illustration of emerging adulthood. The main character, Oscar Grant III, was a 22-year-old man shot and killed by Johannes Mehserle, a police officer for Bay Area Rapid Transit (BART) in 2009. Grant was unarmed and shot on a subway platform. He and a group of friends had been riding on a crowded train with numerous party revelers, when an altercation occurred between two men, one being Grant. Witnesses later reported it was not a life-threatening situation.

Grant and several of his friends then got off the train, by which time BART officers had arrived to respond to reports of a fight. Subway passengers watched in horror and fascination as the incident unfolded on the platform, with officers restraining Grant and Grant insisting he had done nothing wrong. Mehserle, who said he mistook his gun for his taser, then shot Grant. The officer was charged with murder, tried, and convicted of involuntary manslaughter. He served 11 months in prison. The incident as well as the ensuing trial attracted publicity and protests throughout the Bay Area.

As depicted in the film, Grant was a young man who was apparently trying to improve his life after a difficult adolescence and early adulthood, including time spent in prison for drug offenses. Grant lost a job because of chronic tardiness, and he was tempted to go back to selling drugs, though the film shows him throwing a supply into the bay. But Grant had a supportive family, including a mother who encouraged him to continue his education and a four-year-old daughter to whom he gave much attention. His relationship with the girl's mother was becoming increasingly stable, and the two planned to marry. He was technically an adult, but many of his struggles, again as depicted in the movie, suggested that achieving adult status was a challenge.

The concept of emerging adulthood as a developmental stage may hold considerable relevance for explaining antisocial and criminal behavior in individuals who have lived through adolescence but are not full participants in the adult world. Researchers have begun to explore this stage. Following are some of their findings:

- Mental health and substance use problems are often found during this stage (Adams, Knopf, & Park, 2014).
- Decreasing support from institutions (family, educational system) during these years often intensifies such mental disorders as schizophrenia, bipolar disorder, major depressions, and borderline personality disorder (Adams et al., 2014).
- Self-control often increases during this developmental period (Zimmermann & Ivanski, 2014).
- Intimate partner violence (IPV) is negatively associated with the gainful employment of both parties—that is, if both partners are employed, IPV is less likely (Alvira-Hammond, Longmore, Manning, & Giordano, 2014).
- Divorce of parents has a negative effect on emerging adulthood (Arnett, 2014).

Researchers also suggest that ethnic and cultural differences in emerging adulthood should be explored. For example, the stage may be shorter or may not exist at all when individuals are expected to take on responsibility at early age, or may be extended in more protective cultures where the exploration of one's identity is delayed.

Questions for Discussion

1. Is the concept of emerging adulthood a valuable one for understanding the years immediately following adolescence?
2. Is the concept helpful for understanding antisocial or criminal behavior committed by young adults?
3. Provide additional illustrations of emerging adulthood from literature or popular culture. Do they resemble Oscar Grant as depicted in *Fruitvale Station*?
4. Which if any of the research findings summarized above is surprising?

Moffitt et al.'s (2002) finding that some AL offenders continued offending into adulthood has prompted some researchers to hypothesize that there may be still another classification needed to account for the persistent offending found in adults. That is, some persistent offenders begin their antisocial ways during their adolescent years rather than their childhood years. This pattern appears to be especially the case for female offenders (Fontaine et al., 2009). Emerging research now refers to early-onset and adolescent-onset persistent offending. However, it is also important to consider AL offenders who offend into adulthood but stop earlier than the LCP. Thus, we would have four categories of frequent offending: (a) the AL offender, (b) the AL who continues into early adulthood but then stops, (c) the early-onset LCP, and (d) the late-onset LCP. **Table 6-3** summarizes the major differences between LCP and AL offenders.

Other researchers using a developmental perspective have identified more than the early- and late-onset trajectories discussed above. For example, Loeber and Stouthamer-Loeber (1998) and Chung, Hill, Hawkins, Gilchrist, and Nagin (2002) were able to identify five developmental pathways. Nagin and Land (1993), Côté et al. (2001), and Shaw, Gilliom, Ingoldsby, and Nagin (2003)

TABLE 6-3   Major Differences between LCPs and ALs

	Life-Course-Persistent (LCP)	Adolescent Limited (AL)
Crime or antisocial behavior begins	Early (perhaps as early as age three)	Later (usually during the early adolescent years)
Criminal behavior	Continues throughout the offender's life	Usually stops after reaching early adulthood
Types of criminal behaviors	Assortment	Assortment
Developmental backgrounds	Often show neurological problems, ADHD, conduct problems	Usually normal and without neurological problems
Academic skills	Usually below average	Usually average to above average
Interpersonal and social skills	Usually below average	Usually average to above average

have all found four trajectories that lead to antisocial, delinquent, or criminal behavior. Wiesner and Windle (2004) suggest there may be as many as six different developmental pathways to delinquency and crime. Regardless of the number of paths, a distinguishing feature of all developmental models is that the age of onset of the serious antisocial behavior is crucial, as is the severity and persistence of the offending as the child grows into adolescence or young adulthood. As noted above, however, it is important to recognize that even early-onset conduct problems do not destine a child to lifelong antisocial behavior. Furthermore, effective treatment strategies are increasingly available for children and adolescents who may be at significant risk of becoming chronic offenders throughout adulthood. Still to be established are the risk and protective factors that may distinguish the pathways and whether these differ according to gender.

GENDER DIFFERENCES IN DEVELOPMENTAL THEORIES. As mentioned above, Moffitt's theory was formed primarily on the developmental trajectories of males, though Moffitt and Caspi (2001) later reported evidence that the developmental typology fits both genders. However, the LCP pattern of behavior is far more likely to be followed by males than females (approximately 10 males to 1 female), whereas the gender difference is negligible for the AL pattern (approximately 1.5 males to 1 female). These findings are consistent with other studies (Kratzer & Hodgins, 1999; Mazerolle, Brame, Paternoster, Piquero, & Dean, 2000). In other words, the vast majority of female delinquents *appear* to fit the AL pattern. In a study of 820 girls, Côté, Zoccolillo, Tremblay, Nagin, and Vitaro (2001) found that only 1.4 percent of the girls followed the LCP profile. Other researchers have found approximately the same percentage of early-onset, persistent offenders among females (Fontaine et al., 2009).

According to Moffitt (2003), an ongoing association with delinquent peers appears to be an important factor in the onset of delinquency among adolescent girls. An intimate relationship with a male delinquent is also closely connected to delinquency in adolescent girls (Moffitt, Caspi, Rutter, & Silva, 2001).

Although many studies have indicated that only a small percentage of girls become early-onset persistent offenders, a few studies suggest that girls may be more vulnerable to early onset of serious antisocial behavior than previously thought. Brennan, Hall, Bor, Najman, and Williams (2003) found that girls in their sample displayed the same pattern as boys. In the Brennan et al. study, 9 percent of the boys and 7.4 percent of the girls in the high-risk sample were classified as displaying *early-onset* persistent aggressive behavior. However, Silverthorn and Frick (1999) maintain that girls tend to engage in serious antisocial behavior for the first time at later ages—and generally in adolescence—than boys. According to Silverthorn and Frick, antisocial behavior in girls is delayed because of such factors as parental and school-based socialization practices that encourage them to restrict their outward aggressive tendencies during middle childhood. Nevertheless, McCabe, Rodgers, Yeh, and Hough (2004) offer some evidence that a high percentage of antisocial girls began their antisocial behavior before the age of 10. Similar results were reported by Leve and Chamberlain (2004), who found that 23 percent of serious antisocial girls were arrested before age 11, and 71 percent before age 14. These results suggest that perhaps a larger portion of girls can be considered early-onset delinquents than previously believed, and that they may well follow the same developmental trajectory as early-onset boys. These researchers identified parental transitions (separation, divorce, death, incarceration) and biological parental criminality as the strongest predictors of early-onset offending in girls.

Studies further suggest that girls and women who follow an early and persistent trajectory of antisocial behavior exhibit these behaviors throughout the life span and tend to manifest a variety of maladjustment problems in adulthood (Fontaine, 2008; Fontaine et al., 2009; Odgers et al., 2008). Interestingly, there is some evidence to indicate that even girls who begin offending during adolescence may have a life of difficulty. Odgers and her colleagues (2008) report that—although adolescent-onset female offenders do not experience the same degree of problems as the LCP female offenders—they still were at risk of poor outcomes, especially financial, physical health, and mental health difficulties. In sum, persistent antisocial behavior, whether it begins in childhood or adolescence, is often a precursor of other problems well into adulthood.

Gorman-Smith and Loeber (2005) report that, based on extensive data from the National Youth Survey, girls tend to follow the same developmental pathways toward antisocial behavior and delinquency as boys. Although fewer girls than boys engage in such behavior, those that do, show similar pathways to boys. Girls who displayed serious antisocial and delinquent involvement had an early-onset pattern just as boys did. However, Gorman-Smith and Loeber did learn that the risk factors for girls may be somewhat different from those for boys. For example, because girls in general are more invested in interpersonal relationships than boys, they are more likely to get involved in or be affected by parental conflict and transitions, a finding similar to that reported in the Leve and Chamberlain (2004) study. Peer influences may also be different for boys and girls. Girls may be more likely to be pulled into delinquency through involvement in intimate relationships with delinquent males rather than through involvement with delinquent gangs. Therefore, while the developmental pathways may be similar, the family and peer risk factors may be different for boys and girls. Because research so often identifies unique risk factors, it has been argued that the pathways themselves are unique and that girls' and women's pathways to crime should be studied and considered separately from those of boys and men (Salisbury & Van Voorhis, 2009). In fact, Fontaine and colleagues (2009) write, "…the review of the literature suggests that the development of antisocial behavior in females may be more heterogeneous and complex than some theoretical models have suggested" (p. 376).

Steinberg's Dual Systems Model

Over the past decade, many developmental psychologists have been immersed in research on the adolescent brain. The research is highly relevant to antisocial behavior in the teenage years. To summarize briefly, researchers believe that the brain of the typical adolescent matures along two different paths: a cognitive and a socioemotional one. The cognitive control system is found mainly in the prefrontal and parietal regions of the brain (Steinberg, 2010a), while the socioemotional system is located in the limbic system and the midbrain areas, including the amygdala (see Figure 3-1). The socioemotional system is a processing center for reward seeking, social information, and emotional reactions that are more sensitive and easily aroused during puberty (Steinberg, 2007). The cognitive control system is involved in logical reasoning, understanding, and learning.

These systems have come to be known as the **dual systems model** of risk-taking proposed by psychologist Laurence Steinberg (Steinberg, 2004, 2007). Citing considerable evidence from neuroscience, Steinberg and his associates have demonstrated that adolescents as a group reach a peak of logical reasoning (the cognitive brain) at approximately age 16, a time when their psychosocial maturity (the socioemotional) is far less developed. Psychosocial maturity is reflected in such capacities as impulse control, resistance to peer influence, and future orientation. In most individuals, the two paths do not merge until approximately age 25. In other words, the typical person does not reach psychosocial maturity until age 25 or later, although his or her reasoning matures earlier. For example, an adolescent often understands the risk and dangers of drinking-and-driving, but this knowledge does not stop him or her from participating in that behavior under certain circumstances, particularly in the company of friends.

According to this theory, adolescence is a time of taking risks, being susceptible to the influence of peers, and feeling invulnerable. Adolescent risk-taking involves substance abuse, binge drinking, cigarette smoking, reckless driving (often while intoxicated), attempted suicide, and risky sexual behavior. As noted by Sunstein (2008), "adolescent risk-taking leads to seriously impaired lives and even premature deaths" (p. 145). Adolescents are especially vulnerable to considerable risk when they are in a group of their friends or peers, and this vulnerability appears to be the case for both genders. In fact, most crimes committed by adolescents in groups are seldom premeditated (Steinberg, Cauffman, Woolard, Graham, & Banich, 2009). By age 16, their reasoning ability is similar to that of adults, but their decision making is influenced by their immaturity in the socioemotional realm. In other words, there is a temporal gap between the maturation of the two systems (Burt, Sweeten, & Simons, 2014). Steinberg maintains that the socioemotional network of the brain is sensitive to social and emotional stimuli and is "remodeled in early adolescence by the hormonal changes of puberty" (2007, p. 56). The cognitive network "matures gradually over the course of adolescence and young adulthood largely independent of puberty" (p. 56).

The high-level of vulnerability to risk taking is believed to be the result of high levels of sensation or reward seeking and low impulse control, a condition most prevalent during mid-adolescence (Steinberg, 2010a). As teenagers get older, risk-taking behavior slowly decreases, but continues to some extent until around age 25. For some, risk-taking behavior continues.

Coercion Developmental Theory

Similar to Moffitt's theory about the LCP offender, a theory by Gerald Patterson (1982, 1986; Patterson, Forgatch, & DeGarmo, 2010) also proposes that early starters are at greater risk of more serious criminal offending. However, the major difference is that Patterson places a greater emphasis on the role of parenting rather than focusing on the specific characteristics of the child. The **coercion developmental theory** contends that poor parental monitoring of child activities, disruptive family transitions (e.g., divorce), and inconsistent parental discipline are major psychosocial contributors to early-onset delinquency (Brennan et al., 2003; Patterson, 1982). The theory argues that the key predictor of early-onset offending is the family environment in which the child learns to use coercive behaviors, such as temper tantrums and whining, to escape parental discipline and authority. In line with his theory, Patterson and his colleagues conduct ongoing research and family treatment programs to reduce the amount of coercion exercised by parents (Patterson et al., 2010).

Coercion theory acknowledges that some children are more likely than other children to elicit inept parenting strategies. For example, a child with an irritable temperament who is constantly whining is more likely to provoke coercive parenting than a pleasant, even-tempered child. Nevertheless, negative behavior from the child is more likely to emerge after some emotional or physical maltreatment by the parent (Granic & Patterson, 2011). In the coercive cycle, the parent and child each behave in a way that is annoying to the other in an attempt to control the other's behavior. As the child's behaviors increase in intensity and frequency, the parent eventually acquiesces, unwittingly reinforcing the behavior. As the child becomes increasingly irritating, the parent further escalates power-assertion techniques and, presumably, the level of hostility displayed toward the child.

Coercion becomes the child's primary interpersonal strategy, and this generalizes to environments outside the home. According to coercion theory, antisocial behavior is seen as progressing from faulty parent–toddler interactions to similar interactions with teachers, peers, and others in the child's environment. The coercive child—similar to the aggressive child who is characterized as an LCP in Moffitt's theory—is often rejected by noncoercive peers, and as a result he or she associates with peers who are similarly coercive, which contributes to the development of antisocial behavior. The Patterson model, thus, sees a *confluence* between parental and peer influences on delinquency. In further developing the theory, Granic and Patterson (2006) emphasized the dynamic nature of the interactions among the child, parents, and peers. Rather than proceeding on a linear path, feedback continues to occur, something they refer to as the dynamic systems approach.

The coercion developmental model is largely based on social learning theory. According to the theory, "Developmental trajectories for antisocial behavior are initiated, maintained, and diversified as a result of cumulative daily social experiences with parents, siblings, and peers that are highly aversive, inconsistent, and unsupportive" (Snyder, Reid et al., 2003, p. 31).

DEVELOPMENTAL TRAJECTORIES.   The theory identifies two developmental trajectories or pathways toward antisocial behavior, each characterized by an orderly sequence of stages (Patterson & Yoerger, 2002). "One trajectory leads to early arrest (prior to age 14) and adult crime and the other to late-onset arrests and desistance from adult crime" (Patterson & Yoerger, 2002, p. 147). However, the theory takes the position that both the early- and late-start trajectories represent variations of the same basic processes. That is, social-environmental influences, such as divorce, poverty, and

TABLE 6-4 Patterson's Two Developmental Stages of Antisocial Behavior

Early Onset	Late Onset
Begins preschool years	Begins late adolescence
Inept parenting more severe	Inept parenting less severe
High level of social incompetence	Social incompetence, but lower level
Arrest likely high as adult	Desist in offending as adult

parental depression, work in combination with inept parenting and deviant peer socialization to produce two different levels of delinquent and antisocial behavior. There are three variables that separate early- from late-onset trajectories: (1) the early-onset process begins during the preschool years, whereas the late onset begins in mid-adolescence, (2) the inept parenting is more severe for the early onset compared with the late onset, and (3) the levels of social incompetence are more pronounced for the early as compared with the late-onset delinquency (See **Table 6-4**). The inept parenting is often characterized by parents who use ineffective discipline practices, such as physical punishment, and who themselves tend to display antisocial behavior and be plagued by frequent marital transitions and discord.

Because of these differences, early-onset delinquents tend to demonstrate limited levels of social skills, more disruptive peer relations, and lower self-esteem. The late-onset delinquents exhibit similar deficiencies, but not to the degree of early onsets. Basically, late-onset delinquents are less antisocial than the early-onset delinquents but more antisocial than nondelinquents. Research finds that the likelihood of arrest as a young adult for early onsets is high, whereas that for late onsets is relatively low (Patterson & Yoerger, 2002). For example, the majority (71%) of late-onset boys desisted before becoming involved in adult crime (Patterson & Yoerger, 2002), while 74 percent of early-onset offenders are arrested by the time they become young adults (age 21 to 29) (Stattin & Magnusson, 1991).

GENDER DIFFERENCES. According to the coercive development perspective, gender differences in aggression are well in place by age five and persist throughout childhood and adolescence (Snyder, Reid, et al., 2003). These early differences are largely in favor of aggressiveness in boys. The coercive perspective further posits that gender differences in antisocial behavior are the result of the different environmental experiences and reinforcements encountered by boys and girls. Boys and girls evoke different responses from parents, and each gender responds differently to the same parenting conditions. Parents tend to be more coercive toward boys compared with girls, and this difference appears to be more pronounced for highly aggressive boys and girls (Snyder, Reid, et al., 2003). The coercive development model hypothesizes, therefore, that girls display less antisocial behavior because they are less frequently involved in coercive parent–child interactions.

Peer socialization factors begin to play a significant role as the child moves into preschool and kindergarten. Boys and girls demonstrate a strong preference for interaction with same-gender children beginning at age three. Boys tend to ignore girls who try to enter their play groups, even though an individual boy will play with one or two girls. There are more challenges, noncompliance, and rough-and-tumble play among boys, whereas there tends to be more cooperation, verbal exchange, compliance, and mutual accommodation among girls. Unlike for boys, for girls there are fewer highly antisocial, same-gender peers to model or with whom they can associate and exchange deviant talk. Consequently, when girls do begin to show antisocial behavior, it most often occurs during the adolescent years, and appears to be somewhat tied to pubescence. During adolescence, the preference for same-gender peers diminishes and a broad array of peer affiliates becomes available, including antisocial ones.

Callous-Unemotional Trait Theory

Do some people, including children, possess personality traits that render them particularly susceptible to antisocial behavior? Some researchers seem to think so. Among the most carefully studied is a group of traits collectively referred to as **callous-unemotional (CU)**, identified by Paul Frick and his colleagues (Barry et al., 2000; Frick, Barry, & Bodin, 2000; Frick, Ray, Thornton, & Kahn, 2014). These researchers conducted a series of studies to determine whether they could detect childhood precursors to adult psychopathy (discussed in more detail in Chapter 7). They were able to identify a group of children who were diagnosed with conduct disorders but who demonstrated particularly severe and chronic patterns of antisocial behavior beyond what is normally seen in other children with conduct disorders. They found that a subgroup of children and adolescents showed a lack of empathetic concern for others, limited capacity for guilt, and a poverty of emotional expression (Frick, Bodin, & Barry, 2000; Frick, O'Brien, Wootton, & McBurnett, 1994). These traits are highly characteristic of behavioral patterns typically found in adult psychopaths.

A considerable body of contemporary research continues to support the validity and reliability of the CU trait cluster. Contemporary research has found, for example, that children with CU traits are not afraid of being punished for their aggressive actions and view aggression as an effective means for dominating others (Pardini & Byrd, 2012). The CU children in the study tended to minimize the extent to which aggression caused victim suffering, and they openly acknowledged caring little about distress and suffering in others. The title of their research publication captures Pardini and Byrd's findings well: "I'll show you who's boss, even if you suffer and I get into trouble." Additional recent research has found that CU traits in childhood and adolescence are strongly predictive of psychopathy in adulthood (Kahn, Frick, Youngstrom, Findling, & Youngstrom, 2012). Furthermore, CU traits are predictive of severe aggressive patterns of behavior for both boys and girls, and for children as young as ages three and four (Kahn et al., 2012). Perhaps more disturbing, the level of severity of the aggressive behavior found in CU children and adolescents is considerably beyond that typically found for most juvenile offenders. Essentially, CU traits in childhood are predictive of lifelong serious, violent offending.

There is indication that CU traits may be present in some children diagnosed with conduct disorder. For example, in a mental health clinical sample of children and adolescents who were referred because of troubling problems, between 21 and 50 percent of those with diagnosed conduct disorder exhibited CU traits (Kahn et al., 2012). It should be emphasized that a diagnosis of conduct disorder is not a necessary condition for possessing CU traits. For example, some children and adolescents referred to the mental health clinic in the Kahn et al. study exhibited a high level of CU traits but did not have the diagnosis of conduct disorder. Interestingly, cruelty to animals was one of the indicators designating CU traits in the Kahn et al. investigation.

A growing body of research *suggests* that significant and sustained reductions in CU traits in children and adolescents can be accomplished through sophisticated, multimodal cognitive-behavioral treatment approaches (Kolko & Pardini, 2010; Salekin, 2010). This approach, combined with parental factors, such as increased warmth and low levels of harsh discipline, appears to date to offer the most promising results over time (Kolko & Pardini, 2010; Pardini, Lochman, & Powell, 2007).

Despite the above findings, some scholars suggest that the emphasis on CU traits is not warranted, because they offer only weak incremental utility to predicting criminal behavior among juveniles at high risk of serious offending (Skeem, Scott, & Mulvey, 2014). Though these traits do occur in some children and adolescents and should be recognized, they are not overwhelmingly present and, when displayed, they may mask emotions that are felt as a result of abuse or other victimization. We will return to the discussion of CU traits in Chapter 7, because they are highly similar to the core behavioral patterns of psychopathy. They will be particularly pertinent to material on juvenile psychopathy.

PREVENTION, INTERVENTION, AND TREATMENT OF JUVENILE OFFENDING

Treatment and Rehabilitation Strategies

Each year, more than 2 million youth come into contact with the juvenile justice system (Kinscherff, 2012). By some accounts, a substantial number of these youths (65% to 70%) have at least one diagnosable mental health need, and 20–25 percent have serious emotional problems (Kinscherff, 2012; Langton, 2012). One well-cited study (Shufelt & Cocozza, 2006) estimates that 55 percent of males and females involved in the juvenile justice system probably could receive at least two co-occurring mental health diagnoses. In addition, disruptive behavior disorders are diagnosed in approximately 45 percent of the boys and just over half (51%) of the girls who are involved with the juvenile justice system (Kinscherff, 2012). Substance abuse disorders are also common, occurring in at least half of the youth. Research in general has consistently linked substance abuse with serious juvenile offending (Mulvey, Schubert, & Chassin, 2010).

Substance abuse may or may not co-occur with mental health needs, however. Furthermore, it is important to stress that many youth who come into contact with the juvenile justice system do not merit a mental health diagnosis; our main concern in this text are those who do. In addition, we cannot ignore youths who are *at risk* of mental health needs, based on the many risk factors discussed in previous chapters. For example, peer rejection, inadequate parenting, physical abuse, toxic environments, and school failure can lead to serious depression along with antisocial behavior.

The number of prevention, intervention, and treatment programs that have been tried with juvenile offenders and children at risk or already involved in the juvenile justice system is overwhelming. Unfortunately, few programs designed to prevent delinquency or intervene to reduce recidivism have been demonstrated to be effective, although most such programs have not been thoroughly and systematically evaluated (Evans-Chase & Zhou, 2014). Indeed, in an initial pool of 141 studies of intervention programs in the United States for juveniles, only 21 studies met the test of being of high enough quality to merit making conclusions. Quality was measured by such factors as having a control group, and assuring that the intervention intended was actually delivered. The initial pool, it should be noted, included only studies with a control group and those reporting quantitative outcomes, with at least one recidivism measure (e.g., arrest, incarceration). As the Girls Study Group discussed earlier remarked, there are simply not enough resources available to conduct rigorous program evaluations (Zahn, Day, Mihalic, & Tichavsky, 2009; Zahn, Hawkins, et al., 2008). This comment would apply to programs for both boys and girls.

Serious forms of antisocial behavior in school-age children and adolescents have been particularly resistant to change (Borduin et al., 1995; Shaw et al., 2003). Serious juvenile offenders are especially prone to have low motivation for altering their antisocial behaviors and to display a lack of trust, noncompliance, and high levels of anger and impulsiveness (Tarolla et al., 2002). Although programs aimed at their conduct are many, most do not have significant positive effects because they begin too late in the developmental sequence. "By the time children reach these programs, often after referral by court personnel, they are already entrenched in a long history of antisocial interaction with parents, schools, and community that is not easily reversed" (Zigler et al., 1992, p. 997). It is no wonder, then, that the most highly touted programs are those that focus on early intervention, particularly within the context of the family environment (Biglan et al., 2012).

Although the above conclusions are discouraging, it is noteworthy that positive changes have been occurring. Some programs are emerging as highly successful in eliminating antisocial behavior and reducing delinquent behavior, even in children with serious behavior problems and even in institutionalized delinquents. Skeem, Scott, & Mulvey (2014) have observed that both public attitudes toward juveniles and juvenile justice policy are changing in directions that bode well for the rehabilitation of juvenile offenders, shifting from the punitive orientation of the late twentieth century. Nevertheless, in light of the lack of rigor displayed in much evaluation research (Evans-Chase et al., 2014), we cannot confirm the effectiveness of many of the programs with confidence. On the other hand, as Evans-Chase et al. (2014) observe, it cannot be said that the programs are *not* effective, merely that they have not been demonstrated to be.

Characteristics of Successful Programs

Despite concerns about the dearth of high-quality evaluation research, most juvenile justice research coalesces around those features that seem to be essential to a successful program (e.g., Lipsey, 2009; Zahn et al., 2009), particularly those directed at serious juvenile offenders. In some cases, though, programs do not necessarily have to target serious offenders; they may be of benefit to all children. For example, Zigler et al. (1992) concluded in their review that delinquency can be prevented by *early* childhood intervention programs that promote competence (social, interpersonal, and academic) in children across multiple systems in which they are embedded (family, school, peers, and community). These programs can be made available to children in various community settings, such as schools or child-care facilities. By contrast, crisis-oriented programs emphasizing counseling or social casework chiefly to deal with a presenting problem have been ineffective, largely because they focus on a single setting or competency and often are applied too late. Successful and promising prevention and treatment programs have the following characteristics.

THEY BEGIN EARLY.   Seriously antisocial children often can be identified when they are as young as four or five years old on the basis of their aggressive, disruptive, and noncompliant behaviors across home and preschool or school settings. As we learned earlier in the chapter, Terrie Moffitt (1993a; Moffitt et al., 1996) provides convincing evidence that the life-course-persistent delinquent manifests discernible indicators of antisocial behavior as early as age three. Consequently, some researchers (e.g., Guerra, Huesmann, Tolan, Van Acker, & Eron, 1995) recommend that prevention preferably begin no later in life than the first grade and definitely before age eight. Because seriously antisocial children are likely to progress in a spiral of escalating and more severe antisocial and violent behaviors over time, early intervention is critical if it is to be effective (Conduct Problems Prevention Research Group, 2004). In addition, there appears to be a mysterious jump in antisocial behavior between the first and second grade for many children, and, therefore, prevention programs enacted later than the first grade will probably need to be more intensive. Guerra et al. (1995) have observed that aggressive and antisocial behavior begin to develop even earlier in children living in the most economically deprived urban neighborhoods, an observation that appears to hold for both boys and girls (Tolan & Thomas, 1995). In addition, as we learned earlier in the book, there is considerable evidence to suggest that the earlier the signs of antisocial behavior, the more serious or violent the antisocial or criminal behavior will be in later life.

The above is not meant to suggest that all is lost if intervention does not begin early. As we see below, and later in the chapter, treatment that begins in adolescence can be highly successful. Nevertheless, early antisocial indicators often forecast a life of crime. As noted by Rolf Loeber (1990, p. 6), "there is considerable continuity among disruptive and antisocial behavior over time, even though they may manifest themselves differently at different ages." Loeber further finds that as children and adolescents progress toward more serious delinquent behavior, they tend to move toward diversification, rather than moving from one specific deviant behavior to another. Thus, it is clear that without early intervention, many children who are at risk of delinquency are more likely to engage in increasing levels of serious, chronic offending as they grow older, while still exhibiting less serious problems. That is, the adolescent who participates in a gang beating or a drive-by shooting will still use drugs and steal electronic equipment.

THEY FOLLOW DEVELOPMENTAL PRINCIPLES.   Prevention programs that are effective are soundly based on child developmental principles obtained from well-designed research (Dodge, 2001). As we noted earlier in the chapter, different developmental pathways can lead to serious violence and delinquency, and the age of onset of these behaviors can vary considerably. Furthermore, many researchers are drawing attention to the different developmental pathways taken by girls and boys; consequently, gender specific programming should be taken into account (see **Box 6-2**).

RESEARCH FOCUS

BOX 6-2   Gender Responsive Programming

Do girls and boys need different kinds of programs to address their antisocial behavior? Many experts believe they do. As discussed in the chapter, contemporary researchers often focus on similarities and differences between girls and boys—differences and similarities in developmental pathways, in risk factors, in protective factors, and offending history, among many others. It follows that scholars have called for gender responsive programs, defined as programs that respond specifically to the unique needs of girls or of boys (Bloom et al., 2002; Day, Zahn, & Tichavsky, 2014; Hubbard & Matthews, 2008). Additionally, more attention must be given to programming for lesbian, gay, bisexual, transitioning, and transgender youth, all of whom remain invisible in the vast majority of research.

Because girls have traditionally been left out of many evaluation studies, gender responsive programming often focuses on the female population, asking whether programs that have been evaluated for boys are equally adequate and effective for girls. Topics most typically raised are the need to focus on (a) physical and emotional safety, because girls have often been subjected to past abuse; (b) enhancement of self-esteem; and (c) building positive relationships with family and significant others. This is not instead of but rather in addition to the traditional programs that focus on drug and alcohol abuse or mental and physical health.

Margaret Zahn and her colleagues (Zahn, Day, Michalic, & Tichavsky, 2009) reviewed evaluation research of both gender-specific and nongender-specific treatment programs for juveniles. Interestingly, the well-performing programs that were nongender-specific were on the whole equally effective at reducing recidivism for girls and boys. We review some of these programs (e.g., MST, MTFC) later in the chapter. However, programs that were directed only at girls performed well in that they had positive effects on many factors, including self-esteem, parent–child relationships, self-efficacy, and educational achievement. There was, however, lack of evidence for long-term effects on recidivism. Zahn et al. stressed that program evaluation of gender-responsive programming is in its infancy and has limitations, but nothing in the evaluations suggests that such programming is not needed.

Questions for Discussion

1. Why might it be important to develop prevention and treatment programs aimed specifically at girls?
2. Considering the fact that adolescents are often placed in group treatment situations (e.g., substance abuse; alternatives to violence), should the groups be comprised exclusively of one sex or should they be equally dispersed?
3. Find and discuss any one example of a gender-specific program described in the professional literature.

In designing programs to prevent violence and chronic antisocial behavior, it is critical to understand the factors that place youths on a developmental trajectory of serious delinquency. Further, it is equally important to understand how these factors interact with the social environment. As persons move through life, they enter and exit a series of developmental stages (Dahlberg & Potter, 2001). Interestingly, data from the Rochester Youth Study (Thornberry, Huizinga, & Loeber, 1995) indicate that protective factors must be constantly present at transition from early to late adolescence and not simply in place at a single point in childhood or adolescence (Conduct Problems Prevention Research Group, 2004). "Although the negative impact of early risk factors may be buffered by the provision of protective support services during the grade school years, the risk factors themselves may continue to influence developmental trajectories during adolescence" (Conduct Problems Prevention Research Group, 2004, p. 193). This point is especially relevant when the child or adolescent continues to live in a dangerous social, physical, and emotional environment.

In an extensive review, Tremblay, LeMarquand, and Vitaro (1999) examined 50 prevention programs and discovered that 20 of them had been evaluated under carefully designed test conditions. Those programs that were most effective were based on sound child developmental research (Dodge, 2001). Linking the appropriate prevention program with the developmental stage of the youth is paramount for significant, long-term success in delinquency prevention.

THEY FOCUS ON MULTIPLE SETTINGS AND SYSTEMS.   Successful intervention programs should not only begin as early as possible, but must also be skillfully directed at as many causes and negative influences as possible. Targeting multiple potential risk or protective factors rather than one or two in isolation greatly increases the likelihood of positive adjustment and the significant reduction of antisocial and violent behavior (Tedeschi & Kilmer, 2005). Programs that have shown long-term success have taken multipronged approaches concentrating on treating children through their broad social environment, including improving relationships with family and peers and helping them to develop better academic skills for school success (Biglan et al., 2012). One model program, Fast Track, seeks to address the needs of highly aggressive children who display conduct problems from the moment of school entry (1999). The program focuses not only on the child's behavior in the classroom and with peers, but also on parenting skills and teacher class-room management. (see **Box 6-3** later in the chapter). Ongoing research on Fast Track suggests it is effective in reducing aggression (CPPRG, 2002). Furthermore, children in the program had a lower likelihood of arrest in late adolescence than children in a control group who had similar levels of initial risk (CPPRG, 2010). However, a recent analysis suggests that Fast Track did not improve long-term school outcomes, such as academic success in the high school years (Bierman, Coie, et al., 2013).

A focus on multiple settings and systems is important even for those programs that do not begin early in a child's life, however. Therapeutic interventions that provide individual counseling as well as a wide variety of services to adolescents and their families (e.g., employment services, education, family counseling) have received positive reviews (Evans-Chase & Zhou, 2014). We discuss some of these programs later in the chapter.

In addition, effective intervention programs include prenatal and perinatal medical care and intensive health education for pregnant women and mothers with young children (Coordinating Council on Juvenile Justice and Delinquency Prevention, 1996). These services reduce the delinquency risk factors of head and neurological injuries, exposure to toxins, maternal substance abuse, nutritional deficiencies, and perinatal difficulties. For example, research (Dietrich, Ris, Succop, Berger, & Bornschein, 2001; Needleman, McFarland, Ness, Fienberg, & Tobin, 2002) has discovered a strong relationship between high levels of lead in the bones of children and violence and delinquency in adolescence. Recall that in Chapter 2, we emphasized the significance of environmental contamination for healthy brain development.

There is little doubt that living conditions in many neighborhoods, particularly but not exclusively urban areas, are extremely harsh and that—for many children—the daily onslaught of violence, substance abuse, child abuse, and hopelessness is highly disruptive to normal development, even if they experience these conditions only indirectly. For the child who is directly exposed to an adverse family life and inadequate living arrangements with little opportunity to develop even the rudiments of social, interpersonal, and academic skills for dealing effectively with his or her environment, the damage may be almost irreparable. Clearly, the longer a child is exposed to an adverse environment, the more difficult it will be to modify his or her life course away from crime and delinquency. Although our attention is often focused on highly populated urban areas, a child living in suburbia, in a small town, or in a rural, isolated area may also be negatively affected. He may not witness street crime or be subjected to gang influences, but he may witness violence or serious criminal activity in the home, the extended family, or within his circle of peers.

THEY ACKNOWLEDGE AND RESPECT CULTURAL BACKGROUNDS. Although some urban neighborhoods contain numerous risk factors, these same neighborhoods also may be rich in values and traditions that, if acknowledged, would qualify as crucial protective factors. For example, various ethnic and racial groups place great value on the extended family, a particular style of music, or certain holiday traditions and celebrations. The names given to one's children have special meaning in many families, often seeking to retain one's cultural identity. Teachers, clinicians, and service providers do a disservice when they make little effort to correctly pronounce or spell a child's distinctive name. These cultural markers can affect the development of antisocial behavior, sometimes promoting it but often suppressing it. Effective programs, then, are sensitive to a family's cultural background and heritage and they promote its positive aspects.

THEY FOCUS ON THE FAMILY FIRST.   Research has continually shown that the most successful interventions concentrate first on improving parenting and the family system in general, followed by improving peer relations and academic skills. It is clear that certain family relationships and parenting practices strongly promote serious and violent delinquency, while other practices and relationships discourage it (Patterson, Forgatch, & DeGarmo, 2010). Some family characteristics seem to be linked to delinquency regardless of ethnic or socioeconomic status (Gorman-Smith, Tolan, Huesmann, & Zelli, 1996). The family characteristics most closely connected to serious delinquency are poor parental monitoring and supervision of the child's activities, poor and inconsistent discipline, and a lack of family closeness or cohesion.

Recall that in Chapter 2 we discussed risk factors for antisocial behavior, including many associated with the family. In that chapter we emphasized, as well, that contemporary researchers are focusing on the treatment approaches that will foster nurturing, healthy family environments (Biglan et al., 2012). According to Dishion and Andrews (1995), studies have consistently revealed that negative, coercive exchanges between parents or caretakers and children are predictive of child antisocial behavior (e.g., Patterson, 1986), delinquent behavior (e.g., Bank & Patterson, 1992), and adolescent substance abuse (e.g., Dishion & Loeber, 1985). Research also indicates that emotional closeness and family cohesion, where the child receives emotional support, adequate communication, and love, are essential in the prevention of antisocial behavior and delinquency (Gorman-Smith et al., 1996; Schwalbe et al., 2012).

Peer systems are critically important, and research has shown that negative peer associations are significant predictors of both substance abuse and delinquency (O'Donnell, Hawkins, & Abbott, 1995). Thus far, though, intervention programs have been *unsuccessful* in utilizing peer groups as effective change agents in modifying these antisocial behaviors. Interventions that are peer focused can actually have unintended negative effects if they require increased contact with antisocial peers (Vitaro & Tremblay, 1994). Similarly, Dishion and Andrews (1995) found that placing high-risk teens into groups together encouraged escalations in tobacco use and problem behaviors in school. Dishion and Andrews further discovered that bringing high-risk peers together may have actually served to increase contact with deviant peers and, in the long run, exacerbated their antisocial involvement. They recommended that intervention programs that use antisocial peers as change agents be discouraged unless very carefully designed. Likewise, research indicates that group homes for delinquents may increase delinquent behavior (Chamberlain, 1996). The assumption is that antisocial peers tend to model and encourage other antisocial peers.

In summary, effective prevention and treatment programs begin early if possible, are based on child development principles, deal with multiple systems, recognize the cultural influences interacting on the child, and focus on the family and parental skills. When working directly with the developing antisocial child, the effective program focuses on improving positive social and prosocial skills, enhancing academic and learning skills, and promoting self-esteem and confidence.

Classification of Prevention and Treatment Programs

As mentioned earlier, many prevention, intervention, and treatment programs have been tried with children and adolescents, but few have been submitted to rigorous evaluation. Recall that of an initial data base of 141 studies, Evans-Chase and Zhou (2014) found only 21 of these studies passed scrutiny. Other meta-analyses using less strict criteria (e.g., Schwalbe et al., 2012) found that programs with respectable evaluations nonetheless were not demonstrated to be effective at reducing antisocial behavior significantly. In some cases, though, other improvements (e.g., in behavior, self-esteem, or interpersonal relationships) were found. It is also clear that—for those juveniles with substance abuse problems—addressing and treating these problems significantly reduces the likelihood of continued offending (Mulvey, 2011).

Because of the large number of programs available for juveniles, we will only cover those that are well known or that have been notably successful or promising. Some treatment programs targeting specific juvenile offenders (e.g., juvenile sex offenders or juvenile murderers) will be covered in later chapters.

In order to provide some structure to this array of programs, we will organize the remainder of the chapter into three main sections: (1) primary prevention (also called universal prevention in the literature), (2) selective prevention (also called secondary prevention), and (3) treatment or intervention (also called tertiary prevention). These three categories are similar to the public health model of prevention originally proposed by Gordon (1983), and elaborated upon further by Guerra, Tolan, and Hammond (1994) and Mulvey, Arthur, and Reppucci (1993) among others. Although this classification provides structure for the purpose of discussing programs, there is often overlap between these convenient divisions because many programs target a mixture of populations. For example, project Headstart—which was originally designed to provide a "catch-up" educational program for economically disadvantaged families and was considered a primary prevention program—has evolved into a broader program that helps a wider socio-economic spectrum. Furthermore, because some of the children in Headstart may qualify as seriously "at-risk" children, for them, the program could be considered a selective or secondary program. Likewise, Multisystemic Therapy (MST), because it focuses on the family unit, may include both serious delinquents and their siblings who could be considered at risk of future offending.

Primary (or **universal) prevention** is designed to prevent delinquent behavior before any signs of the behavioral pattern emerge. Primary prevention programs are most often implemented early in the developmental sequence of children, preferably before the ages of seven or eight. Typically, they are conducted in the school or preschool setting, and focus on large groups of children, *regardless of possible differences in risk of delinquency*. In most instances, primary prevention programs target all children within a particular geographic area or setting (e.g., a school or school grade) without any further selection criteria (Offord, Chmura Kraemeer, Kazdin, Jensen, & Harrington, 1998). Many of these programs require the promulgation of far-reaching policies and procedures, which often involve legislative authorization and funding. Examples include widespread programs to enhance prenatal care, maternal and infant care and nutrition, and family management programs for preschool children (Committee on Preventive Psychiatry, 1999). Another excellent example of this approach is the development of resilience or protective factors in young children before school entry or soon after entry. We discuss this far-reaching but powerful approach in more detail shortly.

Selective or **secondary prevention** consists of working with *specific* children and adolescents who are at *high risk* and who display some *early signs of antisocial behavior* but have not yet been classified or adjudicated delinquent by the court. The basic assumption in selective prevention is that early detection and early intervention will prevent the youngster from graduating into more serious, habitual offending. A good example of this type of prevention is the Perry Preschool Project started in 1962. The project was an organized educational program directed at the cognitive and social development of young children considered at *high risk* of delinquency and school failure (Berrueta-Clement, Schweinhart, Barnett, & Weikart, 1987). Another well-known example of this prevention strategy is juvenile diversion, which diverts first-time offenders from formal court processing but places them in short-term programs that presumably will discourage them from reoffending. An advantage of selective prevention programs is that they focus on those youth who should benefit most from the services. That is, the effort is more concentrated on those at risk rather than on an entire group of children, many of whom may show no risk factors at all. A disadvantage is that secondary prevention programs isolate and label children as potential problems, possibly creating a self-fulfilling prophecy: "I'm in this special program, therefore I'm different (and bad). So I might as well *be* bad."

The third approach (**tertiary prevention**) is generally referred to as **treatment** (or intervention) in the delinquency literature. We prefer to use the term *treatment*, because it can be argued that primary and selective prevention are also forms of intervention. Furthermore, although there is some overlap between selective prevention and treatment—in the sense that juveniles in selective prevention programs also often receive treatment—we reserve "treatment" to apply to those programs designed to reduce serious, habitual delinquent or antisocial behavior by adjudicated delinquents. Usually, those fully involved delinquents or highly antisocial children have been referred for psychological care in the community or have been placed in residential correctional facilities, training schools, or rehabilitation centers.

Primary Prevention

In the past, prevention and treatment programs tried to focus on reducing or eliminating *risk* factors that children and adolescents face during their formative years. In recent years, however, a discernible shift has taken place that emphasizes the development and enhancement of *protective* factors. While both approaches are important, in this chapter, we focus on protective factors through the development of resilience. We contend that the development of resilience is an extremely effective method for primary and selective prevention of delinquency in children and adolescents and also has enormous potential as an effective treatment strategy. Consequently, we begin the primary prevention section by describing how resilience can come into play across all three classifications of prevention and treatment.

With increasing awareness of the protective factors that promote resilience in children and adolescents, theorists, researchers, and policy makers are now attempting to apply this knowledge toward the prevention of antisocial behavior, particularly in children considered at moderate to high risk. Prevention and treatment programs that are designed to foster and maintain resilience in youth are also known as strength-based programs. It should be emphasized that resilience is made up of ordinary rather than extraordinary processes, and that the average child can be taught to become resilient (Smith, 2006). Prevention programs that promote cognitive and social competencies in the child or adolescent, improve childrearing practices in the family, and foster the development and maintenance of effective social support systems are most likely to be effective in the long run.

Strategies for developing resilience include the enhancement of a child's strengths and interests, as well as the reduction of risk or stressors, and the facilitation of protective processes. Overall, the rallying cry for many programs focusing on enhancing resilience has become, "Every child has talents, strengths, and interests that offer the child potential for a bright future" (Damon, 2004, p. 13). These attitudes reflect a major transformation in conceptualizing the prevention of antisocial behavior and other childhood problems over the past few decades. This is partly because the many risk factors that were described in Chapters 2 and 3 are often very difficult to change, particularly in juvenile treatment programs (Hawkins et al., 2009).

Children who are at risk of engaging in serious antisocial behavior have been exposed to aversive events, which often cannot be reversed. These can include dire economic situations, abuse (physical or emotional), rejection by peers, or trauma such as the sudden loss of a parent or sibling, alone or in combination. This is why some researchers advocate that we must help youth learn how to manage their risk, such as by effectively dealing with the trauma of childhood physical and sexual abuse (Ruffolo, Sarri, & Goodkind, 2004). There is no single means of maintaining equilibrium following highly aversive events, but rather there are multiple pathways to resilience (Bonanno, 2004), as there are multiple pathways on the road to delinquency. For example, McKnight and Loper (2002) found that the most prominent resilience factors in adolescent girls at risk of delinquency were an academic motivation and a desire to go to college, absence of substance abuse, feeling loved and wanted, belief that teachers treat students fairly, parents trusting adolescent children, and religiosity. In a study using ADD Health data, however, Hawkins et al. (2009) found that religiosity was not a protective factor with one exception: girls reporting high levels of religiosity reported lower incidents of selling drugs. Connectedness to school also did not serve as a protective factor, although success in school was protective for some forms of delinquency, such as assault and status offenses. Interestingly, "girls who were successful in school were more likely to commit a property offense during late adolescence and young adulthood" (Hawkins et al., 2009, p. 5). Hawkins et al. also found that the strongest protective factor was the extent to which a girl felt she had caring adults in her life. The presence of caring adults reduced the likelihood that girls would engage in several forms of antisocial behavior.

Waaktaar, Christie, Borge, and Torgerson (2004) conducted a study to explore how resilience or protective factors could be used to help at-risk youths. The youth averaged 12.3 years of age, and slightly over one-third were girls. They represented a medley of cultural and ethnic backgrounds, including the West Indies, Far East, Central Asia, the Arab world, and northeast Africa. All the participants had experienced serious and/or multiple life stresses, and—at the time of the study—they were not receiving "satisfactory help" through "psychiatric" intervention.

The researchers targeted four resilience factors for therapeutic intervention: positive peer relations, self-efficacy, creativity, and coherence. Positive peer relations were defined as prosocial interactions, peer acceptance, and support. Self-efficacy is the belief that one can achieve desired goals through one's own actions (Bandura, 1989, 1997). Hundreds of studies have supported the observation that self-efficacy leads to a range of positive outcomes, and it is regarded as central to resilience (Lightsey, 2006). Creativity in this context refers to individual talent to create an artistic or other communicative product, such as a song, dance, film, play, poem, or short story. This approach requires that children be encouraged to express themselves and their experiences symbolically. Coherence refers to the ways in which people evaluate themselves and their circumstances both cognitively and emotionally. It involves "helping young people to find a coherent meaning to their past, present, and future life through positive thinking, accepting the reality of their bad experiences, avoiding self-blame for uncontrollable circumstances and finding adaptive paths forward" (Waaktaar et al., 2004, p. 173). The researchers discovered that child therapy that focuses on these four concepts has the potential to enhance resilience significantly.

Selective or Secondary Prevention

Selective (or secondary) prevention is directed at children and adolescents who are believed to be "at risk" of engaging in delinquency on the basis of any number of risk factors (e.g., low self-concept, highly dysfunctional family situation, conduct disorder). In a comprehensive review of the research literature, Tremblay and Craig (1995) concluded that selective prevention programs with at-risk youths tend to be successful mainly when the intervention aims at more than one risk factor (e.g., children's disruptive behavior, aggressive behavior, and parenting), lasts for relatively long periods of time (at least one year), and is implemented before adolescence. The time must be quality time, and the more intensive the intervention, the better. Like much of the research alluded to thus far, the programs identified by Tremblay and Craig were especially effective when implemented during the preschool or the early elementary school years. In the case of some selective prevention programs, such as juvenile diversion, such early intervention is not possible.

Nevertheless, diversion programs can be effective, depending on what approach is being taken. Diversion from standard prosecution for both adults and juveniles is now a standard part of the criminal justice process; with respect to juveniles, diversion is often accompanied by substance abuse treatment or mental health treatment. Recall the statistics cited earlier in the chapter regarding juveniles with mental health needs in the juvenile justice system. Concerns about these increasing numbers of juveniles prompted the National Center for Mental Health and Juvenile Justice (NCMHJJ) to fund initiatives to divert these juveniles from prosecution (Colwell, Villarreal, & Espinosa, 2012). Colwell et al. studied juveniles with mental health needs who were assigned to specialized supervision as a diversionary approach and a comparison group of juveniles without the specialized supervision. The youth with mental health needs were significantly less likely to be adjudicated delinquent and were also more likely to improve in problem-solving skills and interpersonal relationships. Although the study was a preliminary one, it suggests an efficient use of this particular diversionary program for juveniles with mental health needs.

There are exceptions, but unfortunately diversion programs as a group have not been found effective in reducing further offending. They may serve primarily to "buy time" for the juvenile until he or she passes through adolescence. They are important in that they give the juvenile a second chance (and in some cases a third or fourth) so that he or she will not have a criminal record. However, *as a group* they do not reduce recidivism. Furthermore, as Schwalbe et al. (2012, p. 28) note, "a cursory review of the literature suggests that emerging data on evidence-based practices has been slow to penetrate diversion program development." Schwalbe et al. conducted a meta-analysis of 28 studies testing juvenile diversion programs and found that diversion's effect on recidivism was nonsignificant. Five types of diversion programming were identified in this group of studies: case management, individual treatment, family treatment, youth court, and restorative justice. Of the five, only family intervention and restorative justice showed a positive effect on recidivism, with evidence-based family intervention having the strongest positive result.

Schwalbe et al., (2012) emphasize that the heterogeneity of diversion programming makes it impossible to conclude that it is an effective approach for juvenile offenders. However, there is much more promise if the programs focus on the family and emphasize restorative justice. Restorative justice is an approach that recognizes the harm done to victims of crime, the accountability of the offender, and the needs of the community. In addition, a focus on evidence-based cognitive-behavior therapy for those programs that rely on individual treatment would be recommended.

Selective prevention programs increasingly are provided primarily to those children identified as showing *early* signs of developing serious and persistent antisocial behavior. It is clear that high-risk children can be identified with reasonable accuracy in early life, at least by the beginning of elementary school (Dodge & Pettit, 2003; Hill, Lochman, Coie, & Greenberg, 2004; Lochman & Conduct Problems Prevention Research Group, 1995). As noted by Dodge and Pettit (2003), the effectiveness of early screening has major consequences for public policy. Schools can play a more active role than they have in the past in identifying young children who could benefit from a prevention program. In addition, selective prevention programs can be more focused, more efficient, and more intensive than universal prevention programs (Hill et al., 2004). It should also be mentioned that prevention with young children offers far more hope than prevention with adolescents who may be already down the path of persistent antisocial behavior. However, prevention methods must span from childhood to adolescence because new risk factors emerge at each new developmental stage (Dodge & Pettit, 2003). That is to say that the child must be followed through his or her developmental years. (See **Box 6-3** for an example of such a program.)

TREATMENT PROGRAM FOCUS

BOX 6-3   The Fast Track Experiment

The Fast Track Project is a multisite, multicomponent prevention program for young children at high risk of long-term antisocial behavior (Conduct Problems Prevention Research Group, 1999). It is based on developmental pathway theory (e.g., Moffitt, 1993a) and is longitudinal in design. The Fast Track Project is guided by developmental theory that posits that multiple influences interact in the development of antisocial behavior (Conduct Problems Prevention Research Group, 2004).

Fast Track is a two-pronged project. Participants in the program include both high-risk children (selective or secondary prevention) and all the children in school grades one to five (primary or universal prevention) within a particular school. The children in the high-risk group began to show persistent and serious antisocial behavior—particularly aggressive behavior—in early childhood (before first grade), as reported by parents and teachers.

The program is divided into two major phases: the elementary school (grades 1 to 5) and adolescent periods (grades 6 to 10). The elementary school phase addresses six areas of risk and protective factors: parenting, child social problem-solving and emotional coping skills, peer relations, classroom atmosphere and curriculum, academic achievement with a focus on reading, and home–school relations (Conduct Problems Prevention Research Group, 2004). In the early grades, Fast Track educational consultants (experienced

teachers with training and expertise working with behaviorally challenged children) make frequent visits to classrooms and meet teachers individually or in small groups to discuss classroom challenges and offer support. Families are invited to participate in weekly parent/child groups, plus home visits, tutoring, and school follow-up. The adolescent phase, middle and secondary school, focuses on four areas associated with successful adolescent adjustment: peer affiliation and peer influence, academic orientation and achievement, social cognition and identity development, and parent and family relationships (Conduct Problems Prevention Research Group, 2004). The protective role of parental supervision and monitoring was also emphasized.

Children in the program were compared with a group of high-risk children (the control group) who did not participate in the program. Early results indicated that the participating children, relative to the children in the control condition, progressed significantly in their acquisition of most of the skills deemed to be critical protective factors (Conduct Problems Prevention Research Group, 1999). The high-risk experimental group children, compared with the control high-risk children, exhibited improvements in their social, emotional, and academic skills, especially their reading skills. Their peer relationships also improved significantly. The results were equally effective for both boys and girls. Parents who

(continued)

participated in the program displayed more warmth, appropriate and consistent discipline, self-efficacy, and positive school involvement. Follow-up research also found that in late adolescence, the experimental group had lower levels of criminal arrest compared with the control group (CPPRG, 2010).

The primary prevention effects of Fast Track were equally impressive. Classrooms that participated in the program were found to have lower peer-rated aggression and lower peer-related hyperactive-disruptive behaviors than were those classrooms that did not participate in the program (the control groups). Ratings by research observers in the classrooms indicated that prevention classrooms had better classroom atmosphere, students were better able to express their feelings appropriately (self-regulation), and the classroom as a whole was better able to stay focused and on task.

Questions for Discussion

1. As noted in the text, recent research (e.g., Bierman et al., 2013) found that the Fast Track Program did not improve long-term school outcomes, such as grades and high school graduation rates. Weigh this finding against the more positive findings and discuss its implications.
2. Fast Track is a continuing, widely watched program. Which aspects of it do you find most appealing? What if any concerns do you have about how it operates?

Treatment Approaches

The effectiveness of most treatment approaches has not been established. In many cases, the treatments have not been empirically investigated or evaluated (Lipsey, Howell, Kelly, Chapman, & Carver, 2010; Zahn et al., 2009). Nevertheless, some meta-analyses are available, and these have added considerably to this body of information (Hanson, Bourgon, Helmus, & Hodgson, 2009). For example, treatment programs that concentrate on self-regulation skills and addressing cognitions hold considerable promise if the treatment programs also include the family, school, peers, and community. It has also become apparent—from a psychological perspective—that the most effective treatment strategies for both juveniles and adults are based on the RNR (risks, needs, responsivity) approach (Andrews, Bonta, & Hoge, 1990; Bonta & Andrews, 2007). Cognitive-behavioral programs fit nicely into RNR principles. We discuss RNR in more detail in Chapter 13.

A wide range of treatment methods have been tried specifically with juvenile delinquents. In a common scenario, the juvenile court refers a persistent delinquent youth to an outpatient mental health clinic or mental health practitioner for counseling and psychotherapy. The traditional approach relied on a one-on-one strategy of providing psychotherapy to an individual, but today group treatment is more likely to occur. Delinquent youth who require a more restrictive setting are usually placed in a residential facility where again group therapy is more common than individual counseling. In recent years, in large part due to limited financial resources, increasingly more juveniles are being allowed to remain in community settings, receiving community treatment services (Skeem, Scott, & Mulvey, 2014).

It is important to realize, though, that research has continually demonstrated that individual-based psychotherapy has not been shown to be effective when used in isolation (Committee on Preventive Psychiatry, 1999; Letourneau et al., 2009; Lipsey et al., 2010; Tarolla et al., 2002). In other words, simply applying any form of psychotherapy to a child or adolescent already on a developmental path leading to serious delinquency without involving the social environment and targeting developmental cascade effects, is in most cases, a waste of time, money, and energy. As Letourneau and Miner (2005, p. 306) observed, "the developmental literature suggests that treatments that focus primarily on changing the individual characteristics (e.g., cognitions and behaviors) of youthful offenders, without also targeting relevant factors with caregivers (e.g., monitoring), peers (e.g., improving ties with prosocial peers), and school (e.g., increasing and improving caregiver-teacher communications) might be of limited usefulness" (p. 306).

Restrictive interventions for serious juvenile offenders, such as residential treatment and incarceration, have also not been effective and are extremely expensive (Henggeler, 1996; Mulvey, 2011). Moreover, any prevention or treatment program that focuses on only one risk factor is unlikely to lead to long-lasting change in delinquency, because multiple other forces and cumulative risk factors act to support antisocial development (Dodge & Pettit, 2003). According to Henggeler (1996, p. 139), "Restrictive out-of-home placements neither address the known determinants of serious antisocial behavior nor alter the natural ecology to which the youth will eventually return. Indeed, data show that incarceration may not even serve a community protection function."

There are some additional points to note before proceeding. The characteristics of treatment programs may be different for those juveniles who receive treatment while confined in an institution compared with those who receive treatment in a noninstitutional setting. Not only is the setting different, but the participants may also differ in terms of offending history and the seriousness of the offending. For example, those offenders who are in an institution are likely to be considered dangerous or a high risk to reoffend. There are likely to be gender and age differences also.

Furthermore, it is difficult to make conclusions about wide-range effectiveness of intervention programs under the auspices of juvenile corrections because there are so many different treatment programs with different policies, procedures, staff training, and outcome measures. For example, Krisberg and Howell (1998) remarked that in juvenile corrections, "there are training schools, detention centers, camps, ranches, wagon trains, environmental institutes, group homes, boot camps, residential programs for emotionally disturbed youths, chemical dependency programs, correctional sailing shills, and independent living arrangements" (p. 347). Juvenile corrections also involve a wide range with respect to size, locations, and security levels.

Not only must effective treatment approaches be multisystemic and address the multidimensional causes of juvenile offending, they must also be intensive and long lasting if they are going to have an impact on juvenile offenders who have already become deeply entrenched into their antisocial behavioral patterns. The behaviors of hard-core juvenile offenders (such as LCP juveniles) are often severe, pervasive, and well learned. While treatment for them is by no means hopeless, LCP delinquents require innovation and extreme patience for the many frustrating setbacks that will certainly occur over the long haul. With the above cautions in mind, we discuss below some of the treatment approaches that have been used with delinquents. We begin with treatments tried in residential settings, and then proceed to those based in the community.

TRADITIONAL RESIDENTIAL TREATMENT.   The traditional form of residential treatment is the juvenile "training school" or "rehabilitation center," where youths are incarcerated for extended periods of time, sometimes even until they reach adulthood. These institutional settings are typically physically secure and may represent the "last stop" for youths with whom less restrictive community settings have been tried. On the other hand, a juvenile found to have committed a one-time serious crime—such as a murder or a rape—and not transferred to adult court may also be placed in such a setting. As a group, youths in residential treatment have high rates of substance abuse, emotional disturbance, and low academic achievement.

The evaluation research on institutional treatment is not encouraging. Studies have even demonstrated that incarcerated juvenile offenders who receive residential treatment have higher rates of criminal involvement after release than their counterparts who received intensive family and community-based treatment (Tarolla et al., 2002).

Lipsey and Wilson (1998) examined the effectiveness of two hundred treatment programs for serious juvenile offenders. The analysis included 83 studies of the effects of treatment with *institutionalized* offenders, 74 of which involved juveniles in the custody of juvenile justice institutions, and nine that involved residential institutions administered by mental health or private agencies. The analysis also included 117 treatment programs for *noninstitutionalized* juveniles, most of whom were on probation or parole. Although the results were mixed and confusing, with no one particular treatment program showing superiority, the average program for both institutionalized and noninstitutionalized offenders produced a 12 percent reduction in subsequent reoffense rates. The most effective programs (e.g., teaching family home, interpersonal skills development, and other broad-based interventions) were able to produce a 40 percent reduction rate, a promising result, while some other programs (e.g., Wilderness/Challenge, vocational programs, milieu therapy) were largely ineffective by most measures. The most effective programs included key components, such as focusing on social skills training, parent management, and family support.

MST AND FFT. In recent years, two forms of intensive treatment for juveniles displaying antisocial behavior—including serious violent offending—have received attention in the research literature. The programs have some similarities but are also based on somewhat different philosophies (Baglivio, Jackowski, Greenwald, & Wolff, 2014). Both programs target juveniles who remain in their own homes or with family caretakers, and both are considered "model programs," having been studied extensively and reviewed positively as being evidence-based.

Multisystemic therapy (MST) was designed and is promoted by Scott Henggeler and his colleagues for serious delinquents, including those with substance abuse and violent offenses (Henggeler & Borduin, 1990; Hengeller et al., 2009; Schaeffer & Borduin, 2005). MST is responsive to the many social systems influencing the youth's delinquent behavior. "Consistent with the known causes of adolescent criminal behavior and substance abuse, MST addresses the multi-determined nature of antisocial behavior in adolescents at individual, family, peer, school, and community levels" (Henggeler, 2011, p. 376). The major focus of MST is the family, all of whose members should be actively involved in the program. In fact, studies have found that siblings of juveniles who were targeted for the program were significantly less likely to be involved in substance use and in criminality as adults than siblings of juveniles who received individual treatment from more traditional programs (Rowland, Chapman, & Henggeler, 2008; Wagner, Borduin, Sawyer, & Dopp, 2014).

MST is an intensive time-limited form of intervention where trained therapists have daily contact with the adolescent and his or her family for approximately 60 hours over four months, though the time span can vary. The therapist's caseload is small, averaging four to six families per counselor. MST therapists identify both strengths and problem areas within the individual, the family, and the other social systems, such as peers, school, social service agencies, and parents' workplace. To a large extent, MST is based on the systems model developed by Bronfenbrenner (1979).

Together, counselors and family collaborate to develop pertinent treatment goals, as well as appropriate plans to meet these goals (Henggeler, 1996). Barriers and impediments to the plan, such as uncooperative family members, teachers, and school administrators, are worked with directly and actively. MST is an action-based treatment program in that it tries to get the involved family members to take "action" (behaviorally do something) rather than just talking. Since its modest beginnings in the late 1970s, there are more than 450 MST programs operating in over 30 states and 11 nations, serving more than 15,000 adolescents with serious antisocial behavioral problems (Henggeler, 2011).

As noted above, MST focuses on the strengths of the family. The program tries to identify family strengths and provide the parent(s) with the resources needed for effective parenting and for developing a better functioning and cohesive family unit. For example, the therapists might work with the parents on improving communication and problem-solving skills, being less susceptible to manipulation by the child, enhancing their consistency in administering discipline and rewards, helping them find ways to reduce stress, and reducing parental drug and alcohol abuse.

MST therapists also work with the targeted youth to remediate deficits in interpersonal skills that hinder acceptance by prosocial peers. Youth and therapist may work on modifying thought processes and coping mechanisms that may interfere with the family, peer, school, and neighborhood microsystems. Other MST strategies include decreasing the teenager's antisocial peer contacts and increasing affiliation with prosocial peers and activities. Another approach is to develop tactics to monitor and promote the youth's school performance. For example, the therapist would work toward opening and maintaining effective communication lines among parents, teachers, and administrators.

Extensive research has been published on the effectiveness of MST, garnering very positive results (Baglivio et al., 2014; Evans-Chase & Zhou, 2014). Henggeler (2011) observed that approximately 21 studies with randomized clinical trials have been published. Most had focused on serious juvenile offenders, such as violent offenders, sex offenders, and drug-abusing offenders, and the vast majority produced favorable results. "Numerous clinical trials have established the capacity of MST to reduce youth criminal behavior, substance abuse, psychiatric symptoms, and out-of-home placements while improving family relations and school performance" (Henggeler, 2011, p. 376).

Although most of the research on MST has been conducted by those associated with the program (e.g., Borduin et al., 1995; Borduin, Schaeffer, & Heiblum, 2009; Henggeler et al., 1993; Schaeffer & Borduin, 2005), studies by independent researchers not associated with MST also have produced favorable results (e.g., Curtis, Ronan, Heiblum, & Crellin, 2009; Glisson et al., 2010; Timmons-Mitchell, Bender, Kishna, & Mitchell, 2006).

Significant follow-up studies (Sawyer & Borduin, 2011; Schaeffer & Borduin, 2005) found that MST participants had significantly lower recidivism rates than did those participants who received individual therapy, even into adulthood. For example, Schaeffer and Borduin found that MST offenders, compared with individually treated offenders, experienced 54 percent fewer arrests and 57 percent fewer days of confinement in adult correctional facilities. Sawyer and Borduin found that after 22 years, the positive impact of the therapy was still significant. More specifically, MST participants were significantly less likely to be arrested for felony crimes than recipients of other therapies (34.8% vs. 54.8%, respectively). Other recent research continues to support the effectiveness of MST with adolescent sex offenders (Borduin, Schaeffer, & Heiblum, 2009; Letourneau et al., 2009).

Despite the above optimistic findings, a meta-analysis of the effectiveness of MST concluded that there were not significant differences between MST and other intensive treatment regimens (Littell, Campbell, Green, & Toews, 2009). Likewise, a study conducted in the Netherlands also found no significant differences with respect to violent behavior, but MST was found more effective in reducing property crimes and addressing some externalizing (disruptive) disorders (Asscher, Dekovic, Manders, van der Laan, & Prins, 2013). **Externalizing disorders** refer to behaviors such as defiance of authority figures, hostility, lying, temper tantrums, intentionally annoying others, and aggression. It is obvious that the program has limitations, but it continues to be regarded as one of the most successful approaches to treating juveniles in a community setting (Baglivio et al., 2014).

Current research has identified two key factors as critical to the program's success for dealing with antisocial behavior: changes in caregiver discipline practices and a reduction in youth associations with deviant peers (Henggeler et al., 2009; Tighe, Pistrang, Casdagli, Baruch, & Butler, 2012). Deković and associates (Deković, Asscher, Manders, Prins, & van der Laan, 2012) found that one of the important aspects targeted by MST for improvement in parental discipline practices is parental sense of competence. The researchers were able to show that increases in parental competence enhance parents' faith in their own ability to parent adequately, especially in terms of warmth, affection, parental supervision, and appropriate discipline. "The increases in sense of competence may motivate parents to be more persistent in attaining their goals, following through their discipline efforts, and thus becoming more consistent in their behavior toward the adolescent" (Deković et al., 2012, p. 10). This chain of events reduced the adolescent's negative and antisocial behavior.

A group of researchers (Robinson, et al., 2014) have studied factors that might influence MST outcomes in a negative direction. Specifically, Robinson et al. wondered what might compromise the positive effects of the parental monitoring and discipline, which is a key goal of MST. The researchers learned that parental monitoring decreased juvenile misbehavior only in neighborhoods that were not plagued by such negative factors as unsupervised youth, drug use, and other crimes such as theft. The socioeconomic status (SES) of the family itself—derived from the occupation and educational level of the caretakers—was not a significant factor. It is important to emphasize that neither neighborhood disadvantage nor SES influenced the parental monitoring; parenting practices improved with the therapy regardless of these factors. However, the effectiveness of monitoring was more limited in disadvantaged neighborhoods. Robinson et al. conclude, "Results of this study are consistent with literature suggesting that parental strategies may be less effective in some neighborhoods than in others…" (p. 108). Interestingly, the authors observe that MST therapists themselves should take steps to increase their own comfort level in working with families in disadvantaged neighborhoods, citing research that therapeutic outcomes may be affected by this discomfort (Glebova et al., 2012). Alternatively, helping the family move to a "better" neighborhood may be a solution. This, though, does nothing to help those families that must remain in the disadvantaged neighborhood and would seem questionable from a social policy viewpoint.

Most recently, follow-up research on siblings of the delinquents has been conducted, again—as noted above—with favorable results. Wagner et al. (2014) focused on 129 siblings of serious and violent juvenile offenders 25 years after the family received MST. Compared with siblings of serious and juvenile offenders who had received individual therapy, the MST siblings were significantly less likely to be arrested. Siblings in the non-MST condition were three times as likely to be convicted of a felony. Likewise, Rowland, Chapman, and Henggeler (2008) found a reduction in substance use among the siblings of substance-abusing juvenile offenders.

Functional Family Therapy (FFT) is a model program with many similarities to MST, and it too has garnered very favorable reviews in the research literature examining both short-term and follow-up recidivism (Alexander, Pugh, Parson, & Sexton, 2000; Gordon, Arbuthnot, Gustafson, & McGreen, 1988). "FFT has an established record of outcome studies that demonstrate its efficacy with a wide variety of adolescent-related problems, including youth violence, drug abuse, and other delinquency-related behavior" (Sexton & Turner, 2010, p. 339).

The evaluation research on FFT is less extensive than that of MST, however. The program focuses on providing intensive treatment services within the family setting. There is less of a widespread systems approach than found in MST, in that FFT therapists do not perform regular advocacy functions with teachers, neighborhoods, or other systems in the target youth's environment. The family system is at the forefront, however. The focus is on developing the inner strengths and self-efficacy of all family members (Sexton & Alexander, 2000). Therapists also work with the family as a unit and try to identify family dynamics that may lead to problematic interactions among various members as well as strengths that would serve as protective factors for the juveniles. According to latest figures, FFT programs exist in more than 300 communities in the United States as well as a few in other nations (Sexton & Turner, 2010).

Both MST and FFT are programs deserving consideration in the treatment of juvenile offenders, including youths who have displayed serious and violent behavior. Of the two, MST appears to be the more broad based, reaching out beyond the youth's family environment to his or her surrounding community, and it has the benefit of a greater cache of supportive research. Not surprisingly, it is also the more expensive to operate according to cost analyses conducted in Washington State (Barnoski, 2009; Lee et al., 2012). There, the cost per participant was placed at about $2,600 for FFT and about $6,400 for MST. Nevertheless, research also has demonstrated that MST treatment produces cost savings to taxpayers as well as crime victims over 25 years following initial treatment (Dopp, Borduin, Wagner, & Sawyer, 2014).

In a recent study comparing the two programs, Baglivio et al. (2014) found no significant differences in recidivism for youths referred to MST and FFT, and found some indication of slightly better results for FFT for certain groups, including girls, and both low-risk and high-risk youth. The results with regard to high-risk offenders are particularly intriguing, because MST is often promoted as the community program of choice for violent offenders. As emphasized by Baglivio and colleagues (2014):

Finding no significant differences in the current study for the sample of all youth referred to MST or FFT, as well as no differences across race, leads to questions regarding the need for a more expensive service. If roughly twice as many youth may be served by the equally effective, cheaper alternative, one would have trouble justifying not pursuing that path in the absence of empirical evidence to the contrary. (p. 1050)

Nevertheless, the researchers were careful about noting the limitations of their research and suggested that additional research on the outcomes of each program, including which juveniles would best benefit from each, was warranted.

SUMMARY AND CONCLUSIONS

The crimes committed by juveniles get considerable media attention, particularly if they are unusual or when they are committed by groups. Gang activity in particular raises public concern, but many gang members have reached the age of adulthood and therefore do not qualify for delinquent status. The unlawful acts committed by youth are usually placed in five categories: unlawful acts against person, unlawful acts against property, drug offenses, offenses against the public order, and status offenses. Of the five, crimes against persons are the least predominant in arrest statistics. Moreover, recent data indicate that all juvenile crimes have decreased in recent years.

We began the chapter with a brief discussion of juvenile status offenses, those behaviors that would not be considered crimes if committed by adults. Researchers have long focused on studying these behaviors. There are gender differences in enforcing them, status offenses often signify deeper problems in a youth's life, and some but not all status offenders move on to commit more serious crimes. Of all the status offenses, running away is probably the most troubling. Both boys and girls run away, but girls are more likely to have run away because of victimization in the home and are also more likely to become involved in prostitution to survive. Research on adult female offenders finds these patterns in many of their backgrounds.

We discussed other gender differences in juvenile offending, noting that girls traditionally have been far less present than boys in juvenile offending statistics. In the 1990s, we began to see a closing of this gender gap, though girls still represent a lower proportion of the delinquency statistics for most offenses, with the exception of runaway. The gender gap for drug offending—and to a lesser extent for violence—is also getting smaller. We reviewed some of the findings of the Girls Study Group (GSG), comprised of scholars and practitioners from different fields, which is conducting ongoing research to identify which girls become delinquent, how they got that way, and what factors are effective in preventing girls' delinquency. Thus far, studies reveal that, although girls and boys share many risk factors for delinquency, certain risk factors are more prevalent for one sex or the other. For example, girls seem to be particularly negatively affected by family disruption and deviant peers, while boys seem to be particularly negatively affected by deficits in self-control.

The chapter is most concerned with serious delinquency and the developmental pathway that leads to that point. Serious delinquents typically begin their antisocial behavior patterns at an early age, and as they grow older, they rarely restrict their behavior to any one offense. As the Pathways study (Mulvey, 2011) demonstrates, however, we cannot assume that even serious offenders do not desist from criminal offending. The developmental theory of Terrie Moffitt is particularly instructive in understanding serious offending. Moffitt's conceptualization of the life-course-persistent (LCP) offender and the adolescent limited (AL) offender has spurred extensive research interest in these two developmental tracks. Later researchers, including Moffitt herself, have recognized that additional tracks are needed to account for offending behavior. Nevertheless, the LCP juvenile is of keen interest from a psychological perspective. LCP offenders have not acquired prosocial and interpersonal skills and are often plagued by psychological problems well into adulthood. Most juveniles, however, confine their offending to their early years and move on to prosocial lives.

Other developmental theories were covered. Patterson's coercion developmental theory attributes much serious delinquency to parenting practices, particularly poor monitoring. Although Patterson does not reject the notion that individual differences in the child affect his or her behavior, he sees the family environment as setting the stage for later antisocial behavior, which is facilitated by the coercive style learned from parents. Patterson and his colleagues continue to offer and evaluate treatment programs for families whose children are at risk of delinquency.

One of the most provocative psychological theories associated with delinquency in recent years is the dual-systems model of risk-taking behavior proposed by Laurence Steinberg. According to this theory, the cognitive capacity of adolescents reaches its peak sooner than their socio-emotive maturity. This is a physiological phenomenon attributed to brain development in humans. A slowly developing emotional system renders adolescents susceptible to peer influence and to risk-taking behavior, even though they "know" they should not take certain actions.

At a time when much of the public fears crime and is skeptical about the prospect of reforming offenders, research results on some approaches to treating even serious juvenile offenders are promising. We highlighted characteristics that programs with good results have in common. Not surprisingly, effective programs begin early in a child's life if at all possible; they are conscious of key principles of child and adolescent development, including gender differences; they focus on multiple settings in a child's life (e.g., the child, family, school); they acknowledge and respect cultural backgrounds; and they focus on the family first—again if possible—with a goal of improving parental skills. With regard to the last characteristic, it is easy to give up on some families that seem highly dysfunctional. However, in many situations, the family is what is familiar to the child. If not sensitive to this, some therapists may overlook or underestimate the love and sense of belonging that exists.

Prevention and intervention programs in juvenile justice were classified according to a tripartite model: primary or universal prevention, secondary or selective prevention, and treatment or intervention (also called tertiary prevention). Primary prevention programs are intended for all children in a given group, whether or not they are "at risk" of engaging in delinquency. Prenatal services, tactics to encourage resilience, and school nutrition programs are examples of such programs. Although research on such programs is positive, because of their universal nature it is difficult to conduct adequate follow-up studies to determine whether children do engage in delinquent behavior. Secondary programs are aimed at "at-risk" children: those with demographic or individual features suggesting that they are likely to engage in delinquency. Diversion is a common secondary prevention program, but studies indicate that only certain types of diversion programs are effective. Another highly watched program is Fast Track, operating out of many public schools.

Treatment, or tertiary prevention, involves numerous programs, few of which have been carefully evaluated. Research on institutional treatment is discouraging at best. The rehabilitation approaches tried have often been simplistic and narrowly focused; alternatively, they have not been submitted to empirical research, so we cannot know whether they were effective. Adolescents who have received either traditional or nontraditional (e.g., boot camps) institutional treatment fare less well than those receiving intensive community treatment. Within the institutions, however, some programs may be more promising than others. Juvenile sex offender treatment is a case in point.

Two promising treatment approaches are Multisystemic Therapy (MST), and Functional Family Therapy (FFT). Each is a community-based, intensive therapy approach for serious offenders, though FFT focuses almost exclusively on the family setting and the psychological needs of the target juvenile and the juvenile's parents and siblings. A fundamental premise of both programs is that youths—even high-risk youth who have committed violent crimes—are better served in their own homes, away from the influences of institutional life. The programs are also used with substance abusers and serious but nonviolent offenders. Studies on both MST and FFT have produced favorable outcomes for a range of offenders, making them "model" programs for the community treatment of juveniles.

Although these community-based programs show good results, it would be naïve to believe that all serious juvenile offenders can be treated in the community. Unless we do away with the juvenile justice system and place all juveniles in the custody of "adult" corrections, there will always be a need to hold some in secure residential settings. The challenge, therefore, is to develop effective treatment programs for the small group of adolescents who cannot benefit from less restrictive community alternatives.

Key Concepts

Adolescent-limited (AL) offenders

Antisocial behavior

Callous-unemotional (CU) traits

Child delinquents

Coercion developmental theory

Conduct disorder

Dual Systems Model

Externalizing disorder

Functional Family Therapy (FFT)

Life-course-persistent (LCP) offenders

Multisystemic therapy (MST)

Primary prevention (universal prevention)

Selective prevention (secondary prevention)

Status offenses

Tertiary prevention (treatment)

Review Questions

1. Summarize the differences between LCP and AL offenders; discuss why more than two tracks or pathways to offending might be needed.

2. Discuss significant findings from the Girls Study Group and from the Pathways to Desistance studies.

3. Describe Gerald Patterson's coercion developmental model.

4. What are status offenses? What has research found relating to gender differences in these offenses?

5. Identify the three categories of delinquency prevention programs and give an illustration of each.

6. What are the strengths of MST and FFT as treatment approaches to serious delinquents?

7

Psychopathy

CHAPTER OBJECTIVES

▪ Present a special type of offender (the criminal psychopath), who differs emotionally, cognitively, and behaviorally from other offenders.

▪ Review the various measures of psychopathy.

▪ Summarize the original four core factors and two new core factors of psychopathy.

▪ Review the evidence for juvenile psychopathy.

▪ Identify the ethical dilemmas that juvenile psychopathy presents.

▪ Examine the neurobiological aspects of psychopathy.

▪ Introduce the dual-process model of psychopathy.

▪ Discuss representative research on treatment strategies used with adult psychopaths and juveniles with psychopathic features.

It is not unusual to read or hear about horrific crimes, accompanied by descriptions of the perpetrator as "a deranged psychopath" or "an evil psychopath," or to hear about the increasing numbers of psychopaths in our midst. "Psychopaths" are also frequently portrayed in the entertainment media and appear increasingly in interactive video games. The common perception of psychopathy is far different from the real construct, which has been studied in psychological research for more than 50 years.

Given its relation to crime and violence, psychopathy is arguably one of the most important psychological constructs in the criminal justice system (Porter et al., 2000, p. 227). More recently, Douglas, Nikolova, Kelley, and Edens (2015) write: "Psychopathy remains one of the most well-studied constructs in the fields of law and psychology, forensic mental health, personality, and criminal justice" (p. 306). Psychologist Paul Frick (2009), a prominent researcher on psychopathy, outlines its broad significance when he writes: "the construct of psychopathy is important to the legal system (for example, defining offenders who are a high risk for recidivism), to the mental health system (for example, defining a group of antisocial people who have unique treatment requirements), and for research attempting to explain the cause of antisocial and aggressive behaviour (for example, defining a group of antisocial people with unique causal processes)" (p. 803). It is no surprise, then, that psychopathy has become a central focus of research in psychology, particularly as it relates to criminal behavior.

In recent years, *juvenile* psychopathy has become the subject of considerable interest and debate. Some researchers question its validity and implications, while others believe it is crucial that we identify psychopathic characteristics in juveniles in order to intervene at an early age. Juveniles who possess psychopathy-like characteristics, such as callous–unemotional traits, are believed to be particularly susceptible to antisocial behavior throughout their lives.

The psychopath is not identical to the sociopath. The latter is a nonclinical label attached to someone who persistently and chronically breaks the law. Neither is the psychopath identical to the person with an antisocial personality disorder (APD), although some researchers and clinicians continue to confuse the two terms (Gacono, Nieberding, Owen, Rubel, & Bodholdt, 2001). Furthermore, definitions of psychopathy and APD are so close as to be virtually indistinguishable. Nevertheless, the fine distinctions are worth maintaining, and we will try to keep them distinct throughout the chapter. Because psychopathy is such an important topic in criminal psychology, we devote an entire chapter to describing the research and clinical characteristics of this interesting behavior.

WHAT IS A PSYCHOPATH?

The term "psychopath" is currently used to describe a person who demonstrates a discernible cluster of psychological, interpersonal, and neurophysiological features that distinguish him or her from the general population. Psychologist Robert Hare (1993), one of the world's leading experts on psychopathy, refers to psychopaths as "social predators who charm, manipulate, and ruthlessly plow their way through life, leaving a broad trail of broken hearts, shattered expectations, and empty wallets. Completely lacking in conscience and empathy, they selfishly take what they want and do as they please, violating social norms and expectations without the slightest sense of guilt or regret" (p. xi).

Hare (1970) proposed a useful scheme to outline three categories of psychopaths: the primary, the secondary or neurotic, and the dyssocial. Only the **primary psychopath** is a "true" psychopath. The primary or "true" psychopath—the main subject of this chapter—has certain identifiable psychological, emotional, cognitive, and biological differences that distinguish him or her from the general and criminal populations. We discuss these differences in some detail throughout the chapter. The other two categories meld a heterogeneous group of antisocial individuals who comprise a large segment of the criminal population. **Secondary psychopaths** commit antisocial or violent acts because of severe emotional problems or inner conflicts. They are sometimes called acting-out neurotics, neurotic delinquents, symptomatic psychopaths, or simply emotionally disturbed offenders. Recent research indicates that the secondary psychopath demonstrates more emotional instability and impulsivity than the primary psychopath, and secondary psychopaths also appear to be more aggressive and violent (Kimonis, Skeem, Cauffman, & Dmitrieva, 2011). The researchers also discovered that the secondary psychopath, compared to the primary psychopath, is more rooted in parental abuse and rejection. The third group, **dyssocial psychopaths**, display aggressive, antisocial behavior they have *learned* from their subculture, like their gangs, terrorist groups, or families. In both cases, the label "psychopath" is misleading, because the behaviors and backgrounds have little, if any, similarity to those of primary psychopaths. Yet, both secondary and dyssocial psychopaths are often confused with primary psychopaths because of their high recidivism rates.

Antisocial Personality Disorder

As noted above, primary psychopathy should be distinguished from **antisocial personality disorder (APD)**. This term is used by psychiatrists and many clinical psychologists to describe "a pervasive pattern of disregard for, and violation of, the rights of others, occurring since age 15..." (American Psychiatric Association, 2013, p. 659). This DSM-5 definition is followed by seven additional criteria, any three or more of which must be met, such as repetitive lying, impulsiveness, and disregard for the safety of others. The individual diagnosed with APD must be at least 18 years old, and there must be evidence that behavioral patterns corresponding to conduct disorder (CD) occurred prior to age 15. Recall that we discussed CD in some detail in Chapter 2. Although not all children diagnosed with CD eventually qualify for APD, persons with APD would have qualified for CD had they been diagnosed.

As we noted, the descriptions of the psychiatric term "antisocial personality disorder" follow very closely the descriptions of the psychological term "psychopathy." Although the DSM-5 states that APD "has also been referred to as psychopathy, sociopathy, or dissocial personality disorder" (p. 659), the features of psychopathy are *not* the same as APD. For example, the definition of APD is narrower than the definition of psychopathy. This is because DSM-5—intended as a diagnostic reference manual for use by clinicians—focuses on behavioral indicators. On the other hand, the contemporary definition of psychopathy includes not only behavioral indicators but also emotional, neurological, and cognitive differences. In addition, APD and psychopathy do not mirror the same underlying psychopathology (Riser & Kosson, 2013). For example, the impairments in cognitive functioning are more pronounced and extensive in psychopaths than in individuals diagnosed with APD (who are sometimes referred to in the literature as ASPs, antisocial personalities). Furthermore, whereas APD by definition always involves criminal behavior, not all psychopaths are criminal, and not all criminals are psychopaths. To illustrate the former, we will meet psychopaths in this chapter who do not commit crime. To illustrate the latter, though approximately 50 to 80 percent of male inmates qualify for criteria for APD (Hare, 1998; Hare, Forth, & Strachan, 1992), only 11 to 25 percent of male inmates meet the criteria for psychopathy (Hare, 1996).

One more important point needs to be emphasized. Recent research clearly indicates that psychopathy is not a category but exists on a continuum (Douglas et al., 2015). That is, "psychopaths differ in degree, not in kind, from nonpsychopaths…" (Douglas et al., 2015, p. 262). The DSM-5 sees the diagnosis of APD as a separate, discrete category. One has or does not have APD. Nevertheless, with each new publication of the American Psychiatric Association's *Diagnostic and Statistical Manual of Mental Disorders*—including the DSM-5—the characteristics used to describe the antisocial personality are increasingly similar to Hare's primary psychopath in behavioral terms. It is easy to understand why clinicians and students often confuse the terms.

This text adopts Hare's scheme, considering "primary psychopath" an empirically and clinically useful designation. It is distinguished from secondary or neurotic psychopaths in its behavioral, cognitive, emotional, and neurophysiological features. From this point on, when we refer to the psychopath, we mean the primary psychopath. He or she is unique: not neurotic, psychotic, or emotionally disturbed, as commonly believed and sometimes portrayed by the entertainment media. Primary psychopaths are usually not volcanically explosive, violent, or extremely destructive, although they certainly can be. They are more apt to be outgoing, charming, and verbally proficient. They may be criminals—in fact, in general, they run in perpetual opposition to the law—but many are not. The term **criminal psychopath** will be used to identify those primary psychopaths who do engage in repetitive antisocial or criminal behavior.

Examples of Primary Psychopaths

The late Ferdinand Waldo Demara Jr., the "Great Impostor," who forged documents and tried dozens of occupations without stopping to obtain a high school education, is a good example of a primary psychopath. A brief description of some of his exploits may help put the psychopath in perspective (see Critchton, 1959, for a more complete version).

Demara frequently came into contact with the law, primarily because he persisted in adopting fake identities. He once obtained the credentials of a Dr. French, who held a Harvard PhD in psychology. Demara was in the U.S. Navy at the time, awaiting a commission on the basis of other forged documents, but when he realized he was in danger of exposure via a routine security check, he decided he would prefer the Dr. French identity. He dramatized a successful suicide by leaving his clothing on the end of a pier with a note stating that "this is the only way out." Navy officials accepted his "death," and Demara became Dr. French. With his impressive credentials in hand, he obtained a dean of philosophy position in a Canadian college, successfully taught a variety of psychology courses, and assumed administrative responsibilities.

He developed a friendship with a physician, Joseph Cyr, and learned the basics of medicine from their long conversations. He eventually borrowed and duplicated Cyr's vital documents—birth, baptism, and confirmation certificates, school records, medical license—and obtained a commission in the Royal Canadian Navy as Dr. Cyr. He read extensively to nurture his growing knowledge of medicine.

During the Korean War, Demara/Cyr was assigned to a destroyer headed for the combat zone. The ship met a small Korean junk carrying many seriously wounded men, who were brought on board for emergency medical care. Three men were in such critical condition that only emergency surgery could save their lives. Although Demara had never seen an operation performed, he hurriedly reviewed his textbooks. With unskilled hands, he operated through the night. By dawn, he had not only saved the lives of the three men, but had also successfully treated 16 others.

Demara/Cyr's deeds were broadcast over the ship's radio and disseminated, along with his photo, by the press. The real Dr. Cyr, shocked to see Demara's visage over his own respected name, immediately exposed him. Demara was discharged from the Canadian Navy, which, to save itself from additional embarrassment, allowed him to leave without prosecution. Demara's biography represents an example of a psychopath who did not engage in serious or lifelong violent crime.

Other psychopaths do commit violent crimes, though, some of them heinous and brutal. Neville Heath—charming, handsome, and intelligent—brutally and sadistically murdered two young English women (Critchley, 1951; Hill, 1960). Like Demara, Heath had an extraordinary career, much of it in the armed forces. Unlike Demara, his brushes with the law were serious and occasionally ended in imprisonment. He was commissioned and dishonorably discharged on three separate occasions, once each in the British Royal Air Force, the Royal Armed Service Corps, and the South African Air Force. He flew in a fighter squadron in the RAF until he was court-martialed for car theft at age 19. He then committed a series of thefts and burglaries and was sentenced to Borstal Prison. Pardoned in 1939, he joined the Royal Armed Service Corps but was dismissed for forgery. On his way home to England, he jumped ship and eventually managed to obtain a commission in the South African Air Force until his past caught up with him. When not in trouble, Heath was regarded as a daring, confident, and highly charming officer—and a rake. After the third court-martial, he developed a taste for sadistic murder.

You may be able to identify other examples of psychopaths at their worst. The notorious Charles Manson, who in the 1960s exhibited an uncanny ability to attract a devout cluster of unresisting followers, is one probable example. The fictional Hannibal Lechter, whose sadistic offenses and deadly charm have captivated readers and screen audiences, is another. It is not advisable, though, to see psychopaths around every corner, despite the frequent usage of this designation in popular media. When the media first heard of Joran Van der Sloot, the "Dutch playboy" charged and ultimately convicted of killing a Peruvian woman and suspected in the disappearance of a U.S. college student in 2010, headlines asked whether he was a psychopath. Every alleged violent criminal is not a psychopath. Moreover, as we noted above, psychopathy exists on a continuum, and it is likely that "full-blown psychopaths" are rare. Throughout the remainder of this chapter, we examine in more detail their behavioral patterns, cognitive processes, interpersonal features, neuropsychological characteristics, and general backgrounds.

BEHAVIORAL DESCRIPTIONS

One pioneering authority on the behavioral characteristics of the psychopath was Hervey Cleckley, a well-known psychiatrist who died in 1984 at the age of 81. A large part of Cleckley's professional recognition came as a result of the nonfiction book, *The Three Faces of Eve*, which he coauthored with Corbett Thigpen. The book, which is about the phenomenon of "multiple personality," was made into a very popular 1957 movie with the same title. However, his major professional contribution to the field of psychiatry can be found in his often-quoted text, *The Mask of Sanity*, first published in 1941. The book describes in clear and empirically useful terms the major behaviors demonstrated by the full-fledged or primary psychopath, as distinct from the other psychopathic types referred to previously. Cleckley was able to identify 16 characteristics he felt described the typical psychopath (see **Table 7-1**). We discuss some of these psychological characteristics identified by both Cleckley and Hare in more detail below. The characteristics proposed by Hare are included in his well-known measure of psychopathy, the *Psychopathy Checklist*, to be discussed later in the chapter. Before we proceed with our description of the behavioral characteristics of the "typical" psychopath, it is important

TABLE 7-1	Psychopathic Behaviors Identified by Hare and Cleckley
Hare PCL Checklist	**Cleckley's Primary Psychopath Description**
Glibness/superficial charm	Superficial charm and good intelligence
Grandiose sense of self-worth	Pathological egocentricity
Pathological lying	Untruthfulness and insincerity
Cunning/manipulative	Manipulative
Lack of remorse or guilt	Lack of remorse or guilt
Shallow affect	General poverty of affective reactions
Callous, lack of empathy	Unresponsiveness in interpersonal relationships
Failure to accept responsibility for actions	Unreliability
Promiscuous sexual behavior	Impersonal sex life
Lack of realistic, long-term goals	Failure to follow any life plan
Poor behavioral controls	Impulsive
High need for stimulation/prone to boredom	Inadequately motivated antisocial behavior
Irresponsibility	Poor judgment Absence of delusions Absence of anxiety Bizarre behavior after drinking alcohol

to note that contemporary research findings reveal that psychopaths—as a group—appear to be more complex than the original Cleckley descriptions. Still, the Cleckley formulations hold for many psychopaths. Therefore, it is instructive to go over them.

Behavioral Characteristics

Superficial charm and average to above-average intelligence are two of the psychopath's main features, according to Cleckley, and they are both especially apparent during initial contacts. It should be emphasized, however, that a large portion of the psychopaths Cleckley worked with were well educated and from middle- or upper-class backgrounds (Hare & Neumann, 2008). Many psychopaths usually impress others as friendly, outgoing, likable, and alert. They often appear well educated and knowledgeable, and they display many interests. They are verbally skillful and can talk themselves out of trouble. In fact, their vocabulary is often so extensive that they can talk at length about anything (Hare, 1991). However, systematic study of their conversation reveals that they often jump "from one topic to another and that much of their speech is empty of real substance, tending to be filled with stock phrases, repetitions of the same ideas, word approximations, abstract terms and jargon used in a superficial or inappropriate fashion, logically inconsistent statements and phrases, and half-formed sentences" (Hare, 1991, p. 57). As Hare (1996, p. 46) notes: "In some respects, it is as if psychopaths lack a central organizer to plan and keep track of what they think and say." However, since psychopaths are so charming and manipulative, these language shortcomings are not readily apparent.

Readers should not conclude that psychopaths as a group are usually verbally and socially skillful at *successfully* manipulating others and the system. In a revealing study that followed a large number of psychopaths from age 8 to 48 (Ullrich, Farrington, & Coid, 2008), it was found that psychopathic traits did not lead to status or wealth, or successful intimate relationships. Apparently, the charm, deception, and impression management used by psychopaths do not usually lead to success in life.

Psychological Testing Differences

Psychometric studies (studies that use standard psychological tests as measures) indicate that psychopaths usually score higher on intelligence tests than the general population (Hare, 1970, 1996), particularly on individually administered tests. In fact, Hare wryly comments, the psychopaths who were the sample for his studies were probably the least intelligent of their ilk, since they were not quite bright enough to avoid being arrested and convicted for their offenses. (Hare has conducted much of his research on imprisoned psychopaths.) Later research (e.g., Ishikawa, Raine, Lencz, Bihrle, & Lacasse, 2001) found that a useful dichotomy of psychopathy may be to divide psychopaths into "successful" psychopaths (those who have committed crimes but avoided arrest and conviction for offenses) and "unsuccessful" psychopaths (those who have been convicted and imprisoned). "Success" should not be equated to "intelligent," however, nor should it be assumed that people convicted of crime are not intelligent. Overall, available research indicates that many psychopaths are bright—as measured by scores on standardized intelligence tests—but some are not (Hare & Neumann, 2008).

Psychopaths and Mental Disorders

Most psychopaths do *not* exhibit severe or disabling mental disorders. Most lack any symptoms of excessive worry and anxiety, psychotic thinking, delusions, severe depressions, or hallucinations. Even under high pressure conditions, they remain cool and calm, as did Ian Fleming's fictitious James Bond, probably a prime example. Feasibly, the doomed psychopath might enjoy a steak dinner (*au poivre*) with gusto just before being executed. The infamous multiple murderer Herman W. Mudget, alias H. H. Holmes, retired at his normal hour the evening before his execution, fell asleep easily, slept soundly, and woke up completely refreshed. "I never slept better in my life," he told his cell guard. He ordered and ate a substantial breakfast an hour before he was scheduled to be hanged. Until the moment of death, he remained remarkably calm and amiable, displaying no signs of depression or fear (Franke, 1975). Later in the chapter we will discuss "boldness" as a possible feature of psychopathy.

Not everyone agrees with the view that psychopaths do not suffer from some mental disorder. Some clinicians argue that psychopathy and schizophrenia are part of the same spectrum of disorders (Hare, 1996), and Cleckley briefly considered psychopathy as a form of masked psychosis. Some forensic clinicians maintain that they occasionally see a mentally disordered offender who qualifies as both a psychopath and a schizophrenic (Hare, 1996). There is some evidence to suggest that it is not uncommon to find psychopaths who seem mentally disordered in maximum-security psychiatric units for highly violent or dangerous patients. Other researchers have reported similar findings (Quinsey, Harris, Rice, & Cormier, 2006; Tengström, Hodgins, Grann, Längström, & Kullgren, 2004; Vitacco, Neumann, & Jackson, 2005). Tengström et al. report that individuals diagnosed with schizophrenia and who demonstrated many of the features of psychopathy had more severe histories of offending and violence than those persons diagnosed with schizophrenia alone.

Psychopaths and Suicide

Cleckley was under the impression that psychopaths rarely—if ever—committed suicide. Recent research and clinical experiences, however, have put Cleckley's observation in doubt. Hare, for instance, knows of several psychopaths who took their own lives when it became clear to them there was no other way out of what they perceived as an intolerable situation (Hare & Neumann, 2008). Intolerable situations include a very long prison term, incurable illness, or being surrounded by the police. "We suspect that at least some cases of 'suicide by cop' involved psychopaths who were trapped and wished to go out in a 'blaze of glory'" (Hare & Neumann, 2008, p. 228).

Verona, Patrick, and Joiner (2001) found that, among male inmates, psychopaths who were especially aggressive and impulsive did show some indicators of suicidality. "Suicidality" is a term used by clinicians to indicate there is a risk of suicide, usually inferred from their self-reported suicidal thoughts or intentions. In another study that examined psychopathy and suicidality in psychiatric patients, youthful offenders, jail detainees, and prison inmates, the researchers also found a significant relationship between psychopathy and suicidality (Douglas, Herbozo, Poythress, Belgrage, & Edens, 2006). However, the researchers also warned that the suicide–psychopathy relationship was highly complex and multifaceted, and required much more research to confidently establish it. In sum, research and clinical experience are beginning to find that some psychopaths who find themselves in desperate situations do commit suicide, especially if they are highly impulsive and violent.

Other Principal Traits

Other principal traits of the psychopath are selfishness and an inability to love or give affection to others. According to Cleckley, egocentricity is *always* present in the psychopath and is essentially unmodifiable. The psychopath is unable to feel genuine, meaningful affection for others. Psychopaths may be likable, but they are seldom able to keep close friends, and they have great difficulty understanding love in others. They may be highly skillful at pretending deep affection, and they may effectively mimic appropriate emotions, but true loyalty, warmth, and compassion are foreign to them. Psychopaths are distinguished by flat emotional reaction and affect. And since psychopaths have so little need to receive or give love, psychopaths, as a group, have relatively little contact with their families, and many change their residences frequently (Hare, 1991). In addition they do not usually respond to acts of kindness. They show capacity only for superficial appreciation. Paradoxically, they may do small favors and appear considerate. One prototype mowed the lawn for his elderly neighbor and brought her comforting drinks when she was ill—the next morning he stole her car.

Psychopaths have a remarkable disregard for truth and are often called "pathological liars." They seem to have no internalized moral or ethical sense and cannot understand the purpose of being honest, especially if dishonesty will bring some personal gain. They have a cunning ability to appear straightforward, honest, and sincere, but their claims to sincerity are without substance.

Psychopaths are unreliable, irresponsible, and unpredictable, regardless of the importance of the occasion or the consequences of their impulsive actions. Impulsivity appears to be a central or cardinal feature of psychopathy (Hart & Dempster, 1997). This pattern of impulsive actions is cyclical, however. Psychopaths may, for months on end, be responsible citizens, faithful spouses, and reliable employees. They may experience great successes, be promoted, and gain honors, as did Demara and Heath. Skillfully as they have attained these socially desirable goals, they have an uncanny knack of suddenly unraveling their lives. They become irresponsible, and may pass bad checks, sabotage the company computers, or go on a drunken spree. They also tend to have a "bad temper" that flares quickly into an argument and attack. Psychopaths may later say they are sorry and plead for another chance—and most will probably get it. Invariably, if the psychopath is a young adult, the irresponsible behavior will return.

Even small amounts of alcohol prompt most psychopaths to become vulgar, domineering, loud, and boisterous and to engage in practical jokes and pranks. Cleckley noted that they choose pranks that have no appeal for most individuals, and that seem bizarre, inappropriate, and cruel. They lack genuine humor and, not surprisingly, the ability to laugh at themselves.

Although often above average in intelligence, psychopaths appear incapable of learning to avoid failure and situations that are potentially damaging to themselves. Some theorists suggest that the self-destructive, self-defeating deeds and attitudes reflect a need to be punished to mitigate the guilt they subconsciously experience, or more simply, that they are driven by a masochistic purpose. However, most researchers and clinicians have difficulty accepting the guilt or masochistic tendencies as valid explanations for the psychopath's periodic self-defeating behavior.

Most experts conclude that a cardinal fault of psychopaths is their absolute lack of remorse or guilt for anything they do, regardless of the severity or immorality of their actions and irrespective of their traumatic effects on others. Since they do not anticipate personal consequences, psychopaths may engage in destructive or antisocial behavior—such as forgery, theft, rape, brawls, and fraud—by taking absurd risks and for insignificant personal gain. When caught, they express no genuine remorse. They may readily admit culpability and take considerable pleasure in the shock these admissions produce in others. Whether they have bashed in someone's head, ruined a car, or tortured a child, psychopaths may well remark they did it "for the hell of it."

When a psychopath drifts into criminal activity, impulsivity will usually prevent him or her from performing like a professional criminal. Psychopaths are more likely to participate in capers and hastily planned frolics, or in spontaneous, serious crimes for immediate satisfaction. The professional criminal has purpose and a plan of action; the psychopath is impulsive and lacks long-range goals.

Psychopaths have little capacity to see themselves as others perceive them. Instead of accepting the facts that would normally lead to insight, they project and externalize blame onto the community and family for their misfortunes. Interestingly, educated psychopaths have been known to speak fluently about the psychopathic personality, quoting the literature extensively and discussing research findings, but they cannot look into their own troublesome antics or mount a reasonable attack on their actions. They articulate their regrets for having done something, but the words are devoid of emotional meaning, a characteristic Cleckley calls **semantic aphasia**. Johns and Quay (1962) remarked that psychopaths "know the words but not the music." Similarly, Grant (1977) notes that the psychopath knows only the book meaning of words, and not the living meaning. Hare (1996, p. 45) concludes, "In short, psychopaths appear to be semantically and affectively shallow individuals."

Another important behavioral characteristic of psychopaths noted by Blair, Peschardt, Budhani, Mitchell, and Pine (2006) is their *excessive* use of instrumental aggression. Instrumental aggression, as discussed in Chapter 5, is purposeful and goal-directed aggression used to achieve a specific goal, such as the possessions of another person. It is distinguished from reactive aggression, which is considered spontaneous, unplanned, and done in response to an event or an action by another individual.

Finally, an important behavioral distinction underlying much of Cleckley's description is what Quay (1965) refers to as the psychopath's profound and pathological stimulation seeking. According to Quay, the actions of the psychopath are motivated by an excessive *neuropsychological* need for thrills and excitement. It is not unusual to see psychopaths drawn to such interests as race car driving, skydiving, and motorcycle stunts. We will examine this alleged need for stimulation in the pages to follow.

In recent years, it has become useful for research purposes to focus on psychopaths who repeatedly commit crimes, collectively called criminal psychopaths. Concentrating on psychopaths who are violent or chronic offenders provides invaluable information about their backgrounds, learning history, and behavioral patterns. Such research also might offer key strategies for how to deal and potentially treat this challenging group of individuals.

THE CRIMINAL PSYCHOPATH

As stated repeatedly above, many psychopaths have no history of serious antisocial behavior, and persistent, serious offenders are not necessarily psychopaths. For our purposes here, the term "criminal psychopath" will be reserved for those psychopaths who demonstrate a wide range of *persistent* and *serious* antisocial behavior. As a group, they tend to be "dominant, manipulative individuals characterized by an impulsive, risk-taking and antisocial lifestyle, who obtain their greatest thrill from diverse sexual gratification and target diverse victims over time" (Porter et al., 2000, p. 220).

As noted above, contemporary theory and research consider psychopathic traits and predispositions as existing on a continuum. The entertainment media often portray the psychopath as an inhuman, vile, despicable person who enjoys violence. One is left with the impression that an individual is either a psychopath or a nonpsychopath. However, psychopathic traits and characteristics in adults and adolescents are best viewed today as occurring along a dimension or continuum, with some people demonstrating more psychopathic tendencies than others. As we will see shortly, someone is labeled as a psychopath after attaining a given cutoff score on tests to measure the construct. The accumulation of psychopathic characteristics is what determines the final diagnosis, and not everyone agrees on the required cutoff point. Therefore, the best perspective to take when studying the following material is that psychopathy exists on different levels rather than viewing people as either psychopaths or nonpsychopaths. Nevertheless, when we refer to percentages of psychopaths in a population, we are referring to the percentages that have met the cutoff criteria as defined by a particular research study.

Prevalence of Criminal Psychopathy

Overall, Robert Hare (1998) estimates that the prevalence of psychopaths in the general population is about 1 percent, whereas in the adult prison population estimates range from 15 to 25 percent. Some researchers (e.g., Simourd & Hoge, 2000) wonder, however, whether these estimates are not somewhat inflated. Simourd and Hoge report only 11 percent of their inmate population could be identified as criminal psychopaths. The inmates used in the Simourd–Hoge study were not simply inmates in a medium-security correctional facility. All 321 were serving a current sentence for violent offending, more than half of them had been convicted of a previous violent offense, and almost all of them had extensive criminal careers. Even so, few qualified as criminal psychopaths. Therefore, percentage estimates of criminal psychopathy within any given prison population should be tempered by the type of facility, as well as the cultural, ethnic, gender, and age mix of the targeted population.

Offending Patterns of Criminal Psychopaths

Criminal psychopaths are believed responsible for a disproportionate amount of crime in society, and they are considered to be the most violent and persistent offenders (Declercq, Willemsen, Audenaert, & Verhaeghe, 2012; Forth & Burke, 1998; Hart & Hare, 1997; Newman, Schmitt, & Voss, 1997; Saltaris, 2002). Gretton, McBride, Hare, O'Shaughnessy, and Kumka (2001, p. 428) point out that criminal psychopaths generally "lack a normal sense of ethics and morality, live by their own rules, are prone to use cold-blooded, instrumental intimidation and violence to satisfy their wants and needs, and generally are contemptuous of social norms and the rights of others." Hare (1996, p. 38) posits, "The ease with which psychopaths engage in...dispassionate violence has very real significance for society in general and for law enforcement personnel in particular." Hare refers to a report by the Federal Bureau of Investigation (1992) that found that nearly half of the law enforcement officers who died in the line of duty were killed by individuals who closely matched the personality profile of the psychopath. Moreover, the unlawful acts of psychopathic sex offenders are likely to be more violent, brutal, unconventional, and sadistic than those of other sex offenders (Hare, Clark, Grann, & Thornton, 2000; Porter, Birt, & Boer, 2001; Woodworth & Porter, 2002). Psychopathic sex offenders appear to be more motivated by thrill seeking and excitement rather than simply sexual arousal (Porter, Woodworth, Earle, Drugge, & Boer, 2003). Psychopaths as a group also appear to be significantly more sadistic than violent nonpsychopaths (Holt, Meloy, & Stack, 1999) and commit more diverse and severe forms of sexual homicides (Firestone, Bradford, Greenberg, & Larose, 1998; Porter et al., 2003). Porter and his colleagues (2003) found that in a sample of the male offenders incarcerated in two Canadian federal prisons for homicide, nearly half could be classified as sexual homicide offenders. (In order to be classified as a sexual homicide, there had to be physical evidence of sexual activity with the victim before, during, or after the homicide.)

Murderers described as excessively sadistic and brutal tend to have many psychopathic features (Hare et al., 2000; Stone, 1998). Serial murderers who exhibit psychopathic features are especially sadistic and brutal in their murders. Collectively, the research suggests that psychopaths may be more likely than other offenders to derive pleasure from both the nonsexual and sexual suffering of others (Porter et al., 2003).

Many of the murders and serious assaults committed by *nonpsychopaths* occurred during domestic disputes or extreme emotional arousal, thereby qualifying as reactive aggression. This pattern of violence is rarely observed for criminal psychopaths (Declercq et al., 2012; Hare, Hart, & Harpur, 1991; Williamson, Hare, & Wong, 1987). Criminal psychopaths frequently engage in violence as a form of revenge or retribution, or during a bout of drinking. Many of the attacks of nonpsychopaths are against women they know well, whereas many of the attacks of criminal psychopaths are directed at men who are strangers. Hare et al. (1991, p. 395) observe that the violence committed by criminal psychopaths was callous and cold-blooded, "without the affective coloring that accompanied the violence of nonpsychopaths." Research also indicates that rapists who have psychopathic characteristics are more likely to have "nonsexual" motivations for their crimes, such as anger, vindictiveness, sadism, and opportunism (Hart & Dempster, 1997).

Recidivism of Criminal Psychopaths

Research studies report that the recidivism rate of criminal psychopaths is very high. **Recidivism** refers to the tendency to return to offending, although studies differ in how it is measured (e.g., arrests, convictions, self-reported crime). In other words, criminal psychopaths commit crimes again and again, regardless of the methods used to stop or rehabilitate them. According to Porter et al. (2000), research suggests that psychopaths reoffend faster, violate parole sooner, and perhaps commit more institutional violence than nonpsychopaths. In one study (Serin, Peters, & Barbaree, 1990), the number of failures of male offenders released on unescorted temporary absence programs (furloughs) was examined. The failure rate for psychopaths was 37.5 percent, while none of the nonpsychopaths failed. The failure rate during parole was also examined. While 7 percent of nonpsychopaths violated parole conditions, 33 percent of the psychopaths violated their conditions. In another study (Serin & Amos, 1995), 299 male offenders were followed for up to eight years after their release from a federal prison. Sixty-five percent of the psychopaths were convicted of another crime within three years, compared with a reconviction rate of 25 percent for nonpsychopaths. Quinsey, Rice, and Harris (1995) found that within six years of release from prison, more than 80 percent of the psychopaths convicted as sex offenders had violently recidivated, compared with a 20 percent recidivism rate for nonpsychopathic sex offenders. Recidivism was measured by either arrests or convictions for a violent offense.

High recidivism rates are also characteristic of psychopathic adolescent male offenders. Later in the chapter, though, we will discuss the controversy over whether juvenile psychopathy even exists, though evidence is mounting that it does. According to Gretton et al. (2001), these offenders are more likely than other adolescent offenders to escape from custody, violate the conditions of probation, and commit nonviolent and violent offenses over a five-year follow-up period. The high recidivism rates among adult and juvenile offenders have prompted some researchers to conclude that there is "nothing the behavioral sciences can offer for treating those with psychopathy" (Gacono et al., 2001, p. 119). Nevertheless, the authors add, "in some cases psychopharmacology may decrease impulsivity and violence" (p. 119). Pessimistic conclusions are drawn partly because psychopaths tend to "be unmotivated to alter their problematic behavior and often lack insight into the nature and extent of their psychopathology" (Skeem, Edens, & Colwell, 2003, p. 26). As we note below, other researchers (e.g., Salekin, Worley, & Grimes, 2010) are more optimistic. Moreover, Salekin et al. (2010) observe that surveys indicate that the bulk of mental health professionals view psychopathy as a treatable condition.

PSYCHOLOGICAL MEASURES OF PSYCHOPATHY

Currently, the dominant psychological instrument for measuring criminal psychopathy is the 20-item **Psychopathy Checklist (PCL-R)** (Hare, 1991, 2003). The PCL-R has been published in a second edition, which includes new information on its applicability in forensic and research settings. The second edition also has been expanded for use with offenders in other countries, and includes updated normative and validation data on male and female offenders. Although several other personality scales for measuring psychopathy have been developed in recent years, the PCL-R is currently the most frequently used instrument for both research and clinical applications; it will be the center of attention for the remainder of this section. As noted by Douglas et al. (2015): "There is little doubt that the PCL family of measures is the most heavily researched, and, as the first widely adopted measurement system on the market, it has been tremendously influential" (p. 263).

"Family of measures" in the above-mentioned quote refers to several instruments that have been derived from the original PCL and that stand alongside it in both research and practice. First, there is a 12-item short-form version, called the **Psychopathy Checklist: Screening Version (PCL:SV)** (Hart, Cox, & Hare, 1995; Hart, Hare, & Forth, 1993). Other additions are the **Psychopathy Checklist: Youth Version (PCL:YV)** (Forth, Kosson, & Hare, 2003) and the **P-Scan: Research Version**. The PCL:YV is beginning to be researched more extensively and is mentioned again in the section on juvenile psychopathy. The P-Scan is a screening instrument that serves as *rough* screen for psychopathic features and as a source of working hypotheses to deal with managing suspects, offenders, or clients. It is designed for use in law enforcement, probation, corrections, civil and forensic facilities, and other areas in which it would be useful to have some information about the possible presence of psychopathic features in a particular person. Of course, the P-Scan needs much more research before its results can be considered definitive. All three checklists are conceptually and—with the exception of the P-Scan—psychometrically similar.

The PCL-R

The PCL scales are largely based on Cleckley's (1976) conception of psychopathy, and were specifically designed to identify psychopaths in male prison, forensic, or psychiatric populations. Cleckley's work was based primarily on psychiatric patients. However, the scales are used to measure psychopathy and psychopathic features, not only in institutionalized populations, but also in clinical settings and among research participants.

The PCL-R assesses the affective (emotional), interpersonal, behavioral, and social deviance facets of psychopathy from various sources, including self-reports, behavioral observations, and collateral sources, such as parents, family members, friends, and arrest and court records which can help to establish the credibility of self-reports (Hare, 1996, 2003; Hare, Hart, & Harpur, 1991). In addition, item ratings from the PCL-R, for instance, require some integration of information across multiple domains, including behavior at work or school; behavior toward family, friends, and sexual partners; and criminal or antisocial behavior (Kosson, Suchy, Mayer, & Libby, 2002). Typically, highly trained examiners use all this information to score each item on a 0–2 scale, depending on the extent to which an individual has the disposition described by each item on the checklist (0 = consistently absent; 1 = inconsistent; 2 = consistently present). Scoring is, however, quite complex and requires substantial time, extensive training, and access to a considerable amount of background information on the individual. Some researchers have obtained PCL-R scores from detailed records, without the interview component. Although there is some support for conducting such reviews (Gretton et al., 2001), it appears that lower scores may result from using this approach (Hare, 2003).

A score of 30 or above usually qualifies a person as a primary psychopath (Hare, 1996). In some research and clinical settings, cutoff scores ranging from 25 to 33 are often used (Simourd & Hoge, 2000). Hare (1991) recommends that persons with scores between 21 and 29 be classified as "middle" subjects, who show many of the features of psychopathy but do not fit all the criteria. As mentioned above, psychopathy is best conceptualized as occurring on a continuum; scores below 21 are considered "nonpsychopaths."

So far, the research has strongly supported the use of the PCL-R for distinguishing criminal psychopaths from criminal nonpsychopaths, and for helping correctional and forensic psychologists involved in risk assessments of offenders (Hare, 1996; Hare & Neumann, 2008; Hare, Forth, & Stachan, 1992). In addition, the instrument provides researchers and mental health professionals with a universal measurement for the assessment of psychopathy that facilitates international and cross-cultural communication concerning theory, research, and eventual clinical practice (Hare et al., 2000). Currently, the PCL-R is increasingly being used as a clinical instrument for the assessment of psychopathy across the globe (Douglas et al., 2015), although it appears to be most powerful in identifying psychopathy among North American white males (Hare et al., 2000).

Criticisms of the PCL-R

Despite its widespread use, the PCL-R has garnered a substantial amount of criticism. Some scholars (e.g., Skeem & Cooke, 2010a, 2010b) believe that the PCL-R has been so overused as representing the definition of psychopathy that the instrument has become confused with the concept of psychopathy itself. The debate centers on the issue of whether criminal behavior is a core feature of psychopathy. In other words, the PCL-R may not be an adequate measure for identifying psychopaths who do not engage in violence or criminal behavior. From the Skeem and Cooke perspective, psychopaths are likely to engage in *antisocial behavior* but not necessarily *criminal behavior*. They define antisocial behavior as "behavior that defeats the interests of the social order" (Skeem & Cooke, 2010a, p. 435). Skeem and Cooke believe that some antisocial behavior seems essential to the interpersonal and emotional core of psychopathy, such as noncriminal manipulation of others for personal gain. Criminal behavior, on the other hand, refers to behavior that is officially forbidden by the legal system. Criminal behavior represents illegal behavior, punishable by criminal sanctions. "Given individual differences in talents and opportunities, psychopathic tendencies may be manifested in one individual's criminality, in another individual's heroism, and in still another's worldly success" (Skeem & Cooke, 2010a, p. 435).

In other words, criminality is not necessarily a core feature psychopathy. Douglas et al. (2015) posit that there are numerous ways to harm others, such as betrayals in relationships, harmful gossip, subterfuge in the workplace, and economic decisions that harm livelihoods or even lives. Very often psychopaths are masters of these behaviors.

Hare and Neumann (2010) disagree with Skeem and Cooke's claim that the measures in the PCL test series imply criminality is an essential core component of psychopathy. They argue that antisocial behavior—not criminal behavior—is central to the concept and measurement of psychopathy. In fact, Hare's statement in 2002 that not all psychopaths were in prison, some were in the boardroom, was widely publicized (Babiak, Neumann, & Hare, 2010), and Hare was not implying that persons with psychopathic characteristics in the corporate world were necessarily acting in a criminal manner. [See **Box 7-1** for discussion of corporate psychopaths.]

RESEARCH FOCUS

BOX 7-1   Corporate Psychopaths

Research on psychopaths has overwhelmingly focused on incarcerated populations, such as prisoners or detained juveniles with psychopathic features. One notable exception is a study by Babiak, Neumann, and Hare (2010), who investigated psychopathy in corporate settings. As noted in the text, Hare was widely quoted in 2002 that not all psychopaths were in prison, some were in the boardroom. Four years later, Paul Babiak and Robert Hare published their book *Snakes in Suits* (2006), and in 2010 the results of their research were published in an academic journal.

Using a sample of 203 corporate professionals from seven companies scattered across the United States, the researchers reviewed records, conducted interviews, and administered the PCL-R (described earlier in the chapter). The records included job applications, resumes, awards and commendations, performance reviews, and background checks, but did not include medical information. The professionals in the sample were managers and executives identified by their companies for participation in a management development program—essentially a program to develop or improve management skills through training and leadership conferences. The great majority were Caucasian males with four-year degrees. All had been identified by the company as having management potential, and almost 50 percent had high management potential.

The researchers found that the prevalence of psychopathic traits was higher than that found in community samples. Psychopathy correlated positively with supervisory ratings such as good communication skills and creativity, but negatively with responsibility and performance—such as being a team player and overall performance. In other words, the persons with psychopathic characteristics were viewed by others as being good communicators, strategic thinkers, and creative, but they also were seen as having poor management styles, and immediate supervisors gave them poor performance appraisals. Even so, as Babiak et al. (2010) noted,

(continued)

some companies viewed psychopathic executives as having leadership potential despite their negative reviews. "Their excellent communication and convincing lying skills, which together would have made them attractive hiring candidates in the first place, apparently continued to serve them well in furthering their careers" (p. 190).

Boldness—a characteristic described in the chapter—and the ability to manipulate and con others emerged as strong factors. As noted by Babiak et al., "being 'tough' or 'strong' (making hard, unpopular decision) or 'cool under fire' (not displaying emotions in the face of unpleasant circumstances) can work in their favor" (p. 191).

Questions for Discussion

1. Assuming that the PCL-R could be legally administered to employees before acceptance into a management training program, should it be done?
2. Very little research has been done on psychopathy in the corporate world. What are possible explanations for this?

Hare and Neuman further assert that "although the PCL-R is not perfect, it works well enough to have generated many hundreds of empirical studies on psychopathy…and to have withstood unusually intense conceptual and statistical scrutiny" (p. 450). However, Douglas et al. (2015) point out that the PCL-R includes a significant amount of questions about criminal behavior, as well as antisocial behavior, which clearly suggest that the measure is based largely on identifying criminality.

It should be noted, as well, that the PCL measures may be used to assess the likelihood of recidivism in criminal offenders. Richards, Casey, and Lucente (2003) found the PCL-R and the PCL:SV measures of persistent offending history, in conjunction with high scores on the PCL-R, are probably two of the most powerful predictors of violent recidivism available anywhere. In fact, the PCL-R is a strong predictor of recidivism even when the offender's criminal history is not known to the examiner (Hemphill & Hare, 2004; Hemphill, Hare, & Wong, 1998).

CORE FACTORS OF PSYCHOPATHY

From the research on the PCL-R, it has become clear that psychopathy is multidimensional in nature. One statistical procedure designed to find different dimensions or factors in test data is **factor analysis**. When expert ratings of psychopathy on the PCL-R were submitted to this statistical method, at least two behavioral dimensions or factors emerged (Hare, 1991; Harpur, Hakstian, & Hare, 1988; Hart, Hare, & Forth, 1993). More recently, many researchers find that more factors have been identified. Lilienfeld and Fowler (2006) even proposed an eight-factor model. Thus, though psychopathy began as a two-factor construct, it has expanded substantially to its dominant status now as comprising at least four factors.

The Two-Factor Position

In the two factor scheme, **Factor 1** reflects the interpersonal and emotional components of psychopathy and consists of items measuring remorselessness, callousness, and selfish use and manipulation of others. The typical psychopath feels no compunctions about using others strictly to meet his or her own needs. **Factor 2** is most closely associated with a socially deviant or antisocial lifestyle, as characterized by poor planning, impulsiveness, an excessive need for stimulation, proneness to boredom, and a lack of realistic goals. Some researchers have found that Factor 1 appears to be associated with planned predatory violence, while Factor 2 appears to be related to spontaneous and impulsive violence (Hart & Dempster, 1997). Factor 1 is also linked to resistance and inability to profit from psychotherapy and treatment programs (Seto & Barbaree, 1999). Factor 2 appears related to socioeconomic status, educational attainment, and cultural/ethnic background, whereas Factor 1 may be more connected to biopsychological influences (Cooke & Michie, 1997). Research also suggests that Factor 1 *may* be a more powerful indicator of psychopathy than Factor 2 (Cooke, Michie, Hart, & Hare, 1999). In addition, while it is quite clear that Factor 1 does a better job of identifying psychopathy in general, there is some evidence that Factor 2 does a better job of predicting general recidivism and violent recidivism (Walters, 2003).

The Three-Factor Position

Psychopathic behavior may be too diverse to be captured in only two dimensions. With increasing sophistication of statistical methods (e.g., confirmatory factor analysis and model-based cluster analysis), contemporary research indicates that there may be at least three core behavioral or personality dimensions that best describe psychopathy (Cooke & Michie, 2001; Cooke, Michie, Hart, & Clark, 2004; Vitacco et al., 2005). The third core factor (**Factor 3**) refers to the emotional shallowness, callousness, and lack of empathy that are characteristic of most psychopaths. In an influential paper, Cooke and Michie (2001) challenged the traditional two-factor explanation of psychopathy and recommended that psychopathy be divided into the following core dimensions:

1. An arrogant and deceptive interpersonal style, which includes a grandiose sense of self-worth, glibness, superficial charm, lying, conning, manipulation, and deceitfulness. (This dimension is also referred to as impression management.)
2. An impulsive and irresponsible behavioral style, including failure to think before acting, a lack of long-term goals, stimulation seeking, unsatisfactory work habits, and a parasitic lifestyle (living off others, including spouses, intimate partners, friends, and parents).
3. Deficient affective or emotional experience characterized by low remorse, low guilt, a weak conscience, the absence of anxiety, fearlessness, callousness, little empathy, and a failure to accept responsibility for one's actions.

The Four-Factor Model

Some researchers (e.g., Hare, 2003; Hare & Neumann, 2008; Salekin, Brannen, Zalot, Leistico, & Neumann, 2006; Vitacco et al., 2005) have asserted that, in addition to disturbances in interpersonal, affective, and behavioral functioning, the definition of psychopathy should also include a fourth factor or dimension: antisocial behavior. Hare and Neumann (2008) write, "A number of recent studies…provide considerable support for a four-factor model of psychopathy across diverse and primarily very large samples of male and female offenders" (p. 232). The **four-factor model** has also been supported across various cultures, ethnic groups, young and adult offenders, and forensic patients (Jackson, Neumann, & Vitacco, 2007; Jones, Cauffman, Miller, & Mulvey, 2006; Neumann, Hare, & Newman, 2007; Neumann, Kosson, Forth, & Hare, 2006).

The argument for a four-factor model is based on the finding that individuals manifesting psychopathic traits often exhibit violence and a large collection of other antisocial behavioral patterns that are more than the poor planning and impulsivity associated with Factor 2. Consequently, the argument contends that researchers and clinicians are missing a critical ingredient in the understanding and definition of the psychopath if measures of antisocial behavior are left out of the equation. It is also argued that much of the predictive power of psychopathy is enhanced if we take into consideration past criminal behavior (Salekin et al., 2006). According to the four-factor perspective, the factors are as follows: (1) interpersonal, such as pathological lying and conning, (2) lifestyle, such as irresponsible behavior, sensation seeking, and impulsiveness, (3) affective (shallow affect or emotional reactions, lack of remorsefulness for their actions), and (4) antisocial tendencies, such as poor self-regulation, and a wide array of antisocial behavior including delinquency. **Table 7-2** summarizes these four factors.

The Boldness Factor

In recent years, scholars have debated whether boldness should be included as a core factor for psychopathy. Interestingly, boldness is not regarded as a negative feature of psychopathy. The **boldness factor** (sometimes referred to as **fearless dominance**) refers to an "interpersonal style that is characterized by fearlessness, being relatively immune to stress or anxiety, and being successful at negotiating social interactions to achieve desired goals" (Douglas et al., 2015, p. 265). Patrick, Fowles, and Krueger (2009) and Skeem et al. (2011) define boldness in the context of psychopathy as the ability to remain calm and focused in pressure or life-threatening situations, and to demonstrate high self-assurance and social efficacy in most social environments. In addition,

TABLE 7-2 Summary of the Four Hypothesized Core Factors of Psychopathy

Factor	Core Features
Interpersonal (F1)	Lying, conning, and manipulating others; superficial charm; grandiose self-worth.
Lifestyle (F2)	Irresponsibility; sensation seeking; lack of realistic goals, poor planning; impulsivity.
Affective (F3)	Shallow emotions, callousness, little empathy; failure to accept responsibility for actions.
Antisocial tendencies (F4)	Poor self-regulation; persistent criminal activity; antisocial behavior; early behavior problems.

boldness reflects the capacity to recover rapidly from stressful events and to seek out unfamiliarity and danger. Note that in absence of the other features described above (e.g., callousness, poor self-regulation, conning, irresponsibility) boldness alone may be a feature to be admired.

In many aspects, a good representative of boldness may be the "corporate psychopath," discussed in **Box 7.1** earlier and described in some detail in Babiak and Hare's book, Snakes in Suits: When Psychopaths Go to Work, published in 2006. Unfortunately, with the exception of the Babiak et al. (2010) research there has been little research done on this topic.

In an interesting study, Lilienfeld and his colleagues (2012) examined the level of boldness (or fearless dominance) found in U.S. presidents. They found that the boldness linked to psychopathy was associated with better presidential performance, leadership, persuasiveness, crisis management, and congressional relations. The authors hastened to add, however, that they certainly did not mean to imply that psychopathic individuals make especially effective presidents, but they do imply that boldness appears to be an effective ingredient for effective political and corporate leadership.

The Meanness Factor

Another factor that some researchers believe should be included as a central element in psychopathy is **meanness** (Patrick et al., 2009). Meanness in this context refers to "deficient empathy, disdain for and lack of close attachments with others, rebelliousness, excitement seeking, exploitativeness, and empowerment through cruelty" (Patrick et al., 2009, p. 927). It can be expressed through extreme arrogance, defiance of authority, destructive excitement seeking, and physical cruelty toward people and animals (Skeem et al., 2011). It is a motivational style in which pleasure and satisfaction are sought without consideration of others. Patrick et al. point out that meanness tends to be a central feature of crime and delinquency that is actively directed at hurting others. Further research is necessary before it can be determined if the boldness and meanness factors should be included as central elements of psychopathy, but preliminary study strongly suggests they should.

THE FEMALE PSYCHOPATH

Overall, research suggests that there are significantly fewer female than male psychopaths, both in the general population and among persons convicted of crime (Bolt, Hare, Vitale, & Newman, 2004; Rogstad & Rogers, 2008). In the general population, the estimated prevalence of psychopathy among males is 1 percent (Hare, 2003), but the prevalence is significantly less among females (Nicholls, Ogloff, Brink, & Spidel, 2005). Salekin, Rogers, and Sewell (1997) reported that the prevalence rate of psychopathy for female offenders in a jail setting was 15.5 percent, compared with the 25 to 30 percent prevalence rate estimated for male offenders. In another study, Salekin, Rogers, Ustad, and Sewell (1998) found, using a PCL-R cutoff score of 29, that 12.9 percent of their sample of 78 female inmates qualified as psychopaths. In a more recent investigation involving 528 adult women incarcerated in the state of Wisconsin, Vitale, Smith, Brinkley, and Newman (2002) report that only 9 percent of their participants could be classified as psychopaths, using the recommended cutoff score of 30 on the PCL-R. Finally, Hare (2003) found that about 7.5 percent of female offenders and 15 percent of male offenders meet the recommended cutoff score of 30 on the PCL-R. All these studies consistently indicate that females generally score lower on the PCL-R than males.

Hare's PCL-R has been developed almost exclusively on white male criminal psychopaths. Some studies using the PCL-R suggest that female criminal psychopaths may demonstrate different behavioral patterns than male criminal psychopaths (Nicholls & Petrila, 2005; Vitale, Smith, Brinkley, & Newman, 2002). Although the data are far from conclusive, female psychopaths, compared with male psychopaths, appear to demonstrate a lack of realistic long-term goals, have numerous marital relationships, engage in a wide range of crime, and show a greater tendency to be sexually promiscuous (Douglas et al., 2015; Grann, 2000; Salekin et al., 1997; Warren et al., 2003). We urge caution in interpreting this last characteristic, because men and women are often judged differently on this criterion. Female psychopaths also may not express the same emotional processing abnormalities as male psychopaths (Sutton, Vitale, & Newman, 2002). It appears that the affective features of psychopathy are especially important in identifying female psychopaths, with high levels of callousness and low levels of empathy clearly distinguishing them from nonpsychopathic women (Jackson, Rogers, Neumann, & Lambert, 2002; Rogstad & Rogers, 2008).

Kreis and Cooke (2011) also found that female psychopaths tend to be more subtle and skillful in their aggression, in their exploitative relationships, and in their manipulation of others, indicating that many of their harmful acts may go largely unnoticed by the authorities. Male psychopaths, on the other hand, are more likely to engage in direct, physical forms of aggression, dominance, and status seeking, which renders their harmful actions more noticeable and more likely to be officially recorded. These findings have led some scholars to propose that female psychopaths may rely more on relational aggression to get their way than male psychopaths (Skeem, Polaschek, Patrick, & Lilienfeld, 2011). Additional research on this issue is certainly required before some conclusions can be developed.

There is also some evidence that female psychopaths have experienced greater levels of environmental deprivation and more sexual and physical victimization compared to male psychopaths (Hicks et al., 2012; Javdani, Sadeh, & Verona, 2011). It is also believed that those who offended began their criminal careers later than male psychopaths (Hart & Hare, 1997). Female psychopaths may also recidivate less often than male psychopaths (Salekin et al., 1998). In fact, the evidence suggests that psychopathic female inmates may have recidivism rates that are no different than the recidivism rates reported for nonpsychopathic female inmates (Salekin et al., 1998).

Similar to gender differences in criminality on the whole, the reported gender distinctions in psychopathy are probably due to a number of social influences and neuropsychological differences that occur across the developmental trajectory of males and females. Women and men arrive at crime via different pathways, and we must often look for different explanations for their crimes (Salisbury & Van Voorhis, 2009). As a result of these differences, females with psychopathic characteristics might rely on different tactics than males to reach the same goals (Nicholls & Petrila, 2005).

The more recent research utilizing the PCL-R shows considerable promise in identifying gender differences in psychopathy, but many researchers and experts urge caution before the instrument is adopted for clinical or diagnostic use with women (Nicholls et al., 2005). Rogers (2000) admonishes that "psychologists are on safest ground if they limit their risk predictions on the PCL-R to White males with criminal histories" (p. 600). For the most part, however, there is emerging evidence that psychopathy as measured by the PCL-R has a significant relationship with antisocial behavior in adult females. To date, though, the research on female juvenile psychopaths is less convincing, as we will see shortly.

RACIAL/ETHNIC DIFFERENCES

The early work on the PCL as a measure of psychopathy was largely conducted using white inmates who were mostly Canadians (Douglas et al., 2015). One of the earliest studies on racial/ethnic differences reported that psychopathy, as measured by Hare's PCL, does exist in black male inmates in a pattern that resembles that of white male inmates (Kosson, Smith, & Newman, 1990). However, Kosson et al. found one important difference. The black criminal psychopaths tended to be less impulsive than white criminal psychopaths. This finding raises some questions as to whether the PCL is entirely appropriate to use with African American inmates. On the other hand, Jennifer Vitale et al. (2002) found no significant racial differences in the scores and distributions of female psychopaths. More specifically, Vitale et al. discovered that 10 percent of the 248 incarcerated Caucasian women who participated in their study reached the cutoff scores of 30 or higher on the PCL-R compared with 9 percent of the 280 incarcerated African American women who had similar scores.

A meta-analysis by Jennifer Skeem, John Edens, Jacqueline Camp, and Lori Colwell (2004) supports the conclusion that the differences between blacks and whites are minimal. They concluded, "Our finding that Blacks and Whites do not meaningfully differ in their levels of core psychopathic traits is consistent with community-based findings for self-report measures of psychopathy and clinical diagnoses of antisocial personality disorder" (p. 505). Additional research suggests that there are no significant differences between blacks and Hispanic inmates compared to white, non-Hispanic inmates (Neumann & Hare, 2008; Vachon, Lynam, Loeber, & Stouthamer-Loeber, 2012). In fact, a majority of studies have found no apparent differences between blacks and whites, convicted or nonconvicted, on PCL:SV scores, indicating that, in general, racial/ethnic difference in psychopathy scores are minimal (Douglas et al., 2015; Vachon et al., 2012).

JUVENILE PSYCHOPATHY

As we have seen, one of the serious shortcomings of the extensive research conducted on psychopathy is that it has focused almost exclusively on white, adult males (Frick, Bodin, & Barry, 2000). Consequently, for many years research on juvenile (adolescent and child) psychopathy was limited. Within the past two decades, however, the field expanded, leading to the general belief that a large amount of empirical research solidly supports the juvenile psychopathy construct (Asscher, van Vugt, Stams, Deković, Eichelsheim, & Yousfi, 2011). Furthermore, specific instruments designed to measure psychopathy in the young, such as a youth version of the PCL-R (PCL:YV) and the Child Psychopathy Scale (CPS; Lynam, 1997), have provided support for measuring the construct. These will be discussed again shortly. There is also substantial evidence that male criminal psychopaths begin their offending patterns at a very early age (Frick, 2009; Rutter, 2005).

Even so, attempts to apply the label "psychopathy" to juvenile populations "raise several conceptual, methodological, and practical concerns related to clinical/forensic practice and juvenile/criminal justice policy" (Edens, Skeem, Cruise, & Cauffman, 2001, p. 54). Some debate has focused on whether psychopathy can or should be applied to juveniles at all. Can features of adult psychopathy be found in children and adolescents in the first place? Others are concerned that—even if psychopathy can be identified in adolescents—the label may have too many negative connotations. More specifically, the label implies that the prognosis for treatment is poor, a high rate of offending and recidivism can be expected, and the intrinsic and biological basis of the disorder means little can be done outside of biological interventions. This may lead those working in the juvenile justice system to give up on the juveniles so labeled, although some experts emphasize that psychopathy can indeed be treated (Salekin et al., 2010). (See **Box 7-2** for illustration of a treatment program for juveniles with psychopathic characteristics.) A third debate contends that psychopathy assessments of youths must achieve a high level of confidence before they can be employed in the criminal justice system (Edens, Campbell, & Weir, 2007; Seagrave & Grisso, 2002). We will discuss these assessments shortly.

Can Juvenile Psychopathy Be Identified?

Another major problem of identifying juvenile psychopaths is that psychopathy—if it exists in this age group—may be very difficult to measure reliably because of the transient and constantly changing developmental patterns across the life span. Many clinicians and researchers have resisted any trend to search for psychopathy in juveniles, noting that features of the adult psychopath simply

TREATMENT PROGRAM FOCUS

BOX 7-2   Treating Adolescents with Psychopathic Features

Offering psychotherapy is not for the faint of heart or the pessimistic. Psychological treatment, often necessary but less often successful, generally does not receive good reviews in the research literature, although evidence-based approaches have been identified. However, as noted by many commentators, it is difficult to gauge "success" because so many variables are involved and so many different outcomes are measured. Does a person show up for appointments? Is the therapist adhering to protocol in delivering the treatment? Do life events—for example, the death of a loved one—interfere with progress in treatment? Should success be measured by graduation from high school? Satisfactory employment? No additional suicide attempts? No more arrests?

As noted in the chapter, treatment for adult psychopaths and juveniles with psychopathic characteristics has been especially discouraging, due largely to the intransigent nature of psychopathy itself. Nevertheless, also as noted in the chapter, there is reason for optimism.

A program with potential is described by Caldwell et al. (2007), who are mental health practitioners and researchers in Mendota, Wisconsin. "The Mendota Juvenile Treatment Center (MJTC) is a 29-bed intensive treatment program intended to provide mental health treatment to the most behaviorally disturbed juvenile boys held in the state's secured correctional facilities" (p. 576). Boys sent to the center failed to adjust in standard correctional institutions for adolescents. Subsequently, they were sent to MJTC even if they might have low IQ, psychosis, neurological deficits, or displayed resistance to treatment.

In this intensive program, the boys typically have several individual counseling sessions each week, as well as group therapy focused on anger management and social skills development. A crucial component of the program is to address defiant resistance to treatment early on. That is, therapists tackle attitudes that can be barriers to change. Although not all boys have psychopathic characteristics, many do.

The study found that youths with psychopathic characteristics responded less favorably than those with nonpsychopathic characteristics, particularly in the short term. However, longer duration in the program (an average of nearly 45 weeks) produced positive change in the psychopathic youth, such as reduced aggression and more engagement in the treatment program. Equally importantly, a four-year follow-up found that the treated youth were significantly less likely to reoffend violently, as measured by rearrest records in the state after release from custody. The MJTC program suggests that "there is a group of youth with pronounced psychopathic features who can respond to appropriate treatment of sufficient duration" (Caldwell et al., 2007, p. 584).

Questions for Discussion

1. The above is an admittedly brief description of a promising program. What more would you want to know about the operation of the program before evaluating its merits?
2. What do you think of the lack of the exclusion criteria mentioned above (e.g., low IQ scores)? Why might the program developers have decided *not* to exclude youth with these features?
3. Comment on the measure of recidivism used in this study.

---

represent normal adolescent development. In other words, adolescents often appear callous and narcissistic, sometimes to hide their own fear and anxiety. They are often impulsive and engage in sensation-seeking behaviors, and many are not particularly good at long-range planning. In reality, these and other psychopathic-like characteristics represent either a passing phase in the difficult transition to adulthood or the adolescent's "cover" to make himself or herself appear noncaring.

For other children, psychopathic-like characteristics might be indicative of physical or sexual abuse. Children in abusive homes often demonstrate an abnormally restricted range of emotions that are similar to the emotional characteristics of psychopathy. Actually, these symptoms are the child's way of coping with a very stressful home environment (Seagrave & Grisso, 2002).

Furthermore, "Some adolescent behavior may...appear psychopathic by way of poor anger control, lack of goals, and poor judgment, but is actually influenced by parallel developmental tasks encountered by most adolescents" (Seagrave & Grisso, 2002, p. 229). Going against the rules is part of many adolescents' attempts to gain autonomy from adult dominance, such as found in adolescent-limited offending.

Nevertheless, certain problem characteristics in children and adolescents—for example, conduct problems, hyperactivity, impulsivity, and attention difficulties—resemble features of the adult psychopath and suggest that the term "juvenile psychopath" may have some validity. On the other hand, these characteristics may simply represent disorders such as conduct disorder (CD) and oppositional defiant disorder (ODD), which are distinct from psychopathy. As Cruise, Colwell,

Lyons, and Baker (2003) have emphasized, to be useful, the construct of juvenile psychopathy must be distinguished from other diagnoses. It appears, though, that current research is rapidly approaching a distinct construct. For example, a multidimensional model that identifies callous and unemotional traits, narcissism, and impulsivity has been proposed and tested as indicative of childhood psychopathy (Barry, Barry, Deming, & Lochman, 2008; Fite, Stoppelbein, & Greening, 2009; Frick, 2009; Pardini & Loeber, 2008).

In a study examining the prevalence rate of psychopathic tendencies in children, Skilling, Quinsey, and Craig (2001) found that 4.3 percent of a sample of over 1,000 boys in grades 4 to 8 could be classified as psychopathic on every measure employed in the study. Dåderman and Kristiansson (2003) found that 59 percent of their sample of violent juvenile offenders qualified as psychopaths. Similarly, Brandt, Kennedy, Patrick, and Curtain (1997), using a sample of incarcerated adolescents with persistent violent offending histories, reported that they could identify 37 percent of the sample as psychopathic. By contrast, Campbell, Porter, and Santor (2004) discovered that only 9 percent of their sample of incarcerated adolescent offenders could be classified as psychopaths. These authors note, though, that the juveniles they studied were primarily nonviolent in nature, with only 15 percent having a history of violent offending. It is clear, therefore, that the sample used in a study, as well as the measuring instrument itself, will strongly influence the number of identifiable psychopathic traits within a given group of adolescents.

Recent studies continually find support for the existence and validity of psychopathy in the young, and it seems to remain stable from age 7 to at least age 24 (Lynam, Caspi, Moffitt, Loeber, & Stouthamer-Loeber, 2007; Lynam et al., 2009). As noted by Skeem et al. (2011): "Put simply, it seems that researchers are capturing something that looks like psychopathy" (p. 125).

Ethical Considerations

On the whole, though, there is considerable concern about misuse of labels suggesting psychopathy by juvenile justice professionals, including judges, youth detention workers, and treatment providers. Because of the widespread assertion that psychopaths are highly resistant to treatment, an adolescent "psychopath" accused of a crime—or even a youth demonstrating psychopathic characteristics—is more likely to be transferred to the adult court system rather than kept in the juvenile system. In the latter, treatment is more likely to be available once the youth has been adjudicated delinquent. Until very recently, a 16- or 17-year-old juvenile who was labeled a psychopath, was more likely than one without such a label to be sentenced to death in some states (Edens, Guy, & Fernandez, 2003). However, in 2005, the U.S. Supreme Court ruled that juveniles who committed their crimes at these ages could not be sentenced to death (*Roper v. Simmons*). The court had previously set 16 as the minimum age at which juveniles were eligible for the death penalty (*Thompson v. Oklahoma*, 1989). Nevertheless, juveniles who are tried in criminal courts continue to be subjected to punitive criminal sanctions, including life sentences, although the Court also has now banned life sentences without the possibility of parole and mandatory life sentences for juvenile offenders (*Graham v. Florida*, 2010; *Miller v. Alabama*, 2012).

Surprisingly, one respectable study found no negative effects associated with the psychopathy label in a juvenile court (Murrie, Boccaccini, McCoy, & Cornell, 2007), but this seems to be the exception. By contrast, Viljoen et al. (2010) found that juveniles whose cases indicated psychopathy received harsher treatment by juvenile courts, including being transferred to adult courts. Viljoen et al. remarked, "psychopathy evidence was commonly used to infer that a youth would be very difficult or impossible to treat" (p. 271).

Even when juveniles are kept in the juvenile system and placed in treatment centers, the label "psychopath" may become a self-fulfilling prophecy with treatment providers who may be unlikely to expend considerable effort on a seemingly hopeless case. Supporters of the construct of juvenile psychopathy argue that treatment providers should have that information at their disposal, both to make management decisions regarding custody and programming and to fashion the type of treatment that could be effective. Others contend that it is important to identify psychopathy as early as possible to avoid the negative consequences to society and to help juveniles with psychopathic characteristics.

Fortunately, researchers are beginning to identify promising treatment (Caldwell, Skeem, Salekin, & Van Rybroek, 2006; Salekin & Lynam, 2010; Spain, Douglas, Poythress, & Epstein, 2004), as we saw in Box 7-2 and discuss again later in the chapter. In essence, if there is a distinct difference between psychopathic youth and nonpsychopathic youth, supporters claim it is critical that knowledge of this difference be communicated to those who work most closely with them. Additionally, it is helpful to identify and promote "protective factors" in a child's developmental sequence that might help insulate him or her from psychopathy (Salekin & Lochman, 2008). Supporters also believe there is wisdom in targeting for early intervention in a subgroup of adolescents who otherwise might become career criminals (Skeem & Cauffman, 2003). This presumes, of course, that youth are correctly identified, which leads to the issue of reliability and validity.

Psychopathic assessments of youths must achieve a high level of confidence before they can be used in the criminal justice system, where individuals face dire consequences (Seagrave & Grisso, 2002). For example, if an assessment instrument is designed to measure juvenile psychopathy, then there must be considerable research to demonstrate that it, in fact, does measure what it says it measures. Many experts maintain that, with reference to "juvenile psychopathy," we are not near that point yet.

Even so, over the past 15 years, knowledge regarding the theoretical and empirical applicability of juvenile "psychopathy" has expanded at a fast pace (Salekin, Leistico, Trobst, Schrum, & Lochman, 2005; Skeem, Polaschek et al., 2011). The research has demonstrated that the diagnostic label is linked to CD (Forth & Burke, 1998; Frick, 1998; Lynam, 1998) and higher levels of delinquency and police contacts (Corrado, Vincent, Hart, & Cohen, 2004; Falkenbach, Poythress, & Heide, 2003; Murrie, Cornell, Kaplan, McConville, & Levy-Elkon, 2004; Salekin, Ziegler, Larrea, Anthony, & Bennett, 2003). Only about 25 percent of juveniles with CDs show psychopathic tendencies (Blair et al., 2006). Forth and Burke (1998) report that children and adolescents with psychopathic traits differ from other antisocial youngsters in terms of the age of onset of their behavior problems, the number of violent acts committed, the seriousness of their offenses, and their recidivism rates. Consequently, it appears that those youth who demonstrate psychopathic characteristics also seem to be heavily involved in antisocial behavior, at least hinting that the psychopathic label may have some validity.

Measures of Juvenile Psychopathy

It is not surprising that the avid interest in psychopathy, including juvenile psychopathy, would lead to the development of a variety of instruments designed to measure it, or at least psychopathic characteristics. Several instruments for measuring juvenile psychopathy have been developed, including the *Psychopathy Screening Device*, or the PSD (Frick & Hare, 2001; Frick, O'Brien, Wootton, & McBurnett, 1994), the *Childhood Psychopathy Scale*, or the CPS (Lynam, 1997), the *Youth Psychopathic Traits Inventory*, or YPI (Andershed, Kerr, Stattin, & Levander, 2002), and the *Psychopathy Checklist: Youth Version*, or the PCL:YV (Forth, Kosson, & Hare, 2003). Although originally developed as research instruments rather than for diagnosis purposes in clinics or for the courts, they are rapidly becoming available to forensic clinical examiners for use in their private practice and their consulting work with the courts and the juvenile justice system.

All the measures are limited by the fact that juvenile psychopaths—if they exist—are unlikely to give accurate or honest self-reports about their emotions, thoughts, or behavior. The PCL:YV relies on an interview with specific questions, plus information from collateral sources and other written data. Because of the interview and collateral data requirement, the PCL:YV necessitates extensive training to administer and is time consuming. In addition, the PCL:YV is more research based and measures four dimensions of psychopathy. In contrast, the PCS and the YPI rely heavily on self-reports, while the APSD and CPS are designed to obtain information from teachers, parents, and the child or adolescent himself or herself.

The PCL:YV (youth version) is a 20-item rating scale adapted from the adult PCL-R (Hare, 1991, 2003) for use with juveniles. It adopts the four-factor model approach, scoring individuals on interpersonal, affective, behavioral, and antisocial factors. The PCL:YV has been subjected to extensive research, which suggests that it has adequate reliability and validity (for a review, see Vincent, 2006). However, caution is urged in its use. In particular, it appears to have limited ability to identify a meaningful relationship between psychopathy and antisocial behavior in adolescent girls (Odgers, Reppucci, & Moretti, 2005; Sevecke, Pukrop, Kosson, & Krischer, 2009; Vincent, Odgers, McCormick, & Corrado, 2008). It appears, therefore, that further investigations into the capacity of the PCL:YV to distinguish psychopathy in girls is critical before it can become a useful forensic tool.

There have been several attempts to compare various measures of juvenile psychopathy in terms of their validity and reliability (Farrington, 2005a). Preliminary research so far indicates that the measures do not have much in common, but more research needs to be done before conclusions can be drawn. One recent study shows considerable promise. Lynam and his colleagues (2007) were interested in discovering whether psychopathy scores on the CPS at age 13 predicted psychopathy scores on PCL:SV (short or screening version) at age 24. They found that the CPS did a decent job of predicting PCL:SV scores. These results suggest that psychopathy not only appears stable across stages of development but also implies that juvenile psychopathy appears similar to adult psychopathy in many ways.

NEUROBIOLOGICAL FACTORS AND PSYCHOPATHY

There is belief among the general public that psychopathic tendencies are caused exclusively by social factors, such as abuse and poor upbringing. However, researchers have implicated a variety of neurobiological factors as well. Contemporary research favors the view that psychopathic behavior results from a complex interaction between neuropsychological and learning or socialization factors. The neurobiological factors are crucial, however, and some research also has indicated that psychopathy may be an inherited condition (Waldman & Rhee, 2006).

Genetic Factors

There is emerging evidence that genetics may play a role in the development of psychopathy (Blonigen, Carlson, Krueger, & Patrick, 2003; Blonigen et al., 2005; Viding, Blair, Moffitt, & Plomin, 2005; Waldman & Rhee, 2006). For example, some evidence suggests that temperament linked to low arousal and fear responses is associated with psychopathy (Frick & Morris, 2004). A temperament of this nature may disrupt the formation of guilt, conscience, or concern about punishment. It is also suggested that youth with psychopathic features may have brain abnormalities (Newman, Curtin, Bertsch, Baskin-Sommers, 2010) and that psychopathy may run in families (Viding & Larsson, 2010). Research extended to psychopathy in children and adolescents, while still relatively new, has thus far found many similarities and some differences (Salekin et al., 2010).

The overall influence of genetics on psychopathy may not be large, but it seems large enough to draw the increasing attention of developmental and genetic researchers, especially those investigators interested in twin studies. Blair et al. (2006) believe that genetic contributions may play a significant role in the emotional dysfunction frequently found in psychopaths. That is, heredity may contribute significantly to the underarousal and low emotional responsiveness of psychopaths. However, at this point in our knowledge, we appear to be a long way from a genetic account of psychopathy. Furthermore, it is highly unlikely that genetics creates psychopathic features in isolation. That is, many factors are likely to interact with genetics along the developmental pathway to psychopathy.

Neuropsychology and Psychopathy

Although research in recent years has focused on the psychometric characteristics of psychopaths, the most current trend is the investigation of neuropsychological factors involved in determining psychopathic behavior (Gao, Glenn, Schug, Yang, & Raine, 2009; Vien & Beech, 2006). Neuropsychological indicators (called **markers**) have been repeatedly found in psychopaths, as reflected in electrodermal (skin conductance) measures and cardiovascular and other nervous system

TABLE 7-3   Major Divisions of the Human Nervous System

I. Central Nervous System (CNS)
   A. Brain
   B. Spinal cord

II. Peripheral Nervous System (PNS)
   A. Somatic nervous system (communicates with voluntary muscles)
   B. Autonomic nervous system
      1. Parasympathetic nervous system (relaxes and deactivates after emergencies)
      2. Sympathetic nervous system (activates for emergencies)

indices (Fishbein, 2001; Morgan & Lilienfeld, 2000). It is important, therefore, to become familiar with additional neuropsychological vocabulary and basic structures of the nervous system, some of which appeared in Chapter 3. The concepts presented here will also lay the foundation for topics in later chapters (e.g., Chapters 12 and 13 on sexual offenses, and Chapter 16 on drugs) as well.

BASIC NEUROPSYCHOLOGICAL CONCEPTS AND TERMINOLOGY.   The human nervous system can be divided into two major parts, either on the basis of structure or function. The structural division—the way it is arranged physically—is perhaps the clearest distinction. The central nervous system (CNS) and the peripheral nervous system (PNS) are the two principal parts. The CNS comprises the brain and spinal cord, and the PNS comprises all nerve cells (called neurons) and nerve pathways located outside the CNS (see **Table 7-3**). In other words, those nerves that leave the spinal cord and brain stem and travel to specific sites in the body belong to the peripheral (outside) nervous system. This includes all the nerves connecting the muscles, skin, heart, glands, and senses to the CNS.

The basic function of the PNS is to bring all the outside information to the CNS, where it is processed. Once the CNS has processed information, it relays the interpretation back to the PNS if action is necessary. When you place your finger on a hot object, the PNS relays this raw datum (it is not yet pain) to the CNS, which interprets the datum as the sensation of pain, and in return, relays a command to the PNS to withdraw the finger. The PNS cannot interpret; it only transmits information to the CNS and carries communications back. In the following pages, we will consider the significance of each of these systems to the diagnosis of psychopathy.

Central Nervous System Differences

Structurally, the CNS consists of the brain and spinal cord (**Table 7-3**). Interpretation, thoughts, memories, and images all occur in the cerebral cortex (the highest center of the brain). It is the processing center for stimulation and sensations received from the outside world and the body via the PNS. The cerebral cortex, which is the outer surface of the human brain, contains more than 100 billion nerve cells (called neurons) (Hockenbury & Hockenbury, 2004). Each neuron has a complicated communication link to numerous other neurons, creating an extremely complex and poorly understood communications network. Although the physical structure of the brain does not directly concern us, the electrical circuitry and arousal properties of the cortex are relevant in understanding the neuropsychological characteristics of the psychopath.

HEMISPHERE ASYMMETRY AND DEFICIENCY.   The human brain can be divided anatomically into two cerebral hemispheres—a right and a left. These two cerebral hemispheres seem to coexist in some sort of reciprocally balanced relationship between cortical functioning and information processing. For most individuals, the right hemisphere specializes in nonverbal functions, whereas the left specializes in verbal or language functions. Furthermore, the left hemisphere processes information in an analytical, sequential fashion. Language, for example, requires sequential cognition, and the left seems to be the best equipped for this operation. The right hemisphere, on the other hand, seems to process information holistically and more globally. For example, the right is involved in the recognition of faces, a complicated process requiring the processing of information all at once or simultaneously. Thus, the right and left hemispheres are two functionally differentiated information processing systems.

In addition to information processing, research is now finding that these two cerebral hemispheres also make different contributions to human emotions (Jacobs & Snyder, 1996; Tomarken, Davidson, Wheeler, & Doss, 1992). The right hemisphere appears to be particularly important in the understanding and communication of emotion (Kosson et al., 2002; Wheeler, Davidson, & Tomarken, 1993). The left seems to be closely tied to self-inhibiting processes, in contrast with the right which appears to be more spontaneous and impulsive (Tucker, 1981). Furthermore, the two hemispheres must have a balance of contribution from each for normal judgment and appropriate self-control (Tucker, 1981), and self-regulation of emotion (Tomarken et al., 1992). These control and judgment processes are especially prevalent in the frontal lobes (front sections of the brain).

Hare (Hare, 1998; Hare & Connolly, 1987; Hare & McPherson, 1984) hypothesizes that criminal psychopaths manifest an abnormal or unusual balance between the two hemispheres, both in language processing and in emotional or arousal states, which he calls **hemisphere asymmetry**. Hare notes that criminal psychopaths are often strikingly inconsistent with their verbalized thoughts, feelings, and intentions. Criminal psychopaths seem to be highly peculiar in the organization of certain perceptual and cognitive processes. Their left hemisphere seems, in some ways, deficient in linguistic processing because they do not rely on the verbal sequential operations to the extent that a majority of individuals do. Hare (1998) also hypothesizes that as the language task increases in complexity, nonpsychopathic persons rely more and more on the left hemisphere to process the information, while psychopaths rely more on the right hemisphere. Subsequent research supports this hypothesis (Lorenz & Newman, 2002).

There is also some research indicating that psychopaths are less accurate than non-psychopaths at reading emotional expressions portrayed by faces. More specifically, psychopaths appear to be less accurate than nonpsychopaths in facial emotional recognition under conditions designed to promote reliance on left-hemisphere processing (Kosson et al., 2002). These data are in support of the *left-hemisphere activation hypothesis* (Kosson, 1998), which states that psychopaths exhibit deficits on a variety of tasks that require activation of the left hemisphere.

Since language plays a very important role in the self-regulation of behavior, one of the contributing factors in the extremely impulsive, episodic behavior of psychopaths may reside in some deficiency in their use of internal language. This characteristic was pointed out some time ago by Flor-Henry (Flor-Henry, 1973; Flor-Henry & Yeudall, 1973), who was convinced that psychopathy is closely linked to left-hemispheric language dysfunction. There has been some research to suggest that the right hemisphere of psychopaths may be deficient as well (Herpertz & Sass, 2000). Research by Day and Wong (1996) and Silberman and Weingartner (1996), for example, suggests that many psychopaths have impairments in the right hemisphere that prevents them from experiencing emotions as strongly as the nonpsychopath population. Other researchers have found evidence that psychopaths exhibit an **emotional paradox**. "That is, psychopaths demonstrate normal appraisal of emotional cues and situations in the abstract (i.e., verbal discussion), but they are deficient in using emotional cues to guide their judgments and behavior in the process of living" (Lorenz & Newman, 2002, p. 91). In other words, psychopaths seem to be able to talk about emotional cues but lack the ability to use them effectively in the real world. This deficiency seems to be due to processing problems located in the left hemisphere (Bernstein, Newman, Wallace, & Luh, 2000; Lorenz & Newman, 2002). Nachshon (Nachshon, 1983; Nachshon & Denno, 1987) points out that many studies have found that a disproportionate percentage of violent, repetitive offenders have left-hemispheric dysfunction. Researchers in Germany had found similar results (Pillmann et al., 1999).

FRONTAL NEUROPSYCHOLOGICAL STUDIES. Some studies suggest that psychopaths may also suffer from frontal lobe problems or dysfunctions (Kiehl, 2006; Morgan & Lilienfeld, 2000; Sellbom & Verona, 2007). This observation is especially the case in many structural brain imaging studies that suggest psychopaths exhibit impairments in this region (Gao et al., 2009). The frontal lobe refers to that section of the cerebral cortex we commonly call the forehead (see **Figure 3-1, page** 67).

The frontal lobes (there are two, left and right) are believed to be responsible for the "higher-level" cognitive functions of abstraction, decision making, cognitive flexibility, foresight, the regulation of impulses, and the control of appropriate behavior (Ishikawa et al., 2001). In other words, the frontal lobes perform the "executive functions" of the human brain. Researchers tend to be more specific in their terminology and focus on the prefrontal cortex, the "front" area of the frontal lobe or cortex. As we learned in Chapter 3, **executive functions** refer to higher-order mental abilities involved in goal-directed behavior. Executive functions include organizing behavior, memory, inhibition processes, and planning strategies. Research has been consistent in demonstrating that prefrontal damage results in poor decision making, reduced autonomic functioning, and a psychopathic-like personality (Yang et al., 2005).

A growing amount of research indicates that psychopaths do appear to have defects in frontal lobe processing (Blair, 2007; Harenski et al., 2010). A comprehensive review by Morgan and Lilienfeld (2000) concluded that psychopaths, as a group, do show executive function deficits, which may result in faulty impulse control, judgment, and planning under certain conditions.

In an interesting study, Cathy Widom (1978) found that psychopaths recruited from newspaper advertisements for her experiment did not demonstrate the same level of frontal lobe deficits as incarcerated psychopaths. Widom speculated that "successful psychopaths" (community-based psychopaths who escaped conviction of their offenses and who answered the ad) probably had better functioning frontal lobes for controlling their behavior than the "unsuccessful" institutionalized psychopaths. Consistent with Widom's results, Ishikawa et al. (2001) discovered that successful psychopaths do not show the same psychophysiological or neuropsychological deficits as unsuccessful psychopaths. Overall, the researchers found that successful psychopaths exhibited stronger and better organized executive functions than either the unsuccessful psychopaths or the controls used in the study.

Despite the increasing number of empirical studies on adult psychopaths, brain imaging studies on children and adolescents who show some psychopathic traits are rare (Gao et al., 2009), but there are exceptions (e.g., Viding & Larsson, 2010, mentioned above). And, the few studies that have been conducted provide "some evidence supporting the speculation that the condition of psychopathy may, in part, be a result of neurodevelopmental abnormalities" (Gao et al., 2009, p. 815). Furthermore, these neurodevelopmental abnormalities appear to occur very early in life. One study, for instance, found that individuals who incurred damage to the prefrontal cortex before the age of 16 months showed considerable similarity to psychopaths (Anderson, Bechara, Damasio, Tranel, & Damasio, 1999). The researchers noted that these patients were "characterized by a pervasive disregard for social and moral standards, consistent irresponsibility and a lack of remorse" (Anderson et al., 1999, p. 1035).

At this point, the evidence suggests that the frontal lobes or prefrontal cortex may play an important role in explaining some of the observed behavioral differences between psychopaths and nonpsychopaths. Furthermore, frontal lobe dysfunction may not be simply limited to psychopaths but may be a feature that is characteristic of many other types of offenders (Raine, 1993, 2013).

AMYGDALA DYSFUNCTION. Psychopaths clearly demonstrate some problems in emotional processing. The frontal lobe is most often associated with this observation, as we have seen. Some researchers are beginning to believe that another neurological structure responsible for this dysfunction may be the amygdala (Crowe & Blair, 2008; Kiehl, 2006). The amygdala is an almond-shaped cluster of neurons in the brain responsible for emotions such as fear, anger, and disgust (see **Figure 3-1, page** 67). The amygdala is also involved in learning and short-term memory, especially in those learning situations involving high emotions. Some researchers have specifically tied the amygdala to psychopathy and the possession of callous–unemotional traits (DeLisi, Umphress, & Vaughn, 2009).

Kiehl et al. (2001) found that psychopaths exhibited lower amygdala activity during an emotional processing task when compared with criminal nonpsychopaths and noncriminal controls. Similar findings were reported by others (Gao et al., 2009; Harenski, Harenski, Kiehl, & Shane, 2010; Jones, Laurens et al., 2009; Marsh et al., 2008; Müller et al., 2003). With further research, the relationship between amygdala and learning might emerge as a highly significant factor in understanding the emotional behavior of the psychopath.

Peripheral Nervous System (PNS) Research

The PNS is subdivided into a *somatic division*, comprising the motor nerves that stimulate the muscles involved in body movement, and an *autonomic division*, which controls heart rate, gland secretion, and smooth muscle activity. Smooth muscles are those muscles found in the blood vessels and gastrointestinal system; they look smooth under a microscope in comparison with the skeletal muscles, which look striped or textured.

The autonomic segment of the PNS is extremely relevant to our discussion of the psychopath, because here, too, research has consistently uncovered a significant difference between the psychopath's and the general population's reactivity or responsiveness to stimuli. The autonomic division is especially important, because it activates emotional behavior and responsivity to stress and tension. It can be subdivided into the *sympathetic* and *parasympathetic systems* (see **Figure 7-1**).

The sympathetic system is responsible for activating or arousing the individual for fight or flight before (or during) fearful or emergency situations. As you will recall, the psychopath displays a James Bond–like coolness, even in stressful situations. We might explain this in one of two ways. Either the sympathetic nervous system does not react sufficiently to stressful stimuli, or the

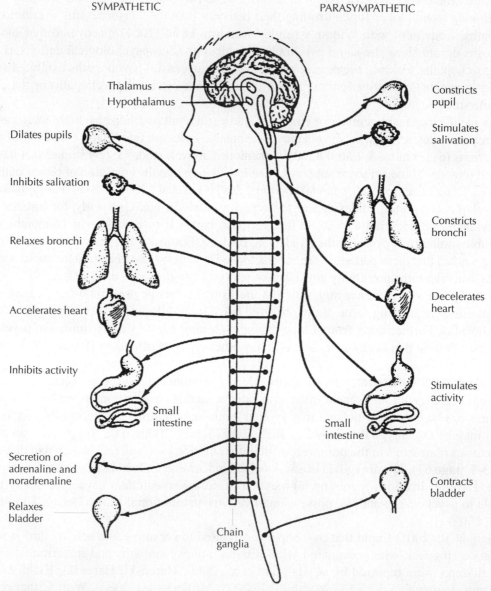

FIGURE 7-1 Illustration of the Sympathetic and Parasympathetic Subdivision of the Autonomic Nervous System

parasympathetic system springs into action in the psychopath more rapidly than in nonpsychopaths. There is research support for both of these positions.

Before discussing in more detail the psychopath's autonomic nervous system, we should note the principles and techniques of measuring autonomic activity. Emotional arousal, which is largely under the control of the autonomic nervous system, can be measured by monitoring the system's activity, such as heart rate, blood pressure or volume, and respiration rate. The most commonly used physiological indicator of emotional arousal, however, is *skin conductance response* (SCR), also known as the *galvanic skin response* (GSR). Since SCR is the label most advocated by researchers (Lykken & Venables, 1971), it will be used throughout this chapter.

SCR is simply a measure of the resistance of the skin to conducting electrical current. Although a number of factors in the skin influence its resistance, perspiration seems to play a major role. Perspiration corresponds very closely to changes in emotional states and has, therefore, been found to be a highly sensitive indicator of even slight changes in the autonomic nervous system. Other things being equal, as emotional arousal increases, perspiration rate increases proportionately. Small changes in perspiration can be detected and amplified by recording devices, known as polygraphs or physiographs. An increase in perspiration lowers skin resistance to electrical conductance. In other words, skin conductance (SC) increases as emotional arousal (anxiety, fear, etc.) increases.

We noted earlier that psychopaths lack the capacity to respond emotionally to stressful or fearful situations. Essentially, they give the impression of being anxiety free, carefree, and cool, and they display a devil-may-care attitude. We would expect, therefore, that compared with the normal population, the psychopath has a comparatively underactive, underaroused autonomic nervous system. What has the research literature revealed? Consistently, investigators have reported low SC arousal in psychopaths (Fishbein, 2001). "Deficits in measures of SC arousal are believed to be associated with low autonomic arousal levels which are, in turn, related to low emotionality, lack of empathy and remorse, and ability to lie easily" (Fishbein, 2001, p. 51). We now turn our attention to the division of the nervous system most responsible for SC arousal.

Autonomic Nervous System Research

A relatively large number of studies focusing on the autonomic nervous system of the psychopath have been conducted (Gao et al., 2009). In a pioneering study, Lykken (1957) hypothesized that since anxiety reduction is an essential ingredient in learning to avoid painful or stressful situations, and since the psychopath is presumed to be anxiety free, then the psychopath should have special difficulty learning to avoid unpleasant things. Recall that two characteristic features of psychopaths are their inability to learn from unpleasant experiences and their very high recidivism. Lykken carefully delineated his research groups according to Cleckley's criteria. His psychopaths (both males and females) were drawn from several penal institutions in Minnesota and were classified as either primary or neurotic psychopaths. College students comprised a third group of normals.

Lykken designed an electronic maze that participants were expected to learn as well as possible in 20 trials. There were 20 choice points in the maze, each with four alternatives, with only one being the correct choice. Although three alternatives were incorrect, only one of these would give the subject a rather painful electric shock. Lykken was primarily interested in discovering how quickly subjects learned to avoid the shock, a process called **avoidance learning**. He reasoned that avoidance learning would be rewarded by the reduction of anxiety on encountering the correct choice point, but since psychopaths are presumably deficient in anxiety, their performance should be significantly worse than that of normals. The hypothesis was supported.

Prior to the maze portion of the experiment, Lykken measured the skin conductance changes of each participant while he or she tried to sit quietly for 30 to 40 minutes. During this time, the person would periodically hear a buzzer and occasionally receive a slight, brief electric shock several seconds after the buzzer. Eventually, the buzzer became associated with the shock. In normal individuals, the sound of the buzzer itself produced an anxiety response in anticipation of the electric shock (classical conditioning) and was reflected by a substantial increase in SCR. Psychopaths, however, were considerably less responsive to this stress. Furthermore, psychopaths were incapable of learning to avoid the painful electric shocks, while the normals learned significantly better.

Lykken's data indicate that psychopaths do in fact have an under responsive autonomic nervous system and, as a result, do not learn to avoid aversive situations as well as most other people. More recent research (with electric shocking no longer part of the protocol) continues to support these findings (Gao et al., 2009; Gottman, 2001; Ogloff & Wong, 1990). Diminished autonomic reactivity has also been discovered in adolescents and children who exhibit psychopathic traits (Fung, Raine, Loeber, Lynam, Steinhauer, Venables, & Stouthamer-Loeber, 2005; Gao et al., 2009). Does this provide at least a partial explanation for why psychopaths continue to get into trouble with the law, despite the threat of imprisonment?

Schachter and Latané (1964) followed up on Lykken's work by using similar apparatus and basic procedures, with the exception of one major revision. Each participant was run through the maze twice, once with an injection of a harmless saline solution, once with an injection of adrenaline, a hormone that stimulates physiological arousal. Participants were prisoners selected on the basis of two criteria: how closely they approximated Cleckley's primary psychopath and how incorrigible they were, as measured by the number of offenses and time in prison. Prisoners high on both criteria were psychopaths; prisoners relatively low were nonpsychopaths.

Injections of adrenaline dramatically improved the performance of the psychopath in the avoidance learning task. In fact, with adrenaline injections, the psychopaths learned to avoid shocks more quickly than did normal prisoners with similar injections. On the other hand, when psychopaths had saline injections, they were as deficient in avoidance learning as Lykken's psychopaths.

Since anxiety is presumed to be a major deterrent to antisocial impulses, the manipulation of arousal or anxiety states by drugs may suggest policy implications for the effective treatment of convicted psychopaths. Specific drugs apparently have the potential to increase the emotional level of psychopaths to a point equivalent to the level of the general population.

Subsequent research by Hare (1965a, 1965b) found that primary psychopaths have significantly lower skin conductance while resting than do nonpsychopaths. As mentioned previously, skin conductance is a measure of how well the skin conducts the passage of a very small electrical current between two electrodes attached to the person. It is most often used as a measure of arousal (the more arousal the better the skin conducts the electrical current) and represents the basic measure of lie detection (polygraph) devices. Other researchers have reported similar results as found by Hare (Herpertz & Sass, 2000; Lorber, 2004). In another major study, Hare (1968) divided 51 inmates at the British Columbia Penitentiary into three groups—primary psychopaths, secondary psychopaths, and nonpsychopaths—and studied them under various conditions, while constantly monitoring their autonomic functioning. The experimental conditions also permitted the observation of a complex physiological response known as the *orienting response* (OR).

The OR is a nonspecific, highly complicated cortical and sensory response to strange, unexpected changes in the environment. The response may take the form of a turning of the head, a dilation of the eye, or a decrease or increase in heart rate. It is made in an effort to determine what the change is. Pavlov referred to the OR as the "what-is-it" reflex. It is an automatic, reflexive accompaniment to any perceptible change, and it can be measured by various physiological indices. The OR produces, among other things, an increase in the analytical powers of the senses and the cortex.

Hare found that not only did psychopaths exhibit very little autonomic activity (skin conductance and heart rate) but also that they gave smaller ORs than did nonpsychopaths. His data suggest that psychopaths are less sensitive and alert to their environment, particularly to new and unusual events.

Hare later reported intriguing data relating to the heart or cardiac activity of the psychopath. The aforementioned conclusions were based on skin conductance data. When cardiovascular variables are considered, however, some apparent anomalies appear. While skin conductance is consistently low, cardiac activity (heart rate) in the psychopath is often as high as that found in the nonpsychopathic population (Hare & Quinn, 1971). Hare comments, "The psychopaths appeared to be poor electrodermal [skin conductance] conditioners but good cardiovascular ones" (Hare, 1976, p. 135). That is, although psychopaths do not learn to react to stimuli as measured by skin variables, it appears that they learn to react autonomically as well as nonpsychopaths when the heart rate is measured. Hare suggests that the psychopath might be more adaptive to stress when "psychophysiological defense mechanisms" are brought into play, thereby reducing the impact of stressful stimuli.

Hare and his colleagues designed experiments in which the heart rate could be monitored throughout the experimental session. In one experiment, a tone preceded an electric shock by about 10 seconds (Hare & Craigen, 1974). In anticipation of the shock, psychopaths exhibited a rapid acceleration of heartbeat, followed by a rapid deceleration of heart rate immediately before the onset of the noxious stimulus (a "normal" reaction is a gradual but steady increase in heart rate until the shock). However, their skin conductance remained significantly lower than that of non-psychopaths. Therefore, psychopaths appear to be superior conditioners when cardiac activity is measured, indicating that they do indeed either learn or inherit autonomic adaptability to noxious stimuli. Hare suggests that this accelerative heart response is adaptive and helps the psychopath tune out or modulate the emotional impact of noxious stimuli. This, he speculates, may be the reason that skin conductance responses are relatively low in the psychopath.

Lykken (1955) also conducted experiments testing the performance of psychopaths on polygraph equipment. If psychopaths are generally underaroused, we would expect that lie detectors would be unable to differentiate their deceptive from their truthful responses, since polygraphs rely on physiological reactivity to questions. Also, psychopaths should have no trouble being deceptive, since they are typically adept at manipulating and deceiving others. Lykken's research confirmed these expectancies. Psychopaths emitted similar skin conductance responses, regardless of whether they were lying or telling the truth. Nonpsychopaths displayed significant differences in reactivity; their lie ratios, reflected by skin conductance, were larger than those of psychopaths. Because of the artificial atmosphere of the laboratory compared with real-life situations, particularly stressful ones, Lykken admonished against uncritical acceptance of his findings until further testing.

Few studies have since directly examined the relationship between psychopathy and lie detection. However, Raskin and Hare (1978) did reexamine the Lykken study, using more sophisticated equipment and better standardization for lie detection. Using 24 psychopathic prisoners and 24 nonpsychopathic prisoners, they found that both groups were equally easily detected at lying about a situation involving a $20 mock theft. This contradictory finding underscores the fact that fine-tuning is still needed if we are to understand the neurophysiological characteristics of the psychopath.

There is evidence, for example, that sufficiently aroused or motivated psychopaths will give physiological responses to interesting events that equal the responses of nonpsychopaths (Hare, 1968). On the other hand, when it comes to highly stressful, serious occasions, psychopaths appear to have incomparable skill at attenuating guilt or aversive reactions (Lykken, 1978). The simulated crime scene in the Raskin–Hare experiment was not only relatively unstressful, it may also have been regarded by the psychopath as an interesting "game." The acid test for the lie detection hypothesis will rest with carefully designed experiments under real-life, highly stressful situations. The present data do not justify firm conclusions.

Christopher Patrick and his colleagues (Patrick, Bradley, & Lang, 1993) conducted a study designed to test in what ways the startle reflex action in psychopaths differs from that of the normal population. An example of a startle response is the eye-blink reflex in response to a puff of air. These researchers note that psychophysiological research on the psychopath has relied almost exclusively on skin conductance and cardiovascular measures. The researchers found that criminal psychopaths (measured by Hare's PCL-R) exhibited much lower startle responses under aversive conditions than nonpsychopaths. Their findings confirm previous research showing that criminal psychopaths give smaller autonomic responses under aversive conditions than do other nonpsychopathic offenders. Hare (1993, 1996) postulates that psychopaths suffer from a general "hypo-emotionality." That is, it appears that psychopaths fail to experience the full impact of any kind of emotion—positive or negative. Psychopaths may be born with this hypoemotionality and that may account for their lack of remorse throughout their lifetimes.

Research studies have continually reported that psychopaths appear to have a lack of fear under a variety of environmental conditions that normally engender fear in nonpsychopaths

(Fowles & Dindo, 2009; Skeem, Polaschek et al., 2011). "On balance, available evidence indicates that fearlessness is a key component of psychopathy but that it is unlikely to account for all of the affective, interpersonal, and behavioral aspects of the condition" (Skeem, Polaschek et al., 2011, p. 113). The fearlessness aspect of psychopathy has prompted the development of the dual-process model, to which we now turn our attention.

The Dual-Process Model of Psychopathy

The **dual-process model** proposes that instead of a single low-fear pathway that accounted for all aspects of psychopathy, there are at least two temperament contributions that interact with social environmental influences to produce developmental pathways that ultimately lead to psychopathy (Fowles & Dindo, 2009). The model hypothesizes—based on recent research—that the two temperament processes involved in the emergence of psychopathy are low-fear temperament and impaired cognitive–executive functioning (Fowles & Dindo, 2009; Patrick & Bernat, 2009). These two temperament contributions appear to be connected to the four core factors of psychopathy discussed earlier in the chapter. Low-fear-temperament component is most closely associated with the affective–interpersonal factors (factors 1 and 2), and impaired cognitive–executive–function component is associated with the liefstyle–antisocial factors (factors 3 and 4).

The low-fear temperament reflects a neurological deficit in the ability to experience fear in situations most people find fearful and anxiety provoking. This deficit appears to be the result of inadequate reactivity in the amygdala and other affiliated brain structures and may account for the boldness and meanness dimensions reported in many psychopaths (Skeem et al., 2011). The second temperament in the model is linked to deficits in the executive functions of the brain, which involve "impulse-control problems of various types, including antisocial behavior and substance abuse" (Skeem et al., 2011, p. 114). The deficit is associated with an impulsive, socially deviant lifestyle. This temperamental propensity is linked to dysfunction in the frontal lobe, which helps regulation in emotion reactions, impulse control, and decision making.

There may be more temperament contributions to psychopathy—such as high anger/irritability or closeness to others (affiliation)—but a rapidly expanding body of contemporary research strongly supports the risk factors of low-fear and impaired executive functioning temperaments for now (Schulreich, Pfabigan, Drentl, & Sailer, 2013; Skeem et al., 2011; Venables & Patrick, 2014; Venables, Hall, Yancey, & Patrick, 2015).

These temperament (or psychobiological) dispositions occur early in childhood but can be influenced significantly by the social environment, such as parents, caregivers, peers, teachers, and other contextual factors (e.g., high-crime neighborhoods and malnutrition). "Interacting with the social environment, the risk factors can contribute to an interpersonally negative antisocial trajectory that culminates, for some individuals, in features that meet criteria for psychopathy (the more severe the risk factors, the less likely it is that parents will have the skills needed to keep the child on a positive trajectory)" (Fowles & Dindo, 2009, p. 182). Elsewhere, Fowles (2011) posits: "The term psychopathy has been valuable in identifying individuals who are distinctive enough to reflect interesting temperament contributions to antisocial behavior, but the construct refers to an outcome from a multidimensional, continuously variable set of etiological factors" (p. 94). Therefore, psychopathy is not caused strictly by psychobiological factors, but rather it is a developmental outcome of many risk factors. Moreover, the influence of psychobiological factors can be mitigated in optimal social environments.

In summary, the research reviewed thus far allows us to make four tentative conclusions about the autonomic functioning of the psychopath. First, psychopaths appear to be both autonomically and cortically underaroused, both under rest conditions and under some specific stress conditions. They are much more physiologically fearless compared to nonpsychopaths. Second, because they lack the necessary emotional equipment, psychopaths appear to be deficient in avoidance learning, which might account partially for their very high recidivism rates. Third, some data suggest that if emotional arousal can be induced, such as by adrenaline, psychopaths can learn from past experiences and avoid normally painful or aversive situations, such as prison, embarrassment, or social censure. And fourth, with adequate incentives, such as monetary rewards, psychopaths can learn from past experiences and avoid aversive consequences as well as anyone.

We noted earlier that psychopaths are often profoundly affected by alcohol, even in small amounts. Alcohol is a general CNS depressant, decreasing arousal levels in the nervous system. Research indicates that underaroused psychopaths are already half asleep and "half in the bag"; alcohol has the general effect of "bagging" them completely. Therefore, we would expect that the psychopath would not only get intoxicated more rapidly than the nonpsychopath of comparable weight but also probably pass out sooner. We would also expect the psychopath to have few sleep difficulties. Steven Smith and Joseph Newman (1990) found that a higher percentage of criminal psychopaths have been polydrug users when compared with criminal nonpsychopaths. In addition, criminal psychopaths were particularly heavy alcohol abusers, and alcohol may have played a very significant role in promoting their extensive antisocial behavior.

Research also has shown that adult psychopaths usually exhibit significant antisocial behavior in their childhoods (Seagrave & Grisso, 2002). It is reasonable, therefore, to expect researchers to begin searching the developmental trajectory of psychopathy in order to identify tomorrow's psychopaths. The next section examines what we currently know about the childhood of the psychopath.

CHILDHOOD OF THE PSYCHOPATH

We have discussed the behavioral descriptions and neuropsychological components of psychopaths. Now, how did they get that way? Criminal behavior and other behavior problems are often assumed to be rooted in the home, usually in homes with conflict, inadequate discipline, or poor models. From our discussion of the biopsychological components of psychopaths, however, it is obvious that the answer is not that simple. Psychopathy seems to be a result of a highly complex interaction of biopsychological, social, and learning factors.

Cleckley (1976) was not convinced that any common precursors exist in the family backgrounds of psychopaths, even though relatively homogeneous classifications of psychopathy do exist. However, even if we accept that neurophysiological factors may be causal factors in the development of psychopathy, this does not mean they are necessarily hereditary. As described earlier, it is possible, though, that psychopaths are born with a biological predisposition to develop the disorder and that this predisposition requires certain psychosocial factors before emerging, such as neglectful or abusive parenting. It could be that psychopaths have a nervous system that interferes with rapid conditioning and association between transgression and punishment. Because of this defect, the psychopath fails to anticipate punishment and, hence, feels no guilt (no conscience). As an alternative to the defect argument, it is possible that certain aspects of the psychopath's nervous system simply have not matured. Another possibility is that genetics, toxicity (e.g., lead paint and other sources of lead or other toxic substances) in utero or early childhood, birth difficulties, temperament, and other early developmental factors may affect certain processes in the nervous system, rendering some children vulnerable to develop conduct problems and psychopathic characteristics. We have learned in the chapter, for example, that early damage to the prefrontal cortex may contribute significantly to psychopathic trait development.

Many researchers believe that psychopathy begins in childhood and continues throughout adulthood (Farrington, 2005b; Forth & Burke, 1998; Lynam, 1998), which has led to the intense interest in juvenile psychopathy, discussed earlier in the chapter (see Salekin & Lochman, 2008). According to the research, the childhood of the psychopath is littered with signals that something is amiss. Marshall and Cooke (1999) found that, compared with nonpsychopaths, psychopaths were more likely to have experienced family difficulties such as parental neglect, abuse, or even antipathy and indifference. They were also more likely to have experienced negative school experiences. Poor parental monitoring and discipline have also been identified in the backgrounds of psychopaths (Tolan, Gorman-Smith, & Henry, 2003). Lynam (1998) reports that children with symptoms of hyperactivity, impulsivity, and attention problems *and* conduct problems closely resemble psychopathic adults. The extensive research of Paul Frick (2009) supports these observations. We hasten to add, however, that while it may appear that all psychopaths have experienced all or some of these problems as children, this is not to say that children with similar problems are necessarily fledgling psychopaths.

"Few researchers have tried to investigate early childhood risk factors that might predict, influence, or cause psychopathy" (Farrington, 2005a, p. 493). And very few researchers have conducted prospective longitudinal investigations of those risk factors (Farrington, 2005a). Some retrospective studies (Koivisto & Haapasalo, 1996; Patrick, Zempolich, & Levenston, 1997) and some longitudinal studies (Lang, af Klinteberg, & Alm, 2002; Weiler & Widom, 1996) have found that PCL-R scores appear to be related to early childhood abuse. In one prospective longitudinal study of 400 London boys, ages 8 to 10 years, it was found that physical neglect, poor parental supervision, a disrupted family, large family size, a convicted parent, a depressed mother, and poverty predicted psychopathy scores at age 48 (Farrington, 2005b).

A fruitful avenue for exploring the childhood of the psychopath would be close examination of the life-course-persistent (LCP) offender described by developmental theorists. Developmental theory postulates that LCP offenders manifest antisocial behaviors across all kinds of conditions and situations in their childhoods. Neurologically, LCPs demonstrate a variety of minor neuropsychological disorders, such as difficult temperaments as infants, attention deficit disorders or hyperactivity as children, and learning problems as adolescents. Socially, LCPs are rejected by peers during their preteen years and are annoying to adults. Emotionally, these children display virtually no empathy or concern for others, show very little bonding to family, and often are sadistic and manipulative. They are highly impulsive and lack insight. A careful reading of LCPs' developmental histories often shows a striking resemblance to the symptomology of criminal psychopaths. It should be emphasized, however, that only a modest number of LCPs probably qualify as full-blown psychopaths.

TREATMENT OF CRIMINAL PSYCHOPATHS

The treatment and rehabilitation of criminal psychopaths has been shrouded with pessimism and discouragement. Hare (1996, p. 41) asserted, "There is no known treatment for psychopathy." He admonished, though, "This does not necessarily mean that the egocentric and callous attitudes and behaviors of psychopaths are immutable, only that there are no methodologically sound treatments or 'resocialization' programs that have been shown to work with psychopaths." A long line of research documents that *adult* psychopaths are not responsive to treatment, whether in prisons, in psychiatric treatment centers, or in the community (e.g., Hare et al., 2000). Some commentary has indicated that psychotherapy or intervention with psychopaths is basically a waste of time. O'Neill, Lidz, and Heilbrun (2003) remarked that "to date, there is no treatment for psychopathy that has been established as effective" (p. 300). In fact, some forms of treatment (e.g., milieu therapy) have been linked to higher rates of violent recidivism in psychopaths (Rice, Harris, & Cormier, 1992). Several studies indicate that psychopaths are either completely nonresponsive to treatment or play the treatment game well, pretending to cooperate but in actuality "conning" the treatment provider (Hare, 1996; Porter et al., 2000; Rice et al., 1992). Farrington (2005a) states that "it seems to be generally believed that psychopaths are difficult to treat because (a) they are an extreme, qualitatively distinct category; (b) psychopathy is extremely persistent throughout life; (c) psychopathy has biological causes which cannot be changed by psychosocial interventions; and (d) the lying, conning, and manipulativeness of psychopaths make them treatment resistant" (pp. 494–495).

Other literature has pushed back on these conclusions, however (Salekin et al., 2010). Many researchers and clinicians believe that untreatability statements concerning the psychopath are unwarranted (Salekin, 2002; Skeem, Monahan, & Mulvey, 2002; Skeem, Poythress, Edens, Lilienfeld, & Cale, 2003; Wong, 2000). It is clear that treating psychopaths is not easy. Skeem et al. (2011) assert that criminal psychopaths—like other high-risk offenders—"tend to be evasive, verbally combative, hostile, prevaricating, disruptive and less ready to change, less committed to adjunct activities such as work and education, and more likely to be removed from or leave treatment prematurely..." (p. 134).

There is some evidence that criminal psychopaths who receive larger "doses" of treatment are less likely to demonstrate subsequent violent behavior than those who receive less treatment (Skeem, Poythress et al., 2003). It should be mentioned that a vast majority of the research has focused on recidivism rates of male psychopathic offenders, and very little is known about the recidivism rates of female psychopathic offenders.

It is usually difficult to evaluate properly the effectiveness of programs designed to treat criminal psychopaths because of their ability to manipulate the system. For example, many psychopaths volunteer for various prison treatment programs, show "remarkable improvement," and present themselves as model prisoners. They are skillful at convincing therapists, counselors, and parole boards that they have changed for the better. Upon release, however, there is a high probability that they will reoffend. In fact, there is some evidence to suggest that psychopaths who participate in therapy are more likely to engage in violent crime following the treatment than those psychopaths who did not receive treatment. Rice et al. (1992) investigated the effectiveness of an intensive therapeutic community program offered in a maximum security facility. The study was retrospective in that the researchers examined records and files 10 years after the program was completed. The results showed that psychopaths who participated in the therapeutic community exhibited higher rates of violent recidivism than did the psychopaths who did not. The results were the reverse for nonpsychopaths. Nonpsychopaths who received treatment were less likely to reoffend than nonpsychopaths who did not receive treatment.

Some critics of this study have remarked that the therapeutic community referred to was highly atypical of treatment programs in correctional facilities and has limited generalizability. Furthermore, the researchers themselves cautioned that the psychopaths used in the study were an especially serious group of offenders. Eighty-five percent had a history of violent crimes. Whether less serious psychopathic offenders will show similar results is unknown. The researchers conclude, "The combined results suggest that a therapeutic community is not the treatment of choice for psychopaths, particularly those with extensive criminal histories" (Rice et al., 1992, p. 408). Hare (1996) suggests that group therapy and insight-oriented treatment programs—both of which were features of the program reviewed above—may help the psychopath develop better ways of manipulating and deceiving others.

Treatment of Children and Adolescents with Psychopathic Features

As we noted in the previous section, the treatment and rehabilitation of adult criminal psychopaths has been cloaked with pessimism and discouragement, less so in more recent years. Unfortunately, little is known about the effectiveness of prevention and treatment methods for child and adolescent psychopathy (Farrington, 2005a, p. 494) or, as many researchers and clinicians prefer to say, children and adolescents with psychopathic tendencies or characteristics. (See again **Box 7-2** for an exception.)

Logically, it makes sense to hypothesize that children and adolescents with psychopathic features would respond more positively than psychopathic adults to prevention and treatment strategies because of their malleability. Consequently, researchers have begun to evaluate the effectiveness of (a) treatment programs designed specifically for juveniles with psychopathic characteristics, and (b) programs for youthful offenders that include those with psychopathic characteristics.

Studies have underscored the observations that children and adolescents with psychopathic features show distinct sets of emotional and cognitive deficits that lead to their violent and antisocial behavior. According to Salekin and Frick (2005), knowledge about these areas may be important for designing more individualized interventions for youths with psychopathic traits. For example, laboratory studies have revealed that children with conduct problems and high levels of callous–unemotional (CU) traits exhibit tendencies to respond better to reward-driven interventions and respond poorly to punishment-driven or fear-induced forms of intervention (Hawes & Dadds, 2005). These findings imply that children displaying high-reward drive and low fearful inhibitions should, compared with conduct-problem children *without* CU traits, respond well to parents who use reward-based strategies for changing behavior (e.g., praise, rewards, reinforcement tokens), but remain insensitive to other parental disciplinary practices (e.g., time-outs, forms of verbal or behavioral punishments, such as scolding or confiscating a favorite game). "The assessment of CU traits in addition to other established risk factors," Hawes and Dadds (2005) conclude, "may allow such children to be targeted with more individualized intervention" (p. 740).

Juveniles with psychopathic characteristics did not fare well in an outpatient *substance abuse* treatment program, however (O'Neill et al., 2003). In this study, youths with higher scores on the PCL:YV were more likely to be rearrested and demonstrated higher attrition from the program, lower quality of participation, and more frequent use of alcohol and drugs while in the treatment program. The treatment program was based on a cognitive-behavioral model, whereby the adolescents would set goals and learn coping skills. They had daily group therapy sessions and twice-weekly one-hour sessions of individual therapy. While youths who scored low on the PCL:YV did benefit from the program, those with high scores did not. The reasons for the failure in this program are unknown.

On a more promising note, Salekin, Rogers, and Machin (2001) in their survey of over five hundred child clinical psychologists discovered that many of these clinicians reported that they were moderately to significantly successful in treating children and adolescents with psychopathic features. The treatment duration for these psychopathic youth averaged about 12 months. "After nearly one year of treatment these youths reportedly made marked improvement on such criteria as violence and recidivism" (Salekin et al., 2001, p. 192). The clinicians estimated that approximately 42 percent of the boys and 45 percent of the girls made moderate-to-marked improvement in reducing their psychopathic symptomatology overall. "These findings are important," Salekin et al. conclude, "and indicate that psychopathy, at least in youth, may be less recalcitrant to treatment than previously thought" (p. 192).

Salekin (2002) also published a comprehensive review of 42 studies specifically directed at treating psychopathy. Despite some methodological shortcomings with many of the studies (e.g., small sample size, diverse definitions of psychopathy), cognitive-behavioral, psychodynamic, and eclectic interventions were shown to be effective. The most notable benefits included a reduction in psychopathic characteristics, such as a decrease in lying, an increase in remorse or empathy, and improved relations with others. Salekin specifically noted that one intensive action-oriented program was highly successful (88%) with youngsters showing psychopathic tendencies. Ingram, Gerard, Quay, and Levison (1970) devised a program specifically designed to address psychopathic behaviors in youth. The program was based on the sensation-seeking model that kept the 20 young participants interested in treatment throughout the sessions. The program was able to decrease institutional aggressive behavior and improved overall adjustment in the community. Those psychotherapies that proved most effective tended to be more intensive and often combined with other programs, such as group psychotherapy, pharmacotherapy, or the involvement of family members. "These results indicate, at least preliminarily," Salekin writes, "that for complex problems such as psychopathy, more elaborate and intensive intervention programs involving individual psychotherapy, treatment of family members, and input from groups (other patients/inmates) are beneficial and may enhance their overall effectiveness" (p. 105). The key for success with psychopaths may be the scope, type, intensity, and duration of the treatment, as well as the training of the staff applying the intervention. Salekin points out that those intervention programs that were less successful were characterized by little input by trained mental health professionals and extremely little one-to-one patient–psychologist contact. He further stated that early intervention is particularly important in working with children exhibiting psychopathic traits. Salekin concludes then, as he has more recently (Salekin & Lynam, 2010; Salekin, Worley, & Grimes, 2010), that the therapeutic pessimism that surrounds the treatment of psychopathy and undermines motivation to search for effective modes of intervention for the disorder is unwarranted.

SUMMARY AND CONCLUSIONS

Psychopathy may well be the most studied construct in psychological criminology. Although psychopaths comprise a minuscule percent of the general population, their numbers are larger among convicted criminals. When psychopaths commit crimes—and they do not always do so—their crimes may be, but again are not necessarily, particularly vicious and brutal. The primary psychopath should be distinguished from people who may be classified as psychotic, neurotic, or emotionally disturbed. The primary psychopath also should be distinguished from the sociopath and from the secondary and dyssocial psychopaths. The diagnostic category "APD" also is distinct from "psychopathy," even though these two terms are often confused by clinicians and researchers. This is understandable, because APD, as defined behaviorally in the DSM-5, has many parallels to Robert Hare's concept of criminal psychopathy.

Psychopaths demonstrate a variety of behavioral and neurophysiological characteristics that differentiate them from other groups of individuals. In this chapter, we are of course most interested in the psychopath who runs afoul of the law, particularly by way of persistent and/or violent offending. In this sense, the criminal psychopath, the sociopath, and the person with APD are very similar in their offending patterns.

Psychopaths most often function in society as charming, daring, witty, intelligent individuals, high on charisma but low on emotional reaction and affect. They appear to lack moral standards or the ability to manifest genuine sensitivity toward others. If criminals, they become the despair of law enforcement officials because their crimes appear to be without discernible or rational motives. Even worse, they show no remorse or desire or ability to be rehabilitated. In recent years, nevertheless, mental health professionals have reported some success in providing psychotherapy to psychopaths in intensive treatment programs of long duration.

Although there are several theoretical approaches to describe psychopathy, the predominant one is the four-factor model, which conceives of psychopathy as a condition defined by interpersonal, lifestyle, affective, and antisocial features. Contemporary researchers suggest additional factors, including boldness and meanness, but for the present the four-factor model remains the most heavily cited. The recently advanced "dual model of psychopathy" proposes that a low-fear temperament and an impaired executive function best characterize most psychopaths. The low-fear temperament component of the model signifies that the psychopath is neurologically unable to experience a level of fear or anxiety that most people experience. The second component of the model represents the psychopath's inability to adequately control his or her impulses for doing inappropriate things.

Various instruments have been devised to measure psychopathy. Chief among them are the PCL, its revision, and its offshoots, developed by Hare and his colleagues. These include screening versions and measures designed specifically for youth. Other researchers also have developed additional scales for youth, including the Child Psychopathy Scale and the Youth Inventory of Psychopathic Traits. While the PCL remains the most heavily researched and most widely used, caution was urged with regard to the populations for which it is used. Furthermore, the use of any measures by nontrained examiners is inadvisable. Being labeled a psychopath has been shown to have negative consequences in the legal system, as well as in some institutional settings.

There are still numerous gaps in our knowledge of the psychopath, one being in the area of gender differences. Research on female psychopaths is scant but has increased in recent years. Some research suggests that behavioral characteristics of female psychopaths are generally similar to those of male psychopaths, with slightly more emphasis among females on sexual acting-out behavior. This probably reflects a cultural bias, however, since women have been traditionally chastised more than men for behavior deemed inappropriate according to sexual mores. However, research on female criminal psychopaths using Hare's PCL-R implies that their behavioral patterns may be somewhat different than those of male criminal psychopaths. Female psychopaths, for example, are believed to be less physically aggressive and more relationally aggressive. They also have been found to have more environmental deprivation and more physical and sexual victimization in their backgrounds than male psychopaths. Some research has found that their criminal careers began later and that they recidivated less than male psychopaths.

A highly controversial area relating to psychopathy has been the measurement and existence of juvenile psychopathy. Researchers are very actively involved in developing scales to assess this construct and in comparing features of juvenile and adult psychopaths. Psychopathic characteristics in juveniles may be deceiving, however. Many youth, for example, are impulsive, seek stimulation, and appear to be noncaring; these features are often part of the normal turmoil of adolescent development. While it is worthwhile to study these characteristics, we must not rush to judgment and assume they are indicative of psychopathy. However, contemporary research has now documented that something very much like psychopathy exists in some children and adolescents, and, more importantly, that successful treatment is possible.

Contemporary research on psychopathy is robust and shows few signs of abating. By now, it is quite clear that Hare's primary psychopath—as measured by the PCL—has many unique features. Psychopathy includes distinctive cognitive and emotional styles and physiological indicators, and there is some research indicating that these psychopathic characteristics may be inherited. Many psychopaths also had childhoods marked by parental deficiency and conduct problems. These features combine to render the adult psychopath highly resistant to treatment. This is particularly frustrating to clinicians working with criminal psychopaths, many of whom know how to play the clinical games that will make it appear that they have changed their behavior. Nevertheless, promising intensive programs have been developed, suggesting that pessimistic conclusions about the possibility of bringing about change in the behavior of the criminal psychopath might have been premature.

Key Concepts

Antisocial personality disorder (APD)
Avoidance learning
Boldness factor (fearless dominance)
Criminal psychopath
Dual-process model
Dyssocial psychopaths
Emotional paradox
Executive functions
Factor analysis
Factor 1
Factor 2
Factor 3

Four-factor model
Hemisphere asymmetry
Markers
Meanness factor
Primary psychopath
Psychopathy Checklist (PCL and PCL-R)
Psychopathy Checklist: Screening Version (PCL:SV)
Psychopathy Checklist: Youth Version (PCL:YV)
P-Scan: Research Version
Recidivism
Secondary psychopaths
Semantic aphasia

Review Questions

1. Briefly describe the core behavioral characteristics of the criminal psychopath.
2. What differences have been found between male and female psychopaths?
3. Name and describe briefly any five instruments used to measure psychopathy.
4. Define each of the following as proposed by Hare: primary psychopath, secondary psychopath, dyssocial psychopath, and criminal psychopath.

5. What has been learned about (a) recidivism and (b) treatment of the criminal psychopath?
6. Identify some of the ethical problems created as a result of labeling a child a "psychopath."
7. Describe the three- and four-factor models of psychopathy.
8. How is the psychopath different from the nonpsychopath on psychophysiology? Thoroughly discuss all relevant features.

8

Crime and Mental Disorders

CHAPTER OBJECTIVES

- Define mental disorders.
- Provide an overview of the *DSM* and the diagnoses that are most relevant to criminal behavior.
- Define and review issues relating to competency to stand trial.
- Review the insanity defense rules and standards.
- Discuss special defenses sometimes raised to absolve defendants of criminal responsibility or mitigate responsibility.
- Discuss the prevalence of mental illness in incarcerated populations.
- Define risk assessment and identify the risk factors employed in assessing violent criminal behavior.
- Explore the relationship between mental disorder and violence.

In 2014, *American Sniper*, a film based on the story of Chris Kyle, was released and eventually nominated for best picture of the year. (It did not win.) Kyle, who had served four tours of duty in the Iraq war, was considered the most lethal sniper in U.S. military history. In 2013, about four years after his honorable discharge, Kyle and his friend Chad Littlefield were murdered at a shooting range in Texas. The shooter, Eddie Ray Routh, a former Marine, pleaded not guilty by reason of insanity (NGRI), saying he was in a psychotic state when he shot his victims. Routh was convicted and sentenced to life in prison without parole.

In January 2011, congresswoman Gabrielle Giffords of Arizona was shot in the head by 23-year-old Jared Loughner, who also killed six other people, including a nine-year-old girl and a federal judge, and wounded 12 people in addition to congresswoman Giffords. The shootings occurred while the congresswoman was meeting with her constituents outside a supermarket in Tucson. The shooter was initially ruled incompetent to stand trial (IST) and was treated for severe mental disorders at a hospital in Missouri. In August 2012, he pled guilty to his crimes, apparently to avoid the death penalty.

James Holmes killed 12 people and injured many others in a Colorado theater in 2012 during a midnight showing of a Batman film. In 2015, he went on trial, pleading NGRI. Holmes had offered to plead guilty in exchange for a life sentence, but prosecutors wanted to try for the death penalty. He was subsequently convicted, but the jury did not sentence him to death. He was sentenced to life without the possibility of parole in August 2015.

Six-year-old Etan Patz was one of the first missing children to be pictured on a milk carton in 1979. In 2012, thirty-three years later, 53-year-old Pedro Hernandez confessed to the boy's abduction and murder. After being interrogated for six hours, he told police he lured the child into the basement of a bodega with the promise of a soda, choked him, stuffed his body in a garbage bag while he was still alive, and then disposed of the body. Hernandez was intellectually disabled and had a history of mental illness. Though defense lawyers argued that his confession was psychologically coerced by police, the judge admitted it into trial, which began in January 2015. He pleaded NGRI. In May 2015, the judge declared a mistrial, because the 12-person jury was unable to reach a verdict after lengthy and careful deliberation that lasted 18 days.

Finally, in another shocking case that cannot be forgotten, 31-year-old Andrea Yates drowned her five children, ages six months to seven years, in a bathtub in 2001. She had a history of mental disorder; she had attempted suicide twice and had been hospitalized at least four times, apparently for depression. At her trial, Yates raised the insanity defense, citing in particular a severe case of postpartum psychosis. Her lawyers said she believed she was possessed by Satan and that her children would suffer in hell because she represented evil. To save them from that fate, she thought it was critical that they die now so that they could go to heaven; she herself would be executed for their deaths, as Satan demanded. Yates was found guilty of the deaths of three of her children, but she was re-tried when an appeals court found significant errors in the prosecution of her case. In her second trial, she was found NGRI. She remains institutionalized today, receiving treatment in a secure hospital setting.

Each of the above cases received national attention, and each has raised troubling questions about the way the U.S. legal system deals with mentally ill individuals who commit serious crimes. The Yates case produced a national debate over the legal standards for determining insanity. The Loughner case, along with others that both preceded it and followed it, questioned the availability of guns to people with mental illness, as well as the process used in bringing them to trial. Loughner was given psychoactive medication against his will to make him competent to be tried for his actions. Holmes was willing to plead guilty, but chose the NGRI route when prosecutors persisted in seeking the death penalty. The Hernandez case was troubling because of the defendant's intellectual disability and long-standing mental illness, as well as concerns that his confession was coerced. Eddie Ray Routh had been diagnosed with posttraumatic stress disorder (PTSD), but lawyers did not use that diagnosis; rather, they argued that he acted under a state of psychosis, believing his victims were "pig assassins," who were sent to kill him. In this chapter, we discuss many of the points and issues brought up by these and other cases.

Despite the tragedy of the above cases, brutal and violent crimes are not usually committed by people who are mentally ill, and the mentally ill do not usually commit such crimes. If they did crime rates would skyrocket: It has been estimated that about 18 percent of the total U.S. adult population has a mental illness, with just over one-fifth of that group having a *serious mental illness* (SMI) (U.S. Department of Health and Human Services, SAMSHA, 2013). It is not uncommon for mass murderers to have demonstrated signs of SMI, as we will discuss in Chapter 10. Other murderers, including serial murderers, are less likely to have done so. Yet, it is a common perception that someone who walks into his workplace and shoots fellow employees must be mentally ill. Likewise, someone who sexually assaults, tortures, and kills a four-year-old child has to be sick. How else could these people do this? Despite this perception, there is not widespread support for an insanity defense (Goldstein et al., 2013). As illustrated in the cases mentioned at the beginning of the chapter, only one—the Yates case—resulted in a successful insanity defense, and it was achieved in a second trial, before a judge and not a jury.

The media have been instrumental in developing the connection between mental disorder and crime, particularly serious violent crime. Along with greed and revenge, mental illness is a basic motivation for criminality in the vast majority of crimes on television and other entertainment media (Surette, 1999). John Monahan (1992) cites an early survey (Gerbner, Gross, Morgan, & Signorielli, 1981) showing that on prime-time American television, 73 percent of all individuals characterized as mentally disordered also displayed some violent behavior. In a later analysis (Shain & Phillips, 1991), 86 percent of all print stories dealing with former mental patients focused on the violence of the patients, especially if the topics dealt with serial or mass murder. The plethora of profiling shows on cable television and the networks today tend to portray violent criminals, particularly murderers, as bizarre, often psychotic, and resistant to the efforts of the profilers to "get into their minds."

Historically, mental illness has challenged society in general, the mental health professions, and the criminal justice system. Individuals exhibiting bizarre behaviors were submitted to strange and sometimes torturous methods. Historians have documented religious ceremonies to rid such individuals of what were believed to be evil spirits; untested techniques like spinning them on stools with wheels and dropping them into icy waters; or simply locking them away in attics or asylums with little attempt to address their behaviors (Rothman, 1975, 1980).

In the twentieth century, these practices were replaced by the introduction of medication intended to manage mental illness. Psychological therapy or treatment would ideally accompany the medication. However, medication was critical because the mental disorders were believed to be physiologically based. The use of medication to address mental illness continues to this day. Medications help people get through the day, but they are rarely the solution to underlying psychological problems.

A major criticism of drug treatment is the side effects they often produce, sometimes including nausea, loss of energy, inability to concentrate, loss of appetite, dizziness, and other equally disturbing symptoms. Nevertheless, medications for mental disorder have improved substantially, and mental health practitioners as a group accept that they are needed, but are concerned nonetheless about overuse. Furthermore, mental health practitioners also emphasize that medication alone is not the solution to mental illness. It is not unusual today for psychiatrists and psychologists to work with a patient as colleagues, the one prescribing medication, and the other offering psychological treatment.

A minority but still forceful position is that taken by the psychiatrist Thomas Szasz, who criticized the psychiatric profession in his classic books, *The Myth of Mental Illness* (1961) and *The Manufacture of Madness* (1970), among numerous other publications and presentations. Szasz believed that deviations in behavior such as those demonstrated in mental disorders should not be regarded as illnesses, primarily because this gave too much power to the medical profession and enabled widespread use of drugs to control behavior of people who acted differently from the general population. He and his followers advocated a therapeutic approach wherein individuals could be taught to take responsibility for their own "problems in living." Szasz, who died in 2012, angered many in the psychiatric profession with his libertarian views, particularly his beliefs that psychiatrists overdiagnosed behaviors and infringed on civil liberties by overprescribing medication.

Today, Szasz's views are in the minority, as medication has become the dominant way of treating mental illness—or if one prefers mental disorder or behavioral disorders. Nevertheless, it cannot be denied that Szasz made significant contributions by challenging the dominance of the psychiatric profession. Even if mental illness is not a myth, its causes and its treatment should continually be scrutinized.

Many researchers distinguish between mental illness in general and *serious mental illness* in particular, and they focus their attention on the latter. As noted earlier, it is estimated that 9.3 million adults experience SMI (U.S. Department of Health and Human Services, 2013). SMI is not always defined the same way, but a common definition is "the class of disorders with psychotic features (e.g., Schizophrenia,...Major Depressive Disorder...) or other symptoms that have the potential to very substantially affect an individual's interpersonal and vocational functioning" (Heilbrun et al., 2012, note 1). It is important to emphasize, as well, that people with SMI—when they do commit crimes—typically commit minor offenses rather than those highlighted at the beginning of the chapter. They are more likely to trespass, shoplift, or commit simple assault than to murder someone. Furthermore, recent research indicates that SMI is not a direct cause of crime (Peterson, Skeem, Kennealy, Bray, & Zvonkic, 2014; see **Box 8-1**) and that risk factors for offending are similar in both mentally ill and nonmentally ill offenders (Skeem, Winter, Kennealy, Louden, & Tatar, 2014).

DEFINING MENTAL ILLNESS

Mental illness is a disorder (some say a disease) of the mind that is judged by experts to interfere substantially with a person's ability to cope with life on a daily basis. It presumably deprives the person of freedom of choice, but it is important to note that there are degrees to this deprivation. In other words, even a seriously disordered individual has some decision-making ability. Mental illness is manifested in behavior that deviates notably from normal conduct. SMI, as we noted above, not only deviates from normal conduct but also severely impedes, or has potential to impede, a person's functioning. However, the word "illness" encourages us to look for etiology, symptoms, and cures and to rely heavily on the medical profession both to diagnose and to treat. An alternative term, **mental disorder**, need not imply that a person is sick, to be pitied, or even necessarily less responsible for his or her actions. Therefore, although "mental illness" is still used in the psychological, psychiatric, and legal literature, as well as in both civil and criminal law, the less restrictive "mental disorder" is also often used. In essence, the two terms have become interchangeable. In fact, the DSM-5, published by the American Psychiatric Association (2013), is the manual of mental *disorders*. This is not to say that medication is not needed, and it is not to say that persons with mental disorder are always responsible for their behavior.

Another term that must be distinguished is **intellectual disability**, formerly known as mental retardation. This is a cognitive deficiency that cannot be cured. Intellectual disability was traditionally measured by standardized "IQ" tests, but these are increasingly being supplemented by other measures and by observations and interviews. Though intellectual disability cannot be cured, intellectually disabled individuals can be provided training and support services to lead productive and independent lives. Even so, they are sometimes charged with primarily minor offenses that result in arrests, being detained in jail, and serving time. Dual diagnoses of intellectual disability and substance abuse have been observed in a significant number of these individuals (Day & Berney, 2001). Misperceptions about the intellectually disabled are perhaps not as strong as misperceptions about the mentally disordered, but they represent a population whose needs may go unrecognized by the criminal justice system. Thus, while the chapter focuses primarily on issues related to the mentally disordered or mentally ill, we will also give attention to unique problems faced by the intellectually disabled.

Mental disorders are manifested in a variety of behaviors, ranging in severity from dangerous, harmful acts to conduct that is essentially innocuous. In a classic work, Morse (1978) preferred the term "crazy behavior," which he characterized as behavior that is obviously strange and unusual *and cannot be logically explained*. The person who walks onto the hotel elevator at the lobby level and faces the rear, staring blankly at the elevator's rear wall, while others are facing the front, is exhibiting strange behavior. However, if the elevator subsequently opens at the "back" door, there is a logical explanation: The person is a hotel guest or an employee who is familiar with the elevator's setup. In the absence of such an explanation, the behavior becomes disconcerting to the other passengers and, if only mildly, "crazy." In this instance, some clinicians—again in the absence of a logical explanation—may see the behavior as symptomatic of an anxiety disorder or a dissociative disorder, depending on other aspects of the individual's behavior. However, the behavior, as described above, is not dangerous. On the other hand, a person who walks into a hotel lobby in a highly agitated state, brandishing a knife, and stating that hotel employees were all trained by Satan and must die for their sins is exhibiting both "crazy" and dangerous behavior. There is obviously a crucial distinction between the above scenarios.

The *DSM*

The concept of mental disorder, therefore, connotes a wide range of bizarre, dramatic, harmful, or mildly unusual behaviors whose classifications are published in the ***Diagnostic and Statistical Manual of Mental Disorders (DSM)***. Compiled by committees appointed by the American Psychiatric Association, the *DSM*—now in its 5th edition (DSM-5; American Psychiatric Association, 2013) is the guidebook for clinicians seeking to define and diagnose specific mental disorders. It is used by mental health professionals to guide diagnosis and to justify third-party reimbursement for treatment. Some prefer to use an alternative classification system, the *International Classification of Disease* (*ICD*)—published by the World Health Organization (WHO)—now in its 10th edition, with an 11th edition scheduled for release in 2015. It is important to note, though, that the DSM-5 is in closer alignment with the structure of the *ICD* than it has been in the past (American Psychiatric Association, 2013). Regardless of the system used, diagnoses often appear in official records, such as court documents and prison files, and they are commonly seen in noncriminal matters such as disability determinations and child custody proceedings. It is noteworthy, however, that psychologists are generally advised not to include clinical diagnoses in their psychological reports unless specifically asked by the courts to provide them (APA, 2013). This is because diagnoses are often misconstrued and misunderstood by persons who are not mental health professionals.

We now turn to the specific mental disorders that are most likely to be associated with criminal conduct, though not necessarily serious criminal conduct. It must be stressed, however, that (1) persons with these disorders are not "crime prone," and (2) even if an individual is diagnosed with these disorders, he or she still can be held responsible for criminal conduct.

We emphasize that the material in this section is intended to provide a cursory overview of specific disorders and their possible relationship to criminal behavior. The DSM-5 and a vast array of psychological and psychiatric literature offer extensive descriptions as well as commentary and treatment recommendations for various forms of mental illness (e.g., Weiner, 2013).

For the present, the categories of mental disorders most relevant are (1) the schizophrenia spectrum and other psychotic disorders, (2) bipolar disorder, (3) major depression, and (4) the personality disorder called "antisocial personality disorder" (APD). Individuals with the first three are overrepresented in the criminal justice system, often detained in jails (Steadman, Osher, Robbins, Case, & Samuels, 2009). APD, as we discuss below, is a catch-all diagnosis often given to individuals with a long history of antisocial behavior. We covered APD briefly in Chapter 7, noting that its behavioral features resemble closely those of psychopathy, though the two are not identical. These four categories of disorders are relevant because they are most likely to be the diagnoses received by individuals charged with serious criminal, or antisocial, behavior, assuming that a mental disorder is at issue. With the exception of APD, they are the disorders most often cited to support an insanity defense to criminal charges or claims of diminished capacity. We review each of these disorders and then assess their relevance to criminal behavior. However, toward the end of the chapter, we discuss less common disorders that, when cited in courts, attract considerable media attention.

Schizophrenia Spectrum and Other Psychotic Disorders

The specific disorders in this category include schizophrenia, other psychotic disorders, and schizotypal (personality) disorder. **Schizophrenia** in particular is the mental disorder that people most often associate with "crazy behavior," since it frequently manifests itself in highly bizarre actions. It is characterized by disturbances in cognition, emotional responses, and behavior. Schizophrenia is a mental disorder that continues to be extremely complex and poorly understood (Andreasen & Carpenter, 1993; Sitnikova, Goff, & Kuperberg, 2009). The disorder generally begins early in life, often leads to social and economic impairment, and leaves traces on its victims for the rest of their lives (Andreasen & Carpenter, 1993). Behavioral manifestations of schizophrenia are varied, but there are some common characteristics. In addition, it has features in common with the other psychotic disorders mentioned above. Specifically, these features are delusions, hallucinations, disorganized thinking, and grossly disorganized or abnormal motor behavior. Recall that Routh, the person convicted of murder in the sniper case, was believed to be psychotic; among other features, he asserted there were "pig people" in his environment, who were trying to kill him. Hernandez, whose case ended in a mistrial, had been diagnosed with a schizotypical personality disorder and had a history of being on antipsychotic medication. In addition, persons with schizophrenia have other negative symptoms that the other disorders herein do not necessarily have, such as diminished emotional expression (American Psychiatric Association, 2013).

Psychoactive drugs to treat these disorders have improved significantly since the time they were first denounced by Szasz and others. They still have side effects, and, like other medication, they often have to be adjusted until the proper dosage is identified. However, without such medication people who have these disorders often experience severe breakdowns in thought patterns, emotions, and perceptions. Spells of extreme social withdrawal from others are also typical. The thoughts and cognitive functioning of the person with schizophrenia become disorganized and fail to correspond to reality, and his or her speech will reflect this. The most common example is a loosening of associations, in which ideas shift between totally unrelated and only obliquely related subjects. Thought becomes fragmented and bizarre, and **delusions**—false beliefs about the world— are common. An example of a delusion is believing an *alien* from another universe is listening in on your cell phone conversations or sending you text messages and ultimately plotting against you.

The person with schizophrenia is typically inappropriate in emotion or affect (e.g., indiscriminate giggling and crying), or reflects emotional flatness, where very little—if any— emotional reaction is exhibited. This may occur even with medication. The voice is monotonous and the face immobile and expressionless. The major disturbances in perception are various forms of **hallucinations**, which involve sensing or perceiving things or events that others do not sense or perceive. The most common hallucinations are auditory, with the individual hearing voices or sounds that no one else in the vicinity hears.

The proportion of violent crimes committed by people with schizophrenia and other psychotic disorders is small; however, when they do commit violent crimes, the level of violence may be higher than that of the "typical" violent offender, particularly with respect to homicide or aggravated assault. At least one of the clinicians who evaluated Jared Loughner—the man who eventually pled guilty in the Arizona "meet and greet" shooting spree mentioned at the beginning of the chapter—diagnosed him schizophrenic, a fact that was revealed at a hearing relative to his competency to stand trial. In a study of 125 homicide offenders diagnosed with schizophrenia (Laajasalo & Häkkänen, 2006), one-third were considered excessively violent. Excessive violence was most common among offenders with hallucination and delusions, rather than one or the other. Delusions, which are improbable beliefs or ideas, particularly persecutory ones, are common in those schizophrenics who commit violent offenses. Other researchers (Marleau, Millaud, & Auclair, 2003; Taylor et al., 1998) also have found that hallucinations alone (without delusions) are rare at the time of crime among homicide offenders. Interestingly, though, the strongest predictors of excessive violence in Laajasalo and Häkkänen's study were the offender's own history of violence and the presence of a co-offender at the scene.

Delusional disorder is now included under the schizophrenia spectrum and other psychotic disorders section in the DSM-5 (American Psychiatric Association, 2013). It is characterized by the presence of one or more *nonbizarre* delusions that persist for at least one month. The judgment of whether the delusion's systems are bizarre or nonbizarre is especially important in deciding between a delusional disorder and schizophrenia. In delusional disorder, the delusions are reasonably believable and not completely farfetched. An example of a nonbizarre delusion is the belief that a neighbor is spying and attempting to poison one's dog, when there is no evidence to that effect. Even so, neighbors sometimes spy and sometimes do try to poison dogs. A bizarre delusion—more characteristic of schizophrenia—is the belief that the neighbor has disguised herself as a large insect and is hovering outside one's window. (Although with the increasing presence of drones, the delusion may not be that bizarre.) Delusional disorder has no psychotic symptoms (American Psychiatric Association, 2013).

Bipolar Disorder

Previously referred to as manic-depressive disorder, bipolar disorder is characterized by episodes of behavior that are alternately characterized by such features as euphoria, hyperenergy, and distractibility (manic phase) and diminished interest or pleasure in all activities and depressed mood (depressive phase). In essence it is a mood disorder. Interestingly, many famous and creative people have been diagnosed with the disorder: Vivien Leigh, Carrie Fisher, Winston Churchill, Ben Stiller,

Virginia Woolf, Jane Pauley, Kurt Cobain, Sting, Rosemary Clooney, among others. In the manic phase, the individual may be excessively involved in activities that have high potential for painful consequences, such as sexual indiscretion or making foolish business investments. The DSM-5 distinguishes between Bipolar I and Bipolar II disorders. As in all other disorders, numerous additional criteria are outlined in diagnostic guidebooks.

Although bipolar disorder is not usually implicated in violent crime, it may be a factor in reckless behavior that leads to criminal activity, such as driving at excessive speed resulting in the death of another individual. Interestingly, lifetime risk of suicide among persons with bipolar disorder is estimated to be at least 15 times that of the general population (American Psychiatric Association, 2013).

Major Depressive Disorder

Major depressive disorder is one of several disorders that now form a category separate from the bipolar disorder mentioned above (American Psychiatric Association, 2013). What they have in common is "the presence of sad empty, or irritable mood, accompanied by somatic and cognitive changes that significantly affect the individual's capacity to function. What differs among them are issues of duration, timing, or presumed etiology" (p. 155). The symptoms of major depressive disorder include an *extremely* depressed state that lasts for at least two weeks and is accompanied by a generalized slowing down of mental and physical activity, gloom, despair, feelings of worthlessness, and perhaps frequent thoughts of suicide. Andrea Yates, the woman who drowned her children, was ultimately found NGRI largely due to evidence of major depression. Everyone has up and down periods, and periods of bereavement have their own form of grief, but the mood changes in major depressive disorder are extreme and the depression is deep and usually long lasting.

The role of depression in the development of criminal behavior has been studied now for many years, but distinctions are often not made between a depressive disorder and situational depression that may not rise to the level of a mental illness. Preliminary data indicate that depression may be strongly associated with delinquency, especially in teenage girls (Kerr et al., 2014; Lanctôt, Hauth-Charlier, & Lemieux, 2015; Obeidallah & Earls, 1999; Teplin, 2000), though it is not clear which comes first—the depression or the delinquency. However, both boys and girls display depressive symptoms (Diamantopoulou, Verhulst, & van der Ende, 2011; Wareham & Dembo, 2007). Depression seems to render teenagers—both boys and girls—indifferent to their own personal safety and the consequences of their actions. They just don't care what happens to them, which may increase the likelihood of gravitating toward delinquency. On the other hand, delinquent behavior may lead to depression—the depression does not come first. In a longitudinal study of 3,604 adolescents (Kofler et al., 2011), the researchers found more support for the former theory—that is, that early depressive symptoms predicted later delinquent behavior. This appeared to be the case especially for girls.

Because depression exists in an individual, this is not meant to say that depression leads to criminal activity, however. In a study of 429 crimes, Peterson et al. (2014) found that only 3 percent related directly to major depression (see **Box 8-1**). Nevertheless, depression likely plays a significant role in mass murders, school shootings, workplace violence, and "suicide-by-cop" incidents in which a person sets up a situation wherein police are essentially forced to shoot. These incidents are discussed in greater detail in Chapter 10.

Antisocial Personality Disorder

The essential feature of a person with **antisocial personality disorder (APD)** is a history of continuous behavior in which the rights of others are violated. As mentioned in Chapter 7, the criteria closely follow Robert Hare's definition of the criminal psychopath. To be diagnosed with APD, the individual must be at least 18 years of age and must have a history of some symptoms of conduct disorder before age 15. Recall that a diagnosis of **conduct disorder** is reserved for children and adolescents. Before a person can be diagnosed with APD, a pervasive

RESEARCH FOCUS

Box 8-1   Does Serious Mental Disorder Cause Crime?

Many people are afraid of those with serious mental disorder, such as individuals with schizophrenia disorders, major depression, and bipolar disorder, each of which is discussed in the text. However, the vast majority of people with these conditions do not commit crimes, and those who do generally do not commit serious crimes. The exceptions, of course, invariably are highlighted in the media, just as we have highlighted them in this chapter for illustrative purposes.

Psychological research overwhelmingly supports the view that the mentally ill as a group—although sometimes exhibiting strange behavior—are no more dangerous than the rest of the population. To add further clarification to this research, Jillian Peterson and her colleagues (2014) examined 429 crimes committed by 143 offenders who had three types of SMI. The researchers interviewed the offenders about the crimes on record as well as other crimes they may have committed over an average of 15 years that did not come to the attention of authorities. Two-thirds of the participants were male, and they were evenly divided between white and black offenders, with 16 percent of other races.

The researchers were interested in learning whether the symptoms of their disorders contributed to their crimes—for example, did someone's delusions cause him to assault a victim? They examined whether the crimes were directly related, mostly or directly related, mostly unrelated, or not at all related to the symptoms of mental disorder. Overall, only 7.5 percent of the crimes were directly related, but adding "mostly related" increased the percentage to 18 percent, or one in five crimes.

Of the three categories, bipolar disorder fared the worst, with 10 percent of the participants with that illness committing crimes that appeared to be a direct result of their symptoms. For participants with major depressive disorders, only 3 percent of the crimes were a direct result of their symptoms, and for participants with symptoms of schizophrenia, only 4 percent were a direct result of their symptoms. For all three categories, the percentages increased when "mostly related" was combined with "directly related," but only for bipolar disorder did the percentage increase significantly (62% vs. 23% for schizophrenia and 15% for depression). The researchers attributed the highest percentage to a possible inflation factor, because 85 percent of the participants also had substance abuse disorders; therefore, their crimes may have been substance abuse related rather than bipolar related, or some combination of both.

The participants reported committing crimes over a 15-year span for reasons similar to reasons cited by offenders who are not mentally disordered, such as unemployment, homelessness, or substance abuse. Overall, consistent with other literature, these researchers found no indication that persons with serious mental disorder were committing repeat crime because of their symptoms.

Questions for Discussion

1. Only one in five crimes were committed directly or mostly as a result of the symptoms of mental disorder. Discuss the importance of this finding.
2. It is noted that 85 percent of the participants also had substance abuse disorders. How might that affect any of the findings reported above?
3. After studying material on the insanity defense, discuss the extent to which this research is relevant to that defense.

pattern of disregard for and the violation of the rights of others must be indicated by at least three of the following behavioral patterns:

1. Failure to conform to social norms or the criminal law, as reflected by frequent performance of acts that are grounds for arrests
2. Irritability and unusual aggressiveness, as indicated by repeated physical fights or assaults
3. Consistent irresponsibility, as reflected in a poor work history or failure to honor financial obligations
4. Impulsivity or a failure to plan ahead (characteristic at all ages)
5. Deceitfulness, as reflected in frequent lying, use of aliases, or conning others for personal profit or pleasure
6. Reckless disregard for the safety of others or self
7. Lack of remorse or guilt for wrongdoings, as indicated by indifference to or rationalization of having hurt, mistreated, or stolen from another

Additional behavioral markers include stealing, fighting, truancy, and resisting authority. Antisocial personalities—often referred to as ASPs in the literature—lack empathy and tend to be callous, cynical, and contemptuous of the feelings, rights, and sufferings of others. Furthermore, they frequently exhibit precocious and aggressive sexual behavior, excessive drinking, and the use of illicit drugs. There is a markedly impaired capacity to maintain lasting, close, warm, and responsible relationships with family, friends, or sexual partners.

On average, ASPs fail to become independent, self-supporting adults. They spend most of their lives in institutions (usually correctional facilities) or remain highly dependent on their families. Other accompanying features include restlessness, an inability to tolerate boredom, and a belief that the world is hostile. ASPs often complain of tension and depression, but they do not usually meet the criteria for a diagnosis of depression. They are often impulsive and unable to plan ahead, and show deficits in executive functioning.

It is estimated that between 0.2 and 3.3 percent of the general population qualifies for an APD diagnosis (American Psychiatric Association, 2013). The disorder occurs more frequently in males than in females, but the DSM-5 suggests it may be underdiagnosed in females because criteria for diagnosis emphasize aggression. The *DSM* also points to a genetic and physiological risk—APD "is more common among first-degree biological relatives of those with the disorder than in the general population" (p. 661). As noted in Chapter 3, recent years many researchers are adopting a biopsychological perspective and finding an interaction between genes and the environment in many behaviors related to offending, including APD (see, e.g., Delisi, Beaver, Vaughn, & Wright, 2009).

Research dating from the 1970s has indicated that APD is a common diagnosis of criminal defendants and offenders. In an early study, Henn and his colleagues conducted an extensive series of investigations on all defendants referred by a St. Louis, Missouri, court for psychiatric assessment over a 10-year period (Henn, Herjanic, & Vanderpearl, 1976a). Focusing on a sample of 1,195 defendants accused of a variety of crimes and referred for psychiatric assessment, Henn and colleagues learned that the most frequent diagnosis was personality disorder, accounting for nearly 40 percent of all the diagnoses.

The pervasiveness of this diagnosis continues today. APD is frequently offered as a diagnosis in criminal courts and in corrections, sometimes serving as a catch-all category. Researchers have noted that when courts press for a diagnosis, many clinicians will oblige by concluding that an individual qualifies for APD (Melton, Petrila, Poythress, & Slobogin, 2007). In correctional facilities, rates of inmates considered APD range from 30 to 50 percent, and it is not unusual to find the diagnosis in over 50 percent of the correctional population (Gacono, Nieberding, Owen, Rubel, & Bodholdt, 2001). APD is such a common diagnosis applied to persons both accused of and convicted of criminal offenses that some jurisdictions specifically exclude it from the list of mental disorders that can support an insanity defense. However, it is important to note that APD does not necessarily appear in isolation. As Skeem et al. (2014) discovered in their research on offenders with mental illness, it is not unusual for offenders with SMI to have troubling personality traits that are also consistent with APD. "As such, they require both psychiatric and correctional treatment" (Skeem et al., 2014, p. 221).

COMPETENCY AND CRIMINAL RESPONSIBILITY

The above psychiatric diagnoses, with the exception of APD, are often those that come into play when decisions must be made as to whether defendants who are mentally disordered are competent to stand trial or, if competent, are culpable enough to be held responsible for the crimes that occurred. In this section, we review these two very important legal constructs.

Incompetency to Stand Trial

Some persons charged with a crime are considered so psychologically or intellectually impaired that—were they to be tried—they would be present in body but not in mind. The U.S. Supreme Court has determined that the trial of such an individual violates the Constitution. Specifically, defendants are competent to stand trial if they have "sufficient present ability to consult with their lawyer with a reasonable degree of rational understanding…and a rational as well as factual understanding of the proceedings" (*Dusky v. United States*, 1960, p. 402). To protect the rights of the individual and to preserve the dignity of the court process, the law states that a person who is incompetent must not be tried.

Incompetence does not refer only to one's overall mental or emotional state, however. It may also refer to a lack of understanding of court proceedings, one's rights, or the functions performed by one's lawyer. Some criminal defendants, for example, may not understand the judge's role and may not know that they do not have to take the witness stand. Words and terms like "self-incrimination," "burden of proof," "stipulate," or, even, "plead" may be perplexing. This is especially, though not exclusively, a problem with relation to juveniles (Rogers et al., 2012). Therefore, some efforts to make individuals competent to stand trial involve educational strategies.

Competency is an important issue in regard to defendants who are intellectually disabled. As Mumley, Tillbrook, and Grisso (2003, p. 343) noted, "Unlike psychotic defendants, persons with mental retardation [sic] often do not show obvious signs of poor understanding or reasoning, so that attorneys may be less capable of identifying those who are in need of AC (adjudicative competence) evaluation." Consequently, we have little information on the extent to which these defendants are referred for competency evaluation, and virtually no information on the proportion of IST defendants who are intellectually disabled.

In addition, the competency issue does not relate only to the actual trial. In fact, some scholars now prefer to use the term **adjudicative competence** rather than **competence to stand trial** (e.g., Bonnie & Grisso, 2000; Mumley et al., 2003; Viljoen & Wingrove, 2007). The former term relates to the ability to participate in a wide variety of court proceedings and court-related activities, including plea bargaining, preliminary hearings, and other pretrial hearings related to one's case. It also encompasses two distinct concepts: (1) the competence to proceed (which implies understanding the purpose of the proceedings and being able to help one's attorney) and (2) decisional competence (which implies the ability to comprehend the significance of various decisions to be made) (Mumley et al., 2003). If a criminal defendant is found incompetent to stand trial, the court has essentially determined that he or she cannot understand the process that is occurring or effectively participate in it. Interestingly, the issue of competence also extends to whether a mentally disordered defendant who is competent to stand trial is necessarily competent to represent himself. In a 2008 case (*Indiana v. Edwards*), the U.S. Supreme Court ruled that a unitary standard for deciding these two issues was inappropriate. Although many questions were left unanswered in that case, for our purposes, it must be emphasized that just because defendants are competent to stand trial, this does not mean that they are competent to serve as their own attorney.

The competency issue can be raised at any time during the actual proceedings. For example, a defendant may be competent up to and into the beginning phases of his trial; during a long and protracted trial, he may become incompetent. A defendant also may be competent before and during trial, but incompetent at the time of sentencing. The Supreme Court recently ruled, though, that a person convicted of crime does not have to be competent during certain appeals processes (*Tibbals v. Carter*, 2013).

Evaluations for competency to stand trial represent the most common referral for criminally related forensic assessments (Cruise & Rogers, 1998; Melton et al., 2007). Most typically, defendants referred for competency evaluation have a history of psychiatric care or institutionalization or exhibited signs of mental disorder at arrest or while detained in jail. Data indicate that approximately 25,000 criminal defendants nationwide, or about one in 15, are evaluated each year by state and federal courts for their competency to stand trial (Cruise & Rogers, 1998; Nicholson & Kugler, 1991). Nationwide, about four out of every five of these evaluated defendants—or roughly 80 percent depending upon the study—are found competent (Grisso, 1986; Nicholson & Kugler, 1991; Pirelli, Gottdiener, & Zapf, 2011; Roesch, Zapf, Golding, & Skeem, 1999). In some cases, multiple competency hearings are held before a defendant is ultimately determined to be competent.

It is important to emphasize the distinction between incompetence to stand trial (IST) and insanity, the legal concept to be discussed below. Although they may be related, the two concepts are distinct and should be assessed by clinicians separately—although this is not always done. In fact, research suggests that at least one-third of competency and sanity evaluations in the

United States are done simultaneously with each other—that is, both competency and sanity are evaluated at the same time (Chauhan et al., 2015). In high-profile cases, competency and sanity are more likely to be kept distinct; for example, in ordering the competency evaluation of Jared Loughner, the judge in the case made it clear that the evaluation was to be limited to the issue of competency, not sanity. Criminal responsibility, which is at the core of the insanity defense, and competency to stand trial refer to a defendant's mental state/capacity at *two different points in time.* If a defendant pleads NGRI, the law asks, "What was the defendant's state of mind at the time the offense was committed?" In competency considerations, the question becomes, "What is the defendant's state of mind at the present time, or at the time of the pretrial proceedings or trial?" An individual who was seriously mentally disordered at the time of an offense and whose criminal responsibility is questionable may have enough mental stability by the time of the trial to be competent to stand trial. On the other hand, a person may be of sound mind during the unlawful act, but may later become disordered or disoriented and be determined incompetent to stand trial.

If found incompetent to stand trial—a decision that must be made by the presiding judge—the defendant is typically sent to a mental institution until rendered competent, as was Loughner. For those defendants who are restored to competency, some research suggests that the average time needed for restoration is about three months (Hoge et al., 1996). In a survey of mental health program directors across the United States, Miller (2003) found that outpatient treatment to restore competency was rare. Outpatient *evaluations* of competency were on the increase, however. Most recently, though, some states are providing for more competency *restoration* in the community, particularly for juveniles who have been found incompetent to participate in court proceedings. In such states, inpatient treatment is considered only as a last resort.

Until the 1970s, the typical procedure for *evaluating* competency required that defendants be confined within a maximum security institution for a lengthy psychiatric–psychological evaluation (usually 60 to 90 days). Following evaluation, the defendant was granted a hearing on the matter of competency. If the court found the defendant unable to understand the charges or the judicial proceedings, or to help counsel in his or her defense, then the defendant would automatically be committed to a secure hospital for an indefinite period of time—until competent. Theoretically, this indefinite time period could extend—and sometimes did—into a lifetime of involuntary commitment.

In 1972, in *Jackson v. Indiana,* the Supreme Court declared that such an indefinite confinement violated the Constitution. While the court allowed the confinement, it specified that if no progress was made toward competence, the individual must be released or must be recommitted under civil, not criminal statutes. Today, individuals found IST with little likelihood of being restored to competency often have their cases dismissed if the charges were not very serious. However, in many jurisdictions, the prosecutor still retains the option of reinstituting charges if the person regains competency at some later time.

In recent years, persons found IST have asserted additional constitutional rights in connection with their status, including the right to the "least restrictive or drastic alternative," specifically the right to be treated in a community setting rather than in an institution. As noted earlier, though, recent research suggests that community treatment is not the typical approach (Miller, 2003). In addition, because treatment is often offered in the form of psychoactive drugs, some defendants ruled IST—like Jared Loughner—have argued that they should not be forced to take these drugs. Psychoactive drugs are "those drugs that exert their primary effect on the brain, thus altering mood or behavior, or that are used in the treatment of mental disorders" (Julien, 1992, p. xii). As noted above, although these drugs have been improved considerably over the past few decades, many have side effects—including in some cases debilitating side effects—and are resisted by many patients.

In a Supreme Court ruling on this matter (*Sell v. United States,* 2003), the Court ruled that, in a case that did not involve violence, courts must be wary of ordering such medication against a defendant's will. Sell, a former dentist charged with insurance fraud, had been found IST and was hospitalized for treatment. He had a history of mental disorder and had prior hospitalizations, during which he had received psychoactive drugs. Psychiatrists again prescribed psychoactive drugs in an effort to render him competent to stand trial, but Sell refused to take them. Both a trial judge and a federal court of appeals ruled against him, but the U.S. Supreme Court did not agree. The Court noted that the trial court had not adequately weighed the advantages and disadvantages of the drugs, and it sent the case back to the trial court to do just that. However, for serious, violent crimes, where the government has a strong interest in bringing a defendant to trial, the Court has been less sympathetic to the defendant, refusing to hear an appeal of an order for involuntary medication (*United States v. Weston*, cert. denied). Russell Eugene Weston, Jr. is the individual charged with the lethal shooting of two Capitol police officers in 1998 and the nonlethal shooting of two other individuals. In light of the nature of the crimes, Weston's long history of SMI (he was a diagnosed paranoid schizophrenic with previous hospitalizations), and the government's strong interest in bringing him to trial, courts ruled in favor of the involuntary medication, saying he could be forced to take the medication. It should be noted, though, that the lower court in Weston's case had given careful consideration to the advantages and disadvantages of ordering the medication. Interestingly, over 15 years after the incident, Weston apparently remains in a federal psychiatric facility and has yet to be brought to trial.

Several studies, including a recent meta-analysis covering 68 studies conducted between 1967 and 2008 (Pirelli et al., 2011), have compared defendants found competent to stand trial to those found incompetent. Competent and incompetent defendants do not differ significantly on demographic variables such as race, gender, or marital status (Nicholson & Kugler, 1991; Riley, 1998; Rosenfeld & Ritchie, 1998). They do differ, not surprisingly, on clinical (psychological or psychiatric) variables. Thus, persons found IST are more likely to be diagnosed with a psychotic disorder or organic mental disorder (mental disorder caused by damage to the brain) (Warren, Rosenfeld, Fitch, & Hawk, 1997) or schizophrenia and affective disorders (Hoge et al., 1997). Pirelli et al. found that those defendants with psychotic disorders were about eight times more likely to be found IST than those without such disorders. Pirellie et al. also established that defendants who were unemployed or had previous psychiatric hospitalizations were about twice as likely to be found IST as those who were employed or without previous psychiatric histories.

Criminal Responsibility

Given the widespread publicity associated with the **insanity defense**, most people are probably far more aware of defendants raising the insanity defense or found NGRI than those raising the question of competency or found incompetent to stand trial. Insanity is a legal term, not a psychiatric or psychological one, and commentators often stress this by referring to "legal insanity," which is redundant. Insanity refers to a person's *state of mind at the time an offense was committed*. When an individual is found NGRI, a judge or jury have determined that he or she was so mentally disordered at the time of the crime that the person should not be held responsible. This was the case for John Hinckley, the man who in 1981 shot President Ronald Reagan, wounding him along with three others, including press secretary James Brady, and for Andrea Yates, in her second trial. By contrast, the jury rejected that verdict in the case of Eddie Ray Routh after less than three hours of deliberation and in the case of James Holmes in Colorado. (As noted above, that jury did not recommend the death sentence, however, apparently because one juror believed his mental status was a mitigating factor in his crimes.) The jury in the Hernandez case deliberated for 18 days, with votes for and against conviction apparently changing over the course of that time period. Ultimately, the jury could not reach unanimity, and a mistrial was declared. In that jury, there was a lone holdout as well. Judging from media interviews, though, that juror seemed more concerned about the possible coerced confession of a vulnerable individual and lack of physical evidence than about the possible "insanity" of the defendant. The law assumes that mental disorder *can* rob an individual of free will or the ability to make appropriate choices. Note that insanity should not be *equated* with mental disorder, even serious mental disorder. That is, a mentally disordered person can still be found responsible for committing a criminal offense. Likewise, an individual who is intellectually disabled can still be held criminally responsible.

Insanity defenses, especially if they are successful, receive extensive media coverage and commentary when the crime was a serious one. When Hinckley was found NGRI by a federal jury, there was widespread public indignation accompanied by numerous demands for repeal of the insanity defense in both federal and state laws. Since the Hinckley acquittal by reason of insanity in June 1982, at least 34 states have made some kind of alteration to their insanity statutes (Steadman et al., 1993). Moreover, in response to the public outcry against the Hinckley acquittal, the U.S. Congress passed the *Insanity Defense Act of 1984*, which is discussed below. Virtually, all these legal changes made it more difficult for defendants who wished to plead NGRI. Hinckley, now 60 years old, remains hospitalized, although he has been allowed to leave the facility for overnight visits to his mother's home for incrementally longer periods, the latest being for 17 days. In May 2015, a court held a seven-day hearing on his application for permanent release, under specific conditions. Mental health professionals have testified that his mental illness is in remission and he is not a danger to society.

In the case of Andrea Yates, public outcry was less vociferous. Recall that she was convicted in her first trial, but that conviction was overturned. She was then found NGRI in a bench trial, which is a trial before a judge rather than a jury. Between the two trials, there was extensive publicity about her background, her past institutionalizations, and the many warning signs about her serious disorder. Although there is no documented evidence to this effect, it is likely that the public had a better appreciation of the dire emotional state that led to the tragic circumstances of her children's deaths. As noted above, she remains hospitalized today.

It is important to note that the number of insanity defenses raised in the United States is believed very small compared with the total number of criminal cases. Furthermore, despite the outcry after the Hinckley verdict, insanity defenses are rarely successful. In addition, we often hear that someone is planning to use the insanity defense, but this does not necessarily come to pass. Amy Bishop, a biology professor at the University of Alabama, Huntsville, opened fire on colleagues in a department meeting in 2010, killing some and wounding others. Although her lawyers had indicated that she would use an insanity defense, she pled guilty on September 11, 2012.

Unfortunately, there are no *systematic, nationwide* data on how often the insanity defense is actually used (McGinley & Paswark, 1989). County, state, and federal levels of government rarely share information about these issues (Steadman et al., 1993). Steadman and his colleagues write, "County level information on insanity pleas, for example, is rarely, if ever, aggregated to the state level, meaning almost nothing is known about the earliest stages of the insanity defense process" (1993, p. 3). However, there are some good estimates based on studies conducted by independent and governmental researchers. These researchers estimate that insanity defenses are used in only 1 percent of all U.S. felony criminal cases (Callahan, Steadman, McGreevy, & Robbins, 1991; Golding, Skeem, Roesch, & Zapf, 1999).

SUCCESS RATE.   The insanity defense rarely succeeds in serious cases. When it is successful, the defendant has virtually always been found to have an SMI that rendered him or her incapable of rational thought at the time of the crime (Goldstein, Morse, & Packer, 2013).

Data on acquittals suggest that the defense is typically not successful. In an eight-state study of 9,000 defendants who pleaded NGRI, Callahan et al. (1991) found a 22 to 25 percent success rate, but this included serious and nonserious cases. In other words, defendants charged with misdemeanor offenses (e.g., trespassing and simple assault) also may raise this defense, and they are more likely to be successful. Other studies have reported wide statewide differences, with a high of 44 percent in Colorado and a low of 2 percent in Wyoming (McGinley & Paswark, 1989). Cirincione and Jacobs (1999) found a mean of only 33.4 insanity acquittals per year across 35 states over the period 1974 to 1995. More importantly, acquittals seem to be closely tied to the diagnosis placed on the defendant and, to some extent, on the crime charged (Cochrane, Grisso, & Frederick, 2001; Warren et al., 1997). Cochrane et al. found that federal defendants with diagnoses of psychotic disorders, affective disorders, and intellectual disability had higher rates of acquittal than those diagnosed with other disorders. Personality disorders were negatively correlated with a finding of insanity. More recently, researchers have found that jurors are favorably disposed toward defendants who provide neurological evidence, particularly evidence of traumatic brain injury (Gurley & Marcus, 2008). Such injury to the brain may be accompanied by increases in aggression, personality changes, and impaired ability to control one's emotions, among other consequences (Gurley & Marcus, 2008).

By contrast, some elements work against a defendant pleading NGRI. For example, recall that many states specifically exclude APD as a mental disorder to support an insanity defense. As we learned in Chapter 7, this is often the diagnosis placed on individuals who are believed to be psychopaths, but it is also placed on chronic offenders. Warren et al. (1997) found that defendants charged with violent crimes against others had the highest acquittal rates, while sex offenders significantly are more likely to be *convicted*. Nevertheless, the research literature strongly indicates that the clinical diagnosis, more than the offense, seems to be the critical factor. This also may explain the low acquittal of sex offenders, because these offenders are often not considered by clinicians to be mentally disordered.

In the United States, acquittals are far more difficult to obtain from juries (jury trials) than from judges (bench trials), a pattern that underscores the pervasive negative attitude the American public has toward the insanity defense. For example, in their eight-state study, Callahan et al. (1991) found that only 7 percent of the acquittals were handed down by juries. In another study, Boehnert (1989) found that 96 percent of defendants found NGRI had gone before a judge. Thus, it seems wise for defendants who plan to use the insanity defense to have a bench trial (where the judge decides) rather than a jury trial. On the other hand, research suggests that, if jurors are informed of the consequences of an NGRI verdict—specifically that the defendant will likely be hospitalized for treatment—they may be more likely to acquit the defendant (Wheatman & Shaffer, 2001).

Callahan et al. (1991) found that successful NGRI defendants, compared with unsuccessful defendants, tended to be older, female, better educated, and single. They also had a history of prior hospitalization and were considered extremely disturbed. Furthermore, 15 percent of the acquitted defendants had not themselves raised the insanity defense, indicating that they were so disordered that an insanity verdict was essentially imposed on them.

CONSEQUENCES OF A SUCCESSFUL DEFENSE.   Defense attorneys generally do not recommend that their clients plead NGRI unless they are charged with a serious offense and the evidence against them is overwhelming. A good case in point is that of James Holmes, the Batman theater shooter. There is no question that Holmes entered the Colorado movie theater and killed 12 persons; he was in fact willing to plead guilty in exchange for being spared the death penalty. However, prosecutors refused to accept the guilty plea. As noted above, the shooter was convicted but was not sentenced to death. Had they lived, other mass shooters with histories of mental disorder, such as those who opened fire at Sandy Hook Elementary School in 2012 and Umpqua Community College in 2015, may well have pleaded NGRI as well.

Nevertheless, it is a mistake to think that defendants charged with misdemeanor offenses do not raise this defense; it is sometimes used to obtain treatment for mentally disordered individuals who might not otherwise be eligible for institutionalization. In many jurisdictions, insanity acquittees are immediately confined to a mental institution, where they are kept for as long as needed to produce substantial improvement in their condition and assure that they are not a danger to themselves or others. In fact, until recently, research indicated that persons found NGRI on average spent at least as much time in mental institutions or treatment facilities as they would have spent in prison if convicted (Golding et al., 1999).

More and more, though, persons found NGRI are being institutionalized for shorter periods of time and then released, typically on a conditional basis, into the community where they can receive specialized treatment services (Vitacco et al., 2008). This is most likely to be the case if the crime was not a serious violent one, though there are exceptions. Dena Schlosser was found NGRI after killing her 11-month-old daughter by amputating her arms. Defense lawyers argued successfully that she was in a state of postpartum psychosis. She was committed to a psychiatric hospital (where her roommate was Andrea Yates), treated for four years, and then released to outpatient care in 2008. Schlosser was rehospitalized in 2010 when found wandering on a street, and released again that same year. Although she changed her name, she was fired from at least one position when her employer (Walmart) learned about her past.

Conditional release of institutionalized persons allows mental health authorities to monitor their progress and assure that they are taking the medication that presumably keeps them stabilized and their mental disorder in remission. Vitacco et al. (2008) found considerable success offering quality services to insanity acquittees in the community. Quality services often included alcohol and drug abuse treatment as well as close monitoring of both mental health symptoms and compliance with medication orders. In other words, someone should assure that the acquittees are "taking their meds" if these have been prescribed. Vitacco et al. found that most individuals who were returned to the institution were more likely to be sent back for rules violations than for criminal charges. In the Schlosser case, the initial crime was extremely serious, but she was not later accused of additional offending after her release.

Community treatment orders are partially in response to a 1992 U.S. Supreme Court decision, *Foucha v. Louisiana*, which placed some limits on the hospital confinement of persons found NGRI. In the *Foucha* case, the Court ruled that insanity acquittees may not be held in psychiatric facilities once they are no longer mentally disordered, even if it could be argued that they are dangerous. Foucha had been hospitalized for four years. While a committee of mental health practitioners found his mental illness to be in remission, they could not certify that he was no longer dangerous. Nevertheless, a divided Supreme Court (5–4) ruled that, if no longer mentally ill, he should be discharged. Critics of the *Foucha* decision maintain that the Court did not sufficiently recognize the recurring quality of serious mental disorders. They note that, while mental disorders may go into remission, persons suffering from them are not necessarily cured (Golding et al., 1999). On the other hand, it is difficult to justify holding an individual whose illness is in remission on the premise that at some point in the future, his or her disorder is likely to reappear and the person will commit a violent crime. Should 60-year-old John Hinckley, who has demonstrated that he could remain in the community for 17-day home visits, be held indefinitely in a hospital setting? This is a difficult question for a judge to answer.

Thus far, we have discussed the consequences of a finding of NGRI. In the following section, we cover a variety of standards that courts use to decide whether a person was insane.

Insanity Standards

The insanity defense has been recognized in English courts for over 700 years (Simon, 1983). Since the American legal system is derived from British law, American courts have generally recognized it as well. It is now accepted in federal courts and in all but four states (Idaho, Kansas, Montana, and Utah). Standards or tests to determine insanity vary widely among the states, but they usually center around one of three broad models: the M'Naghten Rule, the Brawner Rule, or the Durham Rule. Moreover, all the insanity standards are fundamentally based on two criteria: irrationality and compulsion (Morse, 1986). If it can be established that a person was not in control of his or her mental processes (was thinking irrationally) and/or was not in control of his or her behavior (was driven by compulsion) at the time of the offense, then there are grounds for absolving that person of some or all responsibility for the offense. Jurisdictions, however, differ in the extent they accept both these criteria. That is, some jurisdictions accept both criteria, while others will accept only the irrationality component. It is important to note, as well, that in a recent insanity-related decision (*Clark v. Arizona*, 2006), the U.S. Supreme Court made it clear that states could determine their own insanity standards and that the Court would not establish a universal Constitutional standard that would apply to all (DeMatteo, 2007). The Court also refused to say that the insanity defense was a Constitutional right, as it was asked to do in a case that challenged Idaho's rejection of that defense (*Delling v. Idaho*, 2012).

THE M'NAGHTEN RULE.   The **M'Naghten Rule** has been around in some form since at least the nineteenth century. The current rule was formulated in 1843, after Daniel M'Naghten, a Scottish woodcutter, was acquitted of killing a man he believed to be the prime minister. M'Naghten thought he was being persecuted by the Tories and their leader, Prime Minister Sir Robert Peel. He fired a shot into a carriage transporting Peel's secretary, Edward Drumond, thinking Peel himself was in the carriage. There was no question that M'Naghten had committed the act, but the court believed he was so mentally deranged that it would be inhumane to convict him. Applying a "wild beast" test in use at the time, the court concluded it was clear he was not in control of his faculties. He was committed to the Broadmoor Mental Institution, where he remained until his death 22 years later. It was widely believed that M'Naghten "knew" his actions were wrong and that he should have been convicted. Therefore, the law was changed to prevent a similar "miscarriage of justice" in the future. Thus, the rule that bears M'Naghten's name is not the rule under which he was tried.

In 1851, the M'Naghten Rule was adopted in the federal and most state courts in the United States. It is deceptively simple, and therein lies its popularity. It states that a person is not responsible for a criminal act if, "at the time of committing the act, the party accused was labouring under such a defect of reason, from disease of the mind, as not to know the nature and quality of the act he was doing; or if he did know it...he did not know he was doing what was wrong" (*M'Naghten*, 1843, p. 718). Essentially, the rule states that if a person, because of some mental disease, did not know right from wrong at the time of an unlawful act, or did not know that what he or she was doing was wrong, that person cannot be held responsible for his or her actions.

Thus, the M'Naghten Rule, sometimes referred to as the **right and wrong test**, emphasizes the *cognitive elements* of (1) being aware and knowing what one was doing at the time of the illegal act or (2) knowing or realizing right from wrong in the moral sense. The rule recognizes no degree of incapacity. Either you are responsible for the action or you are not. There are no in-betweens.

Some states supplement M'Naghten with an irresistible impulse test, which has similarities to the "wild beast" test applied in the original M'Naghten case. The irresistible impulse test recognizes or assumes that people may realize the wrongfulness of their conduct, be aware of what is right or wrong in a particular set of circumstances, but still be powerless to do right in the face of overwhelming pressures from uncontrollable impulses. In other words, there are conditions under which people presumably cannot help themselves. The M'Naghten Rule alone would not cover those circumstances, since it requires that the person did not know right from wrong.

THE BRAWNER RULE AND THE AMERICAN LAW INSTITUTE RULE.   The **Brawner Rule**, which is largely based on an insanity rule suggested by the Model Penal Code (MPC), is another rule for determining insanity. The MPC was proposed in 1962 by a group of legal scholars associated with the American Law Institute (ALI). The Code was drafted to serve as a model for legislatures seeking to modernize and rationalize their criminal statutes. According to the Brawner Rule, "A person is not responsible for criminal conduct if at the time of such conduct as a result of mental disease or defect, he lacks substantial capacity either to appreciate the criminality [wrongfulness] of his conduct or to conform his conduct to the requirements of the law" (*United States v. Brawner*, 1972, p. 973). It must be demonstrated that the disease or mental defect *substantially* and directly (1) influenced the defendant's mental or emotional processes, or (2) impaired his or her ability to control behavior. The Brawner Rule, unlike M'Naghten, recognizes *partial* responsibility for criminal conduct, as well as the possibility of an irresistible impulse beyond one's control. It also excludes from the definition of mental disease or defect any repeated criminal or otherwise antisocial conduct, an exclusion we referred to earlier in the chapter. This provision (called the **caveat paragraph**) was intended to disallow the insanity defense for criminal psychopaths who persistently violate social mores and the law. Thus, psychopaths and persons with APDs cannot claim that their abnormal condition is a mental disorder, disease, or defect, even if they have been diagnosed with APD.

THE DURHAM RULE: THE PRODUCT TEST.   The **Durham Rule** was created in 1954 in *Durham v. United States* by the same court that later rejected it in favor of the Brawner Rule. Monte Durham, a 26-year-old resident of the District of Columbia, had a long history of mental disorder and petty theft. His crime of the moment was burglary, but he was acquitted because his unlawful act was considered to be "the product of a mental disease or mental defect" (*Durham v. United States*, 1954, p. 874). While the M'Naghten Rule focuses on knowing right from wrong (the mental element in a crime), Durham assumes that one cannot be held responsible if an unlawful action is the product of mental disease or defect.

There is nothing in the Durham Rule that relates directly to the person's mental judgment. If the person has a disease or defect, lack of culpability is easily assumed. The rule was later clarified in *Carter v. United States* (1957), which held that mental illness must not merely have entered into the production of the act; it must have played a necessary role.

Many states were attracted to the apparent simplicity of the Durham Rule, since it seemed more straightforward and comprehensible to juries. However, it soon became apparent that definitions of "mental illness" are vague and subjective, a situation that fostered the widespread discretionary power of psychiatry and considerable misuse of mental health experts during trial. Moreover, virtually any defendant could be excused once mental disease or defect had been established, because even with clarification, it was difficult to decide what was a necessary role. The Durham Rule rapidly lost its popularity.

Until the 1980s, most jurisdictions adopted one of the above rules, with varying degrees of satisfaction. However, the well-publicized Hinckley acquittal sparked a public outcry for the elimination of the insanity defense and prompted legislative bodies and many professional organizations to reexamine it. The American Bar Association and the American Psychiatric Association, for example, proposed new, more restrictive standards (Steadman et al., 1993). Nearly 100 different reforms in 34 jurisdictions occurred soon after Hinckley's acquittal, the most active insanity reform period in American history. In most instances, these reforms reflected a return to the M'Naghten Rule in a modified, more restrictive form (Steadman et al., 1993). As noted above, four states have abolished the insanity defense altogether. (A fifth state, Nevada, attempted to abolish it, but its highest court ruled that abolition violated both the federal and state constitutions (*Finger v. State*, 2001).)

Other changes in insanity law made by states included (1) placing on defendants the burden of proving they were insane (where in the past prosecutors had been required to prove they were not insane), (2) restricting the role of clinical testimony, and (3) requiring persons found NGRI to prove they were no longer mentally ill before being released from a mental institution. Many of these changes were modeled after the federal law discussed below. Recall, though, as mentioned above, the U.S. Supreme Court has given wide latitude to the states in defining insanity and crafting their laws relating to it (DeMatteo, 2007).

THE INSANITY DEFENSE REFORM ACT (IDRA).   Amid public clamors to abolish the insanity defense completely after the Hinckley acquittal, Congress passed the **Insanity Defense Reform Act of 1984 (IDRA)**, which kept the defense in the federal law but modified it in important ways. According to Simon and Aaronson (1988, p. 47), "The Hinckley verdict was unquestionably the decisive influence on congressional modifications to the insanity defense." Essentially, Congress made it more difficult for persons using the insanity defense in federal courts to be acquitted. The IDRA changed the Brawner/ALI Rule—the rule that has been most consistently adhered to in all federal circuits (except the 5th Circuit) since its adoption during the early 1970s—to one patterned more along the lines of the M'Naghten Rule. Specifically, a defendant cannot be held responsible if "at the time of the commission of the acts constituting the offense, the defendant, as a result of a severe mental disease or defect, was unable to appreciate the nature and quality or the wrongfulness of his acts. Mental disease or defect does not otherwise constitute a defense" (18 U.S.C., sec 20[a] [1984]).

In addition, the new federal standard changed the Brawner/ALI Rule in three principal ways (Simon & Aaronson, 1988). First, the act abolished the irresistible impulse test (commonly called

TABLE 8-1	Standards for Criminal Responsibility	
Standard	**Year First Used**	**Description**
M'Naghten Rule	1843	It must be clearly proved that at the time of committing the act, the party accused was laboring under such a defect of reason, from disease of the mind, as not to know the nature and quality of the act he was doing, or if he did know it, that he did not know he was doing what was wrong.
Durham Rule	1954	An accused is not criminally responsible if the unlawful act was the product of mental disease or mental defect.
Brawner/ALI Rule	1972	A person is not responsible for criminal conduct if at the time of such conduct, as a result of mental disease or defect, he lacks substantial capacity to either appreciate the criminality [wrongfulness] of his conduct or conform his conduct to the requirements of the law.
Insanity Defense Reform Act	1984	A person charged with a criminal offense should be found NGRI if it is shown that, as a result of mental disease or mental retardation, he was unable to appreciate the wrongfulness of his conduct at the time of his offense.

the **volitional prong**) of the Brawner/ALI Rule. The inability to control one's actions because of mental defect was no longer acceptable as an excusing condition. Second, the act modified the "cognitive" requirement by replacing the phrase "lacks substantial capacity...to appreciate" with "unable to appreciate." The intention was to tighten the requirement to a total lack of ability to appreciate that what they did was wrong (Simon & Aaronson, 1988). Third, under the new law, the mental disease or defect must be severe, to emphasize that certain behavioral disorders (especially personality disorders) do not qualify as a defense. It should be noted that the federal law also bars mental health clinicians from expressing an opinion as to whether the defendant was insane. Clinicians may testify, report on the findings of their evaluations, and provide a diagnosis, but they may not express an ultimate opinion. This is to emphasize that insanity is a legal determination that must be made by the court. **Table 8-1** summarizes common standards for determining criminal responsibility in mentally disordered defendants.

Guilty but Mentally Ill

Also in response to disenchantment with the insanity defense, some states have introduced a new verdict alternative, **guilty but mentally ill (GBMI)**. Defendants also may enter this as a plea in some states.

Michigan was the first to adopt the GBMI alternative in 1975, and by 1992, 11 other states had followed Michigan's lead. The GBMI option is intended as an alternative to, not a substitute for, the NGRI verdict. States differ in the standards and procedures associated with GBMI, and some use slightly different terminology, such as guilty except insane. In all, though, the major intention of the option is to reduce the number of insanity acquittals (which as we have noted is not large), hold the defendant blameworthy, but still recognize the presence of a mental disorder. Thus, GBMI allows the court to render a "middle-ground" verdict in the case of allegedly mentally disordered defendants. The verdict allows juries, for example, to reconcile their belief that a defendant who commits a crime should be held responsible with the belief that he or she also needs help.

Research on the GBMI laws indicates that the intended purposes may not have been accomplished. An early study in Michigan found that insanity acquittals remained stable while guilty verdicts generally declined (Smith & Hall, 1982). The same finding was reported in other states that adopted the GBMI option (McGinley & Paswark, 1989). Furthermore, defendants found GBMI have received longer sentences and had longer confinements than "sane" defendants found guilty of similar charges (Callahan, McGreevy, Cirincione, & Steadman, 1992; Steadman et al., 1993). In addition, research indicates that those individuals found GBMI are no more likely to receive psychotherapy or rehabilitative services than other mentally disordered defendants in the prison system (Borum & Fulero, 1999; Morse, 1985; Slobogin, 1985; Zapf, Golding, & Roesch, 2006). Thus, the promise of treatment that is implicit in the statutes remains unfulfilled. However, depending upon the wording of the statute, it may be read as creating a *right* to treatment for those defendants found GBMI (Cohen, 2008), although this is not the common approach. Interestingly, there is also evidence that defendants charged with a serious violent crime often elect the GBMI alternative as part of the plea-bargaining process. Defense attorneys may be more willing to accept this option than go to trial and risk their client's life (Steadman et al., 1993). Considering the research strongly suggesting that GBMI statutes do not accomplish what was intended, virtually all of the scholarly writing on this issue has questioned the wisdom and efficacy of these laws (Cohen, 2008; Goldstein et al., 2013; Melton et al., 2007).

UNIQUE DEFENSES AND CONDITIONS

Earlier in the chapter, we discussed some of the psychiatric diagnoses that are most likely to accompany a decision that a defendant is incompetent to stand trial or used to bolster an insanity defense. In this section, we discuss additional disorders or diagnoses that are less common but still cited by defense lawyers, either to absolve defendants completely or to support a claim of diminished capacity or responsibility. At times these conditions are used, not as a separate defense, but to support an insanity defense. In addition, they are often not complete defenses but rather absolve individuals of some degree of responsibility, if they are successful. In addition, these unique conditions may help defendants obtain a more favorable plea bargain or more lenient sentencing. In the following sections, we cover conditions and defenses that have received the most coverage in the research literature.

Posttraumatic Stress Disorder

In the 2014 "American sniper" case, it was widely believed that the defendant's attorneys would use PTSD either to diminish the defendant's responsibility or to support an insanity defense. Routh, a military veteran, had been diagnosed with PTSD, along with psychosis, paranoia, and suicidal tendencies months before the shootings of Kyle and Littlefield. Interestingly, however, the lawyers did not focus on PTSD in making their insanity claim. Psychological and psychiatric experts testifying at his trial for both sides did not believe he had that disorder. Rather, the expert for the defense gave the opinion that he killed during a psychotic episode. As noted earlier in the chapter, the jury convicted him after a short period of deliberation. Routh was eventually sent to a psychiatric facility within the Texas prison system.

According to the DSM-5, the essential feature of **posttraumatic stress disorder (PTSD)** is "the development of characteristic symptoms following exposure to one or more traumatic events" (p. 274). Interestingly, the criteria for PTSD in this latest edition differ significantly from those in the 4th edition, a fact that led to extensive criticism from some mental health professionals during the time the *DSM* was being revised (Friedman et al., 2011). In previous editions, criteria included very negative emotions such as intense fear, terror, or helplessness. According to the latest edition, while these may indeed occur, they are not necessary. The person suffering from PTSD may display it through different mood states, negative cognitions, or dissociative symptoms (symptoms of being separated or detached from normal psychological functioning). Critics of this and other changes were concerned that this could lead to additional problems in diagnosing the disorder, including overdiagnosis.

PTSD was formally recognized as a distinct disorder in the 1980 edition of the DSM-III following efforts by veterans' groups to have mental health professionals recognize a "post-Vietnam syndrome" that led to a variety of disabling symptoms (Appelbaum et al., 1993). Since being formally recognized, PTSD has been broadly applied not only to war veterans but also to survivors of the Holocaust, survivors of major disasters—such as the events of September 11, 2001 or the Boston Marathon bombing of 2013—and victims and survivors of mass shootings, rape, child abuse, spousal abuse, and sexual harassment. Victims of human rights abuses around the globe are also susceptible to the symptoms associated with PTSD. PTSD also may be applied to individuals who have witnessed the events—such as being exposed to war—or threatened with victimization, such as death or sexual violence.

Studies have estimated that between 1 and 7 percent all Americans suffer from PTSD (Elhai, Grubaugh, Kashdan, & Frueh, 2008, 6.8%; Sutker, Uddo-Crane, & Allain, 1991, 1% to 2%). The prevalence of PTSD among military veterans is believed to be considerably higher than the prevalence in the general population, however. Kulka et al. (1991) estimated that PTSD affected 31 percent of all male and 27 percent of all female Vietnam veterans. More recently, it has been estimated that 16.6 percent of soldiers returning from Iraq and Afghanistan met criteria for PTSD within a year of their return (Hoge, Terhakopian, Castro, Messer, & Engel, 2007). Finley et al. (2015) report that PTSD was diagnosed in nearly one-fifth of veterans of recent wars.

The symptoms of PTSD include "flashbacks," recurrent dreams or nightmares, or painful, intrusive memories of the traumatic event. A diminished responsiveness, a don't-care attitude, or psychological "numbing" to the external world are common, particularly during the weeks following the event. Although research (e.g., Hoge et al., 2007) notes that the symptoms of PTSD may not emerge until considerable time has elapsed, six months to a year or more, the DSM-5 indicates that symptoms usually begin within three months of the trauma. However, there is the possibility of delayed expression (formerly called delayed onset) occurring months or years after the event. Feelings of alienation or detachment from the social environment are also characteristic, a pattern that leads to difficulty in developing close, meaningful relationships with others. Other symptoms include sleep problems, being easily startled, considerable difficulty concentrating or remembering, and extreme avoidance of anything that reminds them of the event. Anniversaries of the trauma are enough to precipitate symptoms. Individuals with a diagnosis of PTSD tend to be moody, depressed, and difficult to be around or work with. They often move from job to job, relationship to relationship. In the case of veterans, those with PTSD diagnoses are significantly more likely than those without such diagnoses to be perpetrators of domestic violence and to be arrested for criminal activity (Friel, White, & Hull, 2008).

PTSD has been used to support a defense of NGRI, in both violent and nonviolent cases (Monahan & Walker, 1990, 1994). For example, PTSD has been used as an excusing condition for drug trafficking (e.g., *United States v. Krutschewski*, 1981). Evidence to date, however, shows that—while courts are willing to admit evidence of PTSD—using it to support an insanity defense is not likely to be successful (Appelbaum et al., 1993; Friel et al., 2008; Sparr, 1996). When the PTSD defense has been successful, it usually results in a finding of *diminished responsibility,* rather than the complete absolution of responsibility (NGRI) for the defendant. PTSD has also been cited in plea bargaining and in presentence reports (Monahan & Walker, 1990). That is, prosecutors may be more willing to accept a guilty plea to a reduced charge, and judges more willing to impose a lighter sentence, if evidence of PTSD exists. In a recent U.S. Supreme Court case (*Cone v. Bell*, 2009), the Court vacated the death sentence of a Vietnam veteran because the sentencing jury had not considered the fact that he suffered from PTSD as a mitigating factor in his crime. In cases involving veterans, PTSD may also be used as evidence for diminished responsibility in assigning cases to pretrial diversion, in plea bargaining, and in sentencing (Appelbaum et al., 1993; Christy, Clark, Frei, & Rynearson-Moody, 2012). Indeed, in a study of the attitudes of prosecutors toward veterans with PTSD, Wilson, Brodsky, Neal, and Cramer (2011) found that the prosecutors perceived them as less criminally culpable and were more willing to be lenient, such as by referring these defendants to diversion programs, compared with defendants without PTSD.

The primary legal argument used by the defense is that the defendant was in a PTSD dissociated state when he committed the act. Although PTSD is not regarded as a dissociative disorder in the *DSM* (it is categorized as a trauma- and stressor-related disorder), it can have dissociative symptoms and therefore, some who suffer from it, may at times be in a **dissociated state**. As indicated above, this refers to symptoms in which the individual feels detached from himself or herself and his or her surroundings and basically loses some contact with reality. While in that state, a person typically does not remember what he or she has experienced or even his or her own identity. In *State v. Felde* (1982), the defendant—a Vietnam veteran who shot a police officer—"claimed that he was in a dissociative state and that he believed that he had been captured by the North Vietnamese at the time he shot the officer" (McCord, 1987, p. 65). In *Miller v. State* (1983), the defendant, charged with a prison escape, argued that he thought he was still in Vietnam and his only intention was to get back to the United States.

PTSD has been used to excuse or mitigate criminal responsibility in cases involving battered women who maintain that they have **battered woman syndrome**, sometimes considered a variant of PTSD (Appelbaum et al., 1993). This is a controversial area for several reasons. First, there is not universal agreement in the psychological literature that there exists a battered woman syndrome; its scientific underpinning is questionable (Petrila, 2009). Second, advocates for persons who are victimized by their intimate partners resist the implication that they have a mental disorder or that they are "insane." Third, treating the results of this victimization as a syndrome gives the false impression that everyone experiences battering or similar abuse in the same way, which in turn dissuades treatment providers and the law from dealing with the complexity of this issue (Levesque, 2001).

When PTSD is used as a defense in these situations, though, an abused woman may claim that the abuse was so extensive and brutal that, in a dissociative state brought about by the disorder, she killed the abuser. In this case, she is more likely to claim "temporary insanity" than "insanity," in the hope that acquittal will not be followed by commitment to a mental institution. However, PTSD in a battered woman also may be used to support a claim of self-defense rather than insanity, though courts have not been sympathetic to this approach (Slobogin, 1999). When used in this way, the defendant focuses on other symptoms of PTSD—for example, heightened fear, anxiety, depression—rather than on the dissociative state. She kills in defense of her life, because she lives in a constant state of fear that she will die at the hands of her abuser. In a different context, evidence that a rape victim shows the symptoms of PTSD has been accepted in some courts as proof that the victim has indeed been raped (Appelbaum et al., 1993). Likewise, PTSD has been used in civil suits involving emotional or physical personal injury, such as sexual harassment suits or civil suits against former abusers.

In summary, evidence that an individual is suffering from PTSD is accepted in many courts, but it rarely absolves criminal defendants of total responsibility. In the hands of a sympathetic jury, it could lead to an acquittal. However, it is more likely to support a diversion from prosecution—if the crime is not a serious one—and it may be helpful at the plea bargaining stage or in supporting a claim of diminished capacity. Evidence of PTSD has also contributed to lenience in sentencing.

Until recently, some legal scholars and researchers believed that there was no objective way to assess PTSD—its diagnosis depended almost exclusively on the self-report of the individual or the observations of those close to him or her. Consequently, there was considerable opportunity for malingering or faking the disorder. While malingering remains a concern, clinicians believe they have found better methods of discovering it (Resnick, 1995). In addition, several clinical methods of assessing PTSD itself have been developed and evaluated, including the Clinician-Administered PTSD Scale (CAPS; Blake, Weathers, & Nagy, 1995), which has been referred to as the "gold standard" for assessing the disorder (Friel et al., 2008). With the change in criteria introduced into the DSM-5, however, supplementary methods of assessment will likely be needed.

Dissociation

One of the most fascinating concepts in contemporary psychology is that of dissociation, which is thought to exist on a continuum from the normal to the pathological (Moskowitz, 2004). Most of us probably daydream, which is a "normal" form; in its most severe or pathological form, dissociation can refer to extreme amnesia for past events or even dissociative identity disorder (DID), which was formerly called multiple personality disorder (MPD). Each of these will be discussed in more detail below.

The DSM-5 identifies five different dissociative disorders, including dissociative amnesia and DID. Dissociative disorders are characterized by "a disruption of and/or discontinuity in the normal integration of consciousness, memory, identity, perception, body representation, motor control, and behavior" (American Psychiatric Association, 2013, p. 291). The more extreme or pathological forms of dissociation may be claimed when defendants are charged with violent offenses. As we saw in the section above, persons with PTSD charged with violent crimes may argue that they committed their criminal acts while in a dissociative state.

Dissociative Identity Disorder

The essential feature of **dissociative identity disorder (DID)** is "(a) the presence of two or more distinct personality states or an experience of possession and (b) recurrent episodes of amnesia." The amnesia, or gaps in recall, may occur for everyday events, not just traumatic events, which is a change from DSM-IV criteria. It is not uncommon for persons to experience fugue states, such as by finding themselves at distant locations and not knowing how they got there (American Psychiatric Association, 2013, p. 291). The symptoms of DID may be reported by the individual or observed by others. The change or transition from one personality state to another is often very sudden (seconds to minutes), and is generally triggered by stress or some relevant environmental stimuli. Often, hypnosis can also bring about this shift into another personality state.

Persons who experience DID are highly suggestible and impressionable and can be readily hypnotized either by themselves or by others. Reported cases of what was then called MPD have historically been extremely rare. However, between 1980 and 1989, the number of cases diagnosed in the United States rose dramatically, from 200 to 6,000 (Slovenko, 1989). Part of this increase is due to the American Psychiatric Association officially recognizing the disorder in the DSM-III. In a review of the literature on dissociation and violence, Moskowitz (2004) reported that several prominent studies during that time period found violent "alters" in a significant number of persons who had been diagnosed with DID. Interestingly, however, Moskowitz maintains that varieties of dissociative disorders, not just DID, are often overlooked in criminal justice populations, particularly males.

On occasion, what was then called MPD was used successfully as an excusing condition for criminal responsibility (e.g., *State v. Rodrigues*, 1984; *State v. Milligan*, 1978). In general, however, MPD was not a successful defense (Slovenko, 1989). One of the more well-known cases in which the MPD defense was tried and failed involved serial killer Kenneth Bianchi, known as the Hillside Strangler (*State v. Bianchi*, 1979). The Hillside Strangler was given wide publicity because of the brutality and sadistic quality of his murders. The victims were young women who were raped and strangled, and whose nude bodies were conspicuously displayed on the hillsides in the Los Angeles area. The Hillside Strangler was responsible for at least a dozen murders during a one-year period (1977 to 1978).

Despite considerable evidence against him, Bianchi insisted that he was innocent, arguing that an alter personality, "Steve," had done the killings. He pleaded NGRI. A team of experts appointed by the court found no basis for Bianchi's claim of MPD. Although Bianchi knew the "textbook version" of MPD (probably knowledge gained during a period of his life in which he had impersonated a psychologist), he was less than convincing on the more subtle aspects of the disorder recognized by the experts. The team concluded that Bianchi was a psychopath. Bianchi then quickly changed his plea to guilty in order to avoid the death penalty.

To this day, there is debate among practitioners and scholars as to whether MPD/DID actually exists. Indeed, the criteria for DID in the DSM-5 are markedly different from criteria for MPD in early editions. MPD in particular was referred to as the "UFO of psychiatry" (Ondrovik & Hamilton, 1991). In some instances, DID may be **iatrogenic**—that is, unintentionally caused by clinicians or practitioners themselves. This means that practitioners who firmly believe in and are perceptually sensitive to DID look for and interpret a variety of behaviors as symptoms of the disorder. In effect, the practitioner may develop the syndrome in the patient, and the patient, in turn, learns to believe that he or she is afflicted with it. It has also been argued that implicit and explicit suggestions during hypnosis can shape segments of self into the appearance of MPD (Orne, Dinges, & Orne, 1984). Regardless of whether the syndrome is iatrogenic or whether it is possible for several personality states to "possess" a physical body, an important point must be made. The syndrome is *often subjectively real* to the patient, and the person who allegedly experiences it often plays each of the roles well and convincingly. Martin Orne and his colleagues (Orne et al., 1984, p. 120) observe, "So striking are the behavioral differences between personalities that the assertion is often made that one would need to have the dramatic skills of Sarah Bernhardt or Sir Laurence Olivier, along with a detailed knowledge of psychiatry, to effectively simulate such radically different persons."

In summary, the validity of DID as a viable entity is very much open to debate by both the mental health and legal professions. Supporters of the concept maintain that diagnostic procedures among clinicians are more accurate today than in the past, and clinicians have at their disposal specific diagnostic tests to detect the disorder (Comer, 2004). It is not unusual to be in a roomful of clinicians who seem firmly convinced that DID is a significant problem encountered in their practices and one that mental health practitioners still fail to diagnose. According to this perspective, treatment is a highly complex and multistage process. It involves allowing the alter egos to emerge and enabling the client to confront them. Eventually, the "alters" are left behind, a process that can be frightening to the client. As one therapist commented, after a long period of treatment, the client had successfully confronted her problems and was ready to move on to a normal life. However, she was concerned about how she would handle financial matters, because "Ruth"—one of her alters—was the one who had always balanced the checkbook.

Dissociative Amnesia

Amnesia refers to complete or partial memory loss of an event, series of events, or some segment of life's experiences, either due to physical trauma, neurophysiological disturbance, or psychological factors. It is a topic that is often highlighted in popular movies (e.g., *the Bourne trilogy series, 2002–2007; Memento*, 2000; *The Vow*, 2012). Note that amnesia is one of the criteria for diagnosing DID. It is sometimes classified into retrograde and anterograde amnesia—loss of memory for past events in the first case, inability to form new memories after an event that caused the amnesia in the second case. In the film *Memento*, the main character had anterograde amnesia as a consequence of being victim of a crime, and he wrote notes to himself and even got tattoos so he would not "lose" the new information he obtained in attempting to avenge the crime. In *The Vow*, a far less complicated movie, a young woman loses the memory of her past five years with her husband after coming out of a coma following an automobile accident.

Persons with dissociative amnesia are unable to recall previously learned information or past events. The amnesia may be localized or generalized, with the latter being the rarest form. Localized amnesia is a failure to recall events during a circumscribed period of time, whereas generalized amnesia is a complete loss of memory (DSM-5). Localized amnesia, also referred to as limited amnesia, is "a pathological inability to remember a specific episode, or small number of episodes, from the recent past" (Schacter, 1986, p. 48). It may be caused by emotional shock, alcohol or drug intoxication, or a blow to the head. Therefore, limited amnesia is not ongoing, nor does it involve extensive memory loss. Rather, the loss is temporary and restricted to a specific event or incident. As an example of limited amnesia, the engineer on an Amtrak trail that derailed in Pennsylvania in 2015, killing eight passengers and injuring many others, claimed inability to recall the events leading to and following the derailment.

In general, the courts have not been receptive to amnesia either as a valid condition to support an NGRI defense or as a condition that promotes incompetence to stand trial (Rubinsky & Brandt, 1986). The exception is in cases of brain injury, when a connection can be established between the injury and the memory loss. Finally, with increasing recognition of the reality of traumatic brain injuries in veterans, athletes, or other individuals who have suffered blows to the head, criminal courts may become more sympathetic to defendants who claim that they cannot remember an incident or a chain of incidents because of amnesia related to their physiological conditions.

Pauli (1993) notes that there have been cases in at least 20 states and five federal circuit courts where the court has held that amnesia per se does not render a defendant incompetent. One reason for this judicial "hard-line" approach to amnesia is the suspicion that the defendant may be faking the memory loss. It is easy for people to simply say they cannot remember committing the crime, and it is difficult for psychologists to determine whether a person can or cannot remember. In recent years, though, psychologists have been able to fine-tune a number of instruments designed to measure malingering—or faking—of various symptoms, including symptoms of amnesia (Rogers, 1997). Interestingly, according to the DSM-5, "There is no test, battery of tests, or set of procedures that invariably distinguishes dissociative amnesia from feigned amnesia. Individuals with factitious disorder or malingering have been noted to continue their deception even during hypnotic or barbiturate-facilitated interviews" (American Psychiatric Association, 2013, p. 301). Nevertheless, some psychologists believe that amnesia can be evaluated with recognition tests that are tailored to the information that the client claims not to know (Frederick, 2000).

Amnesia associated with alcoholic intoxication presents a favorite excuse for reprehensible behavior, and is the most commonly invoked excusing condition in criminal cases. "When I drink I go blank about some things" is the usual line. It is intriguing to note that 30 to 65 percent of persons convicted of criminal homicide claim they cannot remember the crime, usually because of alcoholic intoxication at the time of the offense (Schacter, 1986). A similar pattern exists for other violent crimes (e.g., rape) as well.

However, the courts have not been sympathetic to defendants who rely on excuses based on alcohol or other drug intoxication. This is because the courts hold the person blameworthy since he or she should have known, at the outset, the risks involved in drinking alcohol or taking drugs. Thus, attempts to use amnesia in this way have met with strong judicial resistance. For example, one court held that "insanity is the incapacity to discriminate between right and wrong while amnesia is simply the inability to remember" (Rubinsky & Brandt, 1986, p. 30). Therefore, amnesia per se fails to qualify as a mental disorder that robs a person of the ability to distinguish between right and wrong.

MENTAL DISORDER AND VIOLENCE

While the mental disorders described in this chapter may be associated with a variety of criminal offenses, it is the crimes of violence that are most disturbing. The depressed individual may embezzle funds in an effort to obtain a way out of his dire economic situation. The individual with a delusional disorder may break into a building to seek shelter from those who persecute him. The person with an APD may perpetrate a series of economic scams on unsuspecting victims. Publicity is most likely to accompany criminal behavior when it is violent, however, and the public is most fearful of these offenses, despite the fact that we are far more likely to be victims of economic crimes than violent crimes. And as we learned above, the mere presence of a mental illness does not guarantee that a defendant will be found incompetent to stand trial or absolved of criminal responsibility. In some jurisdictions, this is even more true when defendants are accused of violent crimes than when they are accused of property offenses.

It is important to stress that, as a group, individuals who are mentally ill are no more likely to commit crimes than those who are not. Moreover, as documented in recent research and illustrated in **Box 8-1**, serious mental disorder is not a direct cause of crime (Peterson et al., 2014) and risk factors for committing crime are similar for both mentally disordered and nonmentally disordered offenders (Skeem et al., 2014). Nevertheless, mentally disordered individuals do appear with some regularity in arrest records, in jails, in prisons, and on probation and parole caseloads, and they present special challenges to those who supervise them. Recent research indicates that community alternatives, including pretrial diversion into a specialized treatment program, may be a good approach for persons with severe mental illness who have been charged with crimes (Colwell, Villarreal, & Espinosa, 2012; Heilbrun et al., 2012). Colwell et al. found that assignment to such a program significantly reduced the likelihood of future adjudication.

The prevalence of mental disorders is more than three times higher in the criminal justice population than in the general population (Skeem, Emke-Francis, & Louden, 2006). In recent years, researchers have searched for groups or classifications of seriously mentally ill offenders who may be particularly prone to involvement in the criminal justice system. Constantine et al. (2010), for example, found three arrest trajectories patterns for the seriously mentally ill: low chronic, high chronic, and sporadic. Their study of close to 4,000 participants with diagnoses of serious mental disorders did not separate violent from nonviolent offenses, although it did separate felonies from misdemeanors.

Research on the Violence of the Mentally Disordered

Early research literature consistently supported the position that mentally disordered individuals—even the severely mentally disordered—are no more likely to commit serious crimes against others than the general population (Brodsky, 1973, 1977; Henn, Herjanic, & Vanderpearl, 1976a; Monahan, 1981; Rabkin, 1979). Later research (Brennan, Mednick, & Hodgins, 2000; Klassen & O'Connor, 1988, 1990; Monahan, 1992; Silver, 2006) found that a certain subset of the mentally disordered population may be at risk of committing violent crime, leading Heilbrun, Douglas, and Yasuhara (2009, p. 348) to write, "Despite the presence of literally hundreds of studies that address this question, it remains unclear whether mental illness is related to violence." Note that the emphasis is on violence, and the population referred to is a subset of the general population of serious mentally disordered individuals.

Some research indicates that individuals with schizophrenia are at increased risk of violent offending and even at higher risk to commit murder (Naudts & Hodgins, 2005). In addition, when offenders with schizophrenia do commit murder, they most often kill relatives, and many are exhibiting hallucinations and delusions at the time of the offense (Häkkänen & Laajasalo, 2006). The study by Peterson et al. did not include individuals who had committed murder, a rare crime to begin with. In a meta-analysis of 204 studies, psychosis also was found to increase the odds of violence by as much as 50 to 70 percent (Douglas, Guy, & Hart, 2009).

We cannot emphasize enough that a majority of people with mental disorders do *not* commit serious or violent offenses. For example, only 11.3 percent of the men and 2.3 percent of the women who developed schizophrenia committed violent offenses (Tengström, Hodgins, Grann, Långström, & Kullgren, 2004). In addition, those individuals with schizophrenia who commit violent crime constitute a very heterogeneous group. "Some display a history of antisocial behavior from a very early age; others begin engaging in antisocial behavior around the time of schizophrenia onsets; others commit only one violent attack in their lives, while others behave aggressively only when acutely psychotic" (Naudts & Hodgins, 2005, p. 1).

In addition, there is further evidence that men who have both schizophrenia and a substance abuse problem are at an increased risk of violent offending. For instance, Räsänen et al. (1998) report evidence that male schizophrenics with alcohol abuse problems are 25 times more likely to commit violent crimes than males with no mental disorders and no alcohol problems. Follow-up studies of patients with schizophrenia and substance abuse problems have frequently found them to be at risk of committing violent offenses (Appelbaum, Robbins, & Monahan, 2000; Tengström et al., 2004).

John Monahan (1992) stresses two things about the research showing a connection between mental disorders and violence. First, the relationship refers only to people *currently* experiencing a *serious* mental disorder. People who have experienced a serious mental disorder in the past and are not showing symptoms currently are unlikely to engage in violent behavior. Second, it is still a fact that a great majority (over 90%) of the currently mentally disordered are not violent. Finally, it must be emphasized not only that the mental disorder–violence link relates to the seriously mentally disordered but also that the relationship is also stronger for individuals who have a history of violent behavior. Recall that Laajasalo and Häkkänen (2006) found that the strongest predictors of excessive violence among their sample of schizophrenics convicted of homicide were a past history of violent behavior and the presence of a co-offender.

Individuals experiencing affective (mood) psychoses are less likely to be violent. When affective psychoses are associated with violence, they are usually manifested in women within the context of extended suicide, in which the offender kills herself as well as others in the environment, including her immediate family (Blackburn, 1993). However, as will be noted in Chapter 10, mass murders in public settings are often committed by men who feel hopeless and also have the signs of affective psychoses. In most cases, mass murderers plan to die or commit suicide at the site of their crime.

The MacArthur Research Network

Some of the best-known research on the potential violence of the mentally disordered has been conducted by the MacArthur Research Network (Monahan et al., 2001; Steadman et al., 1998). Researchers followed over 1,000 patients discharged from civil psychiatric hospitals in an effort to determine the extent to which they demonstrated aggressive behavior over a one-year period. The patients also had been measured on a wide range of "risk factors"—134 in all—while they were hospitalized. These included such factors as violent fantasies, history of abuse as a child, frequency of parents fighting with each other, and number of negative and positive persons in the social network, to name but a few. The data allowed the MacArthur researchers to develop a risk assessment instrument, The multiple Iterative Classification Tree (ICT), which they believe can help clinicians identify low, average, and high-risk individuals. They emphasize, however, that the instrument was developed on psychiatric inpatients in acute facilities who would soon be discharged, and should not be generalized to other contexts until validated on additional populations. It is worth noting that about half of the discharged patients in this study were in the low-risk group, while the remaining patients were about evenly divided between average and high-risk groups. However, no single risk factor was a significant predictor of violence. As Monahan et al. (2001, p. 142) stated, "The propensity for violence is the result of the accumulation of risk factors, no one of which is either necessary or sufficient for a person to behave aggressively toward others."

In later research, Monahan and his colleagues (Monahan et al., 2005) used a new sample of patients discharged from psychiatric hospitals who had been classified as being at low risk (less than 9% likelihood of violence) or high risk (greater than 37% likelihood of violence). The patients were first assessed and interviewed during their hospitalization for follow-up; all high-risk patients and a random sample of low-risk patients and those who knew them were interviewed in the community at 10 and 20 weeks after the date of discharge. Arrest and rehospitalization records were also reviewed. The expected rates of violence were 1 percent for the low-risk group and 64 percent for the much smaller high-risk group; the observed rates of violence were 9 percent for the low-risk group and 49 percent for the high-risk group.

In sum, then, the research on the mentally disordered and violence allows us to conclude the following:

- Past mental disorder alone, even serious mental disorder, is not necessarily a good predictor of violence.
- The mental disorder most closely associated with violent and serious offenses is schizophrenia.
- Persons with schizophrenia who commit violent crimes—and most do not—consist of a very heterogeneous group.
- Males who develop schizophrenia *and* exhibit antisocial behavior at an *early* age often demonstrate persistent and versatile patterns of criminal offending.
- Violence is associated with *current* serious mental disorder, particularly when a history of violent behavior is also present.

- Risk factors for committing crime (e.g., substance abuse, early onset of offending) are similar for mentally disordered and nonmentally disordered individuals.
- Crimes committed by the seriously mentally ill are generally not a direct result of their illness.
- At least in civilly committed institutionalized patients, the classification system devised by the MacArthur Research Network is an efficient predictor of future violence in the community.
- While researchers have developed some instruments to assess the likelihood that a person will engage in violence, no one factor serves as strong predictor; violent behavior seems to be a result of an accumulation of risk factors, unique to each individual.

Police and the Mentally Disordered

As indicated in the previous section, some research documents that persons who are seriously mentally ill often appear in arrest records, charged with both felony and misdemeanor crimes (Constantine et al., 2010). Early research documented that police may be more apt to arrest the mentally disordered (Teplin, 1984). In her classic study in which trained graduate students in psychology observed 1,382 police–citizen encounters, Teplin found police arrested 20 percent more individuals with symptoms of mental disorders than without such symptoms. Considering that many disordered individuals tend to have annoying symptoms, such as verbal abuse, belligerence, and disrespect, the slightly higher probability of arrest is hardly surprising. To some extent, police also may have taken some of these individuals into custody in order to provide them with shelter. However, police officers failed to recognize the behavior as representing a mental disorder in a large number of cases, believing the individuals were simply being disrespectful and asking for trouble.

In the more than 30 years since Teplin's study, significant changes have occurred nationwide relative to law enforcement's handling of mentally disordered individuals. First, police academies are more likely to offer some training in both recognizing and dealing with mental disorders (Fields, 2006). In some communities, police have taken the initiative to appoint specially trained liaison officers to work with the disordered (Smith, 2002). Nonetheless, researchers continue to identify problems related to police and the mentally disordered. Redlich, Summers, and Hoover (2010), for example, found that persons who are mentally disordered are more likely than those who are not to give "false confessions" to police. In a later study on false confessions (Redlich, Kulich, & Steadman, 2011), it was found that the mentally disordered were asked more questions and were not surprisingly more confused by the interrogation experience. Second, communities across the nation are establishing specialized courts—mental health courts—that provide diversionary options to jailing and prosecuting the mentally disordered—and the intellectually disabled—who are charged with nonviolent offenses, or even minor violent crimes, such as simple assault. Rather than being held in jail, they are offered shelter and treatment or training services. Mental health courts are increasing across the nation and continue to be evaluated for their efficiency, cost-effectiveness, and quality of treatment (see, e.g., Redlich, Liu, Steadman, Callahan, & Robbins, 2012, and references therein).

Mentally Disordered Inmates

Mental disorders in those incarcerated in prison and jail are sometimes cited as evidence of a link between crime and abnormal behavior. Both the prevalence and the nature of disorder among these populations are difficult to determine, however, because statistics and descriptions vary widely. Furthermore, some data are based on the inmates' own self-report, while other data are based on clinical findings. Nonetheless, most contemporary research indicates that the percentage of mentally disordered inmates in the nation's jails and prisons is increasing (Althouse, 2010). In a study by James and Glaze (2006), it was estimated that half of all prison and jail inmates have a mental health problem (James & Glaze, 2006). This does not mean that they are seriously mentally disordered—rather, it suggests that they might benefit

TABLE 8-2	Inmates Identified as Mentally Disordered, by Gender, Race/Hispanic Origin, and Age		
	Percent Identified as Mentally Disordered		
Offender Characteristics	**State Inmates**	**Federal Inmates**	**Jail Inmates**
All inmates	56.2	44.8	64.2
Gender			
Male	55.0	43.60	62.8
Female	73.1	61.2	75.4
Race/Hispanic Origin			
White	62.2	49.6	71.2
Black	54.7	45.9	63.4
Hispanic	46.3	36.8	50.7
Other	61.9	50.3	69.5

Source: Adapted from James, D. J., & Glaze, L. E. (2006, September). Mental health problems of prison and jail inmates. Washington, DC: U.S. Department of Justice, Bureau of Justice Statistics.

from mental health treatment. Female inmates have higher rates of mental health problems than male inmates (see **Table 8-2**). The most common problem reported is major depression, followed by psychotic disorders.

Other researchers have reported that 10 to 15 percent of persons in jails and federal and state prisons have *severe* mental disorders (Lamb, Weinberger, & Gross, 2004). It is difficult to determine to what extent these data include APDs; it is estimated that 40 to 80 percent of inmates carry that diagnosis (Steffan & Morgan, 2005). Nevertheless, both researchers and mental health professionals working with jail and prison inmates report significant increases in *serious* mental health problems in both state and federal facilities (Ashford, Sales, & Reid, 2001; Magaletta, Dietz, & Diamond, 2005).

It is obvious that jail and prison conditions, as well as conditions in juvenile facilities, can have deleterious effects on mental states. Therefore, an individual may become mentally disordered after being institutionalized, which may be reflected in these statistics. However, considerable evidence indicates that many inmates or prisoners were showing signs of mental disorders prior to incarceration (Bureau of Justice Assistance, 2000).

It remains difficult to determine, however, the precise clinical diagnoses associated with these mental disorders. As noted above, many could have been diagnosed with APD. Second, some data were collected by asking the inmates themselves about their mental conditions. Third, the reliability of psychiatric diagnoses, even in the general population, is often in doubt. Finally, we do not know whether the mental disorders reported are the result of being in prison or jail, or whether the individual entered the system with the existing disorder. Regardless, however, if the disorder exists, it is a problem.

In summary, it is very clear that prisons and jails today are facing increasing numbers of mentally disordered inmates whose problems will likely escalate if not sufficiently treated. This may be especially problematic in high-security, supermax facilities where inmates are kept in solitary confinement, sometimes for many years (see, generally, Toch, 2008). Supermax prisons, which exist in every state as well as the federal prison system, are notorious for producing psychological breakdown among inmates who are often confined in individual cells for 23 hours a day. After Dzokhar Tsarrnaev, the Boston Marathon bomber, was convicted, many in the public hoped he would be sentenced to life without parole, because he would be spending the rest of his life in a federal prison, such as ADX, the "supermax" facility in Florence, Colorado. (Jurors sentenced him to death, and it is likely that he will await execution in the federal prison system's "death row," located within a U.S. Penitentiary in Terre Haute, Indiana. Even in the general population of prisons and jails, however, the prevalence of individuals in need of mental health services is sobering.

DANGEROUSNESS AND THE ASSESSMENT OF RISK

Up to this point in the chapter, we have covered a range of situations involving mentally disordered individuals, criminal courts, police, and prisons and jails. In many—but not all—of those situations, the courts and other agents of the criminal justice system were concerned about whether the disordered individual was also a danger to society.

The concept of dangerousness pervades much of the criminal law and appears in civil law as well. Defining dangerous behavior is a challenge faced by legislatures, courts, and clinicians. All states and all courts recognize that behavior that is likely to result in *physical harm* is dangerous. They begin to differ when behaviors that lead to property damage or psychological injury are involved. One example of psychological injury is the effect on victims of stalking, who may be continually shadowed, photographed, contacted online, sent text messages, and otherwise harassed. Some courts have ruled that this type of behavior can cause irreparable emotional damage. They conclude that a threat of "psychological trauma is…as much a menace to the health or safety of others as is possible physical injury" (Developments in the Law, 1974, p. 1237). This form of psychological damage has prompted many state legislatures to pass "stalking laws" that state that persons who continually follow and otherwise harass other individuals, promoting fear, are dangerous and can be charged with a criminal offense.

It is fair to say, though, that dangerousness is used primarily in conjunction with violent behavior. Defendants charged with violent crimes are sometimes denied bail because they are judged dangerous, violent offenders are sentenced to long prison terms to prevent them from committing more crime, and some are sentenced to death because it is feared they will commit more violence. Decisions on whether to parole prisoners convicted of violent crimes are largely based on whether they are dangerous.

Implicit in the above decisions is the belief that it is possible to predict an individual's violent behavior. Although some clinicians believe they can do so with a high degree of confidence, most are far more modest about this ability. Since the 1990s, the research and professional literature have increasingly preferred the term "risk assessment" rather than prediction of dangerousness. Risk assessment suggests that clinicians and researchers are more proficient at *assessing the probability* that a given individual—or group of individuals—will engage in harmful behavior than they are at outrightly predicting that someone is dangerous or will be violent. We will return to this change in terminology shortly.

Controversy over the ability to predict, particularly predict violence, has been longstanding. Not surprisingly, it has often been fueled by highly publicized incidents. The April 2008, shootings at Virginia Tech were perpetrated by a man, who had a history of psychiatric treatment and periodic episodes of violence. A year later, 12 people were killed by a shooter, who entered an immigration center in Binghamton, New York, dedicated to helping immigrants adjust to life in the United States. Individuals who knew him said they were "not surprised," because he was isolated, had continuously voiced his disenchantment with his station in life, and complained that people ridiculed his lack of facility with the English language. Nevertheless, the above could characterize numerous individuals who do not go out and kill others.

Today, the many social media and dark Internet sites allow people to make threats and post rants with little compunction, and often anonymously. In numerous cases, including mass shootings, the perpetrators had given signals through social media that they were on the verge of carrying out a violent act. Sadly, many other people make similar claims, but fortunately they do not act upon them. Although we are all advised to report suspicious behavior or threats to authorities, only mental health professionals are required to do so, under certain conditions.

The Tarasoff Case

A crime that occurred over 30 years ago in California continues to have reverberations among clinicians today. A young woman, Tatiana Tarasoff, was stabbed and killed by Prosenjit Poddar. An outpatient at a University of California, Berkeley, clinic, Poddar had revealed to his psychiatrist his fantasies about harming, or perhaps even killing, a woman whom he had met at a dance. The psychologist, who learned from one of his patient's friends that he planned to purchase a gun, became increasingly concerned. When the patient discontinued therapy, clinic officials wrote to the police requesting their help in getting the individual committed to a mental institution. Police investigated the case, interviewed Poddar, warned him to stay away from the woman, but did not pursue the commitment, apparently because California's new civil commitment law was difficult to interpret. After the murder, the victim's family sued the university clinic, claiming the psychologist had been negligent in not warning the young woman or the family of the danger.

The *Tarasoff* case, undoubtedly familiar to all clinicians, addressed directly the question of what duty therapists owe to third parties in warning them of possible harmful behavior from their clients. The California Supreme Court first ruled that when a therapist determines that a patient is a serious danger to another person, the therapist has a **duty to warn** that individual (*Tarasoff v. Regents*, 1974). Two years later (*Tarasoff v. Regents*, 1976), the duty to warn was redefined as a **duty to protect**. That is, the therapist need not directly warn the individual, but he or she should take some steps to protect the individual from harm. Following the California court's decisions, many other states—either through court decisions or by statute—adopted rules similar to those announced in the *Tarasoff* case. By the early twenty-first century, half the states had done so (Quattrocchi & Schopp, 2005), and two states had explicitly rejected the doctrine (DeMatteo, 2005). Whether or not there exists a statutory duty to warn/protect, many practitioners have interpreted the "spirit" of *Tarasoff* as a standard of practice, believing that the clinician has a professional obligation to take some steps to protect an identifiable potential victim (e.g., Litwack & Schlesinger, 1999). In some states, the laws are broad, such as by requiring clinicians to protect even if information is derived from someone who is a relative of the patient, while in other states the clinician's obligations are no greater than meeting a standard of ordinary care and competence and/or are limited to cases where there is a clearly identifiable potential victim (Quattrocchi & Schopp, 2005).

Courts and legislatures that have adopted duty to warn/protect rules apparently believe that mental health professionals can predict with considerable accuracy who is or will be dangerous and who will not. The law has been relying on predictions of dangerousness for a long time, dating at least as far back as the sixteenth century (Morris & Miller, 1985). Yet, researchers and clinicians have long struggled both to define dangerousness and to predict its occurrence. After the *Tarasoff* case, dangerousness generated more controversy than even the insanity defense (Simon & Cockerham, 1977), and the standard that emerged from that case continues to be criticized in the legal and psychological literature (e.g., Quattrocchi & Schopp, 2005).

Today, as noted above, the psychological literature avoids the term "prediction of dangerousness" and has replaced it with "risk assessment." Clinicians maintain that, at best, they can offer probabilities based on known factors relating to the individual, often based on data obtained from large groups. (Recall our earlier discussion of the MacArthur Risk Assessment Study with civilly committed psychiatric patients.) Regardless of the terminology, it is clear that some attempt at assessing/predicting the likelihood that an individual will commit violence is warranted; what is not clear as a result of the *Tarasoff* case is the steps that should be taken by the clinician, who is also bound by confidentiality in treating his or her patient.

There is little doubt that a person who has been violent in the past and indicates by word or deed that he or she plans to do serious harm to others is—in common terms—dangerous. Someone who has committed a series of murders, mutilations, or rapes, and who attests to planning to do more of the same, is a dangerous individual. Even so, clinicians prefer to stay within the realm of probabilities, such as by calling the person a "high risk." If a person has no history of violence and threatens harm, however, the situation becomes more problematic. Likewise, if a person has been violent in the distant past but has shown no recent signs of violent behavior, the situation is again problematic. In these contexts, clinicians would have difficulty reaching a consensus on who is "dangerous" and who is not. This is why current thinking favors using a list of "risk factors" to determine the likelihood that aggressive behavior will occur. Risk assessment—particularly the assessment of violence risk—is perhaps the most complicated and controversial issue in the entire field of forensic psychology (Borum, 1996). Many researchers and scholars (e.g., Heilbrun et al., 2009; Steadman et al., 1993) consider it one of the most important issues in both criminal and civil matters worldwide. A variety of instruments are available for clinicians engaging in the risk assessment enterprise. As we will see, some of these instruments are chiefly actuarial in nature and may even be filled out just from case files, without an interview, although this is not generally recommended. Other instruments focus more on the interview process, but suggest questions to help the clinician to exercise structured clinical judgment.

Violence Risk Factors and Measures

For over 50 years, scholars have debated the respective merits of statistically based assessment of risk versus the more subjective, clinically based methods, sometimes referred to as unstructured clinical judgment (Douglas & Ogoff, 2003; McGowan, Horn, & Mellott, 2011; Meehl, 1954; Melton et al., 2007). The debate is also referred to as the actuarial versus clinical debate, and when put in these terms, clinical usually loses. For example, as Vitacco et al. (2012) noted, some studies have demonstrated that clinicians relying on unstructured clinical judgment were incorrect in their predictions of violence two out of three times.

Since the late 1990s, however, scholars and clinicians have been discussing **structured professional judgment (SPJ)**, sometimes referred to as structured clinical judgment. This is a combination of clinical and actuarial approaches. SPJ recommends that clinicians abide by established guidelines for conducting a careful assessment of whether an individual is likely to be violent (Douglas et al., 2014). Critical background information is gathered, including the presence of risk and protective factors for the individual being assessed. The clinician weighs the importance of these factors, considers the extent to which the person might be violent and under what circumstances, and also makes recommendations for preventing such violence. SPJ clearly is somewhat subjective in nature, but its proponents argue it is far superior to clinical judgment that is totally unstructured, and it may be a better alternative than actuarial assessment alone (Douglas et al., 2014).

Actuarial measures offer a compilation of risk or needs factors on which the individual is evaluated (e.g., past violence, age, criminal record, early onset of antisocial behavior). Although they are used extensively for assessing risk, they have shortcomings and may be overused. In addition, they should be administered by clinicians who are schooled in psychometric theory (Heilbrun, Marczyk, & De Matteo, 2002). A major advantage of actuarial measures is reduction in subjectivity, or clinical judgment based on hunches or past experience, because the risk factors addressed in the most validated actuarial instruments are objectively assessed. **Table 8-3** outlines weaknesses of unstructured, structured, and actuarial assessment.

Risk measures have gone through four generations of development (Campbell, French, & Gendreau, 2009). *First generation measures* were based on unstructured clinical judgment, with little or no statistical basis. *Second generation measures* offered a more standardized method of assessing risk, using primarily static (nonchanging) variables, such as age, gender, and criminal

---

TABLE 8-3 Chief Weaknesses of Three Approaches to Risk Assessment

Unstructured Clinical
- Highly subjective
- Based only on clinical experience; clinician may have little experience with type of offender
- Unknown as to which factors are taken into account
- Little support in empirical literature

Structured Professional Judgment
- Newer approach, not heavily researched compared with strictly actuarial
- Clinician encouraged to speculate on what conditions might lead to violence
- Subjectivity remains a factor

Actuarial approach
- Focuses on small number of risk factors, may ignore others
- Measures developed on specific populations (e.g., males) may not generalize to others (e.g., females)
- Restrictive definition of violence risk, cannot address duration, severity, or frequency
- Clinician unable to apply professional judgment, such as by weighing importance of risk factors

history. In the *third generation*, developers of risk assessment instruments introduced criminogenic needs into the equation; that is, a way of identifying factors that could respond to treatment, and thus change. Put another way, they identified needs that could be targeted in order to reduce risk of offending. Examples of criminogenic needs are antisocial attitudes or substance use. *Fourth generation instruments* are more attuned to the treatment or rehabilitation process; like third generation tools, they identify both static and dynamic risks and needs, but they also are integrated into the whole process of managing risk and choosing treatment interventions (see Campbell et al., 2009).

Research on the reliability and validity of these various instruments, particularly those of the latest generations, is ongoing. Whether they are equally effective with men and women is a question often posed in the literature. In general, however, as noted above, actuarial instruments have consistently outperformed clinical judgments. In a recent meta-analysis (Ægisdóttir et al., 2006), the researchers found that actuarial risk prediction was 17 percent better than its clinical counterpart. Nevertheless, for many reasons, many mental health practitioners have been and are reluctant to yield their professional judgments to actuarial models. Therefore, the measures that are based on SPJ have been welcomed by many clinicians "as a potentially reasonable, empirically defensible approach to risk assessment that did not have some of the perceived weaknesses of extant actuarial instruments or of unstructured clinical prediction" (Heilbrun et al., 2009, p. 336). (See **Table 8-4** for a representative list of actuarial and SPJ instruments.)

It must be stressed that—although we discuss risk assessment in this chapter— assessment of violence risk is not limited to the mentally disordered. In fact, as **Table 8-4** indicates, most assessment instruments were developed to assess possible violence in general criminal and delinquent populations, such as youth, domestic abusers, and sex offenders. Of the instruments in the table, only the COVR was developed on a population of psychiatric patients. And it must be stressed, again, that the mentally disordered, as a group, are not dangerous. Overall, the best predictor of future behavior is *past behavior*, but even past behavior will not necessarily be repeated. The best predictor of criminal behavior is a history of criminal behavior, and past violence will suggest a probability of future violence. A history of criminal behavior is the best predictor of criminal recidivism regardless of whether the offender is mentally disordered or normal (Bonta, Law, & Hanson, 1998). But again, people change. Furthermore, the more frequently the behavior has occurred in a variety of situations, the more accurate will be the predictions. Someone who frequently manifests violence across many different situations will be far easier to predict than a person who is only occasionally violent in some situations.

Since the 1990s, researchers have made considerable strides in the ability to identify more factors that are associated with violence. In addition to criminal history, recent research strongly indicates that other predictors of criminal recidivism (not limited to violence) include some combination of age, juvenile delinquency, and substance abuse (Andrews & Bonta, 1994; Bonta et al., 1998; Gendreau, Little, & Goggin, 1996). However, researchers have also warned that risk factors are unique for each individual, and that no one factor will necessarily predict violence or serious antisocial behavior in any one individual.

TABLE 8-4 Representative Actuarial and SPJ Assessment Instruments

Examples of Actuarial Risk Assessment Instruments

COVR (Classification of Violence Risk) (Monahan et al., 2005)

LSI-R (Level of Service Inventory—Revised) (Andrews & Bonta, 1995)

ODARA (Ontario Domestic Assault Risk Assessment (Hilton et al., 2008)

SORAG (Sex Offender Risk Appraisal Guide) (Quinsey et al., 2006)

Examples of Structured Professional Judgment Instruments

ERASOR (Estimate of Risk of Adolescent Sexual Offense Recidivism) (Worling & Curwen, 2001)

HCR-20 Version 2 (Historical-Clinical-Risk Management-20) (Webster, Douglas, Eaves, & Hart, 1997)

SARA (Spousal Assault Risk Assessment Guide) (Kropp et al., 1998)

SAVRY (Structured Assessment of Violence Risk among Youth) (Borum et al., 2006)

SUMMARY AND CONCLUSIONS

In this chapter, we focused on the relationship between mentally disordered individuals and crime. In order to understand this relationship, we must go beyond labels, which do not explain why someone behaves in a certain way.

Mental illness (or mental disorder) is a disorder or disease of the mind that interferes substantially with a person's ability to cope with life on a daily basis. Although it deprives someone of freedom of choice, this deprivation is rarely total. As noted in the chapter, even severely disordered individuals can have some decision-making ability. Mental illness should be distinguished from intellectual disability. The former can be treated, cured, or held in remission; the latter cannot, although intellectually disabled individuals can be taught to perform many tasks and should be supported in their desires to be self-sufficient.

We reviewed diagnostic categories that are most often associated with criminal behavior. For example, persons accused of crime may introduce these diagnoses to support an insanity defense. The main categories discussed were schizophrenic and other psychotic disorders, bipolar disorders, major depression, and APD. Schizophrenic and other psychotic disorders and bipolar disorders represent the most concern with respect to serious crime, but even these disorders do not cause criminal behavior. The great majority of individuals with these disorders do not commit crime. Likewise, major depression does not generally lead to criminal activity, though it has been demonstrated in exceptional, high-profile cases like mass murders, workplace violence, or the killing of one's own children. APD is a catch-all diagnosis often placed on chronic offenders. Most courts today do not accept APD to support an insanity defense. The juvenile equivalent of APD is conduct disorder, and it is a frequent diagnosis of adolescents held in detention and treatment facilities.

The chapter also reviewed the legal constructs of competency and insanity. Criminal defendants are found incompetent if they are so disordered or impaired that they cannot understand the proceedings or help their attorneys in their own defense. Adjudicative competence is relevant to a wide range of proceedings, including a variety of pretrial hearings and the trial itself, as well as the sentencing stage and beyond. The law says that an incompetent defendant is not truly present; therefore, before proceeding with prosecution, he or she must be rendered competent. As we noted, the common approach with incompetent defendants is to hospitalize them for treatment until they attain competency; alternatively, the case against them is dismissed, particularly if the crime is not serious. A major issue today relating to incompetent defendants is the extent to which they can be medicated against their will. Courts have generally ruled that when the government has a strong interest in bringing the defendant to trial—such as in a serious crime—involuntary medication will be allowed.

Although it is the competency issue that affects the greatest number of defendants, it is the insanity issue that most intrigues the public. The truly insane individual is not responsible for his or her crime. Successful insanity defenses are rare, but even when they occur, they are no bargain. Persons found NGRI are typically institutionalized, often for longer periods of time than they would have served in prison. We reviewed the various standards for establishing insanity, including the M'Naghten (right/wrong) Rule, the ALI/Brawner Rule, and the Durham Rule (product test), and Insanity Defense Reform Act (IDRA) standard, which is applied in federal courts. Since the 1980s, largely as a result of the acquittal of John Hinckley, many states and the federal government have passed more restrictive insanity statutes, making it even more difficult for defendants to be absolved of criminal responsibility. Some states also have adopted a "guilty but mentally ill" verdict form, which allows a judge or jury to find a defendant guilty, but also acknowledges that he or she needs treatment. Research indicates, though, that the treatment implied in GBMI statutes is rarely provided in correctional facilities.

We also discussed "special defenses" that are sometimes raised in criminal cases, either to absolve a defendant completely or to support a defense of diminished capacity: PTSD, dissociative identity disorder (DID; formerly called multiple personality disorder), and dissociative amnesia. These conditions also may be taken into account in plea bargaining or at sentencing.

Individuals with mental disorders as a group are no more likely than the general population to commit crimes, including violent crimes. If we include the category APD, the likelihood of committing crime increases somewhat. In addition, recent research documents that the subgroup of *currently* mentally disordered male patients, particularly with schizophrenic diagnoses, and who have a *history of violence*, does demonstrate more violence than nondisordered members in the general population.

The visibility of the mentally disordered, as well as publicity given to the occasional sensational case in which a severely disordered individual kills a stranger, has led to questions about dangerousness and our ability to predict it. When the criminal justice system deals with a defendant charged with a violent crime or an offender convicted of one, whether or not the individual is disordered, the system wants to know if he or she is dangerous. For many years, mental health practitioners tried to answer this question with little success. Traditionally, clinicians overestimated the potential violence of this population, engendering debate about the proper criteria for assessing dangerousness.

Recently, this enterprise has shifted to "risk assessment." Rather than trying to predict whether someone is dangerous and will commit a violent act, the clinician is now more likely to identify risk factors that may make it *more likely* that he or she will do so. In other words, the prediction of dangerousness has been transformed to an *assessment of the probability* that violence or other serious offending will occur in the future. Such assessments are made through unstructured clinical judgment, structured professional judgment, or actuarial measures. Strengths and weaknesses of each of these three methods were discussed.

Key Concepts

Adjudicative competence
Amnesia
Antisocial personality disorder (APD)
Battered woman syndrome
Brawner Rule
Caveat paragraph
Competency to stand trial
Conduct disorder
Delusional disorder
Diagnostic and Statistical Manual of Mental Disorders (DSM)
Dissociated state
Dissociative identity disorder (DID) (formerly, multiple personality disorder)
Durham Rule
Duty to protect

Duty to warn
Guilty but mentally ill (GBMI)
Hallucinations
Iatrogenic
Incompetent to stand trial (IST)
Insanity defense
Insanity Defense Reform Act of 1984 (IDRA)
Intellectual disability
Major depressive disorder
Mental illness or mental disorder
M'Naghten Rule (right and wrong test)
Not guilty by reason of insanity (NGRI)
Posttraumatic stress disorder (PTSD)
Schizophrenia
Structured professional judgment (SPJ)
Volitional prong

Review Questions

1. Thoroughly explain the difference between incompetency to stand trial and insanity.
2. What is meant by a "duty to warn" and a "duty to protect"? And to whom does it pertain?
3. What are the conditions under which mentally disordered people may become violent or seriously criminal?
4. Briefly describe four legal standards for insanity and their requirements.
5. Identify and include symptoms of the four diagnostic categories most relevant to criminal behavior.
6. What are guilty but mentally ill statutes? Why do many legal scholars oppose them?
7. Give an example of iatrogenic effects in counseling or psychotherapy.
8. Describe fully and evaluate any three of the unique defenses discussed in the chapter.

9

Homicide, Assault, and Intimate Partner and Family Violence

CHAPTER OBJECTIVES

- Emphasize that criminal homicide is rare compared with other violent offenses.
- Define criminal homicide, negligent manslaughter, and aggravated assault.
- Review the demographics of homicide victims and offenders.
- Review the impact of weapons on crime.
- Introduce a typology of homicide.
- Review what we know about juvenile murderers and their victims.
- Discuss the dynamics of intimate partner violence (IPV).
- Present the research on family violence, its dynamics, and its causes.
- Summarize stereotypical child abduction data.
- Review research on child and elderly abuse.

If the news and entertainment media are reasonably decent barometers of human interest, homicidal violence must be one of Western civilization's most fascinating subjects and, along with sex, the most marketable. Usually, the more bizarre, senseless, or heinous the murder, the more extensive news coverage it receives, followed shortly thereafter by books, television specials, and movies. Unusual mass murders, serial murders, and so-called motiveless killings attract special interest. Yet, on a national level, criminal homicide consistently accounts for only about 1 or 2 percent of all violent crimes reported in the FBI's Uniform Crime Reports (UCR).

As noted at the beginning of this text, homicide is the killing of a human being by another human being. It is not *criminal* homicide if it is justified or excused. Medical examiners often rule a death a homicide, but all homicides are not crimes. However, in this chapter, including the title, we often use the word without the adjective, as do many researchers and statisticians. Thus, when we learn from crime statistics that the number of homicides reached an all-time high of 24,503 in 1991 and then fell quickly to 15,522 in 1999 (Cooper & Smith, 2011), we are referring to criminal homicides. Over the past 15 years, the number of criminal homicides (murder and nonnegligent manslaughter) has continued to decline. A total of 14,196 such homicides were reported in 2013 (Federal Bureau of Investigation, 2014a), representing a murder rate of 4.5 victims per 100,000 population. In the same year, an estimated 1,163,146 violent offenses were reported to law enforcement agencies, representing an estimated 367.9 violent crimes per 100,000 inhabitants. If we consider its percentage distribution among all violent crimes, then criminal homicide represents a minute percent of the total (see **Figure 9-1**).

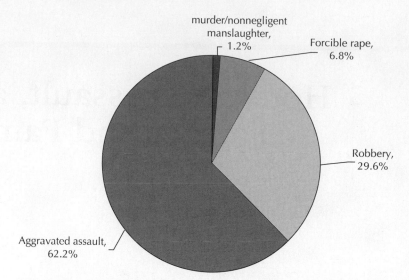

FIGURE 9-1 Violent Crime Distribution in the United States, 2013.
Source: Federal Bureau of Investigation (2014a).

The majority of criminal homicides are cleared by the arrest of one or more individuals, and the majority involve friends, spouses, or acquaintances killing friends, spouses, or acquaintances. During 2013, for example, the relationship between the victims and the perpetrators was known in 54.5 percent of all of the homicides. Within those known relationships, 24.9 percent of the victims were killed by family members and 59.9 percent of the victims were killed by someone else they knew (e.g., neighbors, boyfriends, friends) (Federal Bureau of Investigation, 2014a). This does not make them less serious. It is simply a reminder that homicidal attacks by strangers are not common.

From a psychological perspective, the disproportionate amount of attention paid to criminal homicides may be explained in a variety of ways. Obviously, this is a highly serious crime, with death being the ultimate victimization. However, another reason for the attention may be related to our fascination with the mysterious and the macabre. We crave science fiction, tales of terror, even haunted houses. Perhaps we need a certain amount of excitement and arousal to prevent our lives from becoming too mundane and boring. Psychologists have long known that novelty produces arousal and excitement and breaks monotony (Berlyne, 1960). This human need for stimulation and excitement is greater in some people (extraverts) than others (introverts) (Eysenck, 1967)—and it may partly explain the appeal of roller coasters, skydiving, race car driving, bungee jumping, and gambling. Stimulation seekers also may enjoy films featuring vampires, werewolves, and heavy violence—or these vicarious pleasures might be enjoyed by those not wishing to seek out this type of excitement directly. In any case, tales of murder, fictional or not, are captivating. For the family that has been touched by murder, however, this vicarious response on the part of others is difficult to understand and to accept.

The marketability of murder may also be explained by curiosity or exploratory behavior, which is very closely related to excitement and arousal. One purpose of curiosity is to allow organisms to adjust to their environments (Butler, 1954). An individual or an organism explores a new situation to satisfy this curiosity—which is theorized to be a physiological drive state—and in the process of discovering information, adapts to the new situation. Curiosity about murder might help us prepare for the possibility that a similar event could happen to us. Reading about bizarre, seemingly irrational homicides may help us to identify danger signals. Information about the incident gives clues about who murders, who gets murdered, and under what circumstances. To some extent, we can take preventive measures, even though there is no guarantee that such measures will keep us safe. Obviously, in some situations, and particularly in the case of mass murders, no preventive measures on the part of the victims could have been taken. Preventive measures on the part of society are another matter, and will be addressed in the chapter.

Reactions to depictions of violence—experienced vicariously—may be regarded as adaptive or functional. Extensive exposure to violence also has a dysfunctional side, however. Specifically, it may immunize us from the horror of violence. Many social commentators have advanced cogent arguments that Western civilization has become conditioned or jaded to cruelty and inhumane behavior and that people are desensitized to human suffering. In addition, the constant attention that the news media and politicians give to violence also makes it seem more widespread and frequent than it really is. This phenomenon is called the **availability heuristic** by social psychologists. Heuristics refer to cognitive shortcuts that people use to make quick inferences about their world. When the news media continually show graphic and frightening accounts of violence, people are likely to incorporate these vivid details into cognitive shorthand and have them readily *available* for future reference. When they think of violence at a later time, they remember the most frequently seen and horrific accounts, increasing their fear of violent crime and exaggerating its incidence in their minds. Their availability heuristic, based on media reports, also creates the impression that violence is much more common than it really is.

To speculate about why we are attracted to accounts of murder and violence, or to wonder about the effects of repeated exposure, may not seem to address the main focus of this chapter, which is the violent offender. Speculation becomes relevant, however, when we shift the focus to the individual who is part of a society that seems to have an inordinate need to seek out stimulation or to know details of crimes. When that individual is insensitive to suffering and begins to create his or her own excitement by torturing and murdering, we have a social problem. Psychology, as we will see in this chapter, can offer some suggestions for understanding and solving this problem.

After defining our terms, we examine situational and dispositional factors that occur consistently in homicide and aggravated assault, beginning with statistical data on their incidence and prevalence and their demographic correlates. Thus far in the text, theoretical issues and potential causes of crime have been introduced with minimum application to specific offenses. Beginning here and throughout the remainder of the book, we interweave the research and concepts previously outlined with specific categories of criminal behavior. In this chapter, we focus on criminal homicide and intimate partner and family violence.

DEFINITIONS

In gathering statistics, criminologists separate aggravated assault and homicide, but in explaining these crimes or looking for causes, they often study them together, primarily because they view many aggravated assaults as failed homicide attempts (Doerner, 1988; Doerner & Speir, 1986). Dunn (1976) challenged this practice, noting that the aggravated assault rate was at least 20 times that of homicide. "Given this disparity in rates, it is difficult to imagine that even one-quarter of all aggravated assaults were attempted homicides or would have been homicides except for the intervention of medical care" (Dunn, 1976, p. 10). Therefore, it may be unwarranted to consider aggravated assault as being in the same league as homicide; the two may differ in important variables, including the motives of the perpetrator. A purist, therefore, would try to maintain an aggravated assault–homicide distinction. And, of course, the distinctions are maintained in crime statistics, as well as in criminal law.

Nevertheless, from a psychological perspective it is often difficult to separate aggravated assault from criminal homicide. First, much of the relevant research on offender *characteristics* collapses the categories into one, under the rationale that people who kill usually (but not invariably) have a history of assaultive behavior. Second, the two types of behavior are comparable in many ways because at their core they represent human aggression, the main focus of Chapter 5. On the other hand, certain kinds of homicide offenders—such as juvenile murderers and serial and mass murderers—have distinctive characteristics. Often, though, in the more typical violent crime situation, the weapon used or the quality of medical care available determines the final outcome. The high-powered bullet, as an obvious example, is in most cases far more lethal than the knife, and rapid response to an assault can save a life. A stabbing or even a beating may represent behavior similar to that displayed in homicide with a small firearm. In law, the distinctions between murder and aggravated assault are crucial; in psychology, with exceptions like those mentioned above, they are less so. The individual is displaying highly aggressive behavior in either situation.

Criminal Homicide

Criminal homicide is causing the death of another person without legal justification or excuse. Legally, it is usually divided into two categories: **murder** and **nonnegligent manslaughter**. The term "murder" is reserved for the "unlawful killing of one human being by another with malice aforethought, either expressed or implied" (Black, 1990, p. 1019). "Malice aforethought" refers to premeditation, or the mental state of a person who thinks ahead, plans, and voluntarily causes the death of another, without legal excuse or justification. However, "premeditation" can occur in a very short period of time (even a minute); it does not require weeks of planning.

Homicide laws in most states have additional gradations or degrees. In many jurisdictions, murder is divided into two degrees, a statutory provision that allows courts to impose a more severe penalty for some murders than others. The degree system was once a useful and meaningful method of distinguishing between murder that was punishable by death and that which was not (Gardner, 1985). In more recent times, the distinctions between the degrees have been more blurred. Broadly, state statutes generally posit that murder of the first degree is a homicide that was committed with particularly vicious, willful, deliberate, and premeditated intent. The alleged shooter in the deaths of three Arab-American students in North Carolina in early 2015 was charged with first-degree murder. Murder of the second degree is characterized by the intentional and unlawful killing of another but without the type of malice and premeditation required for first-degree murder. In Baltimore in 2015, a man died after being arrested and transported in a police van. The autopsy showed he had suffered a high energy injury to his neck and spine, and the medical examiner ruled the death a homicide. The officer driving the van was charged with "depraved heart" second degree murder. Other officers in the incident received different charges. Examples of second-degree murder also include "crimes of passion," such as an enraged father who strangles the drunken driver who just killed his son. Although there was no premeditation, the angry father still wanted to kill him. In some jurisdictions, the father would be charged with nonnegligent manslaughter rather than second degree murder.

The *Uniform Crime Reports* include both murder (first and second degree) and nonnegligent manslaughter under the rubric criminal homicide for reporting purposes. Deaths of others that occur as a result of negligence (negligent manslaughter) are not included. The essential difference between murder and nonnegligent manslaughter is that malice aforethought must be present for murder, whereas it must be absent for nonnegligent manslaughter. However, intent to kill is still needed.

Negligent manslaughter—also referred to as involuntary manslaughter—is killing another as a result of recklessness or culpable negligence. Although there is no intent to kill, the law says you should have known that your actions could result in the death of another person. For example, a man who recklessly waves a gun around in jest, and the gun discharges and kills someone, is still responsible for that person's death. In 2015, a man who punched a soccer referee in the neck during an adult league game pleaded guilty to involuntary manslaughter—the referee died two days after the incident. Although the man did not intend to kill the referee, his reckless behavior still caused the death.

The person charged with murder or with nonnegligent manslaughter intended that his victim die. In the case of nonnegligent manslaughter, the *original intent* may not have been to kill the victim. However, the person became so agitated and emotionally upset in a particular situation that he or she lost partial control of his or her self-regulatory system. In some states, nonnegligent manslaughter would be similar to second-degree murder. Indeed, in the referee example above, the individual responsible for the death was first charged with second-degree murder, but as noted he eventually pled guilty to involuntary manslaughter.

As apparent from the above examples, homicide law is complex. Its broad parameters in the United States are highly similar to the laws of homicide found in other countries and cultures (Morawetz, 2002). This similarity is largely because maintaining some semblance of social order in any given society depends greatly on controlling reckless and widespread homicide. As pointed out by Morawetz (2002), "Homicide law ... responds to a universal need to identify, deter, and punish intentional and reckless killings, a need that crosses borders. We all fear annihilation" (p. 400).

In line with UCR classifications, we combine both murder and nonnegligent manslaughter under the general term "criminal homicide" in this chapter, and as noted above we often refer simply to homicide. We are not concerned with suicides, accidental deaths, negligent manslaughter, or homicides that are justified or excused (e.g., in defense of one's life). In other words, from a psychological point of view, these are not illustrative of the aggressive behavior we are concerned about in this chapter. A topic that we do not address is use of excessive force, including lethal force, by law enforcement officers and other agents of government (e.g., prison correction officers). Nor do we address aggression and violence carried out across the globe, allegedly in the interest of national security. Both available statistics and psychological research are lacking on this topic, but anecdotal and media accounts make it clear that such violence is a troubling contemporary social problem.

Aggravated Assault

In most jurisdictions, **assault** is the intentional inflicting of bodily injury on another person, or the attempt to inflict such injury. It is important to qualify this definition, because in past years, assault and battery were considered two discrete crimes: state laws treated the *threat* of physical injury as an assault, and the completed act of physical contact or unlawful touching as battery. Although many states have gotten away from distinguishing the two, in some jurisdictions assault is still the threat of injury, while the actual contact is battery. Furthermore, all jurisdictions continue to recognize some distinction of assault and battery, such as in their definitions of mayhem, malicious wounding, or felonious assault (Bacigal, 2002). For our purposes, we adopt the definitions used in the UCR.

An assault or attack becomes **aggravated assault** when the purpose is to inflict serious bodily injury. Aggravated assault is often accompanied by the use of a deadly or dangerous weapon, such as a gun, knife, axe, or other sharp or blunt instrument. However, the use of one's fists can also consist of aggravated assault. In UCR statistics, even if no actual injury occurs, the crime is counted as an aggravated assault (attempted assault) if a weapon is displayed or threatened. Simple assault is the unlawful, intentional inflicting of less than serious bodily injury without a deadly or dangerous weapon, or the attempt to inflict such bodily injury, again without a deadly or dangerous weapon. Again, though, fists can become a deadly weapon; thus, if a victim is seriously assaulted in this way, the perpetrator will likely be charged with aggravated assault.

Aggravated assault will be illustrated in the sections of the chapter that focus on intimate partner violence (IPV) and family violence—this is often where it occurs. The beginning sections of this chapter will focus on homicide, particularly homicide dealing with a single offender killing one person. Multiple murders (e.g., mass and serial killings) will be covered in Chapter 10. We begin with briefly covering the demographics of homicide offenders and then proceed to the psychological characteristics of people who kill. The demographic characteristics most commonly studied in homicide research are race or ethnic origin, gender, social class, and the victim–offender relationship.

DEMOGRAPHIC AND OTHER FACTORS OF HOMICIDE

Researchers have found that a variety of demographic factors are strongly associated, or correlated, with criminal homicide. These factors may be characteristics of the offenders or the victims. We must emphasize, though, that the factors reported in the literature often refer to *arrests* for murder or nonnegligent manslaughter. Although the minimum standard for an arrest is probable cause that the individual committed a crime or is about to commit a crime, arrests do not necessarily result in conviction, or a finding of guilt. This is an important caveat whenever we consider the official police data which are cited in numerous research studies. As we discuss the demographics of homicide, readers should keep in mind the distinctions between arrests, convictions, and victimizations. In addition to demographic factors, information is often obtained on circumstances of homicide (e.g., during the commission of a felony), relationship between offenders and victims, and the use of weapons, as will be described below.

Race/Ethnicity

One of the most consistent findings reported in the criminology literature is that African Americans in the United States are involved in criminal homicide—both as offenders and victims—at a rate that significantly exceeds their numbers in the general population. Although African Americans make up about 13 percent of the U.S. population, they accounted for approximately 54 percent of all arrests for homicide in 2013 (Federal Bureau of Investigation, 2014a). The reported homicide offending rate for blacks is nearly eight times higher than the rate for whites (Cooper & Smith, 2011). The victimization rate for blacks is six times higher than the rate for whites (Cooper & Smith, 2011).

The disproportionate representation of African Americans in the arrest and conviction data for homicide probably reflects social inequities, such as lack of employment or educational opportunities and racial oppression in its many forms. There is no evidence to suggest that a racial biological or neuropsychological predisposition plays a role in the consistently reported differences in violence rates over the years.

Furthermore, much more research needs to be done on the relationship between racial/ethnic minorities and crime. As noted in Chapter 1, the UCR has only recently begun to distinguish among racial and ethnic groups, and police are discouraged from assuming a particular race or ethnicity. Furthermore, using rigid categories such as black, Latino/Hispanic, Asian, Native Americans, and white represents an oversimplification of the multiethnic and multicultural mixtures across the nation. Cultures and subcultures are highly complex and multidimensional, and meaningful research on the ethnic/minority differences in violence requires a knowledgeable awareness of and sensitivity to this complexity.

Gender

The relationship between homicide and gender is also robust, but once again caution is urged. The gender or sex binary (male–female; man–woman) can no longer be applied to all individuals, because there is increasing evidence of a gender continuum, and groups that have been thus far ignored in crime or victimization statistics (e.g., transgender and transitioning individuals) are asking for more recognition. Official data, and the vast majority of research studies, report male/female statistics, but an unknown number of individuals would not list themselves as either, or would list themselves the opposite of what they are assumed to be. On some college campuses today, for example, students are asked which pronoun should apply to them; it is rare, however, for police to ask persons arrested if they are male or female. We might assume that a low prevalence of individuals who are other than male or female would mean little significant difference in national statistics, but we might also be wrong in this assumption. The Human Rights Campaign reported that 14 transgender women were murdered in 2014—it is assumed that they were counted as women in the official statistics, but we do not know that for sure. Furthermore, we also do not know, *from official data*, the number of transgender individuals who were victims of aggravated assault or other violent offenses.

UCR data consistently reveal that the annual arrest rates for murder run about 90 percent male and 10 percent female (Federal Bureau of Investigation, 2014a). Males represent 78 percent of homicide victims and 90 percent of offenders (Cooper & Smith, 2011; Federal Bureau of Investigation, 2014a). Males accounted for 80 percent of persons arrested for all violent crime in

2013. Although most murders are intraracial (whites kill whites, blacks kill blacks), stranger homicides are more likely to cross racial lines (about 27%). Again, however, given the rich racial and ethnic makeup of contemporary society, these data might not be that significant.

Age

With monotonous regularity, national statistics from all sources continue to underscore the fact that about half of all those arrested for violent crime are between the ages of 20 and 29. Although this statistic refers to all violent crimes, it applies specifically to criminal homicide as well. Approximately one-third of murder victims and almost half of the offenders are under age 25 (Cooper & Smith, 2011; Federal Bureau of Investigation, 2014a).

Socioeconomic Status

Research has consistently shown that children born into an adverse neighborhood and disadvantaged family context are at higher risk for violence, either as offenders or victims, than are children raised in a more propitious environment. As discussed in Chapter 3, poverty places children at risk for violence because of lack of resources, social support, and opportunity, a reality that highlights the crucial importance of social programs. Some researchers have observed that conditions of poverty make it difficult for parents or caregivers to avoid harsh and inconsistent discipline for their young children (Dodge, Greenberg, et al., 2008). Nonetheless, as a general principle, it is important to remember that warm, supportive parenting exists across all social classes. In addition, as we learned in earlier chapters, parenting or caretaking itself is not the only factor to take into account in trying to explain violence. It takes an accumulation of risk factors to fully explain violence. Simplistic explanations usually fall far short of the true picture.

Circumstances

Recent data indicate that interpersonal arguments (including those preceding family violence) are the most frequently cited circumstances for murder (Cooper & Smith, 2011; Federal Bureau of Investigation, 2014a). Second are murders that occur in the process of committing felonies such as forcible rape, robbery, burglary, arson, or drug trafficking (Federal Bureau of Investigation, 2008, 2014a). Thirty-three percent involved other types of circumstances—some also involving felonies—such as brawls, sniper attacks, or juvenile and gang killings (see **Table 9-1** for recent statistics on circumstances accompanying murder).

Weapons

Nationwide data indicate that firearms were used in approximately 69 percent of all homicides in 2013, while knives or cutting instruments were used in less than 12 percent of the homicides (Federal Bureau of Investigation, 2014a). Approximately 68 percent of firearm homicides were committed with handguns, 4 percent with shotguns, 3 percent with rifles, 2 percent with "other" guns, and 23 percent with unspecified firearms.

About every 14 minutes, someone in America dies from a gunshot wound, including suicides. Some deaths are the result of tragic unintentional shootings, as when two children are playing with a loaded weapon. Some intentional shootings may be justified, as when a law enforcement officer uses lethal force to kill an armed suspect, or they may be excused, as when a person kills another in self-defense. These are anecdotes, but they are repeated in many communities across the nation. Despite the fact that not all of these are criminal homicides, it is clear that guns are associated with many deaths.

Guns do not *cause* violent crime, but accessibility of guns facilitates it. Hepburn and Hemenway (2004) found that where there are higher levels of gun ownership, homicides are substantially higher. Of course, where homicides are higher, individuals may be more likely to own guns for protection, and it is understandable that they wish to do this. Furthermore, many people—particularly in more rural areas—own guns for sport, and they clearly have a right to these

TABLE 9-1	Murder Circumstances by Victim's Gender, 2013			
Circumstances	Total Murder Victims	Male	Female	Unknown
Total	**12,253**	**9,523**	**2,707**	**23**
Felony-type total	1,909	1,563	345	1
Rape	20	3	17	0
Robbery	686	605	81	0
Burglary	94	71	23	0
Larceny-theft	18	12	4	0
Motor vehicle theft	27	17	10	0
Arson	37	23	14	0
Prostitution	13	11	2	0
Other sex offenses	9	2	7	0
Narcotic drug laws	386	352	34	0
Gambling	7	6	1	0
Other—not specified	614	461	152	1
Suspected felony type	122	82	40	0
Other than felony-type total	5,782	4,293	1,485	4
Romantic triangle	69	50	19	0
Child killed by babysitter	30	20	10	0
Brawl due to influence of alcohol	93	74	19	0
Brawl due to influence of narcotics	59	42	17	0
Argument over money or property	133	110	23	0
Other arguments	2,889	2,003	885	1
Gangland killings	138	128	10	0
Juvenile gang killings	584	566	18	0
Institutional killings	15	15	0	0
Sniper attack	6	6	0	0
Other—not specified	1,766	1,279	484	3
Unknown	4,440	3,585	837	18

Source: Federal Bureau of Investigation (2014a). Crime in the United States 2013: Uniform Crime Reports. Washington, DC: U.S. Department of Justice.

weapons. It cannot be denied, however, that the availability of firearms is a major reason that homicides occur. In addition, a number of jurisdictions now have "open carry" laws—which allow individuals with registered guns and proper permits to carry their weapons in public places; this is even allowed on some college campuses.

Recall the **weapons effect** discussed in Chapter 5, where the mere sight of an aggressive stimulus can influence behavior. Because weapons are associated with violence, the visible presence of a handgun, a club, or a knife automatically brings violence-related thoughts (cognitions) to mind. The classic study of Berkowitz and LePage (1967) was among the first experiments to

CONTEMPORARY ISSUES

BOX 9-1   Guns, Crime, and Cumulative Risk

Approximately 250 million guns are in private hands in the United States, with about one-third being handguns (Cook, Cukier, & Krause, 2009). In addition, the underground gun market in the United States is a major source of supply to criminals and gangs, including supplying guns to civilians in foreign nations (Cook et al., 2009). At last count, about 10 percent of the millions of firearms produced in the United States were illegally exported.

Between the years 2007 and 2013, an average of 16.4 mass shootings occurred in the United States. (This topic will be covered again in Chapter 10.) In the typical mass murder situation, the perpetrator had stockpiled a variety of weapons, which were found either at the scene of the crime or in the shooter's home or car. Mass murders at Sandy Hook School in 2012, Mother Emanuel Church in 2015, and Umpqua Community College (UCC), also in 2015, are but three illustrations. In the UCC case, for example, it was reported that six weapons were uncovered at the scene and another eight in the perpetrator's home. All the weapons were apparently purchased legally, either by the shooter or by a relative or friend.

Many guns also are in the hands of juveniles. It is a federal offense for any person to sell or transfer a handgun to a person under age 18; it is also a federal crime for a juvenile to possess handgun ammunition. Many states have similar laws. According to 2013 UCR data, 15 percent of the total arrests for the illegal carrying or possession of a firearm were juveniles (under age 18), and 5 percent of the total arrestees were under age 15 (Federal Bureau of Investigation, 2014a). Thirty percent were under age 21.

Restrictions aside, there are obviously multiple ways for juveniles to obtain firearms, and they report being able to do so with ease. For example, gangs often have a "community gun" well hidden on the street but easily accessible to gang members if needed. Some juveniles (about 28%) ask others, such as older siblings or friends, to buy guns for them (Braga & Kennedy, 2001). Juveniles also obtain guns through corrupt licensed dealers, unregulated dealers, gun shows, organized gun rings and fences, and criminal firearms trafficking (Braga & Kennedy, 2001). Theft is also an important source of firearms for juveniles (Wilkinson et al., 2009).

It is estimated that about 500,000 guns are stolen each year, mostly from residences (Braga & Kennedy, 2001; Kleck,

2009). It is further estimated that about 70 percent of the firearms used by offenders (adult and juvenile combined) are obtained through theft (Kleck, 2009; Wright & Rossi, 1994). And, of course, many children have access to weapons that are in their own homes. In the fall of 2015, an 11-year-old boy was charged with murder in the first degree after he killed an 8-year-old girl with a shotgun fired from a window in his home. In other instances, tragic accidents have occurred as a result of children playing with guns.

Gun carrying is far more prevalent in high-poverty neighborhoods (Allen & Lo, 2012; Burgason, Thomas, & Berthelot, 2014; Spano & Bolland, 2013). In addition, it comes as no surprise that drug trafficking youths are far more likely to carry firearms (Allen & Lo, 2012).

Available data (e.g., Decker, Pennel, & Caldwell, 1997; Wilkinson et al., 2009) suggest that more than two-thirds of juveniles who carry weapons say they do so primarily for self-protection. However, a study by Spano, Pridemore, and Bolland (2012) suggests that gun carrying by youths may involve more than simply self-protection. It encompasses myriad factors, such as a lack of dispute settlement skills, being a victim or witnessing violence directed at others, intimidation and control, modeling, status seeking, lack of opportunity, and following a peer street code. In other words, youth gun carrying involves a large collection of cumulative risk factors.

Questions for Discussion

1. The U.S. Supreme Court has interpreted the Second Amendment's right to bear arms as an individual right, at least for protection in one's home (*District of Columbia v. Heller*, 2008). However, governments can place restrictions on ownership or regulate sales and purchases. Discuss and evaluate the various restrictions that have been proposed or placed on gun ownership, gun use, and gun carrying.

2. Respond to the still-often-heard statement, "Guns don't kill people; people do."

3. What is meant by the statement that youth gun carrying involves a collection of cumulative risk factors? How is it relevant to our discussion of criminal behavior thus far?

provide evidence of a strong link between aggressive thoughts engendered by the presence of a weapon and subsequent aggressive behavior. Hepburn and Hemenway's discovery that a high number of available weapons within a neighborhood promote more aggression in a vicious circle of violence may be partially due to the widespread presence of aggressive stimuli. (See **Box 9-1** for additional discussion of guns and crime.)

PSYCHOLOGICAL ASPECTS OF CRIMINAL HOMICIDE

The psychology of criminal homicide is a very complicated subject. There is no universal set of offenders who present developmental risk factors or personality characteristics which predict that they are particularly prone to commit murder or nonnegligent manslaughter. These crimes are multidetermined and are associated with many risk factors, as are other crimes. As we learned in earlier chapters, the risk factors may be social, psychosocial, or even neurobiological in nature. They include early onset of antisocial behavior, peer delinquency, peer rejection or victimization, early indications of conduct disorder, parental neglect or abuse, growing up in violent families and neighborhoods, and even birth complications, to name but a few. To a large extent, criminal homicide—hereafter referred to simply as homicide or murder—is also situation specific. That is, it depends on a number of things, including the availability of a weapon, the amount of alcohol consumption, the nature of the provocation (if provocation is involved), the circumstances, the motivation, and the emotional and mental state of the offender at the time.

Often, a typology is developed to organize complex phenomenon. The term **typology** refers to a particular system for classifying personality, motivations, or other behavioral patterns. Usually the typology is used to organize a wide assortment of factors or variables into a more manageable set of brief descriptions. A typology is not perfect and does not always reflect reality exactly, but it does help in understanding an enormously complex phenomenon such as homicide. Although there have been a number of other homicide typologies developed in an effort to reduce the complexity of homicide, most have focused on the more sensational, "high class" of murderers known as serial or mass killers. Very few typologies or classification systems have been developed on the "underclass" of homicide offenders—the more mundane, single homicide offender, which is the focus of this chapter. One meaningful exception has been the four distinct categories generated by Roberts, Zgoba, and Shahidullah (2007), who analyzed the patterns and motivations of 336 homicide offenders known to the New Jersey Department of Corrections. The four classifications are as follows:

1. Offenders who committed a homicide that was precipitated by a general altercation or argument, such as an argument over money or property, or verbal disputes that escalate into fight. Escalation of aggression refers to progressive increases of hostile or destructive behavior, often to the point of violence. It often stems from the need to reciprocate after being provoked by aggressive behavior from another person. Roberts et al. (2007) discovered that the altercation or argument was often over an exceedingly small amount of money (such as $4) or insignificant value of property (such as a bike). This category represented the largest group, accounting for 45 percent of the total homicide offenders. It is likely that this is the largest group that would be found in other jurisdictions as well.

2. Offenders who committed a homicide during the commission of a felony. In this situation, homicides are committed as a means to commit other crimes, such as robbery, burglary, grand theft, or kidnapping. Roberts et al. (2007) noted that a majority of the offenders in their sample had records of past criminal histories.

3. Offenders who committed a domestic violence-related homicide. The perpetrators in these instances were current or former spouses, cohabiting intimate partners, or girlfriends or boyfriends. The researchers found that these homicides were precipitated by "the complexities and fragilities in relations involving sex, love, and emotion" (Roberts et al., 2007, p. 499). This group represented the second-largest group, accounting for 25 percent of the homicide offenders.

4. Offenders who were charged with a degree of homicide after an accident, usually involving automobiles. In most cases, the fatality was a result of driving under the influence of alcohol or drugs.

We begin with the first two classifications: (1) offenders who committed a homicide precipitated by a general altercation or argument, and (2) offenders who committed a homicide during the commission of a felony. The third classification, offenders who committed a domestic violence-related homicide, will be covered later in the chapter under family violence. The fourth category, offenders who were charged with a degree of homicide after an accident, will not be considered in this chapter. They are distinct from the other groups in that they did not intend to perpetrate harm against their ultimate victims.

General Altercation Homicide

General altercation homicide is a result of hostile aggression. As we learned in Chapter 5, hostile aggression is a form of reactive aggression, and it occurs in response to anger-inducing conditions, such as real or perceived insults, threats, physical attacks, or one's own failures. The ultimate goal is to make a victim or victims suffer. This **reactive violence**, as it is sometimes called, "...is hot blooded, emotionally charged, and enacted quickly for the purpose of harming a perceived provocateur or defending oneself" (Fontaine, 2008, p. 243). It usually involves little instrumental motivation (Fontaine & Dodge, 2006) and consequently is distinct from instrumental aggression or violence. Reactive violence is essentially identical to the Roberts et al. first category which delineates the offender who impulsively and fatally retaliates to a perceived egregious provocation or threat.

Many general altercation offenders probably possess a strong **hostile attribution bias** which promotes violence whenever they perceive provocations and threats, no matter how benign or minor. In other words, they see a threat even when a threat is not intended; they do not walk away. Fontaine (2008) describes these individuals as possessing dysfunctional thinking processes in the interpretation of ambiguous social stimuli. They seem to have a "hair trigger" toward others where the slightest and most benign provocation sets them off. Common descriptions of this behavior include impulsiveness and out-of-control behavior. A not atypical illustration is the office worker who lashes out in anger at a fellow employee for making an off-handed, harmless remark.

Impulsivity is a key concept in understanding violence. In most cases, impulsive violence is a result of faulty or inadequate self-regulation (also known as self-control) compounded by a hostile attribution bias and a simplistic belief of how to deal with perceived hostility or threats. As described in Chapter 2, **self-regulation** is the capacity to control and alter one's behavior and emotions. Note that the definition includes *both* behavioral and emotional control. One of the most important protective factors against developing violent behavior is success in developing self-regulation of emotions, impulses, and behavioral reactions at an early age (Alvord & Grados, 2005).

Recall the discussion of attachment theory in Chapter 2. Fontaine and Dodge (2006) point out that attachment theory is based on the observation that early life events have enduring and considerable influence on beliefs and biases, even more so than do later events. In fact, early events shape the manner in which later events are cognitively represented. It is highly likely that many general altercation offenders demonstrated inadequate self-regulation skills early in their developmental years (Krueger, Caspi, Moffitt, White, & Stouthamer-Loeber, 1996). Clear signs of self-regulation and self-control begin to emerge during the second year of life, as does the concern for others. During the third year, children are expected to become reasonably compliant with parental requests and to internalize the family standards and values for behavior. Girls, on average, tend to show earlier self-regulated compliance during childhood than boys (Feldman & Klein, 2003). Fortunately, most people are able to restrain their aggressive impulses so as to stop violence or severe aggressive behavior. However, alcohol has the property of impairing self-regulation and self-control, even in persons who have a reasonably developed self-regulatory system. Consequently, considerable violence is especially prevalent among those persons who are intoxicated (with alcohol or other substances) and have marginally developed self-regulation skills.

Another key concept in explaining reactive violence is emotional arousal. Emotional arousal is best defined as a state of excitement and readiness for action. Cognitive or thinking processes are greatly impaired at extreme levels of emotional arousal (Zillman, 1979, 1983). Under high excitement, such as anger, behavior normally controlled by reasonable thought becomes controlled by biases and habitual responses. If the individual has the well-learned habit of exploding, lashing out, or otherwise acting in a violent manner, he is especially likely to do this under highly emotional circumstances. High arousal inhibits cognitive processing to the point where one may not think before acting. Therefore, at very high levels of emotional upset, violence is apt to become "impulsive," a term Zillman associated with habit strength. The violent behaviors have been so well learned that they appear quickly and without thought on the part of the individual. They seem to be "mindless" actions.

Felony Commission Homicides

Felony murders are homicides that occur in the process of committing a serious crime and are motivated by instrumental aggression. Instrumental aggression—as we learned in Chapter 6—is aggression for the sake of obtaining some object, rewards, or status possessed by another person—jewelry, money, territory, or influence. It is compared with reactive aggression, which occurs in response to provocation or perceived provocation. When it comes to severe or violent aggression, we will call the term in this section **proactive violence**. Proactive violence is characterized by cold-blooded, nonemotional, and premeditated aggression for the purpose of personal gain, such as a robbery or bullying. This description falls within the category of some offenders who kill during the commission of a felony. However, the term fits only those who anticipated and were accepting of the death of a victim. It does not fit the individual who holds up a liquor store with no intention of killing, but the robbery goes horribly wrong and the robber kills in a state of panic. In that case, the violence is better classified as reactive.

Proactive violence is typified by insensitive, calculated acts of severe violence enacted in the course of a crime, such as robbery, burglary, and drug acquisition. This form of violence is less emotional compared with reactive violence and more likely driven by the expectation of reward (Dodge, Lochman, Harnish, Bates, & Pettit, 1997). Similar to reactive aggressive patterns, proactive forms of violence appear to start early. Dodge et al. (1997) discovered in their research that children who frequently demonstrated reactive aggression seemed not only to have self-regulation problems, but did not expect positive consequences for their behavior. Their reward was in hurting the victim. Proactively aggressive children, on the other hand, anticipated more positive consequences for aggressive actions based on previous social learning. The researchers concluded that "… the proactively violent group might be displaying its violence because of an acquired belief that such violence will lead to positive social consequences for them" (Dodge et al., 1997, p. 49). These findings suggest that reactive violence is thoughtless and emotionally driven, whereas proactive violence is self-regulated and stems from a rewarding learning history. The self-regulation process requires the development and refinement of cognitions and concepts which stem from social learning at an early stage of development, but these children also learn that strongly aggressive actions and bullying lead to the acquisition of goods and status from others.

In conclusion, it should be emphasized that the division separating general altercation homicide offenders from felony commission homicide offenders is used here primarily to present some types of homicide into a manageable set of explanations. There is certainly overlap between the two classifications, as some felony commission offenders during a mugging or armed robbery for example, lose self-control quickly if the victims do not cooperate fully. In addition, we all tend to lose self-regulatory function under certain conditions when we become angry. High levels of emotional arousal take our attention away from our usual internal mechanisms of control. When we become extremely angry, for instance, we often say and do things we later regret. We feel upset, remorseful, and guilty, and we wish we could take back our words or actions. If we had carefully considered and evaluated the consequences of our behavior, we would probably have acted differently. But under the heat of emotion, our self-regulatory system, with all its standards, morality, and values, was held in abeyance. As we get older, however, we generally learn from experience to pay closer attention to our internal control mechanisms, and we engage in fewer impulsive outbursts. This "mellowing" feature may partly account for the lower rates of impulsive violence as age increases.

We should also mention that the Roberts et al. classification scheme does not entirely account for those offenders who have mental or behavioral disorders, such as severe depression and psychosis. In Western countries, it is estimated that 10 to 15 percent of those persons convicted of homicide have some form of psychotic disorders (Hodgins, 2001; Nordström, Dahlgren, & Kullgren, 2006), a topic that was covered in Chapter 8. It is highly likely, therefore, that a significant proportion of the 336 homicide offenders in the Roberts study had one or more psychological disorders. After all, hostile attribution biases are not far from well-developed delusional thinking, and poor self-control or impulse-control deficits are not far from an assortment of disorders characterized by emotional and mental dysfunction.

Nevertheless, we should not overestimate the importance of psychological factors in persons who commit homicide or underestimate other risk factors. In an interesting study, Farrington, Loeber, and Berg (2012) used data from the Pittsburgh Youth Study (PYS) to look back upon the life histories of homicide offenders. They identified 37 PYS males who, up to May 2009, were convicted of homicide as young men, ages 15 to 29. Then they sought to find risk factors in their backgrounds that would explain their later crimes. Most salient were environmental and socioeconomic rather than individual in nature. For example, individual features like callous–unemotional traits, psychopathic characteristics, cruelty, and lack of guilt were not salient; however, prior criminal offenses up to age 14, prior violence, even property offending were. Significant behavioral risk factors in the backgrounds of these convicted offenders were suspension from school, disruptive behavior disorder, and attitudes favoring delinquency. "All combined, the results support the notion that homicide offending is an outcome that is preceded by a history of disruptive, nondelinquent behavior and delinquent acts" (p. 119).

Juvenile Homicide Offenders

In January 2001, two juveniles, aged 16 and 17, arrived at the home of two Dartmouth College professors under the guise of conducting an environmental survey. The husband led them to his study, and proceeded to answer some of their questions, even offering them help in wording them. At some point, the "survey" stopped and the professor was stabbed repeatedly. When his wife came running to his aid, she too was stabbed to death. With the rural New Hampshire community in shock, police began to search for a random killer or possibly even a disgruntled student. Clues at the scene eventually led them to suspect the two juveniles, and a warrant was issued for their arrest. They were located in Michigan after police were notified by a truck driver who had offered them a ride.

The Dartmouth murders—as they have come to be known—were atypical with respect to juvenile murders, most of which are believed to be the result of drive-by shootings or gang-related turf wars. Other juvenile murders are accompanied by severe family dysfunction, such as physical or sexual abuse, or signs of mental illness. In the Dartmouth case, the two boys came from "average" families in their small community and were involved in school activities. The murders were planned—but it is not clear that the professors were the first targets. Neither did robbery appear to be a motive; the boys left the house without taking cash, jewelry, or valuable objects (Powers, 2002). The boys apparently wanted to see if they could successfully carry out a murder; one writer commented that they were going through the "apocalypse of adolescence" (Powers, 2002).

The above incident is atypical, just as are many other cases that receive extensive media attention. The Dartmouth murders do not correspond well with what is known about juvenile homicide offenders (commonly abbreviated as JHOs). For example, studies (Cornell, 1989; Heide, 2003, 2014; Myers, Scott, Burgess, & Burgess, 1995; Shumaker & Prinz, 2000) reveal that a majority of homicide acts by juveniles took place during either general altercation episodes—including gang warfare—or the commission of a felony. These categories, of course, are basically the same as the first two categories outlined by Roberts and his associates. The 2013 UCR data (Federal Bureau of Investigation, 2014a) reveal that 9.7 percent of offenders arrested for homicide were under 18 (2.7% were under 15).

RESEARCH FOCUS

BOX 9-2   Boys, Girls, and Homicide: Why and How Do They Do It?

As noted in the text, Heide and her colleagues have conducted research comparing homicide committed by girls and boys, including very young offenders. In a rare study focused exclusively on female juveniles, Heide and Sellers (2014), using the data from the FBI's SHR, studied 3,556 girls arrested for murder or nonnegligent homicide over a 32-year period. The researchers compared girls aged 12 and younger to those aged 13–17 on a number of variables, including race, region and location arrested, and situation (e.g., single victim and single offender, single victim and multiple offender). In total, 137 girls were between the ages of 6 and 12 and 3,339 between 13 and 17.

Heide and Sellers' report (2014) is rich with data, only some of which are repeated here:

- Girls in both age groups were most likely to be charged as single offenders with one victim, though for approximately 20.0 percent of the younger group and 40 percent of the older group at least one other offender was charged—put another way, they committed the alleged crime with at least one accessory.
- When victims were younger than one year, older girls were charged with killing their own offspring, followed by other family members or acquaintances. In the younger group, nearly all had killed infant family members or acquaintances.
- Older girls were most likely to use guns, while younger girls were more likely to use personal weapons (e.g., fists or hands), fire, or other methods.

In earlier research using the same data base, Sellers and Heide (2012) examined gender differences among 226 very young murderers, ages 6 to 10. Some of these findings were as follows:

- The great majority (88%) of the child offenders were males.
- Boys were more likely to use guns; girls more likely to use personal weapons.
- The victims of boys tended to be older (5 to 13 years), while half of the victims of girls were between 1 and 4.
- A small percentage of boys (about 7%) killed infants younger than one year, while nearly one-quarter of girls had killed infants of that age.
- A small number of boys killed strangers, but no girls did.
- The homicides committed by boys were more likely to be associated with another crime, such as a robbery, while the homicides of girls were more likely to be conflict related, such as in their child-caring capacities.

Questions for Discussion

1. What might be an explanation for younger girls (between 6 and 12) killing infants who were family members or acquaintances?
2. Children below 10 are rarely prosecuted for such serious crimes; rather, in most jurisdictions they are supervised in clinical settings. Discuss the advantages of this approach both for the child and for society. Are there disadvantages?
3. Compare the gender differences found in this research and discuss its importance with respect to preventing these rare crimes and treating these young offenders.

A breakdown of the overall data by gender showed that, in raw numbers, 541 boys aged under 18 were arrested (compared with 73 girls aged under 18) and 53 boys under 15 were arrested (compared with 18 girls under 15). There appears to be significant gender differences when it comes to juvenile murder. Studies reveal that girls, compared to boys, are significantly more likely to kill family members, younger victims, female victims, intimate partners, and their offspring (Heide, Roe-Sepowitz, Solomon, & Chan, 2012). More specifically, "Female JHOs were 9 times more likely than male JHOs to kill intimate partners, 4 times more likely to kill children under age 5, and twice as likely to kill family members and female victims" (Heide et al., 2012, p. 373). Boys are more likely to kill strangers and to be involved in gang-related killings. Female JHOs are more likely to use knives or other weapons, whereas male JHOs prefer guns (Heide et al., 2012; Heide, Solomon, Sellers, & Chan, 2011). When girls kill, they often do so to resolve a conflict; boys are more likely to be involved in crime-related homicides (Heide et al., 2011). (See **Box 9-2** for additional information on research from the Supplementary Homicide Report (SHR).)

Psychological Characteristics of Juvenile Murderers

To obtain more detailed information both about the crimes and about the backgrounds of the offenders, some researchers have conducted studies with small samples of juvenile offenders, typically children and adolescents who are in treatment settings. In general, these offenders have committed the "typical" homicides, and not those of the apparent callousness exhibited in the Dartmouth case discussed above. For example, Myers and Scott (1998) examined 18 male juvenile murderers between the ages of 14 and 17 who met the criteria for conduct disorder at the time of their crimes. The results revealed that 16 of the 18 (89%) juvenile murderers had histories of one or more psychotic episodes (especially paranoid ideation), and other forms of mental disorders. These results were remarkably similar to the prevalence rate in earlier studies examining the psychological characteristics of juvenile murderers (e.g., Lewis et al., 1985, 1988). Interestingly, available literature thus far does not support evidence of psychosis or other serious mental illness in very young child murderers (ages 6 to 10), although the question remains whether some neurological dysfunction may be at issue for this group (Sellers & Heide, 2012).

Research has also revealed that juvenile murderers—and those juveniles who commit violent crimes in general—tend to have a history of severe educational difficulties compared with nonviolent juveniles (Heckel & Shumaker, 2001). Children who begin school with deficits in social and cognitive skills are at high risk to engage in antisocial and violent behavior (Dodge et al., 2008). Myers, Scott, Burgess, and Burgess (1995) report that within their sample of 25 juvenile murderers, 76 percent demonstrated a learning disability and 86 percent had failed at least one grade. Verbal abilities evaluated by intelligence tests have also been found to be associated with antisocial behavior (Moffitt & Caspi, 2001). Significant language handicaps appear to be the most prominent learning problems among juvenile murderers (Heckel & Shumaker, 2001; Myers & Mutch, 1992). Again, though, most research focuses on adolescent and occasionally preadolescent perpetrators, and we cannot assume the same of very young child murderers.

Another prominent factor in the backgrounds of juvenile homicide offenders is lack of parental monitoring. As mentioned in Chapter 2, parental monitoring refers to such things as knowing the child's whereabouts, being involved in the child's school activities and homework, and supervising time allocations for outside activities. Knowing the whereabouts and setting time limits for activities outside the home are especially important during the preteen and teenage years. Roe-Sepowitz (2007) reports that limited parental involvement and lack of supervision were present in many of the adolescent female murderers she followed. Hill, Castellino et al. (2004) report that lack of parental involvement in school during the middle school years also appears to be critical. Other studies have reported that juvenile homicide offenders often have high rates of family abuse (Darby, Allan, Kashani, Hartke, & Reid, 1998; Lansford, Deater-Deckard, Dodge, Bates, & Pettit, 2004), substance use and alcohol abuse (DiCataldo & Everett, 2008; Roe-Sepowitz, 2007), and prior delinquency (Loeber et al., 2005; Roe-Sepowitz, 2007) and peer delinquency (Loeber et al., 2005). Many juvenile murderers also appear to have a variety of neurological abnormalities (Heckel & Shumaker, 2001), similar to what has been reported in the medical histories of life course persistent offenders. Myers and his colleagues (e.g., Myers, 1994; Myers & Mutch, 1992; Myers, Scott, Burgess, & Burgess, 1995) have continually noted the high incidence of conduct disorders in his samples of juvenile murderers, ranging from 84 to 88 percent. ADHD has also been identified with juvenile murderers with some regularity (Heckel & Shumaker, 2001).

In summary, although researchers have made headway in identifying factors that might explain murder committed by juveniles, some cases defy neat explanations. The complexity of crime is illustrated in the bizarre case introduced at the beginning of this section. Nothing seems to fit, with the possible exception of "juvenile psychopathy," a construct we addressed in Chapter 7. In some cases, a serious mental illness may explain the actions of the juvenile murderer; in other cases, it may be a history of abuse. Recall from our discussion of cumulative risk and the dynamic cascade model that the list of risk factors influencing antisocial behavior may be extensive and different for each individual. With reference to homicide, Loeber and his colleagues suggest that the probability of individuals committing it is enhanced by their exposure to an *accumulation* of different risk factors during early development (Loeber et al., 2005). Loeber et al. contend that violence-producing processes do not suddenly emerge; they accumulate over many years. Therefore, the higher the number of risk factors a child experiences, the greater the tendency to engage in violent acts during the life course.

Taking a similar but more dynamic approach, Kenneth Dodge and his colleagues (2008) provide a coherent developmental story of how violent behavior grows across childhood and adolescence in a dynamic cascade, perhaps as one might picture a mud slide or a snowball rolling down a hill accumulating snow with each roll. The model, discussed in Chapter 2, hypothesizes that each risk factor group operates on antisocial and violent outcomes by directly influencing the next factor group in a developmental sequence.

Dodge et al.'s model emphasizes that there are many preventive and therapeutic ways to steer a child away from a developmental trajectory of violence and serious delinquency and crime. Thus, psychological treatment of juveniles who kill may be more realistic than treatment of most adults who commit these crimes. The dynamic cascade model provides specific targets for prevention at specific periods in development. In addition, because new risks arise with each developmental period, prevention and intervention cannot be deemed completed until the child passes through adolescence.

Treatment of Juveniles Who Kill

Juvenile homicide is a perplexing, if rare, phenomenon, and it often defies categorization. Contrast, for example, school shooting cases, the Dartmouth murders, the case of a boy who kills his abusive father, the 13-year-old girl who kills her newborn infant, the gang member in a drive-by shooting, and the 14-year-old who smothers his younger cousin to death in the process of trying to rape her. Some juveniles who kill are mentally disordered or intellectually disabled, and some may have psychopathic traits, but clearly not all do. Very little research is available by which to document the percentages, however. Most of the treatment information of juvenile murderers is from clinical case reports of a few cases referred for treatment (Heide, 2003; Heide et al., 2012). Juveniles who commit homicide—if not transferred to criminal courts—generally are placed in a juvenile facility where they do not always receive treatment tailored to the needs of the offender. In addition, the likelihood of juvenile murderers receiving intensive psychological treatment and intervention decreases as they enter adolescence (Heide, 2003; Myers, 1992). Older adolescent murderers are often placed in adult prisons, where they may be held in protective custody until old enough to be transferred to the general population. Mental health care in juvenile facilities is typically minimal because of financial constraints and limited awareness of the psychological needs of this population (Heide, 2003). Psychiatric hospitalization, although commonly used for young children who kill, is rarely done for adolescent murders (Heide, 2003). There are, of course, exceptions.

Overall, young killers appear to make a satisfactory adjustment in a correctional facility and in the community after release from custody (Heide, 2003). This is especially true for those youths who have killed family members as an isolated act of violence (Hillbrand, Alexandre, Young, & Spitz, 1999). Additionally, as the research by Heide and Sellers (2014) on girls arrested for murder suggests, providing children and adolescents with strategies to cope with stressful events is likely a good approach. On the other hand, hard-core, persistent, violent delinquents who killed in the course of committing other crimes do not make a good adjustment and often continue offending on release. The evidence for successful treatment of those juveniles who committed homicide during an altercation is mixed.

INTIMATE PARTNER VIOLENCE

Intimate partner violence (IPV) is the contemporary term used by researchers to characterize the physical, psychological, and sexual violence perpetrated by individuals in a present or past intimate relationship. This form of abuse has usually been included in studies of family violence or domestic violence, and we might have placed it within that section later in the chapter. However, focusing specifically on the intimate partnership has allowed the research microscope to examine same-sex relationships, dating relationships, and past relationships that may not have been considered in other studies. Since the turn of the twenty-first century, research on IPV has expanded dramatically, perhaps even more than research in other areas of family or domestic violence. For example, most recently researchers have looked at IPV among elder adults (e.g., Dinnen & Cook, 2014; Roberto, McPherson, & Brossoie, 2014) and different cultural groups (e.g., Ammar, Couture-Carron, Alvi, & San Antonio, 2014).

Nevertheless, many criminologists and researchers continue to include IPV as a form of domestic violence, or even more broadly, of family violence. Furthermore, most studies focus on women as victims and men as perpetrators, although female against male violence and same-sex violence are receiving more attention. There is justification for the focus on female victims, because women tend to be experiencing the most—and the most serious—abuse. For example, in the years 1994 to 2010, four out of five victims of IPV were women (Catalano, 2012). In addition, researchers are examining victimization and perpetration of IPV within specific populations and subcultures. We address some of this research below.

Extensive research on IPV makes it clear that it is a complicated topic. The prevalence of IPV is extremely difficult to estimate, with some research noting a prevalence of one in seven relationships for physical violence and close to two-thirds of all partnerships for emotional or psychological abuse. Many studies do not include psychological or emotional abuse in IPV, however. In addition, studies vary according to how questions are asked. For example, some may ask, have you *ever* been physically hurt by an intimate partner? Others ask, have you been hurt within the last two years (or five years, etc.)? Still others ask both. In a recently published study on teen dating (Mumford & Taylor, 2014), 667 adolescents aged 12 to 18 were asked whether they had been victims of physical, sexual, or psychological abuse. Nearly 20 percent of both boys and girls reported themselves to be victims of physical and sexual abuse, and a startling 60 percent said they were both victims and perpetrators of psychological abuse (e.g., insults, accusations). Although psychological abuse may not be considered serious, the researchers noted that these behaviors are not healthy and could lead to serious forms of violence.

Noting that not all IPV is the same, Tinney and Gerlock (2014) observe that it has been studied in four different contexts, and that it is important to recognize the context of any given situation in order to make informed decisions about the victim's safety and how to deal with the offender. They emphasize, though, "It is important to be clear that violence embedded within any of these contexts can be dangerous and lethal. Determining context is not an attempt to minimize the level of risk and danger of IPV. It is not meant to excuse criminal behavior" (p. 402). (See **Table 9-2** for a summary of these contexts.)

TABLE 9-2 Four Contexts of IPV and Associated Features*	
Context	**Features**
IPV with coercive control (battering)	• Ongoing pattern of coercive control • Monitoring of victim's behavior outside the home • Social isolation • Pattern of abuse to wear down victim • Physical and psychological injuries
Reactive violence	• Victim has been abused over time • Victim may use self-defense • Victim may strike first to get violence over with • May be in a rage and retaliation mode
IPV without coercive control	• Atypical violence in retaliation • Follows conflict, such as finances, infidelity
Pathological violence	• May be influenced by psychological problems • May be influenced by brain injury or substance abuse

*Features of contexts may co-occur. For instance, substance abuse may be present in all contexts.

Source: Adapted from Tinney & Gerlock (2014). Intimate partner violence, military personnel, veterans, and their families. Family Court Review, 52, 400-416.

In a special report on IPV based on findings from the NCVS, Catalano (2013) examined non-fatal victimization over the years 1993 to 2011 and found a substantial decrease in both serious and nonserious IPV perpetrated against females (down 72%) and males (down 64%). Serious violence included rape or sexual assault, robbery, and aggravated assault. Simple assault, such as an assault that did not incur great physical damage, or threats of violence, were not included in the serious category, although the report does not indicate that these are of no concern. To the contrary, it emphasizes that repeated nonserious threats or assaults may expose the partner to more severe victimization in the future. Throughout the time period examined, both female and male victims reported more attacks by intimate partners than by non-intimates, the latter including relatives, friends, neighbors, acquaintances, and strangers. Likewise, both females and males reported greater injury in IPV victimizations, as well as greater need for medical treatment. Women were more likely to seek treatment for a serious injury from an intimate partner than men (13.0% compared with 5.4%).

As referred to above, contemporary researchers are beginning to examine IPV among specified populations, including within races, ethnicities, and gender identification. This is done under the general assumption that prevention strategies and public policy approaches to address IPV should be aware of both risk and protective factors that may or may not be unique to subgroups of IPV victims and perpetrators. We provide a few illustrations of this research below.

IPV among Older Adults

Although abuse of older adults will be covered below in a separate section, it is worthwhile to focus specifically here on the issue of IPV among this population. Whereas victimization of older adults by family members, acquaintances, caretakers, and strangers is often acknowledged, less attention is given to their victimization by intimate partners. A recent review of the literature on this topic (Roberto, McPherson, & Brossoie, 2014) makes it clear that IPV among older adults is a significant problem. The review identified 57 empirical studies, mostly published over the past 15 years. Among the common themes were the following:

- Abusers tended to continue their abusive patterns over long periods, even when they themselves were deteriorating in health;
- The prevalence of physical and sexual violence declines, but nonphysical IPV (e.g., emotional abuse) continues in later life;
- Although physical abuse often was replaced by psychological abuse as the years of the partnership increased, in some cases physical abuse continued even when the abuser's health declined;
- Leaving a relationship in later life is complicated not only by financial and emotional risks but also by declining health and concerns about losing social ties to neighborhoods and communities;
- Most health care facilities do not screen older adults for indicators of IPV, particularly physical or sexual violence;
- Isolation of older adults from the community, which is not restricted to rural settings, is a risk factor for IPV.

Older adults do not seem to be at great risk of IPV compared with their risk from other abuse, which will be covered later in the chapter. Many older adults, having lost an intimate partner to death, live alone, with family members, or in community residential settings. Those who continue to live with intimate partners are most at risk if the partnership includes a history of abuse; there is little evidence in the available research that abuse begins suddenly at an advanced age. Nevertheless, there is undoubtedly a good amount of hidden abuse that never comes to the attention of authorities or researchers.

IPV among Hispanics

The Hispanic population in the United States, broadly used to include Latino, refers to individuals whose country of origin includes Mexico, Puerto Rico, Cuba, South or Central America, or other Spanish regions, regardless of race (Catalano, 2013). They are the fastest growing population in the

United States. A national study of cohabiting couples (Caetano et al., 2005) found a higher incidence of IPV among Hispanic couples in comparison to non-Hispanic white couples (14% vs. 6%), even after controlling for socioeconomic status. Female Hispanic victims of IPV have also been found to have poor mental health outcomes compared with female non-Hispanic victims (Bonomi et al., 2009), and female Hispanic victims in one state were found at higher risk of being killed than non-Hispanic victims (Azziz-Baumgartner et al., 2011). In a review of the rapidly growing research in this area, Cummings, Gonzalez-Guarda, and Sandoval (2013) identified 29 published studies that identified risk factors and, to a lesser extent, protective factors relative to IPV among this population.

The risk factors that were consistently found applied to both victims and perpetrators of abuse and included individual, community, and relationship factors. For example, individual factors included history of physical or sexual abuse, unemployment, young age, poor education, and belief in traditional gender roles, to name but a few. Examples of community factors were impoverished and violent neighborhoods and work conditions. Relationship factors included lack of social support and infidelity (for a complete list, see Cummings et al., 2013). Although the researchers did not identify societal risk factors, they emphasized that the 29 studies they reviewed did not analyze them. An example of a societal risk factor would be an immigration policy that places increasing stress on undocumented immigrants, such as denying them access to social services or threatening them with deportation.

It seems clear from the literature thus far available that the Hispanic population is at great risk of both victimization and perpetration of IPV. Cummings et al. (2013) conclude their review by recommending that health and social service providers aim to modify socioeconomic conditions and understand why victims choose to remain in abusive relationships. "Without addressing these underlying circumstances, other interventions (e.g., psychotherapy) may not be successful" (p. 168). Attention also should be given to prevention strategies addressing unique needs of Hispanic youth and their families. Furthermore, more research is needed on different subcultures within the broad Hispanic community, because norms and values of individuals from different countries of origin may vary.

Same Sex or Nonheterosexual IPV

In recent years, the nature and extent of same-sex partnerships has received increased attention. As in other studies of IPV, some researchers have used "domestic violence," or DV, to report their research (Hellemans et al., 2015; Messinger, 2011; Murray & Mobley, 2009; Potoczniak, Mourot, Crosbie-Burnett, & Potoczniak, 2003; Turrell, 2000). With just a few exceptions, most studies have reported similar prevalence of IPV among heterosexual and nonheterosexual populations (Hellemans et al., 2015). Furthermore, much research documents similarity in characteristics of aggressors and victims, in background features (e.g., history of abuse), and in correlates of the violence. For example, Potoczniak et al. (2003) discovered strong similarities in the research literature comparing the violence cycles and stages of abuse between same-sex domestic violence (SSDV) and opposite-sex domestic violence (OSDV). Like OSDV perpetrators, they found SSDV perpetrators to be extremely controlling, threatened by outside influences, highly selfish, and blaming their partners for the abuse. In addition, the SSDV victims show many of the same behavioral and thought characteristics as OSDV victims.

On the other hand, differences in heterosexual and nonheterosexual IPV have been discovered as well. Messinger (2011), using data from the National Violence Against Women survey, reported that women in same-sex relationships were twice as likely to report verbal aggression, controlling behaviors, physical aggression, and sexual aggression in their relationships than were those in heterosexual relationships. In a large study of both heterosexual and nonheterosexual individuals, Hellemans et al. (2015) found that both were equally likely to report physical and psychological IPV, and both men and women reported similar IPV on the whole. However, the female victims of IPV—both heterosexual and nonheterosexual—experienced more frequent psychological IPV. The latter was measured by items asking whether the respondent's partner had engaged in such actions as belittling or humiliating the respondent in front of others, intentionally doing something to scare or intimidate the respondent, or threatening to hurt the respondent or someone he or she loved.

Interestingly, far more research is conducted on female same-sex relationships than on male same-sex relationships, perhaps because victimization of women has received more attention than victimization of men in the literature as a whole. To date, there is a paucity of research on IPV among bisexuals, transitioning, transsexuals, or persons who do not identify themselves with any gender. As noted earlier, studies typically deal with the sex or gender binary (man–woman or male–female) and have barely begun to address the individuals who do not fit neatly into that binary.

IPV within Law Enforcement and Military Families

Law enforcement work is almost universally recognized as among the most stressful of occupations, primarily because of the ever-present possibility of encountering dangerous situations. Interestingly, research on police stress reports indicates that—for most law enforcement personnel—the stress from potential dangers of the job is not as great as that from administrative factors, such as shift work or clashes with supervisory personnel or fellow officers. Nonetheless, regardless of the source of the stress, it may have a spillover effect, where it affects relationships off the job, including within the family.

Some researchers have found higher rates of IPV among law enforcement families than among the general population (Johnson, Todd, & Subramanian, 2005). Regardless of the prevalence compared with other groups, however, stress among law enforcement at all levels (metropolitan, suburban, municipal, rural) and among various agencies (local, county, state, federal) is associated with outcomes that often include violence within the family (Gershon et al., 2009). These negative outcomes are typically attributed to the authoritarian nature of the work, which spills over into the family context. Johnson et al., (2005), found a significant correlation between authoritarianism and domestic violence perpetrated by both male and female police officers.

Anderson and Lo (2011) studied self-reported IPV in a sample of 1,104 full-time urban (Baltimore, Maryland) police officers. (Interestingly, Baltimore was the site of a controversial case in 2015 in which a suspect died in police custody, resulting in six officers being charged with various homicide-related counts.) Nine percent of Anderson and Lo's respondents admitted losing control and becoming physically aggressive toward an intimate partner. As expected, they found significant positive correlations between the IPV and (a) stress (experiencing stressful events on the job), (b) authoritarian spillover (e.g., feeling they need to take control over people in their lives, wanting the final say in the household), and (c) negative emotions (e.g., feeling moody or impatient over job-related problems, given to feelings of depression about work, less interested in pursuing fun activities because of work). Through regression analyses, the researchers examined gender differences (male and female), as well as differences between two racial groups (white and African American). Interestingly, women and non-white officers were likelier than men and white officers to engage in physical aggression. In addition, women and African American officers did not seem to experience the authoritarian spillover effect, while men and white officers did.

Research on IPV in military families (current deployment and veterans) is becoming increasingly available. We include this topic along with the law enforcement IPV research because of the overlap in many features of people who engage in the two occupations. Law enforcement is a paramilitary occupation, with candidates trained in many of the authoritarian militaristic ways. Furthermore, it is not unusual for individuals to come out of the military and seek work in law enforcement positions. To our knowledge, no study on IPV among law enforcement families has controlled for prior military status.

On the other hand, the military alone has features not found in the law enforcement community, such as an increasing likelihood of combat-related conditions such as posttraumatic stress disorder (PTSD) or traumatic brain injuries. Separation from family, unfamiliarity with the culture where one is serving, and the need to readjust after deployment are other features that are unique to military personnel. Those studies that have been conducted have found a positive relationship between PTSD and IPV (e.g., Gerlock, 2004; Sayers, Farrow, Ross, & Oslin, 2009; Taft et al., 2011).

Psychological and Demographic Characteristics of Abusers

Early psychological research on IPV—then usually called domestic violence—almost invariably focused on the characteristics of the person being abused, particularly the woman in heterosexual relationships. It was believed in some quarters that abused women allowed themselves to be battered (Frieze & Browne, 1989) or that victims of spouse abuse were masochistic, consciously and unconsciously precipitating the violence to which they were subjected (Megargee, 1982). Still others have depicted women who were abused as lacking self-esteem, being highly passive and dependent on their husbands, and willing to place greater value on maintaining the marriage above their safety (Megargee, 1982). Many researchers, theorists, and mental health practitioners embraced the concept of the battered woman syndrome (Walker, 1979), which ascribed a number of characteristics that included low self-esteem and learned helplessness. As research on IPV progressed, recognition of its complexity and social as well as psychological correlates became the norm. In addition, researchers shifted their focus to characteristics of abusers.

The early research almost invariably depicted abusers (primarily male) as intent on maintaining power and control in the relationship. They were depicted as extremely possessive and unreasonably jealous men who treated their partners like property coveted by other men. This depiction led to other assumptions about the inadequacy, incompetence, and low self-esteem of these abusive husbands who saw threats to their masculinity everywhere. Although power and control continues to be a theme in IPV literature (Menard et al., 2009), it should not be assumed that all IPV can be explained by this one factor (Kelly & Johnson, 2008). Alcohol abuse and a past history of violence are also seen as major risk factors.

However, efforts to come up with a profile of the batterer based on personality characteristics have seen mixed results. "Indeed, the overwhelming weight of the evidence finds heterogeneity among intimate partner violence perpetrators" (Jackson, 2014, p. 14).

Nevertheless, some research results look promising for a typology that might help in the prevention, intervention, and treatment of abusers. In an extensive review of the research literature, Holtzworth-Munroe and Stuart (1994) identified three primary types of male spouse batterers: Type 1 batterers, who abuse family members only; Type 2 batterers, who abuse family members because of emotional problems; and Type 3 batterers, who are generally violent toward both family members and persons outside the family. Type 1 abusers are the most common, tend to be less aggressive than the other two, and also tend to be more remorseful for their actions. Their violence levels were low compared with the other two groups, and their use of alcohol was low to moderate. Type 2 batterers, labeled borderline/dysphoric, tend to be depressed, inadequate individuals who are emotionally volatile, with high levels of anger, and who display indicators of personality disorders and psychopathology. Type 3 batterers, labeled the generally violent/antisocial group, are individuals who are antisocial, criminally prone, and violent across situations. They are more likely to abuse alcohol and are generally more belligerent toward almost everyone. They are also most likely to be involved in serious violence toward a spouse, which is relevant to this section of the chapter. Later, Holtzworth-Munroe, Stuart, and their colleagues (2003) found a fourth group, which they labeled the low-level antisocial group. This group exhibited higher levels of violence and general antisocial behavior than the family-only group, but lower levels than the general violence group.

Other researchers have focused on pathological personality characteristics of batterers compared with nonbatterers. Chief among these is the batterer's insecure attachment, which has been found correlated with domestic violence and IPV in a number of studies (e.g., Buck et al., 2012; Dutton et al., 1994; Mikulincer & Shaver, 2010). Insecure attachment is believed to relate to such personality attributes as jealousy, low self-esteem, and dependency on the approval of others.

In an attempt to further examine the relationship between IPV and insecure attachment, Buck and her colleagues studied 72 family-only male batterers who were in a court-mandated group treatment program. Both separation anxiety and distrust of partner emerged as attachment-related characteristics, with distrust of partner significantly increasing the risk of battering, even over attachment alone.

Although some headway is made in the search for personality attributes, it is still questionable whether "the" batterer profile exists. The search for demographic variables has been equally mixed and inconclusive (Hotaling & Straus, 1989; Weis, 1989). As noted above, IPV cuts across demographic categories. The abuse of alcohol and drugs seems to play a role as an exacerbator, *but not as a cause,* of the violence. The relationship between IPV and alcohol abuse has been shown repeatedly in the literature (Buck et al., 2012). It is stressed that abusive men with severe alcohol or drug problems are apt to abuse their partners both when drunk and when sober. However, abusive husbands who drink heavily are violent more frequently, and inflict more serious injuries on their partners than do abusive men who do not have a history of alcohol or drug problems (Frieze & Browne, 1989).

FAMILY VIOLENCE

We will begin this section with the good news. As with most other crimes, both crime reports (e.g., UCR reports) and victimization reports (e.g., NCVS) indicate that family violence has gone down since the early 1990s. Recall that incidents of self-reported IPV also have decreased. This can be attributed to numerous factors, and each policy maker likely has his or her preferred explanation. A decline in crime rates is always welcome, but it does not obscure the fact that a significant portion of the population is still subject to victimization from various criminal actions.

As will be made clear throughout this section, research on this topic is extremely fragmented, due in large part to differences in terminology. The above discussion of IPV is a case in point, because much IPV could also be classified as family or domestic violence, and much research has treated it that way. In addition, family violence is also called domestic violence, and within the category of domestic violence researchers refer to child abuse, maltreatment, neglect, sibling violence, and elderly abuse, to name but a few terms. Family violence refers to any assault, intimidation, battery, sexual assault, sexual battery, or any criminal offense resulting in personal injury or death of one family or household member by another who is or was residing in the same single-dwelling unit (Wallace & Seymour, 2001). The term "battering" is often used in a slightly more specific fashion to describe *physical violence* in intimate or family relationships, either during a dating relationship, marriage or partnership, or separation and divorce or in the care of children.

Criminologists and treatment providers are not concerned only with the "violence" aspect, however. Many victims experience psychological harm, and in some cases, what occurs in this area is not necessarily physical harm—it may be only psychological. Stalking—a topic to be discussed in more detail in Chapter 15—is a good illustration; it may involve no physical harm, yet, some researchers include it under the term "domestic violence" (e.g., Perilla, Lippy, Rosales, & Serrata, 2011). To qualify as the criminal offense of stalking, most statutes require that the behavior promote fear in the victim. However, research documents that persons who stalk often do not intend to frighten the victim. Rather, their goal is reunification. Another example of abuse that is not physical is ongoing verbal abuse, which is rarely studied (Perilla et al., 2011). However, as noted in the above section on IPV, psychological abuse is not ignored in that literature. Thus, some researchers define family violence as "an ongoing, debilitating experience of physical, *psychological*, and/or sexual abuse in the home, associated with increased isolation from the outside world and limited personal freedom and accessibility to resources" [italics added] (Wallace & Seymour, 2001, p. 4). Nonetheless, however it is defined or whatever terminology is used, at the heart of family violence is usually the perpetrator's misuse of power, control, and authority (American Psychological Association, 2003).

The conundrum created by using different terms continues to be alluded to in virtually all research on family violence or violence against women and children (see, generally, White, Koss, & Kazdin, 2011). Researchers today try to define their terms very specifically, and they sometimes mint new terms that will better capture what they intend to study. With respect to child abuse, for example, the prominent researcher David Finkelhor (2011, p. 10), notes: "My preferred solution is to call this field *childhood victimization* or *developmental victimology*, using the broader victimization concept instead of the terms *violence* or *abuse*." As Finkelhor observes, the broader term allows us to focus on the areas that professionals are concerned about: conventional crimes against children; acts that violate child welfare statutes—such as neglect or abuse; victimizations of children by nonadults, such as bullying and peer and sibling violence. We will return to Finkelhor's approach below.

For our purposes, we have distinguished IPV as noted above because of the recent explosion of research in this area and the fact that it is not restricted to a family context. In this section, we use the broad term "family violence" because it has traditionally been most often used in the research literature. Nevertheless, virtually all professionals recognize that its victims are not only *physically* harmed, they are harmed psychologically as well. Moreover, sometimes physical harm does not even occur. For example, some victims—both children and adults—are exposed to continual berating and to cruel but non-physical punishments, such as being forced to witness the killing of a pet. And, in the case of corporal punishment—which is clearly violent—it is not the type of violence that raises widespread concern. In other words, despite disavowal of spanking by most professionals, the criminal justice system does not intercede unless it is carried to extremes. As Finkelhor (2011) succinctly states, "it is a crime for a man to hit his wife but not his child" (p. 19). Likewise, in any discussion of family violence, it is important to keep in mind that one form of violence or dysfunction is often accompanied by other forms. For example, child maltreatment and IPV commonly co-occur, with some estimates indicating that half of the families with maltreatment of children also involve IPV (Briggs, Thompson, Ostrowski, & Lekwauwa, 2011).

Prevalence

The ultimate family violence includes the death of one or more individuals. About one of every five murders and nonnegligent manslaughters in the United States—in which the victim–offender relationship is known—involves a family member killing another family member, with a majority (about 50%) involving spouse killing spouse (Durose et al., 2005; Federal Bureau of Investigation, 2011). Similar statistics have also been reported in Canada, although the spousal homicides rate in that country is the lowest reported in three decades (Statistics Canada, 2011). Homicide within the family accounts for 45 percent of all murders in England and Wales (d'Orban & O'Connor, 1989; Home Office, 1986; Mirrless-Black, 1999). A neglected area of research in family violence is homicide followed by suicide, in which a family member kills other family members and then kills him- or herself. One reason for the neglect is that homicide-suicides are relatively rare, accounting for less than 2 percent of all homicides. Yet, they are so sobering that they are almost invariably covered by national media. Research has consistently shown that a high proportion of homicide-suicides (usually well over 50%) involve spouses, especially former spouses.

Victims

Approximately 20 percent of all arrests made for aggravated assaults and 60 percent for simple assault involved family members (Truman & Langton, 2014). Children under 12 comprised 5 percent of victims of family aggravated assault and 4 percent of the victims of family simple assault. Infants (aged under one year) are the most vulnerable victims of family violence. **Figure 9-2** shows the nature of offenses that occurred against infants during the years 2001 to 2003. Most often, the offense committed against infant victims is simple assault, and the second most common is aggravated assault (Federal Bureau of Investigation, 2005). **Figure 9-3** shows the ages of infant victims who were victimized. Although infants make up the majority of victims, sometimes additional

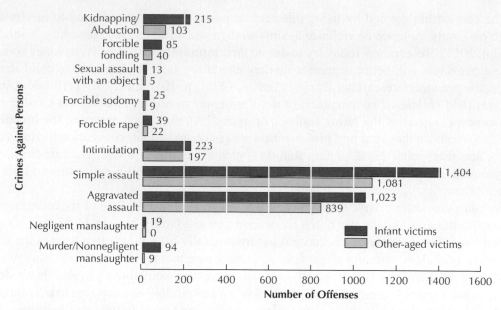

FIGURE 9-2 Offenses Related to Infant Victims *Source:* Federal Bureau of Investigation. (2005). Crime in the United States, 2004: Uniform Crime Reports. Washington, DC: U.S. Department of Justice.

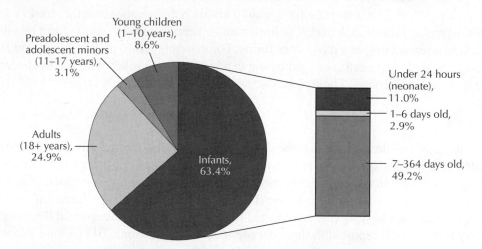

FIGURE 9-3 Age of Victim at Victimization *Source:* Federal Bureau of Investigation (2005, p. 360).

victims of other ages are present at the infant's victimization, demonstrating the multiple aspects of family violence. Infants are rarely the solitary victim in family violence.

Self-report victimization studies also suggest that at least 20 percent of simple or aggravated assaults involve family members (Truman & Langton, 2014). Although these official statistics are woefully incomplete, they still underscore the considerable magnitude of family violence.

Some variant of family violence has probably existed for as long as individuals grouped together as families, both nuclear and extended. However, with the notable exception of intra-familial homicide, domestic or family violence has not traditionally been regarded as serious crime or worthy of criminal prosecution in this country. State governments and the courts have long claimed that family relationships require or deserve special immunity, including the views that parents have a right to discipline children physically, that a husband possesses the right to have sexual access to his wife, or that nagging women or disobedient children often provoke and deserve the beatings they receive (Pleck, 1989). This view has been energetically challenged in recent years by various interest groups attempting not only to acquaint the public with the problem but also to activate lawmakers and the criminal justice system toward more stringent legal and social sanctions.

Coverage of research on family violence will be divided into four major questions: (1) How much family violence is there? (2) What are the common characteristics (or correlates) of the offenders and victims? (3) Is family violence fundamentally different from other kinds of violence (such as street violence)? (4) What are the causes of family violence? We will explore the research in these four areas, keeping in mind the critical problems in definition, sampling, and methodology just described. It should be pointed out that intrafamilial sexual abuse, although mentioned in the following sections, is discussed in greater detail in Chapter 13.

Child Maltreatment

In the United States, about one in seven children (138 per 1,000) are maltreated at some time during their childhood (Finkelhor, Ormrod, Turner, & Hamby, 2005). In one year alone, 1,520 children died from such maltreatment (U.S. Department of Health and Human Services, 2015). Still another sobering statistic is the fact that parents and caretakers account for about one-fifth of all violent crimes committed against children. More than half of these violent crimes are against children aged 2 or younger (Abrams, 2013).

Maltreatment refers to all forms of abuse and/or neglect and can be divided into five types: physical abuse, sexual abuse, emotional abuse, neglect, and abduction (see **Table 9-3**). Finkelhor et al. (2005) discovered that emotional abuse (name calling or denigration by an adult) was the most frequent of the five types. Boys and girls experienced similar rates for maltreatment with the exception of sexual abuse. Girls are four times more likely to be sexually abused. Finkelhor and his associates also conducted a national survey of youths and caretakers regarding the experiences of over 4,500 children from 0 to 17 years. Called the **National Survey of Children Exposed to Violence (NatSCEV)** (Finkelhor, Turner, Ormrod, & Hamby, 2009), the survey is considered one of the most comprehensive nationwide surveys that focused on the incidence and prevalence of children's exposure to violence. The survey discovered that more than one in nine (11%) American youth had been exposed to some form of family violence during the past year and one in four (26%) had been exposed to family violence at some point during their childhood (Hamby, Finkelhor, Turner, & Ormrod, 2011).

TABLE 9-3 Definitions of Child Abuse and Neglect

Type of Abuse	Definition
Physical abuse	Occurs when a parent willfully injures, causes injury, or allows a child to be injured, tortured, or maimed out of cruelty or excessive punishment
Emotional abuse	Chronic pattern of behavior in which the child is belittled, denied love to promote specific behavior, or subjected to extreme and inappropriate punishment
Emotional neglect	Failure to provide a child with appropriate support, attention, and affection
Sexual abuse	Exploitation of a child or adolescent for another person's sexual and control gratification
Child neglect	Chronic failure of a parent or caretaker to provide a child with basic needs such as food, clothing, shelter, medical care, educational opportunity, protection, and supervision
Missing and exploited	Kidnapping a child from a custodial parent, child abduction by strangers, or child sexual exploitation for child pornography, child prostitution

Source: Adapted from Whitcomb (2001). Child victimization. In G. Coleman, M. Gaboury, M. Murray, & A. Seymour (Eds.), 1999 National Victim Assistance Academy. Washington, DC: U.S. Department of Justice.

The project also revealed that almost half of these children had experienced a physical assault in the course of the previous year, often at the hands of their siblings and peers. In fact, research has revealed that sibling aggression and physical assault is the most common form of family violence (Tucker, Finkelhor, Turner, & Shattuck, 2014). Although it has been typically viewed by society as normal and harmless, there is emerging evidence that sibling victimization may have significant psychological effects on many of its victims (Tucker et al., 2013, 2014).

More recently Finkelhor and his colleagues (2014) conducted an update of the first survey, called the Second National Survey of Children Exposed to Violence. The survey obtained maltreatment data from 4,503 children and youth from interviews with caregivers for the children ages 0 to 9 and with the youth themselves for ages 10 to 17. The results of the second survey were somewhat dissimilar from the first survey, largely because the methodology and procedures were different from the original. Overall, though, the survey results did suggest that maltreatment rates appear to be decreasing over the past few years. More importantly, both surveys brought attention to the plight of polyvictims, those children who experience multiple victimizations over the course of their development such as parental abuse, sibling victimization, bullying, physical victimization by caretaker, sexual victimizations. In their national surveys, polyvictims were the youths who had experienced four or more victimizations over the course of a single year. "Analyses have suggested that poly-victimization is the pattern most associated with mental health problems and bad outcomes, and that poly-victims are the kids harboring the greatest amount of distress" (Finkelhor et al., 2011, p. 21). They note that children who experience a single kind of victimization are more able to recover than those who experience multiple kinds from multiple sources. For these latter children, victimization is more a condition than an event (Finkelhor et al., 2011, p. 22).

During 2013, child protection agencies received an estimated 3.5 million maltreatment referrals involving approximately 6.4 million children (U.S. Department of Health and Human Services, 2015). Approximately 61 percent of the 3.5 million referrals that were screened in and required an investigation and protective services. Most of the referrals involved neglect (79.5%) and physical abuse (18%). Approximately 10 percent were sexually abused, and another 8 percent were emotionally (psychologically) abused. There is a high probability that emotional abuse is substantially underreported. Over one-quarter of the victims were victims of more than one type of maltreatment. Definitions for each of these terms are found in **Table 9-3**.

The highest victimization rates were for the 0 to 3 age group, and rates declined as age increased. Child abuse/neglect perpetrators, defined as persons who have maltreated a child while in a caretaking relationship to the child, were mostly female (54%).

In 2013, 1,520 children died from abuse and neglect at a rate of 2.04 per 100,000 children in the population (U.S. Department of Health and Human Services, 2015). More boys died of abuse and neglect (58%) than girls (42%). Over two-thirds (71%) of the victims were neglected, and nearly half (47%) experienced physical abuse either exclusively or in combination with another maltreatment type.

The child fatality figure due to maltreatment is very probably an underestimation, however. The figure is probably closer to 2,000 or more. Determining the actual number of children who die each year from maltreatment is exceedingly difficult. Child fatalities due to maltreatment are probably underreported because *some* deaths labeled as accidents, or sudden infant death syndrome (SIDS), might be attributed to child maltreatment if more comprehensive investigations were conducted.

Interestingly, research has found that pet abuse and child abuse commonly occur together in dysfunctional families (Arkow, 1998). Adults who are cruel and inhumane to children (and their spouses) are often cruel and inhumane to the family pet(s) as well. Abusers often threaten to harm or actually kill a pet to frighten a child into secrecy or to punish the child or to keep the spouse from reporting the abuse to authorities. In one study, more than half of the women at a family shelter reported that their pets had been harmed or killed by their partner, and they delayed coming to the shelter for fear of harm to their pets (Ascione, 1997; Merz-Perez, Heide, & Silverman, 2001).

Missing, Abducted, Runaway, and Thrownaway Children

Each year, thousands of children run away, are abducted, or are "thrown away." A thrownaway youth refers to one whom a parent or caretaker "throws" out of the home. Numerous children—some say a majority—who run away do so to escape neglect or abuse from their current home or living arrangement. Most of the nationwide data on these children are reported in the NISMART Bulletins. NISMART is an acronym for the National Incidence Studies of Missing, Abducted, Runaway, and Thrownaway Children, a large nationwide survey of households, juvenile residential facilities, and law enforcement agencies conducted by the Office of Juvenile Justice and Delinquency Prevention. NISMART consists of several studies designed to estimate the size and nature of the missing children problem in the United States. Much of the information in this section comes from the NISMART-2 report (U.S. Department of Justice, 2002a). A more recent study is—at this writing—currently being conducted which will represent NISMART-3.

In 1999, an estimated 1,682,900 youth had a runaway or thrownaway episode (U.S. Department of Justice, 2002a). In most instances (71%), the runaway/thrownaway youth could have been endangered during the episode by virtue of such "street" factors as substance dependency, use of hard drugs, sexual or physical abuse, and being in places where criminal activity is prevalent. Recall that the UCR is no longer collecting data on runaways as of January 2012, although many states continue to do so. In addition, runaways are often taken into custody for curfew violations, so those statistics reflect the runaway problem to some extent.

Nonstranger child abduction can be another form of child abuse. In many instances, child abduction by a noncustodial parent or other family member from the custodial parent takes place. However, an undetermined number of child abductions are done by a parent who wants to protect the child or children from abuse by the other parent. Even a custodial parent may, in these circumstances, "abduct" the child, if the two parents share joint custody. According to the National Center for Missing and Exploited Children (NCMEC), an estimated 205,000 children were victims of family abduction in 2010 (Douglas, 2011), and nearly half are younger than six years of age (U.S. Department of Justice, 2002a).

Abduction of children by nonfamily members is less frequent. In this type of abduction, a nonfamily perpetrator takes a child by use of physical force or threat of bodily harm or detains the child for a substantial period of time (at least one hour) in an isolated place without lawful authority or parental permission. The primary motivation for this type of abduction is sexual. Nonfamily abductions are not typically the "stereotypical" stranger abductions highlighted in the media, however. They also may occur when a child younger than 15 is taken or detained or voluntarily accompanies a nonfamily person who conceals the child's whereabouts, demands a ransom, or expresses the intention to keep the child permanently. This last would include situations where a 20-year-old persuades his 14-year-old girlfriend to leave the state, or where a family acquaintance takes a child to protect the child from abuse. In 2010, approximately 58,200 children were abducted by nonfamily perpetrators, but this covered a very wide range of circumstances (Douglas, 2011).

STEREOTYPICAL CHILD ABDUCTIONS. Stranger or slight acquaintance abductions—every parent's nightmare—are relatively rare, although any number is too great. These cases are called **stereotypical abductions** because they often end in tragedy, have traumatizing effects on communities, and receive considerable attention from the national media. As we discussed in Chapter 8, 6-year-old Etan Patz was abducted on his way to school in New York City in 1979. His picture was one of the first to appear on a milk carton, intended to prompt anyone knowing anything about his whereabouts to contact police. His body was never found, but in 2015, Pedro Hernandez went on trial for his murder, after he had confessed to killing the boy. The case was widely publicized not only in 1979 when the child first disappeared, but again in 2015. Interestingly, police for many years had suspected another individual of the crime—a person who eventually was convicted of sexual offenses against children and remains imprisoned. In May 2015, a mistrial was declared in the Hernandez case, because the jury was unable to reach a unanimous verdict.

Overall, cases like the above are highly influential in forming public opinion about the risks and frequency of stranger abduction homicides. In every year since 2000, the number of high-profile stereotypical abductions is consistently estimated to be about 115 (Finkelhor, Hammer, & Sedlak, 2002), a number which is also consistent with FBI estimates. Sixteen percent of these children are taken from the home, usually out of their bedroom. The abducted child is frequently sexually assaulted and then killed. Earlier estimates indicated that about 40 percent of all stereotypical abductions result in the death of the child, usually within the first 24 hours (Finkelhor et al., 2002; Hanfland, Keppel, & Weis, 1997; Lord, Boundreaux, & Lanning, 2001). More recently, the FBI has reported a decrease in child abductions committed by strangers, including registered sex offenders (Douglas, 2011), and it is believed that about two-thirds of abducted children are returned without serious physical injury. Sexual motivations appear to be a major factor in stereotypical abductions.

Nearly half of all child victims of these stereotypical kidnappings were sexually assaulted by the perpetrator, and about one-third required medical attention for other injuries (U.S. Department of Justice, 2002a). Over two-thirds of the victims of stereotypical kidnapping are female. The ages of the victims usually range between 6 and 14 years, and preschoolers are rarely targeted. Apparently, the age preference for those abductors who target females is around 11, largely because the abductors find them sufficiently physically mature to be sexually desirable and vulnerable enough to be easily controlled and exploited (Hanfland et al., 1997). In the summer of 2009, the nation was riveted to news that an 11-year-old girl abducted 17 years before was alive and living with her alleged abductor and his wife in a bizarre living arrangement that included a sheltered backyard structure. Now 28, the victim had apparently given birth to children fathered by this individual. In another high-profile similar case in the early 2000s, a teenage boy was found and returned to his family after having lived under an assumed name with his abductor for a number of years. Such returns—after such a long period of time—are unfortunately very rare, however.

Most of the abductions of elementary school children occur in or around the victim's home, with the majority being abducted within one-quarter mile of their residence. The stereotypical abduction of middle school children (ages 11 to 12) often take place in playgrounds, parks, wooded areas, shopping malls, and other areas of recreation. Rarely are children abducted from school grounds. Most children were taken into vehicles (45%) or to the offender's home (28%). Ransom is rarely demanded by the perpetrator(s) (less than 5% of all nonfamily or stereotypical abductions). The vast majority of abductors are under the age of 30, with an average age of 27 (Hanfland et al., 1997). Only 10 percent are over 40. They are predominately unmarried men with poor social skills, marginal work habits, and have very few friends (Lord et al., 2001).

Munchausen Syndrome by Proxy

An unusual but serious type of child abuse identified in the psychological and psychiatric research literature is called **Munchausen syndrome by proxy (MSBP)**. It is important to note that, although MSBP is labeled a "syndrome," it is not a mental disorder listed in the DSM-5. Rather, the DSM-5 refers to the various forms of abuse discussed in this chapter as relational problems or conditions that may be the focus of clinical attention. MSBP is not specifically mentioned in that diagnostic manual.

MSBP is a form of child abuse in which the parent (usually the mother), or parents, *consistently* and *chronically* bring a child in for medical attention with symptoms falsified or directly induced by the parent or parents (Murray, 1997). Like other cases of child abuse, MSBP cases are found in homes of all socioeconomic levels (Pearl, 1995), and the victims are most often children between infancy and eight years of age (Jones et al., 1986). Both male and female children may be victims. Although mothers are almost always the offending parent, the father is often described in case histories as an emotionally distant or physically absent parent (Robins & Sesan, 1991). There does not seem to be a gender preference for the victim, as both male and female children are represented in equal numbers. When several children in the same family are victimized, it is referred to as serial MSBP (Alexander, Smith, & Stevenson, 1990).

Very often, the offending mother is knowledgeable about medical issues, has a fascination with medical details, has her own medical history of fabricated illnesses, and may be a health professional herself. In addition, the mother will be unusually attentive to the child and will be reluctant to leave the child's side during medical examination or treatment. Another important symptom of MSBP is the child's series of reoccurring medical conditions that either do not respond to treatment or follow an unusual course that is persistent, puzzling, and unexplained. Another MSBP symptom is a series of physical or laboratory findings that are highly unusual, discrepant with medical history, or physically or clinically impossible. In extreme cases, the parent may initiate starvation in the child, nearly suffocate the child, inflict vaginal/rectal injuries in order to produce bleeding, add fat to stool collection to produce a lab abnormality, put her blood into child's urine sample before lab testing, or even inject contaminated material intravenously into the child's bloodstream (Murray, 1997; Pearl, 1995; Sheridan, 2003). The extreme forms of abuse certainly can lead to serious injury or even death. Some researchers have reported a mortality rate as high as 6 to 10 percent, particularly when the parent has suffocated or poisoned the child (Ferrara et al., 2013). Unfortunately, the prevalence or incidence of MSBP is unknown at this time, probably partly due to the difficulty of identifying actual illnesses as opposed to the fabricated ones.

In some instances, the family pet may be the victim of MSBP, with the pet owner consistently taking the pet to the veterinarian for a variety of vague or fake symptoms (Tucker, 2002). The pet owner often is trying to get sympathy and attention through the pet's misfortune.

Abusive Head Trauma

Another form of child abuse is abusive head trauma, the preferred term for what was previously called **shaken baby syndrome (SBS)**. In this form, a parent or caretaker, usually in anger, shakes a baby so hard that serious head injury results. Although there are no accurate statistics regarding the frequency of this type of abuse, there is consensus that head trauma is the leading killer of abused children (over 50%) and that shaking is involved in many of these cases (Duhaime, Christian, Rorke, & Zimmerman, 1998; Showers, 1999; Smithey, 1998). Abusive head trauma also can occur when infants are thrown down, such as on the floor, or battered by fists or against a wall. In part because of the difficulty in adequately diagnosing whether the injuries were caused by shaking or by other methods, the more generic term—abusive head trauma—is making its way into the literature. We continue to use SBS in citing studies that use that designation.

Ellis and Lord (2001) estimate that 10 to 12 percent of all deaths due to abuse and neglect are attributable to SBS (see also National Information Support and Referral Service, 1998). Most recently, it was estimated that about 30 percent of children diagnosed with SBS die, and only 15 percent survive with no lasting effects (Russell, 2010). Lasting effects can include significant brain damage resulting in conditions such as cerebral palsy, blindness, deafness, learning disabilities, and coma. Available research suggests that 70 to 80 percent of the perpetrators of SBS are male, and most of the time they are the parent of the child (Child Abuse Prevention Center, 1998; Ellis & Lord, 2001). Both male and female babies appear to be equally victimized.

Available research indicates that childhood abuse and neglect in general increase the odds of future delinquency and adult criminality by 40 percent. More specifically, being abused or neglected as a child increases the likelihood of arrest as a juvenile by over 50 percent, as an adult by 38 percent, and for a violent crime by 38 percent (Widom, 1992). More recent research by Widom (2000) confirms these data further. She states (2000, p. 5), "The odds of arrest for a juvenile offense were 1.9 times higher among abused and neglected individuals than among controls; for crime committed as adult, the odds were 1.6 times higher." In addition, psychological and emotional problems were prevalent among the abused and neglected sample. Specifically, the abused and neglected individuals were significantly more likely than the controls (a comparison group who had not experienced abuse or neglect) to have attempted suicide and to have met the criteria for antisocial personality disorder.

INFANTICIDE

In this section, the focus is on that form of child homicide that occurs when a person intentionally kills a child or infant and *intends that the death occur.* That is, the homicide is not accidental or the incidental result of abuse or neglect. Although the term **infanticide** literally means the killing of an *infant,* it has become synonymous with the killing of a child by a parent.

For a variety of reasons, it is very difficult to maintain accurate statistics on this offense. Cause of death of an infant may be difficult to establish—for example, sudden deaths may be due to sudden infant death syndrome or traumatic brain injury not attributable to the criminal actions of an adult. Some research also has indicated that even if a medical examiner reports grounds for homicide, police may not make a report (Porter & Gavin, 2010). Recall that a homicide is a death caused by another human being; it is not necessarily a crime.

Still, it is estimated that 1,200 to 1,500 children are intentionally killed each year by a parent or other person, representing about 12 to 15 percent of the total criminal homicides in the United States (Child Welfare Information Gateway, 2012) (see **Figures 9-2** and **9-3**). Between 2001 and 2005, 2,402 children under two were killed (Malmquist, 2013) in the United States. In the United States and Canada, about two-thirds of murdered children are killed by family members, mostly parents. For children under five, mothers and fathers are about equally responsible for deaths, but when someone other than a parent is responsible, the majority of cases involve a male offender (Cooper & Smith, 2011).

Several decades ago, Resnick (1970) recommended that the killing of one's children (infanticide) be divided into two separate categories: **neonaticide**, which refers to the killing of the newborn within the first 24 hours after birth, and **filicide**, which refers to the killing of a child older than 24 hours. Resnick's research indicated that neonaticide was more likely to represent an attempt to dispose of a problem, while filicide was more likely a reflection of parental depression or feelings of being overwhelmed. This distinction has disappeared from much of the literature, but social concerns about neonaticide continue. An increasing number of jurisdictions, for example, now have laws that bar the prosecution of parents who leave newborns or infants in "safe harbors" such as hospitals, churches, or synagogues. The assumption is that if the parents have no such safe harbor, they might not sufficiently care for the infants or, worse, take the drastic step of ending their lives. Furthermore, neonaticide is sometimes distinguished from infanticide in the professional literature (Porter & Gavin, 2010).

Neonaticide

The extent of neonaticide is difficult to determine because many go undetected and there is no national data depository for these cases (Beyer, Mack, & Shelton, 2008). The same situation holds for filicide (Koenen & Thompson, 2008), although as children get older their victimization is more likely to be recorded. It is roughly estimated that approximately 150 to 300 incidents of neonaticide occur each year in the United States (Meyer & Oberman, 2001). A similar estimate has been advanced by researchers on filicide (Koenen & Thompson, 2008). In their investigation of existing neonaticide data at the FBI National Center for the Analysis of Violent Crime, Beyer and her colleagues (2008) discovered that many of the 40 women in their study gave birth unassisted to infants of normal birth weight. The women then killed the neonate, disposed of the body, cleaned up the crime scene, and remained undetected. "Many of the offenders are then able to engage in routine activities, immediately following the birth of the child, including attending classes, shopping, eating out, dancing, or returning to work" (Beyer et al., 2008, p. 531).

Beyer et al. found very little evidence that the women who engaged in neonaticide had serious mental or psychological disorders, a finding consistent with previous studies (Dobson & Sales, 2000; Spinelli, 2001). However, several women did show some bizarre behaviors following the neonaticide, such as placing the infant's body in containers, driving around with the infant's body in the trunk of their car, or breastfeeding the dead infant. Such extreme measures likely were indicative of some mental disorder or postpartum psychosis precipitated by hormonal changes associated with the pregnancy and birth.

Beyer et al. report that virtually none of the women in the study had a criminal history, nor were they arrested for crime against a child prior to the homicide. It is also interesting to note that several of the offenders had living biological children (ranging in number from one to four additional children) at the time of the homicide. Killing the newborn appears to reflect a desire to rid oneself of a problem. Most of the women who commit neonaticide are described as being sexually submissive, immature, childlike, and passive (Koenen & Thompson, 2008). However, there is so little research specifically on this topic that firm conclusions are unwarranted.

Filicide

Although severe mental disorders and suicide are rare in neonaticide, this is not the case in filicide. Some researchers contend that a majority of the women who commit filicide are demonstrating symptoms of affective disorders (a prolonged, pervasive disturbance of mood), a psychotic disorder, or a combination of the two (Lewis & Bunce, 2003). Traditionally, women who kill their children have been viewed by the legal system and the mental health profession as suffering from severe emotional problems, rendering them either insane (the legal system) or psychotic (the mental health profession). Men who kill their children are more likely to be viewed as evil and cruel (Wilczynski, 1997). Early research tended to support assumptions of serious mental illness in women (Haapasalo & Petaja, 1999; McKee & Shea, 1998; Resnick, 1969, 1970).

However, recent research questions the assumptions of severe mental illness (Hatters-Friedman & Resnick, 2009) and suggests that other factors are at work. For example, some research has indicated that dropping out of school or anger combined with immaturity were factors associated with the killing of one's child (Krischer, Stone, Sevecke, & Steinmeyer, 2007; Spinelli, 2003). In summary, then, recent research indicates that the majority of child deaths that are caused by the mother are not related to mental illness (Porter & Gavin, 2010).

Still, it is unwarranted to discard completely those cases in which depressive episodes associated with birth may contribute to infanticide. Most often, the clinical diagnosis is "postpartum depression," a depressive episode thought to be brought on by childbirth. However, it is important to realize that three categories of mental or emotional reactions may be apparent after childbirth: (1) postpartum blues, (2) postpartum depression, and (3) postpartum psychosis (Dobson & Sales, 2000). The most frequent category is *postpartum blues*, characterized by crying, irritability, anxiety, confusion, and rapid mood changes. It is estimated that anywhere from 50 to 80 percent of women exhibit some minor features of postpartum blues about one to five days after delivery (Durand & Barlow, 2000). The symptoms may last for a few hours to a few days and are clearly associated with childbirth and the hormonal changes that accompany pregnancy and delivery. The connection between postpartum blues and neonaticide or filicide has not been supported by the research literature (Dobson & Sales, 2000).

The second category, *postpartum depression*, occurs during the weeks or months after childbirth. The symptoms include depression, loss of appetite, sleep disturbances, fatigue, suicidal thoughts, apathy about the newborn, and a general loss of interest in daily living. However, in contrast to postpartum blues, postpartum depression does not appear totally related to childbirth. Rather, it is more a clinical form of depression that is present before childbirth and probably is more a recurring depressive disorder that existed before the delivery; however, it is accelerated by late pregnancy, birth, and the subsequent physical exhaustion and overwhelming responsibility of caring for an infant. This form of mood disorder is usually not linked to filicide.

The third category, *postpartum psychosis*, is a severe mental disorder that is rare, occurring in 1 out of every 1,000 women following delivery. Usually, the psychotic features are strikingly similar to symptoms of serious bipolar depression and appear directly associated with childbirth. Sometimes, this mental disorder is severe enough to lead to the mother's attempted suicide, together with an attempt to kill the infant (Kendall & Hammen, 1995). Dobson and Sales (2000) report that research indicates that many women (estimates range from 20% to 40%) who commit filicide are suffering from postpartum psychosis. In one noteworthy incident that occurred in the 1980s, the new mother had lowered the window shades of her home for several weeks after her baby's birth, sitting in darkened rooms, and resisting entreaties of her husband and other family members to get psychological help. On the day of the killing, she shot her infant to death in his crib. The prosecutor dismissed the case, supposedly because he could not find one clinician who would say she was *not* suffering from a severe form of postpartum psychosis. Other cases have received extensive national publicity (e.g., Andrea Yates and Dena Schlosser mentioned in Chapter 8).

Elderly Abuse

It is now well recognized from Census Data and other statistics that the United States has experienced significant growth in the population of older adults and will continue to do so at least until mid-twenty-first century. In 2010, there were approximately 40 million adults aged 65 and older; approximately 5 million of them were over 85. Projected figures for 2050 were about 90 million for adults aged 65 and over and 19 million for those over 85. The growth in the population of older adults—many of whom do not want to be called "elders," "elderly," or "senior citizens"—has led to a need for medical, clinical, and social service specializations; housing options; and so on. Criminologists also study the population of older adults, not because they are committing crimes (though some do), but because they are often victimized.

It is estimated that approximately 1 to 2 million older Americans are victims of abuse each year (National Center on Elder Abuse, 2013). Elder abuse is said to affect 1 out of 10 older adults as some time in their lives (Acierno et al., 2010). It is generally believed that elder abuse is widely underreported—one estimate is that only 1 in 23 actual incidents are reported (Mosqueda & Olsen, 2015). Most reporting is done to social service agencies, such as Adult Protective Services, rather than to law enforcement communities, and though these agencies investigate reports, perpetrators are rarely referred to law enforcement or turned over for prosecution (Burnes, Rizzo, & Courtney, 2014).

There are many reasons for the underreporting, even to protective service agencies. Although nearly all states require some type of reporting of suspected elderly abuse, there is wide variation about who is required to report and what type of suspected abuse should be reported. For example, persons as varied as mental health professionals, medical personnel, and bank officials may be obliged to report suspected abuse to police or human service agencies, depending upon the state. In addition, though suspected physical abuse involves some mandatory reporting in virtually all states, emotional or financial abuse and neglect are different matters. Additionally, even in cases of physical abuse, because of the frailty associated with aging, bruises and fractures may not be associated with maltreatment. Finally, elder individuals themselves may be reluctant to report abuse that is perpetrated by their caregivers, particularly if these caregivers are spouses, children, or other relatives. There may be fear of retaliation, or fear that the perpetrator will be jailed or in some cases deported. Although medical practitioners today routinely ask patients, "Do you feel safe in your home?" it is likely that some who do not would not be forthright in answering that and similar questions.

Elder abuse is characterized by the infliction of physical, emotional, or psychological harm on the older adult, usually defined as age 65 or older (Marshall, Benton, & Brazier, 2000). Some researchers, including some using very large samples, have used 60 as a minimum age (Acierno et al., 2010). Some researchers include sexual abuse within the general categories of abuse, while others treat it as a separate form of abuse. In addition, financial abuse—such as when someone withdraws sums from an older person's bank accounts or forges his or her signature—may or may not be investigated in the research. In essence, elder abuse can amount to many different actions. "The general concept involved in the numerous definitions of 'elder abuse' is that the victim is injured, neglected, or exploited because of vulnerabilities associated with age, such as impaired physical or mental capacities" (Klaus, 2000, p. 13). Neglect refers to a failure to meet basic needs of the

TABLE 9-4 Percentage of Older Adults Reporting Different Forms of Mistreatment

Type of Abuse	Percentage
Neglect	5.10
Physical	1.60
Financial (by family over past year)	5.20
Financial (by nonfamily over lifetime)	6.50
Emotional	4.60
Sexual	0.60

Source: Adapted from Acierno, Hernandez-Tejada, Muzzy, & Steve (2009). Final report: The National Elder Mistreatment Study. Washington, DC: National Institute of Justice.

individual under one's care, such as providing food, housing, clothing, and health care (Centers for Disease Control and Prevention (CDC), 2013).

Reviewing the data and clinical research on elder abuse, Mosqueda and Olsen (2015) observed that abused elders are more likely to die compared with those who are not abused, and that persons with dementia are more likely to be abused than those without. However, in addition to having dementia, living in a care facility and being female are also risk factors. In general, the research literature documents that victims of this type of elderly abuse have a condition that makes them vulnerable, such as cognitive decline or a physical condition that limits their mobility (Johannesen & LoGiudice, 2013).

Acierno, Hernandez-Tejada, Muzzy, and Steve (2009) used Random Digit Dialing telephone calls to conduct a nationwide survey to determine the prevalence of elder mistreatment, defined generally as physical, sexual, emotional, neglectful, or financial mistreatment of a person age 60 years or above (see Table 9-4). The average age of the 5,777 respondents was 71.5 with a range of 60 to 97 years. The survey was funded by the U.S. Department of Justice. The largest type of abuse was financial, followed closely by neglect. The financial abuse largely was a result of family member spending money without permission, or a stranger forging a signature and spending money without permission.

Family members tend to be the chief perpetrators of elderly abuse—with 90 percent of all incidents being perpetrated by adult children, spouses, or other relative (National Center on Elder Abuse, 2015). After adult children, spouses constitute the second-largest abuser category. Male caretakers are more likely to abuse the elderly physically, while female caretakers are prone to abuse them psychologically or neglect them. However, both men and women are equally likely to exploit them financially.

Although there are similarities between the various types of family abuse, elder mistreatment is a more complex phenomenon that encompasses both aspects of interpersonal violence and the aging process (Wolf, 1992). That is, elder abuse and neglect are often a result of long-standing troubled family dynamics and interpersonal processes that have been highly charged when the dependency relationship is altered, because of either illness or financial needs. Nevertheless, as documented in an important review article (Jackson, 2014), all perpetrators of elder abuse are not alike. Jackson review 19 risk factors across different forms of abuse and discovered that they were extremely variable (e.g., the quality of past relationships with the victim, a desire for access to the victim's belongings, and stress in the caretaker's life from outside sources).

However, while there is no one single causal factor to fully explain why family members abuse their seniors, some explanations have focused on caregiver stress and dependency issues (either the caregiver's or the senior's) (Au Coin, 2003a). Elderly abuse also has been associated with mental disorder or substance abuse among the perpetrators (Jogerst et al., 2012; Mosqueda & Olsen, 2015).

Mosqueda and Olsen (2015) provided a series of "red flags" for mental health clinicians to be attuned to when dealing with elderly clients. Though it is not up to the clinician to investigate, red flags likely signify that a report of suspected abuse is warranted. Examples are unexplained bruising in unusual locations, fearfulness or secretiveness on the part of the client, or cowering or impaired sleep.

The violent crime committed against persons age 65 or older is most likely to be simple assault (Klaus, 2000). Nevertheless, there is ample evidence that they are also victims of more serious violent crimes. Recent statistics from two countries are illustrative. In Canada, 6 percent of the total homicide victims were older Canadians (65 or older), with a family member being responsible for over half of the cases (Au Coin, 2003a). The same statistic (6.4%) was reported in the United States for older Americans (Federal Bureau of Investigation, 2003). The term **eldercide** is usually reserved for the murder of a person age 65 or older. In Canada, when the incident involved a family member, a majority of older women were killed by a spouse or ex-spouse (53%), whereas older men were most often killed by an adult son (43%) (Au Coin, 2003a). The data are similar for American senior citizens (Klaus, 2000). In Canada, the most common cause of death for older victims of family-related homicides was beating (29%) and shooting (28%), followed by stabbing (23%) (Au Coin, 2003a). Although a similar family breakdown is not currently available in the U.S. data, the most common causes of death for all older victims were firearms (45%), followed by stabbing (20%), blunt objects (14%), and beatings with fists or feet (13%) (Federal Bureau of Investigation, 2003).

Sibling-to-Sibling Violence

As mentioned previously, violence between siblings is believed to be the most common form of violence within families, but surprisingly little is known about it (Finkelhor, 2011; Gelles, 1997; Mathis & Mueller, 2015; Wallace, 1996). The violence and abuse a child or adolescent receives from a sibling is often overlooked and trivialized (Simonelli, Mullis, & Rohde, 2005). Sibling conflicts are generally seen as a normal part of growing up (Underwood & Patch, 1999), and some researchers have observed that some level of sibling aggression is normative (Mathis & Muller, 2015). Mothers and fathers display a great tendency to deny the seriousness of the aggressive outburst of siblings or their children—including violence toward themselves—in order to perpetuate a "myth of family harmony" (Harbin & Madden, 1979). Yet, in many cases, sibling conflict and violence involves punching, choking, beating up, threatening to use a weapon, and actually using a weapon. Finkelhor et al. (2006) found that 35 percent of children in their study reported being hit or attacked by a sibling within the past year. In addition, sibling violence appears to be linked to violence in dating relationships, family violence in adulthood, and nonfamily adult violence in general (Hoffman, Kiecolt, & Edwards, 2005). Most recently, Mathis and Mueller (2015) found significant correlations between sibling aggression in childhood (between ages 10 and 14) and one's emotional difficulties and demonstrated aggression as adults. Although their study was exploratory, its findings suggest that aggression between siblings should not be overlooked.

More severe forms of child-to-family violence involve murder, and have specific terms, such as **siblicide** (sibling killing sibling), **patricide** (killing one's father), **matricide** (killing one's mother), **sororicide** (killing one's sister), **fratricide** (killing one's brother), and **parricide** (killing one or more of one's parents).

Over 30 years ago, Steinmetz (1981) reported that two-thirds of the adolescent siblings in the family sample she studied—a sample characterized by family violence—used physical violence to resolve conflict. These findings have been more recently supported by Hoffman et al. (2005), who found 70 percent of the adolescents in their sample (students) had committed at least one violent act against their closest-age sibling during their senior year of high school. Families having only sons consistently experience more sibling violence than do families with only daughters (Hoffman et al., 2005). Hoffman et al. (2005) found that males perpetrated more violent acts against their brothers than against sisters or sisters against their siblings. In 2002, 72 percent of murders by siblings involved a brother killing a brother, and 14 percent involved a brother killing a sister (Durose et al., 2005). An additional 14 percent of siblicides involved a sister killing a brother or sister.

Among the 671 intrafamilial murders reported in 2002, 18 percent (or 119 murders) involved a sibling victim (Durose et al., 2005).

Victims of the more extreme forms of sibling violence tend to be younger siblings. For example, Fehrenbach, Smith, Monastersky, and Deisher (1986) reported that over 40 percent of victims of adolescent sexual assault were younger siblings. Available data also suggest that 85 percent of siblicide offenders and 73 percent of siblicide victims are male (Dawson & Langan, 1994). Approximately one out of every one hundred homicides in the United States is a siblicide (Federal Bureau of Investigation, 2005; Underwood & Patch, 1999). In their analysis, Underwood and Patch (1999) reported that the most common circumstance of sibling homicide was some type of argument between the perpetrator and the victim. Firearms predominated as the weapon of choice.

Child-to-Parent Violence

Child-to-parent violence and abuse has also become an important topic. In one early study (Gelles, 1982), approximately 4 adolescents (ages 15 to 17) in one hundred were reported to kick, bite, punch, hit with an object, beat up, threaten, or use a gun or knife against a parent. Almost one-third of restraining orders issued in Massachusetts were requested by parents against their adolescent children (Pagani et al., 2004). In a study using a nationally representative sample of American children, Ullman and Straus (2003) concluded that 10 percent of the adolescents (ages 10 to 17) participated in child-to-parent violence during the previous 12 months. Sixty percent of these youths had witnessed violence between their parents. In one longitudinal study involving 2,524 Canadian adolescents, Pagani et al. (2004) affirmed that 13 percent of the teenagers engaged in physical aggression toward their mothers, ranging from pushing and shoving, punching or kicking, throwing objects, to using a weapon.

In recent years, attention has been paid to a different group of family offenders, specifically adolescents and young adults who commit "parent abuse" by causing physical, psychological, or financial harm to their parents. Distinctions are drawn between the normal parent–child conflicts of adolescence and abuse in which the adolescent tries to control and coerce the parents (Tew & Nixon, 2010).

In 2013, 16 percent of the family murder victims were killed by their children (Federal Bureau of Investigation, 2014a) (see **Figure 9-4**). The killing of parents is most often committed by sons by a ratio of about 3 to 1 over daughters (Federal Bureau of Investigation, 2005, 2014a). Mothers are killed slightly less often than fathers by both adolescents and adult sons and daughters.

Heide (1993) identifies three types of youth parricide: (1) the severely abused child, (2) the severely mentally ill child, and (3) the dangerously antisocial child. The complex dynamics of families in which parricides occur often include multiassaultive family patterns, easy access to firearms, alcohol and drug abuse, and the youthful offender's strong feelings of helplessness in coping with the stresses at home. Sometimes the adolescent murderer, as well as other family members, feels a sense of relief that the parent(s) is (are) dead.

Although males predominate in the more extreme forms of juvenile violence toward parents, the gender differences disappear at more moderate levels of violence (Pagani et al., 2004). In addition, the risk of violence toward parents gradually increases during adolescence, peaking at age 15 and diminishing thereafter (Pagani et al., 2004). This pattern corresponds to the peak age of adolescent violence toward non-related individuals noted by Loeber and Stouthamer-Loeber (1998). Most violent incidents between child and parents are associated with conflicts about home responsibilities, money, and privilege (Pagani et al., 2004). Children and adolescents who displayed early and chronic forms of aggression and antisocial behavior are most likely to be aggressive toward parents (Pagani et al., 2004). "As adolescents, those described as chronically aggressive by their (annually) different primary school teachers were (9 and 4) times at greater risk of engaging in verbal and physical aggression (respectively) toward their mothers in comparison to their persistently nonaggressive peers" (Pagani et al., 2004, p. 534). In fact, violent predispositions during childhood, measured by teachers, are among the best predictors of later violence toward mothers. "Indeed,"

Expanded Homicide Data Figure

Murder by Relationship[1]
Percent Distribution,[2] Volume by Relationship, 2013

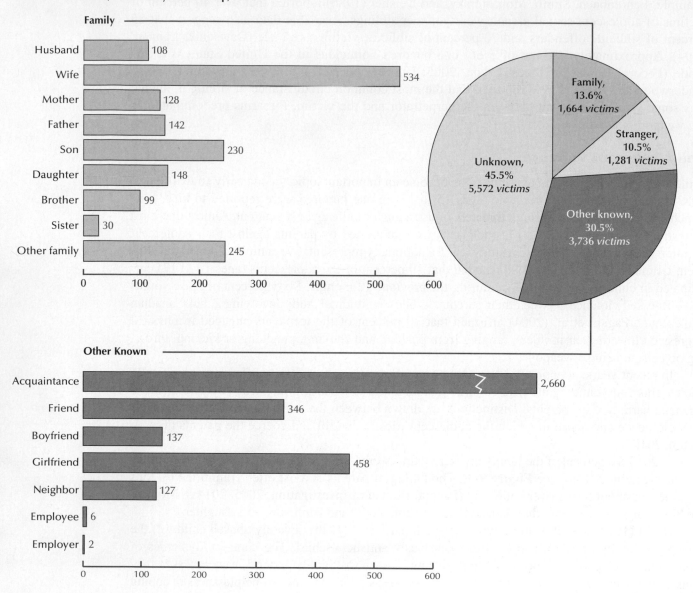

[1]Relationship is that of victim to offender.
[2]Due to rounding, the percentages may not add to 100.0.
Note: Figures are based on 12,253 murder victims for whom supplemental homicide data were received, and includes the 5,572 victims for which the relationship was unknown.

FIGURE 9-4 Murder Distribution by Relationship, 2013 *Source:* Federal Bureau of Investigation (2014a).

Pagani et al. (2004) concluded in their study, "teacher-rated disruptiveness during early childhood predicted the risk of engaging in physical aggression toward mothers during adolescence" (p. 220).

Multiassaultive Families

Some families, referred to as **multiassaultive families**, are characterized by continual cycles of intrafamilial physical aggression and violence. Siblings hit each other, spouses hit each other, parents hit the children, and the older children hit the parents. According to the available data, at least 7 percent of all intact families may be considered multiassaultive (Hotaling & Straus, 1989). As noted previously, child maltreatment often accompanies IPV (Briggs et al., 2011).

Research supports the notion that assault is a generalized pattern in interpersonal relations that crosses settings and is used across targets beyond the immediate family (Hotaling & Straus, 1989). Men in families in which children and wives are assaulted are five times more likely to have also assaulted a nonfamily person than are men in nonassaultive families. A similar pattern holds for women from multiassaultive families, although the relationship is not as strong. Sibling violence is particularly high in families in which child assault and spouse assault are present, with boys displaying significantly more assaultive behavior (Hotaling & Straus, 1989). Moreover, children from multiassaultive families have an inordinately high rate of assault against nonfamily members (Hotaling & Straus, 1989). These children are also more likely to be involved in property crime, to have adjustment difficulties in school, and to be involved with police. It should be carefully noted that it is extremely difficult to tell what is causing what in this complicated web of interrelated variables. Nevertheless, it is quite clear that multiassaultive family members are violent and antisocial across a variety of settings, toward both family members and society in general, and may demonstrate this behavioral pattern throughout most of their lifetimes.

The Cycle of Violence

For some time, the scholarly and popular literature has concluded that both abusive parents and abusive spouses have themselves been the victims of family violence during their childhoods (Megargee, 1982). Some research suggests that highly violent offenders may have been subjected to more severe and frequent physical and psychological abuse and punitive parenting during their childhoods than other offenders (Hämäläinen & Haapasalo, 1996). Individuals grow up to be abusive because they were abused themselves, a belief referred to as the **cycle-of-violence hypothesis**.

According to social learning theory, those who receive harsh discipline learn that physical violence can be used to change the behaviors of others (Schwartz, Hage, Bush, & Burns, 2006). **Coercion theory** proposed by Patterson (1982) and discussed in Chapter 6 also posits that coercive and punitive tactics in parenting increase the likelihood of later aggressive behavior and potential domestic violence. Theories that view domestic violence as a tactic for gaining power and control in relationships are highly consistent with coercion theory. As noted by Schwartz et al. (2006), "Men involved in intimate violence have been found to have demand and/or withdraw patterns of communication with their partners and perceive themselves as lacking power in their relationships" (p. 212). Consequently, abusing spouses and other family members is one way, in the abuser's eyes, of gaining and maintaining control over those in their immediate social environment. There is also accumulating evidence that males who experience parental neglect during their childhoods are more likely to engage in dating violence, a behavior that is a precursor to spousal abuse (Chapple, 2003; Simons, Lin, & Gordon, 1998).

Nevertheless, violence does not necessarily beget violence. The cycle of violence and the presumed overall consequences of abuse and neglect do not take into account the resilience of human beings, which rules out any simple cause-and-effect relationship between maltreatment and future violent behavior (Garbarino, 1989). In many cases, rather than finding that abusive parenting is the logical consequence of being victimized as children, the opposite sequence is likely to take place. Realizing and sensitive to the enormous psychological and social costs of family violence, many victims of child abuse may be unlikely to commit aggressive acts as adults within their families. Garbarino (1989, p. 222), for example, writes, "Many victims of child abuse, probably most, survive it and avoid repeating the pattern in their own child rearing."

On the other hand, children who are maltreated are at risk of further *victimization* as adults; this is particularly true, but not exclusively, of children who were sexually abused. The revictimization is usually through IPV (Briggs et al., 2011). Thus, while the cycle of violence may be broken in the sense that the child victim does not, as adult, victimize others, the thread of violence continues because the child is revictimized as an adult.

The Effects of Family Violence on Children

Domestic violence is recognized as a serious problem in our society today, but how such violence affects the children who are exposed to it did not appear in the research literature until the 1980s. Children who are exposed to violence between adults in their homes have often been referred to as the "silent," "forgotten," and "unintended" victims of domestic violence. These children were initially referred to as simply "witnesses" or "observers," but recent research literature has discovered that some are not only directly involved victims themselves but also suffer some troubling consequences.

Children experience domestic violence through a bewildering array of events. Most often, children see or hear the violence, and they are often directly targeted, sometimes fatally. In a recent incident, a 13-year-old boy was the only survivor in a family mass shooting during which the father shot his mother and two younger siblings before turning the gun on himself. The father had shot at the 13-year-old, but missed. According to news reports, the boy ran around the garage with his hands lifted in the air in a surrender gesture before fleeing to the home of a neighbor. Other children experience family violence by trying to intervene or calling 911 (Edleson, 1999). Additional examples include the assaulter taking the child hostage to force the mother's return, using a child as a physical weapon against the victim, forcing the child to watch the violence, forcing the child to participate in the abuse, and using the child as a spy or questioning the child about the mother's activities (Ganley & Schechter, 1996). In another recent incident, a man tied up and brutally sexually assaulted his wife in front of their three children. Any of these experiences can leave lasting imprints on a child or adolescent.

Experiencing the aftermath of the violence may be equally traumatic for children (Edleson, 1999). Examples include the child seeing the mother with physical injuries and possibly in need of medical help, observing maternal emotions (such as anxiety, depression, stress), and having the family move to a shelter to escape further abuse. If the family has pets, leaving the pet behind can be intensely traumatizing for the child—and often the pet is abused as well. The aftermath of violence can also include a father alternating between physical violence and loving care, as well as police intervention that could result in the removal of the father from the home. In some instances, removal of the children from the home by child welfare agencies is also a terrifying possibility.

The number of children exposed to domestic violence in the United States each year is largely unknown, despite the fact that domestic violence appears to be on the decrease (Finkelhor, 2011). Straus (1991, p. 98) estimates that "at least a third of Americans have witnessed violence between their parents, and most have endured repeated instances." This estimation is based on Straus and Gelles's (1990) national survey that discovered that the 30 percent of parents who admitted domestic violence existed in their home also reported that their children had witnessed at least one violent incident during the length of the marriage.

Research has also found that approximately 14 percent of university students recall witnessing physical violence during their childhood years between their parents (Straus & Michel-Smith, 2014). Police arrest data from five U.S. cities revealed that children were directly involved in adult domestic violence incidents about 27 percent of the time (Fantuzzo, Boruch, Abdullahi, Atkins, & Marcus, 1997). Fantuzzo et al. also found that younger children were disproportionately represented in households where domestic violence occurred.

Explanations about how domestic violence affects a child must include an assortment of already existing risk factors. The child's age, the nature and severity of the violence, socioeconomic status, and parental substance abuse all must be entered into the equation.

The child's behavioral and emotional functioning is the area that has received the most attention from researchers. Overall, these studies report the consistent finding that children exposed to domestic violence exhibit many behavioral and emotional problems when compared with other children. For instance, studies using the Child Behavior Checklist (Achenbach & Edelbrock, 1983) and similar measures have found that children who are exposed to domestic violence display more aggressive and antisocial behaviors, as well as fearful and inhibited behaviors (Fantuzzo et al., 1991; Hughes, 1988; Hughes, Parkinson, & Vargo, 1989), and show lower social competence and interpersonal skills than other children (Adamson & Thompson, 1998; Fantuzzo et al., 1991; Hughes, 1988). More aggressive and antisocial behaviors are often referred to as "externalized" behaviors, while fearful and inhibited behaviors are referred to as "internalized" behaviors (Carlson, 1991; Edleson, 1999; Stagg, Wills, & Howell, 1989).

Domestic violence has also been shown to have dramatic negative effects on children's emotional health and overall adjustment. Both boys and girls in families with spousal violence demonstrate far more depression and aggression (McClosky, Figueredo, & Koss, 1995; Wolfe, Jaffe, Wilson, & Zak, 1985) and lower self-esteem (Hughes & Barad, 1983) compared with other children. In addition, children who are exposed to violence between parents are more likely to show anxiety, depression, trauma symptoms, and temperamental problems (Hughes, 1988; Maker, Kemmelmeier, & Peterson, 1998).

Another consequence of experiencing violence within the home is the overall effects it has on the child's immediate and long-term cognitive functioning and attitudes about how to deal with violence and conflict resolution in their own lives. Many researchers conclude that children's exposure to adult domestic violence may generate attitudes justifying their own use of violence to solve problems and deal with frustrations. For example, Spaccarelli, Coatsworth, and Bowden's (1995) study found support for such an association by showing that, among a sample of 213 adolescent boys incarcerated for violent crimes, those boys who had experienced family violence were more likely to subscribe to the viewpoint that "acting aggressively enhances one's reputation or self-image" (p. 173). And Carlson (1991) reports that in a sample of 101 adolescents, boys who witnessed domestic violence were significantly more likely to approve of violence than were girls who had witnessed domestic violence.

In conclusion, the empirical evidence reveals that children's exposure to domestic violence is a serious and widespread problem. Such violence affects children indirectly through its effect on the parenting relationship, as well as directly affecting children's behavioral, emotional, cognitive, psychological, and social adjustment.

SUMMARY AND CONCLUSIONS

In this chapter, we began to narrow our focus to consider specific offenses. Previous chapters were broader, in that they dealt with general theoretical orientations to crime. Here, we reviewed the data on criminal homicide and summarized empirical and clinical research on juveniles who kill, IPV, and various forms of family violence.

Criminal homicides are rare compared with the total incidence of violent crime. In the United States, violent crime is often committed by young males living in environments that implicitly or explicitly advocate violence for the resolution of conflict. Guns (especially handguns) are commonly used in the crime. Statistics also indicate that, when the relationship of victim and offender is known, the homicide victim and the offender are usually family members, friends, or acquaintances. The relationship is known in between half and two-thirds of the offenses. While assaults are far more common than homicide, the same demographic and psychological features appear, particularly for aggravated assault.

While many of the psychological characteristics of offenders are similar in crimes of assault and homicide, some homicides deserve separate attention. These include the homicides that will be covered in the next chapter and juvenile murders, which were covered here. Murders committed by juveniles are rare, but when they occur, they attract both media and research attention. Researchers have learned that juvenile murderers who act on their own or in a dyad (as opposed to killing as gang activity) often have no significant history of violence, but often come from dysfunctional families, have poor peer relationships, and have emotional and sometimes biological deficiencies—such as brain damage. Clinicians note that juveniles who kill respond favorably to psychological treatment, particularly if they are not placed in adult correctional settings.

Contemporary researchers often prefer to focus on IPV rather than "domestic violence" or, more broadly, "family violence." IPV allows them to consider the prevalence, causes, and prevention of violence directed at intimate partners who may or may not be married or living under the same roof. In addition, IPV researchers are examining violence among subgroups, such as the elderly, racial and ethnic groups, same-sex couples, individuals in dating relationships, and military and law enforcement families. In the chapter we included IPV as a separate section, but readers should keep in mind that material in the family violence section also pertains to many IPV situations.

Family violence is a very broad subject that encompasses child maltreatment, spouse or partner abuse, elder abuse, sibling abuse, and child-to-parent abuse. Abuse comes in many forms, including physical, psychological, or sexual abuse. Family violence is found across ethnic, racial, and socioeconomic classes. Women are disproportionately subject to spousal violence and the dire economic situations that may lead to both victimization and victimizing. Children are particularly vulnerable targets for family violence and maltreatment, enduring physical maltreatment, sexual exploitation, medical and emotional neglect, and psychological trauma—all of which are usually lifelong in their consequences. In this chapter, we focused not only on "typical" forms of child abuse but also on statistics and research relating to child abductions, SBS, MSBP, and infanticide. For the child who survives abuse, the psychological consequences can nevertheless be devastating. Though he or she does not necessarily become an abuser, perpetuating the cycle of abuse, emotional scars relating to one's self-concept, and the ability to trust others are often very deep and longlasting.

In addition to the obvious physical injuries and deaths that result, family violence is often cited in research and clinical studies as contributing to other individual, family, and societal problems. Most of all, family violence and maltreatment highlight the importance of considering a victimological approach for the complete understanding of violent crime, and underscore the fact that the family is far from being a safe haven for many. Factors such as family instability and violence have been consistently found to be prevalent among juveniles who engage in sexually abusive and violent behavior (Righthand & Welch, 2001). Many studies conclude that abused children have trouble recognizing appropriate emotions in others, have less empathy for others, and have difficulty taking another person's perspective (Knight & Prentky, 1993). It is very likely that many of the LCP offenders discussed elsewhere in the text spring from families characterized by abuse, violence, and neglect.

Key Concepts

Assault
Aggravated assault
Availability heuristic
Coercion developmental theory
Criminal homicide
Cycle-of-violence hypothesis
Eldercide
Felony murder
Filicide
Fratricide
General altercation homicide
Hostile attribution bias
Infanticide
Intimate partner violence (IPV)
Matricide
Multiassaultive families
Munchausen syndrome by proxy (MSBP)

Murder
National Survey of Children Exposed to Violence (NatSCEV)
Negligent manslaughter
Nonnegligent manslaughter
Neonaticide
Parricide
Patricide
Proactive violence
Reactive violence
Self-regulation
Shaken baby syndrome
Siblicide
Sororicide
Stereotypical abductions
Typology
Weapons effect

Review Questions

1. What is the availability heuristic? How might it account for our perception of violence?
2. Explain the differences between homicide, murder, nonnegligent manslaughter, and negligent manslaughter.
3. Review research findings on juvenile murderers.
4. Discuss IPV among any *one* special population.
5. What are the psychological effects of (a) child maltreatment and (b) other domestic violence on children?
6. What is the cycle-of-violence hypothesis?
7. Compare and contrast abusive head trauma and Munchausen syndrome by proxy as specific forms of child abuse.
8. Discuss eldercide as a form of family violence, including its prevalence, perpetrators, and victims.

10

Multiple Murder, School and Workplace Violence

CHAPTER OBJECTIVES

▪ Define and review research on investigative psychology and profiling.

▪ Describe the five types of profiling and their relevance to investigating serious crime.

▪ Summarize what is known about serial killers and their victims.

▪ Summarize what is known about mass murderers and their victims.

▪ Discuss crime that can lead to multiple murder, such as school and workplace violence.

• In April 2007, 32 people were killed and approximately 17were wounded during a mass shooting at Virginia Polytechnic Institute and State University.

• In November 2009, 13 were killed and 32 wounded at a military processing center in Fort Hood, Texas.

• In July 2011, 77 people were killed in Norway during a bombing and gun rampage.

• In July 2012, gunfire erupted during a midnight showing of a film in Aurora, Colorado. Twelve people were killed and over 50 others injured.

• In August of the same year, six people were shot and four wounded at a Sikh Temple in Oak Creek, Wisconsin.

• In December 2012, 20 first graders and six staff members were murdered and two were wounded at Sandy Hook Elementary School in Newtown, Connecticut. The perpetrator's mother was shot to death in her home prior to the mass incident

• In September 2013, 12 people were fatally shot and three were injured during a rampage at the Washington, D.C. Naval Yard.

• In August 2015, nine people participating in a church prayer group in Charleston, South Carolina, died after being shot by a man who sat with them calmly for over a half hour before producing a weapon and gunning them down.

• In September 2015, nine students and an instructor at a community college in Oregon were killed, and several others wounded, when a gunman opened fire in a classroom.

The above incidents, most of which will be discussed again in this chapter, illustrate the massive death toll that can be caused by one individual during one incident. Although homicide in general was the topic of Chapter 9, here we examine a very different form of killing, one that implicates different psychological concepts. In each of the above and additional instances to be cited throughout the chapter, the perpetrator planned an offense that would guarantee the death of multiple victims.

In this chapter we revisit criminal homicide, focusing on its exceptional but rare forms, including the mass murders cited above and serial murders, which involve one person killing multiple victims over a period of time. Acts of terrorism that result in many deaths—also a form of mass murder—will be discussed in the following chapter. Finally, because school and workplace violence also can and have resulted in multiple deaths, these are discussed in separate sections.

The homicides covered in this chapter are relatively rare, although there are indications that mass shootings are increasing. . Even though rare, the social and emotional impact they have on a community—and on a society as a whole—is considerable. The fear and terror they engender can alter the lifestyles of thousands. Moreover, they draw extensive media coverage; although it may be accurate with respect to the facts of the case, much of it lacks a solid understanding of the psychosocial aspects involved in the crime. Therefore, it is important that we give attention to what we know—and do not know—about these well-publicized offenses. Due to the serious nature of these offenses, behavioral scientists often try to explain them theoretically or place offenders into categories or typologies. This is done both to provide assistance to law enforcement in identifying the perpetrators—if they are not known—and to predict and prevent future incidents. Although some preventive measures can be taken, predicting who will undertake a multiple murder with a high level of confidence is not possible. Before discussing the various types of multiple murders, it is worthwhile to consider contemporary approaches to studying these crimes.

INVESTIGATIVE PSYCHOLOGY

In recent years, considerable public attention has been given to topics like profiling and investigative psychology. Readers are undoubtedly familiar with popular movies and television shows (e.g., *Silence of the Lambs, Criminal Minds*) that feature these activities. The popular series *Criminal Minds* includes actors portraying behavioral scientists who work within the FBI's Behavioral Science Unit (BSU). Profiling is not restricted to the serious crimes that are the subject of this chapter. Furthermore, it is generally directed at unsolved crimes, such as serial killings, robberies, or burglaries, rather than the mass murders illustrated at the beginning of this chapter, in which the perpetrators soon become known. Nevertheless, psychological profiles of known offenders may be undertaken in an effort to understand what led someone to commit these crimes as well as anticipate further similar events. It must be emphasized that predicting multiple murders is almost impossible, however.

In the professional and academic world, the word "profiling" is often avoided. There are many reasons for this. First, because the activity is unregulated in the United States, persons with minimum degrees or experience can call themselves profilers; some have attained celebrity status, appearing for media interviews and writing in ongoing blogs. At times their "predictions" have been extremely inaccurate, though credible profilers help us understand an event after it occurred or while it is unfolding. Second, many profilers tend to rely on "hunches" rather than on scientific data. While hunches based on clinical experience are understandable, hunches without data to back them up are problematic. We discuss this in more detail below. Third, some profilers in the past have written self-serving personal accounts of their experiences that minimize the imperfect nature of their art. And finally, depictions of profilers in novels or entertainment media too often suggest they are infallible and can solve most crimes. For these reasons, to bring more respectability to the profiling enterprise, some professionals prefer to call themselves "behavioral analysts" or "investigative psychologists" rather than profilers.

Investigative psychology, a term coined by David Canter, the director of the Centre for Investigative Psychology at the University of Liverpool in England, refers to the application of psychological research and principles to the investigation of criminal behavior. Investigative psychology tries to answer three fundamental questions that are crucial in criminal investigations (Canter & Alison, 2000, p. 3):

1. What are the important behavioral features of the crime that may help identify and successfully prosecute the perpetrator?
2. What inferences can be made about the characteristics of the offender that may help identify him or her?
3. Are there any other crimes that are likely to have been committed by the same person?

These questions are central to investigative psychology, and they are rapidly being addressed in the United States, Canada, Australia, the Netherlands, and the United Kingdom. The United Kingdom is where—it is fair to say—this *scientific* approach to criminal investigation—from a psychological perspective—originated. In recent years psychologists worldwide have embraced the need to accumulate data based on empirical research in order to consult with investigators looking to solve crimes. In the United States, for example, members of the Society for Police and Criminal Psychology as well as members of the Police and Public Safety Section of Division 18 of the American Psychological Association conduct research relevant to investigative psychology and consult with the law enforcement community.

In this chapter, because the term "profiling" remains in widespread use, we will retain it in our discussion of the various forms of profiling as well as the research on its effectiveness. However, as in other published work (Bartol & Bartol, 2013), we subdivide profiling into five distinct types. It should be emphasized, though, that the investigation of crime may involve more than one of these forms. Furthermore, the forms summarized below are not equally pertinent to the topic of multiple murder.

FORMS OF PROFILING

Profiling can be divided into five somewhat overlapping categories: (1) psychological profiling; (2) suspect-based profiling; (3) geographical profiling; (4) crime scene profiling; and (5) equivocal death analysis. Although we give attention to each type, the last is the least likely to be relevant to multiple murders.

Each of these profiling methods—and the investigators who employ these methods—rely on different ways to analyze the person, the crime scene, or the incident. Some of the profiling categories rely on either the **clinical** or **actuarial approach**. The clinical approach is *case focused* and tries to infer characteristics of an offender from the analysis of evidence gathered from a specific crime or series of crimes (Alison, West, & Goodwill, 2004). The method concentrates on the description, understanding, and identification of a *single* offender based on the material gathered on an *individual* case. In situations where an offender has not been identified (such as in burglaries, rapes, or some killings), the clinical method hopes to predict if and when the offender will strike again. It is based on the premise that every case is unique, and often emphasizes discovering the motivation for the crime as a basic understanding of the offender. The clinical approach relies heavily on experience and training, and is often supplemented by intuition, subjectivity, and sometimes "gut feelings."

By comparison, the actuarial approach concentrates on a data base gathered from groups of offenders who have committed similar crimes or engaged in similar incidents. This profiling tactic is based on how groups of offenders who have committed similar crimes have acted in the past. The accumulated data from these groups of behavioral patterns are called the base rates. Base rate is defined as "the unconditional, naturally occurring rate of a phenomenon in a population" (VandenBos, 2007, p. 103). If, for example, 65 out of 100 serial killers move the body from the crime scene, the base rate would be 65. The base rate provides an estimation of how many serial killers move the bodies from the crime scene, a helpful indicator for the profiler.

Psychological Profiling

Psychological profiling is an assessment practice designed to help in the identification and prediction of behavior in *known* individuals. As a general concept, it is not limited to negative characteristics. For example, psychological profiling may be used to predict positive characteristics in candidates for law enforcement or even for public office (Bartol & Bartol, 2013). For our purposes, however, we focus on profiling of negative characteristics, such as those that may be associated with criminal behavior. In that sense, psychological profiling consists of two basic approaches: threat assessment and risk assessment. Threat assessment is the process of determining the validity and seriousness of threat being carried out by a person or group of persons. In most cases, the threat has already been made and is generally directed at a person, facility, institution, organization, or group of persons. Therefore, threat assessment might be employed in the case of a high school student who has told peers that he plans to "take out" the school, or an employee who displays uncharacteristic, bizarre behavior.

Risk assessment—which was covered in chapter 8—comes into play even if no direct threat has been made. Risk assessment is a process to evaluate "individuals who have violated social norms or displayed bizarre behavior, particularly when they appear menacing or unpredictable" (Hanson, 2009, p. 172). The primary goal of risk assessment is to estimate the probability that a particular person will harm self or others, and more importantly, to provide what can be done to prevent the harm.

Suspect-Based Profiling

Suspect-based profiling, also known as prospective profiling, refers to identifying the psychological and behavioral features of persons who may commit a particular crime, such as school violence, terrorist activities, stalking, drug trafficking, shoplifting, or skyjacking. For example, is there a "profile" of a school shooter? Suspect-based profiling is built on the systematic collection of behavioral, personality, cognitive, and demographic data on previous offenders who committed similar crimes. Therefore, suspect-based profiling is largely actuarial because it uses statistical methods rather than clinical skills to arrive at conclusions about who is likely to commit the crime.

Suspect-based profiling is often used at airports and border crossings to interdict drugs and out of concern for terrorist activities. In the wake of events of September 11, 2001, the U.S. Transportation Safety Administration has trained behavioral detection officers (BDOs) to observe air passengers for behavior clues—presumably identified by systematic research—that may indicate intentions to harm or bring down aircraft. Unfortunately, this type of profiling is susceptible to racial or ethnic profiling. This is defined as "police-initiated action that relies on the race, ethnicity, or national origin rather than the behavior of an individual or information that leads the police to a particular individual who has been identified as being, or having been, engaged in criminal activity" (Ramirez, McDevitt, & Farrell, 2000, p. 3). Racial profiling is an illegal practice, though difficult to prove that it occurred. However, racial profiling is a practice that accounts in part for the fact that racial and ethnic minorities are disproportionately represented in arrest statistics. Furthermore, racial profiling illustrates the dangers and inaccuracies of the profiling enterprise that could affect anyone in the population. We discuss these issues in more detail in the following chapter.

Geographical Profiling

Geographical profiling is a technique that can help locate where a serial offender resides, or other geographical locations that serve as a base of operations of a serial offender, such as a bar, place of work, or significant other's home. Note that serial offender is not limited to the serial murderers discussed in this chapter; the term can pertain to burglars, sex offenders, arsonists, or other offenders. Geographical profiling depends, in most cases, on sophisticated computer software programs that are continually developed and updated. One of the earliest such programs was Rigel, which developed out of the work of D. Kim Rossmo, who pioneered a *Criminal Geographic Targeting Program* (*CGT*) that was subsequently incorporated into a software application known as Rigel and Rigel Analyst (Rich & Shively, 2004). The *CGT* generates a three-dimensional map that assigns statistical probabilities to various areas that seem to fall into the offender's territory. The three-dimensional map is then placed over a street or topographical map where the crimes have occurred. The program considers known movement patterns, possible comfort zones, and victim-searching patterns of the offender. Ultimately, the objective of the program is to pinpoint the location of the offender's residence and/or base of operations. Another popular geographic profiling package is *Crimestat*, which was developed by Ned Levine and Associates (2000, 2002) and funded by the National Institute of Justice. Still another is *Dragnet*, developed by David Canter (2008).

Geographical profiling can help in any criminal investigation of an unknown offender by locating the approximate area in which he or she lives, or by narrowing the surveillance and stakeouts to places where the next crime by the offender is most likely to occur. The process is usually highly actuarial. This type of profiling basically tries to identify the geographical territory the offender knows well, feels most comfortable in, and prefers to find or take victims in (Rossmo, 1997). Although a *criminal* profile hypothesizes about the demographic, motivational, and psychological features of the crime and offender, a geographic profile focuses on the location of the crime and how it relates to the residence and/or base of operations of the offender. As indicated above, geographical profiling is useful not only in the search for serial violent offenders but also in the search for property offenders, such as serial burglars and serial arsonists.

Crime Scene Profiling

Various terms are used for **crime scene profiling**, which is the process of identifying personality traits, behavioral patterns, geographic habits, cognitive tendencies, and demographic features of an *unknown* offender based on *characteristics of the crime*. It is sometimes called criminal profiling, offender profiling, crime scene analysis, behavioral analysis, or criminal investigative analysis. It can be considered a skill or an activity that is a part of the investigative psychology described earlier. Therefore, while investigative psychology is the broad application of psychological research and principles to solving crimes, crime scene profiling is the narrower activity that focuses on the traits, features, and habits of an unknown offender. Because it is highly relevant to many of the topics in the book, as well as to the material in the present chapter, crime scene profiling will be discussed in some detail here.

Descriptions or profiles of the general characteristics of a person on the basis of a limited amount of information were used long before the FBI employed such methods (Canter & Alison, 2000). In fact, the history of crime scene profiling can be traced back to Jack the Ripper, the serial killer who brutally murdered five prostitutes in separate incidents in London's East End in 1888. Although the case was never solved, the chief forensic pathologist, Dr. George Baxter Phillips, tried to help police investigators by inferring personality characteristics based on the nature of the wounds inflicted on the victims (Turvey, 2012). That is, he noticed that the wounds were inflicted with considerable skill and knowledge, suggesting that the killer had a sophisticated knowledge of human anatomy. Interestingly, the fictional detective Sherlock Holmes, first created by Sir Arthur Conan Doyle in 1887, consistently employed a form of criminal profiling in his intriguing search for the offender. Since then, virtually every detective or mystery novel has the main characters engaging in some variant of criminal profiling.

Crime scene profiling was developed in the United States by the **Behavioral Science Unit** of the FBI during the 1970s. During its early development, it was used primarily to provide investigative assistance to law enforcement in cases of serial homicide and serial rape (Homant & Kennedy, 1998). In 1984, the **National Center for the Analysis of Violent Crime (NCAVC)**—located at the FBI Academy in Quantico, Virginia—was created and within it the **Behavioral Analysis Unit (BAU)** and the **Violent Criminal Apprehension Program (ViCAP)**. Today, most of the crime scene profiling is conducted under the auspices of the BAU, although the BSU remains a separate unit that sponsors research and training, and works closely with the NCAVC. During its early development, crime scene profiling was predominantly clinical in approach.

John Douglas is a former FBI agent and former head of the Behavioral Science Unit of the FBI. He has published extensively on investigative methods and profiling. According to Douglas and Corinne Munn (1992a), three important features of offender behavior may be evident at the scene of a crime: (1) the *modus operandi*, (2) the personation or signature, and (3) staging. *Modus operandi* (the MO) refers to the actions and procedures an offender engages in to commit a crime successfully. It is a behavioral pattern that the offender learns as he or she gains experience in committing the offense. Since the offender generally changes the MO until he or she learns which method is most effective, some professional profilers believe that investigators may make a serious error if they place too much significance on the MO when linking crimes, however (Douglas & Munn, 1992c).

Anything that goes beyond what is necessary to commit the crime is called the **personation** or the **signature**. For example, a serial offender may demonstrate a repetitive, almost ritualistic behavior from crime to crime, an unusual pattern that is not necessary to commit the offense. The signature may involve certain items that are left or removed from the scene, or other symbolic patterns, such as writings on the wall. If the victim is murdered, the signature may include unusual body positions or mutilations. In very rare instances, the signature may involve a "DNA torch," where the offender pours gasoline over a victim and sets the victim and the structure or motor vehicle on fire in an effort to destroy evidence, such as evidence of sexual assault. A signature may also involve the repetitive acts of domination, manipulation, and control used by a serial rapist (Douglas & Munn, 1992b). Or it may be revealed by physical evidence found at the crime scene, such as the type of ligature used or the personal items taken from the victim by a serial rapist. The signature is often thought to be related to the unique cognitive processes of the offender and, in this sense, may be more important to an investigator than the MO. In most cases, signature behaviors often establish the theme of the crime for investigators, as they often reveal the psychological and emotional needs of the offender (Turvey, 2008).

Staging refers to the intentional alteration of a crime scene prior to the arrival of the police, and it is sometimes done by someone other than the perpetrator. As Douglas and Munn (1992a) note, staging is usually done for one of two reasons: either to redirect the investigation away from the most logical suspect, or to protect the victim or the victim's family. Staging is frequently done by someone who has an association or relationship with the victim. For example, staging done by the family with the intent to protect the victim may be seen in autoerotic or other embarrassing fatalities. Autoeroticism, a term coined by Havelock Ellis, refers to self-arousal and self-gratification of sexual desire without a partner.

In some instances, the method of autoeroticism may result in the death of the individual, such as by self-strangulation or hanging. Douglas and Munn (1992a) assert that in about one-third of autoerotic fatalities, the victim is nude, and in about another one-third, the victim is clothed in a costume, such as a male in female clothing. Under these conditions, friends or family members may alter the scene to make the victim more "presentable" to the authorities. In some instances, they may even stage a criminal homicide, including ransacking the house or specific rooms to give the impression of a burglary gone wrong.

In some instances, an offender may engage in **undoing** a behavioral pattern found at the scene in which the offender tries to psychologically "undo" the murder. For example, the offender may wash and dress the victim, or place the body on a bed, placing the head on a pillow and covering the body with blankets. This pattern typically occurs in offenders who become especially distraught about the death of the victim. Very often, the offender has a close association with the victim. In other cases, an offender may try to dehumanize the victim by engaging in actions that obscure the identity of the victim, such as excessive facial battery. Other offenders may employ more subtle acts of dehumanization, such as covering the victim's face with some material or object, or placing the victim facedown. Note that the difference between undoing and staging is the reason behind the action; in staging, the offender or someone else is trying to alter the crime scene in order to divert suspicion. In the classic case, the offender wipes fingerprints from a weapon and positions it close to the body in such a way that a death looks like a suicide.

Crime scenes and offenders are also sometimes classified as organized, disorganized, or mixed (see **Tables 10-1** and **10-2**). As we note shortly, however, this is not necessarily a valid classification as it pertains to offenders, although it is still used in profiling circles. An **organized crime scene** indicates planning and premeditation on the part of the offender. The crime scene shows signs that the offender maintained control of himself and the victim. Often, the victim is moved from the abduction area to another secluded area, and perhaps the body is moved to still another area. Furthermore, the offender in an organized crime usually selects victims according to some personal criteria. The infamous serial killer Ted Bundy, for example, selected young, attractive women who were similar in appearance. He was also successful in the abduction of these young women from highly visible areas, such as beaches, campuses, and ski lodges, indicating considerable planning and premeditation (Douglas, Ressler, Burgess, & Hartman, 1986).

TABLE 10-1	Profile Characteristics of Organized and Disorganized Murderers as Classified by the FBI	
Organized	**Disorganized**	
Average to above-average intelligence	Below average intelligence	
Socially competent	Socially inadequate	
Skilled work preferred	Unskilled work	
High birth order status	Low birth order status	
Father's work stable	Father's work unstable	
Sexually competent	Sexually incompetent	
Inconsistent childhood discipline	Harsh discipline as a child	
Controlled mood during crime	Anxious mood during crime	
Use of alcohol with crime	Minimal use of alcohol	
Precipitating situational stress	Minimal situational stress	
Living with partner	Living alone	
Mobility (car in good condition)	Lives/works near crime scene	
Follows crime in news media	Minimal interest in news media	
May change job or leave town	Significant behavior change	

Source: Federal Bureau of Investigation. (1985, August). Crime scene and profile characteristics of organized and disorganized murders. FBI Law Enforcement Bulletin, 54, 18–25.

TABLE 10-2	Crime Scene Differences between Organized and Disorganized Murderers as Classified by the FBI	
Organized	**Disorganized**	
Planned offense	Spontaneous offense	
Victim a targeted stranger	Victim/location known	
Personalizes victim	Depersonalizes victim	
Controlled conversation	Minimal conversation	
Crime scene reflects control	Crime scene random and sloppy	
Demands submissive victim	Sudden violence to victim	
Restraints used	Minimal use of restraints	
Aggressive acts prior to death	Sexual acts after death	
Body hidden	Body left in view	
Weapon/evidence absent	Weapon/evidence often present	
Transports victim or body	Body left at death scene	

Source: Federal Bureau of Investigation. (1985, August). Crime scene and profile characteristics of organized and disorganized murders. FBI Law Enforcement Bulletin, 54, 18–25.

A **disorganized crime scene** demonstrates that the offender very probably committed the crime without premeditation or planning. The crime scene indicators suggest the individual acted on impulse or in rage, or under extreme excitement. The disorganized offender obtains his victim by chance, often without specific criteria in mind. Generally, the victim's body is found at the scene of the crime. The **mixed crime scene** has ingredients of both organized and disorganized crime aspects. For example, a crime may have begun as carefully planned, but deteriorated into a disorganized crime when things did not go as planned. In fact, the mixed crime scene is likely the most common type.

Although the organized–disorganized classification system seems intuitively logical, it appears to have very limited usefulness as an investigative tool (Canter, Alison, Alison, & Wentink, 2004; Kocsis, Cooksey, & Irwin, 2002). For instance, research has shown that many—if not most—offenders display behavior characteristics of both organized and disorganized in the same offense (Canter et al., 2004; Taylor, Snook, Bennell, & Porter, 2015). Snook, Cullen, Bennell, Taylor, and Gendreau (2008) assert that, at this point, there is no convincing evidence to support the dichotomy. It may be more realistic to assume that crime scenes fall along a continuum, with the organized description at one pole and the disorganized description at the other pole, but with few crimes fitting squarely at either pole.

The practice of crime scene profiling is utilized by police agencies across the world (Snook et al., 2008). Many police investigators and detectives indicate they find it useful in their investigations of certain crime. In one survey reported by Snook et al. (2008), 8 out of 10 police officers in the United Kingdom found criminal profiling helpful in their investigations and said they would seek profiling help again. In an exploratory Internet survey of forensic psychologists and psychiatrists, Torres, Boccaccini, and Miller (2006) found that 40 percent of these professionals thought that criminal profiling was scientifically reliable and valid. Unfortunately these perceptions are not always supported by the research, as we will see shortly.

Profiling appears to be particularly useful in serial sexual offenses, such as serial rape and serial sexual homicides (Pinizzotto & Finkel, 1990). This is because we have a more extensive research base on sexual offending than we do on homicide. In addition, profiling of serial offenders is most successful when the offender demonstrates some form of psychopathology at the crime scene, such as torture, evisceration, postmortem slashing and cutting, and other mutilation (Pinizzotto, 1984). However, profiling is not as effective in the identification of offenders involved in fraud, burglary, robbery, political crimes, theft, and drug-induced crime because of the limited research base, although significant gains in some of these areas (e.g., burglary) have been made in recent years.

RESEARCH ON CRIME SCENE PROFILING.   There has been very little published research on the utility, reliability, and validity of crime scene profiling in general (Alison, Smith, & Morgan, 2003; Woodworth & Porter, 2001), although some studies have attempted to assess its accuracy. One pioneering study was conducted by Pinizzotto and Finkel (1990). The study involved four trained FBI experts, six trained police detectives, six experienced detectives without training, six clinical psychologists naive about crime scene profiling, and six untrained undergraduate students. The results, in general, were not strongly supportive of profile accuracy. Trained experts were somewhat more accurate in profiling the sexual offender, but were not much better than the untrained groups in profiling the homicide offender. The researchers also tried to identify any qualitative differences in the way experts and nonexperts processed the information provided. Overall, the results showed that experts did not process the material any differently than the nonexperts. This finding suggests that the cognitive methods and strategies used by expert profilers are not discernibly different from the way nonexperts process the available information about the crime. The artificiality of the experiment and the quality of information given by the groups may have been influential factors in this observation, however. What the researchers did find is that some trained profilers were more interested and skillful in certain areas than other profilers. Some profilers, for example, were good at gaining information from the medical reports, whereas others were better at gaining clues from the crime scene photos. This finding indicates that group profiling by a team of trained experts may be more effective than utilizing one single profiler.

Despite media portrayals of highly successful and probing profilers employing sophisticated techniques and thoughtful strategies for identifying the offender, reality is far more sobering. Contemporary researchers on profiling (Alison & Canter, 1999; Alison, Bennell, Omerod, &

Mokros, 2002; Snook et al., 2008) point out that there are two basic flaws in modern-day profiling. One flaw is the assumption that human behavior is *consistent* across a variety of *different* situations. The other flaw is the assumption that offense style or evidence gathered at the crime scene is directly related to specific personality characteristics. Psychology has consistently found that behavior varies according to situations or the social context, especially if the social contexts are significantly different. Moreover, there is little empirical data that link crime scene characteristics to personality or other psychological features of the offender. Snook et al. (2008) write,

> Criminal profilers do not seem to recognize that a consensus began to emerge in the psychological literature some 40 years ago that to rely on traits or personality dispositions as the primary explanation for behavior was a serious mistake. Situational factors contribute as much as personality dispositions to the prediction of behavior. (p. 1261)

There are other problems with profiling as well. Some studies point out that a large proportion of the conclusions and predictions contained within profile reports are both ambiguous and unverifiable (Alison, Smith, & Morgan, 2003; Alison, Smith, Eastman, & Rainbow, 2003; Snook, Eastwood, Gendreau, Goggin, & Cullen, 2007). Many of the statements are so vague that they are open to a wide range of interpretations. Compounding the problem is the tendency for police investigators to interpret the ambiguous information contained within the profile report to fit their own biases and hunches about the case or the suspect. They select those aspects of the report that they see as fitting their own cognitive sketch of the suspect while ignoring the conclusions and predictions in the report that do not fit. This powerful tendency is known in psychology as **confirmation bias**. We are all subject to confirmation bias to some extent, but being aware of it may lessen its impact.

The above points underscore the fact that many individuals who call themselves profilers are prone to rely on outdated personality theory and psychological principles, and are basically unfamiliar with the current research literature on profiling and human behavior in general. Some believe that profiling is best done on "gut feelings" and "instinct" based on many years of experience of crime scene investigations. On the other hand, some professional profilers indicate that their profiling strategies are effective and are founded on extensive data bases and clinical expertise (Dern, Dern, Horn, & Horn, 2009). The potential usefulness of crime scene profiling is too critical to be relegated to the entertainment media and questionable applications by law enforcement. It is important, therefore, that we learn how reliable and valid the various profiling methods currently utilized are, and how they can be improved to allow meaningful application in forensic settings.

CONTEMPORARY PERSPECTIVES ON CRIME SCENE OR OFFENDER PROFILING. To summarize the above material, crime scene profiling is not about entering "the evil mind of the serial offender." The primary goal of a professional profiler is to provide information to investigators and law enforcement that is based on solid behavioral science (Rainbow & Gregory, 2011). Profilers are expected to offer advice and information that is based on empirical research on criminal behavior and up-to-date psychological principles. Recent research on profiling finds that it is more helpful to investigators if the profiler focuses on discovering how victims are chosen, how they are treated, the distance and routes traveled by the offender, and the nature of the forensic evidence left at the crime scene, especially if the evidence is unknowingly left by the offender. For example, there is a difference between a **crime scene signature** and a **psychological signature** (Bartol & Bartol, 2013). As described earlier, a serial offender may demonstrate a repetitive, distinguishing behavior from crime to crime, an unusual pattern that is not necessary to commit the offense. The offender *intentionally* engages in this behavioral pattern to leave behind his or her trademark, the crime scene signature. However, there is also a psychological signature left at the scene, which represents a habitual or repetitive behavioral pattern that an offender unknowingly leaves behind. A psychological signature is subtle but distinctive ways of speaking, thinking, behaving, and even problem solving *beyond the person's awareness*. It is the psychological signature that potentially provides important keys to linking crimes and identifying aspects about the offending that ultimately may be helpful to investigators.

David Canter and his associates (Canter, 2000a, 2000b) believe that an offender's style of committing a crime is a reflection of the offender's general lifestyle, not some special, unusual aspect of it. For example, how the offender treats the victim provides critical clues for the profiling process. That is, the manner in which the victim is treated and the role the offender assigns to the victim provides a distinctive pattern of how he treats others in his daily life. Offender actions that exhibit a distinctive theme and that are relatively unusual will provide the best clues for differentiating this crime from those crimes committed by other offenders. More specifically, it is far more helpful to investigators if the offender's behavioral patterns differ from the broad data base committed by other offenders who have committed similar crimes. Before this is possible, however, there must be a significant and systematic data base of similar offender behavioral patterns. Some of the distinguishing clues are so subtle, however, that their identification takes a very skillful and knowledgeable profiler to discover them. Furthermore, there should be some consistencies in the manner in which the offender carries out the crime from one incident to another, regardless of how indistinguishable it seems at first glance. And the consistencies may or may not be found in the *modus operandi*.

In summary, much more research needs to be done on profiling accuracy, usefulness, and processing before any tentative conclusions can be advanced in the area. Some positive steps have been made in that direction in recent years. Contrary to popular perceptions, crime scene profiling is not and should not be restricted to serial murder and serial sexual assaults. It has considerable potential value when applied competently to crimes such as arson, burglary, shoplifting, and robbery. Contemporary research has found situational factors to be critically important in profiling and predicting criminal behavior. Bennell and Canter (2002) and Bennell and Jones (2005) report in their studies of commercial and residential burglary that a high level of consistency exists for crime site selection choices. They found, for instance, that the distance between two crime locations was a very effective linking feature, in that shorter distances between burglaries reliably signaled an increased likelihood that the same person committed the burglaries. Method of entry and items stolen, on the other hand, were not useful as profile indicators. The Bennell research demonstrates that some subsets of behavior do reveal consistent criminal patterns and may be very useful in the development of empirically based profiling methods and typologies.

Equivocal Death Analysis

Equivocal death analysis (EDA) also called **reconstructive psychological evaluation**, is the reconstruction of the emotional life, behavioral patterns, and cognitive features of a deceased person. In this sense, it is a postmortem psychological analysis and therefore is frequently referred to simply as a **psychological autopsy** (Brent, 1989; Ebert, 1987; Selkin, 1987). The psychological autopsy was first used to help medical officials determine the cause of deaths that were classified as ambiguous, uncertain, or equivocal (Shneidman, 1994). Today, equivocal death analysis or the psychological autopsy is most often done to determine whether the death was a suicide, and if it was a suicide, the reasons why the person did it. In other words, the individual conducting the autopsy tries to "reconstruct" what was in the mind of the decedent. In practice, equivocal death analysis usually relies on both clinical and actuarial approaches, depending on the investigator.

EDA is only peripherally relevant to the subject of this chapter. It is usually relevant in the case of *single* murders, if there is question whether an individual committed suicide or was murdered. However, in some mass death situations, psychological autopsies have been conducted on individuals who also died in the incident in an effort to attribute blame or to identify factors that might help in the prevention of future offenses. For example, it is highly likely that psychological autopsies were or would be conducted after the Newtown tragedy and the tragedy in 2015 in which a co-pilot flew a plane into the French Alps, killing all 150 people aboard.

TABLE 10-3	Primary Investigative Methods Used by Five Types of Profiling
Type of Profiling	**Primary Investigative Method**
Crime scene	Information from the scene of the crime
Psychological	Risk assessment methods and procedures
Geographical	Computer models of typical spatial behavioral patterns of offenders
Suspect-based	Base-rate information of previous offenders
Equivocal death analysis	Interviews and background information

Psychological autopsies have yet to gain widespread acceptance among mental health practitioners and researchers, however. A noteworthy illustration is the aftermath of the explosion aboard the USS Iowa in 1989, which caused the death of 47 naval personnel. There was question whether the explosion was accidental or had been deliberately caused by a midshipman, Clayton Hartwig, who was said to have been despondent and purposefully set off a detonation device. A psychological autopsy of Hartwig was conducted, and it was initially concluded that he had committed suicide, taking 46 others with him. Congressional committees, however, heard testimony from other psychologists who expressed concerns about the validity of the psychological autopsy as a procedure. Ultimately, it was determined that Hartwig was not to blame for the unfortunate incident.

In sum, the psychological autopsy involves the discovery and reconstruction of a deceased person's life based on the evidence left behind by that person. It is an investigation that entails revisiting the person's lifestyle, evidence of thought processes, and recent emotional and behavioral patterns prior to his or her death. It can be valuable in various forensic situations and circumstances, including insurance benefit determinations, worker's compensation cases, testamentary capacity cases, product liability determinations, malpractice cases, and criminal investigations. Its importance in criminal investigations refers to determinations of whether a person's death was due to a homicide, an accident, or suicide.

The reliability and validity of the psychological autopsy, however, has yet to be demonstrated and remains open to debate, although process is being made, especially pertaining to attempts to standardize how these autopsies are conducted (Knoll, 2008, 2009; Portzky, Audenaert, & van Heeringen, 2009; Snider, Hane, Berman, 2006). At his point in our knowledge, the quality of the psychological autopsy depends largely on the training, knowledge, experience, and clinical orientation of the investigator (Knoll, 2008).

In summary, the five types of profiling discussed in this section can be extremely helpful to law enforcement investigating crimes. Their primary investigative methods are summarized in **Table 10-3**. The profiling enterprise can be useful in formulating and testing theories of criminal behavior. However, caution is urged before accepting uncritically any form of profiling, as the above research demonstrates.

MULTIPLE MURDERS

One of the most frightening and perhaps incomprehensible types of homicide is the random killing of groups of people, either in one episode or individually over a period of time. Although multiple murders are still rare occurrences, when they do happen, they cannot escape attention, and they remain etched in the public consciousness. The great majority of readers of this text will have heard of the slaughters at Columbine, Sandy Hook, Virginia Tech, Oklahoma City, Aurora, and Fort Hood, among others. Other cases, though decades old, may still be familiar. The murder of 21 patrons at a McDonald's restaurant in San Ysidro, California, in July 1984, and the murders of 22 patrons at Luby's Cafeteria in Killeen, Texas, on October 16, 1991 are cases in point.

Mass murders, facilitated by readily available guns and ammunition, are especially on the increase, though still rare. The list of well-known mass murders can be augmented by more recent incidents—some international, some within the United States—that may not have received nation-wide attention. In 2009, a 19-year-old entered the grounds of a school and killed 16 people, including 13 teachers, in the suburbs of Stuttgart, Germany. In the same week, in the United States, a 28-year-old allegedly killed 10 people, including his mother, relatives, and neighbors before killing himself. Two weeks later, a gunman opened fire in a North Carolina nursing home, killing eight and wounding several others. And in Binghamton, New York, a heavily armed man who had recently lost his job, had relationship difficulties, and claimed to be ridiculed because of his difficulty with the English language, entered a building that served as a community service center for immigrants. He killed 14 people before killing himself. Other individuals barricaded themselves in the basement for several hours before police were able to enter and secure the building and assure that the shooter was no longer at large.

In Norway in July 2011, Anders Breivik killed 77 people in a bombing and gun rampage. Eight were killed by a bomb he planted in Oslo, while 69 were teens and young adults at a Youth Labor Camp on an island. Breivik admitted his actions but refused to plead guilty, claiming that he was defending his country against Muslim immigration and European liberalism. And, in another recent incident in March 2012, staff sergeant Robert Bales allegedly left his barracks on two separate occasions, walked through villages in Afghanistan, and killed 16 Afghan civilians in their homes. Bales pled guilty in military court and was sentenced to life without parole. Breivik was convicted and sentenced to serve the maximum sentence of 21 years in the Norwegian prison system. However, at the end of this time, his sentence could be extended if he is deemed a danger to society.

Serial killings—where one individual carries out a series of murders over an extended period of time—are equally horrifying. Many people still recall the planned, separate murders of 33 young men and boys whose bodies were found in the cellar of the suburban Chicago home of John Wayne Gacy during the late 1970s. Between 1978 and 1991, Jeffrey Dahmer lured at least 17 boys and young men into his apartment in Milwaukee, where he drugged, killed, and dismembered them. The public was shocked to learn the details of how Dahmer ate the victims' flesh and had sex with the corpses. Other notorious serial murderers include David Berkowitz, known as the infamous Son of Sam; Kenneth Bianchi, the Hillside Strangler; Albert DeSalvo, believed to be the Boston Strangler (although this has never been confirmed); Gary Ridgeway, the Green River Killer; Elaine Wuornos, one of the few female serial killers to have been identified and put to death; Donald Harvey, the nursing-care killer; Dennis Rader, the BTK killer; and Theodore Bundy.

England was the setting for the notorious Jack the Ripper and, more recently, Peter Sutcliffe, the Yorkshire Ripper who killed 13 women in the red-light districts of Northern England. Dennis Nilsen became England's first serial killer to prey on gay men, committing at least 15 known murders (Jenkins, 1988).

These are but illustrations of tragic incidences that occurred—sometimes over a short period of time—both in the United States and in other nations. However, as can be seen from the above examples, some of which will be discussed in more detail below, not all multiple murders can be categorized in the same way.

Definitions

Serial murder is usually reserved for incidents in which an individual (or individuals) kills two or more victims in separate events (Federal Bureau of Investigation, 2005a). Some experts and legislation (Protection of Children from Sexual Predators Act, 1998) have defined serial murder as three or more victims in separate incidents, but more recently the FBI has defined it as two or more. The FBI argues that the lower number of victims allows law enforcement more flexibility in committing resources to a potential serial murder investigation (Federal Bureau of Investigation, 2005a). The time interval between serial murders—sometimes referred to as the cooling-off period—may be days or weeks, but it is more likely months or years. The cooling-off period is the main difference between serial murders and other multiple murders. The murders are premeditated and planned (as are most mass murders), and the offender usually selects victims with specific characteristics, such as young age, certain hair color, or occupation.

Another term, **spree murder**, is sometimes used to refer to the killing of three or more individuals without any cooling-off period, usually at two or more locations. A bank robber who kills some individuals within the bank, flees with hostages, and kills a number of people while in flight during a statewide chase would be an example of a spree murderer. However, some experts are not convinced that spree murder represents a meaningful separate category of multiple murders (Federal Bureau of Investigation, 2005a). This is understandable; some murders that would be characterized as spree share characteristics of serial murders; others seem to be more like mass murders, without the single location. Essentially, the spree-murder designation does not provide any real benefit to law enforcement or to psychological study.

Mass murder involves killing four or more persons at a single location with no cooling-off period between murders. Despite the many examples cited in this chapter, it is relatively rare, occurring in less than 1 percent of the thousands of incidents of homicide committed every year (Levin, 2014). There are various kinds of mass murder, including those sponsored by some governmental authority, such as genocide designed to exterminate large groups of people, often on the basis of religion or ethnicity. Another type is mass murder by terrorists, such as occurred in New York City on September 11, 2001, when nearly 3,000 persons were killed. Persons who associate themselves with domestic or international terrorist groups are also responsible for some mass murders, such as the Oklahoma City bombing in 1995 and the Boston Marathon bombing in 2013. Mass murders committed by terrorists will be discussed in more detail in the next chapter.

SERIAL MURDERS

It is believed that the number of serial murders has decreased in the United States over the years 1970 to 2009 (Quinet, 2011). Nevertheless, some have estimated that there are about 35 to 40 serial murderers active at any given point in the United States (Hickey, 2010; Jenkins, 1988). Realistically, though, there are no accurate data on the prevalence and number of serial murderers active at any one time in the United States or internationally (Brantley & Kosky, 2005).

It is equally difficult to estimate the annual number of serial murder victims. Many serial offenders are adept at hiding their victims, and some inflate the number of their victims. Gary Ridgway, the Green River Killer, confessed to killing 48 women, and he skillfully hid their bodies. The long-haul truck driver Keith Hunter Jesperson, known as the Happy Face Killer because of the smiley face he drew on his many letters to the media, claimed to have killed 160 persons in multiple states, although he later recanted these assertions. He took great pride in the fact that he had been killing for over a year before any of the bodies were discovered (Quinet, 2007). In one case of a serial murder described by Wolf and Lavezzi (2007), the offender hid the bodies of eight women in the house inhabited by his parents and sister. Some of the bodies were found in the crawl space of the basement, and others were found comingled in the attic.

Estimating the number of victims is also difficult because, in some criminal homicides, a serial killer may not be suspected. To illustrate, Jenkins (1993) provides the case of Calvin Jackson, who was arrested in 1974 for murder committed in a New York apartment building. Actually, Jackson was a serial murderer, but none of his victims led the police to suspect a serial killer. Jackson's killings took place in a single-occupancy hotel where the guests were poor, socially isolated, largely forgotten, and mostly elderly. Time after time, the police were called to the hotel to deal with cases of death or injury that were apparently attributed to alcohol, drugs, or old age. When foul play was suspected, the police never considered it the work of a serial murderer, because the victims did not fit the stereotypic profile. Since there was no evidence of grotesque sexual abuse of the victim (the victim stereotype), there was little reason for the police to entertain the possibility of a serial murderer. Other serial murderers may set up situations where murders resemble drug-related homicides. Finally, individual murders in different states may not be linked unless law enforcement is sharing information on these crimes. This linkage is more likely to occur today with the advent of computerized systems that allow the sharing of resources and data for solving serious crimes.

Choice of Victims and *Modus Operandi*

Serial killers generally select victims based on availability, vulnerability, and desirability (Morton & Hilts, 2005). *Availability* refers to the lifestyle of the victim or the circumstances in which the victim is involved. In other words, the victim lives a lifestyle that provides many opportunities to be abducted or not missed. In some cases, a victim's disappearance is not noticed; in other cases, they are given up as runaways or adults who have left of their own volition. An examination of the victim selection of known serial murderers reveals that killers prefer the group of people offering easy access, transience, and a tendency to disappear without seeming to cause much alarm or concern. Victims are often prostitutes or runaways, young male drifters, and itinerant farm workers. *Vulnerability* pertains to the degree to which victim is susceptible to attack by the offender. Basically, the serial killer sees them as easy prey. Young women in or near a university or college campus or the elderly and solitary poor are examples. Serial murderers rarely break in and kill strangers in their homes. However, although serial killers begin their murderous careers by selecting highly vulnerable victims, they may, as their killings continue, gain substantially more confidence in their ability to abduct more "challenging" victims.

Desirability refers to the appeal of the victim to the offender; it may involve such victim characteristics as race, gender, ethnicity, age, occupation, hair color, sexual appeal, or other specific features preferred by the offender. It should be emphasized that not all serial killers are sexually motivated. Many other motivations prompt them to kill, such as the thrill of committing the action, financial gain, or attention seeking. Michael Swango, a former U.S. Marine, ambulance worker, and licensed physician, was suspected of poisoning at least 35 and up to 60 patients and colleagues over a period spanning many years. Labeled "Doctor of Death," Swango was convicted of only four of his murders. He was sentenced to three consecutive life terms without possibility of parole and is serving his sentence in the high security federal prison (ADX) in Florence, Colorado. Swango's motivation for the murders was never fully identified, but sexual motivation did not seem to be a factor. He kept a scrap book filled with newspaper and magazine clippings about natural disasters in which many people were killed and also kept a notebook in which he described the joy and thrill he felt during his killings.

Although serial killers are similar in some background characteristics to the single-victim killers discussed in the previous chapter, there are notable differences in the victims they choose and their method of committing the crimes. Single-victim offenders often kill out of anger or lack of control stemming from interpersonal conflict, whereas serial killers often murder in accordance with a carefully thought-out plan, which is frequently but as noted above not always sexually predatory in nature. The murder is typically not precipitated by an interpersonal conflict. The victims of single-victim murderers are most often family, friends, and acquaintances; alternately, they are killed in the process of committing another crime, such as a robbery. Serial murderers most often kill strangers with no apparent consensual relationship between the offender and the victim, and the killing itself is the perpetrator's main goal. However, serial offenders do sometimes lure their victims into their vehicles or homes, such as by offering rides or promising money to juvenile transients in exchange for sexual favors. The lack of a previous relationship in serial murders, compared to single murders, makes identifying suspects especially difficult.

The preferred method of killing also is often different for the two groups. Serial offenders tend to prefer more hands on killing through strangulation or beating with hands or feet, while single-victim offenders prefer guns (Kraemer, Lord, & Heilbrun, 2004). Serial homicide offenders also exhibit more planning by moving the victim or the victim's body from one location to another, by using restraints, and by disposing of the body in a remote location (Kraemer et al., 2004). Single-victim offenders tend to be much less skillful in disposing of the body.

Geographical Location of Serial Killing

Most serial killers have specific preferences for the location of their killings. They frequently commit their crimes within comfort zones that are often defined by an anchor point, such as their residence, employment, or the residence of a relative. Geographical profiling data continue to support this observation. Very few serial murderers travel interstate to kill (Federal Bureau of Investigation, 2005a). Those that do travel interstate for their murders are often truck drivers, those in military service, transients, or itinerant individuals who move from place to place. Hickey (1997) estimates that 14 percent of serial killers use their homes or workplaces as the preferred location, whereas another 52 percent commit their murders in the same general location or region, such as the same neighborhood or city. This tendency suggests that geographical profiling may be an invaluable aid in the identification of serial killers.

Rossmo (1997) developed an interesting typology based on the *modus operandi* of serial killers and serial rapists he studied. Rossmo identified four "hunting patterns" they use in their search for victims: (1) hunter, (2) poacher, (3) troller, and (4) trapper. "Hunters are those criminals who specifically set out from their residence to look for victims, searching through the areas in their awareness space that they believe contain suitable targets" (Rossmo, 1997, p. 167). The hunters are geographically stable in that their crimes usually occur near the offender's residence or neighborhood. Poachers are more transient, traveling some distance from their neighborhood in their search for suitable victims. The troller, on the other hand, does not specifically search for victims but depends on random encounters during the course of other activities. The trapper creates situations (traps) to entice victims to come to him. Beauregard et al. (2007) studied 72 serial sex offenders and did find some support for Rossmo's hunting patterns. To date, however, the typology will require more research before we can confirm or disconfirm its validity.

Ethnic and Racial Characteristics

The widespread belief that only whites are serial killers and blacks and other racial or ethnic groups never commit this type of crime is basically a myth (Morton & Hilts, 2005; Walsh, 2005). Walsh found that approximately 21.8 percent of the serial killers in the United States have been black, and was able to document 90 black serial killers during the post–World War II era. Research on Latino and other minority serial killers is virtually nonexistent.

We may have assumed that serial killings are perpetrated almost exclusively by whites because of how serial murder is identified and investigated. For example, law enforcement agencies may be less prone to investigate African American victims as casualties of serial murderers if they are found in poverty-stricken or high crime neighborhoods. Under these circumstances, law enforcement officials are more likely to conclude that the victim is simply another fatality in the long stream of never-ending violence found in some urban areas.

Also, as Walsh (2005) has observed, the media tend to cover the sensational serial killings by whites but fail to cover in any detail those offenses committed by blacks and other minorities. "The extensive media coverage of Bundy, Gacy, and Berkowitz cases have made these killers almost household names, but African Americans such as Watts, Johnson, Francois, and Wallace are practically unknown, despite having operated within the same general time framework (1980s and 1990s)" (Walsh, 2005, p. 274). Because violent crime, on the whole, is interracial rather than intraracial (Federal Bureau of Investigation, 2005a), it follows that lack of attention might favor the non-white perpetrators of these offenses. However, if black serial killers have been given a "pass," this is highly unrepresentative of how black individuals are routinely treated in many communities across the nation. Racial disparity in both media coverage and enforcement of other crimes has occurred, but it is usually to the disadvantage of the black community. In many communities, it is not unusual to see extensive coverage of the disappearance or murder of a white child and very little attention given to a similar tragedy involving a black victim.

Risk Factors and Psychological Motives

A frequent question asked is: What risk factors predispose a person to become a serial murderer? Serial murderers like all human beings are products of their genetic makeup, their upbringing, their social environment, and ultimately the developmental path that circumstances lead them to take. There is no single identifiable causal factor in the development of a serial killer. As we have discussed throughout the book, criminal behavior develops from a complicated mixture of various factors and influences. The same factors and influences that lead to violence very likely play a significant role in serial homicide, although others are certainly added. For example, and as noted above, the motives of many serial killers appear to be based on some combination of psychological rewards, such as control, domination, media attention, and personal or sexual excitement rather than identifiable material gain. Their actions are predictably planned, organized, and purposeful, and they seem to take delight in playing games with the law enforcement community and the public at large.

Many serial homicide offenders are especially drawn to committing murders that attract media interest, send spine-chilling fear into the community, and are incomprehensible to the public. Keith Hunter Jesperson apparently became so irritated that his killings were not highly publicized that he began writing letters to the media in 1994, signing his letters with a smiling happy face, and thus earning the nickname the Happy Face Killer. Dennis Rader, who could be classified as both a serial and mass murderer, also sent letters to police and newspapers. In his communications, he suggested a number of names for himself; one that eventually stuck was BTK, an abbreviation for "bind, torture and kill."

The evidence does not support any notion that serial killers kill on the basis of some compulsion or irresistible urge. Rather, the murder appears to be more a result of opportunity and the random availability of a suitable victim.

Nor should it be assumed that serial killers are social misfits who have trouble fitting into the local community. Swango, though not a highly successful physician, was able to procure employment with various medical facilities across the country. Dennis Rader was married for 33 years, had two children, and was a Boy Scout leader. He was a long-time and dedicated church member who had held elected office in his church council. He was employed as a local government official and served on several community boards. Gary Ridgway read the Bible at work and tried to save others by talking about religion with coworkers. He liked to hunt, fish, work around the yard, and take trips with his wife in their RV. He had been married three times, had a son, and was married at the time of his arrest. He worked as a truck painter for a company for 32 years. Robert Lee Yates, Jr., worked as a corrections officer in the state Penitentiary in Walla Walla, Washington, and was a well-decorated helicopter pilot during his 19 years of military service. None of these killers stood out as someone considered dangerous, and when their crimes were discovered many who knew them were surprised.

Serial killers have developed versions of the world that facilitate repetitive murder, often in a brutal, demeaning, and cold-blooded manner, but they are not necessarily seriously mentally disordered in the clinical use of this term. This is a difficult concept to comprehend, because most of us are probably attuned to believe that anyone who kills in this manner "must be crazy." However, a vast majority of serial killers fail to qualify as seriously mentally disordered in the traditional diagnostic categories of mental disorders discussed in Chapter 8.

As a group—and there are always exceptions—they would not be diagnosed paranoid schizophrenic, delusional, psychotic, or seriously depressed, for example. However, some would likely qualify as having "antisocial personality disorder," a category that includes many features of psychopathy, which was discussed in Chapter 7.

Research on Backgrounds

The backgrounds of serial killers are varied, which underscores the importance of the many risk factors discussed earlier in the book. Some dysfunction within their immediate families as they were growing up seems common, however. Similar to violent offenders in general, serial killers have frequently experienced considerable abuse and deprivation (Delisi & Scherer, 2006). McKenzie (1995) discovered in her study of 20 serial killers that 80 percent were reared in homes characterized by family violence and severe abuse, and parental alcoholism; 93 percent had been exposed to inconsistent and chaotic parenting.

In his study of serial killers in England, Jenkins (1988) found that—unlike the typical violent individual who demonstrates a propensity for violence at an early age—serial murderers generally begin their careers of repetitive homicide at a relatively late age. He concluded that most started their careers between the ages of 24 and 40. Interestingly, the median age of arrested serial murderers in Jenkins's sample was 36. Arrests typically occurred about four years after they began killing. The serial murderers did have extensive police records, though, but the records reflected a series of petty theft, embezzlement, and forgery, rather than a history of violence (Jenkins, 1988). Surprisingly, they did not have extensive juvenile records. Jenkins concluded that the cases did not provide any early indicators or predictors of eventual murderous behavior. When British serial murderers committed their first murder, about half were married, had a seemingly stable family life, and had usually lived in the same house for many years. A majority had stable jobs, and, disconcertingly, a good number had been former police officers or security guards.

Female Serial Killers

Although female serial killers are rare compared with male serial killers, close to at least three dozen have been identified in U.S. history. Hickey (1991) listed 34 documented female serial murderers, with 82 percent of them acting after 1900.

There are some discernible differences between female and male serial murderers. For example, only about one-third of the female offenders killed strangers, in contrast to male offenders who almost exclusively killed strangers. In a more recent study, Harrison and her colleagues (2015) studied the backgrounds, motive, methods, and mental status of 64 female serial killers active in the United States between the years 1821 and 2008. The victims they targeted had little chance of fighting back—they were typically children, the elderly, or the disabled. Interestingly, the available research indicates that female serial murderers are active longer than the typical male counterpart, averaging around 8 to 11 years (Farrell, Keppel, & Titterington, 2011; Kelleher & Kelleher, 1998). According to Farrell et al., "On average, they operate within a different victim pool, enjoy longer active periods, and amass more victims than their male counterparts" (p. 229). Farrell et al. report that the average number of victims murdered by female serial offenders is nine. However, the average number of victims of male serial killers is unknown, and future studies may reveal that male serial killers murder more than their female counterparts.

Most victims of female serial killers are husbands, former husbands, or suitors (Harrison et al., 2015). For example, Belle Gunness murdered an estimated 14 to 49 husbands or suitors in La Porte, Indiana (Holmes et al., 1991). Nannie Doss killed a combination of 11 husbands and family members in Tulsa, Oklahoma. The second largest group of victims murdered by female serial killers are those who are weak and dependent on them, such as children and the elderly (Farrell et al., 2011; Kelleher & Kelleher, 1998). In April 2015, Megan Huntsman, a 40-year-old Utah woman, pleaded guilty to smothering six of her newborns to death over a 10-year-period. She said she was addicted to methamphetamine and alcohol, suffered from depression, and was in an abusive marriage. She was sentenced to serve both consecutive and concurrent sentences and would not likely be eligible for parole for some 30 years. In New York, Marybeth Tinning was convicted of smothering only one child, a four-month-old daughter, in 1985. However, she was suspected of killing seven or eight of her other children, and she allegedly confessed to killing three of them. She remains imprisoned and has been denied parole at each parole attempt, the last being January 2015.

In the United States, the first known female serial killer was Lucretia Patrica Cannon, who was active in Delaware between 1802 and 1829 (Farrell et al., 2011). Perhaps the most notorious female serial killer in our time was Aileen Wuornos, who killed seven men in Florida in 1989 and 1990, when she was in her thirties. Wuornos had a pathetic, devastating childhood and adolescence, littered with the risk factors we discussed in early chapters. She was pregnant at 13 and became a prostitute at 15. She had a lengthy criminal record, mostly for nonviolent offenses, but she was also frequently victimized. She was generally well known to the criminal justice system even before her first murder. Wuornos is unusual as female serial killers go, because her victims were strangers or brief acquaintances rather than husbands or persons of whom she was in charge. Psychiatrists diagnosed her with borderline personality disorder. She argued that the men she killed had raped her or attempted to rape her, or that her crimes were in self-defense. She was convicted and sentenced to death, and she was executed by lethal injection in October 2002. Wuornos was the subject of several documentaries and the movie *Monster*, in which—despite the film's title—she was portrayed by Charlize Theron as having some humanity.

Traditionally, female serial killers murder primarily for material or monetary gain, such as insurance benefits, will allocations, trusts, and estates. Furthermore, the method of killing is through poisons (usually cyanide) or overdoses of pills. Approximately half of the female serial killers had a male accomplice. Some women murdered because of involvements in cults or with a male serial murderer. For example, Charlene Gallego, the common-law wife of serial killer Gerald Gallego helped him select, abduct, and murder at least 10 individuals (Holmes et al., 1991).

Over the past two decades, several female health care workers who have killed patients have been identified, although males—including at least one physician (Swango)—have also been identified. Some research suggests that as many as 17 percent of female serial killers are nurses (Stark, Paterson, Henderson, Kidd, & Godwin, 1997). A female health worker may have been responsible for the deaths of 28 patients at two hospitals in The Hague, Netherlands. Her victims were either children or elderly patients, and her method of killing involved injections of various substances. She was arrested in December 2001 and was later convicted of four counts of first-degree murder and three counts of attempted murder.

The motivations of health care workers' serial killings are variable: recognition, attention, revenge, power, and control (Brantley & Kosky, 2005). Some of these health care workers admitted that the killings relieved tension, stress, and frustration (Linedecker & Burt, 1990). Some also maintained that they killed to put the patients out of their misery and that these were essentially mercy killings.

Juvenile Serial Killers

Serial murder by children and adolescents is an exceedingly rare event, and scientific information is extremely sparse. Recall that most adult serial murderers did not begin their criminal activity until they were into their thirties. Myers (2004) could only identify six serial cases involving juveniles over the past 150 years, after an exhaustive search of periodicals, newspapers, books, legal references, and Internet sources on crime. According to Myers (2004), serial murders by juveniles are a complex phenomenon, with psychological, family, social, cultural, and biological factors playing a role. Myers believes that many of the same motives manifested by adult serial killers also hold for child and adolescent serial killers. With such a small sample of offenders, however, one cannot even begin to draw conclusions.

MASS MURDERERS

Surprisingly, little research has been directed at mass murderers, especially in comparison with the attention directed at serial murderers. Perhaps this is because mass murder, while frightening, is not as intriguing or mysterious as serial murder. Furthermore, mass murder happens quickly and unpredictably without warning—then the killing is over. It is often clear who the offender is, and his or her life is usually ended on the spot, either when they kill themselves or when they are shot by the police. If they live and are prosecuted, they are almost invariably convicted and receive life sentences or the death penalty. Serial murders, on the other hand, occur over a period of weeks, months, or years, during which time the identity of the offender is unknown.

Investigators have traditionally identified two types of mass murder by individuals: classic and family (Douglas et al., 1986). An example of a **classic mass murder** is when an individual walks into or barricades himself into a public building, such as a fast-food restaurant, mall, or theater, and kills at random (but sometimes selectively). These classic murders also may be called public mass murders, and they occur almost invariably with guns. Family mass murders—sometimes called domestic mass murders—typically involve weapons but also may involve other methods, such as knives, poisonings, or drownings. In a **family mass murder**, at least three family members are killed by another family member. Very often, the perpetrator kills himself or herself, an incident that is classified as a mass murder/suicide. Family murder was discussed in Chapter 9. A third category of mass murders is mass murder by terrorists. It will be covered in the next chapter.

Some mass murders that have features of classic mass murders may require a separate classification. Although the victims may seem to be chosen at random, they may actually be perceived by the perpetrator to belong to a particular group or to be representative of a threatening group, despite the unreasonableness of the threat. The six victims killed at a Sikh temple in 2012 were likely targeted because of their religion. In the Norway killings, Breivik railed against "multicultural forces" and was heard yelling "I will kill you all, Marxists," as he was shooting (Seierstad, 2015). Most of his victims were young people at a camp for members of the Youth Labor Party. Marc Lepine walked into a classroom at the University of Montreal, ordered male students to leave, railed against feminists, and shot female students. Thus, the motivations of these mass killers may include hatred toward certain groups in addition to the many motivations that lead other classic mass murderers to commit their crimes.

In this section we concentrate upon classic mass murders, with or without selected victims. There is no shortage of examples, including many already mentioned. In May 2012, a man walked into a Seattle café, shot to death four people and seriously wounded a fifth, killed a woman and hijacked her car, then shot himself in the head when police were closing in. The 2007 Virginia Tech murders in Blacksburg, Virginia, the 2008 Northern Illinois University killings in Dekalb, the 2009 killings in Binghamton, New York, and the 2015 tragedy in Roseburg, Oregon, are other recent examples of classic mass murder. In these instances, the shooters entered buildings or classrooms claiming most victims at random before killing themselves. To return to the point made above about classification difficulty, however, the Virginia Tech killings could also be classified as spree murders, because they were spread throughout the day, with no "cooling off" period and did not occur in one location. Likewise, the Norway massacre occurred at two separate locations, outside the prime minister's office in Oslo and on a nearby island.

Public Mass Shootings

A public mass shooting—referred to as an active shooter situation—takes place in public circumstances, such as schools, workplaces, malls, restaurants, parking places, and public transit (including aircraft). Over three recent decades (1983 to 2012), there have been approximately 78 public mass shootings in the United States, resulting in 547 deaths (not including the shooters) (Bjelopera, Bagalman, Caldwell, Finlea, & McCallion, 2013). Even if we add the more recent deaths not counted in those figures (e.g., Newtown and Aurora), the numbers do not approach 1,000 over three decades. While shocking, frightening, and tragic, public mass shootings account for a very small proportion of the murders in any given year. In the year 2013 alone, for example, firearms were used to murder 8,454 persons (Federal Bureau of Investigation, 2014a).

Nevertheless, mass shootings are on the rise, according to a special report prepared by the FBI (Barrett, 2014). The government identified 160 shootings from 2000 through 2013, an average of 16.4 "active shooter" incidents a year. Between 2000 and 2006, there was an average of 6.4 a year. Most incidents (73) were in business locations, such as malls, offices, or movie theaters, while educational institutions and government locations followed (39 and 16, respectively). Altogether, the 160 shootings resulted in 486 people being killed and 557 wounded.

A detailed profile that will enable experts and law enforcement to predict the actions of mass murderers does not exist. In retrospect, case studies of mass murderers often identify common risk factors, including in some cases, psychiatric treatment, but in general we cannot identify who will or will not carry out such an event. Many individuals possess these risk factors, and sadly many individuals make threats and post rants on social media sites. Consequently, the major task of law enforcement in a mass murder situation is to reduce the damage perpetrated by an active shooter. However, preventive measures can be addressed. These include alerting authorities if a person makes threats or is known to stockpile weapons, and taking reasonable steps to limit access to guns.

Other characteristics of mass murderers have been identified. Public mass shooters are usually white and male, and they generally act alone. They tend to be frustrated, angry people who feel helpless about their lives—but this can be said of numerous people who do not carry out such terrible attacks. The public shooting may afford them control and domination over others for a brief period of time. Also, they may have grandiose aspirations to achieve fame—believing their names will always be recognized. Like the terrorists who will be discussed in the next chapter, they may also have a desire for significance.

Most mass murderers do not have criminal records or a history of psychiatric hospitalizations (Fox & DeLateur, 2014), despite the fact that some (e.g., Virginia Tech shooter, Aurora theater shooter) have had mental health treatment. They are usually between the ages of 35 and 45, and they are convinced there is little chance that things will get better for them. There are of course exceptions to that age range, illustrated by several cases cited in this chapter. Their personal lives have been a failure by their standards, and they have often suffered some tragic or serious loss, such as a loss of meaningful employment or a significant other. The co-pilot who crashed an airliner into the Alps in 2015 was apparently concerned that depression as well as an eye condition would prevent him from continuing at the work he loved. Anders Breivik, the Norway mass killer, attempted and failed at six business enterprises. He was unsuccessful at building relationships with women, and after being left by a mail-order bride, he moved back in with his mother and lived an online life, mainly in his room, for five years (Seierstad, 2015). The man who killed nine at Umpqua Community College had complained bitterly online that he did not have a girlfriend and another mass shooter left behind rantings that sorority women did not give him sufficient attention.

Mass murders are usually carefully planned, sometimes over very long periods of time, and the crimes are often carried out in calm, systematic fashion. The Aurora theater shooter had equipped himself with a mask and multiple tear-gas canisters along with the deadly weaponry he carried. He also booby-trapped his apartment with incendiary devices that were fortunately detonated before police entered it after the shootings. He kept elaborate notebooks in which he revealed his deliberations about whether he should carry out serial killings or mass murders. The Norwegian shooter rented a farmhouse and meticulously assembled a bomb. The Umpqua Community College shooter came to campus with a flak jacket and multiple weapons and rounds of ammunition. The targets selected by mass murderers are often—perhaps even most often—planned and deliberate. Their preparations often "include where, when, and who to kill, as well as with what weapons they will strike" (Fox & DeLateur, 2014, p. 126). They are determined to accomplish their mission no matter what obstacles and challenges are placed in front of them. The targets are either symbolic of their discontent (such as their workplace) or are hated or blamed for the perpetrator's misfortunes. The level of planning is often so focused and intense that when they do attack, they can maintain a calm composure during the massacre. Fox and DeLateur (2014) write that "Mass murderers have been known to follow a mental script, one that is rehearsed over and over again, to the point where they become comfortable with the mission" (p. 127).

Public mass shooters usually plan to die in the shooting, which characterizes their mission as a mass murder-suicide. Approximately 50 percent of the shooters turn the gun on themselves during the episode and many of the rest are shot by law enforcement officers (Bjelopera et al., 2013).

In recent years, several public mass shooting incidents have occurred in malls. Most mall incidents occur on Sundays. Shooters are usually neither employed by businesses in the mall nor had relationships with mall employees (Federal Bureau of Investigation, 2013). Other incidents have occurred in educational environments, including elementary schools, high schools, and college

TABLE 10-4	Mass Murder Shooting Incidents in the United States with the Highest Casualty Counts as of 2012

- Cinemark Century 16 Theater in Aurora, Colorado:
  70 (12 killed, 58 wounded), July 20, 2012.
- Virginia Polytechnic Institute and State University in Blacksburg, Virginia:
  49 (32 killed, 17 wounded), April 16, 2007.
- Ft. Hood Soldier Readiness Processing Center in Ft. Hood, Texas:
  45 (13 killed, 32 wounded), November 5, 2009.
- Sandy Hook Elementary School and a residence in Newtown, Connecticut:
  29 (27 killed, 2 wounded), December 14, 2012.

Source: Federal Bureau of Investigation. (2013, September 16). A study of active shooter incidents in the United States between 2000 and 2013. Washington, DC: U.S. Department of Justice.

settings. **Table 10-4** provides a list of the four mass shootings with the highest death counts in the United States in recent years. Note that shooting incidents in other nations or terrorist incidents, often not involving shooting, have higher casualty numbers.

Mass murderers often take a very active interest in guns, especially semiautomatics that maximize the number of deaths in a short period of time. Unless one had built a bomb or had a plane at one's disposal, it would be difficult to conceive of a weapon that could take the lives of so many individuals other than one or more semi-automatic weapons. In large measure, the availability of high-powered semiautomatic or automatic weaponry accounts for the increasingly large death toll in recent mass murders.

A Mass Murder Typology

James Alan Fox and Jack Levin (2003) proposed a five-category typology based on the motivations for mass killings. The five categories are revenge, power, loyalty, profit, and terror. According to Fox and Levin, many—if not most—mass killings are motivated by *revenge*, either against specific individuals or specific groups. Usually, the killer seeks to get even with a group of people he dislikes. Fox and Levin bring up the concept of "murder by proxy" in which victims are chosen because they are associated, by the killer, with a primary target against whom revenge is sought. For example, Lépine's long-term hatred against feminists ignited his murderous rampage at the Université de Montréal. Although some of his victims may have not considered themselves feminists, he considered all women, by proxy, feminists.

Another recent example of the revenge mass killer occurred on March 10, 2009, when Michael McLendon, age 28, went on a rampage in southern Alabama. The gunman, who killed 11 people including himself, had a list of people he had worked with who had allegedly done him wrong. He began the day of the shooting by burning down his mother's house (her body and four dead dogs were later found inside), and shot most of his victims at a plant where he had stopped working just days before the rampage.

The second type identified by Fox and Levin (2003) is the killer who seeks *power* and domination over his victims. They enjoy and crave the fear they engender and the immense control they have over their victims. Usually, the need for revenge and power go together. The power killer is seeking both revenge and control over his victims. Fox and Levin observe that the thirst for power and control inspire this type of mass murderer to dress in military fatigues and combat gear, and carry assault weapons packed with considerable firepower. Some investigators refer to them as pseudo-commando killers. James Huberty, the unemployed security guard, put on his camouflage pants and told his wife, "Society has had its chance. I'm going hunting, hunting for humans." As noted above, Huberty also could fit into the revenge category because of his dislike of Hispanics and children. The Umpqua Community College killer in 2015 terrified his victims by having them stand and answer questions, sometimes about their religious affiliation, before shooting them. He demonstrated a callous indifference when some pleaded or even offered sympathy for his plight.

The third type is inspired to kill by a warped sense of love and *loyalty*, usually based on a desire to save their loved ones from misery and hardship. Many family massacres—not discussed in this chapter—stem from this motivation. "Typically, a husband/father is despondent over the fate of the family unit, and takes not only his own life, but also those of his children and sometimes his wife, in order to protect them from pain and suffering in their lives" (Fox & Levin, 2003, pp. 59–60).

The fourth motivation for mass murder is *profit*. The intention in this murder is to eliminate victims and witnesses to a crime, such as a robbery. Drug wars between organized crime groups are also sometimes involved. This type of mass murder also sends the message to other potential witnesses that the same thing could happen to them if they tried to testify to authorities.

The fifth and final motivation for mass murder is *terror*. In this situation, the perpetrator wants to send a message through a horrific murderous rampage. Terror is a motive for the murders to be covered in the following chapter. However, other mass murders not necessarily associated with either domestic or international terrorism also qualify. One of the more infamous examples is represented by Charles Manson, who led a quasi-commune located in southern California in the 1960s. Manson, who likely would qualify as a charismatic psychopath, desired to send a message of terror to communities in southern California. He was a devout listener to Beatles music, and was especially influenced by the song "Helter Skelter," a composition found on the Beatles' *White Album*, which he interpreted as prophesying an apocalyptic war between blacks and whites. In a questionable theory proposed by prosecutor Vincent Bugliosi, and widely circulated ever since, Manson wanted to start a race war by having his followers murder wealthy whites and have the crimes blamed on angry blacks. Manson had the grandiose delusion of world domination (Deal & Hickey, 2003). He believed that once Helter Skelter started, blacks would eventually kill all whites except for himself and his family because they would hide in the desert (Deal & Hickey, 2003). On August 9, 1969, Manson told four of his followers that it was time for Helter Skelter. He instructed them to commit brutal mass murder and to "leave a sign and do something witchy" to ignite fear and terror within the white community. The site they selected was the home of well-known actress Sharon Tate and film director Roman Polanski, located in a prominent Los Angeles neighborhood. The group brutally bludgeoned and stabbed five people at the house that night, including Tate, who was eight and one-half months pregnant. Polanski was out of the country at the time. After the killing, they wrote the message "pig" on the front door of the house in the blood of one of the victims.

The next night, six Manson followers set out—again per Manson's instructions—to murder Leno LaBianca, a wealthy supermarket executive, and his wife Rosemary, a successful dress shop co-owner. After Leno was killed, one of the followers carved "war" on the man's abdomen. The group also left frightening messages in three different places in the house, "death to the pigs," "rise," and "Healter (sic) Skelter," all in the victims' blood. Manson was eventually arrested, convicted of accessory to murder, and sentenced to death. However, his sentence was commuted to life in prison in 1976 after the Supreme Court of California temporarily eliminated that state's death penalty.

One of Manson's followers, Tex Watson, allegedly found God in prison. Another member of the "family," Lynette "Squeaky" Fromme was not present during the murders, but remained visibly loyal to Manson. She received a life sentence for attempting to assassinate President Gerald Ford in 1975, but was paroled in 2009. Still another follower, Susan Atkins, who did participate in the murders, died of cancer in prison in fall of 2009. Other members of the Manson family have been paroled or remain incarcerated.

The Helter Skelter theory, if correct, illustrates mass murder that is terror-motivated. Others have suggested that the crimes were more profit or revenge related, illustrative of a robbery gone wrong or even drug-induced psychoses. As a whole, the typology proposed by Fox and Levin may be of help in trying to understand mass murders, but it is not validated in the research literature. It serves primarily as categories of descriptors that may or may not neatly fit a particular mass murder.

The remainder of the chapter addresses specific offenses that have been, or possess the strong possibility of becoming mass murder. School violence and workplace violence do not necessarily result in death, of course, but when they do, the deaths may be multiple. These crimes have drawn extensive media coverage and research interest in recent years.

SCHOOL VIOLENCE

In the later 1990s a rash of school shootings made headlines. As discussed briefly in Chapter 5, the most infamous case was the mass murder of 12 students and one teacher at Columbine High School in Littleton, Colorado, in April 1999. The two teenage boys who did the shootings committed suicide during the incident. Twenty more students were injured. Although there had been a number of school shootings prior to Columbine (there were at least 10 school shootings between 1996 and 1999), the Columbine shooting prompted a great deal of alarm and concern nationwide. In addition, the media and some experts were quick to make gross generalizations about the school violence problem.

Columbine's death toll was surpassed by the shootings at Virginia Tech in 2007 and Newtown, Connecticut, in 2012. Because the Virginia Tech event happened at a university setting, it is not considered in the same category as a more enclosed high school campus and is treated more as a mass shooting than a "school shooting" in the literature. Likewise, the UCC tragedy in fall 2015 and other college or university incidents do not fit neatly into the "school shooting" terminology. The Newtown massacre is considered a school shooting, although it differed in one significant way from others. It was carried out by an individual in the community but not a student. The typical school shooting is carried out by a student in the school, with fellow students or adult staff as victims.

Even prior to the school shootings of the 1990s, anecdotal and media accounts of children being victimized at school by other children prompted researchers to study the issue to document the magnitude of the problem. Violence in schools is more than school shootings. Violence in schools includes aggravated and simple assaults, sexual assaults, robbery, and some forms of bullying. As long ago as 1974, the U.S. Congress funded a three-year study to evaluate the nature and extent of crime, violence, and disruption in the nation's schools. Periodic studies of school violence have been conducted since that time. The National Center for Education Statistics (Robers, Zhang, Truman, & Snyder, 2012), covering recent years, is illustrative.

That report indicated the following:

- In 2010, the number of students (ages 12 to 18) who reported being victims of crime was 828,000. Keep in mind, however, that the total number of students enrolled in prekindergarten through 12th grade during the 2009–2010 school year was approximately 49 million.
- During the same school year, there were 359, 000 reported violent victimizations, of which 91,400 were serious violent victimizations.
- Of the 33 student, staff, and non-student school-associated violent deaths occurring between July, 2009 and June, 2010, 25 were homicides, 5 were suicides, and 3 were legal interventions (involving a law enforcement officer). During that same time period, 17 of the homicides were school-age youth (ages 5 to 18) while at school.
- In 2009, 8 percent of the students in grades 9 to 12 reported being threatened or injured with a weapon, such as a gun, knife, or club, on school property.
- Eight percent of the secondary school teachers and 7 percent of the elementary school teachers reported being threatened with injury by a student. In addition, 6 percent of elementary school teachers and 2 percent of secondary school teachers reported being physically attacked by a student.
- Six percent of students (ages 12 to 18) reported being cyber-bullied in 2009. (Cyberbullying, to be discussed in Chapter 15, is a much more significant problem today.)

The report also concluded that students were more likely to be victims of serious violence or homicide away from school, occurring at a rate of 12 crimes per 1,000 students away from school. Over the years, the percentage of youth homicides occurring at school remains at less than 2 percent of the total number of youth homicides, indicating youths are more likely to be murdered away from school (Robers et al., 2012). Still, national statistics indicate that about one out of 10 students in secondary schools fear that they will be attacked or harmed while at school (Verlinden, Hersen, & Thomas, 2000). Thus, while an actual attack might not occur, the fear of being harmed is still considerable.

School Shootings

Although mass shootings occur in a variety of settings, the education realm is one that has received the most attention from policy makers, officials, and the public (Bjelopera et al., 2013). The two school shooting incidents that have, so far, drawn the most attention are the above-mentioned 1999 shooting at Columbine High School in Littleton, Colorado, and the 2012 tragedy at Sandy Hook Elementary School in Newtown, Connecticut.

Research has found that school shootings have been a rapidly expanding phenomenon in modern Western societies over the past two decades (Böckler, Seeger, Sitzer, & Heitmeyer, 2013). It should be noted that more school shootings have occurred in the United States than in all other countries combined (Böckler et al., 2013). Nevertheless, as noted below, while mass shootings have increased, the number of *school* shootings has not increased dramatically in recent years. In this country, the term "school shooting" usually refers to those violent incidents that involve a firearm and occur within the school building or on the school grounds. Some argue (e.g., Daniels & Bradley, 2011) that the definition should include one or more fatalities due to firearms that happen "in school, on school property, at school sponsored activities, or to a member of the school community on his or her commute to or from school" (p. 3). Some shootings also involved school board members. Although school shooting is largely a term used in North America, in other parts of the world where there are strong restrictions on the availability of guns, perpetrators of school violence resort to other weapons. In Europe, for example, perpetrators use such weapons as explosives, swords, knives, or axes (Böckler et al., 2013). Even though these incidents are not literally school shootings, the perpetrators exhibit very close similarities to the factors, developments that led up to the attacks, and *modus operandi* of school shooting incidents in North America (Böckler et al., 2013). Even in the United States, though, knives and other weapons are often confiscated from students, and at least one notable incident involving a student slashing fellow students and staff with a knife has occurred. In April 2014, a 16-year-old student in Pennsylvania stabbed 20 students and a security guard before being restrained.

For our purposes, we will restrict our coverage to those school shootings that took place within the school building, or immediately outside the building. In recent years, the incidents that occurred within the school building took place in school classrooms and hallways (Federal Bureau of Investigation, 2013). A few also happened in the school cafeteria.

Although school shootings are understandably frightening and are of deep concern, statistically they are rare. In addition, despite increases in general mass shootings discussed above, studies have found no significant increase in *school* shooting incidents (Bjelopera et al., 2013; Fox & DeLateur, 2014). Nevertheless, as O'Toole (2013) writes: "While these lethal school shootings are rare, when they occur they are devastating, life-changing events, and always leave people shaking their heads" (p. 173). (See **Box 10-1** for one response to school shootings.)

In the 25 school shootings investigated by FBI that occurred between 2000 and 2013, 14 occurred in high schools, 6 occurred in middle schools or junior high schools, 4 occurred in elementary schools, and 1 occurred at a school including grades preK-12 (Federal Bureau of Investigation, 2013). In a majority of the high school and middle school incidents, the shooter was a student at the school. The school shootings at elementary schools, however, did not involve the actions of a student. Shooting incidents in high and middle schools were more likely to occur on Monday but the other days of the school day were not far behind, suggesting that the day of the week is not that significant a factor. Shooting incidents in elementary schools were more likely to take place on Friday, but because there were only four, this tells us little. In most of the school shootings (similar to public mass shootings), the shooter acted alone. The notable exception is Columbine, where two teenage boys carried out the attacks together.

Investigations of school shooters have often found that two characteristics emerge: peer rejection and social rejection. As pointed out by Arluke and Madfis (2014) "School shooters are often students who have been bullied, picked on, and marginalized" (p. 16). One of the Columbine High School shooters wrote in his diary how lonely he was without friends, and he was especially tortured by his failures with girls (Meadows, 2006). The other shooter wrote in his diary how everyone

CONTEMPORARY ISSUES

BOX 10-1   Safety Drills in Schools: Unanticipated Consequences

The terrible tragedy that occurred at Sandy Hook Elementary School in 2012, during which 20 first graders and six staff members lost their lives, produced fear in communities across the nation, particularly among parents and school personnel. Both the Newtown, Connecticut incident and the Columbine incident 13 years earlier were highly atypical, both in their occurrence and in the number of victims. As noted in the chapter, school shootings are still rare events. Furthermore, when they do occur, they generally involve one perpetrator who shoots a small number of victims and is promptly taken down, such as by a teacher, an administrator, other students, or a school safety officer.

After Columbine, but most especially since Newtown, many communities across the country reviewed their safety procedures in the event of a similar crisis. Some schools, as well as some businesses, have initiated general lockdowns or safety drills, and in a small number of states, "active shooter" drills are mandated (Frosch, 2014). Active shooter drills may be conducted by local police or by private consulting companies. They are intended to simulate reality; for example, a person playing the role of a shooter enters the school or business and, in some cases, actually fires blanks. Students and employees are told how to respond. In many schools, however, the drills in public schools are carried out only for teachers and other staff, not while students are present. Furthermore, when students are involved, they are more likely to be high school aged.

Critics of these drills argue that they are far out of proportion to the danger that exists. In addition, they become highly stressful events for the students and employees who are subjected to them. Supporters maintain that simulating an actual event is the best way to prepare for it, and that safeguards are in place for protecting participants. For example, adults are trained ahead in how to disarm a gunman if that is possible before the drill actually begins and the drill is carried out under close supervision.

Thus far, the drills conducted have had numerous consequences, both anticipated and unanticipated. Some participants have felt more secure, while others have experienced severe stress, had nightmares, and have even sued police and school administrators as a result. In communities across the country, parents and guardians have both requested and objected to the drills.

Questions for Discussion

1. What is the difference between a lockdown or safety drill and an active shooter drill? Are both acceptable, unacceptable, or would you support one but not the other? Address this question both in relation to schools and business environments.
2. What psychological reactions might be experienced by students experiencing an active shooter drill?
3. Determine whether the state you reside in (a) requires school lockdown or safety drills in public school, (b) mandates active shooter drills, or (c) neither. If you have participated in such a drill, either in school or the workplace, discuss your reactions to the experience.

continually made fun of him. A vast majority of shooters have poor social and coping skills and felt picked on or persecuted (Verlinden et al., 2000). They expressed anger about being teased or ridiculed and vowed revenge against particular individuals or groups. Moreover, as a group, "they lacked social support and prosocial relationships that might have served as protective factors" (Verlinden et al., 2000, p. 44).

Cruelty to animals was prominent in the backgrounds of at least half of the shooters (Arluke & Madfis, 2014; Verlinden et al., 2000). Moreover, a certain kind of animal foreshadows this kind of violence (Arluke & Madfis, 2014; Levin & Arluke, 2009). The shooters are inclined to abuse socially valued or culturally humanized animals, such as pet dogs and cats. Furthermore, the form of animal abuse is up-close and personal, such as strangulation, bludgeoning, or beating the animal to death. However, not all school shooters show prior histories of unusual cruelty to animals—and animals are abused by youth who never become school shooters. In fact, some shooters display unusual affection, attachment, and empathy toward their pets, probably reflecting how they wish they were treated by peers and others (Arluke & Madfis, 2014).

The backgrounds of school shooters also revealed a keen interest in guns and other weaponry, and they often had easy access to firearms (see **Table 10-5**; see also **Box 9-1** in previous chapter). Most of these assailants expected to be killed or planned suicide during or immediately after the attacks. All the attacks seemed to be carefully planned and thought out beforehand.

TABLE 10-5 School Homicides, 1994–1999		
Type of Weapon	**Number**	**Percent**
Total	**172**	**100**
Firearm	**119**	**69**
Handgun	89	52
Rifle	18	11
Unknown	12	7
Sharp object	31	18
Beating	12	7
Strangulation	5	3
Other	5	3

Source: Perkins, C. A. (2003). Weapon use and violent crime. Washington, DC: U.S. Department of Justice, Bureau of Justice Statistics, p. 11.

In virtually all school shootings, investigators discovered that the violent intentions of the assailants were repeatedly made clear to others, particularly peers, often including the time and place. It is estimated that at least 50 percent of school shooters let their intentions be known to others, a phenomenon that become known by investigators as *leakage*. A vivid example of warning signs took place on December 13, 2013 when an 18-year-old, armed with shotgun, machete, and three Molotov cocktails, began shooting at students in the hallways of Aarapahoe High School in Centennial, Colorado. As he moved through the school and into the library, he fired one additional round and lit a Molotov cocktail, throwing it into a bookcase and causing minor damage. One person was killed (a fellow student) and no one was wounded. The shooter committed suicide as a school resource officer approached him. The shooter kept a chilling diary three months before the shooting about how he wanted to shoot the school up and commit mass murder where he alone would be the judge, jury, and executioner. Among other things, he threatened to kill the head librarian and debate coach in the school parking lot three months prior to the shooting. He provided a series of other warning signs to the point where his mother sought evaluations for him. For example, he showed other students pictures of the gun and machete he had bought. A threat assessment conducted by the school psychologist concluded he was a low level of concern. The shooter's mother also took him to a mental health center several weeks prior to the incident, but therapists apparently determined he was not dangerous.

Documents show that the Columbine school shooters repeatedly dropped hints at school about their murderous intentions (Meadows, 2006). However, peers rarely reported these threats to the authorities. The reasons for this lack of reporting behavior are not well understood, but fear seems to play a major role. A survey by the Safe School Coalition of Washington State (1999) (cited in Verlinden et al., 2000) revealed that fear of not being believed, fear of retribution, or fear for what might happen to the youth threatening the school violence were the most frequently reported concerns of peers. Verlinden et al. (2000) concluded that the risk of school violence is high when there are multiple warning signs and risk factors. "The more signs there are and the greater the opportunity, motivation, and access to weapons, the greater the possibility that the child may commit a violent act" (Verlinden et al., 2000, p. 47).

ADULT PERPETRATORS.   So far, we have talked about school-aged shooters killing classmates and teachers. Adults unaffiliated with the school are also involved in school shootings. In recent years, adult males have barged into school buildings, killing students. Perhaps one of the more horrific murders occurred in West Nickel, Pennsylvania, where, on October 2, 2006, a 32-year-old man carried three guns into Nickel Mines School, an Amish one-room schoolhouse. The gunman took hostages, all girls, and sent the boys and adults outside. He barricaded the doors and then opened fire on a dozen girls, killing five and seriously wounding five before committing suicide.

His motivation was unclear, but he indicated that his actions were not directly related to school or the Amish community, but was driven by events in his childhood. More likely, "he may have viewed himself as powerless or his own life circumstances as hopeless and acted out in a school environment that was simple, peaceful—and completely at his mercy" (Gerler, 2007, p. 2).

A week earlier, a 53-year-old man armed with an assault rifle and carrying a backpack full of explosives, walked into Platte Canyon High School located in Bailey, Colorado. He took six female students hostage and sexually assaulted five of them. He then released four of them. When a SWAT team broke into the classroom, he shot and killed a 16-year-old girl before turning the gun on himself. The other female hostages managed to escape. The motive of this adult attacker remains unclear.

The most horrifying example in recent memory, because of the age of the victims and the number of deaths that occurred, were the murders of 20 first graders and six school staff members at Sandy Hook Elementary School in Newtown, Connecticut in December, 2012. They were carried out by 20-year-old Adam Lanza who lived in the local community with his mother. Before taking his own life, Lanza not only shot his victims within the school but also his mother as she slept in their home.

Psychological Characteristics of School Shooters

It should be emphasized that there is no firmly established school shooter profile, though a school shooter profile is often alluded to in the media. However, many students who fit this so-called profile never engage in violence of any kind, while many students who have planned and committed violent attacks at their school do not match it (Arluke & Madfis, 2014). Put another way, similar to what was said earlier in the chapter about mass murderers, no one general profile fits all, and no general profile firmly identifies the prospective shooter. However, some general observations of psychological characteristics of school shooters can be made, based on research data and expert commentary. We cover the more common observations and findings below.

Leary, Kowalski, Smith, and Phillips (2003) examined the psychological characteristics of juvenile offenders involved in 15 school shootings between 1995 and 2001. They discovered that social rejection was involved in most cases. As mentioned above, peer and social rejection seem very prominent in the backgrounds of the perpetrators. Most of those who were identified as rejected experienced an ongoing pattern of teasing, bullying, or ostracism, and a few were subjected to a recent romantic rejection. In many cases, the victims of the violence were those who rejected or humiliated the shooter.

But social rejection alone did not seem to be enough to ignite killing classmates. In addition to the social rejection, perpetrators showed at least one of the following three risk factors: psychological problems, an interest in guns or explosives, or a morbid fascination with death. The psychological problems centered on low impulse control, lack of empathy for other people, serious depression, aggressiveness, and antisocial behavior. Many of the shooters had been in trouble for aggressive behavior toward peers, and—as noted above—some had abused animals. Depression appears to be especially important in identifying potential school shooters. In one comprehensive study, three-fourths of school shooters had expressed thoughts of suicide or attempts at suicide before the attack (Vossekuil, Fein, Reddy, Borum, & Modzeleski, 2002).

Fascination with firearms, bombs, and explosives is also a common theme. School shooters seem to be comfortable with instruments of destruction. Wike and Fraser (2009) note that police in a community outside of Philadelphia arrested a 14-year-old school dropout who, with his parents' assistance, had collected swords, guns, grenades, bomb-instructional manuals, black powder used in bomb making, and videos of the Columbine massacre. According to police—who acted on a tip from students—this alienated student had plans to attack his former school.

The third observation is that shooters tend to be highly fascinated with death and dark lifestyles and themes. They are not as horrified by sadistic and brutal carnage as most of their peers. On March 12, 2005, Jeffrey Wiese, a 16-year-old at Red Lake High School in Minnesota, killed his grandfather and his grandfather's girlfriend, and then drove to the high school and fatally shot a security guard, a teacher, and five students. He wounded six others before shooting himself. Weise, who had been hospitalized for suicidal behavior, left many dark themes on web sites, dressed in black, and wrote stories about school shootings and zombies (Weisbrot, 2008). However, these dark themes may be more characteristic of depression, thoughts of suicide, and anger at society than a central lifestyle.

In a vast majority of school shootings, the perpetrator apparently had very little attachment or bonding to their schools, teachers, or peers (Wike & Fraser, 2009). School attachment and bonding appear to be crucial in any strategy designed to reduce school violence. Some investigators have found that school attachment plays an important role in producing high levels of academic achievement and in reducing substance use, violence, and high risk sexual behavior (Catalano, Haggerty, Oesterle, Fleming, & Hawkins, 2004; Wike & Fraser, 2009).

In a national study of school violence, Gottfredson, Gottfredson, Payne, and Gottfredson (2005) report that schools in which students find the rules fair and in which discipline is managed consistently experience less violence and disorder. This is regardless of the type of school (e.g., public, private, charter, magnet) and community. They also found that schools characterized by high teacher morale, focus, strong leadership, and high teacher involvement are protected from school crime and violence. Their conclusions: At elementary, middle, and high school levels, the school climate makes a significant difference in reducing the overall crime, disorder, and violence that occur within the school building.

An important study by Daniels and Page (2013) examined the school cultures in those schools where a shooting by a student occurred and those schools where a planned shooting was successfully averted. Four common themes emerged. In those schools where a shooting occurred, there was evidence of (1) an inflexible culture; (2) inequitable disciple; (3) tolerance for disrespectful behavior: and (4) a code of silence. The inflexible culture created among many students a sense of not belonging. Inequitable discipline is when teachers and administrators apply school rules differently to different groups of students. Tolerance for disrespectful behavior refers to "looking the other way," when incidents of bullying, racism, and overt rudeness and aggressiveness happen in the school building and school grounds. The code of silence emerges when students become resistant to reporting threats because of fear of repercussions or lack of an adequate or clearly defined reporting system. It cannot be assumed that school shootings occur only in schools with these negative aspects—some of the schools that have been affected did not have them. Nevertheless, it is worthwhile to take steps to change such a negative culture when it does occur.

Other studies have discovered that one of the most important aspects of a positive school climate is for students to have a sense of school connectedness (Bjelopera et al., 2013). School connectedness is defined as "the belief by students that adults and peers in the school care about their learning as well as about them as individuals" (Centers for Disease Control and Prevention, 2009, p. 3).

WORKPLACE VIOLENCE

Many terms and behaviors have been subsumed under the rubric of workplace violence. In the public mind, workplace violence usually means a worker killing his or her coworkers or supervisors. Commentators, researchers, and experts, on the other hand, have used workplace violence to refer to a wide range of aggressive actions, such as gossip, assaults, sexual assaults, robberies, and murders. For our purpose, it is worthwhile to distinguish between workplace aggression and workplace violence. **Workplace aggression** is "a general term encompassing all forms of behavior by which individuals attempt to harm others at work or their organizations" (Neuman & Baron, 1998, p. 393). Workplace aggression may range from subtle and hidden actions to active confrontations or direct destruction of property (Hepworth & Towler, 2004). Bullying in the workplace also qualifies. **Workplace violence**, on the other hand, refers to incidents in which the offender intends to cause *serious* physical or bodily harm to an individual or individuals within an organization or to the organization itself.

In 2009, 521 persons, age 16 or older, were murdered at the workplace or in the course of their work duties (Harrell, 2011). The highest workplace violence occurs for law enforcement officers, security guards, and bartenders (Harrell, 2011). Persons working in law enforcement and security occupations usually are believed to have the highest annual average rate of workplace violence among government and private-sector employees (Harrell, 2013). However, recent data from the Occupational Safety and Health Administration (OSHA, 2015) indicates that health and social service workers are even more vulnerable to such violence. In 2008, a psychologist was bludgeoned to death in her office in New York City. In 2015, a child protection worker in Vermont was shot to death as she was leaving her office on a Friday afternoon. She was shot by a woman who had recently lost custody of her daughter.

Although the impression derived from media reports over the past two decades is that workplace violence is expanding, it must be emphasized that a large majority of workplace homicides do *not* involve murder between coworkers or supervisors *within* an organization but occur in robberies and related crimes by people *outside* the organization (Barling, Dupré, & Kelloway, 2009) (See **Tables 10-6** and **10-7**). That is, young convenience store clerks or fast-food restaurant workers are often the victims of robbery and other forms of violence while working. Between 2005 and 2009, approximately 28 percent of the workplace homicides involved victims in retail sales and related occupations, and about 17 percent victims were in protective service occupations (e.g., law enforcement officers, security officers) (Harrell, 2011). Shootings accounted for 80 percent of the workplace homicides.

Categories of Workplace Violence

The Occupational Safety and Health Administration (2011) has outlined four categories of workplace violence that describe the relationship between the perpetrator and the target of the workplace violence.

- *Type I—Criminal Intent.* This offender has no legitimate relationship to the workplace or the victim and usually enters the workplace to commit a criminal action such as a robbery or theft. Common victims of Type I offenders are small, late-night retail establishments, including convenience stores and restaurants, and taxi drivers. This type of workplace violence

TABLE 10-6 Workplace Homicides of Victims, Ages 16 or Older, by Known Offender Type, 2005–2009	
Offender Type	**Percentage of Workplace Homicide**
Total	**100.0**
Robbers and other assailants	**70.3**
Robbers	38.3
Other assailants	32.0
Work associates	**21.4**
Coworker, former coworker	11.4
Customer, client	10.0
Relatives	**4.0**
Spouse	2.9
Other relatives	0.8
Other personal acquaintances	**4.3**
Current or former boyfriend or girlfriend	2.0
Other acquaintances	2.3

Source: Harrell, E. (2011, March). Workplace violence, 1993-2009. Washington, DC: U.S. Department of Justice, Bureau of Justice Statistics.

TABLE 10-7	Victim–Offender Relationship for Victims of Workplace Violence, by Sex, 2005–2009	
	Percentage of Workplace Violence	
Victim–Offender Relationship	**Male**	**Females**
Total	**100.0**	**100.0**
Intimate partner	0.8	1.7
Other relatives	0.6	0.7
Well-know/casual acquaintances	11.7	18.9
Work relationships	25.5	31.7
Customer/client	3.9	6.5
Patient	1.5	6.0
Current or former	—	—
Supervisor	1.2	3.3
Employee	2.6	1.7
Coworker	16.3	14.3
Do not know relationship	8.5	6.1
Stranger	52.9	40.9

Source: Harrell, E. (2011, March). Workplace violence, 1993-2009. Washington, DC: U.S. Department of Justice, Bureau of Justice Statistics.

also includes terrorist and hate crimes such as the World Trade Center and Alfred P. Murrah Federal Building bombings, as well as attacks on women's health centers that offer abortions.

- *Type 2—Customer/Client/Patients.* This offender is the recipient of some service provided by the victim or workplace and may be either a current or former client, patient, student, customer, or inmate or person under correctional supervision (e.g., on probation or parole).
- *Type 3—Coworker.* This offender has an employment-related involvement with the workplace. The act of violence is usually committed by a current or former employee, supervisor, or manager who has a dispute with another employee of the workplace. This type of workplace violence offender is usually referred to as the "disgruntled employee" and is often someone who has been fired, demoted, or lost benefits. When death results from the violence, if the victim or victims were of higher authority than the perpetrator, the crime may be called **authority homicide**.
- *Type 4—Personal.* This offender has an indirect involvement with the workplace because of a relationship with an employee. The offender may be a current or former spouse or partner, someone who was in a dating relationship with the employee, or a relative or friend. Typically, violence has been part of the relationship, and the violence follows the employee into the workplace from the outside.

The first of these categories, depicting violence by someone not directly or indirectly connected to workplace, accounts for the vast majority of violence and homicides, perhaps as high as 80 percent of the total (Critical Incident Response Group, 2001). The motive is usually robbery, and in many cases, the offender or offenders are carrying a gun or other weapon, greatly increasing the likelihood that the victim (most often, the victims) will be killed or seriously wounded. For example, in May 2000, two men entered a fast-food restaurant in Flushing, New York, with the intent to rob it. They left with $2,400 in cash after shooting seven employees. Five of the employees died, and two others were seriously wounded. Convenience store clerks, taxi drivers, security guards, and proprietors of "mom-and-pop" stores are also vulnerable to this type of workplace violence. Workers who exchange cash with customers as part of the job, work late-night hours, and work alone are at greatest risk for Type 1 workplace violence.

Type 2 workplace violence usually involves health care workers, police officers, counselors, schoolteachers, college professors, social workers, and mental health workers. An example of Type II workplace violence is provided by the University of Iowa Injury Prevention Research Center (2001, p. 7):

> Rhonda Bedow, a nurse who works in a state-operated psychiatric facility in Buffalo, NY, was attacked by an angry patient who had a history of threatening behavior, particularly against female staff. He slammed Bedow's head down onto a counter after learning that he had missed the chance to go outside with a group of other patients. Bedow suffered a concussion, a bilaterally dislocated jaw, an eye injury, and permanent scarring on her face from the assault.

As noted above, latest figures from OSHA (2015) indicate that health care and social service workers are among the most vulnerable occupations to workplace violence. This is especially the case for those workers providing inpatient psychiatric service, geriatric long-term care settings, high-volume urban emergency departments, and residential and day social services. Child protection workers are also at risk, as illustrated by the 2015 tragedy mentioned above. Although *homicides* may not be as prevalent as in some occupations (e.g., law enforcement), serious personal injury is widespread. Health care workers, for instance, had a 20 percent overall higher rate of workplace violence than all other workers. Moreover, workplace violence in the medical occupations represents about 10 percent of all workplace violence incidents.

The Type 3 workplace violence offender probably is regarded by the media as the most sensational and receives a bulk of its coverage. As noted by the Critical Incident Response Group (2001, p. 11), "mass murders in the workplace by unstable employees have become media-intensive events." In 2013, there were 397 homicides and 270 suicides at the workplace, with shootings being the most common manner of death (U.S. Bureau of Labor Statistics, 2014). These are relatively small in number, but they do receive an inordinate amount of media coverage.

An example of Type 3 violence occurred on August 20, 1986, when a part-time letter carrier, facing possible dismissal after a troubled work history, walked into the Edmond, Oklahoma, post office where he worked and shot 14 people to death before killing himself. In the previous three years, four postal employees were slain by present or former coworkers in separate shootings in South Carolina, Alabama, and Georgia (Critical Incident Response Group, 2001). Similar mass murders in the workplace by emotionally disturbed employees have drawn considerable media scrutiny and—because they initially came to attention with the post office crimes—the term *going postal* was introduced into the American lexicon.

Shortly thereafter, the Critical Incident Response Group (2001) identified a number of additional examples, including four state lottery executives killed in Connecticut by a lottery accountant (1998), seven coworkers killed by a Xerox technician in Honolulu (1999), seven murdered by a software engineer at the Edgewater Technology Company in Massachusetts (2000), four killed by a 66-year-old former forklift driver in Chicago (2001), three killed by an insurance executive at Empire Blue Cross and Blue Shield in New York City (2002), three murdered by a plant worker at a manufacturing plant in Missouri (2003), and six killed by a plant worker at Lockheed–Martin aircraft plant in Mississippi (2003). The Chicago, New York, Mississippi, and Connecticut shooters killed themselves during the incident. The Honolulu and Massachusetts shooters went to trial, both raised the insanity defense, but both were convicted.

The rampage at the Washington, D.C. Naval Yard in September 2013 is a more recent example. Aaron Alexis fatally shot 12 people and injured three others in an early morning shooting spree that lasted just under an hour before he was killed by police. This was the second deadliest mass murder on a military base, after the Fort Hood shootings in 2009, which will be covered in the next chapter as an example of a terrorist attack. Alexis, who had received an honorable discharge from the Navy, was employed as a civilian contractor at the time of the incident. He had had numerous altercations with police and was believed to suffer from mental illness.

Type 4 workplace violence represents a spillover of domestic violence or intimate partner violence into the workplace, and usually women are the victims. As noted earlier, homicide is the leading cause of workplace death for women, accounting for 41 percent of all female worker fatalities (Kelleher, 1997). A good example of Type 4 workplace violence is provided by the University of Iowa Injury Prevention Research Center (2001, p. 11):

> Pamela Henry, an employee of Protocall, an answering service in San Antonio, had decided in the summer of 1997 to move out of the area. The abusive behavior of her ex-boyfriend, Charles Lee White, had spilled over from her home to her workplace, where he appeared one day in July and assaulted her. She obtained and then withdrew a protective order against White, citing her plans to leave the country. On October 17, 1997, White again appeared at Protocall. This time he opened fire with a rifle, killing Henry and another female employee before killing himself.

Perpetrators of Workplace Violence

According to the FBI (Southerland et al., 1997), the workplace homicide offender whose motivation is not robbery is often a disgruntled employee (Type 3) who believes the job is (or was) his life, is a loner, has few friends, and lacks a social support system. The target of the attack may be a person or persons working within a building or structure or for an organization that symbolizes the authority (Douglas et al., 1992). However, it should be emphasized that there is no precise "profile" or litmus test that will provide clear signs that an employee will become violent. Rather, it is important for employees and employers to remain alert to unstable or problematic behavior that, in combination with threatening behavior, could result in violence (see **Table 10-8**).

A vast majority of Type 3 victims are killed (often randomly) by disgruntled employees who were fired or felt mistreated by the company or agency. It seems that a particular autocratic work environment, such as found in large, impersonal bureaucratic organizations, can be a problem. However, as should be clear from the anecdotes cited, no workplace seems immune. As we discussed previously, when an employee feels frustrated and angry, he or she may be more likely to strike out, and this could occur even in a benevolent work environment.

Similar to mass murderers in general, offenders who commit authority homicide—in which a figure in authority, such as a supervisor, is killed—tend to be white males who have few social supports, are socially isolated, and who blame others (externalize) for their problems and misfortune. The offenders often perceive that their performance evaluations were unfair, or that they were treated unjustly (Barling et al., 2009). They are often seriously depressed. Very often, the offender expects to die at the scene, either at his own hands or by the police. Authority offenders also tend to

---

TABLE 10-8   Problematic Behaviors in Workplace that Might Lead to Violence

- Increasing belligerence
- Ominous specific threats
- Hypersensitivity to criticism
- Recent acquisition/fascination with weapons
- Apparent obsession with a supervisor or coworker or employee grievance
- Preoccupation with violent themes
- Interest in recently publicized violent events
- Outbursts of anger
- Extreme disorganization
- Noticeable changes in behavior
- Homicidal/suicidal comments or threats

Source: Critical Incident Response Group. (2001). Workplace violence: Issues in response. FBI Critical Incident Response Group, National Center for the Analysis of Violent Crime, Quantico, VA.

be preoccupied with weapons, accumulating a number of them over a period of time with eventual revenge or "occupational martyrdom" in mind. The weapons are often of maximum lethality, such as automatic or semiautomatic assault weapons. In most instances, the offender is middle aged (over 30 and under 60) (Barling et al., 2009; Kelleher, 1997). There is also evidence that Type 3 workplace offenders tend to have a history of violent behavior, alcohol or drug abuse, and will vocalize, or otherwise act out, their violent intentions prior to the authority homicide (Kelleher, 1997).

In light of increasing sensitivity of employers to the possibility of Type 3 workplace violence, many large organizations contact threat assessment teams to evaluate the probability of a particular employee behaving in a violent manner. Threat assessments were discussed briefly in Chapter 8. A threat assessment specialist may interview the individual, review records, and take statements from other employees. When a significant number of problematic behaviors (**Table 10-8**) have been identified, employers may require that the person seek counseling or, in some situations, may terminate his or her employment. And, as we saw in **Box 10-1**, some businesses, like some schools, conduct safety drills or active shooter drills to prepare employees for possible incidents of violence.

SUMMARY AND CONCLUSIONS

In this chapter, we have taken a closer look at types of homicides that are relatively rare but have significant impact on large numbers of victims, both directly and indirectly. Multiple murders can be divided into three main categories: serial, spree, and mass killings, but the spree murder category is losing favor with criminologists and investigators. Mass killings are divided into classic and family mass murders, as mentioned in Chapter 9. We focused on the classic form here. The deaths that occur as a result of terrorism, a distinct form of mass murder, are discussed in Chapter 11. In addition, the present chapter reviewed school and workplace violence, neither of which necessarily result in death; when it does, it receives intensive public attention.

Many of the crimes that are covered here—particularly serial murders—are often investigated by police with the help of investigative psychology, loosely referred to as "profiling." Because profiling is the commonly used term, we employ it in the chapter, but have divided it into five areas: psychological profiling, suspect-based profiling, geographical profiling, crime scene profiling, and equivalent death analysis. Investigative psychology, which refers to the application of psychological research and principles to the investigation of criminal behavior, is used particularly in crime scene profiling, but it can occur in all forms. It typically includes crime scene investigative methods, such as reviewing features of the modus operandi, the personation or signature, and staging. Crime scene profiling focuses more on the offender, identifying personality traits, behavioral patterns, demographic features, and sometimes geographical habits, such as the distance offenders travel from their homes.

Crime scene profiling is a strategy widely used in law enforcement, particularly for multiple murders or sex crimes. In serial murders, for example, profiling is helpful particularly if the offender demonstrates some psychopathology, such as a specific method of torture. However, it may also be very useful for nonviolent crimes, such as burglaries or arsons. Profiling is a very complex enterprise, though, and unfortunately it is often based on hunches or anecdotal information. However, with increasingly larger data bases made available to professional profilers, along with scientifically rigorous methods applied to the techniques they use, there is hope that the enterprise will gain validity. Rarely does a profile provide the specific identity of an offender, but it is not intended to. As Douglas et al. (1986) noted, profiling tries to narrow the field to a manageable number of suspects.

The form of multiple murder that most terrorizes a community is the serial killing, particularly because it may appear that anyone can be a potential victim. Serial killers generally choose their victims for their specific characteristics, however. For example, victims may be women in their twenties, transients, preadolescent and adolescent boys, prostitutes, or, in the case of the rare female serial killers, husbands or intimate acquaintances, children, or other individuals dependent on them for care. Research indicates that the great majority of serial killers are males; however, prior assumptions that they were invariably white males may be unwarranted. Serial killers are rarely juveniles.

There are many descriptions and illustrations of mass murder but few empirical studies. In the classic form of mass murder, an individual enters a scene and opens fire on a group of people, such as in a restaurant, a place of worship, or a place of work. This form of mass murder is usually carefully planned, and the victims are often symbols of the murderer's discontent. Alternatively, the group of victims includes one or more individuals whom the killer hates or blames for his misfortunes. Mass murderers are typically socially isolated and withdrawn and have inadequate interpersonal and social skills. They may crave the power they gain from their crimes or may have grandiose aspirations to be famous. They also may be searching for significance in their lives.

We discussed unique crimes that have the potential of becoming mass murders, such as school and workplace violence. School violence is a widespread problem in the educational system, although it is not clear that it is on the increase, and it rarely ends in death. In the 1990s, however, an inordinate number of school shootings were reported, the most noteworthy being the Columbine incident in Littleton, Colorado, in 1999. The death toll at Columbine was surpassed by the toll at Sandy Hook, but the latter was distinctive because it was carried out by someone outside the school itself. Despite the fact that school shootings remain rare events, many states mandate safety drills, and a minority mandate "active shooter" drills in their public schools. Investigations of school shootings consistently find that peer rejection and social rejection in general were factors contributing to the eruption of violence. However, other factors, such as cruelty to animals and fascination with guns and other weaponry, often appeared in the background of school shooters. Virtually all had communicated their intentions to other students, sometimes in very specific terms.

The chapter ends with coverage of workplace violence, another phenomenon that may or may not end in mass murder. Offenders are divided into four categories: those having no connection to the workplace but are violent during the commission of another crime, those who have received some service provided by the organization, those who currently or formerly worked there, and those who have some relationship with one or more employees. The vast majority of violence is perpetrated by the first category, those who come into the workplace from the outside, such as the convenience store robber who kills four employees. However, most psychological research has focused on the third type, the disgruntled employee who kills supervisors and/or fellow workers. These individuals are not only angry but also usually socially isolated and seriously depressed. Typically, they expect or plan to die at the scene.

Key Concepts

Actuarial approach to profiling
Authority homicide
Behavioral Analysis Unit (BAU)
Behavioral Science Unit (BSU)
Classic mass murder
Clinical approach to profiling
Confirmation bias
Crime scene profiling
Crime-scene signature
Disorganized crime scene
Equivocal death analysis/Reconstructive psychological evaluation
Family mass murder
Geographical profiling
Investigative psychology
Mass murder
Mixed crime scene

National Center for the Analysis of Violent Crime (NCAVC)
Organized crime scene
Personation
Psychological autopsy
Psychological profiling
Psychological signature
Serial murder
Signature
Spree murder
Staging
Suspect-based profiling (prospective profiling)
Undoing
Violent Criminal Apprehension Program (VICAP)
Workplace aggression
Workplace violence

Review Questions

1. Define investigative psychology.
2. What five categories of profiling are identified? Define each.
3. Briefly describe the difference between an organized and disorganized crime scene, focusing on the characteristics of the offender.
4. List and define the types of multiple murder, and provide an illustration of each.
5. Why is the victimology perspective important in understanding serial murder?
6. Identify and discuss the five-category typology based on the motivations for mass killings provided by Fox and Levin.
7. What are the psychological characteristics of mass murderers, according to the available research?
8. What has research discovered about (a) backgrounds and (b) psychological characteristics of school shooters?
9. List and briefly define each of the four categories of workplace violence.

11

Psychology of Modern Terrorism

CHAPTER OBJECTIVES

- Examine the many definitions of terrorism.
- Evaluate the motives and goals of terrorist groups.
- Introduce a typology of terrorism in order to emphasize the multidimensional features of persons who engage in it.
- Introduce Quest for Significance Theory to explain terrorist motives.
- Introduce Terror Management Theory as another explanation for terrorist motives.
- Describe the lone wolf terrorist.
- Discuss the motives of terrorists and identify psychological concepts that contribute to the understanding of terrorist activity.

- "Terrorist acts are defined to a large degree by their impact, and especially their psychological effects" (Ditzler, 2004, p. 189).
- Without a doubt, "the September 11 attack had achieved its purpose: to create a global psychological state of fear, uncertainty, and terror" (Marsella, 2004, p. 39).
- "Terrorism, like a shark attack, wields tremendous psychological impact" (Victoroff, 2005, p. 33).
- "As a form of intelligible human behavior, terrorism has fundamental psychological aspects" (Kruglanski, Crenshaw, Post, & Victoroff, 2008, p. 98).

As the above quotes indicate, the nature of terrorism is basically psychological; its aim is to create crippling fears and psychological debilitation in a civilian population (Levant, 2002). Given its uniqueness, it is clear that psychology has an important role to play in understanding terrorism, counteracting it, and treating its traumatizing effects (Levant, Barbanel, & DeLeon, 2004). Not until September 11, however, did psychologists demonstrate more than a passing interest in investigating, studying, and writing about this topic (Marsella, 2004).

On that day, an entire nation and much of the world were stunned by the sudden destruction of life and property, when two planes struck the World Trade Center in New York City, a third airliner was flown into the Pentagon outside Washington, and a fourth crashed into a field in Somerset County, Pennsylvania. The plane that crashed in Pennsylvania was believed to be heading for the White House, but passengers on board took over the plane, preventing it from remaining on its original course. At the World Trade Center, 2,823 were killed; at the Pentagon, 184 lives were lost; and all 40 passengers died in the Pennsylvania crash. Nineteen terrorists (all under the age of 35) were directly involved in the airline hijacking (10 at the World Trade Center, 5 at the Pentagon, and 4 in Pennsylvania) (Federal Bureau of Investigation, 2002).

The 9/11 attacks were followed by a number of additional terrorist attacks across the globe. They include, for example, the Bali bombing in 2002, the Madrid bombings of 2004, the London bombing of 2005, the Mumbai attack of 2008, and from 2011 through 2015, attacks throughout the Middle East conducted by Islamic extremists and other terrorist organizations in Iraq, Afghanistan, Syria, and Yemen. During this time, there has been an enormous increase in books, articles, and commentary on the psychological foundations of modern-day terrorism by psychologists, psychiatrists, and other mental health professionals. The slaughter of innocent civilian populations and the destruction of their homes and businesses for some political, religious, or social purpose are considered, by most societies, serious criminal behavior.

 Terrorists are often described as abnormal individuals, sometimes by using terms like evil, psychologically insane, immoral, seriously mentally disordered, or psychopathic killers. Indeed, the outrageous, inhumane attacks on innocent civilians challenge the view that terrorists are rational, emotionally stable individuals. However, there is very little evidence that members of terrorist organizations are mentally unstable, irrational, or psychopathic (Maikovich, 2005; Monahan, 2011; Sarangi & Alison, 2005). In fact, many studies report that terrorists are psychologically much healthier and considerably more stable than other violent criminals (Silke, 2008). There are exceptions, as we will note later in the chapter. Essentially, though, people who demonstrate mental or emotional disorders do not make good terrorists. "They lack the discipline, rationality, self-control and mental stamina needed if terrorists are to survive for any length of time" (Silke, 2008, p. 104). Well-organized terrorist groups immediately expel individuals from their ranks who are emotionally unstable, primarily because they represent a security threat (Post & Gold, 2002). As we learned in Chapter 5, much of the aggression displayed by violent criminals is spontaneous or reactive; terrorist organizations go to great lengths preparing for their attacks, and any breach of their plans seriously compromises their goals. In summary, terrorism is most often a rational behavior based on the belief that violence is morally justified and necessary to further political goals (Ruby, 2002). It is not rational to non-terrorists, but it is rational to the person or group that embraces it.

At this writing, the world is dealing with the emergence of the Islamic State of Iraq and the Levant (ISIL). Many experts prefer to call the terrorist group ISIS, referring to the Islamic State of Iraq and al-Sham. We will use both terms, depending on the reference or quotation. ISIS is a dangerous terrorist organization that has the ambitious goal to solidify and expand its control of territory and govern by implementing its violent interpretation of sharia (Islamic) law (Olson, 2014). The organization believes it requires territory to remain legitimate and follow caliphate rule (Wood, 2015).

The frightening terrorist message of ISIS is promoted by images of extreme violence and brutality and the innovative use of social media, such as for recruitment purposes. However, ISIS and other radical-Islamic groups must not be equated with the practice of Islam as a religion. Muslims across the world are peaceful people and do not support the tactics of radical groups that perpetrate violence in their name. Misunderstanding of Islam—which is one of the world's fastest-growing religions—is demonstrated in a surge in hate crimes against Muslims, as noted earlier in the book.

ISIS has strongly encouraged lone individuals or insular groups in the United States and other Western countries to attack the authority figures and cultural events and symbols in their own countries. These lone terrorist or insular groups that are directly or loosely tied to terrorist organizations in other countries are often referred to as Homegrown Violent Extremists (HVEs). Terrorist attacks by HVEs are quickly becoming the preferred strategy in modern terrorism, often enabled by access to dark sites on the Internet. An example of an HVE attack advocated by foreign terrorist organizations is the 2013 Boston Marathon bombings, which will be discussed later in the chapter.

The plots devised by HVEs are difficult to identify beforehand because they often display few behaviors that law enforcement and intelligence officers usually utilize to detect readiness to commit violence (Rasmussen, 2015). In some cases, those who carry out attacks have been on the radar of government officials, but without sufficient evidence to question or detain them. Moreover, "The perceived success of previous lone offender attacks combined with al-Qaida's, AQAP's, and ISIL's incendiary propaganda promoting individual acts of terrorism has raised the profile of this tactic" (Rasmussen, 2015, p. 4). AQAP is an acronym for "al-Qaeda in the Arabian Peninsula," a Sunni extremist group based in Yemen that has orchestrated numerous terrorist attacks.

ISIS is not the only terrorist organization that presents a serious threat. There are many others as well. The group Boka Haram, an affiliate of al-Qaeda that kidnapped over 200 Nigerian girls in 2014, is responsible for the slaughters of over 5,000 people in that country. In some countries (e.g., Syria and Yemen), groups and individuals are trained in terrorist techniques and sent back to other countries to carry out their crimes. In April 2015, an Ohio man, who trained with a terrorist group in Syria, was charged with returning to the United States, allegedly with instructions to attack a military base or a prison (Shane, 2015). As noted by Mazzetti, Schmidt, and Hubbard (2014), "Beyond the militant groups fighting for control of territory, Syria has become a magnet for Islamic extremists from other nations who have used parts of the country as a sanctuary to plot attacks" (p. A1). Besides al-Qaeda, the terrorist groups of Khorasan and the Nusra Front are also formidable direct threats to the United States (Mazzetti et al., 2014).

DEFINITIONS AND EXAMPLES

Throughout this book, and most particularly in Chapters 9 and 10, we have encountered individuals who terrorized others through their criminal activity. Serial killers, for example, terrorize communities, domestic abusers terrorize members of their household, and a home invader may terrorize a family. However, to terrorize is not to be a terrorist in the context of this chapter. Furthermore, holding a community ransom to fear that still another person will be killed is not to engage in terrorism in the context of this chapter. How then do we define terrorism? According to Sternberg (2003), terrorism is simply "the systematic use of terror, especially as a means of coercion" (p. 299). Hallett (2004) defines the term as a theatrical crime against person or property in which only symbolic or psychological satisfaction to the perpetrators is gained.

In federal law, terrorism is defined as "the unlawful use of force or violence against persons or property to intimidate or coerce a government, the civilian population, or any segment thereof, in furtherance of political or social objectives" (Code of Federal Regulations, 18 U.S.C § 2331(1)). Under federal law, terrorism may be either domestic or international, depending on the origin, base, and objectives of the terrorist organization (U.S. Department of Justice, 2000a). Domestic terrorism refers to the actions of groups or an individual based and operating entirely within the United States or Puerto Rico without clear foreign direction—although there may be foreign influence. A well-known example is the Oklahoma City bombing on April 17, 1995, when a truck bomb destroyed the Alfred P. Murrah Federal Building, killing 167 (19 were children, most of whom were in a day care center on the premises) and injuring 684 persons. Timothy McVeigh, a U.S. citizen and former soldier, was convicted and eventually executed for this crime. His coconspirator, Terry Nichols, pled guilty in both federal and state courts to avoid the death penalty. The Oklahoma City attack remains the deadliest *domestic* terrorist incident ever committed on U.S. soil.

More recently, on November 5, 2009, Army Major Nidal Hasan killed 13 people and wounded 32 others at Fort Hood, Texas. All but two were military personnel. Although we could consider this an illustration of mass murder of the workplace violence variety discussed in Chapter 10, the circumstances of the shooting—including words shouted by Hasan as he opened fire—led the Department of Defense (DoD) to consider this an example of domestic terrorism. As will be mentioned later in the chapter, Hasan also had exchanged email correspondence with a prominent al-Qaeda recruiter. An independent review was undertaken to address possible deficiencies in DoD's force protection and identify employees who could potentially pose credible threats to themselves or others (Monahan, 2011).

Other illustrations of domestic terrorism include actions by members of far-right extremist groups, including political and religious white supremacists, such as Aryan Nations and neo-Nazi organizations. For example, members of the so-called "Army of God" claimed responsibility for the bombings of clinics that provide abortions and an alternative lifestyle nightclub in Atlanta. This form of domestic terrorism is increasingly gaining attention in the scholarly literature (see, generally, Freilich, Chermak, & Caspi, 2009, and the special issues of the *American Psychologist*, October 2013 and September 2011), and many law enforcement authorities consider it a greater threat to national security than international terrorism (Chermak, Freilich, & Shemtob, 2009).

International terrorism refers to violent acts or acts dangerous to human life that are a violation of the criminal laws of the United States or any state and under the direction of a foreign government, group, organization, or person. Although terrorist activities are widespread and affect people throughout the world, the most vivid example of international terrorism and the one most covered by the media and the research literature is that represented by the events that occurred on September 11, 2001. With that exception, most international terrorism aimed at U.S. property or citizens occurs in other countries. For example, in the late twentieth century, groups in Columbia targeted American interests, kidnapped seven U.S. citizens, and carried out multiple bombings against oil pipelines used by American companies (U.S. Department of Justice, 2000a). Another example involves the American embassies in Nairobi, Kenya, and Dar es Salaam, Tanzania, where in August 1998, both embassies were bombed almost simultaneously. The truck bombings killed 224, including 12 American citizens, and injured over 4,500 located in or near the embassies. The attacks on the American consulate in Benghazi in 2012, where four Americans, including Libyan Ambassador Christopher Stevens, were killed, are still another illustration. **Figures 11-1** and **11-2** illustrate data gathered by the National Counterterrorism Center (NCTC) on global attacks in 2008.

Despite these sobering numbers, Americans living or visiting abroad are no more likely to be victimized by terrorist activities than are citizens of other nations. Terrorist activities were a fact of life in other parts of the world long before September 11, and they have continued since then. Japan, the United Kingdom, France, Spain, Indonesia, Israel, Palestine, Sri Lanka, Syria, Yemen, Egypt, and Saudi Arabia, among many others, have all been targeted. On March 11, 2004, a series of coordinated bombings directed at the commuter train system of Madrid, Spain, was carried out by an al-Qaeda–inspired terrorist group. The attacks killed 191 people and injured 1,900. On July 7, 2005, the first Islamist suicide bombings in Europe occurred in London (Silke, 2008). Suicide bombers detonated explosives during the morning rush hour, killing 52 persons and injuring 700 (Silke, 2008). And on October 1, 2005, terrorists believed to be associated with the terrorist network Jemaah Islamiah detonated bombs at two sites in Bali, Indonesia, killing 26 and injuring about 120 persons. In France, on January 7, 2015, the satirical newspaper *Charlie Hebdo* was the site of another attack. Masked gunmen armed with assault rifles and other weapons identified themselves as belonging to al-Qaeda in Yemen (AQAP). They killed 11 people and injured 11 others. *Charlie Hebdo* had been repeatedly threatened for its caricatures of the Prophet Muhammad and other sketches. Also in France, on November 13, 2015, a planned and coordinated terrorist attack at several locations in Paris took the lives of 130 individuals and injured numerous others. Terrorism frightens and touches people worldwide.

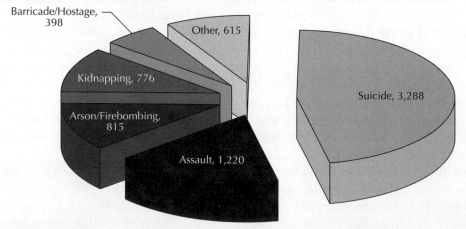

FIGURE 11-1 Deaths by Different Methods in Global Terrorist Attacks, 2008 *Source:* National Counterterrorism Center. (2009, April). 2008 Report on Terrorism. Washington, DC: Office of the Director of National Intelligence.

A quick scan of the literature reveals there are multiple definitions and illustrations of terrorism in addition to those cited above. Victoroff (2005) found at least 109 definitions within the academic literature alone. He asserts that the lack of consensus is probably inescapable, considering the heterogeneity of terrorist behaviors and the wide variety of declared or assumed motivations, justifications, and goals. As Monahan (2011, p. 15) asks succinctly, "(I)s it plausible to expect that the risk factors for joining the Irish Republican Army are the same as the risk factors for joining the Taliban?" Trying to reach a comprehensive definition is complicated by the maxim, "One person's terrorist is another person's freedom fighter" (Marsella, 2004, p. 15).

Despite the vast and sometimes overwhelming array of definitions, Marsella (2004) finds some common ground in all of them, although—as in the definitions above—it may be implicit. "Terrorism is broadly viewed as (a) the use of force or violence (b) by individuals or groups (c) that is directed toward civilian populations (d) and intended to instill fear (e) as a means of coercing individuals or groups to change their political and social positions" (p. 16). These five elements are common to the illustrations used in this chapter. Marsella further notes that any comprehensive definition of terrorism also requires thoughtful consideration of the psychosocial context, motives, and consequences of the act.

Although terrorism is not a new phenomenon, terrorism today offers a much greater threat of violence to the world than ever before. This is because of the globalization of commerce, travel, the Internet, and the consequent rapid flow of information, " ... which puts economic disparities and ideological competition in sharp relief and facilitates cooperative aggression by far-flung but like-minded conspirators" (Victoroff, 2005, p. 3). Victoroff (2005) also notes that, because of this rise in globalization, religious fundamentalism has ascended as an aggrieved competitor with the market-economic, democratic, and secular trends of the rapidly changing modern world. Furthermore, this expanding globalization has been instrumental in the emergence of the first *multinational* terrorist group of the twenty-first century, al-Qaeda (Hellmich, 2008), the group responsible for the attacks of September 11. Multinationalist terrorists train and carry out attacks in many different countries, and they are typically associated with a philosophy that advocates a violent jihad, or duty to be violent. It is important to stress again that the religion of Islam, with which the term is associated, does not advocate violence. To most Muslims the term "jihad" simply means religious duty. However, multinational radical Islamic terrorist groups have given it a violent interpretation—a duty to wage religious war against infidels.

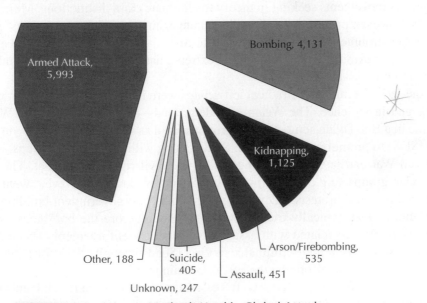

FIGURE 11-2 Primary Methods Used in Global Attacks, 2008 *Source:* National Counterterrorism Center. (2009, April). 2008 Report on Terrorism. Washington, DC: Office of the Director of National Intelligence.

In response to the September 11 attacks, the United States launched strong military forces into Afghanistan in an effort to weed out al-Qaeda cells in that country. Soon thereafter, the United States invaded Iraq on the premise that it contained weapons of mass destruction (WMD) and in apparent pursuit of al-Qaeda–sponsored organizations. Critics argued forcefully—and events since then have documented—that the invasion of Iraq was unjustified. Furthermore, many people believe that such aggressive military responses are rarely successful in preventing future attacks because they do not address the root conditions that spawn terrorism (Marsella, 2004). Instead, "there must be a response to prevent its emergence and its growth and development as an appealing option" (Marsella, 2004, p. 34). "(T)errorism may be contained but never defeated as long as there are real or perceived threats or injustices that foster widespread hatred and revenge. There may be small and large military successes, but eventually there must be coming to grips with the strengths and weaknesses of the human psyche and the cultural milieu in which it is fostered" (Moghaddam & Marsella, 2004b, p. 4).

CLASSIFICATION OF TERRORIST GROUPS

In addition to the domestic and international categories, there are several other ways to classify terrorism and those who engage in it. The FBI classifies terrorists according to political leanings. For example, **right-wing terrorists** are extremist groups or individuals that generally adhere to an antigovernment or racist ideology and often engage in a variety of hate crimes and violence. They may be prompted to become active by the passage of legislation or by government policy in opposition to their beliefs, such as laws placing restrictions on gun ownership or taxation or laws granting civil rights to various groups, such as marriage equality laws or laws applying to the children of undocumented immigrants.

Far-right organizations are receiving considerable research scrutiny. Freilich et al. (2009) note that, though the domestic far right is not easily defined, it is composed of individuals or groups that are fiercely nationalistic, antiglobal, suspicious of centralized federal authority, and reverent of individual liberty, such as an unrestricted right to own guns or be free from taxes. They also believe in conspiracy theories, believe attacks to national sovereignty and/or personal liberty are imminent, and consequently participate in paramilitary training in survival skills.

Left-wing extremist groups have also been prevalent in American history. Although less likely to be labeled "terrorists," their actions may qualify them for that designation when they move from political activism to violent activities. Historically, left-wing extremism developed from working-class movements seeking in theory to eliminate class distinctions. More modern left-wing extremists, however, protest and politically agitate against certain governmental policies, discrimination, and environmental issues. According to Smith and Morgan (1994), the extreme left "… is characterized by extreme egalitarianism, an extreme hatred of racism and capitalism, and an overt opposition to militarism" (p. 44).

In the 1970s, a number of radical left groups were in operation. Some, but not all, were regularly engaged in violence. The Weather Underground—originally called the Weathermen (taken from a line in a Bob Dylan song)—was a group created as an offshoot of Students for a Democratic Society (SDS) to promote social change. SDS—along with many other groups—strongly opposed the Vietnam War and later actively engaged in the civil rights movement. The Weathermen and other similar groups (e.g., the Symbionese Liberation Army) however, went beyond political activism and peaceful protests. They smuggled bombs into government buildings, banks, and restaurants, though they typically tried to warn the public before the bombings. Nevertheless, their members were also associated with assassinations of law enforcement officers, and other deaths sometimes resulted from their criminal activities. (See Burrough, 2015 for a journalistic review of these radical groups and efforts by the FBI to contain them.)

Another powerful and well-known left extremist group was the Black Panther Party, an African American organization that was established to promote black influence through militant-type protests and demonstrations. The Black Panthers also encouraged young African Americans to be proud of their heritage and sponsored various programs to help the black community, including recreational and nutritional programs. The organization was most active in the United States from the mid-1960s to the mid-1970s. Law enforcement organizations were highly suspicious of the group's intentions and went to great lengths to discredit and destroy the organization, despite lack of evidence of violence. Among the most controversial law enforcement activities was the raid on Black Panther headquarters that included the fatal shooting of two Panthers, Fred Hampton and Mark Clark in 1969.

Another FBI classification is **special interest extremists**, whose activities revolve around one issue about which they are passionate. The predominant representatives of this group are violent antiabortion groups that firebombed women's health centers during the 1990s. This category also includes **radical environmental groups**, such as the Earth Liberation Front (ELF). The ELF organization received particular attention during the late 1990s by destroying homes, earth-moving equipment, power lines, computer systems, and buildings that they believed damaged the earth's ecology. In its own words, the organization's primary mission is to "speed up the collapse of industry, to scare the rich, and to undermine the foundations of the state."

During the past several decades, fear of **nuclear/biological/chemical** (abbreviated **NBC**) **terrorism** has apparently accelerated. The thought of being exposed to an invisible or undetectable agent can be more frightening to the general public than the prospect of physical injury or death caused by conventional weapons. Furthermore, the threat of NBC terrorism is more realistic today because terrorists are able to take advantage of the greater availability of information and weapons technology.

Nuclear terrorism includes the use of nuclear bombs or dirty bombs that make use of radioactive material and thus far has not been known to occur. The public is periodically told, however, of thwarted attempts to plant dirty bombs in various global locations. In the spring of 2012, an al-Qaeda plot to place an underwear bomb in an airline departing from Yemen and heading for the United States was stopped; the "terrorist" was apparently a CIA undercover agent who had infiltrated a terrorist training ground and kept U.S. officials apprised of the plan. By design, he was "arrested" before the plot unfolded.

Unknown and unforeseen attacks with chemical agents or biological agents, on the other hand, have happened. The use of sarin, a deadly nerve agent, in the subway system of Tokyo, Japan, in 1995, provides a horrifying example. The attacks were carried out by the doomsday cult Aum Shinrikyo (Supreme Truth Sect) and resulted in the deaths of 11 people and injuries to more than 5,000. It is estimated that about 375 pounds of sarin is enough to kill over 50,000 persons. The use of biological agents in this context is sometimes referred to as **bioterrorism**. It involves the use of bacteria, viruses, germs, and other agents such as anthrax, bubonic plague, and smallpox (Marsella, 2004). A recent example of domestic bioterrorism is represented by the anthrax attacks that occurred in the United States less than a month after 9/11. The bioterrorist(s) sent the anthrax by letter to various persons in the eastern sections of the United States, including the Washington offices of Senators Patrick Leahy and Tom Daschle, and the New York office of former CBS anchor Dan Rather. Anthrax is an acute infectious disease caused by the spore-forming bacterium *Bacillus anthracis*. Although anthrax is most commonly found in hoofed mammals, it can also infect humans. Symptoms of the disease vary depending on how the disease was contracted, but they usually occur within seven days after exposure. The serious forms of human anthrax are inhalation anthrax, cutaneous (skin) anthrax, and intestinal (ingestion) anthrax. Inhalation (pulmonary) anthrax starts with inhalation of anthrax spores and has a mortality rate of around 95 percent, even with treatment. Cutaneous anthrax starts with the spore colonizing the skin through an abrasion, cut, or wound. The mortality rate of the cutaneous anthrax ranges from 20 to 25 percent without treatment, and is less than 1 percent with treatment. Intestinal anthrax, by far the worst, is usually transmitted through eating contaminated meat. It has a mortality rate of 95 percent, even when treated.

The bioterrorist(s) sent letters containing both inhalation and cutaneous anthrax to the victims. (The FBI believes the anthrax mailer was a microbiologist, Dr. Bruce Ivins, who committed suicide on August 1, 2008, before formal charges were filed.) The anthrax spores were mixed with a light powder in the folds of the letters. The first known case of the anthrax letter attack killed a photo editor of a newspaper in Boca Raton, Florida, in October 2001. In total, the bioterrorist letters resulted in at least five deaths due to inhalation anthrax infections; another eight cases of nonfatal cutaneous anthrax infections were reported during 2001. Bioterrorism, if delivered under the right conditions and by using a highly infectious biological agent, could be devastating. The fear of bioterrorism is so intense in some individuals that they entertain its possibility whenever an influenza problem arises. For example, when "swine flu" (H1N1) erupted in Mexico and several states in spring of 2009, radio talk shows and the Internet were flooded with comments that this was the work of bioterrorists. By fall, when H1N1 had reached near-pandemic proportions, the chatter had turned to criticism of the government for not acting swiftly to prevent it.

A TERRORIST TYPOLOGY

In addition to categorizing terrorist groups on the basis of their interest, researchers have also attempted to provide typologies of individuals within the groups based on their motives. In most cases, the motivation can be generalized to the group as a whole. Ditzler (2004) describes a terrorist typology promulgated by the U.S. Army Command and General Staff College (Terrorism Research Center, 1997). The typology also incorporates some of the research conducted at RAND (Hoffman, 1993). The typology identifies three motivational categories: (1) the rationally motivated terrorist, (2) the psychologically motivated terrorist, and (3) the culturally motivated terrorist.

The **rationally motivated terrorists** are those who consider the goals of the organization and the possible consequences of their actions. They develop well-defined and theoretically achievable goals that may involve political, social, economic, or other specific objectives. In many cases, rationally motivated terrorists try to avoid loss of life but focus instead on destroying infrastructures, buildings, and other symbolic structures to get their message across. However, multiple examples of deaths caused by rationally motivated terrorists can be found. Note that this classification does not suggest that the behavior of the group is rational or logical; rather, they believe it is, and they typically carry out carefully planned activities. An example of this motivation is the Weather Underground described earlier.

 Psychologically motivated terrorists are driven by "a profound sense of failure or inadequacy for which the perpetrator may seek redress through revenge" (Ditzler, 2004, p. 202). The attraction to terrorism is usually based on the psychological benefits of group affiliation and collective identity. They are especially drawn to terrorist groups that have a charismatic leader. One variation of the psychologically motivated terrorist, though, is the lone wolf operation, "for whom the validation of the self is not derived through group affiliation, but through the sense of power, mastery, and autonomy that attends to the ability to make unilateral decisions" (Ditzler, 2004, p. 203). A classic example of this type of terrorist may be Theodore Kaczynski, known as the Unabomber. Often, lone wolf terrorists have strong feelings of social alienation, anger, and extreme antigovernment ideology. In most instances, they view themselves as victims of the "system." They also may show signs of serious mental disorder. We will return to the lone wolf terrorist later in the chapter.

Culturally motivated terrorists are driven by fear of irreparable damage to their way of living, national heritage, or culture done by an organization, foreign country, or powerful factions. Most often, religion is the aspect that generates the fervor or passion in the group as well as the individual. National or cultural groups that are largely governed or socially defined by a particular system of faith are often constantly vigilant for forces that may eradicate their religious way of life or cultural identity. Ditzler gives the example of Afghanistan under the Taliban, where "Islam provided not only a system of religious faith as understood in the West, but the entire system of civil and criminal law, political organization, and social behavior" (2004, p. 203). Under such conditions, a perceived threat to the faith would be cause for alarm and a threat to the group's existence. However, as we know from the millions of law-abiding and peaceful Muslims, most members of the religious group do not respond to threats to their way of life with acts of terrorism. One of the most troubling outcomes of the events of September 11 was the widespread and unjustified distrust of those of Islamic faith.

FOLLOWERS AND LEADERS: WHO JOINS AND WHO LEADS

Overall, terrorists are a very heterogeneous group, and the range of people who become involved in terrorism may be placed on a wide spectrum (Silke, 2008). They may differ in educational levels, family background, intelligence, gender, socioeconomic class, and religious conviction. Although young men make up the majority of terrorists, some are women, and a few men are much older than the average group member. In recent years, there have been anecdotal accounts of girls and young women leaving the United States or other Western countries to attempt to join ISIS, but thus far no accurate data are available, and no systematic studies have been conducted to determine the extent of this phenomenon. In his investigation of 242 jihadi terrorists in Europe, Bakker (2006) was able to identify only five women recruits, which seems to be an unrealistically low number. Bakker (2006) also found that most of the terrorists were in their teens to mid-twenties but some were also in their fifties. Over 70 percent of al-Qaeda members were married, including many who carried out suicide attacks (Sageman, 2004; Silke, 2008). Many married al-Qaeda members also had children.

Sageman (2004) found in a survey of extremist Islamist groups, over 60 percent had some higher levels of education, and three-quarters of them came from upper- or middle-class backgrounds. The 9/11 pilots included the middle-aged, middle-class urban planner Mohammad Atta, and the wealthy and educated Ziad Jarrah who enjoyed discos and beer (Victoroff, 2005). Although a significant number of terrorist members come from well-established or well-heeled family backgrounds, many come from the poorer and less-advantaged people of the world (Miller, 2006). Many terrorists come from backgrounds where, "... menial work gives little satisfaction, political freedom is sparse or nonexistent, avenues of recreational escapism are few, and social mobility and hope for a better life is little more than a fantasy" (Miller, 2006, p. 126).

In a summary of the literature on risk factors for terrorism, Monahan (2011) confirms the above. He notes that the mean age for terrorists is between 20 and 29, the preponderance are male, and the majority appear to be unmarried. Their backgrounds indicate no evidence of major mental illness or psychopathology. With respect to social class, "the evidence thoroughly contradicts the common belief that terrorists are disproportionately of lower social class .... In terms of occupation, income, and educational level, terrorists appear to be largely indistinguishable from the local population" (p. 10).

Finally, Monahan (2011) posits, there is no evidence that terrorists have personality disorders or problems with substance abuse. In addition, "The search for personality traits that distinguish terrorists from non-terrorists with any degree of reliability has a long and frustrating history" (p. 12). Citing several researchers, Monahan notes that that search has been more or less abandoned. In essence, research reveals that a specific personality profile that characterizes a terrorist does not exist (Kruglanski et al., 2013).

Why Do They Join?

When people lack the skills and strategies to modify at least some of their social situations, feelings of helplessness usually result. This may explain why some individuals engage in terrorist activities, but by no means all. These feelings are in turn likely to provoke one of two response patterns: approach (attack) or avoidance (withdrawal). The withdrawal response, as theorized by Martin Seligman (1975), is often called **learned helplessness** or **reactive depression**. The person feels there is nothing that can be done about his or her predicament, so why bother? This response pattern is vividly illustrated by powerless people living under dire economic or social conditions, who perceive that they have little opportunity for change—a life without hope. On the other hand, an alternative response is to attack, to lash out in desperation, especially if a person believes this response pattern will be effective in improving his circumstances, or the circumstances of his family or community. If people have next to nothing or little hope for a better future, "the only thing you cannot take away from them is their religious or political or philosophical belief" (Miller, 2006, p. 126). Especially if that belief tells them that, despite their hardships, their God is ultimately just and things will work out for them either in this world or in the next.

It has also been hypothesized that young people lacking self-esteem and a sense of self may be primary candidates for joining terrorist groups. Many Irish and European terrorists, for instance, say they became politically violent primarily to seek a sense of purpose and self-worth (Victoroff, 2005). Young people who are recruited on Internet sites may express the same sentiments. This perspective fits well with Erik Erikson's (1980) theory that adolescents reach a stage of identity formation during which ideologies are most likely to have a significant and potentially lasting impact. Erikson viewed identity and the sense of self as central themes in anyone's life course. Arena and Arrigo (2005) point out that some scholars have suggested that many terrorists have failed to effectively negotiate Erickson's eight stages and consequently have assumed a negative identity. The negative identity encourages these persons to turn to extremist organizations to finally experience purpose and meaning in their lives.

Social learning theory also provides some insight into the psychological processes that influence members to join a terrorist organization. Victoroff (2005) writes, "Teenagers living in hotbeds of political strife may directly witness terrorist behaviors and seek to imitate them or, even more commonly, learn from their culture's public glorification of terrorists—for example, the 'martyr posters' lining the streets of Shi'a regions of Lebanon and Palestinian refugee camps or the songs celebrating the exploits of the PIRA" (p. 18). However, although the theory has strong explanatory power for why they join, it does not completely explain why more young teenagers living within these social contexts do not become terrorists.

Quest for Significance Theory

Although the above perspectives have some validity in explaining how and why someone joins and engages in terrorism, Arie Kruglanski and his colleagues (Kruglanski & Orehek, 2011; Kruglanski, Chen, Dechesne, Fishman, & Orehek, 2009; Kruglanski et al., 2013) have proposed a model that provides a comprehensive framework for explaining the behavior. The model is called the **quest for significance theory**. The motivation to engage in terrorism, the model posits, is the search to be meaningful and recognized as someone significant. The quest for significance represents the "attainment of what the culture says is worth attaining, the kind of competence that the culture deems worthy, and for which one is accorded the admiration of others who matter to oneself" (Kruglanski et al., 2013, p. 561). Moreover, the quest for significance needs to be specifically activated by someone or some event in order for it to influence behavior. This quest may be activated by three events: (1) significant loss; (2) the threat of significant loss; and (3) the opportunity for significant gain.

A loss of significance can occur in a variety of ways, including a failure in some important pursuit (Kruglanski et al., 2013). It also often happens when an individual is demeaned, ostracized, or rendered powerless by another person or social group. The primary way for that individual to regain significance may be to participate in violent or terrorist acts, either by oneself or as a member of a terrorist group. Muslims as a group have been subjected to strong prejudice and disrespect, and radical-Islamic extremists may use this in their efforts to recruit members to their terrorist organization. Sometimes it is the fear of losing power that determines one's engagement in terrorist activities. The racist Ku-Klux-Klan historically recruited members by appealing to their fear that blacks would become a dominant force in society and that they themselves would lose power and status. Furthermore, Bélanger and his colleagues (2014) found evidence to support the observation that individuals who have lost significance will display greater readiness to sacrifice themselves, such as they may do in carrying out terrorist suicidal attacks.

The threat of significant loss may arise when a person fails or refuses to comply with the pressure to engage in terrorism. In other words, if the person resists engaging in suicidal terrorism, he risks the threat of being ostracized from the group.

The opportunity for significant gain may occur when the terrorist goals promise a considerable increase in status and self-esteem. If a person has undergone a series of personal setbacks and has developed a sense of meaninglessness in his life, an organization that comes along and offers the opportunity to become somebody, or to contribute to an important cause, becomes a powerful influence. Kruglanski et al. (2013) describe the tactic of indoctrinating youths into terrorist groups with convincing stories of martyrdom and heroism. This approach reflects the group's attempt to create a promised opportunity for immense significance once they join the cadres of the group's fighters later in their lives.

Once the quest for significance is activated, an ideology (a belief system) has to be put in place for the person to understand what he or she needs to do to obtain significance and life everlasting. Kruglanski et al. (2013) write, "We thus assume that ideology is relevant to radicalization because it identifies such radical activity as violence and terrorism as means to personal significance and justifies it on moral and effectiveness grounds" (p. 564). The ideology may be so demanding that it trumps all other goals, including protecting one's own family. Moreover, the ideology ensures that one be willing to undertake risk and sacrifices on behalf of the group.

Terror Management Theory

Another general model that adds an additional motivational factor for engaging in terrorist activities is **terror management theory** (Jonas & Fritsche, 2013; Pyszczynski, Abdollahi, Greenberg, & Solomon, 2006). The theory was inspired by the works of Ernest Becker (1973, 1975). Similar to quest for significance theory, terror management theory (TMT) offers a useful framework for understanding the motivational forces that help explain why people engage in intergroup conflict, join terrorist organizations, and are willing to sacrifice themselves for a cause. According to the theory, the sacrifice and commitment to a group or cause can be negative (terrorism against innocent people) or positive (a religious commitment toward the betterment of all humankind).

The word "terror" in TMT refers to the high anxiety of eventual death that all humans face. The theory asserts that humans are continually and often keenly aware of their own mortality, and this is accompanied by the consistent threat of personal insignificance. The threat of death brings with it the "nightmare of ending up as 'a speck of insignificant dust in an uncaring universe'" (Kruglanski et al., 2009, p. 335). The basic tenet of TMT is that people construct and maintain cultural worldviews as a way of avoiding the anxiety and fear that comes from the knowledge that death is inevitable (Pyszczynski, Rothschild, & Abdollahi, 2008). "Cultural worldviews are individualized conceptions of reality, derived from the external culture, that provide meaning, purpose, value, and the hope of either literal or symbolic immortality, through either an afterlife or a connection to something greater than oneself that transcends one's mortal existence" (Pyszczynski et al., 2008, p. 318). "The worldview not only provides a canopy under which life makes sense on a grand scale but also prescribes principles to live by and standards for appropriate behavior" (Landau & Sullivan, 2015, p. 210). The worldview is more than merely an outlook on life; it is a formula for immortality (Becker, 1973; Landau & Sullivan, 2015). Reminders of one's own mortality encourage individuals to embrace their group's culture and ideals (Kruglanski et al., 2009). People must believe that "some valued aspect of themselves will continue, either literally or symbolically, after cessation of their biological body" (Burke, Martens, & Faucher, 2010). Literal immortality refers to the form of afterlife existence, whereas symbolic immortality refers to what legacy one leaves behind, such as—in the case of a terrorist—achievements, heroic feats, and martyrdom.

Perceived threats to a group's cultural worldview, in the form of humiliation, domination, and injustice by out-groups, are seen as the root causes underlying terrorist hatred, rage, and violence. On the basis of a growing body of research, Jonas and Fritsche (2013) conclude, "Research has shown that when reminded of death, people become more intolerant and aggressive toward out-group others and more strongly supportive of military action in intergroup conflict" (p. 543). This conclusion applies to terrorist organizations in their quest to terrorize and destroy members of out-groups whom they perceive as serious threats to their beliefs, lifestyle, and worldview. From this perspective, one becomes significant and receives comfort in dealing with death by belonging to an in-group that provides an opportunity for significance and for dealing effectively with death transcendence. It is perhaps comforting to believe that, in order to continue on in some fashion after death, one must fulfill the in-group's requirements for being significant, leading a proper life, and contributing to its ultimate mission.

Overall, the quest for significance theory and terror management theory have a number of similarities but the major difference is the motivational factor. Significance theory contends that people are driven to become significant within a given society or group. Terror management theory contends that people are driven to deal with inevitable death by striving for immortality in the hereafter. Both provide cogent explanations for many terrorist acts.

Suicidal Terrorism

Although most do not, some terrorists volunteer for suicide missions. For Western societies, suicide is often associated with despair, depression, or a disordered mind (Miller, 2006). However, members of terrorist groups are *not* necessarily depressed nor do they necessarily see things as hopeless. Rather, upon entering a terrorist organization, they see themselves doing something worthwhile with their lives; and if they participate in a suicide mission, they see themselves as martyrs, bringing honor to their families and communities (LoCicero & Sinclair, 2008). Terrorists on suicide missions firmly believe that their death is for a just cause and that the act provides a ticket to another form of eternal life. As Kruglanski et al. (2009) note, "the willingness to die in an act of suicidal terrorism may be motivated by the desire to live forever" (p. 336). In the radical jihadist ideology, for instance, martyrdom does not result in an end of individual existence, but rather immortality under highly pleasurable conditions. In addition to paradise, for some insignificant individuals, suicidal terrorism offers the opportunity for a rare shot at immense "stardom" (Kurglanski et al., 2009, p. 349).

Al-Qaeda portrayed martyrdom as a highly desirable goal in the training camps of Afghanistan, and many recruits were willing to volunteer for suicide missions (Busch & Weissman, 2005). After reviewing several studies on the suicidality of terrorists involved in suicide bombings, Monahan (2011) noted that they are not otherwise suicidal—that is, were it not for their mission, they would not likely be candidates for suicide. In addition, the Koran specifically prohibits suicide (Post, McGinnis, & Moody, 2014). "But radical interpretations of the Koran have led to the adoption of suicide terrorism, justifying this as defensive aggression and rationalizing this not as the prohibited suicide, but as martyrdom instead, which is rewarded with a higher place in paradise" (Post et al., 2014, pp. 309–310).

A majority of terrorists lack the early developmental antisocial patterns found in chronic *violent* criminal offenders. They are often young men in their teens or twenties who have been good students, model citizens, and participants in their communities or families, although this tends to be less correct about young, would-be terrorists from Western countries who want to join the cause from afar or hope to flee to training camps. The young persons who join terrorist groups may come from families who may even support their cause and their supreme sacrifice, although others are outcasts and isolated from their communities. Their willingness to sacrifice themselves comes from the rage and resentment they have for the unjust persecutions and humiliations they perceive as originating from outside groups, governments, or societies.

FAIL-SAFE PROCEDURES. Laurence Miller (2006) notes that many terrorist organizations develop a fail-safe procedure to ensure that the suicide mission is completed. Terrorists eventually have the difficult task of coping with the realization that they must kill people, most often innocent men, women, and children. This realization can become psychologically stressful to maintain a terrorist lifestyle during the early stages of membership. Consequently, the organization must focus on intense indoctrination of the members who will carry out the mission, and restrict the tactical details of the mission to the leaders of the organization. As the suicide mission approaches, the organization will have those selected to complete the mission engage in a series of "point-of-no-return rituals" to ensure compliance. "These include having members write last letters to friends and relatives, videotaping a goodbye narrative, saying final prayers, and so on" (Miller, 2006, p. 131). These commitments make it increasingly difficult for the "living martyr" to back out. In those cases where the organization believes the martyr may back out, they arrange for a remote control detonation, just in case (Silke, 2003).

Becoming a Terrorist: The Process of Radicalization

In the context of terrorism, radicalization is defined as an individual's indoctrination to fully embrace a terrorist group's ideology and mission, and to gradually embrace the level of violence necessary to reach the group's goals. Becoming a terrorist is for most people a gradual process (Horgan, 2005). It takes time to become a full-fledged member of a terrorist organization, and the process usually involves many steps, activities, and commitments. The change is frequently achieved by a gradual disengagement of self-censure—in other words, one eventually stops chastising oneself for thinking the excessive violence is wrong. The process usually involves small groups engaging in long periods of intense social interactions (Silke, 2008). Within the group, individuals gradually adopt the beliefs of the extreme members in a psychological process called risky shift (Silke, 2008). **Risky shift** refers to the tendency of groups to develop beliefs and make decisions that are more extreme than the initial inclination of its members. It should be emphasized, however, that group discussions do not usually change the members' initial beliefs into the opposite direction, but serves to shift them into a more extreme worldview in line with their initial views. For example, members may find their opinions regarding the injustices done to their in-group more extreme after group discussions.

Once they formally join the terrorist organization, the process is so gradual, the recruits may not even recognize the transformation they are undergoing (Bandura, 2004). The recruits become deeply immersed in the ideology of the organization, and may even be expected to perform unpleasant acts to discover if they can tolerate hardships and cognitive dissonance without much self-censure. The social modeling of the more experienced peers becomes an integral part of the indoctrination process. "The training not only instills the moral rightness and importance of the cause for militant action; it also creates a sense of eliteness and provides social rewards of solidarity and group esteem for excelling in terrorist exploits" (Bandura, 2004, p. 140).

Another common factor in the backgrounds of many jihadi recruits is social marginalization (Silke, 2008), but, as noted above, this is not necessarily the case. A majority of the recruits who joined al-Qaeda groups were socially isolated from friends, family, and cultural origins at the time they volunteered. One of the major attractions of terrorist groups is the psychological benefits of group affiliation (Ditzler, 2004). In fact, the opportunity to become a member of a meaningful, close-knit organization often holds much stronger attraction than the stated political objectives of the organization.

From a developmental perspective, ease of recruitment may depend to some extent on the fact that the youth being recruited are developmentally less competent decision makers than adults due to both cognitive and psychosocial factors (LoCicero & Sinclair, 2008). Peer influence is often cited as the primary reason for joining a terrorist group (Victoroff, 2005). In April 2015, six Minnesota men, all in their late teens and early twenties, were charged in connection with attempts to join ISIS. A friend of theirs had traveled to Syria and joined the terrorist group and was said to have persuaded his six friends to join him. A U.S. attorney in Minnesota was quoted as follows: "The person radicalizing your son, your brother, your friend may not be a stranger. It may be their best friend right here in town" (Grossman, Kesling, & Audi, 2015, p. 1). Increased social standing among family and friends is also listed as a principal reason, although in many cases, including the Minnesota example above, parents and friends cooperate with authorities and try to prevent or discourage the young people from joining the terrorist group. Once young recruits become members of the group, charismatic leaders have a very strong impact on their decision making as well as on the development of their value system.

One psychological element that may be additionally helpful in understanding why someone would become a terrorist is the cognitive construct. Constructs are mental representations of the social environment; they are our mental summaries of what we know and understand about the world, especially the social world. They are—as described above—an adopted worldview. Cognitive constructs allow flexibility of thought and increase our ability to anticipate future events and to alter a course of action based on unanticipated events. Some people possess more cognitive constructs and knowledge about the world than others. That is, some people are more cognitively complex and their decision making considers all gray areas. People who possess many sophisticated constructs are able to evaluate behavior and world events in more complex ways than people with few, crude constructs. In essence, a construct is an element of knowledge, which varies with age. As experiences and learning with the environment accumulate, the number, quality, and organization of these constructs normally change. It is likely that those who engage in terrorism as followers have fewer sophisticated constructs, but this cannot necessarily be assumed of leaders.

As pointed out by Commons and Goodheart (2007), "Individuals who operate at a more complex stage are less likely to respond with violent, non-empathic behavior" (p. 96). Therefore, leaders of terrorist organizations try to recruit young men who are enthusiastic but who operate at a relatively low level of cognitive complexity. This does not mean they look for individuals with low intelligence, only that they are young, naïve, and idealistic.

Terrorist Leaders

Leaders of terrorist organizations often have some level of charisma (Ditzler, 2004; Staub, 2004). Many are seen by their followers as profoundly significant and influential. Consequently, many recruits of terrorist organizations want to attain some degree of the leader's significance for themselves

(Ditzler, 2004), or submit themselves to powerful leaders (Staub, 2004). In terrorist groups, there is often a strong hierarchy, chain of command, and strong expectation of obedience to authority (Staub, 2004). It is instructive for our purposes in this section to examine in more detail al-Qaeda and its former leader Osama bin Laden, who was captured and killed in 2011.

Al-Qaeda's decentralized, multifaceted organization with multiple, different activities reflected a high level of cognitive complexity in its leader in the domain of organizational competence (LoCicero & Sinclair, 2008) and despite his death this may have continued in his successors. The complicated organizational structure of al-Qaeda—at least in the years immediately following the September 11 attacks—strongly suggests that bin Laden's organizational skills were more advanced than most people realize. Bin Laden was able to organize al-Qaeda on the basis of semiautonomous groups that operated somewhat independently (Staub, 2004). For example, the 19 terrorist hijackers who carried out the attacks of 9/11 were in control of what they were doing and had the power over its execution (LoCicero & Sinclair, 2008). This indicates that the al-Qaeda followers were able to work together without an authoritarian leader and were functioning in a fairly advanced manner. Bin Laden began his quest as a young son of a wealthy Saudi magnate, and at some point decided to commit himself to the Afghan resistance (Borum & Gelles, 2005). With his own wealth, bin Laden hired workers and bought equipment, and with his executive skills created and maintained a sophisticated system to reach and sustain Muslims across the globe to unite in a holy war against communist suppression (Borum & Gelles, 2005).

Together with his friend and confidant Ayman al-Zawahiri, bin Laden began to recognize that Islamic discontent, fueled by globalization, Soviet repression of Islam, and anti-Islamic governmental policies, was brewing in various parts of the world (Borum & Gelles, 2005). Perhaps more importantly, they realized that their greatest and most enduring weapon was its anti-American ideology. From this ideological platform, al-Qaeda eventually was able to progress into a web of affiliated networks that coordinate terrorist recruitment, training, and operations.

Prior to bin-Laden's death, Borum and Gelles (2005) observed that "al-Qaeda has evolved from a group, to an organization, to a network, and ultimately—in its current form—to an international jihadist movement that embraces and promotes a virulent and militant anti-Western ideology" (p. 481). Although observers have remarked that al-Qaeda has been decimated since bin Laden's death, this may be an overly optimistic appraisal. However, his demise may affect the inspirational level of al-Qaeda (DeAngelis, 2011). Nevertheless, the organization remains alive and active.

Hellmich (2008) reports some experts believed bin Laden was a mentally disordered man without any systematic or logical ideology. However, mentally disordered people usually make poor leaders, incapable of complex technical operations, and are usually incompetent communicators (Hellmich, 2008). Perhaps a more realistic appraisal is that bin Laden operated more like a venture capitalist than a simple-minded, hate-filled fanatic (Hoffman, 2002; LoCicero & Sinclair, 2008). Bin Laden succeeded in creating a high degree of unity and cohesion with his network and was able to develop smaller, independent, but loyal cells over a number of continents (Busch & Weissman, 2005).

LONE WOLF TERRORISTS

Although we most often associate terrorism with 9/11, most of the terrorist attacks in the United States have actually been carried out not by international terrorist groups but by one, sometimes two or three individuals who are commonly referred to as "lone wolves." (Interestingly, FBI Director James Comey stated in an interview that he preferred the term "lone rat," because the wolf is far too proud and distinguished an animal to associate with such violence (Graff, 2014). Unfortunately for rodents, they are rarely considered distinguished.)

The United States appears to be especially vulnerable to the **lone wolf terrorist**. Available data suggest that, between the years 1968 and 2007, 42 percent of the identified lone wolf attacks in the world occurred in the United States (COT, 2007). Moreover, the explosion in popularity of all forms of social media, the Internet, and 24/7 cable channels have provided new virtual tools for the recruitment and propaganda platform for terrorist groups to reach out, not only to other like-minded extremists, but also to lonely, isolated young youths without a cause (Post et al., 2014). With these new forms of communication, terrorist groups are now turning to the tactic to empower and motivate individuals to commit violent acts on their own, independent of the terrorist chain of command. Although they act alone, "they see themselves as belonging to a virtual community, a virtual community of hatred" (Post et al., 2014, p. 321). In the following sections we discuss three notable examples.

Boston Marathon Bombers

The team of brothers responsible for the Boston Marathon bombing in April 2013, appear to qualify as lone wolves. Twenty-six-year-old Tamerlan Tsarnaev (known as "Tim" by his friends) and his 19-year-old brother Dzhokhar Tsarnaev (known as "Jahar" or "Joe") planted twin pressure cooker bombs filled with nails, BBs, and explosives hidden in backpacks near rows of spectators close to the marathon finish line. The bombs detonated, killing an eight-year-old boy and two young women, and injuring more than 260 people, including 17 who lost limbs. Shortly after the incident they killed a campus police officer who may have recognized them from descriptions provided to law enforcement officers. As recently as spring of 2015, one bombing victim lost her second leg following a long period of attempted rehabilitation. (See **Box 11-1** for additional discussion of the Marathon bombing.)

CONTEMPORARY ISSUES

BOX 11-1   The Marathon Bombing and Beyond

The annual Boston Marathon has for many years been a popular event attracting runners and spectators, many from across the United States and the world. Many of those who converged on this small city on April 15, 2013, experienced horror and sadness that will likely never be forgotten. As noted in the text, two brothers planted bombs near the marathon finish line that resulted in three deaths and injuries to more than 260 others. As the brothers were leaving the area, they carjacked a vehicle and kidnapped its driver, who ultimately escaped. They also shot to death a campus police officer.

Residents of the city and its surrounding suburbs lived in shock and in fear while the brothers—Tamerlan and Dzhokar Tsarnaev—remained at large. Police released photos of the two captured on video cameras. Images of Dzhokar wearing a white baseball cap backward and nonchalantly purchasing milk at a convenience store after the event were widely circulated, as were images of terrified victims and individuals coming to the victims' aid. At one point when the brothers were being pursued, they engaged in a gun battle with police; in the course of that battle, Tamerlan was killed and Dzhokar escaped. The immediate episode had its bizarre ending four days after the marathon when Dzhokar was found wounded, hiding in a boat in a suburban backyard.

He was ultimately charged with 30 federal criminal counts (e.g., engaging in terrorist activities, murder, kidnapping), 17 of which carried the possibility of a death sentence, and he went to trial in April 2015, two years after the crimes that left the city reeling. Defense lawyers tried unsuccessfully in as many as four pretrial hearings to have the trial moved out of Boston, citing the extensive pretrial publicity about the case.

During 16 days of testimony, prosecutors described the defendant as a terrorist who had been radicalized by online extremist Islamist teachings that call for avenging Muslim deaths (Levitz, 2015). Defense lawyers conceded that the defendant was involved, but attempted to show throughout the proceedings and during the penalty phase that his older brother was the leader. They cited his youth and immaturity at the time of the crime. Tamerlan was a devout follower of radical Islam and was said by the defense to have a strong influence on his brother and to be more responsible for the crimes. A jury rejected those arguments and decided unanimously in May 2015, that Dzhokhar Tsarnaev should be sentenced to death.

Throughout his trial, including the penalty phase when the jury was deciding whether to recommend death or life without parole, Tsarnaev sat stonefaced and showed no remorse. Only once did he express emotion, when a relative testifying on his behalf broke down on the witness stand. An expression of remorse would have been a mitigating factor, although it alone might not have affected the ultimate outcome of the case. It is interesting to observe, also, that had Tsarnaev been just two years younger at the time of the crime (i.e., 17 as opposed to 19), he would have been ineligible for the death sentence.

Questions for Discussion

1. In death penalty cases, juries consider both aggravating and mitigating factors in deciding whether to recommend a death sentence, but one group does not have to outweigh the other. In other words, even two mitigating factors can be enough to spare a person the death penalty, even if there are five aggravating factors. What aggravating and mitigating factors can you identify in this case?
2. The jury in this case was "death qualified," which is a requirement in all capital cases. Psychologists have conducted considerable research on this topic. Discuss the meaning and significance of this term.
3. Does research by Steinberg, cited in earlier chapters, have any relevance to this case? What about research on emerging adulthood, cited in **Box 6-1**?

The younger brother admitted to authorities that the Boston Marathon attack was prompted by the killing of Muslims in Iraq and Afghanistan, primarily by the United States (Reitman, 2013). The brothers were born in republics of the former Soviet Union but were brought to the United States by their parents—who later returned to their native countries. Tamerlan was an aspiring boxer who later became a follower of radical Islam. Dzhokar became a naturalized American citizen on September 11, 2012, seven months before the bombing. At the time he launched the bombing attack with his older brother, he was enrolled as a college student.

The Tsarnaev brothers were not believed to be directly connected to any terrorist group—therefore, the lone wolf designation. They became self-radicalized primarily by using Internet sources to acquire terrorist philosophical beliefs and propaganda. The brothers apparently learned to build their bombs by logging onto an online magazine which was connected to al-Qaeda in Yemen (Cooper, Schmidt, & Schmitt, 2013). The magazine's first issue was published in 2010 and contained detailed bomb making instructions. American investigators indicated that "the two brothers could represent the kind of emerging threat that federal authorities have long feared: angry and alienated young men, apparently self-trained and unaffiliated with any particular terrorist group, able to use the Internet to learn their lethal craft" (Cooper et al., 2013, p. A1).

Fort Hood Shooter

Another example of a terrorist acting alone is Major Nidal Hasan, an Army psychiatrist, who in November 2009, walked into the Soldier Readiness Processing Center at Fort Hood, Texas, and began shooting. He killed 13 people and wounded 30 others before being wounded himself. Hasan passed up several opportunities to shoot civilians, and instead continually targeted military personnel. He was eventually seriously wounded by a civilian police sergeant during the attack and paralyzed from the waist down.

According to the *New York Times*, "Some experts on terrorism said Major Hasan may be the latest example of increasingly common type of terrorist, one who has been self-radicalized with the help of the Internet and who wreaks havoc without support from overseas networks and without having to cross a border to reach his target" (Scott & Dao, 2009, p. A1). Were it not for this, Hasan would qualify as one of the mass killers discussed in Chapter 10. Investigators were able to uncover at least 20 emails Hasan sent to radical cleric Anwar al-Awlaki, outlining his intentions to become an Islamic soldier of Allah. Al-Awlaki, an American born in New Mexico, was a highly influential Islamic extremist who supported a violent jihad and preached a hateful ideology directed at inciting violence against the United States. His videos were widely circulated on the Internet. Some experts believe al-Awlaki was especially appealing to young Muslims who are curious about radical ideas but not yet committed (McKinley, 2009). He was considered a senior talent recruiter and motivator for terrorist operations for the Islamic military group al-Qaeda. He praised Hasan after the Fort Hood shooting. Al-Awlaki was killed in 2011 in a U.S. drone strike in Yemen.

Hasan represents the trend of self-radicalization, which is gaining considerable momentum via the Internet and other social media. Hasan was described by people who knew him as socially isolated. He was sentenced to death in August 2013 and is one of about six inmates on military death row in Leavenworth Penitentiary.

The Times Square Bombing Attempt

On May 1, 2010, Faisal Shahzad parked a sports utility vehicle in crowded Times Square in New York City. The SUV was loaded with propane, gasoline, fireworks, fertilizer, an alarm clock, and electrical wiring (Post et al., 2014). Shahzad wanted to kill as many innocent bystanders as possible to revenge the injustices done to Muslims everywhere. If the bomb went off successfully, he planned to detonate other bombs in various locations in the city a week later. "Shahzad believed that carrying out an act of violent jihad was necessary for the greater good of besieged Muslims everywhere, demonstrating a radical altruism" (Post et al., 2013, p. 318).The device failed to detonate as it was poorly made, and the timer (the clock) was carelessly set for 7 pm rather than the intended 7 am when the number of potential victims was at its highest.

Shahzad was a 31-year-old former budget analyst from Connecticut who was born in Pakistan to a wealthy, well-educated family. He became a U.S. citizen in April 2009. He maintained several contacts with Pakastani Taliban and had received bomb-making training from them. He also told interrogators that he was inspired—via the Internet—by extremist al-Awlaki—mentioned above—to embrace the mission of al-Qaeda. Shahzad plead guilty to a 10-count indictment, including attempting an act of terrorism, and received a mandatory life term under federal sentencing guidelines. At the sentencing, Shahzad defiantly said, "If I am given a thousand lives, I will sacrifice them all for the sake of Allah, fighting this cause, defending our lands, making the work of Allah supreme over any religion or system" (Wilson, 2010, p. A 25). At the end of the judge's sentencing, Shahzad replied "Allahu akbar" ("God is great").

The "lone wolf" terrorists—or homegrown violent extremists—are generally psychologically different from conventional terrorists who belong to a more organized extremist group, network, or organization as discussed above. The lone wolf operators do not rely on group or organization affiliations to validate their mission. They basically operate on their own: They design their own plans, select their own targets, choose their own *modus operandi*, and make their own decisions. Based on their unique interpretations of the world, they perceive injustices that they wish to bring to public attention. Alternately, they adopt the ideological or philosophical leanings of an extremist or outside group, even when the group itself does not engage in terrorist activities.

Table 11-1 summarizes the key characteristics of lone wolf terrorists. Lone wolf terrorists present a greater threat in some ways than conventional terrorist organizations. They are more difficult to track and predict, and gathering intelligence on them is a challenge. Explosives tend to be their main weapon of choice, followed by firearms (COT, 2007), and they principally target civilians. The attacks are premeditated, usually carefully planned, and self-financed. Unlike conventional terrorists who are affiliated with organized groups, they usually do not plan to die during their attacks, and they often escape arrest for long periods of time.

Although the examples we have used thus far are recent and are associated with a violent jihadist philosophy, this is not always the case. In fact, the ideological motivation of most lone wolf attackers in the United States have centered on white supremacy, antiabortion, or antigovernmental issues (COT, 2007). For example, a primary example of a lone wolf terrorist is Theodore Kaczynski, the Unabomber who carried out a campaign of 16 mail bombings over a 17-year period that resulted in three deaths and 23 injuries. He apparently wanted to draw attention to a list of societal problems, including technology, the destruction of the environment, and the worldwide industrial system in general. The targets of his mail bombings, therefore, were usually individuals he identified as involved in some aspect of technology, such as in university research facilities. Kaczynski was a highly educated individual who was a loner throughout his life and eventually withdrew from society and lived simply in a wooded cabin. Though he is widely believed to have been seriously mentally disordered, he ferociously resisted an insanity defense. However, he was apparently persuaded to plead guilty to avoid a death sentence, and he entered into a plea agreement whereby he was sentenced to life in prison with no possibility of parole.

TABLE 11-1 Main Characteristics of Lone Wolf Terrorists

1. They operate individually.
2. They do not belong to an organized terrorist group, network, or organization.
3. They act without the direct influence of a leader or hierarchy.
4. They may *claim* to be acting on behalf of an interest group.
5. Their attacks are premeditated and carefully planned.
6. They are more likely than other terrorists to be emotionally disturbed.
7. They demonstrate poor interpersonal and social skills.

Timothy McVeigh, the Oklahoma City bomber, is often used as another classical example of a lone wolf terrorist, despite the fact that he worked closely with Terry Nichols, who was also convicted. McVeigh, a veteran of the Persian Gulf War, associated himself with the militia movement. Although Nichols and a third man provided tactical support for the Oklahoma City bombing, McVeigh did the planning, target selection, and decision making. As noted above, the 1995 bombing of the Alfred P. Murrah Federal Building in Oklahoma City resulted in the deaths of 168 people and was the deadliest attack of terrorism in the United States prior to the September 11, 2001 attacks. McVeigh's motivation was revenge against what he perceived was a tyrannical U.S. government. He was especially critical of federal intervention in events at Waco, Texas, and Ruby Ridge, Idaho, in the early 1990s. McVeigh was executed by lethal injection in 2001. This was the last execution carried out in the federal system, a fact pointed out by many commentators after Dzhokar Tsarnaev was sentenced to death. The Tsarnaev case is likely to involve a lengthy appeals process.

Another often-cited example of a lone wolf terrorist is Eric Rudolph—also known as the Olympic Park bomber—who committed a series of bombings in Georgia and Alabama in his campaign against gay nightclubs and health centers where abortions were performed. He had no known coconspirators, and apparently planned and carried out the bombings on his own. Rudolph likely identified with antiabortion activist groups and with groups opposed to equal rights regardless of sexual orientation, although the majority of these groups would not condone his actions. He maintained a socially isolated existence and was eventually captured in 2003 near a trash container as he was foraging for food.

In sum, a majority of lone wolf terrorists demonstrate poor interpersonal and social skills and adopt an isolationist attitude, staying away from much direct contact with society. Although conventional terrorists who are affiliated with a terrorist organization do not demonstrate behavioral patterns of emotional instability, the rate of psychological problems appears to be significantly higher among lone wolf terrorists (COT, 2007; Hewitt, 2003).

THE PSYCHOSOCIAL CONTEXT OF TERRORISM

The psychosocial context refers to those social and psychological circumstances that encourage certain behaviors to develop and expand. The psychosocial context is a cognitively constructed world that is sustained through the socialization process associated with each culture. Culture in this sense may be as broad as an entire country or as narrow as a small group of individuals. Thus, there is psychosocial context relevant to both the entire society and to the subcultural components of that society.

Ervin Staub (2004) postulates that certain cultural characteristics are conducive to the emergence of terrorist groups. One characteristic is what he calls **cultural devaluation**, a process that occurs when a group or culture is selected by another group or culture as a scapegoat or an ideological enemy. "It might consist of beliefs that the other is lazy, or of limited intelligence, or manipulative, or morally bad, or a dangerous enemy that intends to destroy society or one's own group" (Staub, 2004, p. 158). The United States itself is often seen this way. Many groups and individuals see the United States as being indifferent to the world's suffering and insensitive to global cultural diversity and local identity (Marsella, 2004). Many are convinced that this indifference contributes to the political suppression of the poor and the disadvantaged on a global basis (Marsella, 2004). In addition, some believe American culture is a real and tangible threat to cultural identities, religious affiliation, and ways of life (Marsella, 2004).

It is also worth noting that in the United States, persons associated with racial, ethnic, or religious groups often believe the "dominant" values of American society are inconsistent with the values of their own subgroups. The vast majority of these individuals either accepts this discrepancy or works within the system to change the dominant views. However, some individuals may take a terrorist approach. Thus, although Staub (2004) discusses what are well recognized as *terrorist groups,* the principle of cultural devaluation can also apply to individuals or groups that engage in terrorist-like activities but who are not always considered terrorists. Persons who in the 1980s and 1990s firebombed women's health clinics where abortions were provided are a case in point.

A second characteristic noted by Staub involves perceptions of *inequality, relative deprivation, and injustice.* Disadvantaged, powerless, and shunned peoples are sometimes more likely to join violent or terrorist groups, not only to get some of their basic needs met, but also to gain a sense of identity and community that the terrorist group offers. In other words, and as discussed earlier, terrorist groups provide the opportunity to satisfy the quest for significance. Staub (2001) calls such situations *difficult life conditions* characterized by hunger, sickness, no sense of community, and lack of shelter for oneself and one's family. "People with few material resources, having little to lose, are prime candidates for joining extremist organizations that promise better living conditions as soon as the haves are removed from power" (Wagner & Long, 2004, p. 211). Not only is there promise of better physical living conditions but also promise of feeling a sense of belonging. Taylor and Louis (2004) make a similar point when they argue that, in addition to disadvantaged economic and political factors, the need for psychological identity draws some individuals into terrorist groups. They assert, "What makes terrorist groups particularly attractive is their simplistic worldview that offers recruits a clear collective identity" (p. 184). To this end, terrorist groups also fill a necessary psychological void. Some individuals, however, may also join because they "have moral principles that lead them to identify with those who are affected by difficult conditions or are unjustly treated" (Staub, 2004, p. 159).

A third characteristic is that many—perhaps most—terrorist groups have a strong hierarchy, sometimes with leaders who are described as all-powerful, convincing, and charismatic. Staub calls this psychosocial characteristic a *strong respect for authority.* Some persons who join simply wish to relinquish their unfulfilled selves and submit themselves to powerful leaders and chain-of-command organizations. They feel most comfortable in hierarchical social structures organized for a challenging or exciting mission. Overall, these real or perceived conditions are apt to be productive areas for terrorist recruitment when promises of a better life beckon.

In summary, terrorism is a learned form of political action that is facilitated by the social and cultural context and maintained by intrinsic rewards, group influences, and indoctrination processes (Ruby, 2002).

TERRORIST MOTIVES AND JUSTIFICATIONS

Despite the efforts discussed earlier in the chapter to neatly classify terrorists and terrorist groups according to motives, there is no single motive for engaging in terrorism. The motives are multiple and complex, ranging from revenge and anger, to attaining paradise, status, respect, and life everlasting (Marsella, 2004). "The roots of terrorism are complex and reside in historical, political, economic, social and psychological factors. Of all of these, psychosocial factors have been among the least studied and the least understood, but arguably the most important" (Moghaddam & Marsella, 2004a, p. xi).

Contemporary researchers are attempting to identify individual risk factors for engaging in terrorism, in an effort to alert investigators to possible activities of this nature. Risk assessment of terrorism is a relatively new enterprise for the psychological community, but several studies have been conducted with this goal in mind. Reviewing this research, Monahan (2011) notes that there is little evidence of risk factors at this point beyond the nontrivial factors (e.g., age, gender) mentioned earlier in the chapter. Risk factors for what Monahan calls "common violence" (e.g., a history of violence) do not typically apply to terrorists. Nevertheless, "promising candidates include ideologies, affiliations, grievances, and moral emotions" (p. 29). That is, the extant research suggests that terrorists have strong beliefs in the rightness of their causes and are willing to act on those beliefs; they associate with other terrorists; they have some grievance against a group or a government; and they experience strong moral emotions, such as contempt or disgust. As Monahan emphasizes, it is premature to assume the validity of these risk factors without additional research.

Bandura (2004) skillfully takes the explanation for motives of terrorism into the cognitive realm. He posits that terrorists justify their horrific acts through **cognitive restructuring**, a psychological process that involves moral justifications, euphemistic language, and advantageous comparisons.

Moral justification enables people to engage in reprehensible conduct by telling themselves that their actions are socially worthy and have an ultimate moral and good purpose. Bandura writes,

The conversion of socialized people into dedicated fighters is achieved not by altering their personality structures, aggressive drives, or moral standards. Rather, it is accomplished by cognitively redefining the morality of killing, so that it can be done free from self-censuring restraints. Through moral sanction of violent means, people see themselves as fighting ruthless oppressors who have an unquenchable appetite for conquest or as protecting their cherished values and way of life, preserving world peace, saving humanity from subjugation to an evil ideology, and honoring their country's international commitments. (2004, p. 124)

The second cognitive restructuring process of **euphemistic language** is based on the well-known research finding that language shapes thought patterns on which people base many of their actions. Importantly, people can display more cruelty or at least can feel better about what they are doing when their conduct is given a sanitized or neutral label. Consequently, they use terms such as "collateral damage" to designate civilians who are killed in bombings. Obviously, euphemistic language is employed in many contexts other than terrorist activities (e.g., wars; drone strikes; control of prisoners). Among the colorful metaphors and euphemisms offered by Bandura to emphasize his point are bombing missions referred to as "serving the target," and bombs themselves called "vertically deployed anti-personal devices."

The third cognitive restructuring process is **advantageous comparison**, where terrorists are convinced that their way of life and fundamental cultural values are superior to those they attack. Advantageous comparison is further advanced when the terrorists are told and come to believe that the enemy engages in widespread cruelties and inhumane treatment of the people the terrorists represent. The United States, for example, is seen by many people in Arab countries as blameworthy for their problems because of a variety of U.S. policies and practices (Staub, 2004), thus providing a fertile atmosphere for terrorist recruitment. Advantageous comparison methods draw heavily on history to justify violence. For example, terrorist leaders will indoctrinate their people about the many oppressive policies and tyrannical tactics their targeted organization or country has employed on them in the past. Many people believe, for example, that the United States has historically and consistently supported repressive governments in the Arab world and elsewhere. Terrorist recruiters take these beliefs a step further and turn them into a hatred of the repressors.

Additional Disengagement Practices

Bandura also states that other disengagement practices are also at play in developing motivations, such as dehumanization, displacement of responsibility, and diffusion of responsibility. **Dehumanization** is based on the premise that mistreating or randomly killing *humanized* or known persons significantly increases the risks of self-condemnation. It is easier to mistreat (and kill) strangers who are divested of human qualities. "Once dehumanized, they are no longer viewed as persons with feelings, hopes, and concerns but as subhuman forms" (Bandura, 2004, p. 136).

In **displacement of responsibility**, terrorists may view their actions as stemming from the dictates of authorities and leaders rather than from their own personal responsibility. Consequently, they avoid self-condemning reactions because they are not personally responsible for their conduct; they are only following orders, perhaps even from their god. Some serial killers have used similar justifications for their actions. **Diffusion of responsibility** is similar to the concept of deindividuation, discussed in Chapter 5. Terrorism often requires the services of many people in the organization, all pulling together to achieve some ultimate purpose. Bandura points out that each person in the organization often performs relatively small, fragmentary jobs that, taken individually, seem harmless, and out of the limelight. The collective sense of identity that results allows members of the group to participate in being part of horrific or heinous actions that individually they may resist doing themselves.

PSYCHOLOGICAL EFFECTS AND NATURE OF TERRORISM

After the attacks of September 11, 44 percent of the adults in a national survey said they experienced significant amount of stress, and 90 percent said they had some degree of stress following the attack (Schuster et al., 2001). However, it has also been shown that ethnic background, gender, and age influence the psychological reactions to terrorism (Walker & Chestnut, 2003). Many participants in the Walker–Chestnut survey thought that the United States has been overly involved in the affairs of other countries and that those countries are now retaliating. In addition, participants felt that the United States has developed a false sense of security in believing terrorist groups would not retaliate for the policies the United States has used on other countries and cultural groups. Today, more than 10 years after the September 11 attacks, the country remains divided over the likelihood of another major international attack on U.S. soil, as well as the wisdom of intervening in conflicts in other countries.

Although psychologists or other mental health professionals provide psychological services to those persons adversely affected by terrorism, it is equally important to try to prevent it. One important point that was made in the beginning of this chapter bears repeating: "The overwhelming majority of evidence indicates that responding to violence with violence only provokes further violence" (Wagner & Long, 2004, p. 215). Aggressive military action is rarely the solution, unless it is in response to an imminent, documented threat to a country and its inhabitants. International terrorism is unlikely to be reduced until the root causes of the violence are addressed and corrected: "These causes often include real or imagined injustice in meeting basic human needs for coping with difficult life conditions, insecurity, lack of self-determination, and disrespect for one's social identity" (Wagner & Long, 2004, p. 219).

Cognitive Restructuring

As mentioned in Chapter 1, social psychologists have observed that many people believe the world is a just place, where one gets what one deserves and deserves what one gets (Lerner, 1980). People who have a just-world bias perceive a connection between what people do, are, or believe in, and what happens to them. According to the just-world bias, for the sake of cognitive consistency, many people cannot believe in a world governed by a schedule of random events. The suffering of innocent or respectable people—those who have done nothing to bring about their own grief—would be too unacceptable and unjust (Lerner & Simmons, 1966). Thus, when tragedy strikes, believers in a just-world tend to blame the victims, concluding that these victims must have deserved their fate in some way. Maikovich (2005) links the same process to the thinking patterns of terrorists. She writes, "When terrorists view the current sociopolitical situation through the lens of a just world bias, their attack victims are not unjustly hurt or killed, but rather deserve these fates either because of what they did personally or, more commonly, because of what their government did" (Maikovich, 2005, p. 383). In this sense, killing the identified enemy is seen as right and moral (Staub, 2004).

Terrorist organizations are typically extremely hierarchical, so that those who actually commit the violent acts can nearly always be said to be following orders of some higher authority (Maikovich, 2005). Psychologists have discovered that many people disengage their personal standards from their conduct when they are told to do something reprehensible by a legitimate authority. Terrorist organizations are designed so that their leaders are unquestionably legitimate, commanding of respect, and powerful (Maikovich, 2005). When someone who possesses legitimate power or perceived power commands someone to do something, the person who is commanded is, in a sense, relieved of personal responsibility for the conduct, even if the conduct is alien to his or her personal standards. This concept is called displacement of responsibility by Bandura (2004), strong respect for authority by Staub (2004), or obedience to authority by Milgram (1974).

Moral Development

One of the most difficult aspects to understand about terrorism is the willingness of supposedly capable leaders to sacrifice the lives, not only of their enemies but also of the individuals they recruit. Often, innocent lives of those close to the recruits are lost as well. For example, in a recent illustration of a suicide bombing, a woman walked into a marketplace with a bomb strapped to her person, holding the hand of her six-year-old daughter. Terrorist groups are known to arm children with explosives that are guaranteed to take the life of the child when detonated. How can a leader who is apparently so skillful at running a complex, multinational organization be able to brutally and, with little empathy, kill so many civilians, including children? How could Timothy McVeigh be willing to bomb a building with a child care center on its premises?

For answers to these questions, some psychologists—in addition to the theories discussed earlier in the chapter—look to the study of moral development, a construct closely related to cognitive complexity and a bit different from the cognitive restructuring discussed above. Moral development refers to the gradual development of a person's concepts of right and wrong, conscience, ethical and religious values, social attitudes, and behavior. A person who is highly cognitively complex is usually at a high level of moral development. However, we are beginning to learn that people who show cognitive complexity and skill in one domain—such as leadership—may not show cognitive complexity (or moral development) in another domain. Nevertheless, it is unlikely that cognitively complex individuals who engage in reprehensible violence against innocent victims can do so unless they are able to justify to themselves the morality of their actions—thus, one would argue that they have convinced themselves of the morality of their cause. In developmental psychology, investigations centering on moral development have been primarily focused on moral judgment and reasoning. The Swiss psychologist Jean Piaget (1948) was an early pioneer in studying how people mentally symbolize social rules and how they make judgments based on the social rules. He hypothesized that morality develops in a series of steps and stages. Each moral stage depends on previous stages, along with the intellectual and cognitive abilities and the social experiences of the individual. The developmental psychologist Lawrence Kohlberg (1976) revised the Piagetian formulation substantially and generated a considerable amount of research interest on the topic. Kohlberg believed that the morality process is fundamentally concerned with justice and fairness, and is a process that continues throughout one's lifetime.

Similar to Piaget, Kohlberg postulated that moral development evolves in a sequence of stages (see **Table 11-2**). The sequence is invariant: each individual must develop the features, skills, and judgments of a lower moral stage before attaining a higher one. Kohlberg identifies three primary stages: preconventional morality, conventional morality, and postconventional morality. Within each primary stage, there are two additional stages, which we will refer to as early and late. During the early preconventional stage, one behaves solely on the basis of obtaining rewards and avoiding punishment. The individual has not yet developed any notion of right or wrong and, therefore, is not moral at all. This orientation toward reward and punishment and unquestioning deference to superior powerful others are principally characteristic of children under age seven, and unfortunately some adults.

During the late preconventional stage, the right action consists of that which satisfies one's own needs. This stage reflects a selfish orientation that considers the needs of others only to the extent that favors will be returned: "You scratch my back and I'll scratch yours." According to Kohlberg (1976), human relationships are viewed similarly to those in a marketplace, not of loyalty,

TABLE 11-2 Kohlberg's Stages and Motives for One's Behavior	
Stage	**Focus**
Early preconventional	Avoid punishment
Late preconventional	Fair exchange; get something in return
Early conventional	Approval from others
Late conventional	Duty, obedience to rules
Early postconventional	Rules important, but can be broken if questionable
Late postconventional	Universal principles of justice and ethics apply

gratitude, or justice, but of using others to gain something. The person develops some understanding that in order to obtain rewards, one has to work with others. Note that the emphasis is still on meeting one's own needs.

The early conventional morality stage is referred to as the "good boy" or "good girl" orientation. The individual's behavior is directed toward gaining social approval and acceptance, and there is much conformity to stereotyped images of what the majority regards as good behavior. During this stage, the conscience, or the ability to feel guilt, begins to emerge. At the late conventional stage, the orientation is to do things out of duty and to respect the authority of others. The person becomes especially aware that certain rules and regulations are necessary to ensure the smooth functioning of society or of terrorist organizations. Socially approved behavior is motivated by anticipation of dishonor and blame if one is derelict in performing one's duty. Guilt feelings arise principally out of doing concrete harm to others. It is at this stage—an average level of moral development—that many young recruits of al-Qaeda and other terrorist organizations probably begin their journey.

The final and highest stage of moral development—the postconventional—is probably reached by only a small sector of the world population. It requires the ability to be reasonably abstract and possess good cognitive ability. During the early postconventional stage, correct action is determined by an understanding of the general rights of the individual as compared with the standards that have been critically examined and agreed upon by the whole society. In this stage, one must also consider the rightness or wrongness of behavior on the basis of personal values. The early postconventional person sees flexibility in the laws of any given society.

The late postconventional person demonstrates an orientation "toward the decision of conscience and toward self-chosen ethical principles appealing to logical comprehensiveness, universality, and consistency" (Kohlberg, 1977, p. 63). The moral principles are abstract and ethical, and they reflect universal principles of justice, of the reciprocity and equality of human rights. These principles also require considerable cognitive complexity. The person relies on his or her own personally developed ethical principles and shows respect for the dignity of human beings as individual persons.

People progress through the stages at different rates and at different ages in their lives, and many never reach the postconventional stage. However, there have been a number of critiques of Kohlberg's theory. Many argue that it emphasizes a justice perspective to the exclusion of empathy or other moral values, such as caring and sensitivity to others. In addition, Kohlberg focused on males to the exclusion of females. It is now established that females outperform males on most measures of moral development, especially pertaining to empathy and prosocial behavior (Spinrad, Eisenberg, & Bernt, 2007). Still, Kohlberg's theory provides an interesting framework for understanding the morality of the leadership and followers of terrorist organizations.

Terrorists often experience considerable social and moral support for their actions among their community. They are often regarded by their in-group as heroic freedom fighters and religious martyrs. Terrorist groups generally assert that their cause is righteous, moral, and that their intentions are noble and just (Stevens, 2005). The morality of al-Qaeda and ISIS, for instance, rests on lofty collection of ideologies that rely on justice to the people, freedom from oppression, duty to God, or retribution for crimes against "our" people (Kruglanski & Fishman, 2006). They rely on moral imperatives to justify their cause and overall mission. And they firmly believe in these values and their own morality. Consequently, they view the world through the lens of their religious beliefs—in their own eyes, and the eyes of their supporters, they are likely high in moral development.

Whether we can apply Kohlberg's stages to their morality is another question. Kohlberg developed his stages of moral development within the social context of Western civilization's concept of justice. To what extent this theory applies to Islamic fundamentalism is debatable and well beyond the scope of currently available empirical evidence. Nevertheless, fundamentalist groups exist in a number of contexts, and a small minority engages in terrorist activities. One of the major approaches of fundamentalism is the dogmatic ability to see the world in black-and-white terms. Al-Qaeda groups tend to have a very narrow definition of what constitutes a proper Muslim, and generally reject Shi'as, Sufi Muslims, and Sunnis (Piazza, 2009). Similar points can be made about other terrorist groups or individuals discussed in this chapter. The Armies of God believe they are right on social issues like abortion and gay marriage, and ecoterrorists believe they must protect the environment by violent means, if necessary.

As we have seen, terrorists justify their acts of violence under the premise that they are accomplishing a greater good, like freeing a society from tyrannical rule or American corruption. Even lone wolf terrorists may adopt this perspective. Persons of high moral development have often broken laws on the basis of ethical principles; in its purest form, for example, civil disobedience involves the breaking of a law that one considers unjust. Henry David Thoreau refused to pay poll taxes, and Martin Luther King, Jr. and countless followers defied laws that prescribed separate water fountains and seats on public buses for racial minorities. In another form, civil disobedience involves breaking a law that is not in itself unjust, but the law is broken to bring attention to what the individual considers a greater evil. Thus, a person may trespass or burglarize in order to gain access to a research facility that injects toxins into monkeys. Although we may not agree with their tactics, we often do not question the moral development of many individuals who practice civil disobedience. However, we tend to draw the line at the use of violence or threats of violence to accomplish one's goals. It is extremely difficult, therefore, to conceptualize terrorists as individuals advanced in moral development, although they believe themselves to be.

SUMMARY AND CONCLUSIONS

In the latter part of the twentieth century, the typical textbook in criminology paid scant attention to the topic of terrorism. The events of September 11, 2001, drastically changed that. Although terrorist activities had been occurring, both in the United States and worldwide, long before the attacks on the World Trade Center and the Pentagon, that date marked a radical shift in public attention and fear, law enforcement activity, and psychological interest. By definition, terrorism involves the unlawful use of force or violence, so by definition, terrorist activities are criminal.

Scholarly literature, government documents, public policy writings, and the media have proposed numerous definitions and categories of terrorism. We adopted the definition used in federal documents, seeing terrorism as unlawful force or violence used to intimidate or coerce a government or population in furtherance of political or social objectives. Terrorism may be either domestic or international, depending on the origin, base, and objectives of the terrorist organization. We covered the FBI's classifications of terrorist *groups*—according to their political leanings—and psychology's classifications of terrorist *motivations*. The groups include the right-wing terrorists, the radical environmental, the special interest extremists, and the nuclear/biological/chemical group. Note that these categories best characterize domestic terrorism; while the al-Qaeda terrorists would probably be classified in the right-wing group, they are far different in organization, skills, and motivations from Timothy McVeigh or Theodore Kaczynski. Classifications of psychological motives are better able to capture terrorism in all its facets, despite the fact that we discussed only three *categories*: rationally motivated, psychologically motivated, and culturally motivated terrorists.

We discussed two recent theories—similar in some ways—that are proposed to explain someone's involvement in terrorist activities: quest for significance and terror management. The major difference between the two is the motivational factor. Quest for significance posits that one of the driving forces in human behavior is to become significant in the eyes of friends, family, or society. The driving force behind terror management is the fear of death and the intense desire to achieve immortality.

The chapter also covered the psychosocial context of terrorism, specifically those social and psychological characteristics of a society or a group that are conducive to the emergence of terrorist groups. When a society or a group devalues another, the devalued other can be seen as a scapegoat or an ideological enemy and thus can become the target of terrorist attacks. Abortion providers became the targets of terrorist attacks because their activities were seen as morally bad. Symbols of power in the United States—the World Trade Center and the Pentagon—were attacked by al-Qaeda because the United States was seen as a dangerous enemy. Perceptions of inequity, relative deprivation, or injustice are also conducive to the emergence of terrorist groups. While most individuals and groups with these perceptions do not terrorize others, those who do terrorize often harbor those perceptions. Finally, the hierarchical command structure evident in many terrorist groups suggests that strong belief in authority and respect of a charismatic leader may facilitate terrorist activity, when the group is already predisposed to that type of action.

A type of terrorist who has received considerable attention in the literature is the lone wolf. This is the person who is self-radicalized and generally acts without support or direct order from more organized terrorist groups. The lone wolf is often sympathetic to the goals of terrorist organizations, however, and may obtain information and guidance from their publications, including increasingly more online sites. The actions of the terrorist who acts alone are premeditated and carefully planned, and these plans are rarely detected before the fact. Unlike the school shooters discussed in Chapter 9, lone wolves do not usually signal to others their intentions to carry out their violent actions. Lone wolves are more likely than other terrorists to be mentally disordered, although many are not. They are generally disaffected, alienated individuals who believe in the rightness of their beliefs and rarely express remorse for their crimes.

While there is no single motive for terrorism, most terrorist acts, because of their horrifying nature, involve some cognitive restructuring. As Bandura has observed, individuals who engage in terrorism justify their actions in a variety of ways. These include using techniques of moral justification, whereby they convince themselves that their actions are socially worthy and have an ultimate moral purpose—the ends justify the means. Terrorists also use euphemistic language and advantageous comparison to restructure their cognitions; thus, their own actions are seen as harmless compared with the actions of the targets of their activities. Finally, terrorists may dehumanize their targets and lose their own identities—and their individual responsibility—by deindividuating. It is the collective not the individual identity that is responsible. The disengagement tactics outlined by Bandura can also apply to criminal behavior in a variety of contexts, not just the violence exhibited by terrorist groups.

Key Concepts

Advantageous comparison	Lone wolf terrorist
Bioterrorism	Moral justification
Cognitive restructuring	Nuclear/biological/chemical (NBC) terrorism
Cultural devaluation	Psychologically motivated terrorists
Culturally motivated terrorists	Quest for Significance Theory
Dehumanization	Radical environmental groups
Diffusion of responsibility	Rationally motivated terrorists
Displacement of responsibility	Right-wing terrorists
Euphemistic language	Risky shift
Learned helplessness (or reactive depression)	Special interest extremists
Left-wing extremist groups	Terror Management Theory

Review Questions

1. How are terrorist groups classified?
2. Summarize the terrorist typology present in the chapter.
3. Compare and contrast Quest for Significance and Terror Management Theory.
4. What are the main characteristics of the lone wolf terrorist?

5. Define the following concepts and explain the role they may play in an individual becoming a terrorist: (a) moral justification; (b) cognitive restricting; (c) advantageous comparison; (d) dehumanization; (e) deindividuation.

12

Sexual Assault

CHAPTER OBJECTIVES

▪ Define rape and other sexual assaults.

▪ Review sexual assault of dates and acquaintances, including campus assault.

▪ Discuss the psychological impact of sexual assault on survivors.

▪ Examine risk factors for sexual assault victimization.

▪ Describe risk factors that influence the development of sexually assaultive behavior.

▪ Discuss research relating to recidivism of sex offenders.

▪ Review attitudes and myths that support rape and other sexual assaults.

▪ Describe the Massachusetts Treatment Center's Classification Systems of rapists.

▪ Describe the Groth typology of rape.

▪ Introduce the Knight and Sims-Knight Three Path Model of sexual offending.

▪ Review principles of effective treatment for adult sex offenders.

Sexual behavior in many societies is a subject fraught with moral codes, taboos, norm expectations, religious injunctions, myths, and unscientific conclusions. In the mid-twentieth century, research published by Albert Kinsey and his colleagues (1948, 1953) helped dispel myths and correct fallacies about sexual behavior in both men and women based on survey reports and interviews. Shortly thereafter, beginning about 1957, William Masters and Virginia Johnson conducted laboratory experiments during which they observed and recorded psychological and physiological sexual behavior in opposite sex couples. Despite these and other efforts to demystify sexual activity, myths and misconceptions still linger, including those about sex offenders, who are frequently and incorrectly viewed as a homogenous class of individuals.

There is no single profile that encompasses even a majority of sex offenders. Research shows that they differ in personal attributes such as age, background, personality, race, religion, beliefs, attitudes, and interpersonal skills (Knight, Rosenberg, & Schneider, 1985; Parent, Guay, & Knight, 2011). The features of their crimes also differ markedly among offenders, including time and place, the gender and age of the victim, the degree of planning the offense, and the amount of violence used or intended (Knight et al., 1985). Nevertheless, there are continuing efforts to find a unifying theory of coercive sexual offending (Knight & Sims-Knight, 2011). In addition, sex offenders often commit a variety of crime beyond sexual offenses, although this is more likely to be the case with rapists than with child molesters (Harris, Mazerolle, & Knight, 2009). Research also indicates that sexual reoffending by sex offenders is not as prevalent as previously assumed. In fact, there is considerable evidence to show that adult sexual offenders are more likely to be convicted for nonsexual offenses than they are for sexual offenses, both before and after a conviction for a sexual offense (Smallbone & Wortley, 2004). Furthermore, whereas sex offending has traditionally been viewed as a male undertaking, it is clear that female sex offending, though less prevalent, is not unusual. Finally, increasing attention has been given to juvenile sex offending. Although this chapter focuses primarily on sex offending by males, female and juvenile sex offending will be covered in the following chapter.

DEFINITIONS AND STATISTICS

In recent years, the term "sexual assault" has often been preferred to the term "rape" in both research and law. **Sexual assault** is more inclusive, encompassing a variety of behaviors that may or may not include penetration. By the beginning of the twenty-first century, about half of the 50 states did not use the word "rape" in their penal code involving sexual assault or sex offenses (Langan, Schmitt, & Durose, 2003), and many contemporary researchers prefer to refer to sexual assault.

As mentioned in Chapter 1, the FBI continues to collect statistics on rape and considers it a major offense. As of December 2013, though, its definition has changed. **Rape** is now defined as the "Penetration, no matter how slight, of the vagina or anus with any body part or object, or oral penetration by a sex organ of another person, without the consent of the victim" (Federal Bureau of Investigation, 2014b, p. 1). A significant change regards the sex of the victim, an acknowledgement that both females and males can be raped. In addition, it is clear from the new definition that the penetration of children as well as adults qualifies as rape. In summary, then, the old definition (which the UCR refers to as the legacy definition) described rape as carnal knowledge of a female forcibly and against her will. The revised definition expands rape to include both male and female victims and offenders, and reflects the various forms of sexual penetration, including nonconsenting acts of sodomy and sexual assaults with objects.

The revised definition further includes instances in which the victim is incapable of giving consent because of temporary or permanent mental or physical incapacity, including due to the influence of drugs or alcohol. Thus, force is presumed, even if the individual does not resist. In essence, the revised definition provides a more accurate portrayal of the scope and volume of rape in the United States. It is important to emphasize that attempted rape is included in the government's rape data.

Sexual assaults that do not qualify as rape are listed as Part II offenses, for which only arrest information is gathered. These other sexual offenses may range from fondling a woman's breast or grabbing a man's genitals, to lewd and lascivious behavior, such as exposing one's sexual organs to passersby. Statutory rape, defined below, is also counted as a Part II offense, under the category sexual assaults.

As also noted in Chapter 1, the UCR program collects offense data through two systems: the Summary Reporting System (SRS) and National Incident-Based Reporting System (NIBRS). The definition change will only affect the SRS because the NIBRS already captures broader sex offense information, including the sex of the person assaulted. Definitions in the NIBRS currently include rape, sexual assault with an object, sodomy, incest, and statutory rape. The NIBRS rape definition refers to the carnal knowledge of a person, without the consent of the victim, including instances where the victim is incapable of giving consent because of his or her age or because of temporary or permanent mental or physical incapacity.

In the NIBRS, sexual assault with an object denotes the use of an object or instrument to unlawfully penetrate, however slightly, the genital or anal opening of the body of another person, without the consent of the victim, including instances where the victim is incapable of giving consent because of age or temporary or permanent mental or physical incapacity. **Sodomy** is defined as oral or anal sexual intercourse with another person, without the consent of victim, including instances where the victim is incapable of giving consent because of age or because of temporary or permanent mental or physical incapacity. **Incest** refers to nonforcible sexual intercourse between persons who are related to each other within the degrees wherein marriage is prohibited by law.

The National Crime Victimization Survey (NCVS) provides an invaluable source of information on sexual victimizations across the United States, and will be referred to frequently throughout the chapter. The NCVS defines rape as the unlawful penetration of a person against the will of the victim, and includes penetration from any foreign object. Sexual assault is defined

TABLE 12-1	Key Components of Definitions of Sex Crimes from SRS, NIBRS, and NCVS	
Source	**Crime**	**Key Components**
SRS of UCR	Rape (new definition)	Penetration without consent by sex organ of another or by an object.
	Rape (legacy definition)	Carnal knowledge of a female against her will.
	Sexual assault	Variety of offenses of a sexual nature; includes statutory rape.
NIBRS	Rape	Carnal knowledge of a person without consent.
	Sexual assault with an object	Unlawful penetration of vaginal or anal opening.
	Sodomy	Oral or anal intercourse without consent.
	Incest	Nonforcible sexual intercourse between persons related to a degree that marriage would prohibit.
	Statutory rape	Consensual intercourse when one party is not of legal age as defined by statute.
NCVS	Rape	Unlawful penetration of a person against his or her will. Includes penetration from an object.
	Sexual assault	Attack involving unwanted sexual contact; may include fondling or grabbing.

as an attack or attempted attack generally involving unwanted sexual contact between the victim and the offender. Sexual assault may or may not involve force and includes grabbing or fondling. It may also include verbal threats. (See **Table 12-1** for key points of definitions from the UCR's SRS, NIBRS, and NCVS.)

Much of our information about sexual assault comes from a large body of research conducted by behavioral and social scientists as well as medical practitioners and published in professional literature. As mentioned above, the trend is to move away from using the term "rape," in favor of the broader "sexual assault." When these researchers study sexual assault, they generally focus on its more extreme forms, particularly rape, attempted rape, and unsolicited sexual contact like forcible touching or fondling. Throughout the chapter, we will use the term "sexual assault", but we will also use the term "rape" if it refers to the government's statistics or if the research we are discussing uses that term.

It is worthwhile to mention a few other terms that appear in the literature on sexual assault, specifically statutory rape, rape by fraud, and marital rape.

Statutory rape is *nonforcible sexual intercourse* with a person who is under the statutory age of consent. In the UCR's SRS, statutory rapes are considered Part II crimes, not rapes, and like other Part II crimes only arrest data are collected. Put another way, a statutory rape will not appear in the summary statistics unless someone has been arrested for that crime. Statutory rape pertains exclusively to consensual intercourse, as opposed to other types of sexual contact (Langan et al., 2003). The critical factor is the age of the victim, an arbitrary legal cutoff point below which a person is believed not to have the maturity to consent to intercourse or understand the consequences.

All states prohibit sex with a minor, but the age of consent varies by state (Troup-Leasure & Snyder, 2005). Most set the limit at 16 or 18. Also, it is generally understood in many states that an age span must exist between the two individuals, typically two to four years. Thus, if an adult male engages in sexual relations with a minor female, he may be convicted of statutory rape, even if he argues that she "consented." Depending on the state, though, an 18-year-old male engaging in sexual relations with a 16-year-old female would not have the same problem.

In addition, some states do criminalize sexual intercourse among peers (Pearlstein, 2010). For example, in New York the age of consent is 17. If a 16-year-old has sex with another 16-year-old, it is illegal—a fact that would surely surprise many adolescents. In California, the age of consent is 18. In March 2015, 12 teenage boys at one high school in that state were arrested for sexual assaults of two girls on school property. The incidents allegedly involved both forced and consensual sex, but all were criminal offenses. In other states, sex between consenting peers below the consenting age is not illegal, but someone above the age of consent may not engage in sexual intercourse with someone below the age of consent.

Critics of statutory rape laws suggest that they are outmoded and unenforceable. Indeed, most adolescent sexual activity that is criminalized by statutory rape laws is never brought to the attention of law enforcement, and that which is rarely results in an arrest (Chaffin, Chenoweth, & Letourneau, in press). National surveys of youth estimate that one-third of 9th graders and two-thirds of 12th graders have had sexual intercourse (Centers for Disease Control and Prevention, 2012). These prevalence rates have been stable for decades, and signify that many statutory rape laws are often not enforced (Chaffin et al., in press).

However, supporters of keeping statutory rape on the books point to law enforcement data indicating that at least half of the male offenders of female victims are six or more years older than their victims (Troup-Leasure & Synder, 2005). The same data also show that more than 75 percent of female offenders with male victims are at least six years older than their victim. Those who advocate the retention of statutory rape laws believe that if states actively enforced them, predatory adults would be inclined not to prey on adolescents, and teenage pregnancy would begin to drop (Pearlstein, 2010). The potential punishments faced by those who commit statutory rape can be severe: "They include prison time and, in many states, lifetime sex offender registration" (Koon-Magnin & Ruback, 2013, p. 1919).

Rape by fraud is having sexual relations with a consenting adult female under fraudulent conditions. Among the most frequently cited examples is that of the psychotherapist who has sexual intercourse with a patient under the guise of offering treatment. Another rape category is **marital rape**, which, as discussed in Chapter 9, is not ignored by criminologists who study IPV. Rape by fraud and marital rape are both counted as rape in the SRS of the UCR. During the past four decades, there have been dramatic changes in marital rape laws in the United States. In 1970, marital rape was essentially legal in all 50 states, but by 1993, all 50 states had passed laws criminalizing it (Martin, Taft, & Resick, 2007). It is estimated that about 10 to 14 percent of married women have experienced marital rape (Martin et al., 2007), but like all sexual assault statistics it is likely that much of it goes unreported. Moreover, as we noted in Chapter 9, sexual assault within an intimate partner relationship transcends the boundaries of marriage, and from a psychological perspective it might not be meaningful to maintain a distinction between women who are assaulted by a partner to whom they are legally married and those who are assaulted by an intimate partner to whom they are not, whether or not they are residing in the same domicile.

Sexual Assault in Date and Acquaintance Relationships

Date and acquaintance rapes are far more common than generally realized, representing as high as 80 percent of all rapes (Planty, Langton, Krebs, Berzofsky, & Smiley-McDonald, 2013). Put another way, it is estimated that strangers commit only about one-fifth of the reported sexual violence in the United States. Both in the literature and in research, the terms "date" and "acquaintance" rapes are often used interchangeably. Technically, though, **date rape** refers specifically to a sexual assault that occurs within the context of a dating relationship. **Acquaintance rape** refers to sexual assaults in which the victim knows the assailant. The perpetrator could be a relative, neighbor, friend, or classmate. About one-third of these assaults are committed by an intimate partner (former or current spouse, girlfriend or boyfriend) (Planty et al., 2013).

Most of the recent research on date and acquaintance rape and sexual assault has concentrated on college women (see **Box 12-1**). Female college students are the most extensively studied populations pertaining to sexual violence (Post et al., 2011), even though they may not be the most representative group of victims.

CONTEMPORARY ISSUES

BOX 12-1 Campus Sexual Assault

Students on virtually every college campus know that sexual assaults happen, and that they are underreported to college officials as well as to police. Sexual assault on college campus is not a new phenomenon. What is new is increased public attention to the issue, prompted by high-profile incidents such as those exposed in a 2015 documentary; empirical research on the topic (e.g., the surveys discussed in this chapter); and national legislation proposed to address it.

The documentary referenced above was *The Hunting Ground*, which premiered at Sundance festival in January 2015 and began appearing in theatres shortly thereafter. A main theme of the documentary is that many campuses do not sufficiently confront the problem of sexual assault. Furthermore, campus sexual assaults are not merely drunken hookups, as commonly assumed. Rather, according to the documentary, predators target victims and carefully plan their attacks. Although the great majority of college males are not predators, those who are predators assault an average of six victims.

Campus crime, including violence, has been addressed in national legislation such as the Clery Act, which requires colleges and universities receiving federal money to submit annual reports on crimes occurring on their campuses. As noted in the text, however, fewer than half of all colleges reported incidents of sexual violence in recent years. The Violence Against Women Act (VAWA; 1994) and its revisions (2002 and 2013) specifically focused on addressing campus safety regarding sexual assault, domestic violence, dating violence, and stalking.

In 2015, U.S. Senators Kirsten Gillibrand (D-NY) and Claire McCaskill (D-MO) cosponsored a revised version of the Campus Accountability and Safety Act (CASA), along with a bipartisan group of additional senators. The proposed law would, among other things: (a) establish resources and support services for survivors of sexual assault; (b) insure due process protections for both survivors and persons accused; (c) initiate a nationwide anonymous survey to gauge the prevalence of sexual assault on campuses; (d) assure that staff meet minimum training standards to address sexual assault complaints; and (e) establish uniform disciplinary process to coordinate responses with local law enforcement.

In addition to the above, some states have taken other measures to improve campus safety on their own campuses. These measures were meant to assure that student disclosures would be treated seriously, and that survivors would be assured confidentiality and respect in discussing details with as few individuals as possible. Some states and some campuses adopted a controversial provision that sexual encounters require affirmative consent of both parties; clear, unambiguous, informed, knowing, and voluntary agreement of all parties is needed to engage in sexual activity. A person's silence or lack of resistance cannot be interpreted as consent, and a person in an intoxicated state cannot provide consent.

Aspects of these affirmative consent policies have been subjected to extensive criticism and ridicule by some students, parents, academicians, and legal scholars, among others. Students asked, "Do I have to ask if every move I make is ok?" The policies were also regarded as unenforceable. Supporters, however, hailed them as a positive step to bring attention to campus sexual assault as well as a possible deterrent to some unwanted—and therefore criminal—sexual activity.

Questions for Discussion

1. Obtain more information about the CASA and discuss its strengths and weaknesses. Would you vote for this act?
2. To what extent is requiring affirmative consent a solution to the problem of campus sexual assault? What are the benefits and drawbacks to such a policy?
3. From a psychological perspective, what personality features are likely to characterize the perpetrator of campus sexual assault? Is it warranted to search for such a personality profile?

During the period 1995 to 2013, females ages 18 to 24 in general had the highest incidence of rape and sexual assault compared to females of any other age group (Sinozich & Langton, 2014). Many of the victims were students enrolled in a college, university, trade school, or vocational school. In 2013, college females were raped or sexually assaulted at a victimization rate of 4.3 per 1,000 compared to the victimization rate of 1.4 victimizations for noncollege females. These victimization rates for students have remained relatively consistent over the eight-year period (1995 to 2013) (Sinozich & Langton, 2014). These researchers also report that the offender was known to the student victim in approximately 80 percent of the incidents, and the offenders were more likely to be friends or acquaintances (50%) than partners in a dating relationship, including intimate partners (24%). Findings such as this suggest that the distinction made between date and acquaintance rape has merit.

In another survey, over one-fourth of college women said they had experienced unwanted sexual contact ranging from kissing and petting to oral, anal, or vaginal intercourse since enrolling in college (Gross, Winslett, Roberta, & Gohm, 2006). This survey found that 41 percent of the offenders were boyfriends, followed by friends (29%), and acquaintances (21%). Date and acquaintance rapists tend to have higher recidivism rates than stranger rapists (Lehmann, Goodwill, Hanson, & Dahle, in press).

According to survey data (NCVS), about 8 out of 10 rape and other sexual victimizations of female students go unreported to the police. The reasons for not reporting the assault are variable, but the most common are the survivor's belief that the assault was a personal matter or they feared reprisal. Self-blame is another common reaction. Furthermore, even when students report their victimization to campus officials such as campus police or counselors, they are not reported outside the campus community. "The actual rate of sexual assault is likely at least an estimated 44% higher than the numbers that universities submit in compliance with the Clery Act" (Yung, 2015, p. 7). As noted in **Box 12-1**, the Clery Act requires higher education institutions to submit yearly data on designated campus crimes to the Department of Education. The Act is named for Jeanne Clery, a 19-year-old college student who was raped and murdered in her college residential hall room in 1986. One reason for the underreporting stems from the belief that "if a school stands out as having a high rate of sexual assault versus peer schools, it risks attracting fewer students and suffering long-term reputational damage" (Yung, 2015, p. 6). The underreporting problem is part of what the proposed CASA (also discussed in **Box 12-1**) is intended to address.

The public attention to campus sexual assault is important, but attention should not be taken away from sexual assaults of people who are not in college settings. Dating patterns have changed dramatically with each generation. Many couples today meet on the Internet, and both women and men initiate a first "date." Whereas males might feel less entitled to "payback" than before—when they paid expenses and provided transportation—other factors (e.g., alcohol, other drugs, sexual mores) can facilitate a sexual assault. These crimes also occur in the context of a casual encounter at a party or a bar. People who are assaulted by acquaintances still often blame themselves for the attack or are blamed by others for placing themselves in vulnerable situations. Thus, the victim is less likely to be believed and more likely to be blamed (Ullman, 1999). As Ullman (2007, p. 412) observes, "These negative reactions are harmful to women's psychological functioning and may lead to or reinforce their own self-blame for being raped."

Incidence and Prevalence of Rape

In many parts of the globe, violence—including violence against women—is underplayed and underreported. Saudi Arabia, Syria, Afghanistan, Somalia, Chile, and India are only some countries where sexual abuse of women and girls may be rampant (UNFPA, 2009). In the United States, an estimated 79,770 rapes (legacy definition) were reported to law enforcement agencies nationwide in 2013 (Federal Bureau of Investigation, 2014a). This figure represents a rate of approximately 25.2 per 100,000 *female* inhabitants. These figures do not represent the new definition of rape, which includes males as victims, because only one year of rape data had been collected under the revised definition. Although these data only include female victims, it has been estimated in previous studies that in about 9 percent of rapes and other sexual assaults, males are the victims (Planty et al., 2013; Sampson, 2011; Turchik & Edwards, 2011).

It is obvious that official data underestimate the extent of the problem, regardless of the sex of the survivor. In addition to the campus sexual assaults discussed above, we have seen numerous examples of unreported assaults in recent years, including in the military (Carbon, 2010; U.S. Department of Defense, 2009, 2015); within organizations such as churches and scouting (Terry, 2008); and in prisons and juvenile facilities. In all of these contexts, sexual assaults rarely come to public attention.

Research data also indicate that 18 percent of women in the United States have been raped at some point in their lifetimes (Kilpatrick, Resnick, Ruggerio, Conoscenti, & McCauley, 2007; Post, Biroscak, & Barboza, 2011). In the United States, children and college students, persons with disabilities, and incarcerated individuals are the most vulnerable to be raped or otherwise sexually assaulted (Carbon, 2010).

In summary, the actual rate of sexual assault is greatly underestimated, partly because of some of the definitional problems listed in the previous sections, and partly because of the ordeal survivors must go through just to report the incident. Victimization studies offer a revealing contrast to the police data. A study based on data collected in the National Violence Against Women Survey (NVAWS) estimates that the number of attempted or completed rapes is four times greater than even the NCVS estimates (Tjaden & Thoennes, 2006).

For the greater part of this chapter we focus on the offenders: their characteristics, possible motivations, and risk factors associated with their behavior. Prior to this focus on the offender, it is important to consider the survivors of sexual assault, particularly the psychological effects they may experience as a result.

IMPACT OF SEXUAL ASSAULT ON SURVIVORS

As noted above, rape and other sexual assaults are most likely to be perpetrated against women and girls; male victims are fewer in number, but the psychological and physical injury they experience cannot be overlooked. Most of the research thus far has focused on female victims, however. Regardless of the gender of the victim, and regardless of the offender's characteristics, motivations, and method of attack or coercion, the social and psychological costs to victims and their families are immeasurable and often devastating.

Having said this, it is important to note that many persons who have been sexually assaulted, particularly as adults, prefer to refer to themselves as survivors rather than victims. Asserting that one is a survivor emphasizes one's strengths and resilience and deemphasizes one's victimhood status. Nevertheless, it is also important to recognize that negative psychological effects from a sexual assault are not uncommon and in some cases can be debilitating.

An early but often-cited survey of 3,132 households in the Los Angeles Epidemiologic Catchment Area (ECA) illustrates this very well. Researchers found that over 13 percent of the individuals interviewed had been victims of sexual assault at least once in their lifetimes (Burnam et al., 1988; Siegel, Sorenson, Golding, Burnam, & Stein, 1987; Sorenson, Stein, Siegel, Golding, & Burnam, 1987). Two-thirds of the sexually assaulted subjects reported two or more assaults. Moreover, lifetime sexual assault was more frequently reported by women (16.7%) than men (9.4%). In a sobering finding, 13 percent of the victims were first assaulted between the ages of 6 and 10, 19 percent between 11 and 15, 34 percent between 16 and 20, and 15 percent between 21 and 25. The experience of being sexually assaulted was associated with substantially higher risks for later onset of serious, self-destructive depression, substance abuse, numerous fears and inhibiting anxieties, and a variety of major interpersonal problems. Overall, the ECA project found that both male and female victims of sexual assault are two to four times more likely than nonvictims to develop serious psychological problems.

Psychological Effects

It is often said that victims of sexual assault are victimized twice, once by the perpetrator and again by the criminal justice system during the investigation of the crime and, if a suspect is arrested, during the prosecution phase. They also may be subjected to scrutiny by the media and by a public that may question whether the incident happened, or denigrate the victims and attribute some blame to them. It is significant that, in incidents of campus sexual assault, the person assaulted is more likely than the perpetrator to withdraw from the college or university.

Self-blame is not an uncommon reaction, and it is a major contributing factor to the psychological damage done by the victimization. Survivors of rape and sexual assault often blame themselves as being responsible for the assault, and "negative reactions from others could strengthen that self-blame" (Sigurvinsdottir & Ullman, 2015, p. 192). Self-blame also plays a major role in the poor adjustment and psychological distress of many sexual assault survivors, and may be a significant factor in exaggerating symptoms of PTSD if it does occur. Recall that PTSD was covered in Chapter 8.

Upon reporting the assault, if it is reported, victims are expected to recall and describe personally stressful and humiliating events in vivid detail for law enforcement personnel. Today, increasingly more police departments take steps to ease the victim's ordeal. These include having victim advocates present, having women officers available for female rape victims, and/or providing rape sensitivity training for both male and female officers. In addition to the interview with representatives of law enforcement, the victim is required to undergo a medical examination to establish physical evidence of penetration, if it was a rape, and use of physical force. It is no wonder that many people who have been assaulted prefer the term "survivor" to "victim" because of its more positive connotation. To be a survivor suggests that one is in control and that the assaulter, the criminal justice system, and the public have not succeeded at totally demolishing one's self-concept.

If the person is able to withstand these stressful conditions, which are sometimes exacerbated by negative reactions from parents, spouses, partners, family members, friends, and even by threats from the assailant, she or he must prepare for the courtroom, where privacy is invaded and credibility may be attacked. Sexual assault trials are usually covered extensively by the press, although many news organizations do not reveal the victims' names. Traditionally, in criminal cases, victim credibility was so much at issue that defense lawyers concentrated on the prior sexual history of a victim. In one highly cited early study, 92 percent of the prosecutors asserted that victim credibility was one of the most important elements in convincing juries to convict for rape (Chappell, 1977). The strategy of disparaging the victim came under attack in the 1970s and 1980s, and many states revised their evidentiary rules in an attempt to limit the use of a victim's sexual history. By the turn of the twenty-first century, virtually all states had enacted "rape shield" laws that restricted, to varying degrees, the admissibility of the victim's sexual history into the courtroom (Kilpatrick, Whalley, & Edmunds, 2000). However, rape shield laws do not always provide the protection for which they were designed (Ross & Bachar, 2002); they vary from state to state (Kinports, 2002). Consequently, many victims are surprised and dismayed when they are asked questions about their social and sexual histories during adjudication, something they believed would not happen (Ross & Bachar, 2002). Fortunately, VAWA, first passed in 1994, revised in 2000 as VAWA-2, and re-authorized in 2013, addressed many of these problems by encouraging more uniformity in rape shield laws and protecting victims of violence nationwide. The 2013 law also includes a number of provisions specifically intended to improve campus safety.

In sum, those who survive sexual assaults may suffer psychological consequences, probably most of which are never addressed in treatment settings. That is, survivors often do not seek psychological help or feel the need to do so, but research documents that the psychological effects of sexual assault are very real. In fact, the psychological damage is usually longer lasting and more damaging than physical injury, resulting in serious depression, extensive fears, and problems of sexual adjustment. In cases where survivors have been severely physically injured, they experience both forms of agony. Women who have been sexually assaulted represent the largest proportion of PTSD sufferers in the United States (Leiner, Kearn, Jackson, Astin, & Rothbaum, 2012). In addition, rape victims are four times more likely than nonvictims to contemplate suicide, and 13 percent of them actually attempt suicide (Carbon, 2011).

Physical Injury

According to the NCVS, on average about 60 percent of the female survivors of sexual assault suffered a physical injury during the incident, such as cuts, bruises, internal injuries, broken bones, and gunshot wounds (Planty et al., 2013). About one-third said they received some form of treatment for their injuries, most of them (80%) in a hospital, doctor's office, or emergency room. The survey also revealed that about 1 in 10 rape or sexual assault victimizations involved a weapon, usually a firearm or a knife.

In the past, women were advised not to resist a rape attempt in order to minimize the risk of other physical harm, possibly even death. With growing evidence that passive resistance was not necessarily related to the amount of harm experienced, advice has changed (Ullman, 2007). Current research supports the use of self-protective measures taken by the victim, including physical resistance, such as yelling, biting, and attacking the attacker if possible. Resistance reduces the risk that the assault will be completed, and does not affect the risk of additional injury (Tark & Kleck, 2014). On the other hand, such strategies as pleading, crying, or trying to reason with the offender have been shown to be largely ineffective in avoiding a completed rape or physical injury (Rosenbaum, Lurigio, & Davis, 1998; Ullman, 2007). However, it should be emphasized that physical resistance is not *required* to demonstrate lack of consent (U.S. Department of Justice, 2012). Resistance may not be possible, and the survivor of a sexual assault should not be judged on the extent to which she attempted to resist the attack.

SEXUAL ASSAULT VULNERABILITY FACTORS

Investigations examining the causes of sexual assault and general violence against women have focused on one of two issues: the behavior, cognitions, and the tactics of offenders, and the risk factors faced by the victims (Siegel & Williams, 2001). It should be emphasized at the onset that the responsibility for the violence clearly rests with the offenders. But it is also important to examine the vulnerability factors that put victims at risk so that prevention and intervention strategies can be implemented. "Vulnerability factors are those that increase women's risk of experiencing sexual assault" (Ullman & Najdowski, 2011, p. 152).

Situational Factors

"Certain places and situations may put women at a greater risk of rape and affect their ability to effectively resist an attacker" (Ullman, 2007, p. 416), and these may differ according to whether the perpetrator is a stranger or an acquaintance. Sexual assaults by acquaintances most often occur indoors or in isolated locations. With respect to strangers, bars are especially risky settings for women if drinking alone. On college campuses, fraternity parties and parties associated with major athletic events often put women at risk. In addition, use of alcohol or drugs by one or both parties, women initiating a date, or men paying expenses associated with a date all are contributing factors in developing a risky situation.

Location

Data from the NCVS indicate that most rape or sexual assault victimizations (55%) occurred at or near the victim's home (Planty et al., 2013). Some (12%) occurred at or near the home of a friend, relative, or acquaintance. Approximately 12 percent occurred while the victim was working, and 7 percent occurred while the victim was attending school. The remainder of the sexual violence occurred while the victim went to work or school, was shopping, or was involved in leisure activities away from home.

Age of Victims

As noted previously, for the period 1995 to 2013, females ages 18 to 24 experienced the highest rate of rape and sexual assault victimizations compared to females in all other age groups (Sinozich & Langton, 2014). However, a significant portion of both females and males are sexually assaulted before the age of 18 (Finkelhor, Shattuck, Turner, & Hamby, 2014). Basile and Smith (2011) report that 71 percent of female victims were first raped before the age of 18 years. Over half of the victims were raped or sexually assaulted by acquaintance peers (Finkelhor et al., 2014). Tjaden and Thoennes (2000) discovered that of the 17.6 percent of all women surveyed, who indicated they had been the victim of a completed or attempted rape at some time in their life, 21.6 percent said they were younger than age 12 when they were first raped. Another 32 percent said they were between the ages of 12 and 17 when first raped. These data are consistent with the ECA study described earlier in the chapter. As noted in Chapter 9, however, sexual assault of older individuals is underreported and understudied.

Relationship Factors

Kilpatrick et al. (2000, p. 12) report cogent evidence that most of those who rape adults are intimate partners and not strangers. They list the following victimization information on adult women gathered from the National Women's Survey:

- 24.4 percent of the assaulters were strangers.
- 21.9 percent were husbands or ex-husbands.
- 19.5 percent were boyfriends or ex-boyfriends.
- 9.8 percent were relatives.
- 14.6 percent were other nonrelatives, such as friends or neighbors.

Consumption of Alcohol

With reference to situational characteristics, alcohol plays a major role in both incapacitated and coerced sexual assaults. Incapacitated sexual assault is defined as "any unwanted sexual contact occurring when a victim is unable to provide consent or stop what is happening because she is passed out, drugged, drunk, incapacitated, or asleep, regardless of whether the perpetrator was responsible for the substance use or whether substances were administered without her knowledge" (Krebs et al., 2007, p. ix). The Campus Sexual Assault Study (Krebs et al., 2007) compared victims who were incapacitated to those who were physically forced but not incapacitated. The vast majority of incapacitated sexual assault victims (82%) reported drinking alcohol and being intoxicated prior to being victimized compared to physically forced victims who reported being intoxicated (13%). Drug use was relatively rare for either incapacitated victims or physically forced victims, at least among college students. Not surprisingly, a large number of incapacitated sexual assault victims said they were at a party when the incident happened.

Alcohol use also plays a significant, multifaceted role in sexually coercive behavior (Knight & Sims-Knight, 2011). The victim is especially vulnerable if she has been drinking heavily (Ullman & Najdowksi, 2011). It should be noted, though, that many researchers have questioned the assumption that campus sexual assault is the result of alcohol fueled hookups. That is to say, survivors are also assaulted on their way to classes, in their residence halls, and other campus buildings, including libraries. When alcohol is a factor, its effect is seen on the offender as well. Alcohol impairs self-control, contributes to communication misinterpretations, and disrupts decision-making ability. In one important study focusing on sexual assault and alcohol consumption, about half of the sexual offenders and one-half the victims had been drinking alcohol prior to the assault (Abbey, Zawacki, Buck, Clinton, & McAuslan, 2004). Alcohol also appears to affect the severity of the assault. Offender alcohol abuse is believed to increase the level of violence for both rapists and child molesters (Abbey, Clinton-Sherrod, McAuslan, Zawacki, & Buck, 2003; Knight & Sims-Knight, 2011).

History of Victimization

For some unexplained reason, having a history of victimization is associated with a woman's vulnerability to sexual assault (Testa, Hoffman, & Livingston, 2010; Ullman & Najdowksi, 2011). More specifically, "… research suggests that child sexual abuse victims who are revictimized as adolescents are more likely than others to experience additional revictimization as adults" (Ullman & Najdowksi, 2011, p. 154). The reasons for this phenomenon appear to be highly complex and multifaceted, and despite the growing research literature on the topic, we have yet to have answers about why it occurs. However, self-blame may be a contributing factor. As noted by Sigurvinsdottir and Ullman (2015), "Many survivors blame themselves in the aftermath of their victimization, and self-blame is related to greater psychological distress and increased risk of revictimization" (p. 193).

Risk Taking Behaviors

The tendency to engage in risky or impulsive sexual behavior such as accepting a ride with a stranger, heavy drinking at parties, or hitchhiking by oneself increases the chance of being sexually assaulted. Risky sexual behavior appears to be especially prevalent at the time of high school graduation and during the first semester of college (Testa et al., 2010). As discussed in the delinquency chapter, adolescents (both males and females) are prone to take unnecessary risks in their daily lives, even though they cognitively know better. Having many prior sexual partners also seems to increase the risk of sexual assault (Testa, VanZile-Tamsen, & Livingston, 2007).

Closely related to risk taking behavior are failures to perceive risk in a situation or the ability to detect danger cues associated with increased vulnerability to sexual assault (Ullman & Najdowski, 2011). Researchers have identified two kinds of risk recognition failure in vulnerable women: global and specific (Gidycz, McNamara, & Edwards, 2006; Nurius, 2000). In **global risk recognition failure**, women are aware of the prevalence of sexual assault, but they believe they are at a significantly lower risk to be victimized than their peers (Norris, Nurius, & Graham, 1999).

In **specific risk failure** (sometimes referred to as situational), some women, for a variety of reasons, do not recognize that the situation they are in poses a threat. Alcohol usually plays a prominent role in this form of risk-recognition failure. In addition, risk recognition is more difficult when the potential offender is an acquaintance or a presumed friend because the threat often emerges incrementally. Also, in these situations there is a high degree of ambiguity because the woman must decide between social, friendship concerns and safety (Nurious, Norris, Young, Graham, & Gaylord, 2000). Training programs designed to help women identify risk factors and to better defend themselves are increasingly being developed, researched, and implemented in recent years (Gidycz et al., 2006). Nevertheless, despite the need to be alert to possible risks, the focus for preventing crimes should be on targeting the person who commits them. For the remainder of the chapter, we will discuss offender characteristics, recidivism, and treatment approaches.

CHARACTERISTICS OF SEXUAL OFFENDERS: WHO OFFENDS?

The causes of sexual offending are neither simple nor straightforward. As the knowledge from systematic study accumulates, it is clear that this behavior is influenced by multiple, interactive factors. Past learning experiences, cognitive expectations and beliefs, conditioning, environmental stimuli, and reinforcement contingencies (both rewards and punishments) are all involved. As indicated at the beginning of this chapter, "Sex offenders are a heterogeneous group, diverse in terms of individual demographics, traits, histories, motivations, and risk to reoffend" (Ennis, Buro, & Jung, in press, p. 1). An individual's propensity to commit sex crimes involves experiencing multiple risk factors during childhood, adolescence, and beyond.

Some studies (e.g., Revitch & Schlesinger, 1988) reveal that many sex offenders are not prone to violence or physical cruelty, but rather are timid, shy, and socially inhibited. This is particularly correct for a large segment of child molesters—those who offend against children—as will be discussed in the next chapter. It is far less likely to be correct with respect to rapists, whose attacks often have strong aggressive features in addition to the violence that defines the act itself. That is, by definition, rape is a violent, aggressive act, but it is often accompanied by additional violence, such as beating, choking, or stabbing the victim, harming a pet, or damaging personal property. Other sex offenders are exhibitionists and never physically touch their victims. Although not all sex offenders are alike, public approbation of sex crimes has produced many punitive laws aimed at deterring sexual offending, such as those limiting where convicted sex offenders can live or requiring them to register their whereabouts. Some of these laws apply to sex offenders as a group rather than to individual types, and, sex offender researchers often emphasize that the dangerousness associated with sex offenders is overpredicted for many of them (Hanson & Morton-Bourgon, 2005; Harris & Lurigio, 2010). This happens even when sex offenders are divided into "levels" of dangerousness, as they typically are.

In this chapter we are most concerned with the crimes of rapists. Recall that rape involves penetration or attempted penetration of any body cavity with the rapist's own body part or an object. Sexual aggression can be divided into at least two major categories: instrumental and expressive. **Instrumental sexual aggression** is when the offender uses just enough coercion to gain compliance from his victim. In **expressive sexual aggression**, the offender's primary aim is to harm the victim physically as well as psychologically. In some cases, the expressive aggression is "eroticized" in that the offender becomes sexually aroused in the presence of physical or psychological brutality. As you will see later in the chapter, these two simple categorizations are not sufficient for understanding the rapist, however, and a number of more complex typologies, some of which will be described below, have been proposed.

What kind of a person rapes? How did he get that way? Why does he do it? Can the "rapist personality" be easily identified? Are rapists mentally disordered? Generally speaking, sexual socialization and social learning play a crucial role in the rapist's perceptions of what the rape accomplishes and what is "masculine" (in the case of a male perpetrator). It is important to realize that sexual socialization (or sexual training) is rarely acquired entirely from home or school; much of it comes from peers, friends, the entertainment media, and experimentation. Some of it may be due to biological factors interacting with developmental influences and the social environment. Most of us, even as children, were fed misconceptions, taboos, and strategies for dealing with others in a sexual manner. Males often learn it is "manly" to take the sexual initiative and to persist, even against resistance. A major problem associated with acquaintance or date rape is that the offender often does not believe he really committed rape.

In this section, we will cover what we know about men who rape, including risk factors. These are environmental, biological, psychological, and other characteristics associated with an increased probability or likelihood that a person will become sexually aggressive and ultimately sexually assaultive. Research in this area does not always distinguish rape from other sexual assaults, however.

Ages of Sex Offenders

The most consistent demographic finding is that rapists in particular tend to be young. According to UCR data for 2013, 42 percent of those *arrested* for rape were under 25 years of age, and 15 percent were under 18 years of age (Federal Bureau of Investigation, 2014b). Six percent of the total arrests for rape and 9 percent of the total arrests for other sex offenses were under 15 years. In Canada, rates of sexual offending were highest among juveniles aged 12 and 17 (Worling & Langton, 2012). The percentage of juvenile arrests for rape has largely been the same for years.

Although the rape arrest patterns indicate that youths dominate the data, we should emphasize that there are many exceptions. For instance, some studies conclude that there are at least three distinct sexual arrest trajectories: one group of offenders peaking at age 25, a second group peaking around age 30, and a third group peaking at age 32 (Francis, Harris, Wallace, Knight, & Soothill, 2014; Freiburger, Marcum, Iannacchione, & Higgins, 2012). Another study (Lussier, Tzoumakis, Cale, & Amirault, 2010) reported that some sex offenders begin their sexual offending around their mid-forties, although many older offenders tend to be child molesters rather than rapists of adult women. Francis et al. (2014) uncovered as many as four trajectories of sexual offending, including one group that "started sexual offending in their teens and persisted at a steady rate of about one sexual offense a year up to age 58" (p. 325). Moreover, they were equally likely to commit rape as child molestation. Age of victim did not matter. It should be noted that the studies cited above, and the research we will cover below, often prefer the broad term "sex offender" to encompass the broad category of rape and sexual assault. In a vast majority of cases, the offender meets the criteria for rape, but as we will learn below, the offender who rapes often engages in a wide assortment of other criminal behaviors.

Recidivism and Offending History

In general, the recorded recidivism rate of sex offenders is less than commonly believed, ranging from 10 to 15 percent over five years (Mann, Hanson, & Thornton, 2010; Zgoba, Miner, Levenson, Knight Letourneau, & Thornton, in press). However, many sex offenders who recidivate reoffend often and generally over a long period of time until they reach a certain age.

In a study of 3,115 rapists released from prison, 1.3 percent of the rapists were rearrested for a new sex crime within six months of release (Langan et al., 2003). At the end of three years after release, 5 percent of the rapists were rearrested for another sex crime (rape or sexual assault).

Forty-one percent were arrested for another, nonsexual crime within three years after release. Fifteen percent were rearrested for a violent crime (other than rape or sexual assault). Thus, rapists in this large sample had a low recidivism rate for *sexual* offenses but a very high rate for offenses *in general*.

Another key point concerning recidivism: If we look at recidivism rates, many studies conclude that the majority of those who do reoffend sexually do not restrict their criminal activities only to sexual offenses (Francis et al., 2014). Rapists in particular consistently commit a broad spectrum of crimes, including nonsexual violent ones. They tend to be criminal career generalists (Parent, Guay, & Knight, 2011). Many men accused of and convicted of rape have been in perpetual conflict with society, long before the current rape offense. Some scholars refer to this broad offending tendency as **general criminality** (Babchishin, Hanson, & Blais, in press). "General criminality includes a global propensity for rule violation, meanness, and impulsivity, and overlaps with the constructs of antisocial personality disorder, psychopathy, and antisocial personality pattern" (Babchishin et al., in press, p. 3). General criminality is best understood as a dimension, with some offenders demonstrating greater criminality than others. In discussing the rapist trajectory across the life span, Francis et al. conclude: "those offenders who specialize in sexual offending are in the minority" (p. 323).

Child molesters, on the other hand, often reoffend, but they generally restrict their offending to sexual crimes and tend to be less violently aggressive (Hamdi & Knight, 2012). However, as a general rule, they tend to commit as many *sexual* offenses over their lifetimes as rapists (Parent et al., 2011).

Different factors predict recidivism for rapists than for child molesters (Parent, Guay, & Knight, 2012), who will be covered in detail in the next chapter. Antisocial and aggressive behaviors—such as anger, planning, sadism—predict recidivism for rapists; whereas isolation, impulsive lifestyle, and intense sexual interests predict recidivism for child molesters.

In summary, general criminality offending is emerging as a critical issue in preventing recidivism. One measure that shows considerable promise for predicting future offending and general criminality is the Static-2002R developed by R. Karl Hanson and David Thornton (2000, 2003) and colleagues. The popularity of the instrument is probably due to its validity, reliability, cost-effectiveness and its applicability to a wide range of sexual offenders. The Static-2002R has a general criminality subscale that contains five items related to criminal history (Babchishin et al., in press). The general criminality subscale, along with the age of the offender, has been found to be an effective predictor of sexual recidivism.

Applying Crime Scene Analysis to Predictions of Recidivism

Some criminologists have taken a different approach to predicting recidivism, one which requires an analysis of the crime scene itself. Crime scene analysis (CSA), a form of the criminal profiling discussed in Chapter 10, focuses on features of the crime that might help determine not only the identity of the offender but also whether the offender is likely to continue the criminal activity. Robert Lehmann and his colleagues (Lehmann, Goodwill, Gallasch-Nemitz, Biedermann, & Dahle, 2013; Lehmann, Goodwill, Hanson, & Dahle, 2014, in press) reasoned that certain characteristics of the rape provide valuable cues for estimating whether the offender will reoffend. CSA involves an examination of the behavioral patterns and qualities of the offender during the crime (the *modus operandi*), including how he interacts with and treats the victim. In an effort to discover what aspects of the rape predict sexual recidivism, Lehmann et al. investigated stranger rape, acquaintance rape, and child molestation. We will cover the stranger and acquaintance rape studies in this section, and present the child molestation project in the next chapter.

In the stranger rape study, Lehmann et al. (2013) explored the recidivistic predictability of three themes: hostility, criminality, and sexual exploitation/involvement. According to previous studies, each theme has been associated with a string of sexual offenses and sexual recidivism. Hostility refers to whether the victim was used as a vehicle for venting the perpetrator's anger and frustration. Usually the attack is sudden and highly aggressive. The **hostility theme** includes verbal violence, insulting or demeaning language, tearing the victim's clothing, and a general tone of violence toward the victim (Bartol & Bartol, 2013).

Criminality denotes general criminality, discussed above. "For the criminal offender, the rape is one among many antisocial behaviors whereas here he steals sexual satisfaction rather than money or property and the victim is solely treated as an object" (Lehmann et al., 2013, p. 243). In the **criminality theme**, the offender regards the victim as an inanimate object that must be restrained and coerced, but the attacker's purpose is to incapacitate more than to demean the victim. Control is a key concept in this theme, and the method of control may include binding, blindfolding, or gagging the victim.

The **sexual exploitation/involvement** (also **labeled pseudo-intimacy**) **theme** represents an attempt by the offender to bond with the victim by showing affection, making apologies, and/or living out some sexual fantasies. In this situation, the victim is treated as a reactive, living person, rather than as merely a sexual object. The offender may kiss the victim and expect the victim to make sexual comments to him. He may also compliment the victim's appearance.

Lehmann et al.'s (2013) results revealed that the criminality theme was significantly predictive of sexual recidivism and was associated with an extensive prior nonsexual and sexual offending history. In addition, stranger rapists scoring high on the criminality theme revealed aspects of organization and planning in their offense. They commonly used weapons and took precautions to avoid being detected or identified. The other two themes—hostility and sexual exploitation—were not good predictors of sexual recidivism, but were associated with certain behavioral characteristics of stranger rapists. The sexual exploitation theme was linked to stranger rapists who applied a low level of aggression and did not have obvious intentions of harming the victim. The theme was also related to a variety of deviant sexual interests. As expected, the hostility theme was characteristic of offenders who were prone to utilize sexual sadism and extreme violence in their attack.

The second Lehmann et al. (2014) study utilized a sample of 247 male acquaintance rapists from Berlin, Germany. The study tested the usefulness of the three themes (criminality, hostility, and pseudo-intimacy) examined in the stranger rape project. The study revealed that the two themes of pseudo-intimacy and hostility predicted sexual recidivism, and "were significantly related to the persistence of sexual offending" (Lehmann et al., 2014, p. 16). Interestingly, these findings were in contrast to the results reported in the stranger rape study where only the criminality theme was predictive of sexual recidivism. According to Lehmann et al., these differences suggest that stranger and acquaintance rape represent different contributing factors. Stranger rapists generally have a strong propensity for antisocial behavior and violent behavior, whereas acquaintance rapists may have "genuine difficulty recognizing their behavior is wrong, believing that their victims wanted or deserved what they got" (Lehmann et al., 2014, p. 16). (See **Table 12-2** for a summary of the themes across stranger and acquaintance rapes.)

In another recent study (Almond, McManus, & Ward, 2014), the three sexual themes were again examined. However, the study focused on male-on-male sexual assault. The study did not investigate the power of the themes to predict sexual recidivism and did not distinguish stranger from acquaintance rapes. However, the researchers did find that a majority of male-on-male assaulters (74%) demonstrated a dominant theme. Specifically, 42 percent were classified as displaying hostility, 23 percent as criminality, and 9 percent as sexual exploitation/involvement. Overall, the study demonstrates that male-on-male sexual assaulters are a heterogeneous group reflecting different themes and reasons in their attacks. Almond et al. conclude: "There are those who gain

TABLE 12-2 Themes Predictive of Recidivism in Stranger and Acquaintance Rapes

Theme	Stranger	Acquaintance
Hostility	Not predictive	Predictive
Criminality	Predictive	Not predictive
Pseudo-intimacy	Not predictive	Predictive

Source: Adapted from Lehmann, R. J. B., Goodwill, A. M., Gallasch-Nemitz, F., Biedermann, J., & Dahl, K- P. (2013). Applying crime scene analysis to the prediction of sexual recidivism in stranger rapes. Law and Human Behavior, 37, 241-254.

intimacy and closeness for the offense, others who use the offense to vent misplaced anger and frustration and those that use the offense as an expression of social dominance" (p. 1293).

Attitudes and Myths That Support Rape and Other Sexual Assaults

Undoubtedly, a major explanatory factor for many sexual assaults of women is the attitudes held by the perpetrators. Some research indicates that these attitudes have been held by many individuals in the general population. Some time ago, Koss and Dinero (1988) surveyed approximately 3,000 male students at 32 U.S. colleges and universities. The students were asked questions about the extent of verbal coercion and physical force they had used to become sexually intimate with women without their consent. They were also questioned about attitudes and habits. The results indicated that highly sexually aggressive men expressed greater hostility toward women, frequently used alcohol, frequently viewed violent and degrading pornography, and were closely involved with peer groups that reinforce highly sexualized and dominating views of women. In addition, the more sexually aggressive the student, the more likely he was to believe that force and coercion are legitimate ways to gain compliance in sexual relationships. The researchers concluded, "In short, the results provided support for a developmental sequence for sexual aggression in which early experiences and psychological characteristics establish conditions for sexual violence" (p. 144).

More recent research provides similar findings, suggesting that men who sexually assault women seem to subscribe to attitudes and ideology that encourage men to be dominant, controlling, and powerful, whereas women are expected to be submissive, permissive, and compliant. For example, one recent study found rape-prone men strongly endorse rape-supportive statements, such as that most women like to be dominated, a woman cannot be raped unless she wants to be, or women who say no are usually lying (Blake & Gannon, 2010).

The role played by fantasy and imagination in the development of sexually aggressive behavior is becoming an increasingly important topic (Knight & Sims-Knight, 2011). Self-reports by sexual offenders find that frequent imagery and fantasy of sexually aggressive scenes are extremely important in motivating and guiding overt sexual aggression. Interestingly, in an SR survey conducted by Greendlinger and Byrne (1987) over one-third of 114 college men indicated they fantasize about aggressively raping a woman and 54 percent fantasize about "forcing a woman to have sex." Nevertheless, it cannot be concluded that having such fantasies will translate to assaultive behavior. Research documenting fantasies in actual offenders is more relevant. Likewise, it is sometimes asserted that many women report fantasies about being forcefully assaulted in a sexual manner; no one is suggesting that they actually want to be raped, however.

RAPE MYTHS.   Rape myths have received considerable research attention during the past four decades. **Rape myths** are "attitudes and beliefs that are generally false but widely and persistently held, and that serve to deny and justify male sexual aggression against women" (Lonsway & Fitzgerald, 1994, p. 134). They stem from the traditional view of masculinity that men should be strong, assertive, sexually dominant, and heterosexual (Davies, 2002). Rape myths essentially are the false beliefs that women must be dominated and coerced into sexual activity. Note that research on rape myths refers to males as aggressors and females as victims, but it is likely to pertain as well to male perpetrators against male victims. It is unclear whether it would pertain to female sex offenders, who are discussed in the following chapter.

Rape myths and misogynistic (hatred of women) attitudes appear to play a major role in sexual assault of women. Many—but not all—rapists and violently sexually aggressive men tend to hold them. Research indicates that men who subscribe to rape myths are hostile toward women in general (Forbes, Adams-Curtis, & White, 2004; Suarez & Gadalla, 2010). Although much of the research cited in this section is older than many college students, both current research and anecdotal evidence of hostility toward women is not difficult to find. In the spring of 2015, a campus fraternity was suspended for a year because its Facebook page included photos depicting drugs and naked, unconscious women. Female political, celebrity, and media figures regularly receive hate-filled emails, and the blogosphere is notorious for its anonymous derisive comments directed toward specific women as well as women in general. Attitudes that promote the denigration of women may be widespread. There is distressing evidence that rapists may reflect the explicit and implicit beliefs held by many others.

A widely used scale today for the purposes of measuring sexual aggression is the revised Sexual Experiences Survey (SES; Koss et al., 2007). It asks specific questions to assess whether and how often a respondent committed a completed rape, attempted rape, sexual coercion, or unwanted sexual contact (Swartout et al., 2014; Swartout et al., in press). Much of the recent research on sexual assault, particularly on college campuses, uses the SES to measure sexual assault.

There is some recent evidence that some false beliefs and rape myths are beginning to change—at least among college students—though incidents such as those cited above remind us that considerable change is still needed. For example, Ferro, Cermele, and Saltzman (2008) report that today's college students are less likely to hold false beliefs about sexual assault, and are generally sympathetic toward survivors. However, the students in the Ferro et al. study still held rape myths concerning marital rape. The participants found it difficult to believe that rape occurs in a married relationship since a higher level of intimacy is expected between married couples. They were also reluctant to believe that the act was a violation of the wife's rights or that she would be psychologically damaged from the experience.

Cognitive-Perceptual Distortions in Communication

Some men have strong cognitive-perceptual biases that lead to misconceptions of women's verbal and nonverbal communications (Knight & Sims-Knight, 2003, 2011). Overall, a subgroup of men who are inclined to be sexually aggressive and coercive, perceive more sexual intent in women's behavior than women perceive in their own behavior or the behavior of other women (Farris, Treat, Viken, & McFall, 2008). For example, some men perceive friendly behavior (verbal and nonverbal) from a woman as seductive and assertive behavior as hostile and attacking. A simple touching of the arm may be interpreted as sexual interest. Furthermore, men who believe that sexual assault is justifiable in certain situations and who blame women for victimization appear to have considerable difficulty distinguishing between when a woman is sexually interested and when she is not (Farris, Viken, Treat, & McFall, 2006). Alcohol certainly compounds the situation by influencing judgment and perceptual processing.

According to Farris et al., these men appear to have particular difficulty decoding rejection when a woman is dressed provocatively—in their perceptions—and sexual interest when a woman is dressed more conservatively. That is, they may assume interest if she is dressed in a way they perceive is provocative and lack of interest if she is dressed more conservatively. The researchers also discovered that sexually aggressive men tend to have particular difficulty making snap judgments. "(I)t appears that provocative clothing was particularly distracting to aggressive men when judgments had to be made quickly" (Farris et al., 2006, p. 874). Using manner of dress to measure "provocativeness" and "conservativeness" presents a minefield for researchers today, however, because typical fashion styles of today lean toward what would have been provocative even a decade ago.

The Influence of Pornography

The relationship between rape and pornography has long been shrouded with confusion and surrounded by debate. In the late twentieth century, two presidential commissions established to study the effect of pornography on crime and human behavior reached opposite conclusions. The first and most comprehensive, established in 1967, was directed not to issue recommendations unless the effects were clear-cut. Because of the complexity it uncovered, the commission could not conclude whether explicit sexual material contributed significantly to sex crimes, prompting then President Richard M. Nixon to remark that the commission was "morally bankrupt." Many have used this conclusion to support their contention that pornography is not harmful. The second National Commission on Obscenity and Pornography, which issued a report in 1984, recommended widespread restrictions of pornographic material. This commission has been extensively criticized for its lack of scientific objectivity. Since then, of course, pornography—including violent and child pornography—has been widely available, including for downloading from the Internet.

Whether pornography contributes to sexual offending may depend both on the type of pornography and the characteristics of the offender. Some researchers also distinguish pornography from erotica, which refers to "sexually explicit material that depicts adult men and women consensually involved in pleasurable, nonviolent, nondegrading, sexual interactions" (Seto, Maric, & Barbaree, 2001, p. 37). Pornography, on the other hand, may be described as depictions of sexual contact where one of the participants is portrayed as powerless or nonconsenting, or is little more than an object for the pleasure of the other participant or participants. In addition, some pornography depicts one or more persons in physically violent or degrading and humiliating situations. In each case, the pornography portrays sexual interactions as impersonal and without affection or consideration of the actors as individuals. Child pornography is a totally different situation because it involves the exploitation of children; possession and distribution of child pornography is illegal and carries prison penalties if convicted. Child pornography will be covered in the next chapter. Overall, Seto et al. (2001) were able to conclude from a critical review of the research literature that there is little support for a direct causal link between pornography use and sexual aggression.

However, some early research evidence suggested that under *certain* conditions, pornography facilitates aggressive, sexual behavior. Studies by Donnerstein (1983) and Malamuth (Malamuth & Check, 1981; Malamuth, Haber, & Feshbach, 1980; Malamuth, Heim, & Feshbach, 1980) indicated, for example, that a general statement that pornography does not negatively influence people needs several qualifiers. In a series of ongoing experiments, Donnerstein found evidence that three factors influence the relationship between pornography and human aggression: (1) the level of arousal elicited by pornographic films, (2) the level of aggressive content, and (3) the reactions of the victims portrayed in these films and photographs. Donnerstein and others (e.g., Meyer, 1972; Zillman, 1971) angered male subjects in a variety of ways, then found that pornography shown to these aroused subjects significantly increased their aggressive behavior toward others. Because of their arousing properties, the pornographic stimuli apparently may promote aggression under certain conditions. This finding accords with Berkowitz's theory (discussed in Chapter 5) on the relationship between arousal and aggression. Anything—sexual or not—that increases the arousal level of an already aroused subject will increase aggressive behavior in situations where aggression is the dominant behavior. The increased arousal may also draw the subject away from his own internal control or self-regulatory mechanisms, thereby allowing him to be less concerned about the consequences of his behavior.

Extremely violent stimuli, both pornographic and nonpornographic, can also facilitate aggression toward women, even in nonangered males, under certain conditions. The level of violence in the film appears significant. Portrayals of women being assaulted, even nonsexually, can increase subsequent aggressive behavior by men toward women, even when the males are not angry. Therefore, highly aggressive and violent acts depicted in the media may facilitate the rape act for some males. Since many rapists regard their act as a direct aggressive attack on women, seeing films where women are physically abused may encourage and support their own violent inclinations. Seto et al. (2001) make the point, though, that individuals who are already predisposed to sexually offend are the most likely to demonstrate the strongest effects of pornographic materials on their sexual and aggressive behavior. Men who are not predisposed toward aggressive sexual behavior are unlikely to be affected by pornographic materials.

The reactions of the victims portrayed in films also seem crucial. Films or photographs that depict the female victim enjoying rape (common in pornography) encourage acceptance of rape myths and promote violence against women (Allen, Emmers, Gebhart, & Giery, 2001; Malamuth & Check, 1981). In fact, Allen and his colleagues (2001) found that as the level of coercion depicted in the pornographic material goes up, so does the acceptance of the rape myth. If, on the other hand, the victim finds the rape both painful and abhorrent (negative aggressive pornography), male observers are disinclined to act aggressively. However, several qualifiers must be attached to this finding. If the male observer is already angered (aroused), seeing the victim suffer may make him more aggressive, since any arousal increase in an already aroused subject will increase subsequent aggressive behavior. The specific content of the film becomes irrelevant, as long as it meets the minimum criterion of being somehow arousing. On the other hand, males who are not upset or aroused before seeing a female victim suffer are less likely to aggress against women.

The above studies were conducted some time ago, but even today the relationship between violent pornography and sexual aggression remains complex and troubling. Some studies continue to indicate that there is a significant relationship between violent pornographic consumption and attitudes supporting violence against women (Hald, Malamuth, & Yuen, 2010). This relationship appears to be especially strong for men who are considered at high risk for sexual aggression and rape (Malamuth, Huppin, & Bryant, 2005; Vega & Malamuth, 2007). Furthermore, the confluence of three factors—attitudes supportive of sexual assault (e.g., acceptance of rape myths), lack of self-control (e.g., through misuse of alcohol), and norms that are conveyed through pornography—has been linked to the likelihood of committing rape (Abbey, Jacques-Tiura, & LeBreton, 2011; Malamuth, Hald, & Koss, 2012; Tharp et al., 2013).

CLASSIFICATION OF RAPE PATTERNS

Since such a wide variety of sexual offenders are involved in rape and sexual assault, several attempts have been made to categorize rapists according to their traits and behavioral-motivational patterns. These classification systems are often referred to as a typology, a key concept described in earlier chapters, where typologies of criminal homicide offenders and batterers were introduced. A typology is used to organize a wide assortment of observations or measurements for research and clinical diagnosis and treatment purposes. The simplest typology used for sex offenders is based on the age of the victim or victims, thereby distinguishing between child molesters and rapists (Ennis et al., in press). For our purposes, we will use the child molester and rapist typology by covering the two types of sexual offenders in separate chapters. However, it should be emphasized that many sex offenders engage in **crossover offending**, meaning they offend against victims regardless of age or other characteristics. Crossover offending refers to the tendency for some offenders to sexually assault victims representing different ages, gender, and relationships, a pattern characteristic of some serial and opportunity offenders (Heil, Ahlmeyer, & Simons, 2003). An opportunity sex offender is one who does not necessarily plan his assault, but rather takes the occasion to sexually assault when a suitable victim is present. Depending on the opportunity, they may select male children or young or older women for sexual assault.

The two most extensively studied sex offender typologies were the ones developed by researchers at the Massachusetts (Bridgewater) Treatment Center (MTC) (Cohen, Garafalo, Boucher, & Seghorn, 1971; Cohen, Seghorn, & Calmas, 1969; Knight & Prentky, 1987; Prentky & Knight, 1986). One typology was developed for rapists and the other for child molesters. The MTC typologies are considered among the most rigorously tested classification systems in sex offender research to date (Goodwill, Alison, & Beech, 2009). The original researchers recognized that sex offending involves both sexual and aggressive features and tried to formulate a behavioral classification system that takes these features into consideration.

The MTC typologies have undergone multiple revisions over the years and currently are in their fourth revision (Knight, 2010; Knight & King, 2012). As research develops, it is becoming clear that some sexual offenders do not fit neatly into the MTC typologies. For example, the usefulness of a typology for sex offenders is beginning to give way to a dimensional approach. That is, rather than placing sex offenders into a variety of pigeon holes, it is becoming more realistic to place them along a variety of dimensions or continua (Guay, Ruscio, Knight, & Hare, 2007; Lehmann et al., 2013). Additionally, and as mentioned above, the MTC typologies disregard "contemporary research that indicates that a significant proportion of sex offenders engage in 'crossover offending' against victims of different ages" (Ennis et al., in press, p. 3). Still, the MTC typologies are very useful for highlighting the multiple types of sex offenders based on the motivational and behavioral characteristics of the offenses. To that extent, we will introduce some of the key offender categories of the MTC typologies. In this chapter we will focus on the typology developed for rapists.

Massachusetts Treatment Center Classification System

The Massachusetts Treatment Center (MTC) originally identified four major categories of rapists: (1) displaced aggression, (2) compensatory, (3) sexual aggressive, and (4) impulsive rapists. Although these major categories still exist—with slight changes in nomenclature—MTC researchers have refined the classification system to include various subcategories, as will be noted shortly. **Displaced aggression rapists** (also called in other classification systems **displaced anger** or **anger-retaliation rapists**) are primarily violent and aggressive in their attack, displaying minimum or total absence of sexual feeling. These men use the act of rape to harm, humiliate, and degrade the woman. This rapist closely tracks the hostility theme discussed earlier in the sexual recidivism section of this chapter. The victim is brutally assaulted and subjected to sadistic acts like biting, cutting, or tearing. In most instances, the victim is a complete stranger who happens to be the best available stimulus for the violence, although she may possess characteristics that attract the assailant's attention. The assault is not sexually arousing for the displaced aggression rapist, and he often demands oral manipulation or masturbation from the victim to become tumescent.

According to Knight and Prentky (1987), an offender must demonstrate the following characteristics during the attack in order to be assigned to the displaced aggression category:

1. The presence of a high degree of nonsexualized aggression or rage expressed either through verbal and/or physical assault that clearly exceeds what is necessary to force compliance of the victim.
2. Clear evidence, in verbalization or behavior, of the intent to demean, degrade, or humiliate the victim.
3. No evidence that the aggressive behavior is eroticized or that sexual pleasure is derived from the injurious acts.
4. The injurious acts are not focused exclusively on parts of the body that have sexual significance.

Although many of these rapists are married, they are usually ambivalent toward the women in their lives (Cohen et al., 1971), and their relationships with women are often characterized by frequent irritation and periodic violence. They perceive women as being hostile, demanding, and unfaithful. In addition, they often select as their targets for sexual assault women whom they consider active, assertive, and independent. The occupational history of these assailants is stable and often shows some level of success. Usually, the work is "masculine," such as truck driving, carpentry, construction, or mechanics. The attack typically follows an incident that has upset or angered the rapist, particularly about women and their behavior. The term *displaced aggression* is derived from the fact that the victim rarely has played any direct role in generating the aggression and arousal. This offender often attributes his offense to "uncontrollable impulses."

Compared with other rapists, the childhood of the displaced aggression offender is often chaotic and unstable. Many were physically and emotionally neglected. A large number were raised in dysfunctional foster or single-parent homes.

Compensatory rapists rape in response to an intense sexual arousal initiated by stimuli in the environment, often quite specific stimuli. This type of rapist is sometimes referred to in the clinical and research literature as the "power-reassurance," "sexual aim," "ego dystonic," or "true" sex offender. Aggression is not a significant feature here; the basic motivation is a desire to prove sexual prowess and adequacy. In their day-to-day lives, compensatory rapists tend to be extremely passive, withdrawn, and socially inept. They live in a world of fantasy that centers on images of eagerly yielding victims who will eventually submit willingly to the attack. The compensatory rapist's fantasies or personal versions of the world may so distort his view of the victim that he may seek further contact with her, even if she strongly resisted the sexual assault. In many respects, the compensatory rapist follows the pseudo-intimacy theme covered earlier in the chapter.

Although his victim is usually a stranger, the compensatory rapist has probably seen her frequently, watched her, or followed her. Specific stimuli associated with her probably excite him.

For example, he may be drawn to college women but may feel the attraction would not be mutual if he approached them via a socially accepted route. He cannot face the prospect of rejection. However, if he can prove his sexual prowess, the victim will appreciate his value. If the victim vigorously resists the compensatory rapist, he is likely to flee; if she submits passively, he will rape without much force or violence. This sexually aroused passive assailant will often ejaculate spontaneously, even on mere physical contact with the victim. In general, he does not demonstrate other kinds of antisocial behavior.

The compensatory rapist is often described by others as a quiet, shy, submissive, lonely nice man. Although he is a reliable worker, his withdrawn, introverted behavior, lack of self-esteem, and low levels of need for achievement usually preclude academic, occupational, or social success. His rapes—or attempts at rape—are efforts to compensate for his sense of inadequacy, hence the category to which he is assigned. Some research by Knight and Prentky (1987) questions the incompetence issue. They found that, compared with the other rapist types, the compensatory rapist evidenced the best heterosexual adaptation and achieved the highest employment skill level. Consequently, the term *compensatory rapist* has been replaced with the term *sexual gratification*, nonsadistic type.

The **sexual aggressive** or **sadistic rapist** is the one in whom sexual and aggressive features seem to coexist at equal or near equal levels. In order for him to experience sexual arousal, it must be associated with violence and pain, which excite him. He rapes, therefore, because of the combination of violence and sexual features in the act. He is convinced that women enjoy being forcefully raped and being dominated and controlled by men. This, he believes, is part of women's nature. Anger and aggression are not always present during the early stages of the assault, which may actually begin as a seduction. In this sense, the sexual aggressive rapist considers the victim's resistance and struggle a game, a form of protesting too much; what she really wants is to be sexually assaulted and raped. This belief appears deeply ingrained and widely accepted in many Western societies (Edwards, 1983).

Sexually aggressive offenders are often married, but because they display little commitment or loyalty, they also often have a history of multiple marriages, separations, and divorces. They also may be frequently involved in domestic violence. In fact, their backgrounds include antisocial behaviors beginning during adolescence or before and ranging from truancy to rape-murder. They have been severe management problems in school. Throughout their childhood, adolescence, and adulthood, they exhibit poor behavior controls and a low frustration tolerance. Their childhoods are characterized by physical abuse and neglect.

In the extreme, these rapists engage in sexual sadism much like the displaced aggression rapists: Their victims may be viciously violated, beaten, and even killed. The difference between the two types is that the sexual aggressive rapist derives intense sexual satisfaction from aggression, pain, and violence. In order to qualify for assignment to this category, the offender needs to demonstrate (1) a level of aggression or violence that clearly exceeds what is necessary to force compliance of the victim, and (2) the explicit, unambiguous evidence that aggression is sexually exciting to him.

A fourth type of rapist, the **impulsive** or **exploitative rapist**, demonstrates neither strong sexual nor aggressive features, but engages in spontaneous rape when the opportunity presents itself. The rape is usually carried out in the context of another crime, such as robbery or burglary. The victims simply happen to be available, and they are sexually assaulted with minimum extra-rape violence or sexual feeling. Generally, this offender has a long history of criminal offenses other than rape. In order to be assigned to this group, the offender must show (1) callous indifference to the welfare and comfort of victim, and (2) the presence of no more force than is necessary to gain the compliance of the victim. The exploitative rapist presents many similarities to the general criminality theme presented earlier in the chapter. We should be cautious in assuming that sexual assaults that accompany a burglary are impulsive, however. In recent years, researchers have begun to focus on **sexual burglary** as a crime that appears to be more than simply an opportunity that occurs as a result of a burglary. (See **Box 12-2**.)

RESEARCH FOCUS

BOX 12-2 Sexual Burglary

Burglary is typically defined in criminal statutes as the unlawful entry into a residence, commercial establishment, or other building for the purposes of committing a felony. When we think of burglary, we usually think of someone entering a home to steal, and most typically when residents are sleeping or are not at home. However, an unknown percentage of burglaries have sexual motives, and the crime the perpetrators intend to commit may range from sexual assault to theft of intimate apparel. In these situations, the burglars are referred to in the literature as sexual burglars.

It is difficult to obtain information about sexual burglaries from official crime statistics, because as noted in the chapter, sexual victimizations are not generally reported to police. In an unknown number of cases, the burglary may be reported but its sexual components not. For example, a victim may tell police someone entered her home and stole cash or jewelry but not add that she was sexually assaulted. With reference to victimization data (e.g., the NCVS), the emphasis will be on the sexual offense, and the burglary component might not be emphasized. Therefore, a very unique type of offense, the sexually motivated burglary, has been left largely unexplored until recently, with but few exceptions. Several studies on this topic have begun to emerge, however (e.g., Deslauriers-Varin & Beauregard, 2010; Harris et al., 2013; Pedneault, Harris, & Knight, 2012; Pedneault, Beauregard, Harris, & Knight, 2014).

Research on burglary in general views it as a rational crime, planned and undertaken by an offender to maximize the profits and minimize the risks (Cornish & Clark, 1987; Nee & Taylor, 2000). In some cases, when a sexual assault accompanies the burglary, the assault has been regarded as opportunistic—that is, the offender burglarizes a residence and happens to find a victim (Scully & Marolla, 1985). In a recent study, though, Pedneault et al. (2014) did not find strong support for this. Rather, they found that those who committed sexual burglary made rational choices and had illegally entered premises with the *primary motivation of committing a sexual offense*.

The researchers reviewed 224 incidents of residential burglary from files of sex offenders, primarily persons convicted of rapes (71%). Their previous research (Pedneault, Harris, & Knight, 2012) had identified three different types of sexual burglars: (1) fetishistic noncontact, (2) versatile contact, and (3) sexually oriented contact. The *fetishistic noncontact burglary* is committed to access property that has a sexually arousing value for the burglar, such as underclothing or other personal items. Usually, these breaking and entering incidents do not involve the sexual assault of a victim. In most cases, the residence is unoccupied.

The *versatile contact burglary* has multiple motivations for entering a residence, and sexual behaviors are only part of the spectrum of motivations. The sexual assault is committed in combination with theft, violence, and the use of weapons.

The *sexually oriented contact* burglary occurs because the offender has the planned, specific goal of gaining access to a sexual victim, without any intent to steal possessions or commit theft or violence other than a sexual assault. Both the fetishistic noncontact and sexually oriented contact burglars were aiming primarily at sexual satisfaction. It should be noted that sexual satisfaction does not negate the probability that anger of hatred of women was also a factor. Further analysis of the 224 incidents (Pedneault, Beauregard et al., 2014) indicated that sexual motivation was predominant among all three groups and, as noted above, there was little support for an opportunistic effect. Moreover, even in the versatile contact burglary, where additional crimes were committed, sexual contact was the primary motivation. As a whole, sexually motivated burglaries took place in occupied residences when the victim was alone. A vast majority occurred at night, most often between midnight and 3 a.m., when the victim was sleeping. The sexual burglars in the study targeted apartments. The researchers speculated that the preference for apartments might be a result of the burglars being more familiar with the layout of the apartment buildings compared to private residences or it being more likely that a victim be alone. Most of the offenders carried weapons, underscoring the fact that they expected the residences to be occupied. The use of weapons, of course, increases the risks for all concerned.

Questions for Discussion

1. Several research findings are different from what researchers have found about nonsexual residential burglaries. For example, nonsexual burglaries usually occur when no one is at home, and weapons are far less frequent. What other differences might be expected?

2. From a psychological perspective, what is the value, if any, in distinguishing contact sexual burglaries from other sexual assaults?

3. Is the sexual burglar likely to be different from the nonsexual burglar in personality characteristics? Is the sexual burglar likely to be different from someone who commits sexual assault on campus or in the community?

The MTC:R3

The Massachusetts Treatment Classification scheme offers a rough framework for conceptualizing and simplifying the behaviors and motives involved in rape. However, it needs refinement and reconstruction, a process the group has been pursuing for a number of years (e.g., Knight, 1999, 2010; Knight & Prentky, 1990). In this section we compare the two latest versions.

After a series of analyses and further development of the classification scheme, Knight and his colleagues decided to classify rape offenders into *four* major types and *nine* subtypes (see **Table 12-3**). Although the basic four offender types discussed above—displaced aggression, sexual gratification (formerly compensatory), sexually aggressive, and impulsive—remained in the equation, the researchers discovered there were subtle differences within them. They then found that identifying four primary *motivations* for rape could improve the MTC's effectiveness significantly: *opportunity*, *pervasive anger*, *sexual gratification*, and *vindictiveness* (Knight, 1999; Knight, Warren, Reboussin, & Soley, 1998). Knight and his colleagues (Knight et al., 1998) concluded that these four motivations appeared to describe enduring behavioral patterns that distinguished most rapists. The **opportunistic types** (Types 1 and 2) are similar to the impulsive rapists described earlier. Their sexual assaults appear to be impulsive, predatory acts as a result of being in a situation where the opportunity for the sexual attack arises, and they are not primarily driven by sexual fantasy or explicit anger at women. However, analysis of offender data showed that the opportunistic type can be subdivided on the basis of their social competence (see **Table 12-3**). Type 1 offenders are higher in social competence and first exhibited their impulsive sexual tendencies in adulthood. Type 2 offenders, on the other hand, are lower in social competence and first demonstrated their impulsive sexual actions during adolescence.

The **pervasively angry type** (Type 3) is similar to displaced aggression rapists but with the difference that his generalized anger pervades all areas of his life. Their pervasive anger is not simply directed at women but at everyone. Consequently, they often have a long history of antisocial, violent behavior of all kinds, and they tend to inflict high levels of physical injury on their victims, especially their rape victims. In many ways, they manifest behaviors similar to the life-course-persistent offender. **Sexual gratification** motivations characterized four subtypes of rapists in the MTC:R3 classification scheme (Types 4, 5, 6, and 7; see **Table 12-3**). The sadistic rapists (Types 4 and 5) are subdivided into overt and muted types on the basis of whether their sexual-aggressive fantasies are directly expressed (overt) in violent attacks or are only fantasized (muted) (Knight et al., 1998). The nonsadistic sexual rapists (Types 6 and 7) are subdivided on the basis of their social competence; they are similar to the compensatory rapist described earlier in the chapter.

The MTC:R3 also includes **vindictive offender types** (Types 8 and 9), characterized by anger directed exclusively at women. These types are also highly similar to the displaced aggressive type described in the original MTC. "The sexual assaults of these men are distinguished by behaviors that are explicitly intended to harm the woman physically, as well as to degrade and humiliate her" (Knight et al., 1998, p. 58). Like the opportunistic and nonsadistic rapists, the vindictive types can be subdivided into high social competence and low social competence people.

Knight et al. (1998) postulate that these nine rape-offender classifications can help substantially in providing additional clues in crime-scene investigations. With refinement and continuing research, the MTC:R3 should ultimately enable investigators to identify "type" based on parameters

TABLE 12-3	Breakdown of MTC:R3 Four Categorizations of Rapist Type into Subtypes Based on Motivation							
Opportunistic		*Pervasively Angry*	*Sexual*				*Vindictive*	
High social competence	Low social competence	Sexual gratification	Sadistic		Nonsadistic		Low Social competence	Moderate social competence
			Overt	Muted	Low social competence	High social competence		
Type 1	Type 2	Type 3	Type 4	Type 5	Type 6	Type 7	Type 8	Type 9

Source: Bartol, Curt R., Bartol, Anne M., Criminal Behavior: A Psychological Approach, 10e, Copyright © 2014. Pearson Education, Upper Saddle River, NJ.

gathered at the crime scene. The MTC:R3 also underscores the multiple strategies and cognitive beliefs possessed by rapists and discourages dogmatic proclamations about why rape occurs. The MTC:R3 increases the understanding of the etiology of sexual offending and helps mental health professions predict recidivism. Knight (1999) cautions, though, that while the MTC:R3 provides a useful way of classifying the many motivations of rapists, it may need considerable refinement and research to establish its validity and ultimate utility. In one study, Goodwill, Alison, and Beech (2009) found that the MTC:R3 does appear to have considerable usefulness in criminal profiling or law enforcement solving of sexual crimes.

MTC Version 4

Knight (2010), in response to studies that have identified several problems with the MTC:R3, recently revised the typological model. In the newly developed MTC:R4 (version 4), Knight deleted subtype 5, the muted sadistic rapist, but all other MTC:R3 subtypes remain.

However, based on previous research (Knight & Sims-Knight, 2003), he emphasizes the importance of three core personality traits that are believed to define three paths that lead to sexual offending in both juveniles and adults: (1) callous unemotionality; (2) antisociality/impulsivity, and (3) hypersexuality/sexualization.

Callous unemotionality is demonstrated by such behaviors as pathological lying, grandiose sense of self-worth, superficial charm, little empathy or compassion for others, and a conning, manipulative behavioral pattern. Antisociality/impulsivity is characterized as exhibiting poor behavioral control, early behavioral problems, and general criminal behavior. This dimension reflects the research findings that many rapists are predominantly criminal generalists and do not specialize in sexual offenses. This path strongly resembles the life-course-persistent offender described by Moffitt (1993a, 1993b), and discussed in earlier chapters. Hypersexuality/sexualization is represented by sexual preoccupation, sexual compulsivity, and sexual coerciveness. Childhood sexual abuse influences this developmental path (see **Figure 12-1**). Childhood sexual abuse appears to be especially prevalent in the backgrounds of juvenile sexual offenders (Zakireh, Ronis, & Knight, 2008). This form of abuse often leads to sexual preoccupation and compulsivity, which increases the risk of aggressive and coercive sexual fantasies and behavior (Knight & Sims-Knight, 2004). It should be emphasized that physical/verbal abuse and sexual abuse do not automatically lead to the traits and associated behaviors described above. As pointed out throughout the book, it takes a combination of risk factors to result in antisocial and criminal offending. Abuse is just one of those risk factors, but it does frequently show up in the backgrounds of sex offenders.

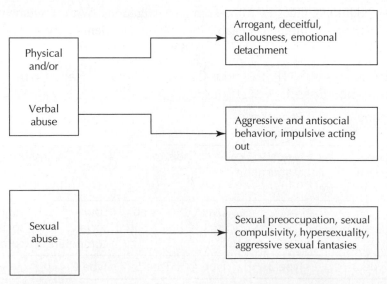

FIGURE 12-1 Knight and Sims-Knight Three Path Model of Sexual Offending

The first two traits are comparable to the two primary factors found in psychopathy. Consequently, the MTC:R4 now includes psychopathy as a main component. According to Knight and Sims-Knight (2004), the traits "play a critical role across the life span for sexually coercive males, are critical in assessing risk of recidivism, and should be targets of therapeutic intervention" (p. 49).

Knight also views each of the three core personality traits as dimensions running from one extreme to another. This approach is in contrast to the strict typological model illustrated by the MTC:R3 model that utilized discrete categories. In the new, revised model, a rapist might fall somewhere between hypersexuality and low sexualization and somewhere between high callousness and unemotionality. The rapist should also fall somewhere between high antisociality and low antisociality. Knight also introduced another twist to the MTC:R4. Rather than illustrating the model by a linear graph, he encompassed the components within a circle that he calls a circumplex. In a circumplex model, factors that are close together in an area of circle are more related than factors that fall further apart in the circle. Those factors furthest apart are opposites, such as psychopathic and nonpsychopathic. At this point, the MTC:R4 needs much more research, development, and refinement before it becomes useful for both researchers and clinicians, but the system holds considerable promise for understanding, preventing, and treating sexual offending.

Research to date indicates that early traumatic physical and sexual abuse play an important role across the board in the development of the personality traits. Early childhood abuses—physical, verbal, and sexual—are hypothesized to intensify these traits in some, but not all individuals. For example, as we will note in the next chapter, childhood sexual abuse appears to be prevalent in the backgrounds of juvenile sexual offenders (Zakireh, Ronis, & Knight, 2008), but we cannot assume that sexually abused children will themselves become abusers.

As noted above, Knight and Sims-Knight (2004) have recommended that these traits should be targets of therapeutic intervention. Moreover, "the consistent predictive potency of this model across criminal and community samples supports the hypothesis that a unified theory of sexual coercion can be generated" (Knight & Sims-Knight, 2011, p. 132). The model, as the authors admit, still needs refinement and perhaps modification. However, this empirically based model holds considerable promise in becoming a unified theory for understanding sexual assault and providing a framework for intervention and treatment.

The Groth Typology

Almost 40 years ago, Groth (1979) developed a typology with many similarities to the MTC scheme, but far less complex. The Groth proposal is based on the presumed motivations and aims that underlie almost all rapes committed by adult males and possibly many other sexual assaults, although the distinction was not then made. Groth considered rape a "pseudo-sexual act" in which sex serves merely as a vehicle for the primary motivations of power and aggression. "Rape is never the result simply of sexual arousal that has no other opportunity for gratification. . . . Rape is always a symptom of some psychological dysfunction, either temporary and transient or chronic and repetitive" (Groth, 1979, p. 5). Furthermore, he stated, "Rape is always and foremost an aggressive act" (p. 12). Consequently, he divided it into three major categories: anger rape, power rape, and sadistic rape. Note that a separate Groth classification based on sexual abuse of children will be discussed in the next chapter.

In **anger rape**, the offender uses more force than necessary for compliance and engages in a variety of sexual acts that are particularly degrading or humiliating to the victim. He also expresses his contempt through abusive and profane language. Thus, for the anger rapist, rape is an act of conscious anger and rage—typically toward women—and he expresses his fury physically and verbally. Sex is actually dirty, offensive, and disgusting to him, and this is why he uses it to defile and degrade the victim. Very often, his attacks are prompted by some previous conflict with or humiliation by a significant woman (often a wife, a boss, or a mother). The assault is characterized by considerable physical brutality.

In **power rape**, the assailant seeks to establish power and control over his victim. Thus, the amount of force and threat used depends on the degree of submission shown by the victim. His goal is sexual conquest, and he will try to overcome any resistance. Sexual penetration is his way of asserting identity, authority, potency, mastery, and domination rather than strictly sexual gratification. Often the victim is kidnapped or held captive in some fashion, and she may be subjected to repeated assaults over an extended period of time. The sexual assault is sometimes disappointing to the power rapist because it fails to live up to his frequent fantasies of rape. The third pattern of rape, **sadistic rape**, includes both sexual and aggressive components. In other words, aggression is eroticized. The sadistic rapist experiences sexual arousal and excitement in the victim's maltreatment, torment, distress, helplessness, and suffering. The assault usually involves bondage and torture, and he directs considerable abuse and injury on various areas of the victim's body. Prostitutes, women he considers promiscuous, or women representing symbols of something he wants to punish or destroy often incur the wrath of the sadistic rapist. The victim may be stalked, abducted, abused, and sometimes murdered.

Groth (1979) reports that over half of the offenders evaluated or treated by his agency (at that time the Connecticut Sex Offender Program) were power rapists, 40 percent were anger rapists, and only 5 percent were sadistic rapists. There are many similarities between Groth's scheme and the MTC original typology. The anger rapist is similar to the displaced aggression rapist, the sadistic rapist is similar to the sexual aggressive rapist, and the power rapist shows many commonalities with the compensatory rapist. However, the MTC typology is far more extensive and based on ongoing research. Nevertheless, references to the Groth typology continually appear in clinical literature, leading to the conclusion that it likely forms the basis for classifying sexual offenders for treatment purposes.

TREATMENT OF SEX OFFENDERS

Many sex offenders are highly resistant to changing their deviant behavioral patterns. A wide variety of treatment programs have been tried, but early reviews were not optimistic. A 1994 survey of therapeutic services for sex offenders revealed that there were 710 adult and 684 juvenile treatment programs (Longo, Bird, Stevenson, & Fiske, 1995) compared to 297 adult and 346 juvenile treatment programs in 1985 (Knopp, Rosenberg, & Stevenson, 1986). Despite the increase in treatment programs, the success ratio remained disappointingly low for many years (Camilleri & Quinsey, 2008; Thakker, Collie, Gannon, & Ward, 2008). One of the most devastating early reviews was produced by Furby, Weinrott, and Blackshaw (1989, p. 27), who concluded after assessing research on a range of therapeutic approaches, "There is as yet no evidence that clinical treatment reduces rates of sex reoffenses in general and no appropriate data for assessing whether it may be differentially effective for different types of offenders." However, and more optimistically, meta-analyses have demonstrated that treatment programs based on cognitive-behavioral approaches have shown positive results.

Today, many clinicians believe that the most effective interventions, or treatment methods for offenders (all offenders, not merely sex offenders), are those that follow the three basic principles of risk, need, and responsivity (RNR), which are frequently cited in the psychological treatment literature (Andrews & Bonta, 2010; Andrews, Bonta, & Hoge, 1990; Bonta & Andrews, 2007). "It is generally accepted in the field of offender rehabilitation that treatment programs that adhere to the principles of effective rehabilitation are more effective for reducing criminal recidivism than are programs that fail to adhere to those principles" (Ennis, Buro, & Jung, in press, p. 2).

The first "R" in the RNR model refers to the **risk principle**. It denotes the importance of assessing what is the likelihood that an offender will reoffend. The major goal of treatment and rehabilitation of sex offenders is to eliminate—or at least—significantly reduce recidivism. The first step in treatment and rehabilitation is to assess the risk of reoffending, commonly referred to as risk assessment. Andrews and Bonta (2010) point out that there are two aspects to the risk principle. The first aspect assumes that criminal behavior can be predicted. The second aspect involves the notion that the levels of treatment should match the risk level of the offender. Recall that we covered factors associated with recidivism earlier in the chapter.

A recent and clinically very useful assessment system for predicting recidivism and treatment needs has been proposed by Liam Ennis, Karen Buro, and Sandy Jung (in press). Using the Static-2002R, the researchers were able to identify three distinct groups of sex offenders prone to reoffend. The three groups were distinguished from one another by using statistically derived risk scores. Offenders with the highest risk of reoffending were labeled moderate to high-risk offenders, abbreviated *Mod-Risk offenders*. This group was characterized by a wide range of problems associated with poor social adjustment and antisocial behavior during childhood and adolescence. Typically, they were exposed to high levels of cumulative risk factors during their development. Not only did they demonstrate a more severe criminal history (general criminality) but they also demonstrated emotional neediness in adulthood, and more planning in their sexual assaults. Ennis et al. write, "From the R-N-R perspective, the Mod-High Risk cluster requires the most intensive treatment programming and the most intensive management efforts in the community" (p. 17).

The second and third groups were termed the low to moderate risk and low risk, abbreviated Low-Mod Risk and Low Risk. The differences between the two groups were not large. Specifically, the Low-Mod Risk group was more than 20 years younger than the offenders in the Low Risk group, and reflected a more severe criminal history. The Low Risk cluster, compared to those offenders in Low-Mod Risk group, demonstrated more deviant sexual interests and began their criminal behavior later in their lives.

The "N" in the RNR model refers to need, which is essentially shorthand for criminogenic need. The **criminogenic need principle** encompasses dynamic risk factors that are likely to lead to criminal behavior. ("Criminogenic" means crime producing.) These risk factors are called "dynamic" because they are changeable, as opposed to static risk factors that cannot be changed. Examples of dynamic risk factors include interpersonal relationships at home, school, or work, or employment status. Associations with criminally prone others and substance abuse would represent other dynamic risk examples. Sexual attitudes and beliefs are additional exemplars. In contrast, examples of static risk factors would be crimes committed in the past or past exposure to sexual abuse while growing up. They occurred and remain in a person's background regardless of what happens, currently or in the future. The word "need" is used by Andrews and Bonta (2010) (in the term "criminogenic need") for practical reasons, primarily because it "carries with it the hope that if criminogenic need factors are reduced, the chances of criminal involvement will decrease" (p. 28). Consequently, effective treatment is predicated on the assumption that the risk is dynamic (Olver et al., 2012). One important point that requires mentioning is that age plays a role in the reduction of sexual crimes—with or without treatment. The research literature underscores the fact that increasing age is "associated with a decline in most, if not all, forms of antisocial activity, including sexual offending" (Olver et al., 2012, p. 399). Criminogenic needs change with age.

The last 'R' in the RNR represents the responsivity principle. The **responsivity principle** involves delivering treatment services in a style and mode that is consistent with the ability and learning style of the offender. Offender characteristics such as interpersonal sensitivity, anxiety, verbal intelligence, and cognitive maturity speak to the appropriateness of different modes and styles of treatment service" (Andrews & Bonta, 2010, p. 50).

According to Andrews and Bonta, the most powerful influential approaches available to clinicians are cognitive-behavioral and cognitive social learning strategies. Cognitive-behavioral programs have fared very well when measured against the responsivity principle because they seek to engage the offender actively in his or her own treatment. In a meta-analysis involving 69 studies and covering close to 10,000 sexual offenders, Lösel and Schmucker (2005; Schmucker & Lösel, 2008) found that treatment programs based on cognitive-behavioral principles had positive effects. Likewise, Hanson et al. (2009) and Olver et al. (2012) found that a program's faithfulness to RNR principles was consistently associated with significantly lower recidivism rates in sex offenders.

Other researchers agree: "A recent comprehensive survey of sex offender treatment programs in North America found that the majority of programs tended to be cognitive behavioral and social learning in orientation ..." (Oliver, Nicholaichuk, Gu, & Wong, 2012, p. 397). Hanson, Bourgon, Helmus, and Hodgson (2009) summarize the RNR approach, "...treatments are most likely to be effective when they treat offenders who are likely to reoffend (moderate or higher risk), target characteristics that are related to reoffending (criminogenic needs), and match treatment to the offenders' learning styles and abilities (responsivity; cognitive-behavioral interventions work best" (p. 867).

Interestingly, offenders who are considered low risks of reoffending are not considered good targets for psychological treatment. This is both because they do not need the intensive attention and because scarce resources can best be applied to offenders who need them the most. Low-risk offenders can benefit from support services in the community (e.g., help with finding employment or improving social skills). Moderate- and high-risk offenders, on the other hand, can benefit by psychological treatment that focuses on their criminogenic needs and match the treatment to the offenders' learning style and abilities (responsivity) (Hanson et al., 2009). In summary, we are beginning to turn the corner on effective treatment of adult sex offenders, and many therapists and researchers are more optimistic than they were in the past. In the next chapter, we will discuss the current status of research and treatment on child molesters, female sex offenders, and juvenile sex offenders.

SUMMARY AND CONCLUSIONS

Sexual assault—a broad term that encompasses rape as well as other sexual offenses—is widely believed to be the most underreported serious crime. When we consider the psychological toll it takes on its victims—or survivors—it is not surprising that the vast majority of sexual assaults never come to the attention of police.

Traditionally, both rape and other sexual assaults have been considered almost exclusively a male enterprise, both in their perpetration and in their victimization. Only in 2013 did the federal government in its UCR summary reports begin to include males as victims. Researchers, however, have for some time examined both female and male victimization, as well as sex offending by women and girls. However, most theory building and typologies have been developed on males.

We reviewed statistics on rape and other sexual assaults, as well as available demographic information about both offenders and victims. Reflecting recent research interest, we covered acquaintance rape and campus sexual assault in some detail. Research indicates that some individuals may be more vulnerable to being assaulted than others, either by nature of their demographic characteristics, such as age, or situational characteristics, such as use of alcohol or victimization history. Despite some interest in studying victimization in this manner, researchers are quick to point out that the blame for sexual assault is on the perpetrator, not the victim.

With respect to offenders, they commit their crimes for a variety of reasons. A major motivation appears to be to harm, derogate, or embarrass the victim. Although sexual satisfaction is a component of the offense, attitudes about sex play a major role in carrying out the crime. Some rapists—likely a minority—interpret their behavior as harmless, believing that victims enjoy being dominated. Nevertheless, the effect is invariably the opposite. The psychological and social damages to the victim are incalculable. Sexual assaults by husbands, dates, and acquaintances are more frequent than commonly supposed and there is indication that the psychological damage to the survivor may be even greater than in stranger rape.

Studies of convicted rapists often show a history of committing sexual assaults and other violent actions. Though recidivism is common, some research has found that repeat crimes are just as likely to be nonsexual offenses. General criminality is often found in their backgrounds. Rape and other sexual behavior appear to be due, in part, to the type of socialization experiences the offender has had. He has constructed, from information received from a variety of sources and models, a belief and value system that encourages and justifies the aggressive behavior. The combination of attitudes supportive of rape myths, norms obtained from peers or the media, and disinhibition enabled by the use of alcohol is often cited as the causal factor for many sexual assaults, particularly those committed by dates, acquaintances, or intimate partners.

Stranger rapes are believed to be the least common of all attacks, but they are most likely to involve weapons. Stranger rapists also are more likely than acquaintance rapists to have a history of general criminality.

Several rapist typologies or classification systems have been developed, the most notable being that proposed by the Massachusetts Treatment Center (MTC). Revisions of the MTC rape classification system (the latest being the MTC:R4) testify to its extensive use and continual research. The system encompasses both types of rapists (e.g., displaced aggression) and their motivations (e.g., vindictiveness). MTC researchers also have developed a three-path model of offending, which identifies personality traits that are associated with sex offenders: sexual preoccupation, antisocial, and callous-unemotional. A second classification system, the Groth system, is less complex, less research based, but still often cited in the literature.

The chapter ended with discussion of the treatment of sex offenders—a topic that will be continued in the next chapter, where child molesters and juvenile and female offenders are covered. With increasing evidence that RNR principles are effective with offenders, including sex offenders, treatment providers are more optimistic about the possibility of preventing future offending than in the past. Nevertheless, of all adult sex offenders, rapists are the most difficult to treat, primarily because their behavior is a reflection of both deeply held attitudes and long-standing, antisocial, violent patterns of behavior.

Key Concepts

Anger rape
Compensatory rapists
Criminality theme
Criminogenic need principle
Crossover offending
Date or acquaintance rape
Displaced aggression rapists/displaced anger/anger-retaliation rapists
Expressive sexual aggression
General criminality
Global risk recognition failure
Hostility theme
Impulsive rapist/exploitative rapist
Incest
Instrumental sexual aggression
Marital rape
Opportunistic types
Pervasive anger rapist

Power rape
Rape
Rape by fraud
Rape myths
Responsivity principle
Risk principle
Sadistic rape
Sexual aggressive rapist/sadistic rapist
Sexual assault
Sexual burglary
Sexual exploitation/involvement theme (also pseudo-intimacy theme)
Sexual gratification rapist
Sodomy
Specific risk recognition failure
Statutory rape
Vindictive offender types

Review Questions

1. What is the difference between rape and sexual assault?
2. Contrast the new definition of rape in the UCR with the legacy definition.
3. Review and discuss vulnerability factors for sexual assault.
4. Review demographic and psychological factors of rapists.
5. Define and provide example of rape myths.
6. Does pornography play a crucial role in sex crimes against women and children? Briefly support your answer with reference to research findings.
7. Compare and contrast the MTC and Groth classifications or rapists.
8. How do RNR principles apply in the treatment of sex offenders?

13

Sexual Abuse of Children and Youth

CHAPTER OBJECTIVES

- Define pedophilia, child sexual abuse, and child sex offending.
- Review the prevalence and forms of child sex abuse.
- Discuss psychological effects on victims.
- Describe the key characteristics of child sex offenders.
- Summarize what is known about recidivism rates of adult and juvenile child sex offenders.
- Review the research literature on classification systems of child sex offenders.
- Review typologies of female child sex offenders.
- Discuss contemporary research on Internet-facilitated child pornography.
- Discuss sex trafficking and its prevention.
- Identify treatment approaches to reducing child sex offender recidivism.

In 2009, the world was shocked at the revelation that an Austrian citizen had held his daughter as a sexual captive in the basement of the family home for 24 years. She had borne seven children, who had apparently been raised as her younger brothers and sisters. Later that year, he confessed to a range of sexual crimes against his daughter and his other children. In the same year, a 28-year-old Sunday school teacher in California was arrested and charged in the abduction and death of an eight-year-old girl; shortly thereafter, child sexual abuse was added to the charges against her. In 2012, reverberations from clergy abuse scandals that were publicized in the 1990s continued, with victims coming forward and more claims made against adults who participated or covered up the crimes. In 2015, a nationally known high school debate coach was charged with possessing, receiving, and producing child pornography after he allegedly obtained nude photos of teenage boys via text messaging and the Internet. As these anecdotes illustrate, sex crimes against children or adolescents run the gamut from rape to solicitation of nude images.

Pedophilia (from the Greek word for child love) is the clinical term that is sometimes used interchangeably with crimes like child molestation and child sexual abuse. We must emphasize at the outset, however, that pedophilia is a clinical condition that is not necessarily accompanied by action. When criminal action *is* involved, even though we may refer to the offender as a "pedophile," this is not the official term. That is, the person is prosecuted for child sexual assault, child molestation, child sexual exploitation, distributing child pornography, or any one of a number of other sexual crimes against children. Essentially, "pedophilia" is a psychological or psychiatric condition that may require treatment. It is included in the DSM-5 as a lifelong mental disorder, though it may fluctuate, increase, or decrease with age (American Psychiatric Association, 2013).

Pedophilia is defined in a variety of ways. The DSM-5 refers to it as a condition in which "over a period of at least 6 months, recurrent, intense sexually arousing fantasies, sexual urges, or behaviors involving sexual activity with a prepubescent child or children (generally age 13 years or younger) occur" (American Psychiatric Association, 2013, p. 697). Note that the definition contains the terms "fantasies" and "urges," which—by themselves—are *not* criminal unless there is an accompanying action (behavior) that is against the law. The DSM-5 further specifies that some pedophiles are sexually attracted only to children (the exclusive type), whereas others are sexually attracted to both children and adults (nonexclusive type).

According to Finkelhor and Araji (1986), pedophilia is an adult's conscious sexual interest in prepubertal children. One of two behaviors signifies that interest. Either the adult has had some sexual contact with a child or the adult has masturbated to sexual fantasies or images involving children. Although the second behavior is not a crime, criminal behavior may have been involved in the procuring of the images, such as downloading child pornography or soliciting the images from a child or adolescent. We will address these topics later in the chapter.

Occasionally, researchers extend the definition of pedophilia to include ages 13 through 15, but most literature uses the term **hebephilia** for sexual contact by adults with young adolescents. However, the distinction between hebephilia and pedophilia does not appear to be clinically meaningful (Blanchard, Klassen, Dickey, Kuban, & Blak, 2001), so hebephilia is usually not considered a distinct, diagnostic category.

Traditionally, most nonclinical definitions of pedophilia were restricted to sexual contact between an adult and child who are not closely related. Sexual acts between members of a family when at least one participant is a minor has traditionally been labeled incest or **intrafamilial** (within the family) **child molestation** and is most commonly perpetrated by men who molest their sexually immature daughters or stepdaughters (Rice & Harris, 2002). Sexual contact with immature family members by individuals from outside the family is called **extrafamilial child molestation**. See **Table 13-1** for terms and definitions.

TABLE 13-1	Terms Used in Research on Child Molestation*
Term	**Definition**
Extrafamilial child molestation	Sexual contact with a minor child by someone *outside* the immediate family.
Infrafamilial child molestation	Sexual contact with a minor child by someone *within* the immediate family.
Pedophilia	For some researchers and clinicians, the term refers to strong sexual *attraction* toward children. Others use the term to refer to sexual *contact* with children.
Pedophile	Someone with strong sexual attraction toward children or someone who has frequent sexual contact with children.
Incest	Sexual activity between individuals of close blood relationship (e.g., brother and sister or parent and biological child) that is prohibited by law or custom.
Child sexual abuse	Refers to any sexual activity involving a child that provides gratification or stimulation to an adult or older adolescent.
Child molester	Largely accepted term for someone who has sexual contact or sexually abuses a minor child. In this context, it is used interchangeably with child sexual offender.
Hebephilia	Sexual contact by adults with young adolescents.
Paraphilia	Sexual disorders in which sexual arousal occurs almost exclusively in the presence of inappropriate objects or unusual sexual practices or fantasies.

*These terms are not necessarily used in statutes or other legal contexts.

A term closely related is the more all-encompassing **paraphilia**, which covers other cognitions and behaviors in addition to those relating to children. Paraphilia denotes any intense and persistent sexual interests other than sexual interest in genital stimulation or preparatory fondling with consenting human partners (American Psychiatric Association, 2013). Examples of paraphilic disorders include repetitive sexual activity involving real or simulated suffering or humiliation, such as whipping or bondage; strong preferences for nonhuman objects, such as animals or underclothing or shoes of the opposite sex; touching or rubbing against a nonconsenting individual (frotteurism); exposing genitals to nonconsenting persons (exhibitionism); or spying on others engaging in private activities (voyeurism).

In this chapter, we will *not* use the clinical term **pedophilia** when referring to illegal sexual actions against children, ranging from sexual touching to penetration. Instead, we will use "child sex offenses" or "child sexual abuse" for these actions. We also cover the exploitation of children and adolescents by accessing child pornography. As emphasized above, it is not illegal to have the disorder that is pedophilia or to have pedophiliac fantasies and thoughts, and it cannot be assumed that pedophiliacs act on these fantasies or urges. However, it is relevant that 40 to 50 percent of those who commit sex crimes against child victims have pedophilic interests (Seto, 2009; Sigre-Leirós, Carvalho, & Nobre, 2015). We will discuss this topic in more detail when we cover **emotional congruence with children** later in the chapter.

INCIDENCE AND PREVALENCE OF CHILD SEX ABUSE

As with sexual offenses in general, a strong caveat pertaining to the statistics is necessary. Data on child sexual abuse are difficult to obtain, because there are no central or national objective recording systems for tabulating sexual offenses against children. Sex crimes as a group have the lowest rates of reporting of all violent crimes (Terry & Tallon, 2004). Furthermore, similar to cases of elder abuse, the alleged sexual abuse of children is often referred to a human service agency and may never appear in official crime statistics.

According to the Department of Health and Human Services (DHHS) (2014), approximately 61,000 children who were believed to be sexually abused received child protective services in 2013. Among these victims, nearly 30 percent were abused at age seven or younger. The DHHS defines sexual abuse as engaging a child in sexual acts that may include fondling, rape, and exposing the child to other sexual activities. The numbers reported by DHHS, however, certainly underestimate the actual number of sexually abused children in the United States.

According to David Finkelhor and his associates (2014), "The experience of sexual abuse/assault in childhood and adolescence is very prevalent" (p. 332). (The terms "abuse" and "assault" are used interchangeably.) The best data available indicate that 1 in 4 girls and 1 in 20 boys in the United States have been sexually abused by the time they reach their 17th birthday. Perhaps more striking is the finding that in most of these assaults, the perpetrators were not adults. Over half of the total estimate of sexual offenses against children and adolescents were at the hands of juvenile perpetrators, many of them acquaintance peers (Finkelhor, Shattuck, Turner, & Hamby, 2014). If only sexual assaults by adults are tabulated, the rate of sexual abuse/assault drops to 1 in 9 girls and 1 in 53 boys.

From a national survey of about 1,200 American males (Finkelhor & Lewis, 1988), it was estimated that between 5 and 10 percent of the male population has engaged in or will engage in child sexual abuse at some time in their lives. In a more recent online survey of both men and women, Wurtele, Simons, and Moreno (2014) discovered that 6 percent of men and 2 percent of women indicated some likelihood of having sex with a child if they were guaranteed they would not be caught or punished. In another anonymous survey, about 4 percent of college-aged men admitted having sexual contact with a prepubescent girl (Ahlers et al., 2011). It is important to note, however, that these figures may include a one-time incident that—although still to be condemned—may not represent the offender's usual behavior and would not qualify him as a child sex abuser for purposes of this chapter. For example, a 14-year-old babysitter who sexually fondles a 3-year-old might never commit another similar offense, but may later self-report that behavior to researchers, either out of guilt or just because anonymity is guaranteed. Nevertheless, these and other data indicate that children are sexually victimized at levels that far exceed those reported for adults (Finkelhor & Dziuba-Leatherman, 1994; Finkelhor et al., 2014).

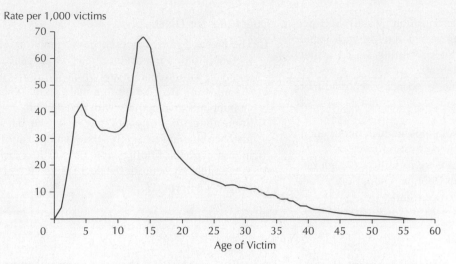

FIGURE 13-1 Age Distribution of Victims of Sexual Assault *Source:* Snyder, H. N. (2000). Sexual assault of young children as reported to law enforcement: Victim, incident, and offender characteristics. Washington, DC: U.S. Department of Justice. Bureau of Justice Statistics.

Nationwide tabulations of the number of victims are equally difficult to obtain. For example, the National Crime Victimization Survey only collects data from victims older than age 12, thus neglecting the victimization of young children. Moreover, only about one-third of the children who are sexually victimized report it to anyone (Finkelhor, 1979). In a nationally representative sample of 2,030 children ages 2 to 17 years, Finkelhor, Ormrod, Turner, and Hamby (2005) discovered that 1 in 12 children or youth had experienced a sexual victimization during the year of the survey (see **Figure 13-1**). And, in recent surveys of juveniles held in public and private correctional facilities, approximately 9 to 12 percent who stayed in a facility from 7 to 12 months reported sexual victimization by peers or staff members (Beck, Cantor, Hartge, & Smith, 2013; Beck, Harrison, & Guerino, 2010). (See **Box 13-1**.)

CONTEMPORARY ISSUES

BOX 13-1   Sexual Abuse: The Shame of Juvenile Corrections

Secure juvenile facilities should be safe harbors for juveniles, even if they were adjudicated for serious crimes. This is far from reality in some juvenile detention and treatment centers nationwide. Both anecdotal accounts and empirical research indicate that assaults, including sexual assaults, happen far too frequently in these institutional settings. Although sexual assaults may be perpetrated by other juveniles, they are also perpetrated by correctional staff.

Sexual contact between adults and juveniles in juvenile facilities is often portrayed as consensual. Whether the juvenile is male or female, he or she may be considered manipulative and eager to obtain favors from his or her captors and thus inclined to initiate the contact. However, with an uneven power relationship, sexual contact between an adult and a confined youth is never truly consensual. In addition, the staff member may groom the adolescent, such as by promising desired items, providing drugs or alcohol, or offering protection from other juveniles.

The *National Survey of Youth in Custody* (Beck, Cantor, Hartge, & Smith, 2013) produced disturbing findings on sexual victimization in state, local, and private juvenile facilities nationwide. As required by law, researchers from the Bureau of Justice Statistics obtained self-reports from 8,707 adjudicated offenders, 91 percent of whom were males.

Among the highlights from the report are the following:

- About 9.5 percent of the youth said they had experienced one or more incidents of sexual victimization by staff or another youth over the past 12 months, a decrease of about 2.5 percent from a similar 2008 to 2009 survey.
- Victimization by staff was higher than victimization by other youth.
- 8.2 percent of males and 2.8 percent of females reported sexual activity with staff.
- Youth-on-youth victimization was far greater (10.3%) for youth who identified as gay, lesbian, bisexual, or other than for heterosexual youth (1.5%).

(continued)

- Of youth who reported victimization by staff, 89.1 percent were males reporting sexual activity with female staff; 3.0 percent were males reporting sexual activity with both male and female staff.
- Most victims of staff sexual misconduct reported more than one incident; nearly 1 in 5 reported 11 or more incidents.
- Of the victims of staff sexual misconduct, about one in five reported physical force or threat of force.
- Thirteen juvenile facilities were identified as high rate; these included facilities in Georgia, Ohio, South Carolina, Arizona, Texas, Iowa, and Illinois.

Questions for Discussion

1. The above figures represent just a small amount of data included in this important report. Obtain the public document and comment on any of its additional findings.
2. Comment on the finding that male youth reported a high amount of sexual activity with female staff.
3. Some allegations of youth may be untrue, but some youth may be reluctant to report sexual victimization. With this in mind, are the findings any more or less disturbing?
4. What might account for the decrease in victimization from the previous report?

The National Incident-Based Reporting System (NIBRS) has the potential to provide better information on the prevalence of sexual assaults of young children. Using NIBRS data between 1991 and 1996, Snyder (2006) found that 34 percent of the victims of sexual assault reported to law enforcement were under age 12. Most disturbing was the finding that one of every seven victims of sexual assault (14% of the victims) was under age six.

It is well recognized in the criminology literature that female adolescents with persistent antisocial behavior as well as adult female offenders have often experienced child sexual abuse (Ullman, 1999, 2007). Among nonoffenders, the figures are also sobering. Russell (1984) surveyed 930 randomly selected female residents of San Francisco during 1978. The purpose of the project was to obtain an estimate of the incidence and prevalence of rape and other forms of sexual assault, including the amount of sexual abuse respondents experienced as children. Twelve percent of the women said they had been sexually abused by a relative before the age of 14. Twenty-nine percent reported at least one experience of sexual abuse by a nonrelative before reaching the age of 14. Overall, 28 percent of the 930 women reported at least one incident of sexual abuse before reaching the age of 14.

Prison data also give us an indication of the extent of the problem. Two-thirds of all prisoners in state prisons convicted of rape or sexual assault had committed their crime against a child or adolescent, and in most cases the victim was female (Greenfeld, 1996). Approximately 60 percent of those convicted of child molestation had victimized children younger than 13 years.

Other data obtained from prisoners point to the extent of the problem and suggest that sex offenders have numerous victims. Some time ago, Abel and his colleagues (Abel, Becker, Murphy, & Flanagan, 1981) reported that incarcerated homosexual child sex offenders (CSOs) had, on the average 31 victims, while heterosexual CSOs had an average of 62 victims. A Dutch study (Bernard, 1975) reported that at least half of its respondents claimed sexual contacts with at least 10 or more children. Fourteen percent of the sample—which included both arrested and nonarrested CSOs—admitted to sexual contacts with more than 50, and 6 percent to contacts with between 100 and 300 children. Fifty-six percent of this sample indicated they had one or more "regular" sexual contacts with children. Fully 90 percent asserted that they did not want to stop their sexual activities against children.

While some of the above studies may appear very dated, nothing in the recent research literature suggests that this problem has been attenuated. In summary, the amount of sexual abuse and violence against children is staggering. In a study of worldwide prevalence, child sexual abuse is estimated to be 11.8 percent, or 118 victims per 1,000 children (Stoltenborgh, van Izendoorn, Euser & Bakermans-Kranenburg, 2011). The global estimated prevalence for girls is 18 percent and about 8 percent for boys. Similar worldwide prevalence rates were reported by Pereda, Guilera, Forns, and Gómez-Benito (2009), who found a child sexual abuse prevalence of 19.2 percent for girls and 9.9 percent for boys.

Although child sex offending is primarily committed by males, it is, by no means, exclusively a male offense. In the United States, national arrest data report that women were involved in 1.9 percent of forcible rape arrests, and 7.8 percent of forcible sexual offense arrests in 2013

(Federal Bureau of Investigation, 2014a). These data very likely underrepresent the "true" proportion and numbers of sexual assaults attributable to women. Although the above statistics refer to all offenses (against both adults and children), a significant number of victims of female offenders are children under age 12 (Johansson-Love & Fremouw, 2009). For example, Vandiver and Walker (2002) reported that 50 percent of the victims in their sample of female sex offenders were between the ages of 11 and 16, and 24 percent were in the 4 to 10 age range. In another study, Ferguson and Cricket Meehan (2005) discovered that 68 percent of the victims in their sample of female sex offenders were between 12 and 16 years of age, and 15 percent of the victims were under the age of 12 years. We will continue to include female CSOs with male CSOs throughout the next few sections of the chapter.

Situational and Victimization Characteristics

In a comprehensive study, Williams and Bierie (2015) examined approximately 20 years' worth of data derived from the NIBRS that included several hundred thousand incidents from thousands of police departments across 37 states. They found that men who sexually abused child victims were more likely to target stepchildren or distant relatives, whereas women were more likely to target their own biological children or children for whom they provide care. Similar findings were also reported by Johansson and Fremouw (2009) and West et al. (2011). Cortoni (2015) notes that, according to stereotyped gender roles, a "normal" woman simply would not wish to hurt a child. The stereotype further assumes that child sexual abuse perpetrated by a female is either the result of male coercion or several mental health problems. "These type of explanations fit comfortably within early theories of female offending more generally that described criminalized women as either emotionally disturbed, maladapted to their feminine role, physiologically or psychologically abnormal, or as choosing to become masculine in rebellion against this 'natural' feminine role" (Cortoni, 2015, p. 232). As Cortoni observes, the notion that sexual offending behavior by women is somehow "unnatural" or "worse" than the identical sexual offending by men must be challenged.

Williams and Bierie (2015) found that women appear to be far less discriminating in the gender of their victims; they commit sex offenses equally against both male and female victims. More specifically, the researchers found that males offended against females in nearly 90 percent of their incidents, whereas, for female sex offenders, half of their victims were female. However, the researchers believe that these findings could partly be explained by the fact that women are, in some instances, coerced to participate by male accomplices. That is, male accomplices frequently impose their own victim preference (females) on the women with whom they offend. Research is beginning to find support for these hypotheses.

For example, a study on solo and co-offending female sex offenders by Vandiver (2006) sheds some light on this topic. Vandiver noted that about half (46%) of female offenders arrested for a sex offense had male co-offenders. Her project included a cross-national sample of 123 female solo offenders and 104 women who were co-offenders. The co-offenders were significantly more likely than the solo offenders to have been arrested for nonsexual offenses prior to the sex offense, and they had sexually offended more than once. Co-offenders also were more likely to abuse female victims compared to male victims. Solo female offenders, on the other hand, were more likely to target male victims. It also appears that the co-offending female is often in an abusive relationship with the co-offender (either a spouse or intimate partner). In many incidents, the male co-offender forces the woman to participate in the behavior, either through fear or threats to withdraw any form of intimacy with her.

Other researchers have found that about one-quarter of female sex offenders fall in this category of being co-offenders with males (Gannon et al., 2014). Wijkman, Bijleveld, and Hendriks (2010, 2014) found that nearly two-thirds of juvenile female sex offenders in their sample were co-offenders. Although most co-offenders of adult female sex offenders are spouses or intimate partners, most co-offenders of the adolescent females were acquaintances or friends.

Still, there are a significant number of female sex offenders without accomplices who target both male and female victims (Gannon et al., 2014; West et al., 2011). One explanation is that solo female sex offenders tend to abuse those with whom they have regular contact (male and/or female), rather than specifically seeking out their victims (West et al., 2011). The mixed-gender offending falls into the category of crossover offending, discussed in the previous chapter.

Researchers describe **crossover** as "engaging in more than one type of sex-offending behavior or victimizing individuals from different relationship categories, genders, or age groups" (Levenson, Becker, & Morin, 2008, p. 44). For example in one early study (Abel, Becker, Cunningham-Rathner, Mittelman, & Rouleau, 1988), 20 percent of the male offenders reported offending against both male and female victims, and 42 percent said they had victims from several age groups (under 14 years old, 14 to 17, and some more than 17). They also selected victims from inside and outside the family. Sim and Proeve (2010) found a considerable amount of crossover in their study of 128 adult male child sexual offenders. More than half of the offenders exhibited crossover in at least one of three domains: victim age, gender, or relationship to the offender. Their data highlight the point that crossovers are not rare among adult offenders who sexually molest children. The researchers discovered the highest degree of crossover (48%) occurred in the victim age domain, similar to the Abel et al. (1988) research. They also found 20 percent crossover for gender type and a 30 percent crossover for relationship to victim. Sim and Proeve conclude: "It is unclear whether crossover in victim type is consistent with offenders' sexual preferences, or that they crossover victim type because their preferred victim type is not available and another type of victim is available" (p. 411). It is clear that crossover research is one area that needs further investigation, as it has implications for understanding CSOs.

GAINING ACCESS TO CHILDREN.   Two important studies on how adult and juvenile CSOs gain access to child victims, arrange to be alone with them, and avoid interference from others were conducted by Wortley and Smallbone (2006) and more recently by Leclerc and Felson (in press). In the Wortley and Smallbone study, subjects were 169 convicted CSOs who admitted their crime and agreed to provide detailed self-report data on their psychosocial/psychosexual histories and their offending behavior. The researchers found that the vast majority of the CSOs (93.5%) sexually abused their own child (intrafamilial offender) or a child they knew (extrafamilial). Wortley and Smallbone identified several strategies adult extrafamilial CSOs used for gaining access to children for sexual contact. The most common approach was to make friends with the parent or caretaker of the child and then spend time with the child while the parent or caretaker was present. Many also volunteered to help the parent or caretaker around the house. Essentially, the CSOs tried to normalize their own presence and therefore disarm parental concern of their intentions (Leclerc & Felson, in press). Eventually, they offered to babysit the child or take the child to a game or playground. Some extrafamilial offenders even tried to establish a romantic relationship with a single mother in an effort to gain access to the child.

Wortley and Smallbone also discovered that adult CSOs most frequently used a "domestic setting" to commit their sexual abuse. They defined a domestic setting as either the home of both the victim and the offender, the home of the victim to which the offender had access, or the home of the offender (or a friend) where the victim had been taken. The study revealed that a vast majority of all child sexual offenses (intrafamilial or extrafamilial) occurred in the home of the child or the offender. Public settings, such as parks, playgrounds, amusement parks, or malls, are rarely used by CSOs for their offending behavior; this disputes the usual concern of parents regarding predatory offenders.

LeClerc and Felson, in their study of adolescent CSOs, followed the model of the Wortley and Smallbone study of adult CSOs. Their sample consisted of 116 adolescent males (ages between 13 and 17) who had committed at least one sexual offense against a child (younger than 12 years of age and at least 3 years younger than themselves). All participants were undergoing treatment for having committed a sexual offense and were told their participation was completely voluntary. Leclerc and Felson found considerable similarity between adolescent and adult CSOs in how they managed to set up the opportunity to sexually abuse the child victim. Adolescent CSOs found victims through babysitting or at a friend's home, and began to spend time with the child through activities (watching TV, playing video games together, walking the child to school) while the parent or caretaker was present or aware of the activity. Similar to the adult offender, the adolescent offender volunteered to help the parent or caregiver around the house and made friends with the parent or caregiver. Adolescent CSOs used their own home or another home for sexual contact, probably taking advantage of parents working or away. As noted by the researchers, the findings emphasize the central role of parental awareness, monitoring, and supervision for preventing child sexual abuse.

Incest

Many parents believe that strangers (rather than family members) pose the greatest threat to their children, but in some cases the perpetrator is the adult male in their own family. Stroebel and her associates (2013) examined the risk factors in father–daughter incest. (Note that incest, as discussed in this section, is different from incest as defined in the UCR. For official recording purposes, the crime involves two adults who would be legally prohibited from marriage because of their relationship. In the UCR, sexual contact involving a child victim is counted as a rape or other sexual assault, depending upon the nature of the attack.)

The Stroebel et al. study collected data from over 2,000 female participants via an anonymous computer-assisted self-interview. The research group identified four potential risk factors that may lead to father–daughter sexual abuse. The strongest risk factor was a relationship between the two parents that is characterized by conflict and abusive behavior. This parental relationship increased the likelihood of father–daughter sexual abuse by five times. Another risk factor was family-tolerated reciprocal father–daughter nudity; this doubled the risk of father–daughter abuse. Two additional risk factors were low maternal affection for the child and low parental affection for one another.

Very little empirical research has been conducted on sibling incest (Griffe et al., in press). Mother against child sexual abuse will be discussed under the sections on the characteristics of female sex offenders.

Types of Sexual Contact

The behavior associated with child sex offending (for both male and female offenders) is usually limited to caressing the child's body, fondling the child's genitals, and/or inducing the child to manipulate the adult's genitals (Peter, 2009; Williams & Bierie, 2015). Penile or inanimate object penetration (vaginal or anal) is apparently involved in only a small proportion of the total number of offenses (Seto, 2008). The form of the sexual contact seems to depend on three factors: (1) the degree to which the offender had previous nonsexual interactions with children; (2) the nature of the relationship between the child and the offender; and (3) the ages of both the child and the offender. Offenders who have had limited interaction with children are more likely to perform or to expect genital–genital and oral–genital contact, rather than to indulge only in caressing or fondling. Furthermore, the more familiar the offender and the victim are with one another, the greater the tendency for genital–genital or oral–genital contact. In reference to age factors, sex offenders often discover their interest in young children during adolescence. Although it is normal for young children to be interested in seeing peers nude, pedophiles and sex offenders remain strongly attracted to young children long after their own childhood.

There is some disagreement about the extent to which CSOs harm the child physically or use physical force. According to most research, CSOs do not usually use overt physical coercion. Male CSOs, for example, tend to use gifts as bribes (Williams & Bierie, 2015). They later justify their behavior by saying the victim did not resist. Female CSOs may take the opportunity to sexually abuse during normal activities of bathing, changing clothes, and other caregiving activities. McCaghy (1967) found no evidence of any kind of coercion, verbal or physical, in three-fourths of the child molestation cases he examined. Research by Groth and his colleagues (Groth, Hobson, & Gary, 1982) supports these findings. Lanyon (1986), summarizing the research, concluded that violence is involved in about 10 to 15 percent of child sexual abuse cases. The research in this area dates back over 25 years, however, and may not reflect the current reality.

PSYCHOLOGICAL EFFECTS OF CHILD SEXUAL VICTIMIZATION

Research indicates strongly that any form of sexual abuse in childhood produces long-term interpersonal, social, and psychological problems in many children, adolescents, and adults (Cantón-Cortés, Cortés, & Cantón, 2015; Domhardt, Münzer, Fegert, & Goldbeck, 2015; Hillberg, Hamilton-Glachritsis, & Dixon, 2011). Some of these behavioral problems even extend to preschoolers (Hébert, Langevin, & Bernier, 2013; Langevin, Hébert, & Cossette, 2015). "The children themselves report more sadness and feeling of isolation compared to non-abused children" (Langevin et al., 2015, p. 2). Some researchers find that male victims may suffer more severe outcomes than female victims (Hillberg et al., 2011; Putnam, 2003; Ullman, 2003). Reports of depression, guilt, feelings of inferiority, substance abuse, suicidality, anxiety, chronic tension, sleep problems, and fears and phobias are common in both male and female victims, however. Depression and PTSD are the symptoms most commonly reported among adolescents and adults who were molested as children (Gospodarevskaya, 2013; Wherry, Baldwin, Junco, & Floyd, 2013). Some research data reveal, for instance, that 30 to 40 percent of individuals who experienced sexual abuse in childhood report a lifetime history of depression, compared with 10 to 20 percent of individuals with no history of child sexual abuse (Musliner & Singer, 2014).

Furthermore, many survivors of child sexual abuse will never tell their stories or will delay revealing the incident(s) (Schönbucher, Maier, Mohler-Kuo, Schnyder, & Landolt, 2012; Tener & Murphy, 2015). Some research (Hébert, Tourigny, Cyr, McDuff, & Joly, 2009) suggests that one in five survivors never disclosed childhood sexual abuse, and approximately 60 percent delayed disclosure for over five years after the first episode.

Research indicates that there are many different reactions to sexual abuse, and some sexually abused individuals retain normal levels of functioning (Domhardt et al., 2015; Negriff, Schneiderman, Smith, Schreyer, & Trickett, 2014). Negriff et al. (2014) also emphasize that there is substantial variability in the sexual abuse experiences of the victims. Moreover, they write: "Clearly, combining all of the sexually abused youth into one group discounts the nuances of their experiences and the impact these different characteristics may have on the development of subsequent problems" (p. 269).

In their careful review of the research literature on child sexual abuse, Browne and Finkelhor (1986) concluded that (1) younger children appear to be somewhat more vulnerable to trauma than older children, (2) the closer the relationship between offender and victim the greater the trauma, and (3) the greater the force used the greater the trauma. They also maintained, however, that there is no conclusive support for the contention that the longer and more frequent the abuse, the greater the trauma. Nor is there any clear evidence that traumas are related to the type of sexual abuse (e.g., penetration, fondling, fellatio, cunnilingus). This suggests that "mild" abuse may be as traumatizing as penetration, especially if the victim is young and closely related to the offender. The Browne and Finkelhor review also suggests that victims of child sexual abuse are more likely than nonvictims to be sexually assaulted again as adults.

CHARACTERISTICS OF CHILD SEX OFFENDERS

Most estimates of the distribution of CSOs in the general population are derived from arrest or prison data, or from anonymous self-report data. In reference to arrest and prison data—and as noted at the beginning of the chapter—offenders may be arrested and prosecuted under a variety of statutes and for a variety of offenses, including child rape, aggravated assault, sodomy, incest, indecent exposure, or lewd and lascivious behavior. In the UCR summary report statistics (SRS), rape of children is now included under rape data, which includes the age of the victim. Other sex offenses against children (e.g., fondling) are counted only if someone is arrested. The NIBRS, however, includes more detailed information about all sex offenses against children (if they come to the attention of police).

Prentky, Knight, and Lee (1997) conclude from their extensive research on the subject that the classification and diagnosis of CSOs are complicated by a high degree of variability among individuals in reference to personal characteristics, life experiences, criminal histories, and reasons or motivations for offending. Some CSOs offend in a persistent and versatile fashion. That is, they offend frequently, and their offending careers extend over many years. Moreover, they may target victims of both genders across all ages. In many ways, they may be similar to Moffitt's life course persistent offender. On the other hand, at the other end of the offending continuum, there are some CSOs who offend infrequently, for brief periods during their offending history, and only target specific gender and age characteristics of their victims. Essentially, there is no single "profile" that accurately describes all CSOs, or for that matter, all sex offenders. In addition, we stress that no one single risk factor described below will necessarily lead to a person becoming a CSO. The best approach is to consider a combination of these factors—cumulative risk—as potentially leading to child sex offending.

Age and Gender

Although there is considerable age variability, it is well documented that adult male CSOs tend to be older, on average, than male rapists whose victims are adults (Hanson, 2001). Henceforth, when we use the term "rapist," it will refer to offenders of adult victims. It should be understood, though, that some CSOs also rape their victims. In their studies of male CSOs, Smallbone and Wortley (2000, 2001) found that the mean self-reported age of first sexual contact with a child was 32 years. By comparison, rapists tend to begin sexually assaulting in their early 20 or younger. Similarly, Francis and his associates (2014) found that CSOs had late adult onset of sexual offending, whereas early-onset sex offending was associated with rapists. One explanation for the late onset of adult male CSOs may be due to the observation that the early thirties is the age when many men are assuming child care responsibilities and other supervisory roles with children, resulting in more opportunity to offend (Wortley & Smallbone, 2006).

Vandiver and Walker (2002) report the majority of female CSOs committed their first sexual offense at around age 31. Again, we stress that there are many exceptions concerning when CSOs begin offending, but, on average, the above data have been supported by the available research.

Juvenile sex offenders (JSOs) also represent a heterogeneous population and defy any unitary profile or simple description. They come from all ethnic, racial, religious, and socioeconomic groups. JSOs (both male and female) mostly victimized children. Several studies show that JSOs account for approximately 20 percent of all sexual assaults and possibly as much as 50 percent of all child sexual abuse cases (Barbaree & Marshall, 2006; Keelan & Fremouw, 2013; Leclerc & Felson, in press).

A number of studies have contrasted juvenile child molesters with juvenile rapists. For example, van Wijk, van Horn, Bullens, Bijleveld, and Doreleijers (2005) discovered that juvenile child molesters demonstrate significantly more social isolation than juvenile rapists because of poorly developed social skills and very limited interactions with peers. This and other research indicates that those youngsters who molest children (individuals at least four or five years younger in age than the perpetrator) are introverted and rejected by peers from an early age. The majority of their victims (more than 60%) are younger than 12 years, and two-thirds of these young victims are younger than six (Veneziano & Veneziano, 2002). Ryan, Miyoshi, Metzner, Krugman, and Fryer (1996) found that 63 percent of the victims of juvenile molesters were younger than nine years. Adolescent rapists, on the other hand, are more likely to select victims their own age or older (Veneziano & Veneziano, 2002).

A study by Daversa and Knight (2007) identified at least two major types of JSOs, which were primarily CSOs. One type denotes those sexually offending adolescents who are described as submissive, sexually inadequate, dependent, interpersonally inadequate, and socially isolated. They are also less aggressive in their sexual encounters with children. The second type refers to adolescent offenders who are coercive and aggressive, and who sexually assault a cross section of children, peer-aged, and adult victims. In many ways, these aggressive, coercive offenders display the characteristics of psychopathy. These psychopathic CSOs tend to be quick tempered and impulsive and are more likely to engage in a variety of antisocial behavior besides sexual offenses. Furthermore, they often have been the victims of far more childhood abuse than adolescent offenders who engage in fondling or nonpenetration sexual contact with children.

Selection of Victims

CSOs tend to be specialists, and rapists tend to be generalists (Seto, Kingston, & Stephens, 2015). In fact, most chronic criminal offenders are generalists rather than specialists (Wortley & Smallbone, 2014). Generalists engage in a variety of sexual and nonsexual crimes; specialists engage mostly in one type of crime. "Specialization in sexual offending refers to the presence of a sustained pattern of offending where sex offences are predominant" (Lussier, Van Den Berg, Bijleveld, & Hendriks, 2012, p. 1576). CSOs, as a group, tend to focus their offending on sexual abuse of children. Some adult sex offenders prefer victimizing adolescents rather than children. However, these offenders often demonstrate crossover sexual patterns. That is, the age of victim makes little difference in their offending patterns, but they still qualify as specialists because their offending is largely sexual in nature.

A majority of JSOs victimize children (Kemper & Kistner, 2007; Seto et al., 2015). There is also evidence indicating that JSOs who sexually victimize peers or adults are more likely to have a more extensive criminal history compared to JSOs who victimize children (Seto et al., 2015). Therefore, peer-victimizing JSOs tend to be generalists in their offending careers.

According to Mann, Hanson, and Thornton (2010), those children targeted by male CSOs do not show physical cues typically indicative of the biological ability to mate and reproduce. "These include maturity in skin texture, degree of body and pubic hair, smell, body shape, musculature, and breast and genital development" (p. 99). Kanters et al. (in press) have proposed that CSOs are not only sexually attracted to the immature physical appearance of children, but they are also drawn to their submissive nature. That is, children are perceived by many CSOs as more reliable, accepting, compliant, and able to be trusted. Using a small sample of child sex abusers, rapists, and nonsexual offenders, the research discovered some support for their hypothesis: CSOs exhibited more sexual preference to submissiveness than rapists. However, considerably more research is warranted before conclusions can be drawn.

Contrary to public belief, CSOs rarely seek children they do not know (Seto et al., 2015). A vast majority of CSOs prefer acquaintances or relatives. Stranger abductions of children for sexual purposes, though extremely frightening, are far less common than assumed.

Backgrounds

Many studies have indicated that rapists with adult victims and male CSOs have distinct developmental, criminal, and clinical histories (Hamdi & Knight, 2012). For example, a frequent finding is that rapists and violent sex offenders have been exposed to a cycle of violence (Harris, Rice, Quinsey, & Cormier, 2015). That is, violent sex offenders commit their offenses because they also have been victims of sexual abuse. Although this appears to be the case for rapists, the evidence confirming the fact that male CSOs were generally sexually abused remains inconclusive or debatable (Harris et al., 2015). Some were abused, but many were not. It is probably safe to conclude, however, that sexual, emotional, and physical abuse probably play some role in the development of child sexual abusive behavior (especially if it violent), but it may only represent some of the many cumulative risk factors that lead to CSO behavior.

Recent findings in other studies indicate that women who become sexual abusers may have experienced more physical, emotional, and sexual abuse than female nonsexual offenders (Levenson, Willis, & Prescott, 2015; Strickland, 2008; van der Put, van Vugt, Stams, & Hendriks, 2014). Some studies have reported that from 70 to 100 percent of female sex offenders have experienced sexual abuse (van der Put et al., 2014). In addition, female sex offenders often come from severely deprived backgrounds, such as poor living conditions, food deprivation, and lack of medical care. Many also come from chaotic and disorganized families, experienced poor parental supervision, and exhibited serious school and mental health problems (Roe-Sepowitz & Krysik, 2008).

These conditions of extreme deprivation and abuse are likely to sharply affect appropriate coping and interpersonal skills, self-regulation skills, emotional maturity, and feelings of self-worth. As noted by Strickland (2008), women who experienced family violence, sexual abuse, and severe deprivation may have greater difficulty in developing and maintaining appropriate interpersonal relationships. Similar findings are found in the backgrounds of male child sex abusers (Simons, Wurtlele, & Durham, 2008). To a large extent, these forms of trauma may induce women who sexually abuse to find intimate relations with young children and adolescents.

Interpersonal and Intimacy Deficits

Prentky et al. (1997) assert that the more an offender's sexual preference is limited to children, the less socially competent the offender tends to be. In this context, social competence refers to the offender's social and sexual relationships with adults. Several early studies (e.g., Hunter, Figueredo, Malamuth, & Becker, 2003; Marshall, Barbaree, & Fernandez, 1995; Marshall & Mazzucco, 1995) revealed that, on average, CSOs are inadequate socially, lack interpersonal skills, arc unasscrtive, and have poor self-esteem. More recent studies have found that many CSOs are characterized by loneliness and fear of intimacy in adult relationships and display a number of inadequate strategies for obtaining emotional closeness (Sigre-Leirós et al., 2015). Researchers studying female sex offenders have found the similar social, interpersonal, self-worth, and confidence factors (Strickland, 2008). Adolescent CSOs are also found to be significantly below average in social skills, compared to other adolescent offenders (Seto & Lalumière, 2010). (See **Table 13-2** for a comparison of CSOs and rapist characteristics.)

A term that has emerged in the research literature in recent years is emotional congruence with children (ECWC). It was introduced to encompass the above-discussed interpersonal and intimacy deficits characteristic of CSOs. ECWC refers to the beliefs and attitudes of many CSOs that relationships with children are more emotionally and socially satisfying than relationships with adults (Mann et al., 2010). Basically, the offender who displays features of ECWC finds children easier to relate to than adults, especially concerning intimacy and sexual needs. They "may seek relationships with children in order to avoid discomfort in social interactions, reduce social and emotional loneliness, or achieve affection and positive self-regard" (McPhail, Hermann, & Nunes, 2013, p. 737). It is not uncommon for CSOs who illustrate features of ECWC to work at jobs or volunteer at activities that bring them into frequent contact with children, such as driving a school bus, coaching, and being a swimming instructor or a Boy Scout leader, although their victims are not necessarily obtained via these jobs and activities. McPhail et al. (2013) also note that CSOs may own a variety of children's recreational equipment and gaming entertainment technology. So far, the ECWC research pertaining to CSOs has focused almost exclusively on males offenders.

TABLE 13-2 General Comparisons between Adult Male Child Sex Offenders and Rapists on Risk Factors		
Common Characteristic*	**Child Sex Offenders**	**Rapists**
Cognitive functioning	Poor or marginal	Average
Interpersonal skills	Below average	Average
Adult intimacy capacity	Low	Average
Callousness–unemotionality	Low	High
Sexual violence	Usually low	Usually high
Sexual self-control	Average	Low
Sexual recidivism	High	High
Offending history	Specialized	Generalized
Offending trajectory	Starts later in life	Begins early

* This table is intended to provide only the typical findings from the available research. It should be emphasized that there are many individual exceptions to these comparisons.

ECWC can be measured by self-report instruments, such as the *Emotional Congruence with Children* scale of the *Children and Sex Questionnaire* (CSQ; Beckett, 1987), or the *Child Identification Scale-Revised* (CIS-R; Wilson, 1999). These self-report inventories include questions concerning how strongly an individual emotionally, cognitively, and socially identifies with and relates to children. Interview data or archival research of case files may also be used.

A growing body of research has discovered that ECWC predicts child sexual recidivism in males and consequently is becoming a key concept in CSO risk assessment and treatment (Hanson & Morton-Bourgon, 2005; Mann et al., 2010; McPhail et al., 2013; McPhail, Hermann, & Fernandez, 2014). It apparently is not useful as predictor for recidivism of rapists (Mann et al., 2010). In their study, McPhail and his colleagues (2013) discovered that ECWC appears to be significantly associated with male CSOs who victimize extrafamilial (outside the family) *male* children. They did not find ECWC useful as a predictor for recidivism involving intrafamilial (within the family) child abuse. The researchers also reported that psychological treatment is effective in decreasing ECWC qualities in extrafamilial CSOs, thereby reducing recidivism of that form of sexual abuse.

Sexual self-control emerges as a critical variable in cognitions of CSOs. As outlined by Hanson (2001), low self-control refers to the tendency to respond impulsively to temptation, have little consideration of the consequences, and engage in high-risk behaviors. However, male CSOs appear to have significantly better self-control than rapists (Hanson, 2001), leading to the conclusion that the argument that CSOs who claim their behavior is outside of their control may have very little validity.

COGNITIVE DISTORTIONS

Theories and research that focus on cognitive aspects appear to be the most promising in explaining child sexual offending, just as treatment based on cognitive principles holds the most promise for preventing criminal recidivism as a whole. Nonetheless, as Walters, Deming, and Elliott (2009, p. 1025) observe, "Cognitive factors have not received the attention they deserve from researchers in the field of sex offending."

In recent years, though, more attention has been given to the cognitions and beliefs of CSOs, and especially to their cognitive distortions. These are similar to the rape myths discussed in Chapter 12. The cognitive distortion hypothesis states that CSOs hold "well-established and generalized offense-related beliefs that facilitate sexual offenses against children" (Gannon & Polaschek, 2006, p. 1001). Mann et al. (2010) refer to this characteristic as offense-supportive attitudes which are defined as beliefs that justify or excuse sexual offending in general. Examples include beliefs that children are fundamentally sexual beings who seek out and enjoy sex, that adult–child sex relationships are instructive to the child, that they are simply demonstrating affection, and that children can be intentionally provocative.

Neurocognitive Functions

Emerging research suggests that problems in executive, neurocognitive functioning and prefrontal processing may play a significant role in explaining the sexually deviant behavior of some CSOs (Eastvold, Suchy, & Strassberg, 2011; Kruger & Schiffer, 2011; Schiffer & Vonlaufen, 2011; Seto et al., 2015). These researchers speculate that neurodevelopmental damage may have occurred at some point early in a CSO's life. In other words, some offenders may commit their crimes against children partly because of poor judgment and sexual impulse control due to problems in brain functioning and cognitive processing. This does not excuse their behavior, but it may help to explain it. Alternatively, individuals with lower cognitive skills or brain deficits may be more likely to be rejected sexually by peers and consequently more likely to turn to children for sexual gratification (Seto & Lalumière, 2010). Lower or defective cognitive processing may limit the individual from appreciating the nature of the sexual assault or its long-term consequences on the victims.

RECIDIVISM AND RISK ASSESSMENT

"Recidivism is one of the most important and most frequently studied aspects of sexual offending" (Harris, Knight, Smallbone, & Dennison, 2011). It should be emphasized that factors that predict recidivism for rapists are generally not the same factors for predicting recidivism for CSOs. For example, antisocial and aggressive behavior, such as anger, planning, and sadism generally predict reoffending for rapists (Parent et al., 2012). Social isolation, intense sexual fixation and interests, and the presence of paraphilias predict reoffending for CSOs (Parent et al., 2012). Moreover, research continually finds that, compared to other sex offenses, lifetime reoffending is highest overall for sexual abuse of children (Langevin & Curnoe, 2012). This reoffending statistic includes extrafamilial child sex abusers, incest offenders, and adult/child mixed offenders.

Sexual preoccupation appears to be a strong predictor for child molesters who are most prone to be repeat offenders (Knight & Thornton, 2007; Mann et al., 2010). "*Sexual preoccupation* refers to an abnormally intense interest in sex that dominates psychological functioning" (Mann et al., 2010, p. 198). Sex is engaged in for itself and defines the self. It is not related to romantic love or intense attraction to any specific person. Interestingly, though, this powerful predictor for child molester recidivism also appears to be a useful predictor of sexual, violent, and general recidivism of all sex offenders (Hanson & Morton-Bourgon, 2004, 2005). Some researchers have concluded that excessive sexual drive and preoccupation are the core, underlying constructs that prompt a wide variety of sexual offending (Zakirek, Ronis, & Knight, 2008).

In some research, offenders who crossed gender lines by offending against both boys and girls had the highest reoffense frequency (Harris et al., 2011). In another study, Dahle et al. (2014) also found that penetration of the child victim predicted a higher incidence of recidivism than other characteristics of the offending pattern. CSOs are more likely than rapists to reoffend sexually. On the other hand, rapists who tend to sexually assault both children and adults are more likely to reoffend by engaging in other criminal actions, often violently (Harris et al., 2011).

Multiple paraphilias appear to predict recidivism in CSOs (Knight & Thornton, 2007; Mann et al., 2010). Multiple paraphilias refer to two or more "rare, unusual, or social deviant sexual interests in persons, objects, or activities" (Mann et al., 2010, p. 200). Examples include intense sexual interests in children (pedophilia), exhibitionism, fetishisms, voyeurism, sexual bondage, and interest in sex that is associated with violence and sadism. The assumption is that CSOs with multiple paraphilias have a stronger propensity to commit further child sexual offenses, though research testing this assumption is sparse.

Like the national recidivism rates for most offenses, however, CSO recidivism rates are difficult to obtain. For example, less than half of the charges against a known sex offender are labeled as sex offenses (Langevin & Curnoe, 2012). The offender is often charged or bargains down to a nonsexual offense. Moreover, the second time around, the CSO is undoubtedly more careful and skillful about avoiding detection. On the other hand, he is also more closely monitored by the criminal justice system or may be in treatment. Interestingly, therefore, some research suggests low repeat offending, particularly for nonviolent CSOs. In general, though, research on recidivism must still be described as uncovering mixed results.

Hanson (2001) examined the recidivism rates of over 4,500 sexual offenders from diverse settings (Canada, the United States, and the United Kingdom). The data revealed a 19 percent sexual recidivism rate for extrafamilial CSOs, compared with a sexual recidivism rate of 17 percent for rapists during an average follow-up time of five years. These figures seem low compared with the findings of other researchers. For example, in a follow-up investigation of 4,295 CSOs released from prison in 1994, Langan, Schmitt, and Durose (2003) found that 39 percent were rearrested within three years after release. However, this figure represents rearrest for any type of offense, not just sexual offenses. If we examine rearrest data for sex crime against a child, only 3.3 percent of the child molesters were rearrested within the three-year follow-up. Thus, Langan's rates are actually lower than those of Hanson. In another study conducted in the United Kingdom, it was found that 12 percent of 413 CSOs had recidivated within two to four years after treatment (Beech, Mandeville-Norden, & Goodwill, 2012). A majority (59%) of the repeat offenders committed sexual offenses, ranging from very serious offenses, such as rape, to less serious (noncontact) sexual offenses, such as indecent exposure. It is unclear, however, how many of the repeat offenders in the study actually had sexual contact with children.

There is also considerable evidence that JSOs who are highly impulsive and demonstrate poor self-regulation are far more likely to reoffend than those JSOs who are evaluated as less impulsive (Waite et al., 2005).

Repeat offending is especially troublesome when CSOs not only demonstrate deviant sexual interests involving children but also exhibit features of psychopathy (Seto, 2008; Strassberg, Eastvold, Kenny, & Suchy, 2012). Strassberg et al. (2012) make the case that their findings suggest two types of CSOs: One is the typical CSO whose main interest is sexual contacts with children, whereas the other is the psychopathic CSO whose main sexual interest is not children. "For those who are self-centered, impulsive, uncaring for others, manipulative, and free of conscience, all typical psychopathic qualities, many kinds of antisocial acts become more likely, including the sexual abuse of children" (Strassberg et al., 2012, p. 381).

Risk Assessment

The assessment of the risk of recidivism—which was discussed in earlier chapters— is an extremely important task for clinicians. It needs to be undertaken prior to treatment and before release into the community. Offenders who are assessed to be low risk can usually be treated and rehabilitated within their local community. Offenders who are assessed moderate to serious risk are best treated in an adult or juvenile correctional facility or kept under close supervision until the risk of recidivism is significantly reduced. This cannot be done once an offender's sentence has been served, however.

Research on sex offending has contributed to the development of several risk assessments instruments for adult and JSOs. As noted above, research indicates that different factors predict recidivism for rapists and for CSOs (Parent et al., 2012). For example, CSOs tend to commit fewer nonsexual offenses than rapists but an equivalent number of sexual offenses (Parent, Guay, & Knight, 2011). Moreover, sexual deviancy measures appear to be more pertinent in measuring recidivism for CSOs, whereas violence measures appear to be more relevant for predicting rapist recidivism. Therefore, recidivism predictions require assessments of a different set of factors for CSOs than rapists.

Parent et al. (2011) ascertained that the *Rapid Risk Assessment for Sex Offender Recidivism* (RRASOR), the Static-99, and the Static-2002 appear to predict quite well recidivism in adult CSOs. Risk assessment instruments designed for adolescents with a history of sexual offending are ERASOR (Worling & Curwen, 2001) and J-SORRAT-II (Epperson et al., 2006). The RRASOR (Hanson, 1997) and the Static-99 (Hanson & Thornton, 2000) are among the most popular recidivism risk assessment scales for sex offenders today In developing the RRASOR, Hanson used data from a large collection of recidivism studies and a sample of 2,592 sex offenders. The instrument contains four items, and its total score ranges from 0 to 6. The four items are (1) prior sexual arrests, (2) age, (3) ever-targeted male victims, and (4) whether any victims were unrelated to the offender.

The Static-99 is a 10-item risk assessment instrument. The items cover static, historical factors, such as the number of prior offenses, victim characteristics, and the offender's age. The items were selected strictly on the basis of empirical relationships with recidivism and ease of administration (Hanson & Morton-Bourgon, 2009). In order to improve upon the accuracy of the Static-99, Hanson and Thornton created the Static-2002. Research continues to indicate that the Static-99 and Static-2002R does improve accuracy in predicting recidivism in CSOs (Hanson, 2010; Hanson et al., in press).

Similar to other sexual offenders, the classification, diagnosis, and assessment of CSOs are complicated by a high degree of variability among individuals in reference to personal characteristics, life experiences, criminal histories, and motives for offending (Prentky et al., 1997). "There is no single 'profile' that accurately describes or accounts for all child molesters" (Prentky et al., 1997, p. v). The best way to highlight the multifaceted nature of CSOs is through a discussion of two well-known classification systems or typologies. Like the rape typologies described in the previous chapter, they were developed by the Massachusetts Research Center and by Groth, with the former being more research based and the latter more clinically based. In addition, like the rapist typologies discussed in the previous chapter, they have been formulated primarily on information gathered on male offenders.

CLASSIFICATION OF MALE CHILD SEX OFFENDER PATTERNS

The Massachusetts Treatment Center (MTC) (Cohen, Seghorn, & Calmas, 1969; Knight, 1988; Knight et al., 1985) has developed a widely cited typology of male CSO behavioral patterns. Four major patterns have been identified: (1) the fixated type, (2) the regressed type, (3) the exploitative type, and (4) the aggressive or sadistic type.

The **fixated** (or **immature**) **sex offender** demonstrates a long-standing, exclusive preference for children as both sexual and social companions. He has never been able to develop a mature relationship with his adult peers, male or female, and he is considered socially immature, passive, timid, and dependent by most people who know him. He feels most comfortable relating to children, whom he seeks out as companions. Sexual contact usually occurs only after the adult and child have become well acquainted. Fixated offenders rarely marry, and their social background lacks much evidence of dating peers or even any sustained, long-term friendship with an adult (outside of relatives). This CSO wishes to touch, fondle, caress, and taste the child. He rarely expects genital intercourse, and very rarely does he use physical force or aggression.

The fixated CSO generally has average intelligence. His work history is steady, although it is often work that is below his ability. His social skills are adequate for day-to-day functioning. Probably most troubling about the fixated or immature CSO is that he is not concerned or disturbed about his exclusive preference for children as companions, nor can he see why others are concerned. Therefore, he is difficult to treat and is most likely to recidivate.

The **regressed sex offender** had a fairly normal adolescence and good peer relationships and sexual experiences, but later developed feelings of masculine inadequacy and self-doubt. Problems in the individual's occupational, social, and sexual lives followed. The regressed child offender's background commonly includes alcohol abuse, divorce, and a poor employment record. Each sexual act is usually precipitated by a significant jolt to the offender's sexual adequacy, either by female or by male peers. For example, the offender may perceive other males as being more successful with women after a female acquaintance rejects him in favor of another man. Unlike the immature (or fixated) child offender, the regressed child offender usually prefers victims who are strangers and who live outside his neighborhood. The victims are nearly always female. Also, unlike the fixated child offender, he seeks genital sex with his victim. Because he feels remorseful and expresses disbelief after that act, clinicians usually find him a good prospect for rehabilitation. As long as stressful events are kept to a minimum and he learns to cope adequately with those he does have, he is unlikely to reoffend. We return to this later in the chapter when we discuss principles of effective treatment.

The **exploitative child sex offender** seeks children primarily to satisfy his sexual needs. He exploits the child's weaknesses any way he can, and tries various kinds of strategies and tricks to get him or her to comply. He is usually unknown to the child and commonly tries to get the child isolated from others and his or her familiar surroundings. If necessary, he will use aggression and physical force to get the child to comply with his wishes. The exploitative offender does not care about the emotional or physical well-being of the child, but only sees the victim as a sexual object.

The exploitative offender exhibits a long history of criminal or antisocial conduct. His relationships with peers are unpredictable and stormy. He is unpleasant to be around and is often avoided by others who know him. He tends to be highly impulsive, irritable, and moody. His markedly defective interpersonal skills may be the principal reason that he chooses children as victims (Knight et al., 1985). Clinicians find him difficult to treat, as his deficiencies extend to all phases of his daily life. Nevertheless, and again as will be discussed later, treatment based on certain principles may be effective.

The **aggressive** (or **sadistic**) **child sex offender** is drawn to children for both sexual and aggressive reasons. Offenders in this group are apt to have a long history of antisocial behavior and poor adaptation to their environments. Since the primary aim is to obtain stimulation without consideration for the victim, this group often assaults the child viciously and sadistically. The more harm and pain inflicted, the more this offender becomes sexually excited. Aggressive or sadistic CSOs are most often responsible for child abductions and murders. Clinicians find this type not only dangerous to children but also among the most difficult to treat. Fortunately, this type is rare. Although rare, this is the type frequently portrayed in the media and is most associated—though wrongfully so—with the image of the child molester.

An example of an aggressive CSO was Albert Fish (1870 to 1936), whose background is discussed by Nash (1975). Fish, called the "Moon Maniac," admitted sexually molesting more than 400 children over a span of 20 years. In addition, he confessed to six child murders and made vague reference to numerous others. He was eventually convicted of murdering a 12-year-old girl and was electrocuted in 1936. Another example is John Wayne Gacy Jr., who, between 1972 and 1978, sadistically murdered at least 33 teenage boys and young men and buried most of the bodies in the cellar of his suburban Chicago home. Gacy was executed by lethal injection in 1994.

These are two examples from somewhat long ago of individuals who committed a multitude of heinous acts over periods of time. Both were subjected to sensational media coverage, as were the child abduction cases referred to in previous chapters. The more typical cases that receive little or no public attention may be less violent but are no less troubling. Persons familiar with court and social service records (e.g., lawyers, social workers, treatment providers, juvenile justice professionals) offer chilling information about the behaviors engaged in by those who sexually assault children and the effects on their victims. An eight-year-old girl told the court about the sexual game her stepfather played on the bed with her and her younger sister every Friday evening. In another incident, a teacher suspected a problem because a young child's leg jumped up and down with great anxiety as the end of the school day approached. It was learned that the child was being sexually abused by an after-school caretaker. Other children are forced to engage in sexual activities with their siblings or are threatened with death or grievous harm if they reveal what is occurring.

The MTC:CM3

Like the MTC classification scheme for rapists (MTC:R3), the MTC classification system of child molesters has undergone some refinement in recent years. In an effort to depict more accurately the complexity involved in classifying CSOs, the MTC:CM3 (referring to Massachusetts Treatment Center: Child Molester, Version 3) includes tentative changes to the original scheme described earlier. Specifically, three significant changes are recommended: (1) Divide the regressed and fixated types into three separate factors—degree of fixation on children, the level of social competence achieved, and the amount of contact an offender has with children, (2) incorporate into the scheme a new narcissistic offender type, and (3) partition the violence of the sexual assault into physical injury and sadistic components (Knight, 1989).

The researchers discovered that, although the regressed offender classification is a valid one, it was also more complicated than originally supposed. Researchers found that the regression classification could be further subdivided into the molester's style of offending, his interpersonal relationships with children, the intensity of the offender's interest, and the level of social competence achieved by the offender. For example, offenders could be classified according to their level of fixation and social competence. Level of fixation refers to the strength of an offender's sexual interest in children (Knight, Carter, & Prentky, 1989). In other words, to what extent are children the major focus of the offender's thought and attention? If children are the central focus of the offender's sexual and interpersonal fantasies and thoughts for more than six months, then the offender qualifies for high fixation. Social competence refers to the degree to which the offender can participate effectively in daily living. An offender would have high social competence if he has demonstrated at least two of the following behaviors: (1) has had a single job lasting three or more years, (2) has had a sexual relationship with an adult for at least one year, (3) has assumed responsibility

TABLE 13-3	Illustration of the Degree of Fixation as a Function of Social Competence Level

Degree of Fixation			
High Fixation		Low Fixation	
Low social competence	High social competence	Low social competence	High social competence
(Type 0)	(Type 1)	(Type 2)	(Type 3)

in parenting a child for three or more years, (4) has been an active member in an adult-oriented organization (e.g., church group, business group) for one or more years, or (5) has had a social friendship with an adult for at least one year. The dimensions of fixation and social competence result in four types of child molesters: high fixation, low social competence (type 0); high fixation, high social competence (type 1); low fixation, low social competence (type 2); and low fixation, high social competence (type 3) (see **Table 13-3**). The regressed type was dropped in MTC:CM3 in favor of the term "low fixation."

Research further revealed that CSOs can also be distinguished on the basis of how much daily contact with children they seek (see **Table 13-4**). A high-contact offender demonstrates regular contact with children in both sexual and nonsexual contexts (Knight et al., 1989). Offenders of high contact often become involved in an occupation or recreation that brings them in considerable contact with children, such as bus drivers, schoolteachers, Boy Scout leaders, or Little League coaches. Research data revealed there are two kinds of offenders who seek more extensive involvement with children beyond their sexual offenses. The first high-contact type, the *interpersonal offender* (type 1), seeks the extensive company of children for both social and sexual needs (**Table 13-4**). He sees the child as an appropriate companion in a relationship, and believes the friendship is mutually satisfying. The second type, the *narcissistic offender* (type 2), solicits the company of children only to increase his opportunities for sexual experiences. Like exploitative offenders, these offenders typically molest children they do not know and their sexual acts with children are typically genitally oriented (Knight, 1989). Furthermore, there is little or no concern about the needs, comfort, or welfare of the child (Knight et al., 1989).

Another group of CSOs are low-contact seekers. Low-contact offenders' only contacts with children are in the context of sexual assault. Low-contact offenders are classified according to the amount of physical injury they administer to their victims. Two types of low-contact seekers tend to administer very little physical injury to their victims: the exploitative type and the muted sadistic type. Low injury refers to the absence of physical injury to victim and the presence of such acts as pushing, shoving, slapping, holding, or verbal threats. None of the acts of low injury results in a lasting injury (e.g., cuts, bruises, contusions). The *exploitative, nonsadistic offender* (type 3) uses no more aggression or violence than is necessary to secure victim compliance. Furthermore, the assault does not reveal evidence that sadistic actions engender sexual arousal in the offender.

TABLE 13-4	Illustration of the Amount of Contact as a Function of Meaning of the Contact and Degree of Physical Injury Experienced by the Child Victim

Amount of Contact					
High Amount of Contact		Low Amount of Contact			
Meaning of Contact: Interpersonal	Meaning of Contact: Narcissistic	Low Physical Injury		High Physical Injury	
↓	↓	Nonsadistic	Sadistic	Nonsadistic	Sadistic
(Type 1)	(Type 2)	(Type 3)	(Type 4)	(Type 5)	(Type 6)

The *muted* or *symbolic sadistic offender* (type 4) engages in a variety of distressing, painful, and threatening acts, none of which causes significant physical injury to the child.

Finally, the MTC:CM3 classifies two offenders who have often administered a high amount of physical injury to their victims: the aggressive offender and the sadistic offender. High injury is characterized by hitting, punching, choking, sodomy, or forcing the child to ingest urine or feces (Knight et al., 1989). The *aggressive, nonsadistic offender* (type 5) is similar to the aggressive CSO described earlier except that sadism is not a primary aim of the assault. This offender is extremely angry about all things in his life and is generally violent toward people in his life, including children. The *sadistic offender* (type 6) obtains sexual pleasure from the pain, fear, and physical harm he inflicts on the child.

The MTC:CM3 helps identify offender type based on crime scene information and perhaps presents a more refined classification system of child molester or predator types. However, research beyond the MTC population is needed before investigators feel comfortable about adopting this promising scheme. Looman, Gauthier, and Boer (2001) were able to replicate the MTC:CM3 Classification System with a Canadian sample of child. In addition, the MTC:CM3 does not include incest offenders and therefore is only applicable to extrafamilial CSOs (Ennis et al., in press). What's more, it does not include crossover CSOs. However, a newly developed MTC:CM4 is currently under revision (Knight & King, 2012).

The Groth Classification Model

In a classification system similar to that of the MTC, Groth (1978; Groth & Burgess, 1977) classifies child offenders on the basis of the longevity of the behavioral patterns and the offender's psychological aims. Like Groth's rape offender groupings discussed in Chapter 12, though, it is less research based compared with the MTC classifications. If the sexual preference for children has existed persistently since adolescence, the person is classified as an *immature* or *fixated child offender.* The fixated child offender has been sexually attracted primarily or exclusively to significantly younger people throughout his life, regardless of what other sexual experiences he has had. Groth believes that this fixation is due to an arresting of psychological maturation, resulting from unresolved formative issues that persist and underlie subsequent development. On the other hand, if the offender has managed to develop some normalcy in his relationships with adults, but resorts to child offending when stressed or after suffering a devastating blow to his self-esteem, he is called a *regressed* child offender.

Groth has also subdivided child offenders according to their intentions or psychological aims. He identifies two basic categories: (1) sex pressure offenders and (2) sex force offenders. In sex pressure offenses, the offender's typical *modus operandi* is to entice children into sexual behavior through persuasion or cajolement, or to entrap them by placing them in a situation in which they feel indebted or obligated. A child may feel he owes something to the person who taught him to swim or bought him a bike. The sex force offense, on the other hand, is characterized by threat of harm and/or the use of physical force in the commission of the offense. The offender either intimidates the child—by exploiting the child's relative helplessness, naiveté, and awe of adults—or attacks and physically overpowers his victim.

Groth finds he can further subdivide the sex force group into the *exploitative type,* in which the threat of force is used to overcome victim resistance, or the *sadistic type,* who derives great pleasure in hurting the child. The exploitative type typically employs verbal threats, restraint, manipulation, intimidation, and physical strength to overcome any resistance on the part of the child. His intent is not necessarily to hurt the child but to obtain compliance. The sadistic type, which fortunately is rare, eroticizes physical aggression and pain. He uses more force than is necessary to overpower the victim and may commit a so-called lust murder. Therefore, the physical and psychological abuse and/or degradation of the child are necessary for him to experience sexual excitement and gratification. Often, the child is beaten, choked, tortured, and violently sexually abused.

Certainly the Groth typology has strong commonalities with the MTC typology. The immature and the regressed child offenders display features of the sex pressure offender, and the aggressive child offender shows strong similarities to the sex force offender. It may be more appropriate at the present time to classify the child offender according to the degree of coercion or force he uses rather than according to personality features. The first method focuses on offender behavior, a criterion that is more objective and clear-cut. The second method focuses on "understanding" the behavior by assuming a variety of personality constructs. We have too little information about child offenders at this point to do that with total confidence.

Female Sex Offender Typology

Vandiver and Kercher (2004) have proposed a clinically useful and research meaningful typology of female sex offenders, which is distinct from the typologies and classifications of male offenders discussed above. Utilizing 471 registered adult female sexual offenders in Texas, the researchers identified six types:

1. Heterosexual nurturers
2. Noncriminal homosexual offenders
3. Female sexual predators
4. Young adult child exploiters
5. Homosexual criminals
6. Aggressive homosexual offenders

Heterosexual nurturers were the largest group. This group victimized only males with an average age of 12. The offenders are generally in mentorship, caretaking, or teacher roles, such as the teacher–lover category in which a teacher engages in a "romantic" relationship with one of her students or a counselor with one of her clients. Many of the offenders in this group do not perceive the relationship as abusive or psychologically damaging to the child. These females appear to be motivated by a desire for intimacy to compensate for unmet emotional and social needs, and may not recognize or want to recognize the inappropriateness of the relationship. This group had a low recidivism rate.

Noncriminal homosexual offenders represented the second largest group. This group primarily preferred early adolescent females as victims (average age of 13). This offender group appeared to have many of the same characteristics as heterosexual nurturers, but their victim preferences were females. Similar to heterosexual nurturers, these offenders were unlikely to have a criminal record or to recidivate.

Female sexual predators victimized both male (60%) and female children (40%) who averaged 11 years of age. This group resembled other female criminals, and their sexual offending may be an offshoot of other criminal activity. In other words, they are repeat offenders committing a variety of crimes. They also had a high probability of committing another sexual offense.

Young adult child exploiters most often committed sexual assault. Their victims were frequently young with an average age of seven and involved both genders. These offenders themselves were the youngest of the six offender groups, with an average age of 28. About half of the victims were related to the offender, sometimes the offender's own child.

The fifth group, homosexual criminals, had an extensive history of antisocial behavior. Their victims were usually female with an average age of 11. Their sexual crimes included indecency with a child and compelling the child into prostitution or child pornography. Most of these offenders are motivated by profit rather than sexual ambitions.

Aggressive homosexual offenders represent the smallest group and were also the oldest. Their victims were generally adult females and therefore are not relevant to the topic of this chapter. They appeared to be representative of homosexual women involved in a domestically violent relationship.

In their sample of 390 female sex offenders in New York State, Sandler and Freeman (2007) also identified six categories. In addition, their sample was very similar to Vandiver and Kercher's on demographic variables, such as offender age and race. However, Sandler and Freeman did not entirely support some of the characteristics reported in the Vandiver and Kercher typology. This is to be expected, considering that typologies that attempt to classify female sex offenders are in early stages of development.

Sandler and Freeman did find support for the heterosexual nurturer and young adult child exploiter categories found by Vandiver and Kercher, but some characteristics of the four other categories were different. One of the major differences was the gender of the victims. Sandler and Freeman discovered that many of the female sex offenders did not *consistently* victimize one gender more than the other. Because the cluster analysis did not highlight a strong victim preference as found in the Vandiver–Kercher analysis, Sandler and Freeman felt it was appropriate to label only one group as homosexual, which they called the homosexual child molester. This group, which emerged as the smallest, almost exclusively targeted female victims (91%).

Some of the differences in results of the two studies may be due to the substantially different criminal codes or registry requirements for sex offenders between states. In addition, the Vandiver and Kercher sample included females who may or may not have served time in prison, and their offenses were considered serious enough to warrant arrest and prosecution (Gannon & Rose, 2008). Although their sample was a forensic population, it represented a very wide range of female sexual offenders.

Although the two studies significantly advance our knowledge pertaining to female sex offenders, neither study was able to obtain additional data relating to co-offenders (Gannon & Rose, 2008). In other words, did the females offend alone or with a co-offender, such as a male partner? Gannon and Rose (2008) emphasize that this shortcoming limits strategies and programs for treating female sex offenders. Recall, however, that Vandiver (2006) conducted further research on female sex offenders as co-offenders, which we covered earlier in the chapter. That study did not focus on the typologies discussed above, however.

The typologies of female sex offenders thus far proposed do not examine psychological variables, such as mental health status or the victimization histories of the offenders themselves. In general, the research on female sexual offenders has focused on the demographics and the very basic details of their offending characteristics, which is extremely helpful. However, as Gannon and Rose (2008) note, there is very little research on the sexual interests, empathy, intimacy deficits, and self-regulation of female sex offenders. This research needs to be done if we are to get a better understanding of the female sex offender.

INTERNET-FACILITATED SEXUAL OFFENDING

In recent years, there has been increasing attention directed at online sexual offending, particularly child pornography offending. As noted by Babchishin, Hanson, and VanZuylen (2015), the Internet is commonly and frequently used for sexual purposes, and pornography is easily accessed. "Approximately three quarters of men and half of women have intentionally viewed pornography over the internet" (Babchishin et al., 2015, p. 45).

Online sexual offending refers to "the use of Internet and related digital technologies to obtain, distribute, or produce child pornography, or to contact potential child victims to create opportunities for sexual offending" (Seto, Hanson, & Babchishin, 2011, p. 125). Criminal sexual behaviors include downloading illegal pornography (such as child pornographic materials) and sexual solicitation of minors for prostitution (Babchishin et al., 2015). The possession, distribution, and production of child pornography is illegal under federal laws and laws in all 50 states (Wolak, Finkelhor, & Mitchell, 2005) and is subject to both criminal and civil penalties.

Who Are the Offenders?

The producers of child pornography are often persons who have legitimate access to the child, such as parents/guardians (22%), relatives (10%), family friends (47%), babysitters, and coaches (U.S. Sentencing Commission, 2012). Two recent examples are described in U.S. Supreme Court cases (*U.S. v. Williams*, 2008; *Paroline v. U.S.*, 2014). In one example, a man offered photographs of men molesting his four-year-old daughter (although he apparently did not deliver them) but did circulate pictures of other children engaging in sexually explicit conduct. A search of his computer yielded additional images, some of which were sadomasochistic. In another case, an eight-year-old girl was raped by her uncle, who videotaped the assault and circulated it on the Internet. Law enforcement officers uncovered more than 35,000 images of the rape in the United States alone.

One of the key goals of researchers in child pornography is to determine the risks that online offenders—those who access these images—pose to actual sexual contact with children. In other words, do those persons interested in child pornography online also seek physical sexual contact with children? Many studies indicate that the majority of online offenders have no prior *official* contact sexual offense history (Seto et al., 2011). Many do not even have any prior criminal history of any kind. However, one study discovered that a majority of online offenders (85%) admitted to contact crimes (unofficially) while undergoing treatment or during a polygraph examination (Bourke & Hernandez, 2009). That study has been criticized for having several serious methodological shortcomings. In a more comprehensive study, conducted by Seto et al. (2011), the data revealed that approximately one in eight online offenders had a known contact sexual offense history, based on official records of arrests, charges, or convictions. The ratio was higher when self-report information (rather than official records) was used, revealing that about a half of the online offenders admitted to a contact sexual offense. Seto and his colleagues conclude: "Many of the online offenders in our study are likely to be sexually interested in children, but only half are known to have acted on these sexual interests" (p. 140). However, the Seto et al. study did find that the recidivism rate for contact sexual offense was quite low (5%) for the majority of online sex offenders.

Although there is no typical profile of the child pornography offender, online offenders are likely to be non-Hispanic white, single, and unemployed (Babchishin, Hanson, & Hermann, 2011). They tend to be slightly younger than contact sex offenders (Babchishin et al., 2011). Moreover, online offenders, compared to contact sexual offenders, appear to have greater empathy for their victims, have greater ability to control acting on their child-oriented sexual interests, and usually restrict their sexual interests to online activity (Seto & Hanson, 2011).

Nevertheless, it is important to emphasize that downloading child pornography is a criminal act which causes harm to its victims. Images of children engaged in sexual activity are not only punishable by prison sentences but also subject to civil penalties under the Crime Victims' Rights Act of 2004. In the case of the eight-year-old girl mentioned above, numerous individuals were jailed and/or fined penalties, ranging from $100 to $3,000 (facts outlined in *Paroline v. U.S.*, 2014).

Who Are the Child Victims?

The emergence of Internet technology lowered the costs of producing commercially circulated pornographic material, substantially increased its availability, and reduced the risk of detection connected to production, distribution, and possession (Quayle & Jones, 2011). The Internet's rapid expansion also has meant more focus on the Internet sex offender (Qualye, 2009). The victims depicted in the commercial child pornographic media are typically white, prepubescent girls (ages 8 to 12 years) (Quayle & Jones, 2011). The second most often used child victim category was Asian prepubescent girls. Nevertheless, no racial or ethnic group is immune from this victimization. Female children outnumber male children in the sexualized photographic media images by about four to one.

In an extensive study called the *National Juvenile Online Victimization Study*, Wolak et al. (2005) examined the information on Internet-related child pornography offenders who had been arrested over a 12-month period, beginning in July 1, 2000. Wolak et al. described 40 percent of offenders as "dual offenders" because they not only had child pornography in their possession but also had a history of sexually abusing minors. Relatively few of the offenders had prior arrests for nonsexual offending (22%). Ninety-one percent of those arrested were non-Hispanic whites.

Eighty-three percent of those arrested had sexual images of children between the ages of 6 and 12, and 39 percent had images of 3- to 5-year-old children. Nineteen percent had images of toddlers or infants younger than three years of age. Sixty-two percent had pictures of mostly girls, and 14 percent possessed pictures of mostly boys. Perhaps more revealing was the finding that 21 percent had images of children in violent scenes, such as bondage, rape, or torture. Most of these graphic photos involved images of children who were gagged, bound, blindfolded, or otherwise enduring some form of sadistic sex. Thirty-nine percent of the arrestees possessed moving images in digital or other videos formats. Considering that these images were discovered by investigators in 2000 and 2001, recent technological advances (e.g., smartphones, ipads, cloud computing, sophisticated encryption formats) making it easier for offenders to collect and store child pornography suggest this problem is far greater today. New technological tools also have enhanced offenders' ability to evade detection by law enforcement (Collins, 2012). In addition, advances in technological communication systems allow persons to find others who share their interests which, in turn, encourage the development of peer, supportive communities.

Online Sex Offenders Interested in Adolescents

Although this section was primarily concerned with online child pornography offenders drawn to prepubescent children, we should briefly describe online offenders who are interested in adolescent pornography or actual sexual encounters with teens. Briggs, Simon, and Simonsen (2011) conducted an exploratory study designed to examine offender differences between noncontact online sexual offenders and those online offenders who activity seek out opportunities to have sex with adolescents. Some online offenders engage in the process of exploitation, luring, and enticement of the teenager to meet with them. The offender may communicate with several adolescents at once via various chat rooms, thinking he is doing so anonymously. However, police officers have been active over the past two decades in their attempts to apprehend these offenders by posing as juveniles online (Mitchell, Wolak, & Finkehor, 2005).

Briggs and his colleagues identified two types of men who use the Internet to gain sexual gratification via adolescent victims. One type utilizes live online chat rooms to entice male or female teenagers into an offline sexual relationship. The other is the fantasy-driven offender who uses the Internet as "a sexual medium to connect with teens for the purpose of cybersex and masturbation" (Briggs et al., 2011, p. 87). For these latter, socially isolated adults, the Internet provides an impersonal social and sexual outlet without the risk of face-to-face rejection. They usually have no interest in an actual physical contact with the teenager.

SEX TRAFFICKING

Human trafficking is the third leading criminal enterprise in the world and is notably one of the fastest growing and most lucrative criminal activities globally (Cecchet & Thoburn, 2014; Rafferty, 2013). Human trafficking is the economic exploitation of an individual through force, fraud, or coercion (Task Force on Trafficking of Women and Girls, 2014; henceforth referred to as Task Force on Trafficking). The vast majority of those trafficked in the United States for labor or commercial sex are women and girls. Girls between the ages of 12 and 16 are heavily sought-after victims in the trafficking trade. It has been reported that the average age of trafficked children has been getting younger, as young as 7 to 10 years of age, however (Wilson & Butler, 2014). Over 80 percent of human trafficking incidents involve sex trafficking, such as forced prostitution and child sex trafficking (Kyckelhahn, Beck, & Cohen, 2009) As such, it is referred to as commercial sexual exploitation (CSE). (See **Table 13-5** for breakdown of types of trafficking.)

Traffickers who recruit, transport, and exploit women and girls for sexual purposes span the continuum from a single individual to organized networks (Task Force on Trafficking, 2014). Interestingly, although organized crime is clearly tied in to human trafficking, it is believed that most traffickers are *not* members of an organized crime group; rather, most are one or two individuals working on their own (Small, Adams, Owen, & Roland, 2008). (This is analogous to research findings that those who commit hate crimes and domestic terrorism are often not affiliated with organized groups.)

The methods used by traffickers are variable. "Traffickers use coercion and psychological abuse, deception and fraud, threats, physical and sexual violence, abusive work and living

TABLE 13-5 Human Trafficking Incidents Opened for Investigation between 2008 and 2010, by Type of Trafficking

Type of Human Trafficking Incident	Total Incidents	
	Number	Percent
All incidents	2,515	100.0
Sex trafficking	2,065	82.1
Adult prostitution	1,218	48.4
Child sex trafficking	1,016	40.4
Sexualized labor*	142	5.6
Other sex trafficking	61	2.4
Labor trafficking	350	13.9
Other/unknown	237	9.4

*Includes exotic dancing and unlicensed massage parlors.

Source: Banks, D., & Kyckelhahn, T. (2011, April). Characteristics of suspected human trafficking incidents, 2008-2010. Washington, DC: U.S. Department of Justice, Bureau of Justice Statistics.

conditions, and coerced substance use to lure, manipulate, and control their victims" (Task Force on Trafficking, 2014, p. 3). In many instances, the trafficker offers false promises for a better life elsewhere (Rafferty, 2013). The typical prior life experiences for victims of CSE have been characterized by violence, and that violence follows them while in the trade and around the time of and following their exit (Wilson & Butler, 2014).

The most effective traffickers are those who can establish trusting relationships with potential victims. Many of the traffickers are women, including former victims who act as suppliers of children to those who will exploit them (Rafferty, 2013). These female traffickers tend to be attractive, nicely dressed, and wear expensive jewelry. They gain the trust of potential victims while using false promises of a better life under their guidance and supervision.

According to some experts (e.g., Cecchet & Thoburn, 2014; Schauer & Wheaton, 2006), the United States ranks as the world's second largest destination country (after Germany) for women and children trafficked for purposes of sexual exploitation in the sex industry. Examples include women who agree to come to this country as food service workers, hotel employees, or exotic dancers, but then are forced into prostitution until they are able to pay off the debt incurred through a smuggling fee. In some countries, parents "sell" their children to traffickers who take them to other parts of the world, including the United States, and profit from their sexual exploitation. Violence, intimidation, and brutality are particularly common with trafficking victims brought in for the sex industry. Children used in the sex trade are often described as seriously hampered in their physical, psychological, and social-emotional development (Cecchet & Thoburn, 2014; Rafferty, 2013). "Most victims meet the criteria for a lifetime diagnosis of PTSD, anxiety, and/or depression, and a substantial proportion continue to experience these symptoms even after obtaining psychological help" (Wilson & Butler, 2014, p. 501).

Those who engage in sexual trafficking are rarely studied by researchers from a psychological perspective. They are more likely to be perceived as economic offenders than as sex offenders. Nevertheless, although the traffickers themselves may not be directly participating in sexual abuse, they are facilitating it and thus arguably could be referred to as sex offenders as well. It is even possible that future research could uncover a link between sexual exploitation of this nature and direct sexual abuse.

TREATMENT OF CHILD SEX OFFENDERS

Over the years, the research literature on the treatment of CSOs (and sex offending in general) has not been overwhelmingly positive about its overall effectiveness to reduce recidivism. For example, Furby, Weinroth, and Blackshaw (1989), after an extensive review of the psychological treatment on sex offenders, concluded: "There is as yet no evidence that clinical treatment reduces rates of sex reoffenses in general and no appropriate data for assessing whether it may be differentially effective for different types of offenders" (p. 27). The Furby et al. review included all types of therapeutic approaches used from the 1960s through the 1980s. In a more recent publication, Camilleri and Quinsey (2008) concluded from their comprehensive review of treatment for CSOs that treatment so far has been largely ineffective. Some scholars have noted that policy makers who lean toward a more punitive criminal justice system welcome research results concluding that treatment is not effective in reducing child sex offending (Grønnerød, Grønnerød, & Grøndahl, 2015).

One reason for these discouraging research results is that many of the evaluation studies have had methodological and design flaws, often due to the difficulty in obtaining a cooperative sizeable treatment group. Even more difficult is trying to obtain a control group of CSOs who did not receive treatment to compare to the group that did. In addition, many studies are conducted within the confines of correctional institutions which may have stringent policies about what can and cannot be done by outside researchers. Another major reason for these disappointing treatment results lies in the fact that CSOs are a very heterogeneous group who differ on a wide range of crucial factors, such as motivations, needs, abilities, cognitions, experiences, and backgrounds. CSOs also vary widely in the frequency and type of sexual activity they engaged in. Obviously, one psychological treatment approach does not fit all.

However, despite the many differences among CSOs, contemporary research has identified some key psychological factors that are important to change in order to reduce sexual reoffending. These are the dynamic risk factors, which we discussed in Chapter 12. The most notable dynamic risk factors of many CSOs are the following: (1) They have problems with emotional regulation when it comes to sexual arousal; (2) they have intimacy and social skill deficits; (3) they have distorted cognitive sexual scripts; and (4) they subscribe to a variety of cognitive distortions.

Contemporary research has also discovered that cognitive-behavioral approaches appear to be the most effective in changing the most relevant dynamic risk factors and thereby reducing recidivism. Cognitive-behavioral therapy is especially effective if it follows the principles of risk-need-responsivity (RNR), discussed in Chapter 12 (Bonta & Andrews, 2010; Hanson, Bourgon, Helmus, & Hodgson, 2009; Walton and Chou, 2015). In line with the RNR principles, the clinician needs to work on reducing criminogenic needs in moderate- to high-risk CSOs and in matching the treatment to the learning style of the offender. Deviant sexual interests and attitudes tolerant of sexually victimizing children are examples of criminogenic needs. The deviant attitudes allow the offender to deny, justify, minimize, and rationalize their actions (Eastman, 2004; Worling & Langton, 2012).

In cognitive-behavioral therapy, the behavioral component focuses on sexual preferences and relapses, while the cognitive component focuses on changing beliefs, fantasies, attitudes, and rationalizations that justify and perpetuate sexually violent behavior. CSOs appear to have far more cognitive distortions than men who sexually assault adult women (Camilleri & Quinsey, 2008). Cognitive-behavior therapy assumes that maladaptive sexual behaviors are learned according to the same rules as normal sexual behavior, by means of classical and/or instrumental conditioning, modeling, reinforcement, generalization, and punishment. They are, therefore, modifiable.

Currently, there is also considerable ongoing research evaluating treatment programs for JSOs (Hanson et al., 2009; Veneziano & Veneziano, 2002). These programs designed for JSOs are different from those that target adult sexual offenders. This is primarily because contemporary research suggests that juveniles are far more changeable than adults, are more influenced by the social and peer environments, and appear to be at lower risk for sexual recidivism. Consequently, multisystemic therapy has been shown to have good effects on reducing recidivism in JSOs, especially if it follows the RNR principles similar to behavioral-cognitive therapy (Hanson et al., 2009).

Worling and Langton (2012), in an article reviewing the assessment and treatment of JSOs in residential settings, note that there have been few published studies in recent years in which researchers used a treatment and a comparison group. However, overall "there is a growing body of evidence that specialized treatment programs result in lower recidivism rates" (p. 827). "Unfortunately," they continue, "there is very little guidance from the published research at this time regarding which treatment components are effective for which youth" (p. 827). Worling and Langton summarize a number of treatment goals that are common to sex offender treatment programs in the United States and Canada. They include, among others, enhancing accountability for one's crimes, enhancing healthy sexual interests, prosocial sexual attitudes, and awareness of victim impact; establishing plans to prevent future offending; and involving parents and caregivers.

Worling and Langton also observe that these confined settings very often produce sexual victimization of both sex offenders and nonsex offenders. They cite the sobering statistic reported by Beck, Harrison, and Guerino (2010) that 2 percent of youth in their survey reported victimization by youth and approximately 12 percent reported victimization by staff within the first year they were held in custody. An alarming 81 percent of the youth who were victimized reported being victimized more than once, and 43 percent had been victimized by more than one individual. The longer the youth was held in custody, the more likely was the sexual victimization. (Recall that the latest report on this issue is highlighted in **Box 13-1** at the beginning of this chapter.)

SUMMARY AND CONCLUSIONS

Following upon the chapter on sexual assaults of adults, the present chapter has focused upon sexual offenses against children. We distinguished child sexual offending from "pedophilia," a clinical term that refers to intense, recurring sexual fantasies and urges relating to children. It may or may not be accompanied by comparable behaviors. By itself, pedophilia is a clinical condition, not a crime. However, if the condition leads to behavior involving child victims, the behavior becomes legally accountable. Despite this distinction, the psychological and criminal justice literatures as well as the media often use terms like "pedophile" and "pedophilia" to describe this group of sexual offenders. Legally, persons suspected of sexually abusing children may be charged with child molestation, child sexual assault, incest, child rape, or a variety of other offenses, depending upon the statutes in a given jurisdiction.

Sexual assaults against children—covering a range of offenses—are disturbingly too common, although accurate statistics are difficult to obtain. Much of our information is derived not only from arrest and conviction data but also from the reports of adults who say they were victimized as children and from the perpetrators themselves. Arrest data indicate that 34 percent of all victims of sexual assault reported to law enforcement in the early 1990s were under age 12. In a related finding, some research indicates that approximately two-thirds of convicted rapists in state prisons committed their crimes against children. By their own accounts, offenders admit to molesting not one but many children, sometimes over a period of years. Other research suggests that from a quarter to a third of all women and one-tenth of men say they were sexually abused during childhood. As we discussed in the chapter, the long-term psychological effects of this victimization are often, if not typically, devastating.

We reviewed a variety of offender characteristics, including both demographic and psychological features. Aggressive child sexual offenders show similarities to men who rape adults, including problems with alcohol, high school failure rates, unstable work history, and low socioeconomic status. As a group, CSOs tend to be older than rapists, although the great majority apparently commits the first offense before age 30. Although increasingly more attention is being given to female CSOs, sexual offending against children is still predominantly a male phenomenon. Nevertheless, contemporary researchers have proposed typologies of female sex offenders and gathered data on their demographic and psychological characteristics.

The cognitive skills of CSOs are typically lower than those of the general population. They often lack social skills and adequate self-control mechanisms, and they often have a background that includes sexual victimization by others. Emotional congruence with children—feeling more comfortable with children than adults, for example—is not uncommon. They rarely take responsibility for their offenses, preferring to attribute their behavior to external forces beyond their control. Interestingly, current research indicates that CSOs actually have greater self-control than rapists.

The Massachusetts Treatment Center (MTC) has developed classification systems for the behavioral patterns of both rapists (discussed in the previous chapter) and child molesters. Both systems have undergone revision to further specify and refine some of their categories and to incorporate crime scene information. We reviewed the MTC systems in some detail, focusing on the MTC:CM3, the latest version. Similar but less elaborate classification systems proposed by Groth for both rapists and child molesters were covered as well. The MTC classification systems are the most widely used and have been the most submitted to empirical research.

We discussed some of the available research on juvenile sex offending, which is clearly a major challenge to the juvenile justice system. Distinctions are often made in the literature between juvenile molesters and juvenile rapists. For example, molesters almost invariably choose children younger than they are as victims, while rapists choose victims of about the same age or older. Juvenile molesters are also more likely than juvenile rapists to have been victims of child sexual abuse and to view themselves as socially inadequate. The topic of female juvenile sex offending is increasingly making an appearance in the literature. These offenders typically have been abused themselves and often commit their abuses while babysitting or otherwise caring for children.

In recent years much attention has been directed at sexual trafficking with children as victims and child sexual abuse facilitated by the Internet. Older children, preadolescents, and adolescents are the most likely victims of both of these offenses. Sexual trafficking may involve vulnerable children sold by their caretakers or naïve adolescents who are promised a better existence. Internet crimes involve primarily the downloading of child pornography or the luring of victims for sexual purposes. The production, distribution, downloading, and possession of child pornography is a federal offense, as is online solicitation of juveniles, but offenders in these category are not typically studied as CSOs.

The chapter ended with a discussion of treatment for CSOs. Although early reviews of the treatment literature were not encouraging, particularly programs aimed at the most serious offenders, there is evidence that treatment of sexual offending can be successful. Treatment strategies must focus not only on the cessation of the antisocial sexual conduct but also on maintenance of prosocial behaviors. Thus, continual monitoring or supervision should be a part of the treatment regimen. Recent meta-analyses indicate that cognitive-behavioral treatment based on the principles of risk-need-responsivity (RNR) is most promising with respect to both sex offenders and offenders in general.

Key Concepts

Aggressive (sadistic) child sex offender

Crossover

Emotional congruence with children

Exploitative child sex offender

Extrafamilial child molestation

Fixated (immature) sex offender

Hebephilia

Intrafamilial child molestation

Paraphilia

Pedophilia

Regressed sex offender

Review Questions

1. What is the distinction between pedophilia and child sex offending?
2. What are the major differences between extrafamilial CSOs and intrafamilial CSOs?
3. Summarize demographic and psychological characteristics of CSOs.
4. Discuss research findings on juvenile sex offenders.
5. Outline child molestation typologies of the MTC and the Groth system. Which is better supported by the research literature?
6. Discuss research findings on female sex offenders.

14

Burglary, Home Invasions, Thefts, and "White-Collar" Offenses

CHAPTER OBJECTIVES

- Provide an overview of offenses that are generally not violent.
- Sketch burglary, including property cues, motives, demographics, and cognitive processes of burglars.
- Discuss the psychological effects of burglary on victims.
- Describe the nature of home invasions.
- Examine motor vehicle theft, including carjacking and the motives and decision making of offenders.
- Describe identity theft and its psychological consequences.
- Discuss the prevalence of shoplifting along with motives and other psychological factors.
- Review the definitions and typologies of "white-collar crime," including Green's categories of occupational crime.

This chapter deals with a wide variety of criminal activity that at first glance would appear to have little in common. However, for the most part, the offenses in this chapter are radically different from the criminal behavior we have discussed up to this point. What they all have in common is a lack of physical aggression—or violence—in carrying out the act. In some cases, though, for example, in some burglaries, carjackings, and home invasions, violence may be a by-product. In addition, corporate offenses may involve actual or potential violence (e.g., when they violate safety standards) or violence to the environment.

The crimes discussed here will implicate psychological concepts we have not discussed extensively thus far. Whereas we have spent considerable time on learning, classical conditioning, self-esteem, frustration, and of course aggression in the previous chapters, we will see a de-emphasis on these concepts in this chapter, despite the fact that they may still be relevant. Burglars and identity thieves still learn how to carry out their crimes. On the other hand, we will place more emphasis on such concepts as self-reinforcement, expectations, justifications, and motivations than was placed in previous chapters.

Most of the crimes discussed here are treated as **property crimes** in official statistics. Property crimes generally involve the illegal acquisition of money and material goods, or the illegal destruction of property for financial gain. According to the UCR, the four major property crimes are burglary, larceny/theft (which includes fraud), motor vehicle theft, and arson. Of the four, arson is the most complex to categorize. Although profit is not *always* the motive in the other property offenses, it is *often not* the motive in arson. For example, it may simply reflect the desire to destroy property, or it may be committed to cover up another crime, even murder. When children and juveniles commit arson, it is called fire-setting and may be considered a psychological disorder. For these reasons, we will discuss arson in the following chapter.

Although the crimes covered here do not typically involve physical aggression, they are similar to the violent offenses discussed in earlier chapters in one important psychological aspect. Most of them involve a dehumanization of the victim, albeit in a different sense from the dehumanization that often occurs in violence. As we have learned, dehumanization occurs when a person or group of persons sees and treats others as objects, rather than as human beings. When a person is not responding to the human qualities of other people, it becomes much more possible to act inhumanely toward them. In crimes like larceny, burglary, and identity theft, for example, the offenders avoid confronting their victims directly. Although there are exceptions, they usually do not directly observe or experience the economic, social, and psychological discomfort of their victims. In the victim's absence, internal values and social constraints are less effective, allowing the offender to repress, deny, or justify the crime more easily. As Gresham Sykes (1956) put it, the individual's internal sentiments are more easily neutralized by the physical absence of the victim. The offender does not have to think of the effects his or her actions have on the victim, because the offender often does not know the victim as a human being, only as a target. This is even more likely to be the case today, when so many fraudulent offenses are committed online. On the other hand, dehumanization is more difficult in carjacking or home invasion cases, particularly the latter.

Table 14-1 gives a percentage breakdown of the UCR property crimes for 2013. As you can see, larceny-theft accounted for about two-thirds of the property crime, followed by burglary at almost one-quarter of these offenses. Like the violent crime rate, the property crime rate has decreased over the past decade. The four property crimes decreased 16.3 percent from 2004 figures and 4.8 percent compared to the 2012 rate. Burglary experienced the greatest decrease from 2012, at 8.6 percent.

In addition to the traditional crimes of burglary, larceny-theft, and motor vehicle theft, the chapter will cover current, specific forms, such as identity theft and carjacking. Identity theft is one of the few official tabulated crimes that has increased in recent years, largely due to online access to data. Carjacking is a unique form of motor vehicle theft that—though relatively rare—has attracted contemporary research attention. We also cover "white-collar" offenses and discuss the difficulty both defining that concept and estimating its prevalence.

Obviously, most offenders engage in property crime for the money or goods they obtain, or for other tangible rewards that meet biological, psychological, or social needs. Sykes (1956) noted long ago, however, that this does not tell us why some people commit these crimes under certain social conditions, while others do not. Explanations based strictly on economic necessity and the satisfaction of basic human needs do not go far enough. Sykes proposed the concept of **relative deprivation** as an additional factor. To assess the economic want associated with property crimes, we should consider not what the person has or is making in personal income, but rather how great the discrepancy is between what he or she has and what he or she would like to have. Specifically, relative deprivation is the psychological distance between what people perceive they have now and what they think they can realistically attain. In another sense, relative deprivation refers to a pervasive sense of injustice that develops between the "haves" and "have nots." It also might apply to

TABLE 14-1	Property Crimes, 2013	
Offense	**Number of Offenses**	**Percent of Property Crimes**
Total property	8,632,512	100.0
Larceny-theft	6,004,453	67.0
Burglary	1,928,465	23.0
Motor vehicle theft	699,594	8.0
Arson	44,840	2.0

Source: Federal Bureau of Investigation (2014a). Crime in the United States 2013: Uniform Crime Reports. Washington, DC: U.S. Department of Justice.

the person who possesses sufficient wealth but believes he or she still needs more to maintain a life-style similar to others. Relative deprivation is an interesting concept, but it would require empirical documentation to make it a likely explanatory factor for criminal behavior.

From a psychological perspective, the crimes discussed in this chapter cannot be simply explained by biological needs, material wants, or relative deprivation. Powerful cognitive motivators must also be considered. These cognitive factors are in the form of outcome expectations and the personal capacity of the individual to predict and appreciate future consequences of his or her behavior. Furthermore, the cognitive forces may be relatively independent of external reinforcements like tangible rewards or even social and status rewards. Self-reinforcements, including self-rewards and self-punishments, may represent a major motivating factor in many of the crimes discussed in this chapter. That it, there may be intrinsic rewards and self-satisfaction in the successful completion of a crime. This is one reason contemporary researchers have begun to focus on expertise in committing certain crimes, such as burglary or carjacking (Nee, 2015).

Cognitive factors are also extremely important in another sense: They allow the offender to justify his or her behavior. A strong theme of this chapter is the tendency of economic offenders—including corporate criminals—to minimize, distort, or deny misconduct or reprehensible behavior. The aforementioned psychological separation from the victim helps them to do this. We expand on these psychological issues of motivation and justification throughout the following pages.

BURGLARY

Burglary is a crime that often affects large segments of the population and can cause extensive economic and emotional distress to victims. Nevertheless, as noted above, official burglary rates have decreased in recent years. Burglary is defined as the unlawful entry of a structure, with or without force, with intent to commit a felony or theft. Recall that in Chapter 12 we covered the topic of sexual burglaries, which were illegal entries with the intent to commit a sexual crime, most notably rape. Because these offenses are better classified as sex crimes than property crimes for our purposes, they are not re-introduced here except as they apply to burglar typologies to be discussed later in the chapter.

The FBI classifies burglary into three categories: (1) forcible entry, (2) unlawful entry where no force is used, and (3) attempted forcible entry. Approximately 1,928,465 burglaries were known to police in 2013, which was a decrease of 8.6 percent from 2012 data (Federal Bureau of Investigation, 2014a). Fifty-nine percent of these involved forcible entry, 34.3 percent were unlawful entry, and 6.4 percent were attempted forcible entry. Most of these (74.0%) were burglaries of residential properties. The average dollar loss per burglary offense was $2,322.

A special report based on NCVS data (Walters, Moore, Berzofsky, & Langton, 2013) investigated household burglaries from 1994 through 2011. During that period, household burglaries decreased 56 percent. Not surprisingly, the *median* dollar value of items and cash stolen was higher in 2011 ($600) than in 1994 ($389). Note that this is lower than the *mean* reported in the FBI statistics. The greatest decreases in burglaries were reported by households in urban areas, households headed by Hispanics, and households with an income of $75,000 or more.

Characteristics of Burglary

As documented in the above data, about one-third of burglaries do *not* involve forced entry. That is, the offenders entered through an unlatched window or unlocked door or used a key "hidden" in an obvious place, such as under a doormat. Fewer than 10 percent of the burglaries were *attempts* at forcible entry.

Consistently, year after year, and also as documented in UCR data, most of the burglaries involve residential property rather than commercial establishments. To be considered residential burglary, the structure entered need not be the house itself. Illegal entry of a garage, shed, or other structure on the premises also constitutes a residential burglary. Burglaries of residences occur more frequently during the daytime, whereas burglaries of businesses and nonresidential property mostly occur at night.

Burglaries are more likely to occur during the warmer months, especially July and August, apparently because people are more likely to be outdoors or away on vacation and are more likely to leave doors and windows open, making their residences vulnerable.

An early study by Langer and Miranksy (1983) reveals that a large segment of the population does not take responsibility for burglary prevention. Approximately half of the New York City residents questioned admitted they did not lock all their doors when away from home, even if they had been burglarized before. Interestingly, while 66 percent believed that burglary could be prevented, 61 percent of these subjects did not use all their locks. They believed that it was the responsibility of others (e.g., the police, the landlord, the building superintendent) to guard the premises, rather than their own personal responsibility. We must be very careful not to blame victims for *any* criminal offenses, however. It is one thing to alert people and make them aware of steps they can take to protect themselves from crime; it is quite another to fault them for not taking the steps. In the above study, those who thought their neighborhoods were unsafe and burglary-prone were less likely to use locks than those who considered their neighborhoods safe and less burglary-prone. Possibly, people in burglary-prone areas are convinced that if someone decides to burglarize their homes, there is not much they can do about it, locks or no locks. Another factor, though, is that good locks and other security devices cost money. If one lives on a tight budget, buying a lock may be seen as a low priority.

Who Commits Burglary?

Like many other criminal offenses, burglary seems to be primarily a crime committed by the young. For example, taking just one year, about 50 percent of those arrested in 2013 were under 25, with the average age being about 22 (Federal Bureau of Investigation, 2014a). Approximately 17 percent were under 18. To some extent, this arrest ratio may reflect the lack of sophistication of younger burglars who, because of their inexperience, are more likely to be detected. However, researchers have noted that, with increasing age, some burglars find they are not as nimble and athletic as they once were. Crawling through small open windows and climbing fences take their toll, and these strenuous activities become more burdensome with age. Thus, many older burglars turn to shoplifting (Cromwell, Olson, & Avary, 1991). Shoplifting—to be discussed again shortly—is considerably easier, less risky, and more cost efficient. Shoplifted items are more easily converted to cash. Furthermore, the criminal penalties are significantly less for shoplifting than they are for burglary.

Burglary is largely a male enterprise, with only 17 percent of those arrested being women in 2013. Although 67.4 percent of those arrested in 2013 were white, nonwhites were overrepresented in proportion to their numbers in the general population (Federal Bureau of Investigation, 2014a).

As noted earlier, about two of every three burglaries are residential, and burglary of residences usually occurs during the daytime and on weekdays. Daytime burglary by juveniles is closely associated with truancy from school (Scott, 2004). Commercial establishments are usually burglarized late at night and on weekends (Cromwell et al., 1991; Pope, 1977b). This is not surprising, since burglary is a passive crime; the offender selects times and places that will minimize the possibility of an encounter with victims. Almost all *experienced* burglars assert they will not even enter a residence when the occupants are believed to be at home (Cromwell et al., 1991; Nee, 2015). Homes occupied during the day most commonly are occupied by a parent providing child care or by retired individuals. However, burglars know that occupants develop predictable patterns regarding the use of discretionary time for the purposes of shopping, errands, or visiting friends or relatives. Individuals who work outside the home during weekdays also show similar patterns on weekends. Parents also usually develop predictable patterns of taking children back and forth to school, nursery programs, and recreational activities.

Of all property crimes, burglary probably offers the greatest probability of success with the least amount of risk. Not only is it a crime without victim contact and probability of identification, but also it does not require weapons. Recall, however, that weapons are involved in most sexual burglaries. Furthermore, the penalties for burglary in which no one is physically harmed usually are less severe than those for robbery, to be covered in the following chapter.

Burglary Cues and Selected Targets

The identification of situational cues is especially important in successful burglary. Nee and Taylor (1988) found that there are at least four broad categories of relevant cues used by experienced residential burglars. They are as follows:

1. *Occupancy cues*, such as letters or newspapers visible in mailbox; motor vehicles present; windows, blinds, and curtains shut or open
2. *Wealth cues*, such as the appearance of the house, the neighborhood, the quality of the landscaping, the make(s) of car(s) driven, and visible furnishings
3. *Layout cues*, such as how easy it would be to gain access to the house or building without detection, as well as escape
4. *Security cues*, such as alarm systems, window locks, and dead bolt locks

Taylor and Nee (1988) designed a study that tested the possible differences in identifying these cues between burglars and home owners. The burglars consisted of a group of 15 experienced burglars serving time in Cork Prison in Ireland, and the home owners consisted of 15 Irish home owners. Each subject was requested to explore a simulated environment made up of slides and maps of five different houses. The researchers found that burglars were better able to discern security provisions and were more concerned about escaping successfully from the scene than were home owners. Most surprising, however, was the high amount of agreement between burglars and home owners on which houses were most vulnerable to burglary.

Burglars tend to prefer single-family homes, primarily because they can be entered directly from the street, and because they often have multiple access and escape points (Bernasco, 2006). Neighborhood residents who are not affiliated with or are isolated from their neighbors (called anonymous environments) are also preferred because the neighbors will less likely be alarmed by unusual or suspicious events (Bernasco, 2006). Corner homes offer an attractive target, as they often have many escape routes, have fewer neighbors nearby, and are more difficult for neighbors to watch (Rengert & Groff, 2011).

Rengert and Groff (2011) note that antiques displayed in a window or somewhere outside are important cues for some burglars. Antiques indicate that the residents are probably collectors, and burglars often assume that they may find valuable coins, stamps, old guns, and other collectibles inside the house.

Table 14-2 provides NCVS data on burglary and occupied versus unoccupied homes at different times of the day. Unless they are entering the home to commit a violent crime or to intimidate their victims, burglars not surprisingly prefer to enter an unoccupied home. Still, as indicated in the table, night-time burglaries occur with some regularity while victims are at home. Burglars have a

TABLE 14-2 Time of Occurrence of Household Burglaries, by Presence of Household Member, 2003–2007

Time of Day	Household Member Not Present		Household Member Present	
	Average Annual Number	Percent	Average Annual Number	Percent
Total	2,683,270	100.0	1,021,430	100.0
Daytime (6 a.m.–6 p.m.)	1,159,450	48.2	336,340	32.9
Nighttime (6 p.m.–6 a.m.)	697,940	26.0	626,150	61.3
Not known	825,880	30.8	58,940	5.8

Source: Catalano, S. M. (2010, September). Victimization during household burglary. Washington, DC: U.S. Department of Justice, Bureau of Justice Statistics.

number of strategies for determining if a targeted house is unoccupied. One strategy, for example, is surveying funeral notices published in newspapers (Rengert & Groff, 2011). "Burglars realize that this is a time when family and friends of the deceased are likely to be at the funeral" (Rengert & Groff, 2011, p. 161). Another method is gathering information about the targeted house while performing a legitimate occupation, such as landscaping and lawn care, sales, or cable television installation. Another method is for the burglar to check Facebook or other online networking portals. Many people post that they are on vacation or are planning to go on vacation, often listing the exact dates. (Interestingly, Facebook postings have worked in the other direction as well: a group of juveniles bragged about their burglarizing exploits on Facebook, and even began posting where they would strike next. Police were waiting for them and caught them in the act.)

Some burglars simply knock on the door. If someone answers the door, they use the excuse that they were looking for directions, were out of gas, or are having car problems. They may also glance around the inside of the house, given the opportunity, to assess whether there is likely to be items worth taking in the future. Leaving the garage door open of an attached garage and no vehicle is sight is a clear invitation to a burglar, but we stress that the burglary, if it occurs, is not the fault of the victim.

Burglar Cognitive Processes

Bennett and Wright (1984) conducted an extensive three-year project involving convicted burglars confined in various prisons throughout southern England. The study is about 30 years old, but it is one of the few qualitative studies that focused on the cognitions of the burglars themselves, through semi-structured interviews. The researchers' primary interest was to learn the decision-making processes and perceptions of the residential burglars at the time of the crime. Although a majority of the burglars had committed a variety of other economic crimes, almost all of them considered burglary their main criminal activity. Therefore, most of them probably qualify as professionals rather than amateurs.

Bennett and Wright discovered that almost all the burglaries were planned. Many other studies have arrived at the same conclusion (Vaughn, DeLisi, Beaver, & Howard, 2008). Very few were the result of spur-of-the-moment decisions, nor were there any constant or irrepressible urges to burglarize. More than likely, though, even those burglaries that appeared to be impulsive or opportunity-driven are probably the result of well-learned cognitive scripts. As described in Chapter 5, **cognitive scripts** are mental images and plans of how one will act and react in certain situations. The more one rehearses these scripts, behaviorally and mentally, the more habitual they become under similar conditions.

The two main aspects that went into the planning of burglars in the Bennett and Wright investigation were the situational cues of surveillability and occupancy. Surveillability cues were related to the amount of cover or openness around the house, whether it was overlooked by neighboring houses, the availability of access to the rear, and the presence or proximity of neighbors. Occupancy cues were similar to the ones reported by Nee and Taylor, such as a car in the driveway, lights on in the house, the presence of mail, whether the walks were shoveled or the lawn was cut, and so forth. Experienced burglars said that "occupancy proxies" were the major deterrents in attempts to burglarize. Specifically, burglar alarms and dogs were extremely important in the prevention of burglary. This was also a consistent finding of Cromwell and colleagues (1991). In fact, Cromwell and colleagues found that the dog does not have to be a large one, and it does not have to be a terrifying breed. Any dog will do, since a large one poses a physical threat, and the small dog will be noisy—yapping papillons come to mind. Cats do not seem to qualify as good property protectors.

Cromwell and his associates also found that dead bolts caused burglars considerable difficulty in entry, even though some of the experienced burglars claimed such locks would not be any problem. However, Cromwell and colleagues not only obtained self-report data from experienced burglars, but also had them demonstrate their claims. Security locks and dead bolts caused all kinds of trouble, even for highly experienced burglars—and even though they had maintained that the locks would not be a deterrent. Much of the research on burglary, on the other hand, finds that increased police patrols and other such strategies have very little influence on decisions to burglarize, or on its success rate. This is primarily because the patrols cannot last indefinitely, and police cannot be everywhere at once. However, curious neighbors—those always peeking out their windows or finding yard chores to do when there is different activity next door—do tend to be strong deterrents for burglars. This observation is supported by both experienced burglars and crime statistics.

RECENT RESEARCH ON OCCUPANCY CUES.   Research data suggest that, although burglary is a "planned" behavior, burglars identify a large number of potential targets, and then select the most vulnerable. Cromwell and his colleagues caution, however, that even though a high percentage of burglars make carefully planned, highly rational decisions based on a detailed evaluation of environmental cues, the critical factor seems to be finding the right opportunity from an array of potential targets. This is related to the expertise required to be a successful burglar (Nee, 2015). Burglary is not generally an impulsive crime, but it isn't usually planned to precise detail either. For example, an offender may target a specific house at a particular time. On the day of the planned burglary, the homeowner is unexpectedly home; the burglar then selects a different target. There is considerable research showing that cues indicating occupancy of the home often act as a deterrent, thus reducing the risk of burglary victimization (Snook, Dhami, & Kavanagh, 2011). There is also contemporary research evidence indicating that professional burglars use less, but more relevant information about their targets than amateur or novice burglars, who are influenced by irrelevant information (Garcia-Retamero & Dhami, 2009). That is, professional burglars make their decisions to burglarize a residence on only one or two cues of occupancy based on their previous experience. For example, if no car is parked outside and the curtains are closed at ground level, these two cues would indicate to the professional the residence is unoccupied. In fact, Snook et al. (2011) found that "vehicle cue" was the most important for burglars in deciding occupancy. Essentially, it seems that professionals do not clutter their minds with complicated strategies compared to novices who tend to rely on more cognitively complex strategies. As emphasized by Snook et al., "this growing body of research on burglars' decision making appears to contradict criminological theories of rational choice that portray offenders as employing compensatory decision strategies that weigh and integrate information" (p. 323). Skillful burglars apparently use simple, fast, and frugal decisions based on previous experiences.

Entry Strategies

Cromwell and his colleagues (1991) found in their systematic study of experienced burglars that one of the most popular entry methods was through sliding glass patio doors. Burglars said that these doors are easily popped out of their sliding tracks by hand or with aid of a crowbar or screwdriver. Unless the doors are armed with security hardware, entry is quick and noiseless. Another common method is to remove, cut, or gently break a windowpane and crawl through the open window. A skillful burglar will carefully remove the pane, crawl through, and then replace the pane in a professional manner. Other commonly preferred methods for residential burglary include forcing the rear door open with a pry tool or kicking it down, or opening the garage door and forcing open the door between the garage and the house.

A more modern entry method for professional burglars is to use a bump key. Most doors can be opened with a bump key—usually made of brass—which fits into the keyway of the lock. Bumping is a method of pin manipulation within the lock by using a key made specifically designed for most commonly used door locks. That is, one bump key is usually sufficient for unlocking a majority of the locks made by a certain manufacturer. Although bump keys are produced for certified locksmiths, a competent professional burglar can purchase online a set of 11 bump keys that fit most of all the commonly used locks. In some cases, a bump hammer must also be purchased. Bump keys allow burglars to enter a house without any signs of damage or signs of entry, and it may be days before anything is noticed missing. The availability of such items as bump keys and hammers is one reason why the unauthorized possession of burglary tools is a crime in most jurisdictions. An electronic keypad would be one way to deter this method of illegal entry.

Once in the house, burglars check easy escape routes in case someone arrives home. Then they usually go to the master bedroom where many valuables are located. As pointed out by Rengert and Groff (2011), the master bedroom also provides a good container for carrying valuables—the pillowcase. After the bedroom, the burglar often turns his or her attention to the dining area, looking for silverware, candlesticks, and silver service. Kitchens are usually avoided. If available, a study is a good place to locate stamp and coin collections, and easily transported electronics.

How Far Do Burglars Travel?

National research data on arrested burglars in the United States indicate that a large proportion commit the offense near their own residence. Both classic and more recent research supports this. The Santa Clara Criminal Justice Pilot Program (1972) found that over one-half of the apprehended offenders traveled no more than a mile from their own home to commit the offenses. More recently, in a study of serial burglars who operated in a small town in southern England, Barker (2000) found that these offenders tended to live surprisingly close to the areas they burglarized. She discovered, however, that the mean home-to-offense distance increased during the later stages of burglary. For example, the average home-to-first-offense distance was 2.16 kilometers, the average distance from home to the middle offense in the series was 3.57 kilometers, and the average distance from home to the last offense in the series was 5.52 kilometers. It is difficult to generalize from these data, however, because apprehended burglars are presumably less skillful and thus more detectable than burglars who succeed. It is possible that successful burglars operate farther away from home. However, in general, burglars are probably less likely to travel distances because they are less familiar with unknown and uncharted territory. Eskridge (1983) found that those who burglarized commercial establishments were more willing to travel much greater distances. Interestingly, Bennell and Jones (2005) found that both commercial and residential burglars select distinct geographical areas to commit their crimes, and they appear to return to those selected areas until they have exhausted the suitable targets. Examination of the geographical patterns of burglars is an important task undertaken by geographical profilers, discussed in Chapter 10, particularly in the case of multiple burglaries that occur in a given community.

Gender Differences in Methods and Patterns

In their study of both male and female burglars, Decker, Wright, Redfern, and Smith (1993) found that the offending patterns of female burglars were very similar to those of males. One major exception was that male burglars often stole cars in addition to burglarizing residences or commercial establishments, whereas the female burglars did not. Decker and his colleagues found that they could divide the female burglars into two major groups: accomplices and partners. Accomplices committed the burglary because of their subservience to others—usually men—during their burglaries. Partners, on the other hand, participated as equals in the commission of burglary. Although some of the females co-offended with males, they did not take orders from them.

Property Taken and Disposed

The items that burglars usually take from homes are jewelry, gold, valuable household ornaments, stamp and coin collections, and computers—now more likely to be laptops and tablets—followed by tools (Schneider, 2005). In recent years, the plethora of handheld communication and video devices found in many homes have been attractive targets. Nongarden-type power tools are especially popular, including cordless drills, saws, snap-on tools, and generators. High-quality televisions, video players, electronic equipment, and all types of alcohol are also desired items. Most recently, prescription medications and even diabetic test strips are in high demand. Burglars usually do not spend the time looking for cash, unless they suspect that there are substantial quantities hidden somewhere in the house. Garden tools that are in good shape, such as mowers, trimmers, and hedge cutters, may be taken if the burglar has readily available transportation. Credit cards and wallets have not traditionally been sought by burglars, but some today intend to commit identity fraud or—more likely—sell these items to someone who plans to do so. (See **Table 14-3** for examples of property stolen in 2013.)

TABLE 14-3	Property Stolen and Recovered, 2013		
	Value of Property		
Type of Property	Stolen	Recovered	Percent Recovered
Total	14,741,818,452	2,832,231,843	19.2
Currency, notes, and so on	2,013,267,402	28,452,259	1.4
Jewelry and precious metals	1,743,673,506	88,475,237	5.1
Clothing and furs	304,670,804	33,542,000	11.0
Locally stolen motor vehicles	3,937,054,674	2,159,429,364	54.8
Office equipment	846,233,329	32,156,043	3.8
Televisions, radios, stereos, and so on	665,750,318	32,632,767	4.9
Firearms	154,826,891	13,693,638	8.8
Household goods	422,439,091	114,868,752	27.2
Consumable goods	231,420,776	14,425,417	6.2
Livestock	16,367,591	1,303,936	8.0
Miscellaneous	4,406,114,070	313,240,430	7.1

Source: Federal Bureau of Investigation (2014a). Crime in the United States 2013: Uniform Crime Reports. Washington, DC: U.S. Department of Justice.

Being easy to sell is the most common reason provided for stealing certain items (Schneider, 2005). Some very expensive items, such as valuable paintings, may be avoided because they may be very difficult to sell. The ease in carrying or removing the item is the second reason for stealing it.

Amateur burglars usually take money or personal items that they need, whereas the professional takes items with excellent resale value (Nee, 2015; Vetter & Silverman, 1978). The professional usually has access to a **fence**, whereas the amateur rarely has that kind of contact. Amateurs usually sell their stolen items to pawn shops or friends. A fence, an integral component in the professional burglary cycle, is a person who knowingly buys stolen merchandise for the purpose of resale. As indicated above, wallets have become saleable items highly desired by identity thieves who do not themselves want to commit burglary (National Center for White Collar Crime, 2015).

The Cromwell and associates (1991) research raises serious questions about the extent to which professional fences are used today, however. In their investigation of experienced burglars operating in an urban Texas metropolitan area of 250,000, they found considerable diversity in the channels through which stolen property was distributed. Some burglars sold their knowingly stolen property to pawnshops, others to friends and acquaintances, and still others traded their property for drugs. Some resold the merchandise to legitimate businesses or strangers. The researchers, therefore, suggest that the "professional fence may have been displaced by a more diverse and readily accessed market for stolen property" (p. 73). Stolen property today, for example, is often disposed of via Internet sites, and purchasers are often not aware that the items were obtained illegally. It is not unusual for persons reporting theft of jewelry to police to be told to check pawnshops, flea markets, and garage sales in their vicinity.

Other research (Schneider, 2005) suggests that selling stolen property to handlers or fences is still the preferred method for disposing of merchandise acquired through burglary, especially by persistent or professional burglars. After fences, the second choice was to sell to friends or trade the stolen items for drugs. In some instances, the burglar keeps the stolen property for himself or herself, but this choice increases the chances of being detected.

Motives

As you might expect, the motives for burglary are varied, but the primary factor for professionals is undoubtedly monetary gain. When performed competently, burglary is a lucrative business with low risks and with monetary rewards far surpassing those the burglar might earn at legitimate work. In addition, burglars make a rough estimation of whether the expected financial gain outweighs the effort and the risk of detection (Bernasco, 2006; Nee, 2015). As noted earlier, however, other researchers indicate that the rational choice argument relative to burglary is overstated (Snook et al., 2011). It appears that, with respect to this issue, far more research is needed before firm conclusions can be drawn.

David (1974) learned that a husband and wife team he interviewed made, on the average, $400 to $500 a day; a solitary offender in his sample made about $500 per week. These figures will obviously be substantially higher in today's market. Many professionals also conceive of their behavior as a challenging skill to be continually developed and refined. Some even said they get a "rush" of excitement during the planning and commission of the crime, especially if they are good at it (Cromwell et al., 1991). In this sense, burglary is highly adaptive and represents an instrumental behavior supported by strong reinforcement. For many burglars, however, a simple conclusion that they participate in their crimes as their sole profession or lucrative business may be unwarranted. A vast majority of burglary is committed, not out of necessity, but rather to supplement the offenders' incomes and to improve their quality of life (Rengert & Wasilchick, 1985). The income gained from burglary enables the offender to buy drugs, alcohol, and expensive goods. Alternatively, it may be used, like the profits from other economic crimes, to finance a college education. Subsistence needs—food, shelter, clothing—are met through other sources of income, such as a regular job, including one that pays only minimum wages.

Some burglars may burglarize the same place again, or even repeatedly, in a pattern called **repeat burglary**. Burglars that participate in repeat burglary do it because of the efficiency in time, planning, and risk involved (Farrell, Phillips, & Pease, 1995). Residential locations are especially vulnerable because residents do not necessarily change the layout or make entry more difficult after a burglary. In other words, the burglar knows the layout of the target well, was successful the first time, and may even have seen valuables the first time around that prompted a return visit. In addition, researchers have identified a phenomenon called **near-repeat offending** (Bernasco, 2008; Sagovsky & Johnson, 2007), which refers to the likelihood of additional burglary in a neighborhood after one house in that neighborhood has been successfully burglarized. Usually, these near repeat crimes occur within the first few weeks of the original crime (Sagovsky & Johnson, 2007). The near repeat phenomenon also has been found for other crimes, such as shootings, robbery, and car theft (Youstin, Nobels, Ward, & Cook, 2011).

The professional burglar, then, is primarily motivated by money but also by self-satisfaction and accomplishment. When self-satisfaction and self-reinforcement are conditioned on certain accomplishments, people are motivated to expend the effort needed to attain the desired goal, perhaps even independently of monetary gain. Walsh (1980), for example, has emphasized the expressive and psychological components of burglary. He posits that, for some burglars, the challenge of the crime is far more rewarding than the material reward. Based on interviews with victims and offenders, Walsh identified three kinds of **expressive burglars**: (1) *the feral threat*, (2) *the riddlesmith*, and (3) *the dominator*. The feral threat burglar engages in destructive, malicious vandalism during the break-in by spilling things, breaking glass, smashing objects, and urinating and defecating in various areas throughout the house. This burglar may slash the clothing in the closets, and vandalize vehicles in the garage. The riddlesmith, on the other hand, tries to demonstrate his or her technical skill to the victims and investigators by setting up puzzles, mysteries, and booby traps throughout the house. The riddlesmith is inventive in the way he or she causes damage, and messages may be left on walls, floors, and mirrors. The dominator enjoys threatening or frightening victims, and therefore breaks into homes that are occupied.

Most burglars are not expressive burglars. For those who are, all three types identified by Walsh are interested in communicating to burglarized victims through a particular style or method of operating. Thus, a burglar who takes great pride in developing ingenious techniques and stumping police is even more likely to continue his illegal conduct. While external reinforcements (tangible rewards) are important, internal reinforcement may be a very powerful motivating and regulating factor. Walsh's study represents an early attempt at formulating a burglar typology. Following are more contemporary approaches.

Burglar Typologies

As mentioned in earlier chapters, researchers often propose typologies of various offenders both for purposes of preventing and solving crimes and for purposes of treating offenders. In previous chapters we covered typologies of batterers, serial murderers, mass murderers, rapists, and child molesters. Although typologies have limitations (e.g., offenders rarely fit neatly into one category), they can offer insight into offending behaviors as well as possible traits shared by offenders.

Michael Vaughn and his colleagues (2008), using a sample of 456 adult career criminals, have empirically identified four classes of burglars: (1) young versatile, (2) vagrant, (3) drug-oriented, and (4) sexual predators. This classification system reveals the underlying motives and behaviors of burglars, some of whom may be considered dangerous. The first group, by far the most common (60%), were young and had committed a variety of offenses. They appear to represent the types of burglars we have described thus far, such as those who plan their offenses and have specific ways to dispose of the stolen property. The second type, the vagrant, made up 22 percent of the sample; they were often charged with various offenses primarily stemming from their transient, vagabond status. They appeared to burglarize primarily for material gain, especially during the winter months. The researchers speculated that many of these burglars may have mental disorders and lack social skills for gaining employment. The drug-oriented group, consisting of 15 percent of the sample, had numerous drug possession and drug-trafficking offenses. They also were likely to carry weapons for protection. In most instances, these offenders tended to burglarize to support their drug habit.

The fourth group, the sexual predator burglars, are the sexual burglars discussed in Chapter 12. In Vaughn et al.'s study they constituted 6 percent of the sample, and they were the most violent. This group had a long criminal career, committing an assortment of offenses, including aggravated assault, robbery, rape, and prostitution/solicitation. According to Vaughn et al., the burglaries committed by this group were at least partially motivated by sexual compulsion and thrills associated with entering dwellings of strangers. In some cases, these offenders were also motivated to sexually assault a person they had been stalking. Although this group represented only a small portion of the total sample, they also accounted for a large majority of the violence reported in burglary, and probably many of the reported home invasions. We will cover home invasions shortly.

Fox and Farrington (2012) developed a typology for burglary that was based on analyzing the crime scene more than the motivations of the offenders, although motivations were sometimes inferred. To conduct their research, they examined files of 405 solved burglary cases in one county of Florida in 2008 and 2009. Their subsequent Statistical Patterns of Offending Typology (SPOT) for burglary identified four offense styles: the opportunistic, the organized, disorganized, and the interpersonal. Each style was accompanied by a description of the offender most likely to characterize it. In the opportunistic style, the crime was not planned, whereas in the organized style the perpetrator came equipped with tools and appeared to be very systematic in his or her approach. The burglary scene was left clean. In the disorganized style, entry was forced and the scene was in disarray. The interpersonal style involved harming or trying to harm someone in an occupied home. In later research, Fox and Farrington (2015) evaluated the usefulness of this four-category profile in a careful experimental study comparing one police agency that used the profile to solve burglaries with three police agencies that did not. During a one-year follow-up, the agency using the profile had a significant increase in burglary arrests compared with departments that did not use the profile. **Table 14-4** summarizes key features of the Fox and Farrington and Vaughn et al. typologies.

TABLE 14-4 Key Features of Two Different Burglar Typologies

Vaughn et al. (2008)

- Sample: 456 adult career criminals, self-reporting their criminal history.
- Young versatile; vagrant; drug-oriented; sexual predator.
- Focused on motivations for each type (e.g., excitement, material gain, support drug habit, sexual satisfaction).
- Most useful for psychological treatment of burglars, but not sufficiently tested.

Fox and Farrington (2012, 2015)

- Sample: 405 files of convicted burglars.
- Opportunistic, organized, disorganized, interpersonal.
- Focused on analysis of behaviors and information from crime scene.
- Most useful for offender profiling to aid law enforcement, but results are preliminary.

These two research-based typologies will likely stimulate considerable research on types of burglary and burglars in the future. Vaughn et al.'s approach offers a sound explanation for the various motivations for some forms of burglary. Fox and Farrington's approach relies less on motivations, but it can offer insight on the offender's behavior and possible traits from analysis of the crime scene itself. Their contribution is more pertinent to offender profiling to solve crimes than to psychological treatment of offenders. Both groups of researchers were careful about noting limitations of their work. Vaughn et al. emphasized that their sample was characterized by extensive criminal careers and may not be entirely representative of professional or amateur burglars who restrict their criminal activity to burglary as a way of financial survival. Fox and Farrington (2015) observed that factors other than the profile they tested may have accounted for the higher arrest rates in the police department trained in SPOT. Nevertheless, the findings suggest that future research on the validity of burglar typologies is warranted.

Psychological Impact of Burglary

The home is a sanctuary: "It is a special place that is central to our daily lives, a place that is at the beginning and end of most of our journeys; it is chosen and personalized" (Merry & Hansent, 2000, p. 36). The manner in which homes are decorated and arranged and the objects within them represent important aspects of our lives and personalities. When our homes are burglarized, therefore, it is an invasion of our intimate space and an attack on our identity, physically and symbolically. Thus, though we may chuckle at the image of the burglar who fell asleep in the home he was burglarizing—an image widely circulated on the Internet—we know that the experience was unsettling for the homeowners.

Some victims describe burglary as a rape of their home, especially when the burglar has disturbed personal photographs, letters, and diaries, leaving the feeling of having been violated or at least "touched" by the intruder (Merry & Hansent, 2000). The distress levels experienced by victims are often more pronounced when the invasion extends to private areas, such as bedrooms, closets, chests-of-drawers, bathrooms, and desks. The invasion also endangers the victims' sense of control and threatens their ability to protect their own personal territory. Many victims, after being burglarized, install security systems such as video cameras, increase and improve the locks, buy dogs, or even move to new homes if they are able to do so. Others, though, no less traumatized, are unable to afford these changes. Overall, the psychological fallout from a burglary can be substantial for many victims and can continue for many years.

For some burglars (e.g., the expressive burglars described by Walsh, 1980), their actions are intended to produce some response from the victim. In other words, they specifically tailor their styles (or signatures) to convey messages to victims and investigators, hoping to induce some strong emotional reactions from the victims. The emotional reactions of burglarized victims often run the gamut from anger and depression to fear and anxiety (Brown & Harris, 1989). In addition, the individual style used by the offender probably reflects something about his character and personality. According to Merry and Hansent (2000), this aspect is referred to as the interpersonal dimension of the crime. It is suggested, therefore, that the victim's feelings of fear and vulnerability are psychological losses that are translated into gains for the offender. In this sense, the burglar gains materially and psychologically from the crime. The interpersonal aspects of the burglary are areas that provide considerable potential for burglary profiling in future research. As noted above, Fox and Farrington (2012) identified the interpersonal style with burglars who caused direct harm to their victims.

Home Invasions

In about 28 percent of residential burglaries, a member of the household is present (Catalano, 2010). These cases are often called **home invasions**, which refers to any crime committed by an individual unlawfully entering a residence while someone is home. It should be noted that home invasion is not a separate crime category in the UCR. In that data base, a home invasion would be counted as a burglary or, more likely, as one of the four violent crimes, depending upon which was the most serious. For example, if a home invader enters the home while everyone is asleep and departs with electronic equipment, this would be a burglary in the UCR. If the home invader entered the home and seriously assaulted the home owner, it would be counted as an aggravated assault. It should be emphasized, though, that even when someone is home, physical harm occurs in about 20 percent of the situations, and it is typically in the form of simple, not aggravated assault (Catalano, 2010).

Home invasion has also been used to "describe a situation where an offender forcibly enters an occupied residence with the specific intent of robbing or harming those inside" (Catalano, 2010, p. 2). In some situations, a household member may become a target either to "settle a score" or because the offender knows the person is vulnerable, such as persons with disabilities or the elderly. In other cases, the offender enters the residence mistakenly believing no one is home, or the household member returns home while a burglary is in process. It is perhaps misleading to refer to these last cases as home invasions, because the perpetrators did not enter the premises with the intent to do harm to the residents.

One of the most horrific and highly publicized, but atypical home invasions of the past decade was the 2007 Connecticut case in which two men entered a home occupied by a man, a woman, and their two daughters, aged 17 and 11. The invaders beat and restrained the man (who eventually escaped and ultimately survived), and sexually assaulted the woman and one of the two daughters. The family was subjected to abuse and cruelty over a lengthy period. At one point during the hours the intruders were at the home, one of them accompanied the woman to a bank and forced her to withdraw funds. Before leaving the home, they poured gasoline over some of the victims and set the house on fire. The mother and the two daughters all perished. The perpetrators were found, convicted, and sentenced to death before the death penalty was repealed by the legislature in that state in 2012. The abolition did not apply to inmates who were already on death row. However, in 2015, the Connecticut Supreme Court found the death penalty was unconstitutional in that state, leaving in question whether the inmates presently on death row would ever be put to death.

As noted above, roughly 20 percent of household burglaries result in violent victimization when the resident was at home, and simple assault was the most common form of violence in these cases. In many of these victimization cases, the burglar was a relative or intimate (current or former) (Catalano, 2010). About a third of the time, the offender was a stranger. Research to date has not allowed us to provide detailed information about the motivations of the burglars whose crimes qualify as home invasions. This is because data on home invasions have been gathered from the National Crime Victimization Survey, which interviews victims about their experiences and is not designed to determine offender motivation or intent for entering an occupied household.

LARCENY AND MOTOR VEHICLE THEFT

McCaghy (1980) refers to the larceny-theft category as a "garbage can" because it is heterogeneous and hard to classify. Larceny-theft is defined as the "unlawful taking, carrying, leading, or riding away of property from the possession or constructive possession of another" (Federal Bureau of Investigation, 1997, p. 430). It differs from burglary in that it does not involve unlawful entry. Larceny includes pickpocketing, purse snatching, shoplifting (which is discussed in a separate section), stealing from vending machines or from motor vehicles, and theft of property left outdoors (bicycles, pedigreed dogs, lawn mowers), and so on. The larceny-theft category does not include identity theft or fraud, each of which is also discussed in a separate section later in the chapter. The larceny-theft offenses in the United States during 2013 accounted for 69.6 percent of the property crime total (Federal Bureau of Investigation, 2014a). More than 23 percent of larceny-thefts were thefts from motor vehicles. (See **Figure 14-1**, p. 421.)

Motor Vehicle Theft

Motor vehicle theft is defined as the theft or attempted theft of a motor vehicle, including the stealing of automobiles, trucks, buses, motorcycles, motor scooters, and snowmobiles. The taking of a motor vehicle for temporary use by persons having lawful access is excluded from the definition (Federal Bureau of Investigation, 2013).

Motor vehicle manufacturers have developed effective and highly sophisticated ways of preventing theft in recent years, making it increasingly difficult for thieves to steal the vehicle by traditional means. Offenders have adapted to these changes by seeking out more effective ways of obtaining keys for the vehicles (Copes & Cherbonneau, 2006). Consequently, there has been a growth in the prevalence of auto theft involving keys (Copes & Cherbonneau, 2006). In addition, obtaining keys minimizes damage done to the vehicle, which will ultimately increase its resale value. Some offenders go to great lengths to steal, find, or manipulate the keys from owners. Others are becoming skillful at manufacturing matching keys themselves.

CARJACKING. A distinct form of motor vehicle theft is **carjacking**, the completed or attempted theft in which a motor vehicle is taken by force or threat of force (Klaus, 1999). Other motor vehicle thefts do not involve the use of force or threat of force against the occupants of the vehicle. The intent of most carjackers is not to harm the occupant, however, and they typically choose individuals who are unlikely to put up a fight. It is believed that most carjackings are done to obtain the vehicle and sell it as quickly as possible—therefore, selecting the target involves judging its potential value and disposability (Topalli, Jacques, & Wright, 2015). Sometimes carjacking is done to enable the perpetrator to obtain transportation, and the driver is released. At other times the driver is forced to remain in the car, in which case the person becomes a hostage. A recent example of the latter situation is the infamous Boston Marathon bombing discussed in Chapter 11, which was perpetrated by the Tsarnaev brothers in 2013. After the bombs were detonated and the brothers were eluding police, they took a vehicle with the driver still in it. The driver testified at trial that he spent a harrowing 90 minutes before seeing a chance to escape while one brother had entered a convenience store.

On average, 34,000 carjacking incidents occur each year in the United States (Klaus, 2004). Approximately a dozen homicides are associated with these carjackings each year; in other words, the driver or a passenger is killed. Though such murders are very rare, in about three-fourths of carjackings the occupants face an armed offender or offenders (Klaus, 2004). In most instances, the carjacker uses a firearm. Victimization surveys indicate that the victim resisted the carjacker in two-thirds of the incidents, which resulted in about 9 percent of the victims receiving serious injury (e.g., gunshot or knife wounds, broken bones, or internal injuries).

Some research suggest that men tend to be victims of carjacking more than women, blacks more than whites, and Hispanics more than non-Hispanics (Klaus, 2004). This may be because carjackings are highly concentrated in particular areas and at particular times. They are highest in urban areas. They occur in parking lots and garages (24%), or in an open area, such as on the street or near public transportation (bus, subway, train station, or airport) (44%). They most often occur at night. Males committed 93 percent of the carjackings, while groups involving both males and females committed 3 percent. Women committed about 3 percent of the incidents.

Although the offense is violent, it appears to contain some elements of short-term planning and decision making and often is directed more at the object (the vehicle) than the person (Jacobs, Topalli, & Wright, 2003). After extensively reviewing literature on this crime, Topalli et al. (2015) concluded that successful carjacking required considerable skill on the part of the offender. They noted that perceptual skills were needed in selecting the appropriate target and procedural skills needed in commandeering the vehicle with minimum of physical force. However, they also note that these skills may be affected by pressures under which the carjackers operate. For example, an offender desperate for money may not use his skills effectively.

Jacobs and his colleagues (2003) interviewed 28 active carjackers who had committed two or more carjackings in the previous year. The researchers discovered that the active carjackers remain in permanent state of "alert opportunism," ready to commit the offense if the chance came their way. Many had gotten away with carjackings in the past, and therefore believed they would succeed when the need for quick cash or quick transportation arose again. In other words, most had developed well-learned cognitive scripts or strategies for how to proceed with their offense. Moreover, each had a preference for the vehicle they sought (gold-spoked wheels, a high-performance engine, or a booming sound system), features that bring a good price on the streets.

FRAUD AND IDENTITY THEFT

Crimes of fraud involve deception used for the purpose of obtaining illegal financial gain. They often involve the misrepresentation of facts and the deliberate intent to deceive with the promise of goods, services, or other benefits that either do not exist or that were never intended to be provided (Deem & Murray, 2000). Examples of fraud include fraud associated with identity theft, elder financial abuse, counterfeiting, mail fraud, bank fraud, and various corporate or organizational wrongdoings. In 2009, Bernard "Bernie" Madoff was convicted of operating a Ponzi scheme that has been called the largest investor fraud ever committed by a single person (Bray, 2009). The "Ponzi scheme" pulled in thousands of investors who lost an estimated $65 billion. Madoff remains in prison today, serving a sentence of 150 years.

Over the last two decades, fraud has increased in awareness with other high-profile cases, such as the savings and loan debacle of the 1980s and the massive Enron and Tyco cases of the early 2000s. In the economic crisis of 2008, corporate practices of banks, credit card companies, and other organizations were scrutinized for possible fraudulent activities. Although many of these practices were questionable and often unethical, they were not always illegal. This is an important distinction from the legal perspective, but from a psychological perspective, it still raises questions about the motives of those responsible. We discuss these issues again later in the chapter.

Identity theft occurs when one individual or a group of individuals misappropriate another person's personal identification information, such as name, Social Security number, date of birth, mother's maiden name, and uses the information to take over existing credit card or bank accounts, apply for a mortgage or car loan, make large purchases, or apply for insurance (Deem & Murray, 2000). (See **Box 14-1** for an illustration of identity theft.) In addition, armed with passwords they may have appropriated, identity thieves can obtain sensitive health information, collect benefits, or even apply to and get accepted into colleges and universities. Two separate elements are involved in this crime: theft occurs when the information is stolen, and fraud occurs when the data are used for illegitimate purposes.

The National Center for White Collar Crime (2015) publishes information on the extent of identity theft along with tips on how to avoid being a victim. The NW3C (2015) reported that from 2005 to 2014, government agencies and other sources had tracked 5,029 data breaches exposing

CONTEMPORARY ISSUES

BOX 14-1 Identity Theft—Anyone Can Be Victimized

Identity theft often occurs without its victims being aware of it, and once they do become aware, putting things to right may involve a long, frustrating, and complicated process. As noted in the chapter, victims of this crime may be children, vulnerable elderly people living alone or under the care of guardians, intellectually or developmentally disabled individuals, and even college students. No one is immune to the possibility of this victimization.

In a not atypical situation, a couple tried to file a 2014 joint tax return electronically—as more and more of us are encouraged to do. When their federal and state tax returns were rejected, they learned they had been scammed. An identity thief apparently had appropriated their identification data, filed a false claim before they themselves filed, and obtained more than $3,000 in federal tax refunds.

As indicated in the chapter, the National Center for White Collar Crime (NW3C, 2015) tries to keep track of identity fraud, and it publishes information on how to avoid being

a victim. Still, personal data have been compromised through sources that were totally out of control of victims. Though victims can file identity theft reports with various agencies, it is unlikely that their cases will be resolved to their satisfaction. Furthermore, as also indicated in the chapter, the perpetrators of identity fraud often are never identified.

Questions for Discussion

1. What techniques of neutralization were likely used by scammers in the above-described case as well as similar cases?
2. Assuming that law enforcement agencies must prioritize cases because of resources, is any of the following fraud cases more or less deserving of investigation: a) theft of a young child's birth and social security data; b) filing a false income tax return and obtaining a refund; c) cashing benefit checks of someone who is deceased.

more than 677 million records. By the end of February 2015, 115 breaches affecting more than 88 million personal records had occurred—in just under two months. This does not mean that fraudulent activity necessarily followed. Though identity fraud cannot occur without identity theft, identity theft is not always followed by fraud (Vieraitis, Copes, Powell, & Pike, 2015). Theft, of course, makes personal data vulnerable to such fraud. Furthermore, the person or persons stealing the identity may then sell it to a third person or group, who then engage in fraud.

Vieraitis and her colleagues (Copes & Vieraitis, 2009; Vieraitis et al., 2015) detail the multiple avenues offenders use to obtain information. These range from simple techniques like stealing wallets and purses from homes, cars, and offices, to sophisticated data mining operations involving online hacking or redirecting victims to fraudulent websites. Many identity thieves have become highly skilled at these activities. "Offenders are seemingly adept at developing new methods as they adapt to target hardening by consumers and businesses and as they identify new sources of data containing valuable information (Vieraitis & Shuryadi, forthcoming)" (p. 12). In many instances, unsuspecting victims have no idea that anything is amiss until they receive phone calls from creditors or have difficulty applying for a job, loan, or mortgage.

In 2007, about 7 percent of the households in the United States (8 million) reported having at least one member become a victim of one or more types of identity theft (see **Table 14-5**) (Langton & Baum, 2010). Credit card theft is the most common type of identity theft. In most cases, persons discover the theft by noticing unfamiliar charges on accounts, or they are contacted by a credit card bureau. The second most common type of identity theft involves the unauthorized use or attempted use of checking or debit bank accounts, or cell phone accounts (Langton & Baum, 2010). The average amount of money lost in identity theft in 2007 was $1,830. According to more recent data, identity theft has increased dramatically over the last two years. For example, in 2011, 11.6 million adults became victims of identity theft, a 13 percent increase from 2010 (Javelin Strategy & Research, 2012). Smartphones, new mobile technologies, and social media (e.g., Facebook) have probably played a major role in this increase. For example, 68 percent of people with public social media profiles shared their birthday information (with 45% revealing month, date, and year), 63 percent revealed their high school name, 18 percent showed their phone number, and 12 percent divulged their pet's name (Javelin Strategy & Research, 2012). These all represent prime examples of personal information that financial institutions use to authenticate a person's identity.

TABLE 14-5	Identity Theft in American Households, 2007		
Did Households Discover Identity Theft in Previous Six Months?	**Number of Households**	**Percent of Households**	**Percent of Victimized Households**
Yes	7,928,500	6.6	100.0
Unauthorized use of existing credit cards	3,894,300	3.3	49.1
Other existing accounts (such as a checking account)	1,917,000	1.6	24.1
Misuse of personal information (to obtain new accounts or loans)	1,031,200	0.9	13.0
Multiple types of theft during the same episode	1,086,100	0.9	13.6
No	108,197,000	90.5	NA
Don't know	3,378,000	2.8	NA

Source: Langton, L., & Baum, K. (2010, June). Identity theft reported by households, 2007—statistical tables. Washington, DC: U.S. Department of Justice, Bureau of Justice Statistics.

Within the past five years, numerous consumers were notified that their personal information had been compromised as a result of data theft. No category of business seems to be immune from hacking. Among the major companies whose computers were breached were Target Corporation, Anthem, Inc., Home Depot, Neiman Marcus, Michaels, PF Chang's China Bistro, UPS, Community Health Systems, Goodwill Industries, JP Morgan Chase, Staples, K-Mart, and SONY. In addition, smaller organizations, such as employee credit unions, community hospitals, or medical practices have reported breaches to their customers and patients. It is important to stress that breaches do not mean that fraud will follow, but it is important for consumers to monitor their credit card activity and health records on a regular basis.

Interestingly, identity theft is known to victimize the deceased and children, two populations that may not come immediately to mind. A local news story recently reported that a woman had kept the body of her deceased relative in an apartment while she cashed the woman's social security checks. According to the NW3C (2012), stealing the identity of a dead person is not unusual. Access to Social Security numbers facilitates the process. Some thieves are acquaintances of the dead person and, like the woman mentioned above, continue receiving their benefits or using their credit cards. Others peruse obituaries and are able to get information, such as where the person worked. They sometimes call relatives of the deceased, pretending they are former coworkers. Provided with enough information, they can make credit card purchases or online purchases, which may not be discovered for months. The victim is deceased and cannot monitor these fraudulent activities and surviving relatives may not notice changes in the various account balances.

The NW3C has also reported that—in research involving more than 40,000 children—it was discovered that Social Security numbers of approximately 10.2 percent had been used for a range of purposes, including obtaining loans or opening credit accounts. Sometimes, the fraudulent transactions are perpetrated by parents or relatives in dire economic straits, but at other times the Social Security numbers have been accessed by strangers. Children, the NW3C notes, have a blank slate, with no history of credit defaults. They have no credit file, thus transactions with their information do not lead to "fraud alerts." Children in foster care are often the targets of identity theft, because their information is broadly shared among various social service and educational institutions. Child identity theft may seem to be a mild form of victimization in comparison to the child abuse victimizations discussed in earlier chapters. Nevertheless, it can have repercussions many years down the line, when adolescents and young adults seek employment or apply for college and other loans. It is likely the most under analyzed form of identity theft.

Information on identity thieves is limited at this time, but some studies have begun to emerge. Copes and Vieraitis (2007, 2009) interviewed 59 identity thieves incarcerated in federal prisons with respect to their backgrounds, methods, and motivations. They were a diverse group. The majority of them were between the ages of 25 and 44 years, had at least some college, and were employed in a wide spectrum of occupations. They were motivated by the quick need for cash and perceived "identity theft as an easy, relatively risk-free way to get it" (Copes & Vieraitis, 2007, p. 2). Approximately a third of the offenders used their employment to carry out their crimes. For example, they worked for mortgage agencies, government agencies, or businesses that have access to credit card numbers and/or Social Security numbers. Many of the thieves possessed considerable knowledge about how banks and credit agencies operate. About two-thirds had prior arrests for such crimes as identity theft, drug use/sales, and property crimes.

Most of the thieves used neutralization techniques to explain their crimes, which also encouraged them to continue offending. For instance, some denied that they caused any real harm to their victims. Others justified their crimes by claiming their actions were done to help others. Considering the fact that the thief assumes someone else's identity, it is likely that dehumanization or denial of the victim is involved. The perpetrator does not have to see what the victim looks like, experience the victim's stress, or know anything about the victim's life, with the exception of financial data.

Vieraitis et al. (2015) also note that developing expertise in identity theft—which is crucial to continuing at this criminal career—helps offenders develop a sense of professionalism. "… (A)s offenders gain a sense of professionalism and develop expertise they are better able to make sense of their crimes, which makes the commission of crime more palatable due to the reduction in fear and anxiety that often accompany felonious activities" (p. 13).

Identity thieves usually gain considerable satisfaction from overcoming challenging barriers that are put in their way. From a psychological perspective then, it is difficult to persuade identity thieves to desist in their fraudulent activity, particularly if they have become experts at beating the system and are able to gain both extrinsic and intrinsic rewards as a result.

Though we know little about the offenders, we do know that the emotional impact of identity theft—and fraud in general—on victims is substantial and should not be underestimated. In addition to having strong feelings of being victimized, feelings emerge that one should blame oneself, can no longer trust one's own ability to handle financial matters, or can no longer trust people. The experience is often described as an emotional rollercoaster, especially involving the long drawn-out ordeal of dealing with challenged credibility, damaged credit, and the feelings of powerlessness and personal vulnerability. According to NW3C (2015), an annual survey of victims of identity theft indicated that half of victims surveyed had not yet seen their cases resolved. Almost 1/3 said their cases were cleared up (e.g., credit reestablished) within six months, but 10 percent said it took up to a year and nearly 3 percent said it took over five years.

SHOPLIFTING

Shoplifting, a form of larceny-theft, is a frequent and costly type of crime. Although shoplifting typically comprises under 20 percent of all larceny-theft (Federal Bureau of Investigation, 2014a), it is obviously very much underreported. In a face-to-face survey of more than 43,000 adults across the nation, Blanco et al. (2008) found that one in ten Americans admitted shoplifting at some point in their lives. The survey also found that shoplifting occurs across all sociodemographic levels. In fact, it was more common among those with higher education and income, indicating that financial considerations are unlikely to be the main motivator for shoplifting.

These data are surprising in light of the rapid improvement in security measures designed to discourage and prevent the crime. For example, most sizeable retail establishments have private security officers on the premises. Furthermore, cameras now are ubiquitous in large retail stores, hidden in clocks, smoke alarms, and pushbars on fire-exit doors (Adler, 2002). In addition, valuable goods are locked in impenetrable cases, and clothing is often accompanied with electronic surveillance devices that need to

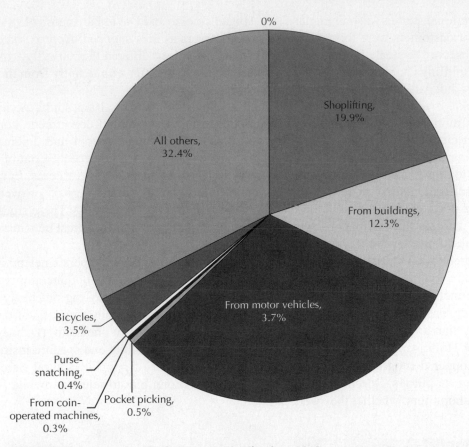

FIGURE 14-1   Larceny-Theft Percent Distribution, 2013   *Source:* Federal Bureau of Investigation (2014a). Crime in the United States 2013: Uniform Crime Reports. Washington, DC: U.S. Department of Justice.

be scanned or with ink tags that can be removed only by store clerks at the time of payment (Eck, 2000). Failure to scan an item sets off an alarm at the door as the customer leaves the store. Ink tags deface the merchandise unless they are removed by the store, thereby destroying the value of the stolen goods. In his review of the research literature, Eck reports that electronic surveillance measures can reduce shoplifting 32 to 80 percent, and are found to be more effective than either security guards or store redesign. However, shoplifting methods have become more sophisticated in recent years. For example, some shoplifters use "tag bags," which are hand baggage filled with materials like polyurethane and aluminum that incapacitate the electronic detection devices located at store entrances and exits (Caputo, 2004). Like identity thieves, many professional shoplifters delight in trying to outfox security measures.

Comprehensive data on all economic crimes are difficult to obtain, but data acquisition for shoplifting offenses is especially difficult, since store personnel exercise wide discretion in reporting offenses. Many years ago, Hindelang (1974) found that whether charges were filed depended on the retail value of the stolen object, what was stolen, and the manner in which it was taken, rather than demographic and personality characteristics of the shoplifter. Specifically, the offender's race did not seem to matter, nor whether the offender was male or female, poor or middle class. What determined referral for arrest was whether the item was expensive, had resale value, or was stolen in a professional, skillful manner.

Later research by Davis, Lundman, and Martinez (1991) found that shoplifters are more likely to be arrested not only when they take expensive items, but also when they resist being apprehended, have no local address, and/or live in poor neighborhoods. In England, on the other hand, store managers consider the age of the shoplifter as well as the value of the stolen item (Farrington & Burrows, 1993). The British study found that, generally, store managers did not report to the police the very young (under age 17) or very old (over 60), the mentally impaired, or those shoplifters in an advanced stage of pregnancy, unless they were caught repeatedly. In a series of observational studies (also in England) by Abigail Buckle and David Farrington (1984), random samples of customers were followed by trained observers as they shopped. Approximately one in 50 was observed to steal. The amount of shoplifting, however, differed dramatically from store to store. Shoplifting characteristics in supermarkets are likely to differ significantly from those exhibited in retail department stores or hardware stores.

Buckle and Farrington (1994) conducted a replication of their 1984 study. Again, trained observers randomly followed approximately 500 customers in a small department store located in another city. The proportion of customers who shoplifted was between 1 and 2 percent, and a majority was male. Most of the shoplifters also purchased goods as they checked out of the store, probably to allay suspicion. In general, the items stolen were small, low-cost items. In contrast to the original study, where there was a preponderance of older shoplifters (age 55 or over), Buckle and Farrington found that most of the shoplifters were young (age 25 or less). These studies underscore the warning that estimations concerning the incidence of shoplifting must be placed within a situational, cultural, and historical context.

Apprehension statistics may tell us more about the store security personnel practices and biases than about the shoplifting population (Klemke, 1992). In fact, it is not uncommon for security personnel to claim that they have developed a "sixth sense" for picking out likely suspects. This "sixth sense" is, in some cases, a bias or stereotype against certain segments of the population more than any all-encompassing, accurate skill. For example, in one study (Dabney, Dugan, Topalli, & Hollinger, 2006) observers who received extensive training and specific instructions to ignore shopper demographics were unable to resist the power of implicit cultural stereotypes in identifying shoplifters. Specifically, the observers had a strong bias to select nonwhite adolescent males as shoplifters, whether they were or not.

Who Shoplifts?

Shoplifting is often considered a behavior that is displayed predominately by juveniles. An analysis of one million juvenile court records across nearly 2,000 jurisdictions reveals that shoplifting is the most common juvenile court referral for youths under age 15 (Kelley, Kennedy, & Homant, 2003). Shoplifting appears to decline, however, both in number of offenses and the number of those engaging in this behavior, as offenders mature and move into early adulthood (Krasnovsky & Lane, 1998; Osgood, O'Malley, Bachman, & Johnstone, 1989). This dropping off appears to be partly due to the crystallization of moral development, as well as to the realization that a young adult is more likely to be charged with an offense than a preteen offender. In other words, the individual tempted to shoplift may believe he or she has more to lose if apprehended.

In a study designed to examine moral development and theft of clothing, Forney, Forney, and Crutsinger (2005) discovered that those juveniles who stole demonstrated a lower moral development than might be expected for someone their age. Their moral reasoning reflected the preconventional ethics of children who were much younger. The preteen juvenile offenders thought their motivations for stealing the clothing were justified. "It is okay as long as no one knows I'm stealing" or "It is okay if no one is watching." The researchers found, however, that there was a discernible shift in the moral reasoning of juvenile delinquents from preteens to teens. For example, teens were more likely to agree with the statement, "It is okay to steal if a friend needs the item."

There is ample evidence that adults as well as juveniles are involved in shoplifting behavior, however. Michele Tonglet (2001) found that contemporary shoplifters, both adolescents and adults, "... were significantly less likely to view shoplifting as bad, dishonest, wrong and stupid, and were less likely to be constrained by moral concerns" (p. 345). Paul Cromwell and Quint Thurman (2003) interviewed 137 apprehended shoplifters who were participants in a court-ordered diversion program for adult first offenders, and they gained interesting insights into how they justified their criminal activity. Participants were promised anonymity in answering such questions as their attitudes toward the victims, and their reasons and justifications for shoplifting. The study was primarily designed to examine the **techniques of neutralization** first proposed by Sykes and Matza (1957). According to Sykes and Matza, people try to neutralize unpleasant feelings of guilt and shame by rationalizing to themselves and others why they committed a deviant or criminal act. Recall that we touched on this topic in pervious chapters as well as in the section on identity theft, noting that identity thieves may dehumanize their victims or deny that they are doing harm.

Techniques of neutralization basically represent different levels of moral rationalizations. For example, a shoplifter might say "I really didn't hurt anybody" or "The store can afford the hit." These two examples describe denial of any injury to the victim. We will discuss in more detail the various forms of neutralization in the white-collar and occupational crime section. The point here, however, is that Cromwell and Thurman learned that 96 percent of the shoplifters used some form of neutralization in rationalizing their criminal behavior of shoplifting. In other words, while not denying their actions, they very rarely took blame or responsibility for them.

Klemke (1992) conducted one of the first comprehensive studies on adolescent shoplifting. He collected self-report data from students in four small town high schools in the Pacific Northwest during the late 1970s. Klemke (1992) discovered that approximately three-fourths of the frequent shoplifters began shoplifting before the age of 10, but then stopped soon after their 18th birthday. However, Blanco and his colleagues (2008), who it will be recalled surveyed more than 43,000 adults, found that although two-thirds of the cases of shoplifting began before age 15, over a third of the shoplifters persisted after that age, many into adulthood. Blanco et al. estimate that 4 percent of the entire American adult population continues to shoplift. If we take into account the entire adult population in the United States, 4 percent represents a substantial number. Interestingly, data from college bookstores indicate that first-year students are more likely to be apprehended for shoplifting than other college students (Klemke, 1992). Readers undoubtedly can think of a variety of explanations for this, ranging from the high minded ("upper-class students are more committed to the college community" or "education decreases the likelihood of committing this crime") to the cynical ("Upper class students don't go near the bookstore any more").

In the Blanco et al. (2008) survey, shoplifters tended to have a higher incidence of additional antisocial behaviors than nonshoplifters. Besides shoplifting, the most common antisocial behavior in this sample was making money illegally or scamming somebody for money.

Psychological disorders were also more common among shoplifters in the Blanco et al. survey, especially those who continued to shoplift into adulthood. Although previous research often reported depression as common among shoplifters—especially female offenders—Blanco et al. found that depression was *not* a major factor. Instead, they discovered the more common disorders were problems in impulse control and self-regulation, similar to what would be reflected in pathological gambling, alcohol dependence, and substance abuse disorders. The authors concluded that "…our findings are most consistent with the understanding of shoplifting as a behavioral manifestation of impaired impulse control" (Blanco et al., 2008, p. 911).

It has also been commonly assumed that shoplifting is committed largely by adolescent girls and women. The most common explanations offered for women's greater involvement are based on the belief that women have greater opportunity to steal small items from merchants than do men. As men join the ranks of frequent shoppers, however, their shoplifting rates are beginning to increase, and the gap between men and women is narrowing. In fact, the Blanco et al. (2008) survey discovered that shoplifting is more common among men than women. Janne Kivivuori (1998) found similar results among Finnish adolescents, and Cromwell and Thurman (2003) report similar results for apprehended adult shoplifters in Wichita, Kansas.

Baumer and Rosenbaum (1984) outline some of the psychological characteristics and behavioral patterns of shoplifters. They note that such things as extreme nervousness, aimless walking up and down the aisles, looking around frequently, glancing up from the merchandise frequently, and leaving the store and returning a number of times are some of the indicators that suggest shoplifting. These behaviors are likely to be exhibited chiefly by first-time shoplifters.

In spite of its traditional prominence in economic crime, shoplifting has received little psychological research attention. The most heavily quoted source on the subject, Mary Owen Cameron's *The Booster and the Snitch: Department Store Shoplifting* (1964), reported data accumulated long ago, in the 1940s and early 1950s. Cameron divided her shoplifters into two groups: Commercial shoplifters were "**boosters**," and amateur pilferers were "**snitches**." All of her data were subsequently explained with reference to this dichotomy. The boosters were professionals, accepted members of the criminal subculture. They stole for substantial financial gain by choosing items from preselected locations. Boosters used a wide range of techniques such as "booster boxes," packages designed for concealing items inserted through hidden slots or hinged openings, or "stalls," containers with hidden compartments (large handbags, coats with hidden pockets). Similar methods are still used today. Snitches, on the other hand, were "respectable" persons who rarely had criminal records. They did not consider themselves thieves, and the idea that they might actually be arrested and prosecuted rarely crossed their minds. Very often, once apprehended, they claimed they stole the item on impulse and did not know what came over them.

Over the years, the term "booster" has survived, particularly in reference to people who make shoplifting a business and tend to work in small groups. "Security specialists call them 'boosting crews,' highly organized teams of thieves who sweep through supermarkets and pharmacies scooping up products such as razor blades, infant formula, meat, seafood and Tide detergent" (Seiler, 2012, p. A3). It appears that boosters have joined forces in what is now regarded as organized retail crime, and they have access to elaborate fencing operations to dispose of the goods they have taken. One local police investigator, noting that retail crime has increased over the past decade, remarked that boosters have become more sophisticated, even knowing on which days stores increase their loss prevention staff and when investigators take their lunch breaks (Seiler, 2012).

Some social science research has focused on elderly shoplifters. Feinberg (1984) found that shoplifting was neither a female-dominated offense nor undertaken for subsistence purposes. Elderly shoplifters, he notes, are neither indigent, lonely, nor victims of poor memory. He attributes their criminal offenses to changes in status that separate the elderly from mainstream society. Often, they must reevaluate their past values and try out different selves and meanings. To what extent Feinberg's research may be generalized to other age groups remains an open question.

Motives

Shoplifting behavior is influenced by a number of factors, including peer pressure, moral development, previous shoplifting experience, economic considerations, self-esteem, and perceptions of apprehension risks (Tonglet, 2001). Shoplifters differ from one another with respect to their skill, use of the stolen goods, motivations, and duration of involvement (Caputo, 2004).

A majority of shoplifters do not consider shoplifting as morally wrong, and generally feel little guilt about the theft (Tonglet, 2001). It appears that many are utilizing the techniques of neutralization referred to above. These are psychological techniques people use to neutralize or turn off their conscience or "inner protest" about committing deviant behavior. Cromwell and Thurman (2003) were able to identify nine such techniques used by shoplifters. In their study, they found that only 5 of 137 apprehended shoplifters did not use a technique of neutralization to justify their behavior. And they didn't use these neutralizations so much to reduce their guilt—because they did not feel guilty—but rather to provide themselves with the necessary justifications for their acts to others.

The motives behind commercial shoplifting may be clearer than those behind the amateur type. Whereas boosters take merchandise of value, snitches tend to take inexpensive items they can use. Some research has noted that male snitches prefer items of more value, such as stereo equipment, and jewelry. Women snitches seem to take clothing, cosmetics, and food. The boosters shoplift for the money; the snitches for more obscure reasons.

Theories concerning the intentions of snitches range from economic ones, like attempts to stretch the family budget (Cameron, 1964), to emotional ones, like attempts to satisfy needs centering around matrimonial stress, loneliness, and depression (Russell, 1973). In recent years, some have concluded that shoplifting often stems from problems with self-regulation, much like gambling and alcoholism. On the other hand, the contention that shoplifting has primarily an economic motivation seems oversimplified. Shoplifting is pursued by different people for different reasons.

Shoplifting by Proxy

Shoplifting by proxy refers to a situation in which people shoplift for someone else because that other person asks or tells them to do so (Kivivuori, 2007). In these instances, the shoplifter follows someone else's orders or suggestions in committing the crime. Essentially, the "offender is a proxy or a substitute for the instigator" (Kivivuori, 2007, p. 817). Kivivuori suggests that shoplifting by proxy can be viewed as existing along a continuum, with strong coercion or explicit threats existing at one pole, and at the other extreme, some form of subtle manipulation or suggestion. Of course, other types of crime may be committed by proxy—especially burglary and other forms of theft—but shoplifting appears to be the most common. Adults sometimes induce juveniles to commit crimes for them because the legal system often does not deal as aggressively with juveniles as with adults. For example, juveniles are more likely to be offered diversion for first-time offenses, and juvenile records are sealed in many jurisdictions.

The incidences of proxy shoplifting may be coercive or may be the result of helping or altruistic behavior. Kivivuori (2007) conducted a self-report study of 6,279 students, age 15 to 16, in the Finland schools. The students were asked to respond anonymously to questions about their shoplifting behavior. Seven percent of the respondents reported having shoplifted for someone else. Males and females were equally involved in shoplifting by proxy. In the vast majority of the cases, the instigator was someone other than a family member, or a boy or girlfriend. In general, the instigator was a peer.

The most common reason provided by the offenders for shoplifting by proxy is that the instigator paid the offender to steal. In one-third of the cases, offenders shoplifted because a peer or peer group pressured them to do so. And in one quarter of the cases, the offenders said they shoplifted so that they would be popular among their peers. The most common reason given by instigators for their actions is that they did not dare to shoplift themselves or were afraid they would get caught.

To what extent other crimes by proxy are committed, such as violence or burglary, is unknown. Certainly, and as noted by Kivivuori (2007), Stanley Milgram's classical experiments on obedience (presented in Chapter 11) might illustrate some of the factors at work in more serious crimes by proxy.

Shoplifting as an Occupation

Gail Caputo and Anna King (2011) conducted qualitative research, interviewing 12 women whose primary criminal offense was shoplifting. Although the sample was extremely small, it provides some insight into shoplifting motivations and methods. The women viewed shoplifting as an occupation that paid quite well and supported their basic needs. They also admitted that the practice supported their drug habit. During the early phases of their shoplifting careers, the women used a number of methods that—while not very efficient—enabled them to make enough to live on. These shoplifting methods included the "exchange for cash," and the "receipt for cash" approaches. In the first method, the shoplifter returns to the retail store with the stolen merchandise and negotiates a merchandise return for cash, indicating that they "lost" or "misplaced" the receipt. The receipt for cash approach was used for retailers with strict policies about returns. The shoplifter would first scour parking lots, sidewalks, and trash containers for discarded receipts, then examine the receipts and decide which merchandise on the lists would be worth shoplifting. She would enter the store, shoplift the selected items, and return to the store with the receipt for a cash refund.

Eventually, the women in Caputo and King's study sought an approach that would lead to more regular income. This required a solid customer base willing to purchase the stolen merchandise, similar to the boosting teams described above. A small neighborhood store, for example, may be willing to purchase grocery products from the shoplifter at a low price, and might then sell them to customers at a higher price, but at a price that was lower than the customer would have to pay at a larger market. As the shoplifters learned and expanded the "trade," their customer bases became larger and more stable. Many of them also employed a "hack," which was usually a male driver who would drive them to retail establishments and wait for them. In most cases, the hack would receive about half of the proceeds.

Methods of Shoplifting

Males tend to favor concealing stolen merchandise in pockets or clothing, while females generally prefer purses or shopping bags. The method of concealment, however, depends not only on the gender of the offender but also on the merchandise and the type of store. In clothing stores, shoplifters would more likely attempt to walk out wearing the clothing after leaving the fitting room, for example. As noted earlier, though, ink tags and electronic surveillance devices limit the extent to which this is possible. Men prefer to hide items beneath their clothing in supermarkets, while pockets are preferred in drug and discount stores. Women tend to prefer purses for concealment in supermarkets or grocery stores, and packages and bags in drug and discount stores. Two things that draw the attention of store security personnel are broken-arm casts (some are false) and large shopping bags obtained from a prior visit. In addition, women with babies in strollers or in carriers often report that they are carefully watched by store personnel even though there is no documentation that these women are any more likely to steal than other customers.

The item most commonly stolen in supermarkets or grocery stores is meat, while in drug stores, baby formula, diabetic test strips, razor blades, and other over-the-counter medications tend to be more common (Johnsen, 2008). The items selected largely depend on the state of the economy at the time. Klemke (1992) notes that some shoplifters prefer to conceal the items, while others do not. Some walk nonchalantly out the door with the item(s) as though nothing is amiss. Some individuals also "graze" while shopping. That is, the shopper openly eats, drinks (commonly soda), or "tastes" while shopping, especially in the fruit section, and fails to pay for the consumed items while checking out. Remnants of the items—wrappers or cans, for example—are either pocketed or left in store aisles. Many individuals who do this do not consider it shoplifting, however, and many stores would not report this type of behavior without first speaking with the individual.

Kleptomania: Fact or Fiction?

Do some people have an irresistible impulse to steal objects they really do not need? Researchers have not found substantial evidence of this phenomenon, which is referred to as kleptomania. However, **kleptomania** is still included as a behavioral disorder in the DSM-5 (American Psychiatric Association, 2013). Identified as a disorder of impulse control, it is estimated to occur in about 4 to 24 percent of persons arrested for shoplifting and only 0.3 to 0.6 percent of the general population. The higher range estimation among persons arrested for shoplifting seems unlikely, though, because shoplifters display very low recidivism rates. Once apprehended, the amateur rarely shoplifts again (Cameron, 1964; Russell, 1973), and as noted above, the same could be said of impulse and occasional offenders. Professional shoplifters, or boosters, who are apparently successful at shoplifting, steal repetitively and for economic reasons; their expertise at this enterprise makes it highly unlikely that irresistible impulse had anything to do with their behavior. If kleptomania is a factor, it would be a factor in a very small percentage of shoplifters.

Lloyd Klemke (1992) suggests that kleptomania is a psychiatric label with roots at the turn of the twentieth century. The label was applied predominantly to women, particularly affluent women. (According to the DSM-5, females outnumber males at a ratio of 3:1). Historically, Klemke notes, the label was intended to ease the guilt of wealthy women who were caught stealing. Merchants did not want to antagonize their affluent clientele and accuse them of theft. Furthermore, affluent families wanted to keep their moral reputations untarnished, and courts did not want to convict "respectable ladies" as common criminals. Thus, kleptomania (the Greek word for "stealing madness," a term presumably coined by Esquirol in 1838) legitimized the actions of the merchants and the courts, allowing them to overlook the actions or dismiss or acquit the "afflicted" woman and excuse her from being held personally responsible for her actions.

In summary, if kleptomania does exist, it seems to be a rare phenomenon. For example, in a study conducted by Sarasalo, Bergman, and Toth (1997), 50 shoplifters (29 males, 21 females) were interviewed immediately after being caught red-handed in central Stockholm, Sweden. None of the persons interviewed fulfilled the DSM criteria for kleptomania. Sarasalo et al., however, did find that many of the shoplifters reported a "thrill" and challenge in connection with the crime.

Much of the literature on the causes of kleptomania focuses on its relationship to anxiety, depression, or sexual disturbances (Goldman, 1991; Sarasalo et al., 1996). Citing sexual disturbances as a cause for kleptomania is primarily based in the psychoanalytic tradition. But as Marcus Goldman (1991, p. 990) notes, "there are no modern data available to refute or confirm these earlier psychoanalytic findings."

On the other hand, research has found *depression* to be a common symptom of people who engage in "nonsensical shoplifting" (Lamontagne, Boyer, Hetu, & Lacerte-Lamontagne, 2000). This term has many similarities to kleptomania with the exception of the compulsion aspect, and indeed the *DSM-5* notes that kleptomania may be associated with compulsive buying and depressive disorders. Yates (1986) observed that 80 percent of those who engaged in nonsensical shoplifting were depressed. McElroy and colleagues (McElroy, Pope, Hudson, Keck, & White, 1991) found that all 20 patients they studied who engaged in nonsensical shoplifting met the then DSM-III-R criteria for a lifetime diagnosis of a major mood (depression) disorder. In addition, many of these patients said they engaged in nonsensical shoplifting far more often when they were depressed. It seems that some depressed people may engage in nonsensical shoplifting as a stimulating, exciting activity that moves them away from feelings of helplessness. Depression could also explain the behavior in elderly shoplifters. In fact, Goldman (1991) finds that depressive states are often reported throughout the literature as precursors to many kinds of theft that are not related to profit.

WHITE-COLLAR AND OCCUPATIONAL CRIME

The term **white-collar crime** was first used by Edwin H. Sutherland in his presidential address to the American Sociological Society in 1939. In his speech, Sutherland urged his fellow sociologists to pay attention to the law-violating behavior of businesses, particularly large corporations. He had uncovered these violations by reviewing government files on 70 large American corporations and had learned that breaking rules was commonplace. In 1949, Sutherland published his now classic book, *White-Collar Crime*, in which he detailed his findings without naming the corporations. A later edition of the book (Sutherland, 1983) did include the names.

Following Sutherland's lead, a considerable amount of pioneering research was done on white-collar crime between 1939 and 1963 (Geis, 1988). This was followed by a decade of inactivity. Since 1975, there has been a revival of interest in studying the area, although criminological literature gives far less attention to white-collar crime than to other forms of criminal behavior. The highly publicized individual and corporate scandals of recent years, like the Enron debacle and the massive fraud perpetrated by the financier Bernard Madoff, have only served to illustrate that this attention is needed. Over the last decade, increasingly more examples of corporate malfeasance and the crimes of the wealthy and/or politically powerful have come to public attention. The roster of those convicted include state and federal legislators, heads of corporations, sports figures, actors, and educational officials, to name but a few professions represented in conviction statistics.

According to Sutherland (1949), "white-collar crime may be defined approximately as a crime committed by a person of respectability and high social status in the course of his occupation" (p. 9). Although Sutherland used the word *crime*, he did not intend it strictly in the legal sense. He recognized that numerous laws and regulations violated by persons of high social status carried civil rather than criminal sanctions, and he wanted these violations to be condemned. In fact, this was a critical factor to Sutherland, who saw a double standard phenomenon at work. The law-violating behavior of the poor carried criminal penalties; the law-violating behavior of the rich often did not. This was so despite the fact that "[t]he financial cost of white-collar crime is probably several times as great as the financial cost of all the crimes which are customarily regarded as 'the crime problem'" (Sutherland, 1949, p. 12).

Although Sutherland's call to study white-collar crime was heeded, his working definition produced numerous problems for subsequent criminologists. Some, most notably Paul Tappan (1947), argued that white-collar "crime" could not really be crime unless it violated the criminal law. The terms *respectability* and *high social status* were considered vague. Over the past four decades, researchers have tried to improve on Sutherland's definition. Marshall Clinard and

Richard Quinney (1980) preferred to dichotomize the concept into (1) occupational crime, committed by an individual for his or her own profit, and (2) corporate crime, committed by the corporation through its agents. This dichotomy is probably the most commonly used by criminologists today. Horning (1970) proposed a threefold division to distinguish the various behaviors that might be at issue. He reserved *white-collar crime* for acts committed by salaried employees in which their place of employment is either the victim or the locale for the commission of an illegal act from which they personally benefit. Embezzlement would be a good example of this. *Corporate crime* refers to illegal acts by employees in the course of their employment that primarily benefit the company or corporation. Illegal dumping of hazardous wastes is an example. *Blue-collar crime* refers to the whole array of illegal acts committed by nonsalaried workers against their place of employment. Thefts of machinery, tools, or paper are examples. Some criminologists also have contended that certain corporate crimes should qualify as violent crimes. James Coleman (1998), for example, cites unsafe working conditions, illegal disposal of toxic waste, and the manufacture of unsafe products as examples of violent crime.

Green's Four Categories of Occupational Crime

Gary Green (1997) made significant contributions to clarifying the definitional dilemmas associated with the term *white-collar crime* by proposing the concept of **occupational crime**. Unfortunately, Green's approach has not been widely adopted, despite its conceptual clarity. To Green, occupational crime encompasses all of the behaviors previously subsumed under white-collar crime, blue-collar crime, and their variants. Occupational crime is "any act punishable by law that is committed through opportunity created in the course of an occupation that is legal" (Green, 1997, p. 15). Green then subdivides occupational crime into four categories: (1) organizational (which includes corporate crime), (2) professional, (3) state-authority, and (4) individual (see **Table 14-6**).

In **organizational occupational crime**, a legal entity such as a company, corporation, firm, or foundation profits by the law-violating behavior. An example would be the chief financial officer of a company falsifying the company's tax records with the tacit approval of its board of directors. Other examples are antitrust violations, overcharging the government for products or services, violations of Occupational Safety and Health Administration (OSHA) standards, and bribery of public officials. **Professional occupational crime** includes illegal behavior by persons such as lawyers, physicians, psychologists, and teachers committed through their occupation. A physician's Medicaid fraud and a lawyer's suborning the perjury of a client are illustrations.

State-authority occupational crime encompasses the wide range of law violation by persons imbued with legal authority; the individual who commits state-authority occupational crime is essentially violating the public trust. Bribe taking by a public official, police unauthorized use of deadly force, and the torture of individuals held in custody are illustrative. However, state-authority occupational crime also includes a broad array of political crimes by agents of government—at times those at the highest levels of government—that are often ignored by social scientists. (See **Box 14-2** for more

TABLE 14-6 Summary of Green's Occupational Crime Typology

Category	Description
Organizational	Law-violating behavior promoted by the corporation or agency and for which the corporation or agency benefit.
Professional	Law-violating behavior facilitated by one's professional status.
State-authority	Law-violating behavior by those in government in their capacity as government representatives.
Individual	Law-violating behavior committed by an individual working for a company or organization, but committed for his or her own advancement or financial gain.

CONTEMPORARY ISSUES

Box 14-2   Political Crimes—Unexamined Issues

For many years psychologists have been interested in political psychology, particularly as it relates to such topics as personality traits of public officials, public attitudes toward politicians and the political system, or voting behavior. Edited books on the topic (e.g., Jost & Sidanius, 2003) as well as peer-reviewed journals (e.g., *Political Psychology*) are available. Psychologists and other social scientists also study crime committed by individuals in power, such as graft, accepting bribes, misappropriation of funds, or embezzlement. In recent years, crimes associated with terrorism—both foreign and domestic—have drawn much attention, as we learned in Chapter 11.

However, psychologists rarely focus on the political crimes that are committed by agents of government—sometimes those at the highest levels—and that affect large segments of society. DeHaven-Smith (2010) refers to these as State Crimes Against Democracy (SCADs). Examples are illegal domestic surveillance, assassinations, illegal arms sales and covert operations, wiretapping, manipulation of elections, or malicious prosecution of individuals or groups, to name but a few. DeHaven-Smith (2010) writes that though perhaps not widespread, these elite crimes deserve more research attention. "The challenge for scholars is to engage in serious, unblinkered study of the subject without contributing to mass paranoia or elite incivility" (p. 7960).

The mass paranoia alluded to refers to the need to avoid encouraging conspiracy theories to run amuck. SCADs are sometimes suspected and sometimes documented in history.

For example, the Watergate break-in in 1972 is a documented SCAD. Highly suspicious, but not as thoroughly documented was the assassination attempt of George Wallace, also in 1972, and assassination attempts on some U.S. senators following the events of 9/11. Many suspect that election tampering in presidential elections in Florida in 2000 and Ohio in 2004 are SCADs (Barstow & Van Natta, 2001; deHaven-Smith, 2010). DeHaven-Smith and others emphasize, though, that these incidents differ from incidents that attract widely circulated but discredited conspiracy theories. For example, a number of 9/11 conspiracy theories posit that the U.S. government knew of the planned attacks ahead of time or even carried out the attacks. There is no evidence to support that belief.

Questions for Discussion

1. The above suggests that psychologists and other social scientists are not sufficiently studying elite political crimes, or those carried out by persons at the highest ranks of political power. If this lack of attention is correct, what could psychologists do to rectify this situation?

2. Review the table of contents of current issues of any three peer-reviewed journals that focus on political psychology or criminal behavior. Is there evidence that political crime in general is being addressed? What about broader state-authority occupational crime, as defined by Green?

discussion of this issue.) Finally, Green uses the category **individual occupational crime** to cover all violations not included in one of the previously discussed categories. The employee who steals equipment from his employer and the person who deliberately underreports income to the IRS are covered in this category.

Green's categories are clearly outlined and offer a good framework for studying certain crimes. They are not mutually exclusive. A prosecutor who withholds evidence that would clear a defendant in order to get a conviction, for example, would fall under both the state-authority and professional categories.

As evident from the above examples, the concept of occupational crime proposed by Green covers a wide variety of offenses, not all of which are economic in nature and not all of which are committed by persons of high social status. A therapist who sexually assaults a patient and a correctional officer who brutalizes an inmate are both committing violent occupational crimes, one in the professional and one in the state-authority category. Neither the therapist's nor the correctional officer's behavior would qualify as white-collar crime in its classic sense.

Green argues convincingly that his four-part division allows us to move away from the conceptual quagmire of "white-collar crime" and study a significant amount of workplace-facilitated illegal behavior in a logical, ordered manner. Although the term "white-collar crime" continues to be widely used, perhaps in deference to Sutherland's contributions to criminology, Green's approach offers an appealing alternative. As noted, however, the approach that seems to be preferred in the criminological literature is the "white-collar" dichotomy proposed by Clinard and Quinney, occupational and corporate crime.

Prevalence and Incidence of Occupational Crime

Regardless of which term is used, the extent of occupationally linked illegal behavior is extremely difficult to measure. The standard methods of measuring crime discussed in Chapter 1 rarely apply. The typical UCR report, for example, does not tell us whether a reported crime or an arrest was related to the perpetrator's occupation. Fraud can be committed by a bank executive, a college student, a Fortune 500 Corporation, a computer hacker working from his bedroom, or a recipient of government benefits. Even when uncovered, the violations we have been discussing are often not reported to law enforcement and recorded in official data. Rather than publicize a theft by an employee, for example, a business might prefer to demand restitution, dismiss the employee, or force a resignation. It does not benefit the company's public image to file a criminal complaint.

When an organization is itself the violator, civil suits are often preferred to criminal charges. The plaintiff in a civil suit is more likely to get some form of restitution, in the form of damages, than the victim in a criminal case. In addition, the government regulatory process is widely acknowledged to be inefficient in preventing, uncovering, and punishing violators. When it comes to the professions, law violation is often shielded from the public, because society authorizes them to police themselves by means of standards, codes of ethics, and licensing.

Nevertheless, some attempts have been made to collect data on "white-collar" offenses, particularly those committed by individuals (Clinard & Quinney's "occupational crime" category). As noted earlier in the chapter, the National White Collar Crime Center (NW3C) collects information, publishes a newsletter, and sponsors training sessions and conferences devoted to this issue. Topics that have recently come to the attention of the NW3C are Internet gambling, financial crimes against seniors, phishing schemes, online child pornography, insurance fraud, and identity theft. Information is available at www.nw3c.org. It should be noted, though, that none of the offenses mentioned above are offenses committed by the businesses; rather they are committed by individuals. The business or its consumers may be the victims; they are not the offenders.

Without settling the difficult definitional morass associated with "white-collar crime," we will nevertheless proceed to discuss in more detail one example of this serious crime problem, specifically, crime committed by corporations and their agents. Sutherland, you will recall, focused on corporations in his original research. Following that discussion, we will consider crimes at the opposite end of the continuum, wherein individual employees victimize their employers. Although not necessarily white-collar crimes, these latter behaviors qualify as individual occupational crimes according to Green's approach.

Corporate Crime

During the 2012 Presidential election cycle, one candidate made the statement, "Corporations are people, my friend." Although the statement was widely interpreted as being insensitive to the inequality between the wealth of corporations and the average citizen, it contained a core of truth, at least in the legal context. For purposes of the criminal law, a corporation is a person. It can be charged, tried, sentenced, and punished. In May of 2015, for example, four major banks—Citicorp, JP Morgan Chase, Barclays, and Royal Bank of Scotland—pled guilty to felony charges of conspiring to regulate the value of world currencies over a five-year period. They were initially fined $5 billion and placed on corporate probation. Corporations can even face "death," by dissolution, although this very seldom occurs.

For our purposes, although a corporation or other organization can be punished, it is *individuals* within that organization who are making decisions that render the corporate behavior a crime. Very rarely are they punished, however. In the above-mentioned bank fraud case and numerous similar cases no individuals have been held accountable. Interestingly, in 2015 the U.S. Justice Department announced it would prioritize the prosecution of white-collar crimes, and put pressure on corporations to turn over evidence against executives who would be subject to both civil and criminal penalties.

In discussing explanations for corporate crime, we will focus on the behavior of persons, despite the fact that the organizational culture as well as the economic structure of society may facilitate and reward the illegal behavior. It could also be argued—and often is, from a sociological perspective—that other crimes covered in this text are best explained from a structural perspective. As stressed throughout the text, however, risk factors for criminal behavior run the gamut from very individual factors to societal.

Corporate crime refers to any criminal offense committed by a corporation. Although people commit the crime, the corporation benefits. Corporate crime covers offenses ranging from price fixing to failure to recall a product known to have a serious defect that could potentially cause physical harm. The offenses are so varied, in fact, that most criminologists who study corporate crime subdivide it into more manageable categories. **Table 14-7** lists categories of corporate crime identified by various research and scholarly literature.

The estimated costs of these corporate offenses—both financial and from a human-suffering standpoint—are staggering. However, up-to-date, reliable, or accurate statistics are nearly impossible to find and are reported primarily by independent watchdog agencies. Mowkiber (2007) reports that the Savings and Loan scandal of the 1980s cost $300 to $500 billion dollars. Auto repairs fraud, $40 billion; securities fraud, $15 billion; health care fraud, $100 to $400 billion. Reiman (1995) has estimated that a conservative total of 90,105 Americans die every year as a result of occupational hazard and disease. Although some would argue that these deaths are not necessarily attributable to corporate malfeasance, others would say that corporations should be held responsible for the harms suffered by their workers.

Public attention to corporate crime has focused primarily on the economic crimes that have been highly publicized. These include a variety of practices that constitute fraud, including but not limited to price-fixing, false advertising, deceptive pricing, and securities fraud. Environmental and health-related crimes such as the illegal disposal of hazardous wastes and others already discussed have also attracted considerable public attention, however. In the 1990s, both the tobacco and the asbestos industry were barraged with lawsuits brought on behalf of individuals who had either died or been seriously harmed by exposure to these hazardous products.

Explanations for corporate criminality often focus on the criminogenic or crime-producing nature of the business environment; that is, in order to survive, law breaking is essential.

TABLE 14-7	Categories of Corporate Crime Identified by Scholars and Researchers
Scholars/Researches	**Categories**
Rosoff, Pontell, & Tillman (1998)	• Crimes against consumers • Crimes against the environment • Institutional corruption • Fiduciary fraud
Coleman (1998)	• Fraud and deception • Manipulating the marketplace • Violating civil liberties • Violent white-collar crime
Albanese (1995)	• Crimes of fraud • Offenses against public administration • Regulatory offenses
Green (1997)	• False and misleading advertising • Defrauding the government • Antitrust crimes • Manufacture and sale of unsafe consumer products • Unfair labor practices • Unsafe working conditions • Crimes against the environment • Political bribe giving

Conklin (1977), for example, argued that law breaking in American business was normative and that executives often believe that some dishonesty or deceit has to be tolerated in the best interest of the company. In response to comments such as these, corporations proclaim that they have entered an era of social responsibility and that the extent of corporate malfeasance is exaggerated. Business schools note that business ethics courses are a requirement in virtually all programs. Gilbert Geis (1997), however, a prominent scholar in the area of white-collar crime, chastises business schools for using "lulling terms, especially 'ethics,' to camouflage what essentially are considerations of criminal behavior" (Geis, 1997, p. xii).

Justifications and Neutralizations

You may recall that in earlier chapters, we referred to strategies people use to neutralize some of their violent conduct and separate it from their personal codes. The strategies, proposed by Bandura (1983), are worth repeating here, even if violence is not involved. Neutralization strategies apply to a wide range of reprehensible conduct, including conduct that qualifies as corporate crime. The strategies, which are considered disengagement or cognitive restructuring, may be used individually or in combination.

In one set of strategies, the individual or group justifies their actions, making them acceptable by associating them with beneficial or moral ends. In other words, a normally reprehensible act becomes personally and socially acceptable when it is associated with beneficial or moral ends. "We did it in the best interest of the company, the employees and their families, and the country."

A second set of neutralizing or dissociative strategies sees the actions themselves as trivial, not bad compared with the actions of others. Similarly, corporate decision makers may regard the laws they are violating as unfair, unjust, or simply not in keeping with good business practices.

This is most likely to be used when no violence has happened, no one has been maimed, no deaths have occurred.

A third strategy uses language, particularly euphemisms, to downplay the effect of the criminal acts. Threatened with exposure of wrongdoing, some businesses have been "restructured" or workers "reassigned" to avoid detection.

A fourth strategy, one frequently used in the corporate world, is the diffusion of responsibility. Many different people were involved in the decision making, and no one person can be held personally responsible. "After considerable deliberation, the Board decided that this would be the best route to take."

A fifth strategy is not to think of the possible consequences of the actions. Closely related to this is to think of the consequences, but calculate their likelihood of occurrence. The classic example of this is the noted Ford motor case of the 1970s, where executives were aware that gas tanks in the Ford Pinto were likely to explode upon impact. Rather than fix the problem, executives weighed the cost of recalling all affected vehicles against the cost of compensating families who lost loved ones in the event an explosion occurred; they decided not to recall the vehicles.

Finally, a sixth strategy involves dehumanizing the victim. This may be as flagrant as indicating that people in third world countries, whose standard of living is already low, so illegally shipping hazardous waste, will not be harmful, or as subtle as quoting the business-mantra of past years, let the buyer beware. A favored comment when products are recalled for safety purposes, for example, is to maintain that the customers did not use the products properly. We saw this strategy in action earlier in this text, when aggressors regarded their victims as less than human. This dehumanizing approach also seems to be a hallmark of prejudice and scapegoating. However, we also saw the strategy used in a slightly different way in property and economic crimes, like burglary and identity theft, where the perpetrator does not have to confront the "personhood" or humanity of the victim.

In sum, through cognitive restructuring supported by corporate norms, decision makers can justify and rationalize behavior that appears reprehensible to outsiders. The restructuring process prevents the manager or executive from labeling himself or herself "criminal." In fact, in some corporations, the extent to which the norms and justifying mechanisms are embraced may well determine how far up the corporate ladder one climbs.

Individual Occupational Crime

When illegal behavior is pursued for the direct benefit of the individual, and the individual is neither a professional nor someone with state authority, Green refers to it as individual occupational crime. In the Clinard-Quinney white-collar crime dichotomy referred to at the beginning of this section, the behavior would simply be "occupational" crime, distinguished from "corporate" crime. The Bernard Madoff case that came to light in 2008 and 2009 is a good example of this category. In this largely solitary pursuit, the offender is guided primarily by his or her own personal justifications and reasoning. An embezzler, for example, is operating outside organizational norms, although he may justify the behavior in much the same way as the corporate criminal may. The dissociation strategies identified by Bandura apply here as well. In other words, an embezzler may convince himself that the activity really is not a crime, since he is merely borrowing the money temporarily and will put it to good use. Later, he will reimburse the company (secretly, of course).

We should note that, with the exception of offering and taking bribes, *political* crimes omitted by individuals are not often studied by researchers. When researchers study "white-collar crime" or offenders, they are typically focusing on individual offenses—usually within the workplace—and separate from their place in either the political or the corporate structure. That is, the white-collar offenders studied in the literature have been convicted of fraud, insider trading, antitrust violations, embezzlement, or such economic crimes. Walters and Geyer (2004) emphasized that white-collar offenders should be subdivided into those who commit only white-collar crimes and those who are versatile in their offending, committing both nonwhite-collar and white-collar offenses. In their study of criminal thinking patterns and lifestyles of these offenders, they discovered that those who committed only white-collar crimes (60% of their male sample) were older, more educated, and less likely to identify themselves as criminals than were those who were more diverse in their offending patterns. However, the white-collar only group was also less likely to justify their behavior. Walters and Geyer's findings were replicated in a later study by Ragatz, Fremouw, and Baker (2012).

Other research has found that white-collar offenders score higher on indicators of depression and alcohol use (Benson & Moore, 1992; Poortinga et al., 2006) and anxiety and narcissism (Blickle et al., 2006) than do nonwhite-collar offenders. However, Ragatz et al. (2012) did not find indication of higher alcohol use in their sample.

Some interesting research has been done examining other personality characteristics of white-collar offenders. Listwan, Piquero, and Van Voorhis (2010) found that offenders who scored high on a "neuroticism" dimension were more likely to repeat their offenses. Ragatz et al. (2012) found that offenders who committed only white-collar crimes were higher on psychopathic characteristics. These findings are intriguing and await replication in research with larger samples and diverse groups of white-collar offenders. However, it seems that the psychological microscope is beginning to be directed at this group of offenders who traditionally have escaped study.

Employee Theft

One common type of illegal behavior in which the workplace is the victim is employee theft, which is an enormous drain on American business. Individually, employees may not take much, but as a group they incur high costs. An early estimate had employee theft costing business and industry $5 to $10 billion a year (Clark & Hollinger, 1983). In a survey of employees from 47 retail, manufacturing, and service organizations, one-third admitted stealing company property (Clark & Hollinger, 1983). The property included merchandise, supplies, tools, and equipment. In addition, almost two-thirds of the employees surveyed reported other types of misconduct, such as sick leave abuse, drug or alcohol use on the job, long lunch and coffee breaks, slow and sloppy workmanship, and falsifying time sheets. Collectively, these are counterproductive behaviors. They do not involve actual removal of material goods from the organization, but they do reduce production and services.

Modern versions of employee theft involve the Internet and electronic payments. For example, the NW3C first reported in 2003 that some employees were taking advantage of the

Automated Clearinghouse (ACH) network to make personal purchases via the telephone or web, using the company's corporate checking account numbers that the employees obtain, often from their own paychecks. Telephone or Internet merchants often accepted the account number without verifying the account ownership. Thus, "some companies remain unaware of the fraudulent entries against their accounts for many months, leading to extended problems in regaining their funds" (The Informant, 2003, p. 14). Other examples of theft and fraud via use of electronic transactions abound.

Explanations for employee theft and counterproductive behaviors are multiple, but most cluster around the themes of age, dissatisfaction, and one's normative group at the workplace. The highest levels of theft and counterproductive behaviors are reported by younger, unmarried male employees (age 16 to mid-20s). Apparently, these younger employees do not feel any commitment or loyalty to the organization, probably because they do not expect to spend their lives in that situation. Many are college and high school students working only until they graduate. High levels of theft and counterproductive behaviors are also found among employees expressing dissatisfaction with some aspect of their employment, especially with their immediate supervisor. Another component of job dissatisfaction is the workers' perception of the company's attitude toward them. If the workers perceive the organization as caring little about them, job dissatisfaction and the concomitant theft and counterproductive behaviors tend to follow. In these situations, the individuals typically know that what they are doing is "wrong," and if caught, they will admit their guilt and hope for a light sentence. Interestingly, financial restitution may involve more than they actually stole. A woman who admitted to ACH debit fraud made unauthorized transactions of $6,661.08 but was sentenced to 24 month probation and restitution of $8,126.56 (The Informant, 2003).

While age and job dissatisfaction are highly correlated with theft and counterproductive behavior, normative support offers a viable explanation. Normative support refers to the standards, perceptions, and values the work group has established for itself, with or without the organization's implicit (or explicit) approval. In short, normative support refers to group norms. For example, the group may consider pilfered material a supplement to one's hourly wages, a fringe benefit. Vocabularies of adjustment are frequently employed. "It goes with the job." "The company expects you to take a little on the side." Another example is the work group verbally neutralizing the societal and organizational prohibitions against theft. "Everyone does it." "No one cares if we take a few things." "This is not really stealing." Sieh (1987) found that garment workers took "only what was owed them" and rarely stole items of substantial value.

Whether the group considers it acceptable to take something and where it decides a line should be drawn ("You can help yourself to pens, but flash drives are hands off"), depends on many variables. For example, the size of the organization is likely to be a factor. Smigel (1970) found that when workers were "forced" (in a questionnaire) to select an organization they would be most inclined to victimize, they first chose large businesses, then government, and lastly, small businesses. They considered large corporations and big government impersonal bureaucratic giants able to absorb losses more easily than smaller organizations.

Regardless of the explanation, employee theft seems to require some subjective justification on the part of the worker. He or she often does not perceive his or her conduct as illegal or even unethical, either because the behavior is in line with group norms, in line with internal standards, or both. From the group's or worker's perspective, the theft or the counterproductive behavior either are expected or they adjust the imbalances inherent in working for the company. It is interesting to note that employee theft diminishes when an organization clarifies for the workforce precisely what constitutes misconduct and what is expected (Clark & Hollinger, 1983). This approach, combined with working conditions that convince employees their organization cares about them, seems to be the most effective in reducing employee theft and counterproductive behavior. Furthermore, improvement in the work environment functions both ways; the worker is also expected to demonstrate loyalty and commitment to the organization, setting up appropriate models for new workers. But loyalty to a company may go too far, as when it represents a higher obligation than commitment to law and ethics. Individual blind loyalty often leads to corporate crime.

SUMMARY AND CONCLUSIONS

At first glance, the offenses discussed in this chapter appear to represent a hodgepodge of unrelated crimes, ranging from petty larceny to corporate crime that claims numerous victims. What they have in common is that they are distinct from the crimes discussed to this point, and, although there are exceptions, they are essentially committed for economic reasons. Their primary distinguishing feature from murder, assault, terrorist activities, and the sexual offenses discussed thus far is a lack of physical aggression or violence against persons. The crimes discussed in this chapter are not, by definition, violent acts. Nevertheless, there may be incidental violence—such as can occur in home invasions, burglaries, and carjackings—or indirect violence—such as would occur when people die as a result of a corporation's malfeasance.

The property offenses of burglary, larceny-theft, and motor vehicle theft make up the greatest proportion of the nation's crime rate in any given year. Put another way, they are reported far more frequently than are violent crimes. We discussed the official and victimization statistics on these crimes, as well as the effects on their victims. We have little information on the characteristics of offenders, however, with the exception of burglars who appear to be more willing than other offenders to share their secrets with researchers. In a number of studies, burglars have described how they choose victims, what tactics they use to gain access to targets, which targets they avoid, and why. Professional burglars seem to carefully plan their offenses and do not seem to consider themselves "real criminals." In addition, researchers study case materials of solved crimes to identify behavioral and crime-scene features. These studies lead to typologies of burglars and can be of help to law enforcement in solving future crimes.

Home invasions are a special category of crimes that have features in common with burglary—they are usually committed for economic reasons—but they also involve direct personal encounters with their victims. In the worst form of home invasion, the perpetrators enter the home with the intention of harming its occupants. To our knowledge, no empirical, psychological research has been conducted on home invaders; those who commit violent acts are likely to possess features of aggressive behavior covered in earlier chapters. Depending on their behavior at the scene, some may possess psychopathic characteristics, such as callous-unemotional traits, discussed in Chapter 7.

In the discussion of motor vehicle theft, we included a section on carjacking, another crime that is of relatively recent origin. We covered information about the behavioral attributes or the motives of carjackers obtained from studies based on interviews with the offenders themselves. Carjackers seem motivated primarily by a need for quick money, or in some cases, a quick ride, or a quick thrill. However, carjackers highlight the expertise needed to carry out their crime successfully.

A fast-growing crime today is identity theft. Persons responsible for this crime may use very simple methods, such as stealing a wallet in someone's office, or complex elaborate methods that make use of the Internet and computer hacking. Cybercrime is covered again in the following chapter.

Shoplifting is a nonviolent offense that presents continuing problems for commercial establishments. Individuals who shoplift do not seem to consider this behavior un-normative. Self-report data indicate that a great majority of juveniles have shoplifted at least once; surprisingly, large numbers of adults also admit to this behavior at some point during their adult lives. Today, there is more evidence of highly organized shoplifting, in which small groups of individuals plan their shoplifting strategy and have access to a network of fencing operations to dispose of their acquisitions. Research does not support the belief that kleptomania—a supposed compulsion to steal—actually exists to the extent that it would explain a significant proportion of shoplifting. While some individuals undoubtedly shoplift to gain attention, get recognition, or embarrass their family, it seems that most do so to obtain goods, go along with peers, or—in the case of some juveniles—on a dare or as initiation into a select group or gang. Furthermore, although there is some suggestion that depressed individuals may engage in "nonsensical shoplifting," the evidence that this is characteristic of large numbers of people is not persuasive.

We discussed white-collar crime and the difficulties in defining this concept. Green's four-part typology, although not often alluded to in the criminology literature, is helpful in considering varieties of crimes committed by individuals in the course of their legal occupations. Not all crimes mentioned by Green would be considered white-collar crime, but all are criminal offenses worthy of consideration. A display of excessive force by a police officer may be considered an aggravated assault, but the police officer's status as a person in authority suggests an additional element that should be taken into consideration in any attempt to understand this behavior. Likewise, a medical doctor's sexual assault of a female patient is still a rape, but the violations of trust and professional ethics add a dimension that render it different, from a psychological perspective, from a date rape or a stranger assault.

The traditional type of white-collar crime is the crime committed by corporations, businesses, or organizations or by individuals within those entities. One of the best explanations for this behavior lies in neutralizing techniques, in which individuals and groups convince themselves that their behavior was not really criminal or that no one was hurt, among other justifications. However, corporate crime is rarely studied by criminal psychologists, psychiatrists, or criminal justice researchers, beyond the gathering of data available from court records or government regulatory agencies. Burglars and rapists get interviewed and participate in studies. Corporate criminals are more likely to write their own books than to cooperate with professionals seeking some insight into their actions. Criminologists have, however, increased their focus on individual white-collar offenders in recent years, finding interesting personality traits, including psychopathic characteristics, and thinking patterns that may distinguish them from nonwhite-collar offenders.

Key Concepts

Boosters
Burglary
Carjacking
Cognitive scripts
Corporate crime
Expressive burglars
Fence
Home invasions
Identity theft
Individual occupational crime
Kleptomania
Near-repeat offending

Occupational crime
Organizational occupational crime
Professional occupational crime
Property crimes
Relative deprivation
Repeat burglary
Shoplifting by proxy
Snitches
State-authority occupational crime
Techniques of neutralization
White-collar crime

Review Questions

1. Define larceny and burglary. How are they different from each other?
2. Identify and contrast the burglar typologies of Vaughn et al. and Fox and Farrington.
3. Discuss identity theft, focusing on a) prevalence; b) characteristics of offenders; and c) impact on victims.
4. In what ways has shoplifting changed since it was first studied by Cameron? What is shoplifting-by-proxy?
5. Define kleptomania and describe the empirical support for the phenomenon.
6. Briefly describe Green's occupational crime typology. Give an example of each. Contrast Green's typology to that of Clinard and Quinney.
7. Describe and illustrate any five neutralization techniques or strategies used by corporate criminals.

15

Violent Economic Crime, Cybercrime, and Crimes of Intimidation

CHAPTER OBJECTIVES

- Define and discuss robbery and the reasons behind the offense.
- Define and distinguish cybercrime, cyberstalking, and cyberbullying.
- Examine the literature on stalking.
- Outline hostage-taking offenses and their characteristics.
- Carefully summarize the literature on arson, with particular emphasis on juvenile firesetting.
- Examine the psychological motives attached to serial arsons.

> *It happened in a supermarket parking lot. It was early evening and I didn't get a good look at him. I wasn't hurt, but he said he had a knife. Only my purse was taken, but he scared me to death. I don't sleep well at night and I don't go food shopping by myself any more, even in the day. It happened two years ago. (62-year-old robbery victim)*

The above may strike some readers as an overreaction to a relatively minor offense in which the victim was not injured. The woman's sleeplessness could be a result of many factors, not just her victimization, and the incident happened so long ago that she should now be able to put it behind her. Nevertheless, it cannot be denied that what occurred left a marked impression on her and affected her perceptions and her lifestyle. This can be said of all of the crimes discussed in this chapter. Even those that seem relatively minor have no small impact on the people they touch, and many are considered very serious crimes.

The chapter focuses primarily on the economic crimes of robbery and arson, but other crimes are also considered. Of robbery and arson, the UCR program considers robbery a violent crime and arson a property crime. We approach both robbery and arson as violent because in both crimes, there is moderate to high level of serious injury or death to the victims, or at least the threat or possibility of such injury. The arsonist who torches a building does not know for sure that someone is not inside, for example. However, from a psychological perspective, many robbers have little in common with those who assault, rape, or kill, because their primary intention is not to harm their victims physically. Likewise, many arsonists have no intention of harming people, even though they are responsible for deaths should they occur.

Cybercrimes, which have been discussed in other contexts in earlier chapters (e.g., downloading child pornography, identity theft), are addressed here as chiefly economic crimes that may produce a large number of victims in a short period of time. Computer intrusion has become a global problem, recognized by virtually all law enforcement agencies, but often with few resources to combat it. A different form of cybercrime, that which involves stalking, is addressed here as well. Cyberstalking is considered a crime of intimidation, just as is stalking that does not necessarily involve electronic means. Crimes of intimidation are intended to frighten, threaten, embarrass, or harass the victim or victims. As we will see later in the chapter, however, all perpetrators do not necessarily have these motives.

Hostage taking is an offense with elements of both violence and extreme intimidation. Although most hostage situations are resolved peacefully, they have the strong potential of resulting in the deaths of the victims.

ROBBERY

Robbery is the taking or attempting to take anything of value from the care, custody, or control of a person or persons by force or threat of force or violence and/or by putting the victim in fear (Federal Bureau of Investigation, 2014a). The major distinctions between robbery and other economic crimes—such as burglary, fraud, or larceny—are the direct contact between the offender and the victim and the threat or use of force. The offender threatens bodily harm if the victim resists or impedes the offender's progress; usually, but not invariably, this threat is backed up by a clearly visible lethal weapon, such as a handgun or a knife.

Similar to other violent offenses, both the number of robberies reported to police and the robbery rate have declined in recent years. For example, while there were 367,832 robberies reported in 2010, reflecting a national robbery rate of 119.1 per 100,000 people (Federal Bureau of Investigation, 2011a), there were 345,031 robberies in 2013, reflecting a rate of 109.1 per 100,000 people (Federal Bureau of Investigation, 2014a). Perhaps more significantly, the number of robberies decreased 15.6 percent from 2009.

Statistics also provide information about the weapons used in reported robberies, when such information is available. In 2013, strong-arm tactics were used slightly more than firearms (43.6% vs. 40.0%). Interestingly, **strong-arm robbery** (without a weapon) is more likely to result in injury to the victim than is robbery with a firearm or knife. Presumably, victims are less fearful (and thus more daring) when confronted by an unarmed individual. In the absence of a gun or other weapon, the victim's resistance to losing valuable personal property is stronger, and he or she is more apt to try to resist or fight off the perpetrator. The tendency to resist, therefore, may partly account for the higher rates of victim injury in these no-weapon situations. On the other hand, the offender is likely to feel more confident, powerful, and in control of the incident when he or she has a weapon. Because of this increase in confidence, the offender is less likely to be anxious and disorganized in response patterns, and thus is better able to think clearly and evaluate the consequences of the actions—provided the offender is not under the influence of drugs.

Like many other crimes, robbery is primarily an offense committed by young adults (under the age of 25), who account for approximately two-thirds of those arrested. The majority of the arrestees (approximately 90%) are males.

Robbery accounts for only about 4 percent of all arrests for economic crimes (but 35% of the violent crimes), but it is highly feared by the general population. This is especially the case for street robbery, which has an edge of desperation to it (Wright, Brookman, & Bennett, 2006). It involves a high probability of physical harm from a stranger, and it can happen to anyone. The highest proportion of robberies (42.5%) in 2013 occurred on streets and highways (see **Figure 15-1**). One in three victims are injured in robbery (also called stickup, holdup, mugging), and one in ten so seriously that he or she requires medical attention (U.S. Department of Justice, 1988). Furthermore, robbery offenders are more likely to use weapons than other violent offenders, although as noted earlier, a surprising number use strong-arm tactics. Yet, despite its dangerousness, robbery is among the criminal offenses least studied by psychologists.

One reason for the lack of research interest on the psychology of robbery is that the crime seems so obvious and straightforward: People rob to obtain money. It is often assumed that the money will be used to buy alcohol or illegal substances, and psychologists as a group may be more interested in studying substance abuse itself rather than delving into the psychology of robbers. The process of committing a robbery is quick, and the potential returns are lucrative. Compared with burglary, however, the risks are great and the penalties substantial. Much of this may be true but, as we have seen, human

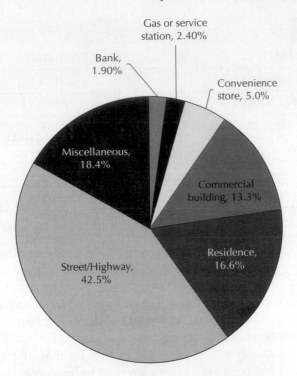

FIGURE 15-1 Percentage Distribution of
Robbery Locations in the United States, 2013
Source: Federal Bureau of Investigation (2014a). Crime
in the United States 2013: Uniform Crime Reports.
Washington, DC: U.S. Department of Justice.

behavior should not be oversimplified. The motives of offenders may be extremely varied. People
behave a certain way because they have convinced themselves that is what works best for them.

Bank Robbery

"A bank robbery is indicated when the crime is robbery and the location is a financial institution" (Federal Bureau of Investigation, 2003). Bank robberies are often the stuff of movies, but
they actually account for a small percentage of all robberies (1.9% in 2013; see **Figure 15-1**).
Although violence is rare, employees and customers are at risk of injury if the robber loses control or becomes violent. During a robbery, bank procedures are highly standardized. Tellers are
instructed to comply quickly with a robber's demands and empty their cash drawers, even if no
violence is threatened or weapons shown. The primary objective of banks is to ensure the safety of
employers and customers. Therefore, the risk to the robber of encountering resistance is low, and
consequently the robbery has a high probability of success during the early stages of the incident.
Bank robbers are typically arrested soon afterward, however, even though most are convinced they
will not get caught (Erickson, 1996; Weisel, 2007). Weisel (2007) reports that 15 percent of bank
robbers are arrested at or near the scene, and one-third of the robberies are solved on the same day.
Overall, 60 to 75 percent of bank robberies are eventually solved (Federal Bureau of Investigation,
2003). Bank robberies have a high rate of being solved because they are reported quickly, have
many witnesses, occur during daylight hours, and are extensively captured on surveillance videos.

According to data collected from the Bank Crime Statistics (BCS) program of the FBI, commercial banks were the most commonly robbed banks in 2014 (see **Table 15-1**). Although clearance rates may be high, the amount of money eventually recovered is quite small, averaging about
20 percent of the total amount taken during the robbery. Bank robbery incidents are most likely
to occur on Fridays. Historically, Friday has been payday for much of the nation, requiring large
amounts of cash to be delivered to the various branch banks. Fridays continue to be the favorite
day, even with the reduction of branch bank offices in recent years and the substantial increase in
direct deposit and other forms of electronic banking.

TABLE 15-1 Bank Robberies by Establishment Robbed, 2014	
Establishment	**Robberies**
Commercial banks	3,430
Mutual savings banks	31
Savings and loans associations	93
Credit unions	312
Armored company	13
Total	**3,961**

Source: Federal Bureau of Investigation, (2014c). Bank Crime Statistics. Washington, DC: U.S. Department of Justice.

Amateurs and Professionals

Most (80%) bank robberies are carried out by a single offender. A vast majority of all bank robbers are males (95%), and most are between the ages of 18 and 29. The majority of bank robbers are amateurs who have *not* been convicted of a bank crime in the past (Federal Bureau of Investigation, 2003). For example, the most recent statistics (2014) indicate that of the persons identified as responsible, only 18 percent had been previously convicted for bank robbery, burglary, or larceny.

An amateur tends to rob a bank on the spur of the moment without much planning, and primarily to fulfill some need, such as to pay for drugs, alcohol, or status-enhancing goods. Basically, they tend to exhibit behavioral indicators of poor self-regulation. They are often under the influence of drugs and alcohol to fortify their nerve. Therefore, amateur bank robberies usually do not involve the meticulously planned caper carried out by a group of highly experienced criminals often portrayed in films. Amateur bank robbers are highly predictable in their behavioral patterns, as they continue to rob because the offense seems to be so easy to carry out. Sometimes they rob other banks on the same day, employing the same *modus operandi* in successive robberies (see **Table 15-2**). They use the same signature repeatedly, such as a distinctively worded note given

TABLE 15-2 *Modus Operandi* Used by Bank Robbers, 2010	
Modus Operandi	**Frequency**
Demand note used	3,142
Firearm used	1,445
Handgun	1,394
Other firearm	78
Other weapon used	126
Weapon threatened	2,461
Explosive device used or threatened	165
Oral demand	3,096
Vault or safe theft	17
Depository trap device	1
Till theft	91
Takeover	333

Source: Bank Crime Statistics (2011). Bank Crime Report: Final 2010. Washington, DC: U.S. Department of Justice, Federal Bureau of Investigation.

to a single teller, and—if they use a disguise—they use it over and over again (Rehder & Dillow, 2003). Interestingly, about half of the amateur bank robbers do not even try to use disguises, and two-thirds are unarmed when they commit their bank robberies (Federal Bureau of Investigation, 2003). In summary, amateur bank robbers tend to commit their crime alone, unarmed, and undisguised (Weisel, 2007).

Violence occurs in a very small percentage of bank robberies. In 2014, for example, only 3 percent of all incidents included violence. There were 63 injuries, 13 deaths (10 of which were the death of the perpetrators), and 31 hostage-taking incidents. Thus, even though a firearm or other weapon may be used or displayed, it is not often used to injure or kill anyone.

Professionals are usually armed and use more than one perpetrator in the robbery. They also often try to disable or obscure surveillance cameras and are more likely to use disguises, such as balaclavas or face-distorting masks. In contrast to amateurs, who usually wait in line with customers before the robbery, try to escape on foot or by bicycle, and usually live near the bank, professionals generally use motor vehicles for escape. A professional, according to the BCS database (Federal Bureau of Investigation, 2003) is a bank robber with a prior criminal record, no matter how unsuccessful he or she has been at bank robbing in the past. Banks that attract amateur bank robbers are very unlikely to attract professionals (Weisel, 2007). In addition, professionals tend to select times when there are few customers, such as at opening time and early in the week; amateurs most often select midday times and Fridays when bank customers are at their highest level. Professionals also select banks that are located at corner locations so that there are multiple choices for vehicle escapes. Professionals prefer to maintain as much control of the situation as possible. Therefore, the displaying of weapons and the presence of few customers increase their control over the robbery scene. They also utilize various kinds of intimidation, physical or verbal threats, and are loud and aggressive. **Table 15-3** contrasts amateur and professional bank robbers.

Assessing skilled robbery, regardless of where it occurs, Peter Letkemann (1973) offered pertinent remarks about the successful robber's confidence and victim "management." Contrasting the robber to the burglar, he noted that burglars do not have to be concerned with people, but professional robbers must be able to maintain control and handle their victims at all times. Professional bank robbers, for example, assert that the keys to a successful heist are confidence and the ability to control people under highly stressful conditions. Confidence, they believe, is reflected in the robber's tone of voice and general behavior. High levels of self-confidence are crucial if robbers are to maintain control of the situation. Successful robbers also note that the posture and physical location of the victims are deliberately designed to enhance the offender's control over them. For example, victims may be told to kneel facing a wall or lie on the floor.

According to Letkemann, professional robbers often express dismay over media treatment of robbery. For example, television and movies often downplay the seriousness of bank robbery, particularly when no one is physically hurt—and recall that injuries are rare. The offenders therefore must work harder to convince their victims that they mean business. The entertainment media also encourage some victims to be heroes; robbers consider heroes irrational and extremely dangerous to their own safety and a threat to the successful outcome to the crime.

TABLE 15-3 Contrasting Features of Amateur and Professional Bank Robbers

Amateurs	Professionals
Lone robber	Two or more robbers
Rob during high customer traffic	Rob during low traffic times
Stand in line	Control the situation, intimidate
Usually not armed	Carry and display weapons
Spur-of-the moment offending when they need money	Careful planning
Getaway by running, or use bikes	Motor vehicles for getaway

Even though there are few actual injuries in bank robberies, some preliminary research reveals that bank workers, such as tellers, take several months to recover psychologically from the trauma of the robbery (Jones, 2002). Returning to the same environment day after day where the traumatic event took place, the victims often continue to experience psychological stress associated with the incident, sometimes for longer than six months. The symptoms may be physical or emotional, and nearly anything that was present during the robbery—sights, smells, textures, sounds—may bring them on. Even bank personnel who were not directly confronted during the robbery may experience stress symptoms. The experience may also have a rippling effect that spreads to family members, friends, and coworkers. These same experiences, of course, are often experienced by victims of other types of robbery and crime in general. People who have experienced workplace violence in other contexts—for example, hospitals, insurance agencies, auto plants, courthouses—may exhibit stress long after the traumatic event has passed.

Commercial Robbery

Approximately 13 percent of all robberies take place in commercial houses, compared with 16 percent in residences. (Recall that entering a residence for the purpose of taking money or goods would qualify as burglary; if the residents are at home and threatened with violence, it becomes a robbery as well as a home invasion, discussed in Chapter 14.) Commercial houses are anywhere where goods are bought and sold. Examples are supermarkets, department stores, restaurants (including fast-food restaurants), financial companies, taverns, and motels and hotels.

Convenience stores accounted for 5.0 percent of robberies in 2013, followed by gas or service stations at 2.4 percent (see **Figure 15-1**). Most convenience stores have no robberies, but a few have many robberies (Eck, 2000). One of the debates concerning prevention of convenience store robbery is whether having two or more clerks in the store, rather than one, reduces the robbery attempts. So far, the evidence is unclear, but the two-clerk experiment does not appear to discourage robberies as much as was anticipated (Eck, 2000). Cameras and silent alarms do not seem to reduce convenience store robberies, but some preliminary evidence suggests that the installation of interactive CCTV (allowing communication between store personnel and security personnel watching a monitor in a remote location) may be effective in reducing store robberies by nearly one-third (Eck, 2000).

Although convenience stores have traditionally been a favorite robbery site, fast-food restaurants are now becoming a preferred target. Many restaurant robberies occur at fast-food restaurants because they are open late, staffed by teenagers, full of cash, and conveniently near a highway. In describing the vulnerability of fast-food restaurants to armed robbery, Schlosser (2001, p. 84) writes, "A couple of sixteen-year-old crew members and a twenty-year-old manager are often the only people locking up a restaurant, long after midnight." About two-thirds of the robberies at fast-food restaurants involve current or former employees as perpetrators, and frequently, the on-duty manager suffers much of the anger and violence administered during the robbery.

The leading fast-food chains have tried to reduce robbery by spending millions on new security measures, including video cameras, panic buttons, drop-safes, burglar alarms, and additional lighting (Schlosser, 2001). But even the most secure restaurant remains highly vulnerable to robbery.

Figure 15-1 indicates that 18.4 percent of robberies in 2013 fell into a miscellaneous category. Examples include robberies in professional offices, churches, union halls, schools, government buildings, subways, and waterways.

Street Robbery

As noted above, the greatest proportion of robberies in the United States occurs on streets and highways (e.g., Federal Bureau of Investigation, 2014a). Street robbery is most common in urban areas, particularly in cities over 250,000 in population. Unlike bank and commercial robbery, street robbery tends to be more based on opportunity than planning, although as noted above the planning done by amateur bank robbers is typically minimal. Street robbery is driven by the culture on the streets, and follows many of the characteristics of carjacking discussed in the previous chapter. Carjackers generally do exhibit more expertise at their crimes, however (Nee, 2015; Topalli, Jacques, & Wright, 2015). Street robbers remain in a state of "alert opportunism," where the motivation to offend is always present. They are in perpetual need of money to buy status-enhancing goods, drugs, and alcohol. When an opportunity to rob occurs, there is little or no time for contemplation; otherwise the opportunity is lost forever. Still, street robbers are most likely to follow well-rehearsed cognitive scripts that have been developed and practiced through offending activities. Even though little contemplation is used when opportunity knocks, their methods and targets have developed through experimentation and tinkering of their own personal approaches or scripts.

Motives and Cultural Influences

Some researchers view robbery as a rational choice driven primarily by the need for money and a desire to minimize the risk of detection. Other researchers believe street robbery represents a cultural pursuit in which the money and risks take second place to the psychological and social rewards toward the offender's lifestyle (Wright et al., 2006).

In a revealing study, Richard Wright and Scott Decker (1997) interviewed 86 individuals who were actively engaged in armed robbery on a regular basis in St. Louis. None of the robbers interviewed were incarcerated or otherwise under supervision of the criminal justice system (e.g., out on bail, on probation, or on parole). Most other studies of armed robbery feature interviews with prisoners who either admit engaging in the offense or have been convicted for robbery.

Wright and Decker tried to determine what factors influenced the robbers as to when, how, and whom to rob. The researchers were also interested in the offenders' thoughts and actions during the commission of the crime. In addition to interviewing, the researchers took 10 of the robbers to the site of a recent holdup for which they had not been apprehended and asked them to reconstruct the crime. Although all age groups were represented, most were between 18 and 29. Most also had committed numerous robberies in their lifetimes—so many in fact that they found it impossible to specify the exact number. Despite the very high number of armed robberies they said they had committed, 60 percent of the sample had never been convicted of armed robbery. Almost all the sample (96%) reported committing many other offenses, particularly theft, burglary, assault, and drug selling. A great majority (85%) typically did their robbery on the street, while 12 percent preferred to rob commercial establishments (e.g., pawnshops, jewelry stores, liquor stores—all of which fall within the "commercial house" category of **Figure 15-1**).

Wright and Decker found that a vast majority of the offenders did not plan the armed robbery. "The reality for many offenders is that crime commission has become so routinized that it emerges almost naturally in the course of their daily lives, often occurring without substantial planning or deliberation" (Wright & Decker, 1997, p. 30). The researchers discovered that, with few exceptions, the decision to rob was strongly influenced by a pressing need for cash to support their hedonistic, carefree lifestyle. The robbers in this sample were deeply enmeshed in the street culture where immediate gratification reigned supreme. Many of them spent their take with reckless abandon without much thought to financial obligations or commitments. The offenders chose armed robbery as a lifestyle because it provides quick cash as the need arises. Armed robbery offered immediate cash compared with the delays inherent in disposing of hot merchandise acquired through burglary, shoplifting, and motor vehicle theft.

One of the favorite targets of the street robbers in this sample were individuals who themselves were involved in lawbreaking, especially drug sellers and wealthy drug users. Drug dealers carry considerable amounts of cash as a result of their illegal activities. Of course, the risks are higher when targeting dealers because they are more likely to be armed, more likely to resist, and are sometimes connected to a powerful drug organization. Wealthy drug users tend to be white persons who come into a neighborhood looking to buy drugs with considerable cash. They can be easily victimized, and like other lawbreakers, they are unlikely to report the robbery to the police.

In a later, more focused examination of street robbery, Wright et al. (2006) discovered that American and United Kingdom **street culture** seem to be a very powerful social force in the commission of these crimes. "American street culture subsumes a number of powerful conduct norms, including, but not limited to, the hedonistic pursuit of sensory stimulation, disdain for conventional living, lack of future orientation and persistent eschewal of responsibility" (Wright et al., 2006, p. 2). The image one presents is paramount and is one of the few sources of status available to most offenders. The same social impetus is present in the United Kingdom street culture. As noted by Katz (1988), while the obvious reason for street robbery is money, the reasons for needing the money are far more revealing.

According to Wright et al. (2006), street robbery accomplishes five things, depending on the needs of the offender:

- Generates quick cash that can be spent quickly and used easily to finance gambling, drug use, and heavy drinking
- Allows purchasing nonessential, status-enhancing items (such as clothing or jewelry) to improve standing in the street culture
- Creates excitement and dominance over victims who are overpowered
- Prompts anger and eagerness to start a fight in those offenders already prone toward fighting and violence
- Achieves a certain measure of informal justice, such as debt collecting or revenge

One of the major findings of the Wright and Decker (1997) and Wright et al. (2006) projects is that there is little psychological mystery behind the motives of armed robbery: These offenders need cash now to support an impulsive lifestyle, and robbery provides the best route to that cash. Some also enjoy dominating their victims and frightening them, seek the "buzz" they receive from the offense, or come across as not to be messed with in the street culture, but these motives are only secondary to cash acquisition. An important point must be emphasized, however. Even though many street robberies appear to be impulsive and hold to the philosophy "strike while the iron is hot," it is highly likely the offender is following his or her favorite cognitive script, developed and perfected over a series of similar street crimes. Furthermore, the script has been formulated most probably through a combination of observation (social learning) and participation with a payoff (instrumental learning). When opportunity knocks, their offending cognitive script immediately comes into play. The script contains information that guides the offending behavior (Ward & Hudson, 2000). "These scripts can be enacted without conscious intention and with minimal awareness of the overall goal" (Ward & Hudson, 2000, p. 197).

Robbery by Groups

Porter and Alison (2006) investigated 116 cases of group robbery (61 commercial and 55 personal) and were able to identify a four-part typology based on the interpersonal behavior between the offenders and their victims. The "group" could be as few as two robbers and as many as six, with a mean group size of three. The researchers examined how the robbers treated the victims, and how the victims, in turn, reacted to the robbers' behavior. The four themes identified were: (1) dominance, (2) submission, (3) cooperation, and (4) hostility.

The interpersonal theme of *dominance* refers to situations in which the group of offenders attempts to control their victims completely. These offenders often use weapons and threaten the victims. In some instances, they bind and gag the victims during the robbery. Dominance is the method most preferred by professional bank robbers.

In the *submission* theme, the offenders allow the victim to make an effort to be in control and are ultimately unsuccessful. That is, the robber group is not forceful or assertive, and the robbery becomes an attempt, with the intended victims taking over the situation. In this scenario, the victims refuse to do as they are told, may struggle with the robbers, and at the end, the robbers run away. Porter and Alison provide the example of a situation in which two youths attempted to rob a store and were physically confronted by both the owner and his wife, who chased off the offenders. "As the offenders left the premises they swore at the couple and made a two-fingered gesture towards the security camera" (Porter & Alison, 2006, p. 336).

In the *cooperation* theme, the behaviors of the robbers are designed to obtain cooperation from the victims. The offenders manipulate the victims to comply with their demands and to participate in the crime. Such participation involves handing over property, opening a safe, providing their PIN for the victim's credit or debit card, filling bags with money, or making sure no additional customers enter the building. The robbers may use a single act of violence or display a weapon, but the intent here is to get cooperation from victims, rather than control them. Many victims tend to comply with the offenders' instructions rather than resist—and as mentioned above, bank employees are typically instructed to cooperate. The researchers discovered that this strategy is the most frequently used in group robberies, and appears to be the most effective.

The interactional theme of *hostility* involves the offenders acting in an aggressive and violent manner toward the victims from the outset. In most cases, the researchers found that a hostile approach by robbers often produces a hostile reaction from victims. Many victims fight back or attempt to flee the scene. In this situation, the offenders are reckless, needlessly attacking victims with violence and verbal threats, and they often use firearms. This method is also most commonly associated with victim resistance. The larger the group, however, the more likely it is that one member will "go rogue" and use violent tactics that were not intended by others in the group. This scenario is depicted, not only in movies, but also in actual court cases where a robber is charged with felony murder because his partner-in-crime killed a victim.

Research by Porter and Alison (2006) indicated that commercial robberies were more associated with the cooperation theme than were personal robberies, and personal robberies also were more hostile than commercial robberies. Personal robberies refer to street robberies, such as at or near an ATM machine. Commercial robberies, as noted above, involve businesses like stores, gas stations, fast-food restaurants, or banks. The researchers also report that personal robbery tends to be more violent than commercial robbery because victims usually are less willing to cooperate and hand over personal property.

Recall that in Chapter 12, we discussed strategies for resisting sexual assault (e.g., Ullman, 2007) and concluded that—as a general principle—forceful resistance is now advocated if possible because it is the least likely to result in a completed rape. When it comes to street robbery, the situation may be quite different. In that case, it is likely wiser to part with one's personal possessions than try to fend off the attacker.

CYBERCRIME

Cybercrime refers to any illegal act that involves a computer system. It is therefore also called computer crime and sometimes, when computers are hacked, computer intrusion. Cybercrime often involves traditional forms of crime, such as fraud, identity theft, accessing and distributing child pornography, and financial theft, discussed in earlier chapters. We also covered cybercrime in Chapter 11, noting that terrorist activities and recruitment are often facilitated through the use of the Internet, including the dark web. The dark web consists of underground websites that often allow people to engage in illegal activities or to discuss them. Accessed with special servers or passwords, the dark web has enabled users to discuss drug dealing and hacking techniques or to recruit would-be terrorists. It also has been used for purposes other than illegal activities, however, such as by persons attempting to avoid repressive regimes.

Although cybercrime is not always a crime of intimidation and does not always involve violence, it is extremely widespread and disruptive. In this chapter we focus primarily on the intimidation aspect of cybercrime, but we also cover more general aspects of the activity—that is, the computer intrusion itself, and some research on characteristics of perpetrators. Cybercrime can be done swiftly, and it has vast numbers of potential victims (Broadhurst, 2006). In one notable operation in 2008 involving stolen debit cards, cyberthieves attacked more than 2,100 ATM machines in at least 280 cities on three continents (see **Box 15-1**). "The cross-national nature of most computer related crimes has rendered many time-honoured methods of policing both domestically and in cross-border situations ineffective even in advanced nations, while the 'digital divide' provides 'safe havens' for cyber-criminals" (Broadhurst, 2006, p. 408).

CONTEMPORARY ISSUES

BOX 15-1   Cybercrime—Heists and Intrusions

It has become increasingly apparent that cybercrime can take many forms and may require complex ability to carry out and to detect and prosecute. Some forms of cybercrime are relatively simple to accomplish, while other forms are carried out with extensive computer knowledge and sophisticated resources.

Computer intrusions—whereby viruses, worms, spyware, and malware are installed on personal, business, and government computers—generally require extensive technical knowledge on the part of the perpetrator. They not only create havoc in private and public spheres, but also are a potential threat to national security.

A recent computer intrusion case involved the hacking group SwaggSec, which carried out a series of computer attacks in 2012 and 2013 against DirecTV, Farmers Insurance, and the Los Angeles Department of Public Works. In April 2015, a member of the hacker group received a three-year prison sentence after admitting to installing a Remote Access Trojan and using it to steal reports, documents, emails, passwords, and health information. The intrusion into the Los Angeles Department compromised records of more than 3,000 people (U.S. Attorney's Office, 2015). The perpetrator was also ordered to pay over two-and-a-half million dollars in restitution to the three entities victimized.

In what the FBI referred to as a complex, carefully planned high-tech heist in 2008, four hackers from different countries (Estonia, Moldova, and Russia) carried out a highly organized attack on 2,100 ATM machines across the globe. One of the hackers had identified a vulnerability in the computer network of a major credit card processing company based in Atlanta, Georgia. They then conspired with thieves who had stolen debit cards, busted into the Atlanta network,

accessed PIN numbers of the stolen cards, and even manipulated codes to increase the maximum amount of money that could be withdrawn. Then, over a 12-hour period, the original thieves—now referred to as "cashiers"—withdrew more than $9 million in cash (FBI, 2009, High-Tech Heist).

In 2011, a two-year FBI investigation, called Operation Ghost Click, ended with the arrest of six Estonians charged with running a sophisticated Internet fraud ring that infected about 4 million computers worldwide, including some 500,000 in the United States (FBI, 2011b). The scheme involved posing as a legitimate business that sold software, but that actually installed malware enabling the perpetrators to redirect users to fraudulent websites purporting to sell products and collect fees. The cyber ring was dismantled through cooperation among law enforcement and private industry internationally.

Questions for Discussion

1. In only one of the above cases is punishment mentioned. Is a three-year-sentence and restitution a fair punishment for the computer intrusions carried out by a member of SwaggSec?
2. With reference to the ATM heist, is it likely that the same psychological factors explain the behavior of the four hackers and the behavior of the "cashiers" who stole the original cards and later withdrew the cash? If yes, why? If no, how might the factors be different?
3. Which, if any, of the following emotions do you experience on reading about the above cyber criminals: admiration, anger, indifference, revulsion, other (specify). Would you experience the same emotions with respect to other cybercrimes mentioned in the chapter?

Advances in computer technology and increased access to personal information via the Internet have created a significant marketplace for worldwide cyber criminals to share stolen information and sophisticated criminal methods (Martinez, 2011). Some law enforcement agencies are making headway into the "digital divide," however. In 2010, the multifaceted strategies of the U.S. Secret Service to combat cybercrime led to the arrests of over 1,200 suspects for cybercrime related violations (Martinez, 2011). The Secret Service investigations discovered over $500 million in actual fraud loss and prevented approximately $7 billion in additional losses. In 2011, government agencies across the globe worked together to crack highly sophisticated cybercrimes involving malware affecting personal and business computers worldwide (see again **Box 15-1**). Despite these successes, numerous challenges to combating cybercrime exist. Today, specially trained cyber squads operate out of FBI headquarters as well as 56 field offices.

The main types of financially related cybercrime are unauthorized access to computers (hacking), mischief to data (virus generation), and theft of communications (see **Table 15-4**). The development and use of malicious software has been especially worrisome for businesses and government. Malware and other computer viruses cause considerable damage to businesses, consumer networks, and governmental systems. In fact, the most recent trend in cybercrime involves

TABLE 15-4 Cybercrime Type Detected by American Businesses, 2005

Type of Incident	Percent
Cyber Theft	**16.4**
Embezzlement	3.8
Fraud	5.5
Theft of intellectual property	3.4
Theft of personal or financial data	3.7
Cyber Attack	**83**
Denial of service	18.4
Vandalism or sabotage	5.3
Computer virus	59.7

Source: Rantala, R. R. (2008, September). Cybercrime against businesses, 2005. Washington, DC: U.S. Department of Justice, Bureau of Justice Statistics.

the ongoing targeting of point of sale systems as well as the compromise of online financial accounts, usually through malware developed explicitly for that purpose.

As illustrated from examples in **Box 15-1**, malware and hacking attacks on financial systems and fraudulent transfers of electronic funds are not only becoming more prevalent but are also affecting every sector of the world economy. In recent years, cyber criminals have concentrated on attacking small and medium-sized business, banks, and data processors as larger organizations have become more adept at developing sophisticated protections (Martinez, 2011). "Phishing" or "spoofing spam" has become increasingly popular. These terms refer to email messages with corresponding web pages designed to appear as existing consumer or business sites. Millions of these fraudulent emails are sent to laptops, tablets, cell phones, and personal computers across the globe, claiming to come from banks, charitable organizations, individuals-in-need, lotteries, or other legitimate-sounding sites in order to persuade people to submit financial, personal, or password data. Cybercrime offenders have developed a growing practice of buying, selling, and trading malicious malware software, credit and debit card data, personal information data, bank account information, brokerage account information, hacking services, and counterfeit identity documents (Martinez, 2011).

In 2006, an FBI agent infiltrated a cybercrime organization website called Darkmarket and was instrumental in shutting it down in 2008, resulting in numerous arrests. It had approximately 2,500 members worldwide at its peak, mostly persons involved in buying and selling stolen financial information, such as credit card data, login information, and equipment to carry out financial crimes (Chabinsky, 2010). Although this website was shut down, many others quickly emerged (Glenny, 2011). Likewise, the now-defunct dark website Silk Road offered a variety of illicit products (e.g., drugs and fake IDs) until its operator was found and arrested in 2013; a successor, Silk Road 2, was shut down in 2014.

Privacy Concerns and Cybercrime Laws

In response to the dramatic increase in computer crimes, the U.S. Congress has attempted to pass laws, such as a 2015 effort to persuade companies to share access to their computer networks with federal investigators. Private companies, the government maintains, do not have sufficient resources to prevent and deal with cyberattacks; only information sharing and a joint effort with the federal government will do this. However, sharing information with the government—or with other companies—raises privacy concerns, and this approach is resisted by many across the political spectrum.

In addition to legislative efforts, various federal agencies (e.g., the FBI, the Department of Defense, and the Department of Homeland Security) have trained agents and opened specialized units to fight cybercrime. The FBI also maintains a "most wanted list" of alleged cyber criminals.

TABLE 15-5	Complaints of Online Crime, 2004–2010
Year	**Complaints Received**
2010	303,809
2009	336,655
2008	275,284
2007	206,884
2006	207,492
2005	231,493
2004	207,449

Source: Internet Crime Complaint Center (2008, 2011).

It is clear that cybercrime is a serious problem that will continue to draw considerable attention from law enforcement agencies across the globe.

At the turn of the twenty-first century, a national initiative to address the problem of Internet fraud was undertaken. The initiative encouraged the FBI to join forces with the NW3C (National White Collar Crime Center, mentioned in the previous chapter) to establish the Internet Fraud Complaint Center for strategic information about and analysis of Internet fraud schemes. The Center was later named the Internet Crime Complaint Center (IC3) to reflect the fact that not all cybercrimes are fraud related and to recognize the considerable overlap between many cybercrimes. (See **Table 15-5** for number of complaints of online crime over a five-year period.)

Psychological Characteristics of Cybercriminals

Research focusing on the psychological characteristics of cybercrime and cybercriminals is just beginning. We do know that cybercriminals are a diverse group in their talents and motivations, but they usually have acquired significant computer technical skills. Some commit the crimes for the thrills of making life miserable for others, whereas others desire the monetary rewards for their efforts. Increasingly, some view themselves as business persons and view cybercrime as their full-time business (Chabinsky, 2010). Some cybercriminals are businesses trying to gain an upper hand in the marketplace by hacking the websites of their competitors; some are rings of criminals wanting to sell personal information; some others are generally young computer-savvy people looking for bragging rights; and still some others are terrorists (FBI, Computer Intrusions, 2015). As the level of profit increases, transnational, violent organized crime groups are becoming progressively more involved in the cybercrime enterprise (Chabinsky, 2010).

It is likely that cybercriminals employ the same techniques of neutralizing their behavior as are employed by other offenders, particularly white collar criminals. These were discussed in earlier chapters, and include such cognitive approaches as dehumanizing victims and minimizing the extent of the harm they do.

Cyberstalking is a serious form of cybercrime that will grow in scope and complexity as more people take advantage of the Internet and other telecommunications and digital technologies. The cyberstalker and the cyberbullyer—both discussed below—are more representative of the general topic of this chapter than the cybercriminals discussed above. Theirs are crimes of intimidation that can take an immense psychological toll on their victims. Both can send repeated and threatening messages by the simple push of a button, and their anonymity leaves them at an advantageous position for avoiding detection. As we will note below, however, a recent U.S. Supreme Court decision (*Elonis v. United States*, 2015) indicates that persons sending threats and perceived threats via the Internet cannot be held criminally liable without proof that they intended to threaten specific targets. We discuss both cyberstalking and cyberbullying in separate sections below, after reviewing research on stalking behavior in general.

STALKING

Many young adults report that they or someone they know well has experienced what they think of as stalking—such as unwelcome, persistent phone calls, text messages, or being followed on the street or into classrooms, stores, bars, and nightclubs. **Stalking** is broadly defined as "a course of conduct directed at a specific person that involves repeated physical or visual proximity, nonconsensual communication, or verbal, written, or implied threats sufficient to cause fear in a reasonable person" (Tjaden, 1997, p. 2). Systematic information on stalking in the United States is somewhat limited, despite the attention it receives from the media and state and federal legislatures (Tjaden, 1997). Early research and attention focused on the stalking of famous persons, entertainment personalities, or politicians, known as "celebrity stalking." However, a substantial increase in the stalking of noncelebrities led to the passage of antistalking laws in all 50 states and the District of Columbia (Tjaden & Thoennes, 1998a). Since that time, social scientists have directed more attention to the causes, correlates, and effects of stalking (e.g., Belknap & Sharma, 2014; Lambert, Smith, Geistman, Cluse-Tolar, & Jiang, 2013; Reyns & Englebrecht, 2012; Sheridan, Scott, & North, 2015).

Legal definitions of stalking vary widely from state to state. While most states define it as the willful, malicious, and repeated following and harassing of another person, some include such activities as lying-in-wait, surveillance, nonconsensual communication, telephone harassment, and vandalism (Tjaden & Thoennes, 1998a). Some states specify that at least two stalking events must occur before the conduct can be considered illegal.

California became the first state to enact antistalking legislation in 1990. The impetus for this legislation was not the stalking/homicide of television actress Rebecca Schaeffer as commonly believed, but rather the intractable problem of domestic violence (Lemon, 1994). A California municipal court judge initiated the development and passage of the antistalking law, following his frustration over existing laws that failed to protect four Orange County women who were killed in different incidents despite the issuance of restraining orders against their assailants. Since 1990, stalking statutes have spread rapidly to all states.

In an attempt to fill in the large gap in our knowledge about stalking, the Center for Policy Research conducted a comprehensive victimization survey of eight thousand women and eight thousand men, 18 years of age or older, on issues relating to violence (Tjaden & Thoennes, 1997). The survey revealed that 8 percent of women and 2 percent of men reported they had been stalked at some point in their lives (Tjaden, 1997). Overall, the survey indicated that approximately 1.4 million Americans are victims of stalkers every year, a surprisingly large number. More recent data indicate that in 2006, an estimated 3.4 million persons age 18 or older were victims of stalking (Baum, Catalano, & Rand, 2009). In most cases, the stalking lasted less than one year, but some people were stalked for over five years. "While individually these acts may not be criminal, collectively and repetitively these behaviors may cause a victim to fear for his or her safety or the safety of a family member" (Baum et al., 2009, p. 1). It is estimated that one out of every 12 women and one out of every 45 men in the United States has been stalked during his or her lifetime (Tjaden & Thoennes, 1998a). Persons between the age of 18 and 24 experience the highest rates of stalking victimization, and the risk of victimization decreases with age (Baum et al., 2009). Individuals who are divorced or separated are also at high risk of stalking victimization by their former partners.

In a recent study, Sheridan et al. (2015) compared various age groups of stalkers via detailed information obtained from their victims. Stalkers were divided into three groups—16 and under, 17 to 59, and 60 and over. Interestingly, there were few significant differences among the stalkers. For example, the three groups were equally violent. Comparisons among the victims—also divided into age groups—were significant, however. Older victims, though suffering from similar effects, were both most likely to be injured and less likely to be taken seriously.

The Center for Policy Research survey (Tjaden & Thoennes) found that the motives of most stalkers were to control, intimidate, or frighten their victims. This observation was made by both male and female victims. Eighty-seven percent of the time the stalker was male, and 80 percent of the time the victim was female. In most stalking incidents, the victims (particularly women) knew their stalker. About half of the female victims were stalked by current or former marital or cohabiting partners, and a majority of these women (80%) had been physically assaulted by that partner either during the relationship, during the stalking episode, or during both. About one in ten victims were stalked by a stranger (Baum et al., 2009). In about one-third of the cases, stalkers vandalized the victim's property, and about 10 percent of the time, the stalker killed or threatened to kill the victim's pet. In nearly half the cases, the stalker made overt threats to the victim. The survey dispels the myth that most stalkers are psychotic or delusional. Only 7 percent of the victims perceived their stalkers as "crazy" or abusers of drugs or alcohol.

Half of all victims reported the stalking to the police, and about one-quarter of the female victims obtained a restraining order. Not surprisingly, 70 percent of all restraining orders were violated by the assailant. About one-quarter of victims in cases where a restraining order was violated pursued prosecution. When prosecution was pursued, most cases resulted in conviction of the stalker and well over half received jail time. Although most of the stalking stopped within two years, the emotional and social effects of being stalked continued for many victims long after the incident. About one-third of the stalking victims sought psychological treatment because of the emotional and social trauma that resulted from the stalking episodes.

Meloy (1998) asserts that stalkers rarely cause serious physical injury to their victims, threaten them with weapons, or use weapons. Sheridan et al. (2015), however, reported that victims were often injured: 29 percent of victims of the mid-group of stalkers (ages 17 to 59) were injured, and 43.1 percent of victims of older stalkers (60 and over) were injured. About half of the younger stalker group (under 17) threatened their victims physically, though just over 7 percent of their victims were injured. Even when not injured, the psychological trauma is often substantial. In a survey of 145 stalking victims (120 females, 25 males), Hall (1998) reports that the experience of being stalked for months or even years is akin to psychological terrorism. A majority of the victims said their entire lives changed as a result of being stalked. "Many move or quit jobs, some change their names, others have gone underground, leaving friends and family in order to escape the terror" (Hall, 1998, p. 134). Some change their physical appearance or wear disguises. Others become exceedingly suspicious of the motives of others, often leading lonely and isolated lives. Many victims constantly worry that the stalker will find them, and that the entire experience will start all over again.

Categories of Stalking

Some researchers have identified categories or typologies of stalking. A prominent example is the four-category classification proposed by Beatty (2001): (1) simple obsession stalking, (2) love obsession stalking, (3) erotomania stalking, and (4) vengeance stalking. **Simple obsession stalking** accounts for the majority of stalking (about 60%), and often represents extensions of previous patterns of domestic violence and psychological abuse. The stalker in these case scenarios usually seeks power and control after a failed relationship with the victim. Simple obsession stalking is perhaps the most dangerous to the victim, since it is often motivated by the stalker's conclusion that "If I can't have you, nobody will." In **love obsession stalking**, the stalker and victim are casual acquaintances or complete strangers. Stalkers in this category are characterized by low self-esteem and tend to select victims they perceive to have certain qualities they believe will raise their self-esteem. Essentially, they seek a love relationship with the object of their obsession, contrary to the wishes of their victim.

Erotomania stalking is considered delusional, and the stalker is often plagued by serious mental disorders. This type of stalker usually targets public figures or celebrities in their misguided attempts to gain self-esteem and status for themselves. Talk show host David Letterman was stalked over a number of years by a woman who apparently believed she was his wife. The woman frequently trespassed on Letterman's property, hid in his home, and even stole his car to go grocery shopping. The delusional woman eventually took her own life. Fortunately, erotomania stalking appears to be relatively rare, and normally the stalker is not violent.

In the 1990s, photographer Sally Mann published a book of photos of her three children, some of which represented the children unclothed. Writing recently (Mann, 2015) in defense of her book, which had been both highly praised and highly criticized, Mann reveals that the family was stalked for about six years by a person who knew their whereabouts and often tried—sometimes posing as a researcher—to obtain information about the children from schools, public records, libraries, and other sources. The stalker, whom she does not name, eventually moved out of the United States. Although he never approached the children directly and never threatened them, the family lived with the fear that he might do so at some point. Mann writes that one of her daughters still has nightmares about the man, many years after the incidents she reports.

Vengeance stalking is quite different from the other three types, because vengeance stalkers do not seek a personal relationship with their targets (Beatty, 2001). Instead, they try to elicit a particular response or change of behavior from the victims. For example, the stalker who wishes to torment those responsible for a perceived injustice or violation of their rights might follow the "guilty parties" day and night until he is fairly compensated.

Other researchers have classified stalkers according to their relationship with the victim. Studying over one thousand male and female stalkers, Mohandie, Meloy, Green-McGowan, and Williams (2006) divided them into intimate stalkers, acquaintance stalkers, public figure stalkers, and private stranger stalkers. The most violence associated with the stalking was perpetrated by intimate stalkers, with the least perpetrated by public figure stalkers. The intimate stalker resembles the simple obsession stalker described above; both are most likely to result in violence.

What terminates stalking? Some stalkers stop their activity toward the current victim when they find a new "love" interest. About 18 percent of the victims in the Center for Policy Research Survey indicated the stalking stopped when their assailant got a new spouse, partner, or boyfriend/girlfriend. Informal law enforcement interventions also seem to help. Fifteen percent said the stalking ceased when the assailant received a warning from the police. More formal interventions such as arrest, conviction, or restraining orders do not appear to be very effective. When it comes to persistent, frightening stalking that creates risks to personal safety, the survey suggests that the most effective method may be to relocate as far away from the offender as possible with no information of whereabouts provided to the offender. This places an unfair burden on the victim, however.

Cyberstalking

Cyberstalking is using the Internet or other forms of electronic communications to threaten or engage in unwanted advances toward another. Virtually every state today has laws criminalizing it. In many laws, a distinction is drawn between **cyberstalking** and **cyberharassment**. Some states have statutes relating to one or the other, others have statutes relating to each, and in other states both behaviors are covered in one statute. The typical state has separate laws for each.

Cyberharassment pertains to threatening or harassing email messages, instant messages, blog entries, or websites dedicated solely to tormenting an individual (NCSL, 2015). When cyberharassment is kept distinct from cyberstalking, the former is not thought to involve a *credible* threat. Although harassment is a milder form of behavior and generally subject to lesser criminal penalties, the effect on the recipient may be substantial, and from a psychological perspective there is little difference between the two activities. In this section we use cyberstalking because it is the more serious offense and has generated the most research, but concepts discussed may also relate to cyberharassment.

It is important to stress that, in some cases, finding someone guilty of communicating threats in cyberspace may be complicated in light of the U.S. Supreme Court's recent ruling in *Elonis v. United States* (2015). After his wife and three children moved out of the house, Elonis had consistently used his Facebook page to post his own rap lyrics using violent language and imagery. Although he made comments about his estranged wife, his coworkers, government officials, and even a kindergarten class, he often included disclaimers that these did not depict real persons. Nevertheless, many individuals, including his boss and his wife, interpreted the posts as threats; his boss fired him and his wife was granted a protection from abuse order. Elonis was convicted under a federal law that makes it a crime to transmit in interstate commerce any communication containing a threat to injure the person of another. The courts had focused on the fact that reasonable persons (e.g., the wife and the boss, among others) had perceived the communication as threats. However, in an 8–0 decision, the U.S. Supreme Court noted that this was not sufficient. In order to be convicted, a person must have the intention to threaten. The specific criteria for establishing intention has yet to be decided, but negligence on the part of the defendant is not enough.

Elonis' behavior on line does not qualify as cyberstalking but may be interpreted as cyber-harassment, which as noted above may or may not be criminally liable depending upon the jurisdiction. If true threats are involved, a person intending to threaten can be punished; how-ever, without that specific intention, successful prosecution is unlikely, despite the fact that others perceive a significant threat.

About one in four stalking victims reported that some form of cyberstalking was used to frighten them (Baum et al., 2009). Online and electronic stalking and harassment may take many forms, but in many ways they are similar to off-line stalking. Although stalkers often wish to estab-lish relationships with the victims, a substantial number seek to terrify and sometimes ultimately harm their victims. In many cases, the cyberstalker and the victim had a prior relationship, and the cyberstalking begins when the victim attempts to break off the relationship (U.S. Department of Justice, 1999). Ultimately, much cyberstalking is designed to control the victim, usually through threats and harassment. As emphasized above, the threat must be intentional.

"Because e-mail is used daily by what some experts say are as many as 35 million people, and it is estimated that there are approximately 200,000 stalkers in the United States, the Internet is a perfect forum with which to terrorize their victims" (Jenson, 1996, p. 1). In the years since that statement was written, opportunities to cyberstalk have expanded dramatically. "Chat rooms," email, social networking sites, cell phones, smart phones, and text messaging provide far-reaching and unregulated outlets for contacting unsuspecting victims. "Today, an estimated 84 percent of American adults use the Internet" (Perrin & Duggan, 2015). An enormous amount of personal information is available through the Internet, and perpetrators can easily and quickly locate private information about a target, similar to the identity thieves discussed in Chapter 14.

One aspect of cyberstalking that should be considered is the process of deindividuation, discussed in earlier chapters. The anonymity offered by the Internet and many forms of elec-tronic communication releases participants from the traditional constraints on their behavior by deindividuating them (Hinduja, 2008). Deindividuation, you will recall, reduces self-awareness and self-regulation. "Individuals who act and interact in cyberspace may feel 'hidden' or immersed among each other (and among the collective of hundreds of millions currently connected online) and more a part of a group than by oneself" (Hinduja, 2008, p. 392). Therefore, some people who cyberstalk or cyberbully may be more inclined to act in a deviant and psychologically damaging manner as a result of the anonymity the Internet provides.

Cyberbullying

Traditional bullying is defined as "systematically and chronically inflicting physical hurt or psychological distress on one or more students" (Diamanduros, Downs, & Jenkins, 2008, p. 693). Although bullying is generally defined and discussed in the context of young people, such as stu-dents in schools, it also can occur among adults, such as in the workplace. As we noted in Chapter 6, bullying can take the form of physical, verbal, and nonverbal actions (Olweus, 1997; Viljoen, O'Neill, & Sidhu, 2005).

Cyberbullying is defined as "sending or posting harmful or cruel text or images using the Internet or other digital communication devices" (Li, 2006, p. 158). These electronic forms of con-tact may include the Internet or cell or smart phones, most often through emails, Instagram, text messaging, and other social media. Even more than those who bully face to face, those who bully online can be daring, vicious, and threatening because they can remain anonymous.

Cyberbullying has become a worldwide problem among students. Estimates of the number of cyberbullied victims are difficult to obtain and have ranged from 4 to 72 percent of all students. There are some research projects that have been well executed and do suggest some accurate data. In Britain, for example, one in four youths between the ages of 11 and 19 said they had been cyberbullied in 2002 (Li, 2006). A similar statistic was found among Canadian youth (Li, 2006, 2007), and among American youth (Hinduja & Patchin, 2008). In a recent publication, Patchin and Hindjuja (2012) report that, based on their best estimate of the research literature, about one in five school-aged youth have been victims of cyberbullying. Girls are most often the victims (Smith et al., 2008). In most instances, cyberbullying is of short duration (a month or less); nevertheless, its effects on the victims can be devastating. Many of the effects of bullying discussed in Chapter 6 apply equally if not more intensely to cyberbullying. As Diamanduros et al. (2008) observed, while the playground or school bus or school hall is where bullying traditionally has occurred, technology has expanded the problem to the borderless cyberworld.

In contrast with traditional bullying, cyberbullies are often anonymous. In one extensive survey of 1,211 students, approximately 40 percent of those who were cyberbullied did not know the identity of the bully, although some students had their suspects (Dehue, Bolman, & Völlink, 2008). "Cyberspace creates an illusion of invisibility because it is faceless" (Mason, 2008, p. 329). This feeling of invisibility eliminates concerns of detection, social disapproval, and punishment. In addition, cyberbullies are not personally confronted with how their victims react to their cyberbullying or the consequences of their actions, which encourages deindividuation (Dehue et al., 2008). However, when the anonymous bullier and the victim attend the same school or otherwise are in contact with one another, the bullier is able to observe the residual effects of his or her behavior. Victims report that not knowing the person behind the cyberattacks is often discouraging; this increases their feelings of powerlessness (Vandebosch & Van Cleemput, 2008). The research literature consistently indicates that the consequences of cyber victimization include low self-esteem, poor academic performance, depression, emotional distress, and even violence and suicide (Mason, 2008).

Those who frequently cyberbully are characterized by the need to feel powerful and in control (Diamanduros et al., 2008). They like to dominate, and they often select victims who are loners (Diamanduros et al., 2008). In many instances, they have been bullied themselves (Barlett & Gentile, 2012; Bauman, 2010; Li, 2007). "In other words, individuals may be motivated to harm others online after receiving such harm, suggesting retaliatory motivations" (Barlett & Gentile, 2012, p. 131). Retaliatory motivations in this context refers to tendency to cyberbully either those who cyberbullied them or other individuals they know. In addition, those who engage in traditional forms of bullying are the same ones who engage in a large amount of the cyberbullying (Bartlett & Gentile, 2012). For instance, Qing Li (2007) discovered that nearly one-third of the cyberbullies in her Canadian research were also traditional bullies. Li also found that 60 percent of cyberbullying victims were females, and a large majority of the cyberbullies in these cases were also females. "This result supports the point that females prefer to use electronic communication medium such as chat-room and email to bully others" (Li, 2007, p. 1787). A majority of the cyberbully victims and those who know about it did not report the incidents to adults. With the exception of the gender differences, Li's research indicates a close tie between bullying and cyberbullying, and suggests that the many effective techniques of combating traditional bullying should also work for dealing with cyberbullying.

The prevalence of this problem among youth is reflected in the fact that as of January 2015, 49 states had enacted bullying prevention legislation, almost all including cyberbullying (Hinduja & Patchin, 2015). Only a handful make cyberbullying itself a criminal offense, but the laws typically require schools to have policies to deal with bullying (Hinduja & Patchin, 2015). Laws must be crafted in such a way as to not infringe on First Amendment protections, however. Bullying usually involves physical victimization, such as shoving, punching, or more serious beatings. Cyberbullying—as disturbing as it is—can be regarded as free speech.

The difficulty enacting laws punishing cyberbullying is illustrated by the fate of the Megan Meier Cyberbullying Prevention Act of 2009, a proposed federal law that would have forbade interstate or foreign digital or electronic communication with intent to coerce, intimidate, harass, or cause substantial emotional distress to a person. The bill was introduced twice into the House of Representatives, but failed to gain support for passage because of concerns that it was overbroad in its coverage and infringed on free speech. Megan Meier was a 14-year-old girl who committed suicide after receiving hostile messages from "Josh Evans," a "boy" she met on MySpace. Ultimately, it was learned that "Josh" was really another girl, an acquaintance of Megan's who lived down the street. The two girls had had disagreements, and the other girl's parents helped her create the fake Josh Evans identity, which she used to send distressing messages to Megan. The girl and her family were themselves subjected to considerable in-person and online harassment when details of the suicide were revealed. Similar suicidal incidents across the country led legislatures to try to craft laws that would criminalize bullying online, particularly when it led to the suicide of the bullied individual. To date, however, punishment for cyberbullying has been limited to suspensions from school, provided the actions significantly disrupted the school environment. However, schools can be sued successfully if they are deliberately indifferent to a bullying problem within the school, including one that involves cyberbullying off school grounds.

HOSTAGE-TAKING OFFENSES

The hostage taker holds victims against their will and uses them to obtain material gain or personal advantage. Typically, this offender threatens to take the lives of the victims if certain demands are not met within a specified time period. Included in the broad hostage-taking category are abductions and kidnappings, skyjackings, and some acts of terrorism. Recall that we gave considerable attention in Chapter 11 to acts of international and domestic terrorism. In this chapter, terrorism is discussed only as it relates specifically to hostage taking. For the most part, however, hostage-taking here refers to perpetrator's behavior out of an international political context.

Instrumental and Expressive Hostage Taking

Some time ago, Miron and Goldstein (1978) divided hostage-taking offenses into two major categories based on the offender's primary motivation: instrumental and expressive hostage taking. The categories continue to be useful today for understanding and responding to hostage-taking scenarios.

In **instrumental hostage taking**, the offender's goal is recognizable—it is chiefly material gain, such as kidnapping a child and holding the child for ransom. The goal also may be to achieve freedom, such as in the classic case wherein a robber holds a hostage until a getaway vehicle is delivered. The goal in **expressive hostage taking** is psychological: the offender wants to become significant and to take control over his or her own fate. Expressive offenders generally feel that they have little control over events in their lives. They want to become important, and they believe the media coverage accompanying their hostage taking will help them to achieve this goal. Alternatively, the hostage taker may be depressed and may use the offense to bring attention to a desperate situation. Hostage-taking offenses sometimes begin as instrumental acts but develop into expressive ones. An offender who initially kidnaps someone for material gain may find that his demands are unrealistic and not likely to be met; in this case, the person may decide to play out the scenario for the attention, significance, and control it affords. Sometimes, both instrumental and expressive motives are clearly involved from the beginning. That is, the offender expects both material and psychological gain from the abduction.

FBI Categories of Hostage Taking

Since the 1970s, the FBI has classified hostage takers into four broad categories: terrorists, prisoners, criminals, and the mentally disordered (Fuselier & Noesner, 1990). Here the focus is less on the motivations of the person and more on their apparent characteristics. Research suggests that over 50 percent of all hostage-taking incidents are perpetrated by mentally disordered individuals (Borum & Strentz, 1993), thus representing the largest category. It should be noted, however, that the categories may overlap, such as when a person holding captives in a domestic violence situation is also mentally disordered.

Early research indicated that the average terrorist hostage taker was not sophisticated (Fuselier & Noesner, 1990) and that training for his or her terrorist activity was marginal or nonexistent. Terrorist hostage takers were usually young males from deprived socioeconomic backgrounds with little formal education. Moreover, they were very willing to kill innocent victims, and were considered more dangerous than the more sophisticated hostage taker.

Over the past two decades, hostage taking by terrorist groups has both increased and become more sophisticated. Attempted negotiation for the release of aid workers, journalists, or government agents have been complex and typically held in highly classified fashion. Few hostages held by al-Qaeda or ISIS have been released, for example, and many have been executed, sometimes in a horrifying manner and seen on videos circulated on the Internet. Negotiation is not an option in active shooter situations, such as the attacks in Paris in November 2015. Terrorists held hostages inside an entertainment venue, and police stormed the concert hall as it became clear that hostages were being executed.

It is doubtful, then, that the following quote from 1990, long before the events of September 11, is still representative today: "(N)egotiation strategies and tactics for terrorist incidents are identical to those that would be used during any hostage or barricade incident, regardless of the political or religious backgrounds of the subjects" (Fuselier & Noesner, 1990, p. 10). For that reason, the FBI's first category—terrorist hostage takers—must be treated very differently from the others and is not addressed in detail here.

Miller (2007) notes that a category of hostage takers similar to the terrorist is the one who has political or religious motives but is not associated with a formal terrorist group. "This is probably one of the most dangerous hostage situations, because many of these perpetrators are quite willing to die and kill others for their cause" (Miller, 2007, p. 66). This type of hostage taker—one we would place in the expressive category above—is likely to be considered a domestic terrorist according to the FBI's scheme.

The other forms of hostage taking have similar features and respond well to knowledgeable negotiation strategies. As Miller (2007) notes, crisis intervention in hostage situations have resolved the situation approximately 95 percent of the time without fatalities to either the hostages or hostage takers.

Criminal and prisoner hostage-taking situations share the most similar features. Both are likely to be instrumental in nature. In the process of committing a bank robbery, for example, the robber may take a hostage as a human shield to assist in the getaway. Likewise, during a prison riot or escape attempt, inmates may take corrections officers or staff as hostages to help earn their way to freedom or aid in their negotiations with prison officials. Such incidents are extremely rare, and the hostages are not usually harmed, but there are exceptions. A riot in the brutal New Mexico Penitentiary in 1980 was extremely violent, and seven of the 12 officers who were taken as hostages were seriously physically injured (Johnson, 1996). However, in the famed Attica uprising of 1971, prisoners in New York's Attica facility held a number of officers hostage but did not harm them (Wicker, 1976). The uprising occurred after many unsuccessful attempts by inmates and advocates to improve conditions within the prison. Most of the deaths of correctional officers and inmates that are associated with that incident occurred when the prison was stormed by law enforcement officers in a controversial move to forego negotiations and end the uprising (Thompson, 2014; Wicker, 1976). That is, most of the deaths were not caused by the prisoners.

The mentally disordered hostage taker—considered the most frequent—also may be the most dangerous, particularly because his or her actions are unpredictable. As Miller (2007) notes, local law enforcement is most likely to come into contact with mentally disordered hostage takers in domestic and workplace hostage situations. "Thus, to be truly effective, negotiators need to wed the art and science of crisis management to the insights on personality and psychopathology offered by mental health professionals" (p. 68). In his useful article, Miller offers specific approaches to take with persons with a variety of disorders, including schizophrenia, paranoia, depression, and antisocial personality disorder, among others.

Strategies for Dealing with Hostage Takers

Experienced negotiators suggest strategies for dealing with hostage takers or barricaded individuals. (A **barricade situation** is one in which an individual has fortified or barricaded himself or herself in a building or residence, and threatens violence, either to self or others.) Many of these strategies are based on psychological concepts (see **Table 15-6**). In addition to these negotiation strategies, however, a basic protocol must be followed (e.g., securing the perimeter, provide for scene control, establish a means of communication) (Miller, 2005).

First, the hostage taker should be denied the excitement and stimulation he or she hopes to initiate; this requires that a potentially chaotic situation be handled as calmly as possible, with minimum media attention. This is difficult to accomplish, because hostage-taking incidents are extremely media worthy. As noted in Chapter 5, very high levels of arousal tend to promote disorganized response patterns and reduce internal thought processes. Under high excitement and chaos, the offender is more likely to revert to "mindless" behavior, which may include violence. The most dangerous phase in most hostage or barricade situations is the first 15 to 45 minutes (Noesner & Dolan, 1992). Miller (2007) emphasizes, however, that two other periods are equally dangerous: during the surrender of the hostage taker, and during tactical assaults to rescue the hostages, if such assaults are undertaken.

With regard to the first 15 to 45 minutes, the first officers on the scene should hold their positions until additional resources, including the negotiation team, arrive at the scene. If possible, the officers who are first on the scene should try to engage the hostage taker in conversation, emphasizing that they wish no harm to the individual. Experienced negotiators believe that conversation distracts the offender from violence and generally calms the situation, especially if the negotiator maintains a calm and steady demeanor.

Second, offenders must be allowed to feel that they are in some control of the situation. Helplessness and powerlessness may have prompted the offense in the first place. If the captors do not feel they have attained any control, they may take steps to prove the opposite, such as shooting one of the hostages.

Third, in hostage or barricade situations, time is usually a strong ally. Once the early stages of a crisis have passed and some stability and calm have been achieved, the passage of time plays a positive role. Time has several effects. After the initial high-arousal state, the body winds down and eventually the offender begins to feel tired, sluggish, and depressed. Under these conditions, the event takes on aversive properties for the hostage taker, and the offender is likely to begin to wish the situation were over. Time also promotes, in the hostage taker, some thought processes and greater reliance on internal standards of conduct. If the offender has incorporated some values of society, he or she may begin to appreciate the ramifications of his or her behavior. However, the hostage taker may also begin to construct justifications. Either process, however, may enable

TABLE 15-6 Guidelines for Hostage Negotiation

- Stabilize and contain the situation.
- Take your time when negotiating.
- Allow the subject to speak: It is more important to be a good listener than a good talker.
- Don't offer the subject anything.
- Avoid directing frequent attention to the victims; do not call them hostages.
- Be as honest as possible; avoid tricks.
- Never dismiss any request as trivial.
- Never say "no."
- Never set a deadline; try not to accept a deadline.
- Do not make alternate suggestions.
- Do not introduce outsiders (non-law enforcement) into the negotiation process.
- Do not allow any exchange of hostages; especially do not exchange a negotiator for a hostage.

Source: Fuselier, G. D., & Noesner, G. W. (1990, July). Confronting the terrorist hostage taker. FBI Law Enforcement Bulletin, 6–11.

the offender to accede more easily to police requests. Experienced negotiators strongly recommend that the negotiator act as spokesperson for the authorities and a conduit of information, emphasizing to the hostage taker that acceding to requests will take time. Consequently, the negotiator should not be a decision maker or in command. Otherwise, if the hostage taker is under the impression that the negotiator (or anyone in the immediate environment) has the power and decision-making authority, he or she will believe that decisions should be made quickly and directly. Under these conditions, any delay generates frustration in the captor and further increases arousal.

Time also affects the relationship with the hostage. According to social psychological research, the more familiar one is with an object or person, the more one tends to become attracted to it (e.g., Freedman, Sears, & Carlsmith, 1978). In many hostage situations, the more the victim and captor get to know one another, the more they begin to accept one another. Furthermore, if the hostage was a stranger to the captor, the hostage takes on human qualities with the passage of time. This is not identical to the Stockholm syndrome, a rare phenomenon in which some hostages and hostage takers develop an attraction to one another.

The Stockholm Syndrome

The attraction between victim and captor is called the **Stockholm syndrome**, after a hostage-taking incident in Sweden in 1973 that resulted in marriage between a female hostage and one of her abductors. Police negotiators have noted that on occasion, the hostage will side with the captor in working out demands. Although this may simply reflect a wish to end the terrifying ordeal as quickly as possible, it may also signify some attraction to or identification with the abductor. When hostages act this way, experts sometimes maintain that they have been brainwashed. An alternate explanation is that they have become attracted to their captors and temporarily identified with their values and goals. In general, though, the Stockholm syndrome is a rare occurrence. According to the FBI's Hostage/Barricade System (HOBAS), a national database that contains data from over 1,200 reported federal, state, and local hostage situations, 92 percent of the victims of such incidents showed no aspect of the Stockholm syndrome (Fuselier, 1999).

Some researchers have suggested that three things must be present before the Stockholm syndrome can take place (Fuselier, 1999). First, the hostage taker and victim must be together for a significant length of time. Second, the hostage must be in direct social contact during the incident. For example, physical separation of the hostages (such as complete isolation in a separate room) from the hostage taker will likely prevent development of the effect. Third, the hostage taker must treat the hostages kindly. In most hostage-taking situations, it is highly unlikely that each of these three conditions will occur.

Rules for Hostages to Follow

Although some experts conclude that the Stockholm effect is unusual and has minimal positive aspects, some disagree. Speckhard, Tarabrina, Krasnov, and Mufel (2005) interviewed 11 of the hostages held for three days in a Moscow theater by suicide terrorists armed with bombs and firearms. The terrorists held over 800 hostages in the incident. The stand-off ended when Russian Special Forces stormed into the theater and killed the terrorists. The core question the researchers posed in their research was, "Is it better to be passive and cooperate with suicide terrorists knowing they are ready and willing to die for their cause, or should one try to find ways to resist?" (Speckhard et al., 2005, p. 138). According to the 11 hostages interviewed (and this is a small number, perhaps unrepresentative of the 800 who were held), those who actively resisted in this situation or were uncooperative were either shot or severely beaten. Those who were cooperative and interacted positively with the hostage takers survived. Although the sample for this study was small, the observations made by the interviewees confirm advice typically given in the event that one is ever held hostage. As emphasized by the researchers, hostage taking events by suicide terrorists are likely to increase across the world in the future, and those who are at risk for hostage taking must be prepared. The researchers advice: "In advising an individual on how best to behave as a hostage it seems wise to teach that positive attachments and passivity are likely to arise in this terrifying state of captivity, and that if one can recognize this reaction when it is occurring and keep it within control it is likely most protective" (p. 138). That is, an individual who can act the part of a cooperative and friendly hostage while maintaining some level of objective detachment is likely to survive.

The above research does not support the existence of the Stockholm syndrome in captives who survived, however. Cooperating with one's captors is not the same as truly liking or identifying with them, which is what the Stockholm syndrome suggests. Moreover, in some cases a captive may "pretend" to identify with the captor or even offer to help, in the belief that this is more likely to save his or her life. Hostage takers are not likely to respond positively to the latter approach, though. Virtually all advice given to hostages is to do nothing that will antagonize the captors, including attempting to ingratiate oneself to them.

Thomas Strentz (1987) also outlines some rules to follow should a person ever be taken hostage, particularly by strangers. His suggestions are based on the psychological reactions of those hostages who survive (survivors) compared with those who do not (succumbers). **Survivors**, Strentz notes, are those "who returned to a meaningful existence with strong self-esteem, and who went on to live healthy and productive lives with little evidence of long-term depression, nightmares, or serious stress-induced illness" (p. 4). Although survivors do not ever forget the hostage experience, the experience does not prevent them from living relatively normal lives. **Succumbers**, on the other hand, are those who either did not live through the ordeal, or upon release or rescue have considerable difficulty dealing with the emotional trauma caused by the ordeal. They have great trouble getting on with their lives.

Strentz emphasizes that the most dangerous phase of any hostage situation is the moment of the abduction and the early minutes thereafter. Arousal levels are extremely high for both the abductors and the hostages. Unpredictable and unforeseen things can happen. Strentz asserts that, without exception, any form of resistance is extremely dangerous and should not be tried. He recommends playing the subordinate role immediately. Furthermore, throughout the entire abduction, maintaining a positive mental attitude that things will be all right in the end is absolutely essential. Feelings of hopelessness, abandonment, and isolation can lead to serious depression. On the other hand, a mature, controlled, and stable appearance—even if one is terrified—also helps settle the hostage taker(s). Anything that calms the situation increases chances of survival for everyone.

Furthermore, hostile feelings toward one's captors must be masked as best as they can, again to keep the situation calm. The hostage should not get into arguments with captors about politics, religion, social issues, or anything else. Strentz refers to the opposite strategy as the **London syndrome**, a behavioral pattern demonstrated during a six-day hostage situation in the Iranian Embassy in London in 1980. One captive, the press secretary, refused to compromise his dedication to his cause, constantly and insistently proclaiming his beliefs, and seemingly intent on martyrdom. Despite the pleas of his fellow hostages for silence, he kept arguing and was eventually killed by his captors. Although we should not fault the secretary for taking this approach—he was not responsible for his own death—potential hostages should be aware of the possible consequences of forceful verbal responses to their captors.

Chances of survival improve greatly if the hostage tries to blend in with fellow captives, if there are any. The individual who stands out in the crowd "by crying, by being overly polite and helpful, or by doing more than the abductors require, is immediately setting himself or herself up as an easy mark to be exploited" (Strentz, p. 6). If a person is more comfortable in the leadership role, he or she should be prepared to take the brunt of the abuse from the captors, and may even be killed as an example to the rest of the hostages. Individuals who have experienced a hostage-taking episode also say that being able to fantasize during the many empty hours is one of the critical factors in dealing with the situation. Some imagine travel to various places or dream about what they plan to do after the episode. Also, trying to keep a normal routine as much as possible will relieve stress. Exercise, personal hygiene, writing letters, or keeping logs—if these things are possible—are examples. Finally, Strentz recommends that no matter what the circumstances, hostages should never blame themselves or ruminate about what they should have done to avoid the abduction.

Rather, they should accept their status, and follow the patterns described here. The possibilities of survival will be greatly enhanced.

In sum, the psychological research on hostage taking focuses more on the effects of the incident on the hostage than on the characteristics of the individual committing the crime. Strategies are offered both to the hostage, for surviving the incident, and to negotiators, for dealing with the hostage taker effectively in order to prevent escalation and to end the crisis.

ARSON

Arson is defined "as any willful or malicious burning or attempt to burn, with or without intent to defraud, a dwelling house, public building, motor vehicle or aircraft, or personal property of another" (Federal Bureau of Investigation, 2014a). According to the UCR guidelines, only fires that law enforcement investigation determined to have been willfully or maliciously set may be classified as arson.

From a psychological perspective, it is more useful to focus on firesetting behavior than on behavior that ultimately qualifies as arson, a criminal act. Most psychological research in this area examines developmental and behavioral characteristics of children, adolescents, and adults who persistently set fires, whether or not they are arrested and convicted of crime. Government data on fires are obtained from agencies such as the U.S. Fire Administration or through the UCR program, if arson is reported. It is noteworthy that the UCR data, to be covered below, do not include fires that are labeled suspicious or of unknown origin. For example, massive wildfires that are suspected to have been deliberately set, but not confirmed as such, are not included in UCR statistics. As for numerous other offenses, there is a large dark figure that is not captured by the official data. Therefore, although we first begin with an overview of the crime of arson, we move quickly to concentrating upon psychological research on firesetting.

Incidence and Prevalence

The U.S. Fire Administration (www.usfa.fema.gov/data/statistics/) is a prominent source of data on fires in the United States. In 2011, over 1 million fires (1,389,500) were reported, a large number but still down 19.5 percent from 2002 statistics. The fires resulted in 3,005 deaths, 17,500 injuries, and a dollar loss of $11.7 billion. Data for the following year, 2012, indicated that about 12 percent of residential fires that involved one or more deaths were intentionally set, and another 12 percent were under investigation. According to a recent report (U.S. Fire Administration, 2011), many communities in the United States are currently experiencing a significant increase in serial arson-related fires. Arson fires may or may not involve death.

UCR data shed additional light on this problem, but again we emphasize that crime statistics capture only a portion of actual firesetting behavior. As in most other crimes, arson has declined in recent years, down 13.5 percent since 2012, and down 25.3 percent since 2004 (FBI, 2014a). Nearly 46 percent of all arson offenses involved structures (residential, storage facilities, public facilities, etc.). About 24 percent involved mobile property such as cars, trucks, and boats, and about 30 percent involved other types of property, such as forests.

Interestingly, juveniles under 18 accounted for about 50 percent of all those arrested for arson in 2004, but a slightly smaller percentage (about 35%) in 2013 (Federal Bureau of Investigation, 2014a). In the U.S. and other parts of the world (e.g., United Kingdom, Australia) young people, particularly males, account for a substantial percent of the total arrests (Lambie, McCardle, & Coleman, 2002; MacKay, Feldberg, Ward, & Marton, 2012). Some studies have found that between 75 and 85 percent of all firesetting is done by males, with increasing percentages of females in the 13 to 17-year-old group (Federal Bureau of Investigation, 2003; Stadolnik, 2000).

In a typical year in the United States, fires set by children and youth claim the lives of approximately 250 to 300 individuals (Putnam & Kirkpatrick, 2005). Children are often the victim of these fires, accounting for 85 percent of the lives lost in the United States (U.S. Fire Administration, 2004). Next to deaths caused by motor vehicle accidents, fires are the leading cause of death among young children (Stickle & Blechman, 2002). Not all these fires, of course, were set with criminal intent or would qualify as arson.

Most fires set by youth go undetected, unreported, or unsolved (Zipper & Wilcox, 2005). It is generally acknowledged, for example, that only a small proportion of fires set by juveniles is reported, probably less than 10 percent (Adler, Nunn, Northam, Lebnan, & Ross, 1994). Zipper and Wilcox (2005) report that of the 1,241 Massachusetts juveniles referred for counseling services because of arson, only 11 percent of the blazes these youths started were reported. No one reported these incidents, apparently because witnesses or caretakers did not consider the behavior danger-ous because no loss of life or significant destruction of property occurred. In these situations, many people also worry that charging juveniles with arson will give them a criminal record that will ham-per their future careers. Finally, children who set fires are often considered emotionally disturbed and thus in need of treatment, not punishment. We address this perception below. Another study of youth from the third to the eighth grades in 15 school districts in Oregon found that 32 percent of the students reported setting fires outside their homes, and 29 percent said they had started fires in their own residences (Zipper & Wilcox, 2005). Because so much attention is given to the topic of firesetting among children, we focus on this in the next section.

Developmental Stages of Firesetting

As indicated at the beginning of this section, **arson** is the legal term that specifically characterizes the willful or malicious setting of fires and defines it as a crime, with or without the intention to defraud. **Firesetting** is the term commonly used in the psychological literature, particularly in the literature on child psychopathology. It is intentional and willful behavior with an understanding of the potential consequences of that behavior. As we note below, if a four-year-old clicks on the bar-becue lighter and sets the outdoor furniture alight, he is not a firesetter. If he continues to do this, though, he is at risk of becoming one. Child firesetters have attracted considerable interest among researchers in psychology.

Gaynor (1996) outlines three developmental phases related to fire: (1) fire interest, (2) fire-play, and (3) firesetting. Fascination and experimentation with fire appears to be a common fea-ture of normal child development. Kafrey (1980) discovered that fascination with fire appears to be nearly universal in children between 5 and 7 years old. Furthermore, this fascination with fire begins even earlier, with one in five children setting fires before the age of three (fire interest). As the child gets older, fireplay (experimentation) may take place between the ages of 5 and 9. In this stage, the child experiments with how a fire starts and what it can do. Children during this phase are especially vulnerable to the hazards of fire because of their more limited ability to under-stand the consequences and their lack of effective strategies for extinguishing the fire once it gets out of control (Lambie et al., 2002). By age 10, and sometimes even earlier, most children have learned the dangers of fire and its consequences; if they continue to set fires at this point, they have reached the firesetting phase. These youths most often demonstrate an intention to use fires to destroy, as a form of excitement, or as a communicative device to draw attention to themselves and their problems.

The literature on persistent firesetting is virtually unanimous in its conclusion that this behav-ior is associated with serious psychological problems. Children who continue to set fires tend to demonstrate poor social skills, inadequate social competence, and impulsiveness compared with their peers (Kolko, 2002; Kolko & Kazdin, 1989). In a national sample of nearly five thousand 12- to 17-year-olds, Chen, Arria, and Anthony (2003) were able to conclude that children rejected by peers were more likely to set fires than those who were not rejected. In fact, in this study, a combination of aggression and peer rejection was significantly related to firesetting. Firesetters as a group—whether they are children, adolescents, or adults—are typically depicted as deficient in many areas, including social maladjustment, educational and social skills, and substance abuse disorders (Doley, Ferguson, & Surette, 2013).

In general, persistent firesetters are also more likely to demonstrate attention deficit hyper-activity disorders and poor impulse control (Forehand, Wierson, Frame, Kemptom, & Armistead,

1991), and many are considered to have "conduct problems" by their teachers. It should be noted that many studies report that conduct disorder is the most frequent diagnosis assigned to juvenile firesetters (MacKay et al., 2006). Lambie et al. (2002) report a similar finding. From their clinical experiences, Lambie et al. found that firesetting is but one part of a more comprehensive set of behavior problems, the motives of which occur for a variety of reasons and typically include impulse control problems and misdirected anger and boredom. There is also some evidence that children who are consistently cruel to animals and other children also tend to engage in consistent firesetting behavior (Slavkin, 2001). Lambie et al. (2002) also point out that adolescent firesetters frequently commit a variety of other crimes, including rape and other sex offenses.

This range of criminal offending has been noted by other researchers as well. It seems that a very large majority of firesetters known to the juvenile justice system have committed many other serious juvenile acts besides arson (Del Bove & Mackay, 2011; Ritvo, Shanok, & Lewis, 1983; Stickle & Blechman, 2002). Stickle and Blechman (2002) found that "firesetting juvenile offenders exhibit a pattern of developmentally advanced, serious antisocial behavior consistent with an early starter or life-course-persistent trajectory" (p. 190), a finding also reported by other researchers (Becker, Stuewig, Herrera, & McCloskey, 2004; Forehand et al., 1991). As might be expected, research has revealed a large portion of the persistent firesetters is boys, probably at a ratio of 9 to 1 to girls (Zipper & Wilcox, 2005).

Nearly all children who set fires beyond the normal fascination and experimental stages tend to have poor relationships with their parents and also appear to be victims of physical abuse (Jackson, Glass, & Hope, 1987) and other forms of maltreatment (Root, MacKay, Henderson, Del Bove, & Warling, 2008). The high rate of maltreatment among firesetting youth is not surprising since maltreatment has been closely associated with self-regulation, academic achievement, attachment, and social skill development (Root et al., 2008). In their investigation of 205 children and youth, ages 4 to 17, and their caregivers, Root et al. (2008) determined that those who were maltreated set more fires, were more versatile regarding ignition sources and targets, and were more likely to continue to set fires. Their primary motive for firesetting was anger.

In their comprehensive review of firesetting, Kolko, Kazdin, and Meyer (1985) suggest that it may be closely associated with parental ineffectiveness and faulty or nonexistent supervision. In a retrospective study by Saunders and Awad (1991), the records of 13 adolescent girls referred to the Toronto Family Court Clinic for setting fires were examined. The authors noted,

> Reading through the 13 charts was a depressing experience even for those of us who have worked for years with families who have many problems and serious difficulties meeting their children's basic needs. These parents had a history of marital problems, separation, violence against the spouse and the children, criminal behaviour, drug and/or alcohol abuse, and inability to take care of the children. (Saunders & Awad, 1991, p. 403)

Interestingly, the prevalence rate of firesetting appears to be significantly higher in children referred to a clinic for psychological problems than children not referred (Kolko & Kazdin, 1989; Lambie et al., 2002). Research suggests that adolescent or adult firesetters usually come from a disadvantaged group who have little or no effective means for influencing their environment and who find themselves in highly undesirable situations (Dadds & Fraser, 2006; Jackson et al., 1987). Juvenile firesetters often come from unstable homes, characterized by parental absence, indifferent or absent fathers, and abuse (Hickle & Roe-Sepowitz, 2010). Some studies describe the parents of firesetters as displaying limited affection, engaging in very little monitoring of their children's behavior, and overall, showing little involvement in their children's lives (McCarty & McMahon, 2005).

Persistent and Repetitive Firesetting among Adults

As suggested from the above, considerable psychological research has focused on the firesetting behavior of children and adolescents. By comparison, far less psychological research has examined the causes of firesetting in adults (Butler & Gannon, 2015), but there are exceptions. Some early attempts at explaining the behavior associated it with various forms of social learning theory, particularly aspects of gaining recognition and reinforcement. For example, repetitive firesetting seems to be precipitated by events that exacerbate feelings of low self-esteem, sadness, and depression (Bumpass, Fagelman, & Birx, 1983). In addition, following a firesetting, many arsonists stay at the scene of the fire, often sound the alarm, and even help fight the fire. In some cases, they take heroic action to save lives. The recognition they receive for these actions probably enhances their self-esteem and instills a sense of control in their lives. Some firesetters also gain internal reinforcement through the sensory stimulation they receive (Fineman, 1995). Jackson et al. (1987) noted that most acts of firesetting by repetitive arsonists progress from small fires to large fires, and the arsonists also become increasingly involved in fighting the fire. Furthermore, repetitive arsonists set fires alone and in secret, with virtually no one aware of their actions until they are caught. If they are caught, their history of firesetting presents an additional opportunity for them to gain attention and recognition from others.

A study of 1,100 patients (Devapriam, Raju, Singh, Collacott, & Bhaumik, 2007) found that persistent firesetting tended to be more frequent among those individuals demonstrating intellectual disabilities. Day and Berney (2001) also noted that firesetting is a common behavioral pattern for the intellectually disabled. Devapriam et al. (2007) discovered that females with intellectual disabilities were as likely to be persistent firesetters as intellectually impaired males. In general, research findings continually find that as a group, those who set fires are inadequate socially and interpersonally, although the exact nature of the inadequacy varies among individuals (Jackson et al., 1987). Research also indicates that firesetting is used as a communicative vehicle in response to conflict and stress (Day & Berney, 2001).The most consistent research finding on the psychology of adult firesetters is that, as a group, they experience and perceive little control over their environment or personal lives. Consequently, they feel worthless and socially ineffective. Some researchers suggest that setting fires may provide conditions whereby the person experiences control or, at least, some influence over the environment.

Female Arsonists

Both statistics and psychological research establish that arson is primarily a male enterprise. Nevertheless, girls and women do engage in this behavior, both on their own and as accomplices to male offenders. Harmon, Rosner, and Wiederlight (1985) studied the psychological and demographic characteristics of 27 women arsonists that were evaluated in the Forensic Psychiatric Clinics for the Criminal and Supreme Courts of New York between 1980 and 1983. Although the sample is small and restricted to a specific geographic area, and the research is quite dated, the findings are still of interest because we have so little data on female arsonists. The researchers found these women were somewhat older than male arsonists (mid-thirties), and with a history of alcohol and drug abuse. Generally, the group was uneducated, unmarried, and relied on public assistance for support. Most often, their motivation was revenge, a consistent finding also reported by Icove and Estepp (1987) for female arsonists. In their revenge, the women tended to act impulsively, responding to a perceived wrong committed against them or a perceived threat to their persons. In their haste, they used whatever flammable material was handy to set the fire. Generally, they set fires to places they lived in—apartments or common, public spaces of their buildings.

Wachi et al. (2007) report similar findings among female serial arsonists in Japan. These researchers discovered that while many of the acts of female firesetters were opportunistic and impulsive and were motivated by emotional distress, most (66%) were motivated by revenge and involved planned and goal-directed behaviors.

In their investigation of 114 female juveniles charged with arson, Hickle and Roe-Sepowitz concluded that the typical female juvenile firesetter comes from a disorganized and unstable home environment, displays difficulties in school, has negative peer relationships, has a history of running away from home, and engages in drug abuse. Their findings are generally similar to those reported for male juvenile firesetters.

Behavioral Typologies and Trajectories

Canter and Fritzon (1988) have developed a typology of firesetters based on the behavioral patterns and crime scene actions of the offender. These investigators learned that firesetting could be distinguished according to two basic behavioral and motivational features. One behavioral pattern was whether the firesetter's actions are directed at a person or persons or at objects, such as buildings or symbolic structures. A second feature—largely based on the motivation for the behavior—is concerned as to whether the actions were expressive or instrumental, much like the expressive and instrumental forms of hostage taking discussed earlier in the chapter, and expressive and instrumental aggression described in Chapter 5.

According to Canter and Fritzon, if the firesetting is intended to draw attention to some underlying emotional distress or feeling, it is expressive. If a specific outcome is desired, such as covering up a crime scene or financial gain, then the firesetting is instrumental. The researchers combined these two features into a four category typology: (1) expressive firesetting directed at a person (expressive person), (2) expressive firesetting directed at an object (expressive object), (3) instrumental firesetting directed at a person (instrumental person), and (4) instrumental firesetting directed at an object (instrumental object).

The **expressive-person pattern**, which is the more common type of firesetting, is often associated with mental disorders and emotional problems, such as depression and feelings of helplessness. Essentially, this firesetting is a cry for help in that the offender seeks to obtain attention from family or persons in authority, such as law enforcement or social services. Unfortunately, the offender may endanger the lives of others as well as himself or herself, but this is not the primary intent. The **expressive-object pattern** is usually characteristic of serial firesetters who set multiple fires. Fortunately, most of these serial firesetters select uninhabited objects to ignite, such as trash bins, barns, abandoned buildings, and deserted houses (Häkkänen, Puolakka, & Santtila, 2004). This suggests that they are not interested in harming or injuring others. Research suggests that these firesetters are using arson as a way of acting out and have a strong fascination with fire (Santtila, Häkkänen, Alison, & Whyte, 2003). These offenders enjoy watching the fire, the fighting activity, and the accompanying excitement.

The **instrumental-person pattern** is most often linked to failed family or ex-companion relationships and their related threats, disagreements, and arguments. In some cases, the firesetting may be directed at someone in authority such as a teacher or church personnel. The target may be a church, a school building, or something associated with school, such as the school bus. The firesetting behavior in this category is motivated by anger and revenge for a perceived wrongdoing against the offender. The overriding intent of the offender in instrumental-person arson is retaliation. The **instrumental-object pattern** is most often associated with young offenders with a serious antisocial history, and is linked with covering traces of other crimes, such as burglary or murder. It may also be directly associated with financial gain, such as burning a building, motor vehicle, or house to gain insurance monies.

Most recently, Gannon and her colleagues (Butler & Gannon, 2015; Gannon et al., 2012) have proposed a multitrajectory theory that sees firesetting as the result of many factors (i.e., developmental, biological, social learning), much like the cumulative factors we have discussed throughout the book. The authors propose five trajectories based on various motives and psychological characteristics. (See **Table 15-7** for a brief summary of the trajectories.)

In addition, Butler and Gannon have published preliminary work on possible scripts associated with these trajectories. For example, they propose that firesetters may hold the following scripts: fire is a powerful messenger (e.g., as a cry for help), fire is the best way to destroy evidence (e.g., to cover up an underlying crime), or fire is soothing (e.g., reduce loneliness). Together with these scripts, they suggest possible treatment methods for firesetters. The authors acknowledge that firesetters are extremely heterogenous, with differing motives and offending styles, and that they may not all hold scripts—just as not all offenders fit neatly into typologies discussed in previous chapters. Nevertheless, the trajectory theory along with the cognitive scripts proposed may suggest treatment strategies for mental health treatment providers.

TABLE 15-7 Examples and Features of Firesetting Trajectories*

Label	Key Features
Antisocial cognition	Person is generally antisocial. Fire is a tool, means to an end (e.g., profit, revenge, vandalizing). Person has problems with self-regulation.
Grievance	No main interest in fire. Fire preferred to gain revenge. Similar to antisocial, but more aggression and hostility.
Fire interest	Fascinated with fire. Thrill seeking or alleviating boredom.
Emotionally expressive/need for recognition	Problems with communicating. Emotionally expressive cry for help. Need for recognition. Wishes to enhance own status.
Multifaceted	General criminality, similar to antisocial cognition. Extremely interested in fire. Problems with self-regulation and communicating.

*Partial information to illustrate proposed trajectories. Original source should be consulted for greater detail.
Source: Bartol, Curt R., Bartol, Anne M., Criminal Behavior: A Psychological Approach, 10e, Copyright © 2014. Pearson Education, Upper Saddle River, NJ.

Psychological Disorders

One of the more fascinating topics associated with firesetting is the possibility that persistent fire-setters are pyromaniacs. **Pyromania** is a psychiatric term for an "irresistible urge" or passion to set fires along with an intense fascination with flames. Before setting the fire, the individual is said to experience a buildup of tension; once the fire is underway, he or she experiences intense pleasure or release (American Psychiatric Association, 2013). The DSM views pyromania as a disorder of impulse control. The person also may frequently be at the scene of fires and even join a volunteer fire department. Although the firesetting urge is believed to be uncontrollable, the individual often provides many clues about his or her intention before setting the fire. Pyromania is believed to be a motive in only a small percentage of all arsons. Furthermore, although firesetting behavior is a problem in children and adolescents, pyromania in that age group appears to be rare (American Psychiatric Association, 2013).

Pyromania does not appear to be a strong explanatory factor for firesetting, but research indicates that many persistent arsonists have a variety of other mental disorders or problems in adjustment (Brett, 2004; Dickens et al., 2009). If not diagnosed with disorders (e.g., antisocial personality disorder; substance abuse disorders), they have psychological problems that could be addressed in treatment, such as the difficulties in communication, low self-concepts, or the deficits in social skills that have been mentioned in the research. In addition, they tend to come from particularly troubled backgrounds and experience difficulties in many areas of life (Lambie & Randell, 2011). Thus, firesetting may be just one component in the constellation of maladaptive behaviors displayed by these individuals. Firesetting may be among these behaviors because of previous experiences with fire. Ritvo et al. (1983) found that a surprisingly large number of firesetters had been burned and maltreated with fire as children. They describe how one frequent firesetter during his early childhood had his feet severely burned by his father as a punishment for lighting fires. Another boy had been beaten on his buttocks with a hot spatula by his father. Still another had his hands held over a lighted stove burner by his mother until they burned as punishment for lighting fires. Ritvo et al. (1983, p. 266) speculate that these punishments may have "conveyed the message that the use of fire was an acceptable mode of retaliation."

In this section, we have concentrated on the repetitive or serial arsonists who set fires primarily for psychological and social gain. This focus is not to imply that a majority of arson fires are set by these individuals. Obviously, firesetting is done for a variety of reasons by a variety of offenders. Much of it is probably committed for monetary gain, such as insurance, or to cover up other crimes or destroy evidence. Recent research concludes that those who persistently and repeatedly set fires are frequently involved in a wide range of other antisocial and criminal behaviors (Del Bove & Mackay, 2011; Lambie & Randall, 2011; Vaughn et al., 2010a). Moreover, persistent arsonists who set multi-point fires and use accelerants are considered especially dangerous (Dickens et al., 2009).

SUMMARY AND CONCLUSIONS

The crimes discussed in the chapter are all either violent or, in most cases, have the potential of doing great physical harm to victims. Even if violence does not occur, however, the crimes typically put the victims in fear. Thus, there is great psychological impact on the victim.

We began with a discussion of robbery, its categories, and its motives. Although financial gain or material gain is the primary reason for robbery, the secondary motive of controlling and instilling fear in a victim does occur, particularly in some street robberies. Bank robberies, in contrast to many depictions in the entertainment media, are rarely carried out by professionals or are well planned. The typical bank robbery is the work of an amateur who undoubtedly sees this as a way of getting quick cash. Commercial robberies are usually carried out against convenience stores or fast-food restaurants. These establishments are seen as more accessible than banks, but they produce smaller return. Nevertheless, they are considered easier targets, generally late at night, when few workers and customers are on the premises. Street robberies are rarely planned; the robber sees the opportunity with a likely target and takes it. Interestingly, the latest data show strong-arm robberies were slightly more frequent than robberies carried out with firearms or knives. Victims also are more likely to be physically harmed during a strong-arm robbery, both because they are more likely to resist and because the perpetrator has less confidence in his ability to control the victim. Professional robbers are a separate group that can conduct any of the above types of robbery but are most likely to be involved in street robbery.

We gave some attention to cybercrime—or computer crime—which is becoming increasingly problematic and which challenges the resources of the law enforcement community. In addition to economically motivated cybercrime, we also discussed cyberstalking and cyberbullying. Both allow the perpetrator to harass the victim while remaining anonymous, and both qualify as crimes of intimidation. To date, we have very little research knowledge about the prevalence of the offenses or the psychological attributes of the offenders.

The most well-known crime of intimidation, stalking, has received increasing public attention since it was first reported as a problem—or first given a name—in the 1980s. It is estimated that one of every 12 women and one of every 45 men has been a victim of stalking. The perpetrator's motive is almost invariably to control, intimidate, and frighten the victim. Restraining orders, sought by about half of the victims who report the crime to police, unfortunately have had little success, since they are ignored by most stalkers. However, some do respond to the restraining order and some do cease stalking when confronted by law enforcement. Many women who are stalked had previously experienced violence at the hands of their stalkers, and future violence is a continuing possibility. Stalking typically stops when the stalker has formed a new relationship, usually within a two-year period.

We also reviewed and provided illustrations of the four major categories of stalking: simple obsession, love obsession, erotomania, and vengeance. Other researchers have classified stalking by the relationship between the stalker and the victim: intimate stalkers, acquaintance stalkers, public figure stalkers, and private stranger stalkers. The first of both classifications (the simple obsession and the intimate stalkers) are the most common, but also the ones most likely to be accompanied by physical harm to the victim. As a group, stalkers are not typically mentally disordered. The exceptions are the erotomania stalkers and the public figure stalkers, who tend to be delusional and plagued with a variety of mental disorders.

Hostage taking is a major crime of intimidation that places its victim in great fear, even though no physical violence may result. Hostage taking by terrorists is a form that does not respond favorably to negotiation strategies. Strategies for law enforcement negotiating with other hostage takers were reviewed as were suggestions for hostages in these terrifying situations. Remaining calm, not challenging the hostage taker, and not bringing attention to oneself (in the case of multiple hostages) were among these suggestions. The Stockholm syndrome—in which the hostage identifies with and becomes emotionally close to the hostage taker—is extremely rare. There is no research evidence that this is a strong phenomenon.

The chapter ended with discussions of arson and persistent firesetting by children and adolescents. Some forms of arson are clearly economically motivated, but firesetting by the young is a conduct problem with significant psychological overtones. Considerable psychological research has studied this behavior. Although most children are fascinated by fire, particularly between the ages of 5 and 7, in a small but very problematic minority, this fascination is accompanied first by experimental firesetting and gradually by continuing and persistent firesetting behavior. Persistent firesetters are usually identified by age 10. They typically have extremely dysfunctional family backgrounds, often lacking parental supervision and plagued by physical abuse and alcohol and other drug problems. Persistent adult arsonists often began their firesetting behavior as children. We reviewed categories of these arsonists and emphasized that very few fall under the term *pyromaniac,* indicating a serious mental disorder characterized by abnormal fascination with fire. It is not unusual, though, to find that persistent firesetters—with the exception of those who commit arson for profit—have other personality disorders.

Key Concepts

Arson
Barricade situation
Cyberbullying
Cybercrime
Cyberharassment
Cyberstalking
Erotomania stalking
Expressive hostage taking
Expressive-object pattern
Expressive-person pattern
Firesetting
Instrumental hostage taking
Instrumental-object pattern

Instrumental-person pattern
London syndrome
Love obsession stalking
Pyromania
Robbery
Simple obsession stalking
Stalking
Stockholm syndrome
Street culture
Strong-arm robbery
Succumbers
Survivors
Vengeance stalking

Review Questions

1. What is the role of street culture and cognitive scripts in the commission of opportunity crimes, such as street robbery?
2. Summarize differences between amateur and professional bank robbers.
3. Define and provide examples of cybercrime, cyberstalking, cyberbullying, and cyberharassment. Is it important to make distinctions between these terms to form a psychological perspective? Why or why not?
4. What categories of stalking are covered in the chapter?
5. What is the difference between instrumental hostage taking and expressive hostage taking?
6. What is the difference between the Stockholm syndrome and the London syndrome?
7. Identify and briefly describe stages leading to firesetting in children.
8. Summarize the five firesetting trajectories proposed by Gannon and Butler.
9. Does the research literature support pyromania? Explain.

16

Substance Abuse and Crime

CHAPTER OBJECTIVES

- Summarize the effects of the psychoactive drugs that have been most connected to crime and delinquency.
- Caution about and emphasize the many individual differences in reactions to illegal drugs and alcohol.
- Define and explain drug tolerance and dependence.
- Examine closely the extent of juvenile substance and alcohol use.
- Explain the tripartite conceptual model and experimental substance use.
- Note the illegal drugs most commonly used in the United States.
- Focus on the effects and extent of marijuana use, because this is the most popular illicit drug today.
- Discuss the sharp increase in the use of synthetic narcotics.
- Sketch the relationship between alcohol abuse and crime and delinquency.

- In May 2015, DEA agents converged on four southern states to arrest 48 persons, including seven physicians, for illegal trafficking in prescription drugs, largely pain medications. With 230 others arrested during the same investigation—which lasted 15 months—this represented the largest DEA operation of its type.
- Marijuana today is often available in a spreadable form—sometimes called "budder"—that has three times the potency of pot that can be smoked.
- Heroin is now available in pill form and can also be crushed into candy.
- LSD and crack cocaine, both highly popular drug in the 1970s and 1980s, are among the least popular illegal drugs on the market today.

The above anecdotes and factoids tell us that the drug market is changing rapidly. During the 1960s and 1970s the United States saw dramatic increases in illicit drug use across the nation (Bukowski, 2015). These increases included heroin, LSD (lysergic acid diethylamide), cocaine, amphetamines, methaqualone, PCP (phencyclidine), and marijuana. Each of these remains available, though in radically different forms. Illegal drugs often lose popularity and then resurface over time; their street names change as well.

Some 40 years ago, the national media and political debate began to focus on a frightening increase in drug abuse and the apparent inability of the government to curtail the rapidly expanding flow of dangerous illegal drugs into the country. As Bukowski (2015) summarizes, rapid increases in theft, robbery, assaults, and other forms of street crime associated with drug use began to spread to both urban and rural areas at an alarming rate. Bukowski writes, "Drug use was demonized in a massive antidrug frenzy that preceded the much-heralded War on Drugs that was yet to come in the mid-1980s" (p. 33).

Since the mid-1980s, the United States has been waging war against individuals who transport, sell, and use a wide variety of illegal substances. While other periods in history have also seen a focus on drugs, it was in the 1980s that the government began to adopt conservative policies in response to perceived epidemics in the trafficking and use of cocaine, crack cocaine, heroin, and marijuana, among others (Walker, 2001). Billions of dollars have been expended on both reducing the supply of drugs and punishing convicted individuals with long prison sentences, resulting in overcrowded conditions in federal penitentiaries and many state prisons. In fall of 2015, recognizing that harsh sentences were not the answer, the federal government announced a change in policy that would allow thousands of prisoners convicted of drug offenses to be released earlier than they had anticipated. Although federal and some state law enforcement priorities shifted toward a "war on terrorism" after September 11, 2001, illicit drugs continue to be a prominent target. In addition, as illustrated by the drug raid mentioned at the beginning of the chapter, illegal trafficking in prescription drugs has taken on a new urgency. (See also **Box 16-1** at page 489.)

Many members of the public believe that a war on drugs is still justified. In this chapter, we review the evidence in support of or against this public perception. Others believe the drug war has been in many ways a colossal failure, neither making significant headway in interdiction nor adequately addressing the widespread problems associated with substance abuse. According to the National Council on Crime and Delinquency (NCCD), substance abuse should be considered "*primarily* [emphasis added] as a health-related problem that should reside in the public health domain" (Rosenbaum, 1989, p. 17). Increasingly, in recent years, we have heard more such calls for addressing the illegal use of drugs as at least as much a health problem as a crime problem. The increasing trend to refer substance abusers to drug courts is indication of this approach; in drug courts, defendants are monitored and provided treatment for substance abuse (Marlowe et al., 2012). Legislatures in many states have decriminalized the possession of small amounts of drugs or made changes in their laws that reflect a health response to the drug problem. In Colorado and Oregon, marijuana is legal and can be purchased in small amounts. In approximately 23 states, marijuana can be legally prescribed to ease pain for a variety of illnesses. Many states also have revised their statutes that had called for severe sentences for drug offenders, though not drug traffickers. Among many other provisions, these laws emphasize the need for treatment services for inmates with substance abuse problems.

In 2010, nearly 22.6 million Americans (9% of the population aged 12 or older) admitted to being current users of illicit drugs (Substance Abuse and Mental Health Services Administration (SAMHSA), 2011), with current use defined as use of an illicit drug during the month prior to the survey. In that same year, 8 million Americans (3% of the population) aged 12 or older needed treatment for illicit drug abuse. As this chapter will illustrate, different substances have markedly different effects on thinking, judgment, decision making, impulse control, and behavioral self-regulation.

Since the early onset of drug and alcohol use is an important risk factor for predicting future substance abuse and—in many cases—involvement in crime, we turn our attention first to juvenile drug use.

JUVENILE DRUG USE

Juvenile illicit drug use is widely regarded as one of today's most important social concerns (Ramirez et al., 2004; Sitnick, Shaw, & Hyde, 2014). Although surveys (e.g., Johnston, O'Malley, Bachman, & Schulenberg, 2011; Johnston, O'Malley, Miech, Bachman, & Schulenberg, 2015; SAMHSA, 2014) indicate an overall decline or leveling off in the use of drugs and alcohol nationwide, a significant proportion of youth continues to be exposed to the deleterious effects of substance abuse (see **Table 16-1**). Approximately 8.8 percent of adolescents between the ages of 12 and 17 and 21.5 percent of young adults between ages 18 and 25 report current illicit drug use (Substance Abuse and Mental Health Services Administration (SAMHSA, 2014)). However, while drug use overall has decreased among teens in recent years, marijuana is by far the most commonly used among this age group (Johnston et al., 2015; SAMHSA, 2014). As we note later in the chapter, it is increasingly available in synthetic form.

TABLE 16-1   Annual Prevalence of Use of Various Drugs in Grades 8, 10, and 12, during the Year 2014

Drug	12th Grade Students	10th Grade Students	8th Grade Students
Any illicit drug other than marijuana	15.9%	11.2%	6.4%
Marijuana/hashish	35.1%	27.3%	11.7%
Synthetic marijuana	5.8%	5.4%	1.3%
OxyContin®	3.3%	3.0%	1.0%
Vicodin®	4.8%	3.4%	1.0%
Ecstasy	3.6%	2.3%	0.9%
Cocaine	2.6%	1.5%	1.0%

Source: Adapted from Johnston, L. D., O'Malley, P. M., Miech, R. A., Bachman, J. G., & Schulenberg, J. E. (2015, February). Monitoring the future: National results on adolescent drug use: Overview of key findings 2014. Ann Arbor: Institute for Social Research, University of Michigan.

In 2014, 38.7 percent of high school seniors admitted using illicit drugs over the year (Johnston et al., 2015). In addition, 29.9 percent of high school sophomores, and 14.6 percent of 8th graders said they had used illicit drugs during 2014. That same 2014 survey found that 5.6 percent of high school seniors reported using illicit drugs on a daily basis, followed by 3.4 percent of sophomores, and 1.0 percent of 8th graders. Marijuana use accounted for a large proportion of the illicit drug use that year (see again **Table 16-1**).

Sitnick and her colleagues (2014) discovered that the pathway to adolescent substance use can begin as early as the toddler period. Conduct problems and antisocial behavioral patterns in early childhood appear to be significant precursors to adolescence substance use and abuse. Peer groups also have strong influence on whether a child or adolescent engages in drug experimentation and abuse. The researchers also found that sensible parental monitoring and knowledge of the child's and adolescent's activities were effective buffers in preventing substance use and abuse. It should be noted that many drugs prescribed for adolescents can also be addictive, provide a "high" or deeply relaxed state, and be abused, although pharmaceutical companies are making serious attempts to remove the high and addictive elements from the prescription drugs.

Drug use and abuse in early adolescence is associated with serious health problems, deviant and antisocial behavior, high-risk behaviors, and poor academic performance. High-level chronic juvenile offenders are far more likely to use drugs and alcohol excessively compared with other juveniles (Wiesner, Kim, & Capaldi, 2005). It should be noted, too, that juveniles (ages 12 to 17) who regularly smoke cigarettes and drink alcohol are far more likely to use a variety of illicit drugs (SAMHSA, 2011, 2014).

The FBI Special Report defines "drug abuse" as including the sale/manufacturing or possession of the illegal drug. In this regard, the FBI data consistently report that most of the arrests of juveniles are for possession of drugs rather than the sale or manufacturing of illegal substances (see **Table 16-2**). With changing methods of producing drugs, however, juveniles also may be increasingly involved in manufacturing and distributing them. For example, "pot butter" is made by soaking marijuana plants in butane, a process that strips the THC off the plant. In those states where marijuana has been legalized, traffickers send it across state lines, sometimes in the form of lollipops or other candies, brownies, and cookies.

When an individual is arrested for a drug abuse violation in the United States, the arresting agency reports to the Department of Justice the type of drug used. The types fall under one of four categories: (1) heroin or cocaine and their derivatives (e.g., morphine, codeine); (2) marijuana; (3) synthetic narcotics, such as synthetic marijuana and controlled prescription drugs (e.g., pain relievers); and (4) dangerous nonnarcotic drugs, such as Demerol and methadone.

TABLE 16-2	Juvenile Drug Arrests by Sale/Manufacturing and Possession by Drug Type, 2009

Drug Type	Number
Total	**130,317**
Sale/Manufacturing	**18,840**
Heroin or cocaine	4,975
Marijuana	9,871
Synthetic narcotics	1,170
Dangerous nonnarcotics	2,824
Possession	**111,477**
Heroin or cocaine	6,208
Marijuana	90,927
Synthetic narcotics	3,385
Dangerous nonnarcotics	10,957

Source: Federal Bureau of Investigation. (2011a). Crime in the United States 2010: Uniform Crime Reports. Washington, DC: U.S. Department of Justice.

Marijuana remains the drug associated with the highest percentage of juveniles arrested for drug abuse. For example, male juveniles arrested for the sale/manufacturing and possession of marijuana combined increased from 55.1 percent of the arrests of male juveniles in 1994 to 74 percent in 2003. We review more up-to-date statistics shortly when we focus on marijuana. Arrests of juveniles for violations involving synthetic narcotics and dangerous nonnarcotics consistently accounted for the lowest percentage of juveniles arrested for drug abuse violations during the 10-year period. Furthermore, these arrests show a downward trend. The percentage of arrests of both male and female juveniles for violations involving opium or cocaine also shows a decline during the 10-year period. Arrests of male juveniles for violations involving opium or cocaine fell from 34.2 percent of the arrests of male juveniles for drugs in 1994 to 13.4 percent in 2003. These data highlight the fact that while the *prevalence* of illicit drug use remains largely the same across generations, the *type* of illicit drug used is continually changing.

The data for the 10 years covered in the FBI Special Report showed that of the number of arrests in 1994 for drug abuse violations involving juveniles under age 10, 83 percent were males and 17 percent were females. A decade later, the percentage of arrests for drug abuse violations of males under age 10 dropped to 78.9 percent, and the percentage of arrests of females increased to 21.1 percent, indicating that there may be a growing trend for female juveniles to be arrested at a younger age for drug abuse violations than male juveniles.

Who Is Selling to Juveniles?

In one comprehensive survey, one in nine high school students reported *selling* drugs during the past year, and most of them said they sold the drugs in school (Steinman, 2005). About 10 percent of the juveniles who bought marijuana said they purchased it at school (Substance Abuse and Mental Health Services Administration, 2005). Another survey found that almost half of high school students (44%) knew a student who sells drugs at school (QEV Analytics, 2012).

Those students most likely to sell drugs on a *regular* basis are also more likely to engage in a variety of delinquent acts, including violence, heavy marijuana use, and other risk behaviors. These youths are often hired by older dealers, especially in cities and metropolitan areas. Moreover, regular juvenile sellers generally do not have a strong relationship with family and prefer to associate with other deviant peers who use and sell drugs. Many are members of gangs that typically include young adults as well as adolescents. However, for the purposes of explaining delinquency, students who *occasionally* sell drugs to friends and relatives should not be placed in the same category as the more routine seller who distributes a variety of substances. Occasional, friend-based sellers rarely are detected by the authorities and do not usually become involved in serious delinquency.

Gender Differences in Juvenile Drug Use

Most research on drug and alcohol abuse and dependence has concentrated on males. Arrest data reveal that juvenile males are arrested nearly five times more frequently for drug violations than are juvenile females (Federal Bureau of Investigation, 2014a). In 2013, 77,022 male juveniles were arrested for drug abuse violations compared to 17,165 female juveniles. The few research studies that have focused on gender differences in alcohol and drug use among adolescents have consistently shown that males consume alcohol and drugs of various kinds more frequently and in higher quantities than females and are prone to experience more drug- and alcohol-related problems (Fothergill & Ensminger, 2006; Webb, Bray, Getz, & Adams, 2002). In addition, there is increasing evidence that males and females experience different substance abuse trajectories and consequences (Fothergill & Ensminger, 2006). Girls who show little commitment to school and academic achievement are at increased risk of later substance abuse problems (Fothergill & Ensminger, 2006).

CONSISTENT FINDINGS ON ILLICIT DRUG USE

Overall, the research literature indicates that alcohol use and illicit drug use increase a person's chances of criminal activity, with drug use having a slightly larger influence (DeMatteo, Filone, & Davis, 2015). We will begin with illicit drug use and crime, and cover alcohol use and crime later in the chapter.

The relationship between drugs and crime may be viewed from two perspectives: (1) the use, sale, manufacture, distribution, and possession of illegal drugs, all of which are themselves crimes, and (2) the pharmacological effects certain drugs have on a user's behavior in promoting criminal actions. Research directed at these two perspectives in recent years has reached the following six conclusions, each of which are discussed in some detail below:

1. More individuals are incarcerated or held in jails and prisons for drug offenses than for any other offense, and this has contributed to burgeoning jail and prison populations.
2. Arrestees frequently test positive for illicit drug use.
3. Arrestees and incarcerated offenders were often under the influence of illicit drugs when they committed their offenses.
4. Some offenders commit property crime to support their drug habit.
5. Drug trafficking often engenders violent crime.
6. The drug–crime relationship is very complex and difficult to identify, measure, and advance conclusions.

The first consistent finding has major implications for jail and prison crowding: More individuals are incarcerated or held in jails and prisons for drug offenses than for any other offense. In recent years many states are making serious attempts to reduce incarceration rates for drug offenders as well as accelerating their release from jails and prisons. As mentioned above, only recently has the federal government done the same. Changes in sentencing laws relating to drug offenses are one method used to do this; another is diversion of substance abusers from standard prosecution, by offering substance abuse treatment in the community in lieu of incarceration. Recent research has also revealed that co-occurring mental and substance use disorders (CODs) are far more common among persons in jails, prisons, and other criminal justice settings than among persons in the general population (Peters, Wexler, & Lurigio, 2015). In other words, these are persons who exhibit *both* a mental disorder and substance abuse problems. Not only are persons with CODs more likely to be arrested but they are also "more likely to violate the conditions of community supervision and to commit acts of violence" (Peters et al., 2015, p. 1). Furthermore, they are more likely to remain in jail or prison longer than those inmates without CODs. As noted by Peters et al., a contributing factor to the development of the combination of mental disorder and substance abuse in some individuals is the finding that substance use can have a "kindling effect" in triggering the onset of various mental disorders. That is, the frequent use of some substance can alter the psycho-neurological functioning of the brain, resulting in permanent damage in mental functioning. On the other hand, persons with serious mental disorders may use illicit or illegal drugs to alleviate their symptoms. Research has shown that incarceration of offenders who have CODs most often leads to poor outcomes, and are usually better served by placement in community treatment and supervision services. In addition, whites in the justice system with CODs are more likely to receive substance abuse or mental health treatment than African Americans or Hispanics with CODs (Hunt, Peters, & Kremling, 2015).

In 2013, 1.5 million people were arrested for drug abuse violations (sales or possession) in the United States (Federal Bureau of Investigation, 2014a) (see **Table 16-3**). Another 280,860 were arrested for liquor law offenses, and nearly 1 million were arrested for driving while intoxicated.

As noted, with growing recognition that substance abuse is a serious health problem that requires intervention and treatment, many communities have established **drug courts**. Initiated in Miami, Florida, in 1989, they are designed to be a first step in diverting nonviolent offenders with drug problems into treatment and other community-based programs. Offenders who go through the drug court model often are expected to undergo long-term treatment and counseling, sanctions, incentives, and frequent court appearances. If they successfully complete their program, they not only avoid jail or prison but also, in many jurisdictions, a criminal record. In 2003, there were 1,424 drug courts in existence or being planned in the United States (Office of National Drug Control Policy, 2003d). Recidivism among drug court participants ranges between 5 and 28 percent and is less than 4 percent for drug court *graduates* (Office of National Drug Control Policy, 2003d). Marlowe et al. (2012) cite six different meta-analyses conducted by independent investigators; the meta-analyses concluded "that drug courts significantly reduced criminal recidivism (typically measured by rearrest rates) by an average of 8 to 26 percentage points" (p. 515).

The *second* consistent finding from the research is that arrestees frequently test positive for illicit drug use. The Arrestees Drug Abuse Monitoring II (ADAM II) survey is a data collection effort covering adult male arrestees in geographically distributed counties in the United States and

TABLE 16-3	Arrests for Drug Abuse Violations by Sale/Manufacturing and Possession by Drug Type, 2013
Drug Type	**Percent**
Total	**100.0**
Sale/Manufacturing	**17.7**
Heroin or cocaine (or derivatives)	6.0
Marijuana	5.6
Synthetic narcotics	1.9
Dangerous nonnarcotics	4.2
Possession	**82.3**
Heroin or cocaine (or derivatives)	16.4
Marijuana	40.6
Synthetic narcotics	4.6
Dangerous nonnarcotics	20.7

Source: Federal Bureau of Investigation (2014a). Crime in the United States 2013: Uniform Crime Reports. Washington, DC: U.S. Department of Justice.

is funded by the Office of National Drug Control. In 2013, the program collected data from more than 13,000 adult male arrestees in five counties in the United States (called sites). Since 2000, ADAM and ADAM II have conducted over 30,000 interviews and over 27,000 urine tests, representing over 300,000 arrests. The ADAM II utilizes both urinalysis and self-report data to identify the level of recent drug use by the arrestees within 48 hours of their arrest. Data collection consists of a 20 to 25 minute face-to-face interview in the booking area of each law enforcement facility, collection of official record information, and the collection of urine samples for drug testing. The arrestees are tested for the presence of 10 drugs.

The ADAM II program continually finds that the level of drug use of arrestees is substantial. Fifty-two to 80 percent (depending on the site) tested positive for the presence of at least one drug in their system at the time of their arrest. Forty-nine percent tested positive for the presence of marijuana. Eleven to 37 percent tested positive for cocaine, and 2 to 18 percent for heroin. As noted by DeMatteo et al. (2015), "Compared to the rate of drug use in the general population, the rate of drug use among criminal offenders is staggering" (p. 326). DeMatteo and his associates find that more than 80 percent of U.S. criminal offenders meet the broad definition of substance use or involvement.

The *third* consistent finding of illicit drug research findings in recent years is that arrestees and incarcerated offenders were often under the influence of illicit drugs when they committed their offenses. In 2004, nearly a third of state and a quarter of federal prisoners committed their offense under the influence of drugs (Mumola & Karberg, 2006).

Furthermore, certain professional criminal groups often prefer one drug over another. Professional pickpockets, shoplifters, and burglars, for example—when they use drugs—have a distinct preference for those that steady their nerves and provide relief from the pressures of their occupation (Inciardi, 1981). Professional pickpockets often consider opiates instrumental in furthering their careers. To some extent, this has a cyclical effect, since their material gain from their crimes is used to obtain the drug.

In reference to the *fourth* point—that some offenders commit property crime to support their drug habit—17 percent of state prisoners and 18 percent of federal prisoners said they committed their current offenses to obtain money for drugs in 2004 (see **Table 16-4**) (Mumola & Karberg, 2006). These figures are actually quite low compared to research and public perceptions that stealing to support a drug habit is widespread. In one recent study (Bennett, Holloway, & Farrington, 2008), the researchers found that the odds of committing a property or income producing crime were between three and four times greater for drug users than nondrug users. In addition, the greatest odds for offending were for crack users (six times greater), and second greatest odds were for heroin users (between three and four times greater).

The *fifth* finding of recent research is that drug trafficking often engenders violent crime. There is considerable evidence that violence accompanies drug distribution in the course of territorial disputes between rival organizations and gangs, or in conflicts between the buyer and the seller (Roth, 1996;

TABLE 16-4 Percent of Prisoners Who Self-Reported that They Committed Offense to Get Money for Drugs

Most Serious Offense	State	Federal
Total[a]	16.6%	18.4%
Violent	9.8	14.8
Property	30.3	10.6
Drug	26.4	25.3
Public Order	6.9	6.8

[a]Includes offenses not shown.

Source: Mumola, C. J., & Karberg, J. C. (2006, October). Drug use and dependence, state and federal prisoners, 2004. Washington, DC: U.S. Department of Justice, Bureau of Justice Statistics.

Walker, 2001). Places where drug deals occur bring together valuable drugs, big money, weapons, and people accustomed to violence. This volatile mix creates a high potential for violence.

The *sixth* and final point is that the drug–crime relationship is difficult to identify and measure. The relationship between drugs and crimes is complicated by a fourfold interaction: (1) the pharmacological effects of the drug, which refer to the chemical impact of the drug on the body; (2) the psychological characteristics of the individual using the drug; (3) the psychosocial conditions under which the drug is taken; and (4) the interactions a particular drug has with other drugs consumed simultaneously. Discussion of pharmacological effects includes features of the nervous system, such as the amount of neurotransmitter substances within neurons, and body weight, blood composition, and other neurophysiological features that significantly influence the chemical effects of the drug. Psychological variables include the mood of the person at the time the drug is consumed, previous experience with the drug, and the person's expectancies about the drug's effects. Psychosocial variables include the social atmosphere under which the drug is taken. The people who are present and their expectations, moods, and behavior all may influence an individual's reactions to a drug. The interaction factor must be considered in any discussion of drug effects because most illegal drugs are taken in combinations, especially with alcohol. For example, it is not unusual to find teenagers and young adults consuming a variety of club drugs in combination with alcohol; more experienced users sometimes combine cocaine powder or crack with heroin (called a "speedball"). More than one-half of the arrestees in 2010 who tested positive for one drug also tested positive for another drug (ADAM II, 2011). Polydrug use is common.

In order to understand the effects of any drug, the pharmacological, psychological, psychosocial, and interacting variables all must be taken into account. Considering the fact that crime is complex to begin with, deciphering the drug–crime connection becomes very difficult, and the conclusions are necessarily that much more elusive and tentative. The relationship between drugs and crime is further complicated by the cultural, subcultural, and ethnographic aspects of drug consumption. The attitudes and perceptions of different age groups and cultures about specific drugs are often in a state of flux. Cultural preferences shift and change depending on drug availability, law enforcement priorities, and changes in cultural attitudes. In addition, demographic studies have shown that drug popularity and epidemics go through four distinct stages: incubation, expansion, plateau, and decline (Golub & Johnson, 1997). During the *incubation* stage, users experiment with the new and emerging drug, learn how to use it, and develop techniques for its use. During the *expansion* stage, prices drop, it becomes easy to use, its availability increases, and word gets around about the drug, all of which contribute to its popularity. During the *plateau* stage, there is a relatively high and constant use of the drug. But during the *decline* stage, the drug is shunned—usually by a new generation of youth—and a new drug emerges in popularity.

Tripartite Conceptual Model

A helpful way of understanding the drug–crime relationship is the **tripartite conceptual model** proposed by Paul Goldstein (1985). Goldstein identifies three main types of drug-related crime: (1) *psychopharmacologically* driven crime, (2) *systemic* crime, and (3) *economically compulsive* crime. Goldstein's psychopharmacological component of the model presupposes that some individuals, as a result of short-term or long-term ingestion of specific drugs or chemical substances, become excitable, and/or irrational and demonstrate violent behavior. In other words, the assumption in this component is that some drugs *cause* some people (even usually nonviolent ones) to become violent and engage in a variety of criminal behaviors. The prevailing view about psychopharmacological violence, however, is that it is rare and attributable mostly to alcohol rather than illicit drugs (MacCoun, Kilmer, & Reuter, 2003).

The *systemic* component of the model hypothesizes that crime arises out of the system of drug trafficking and distribution. Examples of this component include disputes over territory between rival drug dealers and threats, assaults, and murders committed within and by drug-dealing organizations. Essentially, it refers to the violence inherent in the enterprise of drug trafficking and distribution, and is similar to the fifth observation of research noted previously.

Economically compulsive crime refers to criminal behavior that supports an expensive drug addiction. Robbery committed by drug users to support a costly drug habit is an example. Compulsive drug seeking and use is presumably an overwhelming drive, even in the face of negative health and social consequences (MacCoun et al., 2003). The economically compulsive component is similar to the fourth observation discussed earlier in this section. As each of the major drugs is examined in the following sections, the pharmacologically driven aspect as a cause for violence and criminal activity will be, by far, the most difficult to support.

Before entering into this discussion, it is important to stress that we do not, in this text, give more than passing attention to public policy with respect to drugs. As noted at the beginning of the chapter, there is considerable disagreement over the extent to which the government should continue on its present course of being harsh on drug offenders. The events of September 11, 2001, shifted priorities to some extent to a "war on terrorism." In 2009, with a new Presidential administration, the focus again shifted to address rising unemployment rates, bank failures, and a health care crisis, although national security concerns were not ignored. By 2015, the economy was improving but health care, immigration, climate change, distribution of wealth, and national security concerns competed for attention. Nevertheless, drug enforcement and harsh punishments continue, and the individuals who are most often affected are members of racial and economic minority groups. Although this book focuses on the individual behavior of drug users, readers also should be aware of the controversy surrounding public policy on this matter.

MAJOR CATEGORIES OF DRUGS

Four major categories of **psychoactive drugs** will be covered in the chapter: (1) hallucinogens or psychedelics, (2) stimulants, (3) opiate narcotics, and (4) sedative-hypnotics or depressants. A psychoactive drug is a chemical substance that influences a person's mood, perception, mode of thinking, and behavior. To keep the chapter within manageable limits, however, we will focus only on specific drugs within each category that represent a serious risk to public safety or that are most closely associated with criminal activity, such as the illegal manufacturing, selling, and distributing of a controlled substance. A **controlled substance** is any psychoactive drug or chemical substance whose availability is restricted, as designated by state or federal law.

The *Controlled Substances Act* (CSA), Title II of the *Comprehensive Drug Abuse Prevention and Control Act of 1970,* places all substances of potential abuse into one of five schedules. This placement is based on the substance's medical use, potential for abuse, and dependence potential (see **Table 16-5**). The purpose of the act is to control the distribution,

TABLE 16-5	Formal Scheduling as Outlined by the Controlled Substances Act				
Schedule	Potential for Abuse	Accepted Medical Use in United States	Physical Dependence	Psychological Dependence	Examples
I	High	No	High	High	Heroin, LSD, marijuana, Ecstasy, synthetic cannabinoids (Spice), synthetic cathinones (bath salts)
II	High	Yes	High	High	PCP, cocaine, morphine, amphetamines, oxycodone, fentanyl, hydrocodone
III	Medium	Yes	Moderate	High	Certain narcotics containing more than 90 mg codeine, nonnarcotics (ketamine), anabolic steroids
IV	Low	Yes	Low	Low	Valium®, Xanax®, Klonopin®
V	Low	Yes	Low	Low	Cough medicines with codeine

Source: Drug Enforcement Administration. (2015, February). Controlled substance schedule. Washington, DC: U.S. Department of Justice.

classification, sale, and use of psychoactive drugs that have the potential for abuse. Although the term *potential for abuse* is not specifically defined in the CSA, scheduling classifications are based on available evidence that the drugs can create a hazard to health or jeopardize the safety of other individuals, or that there is a significant diversion of the drug from legitimate drug channels. Proceedings to add, delete, or change the schedule of a drug or other substance may be initiated by the Drug Enforcement Administration (DEA) or the Department of Health and Human Services (HHS), or by petition from any interested party (Drug Enforcement Administration, 2000).

The **hallucinogens** or **psychedelics**, which include LSD (lysergic acid diethylamide), mescaline, psilocybin, phencyclidine, ketamine, marijuana, and hashish, will be our first category. So called because they sometimes generate hallucinations, the hallucinogens are chemicals that lead to a change in consciousness involving an alteration of reality. In some respects, they replace the present world with an alternative one, although persons using them can generally attend to their altered state and to reality simultaneously. Marijuana, classified as a hallucinogen, is certainly a mild one for a majority who use it. Because of its widespread use and the public's tendency to mistakenly associate it with crime and bizarre behavior, it will be the main drug covered under the hallucinogens category. We will also include phencyclidine (PCP), a powerful drug that has been linked to crime during the past two decades.

Next we discuss the **stimulants**, so called because they appear to stimulate central nervous system functions. They include amphetamines, clinical antidepressants, cocaine, MDMA (Ecstasy/Molly), caffeine, and nicotine. Again, because of an alleged relationship with crime, the amphetamines, MDMA, and cocaine will be highlighted.

The third group includes the **opiate narcotics**, which generally have sedative (sleep-inducing) and analgesic (pain-relieving) effects. Heroin—a drug whose use appears to be growing at alarming rates in many communities—is featured in this section. The heroin addict appears frequently in crime statistics, since it is believed that he or she often turns to crime—particularly property crime—to finance this expensive habit.

Finally, alcohol and the "club drugs" will represent the **sedative-hypnotic compounds** that depress central nervous system functions. In most instances, the sedative-hypnotics are all capable of sedating the nervous system and reducing anxiety and tension. Examples include alcohol and the benzodiazepines.

Tolerance and Dependence

Before proceeding, we must distinguish two terms that are consistently used in the drug literature: **tolerance** and **dependence**. Drug tolerance is the "state of progressively decreased responsiveness to a drug" (Julien, 1975, p. 29). Tolerance is indicated if the individual requires a larger dose of the drug to reach the same effects he or she has previously experienced. In other words, the person has become psychologically and physiologically used to, or habituated to, the drug.

Dependence may be physical or psychological, or both. In simple terms, physical dependence refers to the physiological distress and physical pain a person suffers if he or she goes without the drug for any length of time. Psychological dependence is difficult to distinguish from physical dependence, but it is characterized by an overwhelming desire to use the drug for a favorable effect. The person is convinced that he or she needs the drug to maintain an optimal sense of well-being. The degree of psychological dependence varies widely from person to person and drug to drug. In its extreme form, the person's life is permeated with thoughts of procuring and using the drug, and he or she may resort to crime to obtain it. In common parlance, the person who is extremely psychologically and/or physically dependent is an addict.

Secondary psychological dependence may also develop. While primary dependence is associated with the reward of the drug experience (positive reinforcement), secondary dependence refers to expectancies about aversive withdrawal or the painful effects that will accompany absence of the drug. Thus, to avoid the anticipated pain and discomfort associated with withdrawal, the individual continues to take the drug (negative reinforcement).

The data reported in this chapter concerning illicit drug use and abuse were primarily gathered from the *National Household Survey on Drug Abuse* (NHSDA) (sponsored by the Substance Abuse and Mental Health Services Administration, 2011); the *2013 National Survey on Drug Abuse and Health* (the updated version of the NDSDA, also sponsored by the Substance Abuse and Mental Health Services Administration, 2014); the Arrestee Drug Abuse Monitoring Program (ADAM II) 2013; Annual Report from the Office of National Drug Control Policy (sponsored by the Office of the President); the National Drug Intelligence Center (NDIC); the Bureau of Justice Statistics (BJS); the University of Michigan's 2014 *Monitoring the Future Study;* the FBI UCR; the Drug Enforcement Administration (DEA); and the National Institute on Drug Abuse. Most of these organizations and agencies maintain up-to-date websites on the Internet.

THE HALLUCINOGENS

Marijuana

This is the most widely available and popular "illegal" drug used in the United States (Drug Enforcement Administration, 2014b). Availability is widespread due to large-scale marijuana importation from Mexico, the large increase of domestic indoor grows, and an increase of the drug cultivated in states that have legalized marijuana or passed legislation approving the drug for medicinal purposes.

In 2013, approximately 4.5 million Americans, aged 12 or older, reported using marijuana on a daily or almost daily basis in the last 12 months (SAMHSA, 2014). In 2014, 35 percent of high school students admitted using marijuana during the past year, and nearly 6 percent indicated they use it daily (Johnston et al., 2015). In the same survey, 27 percent (3.4% daily) of 10th grade students said they used marijuana over the past year, and 3.4 percent said they used it daily. Twelve percent of 8th graders stated they used the drug over the past year and 1 percent of them said they used it daily. These data all indicate that marijuana is a very popular drug in America.

Although marijuana is usually not considered a "hard" and dangerous drug by many experts, it is considered illegal by the federal government and most states, although approximately half have authorized it for medicinal purposes and—at this writing—two allow it to be purchased in small amount for recreational use. Almost everywhere, the use or possession of marijuana can lead to conviction and incarceration. Its heavy use has been linked to a range of poor health outcomes and a variety of mental and cognitive problems (Drug Enforcement Administration, 2014a, 2014b). For example, there was a 62 percent increase in marijuana-related emergency department visits between 2004 and 2011. Marijuana has been found to significantly impair one's ability to safely drive a motor vehicle. In 2009, approximately 28 percent of fatally injured drivers tested positive for marijuana (Drug Enforcement Administration, 2014a). However, marijuana users are often polydrug users, suggesting that many of the assumed links to marijuana-induced behavior is often contaminated by the simultaneous use of other drugs.

At this writing, the Drug Enforcement Administration classifies marijuana as a Schedule I drug under the Controlled Substances Act, primarily because of the high THC content and other chemicals (Drug Enforcement Administration, 2014a). In recent years, many scientists and researchers have identified several chemicals that are useful for treating a range of illnesses, leading many professionals to contend that marijuana should be made legally available for medical purposes. Currently, ongoing research is leading to the development of new pharmaceuticals that harness the therapeutic benefits of these chemicals found in marijuana while reducing or eliminating the harmful side and intoxicating effects of the drug.

In 2013, 46 percent of arrests for drug violations were for marijuana possession, and approximately 6 percent of those arrests were for sales or manufacture of the drug (Federal Bureau of Investigation, 2014a) (see **Table 16-3**). Incarceration for possession, however, is rare, especially for a first offense.

As mentioned at the beginning of this section, marijuana is also one of the most popular illegal drugs used by juveniles, third only to alcohol and tobacco in terms of prevalence of use

(Johnston et al., 2011; Johnston et al., 2015). In 2014, 11.7 percent of 8th graders, 27.3 percent of 10th graders, and 35.1 percent of 12th grades reported using the drug during the past year. In most surveys, a substantial majority of the middle school, high school, and college students all indicated that marijuana is "fairly easy" or "very easy" to obtain. In 2014, for example, 81.3 percent of 12th graders said it was "fairly easy" or "very easy" to get marijuana (Johnston et al., 2015). Perhaps even more startling, 36.9 percent of 8th graders said marijuana was relatively easy to get in 2014.

How Is Marijuana Prepared?

Marijuana, which apparently originated in Asia, is among the oldest and most frequently used intoxicants worldwide. The earliest reference to marijuana was found in a book on pharmacy written by the Chinese emperor Shen Nung in 2737 B.C. (Ray, 1972). It was called the "Liberator of Sin" and was recommended for such ailments as "female weakness," constipation, and absentmindedness. The word marijuana is commonly believed to have derived from "Mary Jane," Mexican slang for cheap tobacco, or from the Portuguese word *mariguano,* meaning intoxicant. Street names for the drug include pot, grass, reefer, weed, Mary Jane, and Acapulco gold.

The drug is prepared from the plant *cannabis,* an annual that is cultivated or grows freely as a weed in both tropical and temperate climates. There are at least three species of cannabis—sativa, indica, and ruderalis—each differing in psychoactive potency. The psychoactive (intoxicating) properties of the plant reside principally in the chemical Delta-9 tetrahydrocannabinol (THC), found mainly in its resin. Thus, the concentration and quality of THC within parts of the plant determine the potency or psychoactive power of the drug. Average marijuana potency has steadily increased over the past 20 years (National Drug Intelligence Center, 2009).

THC content varies from one preparation to another, partly due to the quality of the plant itself, but also due to its environment. The strain of the plant, the climate, and the soil conditions all affect THC content. For example, the resin is believed to retard the dehydration of the flowering elements and thus is produced in greater quantities in hot, tropical climates than in temperate zones. Consequently, cannabis grown in the tropics (Mexico, Columbia, Jamaica, and North Africa) presumably has greater psychoactive potential than American-grown hemp. More recent information suggests, however, that THC potency has become more a feature of the species of the cannabis plant than of geographic area or climatic conditions. Although marijuana produced in Mexico remains the most widely available in the United States, high-potency marijuana also enters the U.S. drug market from Canada (usually grown indoors). Domestically grown marijuana, either grown outdoors or indoors, also represents a substantial proportion of the U.S. drug market. Although domestically produced marijuana has substantially increased in recent years, much of the marijuana available in the United States is foreign-produced, mostly in Mexico and Canada (National Drug Intelligence Center, 2009).

The THC content of marijuana and its derivatives has increased over the years. In 1995, the average THC content was 3.96 percent. In 2013, the average THC content was 12.55 percent (Drug Enforcement Administration, 2014b). In the 1990s, the THC potency of hash oil ranged from 13 to 16 percent. In 2013, the average THC content of hash oil was about 52 percent. One area of concern is the ingestion of marijuana by children through marijuana laced edibles, such as brownies, cookies, peanut butter, candy, and soda drinks.

In the United States, marijuana and hashish are usually smoked most often in hand-rolled cigarettes called "joints," hollowed-out commercial cigars called "blunts," or in pipes or water pipes called "bongs." As noted above, marijuana plants also can be soaked in butane, resulting in a high potency THC. It is still popular to lace the joint or blunt with other drugs, such as phencyclidine (PCP) or crack. A common practice in other countries is to consume cannabis as "tea," or mixed with other beverages or food.

The psychological effects of cannabis are so subjective and depend on such a wide range of variables that any generalizations must be accompanied by the warning that there are numerous exceptions. Reactions to cannabis, like all psychoactive drugs, depend on the complex interactions of both pharmacological and extra-pharmacological factors. As we noted, these include the mood of the user, the user's expectations about the drug, the social context in which it is used, and the user's past experiences with the drug. The strong influence of these extra-pharmacological factors, together with the widespread variation in THC content in any sample of cannabis, makes it exceedingly difficult to obtain comparable research data. Essentially, the effects of cannabis are unique to each individual. Except for increases in heart rate, increases in peripheral blood flow, and reddening of the membranes around the eyes, there are few consistent physiological changes reported for all persons.

Addiction to THC does occur, but only at doses and continued use far above what is now used recreationally. Furthermore, the person who uses marijuana must learn to use the drug to reach a euphoric "stoned" or "high" state. Ray (1983) reports that a three-stage learning process is involved. First, users must inhale the smoke deeply and hold it in their lungs for approximately 20 seconds. Then they must learn to identify and control the effects. Finally, they must learn to label the effects as pleasant.

Synthetic Marijuana

In recent years, a product known as **synthetic marijuana** (synthetic cannabinoids), touted as legal marijuana, has reached the market. The product is sold in small packets under many brand names, including K2, Blaze, fake weed, Genie, Moon Rocks, Panama Red Ball, Skunk, Blueberry Haze, and Spice. On the street it may be known as serenity, wicked spice, black mamba, or fake pot or weed. As for most other drugs, these names are continually in flux.

Synthetic marijuana can be bought on the open market, either online, in head shops, convenience stores, tobacco stores, or gasoline stations, although many states are rushing to make its purchases illegal for juveniles. Synthetic marijuana is produced to mimic the effects of cannabis. The product usually consists of a mixture of dried leaves from herbal plants, and is often laced with synthetic cannabinoids (especially HU-210). It is believed that HU-210 may be hundreds of times more potent that THC, so even traces of the chemical in the product can be potentially effective (U.S. Drug Enforcement Administration, 2009). Some experts refer to HU-210 as "stealth marijuana."

Overdoses of synthetic marijuana have resulted in a sharp rise in visits to emergency rooms and calls to poison control centers nationwide (Schwarz, 2015). Users may be rushed to hospitals experiencing extreme anxiety or violent behavior and delusions, and some of the cases result in death. Synthetic marijuana comes in hundreds of varieties, and new formulations appear monthly, with molecules subtly tweaked to skirt the DEA list of illegal drugs (Schwarz, 2015). It is considered illegal primarily because of its enormous health risk to naïve users. Although the drug appears to resemble marijuana, it can be one hundred times more potent. The chemicals in synthetic marijuana are typically imported from China.

In 2014, 5 percent of high school students and 8th graders (combined) nationwide stated they used synthetic marijuana during the prior 12 months (Johnston et al., 2015). The annual prevalence rate for high school seniors was 11.4 percent. Synthetic marijuana is popular among young people, and it is second only to "real" marijuana in its use among high school seniors (Johnston et al., 2015; National Institute on Drug Abuse, 2012). As the case for most drugs, synthetic marijuana is more popular among boys than girls.

Although the product has been available since 2006, its popularity has increased in recent years. In February 2011, the DEA declared a number of the chemicals used in the product to be Schedule I drugs, and prohibited the product's possession or sale if it contained those chemicals. The temporary ban will continue until the potential safety and health issues of synthetic marijuana can be investigated by the U.S. Department of Health and Human Services. As of this writing, the temporary ban has not been lifted. If taken with alcohol, the person can become very sick, and there are indications that some individuals show psychotic-like symptoms under its influence.

Synthetic Cathinones

Another category of dangerous synthetic drugs are the synthetic cathinones, commonly sold as "bath salts." Recent derivatives are flakka or gravel. They are also falsely marketed as jewelry cleaner, stain remover, plant food or fertilizer, and insect repellent. Synthetic cathinones are sold on the Internet, but also can be purchased at smoke shops, convenience stores, adult book stores, and gas stations. They may be sold in the following forms: powders, crystals, resins, tablets, and capsules. Most often they are ingested by mouth. These drugs can cause powerful negative reactions, including nausea, vomiting, paranoia, hallucinations, delusions, suicidal thoughts, and seizures. Fortunately, only about 1 percent of high school students and 8th graders use synthetic cathinones of any kind on a regular basis.

The dangers posed by synthetic marijuana and the cathinones prompted the passage of the Synthetic Drug Abuse Prevention Act of 2012. The law amended the Federal Controlled Substances Act and placed 26 synthetic drugs into a Schedule I classification.

Salvia

Salvia is a popular perennial in many home gardens—it is a plant in the mint family native to southern Mexico. However, probably unknown to many backyard gardeners, it also can be used to produce hallucinogenic experiences (National Institute on Drug Abuse, 2013c). It is usually ingested by chewing fresh leaves or by drinking its extracted juices, but it can also be smoked in rolled cigarettes, pipes, or inhaled via a vaporizer. Subjective effects of the drug include psychedelic changes in visual perception, mood and body sensations, mood swings, and feelings of detachment. The psychological and physical health effects of Salvia have yet to be systematically investigated. The drug is known by teens, as approximately 2 percent have tried the drug during 2014, but its popularity appears to be declining (Johnston et al., 2015).

Cannabis and Crime

Numerous research projects directed at the effects of cannabis were launched during the 1950s, 1960s, and early 1970s. Many of these studies had methodological shortcomings and did not control for parity of dosage levels, means of administering the drug, and THC content in the drug itself. Psychological factors associated with the subjects were not considered carefully enough, and experimental settings and instructions were haphazard. At first, some of the research suggested a relationship between cannabis use and criminal behavior. However, with more sophisticated statistical analyses that controlled demographic and criminal background variables, the earlier results were found to be spurious (National Commission on Marihuana and Drug Abuse, 1972). To date, no well-executed study has firmly established a general causal link between the use of cannabis (by itself) and violent criminal activity. Of course, this assertion excludes the illegal acts of producing, trafficking, selling, possessing, or using the drug.

Both independent research and investigations conducted by government-sponsored commissions strongly indicated that marijuana does not directly contribute to criminal behavior. After an extensive review of available literature, the National Commission on Marijuana and Drug Abuse (1972, p. 470) came to this conclusion: "There is no systematic empirical evidence, at least that is drawn from the American experience, to support the thesis that the use of marijuana either inevitably or generally causes, leads to or precipitates criminal, violent, aggressive, or delinquent behavior of sexual or nonsexual nature." The Commission Report (p. 470) adds, "If anything, the effects observed suggest that marijuana may be more likely to neutralize criminal behavior and to militate against the commission of aggressive acts."

One of the predominant effects of THC is relaxation and a marked decrease in physical activity (Tinklenberg & Stillman, 1970). THC induces muscular weakness and inability to sustain physical effort, so that the user wishes nothing more strenuous than to stay relatively motionless. As Tinklenberg and Stillman (1970, p. 341) note, "'being stoned' summarizes these sensations of demobilizing lethargy." It is difficult to imagine "stoned" users engaging in assaultive or violent activity. If anything, THC should reduce the likelihood of criminal activity, particularly aggressive conduct, as the Commission suggested. There is some evidence to support this conclusion.

Tinklenberg and Woodrow (1974) found that drug users who use mainly marijuana seem less inclined toward violence and aggression than their counterparts who prefer other drugs, such as alcohol or amphetamines. After examining drug usage among youth, Blumer and his associates (Blumer, Sutter, Ahmed, & Smith, 1967) made the same observation. In fact, they found that marijuana users deliberately shunned aggression and violence; in order to maintain one's status in the group, it was important to remain "cool" and nonaggressive, regardless of provocation.

Although the empirical evidence so far indicates that cannabis does not, as a rule, stimulate aggressive behavior or other criminal actions, whenever we deal with human behavior, there will be some exceptions. Individuals familiar with the effects of cannabis have heard of occasional negative experiences produced by THC. Although the phenomenon is rare, some people do report feelings of panic, hypersensitivity, feelings of being out of contact with their surroundings, and bizarre behavior. Some individuals have experienced rapid, disorganized intrusions of irrelevant thoughts, which prompted them to feel they were losing control of their mind. Under these conditions, it is plausible that one would interpret the actions of others as threatening. It is also possible that these panicked individuals might attack those surrounding them. These examples are likely to become prevalent as the THC levels of the drug continue to increase by enterprising marijuana producers and growers.

Researchers continually find that juvenile offenders and those youths with conduct disorders usually engage in drug and alcohol abuse, including marijuana (Boxmeyer, Lochman, Powell, & Powe, 2015). Usually, juvenile offenders begin experimenting with a variety of drugs and generally do not restrict themselves to any one category. Consequently, it is difficult to pinpoint any one particular drug type as the culprit in generating aggressive behavior or violent crime in adolescents. This especially appears to be the case concerning marijuana. Another point: the early onset of substance use is a significant predictor of future multiple substance abuse.

It should also be noted that marijuana was the drug most commonly admitted when ADAM II adult male arrestees were asked about use in the prior 30 days (Office of National Drug Control Policy, 2014). The admitted prevalence of marijuana use ranged from 39 percent in Atlanta to 58 percent in Sacramento. The rates of use were higher, averaging around 55 percent, among adult male arrestees in the two regions of the country where states legalized use or reduced penalties with marijuana use (e.g., Colorado and California).

Researchers and scientists who investigate cannabis effects usually agree that people who act violently under the influence of the drug were probably *predisposed* to act that way, with or without the drug (National Commission on Marihuana and Drug Abuse, 1972). The evidence indicates that violent marijuana users were violent prior to using cannabis. In other words, they learned the behavioral pattern independently of cannabis. In addition, they have come to expect that the drug will "bring out" aggression or violence in them.

In summary, there is no solid evidence to indicate that cannabis contributes to or encourages violent or property crime, in spite of waning beliefs that this relationship exists. In fact, there is evidence to suggest that cannabis users are less criminally or violently prone under the influence of the drug than users of other drugs, such as alcohol and amphetamines. There are also no supportive data that cannabis is habit forming to the point where the user must get a "fix" and will burglarize or rob to obtain funds to purchase the drug. Marijuana trafficking and distribution are also not fraught with the extensive systematic violence that accompanies other drugs of abuse. For most people, the primary negative effect of marijuana use is diminished psychomotor performance, thereby putting the public safety at risk when someone intoxicated with marijuana drives a motor vehicle or a boat, or operates machinery.

Marijuana generally promotes relaxation and interferes with judgment, and probably makes people more daring and more prone to risk taking. It also alters the experience of reality and often improves mood. The drug is clearly used extensively as a recreation enhancer. There does appear to be significant health risks for heavy, chronic users of the drug. As noted earlier, nearly 50 percent of individuals arrested for a variety of offenses had been using marijuana just prior to or at the time of their offense, and it is also very popular among delinquents. Most likely, arrestees and detainees used the drug to improve their sense of well-being, frequently in combination with other drugs. Although it is illegal to produce, possess, sell, or consume marijuana, there is little evidence that the drug propels nonviolent people to become violent or antisocial, or to engage in some kind of serious criminal behavior.

Phencyclidine (PCP)

PCP may be classified as a central nervous system depressant, anesthetic, tranquilizer, or hallucinogen. It has many effects, but most pronounced is its barbiturate-like downer effect, perceptual distortions and hallucinations, and its amphetamine-like upper effects, such as excitation and hyperactivity. An overdosed person, for example, may show signs of moving from upper to downer effects while having hallucinations.

PCP was first synthesized in 1957, but due to its psychotic and hallucinogenic reactions, it was taken off the market for human consumption in 1965 and limited to veterinary medicine as an animal immobilizing agent. Because of its serious and numerous side effects, it is no longer used even in veterinary medicine. After a decline in abuse during the late 1980s and 1990s, phencyclidine (PCP) re-emerged as a drug of abuse in the late 1990s (Drug Enforcement Administration, 2010a). Recently, its popularity has dropped substantially for teens and currently is rarely used (Johnston et al., 2015). The behavior of some individuals under the influence of PCP is highly unpredictable and may lead to life-threatening situations. Under the spell of PCP psychosis, delusions of superhuman strength, persecution, and grandiosity are not uncommon. In general, PCPs are associated with a number of serious risks, and many experts believe it is one of the most dangerous illicit drugs on the streets. On occasion, individuals under the influence of PCP may use weapons to defend themselves and to commit other acts of violence.

There is wide variation in degree of purity and dosage forms of PCP manufactured in clandestine laboratories. It comes in capsules, tablets, liquids, or powders. It may be administered orally, by inhalation (snorted or smoked), and at times by intravenous injection. If it is smoked, PCP is often applied to leafy material such as mint, parsley, oregano, or marijuana. Users usually combine PCP with other drugs, particularly marijuana and alcohol. In combination with alcohol, PCP increases risk of coma (National Institute on Drug Abuse, 2015). The drug is marketed under a number of other names, including Angel Dust, Supergrass, Killer Weed, Boat, Love Boat, Tic Tac, Embalming Fluid, Zoom, and Rocket Fuel, because of its range of bizarre and volatile effects (Drug Enforcement Administration, 2005).

PCP and Crime

The available evidence clearly indicates that PCP users tend to be multiple illicit drug users (polydrug users). To what extent PCP propels a person toward a life of crime is largely unknown, but it does *not* seem likely that the PCP user regularly engages in crime to support his or her habit. PCPs are inexpensive, easily available, and only marginally addictive after chronic use. PCP users are generally polydrug users who have demonstrated a variety of types of antisocial conduct prior to PCP usage. Polydrug usage is more likely to be one symptom within a complicated matrix of other symptoms found in certain individuals habitually "going against" their environment. Currently, phencyclidine is classified as a Schedule I drug of abuse by the DEA.

THE STIMULANTS

Amphetamines

Amphetamines and cocaine are classified as central nervous system stimulants and have highly similar effects. Amphetamines are part of a group of synthetic drugs known collectively as amines. Cocaine (coke, snow, candy) is a chemical extracted from the coca plant (Erythroxylon coca), an extremely hardy plant native to Peru. The amines in particular produce effects in the sympathetic nervous system, a subdivision of the autonomic nervous system, which arouse the person to actions that might include fighting or fleeing from a frightening situation. Amphetamines are traditionally classified into three major categories: (1) amphetamine (Benzedrine), (2) dextroamphetamine (Dexedrine), and (3) methamphetamine (Methedrine or Desoxyn). Of the three, Benzedrine is the least potent. All may be taken orally, inhaled, or injected, and all act directly on the central nervous system, particularly the reticular activating system.

Methamphetamine

In this section, methamphetamine is the focus of the amphetamine group because it is the drug most preferred by heavy drug users, and carries the most health risks. It is a Schedule II stimulant because it has a high potential for abuse and is available only through a prescription that cannot be refilled (National Institute on Drug Abuse, 2014a). It is an extremely addictive stimulant that can lead to chronic seeking and use. In the past methamphetamine was often prescribed to treat ADHD and other disorders. It is rarely prescribed today because of its strong addictive properties. It is also rarely used by teens. In 2014, the annual prevalence rates was 0.6 percent for 8th graders, 0.8 percent for 10th graders, and 1.0 percent for 12th graders (Johnston et al., 2015). College students show a similar disinterest.

Methamphetamine has traditionally been the drug of preference when the user injects the substance directly into the bloodstream. Although it can be swallowed or snorted, the preferred method of consumption is by smoking, especially the crystallized form of methamphetamine known as ice (Maxwell, 2004). Ice, also known as crank, chalk, fire, crystal, go fast, speed, or crystal meth, is methamphetamine that has been washed in solvent such as alcohol to remove the impurities. Evaporation of the solvent produces crystals that resemble glass shards or ice shavings. Yaba is a Thai name for a colored tablet containing methamphetamine combined with caffeine, which was once popular among young adults (Drug Enforcement Administration, 2010b).

Liquid methamphetamine is becoming a common form of the drug for smuggling across the border because of its ease of concealment (Drug Enforcement Administration, 2014b). The illegal form of the drug is manufactured in clandestine laboratories (meth labs or super labs). In recent years, Mexican drug trafficking organizations have become the primary manufacturers and distributors of methamphetamine in the United States (Drug Enforcement Administration, 2014b; National Institute on Drug Abuse, 2014a). The majority of methamphetamine available in the United States produced in Mexico is highly pure and potent (Drug Enforcement Administration, 2014b). Methamphetamine is relatively easy to produce, and the ingredients can be purchased at local drug stores (Office of National Drug Control Policy, 2003b).

Methamphetamine produces an increase in alertness and a decrease in appetite. The effects may last as long as 12 hours. In high doses, the drug can cause violent behavior, anxiety, insomnia, and symptoms of paranoid behavior, including delusions, hallucinations, and mood swings. Meth alters judgment and self-regulation, prompting some people to engage in highly risky behaviors. Some chronic users develop sores on their bodies from scratching "crank bugs," bugs that, under the user's delusional state, are believed to be crawling under the skin. In studies of chronic users, several structural and functional changes have been found in areas of the brain associated with emotion and memory (National Institute on Drug Abuse, 2014a). These changes may be long-lasting or temporary, but if temporary, it may take up to a year to recover. Methamphetamine is also known to cause severe dental problems, known as "meth mouth."

Other Stimulants with Similar Effects

Methylphenidate, a stimulant known as Ritalin, has a high potential for abuse and produces many of the same effects as methamphetamine. Many children who were diagnosed with attention deficit hyperactivity disorder take Ritalin to stabilize their behavior. Thus, Ritalin is considered easily accessible to children and adolescents who can obtain the drug from classmates or friends who have a prescription for it. In more recent years, Adderall, a mixture of amphetamine salts, has increasingly become the drug of preference for ADHD. It has traditionally been a popular drug of abuse for high school and college students, although its popularity is beginning to level off (SAMHSA, 2009, 2011, 2014).

The amphetamines are synthetic compounds, and, unlike cannabis or cocaine, can be easily produced by self-appointed chemists for large-scale illegal distribution. The manufacture of methamphetamine, for example, requires precursor drugs (drugs that are necessary in the manufacture of another) such as ephedrine or pseudoephedrine, which are widely available in Mexico and are believed to be smuggled into the United States in large quantities (Feucht & Kyle, 1996). Over-the-counter cold medicines containing ephedrine or pseudoephedrine and other materials can also be "cooked" to make methamphetamine (Office of National Drug Control Policy, 1999b). Therefore, it is exceedingly difficult to estimate the quantity of amphetamines consumed each year in the United States. The Comprehensive Methamphetamine Act of 1996 was passed, among other things, to control the sale of ephedrine and pseudoephedrine.

Khat is a flowering evergreen shrub that produces a stimulant-like effect. The drug is native to East Africa and the Arabian Peninsula where it has been used as a tradition in many social occasions. It is chewed like tobacco, and retained in the mouth, or used as a tea or sprinkled on food. The common street names for the drug include Abyssinian Tea, African Salad, Catha, Chat, Kat, and Oat. Khat's health effects and potential for addiction are unknown at this time.

Cocaine and Its Derivatives

Cocaine use has steadily declined since its peak in 2007, especially for young adults (Drug Enforcement Administration, 2014; National Institute on Drug Abuse, 2013a). Teenager cocaine use has declined steadily since the late 1990s. As noted by Johnston and his colleagues (2015), "Over the last fifteen years, use has declined in all three grades; annual 12th grade use stands at a historical low of just 2.6% in 2014, with use by 8th and 10th graders still lower" (p. 20). Approximately one-third of high school seniors said it would be "fairly easy" or "very easy" for them to get cocaine if they wanted to (Johnston et al., 2015). In that same year, about 12 percent of 8th graders indicated that it would be fairly easy or very easy to get powered cocaine or crack if they needed it. In 2013, the percentage of ADAM II arrestees testing positive for cocaine (crack and powder forms) also declined significantly since 2000, decreasing by more than 50 percent (Office of National Drug Control Policy, 2014). Furthermore, arrestees appear to prefer crack cocaine over the powdered cocaine.

In the United States and Canada, cocaine is usually administered nasally (sniffing), intravenously, or by inhaling (smoking). Cocaine taken orally is poorly absorbed because it is hydrolyzed (neutralized) by gastrointestinal secretions. Slang names for powder cocaine include candy sugar, pariba, aspirin, mojo, icing, happy dust, oyster stew, and double bubble. Crack is produced in such a way that the cocaine ingredient can be smoked without destroying its potency. There is no safe way to use cocaine. Any route of administration can lead to toxic amounts, leading to acute cardiovascular or cerebrovascular emergencies that could lead to sudden death, especially in combination with alcohol (National Institute on Drug Abuse, 2015).

Interestingly, it was believed that Coca-Cola contained cocaine as an active ingredient until 1903, when caffeine was substituted (Kleber, 1988). This assertion is vigorously denied by representatives of the company who insist there is no evidence for it. However, around the turn of the century, cocaine *was* used as an important stimulant in some "soft" drinks (such as Kos-Kola, Wiseola, and Care-Cola). It was also used in cigarettes and cigars, various tonics, foods, sprays, and ointments (including hemorrhoid salves) (Smart, 1986). The famous drink "Vin Mariani," so popular among the wealthy at the time, was a combination of vintage French wine and cocaine. However, cocaine began to fall into disfavor when people became concerned about its dangerous and undesirable effects. By 1910, cocaine had become the most hated and feared drug in North America (Kleber, 1988). The Harrison Narcotics Act of 1914 in the United States, and the Propriety and Patents Medicines Act of 1908 in Canada, sharply curtailed or terminated its usage, and the popularity of cocaine correspondingly declined until the 1960s.

Psychological Effects

In small doses, both amphetamines and cocaine increase wakefulness, alertness, and vigilance; improve concentration; and produce a feeling of clear thinking. There is generally an elevation of mood, mild euphoria, increased sociability, and a belief that one can do just about anything. The duration of the stimulant's euphoric effects depends on the route of administration. The faster the absorption into the bloodstream, such as inhaling cocaine vapor into the lungs rather than snorting the powder form, the more rapid and intense the psychoactive effects. Cocaine vapor is usually produced by igniting the powder form of cocaine. In large doses, the effects may be irritability, hypersensitivity, delirium, panic aggression, hallucinations, and psychosis. Hallucinations sometimes include "coke bugs" that appear to be crawling all over the body. Injected at chronically high doses, these drugs may precipitate "toxic psychosis," a syndrome with many of the psychotic features of paranoid schizophrenia. With the metabolization and elimination of the drug, the psychotic episode usually dissipates. Cocaine, like any psychoactive drug, will engender different experiences for different individuals. Some people under the influence will exhibit violent, erratic, paranoid, or even suicidal behavior; others will display peaceful, friendly, sociable behavior.

Adverse Physical Effects

Frequent cocaine use may have some strong adverse effects, depending on how it is administered. Regularly snorting cocaine can lead to a loss of sense of smell, nosebleeds, swallowing problems, hoarseness, and inflammation of the nasal septum (National Institute on Drug Abuse, 2013a). Orally consuming cocaine can cause severe bowel gangrene because of reduced blood flow to the gastrointestinal system. Injecting cocaine can generate some serious allergic reactions, and sometimes results in death. Cocaine is usually processed with a variety of volatile solvents, such as gasoline, benzene, and kerosene, and traces of these toxic substances often remain in the powder form of cocaine.

Cocaine often has a dramatic effect on the cardiovascular system, such as disturbances in heart rhythm and heart attacks. It can adversely affect the respiratory systems, resulting in chest pain or respiratory failure. It can also cause strokes, seizures, blurred vision, nausea, fever, muscle spasms, and coma. Cocaine users who frequently inject the drug are at risk of bacterial infections and other infectious diseases. Sharing needles and using unsterilized drug paraphernalia also put users at considerable risk of HIV, hepatitis, and a variety of other viruses.

There is a potentially very dangerous drug interaction between cocaine and alcohol that should be noted. When the user ingests cocaine and alcohol at once or closely together, the drugs are converted by the body to cocethylene. Cocethylene is substantially more toxic than either drug alone, and available evidence indicates that the mixture of cocaine and alcohol is the most common two-drug combination that results in drug-related death (National Institute on Drug Abuse, 1999, 2015). It should also be noted that the combination of cocaine and heroin (known as a "speedball") carries an even higher risk of death (National Institute on Drug Abuse, 2013a).

Stimulants and Crime

As is the case for all other illegal drugs, possession, production, and trafficking are themselves crime. In the groundbreaking and award-winning cable show, *Breaking Bad*, chemistry teacher Walter White and his former student Jesse became ensnared in a continuing saga of encounters with law enforcement, gangs, and drug kingpins as they cooked crystallized methamphetamine in their desert trailer. White was diagnosed with inoperable lung cancer; his motive—at least initially—was to insure his family's financial future. Jesse, a bright but rudderless young man from a wealthy, distant family, saw the drug operation as an opportunity to become independent and escape his past. Their nemesis was White's brother-in-law Hank, a DEA agent who did not suspect his involvement in drug production for several years.

Although the above clearly illustrates criminal behavior, we are most concerned here with the connection between the use of drugs and other criminal activity, as we have for all other drugs discussed in this chapter.

Heavy users of amphetamines typically prefer to inject methamphetamine directly into the bloodstream, cranking up with several hundred milligrams at one time. During these speed "runs," the user may engage in aggressive or violent behavior. However, it appears that people who behave violently under the effects of amphetamines are very often predisposed to behave violently long before they ingested amphetamines. In other words, there is little evidence to conclude that amphetamines directly *cause* people to behave violently, but they do increase the likelihood that an *already prone* person will behave violently.

High doses of cocaine can engender a temporary case of severe paranoia in which the person loses touch with reality and experiences delusions and auditory hallucinations (National Institute on Drug Abuse, 2013a). However, there is no cogent evidence that cocaine-induced paranoia leads to violence, unless—similar to amphetamines—the person is already prone to be aggressive.

Both amphetamines and cocaine are considered Schedule II drugs by the DEA. In small doses, these drugs increase alertness and concentration. In large doses, they generally produce negative psychological effects. But, to date, virtually no study has shown that stimulants or cocaine facilitate either property crime or violent crime. In an exhaustive review of the literature, the Panel on the Understanding and Control of Violent Behavior concluded, "There is no evidence to support the claim that snorting or injecting cocaine stimulates violent behavior." Morgan and Zimmer (1997) and Vaughn et al. (2010b) also conclude that there is very little convincing evidence that cocaine, either in crack or powder form, causes a nonviolent person to suddenly become violent or dangerous to others. Nor is there any evidence to support the assumption that cocaine, especially crack, causes women to abuse their children. It is more likely the lifestyle of the parent, rather than simply the pharmacologically driven aspect of the drug, that leads to child abuse (Morgan & Zimmer, 1997).

Powder cocaine, however, can be strongly addictive, and the dependence onset can be rapid and severe. It is also expensive, and acquisition of the drug must be accomplished through organized distribution and selling. In other words, powder cocaine is one of the drugs of abuse that encourages systematic violence on a wide scale. In addition, some cocaine abusers may have a difficult time controlling their habit and may rapidly build a tolerance to the drug, requiring larger and larger amounts of the costly drug. Some cocaine users may be forced to engage in shoplifting, theft, drug dealing, and prostitution to support their habit. Furthermore, persistent offenders tend to be polydrug users, as we have found is often the case in drug abuse. Although it is difficult at this point in our knowledge to determine which comes first, drug use or involvement in delinquency or crime, the evidence strongly suggests that persistent offenders have engaged in a variety of illegal activities and troublesome conduct throughout their lifetimes, most probably beginning before the onset of drug or alcohol abuse.

Crack Cocaine

The most common method of cocaine smoking in the United States is freebasing. Freebase is prepared by dissolving cocaine hydrochloride in water, and then adding a strong base such as ammonia or baking soda to the solution. This cocaine freebase is generally dissolved in ether to extract the cocaine, and then the ether is removed by drying the solution. Other methods may be used that bypass the ether method by heating the mixture. The drying process produces crystalline, smokable pellets, or nuggets.

During the 1980s, a purified, high-potency form of freebase cocaine—known as crack—exploded in popularity. It was, according to Howard Abadinsky (1993), the drug abuser's version of fast food. The drug is called "crack" because it makes a crackling sound when smoked. Crack is several times more pure than ordinary street cocaine, and crack smoking generates a very rapid, intense state of euphoria, which peaks in about five minutes. The psychological and physical effects of crack are as powerful as any intravenously injected cocaine. However, the euphoria is short-lived, ending in about 10 to 20 minutes after inhalation, and is followed by depression, irritability, and often an intense craving for more. It is also extremely dangerous to the user and may result in a rapid and irregular heartbeat, respiratory failure, seizures, or a cerebral hemorrhage. Although most users limit themselves to one or two hits, some users seek multiple hits. Crack smokers, in order to stay high, often find a place where crack can be safely smoked, such as a crack house, because the smoke and smell are difficult to hide.

Its popularity probably resided in the instantaneous psychological effects it provides, its inexpensiveness, and its wide availability throughout most major U.S. cities. The drug also provided tremendous profitability for the sellers.

Beginning in the early 1990s, the use of crack cocaine began to decline (Golub & Johnson, 1997). The reasons for the decline are multiple, but the most prominent appear to be its health risks and the changes in attitude among the new generation concerning its use. It continues to show steady declines in use today for both youths and adults. Less than 1 percent of teens used crack during 2014 (Johnston et al., 2015).

Crack and Crime

The relationship between crack and crime remains obscure. One thing that does emerge from the research literature is that crack users, especially persistent users, are often polydrug users. Surveys indicate that virtually all crack users have been frequent users of other drugs, and most also had an extensive history of prior drug use, drug selling, and nondrug criminality (Golub & Johnson, 1997). While it is difficult at this point in our knowledge to determine which comes first, drug use or involvement in crime, the evidence does suggest that persistent offenders have engaged in a variety of illegal activities and troublesome conduct throughout their lifetimes, probably before extensive drug abuse. One thing appears clear, though: Crack use by itself does not appear to cause violent behavior in normally nonviolent people (Golub & Johnson, 1997; Leigey & Backman, 2007; Morgan & Zimmer, 1997; Vaughn, Fu, Perron, Bohnert, & Howard, 2010b).

The association between the crack cocaine black market and systemic violence, on the other hand, is a different matter. The production, distribution, and selling of powder and crack cocaine have been associated with violence for some time, although the amount of violence fluctuates with the illicit market economy.

MDMA (Ecstasy or Molly)

MDMA (3,4-methylenedioxymethamphetamine), more commonly referred to "ecstasy" or "Molly," is a synthetic drug (completely manufactured rather than grown or occurring naturally) that is considered a stimulant, but it also has some strong psychedelic properties similar to methamphetamine and mescaline. "Molly," a purer form of ecstasy, began to be used more commonly by teens in 2013 (Johnston et al., 2015). It is sometimes confused with a similar compound 3,4-methylenedioxyamphetamine, abbreviated MDA. The effects and pharmacological actions of MDA are similar but not identical to MDMA (Maxwell, 2004). Both MDMA and MDA are classified as Schedule I drugs. Other drugs confused with ecstasy include paramethoxyamphetamine (PMA) and p-methylthioamphetamine (MTA). These are substances packaged as ecstasy with similar psychoactive properties and associated with several deaths, especially in Europe (Maxwell, 2004).

The use of ecstasy (also known as Adam, E, X, eccie) increased sharply among teenagers during the late 1990s, in the nightclub scene or at "raves." For several years after the sharp increase, teens lost interest in the drug and its use has declined substantially. Beginning in 2009, however, there has been another upswing in its popularity among teens (Johnston et al., 2011, 2015; National Institute on Drug Abuse, 2013b). In 2014, approximately 3.6 percent of high school seniors indicated they had used MDMA during the past year (Johnston et al., 2015).

The common psychological effects of MDMA include feelings of increased energy, euphoria, emotional warmth and empathy toward others, and distortions in sensory and time perception (National Institute on Drug Abuse, 2013b). Its adverse physical side effects include muscle tension, involuntary clenching of the teeth, nausea, blurred vision, faintness, tremors, sweating, and chills. Baby pacifiers are often used by ecstasy users to prevent danger to or excessive grinding of the teeth. Inhalation of Vicks VapoRub® is also sometimes used to enhance the drug's psychedelic effects. MDMA may also predispose users to participate in high-risk behavior (Moreland, 2000).

The drug's stimulation properties provide an "energy rush" that encourages users to stay physically active for long periods of time, such as dancing all night at rave parties. Although the drug is considered safer than many other illicit drugs, there are physical risks. At very high doses, MDMA can cause the body temperature to rise as high as 110 degrees, leading to muscle breakdown and kidney or cardiovascular failure (National Institute on Drug Abuse, 2000). Also, all-night raves and extensive dancing in crowded and overheated rooms pose the danger of producing not only high body temperatures but also dangerous levels of dehydration. Other adverse side effects of MDMA include hearing and liver damage, strokes, and long-term brain injury (National Institute of Health, 1999).

The majority of MDMA found in the United States comes from clandestine laboratories in Western Europe (primarily the Netherlands and Belgium) and Canada (Drug Enforcement Administration, 2011). MDMA is usually consumed in tablet form, which is sometimes crushed and snorted, occasionally smoked but never injected.

NARCOTIC DRUGS

The word narcotics usually prompts intense negative reactions and very often is quickly associated with crime. Like the word "dope," it is widely misused to denote all illegal drugs. In this chapter, narcotic drugs refer only to the derivatives of or products pharmacologically similar to the products of the opium or poppy plant, *Papaver somniferum.*

The opium plant, an annual, grows to about three to five feet in height. Today, most opium is grown and produced in Afghanistan, a country that supplies at least 90 percent of the world's opium. Burma is the second producer of the world's opium. However, the opium poppies that are of most concern to the United States are grown principally in Columbia and Mexico. Although these two countries together cultivate less than 6 percent of the world's total opium, most of the heroin found in the United States is from Columbian or Mexican suppliers. In fact, Mexico serves as the transit and distribution center for most of the drugs moving into this country.

Narcotic drugs can be divided into three major categories on the basis of the kind of preparation they require: (1) **natural narcotics**, which include the grown opium, (2) **semisynthetic narcotics**, which include the chemically prepared heroin, and (3) **synthetic narcotics**, which are wholly prepared chemically and include methadone, meperidine, and phenazocine. All are narcotics because they produce similar effects: relief of pain, relaxation, peacefulness, and sleep (*narco,* of Greek origin, means "to sleep"). The narcotics are highly addictive for some individuals; they develop a relentless and strong craving for the drug. Many heavy narcotic users, however, lead successful, productive lives, without significant interference in their daily routine. There is no single type of opium user.

Heroin

Heroin was once the most heavily used illegal *narcotic* in the country but its use has steadily declined in past year until 2013. More recently, the use of heroin has shown a slight increase in the United States, especially in the Northeast (New England states, New York, New Jersey) and other Mid-Atlantic states and Great Lakes regions (Drug Enforcement Administration, 2014b). Moreover, law enforcement seizure data suggest substantial increases of heroin availability throughout the nation. The increase in demand for heroin is largely driven by the initial nonmedical use of prescription narcotic pain killers, which eventually become too expensive for users. Studies have indicated, for example, that heroin abuse was 19 times higher among those who had previously abused narcotic pain relievers (Drug Enforcement Administration, 2014b). See **Box 16-1** for more information on this issue.

Data from the 2013 National Survey on Drug Use and Health indicate that only 0.1 percent of Americans, aged 12 and older, are current users of heroin (SAMHSA, 2014). Students and youth in general see heroin to be one of the most dangerous drugs, which largely accounts for its decline. Current youth users of heroin was about 0.4 percent in 2014 (Johnston et al., 2015).

CONTEMPORARY ISSUES

BOX 16-1 Prescription Medications: Fraudulent Distribution

Heroin, cocaine, marijuana—when people think of substance abuse, these are often the drugs that come to mind. Yet the theft, sales, and distribution of medications that are widely available by prescription are growing problems. Medications for pain (e.g., oxycodone, hydrocodone, and Xanax®); medications for mental illness (e.g., Prozac®); and medications for behavioral problems like ADHD or conduct disorders (e.g., Ritalin®, Adderall®) can be abused, sometimes resulting in overdoses and deaths. In addition, as indicated in the chapter, they are often sold on the streets, sometimes by juveniles. Juveniles also may obtain them from medicine cabinets in their own homes.

In May 2015, the DEA announced the arrests of close to 300 people in four southern states, including doctors and pharmacists, who were illegally distributing, prescribing, and dispensing pain medication. Many drugs were dispensed out of pain clinics at which patients reported symptoms but were never examined. Undercover agents posing as patients were sometimes coaxed to report more intense symptoms than they reported (Schwarz, 2015).

The Centers for Disease Control (CDC) reports that about half of the 44,000 accidental drug overdoses in 2013 could be attributed to prescription drugs, primarily though not exclusively painkillers. While many patients benefit from drugs to manage their pain legitimately, health care providers, like those targeted in the above raids, abuse the system by prescribing them when not needed. As a result, individuals often become addicted to the drugs and seek more. Fake prescriptions are reflected in staggering numbers—one pharmacist in the above raid sold close to 100,000 hydrocodone pills for about half a million dollars (Schwarz, 2015). Some of these pills end up on the streets, sold to dealers who in turn prey on persons who are addicted. Others are used directly by patients who are vulnerable to abusing them. Moreover, persons who become addicted to prescription drugs often ease into heroin as a cheap replacement when the prescription drug becomes unavailable.

Questions for Discussion

1. Other than economic benefit, what psychological theory or model could be applied to a health care provider who is involved in the illegal trafficking of prescription medication?
2. Is the person who knowingly and illegally obtains and uses prescription medication less culpable than the person who obtains and uses heroin?
3. Is the physician who illegally prescribes prescription medicine a drug dealer?

Heroin continues to be widely available in almost all areas of the country, although its purity varies considerably from region to region. Most of the white powder heroin east of the Mississippi River comes from South America. Most of the heroin (black tar and brown powder heroin) supplied west of the Mississippi is of Mexican origin (Drug Enforcement Administration, 2014b). Heroin is processed from morphine, which is extracted from the seed pod of certain varieties of poppy plants.

Although its popularity in the United States as a whole has declined, some eastern and midwestern states have reported significant problems, with heroin being available to both high school and middle school students. Also, heroin still reigns as the illicit or "hard drug" of choice in much of the world. Mexican "black tar" heroin has hit the streets in the western states of the United States in recent years. It is a dark brown substance that has the appearance of black tar and is sticky like roofing tar or, in some instances, hard like coal. The color and consistency of black tar heroin is due to the crude processing methods used to manufacture the drug. In many areas, heroin users combine heroin with cocaine powder (HCl) or with crack, and then inject the mixture. As mentioned earlier, this practice is known as "speedballing." In some regions, particularly in the West, users often mix heroin and methamphetamine and then inject. Heroin is rarely taken orally, because the absorption rate is slow and incomplete. It may be administered intramuscularly, subcutaneously ("skin popping"), or intravenously ("mainlining"), or it may be inhaled ("snorted"). Heroin inhalers usually choose to use heroin and crack simultaneously.

In the past, experienced heroin users strongly preferred mainlining because of the sensational thrill, splash, rush, or kick it provided. Injection is probably the most practical and efficient way to administer low-purity heroin. Injection works fast. Intravenous injection provides the most intense and rapid feeling of euphoria, working within seven to eight seconds after injection. Intramuscular injection is slower, taking about five to eight minutes for peak effect. However, in recent years, the dramatic increase in heroin purity has changed the preferred method of administration. The high purity of Columbian heroin available in much of the eastern United States allows the user to snort or sniff the substance like cocaine. In New York, for example, cocaine and heroin are often alternately inhaled, a practice called "criss-crossing." The quality of heroin today also allows it to be smoked.

The effects of heroin depend on the quantity taken, the method of administration, the interval between administrations, the tolerance and dependence of the user, the setting, and the user's expectations. Effects usually wear off in five to eight hours, depending on the user's tolerance. In 1999, heroin-related deaths were rising due to the decreasing price and the potency of the drug, resulting from significant increases in the purity of Columbian heroin.

Like all the narcotics, heroin is a central nervous system depressant. For many users, it promotes mental clouding, dreamlike states, light sleep punctuated by vivid dreams, and a general feeling of "sublime contentment." The body may become permeated with a feeling of warmth, and the extremities may feel heavy. There is little inclination toward physical activity; the user prefers to sit motionless and in a fog.

Heroin and Crime

No other drug group is as closely associated with crime as the narcotics, particularly heroin. The image of the desperate "junkie" looking for a fix is widespread. Furthermore, because of the adverse effects of the drug, it is assumed that the heroin user is bizarre, unpredictable, and therefore dangerous. However, high doses of narcotics produce sleep rather than the psychotic or paranoid panic states sometimes produced by high doses of amphetamines. Therefore, narcotics users rarely become violent or dangerous. Research strongly indicates that addicts do not, as a general rule, participate in violent crimes such as assault, rape, or homicide (Canadian Government's Commission of Inquiry, 1971; National Commission on Marihuana and Drug Abuse, 1973; National Institute on Drug Abuse, 1978; Tinklenberg & Stillman, 1970).

Research evidence does suggest a relationship between heroin addiction and money-producing crime. A study in Miami of 573 narcotics users found that they were responsible for almost 6,000 robberies, 6,700 burglaries, 900 stolen vehicles, 25,000 instances of shoplifting, and 46,000 other events of larceny and fraud (Inciardi, 1986). Self-report surveys find that heroin users report financing their habits largely through "acquisitive crime" (Jarvis & Parker, 1989; Mott, 1986). Parker and Newcombe (1987) studied crime patterns and heroin use in the English community of Wirral, located in northwest England. They found that many heroin users were from the poor sections of the community and were young. The researchers were also able to divide their sample into three groups: (1) the largest group, consisting of young offenders who were not known to be using heroin but were highly criminally active, (2) heroin users who engaged in considerable acquisitive crime, but were involved in this type of crime prior to their heroin addiction, and (3) heroin users who started engaging in acquisitive crime after developing their habit in order to support the habit. The Parker–Newcombe investigation suggests that some heroin addicts do support their habit through crime.

Ball, Shaffer, and Nurco (1983) found that heroin addicts committed more money-producing crime when they were addicted compared with times when they were not. Still, it may be misleading to examine the heroin–crime relationship in isolation without considering the possible interactions between polydrug use and crime, or to conclude that heroin addiction causes crime. All we can say with some confidence at this point is that those who use heroin also seem to be deeply involved in money-producing crime. Heroin users, however, may not be driven to crime by the needs of their addiction. Heroin users, particularly polydrug users, may represent a segment of society that runs counter to society's rules and expectations in multiple ways, drug use and larceny among them. It may well be that most heroin-addicted criminals were involved in crime before they became addicted. Research by Faupel (1991) does support this hypothesis. However, studies also suggest that, although many heroin users have criminal records prior to their addiction, their criminal activity increases substantially during periods of heavy drug consumption (Faupel, 1991). Furthermore, polydrug users tend to switch from drug to drug, depending on what is available and inexpensive at the time, and do not seem physiologically desperate for any one particular drug. They simply substitute one drug for the other. Overall, the relationship between heroin use and criminal behavior is a complex one and varies throughout the addict's career.

Fentanyl

Fentanyl, first synthesized in Belgium in the late 1950s (under the trade name of Sublimaze), is highly similar to heroin in its biological and psychological effects. Fentanyl is a synthetic opiate about 30 to 50 times stronger than heroin (Drug Enforcement Administration, 2014b). In 2013 and 2014, communities in the Northeast and Midwest reported a spike in overdose deaths due to fentanyl and it derivatives (Drug Enforcement Administration, 2014b). Users have overdosed from heroin mixed with fentanyl largely because they believe they are buying only heroin.

Fentanyl is normally produced as a powder, and, on the market, it is often mixed with heroin and to a lesser extent with cocaine. It may be administered by intravenous injection, smoked, or snorted, but intravenous injection is currently the preferred method. An intravenous dose of fentanyl hydrochloride for pain relief is about 45 micrograms, depending on the weight of the user, but careless use can lead to an overdose and possible death. Over 12 different analogues of fentanyl have been produced clandestinely and identified in the U.S. drug traffic trade.

Other Narcotic Drugs

Other drugs that are often classified as narcotics include thebaine, codeine, morphine, hydromorphone, oxycodone, and hydrocodone. Thebaine is chemically similar to both morphine and codeine, but generally produces high rather than depressant effects. It is considered a Schedule II drug. Hydromorphone (Dilaudid®) is a powerful analgesic that is sold in tablet or injectable forms as a painkiller, and may substitute for heroin or morphine. Oxycodone is similar to codeine but more powerful. It is often marketed in combination with aspirin (Percodan®) or acetaminophen (OxyContin®, Percocet®) for the relief of pain. Hydrocodone is an orally active analgesic slightly less powerful than morphine, and is an important ingredient in the opioid pain killers, such as Vicodin®, Lorcet®, and Lortab®.

Although oxycodone products have been illicitly abused for 30 years, the oxycodone-based derivative OxyContin® and the hydrocodone-based derivative Vicodin® have been the two controlled prescription drugs most commonly used in recent years, especially by young people. In 2014, 3.3 percent of high school seniors reported they had taken OxyContin® illegally over the past year, and 4.8 percent said they had taken Vicodin® illegally over the past year (Johnston et al., 2015). The latest available figures indicate that 11 to 12 million Americans (age 12 or older) reported nonmedical use of prescription opioid painkillers in 2010 (Centers for Disease Control and Prevention, 2011a; Wright et al., 2014) (see again **Box 16-1**). Moreover, the opioid analgesics, especially OxyContin® and Vicodin®, were involved in about three of every four pharmaceutical overdose deaths (16,651) in 2010 (Centers for Disease Control and Prevention, 2013b). Some data indicate that opioid painkillers kill more Americans than heroin and cocaine combined (Centers for Disease Control and Prevention, 2011b; Drug Enforcement Administration, 2014b). Because of their importance in the illegal drug market, we will cover the two most common opioid analgesics in more detail in the next section.

OxyContin® and Vicodin®

OxyContin® and Vicodin® are narcotics (opioids) that have the properties of a powerful analgesic for pain control. OxyContin® and Vicodin® are prescription opioid pain medications that have effects similar to heroin when taken in doses or in ways other than prescribed (National Institute on Drug Abuse, 2014b). Both pain medications are drugs that continue to grow in popularity among young people. Most teenagers who abuse prescription drugs are given them for free by a friend or relative (National Institute on Drug Abuse, 2014c).

The drugs are chemically classified as an opiate agonist because they provide pain relief by acting on opioid receptors in the spinal cord and brain. OxyContin® was approved in 1995 by the Food and Drug Administration for use as an analgesic in persons with moderate to severe pain requiring several days of relief or more. It is a semisynthetic opioid synthesized from thebaine which is found in the opium poppy. Vicodin®, although heavily prescribed because of its effectiveness as a pain reducer for moderate to severe pain, has gone through a controversial history with the FDA and has yet to receive approval. Fans of the television show *House* saw the main character, a brilliant but flawed physician, popping the tablets on a consistent basis to manage the pain he experienced from a degenerative disease. Both OxyContin® and Vicodin® come generally in tablet form, but some abusers crush the tablets and sniff the powder or dissolve the tablets in water for injection. Sniffing the drugs is extremely dangerous as it may rapidly cause problems in breathing.

The pharmacological effects of OxyContin® and Vicodin® are highly similar to those of heroin, and consequently tend to be attractive to the same abuser population. However, the direction of abuse often begins with the narcotic pain reducer and then move to the less expensive heroin, as mentioned above. Both drugs are currently classified as Schedule II by the U.S. Drug Enforcement Administration. The estimated number of emergency department visits for nonmedical use of opioids has increased by 81 percent between 2007 and 2011 (Drug Enforcement Administration, 2014b).

OxyContin® and Vicodin® abuse are by far the most prevalent and widespread abuse of all the opioids and prescription drugs in the United States, and they show no signs of declining at this time (Cicero, Inciardi, & Muñoz, 2005; National Institute on Drug Abuse, 2014c). Recent research indicates that Vicodin® is currently far more often prescribed (and probably more abused) than OxyContin® or oxycodone-based drugs (Wright et al., 2014). Part of this observed shift in popularity is probably due to the fact that, in an effort to control the amount of abuse of the drug, OxyContin® was chemically reformulated in 2010 to make it more difficult to abuse and less potent in psychoactive properties for the abuser.

OxyContin®, Vicodin®, and Crime

OxyContin® and Vicodin® abuse have led to a significant increase in the number of pharmacy robberies, thefts, fraudulent prescriptions, and health care fraud incidents during the early 2000s (National Drug Intelligence Center, 2001; Simeone, 2014). In recent years, doctor shopping and prescription diversion of OxyContin® and Vicodin® have increased significantly. The prescriptions are often obtained through what is called "doctor shopping" and improper prescription practices by physicians. Doctor shopping refers to the practice of individuals visiting numerous doctors, sometimes in several states, to acquire large amounts of the drug to use or sell to others. Over the period 2004 to 2011, the number of prescriptions for opioids increased by approximately 146 percent (Simeone, 2014). In 2012 oxycodone-based (mostly OxyContin®) products constituted 32.56 percent of all prescriptions diverted for illegal use (Simeone, 2014). In that same year, hydrocodone-based products (mostly Vicodin®) accounted for 32.70 percent of all prescriptions diverted (Simeone, 2014). Because of the enormous profits involved, transnational criminal organizations, street gangs, and other criminal groups have become increasingly involved in the transportation, distribution, and selling of illegally obtained prescription opioids (Drug Enforcement Administration, 2014b). In addition, "rogue pain management clinics (commonly referred to as 'pill mills') contribute to the extensive availability of illicit pharmaceuticals in the United States (Drug Enforcement Administration, 2014b, p. 6), as illustrated in **Box 16-1**. These operations are largely cash only businesses that do not see patients or perform any kind of medical checkup; they simply hand out pills for cash.

THE CLUB DRUGS: SEDATIVE HYPNOTIC COMPOUNDS

Rohypnol, gamma-hydroxybutyrate (GHB), ecstasy (MDMA), ketamine, and methamphetamine have been considered the "club drugs" in recent years (Maxwell, 2004). They are called "club drugs" because they are most often consumed at teenage and young adult nightclubs, raves, or parties. Although club drugs have attracted considerable national attention, they comprise a relatively small proportion of the drug problem in the United States. Since we covered ecstasy and methamphetamine earlier in the chapter, we shall concentrate on the three sedative hypnotics in this section: ketamine, Rohypnol, and GHB. Although popular during the late 1990s and early 2000s, only a small fraction of teens (less than 1%) consume these three drugs currently (Johnston et al., 2015). However, their popularity may increase again in future years.

Ketamine

Ketamine, also called K, Special K, Super Acid, LA Coke, or cat valium, is a dissociative anesthetic with analgesic and amnestic properties. It was developed in 1962 to replace PCP in veterinary medicine. The drug was first manufactured in the United States in 1960s as Ketalar (Copeland & Dillon, 2005). Use of ketamine as a surgical anesthetic gained significant popularity on the battlefields of Vietnam (Copeland & Dillon, 2005). Much of the ketamine sold on the street in the United States is probably intended for veterinary clinics or is imported from overseas. When sold illicitly, it is often converted from a liquid to a powder—similar in appearance to cocaine and heroin—or tablets. Reports have found that ketamine is increasingly being used in social rather than medical and scientific settings in many parts of the world, especially the United Kingdom and Australia (Copeland & Dillon, 2005). It is often considered a club drug or dance drug because it is used at "raves" or dance parties, a popular scene for teenagers in the late 1990s. Ketamine is also frequently used as a key component in fake MDMA (ecstasy) tablets.

Its chemical structure is similar to PCP but is much less potent and produces less confusion, irrationality, and violent behavior than PCP (Drug Enforcement Administration, 2005). As drug of abuse, ketamine can be administered orally, snorted, or injected. It sometimes is sprinkled on marijuana and smoked. High doses produce analgesia, amnesia, and coma.

Users report sensations ranging from a pleasant feeling of floating or being separated from their bodies (National Institute on Drug Abuse, 2005). It carries slang names such as jet, super acid, cat Valium, and honey oil. Approximately 50 percent of ketamine users have had a bad experience with the drug called the "K-hole" (Copeland & Dillon, 2005).

Ketamine is odorless and tasteless, so it can be added to beverages or food without being detected. Ketamine, along with GHB, are considered "date rape" drugs because it can be given to unsuspecting victims, inducing amnesia and a helpless physical state. Under these conditions, sexual assault can be carried out with the victim being unable to remember the incident.

Gamma Hydroxybutyrate (GHB)

GHB (also known as liquid ecstasy, scoop, liquid X, grievous bodily harm, or Georgia home boy) is a powerful and fast-acting drug most often taken by young users as a pleasure enhancer that produces a rapid state of intoxication. It is usually consumed orally, either as a grainy white- or sandy-colored powder that is often dissolved in alcohol, or as a liquid sold in small bottles. GHB is produced primarily in clandestine laboratories, and consequently there is no guarantee of quality or purity, making its psychoactive effects unpredictable. The drug can be easily produced by combining gamma-butyrolactone (GBL) with either potassium hydroxide or sodium hydroxide in a container. Recipes or kits for making GHB are sold over the Internet. GHB is also marketed as an antidepressant that suppresses feelings of depression and anxiety, and is promoted and sold on the Internet as such. Prior to 1990, the drug was freely available in health food stores across the United States. However, in 1990, the Federal Drug Administration (FDA) banned GHB and does not approve the drug for any use at the present time. However, a pharmaceutical formulation of the drug is currently being developed for the treatment of cataplexy, a serious and debilitating disease.

Psychoactive effects of GHB begin to take effect within 15 to 30 minutes after consumption, and, depending on purity and dosage, may last as long as six hours. It is often used in conjunction with other drugs, especially alcohol. GHB has many severe and unpredictable side effects, such as nausea, drowsiness, vomiting, delusions, depression, vertigo (dizziness), hallucinations, seizures, respiratory distress, loss of consciousness, slowed heart rate, lowered blood pressure, amnesia, and coma (Office of National Drug Control Policy, 1999a). It also interferes with circulation, motor coordination, and balance, and, at higher doses (two to four grams), it produces considerable problems in motor and speech control. At these high doses, GHB usually produces a very deep sleep, resembling a coma. The drug also produces anterograde amnesia, a condition in which events that occurred during the time the drug was in effect are forgotten. In addition, the drug has increasingly been involved in poisonings, overdoses, and fatalities (National Institute on Drug Abuse, 1999).

GHB is tasteless and odorless, and mixes easily with alcohol or any nonalcoholic drink. Because it can be mixed with food and drinks without detection, and because of its ability to sedate and intoxicate unsuspecting victims, GHB has been connected to crime in recent years. It is sometimes used in the commission of sexual assault, and it often plays a role in "date rape." It is also used in some instances to pave the way for robbing heavily sedated or unconscious victims.

Because of GHB's increasing use in sexual assaults, the Date-Rape Drug Prohibition Act was enacted in January 2000, specifically to target GHB. Congress found that the abuse of illicit gamma hydroxybutyrate acid was an imminent hazard to public safety, and moved to amend the federal *Controlled Substances Act* to include the drug as an illegal substance. The act also established a special unit of the Drug Enforcement Administration to assess the abuse of and trafficking in GHB, Rohypnol, ketamine, other controlled substances, and other so-called "designer drugs" whose use has been associated with sexual assault.

Rohypnol

The Drug-Induced Rape Prevention and Punishment Act of 1996 was enacted into federal law specifically in response to the use of Rohypnol (generic name flunitrazepam), another club drug that can be used to sexually assault incapacitated individuals. It can mentally and physically incapacitate the victim. The law makes it a crime to give someone a controlled substance without his or her knowledge and with the intent to commit a crime. The law further imposes a penalty of up to 20 years for the distribution and importation of one gram or more of Rohypnol. Simple possession is punishable by up to three years in prison and a fine.

Since 1999, Rohypnol tablets have been manufactured to turn blue in a drink to increase visibility and thus more visually detectable to potential victims (Office of National Drug Control Policy, 2003a). However, the noncolored tablets continue to be on the market. Furthermore, persons who intend to commit a sexual assault may try to serve blue tropical drinks and punches so that the blue dye in the drug can be inconspicuous.

Slang names for Rohypnol include date-rape drug, circles, roofies, Mexican valium, roach-2, forget-me drug, forget pill, or wolfies. Rohypnol is popular among youth because of its low cost. Rohypnol can be ground into a powder and snorted. Similar to GHB, Rohypnol is tasteless and odorless, and can be dissolved in liquids, but not as easily as GHB, and is also sometimes used by bodybuilders for its alleged anabolic effects. It can be taken orally, snorted, or injected. It is often combined with alcohol or used as a remedy for the depression that often follows a stimulant high. The effects of Rohypnol usually begin in about 15 minutes after administration, and may last for more than 12 hours. In addition, the drug is detectable in urine for up to 72 hours after ingestion (Office of National Drug Control Policy, 2003a).

Lower doses of Rohypnol can cause muscle relaxation. In higher doses, it can cause loss of muscle control, loss of consciousness, and, when combined with alcohol, anterograde amnesia. When combined with alcohol, as is often done, it can be deadly. Chemically, the drug is similar to Valium but 10 times more powerful. Rohypnol is legally manufactured in over 80 countries as a prescribed sedative for the short-term treatment of severe sleep disorders, especially in Europe, but it is neither manufactured nor approved for sale in the United States.

The benzodiazepines include chlordiazepoxide (Librium®), diszepam (Valium®), oxazepam (Serax®), and clorazepate dipotassium (Tranxene®), all of which are marketed legally and prescribed as antianxiety tranquilizers, or to treat muscle spasms or convulsions. The most common side effects are confusion, drowsiness, and loss of coordination.

ALCOHOL

Despite the public concern over the other drug categories, the number one substance of abuse has been, and continues to be, alcohol (ethanol, ethyl alcohol, grain alcohol). It is also the substance most widely used by teenagers (Johnston et al., 2015). "Despite recent declines, two out of every three students (66%) have consumed alcohol more than just a few sips by the end of high school, and over a quarter (27%) have done so by 8th grade" (Johnston et al., 2015, p. 7). Furthermore, in 2014 one half of high school seniors and one in nine 8th graders reported having been drunk at least once in their life. In 2013, rates of binge drinking were 0.8 percent among 12- and 13-year-olds, 4.5 percent for 14- and 15-year-olds, and 13.1 percent for 16- and 17-year olds (SAMHSA, 2014). Binge drinking is defined as having five or more drinks within a very brief period of time or on one occasion. It should be emphasized, however, that although alcohol has been widely used by youth for a very long time in American history, there has been a discernible decline in alcohol abuse by teenagers in recent years. Beginning in 2002 and up to and including 2014, there has been a steady decline in drunkenness and alcohol use by high school students and youth in general.

All 50 states, the District of Columbia, and Puerto Rico have created by law a threshold making it illegal to drive with a BAC of 0.08 or higher. In addition, all 50 states have an age requirement that it is illegal to consume alcohol before reaching the age of 21. However, most underage persons obtain and drink alcohol illegally. In general, legal restrictions on alcohol are less stringent compared to other substances, so legal consequences occur only under specific circumstances, such as driving while intoxicated (Dematteo et al., 2015).

According to the Substance Abuse and Mental Health Services Administration (2014), more than half (52.2%) of Americans, aged 12 or older, are current drinkers of alcohol, representing approximately 136.9 million Americans. Overall, 16.5 million (6.5%) were considered heavy drinkers as defined as binge drinking on five or more days in the past month. Most of the binge and heavy drinkers were young adults between the ages of 18 and 25. Although, alcohol is preferred by teenagers over other drugs, marijuana is a close second.

According to DAWN (Office of Applied Studies, 2004), 23 percent of all drug-related emergency department visits involved the effects of alcohol in persons under age 21 in 2003. Nearly one-third of the alcohol-related visits were because the youth—especially those between the ages of 12 and 17—had combined alcohol with other drugs (SAMHSA, 2014). Marijuana (49%) and cocaine (22%) were the drugs most frequently found in combination with alcohol. Methamphetamine (8%) was also found with some frequency in these visits. There were no gender differences in alcohol-related visits to emergency departments in 2003.

The usual way to determine if an individual is intoxicated is by measuring his or her blood-alcohol concentration, abbreviated BAC. A BAC of 0.10 percent means there are 100 milligrams of alcohol per 100 milliliters of blood. For example, a 165-pound man would reach a BAC of 0.10 percent if he drank about five drinks within one hour on an empty stomach. (A drink is defined as one-and-a-half ounces of liquor, a 12-ounce beer, or a five-ounce glass of wine.)

Alcohol is responsible for more deaths and violence (it is the third major cause of death) than all other drugs combined. In 2012, 10,322 people were killed in alcohol-impaired driving crashes, accounting for nearly one-third (31%) of all traffic-related deaths in the United States (National Highway Traffic Safety Administration, 2013). In addition, in 4,211 of these fatal crashes, the driver was age 16 to 20 and had a BAC in excess of 0.08.

Psychological Effects

The social, psychological, and psychobiological effects of excessive alcohol use can be just as destructive to the individual, his or her family, and society in general, as addictive substance abuse. Similar to the heroin addict, the alcoholic can develop a strong psychological and physical dependence on alcohol. Society's attitudes toward alcohol are dramatically different from its attitudes toward other drugs of abuse, however. In virtually every part of the United States, it is legal and socially acceptable for adults to consume alcohol. In public, drinking behavior is generally unregulated unless it involves heavy intoxication and correspondingly unacceptable conduct (e.g., disturbing the peace or operating a motor vehicle). In private, one can get as drunk as one wishes, a privilege technically not granted with respect to other drugs even though numerous individuals use illegal substances in nonpublic places.

The psychoactive effects of alcohol are extremely complex. Miczek and his colleagues (1994) write that the effects of alcohol depend on "a host of interacting pharmacologic, endocrinologic, neurobiologic, genetic, situational, environmental, social, and cultural determinants" (p. 382). Consequently, we can provide only a cursory review of this complicated topic here. At low doses (e.g., two or four ounces of whiskey), alcohol seems to act as a stimulant on the central nervous system. Initially, it appears to affect the inhibitory chemical process of nervous system transmission, producing feelings of euphoria, good cheer, and social and physical warmth. In moderate and high quantities, however, alcohol begins to depress the excitatory processes of the central nervous system, as well as its inhibitory processes. Consequently, the individual's neuromuscular coordination and visual acuity are reduced, and he or she perceives pain and fatigue. The ability to concentrate is also impaired. Very often, self-confidence increases, and the person becomes more daring, sometimes foolishly so. It is believed that alcohol at moderate levels begins to "numb" the higher brain centers that process cognitive information, especially judgment and abstract thought. It should be emphasized at this point that the levels of intoxication are not necessarily dependent on the amount of alcohol ingested; as for other psychoactive drugs, the effects depend on a myriad of interacting variables.

Alcohol, Crime, and Delinquency

The belief that alcohol is a major cause of crime appears to be deeply embedded in American society. Surveys, for example, suggest that over 50 percent of the population is convinced that alcohol is a major factor in crimes of violence (Critchlow, 1986). This pervasive belief appears to be based on the premise that alcohol instigates aggressive conduct in some individuals, or somehow diminishes the checks and balances of nonaggressive, nonviolent behavior.

As noted by DeMatteo et al. (2015), "Empirical studies examining the relationship between alcohol use and crime typically either use data that are from correctional samples or experimentally manipulate the presence/amount of alcohol consumed by participants in order to observe its effect on behaviors related to criminal activity..." (pp. 334–335). In this section, we will focus on alcohol abuse and dependence found in offenders and prisoners in correctional populations. For example, Fazel, Bains, and Doll (2006) conducted a systematic review of studies that measured the prevalence of drug and alcohol abuse and dependence in male and female prisoners. They examined thirteen different studies with a total of 7,563 prisoners. The researchers found the prevalence for alcohol abuse and dependence ranged from 18 to 30 percent in male prisoners and from 10 to 24 percent in female prisoners, significantly higher than found in the general population.

Roizen (1997), summarizing the research on alcohol and violence, found that up to 86 percent of homicide offenders had been drinking at the time of the offense. Roizen further discovered that 60 percent of sexual offenders, 37 percent of assault offenders, 57 percent of males in marital violence, and 13 percent of child abusers had also been drinking at the time of the crime. **Table 16-6** identifies the percentage of adult offenders who admitted to drinking at the time of their offense (in 1996). Outside of public order crimes, a higher percentage of offenders reported drinking at the time of violent offenses than during the other offense categories. About seven out

TABLE 16-6	Percent of Offenders Drinking at the Time of the Offense, 1996			
Offense	Adults on Probation	Convicted Offenders in Local Jails	Convicted Offenders in State Prisons	Convicted Offenders in Federal Prisons
All offenses	399	395	323	11
Violent offenses	407	406	375	20.4
Property offenses	185	328	318	8.1
Drug offenses	163	288	180	8.2
Public order offenses	751	560	430	13.1

Source: Greenfeld, L. A. (1998, April). Alcohol and crime: An analysis of national data on the prevalence of alcohol involvement in crime. Washington, DC: U.S. Department of Justice.

of 10 alcohol-involved incidents of violence occurred in a residence, and most of the incidents (about two-thirds) are simple assaults. In addition, two-thirds of victims who suffered violence by an intimate reported that alcohol had been a factor. Ninety percent of alcohol-involved incidents of violence occur off campus (Greenfeld, 1998).

Many studies of adolescents have also concluded that alcohol use and violent behavior are linked (Swahn & Donovan, 2004). Several studies also indicate that alcohol use is more common among violent delinquents compared with nonviolent delinquents (Huizinga & Jakob-Chien, 1998; Saner & Ellickson, 1996). Dawkins (1997), on the basis of data collected on 312 youthful offenders at a public juvenile facility, reports that alcohol use is more strongly and consistently related to both violent and nonviolent offenses than is marijuana or other drugs. One study found that even after antecedent peer and family risk factors were adjusted for, young people who abused alcohol were much more likely to engage in violent offenses than those who did not misuse alcohol (Ferguson, Lynskey, & Horwood, 1996). According to Webb et al. (2002), alcohol use and serious delinquency are strongly associated, yet the direction of causality is unclear. Does alcohol cause violence, or do violent adolescents drink alcohol?

Furthermore, numerous other factors must be taken into account. For example, cultural differences may play a significant role in the alcohol-aggression relationship. Cognitive factors, such as a person's expectations or cognitions, also influence how he or she responds to alcohol. Alcohol serves as a cue for acting intoxicated and doing things one normally would not do. In other words, a person may act the way he or she believes alcohol makes one act. It should further be emphasized that not all adolescents who drink heavily engage in violence and aggression. Many adolescents use alcohol experimentally, sometimes frequently, and may binge drink, without engaging in antisocial, violent, or delinquent behavior.

In summary, the evidence is quite clear that approximately one-third of all offenders who commit violent crime were drinking at the time of offense, and many were highly intoxicated. In their careful review of the research literature, Reiss and Roth (1993, p. 185) conclude, "In studies of prison inmates, those classified as 'heavy' or 'problem' drinkers had accumulated more previous arrests for violent crime, and reported higher average frequencies of assaults than did other inmates." The National Institute on Alcohol Abuse and Alcoholism (1990, p. 92) asserts, "In both animals and human studies, alcohol more than any other drug, has been linked with a high incidence of violence and aggression." However, the link does not automatically mean that alcohol causes violence. It is most likely that under the influence of alcohol, individuals prone to be aggressive, violent, and antisocial are more likely to be more aggressive, violent, and antisocial. Alcohol may *facilitate* their aggressive tendencies. The available evidence does not allow cogent conclusions that alcohol makes normally nonviolent people act violently.

SUBSTANCE ABUSE AND VIOLENCE

There is little evidence that alcohol or drug use *cause* violence in adolescent offenders (White, Moffitt, Earls, Robins, & Silva, 1990). Research indicates that aggressive and violent behavior in childhood generally *precedes* the initiation into drug and alcohol abuse, at least in boys. Aggressive behavior in the early school grades and poor school achievement are two of the best predictors of substance abuse later in adolescence and adulthood (Fothergill & Ensminger, 2006). On the other hand, serious male delinquents (including the most violent offenders) by far show the highest rates of consumption of alcohol, marijuana, and other drugs. Girls who are considered shy in early grades are more likely to have high levels of educational attainment and are at low risk of substance or alcohol abuse in adolescence or adulthood (Fothergill & Ensminger, 2006).

Many developmental psychologists contend that substance abuse often takes place in an orderly sequence, starting with tobacco use, followed by marijuana, and then hard drug use as a last step (Kandel, Yamaguichi, & Chen, 1992; White et al., 1990). This gives some credence to those who consider marijuana a "gateway drug" and urge zero tolerance, even for its possession in small amounts. However, before any adolescent becomes dependent on alcohol, tobacco, or any illicit substance, he or she passes through a stage of **experimental substance use** (abbreviated **ESU**)

(Petraitis, Flay, & Miller, 1995). An unknown number of youth experiment but do not continue with regular use. Events and variables that determine who experiments with substances and alcohol during adolescence and who continues are multiple, including the availability of drugs, family history, peer pressures, social attitudes concerning drug use, the social and economic context, and individual differences in biopsychological/psychological makeup. In addition, drug use and experimentation are strongly correlated with cognitions (attitudes and beliefs) about drugs. Adolescent substance and alcohol abuse is not a passive, one-dimensional process caused exclusively by social influence but is strongly influenced by subjective choice made by the youth (Getz & Bray, 2005). For example, rates of drug use are much higher in populations that do not perceive great risk of harm than in populations that do perceive great risk of harm. Thus, explanations for the sustained heavy use of marijuana in adolescents partly center on the belief that there is very little harm in the use of the drug. Due to the enormous complexity involved in ESU, many theories have been proposed to explain the phenomenon. However, very few of them have ever been empirically tested or provided cogent explanations for why some youth experiment with drugs, and others do not.

SUMMARY AND CONCLUSIONS

This chapter reviewed the relationship between crime and a number of drugs commonly associated with criminal behavior. Four major drug categories were identified: (1) the hallucinogens, (2) the stimulants, (3) the opiate narcotics, and (4) the sedative-hypnotics. Rather than discuss most of the drugs in each category, we considered only those commonly believed to be connected with criminal conduct. Moreover, we did not examine the crimes of drug production, possession, or trafficking except to acknowledge that these are critical criminal activities that must be addressed. We are mainly concerned with whether the substance itself facilitates or instigates illegal action, especially violence, and what damage the drug does to the user. In other words, are persons under the influence of marijuana, cocaine, or heroin more violent than they are normally? And how does marijuana affect the health of users? Or, to what extent does alcohol directly contribute to loss of control or reduce self-regulatory mechanisms?

Because juvenile drug use is considered a major social problem, we discussed its prevalence and some of the characteristics of juvenile substance abusers early in the chapter. In addition, throughout the chapter, we distinguished between juvenile and adult drug use when data and research findings were available. Furthermore, we emphasized that juveniles often have access to prescription medication, which may be obtained illegally through pain clinics, physicians, pharmacists, or their home medicine cabinets. Marijuana is the drug for which most juveniles are arrested, but there is troubling use and abuse by juveniles of prescription drugs, inhalants, and "club drugs" as well. There has been a 10-year decline in arrests relating to cocaine and opium use, but synthetic narcotics—particularly synthetic marijuana—may be increasing. Girls are less likely than boys to have drug and alcohol problems, and their experiences with drugs differ. However, their arrest rates for drug-related behaviors are increasing, though it is still far lower than the male rate. Persistent drug use in juveniles is associated with poor academic performance, high-risk behaviors, serious health problems, and delinquency.

Cannabis, which includes marijuana and hashish, is a relatively mild hallucinogen with few psychological or physiological side effects. No significant relationship between cannabis use and crime has been consistently reported in the research literature. If anything, marijuana seems to reduce the likelihood of violence, since its psychoactive ingredient, THC, induces muscle weakness and promotes feelings of lethargy. THC potency also has increased in drugs available today. The use by teenagers is of growing concern because of the mind-altering nature of the drug, its disinhibiting effects, and possible effects on other behaviors, such as driving. Synthetic marijuana is widely available and has outpaced the laws that are intended to control it.

Amphetamines and cocaine (especially crack) represented the stimulant group. Most users do not participate in crime other than the possession or sale of these drugs. Similar to marijuana, amphetamines are plentiful and inexpensive. However, there are some documented cases in which heavy users of amphetamines entered psychological states that presumably predisposed them to violence and paranoia. In addition, several studies have found correlations between violent offenders and a history of amphetamine abuse. As in all correlations, however, it is difficult to determine what contributes to what. Chronic amphetamine use has potential strong dangerous side effects if used improperly, or used in combination with other drugs of abuse. Cocaine, a natural drug that grows only in certain parts of the world, has traditionally been quite expensive. In recent years, the drug has become widely available and its cost less prohibitive. There is no strong evidence that cocaine generally renders one more violent, more out of control, or more likely to engage in property crimes, however.

We discussed heroin as the representative of the opiate narcotics. In recent years, use of heroin has been described as an epidemic in some states. Like most other narcotics, heroin appears to be highly addictive, particularly in the sense that it creates a strong psychological dependency. Narcotics in general are so addictive and so expensive that substantial funds are needed to support a user's habit. Thus, some researchers have found a moderate correlation between narcotics and various income-generating crimes. On the other hand, others have noted that most addicts turned to drugs after they had developed criminal patterns.

Of all the drugs reviewed, alcohol—representing the sedative-hypnotic group—shows the strongest relationship with violent offenses, such as rape, homicide, and assault. At intermediate and high levels, alcohol appears to impair or disrupt the brain operations responsible for self-control. Alcohol may also impair information processing, thereby leading a person to misjudge social cues and encouraging overreactions to a perceived threat. However, it is likely that violent behavior associated with alcohol use is a joint function of pharmacological effects, cognitive expectancies, and situational influences. If the individual expects that alcohol will make him or her act aggressively, and if the social environment provides appropriate cues, aggression or violent behavior will be facilitated. The National Institute on Alcohol Abuse and Alcoholism (1997, p. 4) concluded in its extensive review of the relevant research literature that "alcohol apparently may increase the risk of violent behavior only for certain individuals or subpopulations and only under some situations and social/cultural influences." While the relationship between alcohol and violence clearly exists, the nature of that relationship is largely unknown. Does alcohol cause violence, or are violent people drawn to alcohol? No drug *directly causes* violence simply through its pharmacological action (Morgan & Zimmer, 1997).

In conclusion, the relationships between crime and all the drugs discussed in this chapter are complicated, involving interactions among numerous pharmacological, social, and psychological variables. Additional studies employing well-designed methodology are greatly needed to understand the many possible influences of psychoactive drugs on human behavior, particularly criminal behavior.

At this point in our knowledge, substance abuse appears to be more of a health problem to those who misuse drugs than a "crime problem." On the other hand, we cannot ignore the fact that there is a drug–crime connection, as the tripartite conceptual model proposed by Goldstein (1985) indicates. Goldstein conceived of drug-related crimes as being psychopharmacologically driven, systemic, or economically compulsive. Those who advocate radical changes in government policy—such as decriminalization or legalization of certain drugs—argue that crimes characterized by the systemic and economically compulsive components would likely decrease. This conclusion reflects the continuing controversy over the "right" public policy to adopt with respect to drugs. Although this chapter has not focused on the residual effects of the nation's war on drugs—such as its effect on public health, economically disadvantaged groups, prison populations, and individual civil liberties—these effects also cannot be ignored.

Relating to the psychopharmacologically driven category proposed by Goldstein, we stress that, from the psychological perspective, it is unlikely that drugs "cause" people to engage in criminal activity. On the other hand, some drugs clearly allow some people to disengage from their usual constraints against antisocial conduct, including violence. Individuals who are chronic, persistent criminals often are polydrug users, but again it is unlikely that the drugs they ingest directly cause them to engage in criminal activity. It is more likely they were criminally prone prior to and independent of polydrug use.

Key Concepts

Controlled substance	Psychoactive drugs
Dependence	Sedative-hypnotic compounds
Drug courts	Semisynthetic narcotics
Experimental substance use (ESU)	Stimulants
Hallucinogens	Synthetic marijuana
Natural narcotics	Synthetic narcotics
Opiate narcotics	Tolerance
Psychedelics	Tripartite conceptual model

Review Questions

1. What are the four main categories of drugs discussed in this chapter? List their main effects, and provide one example of a drug from each category.
2. Describe and explain briefly Goldstein's tripartite conceptual model for understanding the drug–crime relationship.
3. Summarize and discuss the six main conclusions researchers have reached in recent years regarding the relationship between drugs and crime. When relevant, provide illustrations from the various categories of drugs.

4. Briefly list the common psychological effects of the following: cocaine, MDMA, heroin, alcohol, methamphetamine.
5. Describe Rohypnol and gamma hydroxybutyrate (GHB). What are they used for? What are some of the effects? How might they be involved in crime?
6. Of all the substances (drugs and alcohol) discussed in the chapter, which substance is most closely connected to crime? Why do you think this is?

GLOSSARY

adjudicative competence The ability to participate in a variety of court proceedings. See also **competency to stand trial.**

adolescent-limited (AL) offenders Individuals who usually demonstrate delinquent or antisocial behavior only during their teen years and then stop offending when they reach adulthood.

advantageous comparison An offender's process of convincing himself that his values and ways of life are superior to those of his victims; used to explain the cognitive restructuring that occurs in terrorism.

aggression, hostile Aggressive behavior characterized by the specific intent to cause the target discomfort or pain.

aggression, instrumental Aggressive behavior characterized by the intent to gain material or financial rewards from the target.

aggression Behavior perpetrated or attempted with the intention of harming one or more individuals physically or psychologically or to destroy an object.

aggressive (sadistic) child sex offender An adult drawn to children for both sexual and aggressive (violent) purposes.

amnesia Complete or partial memory loss of an incident, series of incidents, or some aspects of life's experiences.

amygdala A small almond-shaped group of nerve cells that plays a major role in learning, memory, and the experiencing of emotions; appears to be related to aggression, violence.

anger rape A rape situation, identified by Groth, in which an offender uses more force than necessary for compliance and engages in a variety of sexual acts that are particularly degrading or humiliating to the victim.

antisocial behavior Clinical term reserved for serious habitual behavior, especially that involving direct harm to others.

antisocial personality disorder (APD) A disorder characterized by a history of continuous behavior in which the rights of others are violated.

arson Any willful or malicious burning or attempt to burn, with or without intent to defraud, a dwelling house, public building, motor vehicle, aircraft, or personal property of another.

assault, aggravated Inflicting, or attempting to inflict, bodily injury on another person, with the intent to inflict serious injury.

assault The intentional inflicting of bodily injury on another person, or the attempt to inflict such injury.

attachment theory A theory which states that infants have a strong need to establish close emotional bonds with significant others in their social environments. According to the theory, the nature of this emotional bond determines the quality of social relationships later in life.

attention deficit hyperactivity disorder (ADHD) Traditionally considered a chronic neurobiological condition characterized by developmentally poor attention, impulsivity, and hyperactivity. More contemporary perspectives see the behavioral pattern as resulting in poor interpersonal skills and often in peer rejection.

authoritarian style The approach to parenting that sets a very rigid structure on the family setting and allows little decision making by the child.

authoritative style The approach to parenting that sets firm rules yet encourages the development of autonomy in the child.

authority homicide In the context of workplace violence, the killing of a supervisor or other person in authority by an employee.

avoidance learning A process whereby, if a person responds in time to a warning signal, he or she avoids painful or aversive stimuli.

barricade situation In hostage-taking scenarios, a situation in which an individual has fortified him or herself in a building or residence and threatens violence, typically to the hostages.

battered woman syndrome (BWS) A cluster of behavioral and psychological characteristics believed common to women who have been abused in relationships. Has questionable validity as a "syndrome" characterizing present victims and survivors of abuse. See also IPV.

behavior genetics Investigates the role genes play in the formation and development of behavior.

Behavioral Analysis Unit (BAU) A special unit within the National Center for the Analysis of Violent Crimes dedicated to investigating terrorism and violent crimes against children and adults.

Behavioral Science Unit (BSU) The first behaviorally focused investigative unit in the FBI established in the 1970s to provide assistance to law enforcement. Although the BSU initially was consulting on serial killings and serial rapes, its services were later expanded to cover other offenses.

behaviorism A perspective that focuses on observable, measurable behavior and argues that the social environment and learning arc the key determinants of human behavior.

biopsychologists Psychologists who study the biological aspects of behavior to determine which genetic and neurophysiological variables play a part. They generally see human behavior as the result of a complex interaction between the individual's physiological and social environment.

bioterrorism The category of terrorism that involves the use of bacteria, viruses, germs, and other agents. See also **NBC**.

boldness factor (fearless dominance) In psychopathy research, it is proposed as an additional feature of the psychopathic personality. See also **meanness factor**.

Brawner Rule A standard for evaluating the insanity defense that recognizes that the defendant suffers from a condition that substantially (1) affects mental or emotional processes, or (2) impairs behavior controls. Also called the ALI/Brawner Rule.

burglary The unlawful entry of a structure, with or without force, with intent to commit a felony or theft.

Bystander effect Often referred to as bystander apathy, it refers to the supported hypothesis that people will not interfere in a crime scene if other witnesses are present and able to interfere.

callous-unemotional traits Identified by Paul Frick and colleagues. Refers to a group of personality features indicating little feeling or empathy toward others and resulting in severe and chronic patterns of antisocial behavior.

caveat paragraph A section of the ALI/Brawner Rule that excludes abnormality manifested only by repeated criminal or antisocial conduct. It was specifically designed to disallow the insanity defense for psychopaths or persons diagnosed with antisocial personality disorder.

child delinquents Children between the ages of 7 and 12 who have committed or are accused of committing a criminal act.

classic mass murder A situation in which an individual enters a public place or barricades himself or herself inside a public building, such as a fast-food restaurant, and randomly kills patrons and other individuals.

classical (or Pavlovian) conditioning The process of learning to respond to a formerly neutral stimulus that has been paired with another stimulus that already elicits a response.

classical theory Theory of human behavior that emphasizes free will as a core concept.

clearance rate The proportion of reported crimes that have been "solved" through the arrest and turning over for prosecution of at least one person. Crimes also may be cleared through exceptional means, such as the death of a person about to be arrested.

coercion developmental theory The belief that punitive and coercive tactics employed by parents will encourage children to behave in a coercive manner and increase the likelihood of later aggressive behavior and family violence.

cognitions The internal processes that enable humans to imagine, to gain knowledge, to reason, and to evaluate. The attitudes, beliefs, values, and thoughts that people hold about the environment, relationships, and themselves.

cognitive processes Internal mental processes that enable humans to imagine, gain knowledge, reason, and evaluate information.

cognitive restructuring A psychological process that allows one to justify committing reprehensible actions; typically involves **moral justification, euphemistic language,** and **advantageous comparison.**

cognitive scripts model Rowell Huesmann's theory that social behavior in general and aggressive behavior in particular are controlled largely by cognitive scripts learned through daily experiences.

cognitive scripts Mental images of how one feels he or she should act in a variety of situations.

cognitive-neoassociation model Berkowitz's revision of his frustration-aggression hypothesis, in which the role of cognitions is recognized.

compensatory rapist An offender who rapes in response to an intense sexual arousal initiated by stimuli in the environment, often quite specific stimuli (e.g., dark-haired women). His main motive is to prove his sexual prowess.

competency to stand trial The legal requirement that a defendant is able to understand the proceedings and to help the attorney in preparing a defense.

concordance A term used in genetics to represent the degree to which related pairs of subjects both show a particular behavior or condition. It is usually expressed in percentages.

conduct disorder A diagnostic label used to identify children who demonstrate habitual misbehavior.

confirmation bias Tendency to look for evidence that confirms preexisting expectations or beliefs.

conformity perspective The theoretical position that humans are born basically good and generally try to do the right and just thing.

contagion effect (or copycat effect) A tendency for some people to model or copy a behavior or activity portrayed by the news or entertainment media.

controlled substance Any psychoactive drug or chemical substance whose availability is restricted, as designated by state or federal law.

crime rate In government statistics, the number of crimes known to police per 100,000 population.

crime scene profiling Development of a rough behavioral or psychological sketch of an offender based on clues identified at the crime scene.

crime scene signature Anything deliberately left by the offender at the scene of a crime, usually as a message to investigators. It may be a method of killing (e.g., type of ligature) or an item or behavior (e.g., a small doll; writing on a wall). Contrast to **psychological signature**.

crimes of obedience Illegal acts that are committed under the order of someone in authority.

criminal homicide A term that encompasses both murder and nonnegligent homicide, it is the intentional killing of another human being.

criminal psychopath A primary psychopath who engages in repetitive antisocial or criminal behavior.

criminality theme Applied to rapists, characterizes chronic offenders committing many other crimes and likely to recidivate. Regards victim as an object that must be incapacitated.

criminogenic need principle One of the components of RNR treatment, it refers to the fact that clinicians must identify needs in offenders that make them susceptible to future antisocial behavior. Substance abuse is an example of a criminogenic need.

criminology, psychiatric The branch of criminology that focuses on individual aspects of behavior, particularly internal forces and unconscious drives. Also called **forensic psychiatry.**

criminology, psychological The branch of criminology that examines the individual behavior and especially the mental processes involved in criminal behavior.

criminology, sociological The branch of criminology that examines the demographic, group, and societal variables related to crime.

criminology The multidisciplinary study of crime.

crossover offending Refers to the extent that an offender "crosses over" to selected victims regardless of age, gender, or physical characteristics.

cultural devaluation A process that occurs when a group or culture is selected by another group as a scapegoat or an ideological enemy.

culturally motivated terrorists Terrorists who are driven by fear of irreparable damage to their way of life, heritage, or culture done by an outside entity.

cumulative risk model The model that states that an accumulation of risk factors, rather than any one factor, leads to criminal or antisocial behavior. The factors may be biological, social, or psychological, but the more there are, the more likely an individual will act antisocially.

cyberbullying Sending or posting harmful or cruel text or images using the Internet or other digital communication devices. Primarily a problem with school-aged children and adolescents.

cybercrime Any illegal act that involves a computer system. Examples are hacking, computer intrusions, cyberstalking.

cyberharassment In some statutes, this is defined as communications in cyberspace that do not cross the threshold needed to qualify as cyberstalking; rather, cyberharassment is considered irritating to the receiver and if persistent may lead to civil suits, similar to harassment.

cyberstalking Threatening behavior or unwanted advances directed at another using the Internet or other forms of online communications.

cycle of violence hypothesis The belief that violence is likely to be perpetuated across generations among individuals who have experienced and witnessed violence in their families.

dark figure The number of crimes that go unreported in official crime data reports.

date or acquaintance rape A sexual assault that occurs within the context of a dating relationship or when rapist and victim know one another.

dehumanization To engage in actions that obscure the identity of the victim, such as excessive facial battery, or to see and treat victims like objects rather than human beings.

deindividuation A process by which individuals feel they cannot be identified, primarily because they are disguised or are subsumed within a group.

delusional disorder Mental disorder characterized by a system of false beliefs.

dependence In substance abuse, a condition that may be physical, psychological, or both, whereby a person develops an intense craving for (and feels he or she cannot live without) a drug.

dependent variables The variable that is measured to see how it is changed by manipulations of the independent variable.

deterrence theory The theory that argues that threat of punishment will prevent crime.

developmental approach Examines the changes and influences (risk factors) across a person's lifetime that contribute to the formation of antisocial and criminal behavior or, alternately, that protect individuals with many risk factors in their lives.

developmental cascade model (also dynamic cascade) The model that sees antisocial or criminal behavior being the result of multiple risks along the life path, interacting with one another rather than simply added to one another.

developmental pathway In the study of criminal behavior, these are the various tracks individuals follow that lead to antisocial behavior. Researchers began by identifying two pathways but have now found evidence of more.

Diagnostic and Statistical Manual of Mental Disorders (DSM) The official guidebook or manual, published by the American Psychiatric Association, used to define and diagnose specific mental disorders. Now in its fifth edition (DSM-5).

differential association theory Formulated by Edwin Sutherland, a theory of crime that states that criminal behavior is primarily due to obtaining values or messages from others, including but not limited to those who engage in crime. The critical factors include with whom a person associates, how early, for how long, how frequently, and how personally meaningful the associations are.

differential association-reinforcement (DAR) theory A theory of deviance developed by Ronald Akers that combines Skinner's behaviorism and Sutherland's differential association theory. The theory states that people learn deviant behavior through the reinforcements they receive from the social environment.

Diffusion of responsibility A concept that allows a person to minimize blame for an offense because other individuals were involved in the decision. Often used as a neutralization strategy in corporate and political crimes.

discriminative stimuli According to Akers, social signals or gestures transmitted by subcultural or peer groups to indicate whether certain kinds of behavior will be rewarded or punished within a particular social context.

disorganized crime scene Demonstrates that the offender committed the crime without premeditation or planning. In other words, the crime scene indicators suggest the individual acted on impulse or in rage, or under extreme excitement.

displaced aggression rapists Rapists whose attacks are violent and aggressive, displaying minimum or total absence of sexual feeling. Also called **anger-retaliation rapists.**

displaced aggression theory The theory that some aggression is directed at the target as a replacement for the individual who is the real source of the provocation.

displacement of responsibility A concept that allows an individual to deny responsibility for an action because he or she was told to perform it by someone higher in authority.

disruptive behavioral disorders A pattern that generally includes conduct disorders and oppositional defiant disorders that is characterized by chronic violation of social norms and rights of others.

dissociated state A state of mind during which the person feels detached from self and surroundings.

dissociative identity disorder A psychiatric syndrome characterized by the existence within an individual of two or more distinct personalities, any of which may be dominant at any given moment. Formerly called **multiple personality disorder (MPD).**

drug courts Specialized courts intended to process individuals with substance abuse disorders. Typically limited to first time offenders charged with minor offenses.

dual system model of adolescent risk taking A model that focuses on the differences between the social-emotional systems and the cognitive systems of adolescents. According to the model, cognitive stages progress more rapidly, but the social-emotional system's maturity is delayed, accounting for much adolescent risk taking.

dual-process model A model of psychopathy that proposes two categories of deficits in temperament, a low fear aspect and impaired cognitive-executive functions. The former is associated with factors 1 and 2, and the latter with factors 3 and 4.

Durham Rule A legal standard of insanity that holds that an accused is not criminally responsible if his or her unlawful act was the product of mental disease or defect. Also known as the **Product Rule.**

duty to protect Requirement from the *Tarasoff* case that clinicians must take steps to protect possible victims from serious bodily harm as a result of threats made by the clinicians' clients. The duty to protect does not require that the clinician contact the potential victim.

duty to warn Requirement from the *Tarasoff* case that clinicians must actively warn potential victims of threats of serious bodily harm made by their clients.

eldercide The killing of an older person, usually over 60.

emerging adulthood Developmental stage immediately following adolescence, usually referring to ages 18–24.

emotional congruence with children In some child sex offenders, the tendency to identify with and feel psychologically closer to children than to adults.

emotional paradox The research observation that psychopaths seem to be able to talk about emotional cues but lack the ability to use them effectively in the real world.

enmeshed style A parental style in which the parent takes extraordinary control of the child's life including imposing rigid rules and seeing even trivial, minor behaviors as problematic. Typically results in harsh punishment but inconsistent discipline.

equivocal death analysis (also called **reconstructive psychological evaluation),** it is the profiling method by which the profiler attempts to reconstruct aspects of a person's life after his or her death in order to determine the cause of death. Sometimes referred to as psychological autopsy.

erotomania stalking In this form of stalking, the stalker usually has serious mental disorders and is considered delusional. Public figures are often the targets.

euphemistic language Words used to make something appear more innocuous or less negative than it actually is.

evolutionary psychology The study of the evolution of behavior using the principles of natural selection.

excitation transfer theory Theory explaining how physiological arousal can generalize from one situation to another; based on the assumption that physiological arousal, however produced, dissipates slowly over time.

executive functions Higher order mental abilities involved in goal-directed behavior. They include organizing behavior, memory, inhibition processes, and planning strategies.

expectancy theory A theory of motivation that takes into account both the expectancy of achieving a particular goal and the value placed on it.

experimental substance use (ESU) Experimentation—typically by adolescents—with various psychoactive substances before dependency or addiction to drugs occurs.

expressive hostage taking Hostage-taking situation in which the offender's primary goal is to gain some control over his or her life.

expressive sexual aggression A rape situation in which the offender's primary goal is to gain some control over his life.

expressive-object pattern Relating to firesetting behavior, it is the pattern followed by serial offenders who are fascinated with fire and do not seem to want to harm anyone.

expressive-person pattern Relating to firesetting behavior, it is a common pattern that indicates a desire for attention and cry for help.

extinction The decline and eventual disappearance of a conditioned or learned response when it is no longer reinforced.

extrafamilial child molestation A sex abuser whose victims are outside the immediate or extended family.

Factor 1 A behavioral dimension, identified through factor analysis, representing the interpersonal and emotional aspects of psychopathy.

Factor 2 A behavioral dimension representing the socially deviant lifestyle characteristics of psychopaths.

Factor 3 A behavioral pattern representing shallow emotion, callousness, little empathy, and failure to accept responsibility.

factor analysis A statistical procedure by which underlying patterns, factors, or dimensions are identified among a series of scale items.

Falsification The process of testing a theory whereby if it is discovered that even one of its propositions is found not to be supported, the theory cannot be valid.

family mass murder A situation in which at least three family members are killed (usually by another family member).

FASD (Fetal Alcohol Spectrum Disorder) Broad term for a continuum of conditions that result from alcohol exposure in utero.

felony murder Murder committed during the process of carrying out a felony, such as in a robbery gone wrong.

filicide Killing of one's child older than one year.

firesetting The term used in the literature on child psychopathology for an abnormal fascination with fire accompanied by successful or unsuccessful attempts to start harmful fires.

fixated (immature) sex offender A child sex offender who demonstrates a long-standing, exclusive preference for children as both sexual and social companions.

four-factor model A model of psychopathy that includes **Factors 1, 2, and 3** along with a factor that represents antisocial behavior.

fraternal twins See **dizygotic twins.**

fratricide The killing of one's brother.

frustration An aversive internal state of arousal that occurs when one is prevented from responding in a way that previously produced rewards (or that one believes would produce rewards).

frustration-aggression hypothesis The theory that frustration leads to aggressive behavior. The theory has been revised several times, with most substantial changes coming from the work of Leonard Berkowitz.

Functional Family Therapy An evidence-based approach to treatment based on providing services to the whole family group, usually over an extended period of time.

fundamental attribution error A tendency to underestimate the importance of situational determinates and to overestimate the importance of personality or dispositional factors in identifying the causes of human behavior.

general aggression model An attempt to organize mini-theories of aggression into one unified theory. The model incorporates biological, social, and cognitive processes.

general altercation homicide Death resulting from hostile aggression.

general theory of crime Based on the assumption that lack of self-control is the core factor in criminal behavior.

geographical profiling A type of profiling that focuses on the location of the crime and how it relates to the residence and/or base of operations of the offender.

global risk recognition failure Term used in victimology literature for the tendency of some people to believe they are immune to sexual assault. Compare with specific risk recognition failure, which is the tendency to not recognize certain situations that are likely to put someone in danger of assault.

Guilty but Mentally Ill (GBMI) A verdict alternative in some states that allows mentally disordered defendants to be found guilty while seemingly affording them treatment for mental disorders.

hallucinations Things or events that a mentally disordered person, but no others, see or perceive. Characteristic of schizophrenia and some forms of dementia.

hallucinogens Those psychoactive drugs that sometimes generate hallucinations and lead to changes in perceptions of reality. Also called **psychedelics.**

Hate Crime Statistics Act Federal as well as state laws that require police to track and report crimes motivated by bias or hate against victims based on the race, ethnicity, religion, national origin, gender, or other protected status.

hebephilia The use of young adolescent girls or boys for sexual gratification by adults, usually males.

hemisphere asymmetry An unusual or abnormal balance between the two hemispheres, both in language processing and in emotional states.

hierarchy rule In the UCR program, the rule that requires that only the most serious crime in a series be reported in the crime statistics.

hostile attribution bias The tendency to perceive hostile intent in others even when it is totally lacking.

hostility theme Applied to rapists, characterizes offenders who are particularly brutal in their attacks and who use the victim to vent their anger.

instrumental hostage taking A hostage situation in which the primary goal of the offender is material or monetary gain.

iatrogenic A process whereby mental or physical disorders are unintentionally induced or developed in patients by physicians, clinicians, or psychotherapists.

I-Cubed theory An extension of general aggression theory.

imitational learning See **observational learning.**

impulsive rapist A rapist who demonstrates neither strong sexual nor aggressive features, but engages in spontaneous rape when the opportunity presents itself. The rape is usually carried out in the context of another crime, such as robbery or burglary. Also called **exploitative rapist.**

incest Sexual relations between individuals who are prohibited by law from having such relations, such as brothers and sisters. Incest is rarely prosecuted unless it involves a child, in which case it is prosecuted as child sexual assault or abuse.

independent variables The measure whose effect is being studied, and, in most scientific investigations, that is manipulated by the experimenter in a controlled fashion.

individual offender An offender prompted by a series of intense, long-lasting frustration.

infanticide Although this term literally means the killing of an infant, it has become synonymous with the killing of a child by a parent.

Insanity Defense Reform Act of 1984 (IDRA) A law designed to make it more difficult for defendants using the insanity defense in the federal courts to be acquitted.

instrumental learning A form of learning in which a voluntary response is strengthened or diminished by its consequences. Also called **operant conditioning.**

instrumental sexual aggression When the sexual offender uses just enough coercion to gain compliance from his victim.

instrumental-object pattern Applied to firesetters, this pattern represents a desire to cover up tracks of other crimes or to obtain financial gain (e.g., insurance).

instrumental-person pattern Applied to firesetters, this is anger or vengeance motivated, usually in retaliation against family members, companions, employers, teachers, or other individuals.

intellectual disability Formerly called mental retardation, it refers to limitations in cognitive capacity, determined by IQ tests and a variety of performance measures.

intimate partner violence (IPV) Crimes committed against persons by their current or former spouses, boyfriends, or girlfriends.

intrafamilial child molestation A child sex abuser whose victims are within the immediate or extended family.

investigative psychology The application of psychological research and concepts to the investigation of crime.

just-world hypothesis A belief that one gets what one deserves in this world.

lax style A parental style that does not respond sufficiently to problematic or antisocial behavior in children but rather allows it to occur without disciplinary action. Opposite of the **enmeshed style** and similar to the **permissive.**

learned helplessness (or reactive depression) A learned passive and withdrawing response in the face of perceived hopelessness, as theorized by Martin Seligman (1975).

learning perspective The theoretical position that humans are born basically neutral and behaviorally a blank slate. What they become as individuals depends on their learning experiences rather than innate predispositions.

left-wing extremist groups FBI's category of terrorist groups that hold leftist political positions and carry out violent acts. One example is the Weather Underground responsible for bombings and robberies during the 1970s.

life-course-persistent (LCP) offenders A term introduced by Terrie Moffitt to represent offenders who demonstrate a life-long pattern of antisocial behavior and who are resistant to treatment or rehabilitation.

London syndrome A behavioral pattern observed during a hostage situation at the Iranian Embassy in London. Refers to the explicit and consistent resistance and refusals by hostages to do what is expected by captors. This behavior often results in death or serious injury to the resistors.

Lone wolf terrorist Terrorist who operates alone, or occasionally with one or two others.

love obsession stalking In this form of stalking, the stalker and victim are strangers or casual acquaintances. The stalker seeks a love relationship with the object of his or her obsession.

M'Naghten Rule An insanity standard based on the conclusion that if a defendant has a defect of reason, or a disease of the mind, so as not to know the nature and quality of his or her actions, then he or she cannot be held criminally responsible. Also called **the right and wrong test.**

major depressive disorder General label for symptoms that include an extremely depressed state, general slowing down of mental and physical activity, and feelings of self-worthlessness.

MAOA A gene that appears to play an important role in preventing antisocial behavior in humans.

MAOA-L Known as the "warrior gene," it appears to promote aggressive behavior in humans.

markers A term used for the neurological indicators of a particular phenomenon, such as psychopathy.

mass murder Murdering three or more persons at a single location with no cooling-off period between murders.

matricide The killing of one's mother.

meanness In psychopathy research, meanness is proposed as an additional feature characterizing the psychopathic personality. See also **boldness factor**.

mental illness or disorder Any one or combination of a large group of psychological states that impede health human development to varying degrees.

mixed crime scene Indicates that the nature of the crime demonstrates both organized and disorganized behavioral patterns.

model A graphic or descriptive illustration intended to add clarity to a theory. Examples are the dual-process model of psychopathy, the dynamic or developmental cascade model, and the dual systems model of adolescent development.

models Individuals or groups of individuals in the environment whose behavior is observed and imitated.

molecular genetics Field of biology that studies the structure and function of genes at the level of molecules.

Monitoring the Future (MTF) A self-report survey administered to high school students nationwide focusing on drug use and abuse.

monozygotic twins Twins who developed from one fertilized egg and share the same genes. Also called **identical twins. Distinguished from dizygotic or fraternal twins, who do not share the same genes.**

moral agency The concept that people act in accordance with their value systems.

moral disengagement The process of freeing oneself from one's own moral standards in order to act against those standards. The unacceptable conduct is usually undertaken under orders from someone higher in authority or under high social pressure.

moral justification The process of convincing oneself that one's actions are worthy and have an ultimate moral and good purpose.

multiassaultive families Nuclear families (traditional or nontraditional) characterized by multiple incidents of violence involving more than one perpetrator.

Multisystemic Therapy (MST) An evidence-based treatment approach for serious juvenile offenders that focuses on the family while being responsive to the many other contexts surrounding the family, such as the peer group, the neighborhood, and the school.

Munchausen syndrome by proxy (MSBP) An unusual form of child abuse in which the parent (usually the mother), or parents, consistently bring a child for medical attention with symptoms falsified or directly induced by the parent or parents.

murder The killing of one human being by another with malice aforethought, without justification or excuse.

National Center for the Analysis of Violent Crime (NCAVC) An umbrella federal agency that serves as a resource for investigation of and research on serious criminal offenses throughout the country. See also **Behavioral Analysis Unit** and **ViCAP**.

National Crime Victimization Survey (NCVS) A government-sponsored survey of victims of crime, intended to collect data from the victim's perspective on crimes both reported and not reported to police.

National Incident-Based Reporting System (NIBRS) The FBI's system of collecting *detailed* data from law enforcement agencies on known crimes and arrests. See also **Uniform Crime Reporting.**

National Survey of Children Exposed to Violence (NatSCEV) Survey of youth and caretakers, representing 4500 children, to obtain estimates of victimization. Almost half had been exposed to physical violence over the past year.

natural narcotics Psychoactive substances classified as narcotics that require no chemical preparation.

negative reinforcement See **reinforcement, negative.**

neglecting style Detached and unengaged parental style.

negligent manslaughter The unlawful killing of another through reckless or negligent behavior, without intention to kill.

neonaticide The killing of a newborn, usually under 48 hours.

neurotransmitters Biochemicals directly involved in the transmission of neural impulses and without which communication would not be possible. **Serotonin** is one example.

nonconformist perspective The theoretical perspective that humans will naturally try to get away with anything they can, including illegal conduct, unless social controls are imposed.

nonnegligent manslaughter The killing of a human being without premeditation but with the intention to kill, such as under high emotional states of anger or passion.

nonshared environments An important concept in twin studies, this refers to the living experiences that are different for each twin, such as being raised by different parents.

not guilty by reason of insanity (NGRI) A legal determination that a defendant was so mentally disordered at the time of the crime that he or she cannot be held criminally responsible for his or her actions.

nuclear/biological/chemical (NBC) terrorism Terrorist activities carried out with the use of nuclear, biological, or chemical substances (e.g., anthrax).

obedience to authority Concept is social psychology that posits people will act against their own moral standards if ordered to do so by someone in authority.

observational learning (modeling) The process by which individuals learn patterns of behavior by observing another person performing the action.

occupational crime (1) Any one of a variety of offenses committed by an individual through opportunity created by his or her occupation; divided by Green into four categories: individual, organizational, professional, and state authority. (2) The second category of **white-collar crime** (along with corporate) that refers to crimes committed by individuals for their own benefit.

operant conditioning See **instrumental learning**

opiate narcotics Psychoactive drugs that have sedative (sleep-inducing) and analgesic (pain-relieving) effects.

opportunistic types Refers to rapists whose sexual assaults are impulsive, predatory acts that are controlled by situational and contextual factors, such as a woman being present during the commission of another crime.

oppositional defiant disorder (ODD) A behavior disorder of childhood characterized by frequent disobedience and hostile behavior toward authority figures.

organized crime scene Indicates planning and premeditation on the part of the offender. In other words, the crime scene shows signs that the offender maintained control of himself or herself and of the victim, if it is a crime against a person.

paraphilia The clinical term for a sexual condition exhibited in fantasies, urges, or behaviors involving nonhuman objects, suffering or humiliation of oneself or one's partner, or children or other nonconsenting persons.

parental monitoring Supervision by parents of their children's activities. Poor parental monitoring is a strong risk factor for delinquency.

parental styles Any one of several approaches taken by parents in raising their children. Some examples identified by researchers are lax, negligent, authoritarian, and authoritative.

parricide The killing of a parent.

passive-aggressive behaviors Hostile behaviors that do not directly inflict physical harm, such as refusing to speak to someone against whom one holds a grudge.

patricide The killing of one's father.

pedophilia The clinical term for attraction to children for sexual gratification. Not necessarily accompanied by criminal actions against children.

permissive style A relaxed parenting style characterized by few demands, controls, or limits.

personation See **signature.**

plasticity The characteristic of the brain that allows both its structure and its function to be profoundly responsive to experiences, particularly during early life.

positive reinforcement See **reinforcement, positive.**

positivist theory Theory that argues prior experiences or influences determine present behavior.

posttraumatic stress disorder (PTSD) A cluster of behavioral patterns that result from a psychologically distressing event outside the usual range of human experience.

power rape A rape situation, identified by Groth, in which the assailant seeks to establish power and control over his victim. Thus, the amount of force and threats used depends on the degree of submission shown by the victim.

primary prevention An intervention program designed to prevent behavior or disorders before any signs of the behavioral pattern develops. Also called **universal prevention.**

primary psychopath Robert Hare's classification of the "true" psychopath. That is, the individual who demonstrates those physiological and behavioral features that represent psychopathy—in contrast to **secondary psychopaths,** who commit antisocial acts because of severe emotional problems or inner conflicts, and **dyssocial psychopaths,** who are antisocial because of social learning.

proactive aggression Similar to **instrumental aggression,** actions undertaken to obtain a specific goal. In children, refers to insensitive actions such as bullying, name-calling, and coercive actions.

proactive violence Violence perpetrated as a planned or initial action. Contrast with **reactive violence**.

property crime Any one of many offenses that do not involve direct physical harm to victims. The four major property crime categories in the UCR are burglary, larceny-theft, motor vehicle theft, and arson.

psychoactive drugs Drugs that exert their primary effect on the brain, thus altering mood or behavior.

psychodynamic model The theoretical perspective that argues that human behavior can be best explained through the use of psychological forces and pressures. Also called **hydraulic model.**

psychological autopsy See equivalent death analysis.

psychological criminology See **criminology, psychological.**

psychological profiling Assessing behavioral and psychological characteristics of a person for purposes of determining risk of offending, particularly violent offending. May also be used for positive purposes, such as assessing characteristics for suitability for employment or promotion.

psychological signature A behavioral clue left inadvertently at the scene of a crime that may help investigators identify the offender. An example would be covering a murder victim's face. Contrast with **crime scene signature.**

psychologically motivated terrorists Persons drawn to terrorist activity because of a profound sense of failure or inadequacy. They seek the benefits of affiliation with others and a sense of collective identity.

psychometric approach The perspective that human characteristics, attributes, and traits can be measured and quantified.

psychometric intelligence (PI) A more contemporary designation of intelligence as measured by intelligence or IQ tests. However, the term is not yet widely used in comparison with "IQ."

psychopath An individual who demonstrates a distinct behavioral pattern that differs from the general population in its level of sensitivity, empathy, compassion, and guilt. See also **primary psychopath.**

Psychopathy Checklist (PCL) and Psychopathy Checklist-Revised (PCL-R). Developed by Robert Hare, currently the best-known instrument for the measurement of criminal psychopathy. Additional versions include the **Psychopathy Checklist—Screening Version,** the **P-Scan: Research Version,** and the **Psychopathy Checklist, Youth Version (PCL:YV).**

psychophysiology The study of the dynamic interactions between behavior and the autonomic nervous system.

punishment An event by which a person receives a noxious, painful, or aversive stimulus, usually as a consequence of behavior.

pyromania A psychiatric term for an irresistible urge to set fires along with an intense fascination (usually sexual) with fire. The existence of this behavioral phenomenon has been brought into serious question by the available research.

Quest for Significance theory A recently developed theory that suggests individuals drawn to terrorism are seeking significance in their lives.

radical environmental groups Environmental activists who have used terrorist tactics to draw attention to dangers to the environment.

rape Penetration of the vagina or anus with any body part or object, or oral penetration by a sex organ of another person, without the consent of the victim.

rape by fraud The act of having sexual relations with a supposedly consenting adult under fraudulent conditions, such as when a physician or psychotherapist has sexual intercourse with a patient under the guise of "effective treatment."

rape myths A variety of mistaken beliefs about the crime of rape and its victims held by many men and women.

rationally motivated terrorists Terrorists driven by the goals of their organization, which may be political, social, or economic. Contrast with **psychologically motivated** and **culturally motivated** terrorists.

reactive aggression Spontaneous aggression, possibly in response to provocation. In children, hot-blooded aggressive acts, such as temper tantrums and emotionally driven vengeful hostility.

reactive violence Violence perpetrated in response to provocation, perceived provocation, or an unanticipated occurrence.

recidivism A return to criminal activity (usually measured by arrest) after being convicted of a criminal offense.

regressed sex offender Refers to a child molester who engaged in normal sexual relationships in adolescence and early adulthood, but later developed sexual attraction to children and victimized them.

responsivity principle In RNR treatment, the assessment of the extent to which an individual will cooperate with and benefit from the treatment.

right and wrong test See **M'Naghten Rule.**

right-wing terrorists FBI classification of terrorists with extremely right-leaning political views. An example would be terrorists associated with hate groups.

risk principle In RNR treatment, the assessment of risk factors in a person's life that make the person susceptible to antisocial behavior. An example of a risk factor is conduct disorder as a 6-year-old.

risky shift Tendency of groups to make decisions that are more extreme than if the same decisions were made by individuals.

ritualized aggression The symbolic display of aggressive intentions or strength without actual physical combat or conflict.

robbery The taking or attempt to take anything of value from the care, custody, or control of another by force or the threat of force.

rumination The focused attention on one's own thoughts and feelings that, if excessive, can lead to aggression against others.

sadistic rape A rape situation, identified by Groth, in which the offender experiences sexual arousal and excitement as a result of the victim's torment, distress, helplessness, and suffering. The assault usually involves bondage and torture, and the rapist directs considerable abuse and injury on various areas of the victim's body.

schizophrenia Mental disorder characterized by severe breakdowns in thought patterns, emotions, and perceptions.

sedative-hypnotic compounds Psychoactive drugs that depress central nervous system functioning, generally reducing anxiety and tension.

selective prevention An intervention program designed for individuals who demonstrate early signs or indications of behavioral problems or antisocial behavior. Also called **secondary prevention.**

self-control theory (SCT) A heavily researched theory in criminology that proposes that crime and antisocial behavior are the result of an individual's deficits in ability to control his or her behavior. Controversial aspect of the theory is that self-control is a stable trait and well in place before adolescence is reached.

self-regulation The ability to control one's behavior in accordance with internal cognitive standards.

self-report (SR) data Information about crime and antisocial behavior gathered from the offenders themselves. In recent years many self-report studies focus on substance use and abuse.

semantic aphasia A characteristic found in psychopaths whereby the words they speak are devoid of emotional sincerity.

semisynthetic narcotics See **narcotics.**

serial murder Incidents in which an individual (or individuals) kills a number of individuals (usually a minimum of three) over time.

sexual aggressive rapist A rapist who demonstrates both sexual and aggressive features in his attack. In order for him to experience sexual arousal, it must be associated with violence and pain, which excite him. Also called **sadistic rapist.**

sexual assault Term for any one of various criminal behaviors that involve a sexual attack on the body of another person; has replaced the term "rape" in many criminal statutes. See also **rape.**

sexual burglary A burglary committed with the primary motive of carrying out a sexual assault or obtaining objects supportive of a fetish.

sexual exploitation/involvement theme (also pseudo-intimacy theme) Characterizes the rapist who attempts to bond with the victim, such as by apologizing or attempting to show affection. Treats victim as a person rather than an object.

shaken baby syndrome (SBS) A form of child abuse in which an adult shakes a baby so hard that it causes significant brain damage or death. The preferred term is now abusive head trauma.

shared environments An important concept in twin studies, this refers to the prenatal and life experiences that are common to both twins, such as being raised by the same biological parents.

siblicide The killing of one's brother or sister; **sororicide** is the killing of one's sister; **fratricide** is the killing of one's brother.

simple obsession stalking The form in which the stalker seeks power and control after a failed relationship with the victim; often associated with past domestic violence.

simulation An experimental design that is intended to represent reality in a laboratory environment.

situationism A theoretical perspective that argues that environmental stimuli control behavior.

snitches Amateur shoplifters.

social control theory Theory in criminology that proposes that individuals are prevented from committing antisocial behavior or crime because of bonds they hold to society, such as their attachment to parents or significant others.

social learning theory A theory of human behavior based on learning from watching others in the social environment. This leads to an individual's development of his or her own perceptions, thoughts, expectancies, competencies, and values.

sociological criminology See **criminology, sociological.**

sororicide See **siblicide.**

special interest extremists A category of terrorists defined by the FBI. Their violent activities are driven by dedication to a particular cause, such as animal rights or the environment.

spree murder The killing of three or more individuals without any cooling-off period, usually at two or more locations.

staging The intentional alteration of a crime scene prior to the arrival of the police.

stalking Conduct directed at a specific person that involves repeated physical or visual proximity, nonconsensual communication, or verbal, written, or implied threats sufficient to cause fear in a reasonable person.

Stanford Prison Experiment A classic study conducted by Philip Zimbardo in which participants played roles of guards and prisoners; illustrates social psychological concepts, particularly deindividuation. See also **simulation.**

status offenses A class of illegal behavior that only persons with certain characteristics or status can commit. Used here to refer to the behavior of juveniles. Examples include running away from home, violating curfew, buying alcohol, or skipping school.

statutory rape Rape for which the age of the victim is the crucial distinction, on the premise that a victim below a certain age (usually 16) cannot validly consent to sexual intercourse with an adult.

stereotypical abductions Refer to child abductions that are highly unusual. They often end in the death of the child, are usually committed by strangers, and receive considerable media attention. Nevertheless, they are rare.

stimulants A broad drug classification that refers to those psychoactive drugs that "stimulate" the central nervous system and elevate mood.

stimulus A person, event, or situation that elicits behavior.

Stockholm syndrome A term coined after a hostage situation in Sweden in 1973, it refers to the phenomenon of hostages becoming attracted to their captors. In the original incident, an escaped convict held four bank employees in Stockholm in the bank vault for 131 hours. One of the bank employees eventually married her hostage taker.

strain theory A prominent sociological explanation for crime based on Robert Merton's theory that crime and delinquency occur when there is a perceived discrepancy between the materialistic values and goals cherished and held in high esteem by a society and the availability of the legitimate means for reaching these goals.

street culture A variety of conduct norms, particularly in urban areas, that are conducive to robbery and other street crimes. Examples of these norms are disdain for conventional living, a hedonistic pursuit of sensory stimulation, and lack of future orientation.

strong-arm robbery A robbery in which the main weapon used is one's own body rather than guns, knives, or other weapons.

structured professional judgment An approach to risk assessment that relies on both the assessor's clinical judgment and measures that offer guidance in assessing dangerousness and suggesting steps to prevent violence.

succumbers In hostage-taking situations, refers to those hostages who, after release, have considerable difficulty dealing with the aftereffects of the incident.

survivors In hostage-taking situations, refers to those hostages who are able to return to a meaningful existence with little evidence of long-term depression, nightmares, or serious stress-induced illness; term also preferred by victims of sexual assault.

suspect-based profiling Also called prospective profiling. Prediction of behavioral malintent largely based on base rate data of previous offenders.

synthetic marijuana A relatively recent product widely available on the open market; mimics the effects of cannabis but may be much more potent than THC.

synthetic narcotics See **narcotics.**

temperament A natural mood disposition determined largely by genetic and biological influences.

territoriality The tendency to attack violators of one's personal space.

Terror Management Theory A recent theory of terrorism that posits that individuals who join terrorist organizations do so as a way of dealing with their own high anxiety of eventual death.

tertiary prevention Also treatment. Intervention strategy designed to reduce or eliminate behavioral problems or antisocial behavior that is fully developed in individuals.

theory verification A process whereby a scientific theory is tested through observation and analysis. If the process falsifies the theory, the theory must be revised to account for the observed events. See also **falsification**.

theory An integrated set of principles that describes, predicts, and explains some phenomena and that guides research.

tolerance In substance use, the condition in which only increasing dosages of the drug produce the desired effect.

trait (or disposition) Relatively stable and enduring tendency to behave in a particular way across time and place. Traits are believed by some psychologists to be the basic building blocks of personality.

traumatic brain injury (TBI) Injury to the brain occurring either in utero, during birth, or at any time in an individual's life having a significant effect on functioning. Often associated with accidents or injuries during wartime, and sometimes used as excusing or mitigating condition for aggressive behavior.

tripartite conceptual model Identifies three main categories of drug related crimes. Proposed by Paul Goldstein.

Twins' Early Development Study (TEDS) An ongoing longitudinal study of twins conducted in the United Kingdom. It explores behavioral problems as well as progress in language development, cognition, and academic abilities.

typology In this context, a classification system that finds commonalities among members of groups (e.g., serial murderers; terrorists; sex offenders) to aid in investigating crime and offering treatment services.

undoing A behavioral pattern found at the crime scene whereby the offender tries to psychologically "undo" the murder.

Uniform Crime Reports (UCR) The FBI's system of gathering data from law enforcement agencies on the crimes that come to their attention and on arrests. See also **NIBRS and SRS.**

variable Any entity that can be measured.

vengeance stalking These stalkers do not seek a relationship with their victims but rather are trying to elicit a response or change of behavior from the victim.

victimology The scientific study of the causes, circumstances, individual characteristics, and social contexts associated with crime victims.

vindictive offender types Rapists whose attacks are driven by central and focused hatred of women.

Violent Criminal Apprehension Program (ViCAP) A program within the National Center for the Analysis of Violent Crimes designed to offer support and encourage cooperation among law enforcement agencies in solving serious crimes, particularly those that cross jurisdictional borders. Maintains a large database on violent crimes in the United States.

volitional prong The part of some insanity standards that accepts the possibility that a defendant could not control his or her behavior to conform to the requirements of the law. The volitional prong is not recognized in federal law or the law of many states.

weapons effect Suggestion that the mere presence of a weapon leads a witness or victim to concentrate on the weapon itself rather than other features of the crime.

white-collar crime A broad term, coined in 1939 by Edwin Sutherland, that refers to illegal acts committed by those of high social status in the process of their employment. Contemporary definitions often divide it into corporate crime and individual or occupational crime. See also **occupational crime.**

workplace aggression A term for the conduct, usually on the part of employees or supervisors, that qualifies as emotional harm or minor physical harm to other employees. Distinct from workplace violence.

workplace violence The physically aggressive actions, including assaults and deaths, that occur at the workplace. It is not often caused by those who work within the workplace; most such violence is perpetrated by someone from the outside.

CASES CITED

Baxstrom v. Herold, 383 U.S. 107 (1966).

Carter v. United States, 252 F.2d 608 (D.C. Cir. 1957).

Clark v. Arizona, 548 U.S. 735 (2006).

Cone v. Bell, 556 U.S. 449 (2009).

Delling v. Idaho, cert. denied 133 S.Ct. 504 (2012).

District of Columbia v. Heller, 554 U.S. 570 (2008).

Durham v. United States, 214 F.2d 862 (D.C. Cir. 1954).

Dusky v. United States, 363 U.S. 402 (1960).

Elonis v. United States, ___ U.S. ___ (2015).

Finger v. State, 27 P.3d 66 (Nev. 2001).

Foucha v. Louisiana, 51 Cr.L. 2084 (1992).

Graham v. Florida, 130 S.Ct. 2011 (2010).

Indiana v. Edwards, 554 U.S. 208 (2008).

Jackson v. Indiana, 406 U.S. 715 (1972).

Miller v. Alabama, 132 S.Ct. 2455 (2012).

Miller v. State, 338 N.W.2d 673 (1983).

M'Naghten, 10 Clark & Fin. 200, 210, Eng.Rep 718, 722 (1843).

Paroline v. United States, ___ U.S. ___ 2014

Roper v. Simmons, 543 U.S. 551 (2005).

Sell v. United States, 539 U.S. 166 (2003).

State v. Bianchi, No. 79-10116 (Wash. Super. Ct., October 19, 1979).

State v. Felde, 422 So.2d 370 (La. 1982).

State v. Milligan, No. 77-CR-11-2908 (Franklin Co. Ohio, December 4, 1978).

State v. Rodrigues, 679 P.2d 615 (Hawaii 1984).

Tarasoff v. Regents of the University of California, 529 F.2d 553 (Cal. 1974), vac., reheard en banc, & aff'd 131 Cal. Rptr. 1, 551 P.2d 334 (1976).

Thompson v. Oklahoma, 108 S.Ct. 2687 (1989).

Tibbals v. Carter, 568 U.S. ___ (2013).

United States v. Brawner, 471 F.2d 969 (D.C. Cir. 1972).

United States v. Krutschewski, 509 F.Supp. 1186 (D. Mass. 1981).

United States v. Weston, 255 F.3d 873 (2001); cert. denied.

United States v. Williams, 553 U.S. 285 (2008).

REFERENCES

Abadinsky, H. (1993). *Drug abuse* (2nd ed.). Chicago: Nelson-Hall.

Abbey, A., Clinton-Sherrod, A. M., McAuslan, P., Zawacki, T., & Buck, P. O. (2003). The relationship between the quantity of alcohol consumed and the severity of the sexual assaults committed by college men. *Journal of Interpersonal Violence, 18*, 813–833.

Abbey, A., Jacques-Tiura, A. J., & LeBreton, J. M. (2011). Risk factors for sexual aggression in young men: An expansion of the confluence model. *Aggressive Behavior, 37*, 450–464.

Abbey, A., Zawacki, T., Buck, P. O. Clinton, A. M., & McAuslan, P. (2004). Sexual assault and alcohol consumption: What do we know about their relationship and what types of research are still needed. *Aggression and Violent Behavior, 9*, 271–303.

Abdelouahab, N., Huel, G., Suvorov, A., Foliguet, B., Goua, V., Debotte, G., et al. (2010). Monoamine oxidase activity in placenta in relation to manganese, cadmium, lead, and mercury at delivery. *Neurotoxicology and Teratology, 32*, 256–261.

Abel, G., G., Becker, J. V., Cunningham-Rathner, J., Mittelman, M. S., & Rouleau, J. L. (1988). Multiple paraphilic diagnoses among sex offenders. *Bulletin of the American Academy of Psychiatry and the Law, 16*, 153–168.

Abel, G. G., Becker, J. V., Murphy, W. D., & Flanagan, B. (1981). Identifying dangerous child molesters. In R. B. Stuart (Ed.), *Violent behavior: Social learning approaches to prediction, management and treatment.* New York: Brunner/Mazel.

Abel, G. G., Mittelman, M., Becker, J. V., Rathner, J., & Rouleau, J. (1988). Predicting child molesters' response to treatment. In R. A. Prentky & V. L. Quinsey (Eds.), *Human sexual aggression: Current perspectives* (pp. 223–234). New York: New York Academy of Sciences.

Abrams, D. E. (2013). A primer on criminal child abuse and neglect law. *Juvenile and Family Court, 64*, 1–27.

Achenbach, T. M., & Edelbrock, C. (1983). *Manual for the child behavior checklist and revised child behavior profile.* Burlington, VT: University of Vermont.

Acierno, R. H., Hernandez, M. A., Arnstadter, A. B., Resnick, H. S., Steve, K., Muzzy, W., et al. (2010). Prevalence and correlates of emotional, physical, sexual, and financial abuse and potential neglect in the United States: The National Elder Mistreatment Study. *American Journal of Public Health, 100*, 292–297.

Acierno, R. H., Hernandez-Tejada, M., Muzzy, W., & Steve, K. (2009). *Final report: The National Elder Mistreatment Study.* Washington, DC: National Institute of Justice.

Acoca, L., & Austin, J. (1996). *The hidden crisis: The women offenders sentencing study and alternative sentencing recommendations project.* San Francisco: National Council on Crime and Delinquency.

Acoca, L., & Dedel, K. (1998). *No place to hide: Understanding and meeting the needs of girls in the California juvenile justice system.* San Francisco, CA: National Council on Crime and Delinquency.

Adachi, R. J. C., & Willoughby, T. (2011). The effect of video game competition and violence on aggressive behavior: Which characteristic has the greatest influence? *Psychology of Violence, 1*, 259–274.

ADAM II. (2011). *Annual report: Arrestee drug abuse monitoring.* Washington, DC: Office of National Drug Control Policy.

Adams, D. (1992). Biology does not make men more aggressive than women. In K. Bjorkquist & P. Niemela (Eds.), *Of mice and women: Aspects of female aggression* (pp. 17–25). San Diego, CA: Academic Press.

Adams, S. H., Knopf, D. K., & Park, M. J. (2014). Prevalence and treatment of mental health and substance use problems in the early emerging adult years in the United States: Findings from the 2010 National Survey on Drug Use and Health. *Emerging Adulthood, 2*, 163–172.

Adamson, L. A., & Thompson, R. A. (1998). Coping with interparental verbal conflict by children exposed to spouse abuse from nonviolent homes. *Journal of Family Violence, 13*, 213–232.

Adler, J. (2002, February 25). The "thrill" of theft: It's not just movies stars. *Newsweek*, p. 52.

Adler, R., Nunn, R., Northam, E., Lebnan, V., & Ross, R. (1994). Secondary prevention of childhood firesetting. *Journal of the American Academy of Child and Adolescent Psychiatry, 33*, 1194–1202.

Adshead, G. (2002). Three degrees of security: Attachment and forensic institutions. *Criminal Behaviour and Mental Health, 12,* S31–S45.

Advisory Committee on Childhood Lead Poisoning Prevention (ACCLPP) (2012, January 4). *Low level lead exposure harms children: A renewed call for primary prevention.* Atlanta, GA: Centers for Disease Control and Prevention.

Agnew, R. (1992). Foundation for a General Strain Theory of crime and delinquency. *Criminology, 30,* 47–87.

Agnew, R. (2006). General Strain Theory: Current status and directions for future research. In F. T. Cullen, J. P. Wright, & K. R. Blevins (Eds.), *Taking stock: The status of criminological theory: Vol. 15* (pp. 101–123). New Brunswick, NJ: Transaction.

Ægisdóttir, S., White, M. J., Spengler, P. M., Maugherman, L. A., Cook, R. S., Nichols, C. N., et al. (2006). The meta-analysis of clinical judgment project: Fifty-six years of accumulated research on clinical versus statistical prediction. *The Counseling Psychologist, 34,* 341–382.

Ahler, C. J., Schaefer, G. A., Mundt, I. A., Roll, S., Englert, H., Willich, S. N., et al. (2011). How unusual are the contents of paraphilias? Paraphilia-associated sexual arousal patterns in a community-based sample of men. *Journal of Sexual Medicine, 8,* 1362–1370.

Ainsworth, M. D. (1979). Infant-mother attachment. *American Psychologist, 34,* 932–937.

Ainsworth, M. D., Blehar, M. C., Waters, E., & Wall, S. (1979). *Patterns of attachment: A psychological study of the strange situation.* Hillsdale, NJ: Erlbaum.

Akers, R. L. (1977). *Deviant behavior: A social learning approach* (2nd ed.). Belmont, CA: Wadsworth.

Akers, R. L. (1985). *Deviant behavior: A social learning approach* (3rd ed.). Belmont, CA: Wadsworth.

Akers, R. L., & Cochran, J. K. (1985). Adolescent marijuana use: A test of three theories of deviant behavior. *Deviant Behavior, 6,* 323–346.

Akers, R. L., & Lee, G. (1996). A longitudinal test of social learning theory: Adolescent smoking. *Journal of Drug Issues, 26,* 317–343.

Albanese, J. S. (1995). *White-collar crime in America.* Englewood Cliffs, NJ: Prentice Hall.

Alexander, J. F., Pugh, C., Parsons, B. V., & Sexton, T. L. (2000). Functional family therapy. In D. S. Elliott (Ed.), *Blueprints for violence prevention* (Book 3) (2nd ed., pp. 445–453). Boulder, CO: Center for the Study and Prevention of Violence, Institute of Behavioral Science, University of Colorado.

Alexander, R. A., Smith, W., & Stevenson, R. (1990). Serial Munchausen syndrome by proxy. *Pediatrics, 8,* 581–585.

Alink, L. R. A., & Egeland, B. (2013). The roles of antisocial history and emerging adulthood developmental adaption in predicting adult antisocial behavior. *Aggressive Behavior, 39,* 131–140.

Alison, L. J., & Canter, D. V. (1999). Professional, legal and ethical issues in offender profiling. In D. V. Canter & L. J. Alison (Eds.), *Profiling in policy and practice* (pp. 21–54). Aldershot, UK: Ashgate.

Alison, L., Bennell, C., Ormerod, D., & Mokros, A. (2002). The personality paradox in offender profiling: A theoretical review of the processes involved in deriving background characteristics from crime scene actions. *Psychology, Public Policy, and Law, 8,* 115–135.

Alison, L. J., Smith, M. D., Eastman, O., & Rainbow, L. (2003). Toulmin's philosophy of argument and its relevance to offending profiling. *Psychology, Crime & Law, 9,* 173–183.

Alison, L. J., Smith, M. D., & Morgan, K. (2003). Interpreting the accuracy of offender profiles. *Psychology, Crime & Law, 9,* 185–195.

Alison, L. J., West, A., & Goodwill, A. (2004). The academic and the practitioner: Pragmatists' views of offender profiling. *Psychology, Public Policy, and Law, 10,* 71–101.

Allen, A. N., & Lo, C. C. (2012). Drugs, guns, and disadvantaged youths: Co-occurring behavior and the code of the street. *Crime & Delinquency, 58,* 932–953.

Allen, M., Emmers, T., Gebhardt, L., & Giery, M. A. (2001). Exposure to pornography and acceptance of rape myths. *Journal of Communication, 45,* 5–53.

Allen, N. B., Lewinsohn, P. M., & Seeley, J. R. (1998). Prenatal and perinatal influences on risk for psychopathology in childhood and adolescence. *Development and Psychopathology, 10,* 513–529.

Almond, L., McManus, M. A., & Ward, L. (2014). Male-on-male sexual assaults: An analysis of crime scene actions. *Journal of Interpersonal Violence, 29,* 1279–1296.

Althouse, R. (Ed.). (2010). Standards for psychology services in jails, prisons, correctional facilities, and agencies. Preamble to the Third Edition. *Criminal Justice and Behavior, 37*, 754–756.

Alvira-Hammond, M., Longmore, M. A., Manning, W. D., & Giordano, P. C. (2014). Gainful activity and intimate partner aggression in emerging adulthood. *Emerging Adulthood, 2*, 116–127.

Alvord, M. K., & Grados, J. J. (2005). Enhancing resilience in children: A protective approach. *Professional Psychology: Research and Practice, 3*, 238–245.

American Bar Association. (1979). *Juvenile justice standards project.* Chicago: Author.

American Psychiatric Association. (2013). *Diagnostic and statistical manual of mental disorders—Fifth edition* (*DSM-5*). Washington, DC: Author.

American Psychological Association. (2003). *Violence and the family: Report of the APA Presidential Task Force on Violence and the Family—executive summary.* APA Online. Available: http://www.NNFLP.org/APA_task_force.htm.

American Psychological Association. (2009). APA Board reiterates its stance on interrogations. *Monitor on Psychology, 48*, 10.

American Psychological Association. (2013). Specialty guidelines for forensic psychology. *American Psychologist, 68*, 7–19.

Ammar, N., Couture-Carron, A., Alvi, S., & San Antonio, J. (2014). Experiences of Muslim and non-Muslim battered immigrant women with the police in the United States: A closer understanding of commonalities and differences. *Violence Against Women, 19*, 1449–1471.

Amsel, A. (1958). The role of frustrative nonreward in noncontinuous reward situations. *Psychological Bulletin, 55*, 102–119.

Andershed, H., Kerr, M., Stattin, H., & Levander, S. (2002). Psychopathic traits in non-referred youths: A new assessment tool. In E. Blauuw & L. Sheridan (Eds.), *Psychopaths: Current international perspectives* (pp. 131–158). The Hague, Netherlands: Elsevier.

Anderson, A. S., & Lo, C. C. (2011). Intimate partner violence within law enforcement families. *Journal of Interpersonal Violence, 26*, 1176–1193.

Anderson, C. A. (2004). An update on the effects of playing violent video games. *Journal of Adolescence, 27*, 113–122.

Anderson, C. A., & Bushman, B. J. (2001). Effects of violent games on aggressive behavior, aggressive cognition, aggressive effect, physiological arousal, and prosocial behavior: A meta-analytic review of the scientific literature. *Psychological Science, 12*, 353–359.

Anderson, C. A., & Bushman, B. J. (2002). Human aggression. *Annual Review of Psychology, 53*, 27–51.

Anderson, C. A., & Prot, S. (2011). Effects of playing violent video games. In M. A. Paludi (Ed.), *The psychology of teen violence and victimization: Vols. 1 and 2. From bullying to cyberstalking to assault and sexual violation* (pp. 41–70). Santa Barbara, CA: Praeger?ABC-CLIO.

Anderson, C. A., Sakamoto, A., Gentile, D. A., Ihori, N., Shibuya, A., Yukawa, S., et al. (2008). Longitudinal effects of violent video games on aggression in Japan and the United States. *Pediatrics, 122*, 1067–1072.

Anderson, C. A., Shibuya, A., Ihori, N., Swing, E. L., Bushman, B. J., Sakamoto, A., et al. (2010). Violent video game effects on aggression, empathy, and prosocial behavior in eastern and western countries: A meta-analytic review. *Psychological Bulletin, 136*, 151–173.

Anderson, S. W., Bechara, A., Damasio, H., Tranel, D., & Damasio, A. R. (1999). Impairment of social and moral behavior related to early damage in human prefrontal cortex. *Nature Neuroscience, 2*, 1032–1037.

Andreasen, N. C., & Carpenter, W. T. (1993). Diagnosis and classification of schizophrenia. *Schizophrenia Bulletin, 19*, 199–214.

Andrews, D. A., & Bonta, J. (1994). *The psychology of criminal conduct.* Cincinnati, OH: Anderson.

Andrews, D. A., & Bonta, J. (2010). *The psychology of criminal conduct* (5th ed.). New Providence, NJ: Matthew Bender.

Andrews, D. A., Bonta, J., & Hoge, R. D. (1990). Classification for effective rehabilitation: Rediscovering psychology. *Criminal Justice and Behavior, 17*, 19–52.

Ansary, N. S., & Luthar, S. S. (2009). Distress and academic achievement among adolescents of affluence: A study of externalizing and internalizing problem behaviors and school performance. *Development and Psychopathology, 21*, 319–341.

Ansbro, M. (2008). Using attachment theory with offenders. *Probation Journal, 55*, 231–244.

Apostolou, A., Garcia-Esquinas, E., Fadrowski, J. J., McLain, P., Weaver, V. M., & Navas-Acien, A. (2012). Secondhand tobacco smoke: A source of lead exposure in US children and adolescents. *American Journal of Public Health, 102*, 714–722.

Appelbaum, P. S., Jick, R. Z., Grisso, T., Givelbar, D., Silver, E., & Steadman, H. J. (1993). Use of posttraumatic stress. *Psychiatry, 150*, 229–234.

Appelbaum, P. S., Robbins, P. C., & Monahan, J. (2000). Violence and delusions: Data from the MacArthur Violence Risk Assessment Study. *American Journal of Psychiatry, 157*, 566–572.

Archer, J. (2004). Sex differences in aggression in real-world settings: A meta-analytic review. *Review of General Psychology, 8*, 291–322.

Ardrey, R. (1966). *The territorial imperative*. New York: Athenum.

Arena, M. P., & Arrigo, B. A. (2005). Social psychology, terrorism, and identity: A preliminary re-examination of theory, culture, self, and society. *Behavioral Sciences & the Law, 23*, 485–506.

Arkow, P. (1998). The correlations between cruelty to animals and child abuse and the implications for veterinary medicine. In R. Lockwood & F. R. Ascione (Eds.), *Cruelty to animals and interpersonal violence: Readings in research and application* (pp. 409–414). West Lafayette, IN: Purdue University Press.

Arluke, A., & Madfis, E. (2014). Animal abuse as a warning sign of school massacres: A critique and refinement. *Homicide Studies, 18*, 7–22.

Arnett, J. J. (2000). Emerging adulthood: A theory of development from the late teens through the twenties. *American Psychologist, 55*, 469–480.

Arnett, J. J. (2014). Presidential address: The emergence of emerging adulthood: A personal history. *Emerging Adulthood, 2*, 155–162.

Arrestees Drug Abuse Monitoring Program II. (2011, May). *2010 annual report*. Washington, DC: Executive Office of the President, Office of National Drug Control Policy.

Ascione, R. R. (1997). *Animal welfare and domestic violence*. Logan, UT: Utah State University.

Ashford, J. B., Sales, B. D., & Reid, W. H. (2001). Introduction. In J. B. Ashford, B. D. Sales, & W. H. Reid (Eds.), *Treating adult and juvenile offenders with special needs*. Washington, DC: American Psychological Association.

Asscher, J. J., Dekovic, M., Manders, W. A., van der Laan, P. H., & Prins, P. J. (2013). A randomized controlled trial of the effectiveness of Multisystemic Therapy in the Netherlands: Post-treatment changes and moderator effects. *Journal of Experimental Criminology, 9*, 169–187.

Asscher, J. J., van Vugt, E. S., Stams, G. J. J. M., Deković, M., Eichelsheim, V. I., & Yousfi, S. (2011). The relationship between juvenile psychopathic traits, delinquency, and (violent) recidivism: A meta-analysis. *Journal of Child Psychology and Psychiatry, 52*, 1134–1143.

Au Coin, K. (2003a). Family violence against older adults. *Family violence in Canada: A statistical profile 2003*. Ottawa, ON: Canadian Centre for Justice Statistics.

Ax, R. K., Fagan, T. J., Magaletta, P. R., Morgan, R. D., Nussbaum, D., & White, T. W. (2007). Innovations in correctional assessment and treatment. *Criminal Justice and Behavior, 34*, 893–905.

Azziz-Baumgartner, E., McKeown, L., Melvin, P., Dang, Q., & Reed, J. (2011). Rates of femicide in women of different races, ethnicities, and places of birth: Massachusetts, 1993–2007. *Journal of Interpersonal Violence, 26*, 1077–1090.

Babchishin, K. M., Hanson, R. K., & Blais, J. (in press). Less is more: Using Static-200R subscales to predict violent and general recidivism among sexual offenders. *Sexual Abuse: A Journal of Research and Treatment*.

Babchishin, K. M., Hanson, R. K., & Hermann, C. A. (2011). The characteristics of online sex offenders: A meta-analysis. *Sexual Abuse: A Journal of Research and Treatment, 23*, 92–123.

Babchishin, K. M., Hanson, R. K., & VanZuylen, H. (2015). Online child pornography offenders are different: A meta-analysis of the characteristics of online and offline sex offenders against children. *Archives of Sexual Behavior, 44*, 45–66.

Babiak, P., & Hare, R. D. (2006). *Snakes in suits: When psychopaths go to work*. New York: Regan Books.

Babiak, P., Neumann, C. S., & Hare, R. D. (2010). Corporate psychopathy: Talking the walk. *Behavioral Sciences & the Law, 28*, 174–193.

Bacigal, R. J. (2002). Assault and battery. In K. L. Hall (Ed.), *The Oxford companion to American law* (p. 43). New York: Oxford University Press.

Baglivio, M. T., Jackowski, K., Greenwald, M. A., & Wolff, K. T. (2014). Comparison of Multisystemic Therapy and Functional Family Therapy effectiveness. *Criminal Justice and Behavior, 41*, 1033–1056.

Bagwell, C. L. (2004). Friendships, peer networks, and antisocial behavior. In J. B. Kupersmidt & K. A. Dodge (Eds.), *Children's peer relations: From development to intervention* (pp. 37–57). Washington, DC: American Psychological Association.

Baird, K. A. (2007). A survey of clinical psychologists in Illinois regarding prescription privileges. *Professional Psychology: Research and Practice, 38*, 196–202.

Bakker, E. (2006). *Jihadi terrorists in Europe, their characteristics and the circumstances in which they joined the jihad: An exploratory study*. The Hague: Clingendael Institute.

Ball, J. C., Shaffer, J. W., & Nurco, D. N. (1983). The day-to-day criminality of heroin addicts in Baltimore—a study in the continuity of offense rates. *Drug and Alcohol Dependence, 12*, 119–142.

Bandura, A. (1965). Influence of models' reinforcement contingencies on the acquisition of imitative responses. *Journal of Personality and Social Psychology, 1*, 589–595.

Bandura, A. (1973a). *Aggression: A social learning analysis*. Englewood Cliffs, NJ: Prentice Hall.

Bandura, A. (1973b). Social learning theory of aggression. In J. F. Knutson (Ed.), *The control of aggression* (pp. 1–32). Chicago: Aldine.

Bandura, A. (1983). Psychological mechanisms of aggression. In R. G. Geen & E. I. Donnerstein (Eds.), *Aggression: Theoretical and empirical reviews: Vol. 1*. New York: Academic Press.

Bandura, A. (1989). Human agency in social cognitive theory. *American Psychologist, 44*, 1175–1184.

Bandura, A. (1990). Selective activation and disengagement of moral control. *Journal of Social Issues, 46*, 27–46.

Bandura, A. (1991). Social cognitive theory or moral thought and action. In M. W. Kurtines & J. L. Gewirtz (Eds.), *Handbook of moral behavior and development: Vol. I. Theory*. Hillsdale, NJ: Erlbaum.

Bandura, A. (1997). *Self-efficacy: The exercise of control*. New York: Freeman.

Bandura, A. (1999). Moral disengagement in the perpetration of inhumanities. *Personality and Social Psychology Review, 3*, 193–209.

Bandura, A. (2001). Social cognitive theory: An agentic perspective. *Annual Review of Psychology, 52*, 1–26.

Bandura, A. (2004). The role of selective moral disengagement in terrorism and counterterrorism. In F. M. Moghaddam & A. J. Marsella (Eds.), *Understanding terrorism: Psychosocial roots, consequences, and interventions* (pp. 121–150). Washington, DC: American Psychological Association.

Bandura, A., Barbaranelli, C., Caprara, G. V., & Pastorelli, C. (1996). Mechanisms of moral disengagement in the exercise of moral agency. *Journal of Personality and Social Psychology, 71*, 364–374.

Bandura, A., Caprara, G. V., Barbaranelli, C., Pastorelli, C., & Regalia, C. (2001). Sociocognitive self-regulatory mechanisms governing transgressive behavior. *Journal of Personality and Social Psychology, 80*, 125–135.

Bandura, A., & Huston, A. (1961). Identification as a process of incidental learning. *Journal of Abnormal and Social Psychology, 63*, 311–318.

Bandura, A., Ross, D., & Ross, S. (1963). Vicarious reinforcement and imitative learning. *Journal of Abnormal and Social Psychology, 67*, 601–607.

Bandura, A., & Walters, R. H. (1959). *Adolescent aggression*. New York: Ronald Press.

Bank Crime Statistics. (2011). *Bank Crime Report: Final 2010*. Washington, DC: U.S. Department of Justice, Federal Bureau of Investigation.

Bank, L., & Patterson, G. R. (1992). The use of structural equation modeling in combining data from different types of assessment. In J. C. Rosen & P. McReynolds (Eds.), *Recent advances in psychological assessment: Vol. 8* (pp. 41–74). New York: Plenum Press.

Banks, D., & Kyckelhahn, T. (2011, April). *Characteristics of suspected human trafficking incidents, 2008–2010*. Washington, DC: U.S. Department of Justice, Bureau of Justice Statistics.

Bao, Q. S., Lu, C-Y., Song, H., Wang, M., Ling, W., Chen, W-Q., et al. (2009). Behavioural development of school-aged children who live around a multi-metal sulphide mine in Guangdong province, China: A cross-sectional study. *BMC Public Health, 9*, 1–8.

Barash, J., Tranel, D., & Anderson, S. W. (2000). Acquired personality disturbances associated with bilateral damage to the ventromedial prefrontal region. *Developmental Neuropsychology, 18*, 355–381.

Barbaree, H. E., & Marshall, W. L. (Eds.). (2006). *The juvenile sex offender* (2nd ed.). New York: Guilford Press.

Bardone, A. M., Moffitt, T. E., & Caspi, A. (1996). Adult mental health and social outcomes of adolescent girls with depression and conduct disorder. *Development and Psychopathology, 8*, 811–829.

Barker, M. (2000). The criminal range of small-town burglars. In D. Canter & L. Alison (Eds.), *Profiling property crimes* (pp. 57–74). Dartmouth, UK: Ashgate.

Barlett, C. P., & Gentile, D. A. (2012). Attacking others on line: The formation of cyberbullying in late adolescence. *Psychology of Popular Media Culture, 1*, 123–133.

Barling, J., Dupré, K. E., & Kelloway, E. K. (2009). Predicting workplace aggression and violence. *Annual Review of Psychology, 60*, 672–692.

Barnes, J. C., Beaver, K. M., & Boutwell, B. B. (2011). Examining the genetic underpinnings to Moffitt's developmental taxonomy: A behavioral genetic analysis. *Criminology, 49*, 923–954.

Barnoski, R. (2009). *Providing evidence-based programs with fidelity in Washington State juvenile courts: Cost analysis* (Document No. 09-12-1201). Olympia, WA: Washington State Institute for Public Policy.

Baron, R. A. (1977). *Human aggression.* New York: Plenum.

Baron, R. A. (1983). The control of human aggression: An optimistic perspective. *Journal of Social and Clinical Psychology, 1*, 97–119.

Baron, R. A., & Byrne, D. (1977). *Social psychology* (2nd ed.). Boston: Allyn and Bacon.

Barrett, D. (2014, September 25). Mass shootings on the rise. *The Wall Street Journal,* p. A3.

Barrett, D. E., Ju, S., Katsiyannis, A., & Zhang, D. (2015). Females in the juvenile justice system: Influences on delinquency and recidivism. *Journal of Child and Family Studies, 24*, 427–433.

Barry, C. T., Frick, P. J., DeShazo, T. M., McCoy, M. G., Ellis, M., & Loney, B. R. (2000). The importance of callous-unemotional traits for extending the concept of psychopathy to children. *Journal of Abnormal Psychology, 109*, 335–340.

Barry, T. D., Barry, C. T., Deming, A. M., & Lochman, J. E. (2008). Stability of psychopathic characteristics in childhood. *Criminal Justice and Behavior, 35*, 244–262.

Barstow, D., & Van Natta, D., Jr. (2001, July 15). How Bush took Florida: Mining the overseas absentee vote. *The New York Times,* Section 1, p. 1.

Bartholow, B. D., Sestir, M. A., & Davis, E. B. (2005). Correlates and consequences of exposure to video game violence: Hostile personality, empathy, and aggressive behavior. *Personality and Social Psychology Bulletin, 31*, 1573–1586.

Bartol, C. R., & Bartol, A. M. (2013). *Criminal and behavioral profiling.* Thousand Oaks, CA: Sage.

Basile, K. C., & Smith, S. G. (2011). Sexual violence victimization of women: Prevalence, characteristics, and the role of public health and prevention. *American Journal of Lifestyle Medicine, 5*, 407–417.

Bates, J. E., & McFadyen-Ketchum, S. (2000). Temperament and parent-child relations as interacting factors in children's behavioral adjustment. In V. Molfese & D. L. Molfese (Eds.), *Temperament and personality development across the life span* (pp. 71–94). Mahway, NJ: Lawrence Erlbaum Associates.

Bates, J. E., Pettit, G. S., Dodge, K. A., & Ridge, B. (1998). Interaction of temperamental resistance to control and restrictive parenting in the development of externalizing behavior. *Developmental Psychology, 34*, 982–995.

Baum, K., Catalano, S., & Rand, M. (2009, January). *Stalking victimization in the United States.* Washington, DC: U.S. Department of Justice, Bureau of Justice Statistics.

Bauman, S. (2010). Cyberbullying in a rural intermediate school: An exploratory study. *Journal of Early Adolescence, 30*, 803–833.

Baumer, T. L., & Rosenbaum, D. P. (1984). *Combating retail theft: Programs and strategies.* Boston: Butterworth.

Baumrind, D. (1991a). Parenting styles and adolescent development. In J. Brooks-Gunn, R. Lerner, & A. C. Petersen (Eds.), *The encyclopedia of adolescence.* New York: Garland.

Baumrind, D. (1991b). The influence of parenting style on adolescent competence and substance use. *Journal of Early Adolescence, 11*, 56–95.

Beaman, A., Barnes, P. J., Klentz, B., & McQuirk, B. (1978). Increasing helping rates through information dissemination: Teaching pays. *Personality and Social Psychology Bulletin, 105*, 113–121.

Beatty, D. (2001). Stalking. In G. Coleman, M. Gaboury, M. Murray, & A. Seymour (Eds.), *1999 National Victim Assistance Academy.* Washington, DC: U.S. Department of Justice.

Beauchaine, T. P., Hinshaw, S. P., & Pang, K. L. (2010). Comorbidity of attention-deficit/hyperactivity disorder and early-onset conduct disorder: Biological, environmental, and developmental mechanisms. *Clinical Psychology: Science and Practice, 17*, 327–336.

Beauregard, E., Proulx, J., Rossmo, K., Leclerc, B., & Allaire, J-F. (2007). Script analysis of the hunting process of serial sex offenders. *Criminal Justice and Behavior, 34*, 1069–1084.

Beck, A. J., Cantor, D., Hartge, J., & Smith, T. (2013, June). *Sexual victimization in juvenile facilities reported by youth, 2012.* Washington, DC: U.S. Department of Justice, Bureau of Justice Statistics.

Beck, A. J., Harrison, P. M., & Guerino, P. (2010). *Sexual victimization in juvenile facilities reported by youth, 2008–2009.* Washington, DC: U.S. Department of Justice, Office of Justice Programs, Bureau of Justice Statistics.

Becker, E. (1973). *The denial of death.* New York: Free Press.

Becker, E. (1975). *Escape from evil.* New York: Free Press.

Becker, K. D., Stuewig, J., Herrera, V. M., & McCloskey, L. A. (2004). A study of firesetting and animal cruelty in children: Family influences and adolescent outcomes. *Journal of the American Academy of Child and Adolescent Psychiatry, 43*, 905–913.

Beckett, R. C. (1987). *Children and Sex Questionnaire.* Oxford, UK: Oxford Forensic Services.

Beech, A. R., Mandeville-Norden, R., & Goodwill, A. (2012). Comparing recidivism rates of treatment responders/nonresponders in a sample of 413 child molesters who had completed community-based sex offender treatment in the United Kingdom. *International Journal of Offender Therapy and Comparative Criminology, 56*, 29–49.

Belknap, J., & Sharma, N. (2014). The significant frequency and impact of stealth (nonviolent) gender-based abuse among college women. *Trauma, Violence, and Abuse, 15*, 181–190.

Bennell, C., & Canter, D. V. (2002). Linking commercial burglaries by modus operandi: Tests using regression and ROC analysis. *Science and Justice, 42*, 153–162.

Bennell, C., & Jones, N. J. (2005). Between a ROC and a hard place: A method for linking serial burglaries using an offender's modus operandi. *Journal of Investigative Psychology and Offender Profiling, 2*, 23–41.

Bennett, D. S., Bendersky, M., & Lewis, M. (2002). Children's intellectual and emotional-behavioral adjustment at 4 years as a function of cocaine exposure, maternal characteristics, and environmental risk. *Developmental Psychology, 38*, 648–658.

Bennett, T., Holloway, K., & Farrington, D. (2008). The statistical association between drug misuse and crime: A meta-analysis. *Aggression and Violent Behavior, 13*, 107–118.

Bennett, T., & Wright, R. (1984). *Burglars on burglary: Prevention and the offender.* Brookfield, VT: Gower.

Benson, M. L., & Moore, E. (1992). Are white-collar and common offenders the same? An empirical and theoretical critique of a recently proposed general theory of crime. *Journal of Research in Crime and Delinquency, 29*, 251–272.

Berkowitz, L. (1962). *Aggression: A social-psychological analysis.* New York: McGraw-Hill.

Berkowitz, L. (1969). The frustration-aggression hypothesis revisited. In L. Berkowitz (Ed.), *Roots of aggression.* New York: Atherton Press.

Berkowitz, L. (1973). Words and symbols as stimuli to aggressive responses. In J. F. Knutson (Ed.), *The control of aggression.* Chicago: Aldine.

Berkowitz, L. (1983). The experience of anger as a parallel process in the display of impulsive, "angry" aggression. In R. G. Geen & E. I. Donnerstein (Eds.), *Aggression: Theoretical and empirical reviews: Vol. 1.* New York: Academic Press.

Berkowitz, L. (1989). Frustration-aggression hypothesis: Examination and reformulation. *Psychological Bulletin, 106*, 59–73.

Berkowitz, L. (1994). Guns and youth. In L. E. Eron, J. H. Gentry, & P. Schlegel (Eds.), *Reason to hope: A psychosocial perspective on violence and* *youth* (pp. 251–280). Washington, DC: American Psychological Association.

Berkowitz, L., & LePage, A. (1967). Weapons as aggression-eliciting stimuli. *Journal of Personality and Social Psychology, 7*, 202–207.

Berlyne, D. E. (1960). *Conflict, arousal, and curiosity.* New York: McGraw-Hill.

Bernard, F. (1975). An inquiry among a group of pedophiles. *Journal of Sex Research, 11*, 242–255.

Bernasco, W. (2006). Co-offending and the choice of target areas in burglary. *Journal of Investigative Psychology and Offending Profiling, 3*, 139–155.

Bernasco, W. (2008). Then again? Same-offender involvement in repeat and near repeat burglaries. *European Journal of Criminology, 5*, 411–431.

Bernstein, A., Newman, J. P., Wallace, J. F., & Luh, K. E. (2000). Left hemisphere activation and deficient response modulation in psychopaths. *Psychological Science, 11*, 414–418.

Burchard (1987). The effects of early educational intervention in adolescence and early adulthood. In J. D. Burhcard & S. N. Burchard (Eds.), *Prevention of delinquent behavior.* Newbury Park, CA: Sage.

Bettencourt, B. A., Talley, A., Benjamin, A. J., & Valentine, J. (2006). Personality and aggressive behavior under provoking and neutral conditions: A meta-analytic review. *Psychological Bulletin, 132*, 731–777.

Beyer, K., Mack, S. M., & Shelton, J. L. (2008). Investigative analysis of neonaticide: An exploratory study. *Criminal Justice and Behavior, 35*, 522–535.

Beyers, J. M., Bates, J. E., Pettit, G. S., & Dodge, K. A. (2003). Neighborhood structure, parenting processes, and the development of youths' externalizing behaviors: A multilevel analysis. *American Journal of Community Psychology, 31*, 35–53.

Bierman, K. L., Coie, J., Dodge, K., Greenberg, M., Lochman, J., McMohan, R., Pinderhughes, E., & Conduct Problems Prevention Research Group. (2013). School outcomes of aggressive-disruptive children: Prediction from kindergarten risk factors and impact of the Fast Track Prevention Program. *Aggressive Behavior, 39*, 114–130.

Biglan, A., Flay, B. R., Embry, D. D., & Sandler, I. N. (2012). The critical role of nurturing environments for promoting human well-being. *American Psychologist, 63*, 257–271.

Binelli, M. (2015, March 26). Inside America' toughest federal prison. *New York Times Magazine*, pp. 12–14.

Bjelopera, J. P., Bagalman, E., Caldwell, S. W., Finklea, K. M., & McCallion, G. (2013, March 18). *Public mass shootings in the United States: Selected implications for federal public health and safety policy.* Washington, DC: Congressional Research Service.

Bjorklund, D. F., & Hawley, P. H. (2014). Aggression grows up: Looking through an evolutionary developmental lens to understand the causes and consequences of human aggression. In T. K. Shackelford & R. D. Hansen (Eds.), *The evolution of violence. Evolutionary psychology* (pp. 159–186). New York: Springer Science and Business Media.

Björkqvist, K., Lagerspetz, M. J., & Kaukianinen, A. (1992). Do girls manipulate and boys fight? Developmental trends in regard to direct and indirect aggression. *Aggressive Behavior, 18*, 117–127.

Black, H. C. (1990). *Black's law dictionary.* St. Paul, MN: West Publishing.

Black, M. S., & Pettway, C. (2001, December). *Profile of ODRC offenders assessed at the sex offender risk reduction center.* Columbus, OH: Ohio Office of Policy, Bureau of Research.

Blackburn, R. (1993). *The psychology of criminal conduct: Theory, research and practice.* Chichester, UK: Wiley.

Blackburn, R. (1998). Criminality and the interpersonal circle in mentally disordered offenders. *Criminal Justice and Behavior, 25*, 155–176.

Blair, C., & Raver, C. C. (2012). Child development in the context of adversity: Experiential canalization of brain and behavior. *American Psychologist, 67*, 309–318.

Blair, R. J. R., Peschardt, K. S., Budhani, S., Mitchell, D. G. V., & Pine, D. S. (2006). The development of psychopathy. *Journal of Child Psychology and Psychiatry, 47*, 262–275.

Blake, D. D., Weathers, F. W., & Nagy, L. M. (1995). The development of a clinician-administered PTSD scale. *Journal of Traumatic Stress, 8*, 75–90.

Blake, E., & Gannon, T. A. (2010). The implicit theory of rape-prone men: An information-processing investigation. *International Journal of Offender Therapy and Comparative Criminology, 54*, 895–914.

Blanchard, R., Klassen, P., Dickey, R., Kuban, M. E., & Blak, T. I. (2001). Sensitivity and specificity of the phallometric test for pedophilia in nonadmitting sex offenders. *Psychological Assessment, 13*, 118–126.

Blanchard, R., Watson, M. S., Choy, A., Dickey, R., Klassen, P., Kuban, M., & Ferren, D. J. (1999). Pedophiles: Mental retardation, maternal age, and sexual orientation. *Archives of Sexual Behavior, 28*, 111–127.

Blanco, C., Grant, J., Petry, N. M., Simpson, H. B., Alegria, A., Liu, S-M., et al. (2008). Prevalence and correlates of shoplifting in the United States: Results from the National Epidemiologic Survey on Alcohol and Related Conditions (NESARC). *American Journal of Psychiatry, 155*, 905–913.

Blandon, A. Y., Calkins, S. D., Grimm, K. J. Keane, S. P., & O'Brien, M. (2010). Testing a developmental cascade model of emotional and social competence and early peer acceptance. *Development and Psychopathology, 22*, 737–748.

Blass, T. (2009). From, New Haven to Santa Clara: A historical perspective on the Milgram obedience experiments. *American Psychologist, 64*, 37–45.

Blickle, G., Schlegel, A., Fassbender, P., & Klein, V. (2006). Some personality correlates of business white-collar crime. *Applied Psychology: An International Review, 55*, 220–233.

Blitstein, J. L., Murray, D. M., Lytle, L. A., Birnbaum, A. S., & Perry, C. L. (2005). Predictors of violent behavior in an early adolescent cohort: Similarities and differences across genders. *Health Education and Behavior, 32*, 175–194.

Blonigen, D. M., Carlson, S. R., Krueger, R. F., & Patrick, C. J. (2003). A twin study of self-reported psychopathic traits. *Personality and Individual Differences, 35*, 179–197.

Blonigen, D. M., Hicks, B. M., Krueger, R. F., Iacono, W. G., & Patrick, C. J. (2005). Psychopathic personality traits: Heritability and genetic overlap with internalizing and externalizing psychopathology. *Psychological Medicine, 35*, 637–648.

Bloom, B., Owen, B., Deschenes, E. P., & Rosenbaum, J. (2002). Moving toward justice for female juvenile offenders in the new millennium: Modeling gender-specific policies and programs. *Journal of Contemporary Criminal Justice, 18*, 37–56.

Blumenthal, D. R. (1999). *The banality of good and evil: Moral lessons from the Shoah and Jewish tradition.* Washington, DC: Georgetown University Press.

Blumer, H., Sutter, A., Ahmed, S., & Smith, R. (1967). *ADD center final report: The world of youthful drug use.* Berkeley, CA: University of California Press.

Böckler, N., Seeger, T., Sitzer, P., & Heitmeyer, W. (2013). School shootings: Conceptual framework and international empirical trends. In N. Böckler, T. Seeger, P. Sitzer, & W. Heitmeyer (Eds.), *School shootings: International research, case studies, and concepts for prevention* (pp. 1–26). New York: Springer.

Boehnert, C. E. (1989). Characteristics of successful and unsuccessful insanity pleas. *Law and Human Behavior, 13*, 31–39.

Bolt, D. M., Hare, R. D., Vitale, J. E., & Newman, J. P. (2004). A multigroup item response theory analysis of the Psychopathy Checklist—Revised. *Psychological Assessment, 16*, 155–168.

Bonanno, G. A. (2004). Loss, trauma, and human resilience: Have we underestimated the human capacity to thrive after extremely aversive events? *American Psychologist, 59*, 20–28.

Bongers, I. L., Koot, H. M., van der Ende, J., & Verhulst, F. C. (2003). The normative development of child and adolescent problem behavior. *Journal of Abnormal Psychology, 112*, 179–192.

Bonnie, R. J., & Grisso, T. (2000). Adjudicative competence and youthful offenders. In T. Grisso & R. G. Schwartz (Eds.), *Youth on trial.* Chicago: University of Chicago Press.

Bonomi, A. E., Anderson, M. L., Cannon, E. A., Slesnick, N., & Rodriguez, M. A. (2009). Intimate partner violence in Latina and non-Latina. *American Journal of Preventive Medicine, 36*, 43–48.

Bonta, J., & Andrews, D. A. (2007). *Risk-need-responsivity model for offender assessment and rehabilitation (corrections research user report no. 2007–06).* Ottawa, ON: Public Safety Canada.

Bonta, J., Law, M., & Hanson, K. (1998). The prediction of criminal and violent recidivism among mentally disordered offenders: A meta-analysis. *Psychological Bulletin, 123*, 123–142.

Borduin, C. M., Mann, B. J., Cone, L. T., Henggeler, S. W., Fucci, B. R., Blaske, D. M., et al. (1995). Multisystemic treatment of serious juvenile offenders: Long-term prevention of criminality and violence. *Journal of Consulting and Clinical Psychology, 63*, 569–578.

Borduin, C. M., Schaeffer, C. M., & Heiblum, N. (2009). A randomized clinical trial of multisystemic therapy with juvenile sexual offenders: Effects on youth social ecology and criminal activity. *Journal of Consulting and Clinical Psychology, 77*, 26–37.

Borum, R. (1996). Improving the clinical practice of violence risk assessment. *American Psychologist, 51*, 945–956.

Borum, R., Bartel, P., & Forth, A. (2006). *Manual for the Structured Assessment of Violence Risk in Youth (SAVRY).* Odessa, FL: Psychological Assessment Resources.

Borum, R., & Fulero, S. M. (1999). Empirical research on the insanity defense and attempted reforms: Evidence toward informed policy. *Law and Human Behavior, 23*, 375–394.

Borum, R., & Gelles, M. (2005). Al-Qaeda's operational evolution: Behavioral and Organizational Perspectives. *Behavioral Sciences & the Law, 23*, 467–483.

Borum, R., & Strentz, T. (1993, April). The borderline personality: Negotiation strategies. *FBI Law Enforcement Bulletin*, 6–10.

Bourke, M. L., & Hernandez, A. E. (2009). The "Butner Study" redux: A report of the incidence of hands-on child victimization by child pornography offender. *Journal of Family Violence, 24*, 183–191.

Bowlby, J. (1969). *Attachment and loss: Vol. 1. Attachment.* New York: Basic Books.

Boxmeyer, C. L., Lochamn, J. E., Powell, N. P., & Powe, C. E. (2015). Preventing conduct disorders and related problems. In L. M. Scheier (Ed.), *Handbook of adolescent drug use prevention: Research, intervention strategies, and practice* (pp. 103–119). Washington, DC: American Psychological Association.

Braga, A. A., & Kennedy, D. M. (2001). The illicit acquisition of firearms by youth and juveniles. *Journal of Criminal Justice, 29*, 397–388.

Brandt, J. R., Kennedy, W. A., Patrick, C. J., & Curtain, J. J. (1997). Assessment of psychopathy in a population of incarcerated adolescent offenders. *Psychological Assessment, 9*, 429–435.

Brantley, A. G., & Kosky, R. H., Jr. (2005, January). Serial murder in the Netherlands: A look at motivation, behavior, and characteristics. *FBI Law Enforcement Bulletin*, 26–32.

Bray, C. (2009, March 12). Madoff pleads guilty to massive fraud. *The Wall Street Journal*, pp. A1, A9.

Brennan, P. A., Grekin, E. R., & Mednick, S. A. (1999). Maternal smoking during pregnancy and adult male criminal outcomes. *Archives of General Psychiatry, 56*, 215–219.

Brennan, P. A., Hall, J., Bor, W., Najman, J. M., & Williams, G. (2003). Integrating biological and social processes in relation to early-onset persistent aggression in boys and girls. *Developmental Psychology, 39*, 309–323.

Brennan, P. A., Mednick, S. A., & Hodgins, S. (2000). Major mental disorders and criminal violence in a Danish birth cohort. *Archives of General Psychiatry, 53*, 1033–1039.

Brenner, V., & Fox, R. A. (1999). An empirically derived classification of parenting practices. *The Journal of Genetic Psychology, 160*, 343–356.

Brent, D. A. (1989). The psychological autopsy: Methodological issues for the study of adolescent suicide. *Suicide and Life Threatening Behavior, 19*, 43–57.

Brett, A. (2004). 'Kindling theory' in arson: How dangerous are firesetters? *Australian and New Zealand Journal of Psychiatry, 38*, 419–425.

Breuer, J., Scharkow, M., & Quandt, T. (2015). Sore losers? A reexamination of the frustration-aggression hypothesis for colocated video game play. *Psychology of Popular Media Culture, 4*, 126–137.

Brier, N. (1989). The relationship between learning disability and delinquency: A review and reappraisal. *Journal of Learning Disabilities, 22*, 546–553.

Briere, J., Malamuth, N., & Ceniti, J. (1981). *Self-assessed rape proclivity: Attitudinal and sexual correlates.* Paper presented at APA Meeting, Los Angeles, CA.

Briggs, E. C., Thompson, R., Ostrowski, S., & Lekwauwa, R. (2011). Psychological, health, behavioral, and economic impact of child maltreatment. In J. W. White, M. P. Koss, & A. E. Kasdin (Eds.), *Violence against women and children: Vol. 1. Mapping the terrain* (pp. 77–97). Washington, DC: American Psychological Association.

Briggs, P., Simon, W. T., & Simonsen, S. (2011). An exploratory study of Internet-initiated sexual offenses and the chat room sex offender: Has the Internet enabled a new typology of sex offender. *Sexual Abuse: A Journal of Research and Treatment, 23*, 72–91.

Broadhurst, R. (2006). Developments in the global law enforcement of cyber-crime. *Policing: An International Journal of Police Strategies and Management, 29*, 408–433.

Brodsky, S. L. (1973). *Psychologists in the criminal justice system.* Urbana, IL: University of Illinois Press.

Brodsky, S. L. (1977). Criminal and dangerous behavior. In D. Rimm & J. Somervill (Eds.), *Abnormal psychology.* New York: Academic Press.

Broidy, L. M., Nagin, D. S., Tremblay, R. E., Bates, J. E., Brame, B., Dodge, K. A., et al. (2003). Developmental trajectories of childhood disruptive behaviors and adolescent delinquency: A six-site, cross-national study. *Developmental Psychology, 39*, 222–245.

Bronfenbrenner, U. (1979). *The ecology of human development: Experiments by design and nature.* Cambridge, MA: Harvard University Press.

Bronte-Tinkew, J., Moore, K. A., & Carrano, J. (2006). The father-child relationship, parenting styles, and adolescent risk behaviors in intact families. *Journal of Family Issues, 27*, 850–881.

Brown, B. B., & Harris, P. B. (1989). Residential burglary victimization: Reactions to the invasion of a primary territory. *Journal of Environmental Psychology, 9*, 119–132.

Brown, J. S., & Farber, I. E. (1951). Emotions conceptualized as intervening variables—with suggestions toward a theory of frustration. *Psychological Bulletin, 48*, 465–495.

Brown, N. N., Connor, P. D., & Adler, R. S. (2012). Conduct-disordered adolescents with fetal alcohol spectrum disorder: Intervention in secure treatment settings. *Criminal Justice and Behavior, 39*, 770–793.

Browne, A., & Finkelhor, D. (1986). Impact of child sexual abuse: A review of the research. *Psychological Bulletin, 99*, 66–77.

Brownlie, E. B., Beitchman, J. J., Escobar, M., Young, A., Atkinson, L., Johnson, C., et al. (2004). Early language impairment and young adult delinquent and aggressive behavior. *Journal of Abnormal Child Psychology, 32*, 453–467.

Bryant, J., & Zillmann, D. (Eds.). (2002). *Media effects: Advances in theory and research* (2nd ed.). Mahwah, NJ: Erlbaum.

Buck, N. M. L., Leenaars, E. P. E. M., Emmelkamp, P. M. G., & van Marle, H. J. C. (2012). Explaining the relationship between insecure attachment and partner abuse: The role of personality characteristics. *Journal of Interpersonal Violence, 27*, 3149–3170.

Buckle, A., & Farrington, D. P. (1984). An observational study of shoplifting. *British Journal of Criminology, 24*, 63–73.

Buckle, A., & Farrington, D. P. (1994). Measuring shoplifting by systematic observation: A replication study. *Psychology, Crime & Law, 1*, 133–141.

Buist, K. L. (2010). Sibling relationship quality and adolescent delinquency: A latent growth curve approach. *Journal of Family Psychology, 24*, 400–410.

Bukowski, W. (2015). A history of drug abuse prevention science. In L. M. Scheier (Ed.), *Handbook of adolescent drug use prevention: Research, intervention strategies and practice* (pp. 31–48). Washington, DC: American Psychological Association.

Bumpass, E. R., Fagelman, F. D., & Birx, R. J. (1983). Intervention with children who set fires. *American Journal of Psychotherapy, 37*, 328–345.

Bureau of Justice Assistance. (2000, April). *Emerging judicial strategies for the mentally ill in the criminal caseload: Mental health courts.* Washington, DC: U.S. Department of Justice.

Bureau of Justice Statistics. (2000, June). *Drugs and crime facts: Drug use and crime.* Washington, DC: Author.

Bureau of Justice Statistics. (2012, May 3). *Number of violent victimizations, 2006–2010.* Generated using the NCVS Victimization Analysis Tool at www.bjs.gov.

Burgason, K. A., Thomas, S. A., & Berthelot, E. R. (2014). The nature of violence: A multilevel analysis of gun use and victim injury in violent interpersonal encounters. *Journal of Interpersonal Violence, 29*, 371–393.

Burger, J. M. (2009). Replicating Milgram: Would people still obey today? *American Psychologist, 64*, 1–11.

Burgess, R. L., & Akers, R. L. (1966). A differential association-reinforcement theory of criminal behavior. *Social Problems, 14*, 128–147.

Burke, B. L., Martens, A., & Faucher, E. H. (2010). Two decades of terror management theory: A meta-analysis of mortality salience research. *Personality and Social Psychology Review, 14*, 155–195.

Burke, J. D., Boylan, K., Rowe, R., Duku, E., Stepp, S. D., Hipwell, A. E., & Waldman, I. D. (2014). Identifying the irritability dimension of ODD: Application of a modified bifactor model across five large community samples of children. *Journal of Abnormal Psychology, 123*, 841–851.

Burke, J. D., Waldman, I., & Lahey, B. B. (2010). Predictive validity of childhood oppositional defiant disorder and conduct disorder: Implications for the DSM-V. *Journal of Abnormal Psychology, 119*, 739–751.

Burnam, M. A., Stein, J. A., Golding, J. M., Siegel, J. M., Sorenson, S. B., Forsythe, A. B., et al. (1988). Sexual assault and mental disorders in a community population. *Journal of Consulting and Clinical Psychology, 56*, 843–850.

Burnes, D. P. R., Rizzo, V. M., & Courtney, E. (2014). Elder abuse and neglect risk alleviation in protective services. *Journal of Interpersonal Violence, 29*, 2091–2113.

Burrough, B. (2015). *Days of rage: America's radical underground, the FBI, and the forgotten age of revolutionary violence.* New York: Penguin.

Burt, C., Sweeten, G., & Simons, R. L. (2014). Self-control through emerging adulthood: Instability, multidimensionality, and criminological significance. *Criminology, xxx*, 1–38.

Burt, S. A. (2009). Are there meaningful etiological differences within antisocial behavior? Results of a meta-analysis. *Clinical Psychological Review, 29*. 163–178.

Busch, K. G., & Weissman, S. H. (2005). The intelligence community and the war on terror: The role of behavioral science. *Behavioral Sciences & the Law, 23*, 559–571.

Bushman, B. J., & Anderson, C. A. (2001). Is it time to pull the plug on the hostile versus instrumental aggression dichotomy. *Psychological Review, 108*, 273–279.

Bushman, B. J., Bonacci, A. M., Pederson, W. C., Vasquez, E. A., & Miller, N. (2005). Chewing on it can chew you up: Effects of rumination on triggered displaced aggression. *Journal of Personality and Social Psychology, 88*, 969–983.

Bushman, B. J., Gollwitzer, M., & Cruz, C. (2015). There is broad consensus: Media researchers agree that violent media increase aggression in children, and pediatricians and parents concur. *Psychology of Popular Media Culture, 4*, 200–214.

Buss, A. H. (1971). Aggression pays. In J. L. Singer (Ed.), *The control of aggression and violence.* New York: Academic Press.

Butler, H., & Gannon, T. A. (2015). The scripts and expertise of firesetters: A preliminary conceptualization. *Aggression and Violent Behavior, 20*, 72–81.

Butler, R. A. (1954). Curiosity in monkeys. *Scientific American* (Reprint #426). San Francisco: W. H. Freeman.

Cacioppo, J. T., Berntson, G. G., Sheridan, J. F., & McClintock, M. K. (2000). Multilevel integrative analyses of human behavior: Social neuroscience and the complementing nature of social and biological approaches. *Psychological Bulletin, 6*, 829–843.

Caetano, R., Field, C. A., Ramisetty-Mikler, S., & McGrath, C. (2005). The 5-year course of intimate partner violence among White, Black, and Hispanic couples in the United States. *Journal of Interpersonal Violence, 20*, 1039–1057.

Cairns, R. B., Cairns, B. D., Neckerman, H. J., Ferguson, L. L., & Gariépy, J. L. (1989). Growth and aggression: I. Childhood to early adolescence. *Developmental Psychology, 25*, 320–330.

Caldwell, M. F., McCormick, D. J., Umstead, D., & Van Rybroek, G. J. (2007). Evidence of treatment progress and therapeutic outcomes among adolescents with psychopathic features. *Criminal Justice and Behavior, 34*, 573–587.

Caldwell, M. F., Skeem, J. L., Salekin, R., & Van Rybroek, G. (2006). Treatment response of adolescent offenders with psychopathy features: A 2-year follow up. *Criminal Justice and Behavior, 33*, 571–596.

California Division of Occupational Safety and Health. (1995). *Guidelines for workplace security.* San Francisco: California Department of Industrial Relations.

Callahan, L. A., McGreevy, M. A., Circincione, C., & Steadman, H. J. (1992). Measuring the effects of guilty but mentally ill (GBMI) verdict. *Law and Human Behavior, 16*, 447–462.

Callahan, L. A., Steadman, H. J., McGreevy, M. A., & Robbins, P. C. (1991). The volume and characteristics of insanity defense pleas: An eight-state study. *Bulletin of Psychiatry and the Law, 19*, 331–338.

Cameron, M. O. (1964). *The booster and the snitch.* New York: Free Press.

Camilleri, J. A., & Quinsey, V. L. (2008). Pedophilia: Assessment and treatment. In D. R. Laws & W. T. O'Donohue (Eds.), *Sexual deviance: Theory, assessment, and treatment* (pp. 183–212). New York: Guilford.

Campbell, A. (1993). *Men, women, and aggression.* New York: Basic Books.

Campbell, A. (2006). Sex differences in direct aggression: What are the psychological mediators. *Aggression and Violent Behavior, 22*, 237–264.

Campbell, M. A., French, S., & Gendreau, P. (2009). The prediction of violence in adult offenders: A meta-analytic comparison of instruments and methods of assessment. *Criminal Justice and Behavior, 36*, 567–590.

Campbell, M. A., Porter, S., & Santor, D. (2004). Psychopathic traits in adolescent offenders: An evaluation of criminal history, clinical, and psychosocial correlates. *Behavioral Sciences & the Law, 22*, 23–47.

Canadian Government's Commission of Inquiry. (1971). *The non-medical use of drugs: Interim report.* London: Penguin Books.

Canter, D. V. (2000a). Offender profiling and criminal differentiation. *Legal and Criminological Psychology, 5*, 23–46.

Canter, D. V. (2000b). *Criminal shadows: The inner narratives of evil.* Irving, TX: Authorlink Press.

Canter, D. (2008). Geographical profiling of criminals. In D. Canter & D. Youngs (Eds.), *Principles of geographical offender profiling* (pp. 197–219). Burlington, VT: Ashgate.

Canter, D., & Alison, L. (2000). Profiling property crimes. In D. Canter & L. Alison (Eds.), *Profiling property crimes* (pp. 1–30), Burlington, VT: Ashgate.

Canter, D. V., Alison, L. J., Alison, E., & Wentink, N. (2004). The organized/disorganized typology of serial murder: Myth or model? *Psychology, Public Policy, and Law, 10*, 293–320.

Canter, D. V., & Fritzon, K. (1998). Differentiating arsonists: A model of firesetting actions and characteristics. *Legal and Criminological Psychology, 3*, 73–96.

Cantón-Cortés, D., Cortés, M. R. & Cantón, J. (2015). Child sexual abuse, attachment style, and depression: The role of the characteristics of abuse. *Journal of Interpersonal Violence, 30*, 420–436.

Caprara, G. V., Tisak, M. S., Alessandri, G., Fontaine, R. G., Fida, R., & Paciello, M. (2013). The contribution of moral disengagement in mediating individual tendencies toward aggression and violence. *Developmental Psychology, 50*, 71–85.

Caputo, G. A. (2004). Treating sticky fingers: An evaluation of treatment and education for shoplifters. *Journal of Offender Rehabilitation, 38*, 49–68.

Caputo, G. A., & King, A. (2011). Shoplifting: Work, agency, and gender. *Feminist Criminology, 63*, 159–177.

Carbon, S. B. (2010, September 14). *Rape in the United States: The chronic failure to report and investigate rape cases. Statement of Susan B. Carbon, Director, Office on Violence Against Women before the Subcommittee on Crime and Drugs, Committee on the Judiciary, United States Senate.* Washington, DC: U.S. Senate.

Carlson, B. E. (1991). Outcomes of physical abuse and observation of marital violence among adolescents in placement. *Journal of Interpersonal Violence, 6*, 526–534.

Carlson, M., Marcus-Newhall, A., & Miller, N. (1990). Effects of situational aggression cues: A quantitative review. *Journal of Personality and Social Psychology, 58*, 622–633.

Carraher, T. N., Carraher, D., & Schliemann, A. D. (1985). Mathematics in the streets and schools. *British Journal of Developmental Psychology, 3*, 21–29.

Carsten, M. K., & Uhl-Bien, M. (2013). Ethical fellowship: An examination of followership beliefs and crimes of obedience. *Journal of Leadership & Organizational Studies, 20*, 49–61.

Casey-Cannon, S., Hayward, C., & Gowen, K. (2001). Middle-school girls' reports of peer victimization: Concerns, consequences, and implications. *Professional School Counseling, 5*, 138–148.

Casillas, A., Robbins, S., Allen, J., Kuo Y-L., Hanson, M. A., & Schmeiser, C. (2012). Predicting early academic failure in high school from prior academic achievement, psychosocial characteristics, and behavior. *Journal of Educational Psychology, 104*, 407–420.

Caspi, A., Wright, B. R. E., Moffitt, T. E., & Silva, P. A. (1998). Early failure in the labor market: Childhood and adolescent predictors of unemployment in the transition to adulthood. *American Sociological Review, 63,* 424–451.

Catalano, R., Haggerty, K., Oesterle, S., Fleming, C., & Hawkins, J. D. (2004). The importance of bonding to school for healthy development: Findings from the Social Development Research Group. *Journal of School Health, 74,* 252–261.

Catalano, S. M. (2010, September). *Victimization during household burglary.* Washington, DC: U.S. Department of Justice, Bureau of Justice Statistics.

Catalano, S. M. (2012). *Intimate partner violence, 1993–2010.* Washington, DC: U.S. Department of Justice, Office of Justice Programs, Bureau of Justice Statistics.

Catalano, S. M. (2013). *Intimate partner violence: Attributes of victimization, 1993–2011.* Washington, DC: U.S. Department of Justice, Office of Justice Program, Bureau of Justice Statistics.

Cecchet, S. J., & Thoburn, J. (2014). The psychological experience of child and adolescent sex trafficking in the United States: Trauma and resilience in survivors. *Psychological Trauma, Theory, Research, Practice, and Policy, 6,* 482–491.

Centers for Disease Control and Prevention. (2009). *School connectedness: Strategies for increasing protection factors among youth.* Atlanta, GA: Department of Health and Human Services.

Centers for Disease Control and Prevention. (2011a, November). *Vitalsigns: Prescription painkiller overdoses in the US.* Atlanta, GA: Author.

Centers for Disease Control and Prevention. (2011b, November 1).Press release: Prescription painkiller overdoses at epidemic levels. Atlanta, GA: Author.

Centers for Disease Control and Prevention. (2012). *Youth risk behavior surveillance—United States, 2011* (Table 64, page no. 111). Atlanta, GA: Author.

Centers for Disease Control and Prevention. (2013b, February 20). *Press release: Opiods drive continued increase in drug overdose deaths.* Atlanta, GA: Author.

Centers for Disease Control and Prevention. (2014, October 16). *Facts about ADHD.* Atlanta, GA: Author.

Centers for Disease Control and Prevention. (2015, February 6). *Secondhand smoke (SHS) facts.* Atlanta, GA: Author.

Chabinsky, S. R. (2010, March 23). *The cyber threat: Who's doing what to whom? Key Note address at the GovSec/FOSE Conference.* Washington, DC: Government Security Conference.

Chaffin, M., Chenoweth, S., & Letourneau, E. J. (in press). Same sex and race-based disparities in statutory rape arrests. *Journal of Interpersonal Violence.*

Chamberlain, P. (1996). Treatment foster care for adolescents with conduct disorders and delinquency. In P. S. Jensen & D. Hibbs (Eds.), *Psychological treatment with research with children and adolescents.* Rockville, MD: National Institute of Mental Health.

Chappell, D. (1977). *Forcible rape: A national survey of the response by prosecutors.* Washington, DC: USGPO.

Chappell, A. T., & Piquero, A. R. (2004). Applying social learning theory to police misconduct. *Deviant Behavior, 25,* 89–108.

Chapple, C. L. (2003). Examining intergenerational violence: Violent role modeling or weak parental controls? *Violence and Victims, 18,* 143–159.

Chauhan, P., Warren, J., Kois, L., & Well-beloved-stone, J. (2015). Significance of combining evaluations of competency to stand trial and sanity at the time of the offense. *Psychology, Public Policy and Law, 21,* 56–59.

Chen, N., Deater-Deckard, K., Bell, M. A. (2014). The role of temperament by family environment interactions in child maladjustment. *Journal of Abnormal Child Psychology, 42,* 1251–1262.

Chen, Y-H., Arria, A., & Anthony, J. C. (2003). Firesetting in adolescents and being aggressive, shy, and rejected by peers: New epidemiologic evidence from a national sample survey. *Journal of the American Academy of Psychiatry and Law, 31,* 44–52.

Chermak, S. M., Freilich, J. D., & Shemtob, Z. (2009). Law-enforcement training and the domestic far right. *Criminal Justice and Behavior, 36,* 1305–1322.

Chesney-Lind, M. (2002). Criminalizing victimization: The unintended consequences of pro-arrest policies for girls and women. *Criminology and Public Policy, 2,* 81–90.

Chesney-Lind, M., & Shelden, R. (1998). *Girls, delinquency, and juvenile justice* (2nd ed.). Belmont, CA: West/Wadsworth.

Child Abuse Prevention Center. (1998). *Shaken baby syndrome fatalities in the United States.* Ogden, UT: Author.

Child Welfare Information Gateway. (2012, May). *Child abuse and neglect fatalities 2010: Statistics and interventions.* Washington, DC: Children's Bureau.

Chilosi, A. M., Cipriani, P., Pecini, C., Brizzolara, D., Blagi, L., Montanaro, D., et al. (2008). Acquired focal brain lesions in childhood: Effects on development and reorganization of language. *Brain & Language, 106,* 211–225.

Choe, D. E., Lane, J. D., Grabell, A. S., & Olson, S. L. (2013). Developmental precursors of young school-age children's hostile attribution bias. *Developmental Psychology, 49,* 2245–2256.

Christiansen, K. O. (1977). A review of studies of criminality among twins. In S. Mednick & K. O. Christiansen (Eds.), *Biosocial bases of criminal behavior* (pp. 45–88). New York: Gardiner Press.

Christy, A., Clark, C., Frei, A., & Rynearson-Moody, S. (2012). Challenges of diverting veterans to trauma informed care: The heterogeneity of Intercept 2. *Criminal Justice and Behavior, 39,* 461–474.

Chung, I-J, Hill, K. G., Hawkins, J. D., Gilchrist, L. D., & Nagin, D. S. (2002). Childhood predictors of offense trajectories. *Journal of Research in Crime and Delinquency, 39,* 60–90.

Cicero, T. J., Inciardi, J. A., & Muñoz, A. (2005). Trends in abuse of OxyContin® and other opioid analgesics in the United States: 2002–2004. *The Journal of Pain, 6,* 662–672.

Cillessen, A. H. N., Lansu, T. A. M., & Van Den Berg, Y. (2014). Aggression, hostile attributions, status, and gender: A continued quest. *Development and Psychopathology, 26,* 635–644.

Cillessen, A. H. N., & Mayeux, L. (2004). Sociometric status and peer group behavior: Previous findings and current directions. In J. B. Kupersmidt & K. A. Dodge (Eds.), *Children's peer relations: From development to intervention* (pp. 3–20). Washington, DC: American Psychological Association.

Cirincione, C., & Jacobs, C. (1999). Identifying insanity acquittals: Is it easier? *Law and Human Behavior, 23,* 487–497.

Claridge, G. (1973). Final remarks. In G. Claridge, S. Canter, & W. I. Hume (Eds.), *Personality differences and biological variations.* Oxford, UK: Pergamon Press.

Clark, J. P., & Hollinger, R. C. (1983). *Theft by employees in work organizations.* Washington, DC: USGPO.

Clay, R. A. (2013). Easing ADHD without meds. *Monitor on Psychology, 44,* 45–47.

Cleckley, H. (1976). *The mask of sanity* (5th ed.). St. Louis, MO: Mosby.

Clinard, M. B., & Quinney, E. R. (1980). *Criminal behavior systems: A typology.* New York: Holt, Rinehart & Winston.

Coatsworth, J. D. (nd). *A developmental psychopathology and resilience perspective on 21st century competences.* State College, PA: Pennsylvania State University, Department of Human Development and Family Studies.

Cochrane, R. E., Grisso, T., & Frederick, R. I. (2001). The relationship between criminal charges, diagnoses, and psychological opinions among federal defendants. *Behavioral Sciences & the Law, 19,* 565–582.

Cohen, D., & Strayer, J. (1996). Empathy in conduct-disordered and comparison youth. *Developmental Psychology, 32,* 988–998.

Cohen, F. (2008). *The mentally disordered inmate and the law* (2nd ed.). Kingston, NJ: Civic Research Institute.

Cohen, M., Seghorn, T., & Calmas, W. (1969). Sociometric study of the sex offender. *Journal of Abnormal Psychology, 74,* 249–255.

Cohen, M. L., Garafalo, R., Boucher, R., & Seghorn, T. (1971). The psychology of rapists. *Seminars in Psychiatry, 3,* 307–327.

Cohen, N. J., Menna, R., Vallance, D. D., Barwick, M., Im, N., & Horodezky, N. B. (1998). Language, social cognitive processing, and behavioral characteristics of psychiatrically disturbed children with previously identified and suspected language impairments. *Journal of Child Psychology and Psychiatry, 39,* 853–864.

Coie, J. D. (2004). The impact of negative social experience on the development of antisocial behavior. In J. B. Kupersmidt & K. A. Dodge (Eds.), *Children's peer relations: From development to intervention.* Washington, DC: American Psychological Association.

Coie, J. D., Belding, M., & Underwood, M. (1988). Aggression and peer rejection in childhood. In B. Lahey & A. Kazdin (Eds.), *Advances in clinical child psychology: Vol. 2.* New York: Plenum.

Coie, J. D., & Dodge, K. A. (1998). Aggression and antisocial behavior. In N. Eisenberg & W. Damon (Eds.), *Handbook of child psychology: Vol. 3. Social, emotional and personality development* (5th ed., pp. 779–862). New York: Wiley.

Coie, J. D., Dodge, K., & Kupersmith, J. (1990). Peer group behavior and social status. In S. R. Asher & J. D. Coie (Eds.), *Peer rejection in childhood.* Cambridge, UK: Cambridge University Press.

Coie, J. D., & Miller-Johnson, S. (2001). Peer factors and interventions. In R. Loeber & D. P. Farrington (Eds.), *Child delinquents: Development, intervention, and service needs.* Thousand Oaks, CA: Sage.

Colantonio, A., Kim, H., Allen, S., Asbridge, M., Petgrave, J., & Brochu, S. (2014). Traumatic brain injury and early life experiences among men and women in a prison population. *Journal of Correctional Health Care, 20*(4), 271–279.

Cole, C., & Winsler, A. (2010). Protecting children for exposure to lead: Old problem, new data, and new policy needs. *Social Policy Report, 24*(1), 1–23.

Coleman, J. W. (1998). *The criminal elite* (4th ed.). New York: St. Martin's Press.

Coley, R. J., & Barton, P. E. (2006). *Locked up and locked out: An educational perspective on the U.S. prison population.* Princeton, NJ: Educational Testing Service.

Collins, M. (2012, February 15). *Federal child pornography offenses. Testimony of Michelle Collins of the National Center for Missing & Exploited Children before the U.S. Sentencing Commission.* Washington, DC: U.S. Sentencing Commission.

Colwell, B., Villarreal, S. F., & Espinosa, E. M. (2012). Preliminary outcomes of a pre-adjudication diversion initiative for juvenile justice involved youth with mental health needs in Texas. *Criminal Justice and Behavior, 39,* 447–460.

Colwell, M. J., Pettit, G. S., Meece, D., Bates, J. E., & Dodge, K. A. (2001). Cumulative risk and continuity in nonparental care from infancy to early adolescence. *Merrill-Palmer Quarterly, 47,* 207–234.

Comer, R. J. (2004). *Abnormal psychology* (5th ed.). New York: Worth.

Committee on Preventive Psychiatry. (1999). Violent behavior in children and youth: Preventive intervention from a psychiatric perspective. *Journal of the American Academy of Child and Adolescent Psychiatry, 38,* 235–241.

Commons, M. L., & Goodheart, E. A. (2007). Consider stages of development in preventing terrorism: Does government building fail and terrorism result when developmental stages of governance are skipped? *Journal of Adult Development, 14,* 91–111.

Conduct Problems Prevention Research Group (CPPRG). (1999). Initial impact of the Fast Track prevention trial for conduct problems: I. The high-risk sample. *Journal of Consulting and Clinical Psychology, 67,* 631–647.

Conduct Problems Prevention Research Group (CPPRG). (2002). Evaluation of the first three years of the Fast Track Prevention Trial with children at high risk for adolescent conduct problems. *Journal of Abnormal Child Psychology, 30,* 19–35.

Conduct Problems Prevention Research Group. (2004). The fast track experiment: Translating the developmental model into a prevention design. In J. B. Kupersmidt & K. A. Dodge (Eds.), *Children's peer relations: From development to intervention* (pp. 181–208). Washington, DC: American Psychological Association.

Conduct Problems Prevention Research Group (CPPRG). (2010). Fast Track intervention effects on youth arrests and delinquency. *Journal of Experimental Criminology, 6,* 131–157.

Conklin, J. E. (1977). *Illegal but not criminal: Business crime not criminal.* Englewood Cliffs, NJ: Prentice Hall.

Connor, D. F., Ford, J. D., Chapman, J. F., & Banga, A. (2012). Adolescent attention deficit hyperactivity disorder in the secure treatment setting. *Criminal Justice and Behavior, 39,* 725–747.

Constantine, R. J., Petrila, J., Andel, R., Givens, E. M., Becker, M., Robst, J., et al. (2010). Arrest trajectories of adult offenders with a serious mental illness. *Psychology, Public Policy, and Law, 16,* 319–339.

Cook, K. (2014). *Kitty Genovese: The murder, the bystander, the crime that changed America.* New York: W. W. Norton.

Cook, P. J., Cukier, W., & Krause, K. (2009). The illicit firearms trade in North America. *Criminology and Criminal Justice, 9,* 265–286.

Cooke, D. J., & Michie, C. (1997). An item response theory analysis of the Hare Psychopathy Checklist-Revised. *Psychological Assessment, 9,* 3–14.

Cooke, D. J., & Michie, C. (2001). Refining the construct psychopathy: Toward a hierarchical model. *Psychological Assessment, 13,* 171–188.

Cooke, D. J., Michie, C., Hart, S. D., & Clark, D. A. (2004). Reconstructing psychopathy: Clarifying the significance of antisocial and socially deviant behavior in the diagnosis of psychopathic personality disorder. *Journal of Personality Disorders, 18,* 337–357.

Cooke, D. J., Michie, C., Hart, S. D., & Hare, R. D. (1999). Evaluation of the screening version of the Hare Psychopathy Checklist– Revised (PCL:SV): An item response theory analysis. *Psychological Assessment, 11,* 3–13.

Cooper, M., Schmidt, M. S., & Schmitt, E. (2013, April 24). Boston suspects are seen as self-taught and fueled by Web. *The New York Times,* p. A1.

Cooper, A., & Smith, E. L. (2011, November). *Homicide trends in the United States, 1980–2008: Annual rates for 2009 and 2010.* Washington, DC: U.S. Department of Justice, Bureau of Justice Statistics.

Coordinating Council on Juvenile Justice and Delinquency Prevention. (1996). *Combating violence and delinquency: The national juvenile justice action plan.* Washington, DC: USGPO.

Copeland, J., & Dillon, P. (2005). The health and psycho-social consequences of ketamine use. *International Journal of Drug Policy, 16,* 122–131.

Copes, H., & Cherbonneau, M. (2006). The key to auto theft. *British Journal of Criminology, 46,* 1–18.

Copes, H., & Vieraitis, L. (2007, July). *Identity theft: Assessing offenders' strategies and perceptions of risks.* Washington, DC: U.S. Department of Justice, National Institute of Justice.

Copes, H, & Vieraitis, L. (2009). Understanding identity theft: Offenders' accounts of their lives and crimes. *Criminal Justice Review, 34,* 329–349.

Cornell, D. G. (1989). Causes of juvenile homicide: A review of the literature. In E. P. Benedek & D. G. Cornell (Eds.), *Juvenile homicide.* Washington, DC: American Psychiatric Press.

Cornish, D. B., & Clarke, R. V. (1987). Understanding crime displacement: An application of rational choice theory. *Criminology, 25,* 933–947.

Corrado, R. R., Vincent, G. M., Hart, S. D., & Cohen, I. M. (2004). Predictive validity of the Psychopathy Checklist: Youth Version for general and violent recidivism. *Behavioral Sciences & the Law, 22,* 5–22.

Cortoni, F. (2015). What is so special about female sexual offenders? Introduction to the special issue on female sexual offenders. *Sexual Abuse: A Journal of Research and Treatment, 27,* 232–234.

Coscina, D. V. (1997). The biopsychology of impulsivity: Focus on brain serotonin. In C. D. Webster & M. A. Jackson (Eds.), *Impulsivity: Theory, assessment, and treatment.* New York: Guilford Press.

COT. (2007, June 7). *Lone-wolf terrorism.* The Hague, Netherlands: COT, Instituut voor Veiligheids- en Crisismanagement.

Côté, S., Zoccolillo, M., Tremblay, R. E., Nagin, D., & Vitaro, F. (2001). Predicting girls' conduct disorder in adolescence from childhood trajectories of disruptive behaviors. *Journal of the American Academy of Child & Adolescent Psychiatry, 40,* 678–684.

Cowan, P. A., & Cowan, C. P. (2004). From family relationships to peer rejection to antisocial behavior in middle childhood. In J. B. Kupersmidt & K. A. Dodge (Eds.), *Children's peer relations: From development to intervention* (pp. 159–178). Washington, DC: American Psychological Association.

Cowley, G. (1993, July 26). The not-young and the restless. *Newsweek,* pp. 48–49.

Cressey, D. R. (1953). *A study in the social psychology of embezzlement: Other people's money.* Glencoe, IL: Free Press.

Crick, N. R. (1995). Relational aggression: The role of intent attributions, feelings of distress, and provocation type. *Development and Psychopathology, 7,* 313–322.

Crick, N. R., & Grotpeter, J. K. (1995). Relational aggression, gender, and social-psychological adjustment. *Child Development, 66,* 710–722.

Crick, N. R., & Zahn-Waxler, C. (2003). The development of psychopathology in females and males: Current progress and future challenges. *Development and Psychopathology, 15,* 719–742.

Critchley, M. (1951). *The trial of Neville George Clevely Heath.* London: William Hodge.

Critchlow, B. (1986). The powers of John Barleycorn: Beliefs about the effects of alcohol on social behavior. *American Psychologist, 41,* 751–764.

Critchton, R. (1959). *The great imposter.* New York: Random House.

Critical Incident Response Group. (2001). *Workplace violence: Issues in response.* FBI Critical Incident Response Group, National Center for the Analysis of Violent Crime, Quantico, VA.

Crocker, A. G., & Hodgins, S. (1997). The criminality of noninstitutionalized mentally retarded persons: Evidence from a birth cohort followed to age 30. *Criminal Justice and Behavior, 24,* 432–454.

Cromwell, P. F., Olson, J. F., & Avary, D. W. (1991). *Breaking and entering: An ethnographic analysis of burglary.* Newbury Park, CA: Sage.

Cromwell, P. F., & Thurman, Q. (2003). The devil made me do it: Use of neutralizations by shoplifters. *Deviant Behavior, 24,* 535–550.

Crowe, R. R. (1974). An adoptive study of antisocial personality. *Archives of General Psychiatry, 31,* 785–791.

Crowe, S. L., & Blair, R. J. R. (2008). The development of antisocial behavior: What can we learn from functioning neuroimaging studies? *Development and Psychopathology, 20,* 1145–1159.

Cruise, K. R., Colwell, L. H., Lyons, P. M., & Baker, M. D. (2003). Prototypical analysis of adolescent psychopathy: Investigating the juvenile justice perspective. *Behavioral Sciences & the Law, 21,* 829–846.

Cruise, K. R., & Rogers, R. (1998). An analysis of competency to stand trial: An integration of case law and clinical knowledge. *Behavioral Sciences & the Law, 16,* 35–50.

Culberton, F. M., Feral, C. H., & Gabby, S. (1989). Pattern analysis of Wechsler Intelligence Scale for Children-Revised profiles of delinquent boys. *Journal of Clinical Psychology, 45,* 651–660.

Cummings, A., Gonzalez-Guarda, R. M., & Sandoval, M. F. (2013). Intimate partner violence among Hispanics: A review of the literature. *Journal of Family Violence, 28,* 153–171.

Curtis, N. M., Ronan, K. R., Heiblum, N., & Crellin, K. (2009). Dissemination and effectiveness of multisystemic treatment in New Zealand: A benchmarking study. *Journal of Family Psychology, 23,* 119–129.

Cusimano, M. D., Holmes, S. A., Sawicki, C., & Topolovec-Vranic, J. (2014). Assessing aggression following traumatic brain injury: A systematic review of validated aggression scales. *Journal of Head Trauma Rehabilitation, 29,* 172–184.

Dabney, D. A., Dugan, L., Topalli, V., & Hollinger, R. C. (2006). The impact of implicit stereotyping on offender profiling: Unexpected results from an observational study of shoplifting. *Criminal Justice and Behavior, 33,* 646–674.

Dadds, M. R., & Fraser, J. A. (2006). Fire interest, fire setting and psychopathology in Australian children: A normative study. *Australian and New Zealand Journal of Psychiatry, 40,* 581–586.

Dåderman, A. M., & Kristiansson, M. (2003). Degree of psychopathy: Implications for treatment in male juvenile delinquents. *International Journal of Law and Psychiatry, 26,* 310–315.

Dahlberg, L. L., & Potter, L. B. (2001). Youth violence: Developmental pathways and prevention challenges. *American Journal of Preventive Medicine, 20*(1s), 3–14.

Dahle, K-P., Biederman, J., Lehmann, R. J. B., & Gallasch-Nemitz, F. (2014). The development of the Crime Scene Behavior Risk measure for sexual offense recidivism. *Law and Human Behavior, 38,* 569–579.

Dalbert, C. (1999). The world is more just for me than generally: About the Personal Belief in a Just World Scale's validity. *Social Justice Research, 12,* 79–98.

Dalbert, C., & Filke, E. (2007). Belief in a personal just world, justice judgments, and their functions for prisoners. *Criminal Justice and Behavior, 34,* 1516–1527.

Damon, W. (2004). What is positive youth development? *Annals, AAPSS, 591,* 13–24.

Daniels, D. N., & Gilula, M. F. (1970). Violence and the struggle for existence. In D. Daniels, M. Gilula, & F. Ochberg (Eds.), *Violence and the struggle for existence.* Boston: Little, Brown.

Daniels, J. A., & Bradley, M. C. (2011). *Preventing lethal school violence.* New York: Springer.

Daniels, J. A., & Page, J. W. (2013). Averted school shootings. In N. Böckler, T. Seeger, P. Sitzer, & W. Heitmeyer (Eds.), *School shootings: International research, case studies, and concepts for prevention* (pp. 421–440). New York: Springer.

Darby, P. J., Allan, W. D., Kashani, J. H., Hartke, K. L., & Reid, J. C. (1998). Analysis of 112 juveniles who committed homicide: Characteristics and a closer look at family abuse. *Journal of Family Violence, 13,* 365–375.

Darling, N., & Steinberg, L. (1993). Parenting style as context: An integrative model. *Psychological Bulletin, 113*, 487–496.

Daversa, M. T., & Knight, R. A. (2007). A structural examination of the predictors of sexual coercion against children in adolescent sexual offenders. *Criminal Justice and Behavior, 34*, 1313–1333.

David, P. R. (1974). *The world of the burglar.* Albuquerque, NM: University of New Mexico Press.

Davies, M. (2002). Male sexual assault victims: A selected review of the literature and implications for support services. *Aggression and Violent Behavior, 7*, 203–214.

Davis, M. G., Lundman, R. J., & Martinez, R. (1991). Private corporate justice: Store police, shoplifters, and civil recovery. *Social Problems, 38*, 395–411.

Dawkins, M. P. (1997). Drug use and violent crime among adolescents. *Adolescence, 32*, 395–405.

Dawson, J. M., & Langan, P. A. (1994). *Murder in families.* Washington, DC: Bureau of Justice Statistics.

Day, J. C., Zahn, M. A., & Tichavsky, L. P. (2014). What works for whom? The effects of gender responsive programming on girls and boys in secure detention. *Journal of Research in Crime and Delinquency, XX*, 1–37.

Day, K., & Berney, T. (2001). Treatment and care for offenders with mental retardation. In J. B. Ashford, B. D. Sales, & W. H. Reid (Eds.), *Treating adult and juvenile offenders with special needs* (pp. 199–220). Washington, DC: American Psychological Association.

Day, R., & Wong, S. (1996). Anomalous perceptual asymmetrics for negative emotional stimuli in the psychopath. *Journal of Abnormal Psychology, 105*, 648–652.

Deal, M. M., & Hickey, E. W. (2003). Helter-Skelter. In E. Hickey (Ed.), *Encyclopedia of murder & violent crime.* Thousand Oaks, CA: Sage.

DeAngelis, T. (2011, September). Bin Laden's death: What does it mean? *APA Monitor on Psychology*, pp. 77–78.

Decker, S. H., Pennel, S., & Caldwell, A. (1997). *Illegal firearms: Access and use by arrestees.* Washington, DC: U.S. Department of Justice, National Institute of Justice.

Decker, S. H., Wright, R., Redfern, A., & Smith, D. (1993). A woman's place is in the home: Females and residential burglary. *Justice Quarterly, 10*, 143–163.

Declercq, F., Willemsen, J., Audenaert, K., & Verhaeghe, P. (2012). Psychopathy and predatory violence in homicide, violent, and sexual offenses: Factor and facet relations. *Legal and Criminological Psychology, 17*, 59–74.

Deem, D., & Murray, M. (2000). Financial crime. In G. Coleman, M. Gaboury, M. Murray, & A. Seymour (Eds.), *1999 National Victim Assistance Academy.* Washington, DC: U.S. Department of Justice.

deHaven-Smith, L. (2010). Beyond conspiracy theory: Patterns of high crime in American government. *American Behavioral Scientist, 53*, 795–825.

Dehue, F., Bolman, C., & Völlink, T. (2008). Cyberbullying: Youngsters' experiences and parental perception. *Cyberpsychology & Behavior, 11*, 217–223.

de Kemp, R. A. T., Overbeek, G., de Wied, M., Engels, R. C. M. E., & Scholte, R. H. J. (2007). Early adolescent empathy, parental support, and antisocial behavior. *The Journal of Genetic Psychology, 168*, 5–18.

Deković, M., Asscher, J. J., Manders, W. A., Prins, P. J. M., & van der Laan, P. (2012). Within-intervention change: Mediators of intervention effects during multisystemic therapy. *Journal of Consulting and Clinical Psychology, 80*, 574–587.

Dekovic, M., Janssens, J. M. A. M., & Van As, N. M. C. (2003). Family predictors of antisocial behavior in adolescence. *Family Process, 42*, 223–235.

DeLisi, M. (2009). Introduction to special issues on biosocial criminology. *Criminal Justice and Behavior, 36*, 1111–1112.

DeLisi, M., Beaver, K. M., Vaughn, M. G., & Wright, J. P. (2009). All in the family: Gene X environment interaction between DRD2 and criminal father is associated with five antisocial phenotypes. *Criminal Justice and Behavior, 36*, 1177–1187.

Delisi, M., & Scherer, A. M. (2006). Multiple homicide offenders: Offense characteristics, social correlates, and criminal careers. *Criminal Justice and Behavior, 33*, 367–391.

DeLisi, M., Umphress, Z. R., & Vaughn, M. G. (2009). The criminology of the amygdala. *Criminal Justice and Behavior, 36*, 1231–1242.

Del Bove, G., & Mackay, S. (2011). An empirically derived classification system for juvenile firesetters. *Criminal Justice and Behavior, 38,* 796–817.

DeMatteo, D. (2005, Winter). Legal update: An expansion of Tarasoff's duty to protect. *American Psychology-Law News, 25*(2), 1, 6.

DeMatteo, D. (2007a, Winter). The Supreme Court rules on the insanity defense and capital sentencing procedures. *American Psychology-Law News, 27*(1), 1, 5.

DeMatteo, D. (2007b). Legal update: The Supreme Court rules on the insanity defense and capital sentencing procedures. *American Psychology-Law Society Newsletter, 27*(1), 1, 5.

DeMatteo, D., Filone, S., & Davis, J. (2015). Substance use and crime. In B. L. Cutler & P. A. Zapf (Eds.), *APA handbook of forensic psychology: Vol.1. Individual and situational influences in criminal and civil contexts* (pp. 325–349). Washington, DC: American Psychological Association.

Department of Health and Human Services. (2014). *Child maltreatment 2013.* Washington, DC: Administration on Children, Youth, and Families.

Dern, H., Dern, C., Horn, A., & Horn, U. (2009). The fire behind the smoke: A reply to Snook and colleagues. *Criminal Justice and Behavior, 36,* 1085–1090.

Deslauriers-Varin, N., & Beauregard, E. (2010). Victim's routine activities and sex offenders' target selection scripts: A latent class analysis. *Sexual Abuse: A Journal of Research and Treatment, 22,* 315–342.

Devapriam, J., Raju, L. B., Singh, N., Collacott, R., & Bhaumik, S. (2007). Arson: Characteristics and predisposing factors in offenders with intellectual disabilities. *The British Journal of Forensic Practice, 9,* 23–27.

Developments in the Law. (1974). Civil commitment of the mentally ill. *Harvard Law Review, 87,* 1190–1406.

DeWall, C. N., & Anderson, C. A. (2011). The General Aggression Model. In P. R. Shaver & M. Mikulincer (Eds.), *Human aggression and violence: Causes, manifestations, and consequences* (pp. 15–33). Washington, DC: American Psychological Association.

DeWall, C. N., Anderson, C. A., & Bushman, B. J. (2011). The General Aggression Model: Theoretical extension to violence. *Psychology of Violence, 1,* 245–258.

DeWall, C. N., Twenge, J. M., Gitter, S. A., & Baumeister, R. F. (2009). It's the thought that counts: The role of hostile cognition in shaping aggressive responses to social exclusion. *Journal of Personality and Social Psychology, 96,* 45–59.

Diamanduros, T., Downs, E., & Jenkins, S. J. (2008). The role of school psychologists in the assessment, prevention, and intervention of cyberbullying. *Psychology in the Schools, 45,* 693–704.

Diamantopoulou, S., Verhulst, F. C., & van der Ende, J. (2011). Gender differences in the development and adult outcome of co-occurring depression and delinquency in adolescence. *Journal of Abnormal Psychology, 120,* 644–655.

DiCataldo, F., & Everett, M. (2008). Distinguishing juvenile homicide from violent juvenile offending. *International Journal of Offender Therapy and Comparative Criminology, 52,* 158–174.

Dick, D. M., & Rose, R. J. (2002). Behavior genetics: What's new? What's next? *Current Directions in Psychological Science, 11,* 70–74.

Dickens, G., Sugarman, P., Edgar, S., Hofberg, K., Tewari, S., & Ahmad, F. (2009). Recidivism and dangerousness in arsonists. *Journal of Forensic Psychiatry & Psychology, 20,* 621–639.

Diener, E. (1980). Deindividuation: The absence of self-awareness and self-regulation in group members. In P. Paulus (Ed.), *The psychology of group influence* (pp. 90–106). Hillsdale, NJ: Erlbaum.

Dietrich, K. N., Ris, M. D., Succop, P. A., Berger, O. G., & Bornschein, R. L. (2001). Early exposure to lead and juvenile delinquency. *Neurotoxicology and Teratology, 23,* 511–518.

Dill, K. E., Anderson, C. A., Anderson, K. B., & Deuser, W. E. (1997). Effects of aggressive personality on social expectations and social perceptions. *Journal of Research in Personality, 31,* 272–292.

Dill, K. E., & Dill, J. C. (1998). Video game violence: A review of the empirical literature. *Aggression and Violent Behavior, 3,* 407–428.

Dionne, G. (2005). Language development and aggressive behavior. In R. E. Tremblay, W. W. Hartup, & J. Archer (Eds.), *Developmental origins of aggression* (pp. 330–352). New York: Guilford Press.

Diserens, C. M. (1925). Psychological objectivism. *Psychological Review, 32,* 121–152.

Dishion, T. J., & Andrews, D. W. (1995). Preventing escalation in problem behaviors with high-risk young adolescents: Immediate and 1-year outcomes. *Journal of Consulting and Clinical Psychology, 63*, 538–548.

Dishion, T. J., & Loeber, R. (1985). Male adolescent marijuana and alcohol use: The role of parents and peers revisited. *American Journal of Drug and Alcohol Abuse, 11*, 11–25.

Ditzler, T. F. (2004). Malevolent minds: The teleology of terrorism. In F. M. Moghaddam & A. J. Marsella (Eds.), *Understanding terrorism: Psychosocial roots, consequences, and interventions* (pp. 3–8). Washington, DC: American Psychological Association.

Doan, S. N., Dich, N., & Evans, G. W. (2014). Childhood cumulative risk and later allostatic load: Mediating role of substance abuse. *Health Psychology, 33*, 1402–1409.

Doan, S. N., Fulller-Rowell, T. E., & Evans, G. W. (2012). Cumulative risk and adolescent's internalizing and externalizing problems: The mediating roles of maternal responsiveness and self-regulation. *Developmental Psychology, 48*, 1529–1539.

Dobson, V., & Sales, B. (2000). The science of infanticide and mental illness. *Psychology, Public Policy, and Law, 6*, 1098–1112.

Dodge, K. A. (1986). A social information processing model of social competence in children. In M. Perlmutter (Ed.), *The Minnesota symposium on child psychology*. Hillsdale, NJ: Erlbaum.

Dodge, K. A. (1991). The structure and function of reactive and proactive aggression. In D. J. Pepler & K. H. Rubin (Eds.), *The development and treatment of childhood aggression*. Hillsdale, NJ: Erlbaum.

Dodge, K. A. (1993a). The future of research on the treatment of conduct disorder. *Development and Psychopathology, 5*, 311–319.

Dodge, K. A. (1993). Social-cognitive mechanisms in the development of conduct disorder and depression. *Annual Review of Psychology, 44*, 559–584.

Dodge, K. A. (2001). The science of youth violence prevention: Progressing from developmental epidemiology to efficacy to effectiveness in public policy. *American Journal of Preventive Medicine, 20*(1s), 63–70.

Dodge, K. A. (2003). Do social information-processing patterns mediate aggressive behavior? In B. B. Lahey, T. E. Moffitt, & A. Caspi (Eds.), *Causes of conduct disorder and juvenile delinquency* (pp. 254–276). New York: Guilford Press.

Dodge, K. A. (2011). Social information processing patterns as mediators of the interaction between genetic factors and life experiences in the development of aggressive behavior. In P. R. Shaver & M. Mikulincer (Eds.), *Human aggression and violence: Causes, manifestations, and consequences* (pp. 165–185). Washington, DC: American Psychological Association.

Dodge, K. A., Bates, J. E., & Pettit, G. S. (1990). Mechanisms in the cycle of violence. *Science, 250*, 1678–1683.

Dodge, K. A., & Coie, J. D. (1987). Social information processing factors in reactive and proactive aggression in children's peer groups. *Journal of Personality and Social Psychology, 53*, 1146–1158.

Dodge, K. A., Coie, J. D., & Lynam, D. (2006). Aggression and antisocial behavior in youth. In D. Damon & R. M. Lerner (Series Eds.), & N. Eisenberg (Vol. Ed.), *Handbook of child psychology: Vol. 3. Social, emotional, and personality development* (6th ed., pp. 505–570). New York: Wiley.

Dodge, K. A., Greenberg, M. T., Malone, P. S., & Conduct Problems Prevention Research Group. (2008). Testing an idealized dynamic cascade model of the development of serious violence in adolescence. *Child Development, 79*, 1907–1927.

Dodge, K. A., Laird, R., Lochman, Zelli, A., & Conduct Problems Prevention Research Group. (2002). Multidimensional latent construct analysis of children's social information-processing patterns: Correlations with aggressive behavior problems. *Psychological Assessment, 14*, 60–73.

Dodge, K. A., Lochman, J. E., Harnish, J. D., Bates, J. E., & Pettit, G. S. (1997). Reactive and proactive aggression in school children and psychiatrically impaired chronically assaultive youth. *Journal of Abnormal Psychology, 106*, 37–51.

Dodge, K. A., & Pettit, G. S. (2003). A biopsychological model of the development of chronic conduct problems in adolescence. *Developmental Psychology, 39*, 349–371.

Doerner, W. G. (1988). The impact of medical resources on criminally induced lethality: A further examination. *Criminology, 26*, 171–179.

Doerner, W. G., & Speir, J. C. (1986). Stitch and sew: The impact of medical resources upon criminally induced lethality. *Criminology, 24*, 319–330.

Doley, R., Ferguson, C., & Surette, R. (2013). Copycat firesetting: Bridging two research area. *Criminal Justice and Behavior, 40,* 1472–1491.

Dollard, J., Doob, L. W., Miller, N. E., Mowrer, O. H., & Sears, R. R. (1939). *Frustration and aggression.* New Haven, CT: Yale University Press.

Domhardt, M., Munzer, A., Fegert, J. M., & Goldbeck, L. (2015). Resilience in survivors of child sexual abuse: A systematic review of the literature. *Trauma, Violence, Abuse, 16,* 476–493.

Donnerstein, E. (1983). Erotica and human aggression. In R. G. Geen & E. I. Donnerstein (Eds.), *Aggression: Theoretical and empirical reviews: Vol. 2.* New York: Academic Press.

Dopp, A. R., Borduin, C. M., Wagner, D. V., & Sawyer, A. M. (2014). The economic impact of Multisystemic Therapy through midlife: A cost-benefit analysis with serious juvenile offenders and their siblings. *Journal of Consulting and Clinical Psychology, 82,* 694–705.

d'Orban, P. T., & O'Connor, A. (1989). Women who kill their parents. *British Journal of Psychiatry, 154,* 27–33.

Doren, D. M. (2002). *Evaluating sex offenders.* Thousand Oaks, CA: Sage.

Douglas, A-J. (2011, August). Child abductions: Known relationships are the greater danger. *FBI Law Enforcement Bulletin, 80*(8), 8–9.

Douglas, J. E., Burgess, A. W., Burgess, A. G., & Ressler, R. K. (1992). *Crime classification manual.* New York: Lexington Books.

Douglas, J. E., Burgess, A. W., Burgess, A. G., & Ressler, R. K. (2006). Psychopathy and suicide: A multisample investigation. *Crime classification manual* (2nd ed.). San Francisco: Jossey-Bass.

Douglas, J. E., & Munn, C. (1992a). The detection of staging and personation at the crime scene. In J. E. Douglas, A. W. Burgess, A. G. Burgess, & R. K. Ressler (Eds.), *Crime classification manual* (pp. 249–258). New York: Lexington Books.

Douglas, J. E., & Munn, C. (1992b). Modus operandi and the signature aspects of violent crime. In J. E. Douglas, A. W. Burgess, A. G. Burgess, & R. K. Ressler (Eds.), *Crime classification manual* (pp. 259–268). New York: Lexington Books.

Douglas, J. E., & Munn, C. (1992c, February). Violent crime scene analysis. *FBI Law Enforcement Bulletin,* 1–10.

Douglas, J. E., Ressler, R. K., Burgess, A. W., & Hartman. C. R. (1986). Criminal profiling from crime scene analysis. *Behavioral Sciences & the Law, 4,* 401–421.

Douglas, K. S., Guy, L. L., & Hart, S. D. (2009). Psychosis as a risk factor for violence to others: A meta-analysis. *Psychological Bulletin, 135,* 679–706.

Douglas, K. S., Hart, S. D., Groscup, J. L., & Litwack, T. R. (2014). Assessing violence risk. In I. B. Weiner & R. K. Otto (Eds.), *The handbook of forensic psychology* (4th ed., pp. 385–441). Hoboken, NJ: Wiley.

Douglas, K. S., Herbozo, S., Poythress, N. G., Belfrage, H., & Edens, J. F. (2006). *Psychological Services, 3,* 97–116.

Douglas, K. S., Nikolova, N. L., Kelley, S. E., & Edens, J. E. (2015). Psychopathy. In B. L. Cutler & P. A. Zapf (Eds.), *APA handbook in forensic psychology: Vol. I. Individual and situational influences in criminal and civil contexts* (pp. 257–323). Washington, DC: American Psychological Association.

Douglas, V. I. (2004). Cognitive deficits in children with attention deficit hyperactivity disorder: A long-term follow up. *Canadian Psychology, 46,* 23–31.

Drug Enforcement Administration. (2000). *Drugs of abuse.* Washington, DC: U.S. Department of Justice. Available: www.usdoj.gov/dea/concern/abuse.

Drug Enforcement Administration. (2005). *Drugs of abuse, 2005 edition.* Washington, DC: U.S. Department of Justice.

Drug Enforcement Administration. (2010a, April). *Phencyclidine.* Washington, DC: U.S. Department of Justice, Author.

Drug Enforcement Administration. (2010b, May). *Methamphetamine.* Washington, DC: Department of Justice, Author.

Drug Enforcement Administration. (2011). *Drugs of abuse, 2011 edition.* Washington, DC: U.S. Department of Justice.

Drug Enforcement Administration. (2014a, May). *The dangers and consequences of marijuana abuse.* Washington, DC: U.S. Department of Justice.

Drug Enforcement Administration. (2014b, November). *2014 National drug assessment summary.* Washington, DC: U.S. Department of Justice.

Drug Enforcement Administration. (2015, February). *Controlled substance schedule*. Washington, DC: U.S. Department of Justice.

Duhaime, A., Christian, C. W., Rorke, L. B., & Zimmerman, R. A. (1998). Nonaccidental head injury in infants: The "shaken-baby syndrome." *New England Journal of Medicine, 338,* 1822–1829.

Duke, A. A., Bègue, L., Bell, R., & Eisenlohr-Moul, T. (2013). Revisiting the serotonin-aggression relation in humans: A meta-analysis. *Psychological Bulletin, 139,* 1148–1172.

Duncan, G. J. (2012). Give us this day our daily breath. *Child Development, 83,* 6–15.

Duncan, G. J., Dowsett, C. J., Claessens, A., Magnusson, K., Huston, A. C., Klebanov, P., **et al.** (2007). School readiness and later achievement. *Developmental Psychology, 43,* 1428–1446.

Dunn, C. S. (1976). *The patterns and distribution of assault incident characteristics among social areas.* Albany, NY: Criminal Justice Research Center, Analytic Report 14.

Durand, V. M., & Barlow, D. H. (2000). *Abnormal psychology: An introduction.* Belmont, CA: Wadsworth.

Durose, M. R., Harlow, C. W., Langan, P. A., Motivans, M., Rantala, R. R., & Smith, E. L. (2005, June). *Family violence statistics: Including statistics on strangers and acquaintances.* Washington, DC: U.S. Department of Justice, Bureau of Justice Statistics.

Dutton, M. A., Holnecker, L. C., Halle, P. M., & Burghardt, K. J. (1994). Traumatic responses among battered women who kill. *Journal of Traumatic Stress, 7,* 549–564.

Eastman, B. J. (2004). Assessing the efficacy of treatment for adolescent sex offenders: A cross-over longitudinal study. *Prison Journal, 84,* 472–485.

Eastvold, A., Suchy, Y., & Strassberg, D. (2011). Executive function profiles of pedophilic and nonpedophilic child molesters. *Journal of the International Neuropsychological Society, 17,* 295–307.

Eaton, J., & Polk, K. (1961). *Measuring delinquency.* Pittsburgh, PA: University of Pittsburgh Press.

Ebert, B. W. (1987). Guide to conducting a psychological autopsy. *Professional Psychology: Research and Practice, 18,* 52–56.

Eck, J. (2000). Preventing crime at places. In L. W. Sherman, D. Gottfresson, D. MacKenzie, J. Eck, P. Reuter, & S. Bushway (Eds.), *Preventing crime: What works, what doesn't, what's promising.* A Report to the United State Congress. Available: www.ncjrs.org/works.

Eddy, J. M. (2003). *Conduct disorders: The latest assessment and treatment strategies.* Kansas City, MO: Compact Clinicals.

Edens, J. F., Campbell, J., & Weir, J. (2007). Youth psychopathy and criminal recidivism: A meta-analysis of the psychopathy checklist measures. *Law and Human Behavior, 31,* 53–75.

Edens, J. F., Guy, L. S., & Fernandez, K. (2003). Psychopathic traits predict attitudes toward a juvenile capital murderer. *Behavioral Sciences & the Law, 21,* 807–828.

Edens, J. F., Petrila, J., & Buffington-Vollum, J. K. (2001). Psychopathy and the death penalty: Can the Psychopathy Checklist-Revised identify offenders who represent "a continuing threat to society?" *Journal of Psychiatry and Law, 29,* 433–481.

Edens, J. F., Skeem, J. L., Cruise, K. R., & Cauffman, E. (2001). Assessment of "juvenile psychopathy" and its association with violence: A critical review. *Behavioral Sciences & the Law, 19,* 53–80.

Edleson, J. L. (1999). Children's witnessing of adult domestic violence. *Journal of Interpersonal Violence, 14,* 839–870.

Edwards, S. (1983). Sexuality, sexual offenses, and conception of victims in the criminal justice process. *Victimology: An International Journal, 8,* 113–128.

Efran, M. G., & Cheyne, J. A. (1974). Affective concomitants of the invasion of shared space: Behavioral, physiological, and verbal indicators. *Journal of Personality and Social Psychology, 29,* 219–226.

Egger, H. L., Kondo, D., & Angold, A. (2006). The epidemiology and diagnostic issues in preschool attention-deficit/hyperactivity disorder—a review. *Infants and Young Children, 19,* 109–122.

Eisenberg, N., & Fabes, R. A. (1998). Prosocial development. In W. Damon (Series Ed.), & N. Eisenberg (Vol. Ed.), *Handbook of child psychology: Vol 3. Social, emotional and personality development* (5th ed.). New York: Wiley.

Eisenhower, M. S. (Chairman). (1969). *Commission statement on violence in television entertainment programs.* Washington, DC: USGPO.

Elhai, J. D., Grubaugh, A. L., Kashdan, T. B., & Frueh, B. C. (2008). Empirical examination of a proposed refinement to DSM-IV posttraumatic stress disorder symptom criteria using the National Comorbidity Survey Replication data. *Journal of Clinical Psychiatry, 69,* 597–602.

Ellingsen, D. G., Kusraeva, Z., Bast-Pettersen, R., Zibarev, E., Chashchin, M., Thomassen, Y., et al. (2014). The interaction between manganese exposure and alcohol on neurobehavioral outcomes in welders. *Neurotoxicology and Teratology, 41,* 8–15.

Elliott, D. S. (1989). Criminal justice procedures in family violence crimes. In L. Ohlin & M. Tonry (Eds.), *Family violence (Vol. 11).* Chicago: University of Chicago Press.

Elliott, D. S., Dunford, T. W., & Huizinga, D. (1987). The identification and prediction of career offenders utilizing self-reported and official data. In J. D. Burchard & S. N. Burchard (Eds.), *Prevention of delinquent behavior.* Newbury Park, CA: Sage.

Ellis, C. A., & Lord, J. (2001). Homicide. In G. Coleman, M. Gaboury, M. Murray, & A. Seymour (Eds.), *1999 National victim assistance academy.* Washington, DC: U.S. Department of Justice.

Else-Quest, N. M., Hyde, J. S., Goldsmith, H. H., & Van Hulle, C. A. (2006). Gender differences in temperament: A meta-analysis. *Psychological Bulletin, 132,* 33–72.

Elson, M., & Ferguson, C. J. (2014). Twenty-five years of research on violence in digital games and aggression. *European Psychologist, 19,* 33–46.

Ennis, L., Buro, K., & Jung, S. (in press). Identifying male sexual offender subtypes using cluster analysis and the Static-200R. *Sexual Abuse: A Journal of Research and Treatment.*

Environmental Protection Agency. (2000). *Cadmium compounds.* Washington, DC: Author.

Environmental Protection Agency. (2007, October). *Manganese.* Washington DC: Author.

Epperson. D., Ralston, C., Fowers, D., DeWitt, J., & Gore, K. (2006). Juvenile Sex Offense Recidivism Rate Assessment Tool—II (J-SORRAT-II). In D. Prescott (Ed.), *Risk assessment of youth who have sexually abused.* Oklahoma City, OK: Wood N' Barnes Publishing.

Erhardt, D., & Hinshaw, S. P. (1994). Initial sociometric impressions of attention-deficit hyperactivity disorder and comparison boys: Predictions from social behaviors and from nonbehavioral variables. *Journal of Consulting and Clinical Psychology, 62,* 833–842.

Erickson, R. (1996). *Armed robbers and their crimes.* Seattle, WA: Athena Research Corporation.

Ericson, J. E., Crinella, F. M., Clarke-Stewart, K. A., Allhusen, V. D., Chan, T., & Robertson, R. T. (2007). Prenatal manganese levels linked to child behavioral inhibition. *Neurotoxicology and Teratology, 29,* 181–187.

Ericson, N. (2001, June). *Addressing the problem of juvenile bullying.* Washington, DC: U.S. Department of Justice, Office of Juvenile Justice and Delinquency Prevention.

Erikson, E. (1980). Identity and the life cycle. New York: Norton.

Eron, L. D., & Huesmann, L. P. (1984). The relation of prosocial behavior to the development of aggression and psychopathology. *Aggressive Behavior, 10,* 201–211.

Eron, L. D., & Slaby, R. G. (1994). Introduction. In L. D. Eron, J. H. Gentry, & P. Schlegel (Eds.), *Reason to hope: A psychosocial perspective on violence and youth* (pp. 1–24).Washington, DC: American Psychological Association.

Eskridge, C. W. (1983). Prediction of burglary: A research note. *Journal of Criminal Justice, 11,* 67–75.

Evans, G. W. (2004). The environment of childhood poverty. *American Psychologist, 59,* 77–92.

Evans, G. W., Li, D., & Whipple, S. S. (2013). Cumulative risk and child development. *Psychological Bulletin, 139,* 1342–1396.

Evans-Chase, M., & Zhou, H. (2014). A systematic review of the juvenile justice intervention literature: What it can (and cannot) tell us about what works with delinquent youth. *Crime & Delinquency, 60,* 451–470.

Eysenck, H. J. (1967). *The biological basis of personality.* Springfield, IL: Charles C Thomas.

Fabiano, G. A., Pelham, W. E., Coles, E. k., Gnagy, E. M., Chronis-Tuscano, A., & O'Connor, B. O. (2009). A meta-analysis of behavioral treatments for Attention-Deficit Hyperactivity Disorder. *Clinical Psychology, 29,* 129–140.

Falkenbach, D. M. Poythress, N. G., & Heide, K. M. (2003). Psychopathic features in a juvenile diversion population: Reliability and predictive validity of two self-report measures. *Behavioral Sciences & the Law, 21*, 787–805.

Fantuzzo, J. W., Boruch, R., Abdullahi, B., Atkins, M., & Marcus, S. (1997). Domestic violence and children: Prevalence and risk in five major U.S. cities. *Journal of American Academy of Child and Adolescent Psychiatry, 36*, 116–122.

Fantuzzo, J. W., DesPaola, L. M., Lambert, L., Martino, T., Anderson, G., & Sutton, S. (1991). Effects of interparental violence on the psychological adjustment and competencies of young children. *Journal of Consulting and Clinical Psychology, 59*, 258–265.

Farrell, A. L., Keppel, R. D., & Titterington, V. B. (2011). Lethal ladies: Revisiting what we know about female serial murderers. *Homicide Studies, 15*, 228–252.

Farrell, G., Phillips, C., & Pease, K. (1995). Like taking candy, why does repeat victimization occur? *British Journal of Criminology, 35*, 384–399.

Farrington, D. P. (1991). Childhood aggression and adult violence: Early precursors and later life outcomes. In D. J. Pepler & K. H. Rubin (Eds.), *The development and treatment of childhood aggression*. Hillsdale, NJ: Erlbaum.

Farrington, D. P. (1995). Crime and physical health: Illnesses, injuries, accidents, and offending in the Cambridge study. *Criminal Behaviour and Mental Health, 5*, 278.

Farrington, D. P. (2005a). The importance of child and adolescent psychopathy. *Journal of Abnormal Child Psychology, 33*, 489–497.

Farrington, D. P. (2005b). Family background and psychopathy. In C. J. Patrick (Ed.), *Handbook of psychopathy*. New York: Guilford.

Farrington, D. P., & Burrows, J. N. (1993). Did shoplifting really decrease? *British Journal of Criminology, 33*, 57–59.

Farrington, D. P., Loeber, R., & Berg, M. T. (2012). Young men who kill: A prospective longitudinal examination from childhood. *Homicide Studies, 16*, 99–128.

Farrington, D. P., Ttofi, M. M., & Coid, J. W. (2009). Development of adolescence-limited, late-onset, and persistent offenders from age 8 to age 48. *Aggressive Behavior, 35*, 150–163.

Farris, C., Treat, T. A., Viken, R. J., & McFall, R. M. (2008). Sexual coercion and the misperception of sexual intent. *Clinical Psychology Review, 28*, 48–66.

Farris, C., Viken, R. J., Treat, T. A., & McFall, R. M. (2006). Heterosocial perceptual organization: Application of the choice model to sexual coercion. *Psychological Science, 17*, 869–875.

Faupel, C. E. (1991). *Shooting dope: Career patterns of hard-core heroin users.* Gainesville, FL: University of Florida Press.

Fazel, S., Bains, P., & Doll, H. (2006). Substance abuse and dependence in prisoners: A systematic review. *Addiction, 101*, 181–191.

Federal Bureau of Investigation. (1985, August). Crime scene and profile characteristics of organized and disorganized murders. *FBI Law Enforcement Bulletin, 54*, 18–25.

Federal Bureau of Investigation. (1992). *Killed in the line of duty: A study of selected felonious killings of law enforcement officers.* Washington, DC: U.S. Department of Justice.

Federal Bureau of Investigation. (1997). *Uniform Crime Reports—1996.* Washington, DC: U.S. Department of Justice.

Federal Bureau of Investigation. (2002). *Uniform Crime Reports—2001.* Washington, DC: U.S. Department of Justice.

Federal Bureau of Investigation. (2003). Special report: Bank robbery in the United States. *Uniform Crime Reports—2002.* Washington, DC: U.S. Department of Justice.

Federal Bureau of Investigation. (2005a). *Serial murder: Multi-disciplinary perspectives for investigators.* Washington, DC: Behavioral Analysis Unit-2, National Center for the Analysis of Crime.

Federal Bureau of Investigation. (2005b). *Crime in the United States 2004: Uniform Crime Reports.* Washington, DC: U.S. Department of Justice.

Federal Bureau of Investigation. (2008). *Crime in the United States 2007: Uniform Crime Reports.* Washington, DC: U.S. Department of Justice.

Federal Bureau of Investigation. (2009). *High tech-heist.* Accessed 4/21/15. Available: www.fbi.gov/news/stories/2009/november/atm.

Federal Bureau of Investigation. (2011a). *Crime in the United States 2010: Uniform crime reports.* Washington, DC: U.S. Department of Justice.

Federal Bureau of Investigation. (2011b). *Operation ghost click.* Accessed 4/21/15. Available: www.fbi. gov/news/stories/2011/november/malware.

Federal Bureau of Investigation. (2013, September 16). *A study of active shooter incidents in the United States between 2000 and 2013.* Washington, DC: U.S. Department of Justice.

Federal Bureau of Investigation. (2014a). *Crime in the United States 2013: Uniform crime reports.* Washington, DC: U.S. Department of Justice.

Federal Bureau of Investigation. (2014b). *Crime in the United States 2013. Rape addendum.* Washington, DC: U.S. Department of Justice.

Federal Bureau of Investigation. (2014c). *Bank crime statistics: Federally insured financial institutions.* Washington, DC: U.S. Department of Justice.

Federal Bureau of Investigation. (2015). *Computer intrusions.* Accessed 4/20/15. Available: www.fbi.gov/ about-us/investigate/cyber/computer-intrusions.

Federal Interagency Forum on Child and Family Statistics. (2005). *America's children: Key national indicators of well-being 2005.* Washington, DC: Author.

Fehrenbach, P. A., Smith, W., Monastersky, C., & Deisher, R. W. (1986). Adolescent sexual offenders: Offender and offense characteristics. *American Journal of Orthopsychiatry, 56,* 225–233.

Feinberg, G. (1984). Profile for the elderly shoplifter. In E. S. Newman, D. J. Newman, & M. L. Gewirtz (Eds.), *Elderly criminals.* Cambridge, MA: Oelgeschlager, Gunn & Hain.

Feldman, R., & Klein, P. S. (2003). Toddler's self-regulated compliance to mothers, caregivers, and fathers: Implications for theories of socialization. *Developmental Psychology, 39,* 680–692.

Ferguson, C. A., Rueda, S. M., Cruz, A. M., Ferguson, D. E., Fritz, S., & Smith, S. M. (2008). Violent video games and aggression: Causal relationship or byproduct of family violence and intrinsic violence motivation? *Criminal Justice and Behavior, 35,* 311–332.

Ferguson, C. J., & Cricket Meehan, D. (2005). An analysis of females convicted of sex crime in the state of Florida. *Journal of Child Sexual Abuse, 14,* 75–89.

Ferguson, D. M., Lynskey, M. T., & Horwood, I. J. (1996). Factors associated with continuity and change in disruptive behavior patterns in childhood and adolescence. *Journal of Abnormal Child Psychology, 24,* 533–553.

Fergusson, D. M., Boden, J. M., Horwood, L. J., Miller, A., & Kennedy, M. A. (2012). Moderating role of the MAOA genotype in antisocial behaviour. *British Journal of Psychiatry, 200,* 116–123.

Ferrara, P., Vitelli, O., Bottaro, G., Gatto, A., Liberatore, P., Binetti, P., et al. (2013). Factitious disorders and Munchausen syndrome: The tip of the iceberg. *Journal of Child Health Care, 17,* 366–374.

Ferro, C., Cermele, J., & Saltzman, A. (2008). Current perceptions of marital rape: Some good and not-so-good news. *Journal of Interpersonal Violence, 23,* 764–779.

Feshbach, S. (1964). The function of aggression and the regulation of aggressive drive. *Psychological Review, 71,* 257–272.

Festinger, L., Pepitone, A., & Newcomb, T. (1952). Some consequences of de-individuation in a group. *Journal of Abnormal and Social Psychology, 47,* 382–389.

Feucht, T. W., & Kyle, G. M. (1996, November). Methamphetamine use among adult arrestees: Findings of the DUF program. *NIJ Research in Brief.* Washington, DC: U.S. Department of Justice.

Fields, G. (2006, September 26). Police are changing how they confront the mentally ill. *The Wall Street Jorunal,* pp. A1, A11.

Finckenauer, J. O., & Schrock, J. (2000). *Human trafficking: A growing criminal market in the U.S.* Washington, DC: National Institute of Justice, International Center.

Fineman, K. R. (1995). A model for the qualitative analysis of child and adult fire deviant behavior. *American Journal of Forensic Psychology, 13,* 31–60.

Finkelhor, D. (1979). *Sexually victimized children.* New York: Free Press.

Finkelhor, D. (2011). Prevalence of child victimization, abuse, crime, and violence exposure. In J. W. White, M. P. Koss, & A. E. Kasdin (Eds.), *Violence against women and children: Vol. 1. Mapping the terrain* (pp. 9–29). Washington, DC: American Psychological Association.

Finkelhor, D., & Araji, S. (1986). Explanations of pedophilia: A four factor model. *The Journal of Sex Research, 22,* 145–161.

Finkelhor, D., & Dziuba-Leatherman, J. (1994). Children as victims of violence: A national survey. *Pediatrics, 94*, 413–420.

Finkelhor, D., Hammer, H., & Sedlak, A. J. (2002, October). *Nonfamily abducted children: National estimates and characteristics*. Washington, DC: U.S. Department of Justice.

Finkelhor, D., & Lewis, I. A. (1988). An epidemiologic approach to the study of child molestation. In R. A. Prentky & V. L. Quinsey (Eds.), *Human sexual aggression: Current perspectives*. New York: New York Academy of Sciences.

Finkelhor, D., Ormrod, R., Turner, H., & Hamby, S. L. (2005). The victimization of children and youth: A comprehensive, national survey. *Child Maltreatment, 10*, 5–25.

Finkelhor, D., Shattuck, A., Turner, H. A., & Hamby, S. L. (2014). The lifetime prevalence of child sexual abuse and sexual assault assesses in late adolescence. *Journal of Adolescent Health, 55*, 329–333.

Finkelhor, D., Turner, H., & Ormrod, R. (2006). Kid's stuff: The nature and impact of peer and sibling violence on younger and older children. *Child Abuse & Neglect, 30*, 1401–1421.

Finkelhor, D., Turner, H. A., Ormrod, R., & Hamby, S. L. (2009). Violence, abuse, and crime exposure in a national sample of children and youth. *Pediatrics, 124*, 1411–1423.

Finkelhor, D., Turner, H., Hamby, S., & Ormrod, R. (2011, October). *Polyvictimization: Children's exposure to multiple types of violence, crime, and abuse*. Washington, DC: U. S. Department of Justice, Office of Juvenile Justice and Delinquency Prevention.

Finkelhor, D., Vanderminden, J., Turner, H., Hamby, S., & Shattuck, A. (2014). Child maltreatment rates assessed in a national household survey of caregivers and youth. *Child Abuse & Neglect, 38*, 1421–1435.

Finley, E. P., Garcia, H. A., Ketchum, N. S., McGeary, D. D., McGeary, C. A., Stirman, S. W., et al. (2015). Utilization of evidence-based psychotherapies in veterans' affairs posttraumatic stress disorder outpatient clinics. *Psychological Services, 12*, 73–82.

Finley, J. W. (1999). Manganese absorption and retention by young women is associated with serum ferritin concentration. *American Journal of Clinical Nutrition, 70*, 37–43.

Firestone, P., Bradford, J. M., Greenberg, D. M., & Larose, M. R. (1998). Homicidal sex offenders: Psychological, phallometric, and diagnostic features. *Journal of the American Academy of Psychology and Law, 26*, 537–552.

Fischer, P., Greitemeyer, T., Pollozek, F., & Frey, D. (2006). The unresponsive bystander: Are bystanders more responsive in dangerous emergencies? *European Journal of Social Psychology, 36*, 267–278.

Fischer, P., Krueger, J. I., Greitemeyer, T., Vogrincic, C., Kastenmüller, A., Frey, D., et al. (2011). The bystander-effect: A meta-analytic review on bystander intervention in dangerous and non-dangerous emergencies. *Psychological Bulletin, 137*, 517–537.

Fishbein, D. (2001). *Biobehavioral perspectives in criminology*. Belmont, CA: Wadsworth/Thomson Learning.

Fisher, B. S., Cullen, F. T., & Turner, M. G. (2000). *Sexual victimization of college women*. Washington, DC: U.S. Department of Justice, National Institute of Justice.

Fite, P. J., Stoppelbein, L., & Greening, L. (2009). Proactive and reactive aggression in a child psychiatric inpatient population: Relations to psychopathic characteristics. *Criminal Justice and Behavior, 36*, 481–493.

Flannery, D. J., Williams, L. L., & Vazsonyi, A. T. (1999). Who are they with and what are they doing? Delinquent behavior, substance abuse, and early adolescence after school time. *American Journal of Orthopsychiatry, 69*, 247–253.

Flor-Henry, P. (1973). Psychiatric syndromes considered as manifestations of lateralized temporal-limbic dysfunction. In L. V. Latiner & K. E. Livingston (Eds.), *Surgical approaches in psychiatry*. Lancaster, UK: Medical and Technical Publishing.

Flor-Henry, P., & Yeudall, L. T. (1973). Lateralized cerebral dysfunction in depression and in aggressive criminal psychopathy. *International Research Communications, 7*, 31.

Flynn, E. E. (1983). Crime as a major social issue. *American Behavioral Scientist, 27*, 7–42.

Fontaine, N., Carbonneau, R., Vitaro, F., Barker, E. D., & Tremblay, R. E. (2009). Research review: A critical review of studies on the developmental trajectories of antisocial behavior in females. *Journal of Child Psychology and Psychiatry, 50*, 363–385.

Fontaine, R. G. (2008). Reactive cognitive, reaction emotion: Toward a more psychologically-informed understanding of reactive homicide. *Psychology, Public Policy, and Law, 14*, 243–261.

Fontaine, R. G., & Dodge, K. A. (2006). Real-time decision making and aggressive behavior in youth: A heuristic model of response evaluation and decision (RED). *Aggressive Behavior, 32*, 604–624.

Fontaine, N. M. G., McCrory, E. J. P., Boivin, M., Moffitt, T. E., & Viding, E. (2011). Predictors and outcomes of joint trajectories of callous-unemotional traits and conduct problems in childhood. *Journal of Abnormal Psychology, 120*, 730–742.

Forbes, G. B., Adams-Curtis, L. E., & White, K. B. (2004). First- and second-generation measures of sexism, rape myths and related beliefs, and hostility toward women. *Violence Against Women, 10*, 236–261.

Forehand, R., Wierson, M., Frame, C. L., Kemptom, T., & Armistead, L. (1991). Juvenile firesetting: A unique syndrome or an advanced level of antisocial behavior? *Behavioral Research and Therapy, 29*, 125–128.

Forney, W. S., Forney, J. C., & Crutsinger, C. (2005). Developmental stages of age and moral reasoning as predictors of juvenile delinquents' behavioral intention to steal clothing. *Family and Consumer Sciences Research Journal, 34*, 110–126.

Forth, A. E., & Burke, H. C. (1998). Psychopathy in adolescence: Assessment, violence, and developmental precursors. In D. J. Cooke, A. E. Forth, & R. D. Hare (Eds.), *Psychopathy: Theory, research and implications for society*. Boston: Kluwer Academic.

Forth, A. E., Kosson, D. S., & Hare, R. D. (2003). *Psychopathy Checklist-Youth Version: Technical manual*. Toronto, ON: Multi-Health Systems.

Fosco, G. M., Stromshak, E. A., Dishion, T. J., & Winter, C. E. (2012). Family relationships and parental monitoring during middle school as predictors of early adolescent problem behavior. *Journal of Clinical Child & Adolescent Psychology, 42*, 202–213.

Fothergill, K. E., & Ensminger, M. E. (2006). Childhood and adolescent antecedents of drug and alcohol problems: A longitudinal study. *Drug and Alcohol Dependence, 82*, 61–76.

Fowles, D. C. (2011). Current scientific views of psychopathy. *Psychological Science in the Public Interest, 12*, 93–94.

Fowles, D. C., & Dindo, L. (2009). Temperament and psychopathy: A dual-pathway model. *Current Directions in Psychological Science, 18*, 179–183.

Fox, B. H., & Farrington, D. P. (2012). Creating burglary profiles using latent class analysis: A new approach to offender profiling. *Criminal Justice and Behavior, 39*, 1582–1611.

Fox, B. H., & Farrington, D. P. (2015). An experimental evaluation on the utility of burglary profiles applied in active police investigations. *Criminal Justice and Behavior, 42*, 156–175.

Fox, J. A., & DeLateur, M. J. (2014). Mass shootings in America: Moving beyond Newtown. *Homicide Studies, 18*, 125–145.

Fox, J. A., & Levin, J. (2003). Mass murder: An analysis of extreme violence. *Journal of Applied Psychoanalytic Studies, 5*, 47–64.

Francis, B., Harris, D. A., Wallace, S., Knight, R. A., & Soothill, K. (2014). Sexual and general offending trajectories of men referred for civil commitment. *Sexual Abuse: A Journal of Research and Treatment, 26*, 311–329.

Franke, D. (1975). *The torture doctor*. New York: Avon.

Frederick, R. I. (2000). Mixed group validation: A method to address the limitations of criterion group validation in research on malingering detection. *Behavioral Sciences & the Law, 18*, 693–718.

Freedman, J. L., Sears, D. O., & Carlsmith, J. J. (1978). *Social psychology* (3rd ed.). Englewood Cliffs, NJ: Prentice Hall.

Freiburger, T., Marcum, C., Iannacchione, B., & Higgins, G. (2012). Sex offenders and criminal recidivism: An exploratory trajectory analysis using a Virginia sample. *Journal of Crime and Justice, 35*, 365–375.

Freilich, J. D., Chermak, S. M., & Caspi, D. (2009). Critical events in the life trajectories of domestic extremist white supremacist groups: A case study analysis of four violent organizations. *Criminology and Public Policy, 8*, 497–530.

Freire, C., Ramos, R., Lopez-Espinosa, M-J., Díez, S., Vioque, J., Ballester, F., et al. (2010). Hair mercury levels, fish consumption, and cognitive development in preschool children from Granada, Spain. *Environmental Research, 110*, 96–104.

Frick, P. J. (1998). Callous-unemotional traits and conduct problems: Applying the two-factor model of psychopathy to children. In D. J. Cooke, A. E. Forth, & R. D. Hare (Eds.), *Psychopathy: Theory, research and implications for society*. Boston: Kluwer Academic.

Frick, P. J. (2006). Developmental pathways to conduct disorder. *Child and Adolescent Psychiatric Clinics of North America, 15*, 311–331.

Frick, P. J. (2009). Extending the construct of psychopathy to youth: Implications for understanding, diagnosing, and treating antisocial children and adolescents. *Canadian Journal of Psychiatry, 54*, 803–812.

Frick, P. J., Barry, C. T., & Bodin, S. D. (2000). Applying the concept of psychopathy to children: Implications for the assessment of antisocial youth. In C. B. Gacono (Ed.), *The clinical and forensic assessment of psychopathy* (pp. 3–24). Mahwah, NJ: Erlbaum.

Frick, P. J., Bodin, S. D., & Barry, C. T. (2000). Psychopathic traits and conduct problems in community and clinic-referred samples of children: Further development of the psychopathy screening device. *Psychological Assessment, 12*, 382–393.

Frick, P. J., & Hare, R. D. (2001). *The Antisocial Process Screening Device*. Toronto, ON: Multi-Health Systems.

Frick, P. J., & Morris, A. S. (2004). Temperament and developmental pathways to conduct problems. *Journal of Clinical Child and Adolescent Psychology, 33*, 54–68.

Frick, P. J., & Nigg, J. T. (2012). Current issues in the diagnosis of attention deficit hyperactivity disorder, oppositional defiant disorder, and conduct disorder. *Annual Review of Clinical Psychology, 8*, 77–107.

Frick, P. J., O'Brien, B. S., Wootton, J., & McBurnett, K. (1994). Psychopathy and conduct problems in children. *Journal of Abnormal Psychology, 103*, 700–707.

Frick, P. J., Ray, J. V., Thornton, L. C., & Kahn, R. E. (2014). Can callous-unemotional traits enhance the understanding, diagnosis, and treatment of serious conduct problems in children and adolescents? A comprehensive review. *Psychological Bulletin, 140*, 1–57.

Frick, P. J., & White, S. F. (2008). Research review: The importance of callous-unemotional traits for developmental models of aggressive and antisocial behavior. *Journal of Child Psychology and Psychiatry, 49*, 359–375.

Friedman, M. J., Resick, P. A., Bryant, R. A., Strain, J., Horowitz, M., & Spiegel, D. (2011). Classification of trauma and stress-related disorders in DSM-5. *Depression and Anxiety, 28*, 737–749.

Friel, A., White, T., & Hull, A. (2008). Posttraumatic stress disorder and criminal responsibility. *The Journal of Forensic Psychiatry & Psychology, 19*, 64–85.

Frieze, I. H., & Browne, A. (1989). Violence in marriage. In L. Ohlin & M. Tonry (Eds.), *Family violence: Vol. 11*. Chicago: University of Chicago Press.

Frosch, D. (2014). Fake gunmen, real terror. *The Wall Street Journal*, September 4, 2014, p. A4.

Fung, M. T., Raine, A., Loeber, R., Lynam, D. R., Steinhauser, S. R., Venables, P. H., et al. (2005). Reduced electrodermal activity in pychopathy-prone adolescents. *Journal of Abnormal Psychology, 114*, 187–196.

Funk, J. B., Baldacci, H. B., Pasold, T., & Baumgarnder, J. (2004). Violence exposure in real-life, video games, television, movies, and the internet: Is there desensitization? *Journal of Adolescence, 27*, 23–39.

Furby, L., Weinrott, M. R., & Blackshaw, L. (1989). Sex offender recidivism: A review. *Psychological Bulletin, 105*, 3–30.

Fuselier, G. D. (1999, July). Placing the Stockholm syndrome in perspective. *FBI Law Enforcement Bulletin*, 9–12.

Fuselier, G. D., & Noesner, G. W. (1990, July). Confronting the terrorist hostage taker. *FBI Law Enforcement Bulletin*, 6–11.

Gabrielli, W. F., & Mednick, S. A. (1983). Genetic correlates of criminal behavior. *American Behavioral Scientist, 27*, 59–74.

Gacono, C. B., Nieberding, R. J., Owen, A., Rubel, J., & Bodholdt, R. (2001). Treating conduct disorder, antisocial, and psychopathic personalities. In J. B. Ashford, B. D. Sales, & W. H. Reid (Eds.), *Treating adult and juvenile offenders with special* needs (pp. 99–130). Washington, DC: American Psychological Association.

Galler, J. R., Bryce, C. P., Waber, D. P., Hock, R. S., Harrison, R., Eaglesfield, G. D., & Fitzmaurice, G. (2012). Infant malnutrition predicts conduct problems in adolescents. *Nutritional Neuroscience, 15*, 186–192.

Galler, J. R., Bryce, C. P., Waber, D. P., Medford, G., Eaglesfield, D. G., & Fitzmaurice, G. (2011). Early malnutrition predicts parent reports of externalizing behaviors at ages 9–17. *Nutrtional Neuroscience, 14*, 138–144.

Gallitto, E. (2014). Temperament as a moderator of the effects of parenting on children's behavior. *Development and Psychopathology,* 1–17.

Ganley, A. L., & Schechter, S. (1996). *Domestic violence: A national curriculum for children's protective services.* San Francisco: Family Violence Prevention Fund.

Gannon, T. A., O'Ciardha, C., Doley, R., & Alleyne, E. (2012). The multi-trajectory theory of adult firesetting (M-TTAF). *Aggression and Violent Behavior, 17,* 107–121.

Gannon, T. A., & Polaschek, D. L. L. (2006). Cognitive distortions in child molesters: A re-examination of key theories and research. *Clinical Psychology Review, 26,* 1000–1019.

Gannon, T. A., & Rose, M. R. (2008). Female child sexual offenders: Towards integrating theory and practice. *Aggression and Violent Behavior, 13,* 442–461.

Gannon, T. A., Waugh, G., Taylor, K., Blanchette, K., O'Connor, A., Blake, E., et al. (2014). Women who sexually offender display three main offense styles: A reexamination of the descriptive model of female sexual offending. *Sexual Abuse: A Journal of Research and Treatment, 26,* 207–224.

Gao, Y., Glenn, A. L., Schug, R. A., Yang, Y., & Raine, A. (2009). The neurobiology of psychopathy: A neurodevelopmental perspective. *The Canadian Journal of Psychiatry, 54,* 813–823.

Garbarino, J. (1989). The incidence and prevalence of child maltreatment. In L. Ohlin & M. Tonry (Eds.), *Family violence: Vol. 11.* Chicago: University of Chicago Press.

Garbarino, J., & Asp, C. E. (1981). *Successful schools and competent students.* Lexington, MA: Lexington Books.

Garcia, M. M., Shaw, D. S., Winslow, E. B., & Yaggi, K. E. (2000). Destructive sibling conflict and the development of conduct problems in young boys. *Developmental Psychology, 36,* 44–53.

Garcia-Retamero, R., & Dhami, M. K. (2009). Take-the-best in expert-novice decision strategies for residential burglary. *Psychonomic Bulletin & Review, 16,* 163–169.

Gardner, T. J. (1985). *Crime law: Principles and cases.* St. Paul, MN: West Publishing.

Garofalo, J. (1977). *Public opinion about crime: The attitudes of victims and nonvictims in selected cities.* Washington, DC: USGPO.

Garside, R. B., & Klimes-Dougan, B. (2002). Socialization of discrete negative emotions: Gender differences and links with psychological distress. *Sex Roles: A Journal of Research, 14,* 115–129.

Gaynor, J. (1996). Firesetting. In M. Lewis (Ed.), *Child and adolescent psychiatry: A comprehensive textbook.* Baltimore, MD: Williams & Wilkins.

Geis, G. (1988). From Deuteronomy to deniability: A historical perlustration on white-collar crime. *Justice Quarterly, 5,* 7–32.

Geis, G. (1997). Preface. In G. Green, *Occupational crime* (2nd ed.). Chicago: Nelson-Hall.

Gelles, R. J. (1982). Domestic criminal violence. In M. E. Wolfgang & N. A. Weiner (Eds.), *Criminal violence.* Beverly Hills, CA: Sage.

Gelles, R. J. (1997). *Intimate violence in families.* Thousand Oaks, CA: Sage.

Gendreau, P., Little, T., & Goggin, C. (1996). A meta-analysis of the predictors of adult offender recidivism: What works! *Criminology, 34,* 575–607.

Gentile, D. A., & Walsh, D. A. (2002). A normative study of family media habits. *Journal of Applied Developmental Psychology, 23,* 157–178.

Gerbner, G., Gross, L., Morgan, M., & Signorielli, N. (1981). Health and medicine on television. *The New England Journal of Medicine, 305,* 901–904.

Gerler, E. R., Jr. (2007). What the Amish taught us. *Journal of School Violence, 6,* 1–2.

Gerlock, A. A. (2004). Domestic violence and post-traumatic stress disorder severity for participants of a domestic violence rehabilitation program. *Military Medicine, 169,* 470–474.

Gershon, R. R. M., Barocas, B., Canton, A. N., Li, X., & Vlahov, D. (2009). Mental, physical and behavioral outcomes associated with perceived work stress in police officers. *Criminal Justice and Behavior, 36,* 275–289.

Getlen, L. (2014, February 16). Debunking the myth of Kitty Genovese. *New York Post.* Available: http://nypost.com/2014/02/16/book-reveals-real-story-behind-the-kitty-genovese-murder/.

Getz, J. G., & Bray, J. H. (2005). Predicting heavy alcohol use among adolescents. *American Journal of Orthopsychiatry, 75,* 102–116.

Gibbons, D. C. (1977). *Society, crime and criminal careers* (3rd ed.). Englewood Cliffs, NJ: Prentice Hall.

Giddan, J. J., Milling, L., & Campbell, N. B. (1996). Unrecognized language and speech deficits in preadolescent psychiatric patients. *American Journal of Orthopsychiatry, 66,* 85–92.

Gidycz, C. A., McNamara, J. R., & Edwards, K. M. (2006). Women's risk perception and sexual victimization: A review of the literature. *Aggression and Violence Behavior, 11,* 441–456.

Gini, G. (2006). Social cognition and moral cognition in bullying: What's wrong? *Aggressive Behavior, 32,* 528–539.

Glebova, T., Foster, S. L., Cunningham, P. B., Brennan, P. B., & Whitmore, E. (2012). Development and evaluation of the Therapist Comfort Scale. *Psychotherapy, 49,* 52–61.

Glenny, M. (2011). *Darkmarket: Cyberthieves, cybercops, and you.* New York: Knopf.

Glisson, C., Schoenwald, S. K., Hemmelgarn, A., Green, P., Dukes, D., Armstrong, K. S., et al. (2010). Randomized trial of MST and ARC in a two-level evidence-based treatment implementation strategy. *Journal of Consulting and Clinical Psychology, 78,* 537–550.

Glueck, S., & Glueck, E. (1950). *Unraveling juvenile delinquency.* New York: Harper & Row.

Gold, L. H. (1962). Psychiatric profile of the firesetter. *Journal of Forensic Sciences, 7,* 404–417.

Golding, S. L., Skeem, J. L., Roesch, R., & Zapf, P. A. (1999). The assessment of criminal responsibility: Current controversies. In I. B. Weiner & A. K. Hess (Eds.), *Handbook of forensic psychology* (2nd ed., pp. 379–408). New York: Wiley.

Goldman, M. J. (1991). Kleptomania: Making sense of the nonsensical. *American Journal of Psychiatry, 148,* 986–995.

Goldstein, A. M., Morse, S. J., & Packer, I. K. (2013). Evaluation of criminal responsibility. In I. B. Weiner (Ed.), *Handbook of psychology* (2nd ed., pp. 440–472). Hoboken, NJ: Wiley.

Goldstein, J. H. (1975). *Aggression and crimes of violence.* New York: Oxford University Press.

Goldstein, N. E., Arnold, D. H., Rosenberg, J. L., Stowe, R. M., & Ortiz, C. (2001). Contagion of aggression in day care classrooms as a function of peer and toddler responses. *Journal of Educational Psychology, 93,* 708–719.

Goldstein, P. J. (1985). The drugs-violence nexus: A tri-partite conceptual framework. *Journal of Drug Issues, 15,* 493–506.

Golub, A. L., & Johnson, B. D. (1997, July). *Crack's decline: Some surprises across U.S. cities.* NIJ Research in Brief. Washington, DC: U.S. Department of Justice.

Goodwill, A. M., Alison, L. J., & Beech, A. R. (2009). What works in offender profiling? A comparison of typological, thematic, and multivariate models. *Behavioral Sciences & the Law, 27,* 507–529.

Gooren, E. M. J. C., van Lier, P. A. C., Stegge, H., Terwogt, M. M., & Koot, H. M. (2011). The development of conduct problems and depressive symptoms in early elementary school children: The role of peer rejection. *Journal of Criminal Child & Adolescent Psychology, 40,* 245–253.

Gordon, D. A., Arbuthnot, J., Gustafson, K. E., & McGreen, P. (1988). Home-based behavioral-systems family therapy with disadvantaged juvenile delinquents. *The American Journal of Family Therapy, 16,* 243–255.

Gordon, R. (1983). An operational definition of prevention. *Public Health Reports, 98,* 107–109.

Gorman-Smith, D., & Loeber, R. (2005). Are developmental pathways in disruptive behaviors the same for girls and boys? *Journal of Child and Family Studies, 14,* 15–27.

Gorman-Smith, D., Tolan, P. H., Huesmann, L. R., & Zelli, A. (1996). The relation of family functioning to violence among inner-city minority youths. *Journal of Family Psychology, 10,* 115–129.

Gospodarevskaya, E. (2013). Post-traumatic stress disorder and quality of life in sexually abuse Australian children. *Journal of Child Sexual Abuse, 22,* 277–296.

Gottfredson, G. D., Gottfredson, D. C., Payne, A. A., & Gottfredson, N. C. (2005). School climate predictors of school disorder: Results from a national study of delinquency prevention in schools. *Journal of Research in Crime and Delinquency, 42*, 412–444.

Gottfredson, M., & Hirschi, T. (1990). *A general theory of crime.* Stanford, CA: Stanford University Press.

Gottman, J. M. (2001). Crime, hostility, wife battering, and the heart: On the Meehan et al. (2001) failure to replicate the Gottman **et al**. (1995) typology. *Journal of Family Psychology, 15*, 409–414.

Graff, G. M. (2014, September). Comey island. *Politico Magazine* (on-line).

Grafman, J., Schwab, K., Warden, D., Pridgen, A., Brown, H. R., & Salazar, A. M. (1996). Frontal lobe injuries, violence and aggression: A report of the Vietnam Head Injury Study. *Neurology, 46*, 1231–1238.

Grandjean, P., Weihe, P., Debes, F., Choi, A. L., & Budtz-Jørgensen, E. (2014). Neurotoxicity from prenatal and postnatal exposure to methylmercury. *Neurotoxicology and Teratology, 43*, 39–44.

Granic, I., & Patterson, G. R. (2006). Toward a comprehensive model of antisocial development: A dynamic systems approach. *Psychological Review, 113*, 101–131.

Grann, M. (2000). The PCL-R and gender. *European Journal of Psychological Assessment, 16*, 147–149.

Grant, V. (1977). *The menacing stranger.* New York: Dover.

Green, G. S. (1997). *Occupational crime* (2nd ed.). Chicago: Nelson-Hall.

Greendlinger, V., & Byrne, D. (1987). Coercive sexual fantasies of college men as predictors of self-reported likelihood to rape and overt sexual aggression. *Journal of Sex Research, 23*, 1–11.

Greenfeld, L. A. (1996, March). *Child victimization: Violent offenders and their victims.* Washington, DC: U.S. Department of Justice, Bureau of Justice Statistics.

Greenfeld, L. A. (1998, April). *Alcohol and crime: An analysis of national data on the prevalence of alcohol involvement in crime.* Washington, DC: U.S. Department of Justice.

Gretton, H. M., McBride, M., Hare, R. D., O'Shaughnessy, R., & Kumka, G. (2001). Psychopathy and recidivism in adolescent sex offenders. *Criminal Justice and Behavior, 28*, 427–449.

Griffe, K., Swindell, S., O'Keefe, S. L., Stroebel, S. S., Beards, K. W., Kuo, S-Y., et al. (in press). Ecological risk factors for sibling incest: Data from an anonymous computer-assisted self interview. *Sexual Abuse: A Journal of Research and Treatment.*

Griggs, R. A. (2014). Coverage of the Stanford Prison Experiment in introductory psychology textbooks. *Teaching of Psychology, 41*, 195–203.

Griggs, R. A., & Whitehead III, G. I. (2014). Coverage of the Stanford Prison Experiment in introductory social psychology textbooks. *Teaching of Psychology, 41*, 318–324.

Grimes, T., & Bergen, L. (2008). The epistemological argument against a causal relationship between media violence and sociopathic behavior among psychologically well viewers. *American Behavioral Scientist, 51*, 1137–1154.

Grisso, T. (1986). *Evaluating competencies: Forensic assessments and instruments.* New York: Plenum.

Grønnerød, C., Grønnerød, J. S., & Grøndahl, P. (2015). Psychological treatment of sexual offenders against children: A meta-analytical review of treatment outcome studies. *Trauma, Violence, & Abuse, 16*, 401–417.

Gross, A. M., Winslett, A., Roberts, M., & Gohm, C. L. (2006). An examination of sexual violence against women. *Violence against Women, 12*, 288–300.

Grossman, A., Kesling, B., & Audi, T. (2015, April 21). Six held for trying to join militants. *The Wall Street Journal*, p. 1.

Groth, A. N. (1978). Patterns of sexual assault against children and adolescents. In A. W. Burgess, A. N. Groth, L. L. Holmstrom, & S. M. Sgroi (Eds.), *Sexual assault of children and adolescents.* Lexington, MA: Lexington Books.

Groth, A. N. (1979). *Men who rape: The psychology of the offender.* New York: Plenum.

Groth, A. N., & Burgess, A. W. (1977). Motivational intent in the sexual assault of children. *Criminal Justice and Behavior, 4*, 253–271.

Groth, A. N., Hobson, W. F., & Gary, T. S. (1982). The child molester: Clinical observation. *Journal of Social Work and Human Sexuality, 1*, 129–144.

Guay, J., Ruscio, J., Knight, R. A., & Hare, R. D. (2007). A taxometric analysis of the latent structure of psychopathy: Evidence for dimensionality. *Journal of Abnormal Psychology, 116*, 701–716.

Guerra, N. G., Huesmann, L. R., Tolan, P. H., Van Acker, R., & Eron, L. D. (1995). Stressful events and individual beliefs as correlates of economic disadvantage and aggression among urban children. *Journal of Consulting and Clinical Psychology, 63,* 518–528.

Guerra, N., Tolan, P. H., & Hammond, W. R. (1994). Prevention and treatment of adolescent violence. In L. R. Eron, J. H., Gentry, & P. Schlegel (Eds.), *Reason to hope: A psychological perspective on violence and youth* (pp. 383–404). Washington, DC: American Psychological Association.

Gunter, B. (2008). Media violence: Is there a case for causality? *American Behavioral Scientist, 51,* 1061–1122.

Gurley, J. R., & Marcus, D. K. (2008). The effects of neuroimaging and brain injury on insanity defenses. *Behavioral Sciences & the Law, 26,* 85–97.

Guymer, A. C., Mellor, D., Luk, E. S., & Pearse, V. (2001). The development of a screening questionnaire for childhood cruelty to animals. *Journal of Child Psychology and Psychiatry, 42,* 1057–1063.

Haider, S., Anis, L., Batool, Z., Sajid, I., Naqvi, F., Khaliq, S., & Ahmed, S. (2014). Short term cadmium administration dose dependently elicits immediate biochemical, neurochemical and neurobehavorial dysfunction in male rates. *Metabolic Brain Disease, 30,* 83–92.

Häkkänen, H., & Laajasalo, T. (2006). Homicide crime scene behaviors in a Finnish sample of mentally ill offenders. *Homicide Studies, 10,* 33–54.

Häkkänen, H., Puolakka, P., & Santtila, P. (2004). Crime scene actions and offender characteristics in arsons. *Legal and Criminological Psychology, 9,* 197–214.

Hald, G. M., Malamuth, N. M., & Yuen, C. (2010). Pornography and attitudes supporting violence against women: Revisiting the relationship in nonexperimental studies. *Aggressive Behavior, 36,* 14–20.

Hall, D. M. (1998). The victims of stalking. In J. R. Meloy (Ed.), *The psychology of stalking: Clinical and forensic perspectives.* San Diego, CA: Academic Press.

Hallett, B. (2004). Dishonest crimes, dishonest language: An argument about terrorism. In F. M. Moghaddam & A. J. Marsella (Eds.), *Understanding terrorism: Psychosocial roots, consequences, and interventions* (pp. 49–68). Washington, DC: American Psychological Association.

Hämäläinen, T., & Haapasalo, J. (1996). Retrospective reports of childhood abuse and neglect among violent and property offenders. *Psychology, Crime & Law, 3,* 1–13.

Hamby, S., Finkelhor, D., Turner, H., & Ormrod, R. (2011). *Children's exposure to intimate partner violence and other family violence.* Washington, DC: U.S. Department of Justice.

Hamdi, N. R., & Knight, R. A. (2012). The relationships of perpetrator and victim substance use to the sexual aggression of rapists and child molesters. *Sexual Abuse: A Journal of Research and Treatment, 24,* 307–327.

Hammond, W. R., & Yung, B. (1994). African Americans. In L. D. Eron, J. H. Gentry, & P. Schlegel (Eds.), *Reason to hope: A psychosocial perspective on violence and youth* (pp. 105–118). Washington, DC: American Psychological Association.

Haney, C. W. (1983). The good, the bad, and the lawful: An essay on psychological injustice. In W. S. Laufer & J. M. Day (Eds.), *Personality theory, moral development, and criminal behavior.* Lexington, MA: Lexington Books.

Haney, C., & Zimbardo, P. (1998). The past and future of U.S. prison policy: Twenty-five years after the Stanford prison experiment. *American Psychologist, 53,* 709–727.

Hanfland, K. A., Keppel, R. D., & Weis, J. G. (1997, May). *Case management for missing children homicide investigation.* Washington, DC: U.S. Department of Justice, Office of Justice Programs.

Hanson, R. K. (1997). *The development of a brief actuarial risk scale for sexual offense recidivism.* Ottawa, ON: Office of the Solicitor General Canada.

Hanson, R. K. (2001). *Age and sexual recidivism: A comparison of rapists and child molesters.* Ottawa, ON: Solicitor General Canada.

Hanson, R. K. (2009). The psychological assessment of risk for crime and violence. *Canadian Psychology, 50,* 172–182.

Hanson, R. K., Bourgon, G., Helmus, L., & Hodgson, S. (2009). The principles of effective correctional treatment also apply to sexual offenders: A meta-analysis. *Criminal Justice and Behavior, 36,* 865–891.

Hanson, R. K., & Morton-Bourgon, K. E. (2004). *Predictors of sexual recidivism: An updated meta-*

analysis (Corrections User Report No. 2004-02). Ottawa, ON: Public Safety Canada.

Hanson, R. K., & Morton-Bourgon, K. E. (2005). The characteristics of persistent sexual offenders: A meta-analysis of recidivism studies. *Journal of Consulting and Clinical Psychology, 73,* 1154–1163.

Hanson, R. K., & Thornton, D. (2000). Improving risk assessment for sex offenders: A comparison of three actuarial scales. *Law and Human Behavior, 24,* 119–136.

Hanson, R. K., & Thornton, D. (2003). *Notes on the development of the Static-2002* (Corrections Research User Report No. 2003-01). Ottawa, ON: Department of the Solicitor General of Canada.

Hanson, R. K., Thornton, D., Helmus, L-M., & Babchishin, K. M. (in press). What sexual recidivism rates are associated with Static-99R and Static-2002R scores? *Sexual Abuse: A Journal of Research and Treatment.*

Harbin, H. T., & Madden, D. J. (1979). Battered parents: A new syndrome. *American Journal of Psychiatry, 136,* 1288–1291.

Hare, R. D. (1965a). A conflict and learning theory analysis of psychopathic behavior. *Journal of Research in Crime and Delinquency, 2,* 12–19.

Hare, R. D. (1965b). Acquisition and generalization of a conditioned-fear response in psychopathic and nonpsychopathic criminals. *Journal of Psychology, 59,* 367–370.

Hare, R. D. (1968). Psychopathy, autonomic functioning, and the orienting response. *Journal of Abnormal Psychology, 73,* 1–24.

Hare, R. D. (1970). *Psychopathy: Theory and research.* New York: Wiley.

Hare, R. D. (1976). Anxiety, stress and psychopathy. In G. Shean (Ed.), *Dimensions in abnormal psychology.* Chicago: Rand McNally.

Hare, R. D. (1991). *The Hare Psychopathy Checklist-Revised.* Toronto, ON: Multi-Health Systems.

Hare, R. D. (1993). *Without conscience: The disturbing world of the psychopaths among us.* New York: Pocket Books.

Hare, R. D. (1996). Psychopathy: A clinical construct whose time has come. *Criminal Justice and Behavior, 23,* 25–54.

Hare, R. D. (1998). Emotional processing in psychopaths. In D. J. Cooke, R. D. Hare, & A. Forth (Eds.), *Psychopathy: Theory, research, and implications for society.* The Netherlands: Kluwer Academic Publishers.

Hare, R. D. (2003). *The Hare Psychopathy Checklist—Revised* (2nd ed.). Toronto, ON: Multi-Health Systems.

Hare, R. D., Clark, D., Grann, M., & Thornton, D. (2000). Psychopathy and the predictive validity of the PCL-R: An international perspective. *Behavioral Sciences & the Law, 18,* 623–645.

Hare, R. D., & Connolly, J. F. (1987). Perceptual asymmetries and information processing in psychopaths. In S. A. Mednick, T. E. Moffitt, & S. A. Stack (Eds.), *The causes of crime: New biological approaches.* Cambridge, UK: Cambridge University Press.

Hare, R. D., & Craigen, D. (1974). Psychopathy and physiological activity in a mixed-motive game. *Psychophysiology, 11,* 197–206.

Hare, R. D., Forth, A. E., & Stachan, K. E. (1992). Psychopathy and crime across the life span. In R. D. Peters, R. J. McMahon, & V. L. Quinsey (Eds.), *Aggression and violence throughout the life span.* Newbury Park, CA: Sage.

Hare, R. D., Hart, S. D., & Harpur, T. J. (1991). Psychopathy and the DSM-IV criteria for antisocial personality disorder. *Journal of Abnormal Psychology, 100,* 391–398.

Hare, R. D., & McPherson, L. M. (1984). Violent and aggressive behavior by criminal psychopaths. *International Journal of Law and Psychiatry, 7,* 35–50.

Hare, R. D., & Neumann, C. S. (2008). Psychopathy as a clinical and empirical construct. *Annual Review of Clinical Psychology, 4,* 217–246.

Hare, R. D., & Quinn, M. (1971). Psychopathy and autonomic conditioning. *Journal of Abnormal Psychology, 77,* 223–239.

Harenski, C. L., Harenski, K. A., Kiehl, K. A., & Shane, M. S. (2010). Aberrant neural processing of moral violations in criminal psychopaths. *Journal of Abnormal Psychology, 119,* 863–874.

Harlow, C. W. (2003). *Education and correctional populations.* Washington, DC: U.S. Department of Justice, Office of Justice Programs.

Harmon, R. B., Rosner, R., & Wiederlight, M. (1985). Women and arson: A demographic study. *Journal of Forensic Sciences, 10*, 467–477.

Harpur, T. J., Hakstian, A., & Hare, R. D. (1988). Factor structure of the Psychopathy Checklist. *Journal of Consulting and Clinical Psychology, 56*, 741–747.

Harrell, E. (2011, March). *Workplace violence, 1993–2009.* Washington, DC: U.S. Department of Justice, Bureau of Justice Statistics.

Harrell, E. (2013, April). *Workplace violence against government employees, 1994–2011.* Washington, DC: U.S. Department of Justice, Bureau of Justice Statistics.

Harris, A. J., & Lurigio, A. J. (2010). Special Issue: Sex offenses and offenders: Toward evidence-based public policy. *Criminal Justice and Behavior, 37*, 503–519.

Harris, D. A. (1999, June). *Driving while Black: Racial profiling on our nation's highways.* New York: American Civil Liberties Union.

Harris, D. A., Knight, R. A., Smallbone, S., & Dennison, S. (2011). Postrelease specialization and versatility in sexual offenders referred for civil commitment. *Sexual Abuse: A Journal of Research and Treatment, 23*, 243–259.

Harris, D. A., Mazerolle, P., & Knight, R. A. (2009). Understanding male sexual offending: A comparison of general and specialist theories. *Criminal Justice and Behavior, 36*, 1051–1069.

Harris, D. A., Pedneault, A., & Knight, R. A. (2013). An exploration of burglary in the criminal histories of sex offenders referred for civil commitment proceedings. *Psychology, Crime and the Law, 19*, 765–781.

Harris, G. T., Rice, M. E., Quinsey, V. L., & Cormier, C. A. (2015). Sex offenders. In G. T. Harris, M. E. Rice, V. L. Quinsey, & C. A. Cormier (Eds.). *Violent offenders: Appraising and managing risk* (3rd ed., pp. 93–118). Washington, DC: American Psychological Association.

Harrison, M. A., Murphy, E. A., Ho, L. Y., Bowers, T. G., & Flaherty, C. V. (2015). Female killers in the United States: Means, motives, and makings. *Journal of Forensic Psychiatry & Psychology, 26*, 383–406.

Hart, S. D., Cox, D. N., & Hare, R. D. (1995). *The Hare Psychopathy Checklist: Screening Version.* Toronto, ON: Multi-Health Systems.

Hart, S. D., & Dempster, R. J. (1997). Impulsivity and psychopathy. In C. D. Webster & M. A. Jackson (Eds.), *Impulsivity: Theory, assessment and treatment.* New York: Guilford.

Hart, S. D., & Hare, R. D. (1997). Psychopathy: Assessment and association with criminal conduct. In D. M. Stoff, J. P. Maser, & J. Breiling (Eds.), *Handbook of antisocial behavior.* New York: Wiley.

Hart, S. D., Hare, R. D., & Forth, A. E. (1993). Psychopathy as a risk marker for violence: Development and validation of a screening version of the Revised Psychopathy Checklist. In J. Monahan & H. Steadman (Eds.), *Violence and mental disorder: Development in risk assessment.* Chicago: University of Chicago Press.

Hart, C. H., Nelson, A. A., Robinson, C. C., Olsen, S. F., & McNeilly-Choque, M. K. (1998). Overt and relational aggression in Russian nursery-school-age children: Parenting style and marital linkages. *Developmental Psychology, 34*, 687–697.

Haslam, S. A., & Reicher, S. D. (2012). When prisoners take over the prison: A social psychology of resistance. *Personality and Social Psychology Review, 16*, 154–179.

Hastings, P. D., Zahn-Waxler, C., Usher, B., Robinson, J., & Bridges, D. (2000). The development of concern for others in children with behavior problems. *Developmental Psychology, 36*, 531–546.

Hatters-Friedman, S., & Resnick, P. (2009). Neonaticide: Phenomenology and considerations for prevention. *International Journal of Law and Psychiatry, 32*, 43–47.

Hawes, D. J., & Dadds, M. R. (2005). The treatment of conduct problems in children with callous-unemotional traits. *Journal of Consulting and Clinical Psychology, 73*, 737–741.

Hawes, D. J., & Dadds, M. R. (2012). Revisiting the role of empathy in childhood pathways to antisocial behavior. In R. Langdon & C. MacKenzie (Eds.), *Emotions, imagination, and moral reasoning* (pp. 45–70). New York: Psychology Press.

Hawkins, D. L., Pepler, D. J., & Craig, W. M. (2001). Naturalistic observations of peer interventions in bullying. *Social Development, 10*, 512–527.

Hawkins, S. R., Graham, P. W., Williams, J., & Zahn, M. A. (2009, January). *Resilient girls: Factors that protect against delinquency.* Washington, DC: U.S. Department of Justice, Office of Justice Programs.

Haworth, C. M. A., Davis, O. S. P., & Plomin, R. (2012). Twins early development study (TEDS): A genetically sensitive investigation of cognitive and behavioral development from childhood to young adulthood. *Twin Research and Human Genetics, 16*, 117–125.

Hebb, D. O. (1955). Drives and the C.N.S. (Conceptual Nervous System). *Psychological Review, 62*, 243–254.

Hébert, M., Langevin, R., & Bernier, M. J. (2013). Self-reported symptoms and parents' evaluation of behavior problems in preschoolers disclosing sexual abuse. *International Journal of child, Youth, and Family Studies, 4*, 467–483.

Hébert, M., Tourigny, M., Cyr, M., McDuff, P., & Joly, J. (2009). Prevalence of childhood sexual abuse and timing of disclosure in a representative sample of adults from Quebec. *Canadian Journal of Psychiatry, 54*, 631–636.

Heckel, R. V., & Shumaker, D. M. (2001). *Children who murder: A psychological perspective.* Westport, CT: Praeger.

Heide, K. (1993). Adolescent parricide offenders: Synthesis, illustration and future directions. In A. V. Wilson (Ed.), *Homicide—the victim/offender connection.* Cincinnati, OH: Anderson.

Heide, K. M. (2003). Youth homicide: A review of the literature and blueprint for action. *International Journal of Offender Therapy and Comparative Criminology, 47*, 6–36.

Heide, K. M. (2014). Juvenile homicide: Trends, correlates, causal factors, and outcomes. In C. A. Pietz & C. A. Mattson (Eds.), *Violent offenders: Understanding and assessment* (pp. 127–150). New York, NY: Oxford University Press.

Heide, K. M., Roe-Sepowitz, D., Solomon, E. P., & Chan, H. C. (2012). Male and female juveniles arrested for murder: A comprehensive analysis of U.S. data by offender gender. *International Journal of Offender Therapy and Comparative Criminology, 56*, 356–384.

Heide, K. M., & Sellers, B. G. (2014). Girls arrested for murder: An empirical analysis of 32 years of U.S. data by offender age groups. *Behavioral Sciences & the Law, 32*, 467–482.

Heide, K. M., Solomon, E. P., Sellers, B. G., & Chan, H. C. (2011). Male and female juvenile homicide offenders: An empirical analysis of U.S. arrests by offender age. *Feminist Criminology, 6*, 3–31.

Heil, P., Ahlmeyer, S., & Simons, D. (2003). Crossover sexual offenses. *Sexual Abuse: A Journal of Research and Treatment, 15*, 221–236.

Heilbrun, K., DeMatteo, D., Yasuhara, K., Brooks-Holliday, S., Shah, S., King, C., et al. (2012). Community-based alternatives for justice-involved individuals with severe mental illness: Review of the relevant research. *Criminal Justice and Behavior, 39*, 351–419.

Heilbrun, K., Douglas, K. S., & Yasuhara, K. (2009). Violence risk assessment: Core controversies. In J. L. Skeem, K. S. Douglas, & S. O. Lilienfeld (Eds.), *Psychological science in the courtroom: Consensus and controversies* (pp. 333–357). New York: The Guilford Press.

Heilbrun, K., Marczyk, G. R., & DeMatteo, D. (2002). *Forensic mental health assessment: A casebook.* New York: Kluwer Academic.

Hellemans, S., Loeys, T., Buysse, A., Dewaele, A., & De Smet, O. (2015). Intimate partner violence victimization among non-heterosexuals: Prevalence and associations with mental and sexual well-being. *Journal of Family Violence, 30*, 71–188.

Hellmich, C. (2008). Creating the ideology of Al Qaeda: From hypocrites to Salafi-Jihadists. *Studies in Conflict & Terrorism, 31*, 111–124.

Hemphill, J. F., & Hare, R. D. (2004). Some misconceptions about the Hare PCL-R and risk assessment: A reply to Gendreau, Goggin, and Smith. *Criminal Justice and Behavior, 31*, 203–243.

Hemphill, J. F., Hare, R. D., & Wong, S. (1998). Psychopathy and recidivism: A review. *Legal and Criminological Psychology, 3*, 139–170.

Hendricks, N. J., Ortiz, C. W., Sugie, N., & Miller, J. (2007). Beyond the numbers: Hate crimes and cultural trauma within Arab American immigrant communities. *International Review of Victiminology, 14*, 95–113.

Henggeler, S. W. (1996). Treatment of violent juvenile offenders—we have the knowledge. *Journal of Family Psychology, 10*, 137–141.

Henggeler, S. W. (2011). Efficacy studies to large-scale transport: The development and validation of multisystemic therapy programs. *Annual Review of Clinical Psychology, 7*, 351–381.

Henggeler, S. W., & Borduin, C. M. (1990). *Family therapy and beyond: A multisystemic approach* *to treating the behavior problems of children and adolescents.* Pacific Grove, CA: Brooks/Cole.

Henggeler, S. W., Letourneau, E. J., Chapman, J. E., Borduin, C. M., Schewe, P. A., & McCart, M. R. (2009). Mediators of change for multisystemic therapy with juvenile sex offenders. *Journal of Consulting and Clinical Psychology, 77,* 451–462.

Henggeler, S. W., Melton, G. B., & Smith, L. A. (1992). Family preservation using multisystemic therapy—an effective alternative to incarcerating serious juvenile offenders. *Journal of Consulting and Clinical Psychology, 60,* 953–961.

Henggeler, S. W., Melton, G. B., Smith, L. A., Schoenwald, S. K., & Hanley, J. (1993). Family preservation using multisystemic therapy: Long-term follow-up to a clinical trial with serious juvenile offenders. *Journal of Child and Family Studies, 2,* 283–293.

Henggeler, S. W., Schoenwald, S. K., Borduin, C. M., Rowland, M. D., & Cunningham, P. B. (2009). *Multisystemic therapy of antisocial behavior in children and adolescents* (2nd ed.) New York, NY: Guilford.

Henker, B., & Whalen, C. K. (1989). Hyperactivity and attention deficits. *American Psychologist, 44,* 216–244.

Henn, F. A., Herjanic, M., & Vanderpearl, R. H. (1976a). Forensic psychiatry: Profiles of two types of sex offenders. *American Journal of Psychiatry, 133,* 694–696.

Henn, F. A., Herjanic, M., & Vanderpearl, R. H. (1976b). Forensic psychiatry: Diagnosis of criminal responsibility. *The Journal of Nervous and Mental Disease, 162,* 423–429.

Henneberger, A. K., Tolan, P. H., Hipwell, A. E., & Keenan, K. (2014). Delinquency in adolescent girls: Using a confluence approach to understand the influences of parents and peers. *Criminal Justice and Behavior, 41,* 1327–1337.

Henry, B., Caspi, A., Moffitt, T. E., & Silva, P. A. (1996). Temperament and familial predictors of violent and nonviolent criminal conviction: Age 3 to age 18. *Developmental Psychology, 32,* 614–623.

Henry, B. C., & Sanders, C. E. (2007). Bullying and animal abuse: Is there a connection? *Society and Animals, 15,* 107–126.

Hepburn, L. M., & Hemenway, D. (2004). Firearm availability and homicide: A review of the literature. *Aggression and Violent Behavior, 9,* 417–429.

Hepworth, W., & Towler, A. (2004). The effects of individual differences and charismatic leadership on workplace aggression. *Journal of Occupational Health Psychology, 9,* 176–185.

Herpertz, S. C., & Sass, H. (2000). Emotional deficiency and psychopathy. *Behavioral Sciences & the Law, 18,* 567–580.

Herzberg, J. L., & Fenwick, P. B. C. (1988). The aetiology of aggression in temporal lobe epilepsy. *British Journal of Psychiatry, 153,* 50–55.

Hetherington, E. M., & Parke, R. D. (1975). *Child psychology: A contemporary viewpoint.* New York: McGraw-Hill.

Hewitt, C. (2003). *Understanding terrorism in America: From the Klan to al Qaeda.* New York: Routledge.

Hickey, E. (1991). *Serial killers and their victims.* Pacific Grove, CA: Brooks/Cole.

Hickey, E. W. (1997). *Serial murderers and their victims* (2nd ed.). Belmont, CA: Wadsworth.

Hickey, E. W. (2010). *Serial murderers and their victims* (5th ed.). Belmont, CA: Wadsworth.

Hickle, K. E., & Roe-sepowitz, D. E. (2010). Female juvenile arsonists: An exploratory look at characteristics and solo and group arson offences. *Legal and Criminological Psychology, 15,* 385–399.

Hicks, B. M., Carlson, M. D., Blonigen, D. M., Patrick, C. J., Iacono, W. G., & McGue, M. (2012). Psychopathic personality traits and environmental contexts: Differential correlates, gender differences, and genetic mediation. *Personality Disorders: Theory, Research, and Treatment, 3,* 209–227.

Higgins, G. E., Piquero, N. L., & Piquero, A. R. (2011). General Strain Theory, peer rejection, and delinquency/crime. *Youth & Society, 43,* 1272–1297.

Hill, H. M., Soriano, F. I., Chen, S. A., & LaFromboise, T. D. (1994). Sociocultural factors in the etiology and prevention of violence among ethnic minority youth. In L. D. Eron, J. H. Gentry, & P. Schlegel (Eds.), *Reason to hope: A psychosocial perspective on violence and youth* (pp. 59–100). Washington, DC: American Psychological Association.

Hill, L. G., Lochman, J. E., Coie, J. D., & Geenberg, M. T. (2004). Effectiveness of early screening for externalizing problems: Issues of screening accuracy and utility. *Journal of Consulting and Clinical Psychology, 72,* 809–820.

Hill, N. E., Castellino, D. R., Lansford, J. E., Nowlin, P., Dodge, K. A., Bates, J. E., et al. (2004). Parent-academic involvement as related to school behavior, achievement, and aspirations: Demographic variations across adolescence. *Child Development, 75*, 1491–1509.

Hill, P. (1960). *Portrait of a sadist*. New York: Avon.

Hill, R. W., Langevin, R., Paitich, D., Handy, L., Russon, A., & Wilkinson, L. (1982). Is arson an aggressive act or a property offense? *Canadian Journal of Psychiatry, 27*, 648–654.

Hillberg, T., Hamilton-Giachrisis, C., & Dixon, L. (2011). Review of meta-analyses on the association between child sexual abuse and adult mental health difficulties: A systematic approach. *Trauma, Violence, & Abuse, 12*, 38–49.

Hillbrand, M., Alexandre, J. W., Young, J. L., & Spitz, R. T. (1999). Parricide: Characteristics of offenders and victims, legal factors, and treatment issues. *Aggression and Violent Behavior, 4*, 179–190.

Hilton, N. Z., Harris, G. T., Rice, M. E., Houghton, R. E., & Eke, A. W. (2008). An in-depth actuarial assessment for wife assault recidivism: The domestic violence risk appraisal guide. *Law and Human Behavior, 32*, 150–163.

Hindelang, M. J. (1974). Decisions of shoplifting victims to invoke the criminal justice process. *Social Process, 21*, 580–593.

Hindelang, M. J., Dunn, C. S., Sutton, L. P., & Aumick, A. (1976). *Sourcebook of criminal justice statistics, 1975*. Washington, DC: USGPO.

Hinduja, S. (2008). Deindividuation and Internet software piracy. *Cybercrime and Behavior, 11*, 391–398.

Hinduja, S., & Patchin, J. W. (2008). Cyberbullying: An exploratory analysis of factors related to offending and victimization. *Deviant Behavior, 29*, 129–156.

Hindujua, S., & Patchin, J. (2012). *A brief review of state cyberbullying laws and policies*. Cyberbullying Research Center. Available: www.cyberbullying.us

Hinduja, S., & Patchin, J. W. (2015). *Cyberbullying legislation and case law: Implications for school policy and practice*. On-line, Cyberbullying Research Center fact sheet. Available: www.cyberbullying.us.

Hinshaw, S. P. (1992). Externalizing behavior problems and academic underachievement in childhood and adolescence: Causal relationships and underlying mechanisms. *Psychological Bulletin, 111*, 127–155.

Hipwell, A. E., Loeber, R., Stouthamer-Loeber, M., Keenan, K., White, H. R., & Krone-Man, L. (2002). Characteristics of girls with early onset disruptive and antisocial behaviour. *Criminal Behaviour and Mental Health, 12*, 99–118.

Hirschi, T. (1969). *Causes of delinquency*. Berkeley: University of California Press.

Hirschi, T., & Hindelang, M. J. (1977). Intelligence and delinquency. *American Sociological Review, 42*, 571–587.

Hochstedler, E. (Ed.). (1984). *Corporations as criminals*. Beverly Hills, CA: Sage.

Hockenberry, S., & Puzzanchera, C. (2014). *Delinquency cases in juvenile court 2011*. Washington, DC: U.S. Department of Justice, Office of Juvenile Justice and Delinquency Prevention.

Hockenberry, S., & Puzzanchera, C. (2015, July). *Juvenile court statistics 2013*. Pittsburgh, PA: National Center for Juvenile Justice.

Hockenbury, D. H., & Hockenbury, S. E. (2004). *Discovering psychology* (3rd ed.). New York: Worth.

Hodgins, S. (2001). The major mental disorders and crime: Stop debating and start treating and preventing. *International Journal of Law and Psychiatry, 24*, 427–446.

Hoeve, M., Smeenk, W., Loeber, R., Stouthamer-Loeber, M., van der Laan, P. H., Gerris, J. R. M., et al. (2007). Long-term effects of parenting and family characteristics on delinquency of male young adults. *European Journal of Criminology, 4*, 161–194.

Hoffman, B. (1993). *"Holy terror": The implications of terrorism motivated by a religious imperative* (RAND Research Paper P-7834). Santa Monica, CA: RAND.

Hoffman, B. (2002). Rethinking terrorism and counterterrorism since 9/11. *Studies in Conflict and Terrorism, 25*, 303–316.

Hoffman, K. L., Kiecolt, K. J., & Edwards, J. N. (2005). Physical violence between siblings: A theoretical and empirical analysis. *Journal of Family Issues, 26*, 1103–1130.

Hoge, C. W., Terhakopian, A., Castro, C. A., Messer, S. C., & Engel, C. C. (2007). Association of posttraumatic stress disorder with somatic symptoms, heath care visits, and absenteeism among Iraq war veterans. *American Journal of Psychiatry, 164*, 150–153.

Hoge, S. K., Poythress, N., Bonnie, R., Monahan, J., Eisenberg, M., & Feucht-Haviar, T. (1997). The MacArthur adjudicative competence study: Diagnosis, psychopathology, and competence-related abilities. *Behavioral Sciences & the Law, 15*, 329–345.

Hoge, S. K., Poythress, N., Bonnie, R., Eisenberg, M., Monahan, J., Feucht-Haviar, T., & Oberlander, L. (1996). Mentally ill and non-mentally ill defendants' abilities to understand information relevant to adjudication: A preliminary study. *Bulletin of the American Academy of Psychiatry and the Law, 24*, 187–197.

Holder, E. (2012, January). Attorney General Eric Holder announces revisions to the Uniform Crime Report's definition of rape. *FBI National Press Release.*

Hollinger, R. (1986). Acts against the workplace: Social bonding and employee deviance. *Deviant Behavior, 7*, 53–75.

Hollister-Wagner, G. H., Foshee, V. A., & Jackson, C. (2001). Adolescent aggression: Models of resilience. *Journal of Applied Social Psychology, 31*, 445–466.

Holmes, C. T. (1989). Grade level retention effects: A meta-analysis of research studies. In L. A. Shepard & M. L. Smith (Eds.), *Flunking grades: Research and policies on retention.* Philadelphia: Falmer Press.

Holmes, S. T., Hickey, E., & Holmes, R. M. (1991). Female serial murderesses: Constructing differentiating typologies. *Journal of Contemporary Criminal Justice, 7*, 245–256.

Holt, S. E., Meloy, J. R., & Stack, S. (1999). Sadism and psychopath in violent and sexual violent offenders. *Journal of the American Academy of Psychiatry and Law, 27*, 23–32.

Holtzworth-Munroe, A., Meehan, J. C., Herron, K., Rehman, U., & Stuart, G. L. (2003). Do subtypes of martially violent men continue to differ over time? *Journal of Consulting and Clinical Psychology, 71*, 728–740.

Holtzworth-Munroe, A., & Stuart, G. L. (1994). Typologies of male batterers: Three subtypes and the differences among them. *Psychological Bulletin, 116*, 476–497.

Homant, R. J., & Kennedy, D. B. (1998). Psychological aspects of crime scene profiling: Validity research. *Criminal Justice and Behavior, 25*, 319–343.

Home Office. (1986). *Criminal statistics: England and Wales 1985.* London: HMSO.

Honomichl, R. D., & Donnellan, M. B. (2012). Dimensions of temperament in preschoolers predict risk taking and externalizing behaviors in adolescents. *Social Psychological and Personality Science, 3*, 14–22.

Horgan, J. (2005). *The psychology of terrorism.* London: Routledge.

Horning, D. N. M. (1970). Blue-collar theft: Conceptions of property, attitudes toward pilfering, and work group norms in a modern industrial plant. In E. O. Smigel & H. L. Ross (Eds.), *Crimes against bureaucracy.* New York: Van Nostrand Reinhold.

Hotaling, G. T., & Straus, M. A. (1989). Intrafamily violence, and crime and violence outside the family. In L. Ohlin & M. Tonry (Eds.), *Family violence: Vol. 11.* Chicago, IL: University of Chicago Press.

Hou, J., Chen, Z., Natsuaki, M. N., Li, X., Yang, X., Zhang, J., et al. (2013). A longitudinal investigation of the associations among parenting, deviant peer affiliation, and externalizing behaviors: A monozygotic twin differences design. *Twin Research and Human Genetics, 16*, 698–706.

Hoza, B., Mrug, S., Hinshaw, S. P., Bukowski, W. M., Gold, J., A., et al. (2005). What aspects of peer relationships are impaired in children with ADHD? *Journal of Consulting and Clinical Psychology, 73*, 411–423.

Hubbard, D. J., & Matthews, B. (2008). Reconciling the differences between the "gender-responsive" and the "what works" literatures to improve services for girls. *Crime & Delinquency, 54*, 225–258.

Hubbard, J. A., Dodge, K. A., Cillessen, A. H. N., Coie, J. D., & Schwartz, D. (2001). The dyadic nature of social information processing in boys' reactive and proactive aggression. *Journal of Personality and Social Psychology, 80*, 268–280.

Hubbs-Tait, L., Nation, J. R., Krebs, N. F., & Bellinger, D. C. (2005). Neurotoxicants, micronutrients, and social environments. *Psychological Science in the Public Interest, 6*, 57–121.

Hudson, M. I. (1986). Elder maltreatment: Current research. In K. A. Pillemer & R. S. Wolf (Eds.), *Elder abuse: Conflict in the family.* Dover, MA: Auburn House.

Huesmann, L. R. (1988). An information processing model for the development of aggression. *Aggressive Behavior, 14*, 13–24.

Huesmann, L. R. (1997). Observational learning of violent behavior: Social and biosocial processes. In A. Raine, P. A. Brennan, D. P. Farrington, & S. A. Mednick (Eds.), *Biosocial bases of violence.* New York: Plenum.

Huesmann, L. R. (1998). The role of social information processing and cognitive schema in the acquisition and maintenance of habitual aggressive behavior. In R. G. Geen & E. Donnerstein (Eds.), *Human aggression: Theories, research, and implications for social policy.* San Diego, CA: Academic Press.

Huesmann, L. R. (2007). The impact of electronic media violence: Scientific theory and research. *Journal of Adolescent Health, 41*, Supplement, S6–S13.

Huesmann, L. R., Dubow, E. F., & Boxer, P. (2011). The transmission of aggressiveness across generations: Biological, contextual, and social learning processes. In P. R. Shaver & M. Mikulincer (Eds.), *Human aggression and violence: Causes, manifestations, and consequences* (pp. 123–142). Washington, DC: American Psychological Association.

Huesmann, L. R., Moise-Titus, J., Podolski, C., & Eron, L. D. (2003). Longitudinal relations between children's exposure to TV violence and their aggressive and violent behavior in young adulthood: 1977–1992. *Developmental Psychology, 39*, 201–221.

Hughes, H. M. (1988). Psychological and behavioral correlates of family violence in child witnesses and victims. *American Journal of Orthopsychiatry, 58*, 77–90.

Hughes, H. M., & Barad, S. J. (1983). Psychological functioning of children in a battered women's shelter: A preliminary investigation. *American Journal of Orthopsychiatry, 53*, 525–531.

Hughes, H. M., Parkinson, D., & Vargo, M. (1989). Witnessing spouse abuse and experiencing physical abuse: A "double whammy"? *Journal of Family Violence, 4*, 197–209.

Huizinga, D., & Jakob-Chien, C. (1998). The contemporaneous co-occurrence of serious and violent juvenile offending and other problem behaviors. In R. Loeber & D. P. Farrington (Eds.), *Serious & violent juvenile offenders: Risk factors and successful interventions.* Thousand Oaks, CA: Sage.

Hunt, E., Peters, R. H., & Kremling, J. (2015). Behavioral health treatment history among persons in the justice system: Findings from the arrestee drug abuse monitoring II program. *Psychiatric Rehabilitation Journal, 38*, 7–15.

Hunt, P. M. (2010). Are you kynd? Conformity and deviance within the jamband culture. *Deviant Behavior, 31*, 521–551.

Hunter, J. A., Figueredo, A. J., Malamuth, N. M., & Becker, J. V. (2003). Juvenile sex offenders: Toward the development of a typology. *Sexual Abuse: A Journal of Research and Treatment, 15*, 27–48.

Hutchings, B., & Mednick, S. A. (1975). Registered criminality in the adoptive and biological parents of registered male criminal adoptees. In R. R. Fieve, D. Rosenthal, & H. Brill (Eds.), *Genetic research in psychiatry.* Baltimore, MD: Johns Hopkins University Press.

Icove, D. J., & Estepp, M. H. (1987, April). Motive-based offender profiles of arson and fire-related crime. *FBI Law Enforcement Bulletin*, 17–23.

Inciardi, J. A. (1981). Crime and alternative patterns of substance abuse. In S. E. Gardner (Ed.), *Drug and alcohol abuse.* Rockville, MD: National Institute on Drug Abuse.

Inciardi, J. A. (1986). *The war on drugs: Heroin, cocaine, crime and public policy.* Palo Alto, CA: Mayfield Publishing.

The Informant. (2003). *Newsletter of national white collar crime center*(August issue). Richmond, VA: National White Collar Crime Center.

Ingram, G. L., Gerard, R. E., Quay, H. C., & Levison, R. B. (1970). An experimental program for the psychopathic delinquent: Looking in the "correctional wastebasket." *Journal of Research in Crime and Delinquency, 7*, 24–30.

Innocence Project. (2014). http://www.innocenceproject.org/news-events-national-registry-reports-record-number-of-exonerations-in-2014.

Internet Crime Complaint Center. (2008). *Annual report on Internet crime.* Available: www.Ic3.gov.

Internet Crime Complaint Center. (2011). *Annual report on Internet crime.* Washington, DC: U.S. Department of Justice.

Ishikawa, S. S., & Raine, A. (2004). Prefrontal deficits and antisocial behavior: A causal model. In B. B. Lahey, T. E. Moffitt, & A. Caspi (Eds.), *Causes of conduct disorder and juvenile delinquency* (pp. 277–304). New York: Guilford.

Ishikawa, S. S., Raine, A., Lencz, T., Bihrle, S., & Lacasse, L. (2001). Autonomic stress reactivity and executive functions in successful and unsuccessful criminal psychopaths from the community. *Journal of Abnormal Psychology, 110,* 423–432.

Jackson, C., & Foshee, V. A. (1998). Violence-related behaviors of adolescents: Relations with responsive and demanding parenting. *Journal of Adolescent Research, 13,* 343–359.

Jackson, H. F., Glass, C., & Hope, S. (1987). A functional analysis of recidivistic arson. *British Journal of Clinical Psychology, 26,* 175–185.

Jackson, R. L., Neumann, C. S., & Vitacco, M. J. (2007). Impulsivity, anger, and psychopathy: The moderating effect of ethnicity. *Journal of Personality Disorders, 21,* 289–304.

Jackson, R. L., Rogers, R., Neumann, C. S., & Lambert, P. L. (2002). Psychopathy in female offenders: An investigation of its underlying dimensions. *Criminal Justice and Behavior, 29,* 692–704.

Jackson, S. L. (2014). All elder abuse perpetrators are not alike: The heterogeneity of elder abuse perpetrators and implications for intervention. *International Journal of Offender Therapy and Comparative Criminology, 58,* 1–21.

Jacobs, B. A., Topalli, V., & Wright, R. (2003). Carjacking, streetlife and offender motivation. *British Journal of Criminology, 43,* 673–688.

Jacobs, G. D., & Snyder, D. (1996). Frontal brain asymmetry predicts affective style in men. *Behavioral Neuroscience, 110,* 3–6.

Jaffee, S. R., Caspi, A., Moffitt, T. E., Dodge, K. A., Rutter, M., Taylor, A., et al. (2005). Nature x nurture: Genetic vulnerabilities interact with physical maltreatment to promote conduct problems. *Development and Psychopathology, 17,* 67–84.

Jaffee, S. R., & Odgers, C. L. (2013). Conduct disorder across the life course. In K. C. Loenen, S. Rudenstine, E. Susser, & S. Galea (Eds.), *Life course approach to mental disorders* (pp. 165–172). New York, NY: Oxford University Press.

Jaffee, S. R., Strait, L. B., & Odgers, C. L. (2012). From correlates to causes: Can quasi-experimental studies and statistical innovations bring us close to identifying the causes of antisocial behavior. *Psychological Bulletin, 136,* 279–295.

James, D. J., & Glaze, L. E. (2006, September). *Mental health problems of prison and jail inmates.* Washington, DC: U.S. Department of Justice, Bureau of Justice Statistics.

Jarvis, G., & Parker, H. (1989). Young heroin users and crime. *British Journal of Criminology, 29,* 175–185.

Javdani, S., Sadeh, N., & Verona, E. (2011). Expanding our lens: Female pathways to antisocial behavior in adolescence and adulthood. *Clinical Psychology Review, 31,* 1324–1348.

Javelin Strategy & Research. (2012, February 22). *2011 Identity fraud survey report.* Pleasanton, CA: Author.

Jeffrey, C. R. (1965). Criminal behavior and learning theory. *Journal of Criminal Law, Criminology and Police Science, 56,* 294–300.

Jenkins, P. (1988). Serial murder in England 1940–1985. *Journal of Criminal Justice, 16,* 1–15.

Jenkins, P. (1993). Chance or choice: The selection of serial murder victims. In A. V. Wilson (Ed.), *Homicide: The victim/offender connection.* Cincinnati, OH: Anderson.

Jenson, B. (1996 May). *Cyberstalking: Crime, enforcement and personal responsibility in the on-line world.* Available: www.law.ucla.edu/Classes/Archive. S96/340/cyberlaw.htm.

Jogerst, G. J., Daly, J. M., Galloway, L. J., Zheng, S., & Xu, Y. (2012). Substance abuse associated with elder abuse in the United States. *The American Journal of Drug and Alcohol Abuse, 38,* 63–69.

Johannesen, M., & LoGiudice, D. (2013). Elder abuse: A systematic review of risk factors in community-dwelling elders. *Age and Ageing, 42,* 292–298.

Johansson-Love, J., & Fremouw, W. (2009). Female sex offenders: A controlled comparison of offender and victim/crime characteristics. *Journal of Family Violence, 24,* 367–376.

Johns, J. H., & Quay, H. C. (1962). The effect of social reward on verbal conditioning in psychopathic military offenders. *Journal of Consulting Psychology, 26,* 217–220.

Johnsen, M. (2008, October 20). Pinched by economy retail crime on the rise. *Drug Store News,* pp. 1, 6, 42.

Johnson, L. B., Todd, M., & Subramanian, G. (2005). Violence in police families: Work-family spillover. *Journal of Family Violence, 20,* 3–12.

Johnson, R. (1996). *Hard time: Understanding and reforming the prison* (2nd ed.). Belmont, CA: Wadsworth.

Johnson, W. (2007). Genetic and environmental influences on behavior: Capturing all the interplay. *Psychological Review, 114,* 424–440.

Johnson, W., Turkheimer, E., Gottesman, I. I., & Bouchard, T. J., Jr. (2009). Beyond heritability: Twin studies in behavioral research. *Current Directions in Psychological Science, 18,* 217–220.

Johnston, L. D., O'Malley, P. M., Bachman, J. G., & Schulenberg, J. E. (2011, December). *Monitoring the future: National results on adolescent drug use: Overview of key findings 2011.* Ann Arbor, MI: Institute for Social Research, University of Michigan.

Johnston, L. D., O'Malley, P. M., Miech, R. A., Bachman, J. G., & Schulenberg, J. E. (2015, February). *Monitoring the future: National results on adolescent drug use: Overview of key findings 2014.* Ann Arbor: Institute for Social Research, University of Michigan.

Jolliffe, D., & Farrington, D. P. (2007). Examining the relationship between low empathy and self-reported offending. *Legal and Criminological Psychology, 12,* 265–286.

Jonas, E., & Frische, I. (2013). Destined to die but not to wage war: How existential threat can contribute to escalation or de-escalation of violent intergroup conflict. *American Psychologist, 68,* 543–558.

Jones, C. A. (2002). Victim perspective of bank robbery trauma and recovery. *Traumatology, 8,* 191–204.

Jones, J. G., Butler, H. L., Hamilton, B., Perdue, J. D., Stern, H. P., & Woody, R. C. (1986). Munchausen syndrome by proxy. *Child Abuse and Neglect, 10,* 33–40.

Jones, S., Cauffman, E., Miller, J. D., & Mulvey, E. (2006). Investigating different factor structures of the Psychopathy Checklist: Youth Version (PCL:YV) confirmatory factor analytic findings. *Psychological Assessment, 18,* 33–48.

Jones, A. P., Laurens, K. R., Herba, C. M., Barker, G. J., & Viding, E. (2009). Amygdala hypoactivity to fearful faces in boys with conduct problems and callous-unemotional traits. *American Journal of Psychiatry, 166,* 95–102.

Jost, J., & Sidanius, J. (2003). *Political psychology: Key readings.* London: Psychology Press.

Julien, R. M. (1975). *A primer of drug action.* San Francisco: W. H. Freeman.

Julien, R. M. (1992). *A primer of drug action* (6th ed.). New York: W. H. Freeman.

Kafrey, D. (1980). Playing with matches: Children and fire. In D. Canter (Ed.), *Fires and human behaviour.* Chichester, UK: Wiley.

Kahn, R. E., Frick, P. J., Youngstrom, E., Findling, R. L., & Youngstrom, J. K. (2012). The effects of including a callous-unemotional specifier for the diagnosis of conduct disorder. *Journal of Child Psychology and Psychiatry, 53,* 271–282.

Kakihara, F., Tilton-Weaver, L. C., Kerr, M., & Stattin, H. (2010). The relationship of parental control to youth adjustment: Do youths' feelings about their parents play a role? *Journal of Youth and Adolescence, 39,* 1442–1456.

Kandel, D., Yamaguchi, K., & Chen, K. (1992). Stages of drug involvement from adolescence to adulthood: Further evidence for the gateway theory. *Journal of Studies on Alcohol, 53,* 447–457.

Kandel, E., Mednick, S. A., Kirkegaard-Sorenson, L., Hutchings, B., Knop, J., Rosenberg, R., & Schulsinger, F. (1988). IQ as a protective factor for subjects at high risk for antisocial behavior. *Journal of Consulting and Clinical Psychology, 56,* 224–226.

Kanters, T., Hornsveld, R. H. J., Nunes, K. L., Huijding, J., Zwets, A. J. Snowden, R. J., et al. (in press). Are child abusers sexually attracted to submissiveness? Assessment of sex-related cognition with the Implicit Association Test. *Sexual Abuse: A Journal of Research and Treatment.*

Karagas, M. R., Choi, A. L., Oken, E., Horvat, M., Schoeny, R., Kamai, E., et al. (2012). Evidence of the human health effects of low-level methylmercury exposure. *Environmental Health Perspectives, 120,* 799–806.

Karmen, A. (2009). *Crime victims: An introduction to victimology* (7th ed.). Florence, KY: Cengage Learning.

Katz, J. (1988). *Seduction of crime: Moral and sensual attractions in doing evil.* New York: Basic Books.

Kazdin, A. E. (1989). Developmental psychopathology: Current research, issues, and directions. *American Psychologist, 44,* 180–187.

Keelan, C. M., & Fremouw, W. J. (2013). Child versus peer/adult offenders: A critical review of the juvenile sex offender literature. *Aggression and Violent Behavior, 18*, 732–744.

Keenan, K., Hipwell, A., Chung, T., Stepp, S., Stouthamer-Loeber, M., Loeber, R., et al. (2010). The Pittsburgh girls study: Overview and initial findings. *Journal of Clinical Child & Adolescent Psychology, 39*, 506–521.

Kelleher, M. D. (1997). *Profiling the lethal employee: Case studies of violence in the workplace.* Westport, CT: Praeger.

Kelleher, M. D., & Kelleher, C. L. (1998). *Murder most rate: The female serial killer.* Westport, CT: Dell Publishing.

Kelley, T. M., Kennedy, D. B., & Homant, R. J. (2003). Evaluation of an individualized treatment program for adolescent shoplifters. *Adolescence, 38*, 725–733.

Kelman, H. C., & Hamilton, V. L. (1989). *Crimes of obedience: Toward a social psychology of authority and responsibility.* New Haven, CT: Yale University Press.

Kemper, T. S., & Kistner, J. A. (2007). Offense history and recidivism in three victim-age-based groups of juvenile sexual offenders. *Sexual Abuse: A Journal of Research and Treatment, 19*, 409–424.

Kendall, P. C., & Hammen, C. (1995). *Abnormal psychology.* Boston: Houghton Mifflin.

Kendler, K. S., Prescott, C. A., Myers, J., & Neale, M. C. (2003). The structure of genetic and environmental risk factors for common psychiatric and substance use disorders in men and women. *Archives of General Psychiatry, 60*, 929–937.

Kerlinger, F. (1973). *Foundations of behavioral research* (2nd ed.). New York: Holt, Rinehart & Winston.

Kerr, D. C. R., DeGarmo, D. S., Leve, L. D., & Chamberlain, P. (2014). Juvenile justice girls' depressive symptoms and suicidal ideation 9 years after multidimensional treatment foster care. *Journal of Consulting and Clinical Psychology, 82*, 684–693.

Kessler, R. C., Adler, L., Barkley, R., Biedereman, J., Conners, C. K., Demler, O., et al. (2006). The prevalence and correlates of adult ADHD in the United States: Results from the National Comorbidity Survey Replication. *American Journal of Psychiatry, 163*(4), 716–723.

Kiehl, K. A. (2006). A cognitive neuroscience perspective on psychopathy: Evidence for paralimbic system dysfunction. *Psychiatry Research, 142*, 107–128.

Kiehl, K. A., Smith, A. M., Hare, R. D., Mendrek, A., Forster, B. B., Brink, J., et al. (2001). Limbic abnormalities in affective processing by criminal psychopaths as revealed by functional magnetic resonance imaging. *Biological Psychiatry, 50*, 677–684.

Kilgore, K., Snyder, J., & Lentz, C. (2000). The contribution of parental discipline, parental monitoring, and school risk to early-onset conduct problems in African American boys and girls. *Developmental Psychology, 36*, 835–845.

Kilpatrick, D. G., Resnick, H. S., Ruggiero, K. J., Conoscenti, L. M., & McCauley, J. (2007, February). *Drug-facilitated, incapacitated, and forcible rape: A national study.* Charleston, SC: Medical University of South Carolina.

Kilpatrick, D. G., Whalley, A., & Edmunds, C. (2000). Sexual assault. In A. Seymour, M. Murray, J. Sigmon, M. Hook, C. Edmunds, M. Gaboury, & G. Coleman (Eds.), *2000 National Victim Assistance Academy.* Washington, DC: U.S. Department of Justice.

Kim-Cohen, J., Caspi, A., Taylor, A., Williams, B., Newcombe, R., & Craig, I. W. (2006). MAOA, maltreatment, and gene-environment interaction predicting children's mental health: New evidence and a meta-analysis. *Molecular Psychiatry, 11*, 903–913.

Kim-Cohen, J., & Gold, A. L. (2009). Measured gene-environment interactions and mechanisms promoting resilient development. *Current Directions in Psychological Science, 18*, 138–142.

Kimonis, E. R., Skeem, J. L., Cauffman, E., & Dimitrieva, J. (2011). Are secondary variants of juvenile psychopathy more reactively violent and less psychosocially mature than primary variants? *Law and Human Behavior, 35*, 381–391.

Kinports, K. (2002). Sex offenses. In K. L. Hall (Ed.), *The Oxford companion to American law* (pp. 176–178). New York: Oxford University Press.

Kinscherff, R. (2012, January). *A primer for mental health practitioners working with youth involved in the juvenile justice system.* Washington, DC: Technical Assistance Partnership for Child and Family Mental Health.

Kinsey, A. C., Pomeroy, W. B., & Martin, C. E. (1948). *Sexual behavior in the human male.* Oxford, England: Saunders.

Kinsey, A. C., Pomeroy, W. B., Martin, C. E., & Gebhard, P. H. (1953). *Sexual behavior in the human female.* Oxford, England: Saunders.

Kivivuori, J. (1998). Delinquent phases: The case of temporally intensified shoplifting behaviour. *British Journal of Criminology, 38,* 663–680.

Kivivuori, J. (2007). Crime by proxy: Coercion and altruism in adolescent shoplifting. *British Journal of Criminology, 47,* 817–833.

Klassen, D., & O'Connor, W. (1988). Crime, inpatient admissions, and violence among male mental patients. *International Journal of Law and Psychiatry, 11,* 305–312.

Klassen, D., & O'Connor, W. (1990). Assessing the risk of violence in released mental patients: A cross-validation study. *Psychological Assessment: A Journal of Consulting and Clinical Psychology, 1,* 75–81.

Klaus, P. (1999, March). *Carjackings in the United States, 1992–1996.* Washington, DC: U.S. Department of Justice, Bureau of Justice Statistics.

Klaus, P. (2000, January). *Crimes against persons age 65 or older, 1992–97* (NCJ 176352). Washington, DC: U.S. Department of Justice, Bureau of Justice Statistics.

Klaus, P. (2004, July). *Carjacking, 1993–2002.* Washington, DC: U.S. Department of Justice, National Crime Victimization Survey.

Kleber, H. D. (1988). Epidemic cocaine abuse: America's present, Britain's future. *British Journal of Addiction, 83,* 1359–1371.

Kleck, G. (2009). Mass shootings in schools: The worst possible case for gun control. *American Behavioral Scientist, 52,* 1447–1464.

Klemke, L. W. (1992). *The sociology of shoplifting: Boosters and snitches today.* Westport, CT: Praeger.

Knight, R. A. (1988). A taxonomic analysis of child molesters. In R. A. Prentky & V. L. Quinsey (Eds.), *Human sexual aggression: Current perspectives.* New York: New York Academy of Science.

Knight, R. A. (1989). An assessment of the concurrent validity of a child molester typology. *Journal of Interpersonal Violence, 4,* 131–150.

Knight, R. A. (1999). Validation of a typology for rapists. *Journal of Interpersonal Violence, 14,* 303–330.

Knight, R. A. (2010). Typologies for rapists—The generation of a new structural model. In A. Schlank (Ed.), *The sexual predator: Legal issues assessment treatment: Vol. IV* (pp. 17.2–17.24). Kingston, NJ: Civic Research Institute.

Knight, R. A., Carter, D. L., & Prentky, R. A. (1989). A system for the classification of child molesters: Reliability and application. *Journal of Interpersonal Violence, 4,* 3–23.

Knight, R. A., & King, M. W. (2012). Typologies for child molesters: The generation of a new structural model. In B. K. Schwartz (Ed.), *The sexual offender: Vol. 7* (pp. 5.2–5.27). Kingston, NJ: Civic Research Institute.

Knight, R. A., & Prentky, R. A. (1987). The developmental antecedents and adult adaptations of rapist subtypes. *Criminal Justice and Behavior, 14,* 403–426.

Knight, R. A., & Prentky, R. A. (1990). Classifying sexual offenders: The development and corroboration of taxonomic models. In W. L. Marshall, D. R. Laws, & H. E. Barbaree (Eds.), *The handbook of sexual assault: Issues, theories, and treatment of the offender.* New York: Plenum.

Knight, R. A., & Prentky, R. A. (1993). Exploring characteristics for classifying juvenile sex offenders. In H. E. Barbaree, W. L. Marshall, & S. M. Hudson (Eds.), *The juvenile sex offender.* New York: Guilford.

Knight, R. A., Rosenberg, R., & Schneider, B. A. (1985). Classification of sexual offenders: Perspectives, methods, and validation. In A. W. Burgess (Ed.), *Rape and sexual assault.* New York: Garland.

Knight, R. A., & Sims-Knight, J. E. (2003). The development of antecedents of sexual coercion against women: Testing alternative hypotheses with structural equation modeling. *Annuals of the New York Academy of Science, 989,* 72–85.

Knight, R. A., & Sims-Knight, J. E. (2004). Testing an etiological model for male juvenile sexual offending against females. *Journal of Child Sexual Abuse, 13,* 33–55.

Knight, R. A., & Sims-Knight, J. (2011). Risk factors for sexual violence. In J. W. White, M. R. Koss, & A. F. Kazdin (Eds.), *Violence against women and children: Vol. 1. Mapping the terrain* (pp. 125–150). Washington, DC: American Psychological Association.

Knight, R. A., & Thornton, D. (2007). *Evaluating and improving risk assessments schemes for sexual* *recidivism: A long-term follow-up of convicted sexual offenders* (Document No. 217618). Washington, DC: U.S. Department of Justice.

Knight, R. A., Warren, J. I., Reboussin, R., & Soley, B. J. (1998). Predicting rapist type from crime-scene variables. *Criminal Justice and Behavior, 25*, 46–80.

Knoll, J. L. (2008). The psychological autopsy, Part I: Applications and methods. *Journal of Psychiatric Practice, 14*, 393–397.

Knoll, J. L. (2009). The psychological autopsy, Part II: Toward a standardized protocol. *Journal of Psychiatric Practice, 15*, 52–59.

Knopp, F. H., Rosenberg, J., & Stevenson, W. (1986). *Report on nationwide survey of juvenile and adult sex-offender treatment programs and providers.* Syracuse, NY: Safer Society Press.

Kochanska, G., Friesenborg, A. E., Lange, L. A., & Martel, M. M. (2004). Parents' personality and infants' temperament as contributors to their emerging relationship. *Journal of Personality and Social Psychology, 86*, 744–759.

Kocsis, R. N., Cooksey, R. W., & Irwin, H. J. (2002). Psychological profiling of offender characteristics from crime behaviors in serial rape offenses. *International Journal of Offender Therapy and Comparative Criminology, 46*, 144–169.

Koenen, K. C., Caspi, A., Moffitt, T. E., Rijsdijk, F., & Taylor, A. (2006). Genetic influences on the overlap between low IQ and antisocial behavior in young children. *Journal of Abnormal Psychology, 115*, 787–797.

Koenen, M. A., & Thompson, J. W. (2008). Filicide: Historical review and prevention of child death by parent. *Infant Mental Health Journal, 29*, 61–75.

Kofler, M. J., McCart, M. R., Zajac, K., Ruggiero, K. J., Saunders, B. E., & Kilpatrick, D. G. (2011). Depression and delinquency covariation in an accelerated longitudinal sample of adolescents. *Journal of Consulting and Clinical Psychology, 79*, 458–469.

Koger, S. M., Schettler, T., & Weiss, B. (2005). Environmental toxicants and developmental disabilities: A challenge for psychologists. *American Psychologist, 60*, 243–255.

Kohlberg, L. (1976). Moral stages and moralization: The cognitive development approach. In T. Licona (Ed.),

Moral development and behavior. New York: Holt, Rinehart, & Winston.

Kohlberg, L. (1977). The child as a moral philosopher. In CRM, *Readings in developmental psychology today.* New York: Random House.

Koivisto, H., & Haapasalo, J. (1996). Childhood maltreatment and adulthood in psychopathy in light of file-based assessments among mental state examinees. *Studies on Crime and Crime Prevention, 5*, 91–104.

Kokko, K., & Pulkkinen, L. (2005). Stability of aggressive behavior from childhood to middle age in women and men. *Aggressive Behavior, 31*, 485–497.

Kolko, D. (Ed.). (2002). *Handbook on firesetting in children and youth.* Boston: Academic Press.

Kolko, D. J., & Kazdin, A. E. (1989). The children's firesetting interview with psychiatrically referred and nonreferred children. *Journal of Abnormal Child Psychology, 17*, 609–624.

Kolko, D. J., Kazdin, A. E., & Meyer, E. C. (1985). Aggression and psychopathology in childhood firesetters: Parent and child reports. *Journal of Consulting and Clinical Psychology, 53*, 377–385.

Kolko, D., & Pardini, D. A. (2010). ODD dimensions, ADHD, and callous-emotional traits as predictors of treatment respond in children with disruptive behavior disorders. *Journal of Abnormal Psychology, 119*, 713–725.

Koon-Magnin, S., & Ruback, R. B. (2013). The perceived legitimacy of statutory rape laws: The effects of victim age, perpetrator age, and age span. *Journal of Applied Social Psychology, 43*, 1918–1930.

Kornhauser, R. R. (1978). *Social sources of delinquency.* Chicago: University of Chicago Press.

Koson, D. F., & Dvoskin, J. (1982). Arson: A diagnostic study. *Bulletin of the American Academy of Psychiatry and the Law, 10*, 39–49.

Koss, M. P., Abbey, A., Campbell, R., Cok, S., Norris, J., Testa, M., et al. (2007). Revising the SES: A collaborative process to improve assessment of sexual aggression and victimization. *Psychology of Women Quarterly, 31*, 357–370.

Koss, M. P., & Dinero, T. E. (1988). Predictors of sexual aggression among a national sample of male college students. In R. A. Prentky & V. L. Quinsey (Eds.), *Human sexual aggression: Current perspectives* (pp. 133–147). New York: New York Academy of Sciences.

Kosson, D. S. (1998). Divided visual attention to psychopathic and nonpsychopathic offenders. *Personality and Individual Differences, 24,* 373–391.

Kosson, D. S., Smith, S. S., & Newman, J. P. (1990). Evaluating the construct validity of psychopathy in black and white male inmates: Three preliminary studies. *Journal of Abnormal Psychology, 99,* 250–259.

Kosson, D. S., Suchy, Y., Mayer, A. R., & Libby, J. (2002). Facial affect recognition in criminal psychopaths. *Emotion, 2,* 398–411.

Kozol, H. L., Boucher, R. L., & Garofalo, P. F. (1972). The diagnosis and treatment of dangerousness. *Crime and Delinquency, 8,* 371–392.

Kraemer, G. W., Lord, W. D., & Heilbrun, K. (2004). Comparing single and serial homicide offenses. *Behavioral Sciences & the Law, 22,* 325–343.

Krahé, B., & Möller, I. (2004). Playing violent electronic games, hostile attributional style, and aggression-related norms in German adolescents. *Journal of Adolescence, 27,* 53–69.

Krasnovsky, T., & Lane, R. (1998). Shoplifting: A review of the literature. *Aggression and Violence Behavior, 3,* 219–235.

Kratzer, L., & Hodgins, S. (1999). A typology of offenders: A test of Moffitt's theory among males and females from childhood to age 30. *Criminal Behaviour and Mental Health, 9,* 57–73.

Krebs, C. P., Lindquist, C. H., Warner, T. D., Fisher, B. S., & Martin, S. L. (2007, December). *The Campus Sexual Assault (CSA) study: Final report.* Washington, DC: National Institute of Justice.

Kreis, M. K. F., & Cooke, D. J. (2011). Capturing the psychopathic female: A prototypicality analysis of the Comprehensive Assessment of Psychopathic Personality (CAPP) across gender. *Behavioral Sciences & the Law, 29,* 634–648.

Krisberg, B. (1992). Youth crime and its prevention: A research agenda. In I. M. Schwartz (Ed.), *Juvenile justice and public policy.* New York: Lexington Books.

Krisberg, B. (1995). The legacy of juvenile corrections. *Corrections Today, 57,* 122–126.

Krisberg, B., & Howell, J. C. (1998). The impact of the juvenile justice system and prospects for graduated sanctions in a comprehensive strategy. In R. Loeber & D. P. Farrington (Eds.), *Serious & violent juvenile offenders: Risk factors and successful interventions.* Thousand Oaks, CA: Sage.

Krisberg, B., & Schwartz, I. (1983). Rethinking juvenile justice. *Crime and Delinquency, 29,* 333–364.

Krischer, M., Stone, M., Sevecke, K., & Steinmeyer, E. (2007). Motives for maternal filicide: Results from a study with female forensic patients. *International Journal of Law and Psychiatry, 30,* 191–200.

Krohn, M. D., Akers, R. L., Radosevich, M. J., & Lanza-Kaduce, L. (1982). Norm qualities and adolescent drinking and drug behavior: The effects of norm quality and reference group on using and abusing alcohol and marijuana. *Journal of Drug Issues, 4,* 343–360.

Kropp, P. R., Hart, S. D., Webster, C. E., & Eaves, D. (1998). *Spousal Assault Risk Assessment: User's guide.* Toronto, ON: Multi-Health Systems.

Krueger, R. F., Caspi, A., Moffitt, T. E., White, J., & Stouthamer-Loeber, M. (1996). Delay of gratification, psychopathology, and personality: Is low self-control specific to externalizing problems? *Journal of Personality, 64,* 107–129.

Kruger, T. H. C., & Schiffer, B. (2011). Neurocognitive and personality factors in homo- and heterosexual pedophiles and controls. *Journal of Sexual Medicine, 8,* 1650–1659.

Kruglanski, A. W., Bélanger, J. J., Gelfand, M., Gunaratma, R., Hettiarachchi, M., Reinares, F., et al. (2013). Terrorism—A (self) love story. *American Psychologist, 68,* 559–575.

Kruglanski, A. W., Chen, X., Dechesne, M., Fishman, S., & Orehek, E. (2009). Fully committed: Suicide bombers' motivation and the quest for personal significance. *Political Psychology, 30,* 331–357.

Kruglanski, A. W., Crenshaw, M., Post, J. M., & Victoroff, J. (2008). What should this fight be called? Metaphors of counterterrorism and their implications. *Psychological Science in the Public Interest, 8,* 97–133.

Kruglanski, A. W., & Fishman, S. (2006). The psychology of terrorism: "Syndrome" versus "tool" perspectives. *Terrorism and Political Science, 18,* 193–215.

Kruglanski, A. W., & Orehek, E. (2011). The role of the quest for personal significance in motivating terrorism. In J. P. Forgas, A. W. Kruglanski, &. K. D. Williams (Eds.), *The psychology of social conflict and aggression* (pp. 153–164). New York: Psychology Press.

Kulka, R. A., Schlenger, W. E., Fairbank, J. A., Jordan, B. K., Hough, R. L., Marmar, C. R., et al. (1991). Assessment of post-traumatic stress disorder in the community: Prospects and pitfalls from recent studies of Vietnam veterans. *Psychological Assessment: A Journal of Consulting and Clinical Psychology, 4*, 547–560.

Kyckelhahn, T., Beck, A. J., & Cohen, T. H. (2009, January). *Characteristics of suspected human trafficking incidents, 2007–2008*. Washington, DC: U.S. Department of Justice, Bureau of Justice Statistics.

Laajasalo, T., & Häkkänen, H. (2006). Excessive violence and psychotic symptomatology among homicide offenders with schizophrenia. *Criminal Behaviour and Mental Health, 16*, 242–253.

Lacourse, E., Nagin, D., Tremblay, R. E., Vitaro, F., & Claes, M.
(2003). Developmental trajectories of boys' delinquent group membership and facilitation of violent behaviors during adolescence. *Developmental and Psychopathology, 15*, 183–197.

Lahey, B. B., Loeber, R., Hart, E. L., Frick, P. J., Applegate, B., Zhang, Q., et al. (1995). Four-year longitudinal study of conduct disorder in boys: Patterns and predictors of persistence. *Journal of Abnormal Psychology, 104*, 83–93.

Lahey, B. B., & Waldman, I. D. (2003). A developmental propensity model of the origins of conduct problems during childhood and adolescence. In B. B. Lahey, T. E. Moffitt, & A. Caspi (Eds.), *Causes of conduct disorder and juvenile delinquency* (pp. 76–117). New York: Guilford.

Laird, R. D., Jordan, K., Dodge, K. A., Pettit, G. S., & Bates, J. E. (2001). Peer rejection in childhood, involvement with antisocial peers in early adolescence, and the development of externalizing problems. *Development and Psychopathology, 13*, 337–354.

Laird, R. D., Pettit, G. S., Bates, J. E., & Dodge, K. A. (2003). Parents' monitoring—relevant knowledge and adolescents' delinquent behavior: Evidence of correlated developmental changes and reciprocal influences. *Child Development, 74*, 752–768.

Laird, R. D., Pettit, G. S., Dodge, K. A., & Bates, J. E. (2005). Peer relationship antecedents of delinquent behavior in late adolescence: Is there evidence of demographic group differences in developmental processes. *Development and Psychopathology, 17*, 127–144.

Lamb, H. R., Weinberger, L. E., & Gross, B. H. (2004). Mentally ill persons in the criminal justice system: Some perspectives. *Psychiatric Quarterly, 75*, 107–126.

Lambert, E. G., Smith, B., Geistman, J., Cluse-Tolar, T., & Jiang, S. (2013). Do men and women differ in their perceptions of stalking: An exploratory study among college students. *Violence and Victims, 28*, 195–209.

Lambie, I., McCardle, S., & Coleman, R. (2002). Where there's smoke there's fire: Firesetting behaviour in children and adolescents. *New Zealand Journal of Psychology, 31*, 73–79.

Lambie, I., & Randell, I. (2011). Creating a firestorm: A review of children who deliberately light fires. *Clinical Psychology Review, 31*, 307–327.

Lambie, L., Randell, I., & McDowell, H. (2014). "Inflaming your neighbors": Copycat firesetting in adolescents. *International Journal of Offender Therapy and Comparative Criminology, 58*, 1020–1032.

Lamontagne, Y., Boyer, R., Hetu, C., & Lacerte-Lamontagne, C. (2000). Anxiety, significant losses, depression, and irrational beliefs in first-offence shoplifters. *Canadian Journal of Psychiatry, 45*, 63–66.

Lanctôt, N., Hauth-Charlier, S., & Lemieux, A. (2015). Do depressive symptoms in justice-involved girls reduce the effects of a cognitive-behavioral program on their disruptive and delinquent behaviors? *International Journal of Social Welfare, 24*, 193–203.

Landau, M. J., & Sullivan, D. (2015). Terror management motivation at the core of personality. In M. Mikulincer & P. R. Shaver (Eds.), *APA handbooks of personality and social psychology: Vol. 4. Personality processes and individual differences* (pp. 209–250). Washington, DC: American Psychological Association.

Lang, S., Klinteberg, B., & Alm, P. O. (2002). Adult psychopathy and violent behavior in males with early neglect and abuse. *Acta Psychiatrica Scandinavica, 106*, 93–100.

Lange, J. (1929). *Verbrechen als sochicksal* (Crime as destiny). Leizig, Germany: Georg Thieme Verlag.

Langan, P. A., Schmitt, E. L., & Durose, M. R. (2003, November). *Recidivism of sex offenders released from prison in 1994*. Washington, DC: U.S. Department of Justice, Bureau of Justice Statistics.

Langer, E. J., & Miransky, J. (1983). Burglary (non) prevention. In E. J. Langer (Ed.), *The psychology of control.* Beverly Hills, CA: Sage.

Langevin, R., & Curnoe, S. (2012). Lifetime criminal history of sex offenders seen for psychological assessment in five decades. *International Journal and Comparative Criminology, 56*, 997–1021.

Langevin, R., Hebert, M., & Cossette, L. (2015). Emotion regulation as a mediator of the relation between sexual abuse and behavior problems in children. *Child Abuse and Neglect, 46*, 16–26.

Langton, C. M. (2012). Introduction to the special issue: Treatment considerations for aggressive adolescents in secure settings. *Criminal Justice and Behavior, 39*, 685–693.

Langton, L., & Baum, K. (2010, June). *Identity theft reported by households, 2007—statistical tables.* Washington, DC: U.S. Department of Justice, Bureau of Justice Statistics.

Langton, L., & Planty, M. (2011). *Hate crime, 2003–2009: Special Report.* Washington, DC: U.S. Department of Justice, Office of Justice Programs, Bureau of Justice Statistics.

Lansford, J. E., Deater-Deckard, K., Dodge, K. A., Bates, J. E., & Pettit, G. S. (2004). Ethnic differences in the link between physical discipline and later adolescent externalizing behaviors. *Journal of Child Psychology and Psychiatry, 45*, 801–812.

Lansford, J. E., Dodge, K. A., Pettit, G. S., Bates, J. E., Crozier, I., & Kaplow, J. (2002). Long-term effects of early child physical maltreatment on psychological, behavioral, and academic problems in adolescence: A 12-year prospective study. *Archives of Pediatrics and Adolescent Medicine, 156*, 824–830.

Lansford, J. E., Malone, P. S., Dodge, K. A., Pettit, G. S., & Bates, J. E. (2010). Developmental cascades of peer rejection, social information processing biases, and aggression during middle childhood. *Development and Psychopathology, 22*, 593–602.

Lanyon, R. I. (1986). Theory and treatment in child molestation. *Journal of Consulting and Clinical Psychology, 54*, 176–182.

Larkin, R. W. (2009). The Columbine legacy: Rampage shootings as political acts. *American Behavioral Scientist, 52*, 1309–1326.

Latané, B., & Darley, J. M. (1970). *The unresponsive bystander: Why doesn't he help?* New York: Appleton-Century-Crofts.

Laws, D. R., & Marshall, W. L. (1990). A conditioning theory of the etiology and maintenance of deviant sexual preference and behavior. In W. L. Marshall, D. R. Laws, & H. E. Barbaree (Eds.), *Handbook of sexual assault.* New York: Plenum.

Leach, E. (1973). Don't say "boo" to a goose. In A. Montagu (Ed.), *Man and aggression* (2nd ed.). London: Oxford University Press.

Leadbetter, B. J., & Homel, J. (in press). Irritable and defiant sub-dimensions of ODD: Their stability and prediction of internalizing symptoms and conduct problems from adolescence to young adulthood. *Journal of Abnormal Child Psychology.*

Leary, M. R., Kowalski, R. M., Smith, L., & Phillips, S. (2003). Teasing, rejection, and violence: Case studies of the school shootings. *Aggressive Behavior, 29*, 202–214.

Le Blanc, M., & Loeber, R. (1998). Developmental criminology updated. In M. Tonry (Ed.), *Crime and justice: A review of research* (pp. 115–198). Chicago: The University of Chicago Press.

LeClair, J. A., & Quig, D. W. (2001). Mineral status, toxic metal exposure and children's behavior. *Journal of Orthomolecular Medicine, 16*, 13–32.

Leclerc, B., & Felson, M. (in press). Routine activities preceding adolescent sexual abuse of children. *Sexual Abuse: A Journal of Research and Treatment.*

Lee, J. K. P., Jackson, H. J., Pattison, P., & Ward, T. (2002). Developmental risk factors for sexual offending. *Child Abuse and Neglect, 26*, 73–92.

Lee, S., Aos, S., Drake, E., Pennucci, A., Miller, M., & Anderson, L. (2012). *Return on investment: Evidence-based options to improve statewide outcomes.* Olympia, WA: Washington State Institute for Public Policy.

Lee, S. S., & Hinshaw, S. P. (2004). Severity of adolescent delinquency among boys with and without attention deficit hyperactivity disorder: Prediction from early antisocial behavior and peer status. *Journal of Clinical Child and Adolescent Psychology, 33*, 705–716.

Legras, A. M. (1932). *Psychose en criminaliteit bij tweelingen* (Psychoses and criminality in twins). Utrecht, Netherlands: Keminkeen ZOON N. V.

Lehmann, R. J. B., Goodwill, A. M., Gallasch-Nemitz, F., Biedermann, J., & Dahl, K- P. (2013). Applying crime scene analysis to the prediction of sexual recidivism in stranger rapes. *Law and Human Behavior, 37*, 241–254.

Lehmann, R. J. B., Goodwill, A. M., Hanson, R. K., & Dahle, K-P. (2014). Crime scene behaviors indicate risk-relevant propensities of child molesters. *Criminal Justice and Behavior, 41*, 1008–1028.

Lehmann, R. J. B., Goodwill, A. M., Hanson, R. K., & Dahle, K-P. (in press). Acquaintance rape: Applying crime scene analysis to the prediction of sexual recidivism. *Sex Abuse: A Journal of Research and Treatment.*

Leigey, M. E., & Bachman, R. (2007). The influence of crack cocaine on the likelihood of incarceration for a violent offense: An examination of a prison sample. *Criminal Justice Policy Review, 18*, 335–352.

Leiner, A. S., Kearns, M. C., Jackson, J. L., Astin, M. C., & Rothbaum, B. O. (2012). Avoidant coping and treatment outcome in rape-related posttraumatic stress disorder. *Journal of Consulting and Clinical Psychology, 80*, 317–321.

Lemann, N. (2014, March 10). A call for help: What the Kitty Genovese story really means. *The New Yorker.* Accessed 1/12/2015. Available: http://www.newyroker.com/magazine/2014/03/10a-call-for-help.

Lemon, N. K. D. (1994, December). *Domestic violence & stalking: A comment on the model anti-stalking code proposed by the National Institute of Justice.* Duluth, MN: Battered Women's Justice Project.

Lenhart, A., Kahne, J., Middaugh, E., Macgill, A. R., Evans, C., & Vitak, J. (2008). *Teens, video games, and civics.* (Report No. 202-415-4500). Washington, DC: Pew Internet and American Life Project.

Lerner, M. J. (1980). *The belief in a just world: A fundamental delusion.* New York: Plenum.

Lerner, M. J., & Miller, D. T. (1978). Just world research and the attribution process: Looking back and ahead. *Psychological Bulletin, 85*, 1030–1051.

Lerner, M. J., & Simmons, C. H. (1966). Observer's reaction to the "innocent victim": Compassion or rejection? *Journal of Personality and Social Psychology, 4*, 203–210.

Lesch, K. P., & Merschdorf, U. (2000). Impulsivity, aggression, and serotonin: A molecular psychobiological perspective. *Behavioral Sciences & the Law, 18*, 581–604.

Letkemann, P. (1973). *Crime as work.* Englewood Cliffs, NJ: Prentice Hall.

Letourneau, E. J., Henggeler, S. W., Borduin, C. M., Schewe, P. A., McCart, M. R., & Chapman, J. E. (2009). Multisystemic therapy for juvenile sexual offenders: 1-year results from a randomized effectiveness trial. *Journal of Family Psychology, 23*, 89–102.

Letourneau, E. J., & Miner, M. H. (2005). Juvenile sex offenders: A case against the legal and clinical status quo. *Sexual Abuse: A Journal of Research and Treatment, 17*, 293–312.

Levant, R. F. (2002). Psychology responds to terrorism. *Professional Psychology: Research and Practice, 33*, 507–509.

Levant, R. F., Barbanel, L., & DeLeon, P. H. (2004). Psychology's response to terrorism. In F. M. Moghaddam & A. J. Marsella (Eds.), *Understanding terrorism: Psychosocial roots, consequences, and interventions* (pp. 265–282). Washington, DC: American Psychological Association.

Leve, L. D., & Chamberlain, P. (2004). Female juvenile offenders: Defining an early-onset pathway for delinquency. *Journal of Child and Family Studies, 13*, 439–452.

Levenson, J. S., Becker, J., & Morin, J. W. (2008). The relationship between victim age and gender crossover among sex offenders. *Sexual Abuse: A Journal of Research and Treatment, 20*, 43–60.

Levenson, J. S., Willis, G. M., & Prescott, D. S. (2015). Adverse childhood experiences in the lives of female sex offenders. *Sexual Abuse: A Journal of Research and Treatment, 27*, 258–283.

Levesque, R. J. R. (2001). *Culture and family violence: Fostering change through human rights law.* Washington, DC: American Psychological Association.

Levin, J. (2014). Mass murder in perspective: Guest editor's introduction. *Homicide studies, 18*, 3–6.

Levin, J., & Arluke, A. (2009). Refining the link between animal abuse and subsequent violence. In A. Linzey (Ed.), *The link between animal abuse and violence* (pp. 163–171). Eastbourne, UK: Sussex Academic Press.

Levine, N. (2000). *CrimeStat: A spatial statistics program for the analysis of crime incident locations.* Annadale, VA: Ned Levine & Associates. Also available: Washington, DC: National Institute of Justice.

Levine, N. (2002). *CrimeStat II: A spatial statistics program for the analysis of crime incident locations.* Houston, TX: Ned Levine & Associates.

Levitz, J. (2015, April 9). Marathon bomber convicted. *The Wall Street Journal,* p. A3.

Lewis, C. F., & Bunce, S. C. (2003). Filicidal mothers and the impact of psychosis on filicide. *Journal of the American Academy of Psychiatry and the Law, 31,* 459–470.

Lewis, D. O., Lovely, R., Yeager, C., Ferguson, G., Friedman, M., Sloane, G., et al. (1988). Intrinsic and environmental characteristics of juvenile murderers. *Journal of the American Academy of Child and Adolescent Psychiatry, 27,* 582–587.

Lewis, D. O., Moy, E., Jackson, L. D., Aarsonson, R., Restifo, N., Serra, S., et al. (1985). Biopsychological characteristics of children who later murder: A prospective study. *American Journal of Psychiatry, 142,* 1161–1167.

Li, Q. (2006). Cyberbullying in schools: A research on gender differences. *School Psychology International, 27,* 157–170.

Li, Q. (2007). New bottle but old wine: A research of cyberbullying in schools. *Computers in Human Behavior, 23,* 1777–1791.

Lidzba, K., & Staudt, M. (2008). Development and (re) organization of language after early brain lesions: Capacities and limitation of early brain plasticity. *Brain & Language, 106,* 165–166.

Lightsey, O. R., Jr. (2006). Resilience, meaning, and well-being. *Counseling Psychologist, 34,* 96–107.

Lilienfeld, S. O., & Fowler, K. A. (2006). The self-report assessment of psychopathy. In C. J. Patrick (Ed.), *Handbook of psychopathy* (pp. 107–132). New York: Guilford.

Lilienfeld, S. O., Waldman, I. D., Landfield, K., Watts, A. L., Rubenzer, S., & Faschingbauer, T. R. (2012). Fearless dominance and the U.S. presidency: Implications of psychopathic personality traits for successful and unsuccessful political leadership. *Journal of Personality and Social Psychology, 103,* 489–505.

Linedecker, C., & Burt, W. (1990). *Nurses who kill.* New York: Pinnacle Books.

Lipsey, M. W. (2009). The primary factors that characterize effective interventions with juvenile offenders: A meta-analytic overview. *Victims and Offenders, 4,* 124–147.

Lipsey, M. W., Howell, J. C., Kelly, M. R., Chapman, G., & Carver, D. (2010). *Improving the effectiveness of juvenile justice programs: A new perspective on evidence-based practice.* Washington, DC: Center for Juvenile Justice Reform.

Lipsey, M. W., & Wilson, D. B. (1998). Effective interventions with serious juvenile offenders: A synthesis of research. In R. Loeber & D. P. Farrington (Eds.), *Serious and violent juvenile offenders: Risk factors and successful intervention* (pp. 313–345). Thousand Oaks, CA: Sage.

Listwan, S. J., Piquero, N. L, & Van Voorhis, P. (2010). Recidivism among a white-collar sample: Does personality matter? *Australian and New Zealand Journal of Criminology, 43,* 156–174.

Littell, J. H., Campbell, M., Green, S., & Toews, B. (2009). Multisystemic therapy for social, emotional, and behavioral problems in youth aged 10–17 (Review). *The Cochrane Collaboration.* New York: Wiley.

Litwack, T. R., & Schlesinger, L. B. (1999). Dangerous risk assessments: Research, legal, and clinical considerations. In A. K. Hess & I. B. Weiner (Eds.), *The handbook of forensic psychology* (2nd ed., pp. 171–217). New York: Wiley.

Liu, J., Raine, A., Venables, P. H., & Mednick, S. A. (2004). Malnutrition at age 3 years and externalizing behavior at ages 8, 11, and 17 years. *American Journal of Psychiatry, 161,* 2005–2013.

Lochman, J. G., & Conduct Problems Prevention Research Group. (1995). Screening of child behavior problems for prevention programs at school entry. *Journal of Consulting and Clinical Psychology, 63,* 549–559.

LoCicero, A., & Sinclair, S. J. (2008). Terrorism and terrorist leaders: Insights from developmental and ecological psychology. *Studies in Conflict & Terrorism, 31,* 227–250.

Loeber, R. (1990). Development and risk factors of juvenile antisocial behavior and delinquency. *Clinical Psychology Review, 10,* 1–41.

Loeber, R., Farrington, D. P., & Petechuk, D. (2003, May). Child delinquency: Early intervention and prevention. *Child Delinquency Bulletin Series.* Washington, DC: U.S. Department of Justice, Office of Juvenile Justice and Delinquency Prevention.

Loeber, R., Farrington, D. P., Stouthamer-Loeber, M., & Van Kammen, W. B. (1998). *Antisocial behavior* *and mental health problems: Explanatory factors in childhood and adolescence.* Mahmah, NJ: Lawrence Erlbaum.

Loeber, R., Lahey, B. B., & Thomas, C. (1991). The diagnostic conundrum of oppositional defiant disorder and conduct disorder. *Journal of Abnormal Psychology, 100*, 379–390.

Loeber, R., Pardini, D., Homish, D. L., Wei, E. H., Crawford, A. M., Farrington, D., et al. (2005). The prediction of violence and homicide in young men. *Journal of Consulting and Clinical Psychology, 73*, 1074–1088.

Loeber, R., & Stouthamer-Loeber, M. (1998). Development of juvenile aggression and violence: Some common misconceptions and controversies. *American Psychologist, 53*, 242–259.

Loehlin, J. C. (1992). *Genes and environment in personality development.* Newbury Park, CA: Sage.

Lombardo, V. S., & Lombardo, E. F. (1991). The link between learning disabilities and juvenile delinquency: Fact or fiction? *International Journal of Biosocial and Medical Research, 13*, 112–117.

Lombroso, C. (1876). *L'uomo delinquente.* Milan, Italy: Turin.

Longo, R. F., Bird, S., Stevenson, W. F., & Fiske, J. A. (1995). *1994 nationwide survey of treatment programs and models.* Brandon, VT: Safer Society Program and Press.

Lonsway, K. A., & Fitzgerald, L. F. (1994). Rape myths: In review. *Psychology of Woman Quarterly, 18*, 133–164.

Looman, J., Gauthier, C., & Boer, D. (2001). Replication of the Massachusetts Treatment Center child molester typology in a Canadian sample. *Journal of Interpersonal Violence, 16*, 753–767.

Lorber, M. F. (2004). Psychophysiology of aggression, psychopathy, and conduct problems: A meta-analysis. *Psychological Bulletin, 130*, 531–552.

Lord, W. D., Boudreaux, M. C., & Lanning, K. V. (2001, April). Investigating potential child abduction cases: A developmental perspective. *FBI Law Enforcement Bulletin*, 1–10.

Lorenz, A. R., & Newman, J. P. (2002). Deficient response modulation and emotion processing in low-anxious caucasian psychopathic offenders: Results from a lexical decision task. *Emotion, 2*, 91–104.

Lorenz, K. (1966). *On aggression.* New York: Harcourt Brace Jovanovich.

Lösel, F., & Schmucker, M. (2005). The effectiveness of treatment for sexual offenders: A comprehensive meta-analysis. *Journal of Experimental Criminology, 1*, 117–146.

Lottes, I. L. (1988). Sexual socialization and attitudes toward rape. In A. W. Burgess (Ed.), *Rape and sexual assault II.* New York: Garland Publishing.

Loukas, A., Zucker, R. A., Fitzgerald, H. F., & Krull, J. L. (2003). Developmental trajectories of descriptive behavior problems among sons of alcoholics: Effects of parent psychopathology, family conflict, and child under control. *Journal of Abnormal Psychology, 112*, 119–131.

Lucia, S., & Killias, M. (2011). Is animal cruelty a marker of interpersonal violence and delinquency? Results of a Swiss national self-report study. *Psychology of Violence, 1*, 93–105.

Lumley, V. A., McNeil, C. B., Herschell, A. D., & Bahl, A. B. (2002). An examination of gender differences among young children with disruptive behavior disorders. *Child Study Journal, 32*, 89–100.

Lussier, P., Tzoumakis, S., Cale, J., & Amirault, J. (2010). Criminal trajectories of adult sexual aggressors and the prediction of reoffending: Examining the aging-effect. *International Criminal Justice Review, 20*, 147–168.

Lussier, P., Van Den Berg, C., Bijeveld, C., & Hendriks, J. (2012). A developmental taxonomy of juvenile sex offenders for theory, research, and prevention: The adolescent-limited and the high-rate slow desister. *Criminal Justice and Behavior, 39*, 1559–1581.

Lykken, D. T. (1955). *A study of anxiety in the sociopathic personality* (Doctoral dissertation, University of Minnesota). Ann Arbor, MI: University Microfilms, No. 55–944.

Lykken, D. T. (1957). A study of anxiety in the sociopathic personality. *Journal of Abnormal and Social Psychology, 55*, 6–10.

Lykken, D. T. (1978). The psychopath and the lie detector. *Psychophysiology, 15*, 137–142.

Lykken, D. T., & Venables, P. H. (1971). Direct measurement of skin conductance: A proposal for standardization. *Psychophysiology, 8*, 856–872.

Lynam, D. R. (1997). Pursuing the psychopath: Capturing the fledging psychopath in a nomological net. *Journal of Abnormal Psychology, 106*, 425–438.

Lynam, D. R. (1998). Early identification of the fledgling psychopath: Locating the psychopathic child in the current nomenclature. *Journal of Abnormal Psychology, 107*, 566–575.

Lynam, D. R., Caspi, A., Moffitt, T. E., Loeber, R., & Stouthamer-Loeber, M. (2007). Longitudinal evidence that psychopathy scores in early adolescence predict adult psychopathy. *Journal of Abnormal Psychology, 116*, 155–165.

Lynam, D. R., Charnigo, R., Moffitt, T. E., Raine, A., Loeber, R., & Stouthamer-Loeber, M. (2009). The stability of psychopathy across adolescence. *Developmental and Psychopathology, 21*, 1133–1153.

Lynam, D. R., Moffitt, T., & Stouthamer-Loeber, M. (1993). Explaining the relation between IQ and delinquency: Class, race, test motivation, school failure, or self control? *Journal of Abnormal Psychology, 102*, 187–196.

Lynne-Landsman, S. D., Bradshaw, C. P., & Ialongo, N. S. (2010). Testing a developmental cascade model of adolescent substance use trajectories and young adult adjustment. *Development and Psychopathology, 22*, 933–948.

Maccoby, E. E. (1986). Social groupings in childhood. In D. Olweus, J. Block, & M. Radke-Yarrow (Eds.), *Development of antisocial and prosocial behavior: Research, theories, and issues.* New York: Academic Press.

MacCoun, R., Kilmer, B., & Reuter, P. (2003, July). *Research on drugs-crime linkages: The next generation. NIJ Special Report: Toward a drug and crime research agenda for the 21st century.* Washington, DC: National Institute of Justice.

MacKay, S., Feldberg, A., Ward, A. K., & Marton, P. (2012). Research and practice in adolescent firesetting. *Criminal Justice and Behavior, 39*, 842–864.

MacKay, S., Henderson, J., Del Bove, G., Marton, P., Warling, D., & Root, C. (2006). Fire interest and antisociality as risk factors in the severity and persistence of juvenile firesetting. *Journal of the American Academy of Child and Adolescent Psychiatry, 45*, 1077–1084.

MacKenzie, D. L., & Hebert, E. (Eds.). (1995). *Correctional boot camps: A tough intermediate sanction.* Washington, DC: National Institute of Justice.

Maes, H. H., Silberg, J. L., Neale, M. C., & Eaves, L. J. (2006). Genetic and cultural transmission of antisocial behavior: An extended twin parent model. *Twin Research and Human Genetics, 10*, 136–150.

Maikovich, A. K. (2005). A new understanding of terrorism using cognitive dissonance principles. *Journal for the Theory of Social Behaviour, 35*, 373–397.

Maker, A. H., Kemmelmeier, M., & Peterson, C. (1998). Long-term psychological consequences in women witnessing parental physical conflict and experiencing abuse in childhood. *Journal of Interpersonal Violence, 13*, 574–589.

Malamuth, N. M. (1981). Rape proclivity among males. *Journal of Social Issues, 37*, 138–157.

Malamuth, N. M. (1989). The attraction to sexual aggression scale: Part one. *Journal of Sex Research, 26*, 26–49.

Malamuth, N. M., & Check, J. V. P. (1981). The effects of violent-sexual movies: A field experiment. *Journal of Research in Personality, 15*, 436–446.

Malamuth, N. M., Check, J. V. P., & Briere, J. (1986). Sexual arousal in response to aggression: Ideological, aggressive, and sexual correlates. *Journal of Personality and Social Psychology, 50*, 330–340.

Malamuth, N. M., Haber, S., & Feshbach, S. (1980). Testing hypothesis regarding rape: Exposure to sexual violence, sex differences, and the "normality" of rape. *Journal of Research in Personality, 14*, 121–137.

Malamuth, N. M., Hald, G., & Koss, M. (2012). Pornography, individual differences in risk and men's acceptance of violence against women in a representative sample. *Sex Roles, 66*, 427–439.

Malamuth, N. M., Heim, M., & Feshbach, S. (1980). The sexual responsiveness of college students to rape depictions: Inhibitory and disinhibitory effects. *Journal of Personality and Social Psychology, 38*, 399–408.

Malamuth, N. M., Huppin, M., & Bryant, P. (2005). Sexual coercion. In D. M. Buss (Eds.), *The handbook of evolutionary psychology* (pp. 394–418). Hoboken, NJ: Wiley.

Maldonado, R. C., DiLillo, D., & Hoffman, L. (2015). Can college students use emotion regulation strategies to alter intimate partner aggression-risk behaviors? An examination using I^3 theory. *Psychology of Violence, 5*, 46–55.

Mallett, C. A. (2014). Youthful offending and delinquency: The comorbid impact of maltreatment, mental health problems, and learning disabilities. *Child & Adolescent Social Work Journal, 31,* 369–392.

Malmquist, C. P. (2013). Infanticide/neonaticide: The outlier situation in the United States. *Aggression and Violent Behavior, 18,* 399–408.

Mann, R. E., Hanson, R. K., & Thornton, D. (2010). Assessing risk for sexual recidivism: Some proposals on the nature of psychologically meaningful risk factors. *Sexual Abuse: A Journal of Research and Treatment, 22,* 191–217.

Mann, S. (2015, April 16). Sally Mann's exposure: What an artist captures, what a mother knows and what the public sees can be dangerously different things. *New York Times Magazine.*

Manning, R., Levine, M., & Collins, A. (2007). The Kitty Genovese murder and the social psychology of helping: The parable of the 38 witnesses. *American Psychologist, 62,* 555–562.

Marleau, J. D., Millaud, F., & Auclair, N. (2003). A comparison of parricide and attempted parricide: A study of 39 psychotic adults. *International Journal of Law and Psychiatry, 26,* 269–279.

Marlowe, D. B., Festinger, D. S., Dugosh, K. L., Benasutti, K. M., Fox, G., & Croft, J. R. (2012). Adaptive programming improves outcomes in drug court: An experimental trial. *Criminal Justice and Behavior, 39,* 514–532.

Marsella, A. J. (2004). Reflections on international terrorism: Issues, concepts, and directions. In F. M. Moghaddam & A. J. Marsella (Eds.), *Understanding terrorism: Psychosocial roots, consequences, and interventions* (pp. 11–48). Washington, DC: American Psychological Association.

Marsh, A. A., Finger, E. C., Mitchell, D. G., Reid, M. E., Sims, C., Kosson, D. S., et al. (2008). Reduced amygdala response to fearful expressions in children and adolescents with callous-unemotional traits and disruptive behavior disorders. *American Journal of Psychiatry, 165,* 712–720.

Marshall, A. D., Martin, E. K., Warfield, G. A., Doron-Lamarca, S., Niles, B. L., & Taft, C. T. (2010). The impact of antisocial personality characteristics on anger management treatment for veterans with PTSD. *Psychological Trauma: Theory, Research, Practice, and Policy, 2,* 224–231.

Marshall, C. E., Benton, D., & Brazier, J. M. (2000). Elder abuse: Using clinical tools to identify clues of mistreatment. *Geriatrics, 55,* 42–53.

Marshall, L. A., & Cooke, D. J. (1999). The childhood experiences of psychopaths: A retrospective study of familial and societal factors. *Journal of Personality Disorders, 13,* 211–225.

Marshall, L. E. & Marshall, W. L. (2011). Empathy and antisocial behavior. *Journal of Forensic Psychiatry & Psychology, 22,* 742–759.

Marshall, W. L., Barbaree, H. E., & Fernandez, M. (1995). Some aspects of social competence in sexual offenders. *Sexual Abuse, 7,* 113–127.

Marshall, W. L., & Mazzucco, A. (1995). Self-esteem and parental attachments in child molesters. *Sexual Abuse, 7,* 229–285.

Martin, E. K., Taft, C. T., & Resick, P. A. (2007). A review of marital rape. *Aggression and Violent Behavior, 12,* 329–347.

Martinez, P. A. (2011, September 7). *Cybercrime: Updating the computer fraud and abuse act to protect cyberspace and combat emerging threats.* Comments of Pablo A. Martinez, Deputy Special Agent in Charge, Criminal Investigative Division, U.S. Secret Service, before the U.S. Senate Committee on the Judiciary. Available: http://www.dhs.gov/ynews/testimony/20110907-Martinez-cybercrime-computer-fraud.shtm.

Maslow, A. H. (1954). *Motivation and personality.* New York: Harper.

Mason, K. L. (2008). Cyberbullying: A preliminary assessment for school personnel. *Psychology in the Schools, 45,* 323–348.

Masten, A. S. (2006). Developmental psychopathology: Pathways to the future. *International Journal of Behavioral Development, 30,* 47–54.

Masten, A. S. (2014). *Ordinary magic: Resilience in development.* New York: Guilford Press.

Masten, A. S., & Cicchetti, D. (2010). Developmental cascades. *Development and Psychopathology, 22,* 491–495.

Matheny, A. P. (1989). Children's behavioral inhibition over age and across situations: Genetic similarity for a trait during change. *Journal of Personality, 57,* 215–235.

Mathews, J. K., Hunter, J. A., & Vuz, I. (1997). Juvenile female sexual offenders: Clinical characteristics and treatment issues. *Sexual Abuse: A Journal of Research and Treatment, 9*, 187–199.

Mathis, G., & Mueller, C. (2015). Childhood sibling aggression and emotional difficulties and aggressive behavior in adulthood. *Journal of Family Violence, 30*, 315–327.

Maughan, B., Rowe, R., Messer, J., Goodman, R., & Meltzer, H. (2004). Conduct disorder and oppositional defiant disorder in a national sample: Developmental epidemiology. *Journal of Child Psychology and Psychiatry, 45*, 609–621.

Maxwell, J. C. (2004). *Patterns of club drug use in the U.S., 2004.* Austin, TX: The Center for Excellence in Drug Epidemiology, The Gulf Coast Addition Technology Transfer Center, University of Texas.

Mayes, L. C. (1999). Developing brain and in utero cocaine exposure: Effects on neural ontogeny. *Development and Psychopathology, 11*, 685–714.

Mazerolle, P., Brame, R., Paternoster, R., Piquero, A., & Dean, C. (2000). Onset age, persistence, and offending versatility: Comparisons across gender. *Criminology, 38*, 1143–1172.

Mazulis, A. H., Hyde, J. S., & Clark, R. (2004). Father involvement moderates the effect of maternal depression during a child's infancy on child behavior problems in kindergarten. *Journal of Family Psychology, 18*, 575–588.

Mazzetti, M., Schmidt, M. S., & Hubbard, B. (2014, September 20). U.S. suspect more direct threats beyond ISIS. *New York Times*, p. A1.

McCabe, K. M., Hough, R., Wood, P. A., & Yeh, M. (2001). Childhood and adolescent onset conduct disorder: A test of the developmental taxonomy. *Journal of Abnormal Child Psychology, 29*, 305–316.

McCabe, K. M., Rodgers, C., Yeh, M., & Hough, R. (2004). Gender differences in childhood onset conduct disorder. *Development and Psychopathology, 16*, 179–192.

McCaghy, C. H. (1967). Child molesters: A study of their careers as deviants. In M. Clinard & R. Quinney (Eds.), *Criminal behavior systems: A typology.* New York: Holt, Rinehart & Winston.

McCaghy, C. H. (1980). *Crime in American society.* New York: Macmillan.

McCarthy, J. (2003, November 29). Police link 2 shootings on stretch of highway. *Boston Globe*, pp. 1, 13.

McCarty, C. A., & McMahon, R. J. (2005). Domains of risk in the developmental continuity of fire setting. *Behavior Therapy, 36*, 185–195.

McClearn, G. E., & DeFries, J. C. (1973). *Introduction to behavioral genetics.* San Francisco: W. H. Freeman.

McClosky, L. A., Figueredo, A. J., & Koss, M. P. (1995). The effects of systemic family violence on children's mental health. *Child Development, 66*, 1239–1261.

McCord, D. (1987). Syndromes, profiles and other mental exotica: A new approach to the admissibility of nontraditional psychological evidence in criminal cases. *Oregon Law Review, 66*, 19–108.

McCord, W., McCord, J., & Zola, I. K. (1959). *Origins of crime: A new evaluation of the Cambridge-Somerville Youth Study.* New York: Columbia University Press.

McDermott, R., Tingley, D., Cowden, J., Frazzetto, G., & Johnson, D. D. P. (2009). Monoamine oxidase A gene (MAOA) predicts behavioral aggression following provocation. *Proceedings of the National Association of Sciences, 106*, 2118–2123.

McElroy, S. L., Pope, H. G., Hudson, J. I., Keck, P. E., & White, K. L. (1991). Kleptomania: A report of 20 cases. *American Journal of Psychiatry, 148*, 652–657.

McGinley, H., & Paswark, R. A. (1989). National survey of the frequency and success of the insanity plea and alternate pleas. *Journal of Psychiatry and Law, 17*, 205–221.

McKee, G. R., & Shea, S. J. (1998). Maternal filicide: A cross-national comparison. *Journal of Clinical Psychology, 54*, 679–687.

McKenzie, C. (1995). A study of serial murder. *International Journal of Offender Therapy and Comparative Criminology, 39*, 3–10.

McKinley, J. C., Jr. (2009, November 10). U.S. knew of suspect's tie to radical cleric. *The New York Times*, p. A1.

McKnight, L. R., & Loper, A. B. (2002). The effect of risk and resilience factors on the prediction of delinquency in adolescent girls. *School Psychology International, 23*, 186–198.

McMahon, R. J., Witkiewitz, K., Kotler, J. S., & The Conduct Problems Prevention Research Group. (2010). Predictive validity of callous-emotional traits measured in early adolescence with respect to multiple antisocial outcomes. *Journal of Abnormal Psychology, 119*, 752–763.

McPhail, I. V., Hermann, C. A., & Fernandez, Y. M. (2014). Correlates of emotional congruence with children in sexual offenders against children: A test of theoretical models in an incarcerated sample. *Child Abuse & Neglect, 38*, 336–346.

McPhail, I. V., Hermann, C. A., & Nunes, K. L. (2013). Emotional congruence with children and sexual offending against children: A meta-analytic review. *Journal of Consulting and Clinical Psychology, 81*, 737–749.

McShane, D. A., & Plas, J. M. (1984a). Response to a critique of the McShane & Plas review of American Indian performance on the Wechsler Intelligence Scales. *School Psychology Review, 13*, 83–88.

McShane, D. A., & Plas, J. M. (1984b). The cognitive functioning of American Indian children: Moving from the WISC to the WISC-R. *School Psychology Review, 13*, 61–73.

McWhirter, P. T., & McWhirter, J. J. (2010). Community and school violence and risk reduction: Empirically supported prevention. *Group Dynamics, Theory, Research, and Practice, 14*, 242–256.

Meadows, S. (2006, July 17). Murder on their minds. *Newsweek*, pp. 28–29.

Mechoulam, R. (1970). Marihuana chemistry. *Science, 168*, 1159–1166.

Mednick, S. A., Gabrielli, W. F., & Hutchings, B. (1984). Genetic influences in criminal convictions: Evidence from an adoption cohort. *Science, 234*, 891–894.

Mednick, S. A., Gabrielli, W. F., & Hutchings, B. (1987). Genetic factors in the etiology of criminal behavior. In S. A. Mednick, T. E. Moffitt, & S. A. Stack (Eds.), *The causes of crime: New biological approaches*. Cambridge, UK: Cambridge University Press.

Megargee, E. I. (1982). Psychological determinants and correlates of criminal violence. In M. E. Wolfgang & N. A. Weinder (Eds.), *Criminal violence*. Beverly Hills, CA: Sage.

Meier, M. H., Slutske, W. S., Heath, A. C., & Martin, N. G. (2009). The role of harsh discipline in explaining sex differences in conduct disorder: A study of opposite-sex twin pairs. *Journal of Abnormal Child Psychology, 37*, 653–664.

Meloy, J. R. (1998). The psychology of stalking. In J. R. Meloy (Ed.), *The psychology of stalking: Clinical and forensic perspectives*. San Diego, CA: Academic Press.

Melton, G. B., Petrila, J., Poythress, N. G., & Slobogin, C. (1997). *Psychological evaluations for the courts: A handbook for mental health professionals and lawyers* (2nd ed.). New York: Guilford.

Melton, G. B., Petrila, J., Poythress, N., & Slobogin, C. (2007). *Psychological evaluations for the courts: A handbook for attorneys and mental health professionals* (3rd ed.). New York: Guilford Press.

Menard, K. S., Anderson, A. L., & Goldboldt, S. M. (2009). Gender differences in intimate partner recidivism: A 5-year follow-up. *Criminal Justice and Behavior, 36*, 61–76.

Mercy, J., & Salzman, L. (1989). Fatal violence among spouses in the United States, 1986–1987. *American Journal of Public Health, 79*, 595–599.

Merry, S., & Hansent, L. (2000). Intruders, pilferers, raiders, and invaders: The interpersonal dimension of burglary. In D. Canter & L. Alison (Eds.), *Profiling property crimes*. Dartmouth, UK: Ashgate.

Merton, R. K. (1957). *Social theory and social structure* (Rev. ed.). New York: The Free Press.

Merz-Perez, L., Heide, K. M., & Silverman, I. J. (2001). Childhood cruelty to animals and subsequent violence against humans. *International Journal of Offender Therapy and Comparative Criminology, 45*, 556–573.

Messinger, A. M. (2011). Invisible victims: Same-sex IPV in the National Violence Against Women Survey. *Journal of Interpersonal Violence, 26*, 2228–2243.

Messner, S., & Rosenfeld, R. (1994). *Crime and the American dream*. Belmont, CA: Wadsworth.

Meyer, C. L., & Oberman, M. (2001). *Mothers who kill their children: Understanding the acts of moms from Susan Smith to the "prom mom."* New York: University Press.

Meyer, T. P. (1972). The effects of sexually arousing and violent films on aggressive behavior. *Journal of Sex Research, 8*, 324–333.

Miczek, K. A., DeBold, J. F., Haney, M., Tidey, J., Vivian, J., & Weerts, E. M. (1994). Alcohol, drugs of abuse, aggression, and violence. In A. J. Reiss & J. A. Roth (Eds.), *Understanding and preventing violence: Vol. 3. Social influences* (pp. 377–468). Washington, DC: National Academy Press.

Mikulincer, M., & Shaver, P. R. (2010). *Attachment in adulthood: Structure, dynamics, and change*. New York, NY: Guilford.

Milgram, S. (1963). Behavioral study of obedience. *Journal of Abnormal and Social Psychology, 67,* 371–378.

Milgram, S. (1974). *Obedience to authority.* New York: Harper & Row.

Milgram, S. (1977). *The individual in a social world.* Reading, MA: Addison-Wesley.

Miller, J. L. (1991). Prostitution in contemporary American society. In E. Graverholtz & M. A. Koralewski (Eds.), *Sexual coercion: A sourcebook on its nature, causes, and prevention.* Lexington, MA: Lexington Books.

Miller, L. (2005). Hostage negotiation: Psychological principles and practices. *International Journal of Emergency Mental Health, 7,* 277–298.

Miller, L. (2006). The terrorist mind I: A psychological and political analysis. *International Journal of Offender Therapy and Comparative Criminology, 50,* 121–138.

Miller, L. (2007). Negotiating with mentally disordered hostage takers: Guiding principles and practical strategies. *Journal of Police Crisis Negotiations, 7,* 63–83.

Miller, N., Pedersen, W. C., Earleywine, M., & Pollack, V. E. (2003). A theoretical model of triggered displaced aggression. *Personality and Social Psychology Review, 7,* 75–97.

Miller, P. A., & Eisenberg, N. (1988). The relation of empathy to aggressive and externalizing antisocial behavior. *Psychological Bulletin, 103,* 324–344.

Miller, R. D. (2003). Hospitalization of criminal defendants for evaluation of competence to stand trial or for restoration of competence: Clinical and legal issues. *Behavioral Sciences & the Law, 21,* 369–391.

Miller, S., Loeber, R., & Hipwell, A. (2009). Peer deviance, parenting and disruptive behavior among young girls. *Journal of Abnormal Child Psychology, 37,* 139–152.

Miller-Johnson, S., Coie, J. D., Maumary-Gremaud, A., Bierman, K., & The Conduct Problems Prevention Research Group. (2002). Peer rejection and aggression and early starter models of conduct disorder. *Journal of Abnormal Child Psychology, 30,* 217–230.

Min, M. O., Singer, L. T., Kirchner, H. L., Minnes, S., Short, E., Hussain, Z., & Nelson, S. (2009). Cognitive development and low-level lead exposure in poly-drug exposed children. *Neurotoxicology and Teratology, 31,* 225–231.

Miron, M. S., & Goldstein. A. P. (1978). *Hostage.* Kalamazoo, MI: Behaviordelia.

Mirrless-Black, C. (1999). *Domestic violence: Findings from a new British crime survey self-completion questionnaire.* London: Great Britain Home Office Research Development and Statistics Directorate.

Mischel, W. (1976). *Introduction to personality* (2nd ed.). New York: Holt, Rinehart & Winston.

Mitchell, K. J., Wolak, J., & Finkelhor, D. (2005). Police posing as juveniles online to catch sex offenders. Is it working? *Sexual Abuse: A Journal of Research and Treatment, 17,* 241–267.

Moffitt, T. E. (1990b). Juvenile delinquency and attention deficit disorder: Boys' developmental trajectories from age 13 to age 15. *Child Development, 61,* 893–910.

Moffitt, T. E. (1993a). Adolescence-limited and life-course-persistent antisocial behavior: A developmental taxonomy. *Psychological Review, 100,* 674–701.

Moffitt, T. E. (1993b). The neuropsychology of conduct disorder. *Development and Psychopathology, 5,* 135–151.

Moffitt, T. E. (2003). Life-course-persistent and adolescent-limited antisocial behavior: A 10-year research review and research agenda. In B. B. Lahey, T. E. Moffitt, & A. Caspi (Eds.), *Causes of conduct disorder and juvenile delinquency.* New York: Guilford.

Moffitt, T. E. (2005a). The new look of behavioral genetics in developmental psychopathology: Gene-environment interplay in antisocial behaviors. *Psychological Bulletin, 131,* 533–534.

Moffitt, T. E. (2005b). Genetic and environmental influences on antisocial behaviors: Evidence from behavioral-genetic research. *Advances in Genetics, 55,* 41–104.

Moffitt, T. E. (2006). Life-course-persistent versus adolescence-limited antisocial behavior. In D. Cicchetti & D. J. Cohen (Eds.), *Developmental psychopathology: Vol. 3. Risk, disorder, and adaptation* (2nd ed.). Hoboken, NJ: Wiley.

Moffitt, T. E., & Caspi, A. (2001). Childhood predictors differentiate life-course persistent and adolescence-limited antisocial pathways among males and females. *Development and Psychopathology, 13,* 355–375.

Moffitt, T. E., Caspi, A., Dickson, N., Silva, P., & Stanton, W. (1996). Childhood-onset versus adolescent-onset antisocial conduct problems in males: Natural history from age 3 to age 18. *Development and Psychopathology, 8*, 399–424.

Moffitt, T. E., Caspi, A., Fawcett, P., Brammer, G. L., Raleigh, M., Yuwiler, A., et al. (1997). Whole blood serotonin and family background relate to male violence. In A. Raine, P. A. Brennan, D. P. Farrington, & S. A. Mednick (Eds.), *Biological bases of violence.* New York: Plenum.

Moffitt, T. E., Caspi, A., Harrington, H., & Milne, B. J. (2002). Males on the life-course-persistent and adolescence-limited antisocial pathways: Follow-up at age 26 years. *Development and Psychopathology, 14*, 179–207.

Moffitt, T. E., Caspi, A., Rutter, M., & Silva, P. A. (2001). *Sex differences in antisocial behaviour: Conduct disorder delinquency, and violence in the Dunedin Longitudinal Study.* New York: Cambridge University Press.

Moffitt, T. E., Lynam, D. R., & Silva, P. A. (1994). Neuropsychological tests predicting persistent male delinquency. *Criminology, 33*, 111–139.

Moffitt, T. E., & Silva, P. A. (1988). Self-reported delinquency, neuropsychological deficit, and history of attention deficit disorder. *Journal of Abnormal Child Psychology, 16*, 553–569.

Moghaddam, F. M., & Marsella, A. J. (2004a). Preface. In F. M. Moghaddam & A. J. Marsella (Eds.), *Understanding terrorism: Psychosocial roots, consequences, and interventions.* Washington, DC: American Psychological Association.

Moghaddam, F. M., & Marsella, A. J. (2004b). Introduction. In F. M. Moghaddam & A. J. Marsella (Eds.), *Understanding terrorism: Psychosocial roots, consequences, and interventions* (pp. 3–8). Washington, DC: American Psychological Association.

Mohandie, K., Meloy, J. R., Green-McGowan, M., & Williams, J. (2006). The RECON typology of stalking: Reliability and validity based upon a large sample of North American stalkers. *Journal of Forensic Sciences, 51*, 147–155.

Molina, B. S. G., & Pelham, W. E., Jr. (2014). Attention-deficit/hyperactivity disorder and risk of substance use disorder: Developmental considerations, potential pathways, and opportunities for research. *Annual Review of Clinical Psychology, 10*, 607–619.

Monahan, J. (1981). *Predicting violent behavior.* Beverly Hills, CA: Sage.

Monahan, J. (1992). Mental disorder and violent behavior: Perceptions and evidence. *American Psychologist, 47*, 511–521.

Monahan, J. (2012). The individual risk assessment of terrorism. *Psychology, Public Policy, and Law, 18*, 167–205.

Monahan, J., Steadman, H., Robbins, P. C., Appelbaum, P., Banks, S., Grisso, T., et al. (2005). An actuarial model of violence risk assessment for persons with mental disorders. *Psychiatric Services, 56*, 810–815.

Monahan, J., Steadman, H. J., Silver, E., Appelbaum, P. S., Robbins, P. C., Mulvey, E. P., et al. (2001). *Rethinking risk assessment: The MacArthur study of mental disorder and violence.* New York: Oxford University Press.

Monahan, J., & Walker, L. (1990). *Social science and law: Cases and materials* (2nd ed.). Westbury, NY: Foundation Press.

Monahan, J., & Walker, L. (1994). *Social science and law: Cases and materials* (3rd ed.). Waterbury, NY: Foundation Press.

Monahan, T. P. (1957). Family status and the delinquent child: A reappraisal and some new findings. *Social Forces, 35*, 250–258.

Montagu, A. (1973). *Man and aggression* (2nd ed.). London: Oxford University Press.

Montagu, A. (1976). *The nature of human aggression.* New York: Oxford University Press.

Moore, R. H. (1984). Shoplifting in middle America: Patterns and motivational correlates. *International Journal of Offender Therapy and Comparative Criminology, 28*, 53–64.

Morawetz, T. H. (2002). Homicide. In K. L. Hall (Ed.), *The Oxford companion to American law.* New York: Oxford University Press.

Moreland, J. (2000). Toxicity of drug abuse—amphetamine designer drugs (ecstasy): Mental effects and consequences of a single dose. *Toxicology Letters,* 147–152.

Morgan, A. B., & Lilienfeld, S. O. (2000). A meta-analytic review of the relation between antisocial behavior and neuropsychological measures of executive function. *Clinical Psychology Review, 20,* 113–146.

Morgan, J. P., & Zimmer, L. (1997). The social pharmacology of smokeable cocaine: Not all it's cracked up to be. In C. Reinarman & H. G. Levine (Eds.), *Crack in America: Demon drugs and social justice.* Berkeley, CA: University of California Press.

Morin, J. W., & Levenson, J. S. (2008). Exhibitionism: Assessment and treatment. In D. R. Laws & W. T. O'Donohue (Eds.), *Sexual deviance: Theory, assessment, and treatment* (pp. 76–107). New York: Guilford.

Morris, D. (1967). *The naked ape.* New York: McGraw-Hill.

Morris, N., & Miller, M. (1985). Prediction of dangerousness. In M. Tonry & N. Morris (Eds.), *Crime and justice: An annual review of research.* Chicago: University of Chicago Press.

Morris, R. G., Gerber, J., & Menard, S. (2011). Social bonds, self-control, and adult criminality: A nationally representative assessment of Hirschi's revised self-control theory. *Criminal Justice and Behavior, 38,* 584–599.

Morrissey, T. W. (2009). Multiple child-care arrangements and young children's behavioral outcomes. *Child Development, 80,* 59–76.

Morse, S. J. (1978). Behavior, morals, and science: An analysis of mental health law. *Southern California Law Review, 51,* 527–654.

Morse, S. J. (1985). Excusing the crazy: The insanity defense reconsidered. *Southern California Law Review, 58,* 777–836.

Morse, S. J. (1986). Why amnesia and the law is not a useful topic. *Behavioral Sciences & the Law, 4,* 99–102.

Morton, R. J. & Hilts, M. A. (Eds.). (2005). *Serial murder: Multidisciplinary perspectives for investigators.* Washington, DC: U.S. Department of Justice, Federal Bureau of Investigation.

Moskowitz, A. (2004). Dissociation and violence: A review of the literature. *Trauma, Violence, & Abuse, 5,* 21–46.

Mosqueda, L., & Olsen, B. (2015). Elder abuse and neglect. In P. A. Lichtenberg, B. T. Mast, B. D. Carpenter, & J. Loebach Wetherell (Eds.), *APA handbook of clinical geropsychology: Vol. 2.*

Assessment, treatment, and issues of later life (pp. 667–686). Washington, DC: American Psychological Association.

Mott, J. (1986). Opioid use and burglary. *British Journal of Addiction, 81,* 671–677.

Mounts, N. S. (2002). Parental management of adolescent peer relationships in context: The role of parenting style. *Journal of Family Psychology, 16,* 58–69.

Mowkiber, R. (2007). Twenty things you should know about corporate crime. *Corporate Crime Reporter.* Washington, DC: Corporate Crime Reporter.

Müller, J. L., Sommer, M., Wagner, V., Lange, K., Taschler, H., Röder, C. H., et al. (2003). Abnormalities in emotion processing within cortical and subcortical regions in criminal psychopaths: Evidence from a functional magnetic resonance imaging study using pictures with emotional content. *Biological Psychiatry, 54,* 152–162.

Mulvey, E. P. (2011). Highlights from Pathways to Desistance: A longitudinal study of serious adolescent offenders. (Fact Sheet). Washington: DC: U.S. Department of Justice. Office of Justice Programs. Office of Juvenile Justice and Delinquency Prevention.

Mulvey, E. P., Arthur, M. W., & Reppucci, N. D. (1993). The prevention and treatment of juvenile delinquency: A review of the research. *Clinical Psychology Review, 13,* 133–167.

Mulvey, E. P., Schubert, C. A., & Chassin, L. (2010). *Substance use and offending in serious adolescent offenders.* Washington, DC: U.S. Department of Justice, Office of Justice Programs, Office of Juvenile Justice and Delinquency Prevention.

Mumford, E., & Taylor, B. (2014). *National Survey on Teen Relationships and Intimate Violence.* Chicago: National Opinion Research Center, University of Chicago.

Mumley, D. L., Tillbrook, C. E., & Grisso, T. (2003). Five year research update (1996–2000): Evaluations for competence to stand trial (adjudicative competence). *Behavioral Sciences & the Law, 21,* 329–350.

Mumola, C. J., & Karberg, J. C. (2006, October). *Drug use and dependence, state and federal prisoners, 2004.* Washington, DC: U.S. Department of Justice, Bureau of Justice Statistics.

Murray, C. E., & Mobley, A. K. (2009). Empirical research about same-sex intimate partner violence: A methodological review. *Journal of Homosexuality, 56,* 361–386.

Murray, J. B. (1997). Munchausen syndrome/Munchausen syndrome by proxy. *The Journal of Psychology, 131,* 343–350.

Murray, J. P. (2008). Media violence: The effects are both real and strong. *American Behavioral Scientist, 51,* 1212–1230.

Murrie, D. C., Boccaccini, M. T., McCoy, W., & Cornell, D. G. (2007). Diagnostic labeling in juvenile court: How do descriptions of psychopathy and conduct disorder influence judges? *Journal of Clinical Child and Adolescent Psychology, 36,* 228–241.

Murrie, D. C., Cornell, D. G., Kaplan, S., McConville, D., & Levy-Elkon, A. (2004). Psychopathy scores and violence among juvenile offenders: A multi-measure study. *Behavioral Sciences & the Law, 22,* 49–67.

Murray-Close, D., Hoza, B., Hinshaw, S. P., Arnold, L. E., Swanson, J., Jensen, P. S., et al. (2010). Developmental processes in peer problems of children with attention-deficit/hyperactivity disorder in The Multimodel Treatment Study of Children with ADHD: Developmental cascades and vicious cycles. *Development and Psychopathology, 22,* 785–802.

Musliner, K. L., & Singer, J. B. (2014). Emotional support and adult depression in survivors of childhood sexual abuse. *Child Abuse & Neglect, 38,* 1331–1340.

Myers, D. G. (1996). *Social psychology* (5th ed.). New York: McGraw-Hill.

Myers, W. C. (1992). What treatments do we have for children and adolescents who have killed. *Bulletin of the American Academy of Psychiatry and Law, 20,* 47–58.

Myers, W. C. (1994). Sexual homicide by adolescents. *Journal of the American Academy of Child and Adolescent Psychiatry, 33,* 962–969.

Myers, W. C. (2004). Serial murder by children and adolescents. *Behavioral Sciences & the Law, 22,* 357–374.

Myers, W. C., & Mutch, P. J. (1992). Language disorders in disruptive behaviour disordered homicidal youth. *Journal of Forensic Sciences, 37,* 919–922.

Myers, W. C., & Scott, K. (1998). Psychotic and conduct disorder symptoms in juvenile murderers. *Homicide Studies, 2,* 160–175.

Myers, W. C., Scott, K., Burgess, A. W., & Burgess, A. G. (1995). Psychopathology, biopsychosocial factors, crime characteristics, and classification of 25 homicidal youths. *Journal of the American Academy of Child and Adolescent Psychiatry, 34,* 1483–1489.

Nachshon, I. (1983). Hemisphere dysfunction in psychopathy and behavior disorders. In M. Myslobodsky (Ed.), *Hemisyndromes: Psychobiology, neurology, psychiatry.* New York: Academic Press.

Nachshon, I., & Denno, D. (1987). Violent behavior and cerebral hemisphere function. In S. A. Mednick, T. E. Moffitt, & S. A. Stack (Eds.), *The causes of crime: New biological approaches.* Cambridge, UK: Cambridge University Press.

Nagin, D. (2007). Moving choice to center stage in criminological research. *Criminology, 45,* 259–272.

Nagin, D. S., & Land, K. C. (1993). Age, criminal careers, and population heterogeneity: Specification and estimation of a nonparametric mixed Poisson model. *Criminology, 31,* 163–189.

Narag, R. E., Pizarro, J., & Gibbs, C. (2009). Lead exposure and its implications for criminological theory. *Criminal Justice and Behavior, 36,* 954–973.

Nash, J. R. (1975). *Bloodletters and badmen: Book 3.* New York: Warner Books.

National Cable Television Association. (1998). *National television violence study: Vol. 3.* Thousand Oaks, CA: Sage.

National Center for Juvenile Justice. (2003, July). *Juvenile court statistics 1999.* Washington, DC: U.S. Department of Justice, Office of Juvenile Justice and Delinquency Prevention.

National Center for White Collar Crime. (2015). Key actions to take in the wake of identity theft. *NW3C News* (March 4). Available: www.nw3c.org/News/article/Fulltext/2015/03/04.

National Commission on Marihuana and Drug Abuse. (1972). *Marihuana: A signal of misunderstanding* (Appendix, Vol. 1). Washington, DC: USGPO.

National Commission on Marihuana and Drug Abuse. (1973). *Drug use in America: Problem in perspective* (2nd report). Washington, DC: USGPO.

National Conference of State Legislatures. (2015). State cyberstalking and cyberharassment laws. Accessed 4/22/15. Available: www.ncsl.org/research/telecommunications-and-information-technology/cyberstalking.

National Drug Intelligence Center. (2001, January). *OxyContin diversion and abuse.* Washington, DC: Author.

National Drug Intelligence Center. (2009, July). *Domestic cannabis cultivation assessment: 2009.* Washington, DC: U.S. Department of Justice.

National Highway Traffic Safety Administration. (2005, March). *Alcohol involvement in fatal motor vehicle traffic crashes, 2003.* Springfield, VA: Author.

National Highway Traffice Safety Administration (NHTSA). (2013, December). *Traffic safety facts 2012: Alcohol-impaired driving.* Washington, DC: Department of Transportation.

National Information Support and Referral Service. (1998, Winter). *Shaken baby syndrome.* Ogden, UT: Child Abuse Prevention Center of Utah.

National Institute of Health. (1999, June). *NIDA news release: Long-term brain injury from use of "ecstasy."* Rockville, MD: National Institute of Drug Abuse. Available: www.nida.nih.gov/ MedAdv/99/NR-614b. html.

National Institute on Alcohol Abuse and Alcoholism. (1990). *Alcohol and health: Neuroscience.* Rockville, MD: USGPO.

National Institute on Alcohol Abuse and Alcoholism. (1997, October). Alcohol, violence, and aggression. *Alcohol Alert.* Rockville, MD: USGPO.

National Institute on Drug Abuse. (1978). Drug abuse and crime. In L. D. Savitz & N. Johnson (Eds.), *Crime in society.* New York: Wiley.

National Institute on Drug Abuse. (1999, May). *Cocaine: Abuse and addiction.* Rockville, MD: USGPO. Available: www.nida.nih.gov/ researchreports/cocaine/cocaine.html.

National Institute on Drug Abuse. (2000, June). *Epidemiologic trends in drug abuse.* Rockville, MD: USGPO. Available: www.nida.gov/CEWG/ AdvancedRep/6_20ADV/0600adv.html.

National Institute on Drug Abuse. (2005). *Hallucinogens and dissociative drugs.* Rockville, MD: U.S. Department of Health and Human Services.

National Institute on Drug Abuse. (2012, December). *Drugfacts: Spice (synthetic marijuana).* Rockville, MD: U.S. Department of Health and Human Services.

National Institute on Drug Abuse. (2013a, April). *Drugfacts: Cocaine.* Rockville, MD: U.S. Department of Health and Human Services.

National Institute on Drug Abuse. (2013b, September). *Drugs of abuse: MDMA (ecstasy/Molly).* Rockville, MD: U.S. Department of Health and Human Services.

National Institute on Drug Abuse. (2013c, April). *Drugfacts: Salvia.* Rockville, MD: U.S. Department of Health and Human Services.

National Institute on Drug Abuse. (2014a, January). *Drugfacts: Methamphetamine.* Rockville, MD: U.S. Department of Health and Human Services.

National Institute on Drug Abuse. (2014b, October). *Drugfacts: Heroin.* Rockville, MD: U.S. Department of Health and Human Services.

National Institute on Drug Abuse. (2014c, December). *Drugfacts: Prescription and over-the-counter medications.* Rockville, MD: U.S. Department of Health and Human Services.

National Institute on Drug Abuse. (2015, February). *Commonly abused drugs.* Rockville, MD: U.S. Department of Health and Human Services.

National Institute on Drug Abuse and University of Michigan. (2005, December). *Monitoring the Future National Survey results on drug use, 1975–2003. Volume II: College students & Adults ages 19–45.* Washington, DC: National Institute on Drug Abuse.

Naudts, K., & Hodgins, S. (2006). Neurobiological correlates of violent behavior among persons with schizophrenia. *Schizophrenia Bulletin, 32,* 562–572.

Nee, C. (2015). Understanding expertise in burglars: From pre-conscious scanning to action and beyond. *Aggression and Violent Behavior, 20,* 53–61.

Nee, C., & Taylor, M. (1988). Residential burglary in the Republic of Ireland: A situational perspective. *Howard Journal, 27,* 105–116.

Nee, C., & Taylor, M. (2000). Examining burglars' target selection: Interview, experiment or ethnomethodology? *Psychology, Crime & Law, 6,* 45–59.

Needleman, H. L. (2004). Lead poisoning. *Annual Review of Medicine, 56,* 209–222.

Needleman, H. L., McFarland, C., Ness, R. B., Fienberg, S. E., & Tobin, M. J. (2002). Bone lead levels in adjudicated delinquents: A case control study. *Neurotoxicology and Teratology, 24,* 711–717.

Negriff, S., Schneiderman, J. U., Smith, C., Schreyer, J. K., & Trickett, P. K. (2014). Characterizing the sexual abuse experiences of young adolescents. *Child Abuse & Neglect, 38*, 261–270.

Neisser, U., Boodoo, G., Bouchard, T., Boykin, A. W., Brody, N., Ceci, S. J., et al. (1996). Intelligence: Knowns and unknowns. *American Psychologist, 51*, 77–101.

Nelson, C. A., & Bloom, F. E. (1997). Child development and neuroscience. *Child Development, 68*, 970–987.

Nelson, D. R., Hammen, C., Brennan, P. A., & Ullman, J. B. (2003). The impact of maternal depression in adolescent adjustment: The role of expressed emotion. *Journal of Consulting and Clinical Psychology, 71*, 935–944.

Neugebauer, R., Hoek, H. W., & Susser, E. (1999). Prenatal exposure to wartime famine and development of antisocial personality disorder in early adulthood. *Journal of the American Medical Association, 4*, 479–481.

Neuman, J. H., & Baron, R. A. (1998). Workplace violence and workplace aggression: Evidence concerning specific forms, potential causes, and preferred targets. *Journal of Management, 24*, 391–419.

Neumann, C. S., & Hare, R. D. (2008). Psychopathic traits in a large community sample: Links to violence, alcohol use, and intelligence. *Journal of Consulting and Clinical Psychology, 76*, 893–899.

Neumann, C. S., Hare, R. D., & Newman, J. P. (2007). The superordinate nature of Psychopathy Checklist-Revised. *Journal of Personality Disorders, 21*, 102–107.

Neumann, C. S., Kosson, D. S., Forth, A. E., & Hare, R. D. (2006). Factor structure of the Hare Psychopathy Checklist: Youth Version (PCL:YV) in incarcerated adolescents. *Psychological Assessment, 18*, 142–154.

Nevin, R. (2000). How lead exposure relates to temporal changes in IQ, violent crime, and unwed pregnancy. *Environmental Research, 83*, 1–22.

Nevin, R. (2007). Understanding international crime trends: The legacy of preschool lead exposure. *Environmental Research, 104*, 315–336.

Newcomb, A. F., Bukowksi, W. M., & Pattee, L. (1993). Children's peer relations: A meta-analytic review of popular, rejected, neglected, controversial and average sociometric status. *Psychological Bulletin, 113*, 99–128.

Newman, J. P., Curtin, J. J., Bertsch, J. D., & Baskin-Sommers, A. R. (2010). Attention moderates the fearlessness of psychopathic offenders. *Biological Psychiatry, 67*, 66–70.

Newman, J. P., Schmitt, W. A., & Voss, W. D. (1997). The impact of motivationally neutral cues on psychopathic individuals: Assessing the generality of the response modulation hypothesis. *Journal of Abnormal Psychology, 106*, 563–575.

Nicholls, T. L., & Petrila, J. (2005). Gender and psychopathy: An overview of important issues and introduction to the special issue. *Behavioral Sciences & the Law, 23*, 729–741.

Nicholls, T. L., Ogloff, J. R. P., Brink, J., & Spidel, A. (2005). Psychopathy in women: A review of its clinical usefulness for assessing risk for aggression and criminality. *Behavioral Sciences & the Law, 23*, 779–802.

Nicholson, I. (2011). "Torture at Yale": Experimental subjects, laboratory torment and the "rehabilitation" of Milgram's "obedience to authority." *Theory & Psychology, 2*, 737–761.

Nicholson, R. A., & Kugler, K. E. (1991). Competent and incompetent criminal defendants: A quantitative review of comparative research. *Psychological Bulletin, 109*, 355–370.

Nietzel, M. T. (1979). *Crime and its modification: A social learning perspective.* New York: Pergamon.

Nigg, J. T., & Huang-Pollock, C. L. (2003). An early-onset model of the role of executive functions and intelligence in conduct disorder/delinquency. In B. B. Lahey, T. E. Moffitt, & A. Caspi (Eds.), *Causes of conduct disorder and juvenile delinquency.* New York: Guilford.

Nisbett, R. E. (2005). Heredity, environment, and race differences in IQ. *Psychology, Public Policy, and Law, 11*, 302–310.

Noesner, G. W., & Dolan, J. T. (1992, August). First responder negotiation training. *FBI LawEnforcement Bulletin*, 1–4.

Nordström, A., Dahlgren, L., & Kullgren, G. (2006). Victim relations and factors triggering homicides committed by offenders with schizophrenia. *Journal of Forensic Psychiatry & Psychology, 17*, 192–203.

Norris, J., Nurius, P. S., & Graham, T. L. (1999). When a date changes from fun to dangerous: Factors influencing women ability to distinguish. *Violence Against Women, 5*, 230–250.

Nurius, P. S. (2000). Risk perception for acquaintance sexual aggression: A social-cognitive perspective. *Aggression and Violent Behavior, 5*, 63–78.

Nurius, P. S., Norris, J., Young, D. S., Graham, T. L., & Gaylord, J. (2000). Interpreting and defensively responding to threat: Examining appraisals and coping with acquaintance sexual aggression. *Violence and Victims, 15*, 187–298.

Obeidallah, D. A., & Earls, F. J. (1999). *Adolescent girls: The role of depression in the development of delinquency.* Washington, DC: National Institute of Justice.

Occupational Safety and Health Administration. (2011, September). *OSHA instruction.* Washington, DC: U.S. Department of Labor, Occupational Safety and Health Administration.

Occupational Safety and Health Administration. (2014). *Safety and health topics: Cadmium.* Washington, DC: U.S. Department of Labor, Occupational Safety and Health Administration.

Occupational Safety and Health Administration. (2015). *Guidelines for preventing workplace violence for healthcare and social service workers.* Washington, DC: U.S. Department of Labor, Occupational Safety and Health Administration.

Odgers, C. L., Moffitt, T. E., Broadbent, J. M., Dickson, N., Hancox, R. J., Harrington, H., et al. (2008). Female and male antisocial trajectories: From childhood origins to adult outcomes. *Development and Psychopathology, 20*, 673–716.

Odgers, C. L., Reppucci, N. D., & Moretti, M. M. (2005). Nipping psychopathy in the bud: An examination of the convergent, predictive, and theoretical utility of the PCL-YV among adolescent girls. *Behavioral Sciences & the Law, 23*, 743–763.

O'Donnell, J., Hawkins, J. D., & Abbott, R. D. (1995). Predicting serious delinquency and substance abuse among aggressive boys. *Journal of Consulting and Clinical Psychology, 63*, 529–537.

Office of Applied Studies. (2004). *Drug abuse warning network, 2003.* Rockville, MD: U.S. Department of Health and Human Services.

Office of National Drug Control Policy. (1999a, November). *Gamma hydroxybutyrate (GHB).* Washington, DC: Executive Office of the President. Available: www.whitehousedrugpolicy.gov.

Office of National Drug Control Policy. (1999b, May). *Methamphetamine.* Washington, DC: Executive Office of the President. Available: www.whitehousedrugpolicy.gov.

Office of National Drug Control Policy. (2003a, February). *Rohypnol.* Washington, DC: Executive Office of the President. Available: www.whitehousedrugpolicy.gov.

Office of National Drug Control Policy. (2003b, November). *Methamphetamine.* Washington, DC: Author.

Office of National Drug Control Policy. (2003d, November). *Drug data summary.* Washington, DC: Author.

Office of National Drug Control Policy. (2006b, July). *Methamphetamine.* Washington, DC: Author.

Office of National Drug Control Policy. (2014, January). *2013 Annual Report, Arrestee Drug Abuse Monitoring Program II.* Washington, DC: Executive Office of the President.

Offord, D. R., Boyle, M. C., & Racine, Y. A. (1991). The epidemiology of antisocial behavior in childhood and adolescence. In D. J. Pepler & K. H. Rubin (Eds.), *The development and treatment of childhood aggression.* Hillsdale, NJ: Erlbaum.

Offord, D. R., Chmura Kraemeer, H., Kazdin, A. E., Jensen, P. S., & Harrington, R. (1998). Lowering the burden of suffering from child psychiatric disorder: Trade-offs among clinical, targeted, and universal interventions. *Journal of the American Academy of Child & Adolescent Psychiatry, 37*, 686–694.

Ogloff, J. R., & Wong, S. (1990). Electrodermal and cardiovascular evidence of a coping response in psychopaths. *Criminal Justice and Behavior, 17*, 231–245.

Ohlin, L. E., & Tonry, M. (1989). Family violence in perspective. In L. Ohlin & M. Tonry (Eds.), *Family violence: Vol. 11.* Chicago: University of Chicago Press.

Oken, E., Choi, A. L., Karagas, M. R., Mariën, K., Rheinberger, C. M., Schoeny, R., et al. (2012). Which fish should I eat? Perspectives influencing fish consumption choices. *Environmental Health Perspectives, 120*, 790–798.

Oken, E., Redesky, J. S., Wright, R. O., Bellinger, D. C., Amarasiriwardena, C. J., Kleinman, K. P., et

al. (2008). Maternal fish intake during pregnancy, blood mercury levels, and child cognition at age 3 years in a U.S. cohort. *American Journal of Epidemiology, 167*, 1171–1181.

Oliver, B. R., & Plomin, R. (2007). Twins' early development study (TEDS): A multivariate, longitudinal genetic investigation of language, cognition and behavior problems from childhood through adolescence. *Twin Research and Human Genetics, 10*, 96–105.

Olson, C. K. (2004). Media violence research and youth violence data: Why do they conflict? *Academic Psychiatry, 28*, 144–150.

Olson, S. L., Sameroff, A. J., Kerr, D. C. R., Lopez, N. L., & Wellman, H. M. (2005). Developmental foundations of externalizing problems in young children: The role of effortful control. *Development and Psychopathology, 17*, 25–45.

Olson, M. G. (2014, September 17). *Worldwide threats to the homeland*. Hearing before the Senate Committee on Homeland Security. McLean, VA: National Counterterrorism Center.

Olver, M. E., Nicholaichuk, T. P., Gu, D., & Wong, S. C. P. (2012). Sex offender treatment outcome, actuarial risk, and the aging sex offender in Canadian corrections: A long-term follow-up. *Sexual Abuse: A Journal of Research and Treatment, 25*, 396–422.

Olweus, D. (1997). Bully/victim problems in school: Facts and intervention. *European Journal of Psychology of Education, 12*, 495–510.

Olympio, K. P. K., Gonçalves, C., Günther, W. M. R., & Bechara, E. J. H. (2009). Neurotoxicity and aggressiveness triggered by low-level lead in children—a review. *Pan American Journal of Public Health, 26*, 266–275.

Olympio, K. P. K., Oliveira, P. V., Naozuka, J., Cardoso, M. R. A., Marques, A. F., Günther, W. M. R., & Bechara, E. J. H. (2010). Surface dental enamel levels and antisocial behavior in Brazilian adolescents. *Neurotoxicology and Teratology, 32*, 273–279.

Ondrovik, J., & Hamilton, D. (1991). Credibility of victims diagnosed as multiple personality: A case study. *American Journal of Forensic Psychology, 9*, 13–17.

O'Neill, M. L., Lidz, V., & Heilbrun, K. (2003). Adolescents with psychopathic characteristics in a substance abusing cohort: Treatment process and outcomes. *Law and Human Behavior, 27*, 299–313.

Orne, M. T., Dinges, D. F., & Orne, E. C. (1984). On the differential diagnosis of multiple personality in the forensic context. *International Journal of Clinical and Experimental Hypnosis, 32*, 118–169.

Osgood, W. D., O'Malley, P. M., Bachman, G. G., & Johnstone, L. D. (1989). Time trends and urge trends in arrests and self-reported illegal behavior. *Criminology, 27*, 389–415.

Osofsky, M. J., Bandura, A., & Zimbardo, P. G. (2005). The role of moral disengagement in the executive process. *Law and Human Behavior, 29*, 371–393.

O'Toole, M. E. (2013). Jeffrey Weise and the shooting at Red Lake Minnesota High School: A behavioral perspective. In N. Böckler, T. Seeger, P. Sitzer, & W. Heitmeyer (Eds.), *School shootings: International research, case studies, and concepts for prevention* (pp. 177–188). New York: Springer.

Outhall, A. (2014, September 12). T.J. Lane, killer in school shooting, is caught after prison escape in Ohio. *The New York Times*, p. A3.

Paciello, M., Fida, R., Tramontano, C., Lupinetti, C., & Caprara, G. V. (2008). Stability and change of moral disengagement and its impact on aggression and violence in late adolescence. *Child Development, 79*, 1288–1309.

Pagani, L. S., Tremblay, R. G., Nagin, D., Zoccolilo, M., Vitaro, F., & McDuff, P. (2004). Risk factor models for adolescent verbal and physical aggression toward mothers. *International Journal of Behavioral Development, 28*, 528–537.

Pardini, D., & Byrd, A. L. (2012). Perceptions of aggressive conflicts and others' distress in children with callous-unemotional traits: "I'll show you who's boss, even if you suffer and I get in trouble." *Journal of Child Psychology and Psychiatry, 53*, 283–291.

Pardini, D., Lochman, J. E., & Powell, N. (2007). The development of callous-unemotional traits and antisocial behavior in children: Are there shared and/or unique predictors. *Journal of Clinical Child and Adolescent Psychology, 36*, 319–333.

Pardini, D., & Loeber, R. (2008). Interpersonal callousness trajectories across adolescence: Early social influences and adult outcomes. *Criminal Justice and Behavior, 35*, 173–196.

Parent, G., Guay, J-P., & Knight, R. A. (2011). An assessment of long-term risk of recidivism by adult sex offenders: One size doesn't fit all. *Criminal Justice and Behavior, 38*, 188–209.

Parent, G., Guay, J-P., & Knight, R. A. (2012). Can we do better? The assessment of risk of recidivism by adult sex offenders. *Criminal Justice and Behavior, 39*, 1647–1667.

Parents Television Council. (2007, January). *Dying to entertain: Violence on prime time broadcast television 1998 to 2006*. Lost Angeles, CA: Author.

Parker, H., & Newcombe, R. (1987). Heroin use and acquisitive crime in an English community. *British Journal of Sociology, 38*, 331–350.

Parker, J. G., & Asher, S. R. (1987). Peer relations and later personal adjustment: Are low-accepted children at risk? *Psychological Bulletin, 102*, 357–389.

Parker, J. S., & Morton, T. L. (2009). Distinguishing between early and late onset delinquents: Race, income, verbal intelligence and impulsivity. *North American Journal of Psychology, 11*, 273–284.

Paschal, D. C., Burt. V., Caudill, S. P., Gunter, E. W., Pirkle, J. L.,& Jackson, R. J. (2000). Exposure of the U.S. population aged 6 years and older to cadmium: 1988–1994. *Archives of Environmental Contamination and Toxicology, 38*, 377–283.

Patchin, J. W., & Hinduja, S. (2006). Bullies move beyond the schoolyard: A preliminary look at cyberbullying. *Youth Violence and Juvenile Justice, 4*, 148–169.

Patchin, J. W., & Hinduja, S. (2012). Cyberbullying: An update and synthesis of the research. In J. W. Patchin & S. Hinduaj (Eds.), *Cyberbullying Prevention and Response: Expert Perspectives* (pp. 13–35). New York: Routledge.

Patrick, C. J., & Bernat, E. M. (2009). Neurobiology of psychopathy: A two-process theory. In G. G. Berntson & J. T. Cacioppo (Eds.), *Handbook of neuroscience for the behavioral sciences* (pp. 1110–1131). New York: Wiley.

Patrick, C. J., Bradley, M. M., & Lang, P. J. (1993). Emotion in the criminal psychopath: Start reflex modulation. *Journal of Abnormal Psychology, 102*, 82–92.

Patrick, C. J., Fowles, D. C., & Krueger, R. F. (2009). Triarchic conceptualization of psychopathy: Developmental origins of disinhibition, boldness, and meanness. *Development and Psychopathology, 21*, 913–938.

Patrick, C. J., Zempolich, K. A., & Levenston, G. K. (1997). Emotionality and violent behavior in psychopaths: A biosocial analysis. In A. Raine, P. A. Brennan, D. P. Farrington, & S. A. Mednick (Eds.), *Biosocial bases of violence*. New York: Plenum.

Patterson, G. R. (1982). *Coercive family processes*. Eugene, OR: Castalia Press.

Patterson, G. R. (1986). Performance models for antisocial boys. *American Psychologist, 41*, 432–444.

Patterson, G. R., Forgatch, M. S., & DeGarmo, D. S. (2010). Cascading effects following intervention. *Development and Psychopathology, 22*, 949–970.

Patterson, G. R., & Yoerger, K. (2002). A developmental model for early- and late-onset delinquency. In J. B. Reid, G. R. Patterson, & J. J. Snyder (Eds.), *Antisocial behavior in children and adults: A developmental analysis and the Oregon model for intervention*. Washington, DC: American Psychological Association.

Paull, D. (1993). *Fitness to stand trial*. Springfield, IL: C C Thomas.

Pearl, P. T. (1995). Identifying and responding to Munchausen syndrome by proxy. *Early Child Development and Care, 106*, 177–185.

Pearlstein, L. (2010, winter). Walking the tightrope of statutory rape law: Using international standards to serve the best interest of juvenile offenders and victims. *American Criminal Law Review, 47*, 109–128.

Pedneault, A., Beauregard, E., Harris, D. A., & Knight, R. A. (2015). Rationally irrational: The case of sexual burglary. *Sexual Abuse: A Journal of Research and Treatment, 26*, 34–57.

Pedneault, A., Harris, D. A., & Knight, R. A. (2012). Toward a typology of sexual burglary: Latent class findings. *Journal of Criminal Justice, 40*, 278–284.

Pelonero, C. (2014). *Kitty Genovese: A true account of a public murder and its private consequences*. New York: Skyhorse Publishing.

Penrod, S. (1983). *Social psychology*. Englewood Cliffs, NJ: Prentice Hall.

Pepler, D. J., & Slaby, R. G. (1994). Theoretical and development perspectives on youth and violence. In L. D. Eron, J. H. Gentry, & P. Schlegel (Eds.), *Reason to hope: A psychosocial perspective on violence and youth* (pp. 27–58). Washington, DC: American Psychological Association.

Pereda, N., Guilera, G., Forns, M., & Gómez-Benito, J. (2009). The prevalence of child sexual abuse in community and student samples: A meta-analysis. *Clinical Psychology Review, 29*, 328–338.

Perilla, J. L., Lippy, C., Rosales, A., & Serrata, J. V. (2011). Prevalence of domestic violence. In J. W. White, M. P. Koss, & A. E. Kasdin (Eds.), *Violence against women and children: Vol. 1. Mapping the terrain* (pp. 199–220). Washington, DC: American Psychological Association.

Perkins, C. A. (2003). *Weapon use and violent crime.* Washington, DC: U.S. Department of Justice, Bureau of Justice Statistics.

Perrin, A., & Duggan, M. (2015, June 26). Americans' Internet access: 2000–2015. Washington, DC: Pew Research Center.

Peter, T. (2009). Exploring taboos: Comparing male- and female-perpetrated child sexual abuse. *Journal of Interpersonal Violence, 24*, 1111–1128.

Peters, R. H., Wexler, H. K., & Lurigio, A. J. (2015). Co-occurring substance use and mental disorders in the criminal justice system: A new frontier of clinical practice and research. *Psychiatric Rehabilitation Journal, 38*, 1–6.

Petersen, I. T., Bates, J. E., D'Onofrio, B. M., Lansford, J. E., Dodge, K. A., Pettit, G. S., & Van Hulle, C. A. (2013). Language ability predicts the development of behavior problems in children. *Journal of Abnormal Psychology, 122*, 542–557.

Peterson, C. (2006). *A primer in positive psychology.* New York, NY: Free Press.

Peterson, J. K., Skeem, J., Kennealy, P., Bray, B., & Zvonkovic, A. (2014). How often and how consistently do symptoms directly precede criminal behavior among offenders with mental illness? *Law and Human Behavior, 38*, 439–449.

Petraitis, J., Flay, B. R., & Miller, T. Q. (1995). Reviewing theories of adolescent substance abuse: Organizing pieces in the puzzle. *Psychological Bulletin, 117*, 67–86.

Petras, H., Schaeffer, C. M., Ialongo, N., Hubbard, S., Muthén, B., Lambert, S. F., et al. (2004). When the course of aggressive behavior in childhood does not predict antisocial behavior outcomes in adolescence and young adulthood: An examination of potential explanatory variables. *Development and Psychopathology, 16*, 919–941.

Petrila, J. P. (2009). Finding common ground between scientific psychology and the law. In J. L. Skeem, K. S. Douglas, & S. O. Lilienfeld (Eds.), *Psychological science in the courtroom* (pp. 387–407). New York: Guilford Press.

Pettit, G. S., Laird, R. D., Bates, J. E., & Dodge, K. A. (1997). Patterns of after-school care in middle childhood: Risk factors and developmental outcomes. *Merrill-Palmer Quarterly, 43*, 515–538.

Pfiffner, L. J., McBurnett, K., Rathouz, P. I., & Judice, S. (2005). Family correlates of oppositional and conduct disorder in children with attention deficit/hyperactivity disorders. *Journal of Abnormal Child Psychology, 33*, 551–563.

Piaget, J. (1948). *The moral judgment of the child.* New York: Free Press.

Piazza, J. A. (2009). Is Islamist terrorism more dangerous? An empirical study of group of ideology, organization, and goal structure. *Terrorism and Political Violence, 21*, 62–88.

Piccolino, A. L., & Solberg, K. B. (2014). The impact of traumatic brain injury on prison health services and offender management. *Journal of Correctional Health Care, 20*(3), 203–212.

Pidd, H. (2012, April 19). Anders Breivik "trained" for shooting attacks by playing call of duty. *The Guardian.* Available: www.Guardian.co.uk/world/2012/apr/19/anders-breivik-call-of-duty.

Piehler, T. F., Bloomquist, M. L., August, G. J., Gewirtz, A. H., Lee, S. S., & Lee, W. S. C. (2014). Executive functioning as a mediator of conduct problems prevention in children of homeless families residing in temporary supportive housing: A parallel process latent growth modeling approach. *Journal of Abnormal Child Psychology, 42*, 681–692.

Pihl, R. O., & Benkelfat, C. (2005). Neuromodulators in the development and expression of inhibition and aggression. In R. E. Tremblay, W. W. Hartup, & J. Archer (Eds.), *Developmental origins of aggression* (pp. 261–280). New York: Guilford Press.

Pillmann, F., Rohde, A., Ullrich, S., Draba, S., Sannemueller, U., & Marnerous, A. (1999). Violence, criminal behavior, and the EEG: Significance of left hemispheric focal abnormalities. *Journal of Neuropsychiatry & Clinical Neurosciences, 11*, 454–457.

Pinizzotto, A. J. (1984). Forensic psychology: Criminal personality profiling. *Journal of Police Science and Administration, 12*, 32–40.

Pinizzotto, A. J., & Finkel, N. J. (1990). Criminal personality profiling: An outcome and process study. *Law and Human Behavior, 14*, 215–234.

Pinker, S. (2014). Foreword. In T. K. Shackelford & R. D. Hansen (Eds.), *The evolution of violence* (pp. ix–xii). New York: Springer Science and Business Media.

Piquero, A. R., Connell, N. M., Leeper, N., Farrington, D. P., & Jennings, W. G. (2013). Does adolescent bullying distinguish between male offending trajectories in late middle age. *Journal of Youth and Adolescence, 42*, 444–453.

Piquero, A. R., Farrington, D. P., & Blumstein, A. (2003). *The criminal career paradigm. Crime and justice: A review of research.* Chicago: University of Chicago Press.

Pirelli, G., Gottdiener, W. H., & Zapf, P. A. (2011). A meta-analytic review of competency to stand trial research. *Psychology, Public Policy, and Law, 17*, 1–53.

Planty, M., Langton, L., Krebs, C., Berzofsky, M., & Smiley-McDonald, H. (2013, March). *Female victims of sexual violence, 1994–2010.* Washington, DC: U.S. Department of Justice, Bureau of Justice Statistics.

Pleck, E. (1989). Criminal approaches to family violence, 1640–1980. In L. Ohlin & M. Tonry (Eds.), *Family violence: Vol. 11.* Chicago: University of Chicago Press.

Plomin, R. (1986). *Development, genetics, and psychology.* Hillsdale, NJ: Erlbaum.

Plummer, D. L., & Graziano, W. G. (1987). Impact of grade retention on the social development of elementary school children. *Developmental Psychology, 23*, 267–275.

Poortinga, E., Lemmen, C., & Jibson, M. D. (2006). A case control study: White-collar defendants compared with defendants charged with other nonviolent theft. *Journal of the American Academy of Psychiatry and the Law, 34*, 82–89.

Pope, C. E. (1977). *Crime-specific analysis: The characteristics of burglary incidents (LEAA).* Washington, DC: USGPO.

Popper, K. R. (1968). *The logic of scientific discovery.* New York: Harper & Row.

Porter, C. L., Hart, C. H., Yang, C., Robinson, C. C., Olsen, S. F., Zeng, Q., et al. (2005). A comparative study of child temperament and parenting in Beijing, China and the western United States. *International Journal of Behavioral Development, 29*, 541–551.

Porter, L. E., & Alison, L. J. (2006). Behavioural coherence in group robbery: A circumplex model of offender and victim interactions. *Aggressive Behavior, 32*, 330–342.

Porter, S., Birt, A. R., & Boer, D. P. (2001). Investigation of the criminal and conditional release histories of Canadian federal offenders as a function of psychopathy and age. *Law and Human Behavior, 25*, 647–661.

Porter, S., Fairweather, D., Drugge, J., Herve, H., Birt, A. R., & Boer, D. (2000). Profiles of psychopathy in incarcerated sexual offenders. *Criminal Justice and Behavior, 27*, 216–233.

Porter, S., Woodworth, M., Earle, J., Drugge, J., & Boer, D. (2003). Characteristics of sexual homicides committed by psychopathic and nonpsychopathic offenders. *Law and Human Behavior, 27*, 459–470.

Porter, T., & Gavin, H. (2010). Infanticide and neonaticide: A review of 40 years of research literature on incidence and causes. *Trauma, Violence, & Abuse, 11*, 99–112.

Portzky, G., Audenaert, K., & van Heeringen, K. (2009). Psychological and psychiatric factors associated with adolescent suicide: A case-control psychological autopsy study. *Journal of Adolescence, 32*, 849–862.

Posner, J. K., & Vandell, D. L. (1999). After-school activities and the development of low-income urban children: A longitudinal study. *Developmental Psychology, 35*, 868–879.

Post, J. M., & Gold, S. N. (2002). The psychology of the terrorist: An interview with Jerrold M. Post. *Journal of Trauma Practice, 1*, 83–100.

Post, J. M., McGinnis, C., & Moody, K. (2014). The changing face of terrorism in the 21st century: The communications of revolution and the virtual community of hatred. *Behavioral Sciences & the Law, 32*, 306–334.

Post, L. A., Biroscak, B. J., & Barboza, G. (2011). Prevalence of sexual violence. In J. W. White, M. P. Koss, & A. F. Kazdin (Eds.), *Violence against women and children: Vol. 1. Mapping the terrain* (pp. 101–123). Washington, DC: American Psychological Association.

Postmes, T., & Spears, R. (1998). Deindividuation and antinormative behavior: A meta-analysis. *Psychological Bulletin, 123*, 238–259.

Potoczniak, M. J., Mourot, J. E., Crosbie-Burnett, M., & Potoczniak, D. J. (2003). Legal and psychological perspectives on same-sex domestic violence: A multisystematic approach. *Journal of Family Violence, 17*, 252–259.

Poulin, F., & Boivin, M. (2000). Reactive and proactive aggression: Evidence of a two-factor model. *Psychological Assessment, 12*, 115–122.

Power, R. (2000, Spring). 2000 CSI/FBI computer crime and security survey. *Computer Security: Issues & Trends, 6*(1).

Powers, R. (2002, March). Apocalypse of adolescence. *Atlantic Monthly*, pp. 58, 60–65.

Prentky, R. A., & Knight, R. A. (1986). Impulsivity in the life style and criminal behavior of sexual offenders. *Criminal Justice and Behavior, 13*, 141–164.

Prentky, R. A., Knight, R. A., & Lee, A. F. S. (1997). *Child sexual molestation: Research issues*. NIJ Research Report. Rockville, MD: National Criminal Justice Reference Service. Available: www.ncjrs.org/txtfiles/163390.txt.

Prinstein, M. J., Boergers, J., & Vernberg, E. M. (2001). Overt and relational aggression in adolescents: Social-psychological adjustment of aggressors and victims. *Journal of Clinical Child Psychology, 30*, 479–491.

Prinstein, M. J., & La Greca, A. M. (2004). Childhood peer rejection and aggression predictors of adolescent girls' externalizing and health risk behaviors: A 6-year longitudinal study. *Journal of Consulting and Clinical Psychology, 72*, 103–112.

Protection of Children from Sexual Predators Act. (1998, October 30). United States Congress, Pub. L. No. 105-314 § & 701. Washington, DC: U.S. Government Printing Office.

Pullman, M. D. (2010). Predictors of criminal charges for youth in public mental health during the transition to adulthood. *Journal of Child and Family Studies, 19*, 483–491.

Putnam, C. T., & Kirkpatrick, J. T. (2005, May). Juvenile firesetting: A research overview. *Juvenile Justice Bulletin* (NCJ 207606). Washington, DC: U.S. Department of Justice, Office of Juvenile Justice and Delinquency Prevention.

Putnam, F. W. (2003). Ten-year research update review: Child sexual abuse. *Journal of American Academy of Child and Adolescent Psychiatry, 42*, 269–278.

Puzzanchera, C. M. (2009, April). *Juvenile arrests 2007*. Washington, DC: U.S. Department of Justice, Office of Juvenile Justice and Delinquency Prevention.

Puzzanchera, C. M., & Adams, B. (2011, December). *Juvenile arrests, 2009. National Report Series Bulletin*. Washington, DC: U.S. Department of Justice, Office of Juvenile Justice and Delinquency Prevention.

Puzzanchera, C., Adams, B., & Sickmund, M. (2011). *Juvenile Court Statistics, 2008*. Pittsburgh, PA: National Center for Juvenile Justice.

Puzzanchera, C. M., & Addie, S. (2014, February). *Delinquency cases waived to criminal court, 2010*. Washington, DC: U.S. Department of Justice, Office of Juvenile Justice and Delinquency Programs.

Puzzanchera, C., & Hockenberry, S. (2013). *Juvenile court statistics 2010*. Washington, DC: U.S. Department of Justice, Office of Juvenile Justice and Delinquency Prevention.

Pyszczynski, T., Abdollahi, A., Greenberg, J., & Solomon, S. (2006). Crusades and Jihads: An existential psychological perspective on the psychology of terrorism and political extremism. In J. Victoroff (Ed.), *Tangled roots: Social and psychological factors in the genesis of terrorism* (pp. 85–97). Amsterdam, the Netherlands: IOS Press.

Pyszczynski, T., Rothschild, Z., & Abdollahi, A. (2008). Terrorism, violence, and hope for peace: A terror management perspective. *Current Directions in Psychological Science, 17*, 318–322.

QEV Analytics. (2012, August). *National survey of American attitudes on substance abuse XVII: Teens*. New York: National Center on Addiction and Substance Abuse at Columbia University.

Quattrocchi, M. R., & Schopp, R. F. (2005). Tarasaurus Rex: A standard of care that could not adapt. *Psychology, Public Policy, and Law, 11*, 109–137.

Quay, H. C. (1965). Psychopathic personality: Pathological stimulation-seeking. *American Journal of Psychiatry, 122*, 180–183.

Quayle, E. (2009). Child pornography. In Y. Jewkes & M. Yars (Eds.), *Handbook of Internet crime* (pp. 343–368). Cullompton, UK: Willan Publishing.

Quayle, E., & Jones, T. (2011). Sexualized images of children on the Internet. *Sexual Abuse: A Journal of Research and Treatment, 23*, 7–21.

Quinet, K. (2007). The missing missing: Toward a quantification of serial murder victimization in the United States. *Homicide Studies, 11*, 319–339.

Quinet, K. (2011). Prostitutes as victims of serial homicide: Trends and case characteristics, 1970-2009. *Homicide Studies, 15*, 74–100.

Quinsey, V. L., Harris, G. T., Rice, M. E., & Cormier, C. (2006). *Violent offenders: Appraising and managing risk* (2nd ed.). Washington, DC: American Psychological Association.

Quinsey, V. L., Rice, M. E., & Harris, G. T. (1995). Actuarial prediction of sexual recidivism. *Journal of Interpersonal Violence, 10*, 85–105.

Rabkin, J. G. (1979). Criminal behavior of discharged mental patients: A critical appraisal of the research. *Psychological Bulletin, 86*, 1–27.

Rafferty, Y. (2013). Child trafficking and commercial sexual exploitation: A review of promising prevention policies and programs. *American Journal of Orthopsychiatry, 83*, 559–573.

Ragatz, L. L., Fremouw, W., & Baker, E. (2012). The psychological profile of white-collar offenders: Demographics, criminal thinking, psychopathic traits, and psychopathology. *Criminal Justice and Behavior, 39*, 978–997.

Rainbow, L., & Gregory, A. (2011). What behavioural investigative advisers actually do. In L. Alison & L. Rainbow (Eds.), *Professionalizing offender profiling* (pp. 18–34). London: Routledge.

Raine, A. (1993). *The psychopathology of crime: Criminal behavior as a clinical disorder.* San Diego, CA: Academic Press.

Raine, A. (2002). Biosocial studies of antisocial and violent behavior in children and adults: A review. *Journal of Abnormal Child Psychology, 30*, 311–326.

Raine, A. (2008). From genes to brain to antisocial behavior. *Current Directions in Psychological Science, 17*, 323–328.

Raine, A. (2013). *The anatomy of violence: The biological roots of crime.* New York: Vintage Books.

Raine, A., Buschsbaum, M., & LaCasse, L. (1997). Brain abnormalities in murderers indicated by positron emission tomography. *Biological Psychiatry, 42*, 495–508.

Raine, A., Venables, P. H., & Williams, M. (1995). High autonomic arousal and electrodermal orienting at age 15 years as protective factors against criminal behavior at age 29 years. *American Journal of Psychiatry, 152*, 1595–1600.

Raine, A., Venables, P. H., & Williams, M. (1996). Better autonomic arousal and faster electrodermal half-recovery time at age 15 years as possible protective factors against crime at age 29 years. *Developmental Psychology, 32*, 624–630.

Ramirez, D., McDevitt, J., & Farrell, A. (2000, November). *A resource guide on racial profiling data collection systems: Promising practices and lessons learned.* Boston: Northeastern University Press. Available: www.usdoj.gov.

Ramirez, J. R., Crano, W. D., Quist, R., Burgoon, M., Alvaro, E. M., & Grandpre, J. (2004). Acculturation, familism, parental monitoring, and knowledge as predictors of marijuana and inhalant use in adolescents. *Psychology of Addictive Behavior, 18*, 3–11.

Rantala, R. R. (2008, September). *Cybercrime against businesses, 2005.* Washington, DC: U.S. Department of Justice, Bureau of Justice Statistics.

Räsänen, P., Tiihonen, J., Isohanni, M., Rantakallio, P., Lehtonen, J., & Moring, J. (1998). Schizophrenia, alcohol abuse, and violent behavior: A 26-year follow-up study of an unselected birth cohort. *Schizophrenia Bulletin, 24*, 432–441.

Raskin, D. C., & Hare, R. D. (1978). Psychopathy and detection of deception in a prison population. *Psychophysiology, 15*, 126–136.

Rasmussen, N. J. (2015, February 15). *Current terrorist threat to the United States.* Hearing before the Senate Select Committee on Intelligence. McLean, VA: National Counterterrorism Center.

Ray, O. (1972). *Drugs, society and human behavior.* St. Louis, MO: C. V. Mosby.

Ray, O. (1983). *Drugs, society and human behavior* (3rd ed.). St. Louis, MO: C. V. Mosby.

Redding, R. E. (2010, June). *Juvenile transfer laws: An effective deterrent to delinquency?* Washington, DC: U.S. Department of Justice, Office of Justice Programs, Office of Juvenile Justice and Delinquency Prevention.

Redlich, A. D., Liu, S., Steadman, H. J., Callahan, L., & Robbins, P. C. (2012). Is diversion swift? Comparing mental health court and traditional criminal justice processing. *Criminal Justice and Behavior, 39*, 420–433.

Redlich, A. D., Summers, A., & Hoover, S. (2010). Self-reported false confessions and false guilty pleas among offenders with mental illness. *Law and Human Behavior, 34*, 79–90.

Rehder, W., & Dillow, G. (2003). *Where the money is: True tales from the bank robbery capital of the world.* New York: Norton.

Reicher, S. D., Haslam, S. A., & Smith, J. R. (2012). Working toward the experimenter: Reconceptualizing obedience within the Milgram paradigm as identification-based fellowship. *Perspectives on Psychological Science, 7*, 315–324.

Reid, J. B. (1993). Prevention of conduct disorder before and after school entry: Relating interventions to developmental findings. *Development and Psychopathology, 5*, 243–262.

Reiman, J. (1995). *The rich get richer and the poor get prison* (4th ed.). Needham Heights, MA: Allyn & Bacon.

Reiss, A. J., & Roth, J. A. (Eds.). (1993). *Understanding and preventing violence.* Washington, DC: National Academy Press.

Reitman, J. (2013, July 17). Jahar's world. *Rolling Stone.* Available: www.rollingstone.com/culture/news/jahars-world-20130717.

Rengert, G. F., & Groff, E. (2011). *Residential burglary: How the urban environment and our lifestyles play a contributing role* (3rd ed.). Springfield, IL: Charles C Thomas.

Rengert, G., & Wasilchick, J. (1985). *Suburban burglary: A time and place for everything.* Springfield, IL: Charles C Thomas.

Rennison, C. M. (2003, February). *Intimate partner violence, 1993–2001* (NCJ 197838). Washington, DC: U.S. Department of Justice, Bureau of Justice Statistics.

Rennison, C. M., & Rand, M. R. (2003, August). *Criminal victimization, 2002.* Washington, DC: U.S. Department of Justice, Bureau of Justice Statistics.

Rennison, C. M., & Welchans, S. (2000, May). *Intimate partner violence.* Washington, DC: U.S. Department of Justice.

Resnick, P. J. (1969). Child murder by parents. *American Journal of Psychiatry, 126*, 325–334.

Resnick, P. J. (1970). Murder of the newborn: A psychiatric review of neonaticide. *American Journal of Psychiatry, 126*, 1414–1420.

Resnick, P. J. (1995). Guidelines for the evaluation of malingering in posttraumatic stress disorder. In R. I. Simon (Ed.), *Posttraumatic stress disorder in litigation guidelines for forensic assessment* (pp. 309–329). Washington, DC: American Psychiatric Association.

Revitch, E., & Schlesinger, L. B. (1988). Clinical reflections on sexual aggression. In R. A. Prentky & V. L. Quinsey (Eds.), *Human sexual aggression: Current perspectives.* New York: New York Academy of Sciences.

Reyns, B. W., & Englebrecht, C. M. (2012). The fear factor: Exploring predictors of fear among stalking victims throughout the stalking encounter. *Crime & Delinquency, 59*, 788–808.

Rhee, S. H., & Waldman, I. D. (2002). Genetic and environmental influences on antisocial behavior: A meta-analysis of twin and adoption studies. *Psychological Bulletin, 128*, 490–529.

Rhee, S. H., & Waldman, I. D. (2011). Genetic and environmental influences on aggression. In P. R. Shaver & M. Mikulincer (Eds.), *Human aggression and violence: Causes, manifestations, and consequences* (pp. 143–163). Washington, DC: American Psychological Association.

Rhoads, J. M., & Borjes, E. D. (1981). The incidence of exhibitionism in Guatemala and U.S. *British Journal of Psychiatry, 139*, 242–244.

Ribeaud, D., & Eisner, M. (2010). Risk factors for aggression in pre-adolescence: Risk domains, cumulative risk and gender differences—Results for a prospective longitudinal study in a multi-ethnic urban sample. *European Journal of Criminology, 7*, 440–498.

Rice, M. E., & Harris, G. T. (2002). Men who molest their sexually immature daughters: Is a special explanation required? *Journal of Abnormal Psychology, 111*, 329–339.

Rice, M. E., Harris, G. T., & Cormier, C. A. (1992). An evaluation of a maximum security therapeutic community for psychopaths and other mentally disordered offenders. *Law and Human Behavior, 16*, 399–412.

Rich, T., & Shively, M. (2004, December). *A methodology for evaluating geographic profiling software.* Cambridge, MA: Abt Associates.

Richards, H., Casey, J., & Lucente, S. (2003). Psychopathy and treatment response to incarcerated female substance abusers. *Criminal Justice and Behavior, 30*, 251–276.

Richardson, D. S. (2005). The myth of female passivity: Thirty years of revelations about female aggression. *Psychology of Women Quarterly, 29*, 238–247.

Richardson, D. S. (2014). Everyday aggression takes many forms. *Psychological Science, 23*, 220–224.

Righthand, S., & Welch, C. (2001, March). *Juveniles who have sexually offended: A review of the professional literature.* Washington, DC: Office of Juvenile Justice and Delinquency Prevention.

Riley, S. (1998). Competency to stand trial adjudication: A comparison of female and male defendants. *Journal of the American Academy of Psychiatry and the Law, 26*, 223–240.

Risen, J. (2014). *Pay any price: Greed, power, and endless war.* New York: Houghton Mifflin Harcourt Publishing.

Riser, R. E., & Kosson, D. S. (2013). Criminal behavior and cognitive processing in male offenders with antisocial personality disorder with and without comorbid psychopathy. *Personality Disorders: Theory, Research, and Treatment, 4*, 332–340.

Ritvo, E., Shanok, S. S., & Lewis, D. O. (1983). Firesetting and nonfiresetting delinquents. *Child Psychiatry and Human Development, 13*, 259–267.

Robbins, T. (2015, February 28). A brutal beating wakes Attica's ghosts. *The New York Times,* p. A1.

Robbins, E., & Robbins, L. (1964). Arson with special reference to pyromania. *New York State Journal of Medicine, 2*, 795–798.

Robers, S., Zhang, J., Truman, J., & Snyder, T. D. (2012, February). *Indicators of school crime and safety: 2011.* Washington, DC: National Center for Educational Statistics, Bureau of Justice Statistics.

Roberto, K. A., McPherson, M. C., & Brossoie, N. (2014). Intimate partner violence in late life: A review of the empirical literature. *Violence Against Women, 19*, 1538–1558.

Roberton, T., Daffern, M., & Bucks, R. S. (2015). Beyond anger control: Difficulty attending to emotions also predicts aggression in offenders. *Psychology of Violence, 5*, 74–83.

Roberts, A. R. (2002). Preface. In A. R. Roberts (Ed.), *Handbook of domestic violence intervention strategies: Policies, programs, and legal remedies.* New York: Oxford University Press.

Roberts, A. R., Zgoba, K. M., & Shahidullah, S. M. (2007). Recidivism among four types of homicide offenders: An exploratory analysis of 336 homicide offenders in New Jersey. *Aggression and Violent Behavior, 12*, 493–507.

Robins, P. M., & Sesan, R. (1991). Munchausen syndrome by proxy: Another women's disorder. *Professional Psychology: Research and Practice, 22*, 285–290.

Robinson, M., McLean, N. J., Oddy, W. H., Mattes, E., Bulsara, M., Li, J., & Newnham, J. P. (2010). Smoking cessation in pregnancy and the risk of child behavioural problems: A longitudinal perspective. *Journal of Epidemiology and Community Health, 64*, 622–629.

Robinson, B. A., Winiarski, D. A., Brennan, P. A., Foster, S. L., Cunningham, P. B., & Whitmore, E. A. (2015). Social context, parental monitoring, and Multisystemic Therapy outcomes. *Psychotherapy, 52*, 103–110.

Roche, T. (2006, July 7). Andrea Yates: More to the story. *Time.* Available: www.time.com/time/ nation/article/0,8599,218445,00html.

Rodman, H., & Grams, P. (1967). *Juvenile delinquency and the family: A review and discussion.* Task Force Report: Juvenile delinquency and youth crime. Washington, DC: USGPO.

Roesch, R., Zapf, P. A., Golding, S. L., & Skeem, J. L. (1999). Defining and assessing competency to stand trial. In A. K. Hess & I. B. Weiner (Eds.), *The handbook of forensic psychology* (2nd ed., pp. 327–349). New York: Wiley.

Roe-Sepowitz, D. (2007). Adolescent female murderers: Characteristics and treatment implications. *American Journal of Orthopsychiatry, 77*, 489–496.

Roe-Sepowitz, D., & Krysik, J. (2008). Examining the sexual offenses of female juveniles: The relevance of childhood maltreatment. *American Journal of Orthopsychiatry, 78*, 405–417.

Rogers, P., & Davies, M. (2007). Perceptions of victims and perpetrators in a depicted child sexual abuse case: Gender and age factors. *Journal of Interpersonal Violence, 22*, 566–584.

Rogers, R. (1997). *Clinical assessment of malingering and deception* (2nd ed.). New York: Guilford.

Rogers, R. (2000). The uncritical acceptance of risk assessment in clinical practice. *Law and Human Behavior, 24*, 595–605.

Rogers, R., Blackwood, H. L., Fiduccia, C. E., Steadham, J. A., Drogin, E. Y., & Rogstad, J. E. (2012). Juvenile Miranda warnings: Perfunctory rituals or procedural safeguards? *Criminal Justice and Behavior, 39*, 229–249.

Rogstad, J. E., & Rogers, R. (2008). Gender differences in contributions of emotion to psychopathy and antisocial personality disorder. *Clinical Psychology Review, 28*, 1472–1484.

Roizen, J. (1997). Epidemiological issues in alcohol-related violence. In M. Galanter (Ed.), *Recent developments in alcoholism: Vol. 13*. New York: Plenum.

Romer, D. (2010). Adolescent risk taking, impulsivity, and brain development: Implications for prevention. *Developmental Psychobiology, 52*, 263–276.

Romer, D., Betancourt, L. M., Brodsky, N., Giannetta, J. M., Yang, W., & Hurt, H. (2011). Does adolescent risk taking imply weak executive function? A prospective study of relations between working memory performance, impulsivity, and risk taking in early adolescence. *Developmental Science, 14*, 1119–1133.

Root, C., MacKay, S., Henderson, J., Del Bove, G., & Warling, D. (2008). The link between maltreatment and juvenile firesetting: Correlates and underlying mechanisms. *Child Abuse & Neglect, 32*, 161–176.

Rose, A. J., Swenson, L. P., & Waller, E. M. (2004). Overt and relational aggression and perceived popularity: Developmental differences in concurrent and prospective relations. *Developmental Psychology, 40*, 378–387.

Rosenbaum, D. P., Lurigio, A. J., & Davis, R. C. (1998). *The prevention of crime: Social and situational strategies*. Belmont, CA: West/Wadsworth.

Rosenbaum, M. (1989). *Just saw what? An alternative view on solving America's drug problem*. San Francisco: National Council of Crime and Delinquency.

Rosenfeld, B., & Ritchie, K. (1998). Competence to stand trial: Clinician reliability and the role of offense severity. *Journal of Forensic Sciences, 43*, 151–157.

Rosenthal, D. (1970). *Genetic theory and abnormal behavior*. New York: McGraw-Hill.

Rosenthal, D. (1971). *Genetics of psychopathology*. New York: McGraw-Hill.

Rosoff, S. M., Pontell, H. N., & Tillman, R. (1998). *Profit without honor: White-collar crime and the looting of America*. Upper Saddle River, NJ: Prentice Hall.

Ross, M. P., & Bachar, K. J. (2002). Rape. In D. Levinson (Ed.), *Encyclopedia of crime and punishment: Vol. 3*. Thousand Oaks, CA: Sage.

Rossmo, D. K. (1997). Geographic profiling. In J. L. Jackson & D. A. Bekerain (Eds.), *Offender profiling: Theory, research, and practice*. Chichester, UK: Wiley.

Roth, J. A. (1996). *Psychoactive substances and violence*. Washington, DC: U.S. Department of Justice. Available: www.ncjrs.org/txtfile/psycho.txt.

Rothman, D. J. (1980). *Conscience and convenience*. Boston: Little, Brown.

Rowe, D. C., & Gulley, B. (1992). Sibling effects on substance abuse and delinquency. *Criminology, 35*, 217–233.

Rowland, M. D., Chapman, J. E., & Henggeler, S. W. (2008). Sibling outcomes from a randomized trial of evidence-based treatments with substance abusing juvenile offenders. *Journal of Child and Adolescent Substance Abuse, 17*, 11–26.

Roza, S. J., Verburg, B. O., Jaddoe, V. W. V., Hofman, A., Mackenbach, J. P., Steegers, E. A. P., & Tiemeier, H. (2007). Effects of maternal smoking pregnancy on prenatal brain development: The Generation R Study. *European Journal of Neuroscience, 25*, 611–617.

Rubin, B. (1972). Predictions of dangerousness in mentally ill criminals. *Archives of General Psychiatry, 27*, 397–407.

Rubin, K. H., Bukowski, W., & Parker, J. G. (1998). Peer interactions, relationships, and groups. In W. Damon (Series Ed.), & N. Eisenberg (Vol. Ed.), *Handbook of child psychology: Vol. 3. Social, emotional, and personality development* (5th ed.). New York: Wiley.

Rubin, K. H., Burgess, K. B., Dwyer, K. M., & Hastings, P. D. (2003). Predicting preschoolers' externalizing behaviors from toddler temperament, conflict, and maternal negativity. *Developmental Psychology, 39*, 164–176.

Rubinsky, E. W., & Brandt, J. (1986). Amnesia and criminal law: A clinical overview. *Behavioral Sciences & the Law, 4*, 27–46.

Rubinstein, M., Yeager, C. A., Goodstein, C., & Lewis, D. O. (1993). Sexually assaultive male juveniles: A follow-up. *American Journal of Psychiatry, 150*, 262–265.

Ruby, C. L. (2002). Are terrorists mentally deranged? *Analyses of Social Issues and Public Policy, 2*, 15–26.

Ruchkin, V. (2002). Family impact on violent youth. In R. R. Corrado, R. Roesch, S. D. Hart, & J. K. Gierowski (Eds.), *Multi-problem violent youth: A foundation for comparative research on needs, interventions, and outcomes.* Amsterdam: IOS Press.

Rucklidge, J. J., McLean, A. P., & Bateup, P. (2009). Criminal offending and learning disabilities in New Zealand youth: Does reading comprehension predict recidivism. *Crime & Delinquency, 59*, 1263–1286.

Ruffolo, M. C., Sarri, R., & Goodkind, S. (2004). Study of delinquent, diverted, and high-risk adolescent girls: Implications for mental health intervention. *Social Work Research, 28*, 237–245.

Rulison, K. L., Kreager, D. A., & Osgood, D. W. (2014). Delinquency and peer acceptance in adolescence: A within-person test of Moffitt's hypotheses. *Developmental Psychology, 50*, 2437–2448.

Russell, A., Hart, C. H., Robinson, C. C., & Olsen, S. F. (2003). Children's sociable and aggressive behaviour with peers: A comparison of the US and Australia, and contributions of temperament and parental styles. *International Journal of Behavioral Development, 27*, 74–86.

Russell, B. S. (2010). Revisiting the measurement of shaken baby syndrome awareness. *Child Abuse & Neglect, 34*, 671–676.

Russell, D. (1973). Emotional aspects of shoplifting. *Psychiatric Annals, 3*, 77–86.

Russell, D. E. H. (1975). *The politics of rape: The victim's perspective.* New York: Stein & Day.

Russell, D. E. H. (1983). The prevalence and incidence of forcible rape and attempted rape of females. *Victimology: An International Journal, 7*, 81–93.

Russell, D. E. H. (1984). *Sexual exploitation.* Beverly Hills, CA: Sage.

Rutter, M. (1979). Maternal deprivation, 1972–1978: New findings, new concepts, new approaches. *Child Development, 50*, 283–305.

Rutter, M. (1997). Individual differences and levels of antisocial behavior. In A. Raine & P. A. Brennan (Eds.), *Biological bases of violence.* New York: Plenum.

Rutter, M. (2005). Commentary: What is the meaning and utility of the psychopathy concept? *Journal of Abnormal Child Psychology, 33*, 499–503.

Rutter, M., Giller, H., & Hagell, A. (1998). *Antisocial behavior by young people.* Cambridge, UK: Cambridge University Press.

Ryan, G., Miyoshi, T. J., Metzner, J. L., Krugman, R. D., & Fryer, G. E. (1996). Trends in a national sample of sexually abusive youths. *Journal of the American Academy of Child and Adolescent Psychiatry, 33*, 17–25.

Sageman, M. (2004). *Understanding terrorist networks.* Philadelphia: University of Pennsylvania Press.

Sagovsky, A., & Johnson, S. D. (2007). When does repeat burglary victimization occur? *Australian and New Zealand Journal of Criminology, 40*, 1–26.

Salekin, R. T. (2002). Psychopathy and therapeutic pessimism: Clinical lore or clinical reality? *Clinical Psychology Review, 22*, 79–112.

Salekin, R. T. (2010). Treatment of child and adolescent psychopathy: Focusing on change. In R. T. Salekin & D. R. Lyman (Eds.), *Handbook of child and adolescent psychopathy* (pp. 343–373). New York: Guilford.

Salekin, R. T., Brannen, D. N., Zalot, A. A., Leistico, A-M., & Neumann, C. S. (2006). Factor structure of psychopathy in youth: Testing the applicability of the new four-factor model. *Criminal Justice and Behavior, 33*, 135–157.

Salekin, R. T., & Frick, P. J. (2005). Psychopathy in children and adolescents: The need for a developmental perspective. *Journal of Abnormal Child Psychology, 33*, 403–409.

Salekin, R. T., Leistico, A-M. R., Trobst, K. K., Schrum, C. L., & Lochman, J. E. (2005). Adolescent psychopathy and personality theory—the interpersonal circumplex: Expanding evidence of a nomological net. *Journal of Abnormal Child Psychology, 33*, 445–460.

Salekin, R. T., & Lochman, J. E. (2008). Child and adolescent psychopathy: The search for protective factors. *Criminal Justice and Behavior, 35*, 159–172.

Salekin, R. T., & Lynam, D. R. (2010). (Eds.). *Handbook of child and adolescent psychopathy.* New York: Guilford Press.

Salekin, R. T., Rogers, R., & Machin, D. (2001). Psychopathy in youth: Pursuing diagnostic clarity. *Journal of Youth and Adolescence, 30*, 173–195.

Salekin, R. T., Rogers, R., & Sewell, K. W. (1997). Construct validity of psychopathy in a female offender sample: A multitrait-multimethod evaluation. *Journal of Abnormal Psychology, 106*, 576–585.

Salekin, R. T., Rogers, R., Ustad, K. L., & Sewell, K. W. (1998). Psychopathy and recidivism among female inmates. *Law and Human Behavior, 22*, 109–128.

Salekin, R. T., Worley, C., & Grimes, R. D. (2010). Treatment of psychopathy: A review and brief introduction to the mental model approach for psychopathy. *Behavioral Sciences and the Law, 28*, 235–266.

Salekin, R. T., Ziegler, T. A., Larrea, M. A., Anthony, V. L., & Bennett, A. D. (2003). Predicting psychopathy with two Millon Adolescent Psychopathy scales. The importance of egocentric and callous traits. *Journal of Personality Assessment, 80*, 154–163.

Salerno, J. M., Najdowski, C. J., Bottoms, B. L., Harrington, E., Kemner, G., & Dave, R. (2015). Excusing murder? Conservative jurors' acceptance of the gay-panic defense. *Psychology, Public Policy, and Law, 21*, 24–34.

Salisbury, E. J., & Van Voorhis, P. (2009). Gendered pathways: An empirical investigation of women probationers' paths to incarceration. *Criminal Justice and Behavior, 35*, 541–566.

Saltaris, C. (2002). Psychopathy in juvenile offenders: Can temperament and attachment be considered as robust developmental precursors? *Clinical Psychology Review, 22*, 729–752.

Samek, D. R., & Rueter, M. A. (2011). Considerations of elder sibling closeness in predicting younger sibling substance use: Social learning versus social bonding explanations. *Journal of Family Psychology, 25*, 931–941.

Sameroff, A. J., Peck, S. C., & Eccles, J. S. (2004). Changing ecological determinants of conduct problems from early adolescence to early childhood. *Development and Psychopathology, 16*, 873–896.

Sampson, R. (2011, August). *Acquaintance rape of college students: Problem-oriented guides for police problem-specific guides, No. 17*. Washington, DC: Office of Community Oriented Policing Services, U.S. Department of Justice.

Sampson, R. J. (2012). *Great American city: Chicago and the enduring neighborhood effect*. Chicago: University of Chicago Press.

Sampson, R. J., & Lauritsen, J. L. (1994). Violent victimization and offending: Individual, situational and community-level risk factors. In A. T. Reiss Jr. & J. Roth (Eds.), *Understanding and preventing violence: Social Influences: Vol. 3* (pp. 1–14). Washington, DC: National Academy Press.

Sampson, R. J., Morenoff, J. D., & Gannon-Rowley, T. (2002). Assessing neighborhood effects: Social processes and new directions in research. *Annual Review of Sociology, 28*, 443–478.

Sandler, J. C., & Freeman, N. J. (2007). Typology of female sex offenders: A test of Vandiver and Kercher. *Sexual Abuse: Journal of Research and Treatment, 19*, 73–89.

Saner, H., & Ellickson, P. (1996). Concurrent risk factors for adolescent violence. *Journal of Adolescent Health, 19*, 94–103.

Sanneh, K. (2015, February 9). Don't be like that: Does black culture need to be reformed? Book Review. *The New Yorker*, pp. 62–67.

Santa Clara Criminal Justice Pilot Program. (1972). *Burglary in San Jose*. Springfield, VA: U.S. Department of Commerce.

Santtila, P., Häkkänen, H., Alison, L., & Whyte, C. (2003). Juvenile firesetters: Crime scene actions and offender characteristics. *Legal and Criminological Psychology, 8*, 1–20.

Sarangi, S., & Alison, L. (2005). Life story accounts of left wing terrorists in India. *Journal of Investigative Psychology and Offender Profiling, 2*, 69–86.

Sarasalo, E., Bergman, B., & Toth, J. (1996). Personality traits and psychiatric and somatic morbidity among kleptomaniacs. *Acta Psychiatrica Scandinavica, 94*, 358–364.

Sarasalo, E., Bergman, B., & Toth, J. (1997). Kleptomania-like behaviour and psychosocial characteristics among shoplifters. *Legal and Criminological Psychology, 2*, 1–10.

Sarbin, T. R. (1979). The myth of the criminal type. In T. R. Sarbin (Ed.), *Challenges to the criminal justice system: The perspective of community psychology*. New York: Human Services Press.

Satterfield, J. H., Swanson, J., Schell, A., & Lee, F. (1994). Prediction of antisocial behavior in attention-deficit hyperactivity disorder boys from aggression/defiance scores. *Journal of the American Academy of Child and Adolescent Psychiatry, 33*, 185–191.

Saulnier, K., & Perlman, D. (1981). The actor-observer bias is alive and well in prison: A sequel to Wells. *Personality and Social Psychology, 7*, 559–564.

Saunders, D. G., & Azar, S. T. (1989). Treatment programs for family violence. In L. Ohlin & M. Tonry (Eds.), *Family violence: Vol. 11*. Chicago: University of Chicago Press.

Saunders, E. B., & Awad, G. A. (1991). Adolescent female firesetters. *Canadian Journal of Psychiatry, 36*, 401–404.

Savage, C. (2014, June 24). Court releases large part of memo approving killing of American in Yemen. *The New York Times*, p. A17.

Savage, J. (2008). The role of exposure to media violence in the etiology of violent behavior: A criminologist weighs in. *American Behavioral Scientist, 51*, 1123–1136.

Savage, J., & Yancey, C. (2008). The effects of media violence exposure on criminal aggression: A meta-analysis. *Criminal Justice and Behavior, 35*, 772–791.

Sawyer, A. M., & Borduin, C. M. (2011). Effects of multisystemic therapy through midlife: A 21.9-year follow-up to a randomized clinical trial with serious and violent juvenile offenders. *Journal of Consulting and Clinical Psychology, 79*, 643–652.

Sayers, S. L., Farrow, V. A., Ross, J., & Oslin, D. W. (2009). Family problems among recently returned military veterans referred for a mental health evaluation. *Journal of Clinical Psychiatry, 70*, 163–170.

Scaret, D., & Wilgosh, L. (1989). Learning disabilities and juvenile delinquency: A causal relationship? *International Journal for the Advancement of Counselling, 12*, 113–123.

Schachter, S., & Latane, B. (1964). Crime, cognition, and the autonomic nervous system. In M. R. Jones (Ed.), *Nebraska symposium on motivation*. Lincoln, NE: University of Nebraska Press.

Schacter, D. L. (1986). On the relation between genuine and simulated amnesia. *Behavioral Sciences & the Law, 4*, 47–64.

Schaeffer, C. M., & Borduin, C. M. (2005). Long-term follow-up to a randomized clinical trial of multisystemic therapy with serious and violent juvenile offenders. *Journal of Consulting and Clinical Psychology, 73*, 445–453.

Schaffer, M., Clark, S., & Jeglic, E. L. (2009). The role of empathy and parenting style in the development of antisocial behaviors. *Crime & Delinquency, 55*, 586–588.

Schauer, E. J., & Wheaton, E. M. (2006). Sex trafficking into the United States: A literature review. *Criminal Justice Review, 31*, 146–169.

Schiffer, B., & Vonlaufen, C. (2011). Executive dysfunctions in pedophilic and nonpedophilic child molesters. *Journal of Sexual Medicine, 8*, 1975–1984.

Schlosser, E. (2001). *Fast food nation: The dark side of the all-American meal.* Boston: Houghton Mifflin.

Schmucker, M., & Lösel, F. (2008). Does sexual offender treatment work? A systematic review of outcome evaluation. *Psicothema, 20*, 10–19.

Schneider, J. L. (2005). Stolen-goods markets. *British Journal of Criminology, 45*, 129–140.

Scholtz, D. C., Girard, M. L., & Vanderpool, M. A. (2008). *The development of a psychological screening program for sniper selection.* Ottawa, ON: Director Human Resources Research and Evaluation, National Defence Headquarters.

Schönbucher, V., Maier, T., Mohler-Kuo, M., Schnyder, U., & Landolt, M. A. (2012). Disclosure of child sexual abuse by adolescents: A qualitative in-depth study. *Journal of Interpersonal Violence, 27*, 3486–3513.

Schulreich, S., Pfabigan, D. M., Derntl, B., & Sailer, B. (2013). Fearless dominance and reduced feedback-related negativity amplitudes in time-estimation task—Further neuroscientific evidence for dual-process models of psychopathy. *Biological Psychology, 93*, 352–363.

Schulsinger, F. (1972). Psychopathy: Heredity and environment. *International Journal of Mental Health, 1*, 190–206.

Schuster, M. A., Stein, B. D., Jaycox, L. H., Collins, R. L., Marshall, G. N., & Elliott, M. N. (2001). A national survey of stress reactions after the September 11, 2001, terrorist attacks. *New England Journal of Medicine, 345*, 1507–1512.

Schwalbe, C. S., Gearing, R. E., MacKenzie, M. J., Brewer, K. B., & Ibrahim, R. (2012). A meta-analysis of experimental studies of diversion programs for juvenile offenders. *Clinical Psychology Review, 32*, 26–33.

Schwartz, I. M. (1989). *(In) Justice for juveniles: Rethinking the best interests of the child.* Lexington, MA: Lexington Books.

Schwartz, J. P., Hage, S. M., Bush, I., & Burns, L. K. (2006). Unhealthy parenting and potential mediators as contributing factors to future intimate violence: A review of the literature. *Trauma, Violence, & Abuse, 7,* 206–221.

Schwarz, A. (2015, April 25). Potent synthetic drug fuels rise in visits to emergency room. *The New York Times,* p. A10.

Sciutto, M. J. (2015). ADHD knowledge, misconceptions, and treatment acceptability. *Journal of Attention Disorders, 19,* 91–98.

Scott, C., McKinlay, A., McLellan, T., Britt, E., Grace, R., & MacFarlande, M. (2015). A comparison of adult outcomes for males compared to females following pediatric traumatic brain injury. *Neuropsychology, 29,* 501–508.

Scott, M. S. (2004, January). *Burglary of single-family houses in Savannah, Georgia.* Washington, DC: U.S. Department of Justice.

Scott, S., & Dao, J. (2009, November 15). Investigators study tangle of clues on Fort Hood suspect. *The New York Times,* p. A1.

Scully, D., & Marolla, J. (1985). Rape and vocabularies of motive: Alternative perspectives. In A. W. Burgess (Ed.), *Rape and sexual assault.* New York: Garland Publishing.

Seagrave, D., & Grisso, T. (2002). Adolescent development and measurement of juvenile psychopathy. *Law and Human Behavior, 26,* 219–239.

Sears, R., Maccoby, E., & Levin, H. (1957). *Patterns of child rearing.* Evanston, IL: Row, Peterson.

Séguin, J. R., Nagin, D., Asaad, J-M., & Tremblay, R. E. (2004). Cognitive-neuropsychological function in chronic physical aggression and hyperactivity. *Journal of Abnormal Psychology, 113,* 603–613.

Seierstad, A. (2015). *One of us: The story of Anders Breivik and the massacre in Norway.* New York: Farrar, Straus and Giroux.

Seiler, C. (2012, June 6). Bills would fight "shoplifting on steroids." *Albany Times Union,* p. A3.

Seligman, M. E. (1975). *Helplessness: On depression, development, and death.* San Francisco: W. H. Freeman.

Seligman, M. E. P., & Csikszentmihalyi, M. (2000). Positive psychology: An introduction. *American Psychologist, 55,* 5–14.

Selkin, J. (1987). *Psychological autopsy in the courtroom.* Denver, CO: Author.

Selkin, J. (1994). Psychological autopsy: Scientific psychohistory or clinical intuition? *American Psychologist, 49,* 74–75.

Sellbom, M., & Verona, E. (2007). Neuropsychological correlates of psychopathic traits in a non-incarcerated sample. *Journal of Research in Personality, 41,* 276–294.

Sellers, B. G., & Heide, K. M. (2012). Male and female child murderers: An empirical analysis of U.S. arrest data. *International Journal of Offender Therapy and Comparative Criminology, 56,* 691–714.

Sellin, T. (1970). A sociological approach. In M. E. Wolfgang, L. Savitz, & N. Johnson (Eds.), *The sociology of crime and delinquency* (2nd ed.). New York: Wiley.

Serin, R. C., & Amos, N. L. (1995). The role of psychopathy in the assessment of dangerousness. *International Journal of Law & Psychiatry, 18,* 231–238.

Serin, R. C., Peters, R. D., & Barbaree, H. E. (1990). Predictors of psychopathy and release outcome in a criminal population. *Psychological Assessment, 2,* 419–422.

Serin, R. C., & Preston, D. L. (2001). Managing and treating violent offenders. In J. B. Ashford, B. D. Sales, & W. H. Reid (Eds.), *Treating adult and juvenile offenders with special needs.* Washington, DC: American Psychological Association.

Seto, M. C. (2008). Pedophilia: Psychopathology and theory. In D. R. Laws & W. T. O'Donohue (Eds.), *Sexual deviance: Theory, assessment, and treatment* (2nd ed., pp. 164–182). New York: Guilford.

Seto, M. C. (2009). Pedophilia. *Annual Review of Clinical Psychology, 5,* 391–407.

Seto, M. C., & Barbaree, H. E. (1999). Psychopathy, treatment behavior, and sex offender recidivism. *Journal of Interpersonal Violence, 14,* 1235–1248.

Seto, M. C., & Hanson, R. K. (2011). Introduction to special issue on Internet-facilitated sexual offending. *Sexual Abuse: A Journal of Research and Treatment, 23,* 3–6.

Seto, M. C., Hanson, R. K., & Babchishin, K. M. (2011). Contact sexual offending by men with online sexual offenses. *Sexual Abuse: A Journal of Research and Treatment, 23*, 124–145.

Seto, M. C., Kingston, D. A., & Stephens, S. (2015). Sexual offending. In B. L. Cutler & P. A. Zapf (Eds.), *APA handbook of forensic psychology: Vol. 1. Individual and situation influences in criminal and civil contexts* (pp. 351–379). Washington, DC: American Psychological Association.

Seto, M. C., & Lalumière, M. L. (2010). What is so special about male adolescent sexual offending? A review and test of explanations through meta-analysis. *Psychological Bulletin, 136*, 526–575.

Seto, M. C., Maric, A., & Barbaree, H. E. (2001). The role of pornography in the etiology of sexual aggression. *Aggression and Violent Behavior, 6*, 35–53.

Sevecke, K., Pukrop, R., Kosson, D. S., & Krischer, M. K. (2009). Factor structure of the Hare Psychopathy Checklist: Youth Version in German female and male detainees and community adolescents. *Psychological Assessment, 21*, 45–56.

Sexton, T. L., & Alexander, J. F. (2000). *Functional Family Therapy* (Juvenile Justice Bulletin Series). Washington, DC: Office of Juvenile Justice and Delinquency Prevention.

Sexton, T. L., & Turner, C. W. (2010). The effectiveness of Functional Family Therapy for youth with behavioral problems in a community practice setting. *Journal of Family Psychology, 3*, 339–348.

Seymour, A. (2001). Victimization of the elderly. In G. Coleman, M. Gaboury, M. Murray, & A. Seymour (Eds.), *1999 National Victim Assistance Academy.* Washington, DC: U.S. Department of Justice.

Shah, N. R., & Bracken, M. B. (2000). A systematic review and meta-analysis of prospective studies on the association between maternal cigarette smoking and preterm delivery. *American Journal of Obstetrics and Gynecology, 182*, 465–472.

Shain, R., & Phillips, J. (1991). The stigma of mental illness: Labeling and stereotyping in the news. In L. Wilkins & P. Patterson (Eds.), *Risky business: Communicating issues of science, risk, and public policy.* Westport, CT: Greenwood Press.

Shane, S. (2015, April 17). Ohio man trained in Syria is charged with planning terrorism in U.S., *The New York Times*, p. A1.

Shaver, P. R., & Mikulincer, M. (2011). Introduction. In P. R. Shaver & M. Mikulincer (Eds.), *Human aggression and violence: Causes, manifestations, and consequences* (pp. 3–11). Washington, DC: American Psychological Association.

Shaw, D. S., Gilliom, M., Ingoldsby, E. M., & Nagin, D. S. (2003). Trajectories leading to school-age conduct problems. *Developmental Psychology, 39*, 189–200.

Shaw, D. S., Owens, E. B., Giovannelli, J., & Winslow, E. B. (2001). Infant and toddler pathways leading to early externalizing disorders. *Journal of the American Academy of Child and Adolescent Psychiatry, 40*, 36–43.

Shaw, D. S., & Shellbey, E. C. (2014). Early-starting conduct problems: Intersection of conduct problems and poverty. *Annual Review of Clinical Psychology, 10*, 503–528.

Sheridan, L., Scott, A. J, & North, A. C. (2015). Stalking and age. *Journal of Threat Assessment and Management, 1*, 262–273.

Sheridan, M. S. (2003). The deceit continues: An updated literature review of Munchausen syndrome by proxy. *Child Abuse & Neglect, 27*, 431–451.

Shiroma, E. J., Ferguson, P. L., & Pickelsimer, E. E. (2010). Prevalence of traumatic brain injury in an offender population: A metal-analysis. *Journal of Correctional Health Care, 16*(2), 147–159.

Shneidman, E. S. (1994). The psychological autopsy. *American Psychologist, 49*, 75–76.

Shorey, R. C., Seavey, A. E., Quinn, E., & Cornelius, T. L. (2014). Partner-specific anger management as a mediator of the relation between mindfulness and female perpetrated dating violence. *Psychology of Violence, 4*, 51–64.

Short, J. F., & Nye, I. (1957). Reported behavior as a criterion of deviant behavior. *Social Problems, 5*, 207–213.

Showers, J. (1999). *Never never never shake a baby: The challenges of shaken baby syndrome.* Alexandria, VA: National Association of Children's Hospitals and Related Institutions.

Shufelt, J. L., & Cocozza, J. J. (2006). *Youth with mental health disorders in the juvenile justice system: Results from a multi-state prevalence study.* Delmar, NY: National Center for Mental Health and Juvenile Justice.

Shulman, E. P., Cauffman, E., Piquero, A. R., & Fagan, J. (2011). Moral disengagement among serious juvenile offenders: A longitudinal study of the relations between morally disengaged attitudes and offending. *Developmental Psychology, 47,* 1619–1632.

Shumaker, D. M., & Prinz, R. J. (2000). Children who murder: A review. *Clinical Child and Family Psychology Review, 3,* 97–115.

Sibley, M. H., Pelham, W. E., Molina, B. S. G., Gnagy, E. M., Waschbusch, D. A., Biswas, A., et al. (2011). The delinquency outcomes of boys with ADHD with and without comorbidity. *Journal of Abnormal Child Psychology, 39,* 21–32.

Siegel, A., & Kohn, L. (1959). Permissiveness, permission, and aggression: The effect of adult presence or absence on aggression in children's play. *Child Development, 30,* 131–141.

Siegel, J. A., & Williams, L. M. (2001, July). *Risk factors for violent victimization of women: A prospective study.* Washington, DC: U.S. Department of Justice.

Siegel, J. M., Sorenson, S. B., Golding, J. M., Burnam, M. A., & Stein, J. A. (1987). The prevalence of childhood sexual assault: The Los Angeles Epidemiological Catchment Area Project. *American Journal of Epidemiology, 126,* 1141–1153.

Sieh, E. W. (1987). Garment workers: Perceptions of inequity and employee theft. *British Journal of Criminology, 27,* 174–190.

Siever, L. J. (2008). Neurobiology of aggression and violence. *American Journal of Psychiatry, 165,* 429–442.

Sigre-Leirós, V., Carvalho, J., & Nobre, P. (2015). Cognitive schemas and sexual offending: Differences between rapists, pedophilic and nonpedophilic child molesters, and nonsexual offenders. *Child Abuse & Neglect, 40,* 81–92.

Sigurvinsdottir, R., & Ullman, S. E. (2015). Social reactions, self-blame, and problem drinking in adult sexual assault survivors. *Psychology of Violence, 5,* 192–198.

Silberman, E. K., & Weingartner, H. (1996). Hemispheric lateralization of functions related to emotion. *Brain and Cognition, 5,* 322–353.

Silke, A. (2003). The psychology of suicidal terrorism. In A. Silke (Ed.), *Terrorists, victims and society: Psychological perspectives on terrorism and its consequences.* Chichester, UK: Wiley.

Silke, A. (2008). Holy warriors: Exploring the psychological processes of Jihadi radicalization. *European Journal of Criminology, 5,* 99–123.

Silver, E. (2006). Understanding the relationship between mental disorder and violence: The need for a criminological perspective. *Law and Human Behavior, 30,* 685–706.

Silverthorn, P., & Frick, P. J. (1999). Developmental pathways to antisocial behavior: The delayed-onset pathway in girls. *Development and Psychopathology, 11,* 101–126.

Sim, D. J., & Proeve, M. (2010). Crossover and stability of victim type in child molesters. *Legal and Criminological Psychology, 15,* 401–413.

Simeone, R. (2014, August 14). *Doctor shopping behavior and the diversion of opioid analgesics: 2008-2012.* Albany, NY: Simeone Associates, Inc.

Simon, R. J. (1983). The defense of insanity. *Journal of Psychiatry and Law, 11,* 183–201.

Simon, R. J., & Aaronson, D. E. (1988). *The insanity defense.* New York: Praeger.

Simon, R. J., & Cockerham, W. (1977). Civil commitment, burden of proof, and dangerous acts: A comparison of the perspectives of judges and psychiatrists. *Journal of Psychiatry and Law, 5,* 571–594.

Simonelli, C. J., Mullis, T., & Rohde, C. (2005). Scale of negative family interactions: A measure of parental and sibling aggression. *Journal of Interpersonal Violence, 20,* 792–803.

Simonoff, E., Elander, J., Holmshaw, J., Pickels, A., Murray, R., & Rutter, M. (2004). Predictors of antisocial personality: Continuities from childhood to adult life. *British Journal of Psychiatry, 184,* 118–127.

Simons, D. A., Wurtele, S. K., & Durham, R. L. (2008). Developmental experiences of child sexual abusers and rapists. *Child Abuse & Neglect, 32,* 549–560.

Simons, R. L., Lin, K. H., & Gordon, L. C. (1998). Socialization in the family of origin and male dating violence: A prospective study. *Journal of Marriage and the Family, 60,* 467–478.

Simourd, D. J., & Hoge, R. D. (2000). Criminal psychopathy: A risk-and-need perspective. *Criminal Justice and Behavior, 27,* 256–272.

Sinozich, S., & Langton, L. (2014, December). *Rape and sexual assault victimization among college-age females, 1995-2013.* Washington, DC: U.S. Department of Justice, Bureau of Justice Statistics.

Sitnick, S. L., Shaw, D. S., & Hyde, L. W. (2014). Precursors of adolescent substance use from early childhood and early adolescence: Testing a developmental cascade model. *Development and Psychopathology, 26,* 125–140.

Sitnikova, T., Goff, D., & Kuperberg, G. R. (2009). Neurocognitive abnormalities during comprehension of real-world, goal-directed behaviors in schizophrenia. *Journal of Abnormal Psychology, 118,* 256–277.

Sjöwall, D., Backman, A., & Thorell, L. B. (2015). Neuropsychological heterogeneity in preschool ADHD: Investigation the interplay between cognitive, affective and motivation-based forms of regulation. *Journal of Abnormal Child Psychology, 43,* 669–680.

Skeem, J. L., & Cauffman, E. (2003). Views of the downward extension: Comparing the youth version of the Psychopathy Checklist with the Youth Psychopathic Traits Inventory. *Behavioral Sciences & the Law, 21,* 737–770.

Skeem, J. L., & Cooke, D. J. (2010a). Is criminal behavior a central component of psychopathy? Conceptual directions for resolving the debate. *Psychological Assessment, 22,* 433–445.

Skeem, J. L. & Cooke, D. J. (2010b). One measure does not a construct make: Directions toward reinvigorating psychopathy research—reply to Hare and Neuman (2010). *Psychological Assessment, 22,* 455–459.

Skeem, J. L., Edens, J. F., Camp, J., & Colwell, L. H. (2004). Are there ethnic differences in levels of psychopathy? A meta-analysis. *Law and Human Behavior, 28,* 505–527.

Skeem, J. L., Edens, J. F., & Colwell, L. H. (2003, April). Are there racial differences in levels of psychopathy? A meta-analysis. *Paper presented at the 3rd annual conference of the International Association of Forensic Mental Health Services,* Miami, FL.

Skeem, J. L., Emke-Francis, P., & Louden, J. L. (2006). Probation, mental health, and mandated treatment: A national survey. *Criminal Justice and Behavior, 33,* 158–184.

Skeem, J. L., Monahan, J., & Mulvey, E. P. (2002). Psychopathy, treatment involvement, and subsequent violence among civil psychiatric patients. *Law and Human Behavior, 26,* 577–603.

Skeem, J. L., Polaschek, D. L. L., Patrick, C. J., & Lilienfeld, S. O. (2011). Psychopathic personality: Bridging the gap between scientific evidence and public policy. *Psychological Science in the Public Interest, 12,* 95–162.

Skeem, J. L., Poythress, N., Edens, J., Lilienfeld, S., & Cale, E. (2003). Psychopathic personality or personalities? Exploring potential variants of psychopathy and their implications for risk assessment. *Aggression and Violent Behavior, 8,* 513–546.

Skeem, J. L., Scott, E., & Mulvey, E. P. (2014). Justice policy reform for high-risk juveniles: Using science to achieve large-scale crime reduction. *Annual Review of Clinical Psychology, 10,* 709–739.

Skeem, J. L., Winter, E., Kennealy, P. J, Louden, J. E., & Tatar, J. R. II. (2014). Offenders with mental illness have criminogenic needs, too: Toward recidivism reduction. *Law and Human Behavior, 38,* 212–224.

Skilling, T. A., Quinsey, V. L., & Craig, W. M. (2001). Evidence of a tax on underlying serious antisocial behavior in boys. *Criminal Justice and Behavior, 28,* 450–470.

Skinner, B. F. (1964). Behaviorism at fifty. In T. W. Wann (Ed.), *Behaviorism and phenomenology.* Chicago: University of Chicago Press.

Slavkin, M. L. (2001). Enuresis, firesetting, and cruelty to animals: Does the ego triad show predictive validity? *Adolescence, 36,* 461–467.

Slesnick, N., Reed, S., Letcher, A., Katafiasx, H., Jones, T., & Buettner, C. (2012). Predictors of parental monitoring among families with a runaway adolescent. *American Journal of Orthopsychiatry, 82,* 10–18.

Slobogin, C. (1985). The guilty but mentally ill verdict: An idea whose time should not have come. *George Washington Law Review, 53,* 494–580.

Slobogin, C. (1999). The admissibility of behavioral science information in criminal trials: From primitivism to *Daubert* to voice. *Psychology, Public Policy, and Law, 5,* 100–119.

Slotter, E. B., & Finkel, E. J. (2011). I³ theory: Instigating, impelling, and inhibiting factors in aggression. In P. R. Shaver & M. Mikulincer (Eds.), *Human aggression and violence: Causes,* *manifestations, and consequences* (pp. 35–52). Washington, DC: American Psychological Association.

Slovenko, R. (1989). The multiple personality: A challenge to legal concepts. *The Journal of Psychiatry and Law, 17,* 681–719.

Small, K., Adams, W., Owens, C., & Roland, K. (2008). *An analysis of federally prosecuted CSEC cases since the passage of the Victims of Trafficking and Violence Prevention Act of 2000.* Washington, DC: Urban Institute Justice Policy Center.

Smallbone, S. W., & Wortley, R. K. (2000). *Child sexual abuse in Queensland: Offender characteristics and modus operandi.* Brisbane, Australia: Queensland Crime Commission.

Smallbone, S. W., & Wortley, R. K. (2001). *Child sexual abuse: Offender characteristics and modus operandi* (Australian Institute of Criminology Trends and Issues in Crime and Criminal Justice, No. 193). Canberra: Australian Institute of Criminology.

Smallbone, S. W., & Wortley, R. K. (2004). Criminal diversity and paraphilic interests among adult males convicted of offenses against children. *International Journal of Offender Therapy and Comparative Criminology, 48,* 175–188.

Smart, R. G. (1986). Cocaine use and problems in North America. *British Journal of Criminology, 28,* 109–128.

Smigel, E. O. (1970). Public attitudes toward stealing as related to the size of the victim organization. In E. O. Smigel & H. L. Ross (Eds.), *Crimes against bureaucracy.* New York: Van Nostrand Reinhold.

Smith, B. L., & Morgan, K. D. (1994). Terrorists right and left: Empirical issues in profiling American terrorists. *Studies in Conflict and Terrorism, 17,* 39–57.

Smith, D. (2002, June). Helping mentally ill offenders. *Monitor on Psychology, 33,* 64.

Smith, E. J. (2006). The strength-based counseling model. *The Counseling Psychologist, 34,* 13–79.

Smith, G. A., & Hall, J. A. (1982). Evaluating Michigan's guilty but mentally ill verdict: An empirical study. *Michigan Journal of Law Reform, 16,* 75–112.

Smith, P. K., Mahdavi, J., Carvalho, M., Fisher, S., Russell, S., & Tippett, N. (2008). Cyberbullying: Its nature and impact in secondary school pupils. *Journal of Child Psychology and Psychiatry, 49,* 376–385.

Smith, S. S., & Newman, J. P. (1990). Alcohol and drug abuse-dependence disorder in psychopathic and nonpsychopathic criminal offenders. *Journal of Abnormal Psychology, 99,* 430–439.

Smithey, M. (1998). Infant homicide: Victim-offender relationship and causes of death. *Journal of Family Violence, 13,* 285–287.

Snider, J. F., Hane, S., & Berman, A. L. (2006). Standardizing the psychological autopsy: Addressing the Daubert standard. *Suicide and Life-Threatening Behavior, 36,* 511–518.

Snook, B., Cullen, R. M., Bennell, C., Taylor, P. J., & Gendreau, P. (2008). The criminal profiling illusion: What's behind the smoke and mirrors? *Criminal Justice and Behavior, 35,* 1257–1276.

Snook, B., Dhami, M. K., & Kavanagh, J. M. (2011). Simply criminal: Predicting burglars' occupancy decisions with a simple heuristic. *Law and Human Behavior, 35,* 316–326.

Snook, B., Eastwood, J., Gendreau, P., Goggin, C., & Cullen, R. M. (2007). Taking stock of criminal profiling: A narrative review and meta-analysis. *Criminal Justice and Behavior, 34,* 437–453.

Snyder, H. N. (2006, December). *Juvenile arrests 2004.* Washington, DC: U.S. Department of Justice, Office of Juvenile Justice and Delinquency Prevention.

Snyder, H. N. (2008, August). *Juvenile arrests 2005.* Washington, DC: U.S. Department of Justice, Office of Juvenile Justice and Delinquency Prevention.

Snyder, H. N., Espiritu, R. C., Huizinga, D., Loeber, R., & Petechuk, D. (2003, March). Prevalence and development of child delinquency. *Child Delinquency Bulletin Series* (NCJ193411). Washington, DC: U.S. Department of Justice, Office of Juvenile Justice and Delinquency Prevention.

Snyder, H. N., Sickmund, M., & Poe-Yamagata, E. (2000). *Juvenile transfer to criminal court in the 1990s: Lessons learned from four studies.* Washington, DC: Office of Juvenile Justice and Delinquency Prevention.

Snyder, J., & Patterson, G. (1987). Family interaction and delinquent behavior. In H. C. Quay (Ed.), *Handbook of juvenile delinquency.* New York: Wiley.

Snyder, J., Reid, J., & Patterson, G. (2003). A social learning model of child and adolescent antisocial behavior. In B. B. Lahey, T. E. Moffitt, & A. Caspi (Eds.), *Causes of conduct disorder and juvenile delinquency* (pp. 27–48). New York: Guilford.

Sorenson, S. B., Stein, J. A., Siegel, J. M., Golding, J. M., & Burnam, M. A. (1987). The prevalence of adult sexual assault: The Los Angeles Epidemiological Catchment Area Project. *American Journal of Epidemiology, 126*, 1154–1164.

Sorge, G. B., Skilling, T. A., & Toplak, M. E. (in press). Intelligence, executive functions, and decision making as predictors of antisocial behavior in an adolescent sample of justice-involved youth and community comparison group. *Journal of Behavioral Decision Making*.

Southerland, M. D., Collins, P. A., & Scarborough, K. E. (1997). *Workplace violence.* Cincinnati, OH: Anderson.

Spaccarelli, S., Coatsworth, J. D., & Bowden, B. S. (1995). Exposure to serious family violence among incarcerated boys: Its association with violent offending and potential mediating variables. *Violence and Victims, 10*, 163–182.

Spain, S. E., Douglas, K. S., Poythress, N. G., & Epstein, M. (2004). The relationship between psychopathic features, violence, and treatment outcomes: The comparison of three youth measures of psychopathic features. *Behavioral Sciences & the Law, 22*, 85–102.

Spallone, P. (1998). The new biology of violence: New geneticisms for old? *Body and Society, 4*, 47–65.

Spano, R., & Bolland, J. (2013). Disentangling the effects of violent victimization, violent behavior, and gun carrying for minority inner-city youth living in extreme poverty. *Crime & Delinquency, 59*, 191–213.

Spano, R., Pridemore, W. A., & Bolland. J. (2012). Specifying the role of exposure to violence and violent behavior on initiation of gun carrying: A longitudinal test of three models of youth gun carrying. *Journal of Interpersonal Violence, 27*, 158–176.

Sparr, L. F. (1996). Mental defenses and posttraumatic stress disorder: Assessment of criminal intent. *Journal of Traumatic Stress, 9*, 405–425.

Speckhard, A., Tarabrina, N., Krasnov, V., & Mufel, N. (2005). Stockholm effects and psychological responses to captivity in hostages held by suicide terrorists. *Traumatology, 11*, 121–140.

Spinelli, M. G. (2001). A systematic investigation of 16 cases of neonaticide. *American Journal of Psychiatry, 158*, 811–813.

Spinelli, M. G. (2003). *Infanticide: Psychosocial and legal perspectives on mothers who kill.* Washington, DC: American Psychiatric Publishing.

Spinrad, T. L., Eisenberg, N., & Bernt, F. (2007). Introduction to the special issues on moral development: Part I. *The Journal of Genetic Psychology, 168*, 101–104.

Stadolnik, R. F. (2000). *Drawn to the flame: Assessment and treatment of juvenile firesetting behavior.* Sarasota, FL: Professional Resources Press.

Stagg, V., Wills, G. D., & Howell, M. (1989). Psychopathology in early childhood witnesses of family violence. *Topics in Early Childhood Special Education, 9*, 73–87.

Staller, J. A. (2006). Diagnostic profiles in outpatient child psychiatry. *American Journal of Orthopsychiatry, 76*, 98–102.

Stanger, C., Achenbach, T. M., & Verhulst, F. C. (1997). Accelerated longitudinal comparisons of aggressive versus delinquent syndromes. *Development and Psychopathology, 9*, 43–58.

Stark, C., Paterson, B., Henderson, T., Kidd, B., & Godwin, M. (1997). Counting the dead. *Nursing Times, 93*, 34–37.

Statistics Canada. (2011). *Family violence in Canada: A statistical profile.* Ottawa, ON: Canadian Centre for Justice Statistics.

Stattin, H., & Klackenberg-Larsson, I. (1993). Early language and intelligence development and their relationship to future criminal behavior. *Journal of Abnormal Psychology, 102*, 369–378.

Stattin, H., & Magnusson, D. (1991). Stability and change in criminal behaviour up to age 30. *The British Journal of Criminology, 31*, 327–346.

Staub, E. (2001). Genocide and mass killing: Their roots and prevention. In D. J. Christie, R. V. Wagner, & D. D. Winter (Eds.), *Peace, conflict, and violence: Peace psychology for the 21st century.* Upper Saddle River, NJ: Prentice-Hall.

Staub, E. (2004). Understanding and responding to group violence: Genocide, mass killing, and terrorism. In F. M. Moghaddam & A. J. Marsella (Eds.), *Understanding terrorism: Psychosocial roots, consequences, and interventions* (pp. 151–168). Washington, DC: American Psychological Association.

Steadman, H. J., McGreevy, M. A., Morrissey, J. P., Callahan, L. A., Robbins, P. C., & Cirincione, C. (1993). *Before and after Hinckley: Evaluating insanity defense reform.* New York: Guilford Press.

Steadman, H. J., Mulvey, E. P., Monahan, J., Robbins, P. C., Appelbaum, P. S., Grisso, T., et al. (1998). Violence by people discharged from acute psychiatric inpatient facilities and by others in the same neighborhoods. *Archives of General Psychiatry, 55,* 393–401.

Steadman, H. J., Osher, F. C., Robbins, P. C., Case, B., & Samuels, S. (2009). Prevalence of serious mental illness among jail inmates. *Psychiatric Services, 60,* 761–765.

Steffan, J. S., & Morgan, R. D. (2005, February). Meeting the needs of mentally ill offenders: Inmate service utilization. *Corrections Today,* pp. 38–43.

Steinberg, L. (2004). Risk-taking in adolescence: What changes, and why? *Annals of the New York Academy of Sciences, 1021,* 51–58.

Steinberg, L. (2007). Risk-taking in adolescence: New perspectives from brain and behavioral science. *Current Perspectives in Psychological Sciences, 16,* 55–59.

Steinberg, L. (2008). A social neuroscience perspective on adolescent risk taking. *Developmental Review, 28,* 78–106.

Steinberg, L. (2010). A dual system model of adolescent risk taking. *Developmental Psychobiology, 52,* 216–224.

Steinberg, L, Albert, D., Cauffman, E., Banich, M., Graham, S., & Woolard, J. (2008). Age differences in sensation seeking and impulsivity as indexed by behavior and self-report: Evidence for a dual systems model. *Developmental Psychology, 44,* 1764–1778.

Steinberg, L., Cauffman, E., Woolard, J., Graham, S., & Banich, M. (2009). Are adolescents less mature than adults? *American Psychologist, 64,* 583–594.

Steinman, K. J. (2005). Drug selling among high school students: Related risk behaviors and psychosocial characteristics. *Journal of Adolescent Health, 36,* 71–79.

Steinmetz, S. K. (1981). A cross-cultural comparison of sibling violence. *International Journal of Family Psychiatry, 2,* 337–351.

Steketee, M., Junger, M., & Junger-Tas, J. (2013). Sex differences in the predictors of juvenile delinquency: Females are more susceptible to poor environments; Males are influenced more by low self-control. *Journal of Contemporary Criminal Justice, 29,* 88–105.

Stern, K. R. (2001, May). A treatment study of children with attention deficit hyperactivity disorder. *OJJDP Fact Sheet.* Washington, DC: U.S. Department of Justice, Office of Juvenile Justice and Delinquency Prevention.

Sternberg, R. J. (2003). A duplex theory of hate: Development and application of terrorism, massacres, and genocide. *Review of General Psychology, 7,* 299–328.

Sternberg, R. J., Grigorenko, E. L., & Kidd, K. K. (2005). Intelligence, race, and genetics. *American Psychologist, 60,* 46–59.

Stevens, M. J. (2005). What is terrorism and can psychology do anything to prevent it? *Behavioral Sciences & the Law, 23,* 507–526.

Stickle, T., & Blechman, E. (2002). Aggression and fire: Antisocial behavior in firesetting and nonfiresetting juvenile offenders. *Journal of Psychopathology and Behavioral Assessment, 24,* 177–193.

Stillwell, R. (2009). *Public school graduates and dropouts from the common core of data: School year 2006–07* (NCES 2010-313). Washington, DC: National Center for Education Statistics, Institute of Education Sciences, U.S. Department of Education.

Stoltenborgh, M., van Ijzendoorn, M. H., Euser, G. M., & Bakermans-Kranenburg, M. J. (2011). A global perspective on child sexual abuse: Meta-analysis of prevalence around the world. *Child Maltreatment, 16,* 79–101.

Stone, M. H. (1998). Sadistic personality in murders. In T. Millon, E. Simonsen, M. Burket-Smith, & R. Davis (Eds.), *Psychopathy: Antisocial, criminal, and violent behavior.* New York: Guilford.

Stouthamer-Loeber, M., Loeber, R., Wei, E., Farrington, D., & Wilkström, P. H. (2002). Risk and promotive effects in the explanation of persistent serious delinquency in boys. *Journal of Consulting and Clinical Psychology, 70,* 111–123.

Stouthamer-Loeber, M. Wei, E., Loeber, R., & Masten, A. S. (2004). Desistence from persistent serious delinquency in the transition to adulthood. *Development and Psychopathology, 16,* 897–918.

Strassberg, D. S., Eastvold, A., Kenny, J. W., & Suchy, Y. (2012). Psychopathy among pedophilic and nonpedophilic child molesters. *Child Abuse & Neglect, 36,* 379–382.

Straus, M. (1991). Discipline and deviance: Physical punishment of children and violence and other crime in adulthood. *Social Problems, 38,* 133–154.

Straus, M. A., & Gelles, R. J. (1990). *Physical violence in American families.* New Brunswick, NJ: Transaction Publishers.

Straus, M. A., & Michel-Smith, Y. (2014). Mutuality, severity, and chronicity of violence by father-only, mother-only, and mutually violent parents as reported by university students in 15 nations. *Child Abuse & Neglect, 38,* 664–676.

Strentz, T. (1987, November). A hostage psychological survival guide. *FBI Law Enforcement Bulletin,* 1–7.

Strickland, S. M. (2008). Female sex offenders: Exploring issues of personality, trauma, and cognitive distortions. *Journal of Interpersonal Violence, 23,* 474–489.

Stroebel, S. S., Kuo, S-Y., O'Keefe, S. L., Beard, K. W., Swindell, S., & Kommor, M. J. (2013). Risk factors for father-daughter incest: Data from an anonymous computerized survey. *Sexual Abuse: A Journal of Research and Treatment, 25,* 583–605.

Suarez, E., & Gadalla, T. M. (2010). Stop blaming the victim: A meta-analysis on rape myths. *Journal of Interpersonal Violence, 25,* 2010–2035.

Substance Abuse and Mental Health Services Administration (SAMHSA). (2005, September). *2004 National Survey on Drug Abuse and Mental Health.* Rockville, MD: U.S. Department of Health and Human Services, Author.

Substance Abuse and Mental Health Services Administration (SAMHSA). (2009, April). *Nonmedical use of Adderall® among full-time college students.* Rockville, MD: U.S. Department of Health and Human Services, Author.

Substance Abuse and Mental Health Services Administration (SAMHSA). (2011, September). *Results from the 2010 National Survey of Drug Use and Health: Summary of national findings.* Rockville, MD: U.S. Department of Health and Human Services, Author.

Substance Abuse and Mental Health Services Administration (SAMHSA). (2014, September). *Results from the 2013 National Survey of Drug Use and Health: Summary of national findings.* Rockville, MD: U.S. Department of Health and Human Services, Author.

Sunstein, C. R. (2008). Adolescent risk-taking and social meaning: A commentary. *Developmental Review, 28,* 145–152.

Surette, R. (1999). *Media, crime, and criminal justice* (2nd ed.). Belmont, CA: West/Wadsworth.

Surette, R. (2014). Estimating the prevalence of copycat crime: A research note. *Criminal Justice Policy Review, 25,* 703–718.

Surette, R., & Maze, A. (2015). Video game play and copycat crime: An exploratory analysis of an inmate population. *Psychology of Popular Media Culture, 4,* 360–374.

Sutherland, E. H. (1947). *Principles of criminology* (4th ed.). Philadelphia: Lippincott.

Sutherland, E. H. (1949). *White-collar crime.* New York: Holt, Rinehart & Winston.

Sutherland, E. H. (1983). *White-collar crime: The uncut version.* New Haven, CT: Yale University Press.

Sutherland, E. H., & Cressey, D. R. (1974). *Criminology* (9th ed.). Philadelphia: Lippincott.

Sutherland, E. H., & Cressey, D. R. (1978). *Criminology* (10th ed.). Philadelphia: Lippincott.

Sutherland, E. H., Cressey, D. R., & Luckenbill, D. F. (1992). *Principles of criminology* (11th ed.). Dix Hills, NY: General Hall.

Sutker, P. B., Uddo-Crane, M., & Allain, A. N. (1991). Clinical and research assessment of posttraumatic stress disorder: A conceptual overview. *Psychological Assessment: A Journal of Consulting and Clinical Psychology, 3,* 520–530.

Sutton, R. M., & Douglas, K. M. (2005). Justice for all, or all for me? More evidence of the importance of the self-other distinction in just-world beliefs. *Personality and Individual Differences, 39,* 637–645.

Sutton, S. K., Vitale, J. E., & Newman, J. P. (2002). Emotion among women with psychopathy during picture perception. *Journal of Abnormal Psychology, 111,* 610–619.

Suzuki, L. A., Naqvi, S., & Hill, J. S. (2014). Assessing intelligence in a cultural context. In F. Leong, L.

Comas-Diaz, G. Nagayama Hall, V. C. McLoyd, & J. Trimble (Eds.,), *APA handbook of multicultural psychology: Vol. 1. Theory and research* (pp. 247–266). Washington, DC: American Psychological Association.

Swahn, M. H., & Donovan, J. E. (2004). Correlates and predictors of violent behavior among adolescent drinkers. *Journal of Adolescent Health, 34,* 480–492.

Swartout, K., Koss, M., Bellis, A., Thompson, M., White, J., & Abbey, A. (2014). Trajectories of sexual assault by college men: A test of the serial rapist hypothesis. *21st International Society for Research on Aggression World Meeting*, July 15–19, Atlanta, Georgia.

Swartout, K. M., Koss, M. P., & Su, N. (in press). What is the best way to analyze less frequent forms of violence? The case of sexual aggression. *Psychology of Violence.*

Sykes, G. M. (1956). *Crime and society.* New York: Random House.

Sykes, G. M., & Matza, D. (1957). Techniques of neutralization: A theory of delinquency. *American Sociological Review, 22,* 664–670.

Syngelaki, E. M., Moore, S. C., Savage, J. C., Fairchild, G. E., & Van Goozen, S. H. M. (2009). Executive functioning and risky decision making in young male offenders. *Criminal Justice and Behavior, 36,* 1213–1227.

Szasz, T. S. (1961). The use of naming and the origin of the myth of mental illness. *American Psychologist, 16,* 59–65.

Szasz, T. S. (1970). *Ideology and insanity: Essays on the psychiatric dehumanization of man.* Oxford, England: Doubleday.

Taft, C. T., Watkins, L. E., Stafford, J., Street, A. E., & Monson, C. M. (2011). Posttraumatic stress disorder and intimate relationship problems: A meta-analysis. *Journal of Consulting and Clinical Psychology, 79,* 22–33.

Tappan, P. W. (1947). Who is the criminal? *American Sociological Review, 12,* 100–110.

Tark, J., & Kleck, G. (2014). Resisting rape: The effects of victim self-protection on rape completion and injury. *Violence Against Women, 20,* 270–292.

Tarolla, S. M., Wagner, E. F., Rabinowitz, J., & Tubman, J. G. (2002). Understanding and treating juvenile offenders: A review of current knowledge and future directions. *Aggression and Violent Behavior, 7,* 125–143.

Task Force on Trafficking of Women and Girls. (2014). *Report of the Task Force on Trafficking of Women and Girls.* Washington, DC: American Psychological Association.

Taylor, J., Iacono, W. G., & McGue, M. (2000). Evidence for a genetic etiology of early-onset delinquency. *Journal of Abnormal Psychology, 109,* 634–643.

Taylor, P. J., Leese, M., Williams, D., Butwell, M., Daly, R., & Larkin, E. (1998). Mental disorder and violence: A special (high security) hospital study. *British Journal of Psychiatry, 172,* 477–484.

Taylor, D. M., & Louis, W. (2004). Terrorism and the quest for identity. In F. M. Moghaddam & A. J. Marsella (Eds.), *Understanding terrorism: Psychosocial roots, consequences, and interventions* (pp. 169–186). Washington, DC: American Psychological Association.

Taylor, B. G., & Mumford, E. (in press). A national descriptive portrait of adolescent relationship abuse: Results from the National Survey on Teen Relationships and Intimate Violence. *Journal of Interpersonal Violence.*

Taylor, M., & Nee, C. (1988). The role of cues in simulated residential burglary. *British Journal of Criminology, 28,* 396–401.

Taylor, P. J., Snook, B., Bennell, C., & Porter, L. (2015). Investigative psychology. In B. L. Cutler, & P. A. Zapf (Eds.), *APA handbook of forensic psychology: Vol. 2. Criminal investigation, adjudication, and sentencing outcomes* (pp. 165–186). Washington, DC: American Psychological Association.

Tedeschi, R. G., & Kilmer, R. P. (2005). Assessing strengths, resilience, and growth to guide clinical interventions. *Professional Psychology: Research and Practice, 36,* 230–237.

Tener, D., & Murphy, S. (2015). Adult disclosure of child sexual abuse: A literature review. *Trauma, Violence, Abuse, 16,* 391–400.

Tengström, A., Hodgins, S., Grann, M., Långström, N., & Kullgren, G. (2004). Schizophrenia and criminal offending: The role of psychopathy and substance use disorders. *Criminal Justice and Behavior, 31,* 367–391.

Teplin, L. (1984). Criminalizing mental disorder. *American Psychologist, 39,* 794–803.

Teplin, L. (2000, October). Psychiatric disorders in youthful offenders. *National Institute of Justice Journal,* 30–32.

Terrorism Research Center. (1997). *The basics: Combating terrorism.* Alexandria, VA: Author.

Terry, K. J. (2008). Stained glass: The nature and scope of child sexual abuse in the Catholic church. *Criminal Justice and Behavior, 35,* 549–569.

Terry, K. J., & Tallon, J. (2004). *Child sexual abuse.* New York: John Jay College Research Team, John Jay College of Criminal Justice.

Testa, M., Hoffman, J. H., & Livingston, J. A. (2010). Alcohol and sexual risk behaviors as mediators of the sexual victimization-revictimization relationship, *Journal of Consulting and Clinical Psychology, 78,* 249–259.

Testa, M., VanZile-Tamsen, C., & Livingston, J. A. (2007). Prospective prediction of women's sexual victimization by intimate and nonintimate male perpetrators. *Journal of Consulting and Clinical Psychology, 75,* 52–60.

Tew, J., & Nixon, J. (2010). Parent abuse: Opening up a discussion of a complex instance of family power relations. *Social Policy and Society, 9,* 579–589.

Thakker, J., Collie, R. M., Gannon, T., & Ward, T. (2008). Rape: Assessment and treatment. In D. R. Laws & W. T. O'Donohue (Eds.), *Sexual deviance: Theory, assessment, and treatment* (pp. 356–383). New York: Guilford.

Tharp, A. T., DeGue, S., Valle, L. A., Brookmeyer, K. A., Massetti, G. M., & Jatjasko, J. L. (2013). A systematic qualitative review of risk and protective factors for sexual violence perpetration. *Trauma, Violence, & Abuse, 14,* 133–167.

Thomas, A., & Chess, S. (1977). *Temperament and development.* New York: Brunner/Mazel.

Thompson, H. A. (2014). *Empire state disgrace: The dark, secret history of the Attica prison tragedy.* Salon.com, posted online May 25, 2014.

Thompson, R. A., & Nelson, C. A. (2001). Developmental science and the media: Early brain development. *American Psychologist, 56,* 5–15.

Thornberry, T. P., & Burch, J. H. H. (1997). *Gang membership and delinquent behavior.* Washington, DC: U.S. Department of Justice, Office of Juvenile Justice and Delinquency Prevention.

Thornberry, T. P., Huizinga, D., & Loeber, R. (1995). The prevention of serious delinquency and violence: Implication from the program of research on the causes and correlates of delinquency. In J. C. Howell, B. Krisberg, J. D. Hawkins, & J. Wilson (Eds.), *Sourcebook on serious violent and chronic juvenile offenders.* Thousand Oaks, CA: Sage.

Thornberry, T. P., & Krohn, M. D. (2005). Applying interactional theory to the explanation of continuity and change in antisocial behavior. In D. P. Farrington (Ed.), *Integrated developmental and life-course theories of offending.* New Brunswick, NJ: Transaction.

Tighe, A., Pistrang, N., Casdagli, L., Baruch, G., & Butler, S. (2012). Multisystemic therapy for young offenders: Families' experiences of therapeutic processes and outcomes. *Journal of Family Psychology, 26,* 187–197.

Tilton-Weaver, L., Burk, W. J., & Kerr, M., & Stattin, H. (2013). Can parental monitoring and peer management reduce the selection or influence of delinquent peers? Testing the question using a dynamic social network approach. *Developmental Psychology, 49,* 2057–2070.

Timmons-Mitchell, J., Bender, M. B., Kishna, M. A., & Mitchell, C. C. (2006). An independent effectiveness trial of multisystemic therapy with juvenile justice youth. *Journal of Clinical Child and Adolescent Psychology, 35,* 227–236.

Tinklenberg, J. R., & Stillman, R. C. (1970). Drug use and violence. In D. Daniels, M. Gilula, & F. Ochberg (Eds.), *Violence and the struggle for existence.* Boston: Little, Brown.

Tinklenberg, J. R., & Woodrow, K. M. (1974). Drug use among youthful assaultive and sexual offenders. In S. H. Frazier (Ed.), *Aggression.* Baltimore, MD: Williams & Wilkins.

Tinney, G., & Gerlock, A. A. (2014). Intimate partner violence, military personnel, veterans, and their families. *Family Court Review, 52,* 400–416.

Tittle, C. R. (1980). *Sanctions and social deviance: The question of deterrence.* New York: Praeger.

Tjaden, P. (1997, November). *The crime of stalking: How big is the problem?* NIJ Research Preview. Washington, DC: U.S. Department of Justice.

Tjaden, P., & Thoennes, N. (1997). *Stalking in America: Findings from the National Violence Against Women Survey.* Denver, CO: Center for Policy Research.

Tjaden, P., & Thoennes, N. (1998a). *Stalking in America: Findings from the National Violence Against Women Survey.* Washington, DC: U.S. Department of Justice.

Tjaden, P., & Thoennes, N. (2000, November). *Full report of prevalence, incidence, and consequences of violence against women: Findings from National Violence against Women Survey.* Washington, DC: National Institute of Justice.

Tjaden, P., & Thoennes, N. (2006, January). *Extent, nature, and consequences of rape victimization: Findings from the National Violence Against Women Survey.* Washington, DC: U.S. Department of Justice.

Toch, H. (2008). (Ed.), Special issue: The disturbed offender in confinement. *Criminal Justice and Behavior, 35.*

Tolan, P. H., Gorman-Smith, D., & Henry, D. B. (2003). On developmental ecology of urban males' youth violence. *Developmental Psychology, 39,* 274–279.

Tolan, P. H., & Thomas, P. (1995). The implications of age of onset for delinquency II: Longitudinal data. *Journal of Abnormal Child Psychology, 23,* 157–169.

Tomarken, A. J., Davidson, R. J., Wheeler, R. E., & Doss, R. C. (1992). Individual differences in anterior brain asymmetry and fundamental dimensions of emotion. *Journal of Personality and Social Psychology, 62,* 676–687.

Tonglet, M. (2001). Consumer misbehaviour: An exploratory study of shoplifting. *Journal of Consumer Behaviour, 1,* 336–354.

Topalli, V., Jacques, J., & Wright, R. (2015). "It takes skills to take a car": Perceptual and procedural expertise in carjacking. *Aggression and Violent Behavior, 20,* 19–25.

Torres, A. N., Boccaccini, M. T., & Miller, H. A. (2006). Perceptions of the validity and utility of criminal profiling among forensic psychologists and psychiatrists. *Professional Psychology: Research and Practice, 37,* 51–58.

Tran, H., & Weinraub, M. (2006). Child care effects in context. Quality, stability, and multiplicity in nonmaternal child care arrangements during the first 15 months of life. *Developmental Psychology, 42,* 566–582.

Tremblay, R. E. (2003). Why socialization fails: The case of chronic physical aggression. In B. B. Lahey, T. W. Moffitt, & A. Caspi (Eds.), *Causes of conduct disorder and juvenile delinquency* (pp. 182–226). New York; Guilford.

Tremblay, R. E., & Craig, W. (1995). Developmental crime prevention. In M. Tonry & D. P. Farrington (Eds.), *Building a safer society: Strategic approaches to crime prevention.* Chicago: University of Chicago Press.

Tremblay, R. E., LeMarquand, D., & Vitaro, F. (1999). The prevention of oppositional defiant disorder and conduct disorder. In H. C. Quay & A. F. Hogan (Eds.), *Handbook of disruptive behavior disorders.* New York: Kluwer Academic/Plenum Publishers.

Tremblay, R. E., Vitaro, F., Gagnon, C., Piche, C., & Royer, N. (1992). A prosocial scale for the Preschool Behaviour Questionnaire: Concurrent and predictive correlates. *International Journal of Behavioral Development, 15,* 227–245.

Trentacosta, C. J., & Shaw, D. S. (2009). Emotional self-regulation, peer rejection, and antisocial behavior: Developmental associations from early childhood to early adolescence. *Journal of Applied Developmental Psychology, 30,* 356–365.

Troup-Leasure, K., & Synder, H. N. (2005, August). *Statutory rape known to law enforcement.* Washington, DC: U.S. Department of Justice, Office of Juvenile Justice and Delinquency Prevention.

Trouton, A., Spinath, F. M., & Plomin, R. (2002). Twins Early Development Study (TEDS): A multivariate, longitudinal genetic investigation of language, cognition and behavior problems in childhood. *Twin Research, 5,* 444–448.

Truman, J. L. (2011, September). *National Crime Victimization Survey: Criminal Victimization, 2010.* Washington, DC: U.S. Department of Justice, Bureau of Justice Statistics.

Truman, J. L., & Langton, L. (2014). *Criminal victimization, 2013.* Washington, DC: U. S. Department of Justice, Bureau of Justice Statistics.

Tsang, J. (2002). Moral rationalization and the integration of situational factors and psychological processes in immoral behavior. *Review of General Psychology, 6,* 25–50.

Tucker, C. J., Finkelhor, D., Turner, H., & Shattuck, A. M. (2013). Association of sibling aggression with child and adolescent mental health. *Pediatrics, 132,* 79–84.

Tucker, C. J., Finkelhor, D., Turner, H., & Shattuck, A. M. (2014). Family dynamics and young children's sibling victimization. *Journal of Family Psychology, 28*, 625–633.

Tucker, D. M. (1981). Lateral brain function, emotion and conceptualization. *Psychological Bulletin, 89*, 19–46.

Tucker, H. S. (2002). Some seek attention by making pets sick. *Archives of Disease in Childhood, 87*, 263.

Turchik, J. A., & Edwards, K. M. (2011). Myths about male rape: A literature review. *Psychology of Men & Masculinity, 12*, 1–16.

Turrell, S. C. (2000). A descriptive analysis of same-sex relationship violence for a diverse sample. *Journal of Family Violence, 15*, 281–293.

Turvey, B. E. (2008). *Criminal profiling: An introduction to behavioral evidence analysis* (3rd ed.). San Diego, CA: Elsevier.

Turvey, B. E. (2012). *Criminal profiling: An introduction to behavioral evidence analysis* (4th ed.). San Diego, CA: Elsevier.

Tuvblad, C., Eley, T. C., & Lichtenstein, P. (2005). The development of antisocial behaviour from childhood to adolescence: A longitudinal twin study. *European Child and Adolescent Psychiatry, 14*, 216–225.

Ullman, S. E. (1999). Social support and recovery from sexual assault: A review. *Aggression and Violent Behavior: A Review Journal, 4*, 343–358.

Ullman, S. E. (2003). Social reactions to child sexual abuse disclosures: A critical review. *Journal of Child Sexual Abuse, 12*, 89–121.

Ullman, S. E. (2007). A 10-year update of "Review and critique of empirical studies of rape avoidance." *Criminal Justice and Behavior, 34*, 411–429.

Ullman, S. E., & Najdowski, C. J. (2011). Vulnerability and protective factors for sexual assault. In J. W. White, M. R. Koss, & A. F. Kazdin (Eds.), *Violence against women and children: Vol. 1. Mapping the terrain* (pp. 151–163). Washington, DC: American Psychological Association.

Ullman, A., & Straus, M. A. (2003). Violence by children against mothers in relation to violence between parents and corporal by parents. *Journal of Comparative Family Studies, 34*, 41–64.

Ullrich, S., Farrington, D. P., & Coid, J. W. (2008). Psychopathic personality traits and life-success. *Personality and Individual Differences, 44*, 1162–1171.

Underwood, R. C., & Patch, P. C. (1999). Siblicide: A descriptive analysis of sibling homicide. *Homicide Studies, 3*, 333–348.

UNFPA. (2009). *Programming to address violence against women: 8 case studies*. New York: Author.

University of Iowa Injury Prevention Research Center. (2001). *Workplace violence: A report to the nation*. Iowa City: Author.

U.S. Attorney's Office. (2015). Member of hacking group sentenced to three years in prison for intrusions into corporate and governmental computer systems. Accessed 4/21/15. Available: www.fbi.gov/losangeles/press-releases/2015.

U.S. Bomb Data Center. (2008). *Fact sheet*. Washington, DC: Bureau of Alcohol, Tobacco, Firearms, and Explosives.

U.S. Bureau of Labor Statistics. (2014, September). *Census of fatal occupational injuries summary, 2013*. Washington, DC: Author.

U.S. Bureau of the Census. (2014, August). *Child care: An important part of American life*. Washington, DC: U.S. Department of Commerce, Bureau of Census.

U.S. Department of Defense. (2009, March). *Report on sexual assault in the military, FY 2009*. Washington, DC: U.S. Department of Defense, Sexual Assault and Response Office.

U.S. Department of Defense SAPR. (2015, May). *The fiscal year 2014 annual report on sexual assault in the military*. Washington, DC: Department of Defense, Sexual Assault Prevention and Response.

U.S. Department of Health and Human Services. (2013). *SAMSHA: 2013 Behavioral Health Barometer*. Center for Behavioral Health Statistics and Quality.

U.S. Department of Health & Human Services. (2015). *Child maltreatment 2013*. Washington, DC: Administration for Children and Families, Administration on Children, Youth and Families, Children's Bureau.

U.S. Department of Justice. (1988). *Report to the nation on crime and justice: The data* (2nd ed.). Washington, DC: USGPO.

U.S. Department of Justice. (1999). *Cyberstalking: A new challenge for law enforcement and industry*. Washington, DC: Author. Available: www.usdoj.gov/criminal/cybercrime/cyberstalking.htm.

U.S. Department of Justice. (2000a). *Terrorism in the United States–1998.* Washington, DC: Author.

U.S. Department of Justice. (2002a, October). *Highlights from the NISMART Bulletin.* Washington, DC: U.S. Department of Justice, Office of Juvenile Justice and Delinquency Prevention.

U.S. Drug Enforcement Administration. (2009, March). "Spice" – plant material(s) laced with synthetic cannabinoids or cannabinoid mimicking compounds. *Microgram Bulletin.* Washington, DC: Author.

U.S. Fire Administration. (2004). *Arson and juveniles: Responding to the violence.* Washington, DC: Federal Emergency Management Agency, National Fire Data Center.

U.S. Fire Administration. (2009, November). Intentionally set fire. *Topical Fire Report Series, 9*(5), 1–8.

U.S. Fire Administration. (2011, March 11). *USFA announces the 2011 arson awareness week theme.* Emmitsburg, MD: Author.

Vachon, D. D., Lynam, D. R., & Johnson, J. A. (2014). The (non)relation between empathy and aggression: Surprising results from a meta-analysis. *Psychological Bulletin, 140*, 751–773.

Vachon, D. D., Lynam, D. R., Loeber, R., & Stouthamer-Loeber, M. (2012). Generalizing the nomological network of psychopathy across populations differing on race and conviction status. *Journal of Abnormal Psychology, 121*, 263–269.

Valenstein, E. S. (1973). *Brain control.* New York: Wiley.

van Beijsterveldt, C. E. M., Bartels, M., Hudziak, J. J., & Boomsma, D. I. (2003). Causes of stability of aggression from early childhood to adolescence: A longitudinal genetic analysis in Dutch twins. *Behavior Genetics, 33*, 591–605.

van Bommel, M., van Prooijen, J., Elffers, H., & van Lange, P. A. M. (2014). Intervene to be seen: The power of a camera in attenuating the bystander effect. *Social Psychological and Personality Science, 5*, 459–466.

Vandebosch, H., & Van Cleemput, K. (2008). Defining cyberbullying: A qualitative research into the perceptions of youngsters. *Cyberpsychology & Behavior, 11*, 499–503.

Vandell, D. L., & Posner, J. K. (1999). Conceptualization and measurement of children's after-school environments. In S. L. Freidman & T.

D. Wachs (Eds.), *Measuring environment across the life-span: Emerging methods and concepts.* Washington, DC: American Psychological Association.

VandenBos, G. R. (Ed.). (2007). *APA dictionary of psychology.* Washington, DC: American Psychological Association.

Vandiver, D. M. (2006). Female sex offenders: A comparison of solo offenders and co-offenders. *Violence and Victims, 21*, 339–354.

Vandiver, D. M., & Kercher, G. (2004). Offender and victim characteristics of registered female sexual offenders in Texas: A proposed typology of female sexual offenders. *Sexual Abuse: A Journal of Research and Treatment, 16*, 121–137.

Vandiver, D. M., & Walker, J. T. (2002). Female sex offenders: An overview and analysis of 40 cases. *Criminal Justice Review, 27*, 284–300.

van Langen, M. A. M., Wissink, I. B., van Vugt, E. S., Van der Stouwe, T., & Stams, G. J. J. M. (2014). The relation between empathy and offending: A meta-analysis. *Aggression and Violent Behavior, 19*, 179–189.

van Lier, P. A. C., Vuijk, P., & Crijen, A. M. (2005). Understanding mechanisms of change in the development of antisocial behavior: The impact of a universal intervention. *Journal of Abnormal Psychology, 33*, 521–533.

van Lier, P. A. C., Wanner, B., & Vitaro, F. (2007). Onset of antisocial behavior affiliation with deviant friends and childhood maladjustment: A text of the childhood- and adolescent-onset models. *Development and Psychopathology, 19*, 167–185.

Van Wijk, A., van Horn, J., Bullens, R., Bijleveld, C., & Doreleijers, T. (2005). Juvenile sex offenders: A group on its own? *International Journal of Offender Therapy and Comparative Criminology, 49*, 25–36.

Van Vugt, E., Gibbs, J., Stams, G. J., Bijleveld, C., Hendricks, J., & Van der Laan, P. (2011). Moral development and recidivism: A meta-analysis. *International Journal of Offender Therapy and Comparative Criminology, 55*, 1234–1250.

Vaughn, M. G., DeLisi, M., Beaver, K. M., & Howard, M. O. (2008). Toward a quantitative typology of burglars: A latent profile analysis of career offenders. *Journal of Forensic Sciences, 53*, 1387–1392.

Vaughn, M. G., DeLisi, M., Beaver, K. M., & Wright, J. P. (2009). DAT1 and 5HTT are associated with pathological criminal behavior in a nationally representative sample of youth. *Criminal Justice and Behavior, 36*, 1113–1124.

Vaughn, M. G., Fu, Q., DeLisi, M., Wright, J. P., Beaver, K. M., Perron, B. E., & Howard, M. O. (2010a). Prevalence and correlates of fire-setting in the United States: Results from the National Epidemiological Survey on Alcohol and Related Conditions. *Comprehensive Psychiatry, 51*, 217–233.

Vaughn, M. G., Fu, Q., Perron, B. E., Bohnert, A. S. B., & Howard, M. O. (2010b). Is crack cocaine use associated with greater violence than powdered cocaine use? Results from a national sample. *American Journal of Drug and Alcohol Abuse, 36*, 181–186.

Veenstra, R., Lindenberg, S., Oldehinkel, A. J., De Winter, A. F., & Ormel, J. (2006). Temperament, environment, and antisocial behavior in a population sample of preadolescent boys and girls. *International Journal of Behavioral Development, 30*, 422–432.

Vega, V., & Malamuth, N. M. (2007). Predicting sexual aggression: The role of pornography in the context of general and specific risk factors. *Aggressive Behavior, 33*, 104–117.

Venables, N. C., Hall, J. R., Yancey, J. R., & Patrick, C. J. (2015). Factors of psychopathy and electrocortical response to emotional pictures: Further evidence for a two-process theory. *Journal of Abnormal Psychology, 124*, 319–328.

Venables, N. C., & Patrick, C. J. (2014). Reconciling discrepant findings for P3 brain response in criminal psychopathy through reference to the concept of externalizing proneness. *Psychophysiology, 51*, 427–436.

Veneziano, C., & Veneziano, L. (2002). Adolescent sex offenders: A review of the literature. *Trauma, Violence, & Abuse, 3*, 247–260.

Verlinden, S., Hersen, M., & Thomas, J. (2000). Risk factors in school shootings. *Clinical Psychology Review, 20*, 3–56.

Verona, E., Joiner, T. E., Johnson, F., & Bender, T. W. (2006). Gender specific gene-environment interactions on laboratory-assessed aggression. *Biological Psychology, 71*, 33–41.

Verona, E., Patrick, C. J., & Joiner, T. E. (2001). Psychopathy, antisocial personality, and suicide risk. *Journal of Abnormal Psychology, 110*, 462–470.

Vespa, J., Lewis, J. M., & Kreider, R. M. (2013, August). *America's families and living arrangements: 2012*. Washington, DC: U.S. Census Bureau.

Vetter, H. J., & Silverman, I. J. (1978). *The nature of crime*. Philadelphia, PA: W. B. Saunders.

Victoroff, J. (2005). The mind of the terrorist: A review and critique of psychological approaches. *Journal of Conflict Resolution, 49*, 3–42.

Viding, E., Blair, R., James, R., Moffitt, T. E., & Plomin, R. (2005). Evidence for substantial genetic risk for psychopathy in 7-year-olds. *Journal of Child Psychology and Psychiatry, 46*, 592–597.

Viding, E., & Larsson, H. (2010). Genetics of child and adolescent psychopathy. In R. T. Salekin & D. R. Lynam (Eds.), *Handbook of child and adolescent psychopathy* (pp. 113–134). New York: Guilford Press.

Vien, A., & Beech, A. R. (2006). Psychopathy: Theory, measurement, and treatment. *Trauma, Violence, & Abuse, 7*, 155–174.

Vieraitis, L. M., & Shuryadi, A. (2014). Identity theft. In M. Tonry (Ed.), *Oxford handbooks online*. New York: Oxford University Press.

Vieraitis, L. M., Copes, H., Powell, Z. A., & Pike, A. (2015). A little information goes a long way: Expertise and identity theft. *Aggression and Violent Behavior, 20*, 10–18.

Viljoen, J. L., & Grisso, T. (2007). Prospects for remediating juveniles' adjudicative incompetence. *Psychology, Public Policy, and Law, 13*, 87–114.

Viljoen, J. L., MacDougall, E. A. M., Gagnon, N. C., & Douglas, K. S. (2010). Psychopathy evidence in legal proceedings involving adolescent offenders. *Psychology, Public Policy, and Law, 16*, 254–283.

Viljoen, J. L., McLachlan, K., Wingrove, T., & Penner, E. (2010). Defense attorneys' concerns about the competence of adolescent defendants. *Behavioral Sciences & the Law, 28*, 630–646.

Viljoen, J. L., O'Neill, M. L., & Sidhu, A. (2005). Bullying behaviors in female and male adolescent offenders: Prevalence, types, and association with psychosocial adjustment. *Aggressive Behavior, 31*, 521–536.

Viljoen, J. L., & Wingrove, T. (2007). Adjudicative competence in adolescent defendants: Judges' and defense attorneys' views of legal standards for adolescents in juvenile and criminal court. *Psychology, Public Policy, and Law, 13*, 204–229.

Vincent, G. (2006). Psychopathy and violence risk assessment in youth. *Child and Adolescent Psychiatric Clinics of North America, 15*, 407–428.

Vincent, G. M., Guy, L. S., & Grisso, T. (2012). *Risk assessment in juvenile justice: A guidebook for implementation*. Chicago: MacArthur Foundation.

Vincent, G. M., Odgers, C. L., McCormick, A. V., & Corrado, R. R. (2008). The PCL:YV and recidivism in male and female juveniles: A follow-up into young adulthood. *International Journal of Law and Psychiatry, 31*, 287–296.

Vitacco, M. J., Erickson, S. K., Kurus, S., & Apple, B. N. (2012). The role of the Violence Risk Appraisal Guide and Historical, Clinical, Risk-20 in U.S. courts: A case law survey. *Psychology, Public Policy, and Law, 18*, 361–391.

Vitacco, M. J., Neumann, C. S., & Jackson, R. L. (2005). Testing a four-factor model of psychopathy and its association with ethnicity, gender, intelligence, and violence. *Journal of Consulting and Clinical Psychology, 73*, 466–476.

Vitacco, M. J., Van Rybroek, G. J., Rogstad, J. E., Erickson, S. K., Tripp, A., Harris, L., et al. (2008). Developing services for insanity acquittees conditionally released into the community: maximizing success and minimizing recidivism. *Psychological Services, 5*, 118–125.

Vitale, J. E., Newman, J. P., Serin, R. C., & Bolt, D. M. (2005). Hostile attributions in incarcerated adult male offenders: An exploration of diverse pathways. *Aggressive Behavior, 31*, 99–115.

Vitale, J. E., Smith, S. S., Brinkley, C. A., & Newman, J. P. (2002). The reliability and validity of the Psychopathy Checklist-Revised in a sample of female offenders. *Criminal Justice and Behavior, 29*, 202–231.

Vitaro, F., & Brendgen, M. (2005). Proactive and reactive aggression: A developmental perspective. In R. E. Tremblay, W. W. Hartrup, & J. Archer (Eds.), *The developmental origins of aggression*. New York: Guilford.

Vitaro, F., Brendgen, M., & Barker, E. D. (2006). Subtypes of aggressive behaviors: A developmental perspective. *International Journal of Behavioral Development, 30*, 12–19.

Vitaro, F., & Tremblay, R. P. (1994). Impact of a prevention program on aggressive children's friendships and social adjustment. *Journal of Abnormal Child Psychology, 22*, 457–476.

Vold, G. B. (1958). *Theoretical criminology*. New York: Oxford University Press.

Vossekuil, B., Fein, R., Reddy, M., Borum, R., & Modzeleski, W. (2002). *The final report and findings of the Safe School Initiative: Implications for the prevention of school attacks in the United States*. Washington, DC: U.S. Secret Service and Department of Education.

Waaktaar, T., Christie, H. J., Borge, A. I. H., & Torgerson, S. (2004). How can young people's resilience be enhanced? Experiences from a clinical intervention project. *Clinical Child Psychology and Psychiatry, 9*, 167–183.

Waber, D. P., Bryce, C. P., Fitzmaurice, G. M., Zichlin, M. L., McGaughy, J., Girard, J. M., & Galler, J. R. (2014). Neuropsychological outcomes at midlife following moderate to severe malnutrition in infancy. *Neuropsychology, 28*, 530–540.

Wachi, T., Watanabe, K., Yokota, K., Suzuki, M., Hoshino, M., Sato, A., et al. (2007). Offender and crime characteristics of female serial arsonists in Japan. *Journal of Investigative Psychology and Offender Profiling, 4*, 29–52.

Wade, M., Browne, D. T., Plamondon, A., Daniel, E., & Jenkins, J. M. (in press). Cumulative risk disparities in children's neurocognitive functioning: A developmental cascade model. *Developmental Science*.

Wagner, D. V., Borduin, C. M., Sawyer, A. M., & Dopp, A. R. (2014). Long-term prevention of criminality in siblings of serious and violent juvenile offenders: A 25-year follow-up to a randomized clinical trial of Multisystemic Therapy. *Journal of Consulting and Clinical Psychology, 82*, 492–499.

Wagner, R. V., & Long, K. R. (2004). Terrorism from a peace psychology perspective. In F. M. Moghaddam & A. J. Marsella (Eds.), *Understanding terrorism: Psychosocial roots, consequences, and interventions* (pp. 207–220). Washington, DC: American Psychological Association.

Waite, D., Keller, A., McGarvey, E. L., Wieckowski, E., Pinkerton, R., & Brown, G. L. (2005). Juvenile sex offender re-arrest rates for sexual, violent nonsexual, and property crimes. *Sexual Abuse: A Journal of Research and Treatment, 17*, 313–331.

Wakschlag, L. S., & Hans, S. L. (2002). Maternal smoking during pregnancy and conduct problems in high-risk youth: A developmental framework. *Development and Psychopathology, 14*, 351–369.

Wald, M. M., Helgeson, S. R., Langlois, J. A. (2008). Traumatic brain injury among prisoners. *Brain Injury Professional, 5*, 22–25.

Waldman, I., & Rhee, H. S. (2006). Genetic and environmental influences on psychopathy and antisocial behavior. In C. J. Patrick (Ed.), *Handbook of psychopathy* (pp. 205–228). New York: Guilford.

Walker, K. L., & Chestnut, D. (2003). The role of ethnocultural variables in response to terrorism. *Cultural Diversity and Ethnic Minority Psychology, 9*, 251–262.

Walker, L. E. (1979). *The battered woman.* New York: Harper Colophon Books.

Walker, S. (2001). *Sense and nonsense about crime and drugs* (5th ed.). Belmont, CA: Wadsworth/Thomson Learning.

Wallace, H. (1996). *Family violence: Legal, medical, and social perspectives.* Boston: Allyn & Bacon.

Wallace, H., & Seymour, A. (2001). Domestic violence. In G. Coleman, M. Gaboury, M. Murray, & A. Seymour (Eds.), *1999 National Victim Assistance Academy.* Washington, DC: U.S. Department of Justice.

Wallerstein, J. S., & Wyle, J. (1947). Our law-abiding law breakers. *Probation, 25*, 107–112.

Walsh, A. (2005). African Americans and serial killing in the media. *Homicide Studies, 9*, 271–291.

Walsh, D. (1980). *Break-ins: Burglary from private homes.* London: Constable.

Walters, G. C., & Grusec, J. E. (1977). *Punishment.* San Francisco: W. H. Freeman.

Walters, G. D. (2003). Predicting institutional adjustment and recidivism with the Psychopathy Checklist factor scores: A meta-analysis. *Law and Human Behavior, 27*, 541–558.

Walters, G. D. (2013). Testing the specificity postulate of the violence graduation hypothesis: Meta-analysis of the animal cruelty-offense relationship. *Aggression and Violent Behavior, 18*, 797–802.

Walters, G. D. (2014). Testing the direct, indirect, and moderated effects of childhood cruelty on future aggressive and non-aggressive offending. *Aggressive Behavior, 40*, 238–249.

Walters, G. D., Deming, A., & Elliott, W. N. (2009). Assessing criminal thinking in male sex offenders with the Psychological Inventory of Criminal Thinking Styles. *Criminal Justice and Behavior, 36*, 1025–1036.

Walters, G. D., & Geyer, M. D. (2004). Criminal thinking and identity in male white-collar offenders. *Criminal Justice and Behavior, 31*, 263–281.

Walters, J. H., Moore, A., Berzofsky, M., & Langton, L. (2013, June). *Household burglary, 1994-2011.* Special Report. U.S. Department of Justice, Office of Justice Programs, Bureau of Justice Statistics.

Walton, J. S., & Chou, S. (2015). The effectiveness of psychological treatment for reducing recidivism of child molesters: A systematic review of randomized and nonrandomized studies. *Trauma, Violence, Abuse, 16*, 401–417.

Ward, T., & Hudson, S. M. (2000). Sexual offenders' implicit planning: A conceptual model. *Sexual Abuse: A Journal of Research and Treatment, 12*, 189–202.

Ward. T., Hudson, S. M., Marshall, W. L., & Siegert, R. (1995). Attachment style and intimacy deficits in sexual offenders: A theoretical framework. *Sexual Abuse: A Journal of Research and Treatment, 7*, 317–335.

Wareham, J., & Dembo, R. (2007). A longitudinal study of psychological functioning among juvenile offenders: A latent growth model. *Criminal Justice and Behavior, 34*, 259–273.

Warren, J. I., Burnette, M. L., South, S. C., Chauhan, P., Bale, R., Friend, R., et al. (2003). Psychopathy in women: Structural modeling and comorbidity. *International Journal of Law and Psychiatry, 26*, 223–242.

Warren, J. I., Rosenfeld, B., Fitch, W. L., & Hawk, G. (1997). Forensic mental health clinical evaluation: An analysis of interstate and intersystemic differences. *Law and Human Behavior, 21*, 377–390.

Wasserman, G. A., & Seracini, A. M. (2001). Family risk factors and interventions. In R. Loeber & D. P. Farrington (Eds.), *Child delinquents: Development, intervention, and service needs* (pp. 165–190). Thousand Oaks, CA: Sage.

Watson, R. I. (1973). Investigation into deindividuation using a cross-cultural survey technique. *Journal of Personality and Social Psychology, 25*, 342–345.

Webb, J. A., Bray, J. H., Getz, J. G., & Adams, G. (2002). Gender, perceived parental monitoring, and behavioral adjustment: Influences on adolescent alcohol use. *American Journal of Orthopsychiatry, 72*, 392–400.

Webster, C. D., Douglas, K. S., Eaves, D., & Hart, S. D. (1997). Assessing risk to violence to others. In C. D. Webster & M. A. Jackson (Eds.), *Impulsivity: Theory, assessment and treatment.* New York: Guilford.

Weiler, B. L., & Widom, C. S. (1996). Psychopathy and violent behaviour in abused and neglected young adults. *Criminal Behaviour and Mental Health, 6*, 253–271.

Weiner, J. B. (2013). The assessment process. In J. R. Graham, J. A. Naglieri, & I. B. Weiner (Eds.), *Handbook of psychology: Vol 10. Assessment psychology* (2nd ed., pp. 3–25). Hoboken, NJ: Wiley.

Weis, J. G. (1989). Family violence methodology and design. In L. Ohlin & M. Tonry (Eds.), *Family violence: Vol. 11.* Chicago: University of Chicago Press.

Weis, J. G., & Sederstrom, J. (1981). *The prevention of serious delinquency. What to do?* Washington, DC: U.S. Department of Justice.

Weisbrot, D. M. (2008). Prelude to school shooting? Assessing threatening behaviors in childhood and adolescence. *Journal of the American Academy of Child & Adolescent Psychiatry, 47*, 847–852.

Weisel, D. L. (2007, March). *Bank robbery.* Washington, DC: U.S. Department of Justice, Office of Community Oriented Policing Services.

West, S. G., Friedman, S. H., & Kim, K. D. (2011). Women accused of sex offenses: A gender–based comparison. *Behavioral Sciences & the Law, 29*, 728–740.

Wheatman, S. R., & Shaffer, D. R. (2001). On finding for defendants who plead insanity: The crucial impact of dispositional instructions and opportunity to deliberate. *Law and Human Behavior, 25*, 167–183.

Wheeler, R. W., Davidson, R. J., & Tomarken, A. J. (1993). Frontal brain asymmetry and emotional reactivity: A biological substrate of affective style. *Psychophysiology, 30*, 82–89.

Wherry, J. N., Bladwin, S., Junco, K., & Floyd, B. (2013). Suicidal thoughts/behaviors in sexually abused children. *Journal of Child Sexual Abuse, 22*, 534–551.

Whitcomb, D. (2001). Child victimization. In G. Coleman, M. Gaboury, M. Murray, & A. Seymour (Eds.), *1999 National Victim Assistance Academy.* Washington, DC: U.S. Department of Justice.

White, J. L., Moffitt, T. E., Earls, F., Robins, L., & Silva, P. A. (1990). How early can we tell? Predictors of childhood conduct disorder and delinquency. *Criminology, 28*, 507–533.

White, J. W., Koss, M. P., & Kazdin, A. E. (Eds.). 2011. *Violence against women and children. Vol 1. Mapping the terrain.* Washington, DC: American Psychological Association.

Whiteman, S. D., Jensen, A. C., & Maggs, J. L. (2014). Similarities and differences in adolescent siblings' alcohol-related attitudes, use, and delinquency: Evidence for convergent and divergent influence processes. *Journal of Youth and Adolescence, 43*, 687–697.

Whitson, M. L., Bernard, S., & Kaufman, J. S. (2013). The effects of cumulative risk and protection on problem behaviors for youth in an urban school-based system of care. *Community Mental Health, 49*, 576–586.

Wicker, T. (1976). *A time to die.* New York: Ballatine.

Widom, C. S. (1978). A methodology for studying non-institutionalized psychopaths. In R. D. Hare & D. Schalling (Eds.), *Psychopathic behavior: Approaches to research.* Chichester, UK: Wiley.

Widom, C. S. (1992, September). The cycle of violence. *Research in Brief.* Washington, DC: U.S. Department of Justice.

Widom, C. S. (2000, January). Childhood victimization: Early adversity, later psychopathology. *National Institute of Justice Journal*, 3–9.

Wiesner, M., Kim, H. K., & Capaldi, D. M. (2005). Developmental trajectories of offending: Validation and prediction to young adult alcohol use, drug use, and depressive symptoms. *Development and Psychopathology, 17*, 251–270.

Wiesner, M., & Windle, M. (2004). Assessing covariates of adolescent delinquency trajectories: A latent growth mixture modeling approach. *Journal of Youth and Adolescence, 33*, 431–432.

Wijkman, M., Bijleveld, C., & Hendriks, J. (2010). Women don't do such things! Characteristics of female sex offender and offender types. *Sexual Abuse: A Journal of Research and Treatment, 22*, 135–156.

Wijkman, M., Bijleveld, C., & Hendriks, J. (2014). Juvenile sex offenders: Offender and offence characteristics. *European Journal of Criminology, 11*, 23–28.

Wike, T. L., & Fraser, M. W. (2009). School shootings: Making sense of the senseless. *Aggression and Violent Behavior, 14*, 162–169.

Wilczynski, A. (1997). Mad or bad? Child-killers, gender, and the courts. *British Journal of Criminology, 37*, 419–436.

Wilkinson, D. L., McBryde, M. S., Williams, B., Bloom, S., & Bell, K. (2009). Peers and gun use among urban adolescent males: An examination of social embeddedness. *Journal of Contemporary Criminal Justice, 25*, 20–44.

Williams, F. P., & McShane, M. D. (2004). *Criminological theory* (4th ed.). Upper Saddle River, NJ: Prentice Hall.

Williams, K. S., & Bierie, D. M. (2015). An incident-based comparison of female and male sexual offenders. *Sexual Abuse: A Journal of Research and Treatment, 27*, 235–257.

Williamson, S., Hare, R. D., & Wong, S. (1987). Violence: Criminal psychopaths and their victims. *Canadian Journal of Behavioral Science, 19*, 454–462.

Willoughby, T., Adachi, P. J. C., & Good, M. (2011, October 31). A longitudinal study of association between violent video game play and aggression among adolescents. *Developmental Psychology*. Advance online publication. DOI: 10.1037/a0026046.

Wilson, B., & Butler, L. D. (2014). Running a gauntlet: A review of victimization and violence in the pre-entry, post-entry, and peri-/post-exit periods of commercial sexual exploitation. *Psychological Trauma: Theory, Research, Practice, and Policy, 6*, 494–504.

Wilson, J. K., Brodsky, S. L., Neal, T. M. S., & Cramer, R. J. (2011). Prosecutor pretrial attitudes and plea-bargaining behavior toward veterans with Posttraumatic Stress Disorder. *Psychological Services, 8*, 319–331.

Wilson, M. (2010, October 6). Shahzad gets life term for Times Square bombing attempt. *The New York Times*, p. A25.

Wilson, R. J. (1999). Emotional congruence in sexual offenders against children. *Sexual Abuse: A Journal of Research and Treatment, 11*, 33–47.

Winsper, C., & Wolke, D. (2014). Infant and toddler crying, sleeping and feeding problems and trajectories of dysregulation behavior across childhood. *Journal of Abnormal and Child Psychology, 42*, 831–843.

Wolak, J., Finkelhour, D., & Mitchell, K. (2005). *Child pornography possessors and the Internet: A national study*. Arlington, VA: National Center for Missing & Exploited Children.

Wolf, B. C., & Lavezzi, W. A. (2007). Paths to destruction: The lives and crimes of two serial killers. *Journal of Forensic Science, 52*, 199–203.

Wolf, R. S. (1992). Victimization of the elderly: Elder abuse and neglect. *Reviews in Clinical Gerontology, 2*, 269–276.

Wolfe, D. A., Jaffe, P. G., Wilson, S. K., & Zak, L. (1985). Children of battered women: The relation of child behavior to family violence and maternal stress. *Journal of Consulting and Clinical Psychology, 53*, 657–665.

Wong, M. T. H., Lumsden, J., Fenton, G. W., & Fenwick, P. B. C. (1994). Epilepsy and violence in mentally abnormal offenders in a maximum security mental hospital. *Journal of Epilepsy, 7*, 253–258.

Wong, S. (2000). Psychopathic offenders. In S. Hodgins & R. Muller-Isberner (Eds.), *Violence, crime and mentally disordered offenders: Concepts and methods for effective treatment and prevention*. New York: Wiley.

Wood, G. (2015, March). What ISIS really wants. *The Atlantic*. Available: http://www.theatlantic.com/features/archive/2015/02what-isis-really-wants/384980.

Wood, J. J., Cowan, P. A., & Baker, B. L. (2002). Behavior problems and peer rejection in preschool boys and girls. *Journal of Genetic Psychology, 163*, 72–89.

Woodworth, M., & Porter, S. (2001). Historical foundations and current applications of criminal profiling in violent crime investigations. *Expert Evidence, 7*, 241–264.

Woodworth, M., & Porter, S. (2002). In cold blood: Characteristics of criminal homicides as a function of psychopathy. *Journal of Abnormal Psychology, 111*, 436–445.

Worling, J. R., & Langton, C. M. (2012). Assessment and treatment of adolescents who sexually offend: Clinical issues and implications for secure settings. *Criminal Justice and Behavior, 39*, 814–841.

Wortley, R., & Smallbone, S. (2006). Applying situational principles to sexual offenses against children. In R. Wortley & S. Smallbone (Eds.), *Crime prevention studies: Vol, 19. Situational prevention of child sexual abuse* (pp. 7–35). Monsey, NY: Criminal Justice Press.

Wortley, R., & Smallbone, S. (2014). A criminal careers typology of child sexual abusers. *Sexual Abuse: A Journal of Research and Treatment, 26,* 569–585.

Wright, J. P., & Boisvert, D. (2009). What biosocial criminology offers criminology. *Criminal Justice and Behavior, 36,* 1228–1240.

Wright, R., Brookman, F., & Bennett, T. (2006). The foreground dynamics of street robbery in Britain. *British Journal of Criminology, 46,* 1–15.

Wright, R. T., & Decker, S. (1997). *Armed robbers in action: Stickup and street culture.* Boston: Northeastern University Press.

Wright, J. P., Dietrick, K. N., Ris, M. D., Hornung, R. W., Wessel, S. D., Lanpher, B. P., et al. (2008). Association of prenatal and childhood blood lead concentrations with criminal arrests in early adulthood. *PLos Medicine, 5,* 732–740.

Wright, J., & Hensley, C. (2003). From animal cruelty to serial murder: Applying the graduation hypothesis. *International Journal of Offender Therapy and Comparative Criminology, 47,* 71–88.

Wright, J. C., Huston, A. C., Vandewater, E. A., Bickman, D. S., Scantlin, R. M., Kotler, J. A., et al. (2001). American children's use of electronic media in 1997: A national survey. *Applied Developmental Psychology, 22,* 31–47.

Wright, E. R., Kooreman, H. E., Greene, M. S., Chambers, R. A., Banerjee, A., & Wilson, J. (2014). The iatrogenic epidemic of prescription drug abuse: County-level determinants of opioid availability and abuse. *Drug and Alcohol Dependence, 138,* 209–215.

Wright, J. D., & Rossi, P. H. (1994). *Armed and considered dangerous: A survey of felons and their firearms.* New York: Aldine De Gruyter.

Wurtele, S. K., Simons, D. A., & Moreno, T. (2014). Sexual interest in children among an online sample of men and women: Prevalence and correlates. *Sexual Abuse: A Journal of Research and Treatment, 26,* 546–568.

Xie, H., Farmer, T. W., & Cairns, B. D. (2003). Different forms of aggression among inner-city African-American Children: Gender, configurations, and school social networks. *Journal of School Psychology, 41,* 355–375.

Yang, Y., Raine, A., Lencz, T., Bihrle, S., LaCasse, L., & Colletti, P. (2005). Volume reduction in prefrontal gray matter in unsuccessful criminal psychopaths. *Biological Psychiatry, 57,* 1103–1108.

Yates, E. (1986). The influence of psychosocial factors on nonsensical shoplifting. *International Journal of Offender Therapy and Comparative Criminology, 30,* 203–211.

Yolton, K., Cornelius, M., Ornoy, A., McGough, J., Makris, S., & Schantz, S. (2014). Exposure to neurotoxicants and the development of attention deficit hyperactivity disorder and its related behaviors in childhood. *Neurotoxicology and Teratology, 44,* 30–45.

Yoshikawa, H., Aber, J. L., & Beardslee, W. R. (2012). The effects of poverty on the mental, emotional, and behavioral health of children and youth: Implications for prevention. *American Psychologist, 67,* 272–284.

Young, S., Fox, N. A., & Zahn-Waxler, C. (1999). Relations between temperament and empathy. *Developmental Psychology, 35,* 1189–1197.

Youstin, T. J., Nobles, M. R., Ward, J. T., & Cook, C. L. (2011). Assessing the generalizability of the near repeat phenomenon. *Criminal Justice and Behavior, 38,* 1042–1063.

Yung, C. R. (2015). Concealing campus sexual assault: An empirical examination. *Psychology, Public Policy, and Law, 21,* 1–9.

Zahn, M. A., Agnew, R., Fishbein, D., Miller, S., Winn, D., Dakoff, G., et al. (2010). *Causes and correlates of girls' delinquency.* Washington, DC: Office of Juvenile Justice and Delinquency Prevention.

Zahn, M. A., Brumbaugh, S., Steffensmeier, D., Feld, B. C. Morash, M., Chesney-Lind, M., et al. (2008, May). *Violence by teenage girls: Trends and context.* Washington, DC: U.S. Department of Justice, Office of Juvenile Justice and Delinquency Prevention.

Zahn, M. A., Day, J. C., Mihalic, S. F., & Tichavsky, L. (2009). Determining what works for girls in the juvenile justice system: A summary of evaluation evidence. *Crime & Delinquency, 55,* 266–293.

Zahn, M. A., Hawkins, S. R., Chiancone, J., & Whitworth, A. (2008, October). *The Girls Study Group—Charting the way to delinquency prevention for girls.* Washington, DC: U.S.

Department of Justice, Office of Juvenile Justice and Delinquency Prevention.

Zakireh, B., Ronis, S. T., & Knight, R. A. (2008). Individual beliefs, attitudes, and victimization histories of male juvenile sexual offenders. *Sexual Abuse: Journal of Research and Treatment, 20*, 323–351.

Zapf, P. A., Golding, S. L. & Roesch, R. (2006). Criminal responsibility and the insanity defense. In I. B. Weiner & A. K. Hess (Eds.), *The handbook of forensic psychology* (3rd ed., pp. 332–363). Hoboken, NJ: Wiley.

Zgoba, K. M., Miner, M., Levenson, J., Knight, R., Letourneau, E., & Thornton, R. (in press). The Adam Walsh Act: An examination of sex offender risk classification systems. *Sexual Abuse: A Journal of Research and Treatment.*

Zigler, E., Taussig, C., & Black, K. (1992). Early childhood intervention: A promising prevention for juvenile delinquency. *American Psychologist, 47*, 997–1006.

Zillmann, D. (1971). Excitation transfer in communication-mediated aggressive behavior. *Journal of Experimental Social Psychology, 7*, 419–434.

Zillmann, D. (1979). *Hostility and aggression.* Hillsdale, NJ: Erlbaum.

Zillmann, D. (1983). Arousal and aggression. In R. G. Geen & E. I. Donnerstein (Eds.), *Aggression: Theoretical and empirical reviews: Vol. 1.* New York: Academic Press.

Zillmann, D. (1988). Cognitive-excitation interdependencies in aggressive behavior. *Aggressive Behavior, 14*, 51–64.

Zimbardo, P. G. (1970). The human choice. Individuation, reason, and order versus deindividuation, impulse, and chaos. In W. J. Arnold & D. Levine (Eds.), *Nebraska symposium on motivation 1969.* Lincoln, NE: University of Nebraska Press.

Zimbardo, P. G. (1973). The psychological power and pathology of imprisonment. In E. Aronson & R. Helmreich (Eds.), *Social psychology.* New York: Van Nostrand.

Zimbardo, P. G. (2007). Thoughts on psychologists, ethics, and the use of torture in interrogations: Don't ignore varying roles and complexities. *Analyses of Social Issues and Public Policy, 7*, 65–73.

Zimmermann, P., & Iwanski, A. (2014). Emotion regulation from early adolescence to emerging adulthood and middle adulthood: Age differences, gender differences, and emotion-specific developmental variations. *International Journal of Behavior Development, 38*, 182–194.

Zipper, P., & Wilcox, D. K. (2005, April). The importance of early intervention. *FBI Law Enforcement Bulletin, 74*, 3–9.

Zucker, R. A., Fitzgerald, H. E., Refior, S. K., Puttler, L. I., Pallas, D. M., & Ellis, D. A. (2000). The clinical and social ecology of childhood for children of alcoholics: Description of a study and implications for a differentiated social policy. In H. E. Fitzgerald, B. M. Lester, & B. S. Zuckerman (Eds.), *Children of addiction: Research, health, and public policy issues.* New York: RoutledgeFalmer.

AUTHOR INDEX

Colwell, L. H., 187, 194
Colwell, M. J., 37
Comer, R. J., 235
Commons, M. L., 335
Conc, L. T., 148
Conklin, J. E., 431
Connolly, J. F., 200
Connor, D. F., 53, 54
Connor, P. D., 70
Conoscenti, L. M., 353
Constantine, R. J., 237, 239
Cook, C. L., 412
Cook, K., 107, 263
Cook, P. J., 255
Cooke, D. J., 189, 190, 191, 193, 207
Cooksey, R. W., 295
Cooper, A., 247, 252, 253, 276
Copeland, J., 493
Copes, H., 416, 418, 420
Cormier, C. A., 208
Cormier, C., 183
Cornelius, M., 71
Cornelius, T. L., 78
Cornell, D. G., 196, 197, 259
Cornish, D. B., 368
Corrado, R. R., 197, 198
Cortoni, F., 381
Coscina, D. V., 80
COT, 336, 339, 340
Côté, S., 155, 156
Courtney, E., 278
Couture-Carron, A., 263
Cowan, C. P., 34
Cowan, P. A., 34, 132
Cowden, J., 66
Cowley, G., 52
Cox, D. N., 188
Craig, W. M., 129, 132, 196, 205
Craig, W., 168
Craigen, D., 205
Cramer, R. J., 232
Crellin, K., 173
Cressey, D. R., 92, 93
Crick, N. R., 35, 133
Crijen, A. M., 152
Critchley, M., 181
Critchlow, B., 502
Critchton, R., 180
Crocker, A. G., 51
Cromwell, P. F., 406, 408, 409, 411, 412, 422, 423, 424
Crosbie-Burnett, M., 265
Crowe, R. R., 64, 65
Crowe, S.L., 201
Cruise, K. R., 194, 195, 222
Crutsinger, C., 422
Cruz, A. M., 134
Csikszentmihalyi, M., 4
Culberton, F. M., 50
Cullen, R. M., 295, 296
Cummings, A., 265
Cunningham-Rathner, J., 382
Curtain, J. J., 196

Curtin, J. J., 198
Curtis, N. M., 173
Cusimano, M. D., 78

D

d'Orban, P. T., 269
Dabney, D. A., 422
Dadds, M. R., 47, 209, 210, 461
Dåderman, A. M., 196
Daffern, M., 128
Dahl, K- P., 353, 360
Dahlberg, L. L., 151, 163
Dahle, K-P., 353, 360, 389
Dahlgren, L., 259
Dalbert, C., 3
Damasio, A. R., 201
Damasio, H., 201
Damon, W., 167
Daniels, D. N., 117
Daniels, J. A., 311, 315
Dao, J., 338
Darby, P. J., 261
Darling, N., 41
Daversa, M. T., 385
David, P. R., 412
Davidson, R. J., 200
Davies, J., 471
Davies, M., 362
Davis, E. B., 139
Davis, J., 429
Davis, M. G., 421
Davis, O.S.P., 63
Davis, R. C., 356
Dawkins, M. P., 497
Dawson, J. M., 281
Day, J. C., 161, 163
Day, K., 216, 462
Day, R., 200
de Kemp, R. A. T., 47
de Wied, M., 47
De Winter, A. F., 69
Deal, M. M., 309
Dean, C., 156
DeAngelis, T., 336
Deater-Deckard, K., 261
Debotte, G., 73
Decker, S. H., 255, 410
Decker, S., 443, 444
Declercq, F., 186
Declercq, F., 186
Dedel, K., 149
Deem, D., 417
DeFries, J. C., 62
DeGarmo, D. S., 158, 165
deHaven- Smith, L., 429
Dehue, F., 453
Deisher, R. W., 281
Deković, M., 69, 173, 194
Del Bove, G., 461, 465
DeLeon, P. H., 323
DeLisi, M., 5, 67, 79, 80, 201, 221, 304, 408
DeMatteo, D., 227, 229, 242, 471

SUBJECT INDEX

Note: 'b', 'f' and 't' refer to boxes, figures and tables